This Is Who We Were
In The 1970s

This Is Who We Were
In The 1970s

Based on material from Grey House Publishing's
Working Americans Series by Scott Derks

Grey House
Publishing

PUBLISHER: Leslie Mackenzie
EDITORIAL DIRECTOR: Laura Mars
EDITORIAL ASSISTANT: Melissa Rose
PRODUCTION MANAGER: Kristen Thatcher
MARKETING DIRECTOR: Jessica Moody
COMPOSITION: David Garoogian

Grey House Publishing, Inc.
4919 Route 22
Amenia, NY 12501
518.789.8700
FAX 845.373.6390
www.greyhouse.com
e-mail: books @greyhouse.com

While every effort has been made to ensure the reliability of the information presented in this publication, Grey House Publishing neither guarantees the accuracy of the data contained herein nor assumes any responsibility for errors, omissions or discrepancies. Grey House accepts no payment for listing; inclusion in the publication of any organization, agency, institution, publication, service or individual does not imply endorsement of the editors or publisher.

Errors brought to the attention of the publisher and verified to the satisfaction of the publisher will be corrected in future editions.

TABLE OF CONTENTS

Section One: Profiles

This section contains 28 profiles of individuals and families living and working in the 1970s. It examines their lives at home, at work, and in their neighborhoods. Based upon historic materials, personal interviews, and diaries, the profiles give a sense of what it was like to live in the years 1970 to 1979.

Section Two: Historical Snapshots

This section includes lists of important "firsts" in America, from technical advances and political events to new products and top-selling books. Combining American history with fun facts, these snapshots present an easy-to-read overview of what happened in the 1970s.

Section Three: Economy of the Times

This section looks at a wide range of economic data, including prices for food, clothing, transportation, and housing, plus reprints of actual advertisements for products and services of the time. It includes comparable figures for expenditures, income, and prices, plus a valuable year-by-year listing of the value of a dollar.

Section Four: All Around Us—What We Saw, Wrote, Read & Listened To

This section includes reprints of newspaper and magazine articles, speeches, and other items designed to help readers focus on what was on the minds of Americans in the 1970s. These 39 original pieces show how popular opinion was formed, and how American life was affected.

Section Five: Census Data

This section includes state-by-state comparative tables and reprints from the 1980 Census.

ESSAY ON THE 1970s

The 1970s was a decade of opposites. The Vietnam War finally came to a long-awaited end, only to spawn spiraling costs and several waves of inflation. Battles on the education front over the forced busing of school children to attain integration resulted in violence and dramatic headlines. Asian-Americans began to capture the public's attention because of their quality performance in school and striking lack of upward mobility after graduation. Technology within the classroom was innovative, but often controversial. And television programming, famously called a "wasteland," started focusing on the education of preschoolers, resulting in *Sesame Street*.

Economy

President Richard Nixon was forced in 1971 to devalue the U.S. dollar against foreign currencies and allow its previously fixed value to "float" according to changing economic conditions. By the end of 1971, the money paid for foreign goods exceeded that spent on U.S. exports for the first time in the century. Two years later, during the Yom Kippur War between Israel and its Arab neighbors, Arab oil producers declared an embargo on oil shipments to the United States, setting off gas shortages, a dramatic rise in the price of oil, and gas rationing for the first time in 30 years. The sale of automobiles plummeted, unemployment and inflation nearly doubled, and the buying power of Americans fell dramatically. The economy did not fully recover for more than a decade, while the fast-growing economies of Japan and Western Europe mounted competitive challenges to American manufacturers. The value of imported manufactured goods skyrocketed. The inflationary cycle and recession returned in 1979 to disrupt markets, put thousands out of work, and prompt massive downsizing of companies. A symbol of the era was the pending bankruptcy of Chrysler Corporation, who could not compete against Japanese imports. The federal government was forced to extend loan guarantees to the company to prevent bankruptcy and the loss of thousands of jobs.

Late in the decade, Federal Reserve Chairman Paul Volcker slammed on the economic brakes, restricted the growth of the money supply, and curbed inflation. As a result, interest rates rose to nearly 20 percent—their highest level since the Civil War—and the sale of big ticket items decreased.

Music

By 1975, disco was firmly established as the music genre of the 1970s. First appearing in dance clubs, disco was popularized by the movie *Saturday Night Fever*, released in December 1977. The soundtrack to the movie became the best-selling album of all time. The 1970s also saw the emergence of hard rock, personified by Alice Cooper, Lynyrd Skynyrd, Aerosmith, and Kiss. But it was Don McLean's 1971 song "American Pie," inspired by the death of musician Buddy Holly, that became one of the most recognizable songs of the era.

Jobs

In the 1970s, the shift of manufacturing facilities to the South from the Northeast and Midwest accelerated. The Sunbelt became the new darling of corporate America. By the late 1970s, the South had gained more than a million manufacturing jobs, while the Northeast and the Midwest lost nearly two million. Rural North Carolina had the highest percentage of manufacturing of any state in the nation, along with the lowest blue-collar wages, and the lowest unionization rate in the country. The Northeast lost more than traditional manufacturing jobs, however. Computerization of clerical work made it possible for big firms such as Merrill Lynch, American Express, and Citibank to shift operations to the South and West.

Social Change

One of the most striking of all social actions of the 1970s was the Women's Liberation Movement, which reshaped American society. Since the late 1950s, a small group of American women had attempted to convince Congress and the courts to bring about equality between the sexes. By the 1970s, the National Organization for Women (NOW) multiplied in size, the first issue of *Ms. Magazine* sold out in a week, and women began demanding economic equality, the legalization of abortion, and the improvement of women's roles in society.

Although the women's movement was big, there were others. A report by the Department of Health, Education, and Welfare commented: "All authority in our society is being challenged. Professional athletes challenge owners, journalists challenge editors, consumers challenge manufacturers, and young blue-collar workers, who have grown up in an environment in which equality is called for in all institutions, are demanding the same rights and expressing the same values as university graduates."

The decade also included the maturation of the National Welfare Rights Organization (NWRO), founded in 1966, which resulted in millions of urban poor demanding additional rights. The environmental movement gained recognition and momentum, starting with the first Earth Day celebration in 1970 and the subsequent passage of the federal Clean Air and Clean Water acts. Also notable was the growing opposition to the use of nuclear power, which peaked after the near calamity at Three Mile Island nuclear power plant in Pennsylvania in 1979.

The decade also was marred by the deep divisions caused by the Vietnam War. For more than 10 years, the war had been fought on two fronts: at home and abroad. As a result, U.S. policymakers conducted the war with one eye always focused on national opinion. The Vietnam War was the longest war in American history. It cost $118 billion, resulted in 56,000 Americans killed, 30,000 Americans wounded, 3.8 million Vietnamese dead, and the loss of American prestige abroad.

Back at home, California created a no-fault divorce law, and Massachusetts introduced no-fault insurance. Health food was growing in popularity, with sales reaching $3 billion. By 1975, the so-called "nuclear" family—working father, stay-at-home mother, and two children—represented only 7 percent of the population, and the average family size went from 4.3 persons in 1920 to 3.4.

INTRODUCTION

This Is Who We Were In The 1970s is an offspring of our 13-volume *Working Americans* series, which is devoted, volume by volume, to Americans by class, occupation, or social cause. This new edition is devoted to the 1970s. It represents various economic classes, dozens of occupations, and all regions of the country. This comprehensive look at this decade is through the eyes and ears of everyday Americans, not the words of historians or politicians.

This Is Who We Were In The 1970s presents 28 profiles of individuals and families—their lives at home, on the job, and in their neighborhood—with lots of photos and historical images. These stories portray both struggling, and successful Americans, and capture a wide range of thoughts and emotions. From the many government surveys, social worker histories, economic data, family diaries and letters, and newspaper and magazine features, this unique reference assembles a remarkable personal and realistic look at the lives of a wide range of Americans between the years 1970-1979.

The profiles, together with additional sections outlined below, present a complete picture of what it was like to live in America in the 1970s.

Section One: Profiles

Each of the 28 profiles in Section One begins with a brief introduction. Each profile is arranged in three categories: Life at Home; Life at Work; Life in the Community. Photographs and original advertisements support each chapter, and many include industry or social timelines and contemporary articles.

Section Two: Historical Snapshots

Section Two is made up of three long, bulleted lists of significant events and milestones. In chronological order—Early 1970s, Mid 1970s, and Late 1970s—these offer an amazing range of firsts and turning points in American history, including a few "can you believe it?" facts.

Section Three: Economy of the Times

One of the most interesting things about researching an earlier time is learning how much things cost and what people earned. This section offers this information in three categories—Consumer Expenditures, Annual Income of Standard Jobs, and Selected Prices—with actual figures from three specific years for easy comparison and study.

At the end of Section Three is a Value of a Dollar Index that compares the buying power of $1.00 in 2014 to the buying power of $1.00 in every year prior, back to 1860, helping to put the economic data in *This Is Who We Were In The 1970s* into context.

Section Four: All Around Us

There is no better way to put your finger on the pulse of a country than to read its magazines and newspapers. This section offers 39 original articles, book excerpts, speeches, and advertising copy that influenced American thought from 1970-1979.

Section Five: Census Data

This section includes invaluable data to help define the 1970s such as State-by-State comparative tables, and actual reprints from the Census of Population, including a Census of Housing and Report on Housing Inventory. Here you will find detailed population, social and economic characteristics, plus structural characteristics of the housing stock. This section also includes dozens of maps and charts for easy analysis.

This Is Who We Were In The 1970 ends with a comprehensive Bibliography, arranged by thoughtful topics, and a detailed Index.

The editors thank all those who agreed to be interviewed and share their personal photos for this book. We also gratefully acknowledge the Prints & Photographs Collections of the Library of Congress.

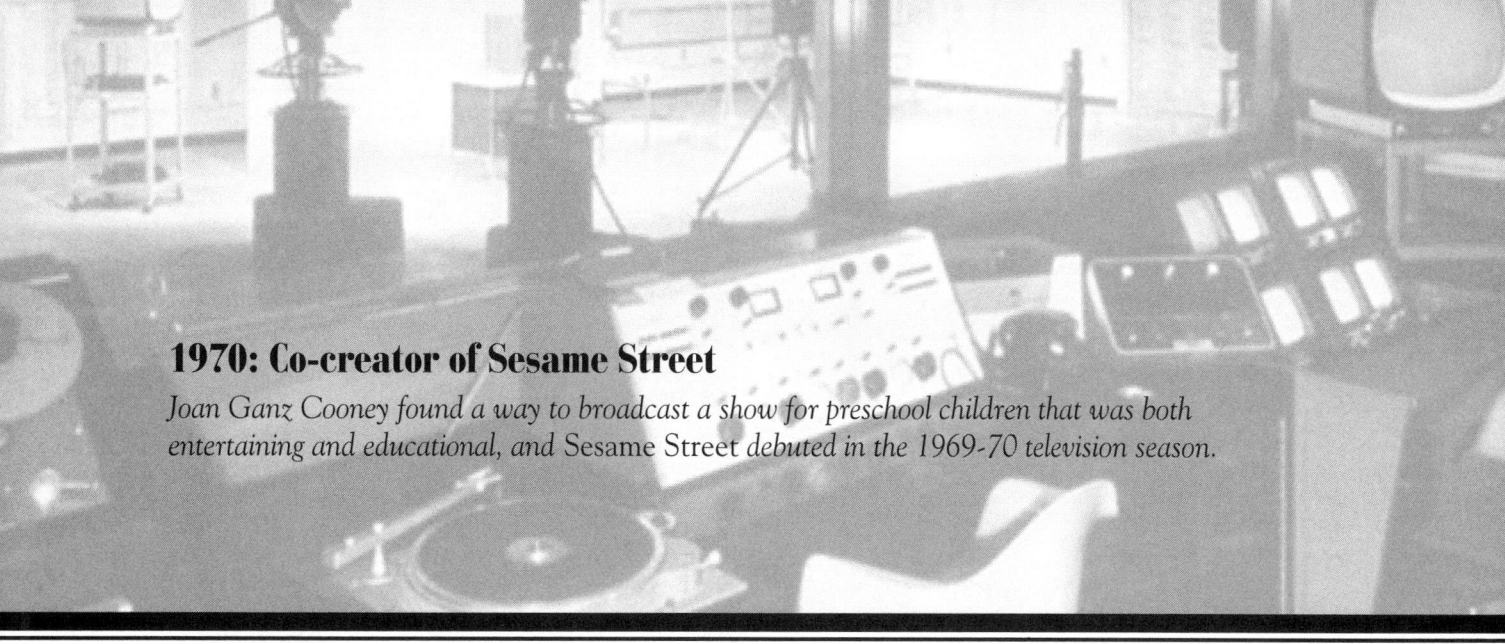

1970: Co-creator of Sesame Street

Joan Ganz Cooney found a way to broadcast a show for preschool children that was both entertaining and educational, and Sesame Street debuted in the 1969-70 television season.

Life at Home

- Joan Ganz Cooney was born November 30, 1929, in Phoenix, Arizona, to a wealthy banking family with both Jewish and Catholic heritage.
- Her grandfather, Emil Ganz, was a German Jew who came to America just before the Civil War, moved to Georgia and fought with the Confederate Army.
- After the war, he moved west and settled in Phoenix, where he opened a liquor store and later became president of a local bank.
- He was a Democrat who was elected mayor of Phoenix three times.
- Joan's mother, Pauline Reardon Ganz, was a Catholic from Michigan; her father, Sylvan Cleveland Ganz, was president of his father's bank for 44 years.
- "I was raised in the most conventional way," Joan said, "raised to be a housewife and mother, to work in an interesting job when I got out of college, and to marry at the appropriate time, which would have been 25."
- Joan grew up within a "countryclub atmosphere," but she became concerned about poverty in high school.
- She was inspired by Father James Keller, a Maryknoll priest who founded The Christophers, a group that encouraged people to use their God-given talents to make a positive difference in the world.
- The movement borrowed an ancient Chinese proverb: "It's better to light one candle than to curse the darkness."
- She went to the Dominican College of San Raphael, a Catholic college in California, but transferred to the University of Arizona, where she graduated with a bachelor's degree in education in 1951.
- Joan had no interest in teaching.
- So right after college, she and a friend moved to Washington, DC, to work as clerks using a typewriter to create letters and other documents for the State Department.
- "I just wanted to see what it was like to live in Washington and work for the federal government."

Joan Cooney's passion for educational TV helped put Sesame Street *on the air.*

1

- She returned to Phoenix for a year to work on the local newspaper, The Arizona Republic, and save money for her next goal: moving to New York City.
- Her mother said: "You know you are a big fish in a little pond in Phoenix; why do you want to be a little fish in a big pond?"
- Joan's response: "How do you know I won't be a big fish in a big pond?"
- Joan was 23 when she arrived in New York in the fall of 1953.
- "When I came to New York I thought I would probably work in print, but of course this great new medium of television was blossoming."
- Her newspaper work helped her get an entry-level job in RCA's publicity department, which quickly led to her getting a job making $65 a week writing summaries of soap operas for the NBC television network.
- In 1954, she stepped up to a job as a publicist for U.S. Steel Corporation on their show, The U.S. Steel Hour (ABC, 1953-55; CBS, 1955-63), which aired a variety of critically praised dramas.

New York City was exciting for Joan.

- She was aware of the emergence of educational television, and became "obsessed" with being part of it.
- "It just hit me as exactly what I wanted to do with my life," she said.
- "I wanted to see the medium do constructive things, and I could see that that was really the way."
- When WNDT, Channel 13, established a public television station in New York in 1962, she jumped at the opportunity to join, even though she knew it meant a cut in pay.
- She tried to get a job as a publicist, but the general manager said they didn't need publicists; they needed producers, particularly one for a weekly live debate show called Court of Reason.
- She had no experience as a producer, but was undeterred.
- She told the general manager: "I don't know all the people personally that you would have on the air, but I know what the issues are and I know who the people are who espouse what positions on what issues. I can do that show."
- She was hired-and her yearly pay fell from $12,000 at U.S. Steel to $9,000 on Channel 13.
- "I had a thousand dollars in the bank," she said; "I figured I would need a hundred dollars more a month to live, but by the time I ran out of money, I would get a raise, and that's just the way it worked out."
- Joan graduated to short documentaries.
- One of her suppliers for ideas was Tim Cooney, director of public relations for the New York City Department of Labor.
- He called her in 1964 to alert her to an experimental reading program underway with four-yearolds in Harlem.
- This experiment-like one being conducted by psychologist Susan Gray in Tennessee-would become a model for the inception of Head Start that year.
- Joan met with researchers Lillian and Martin Deutsch and produced a documentary called *A Chance at the Beginning.*

- After Head Start was launched, the federal program bought 125 prints of the documentary to use as training films for their teachers.
- Joan married Cooney in February 1964.
- Her June 1965 documentary called *Poverty, Anti-Poverty and the Poor* caught the attention of Jack Gould, an influential television critic for *The New York Times*.
- He described the format as similar to a "teach-in" held earlier in Washington, DC, joining public officials, experts and the general public.

Joan's documentary was used to train Head Start teachers.

- "The floor participants queued up before microphones in the aisles and let fly with statements, criticisms, challenges and, occasionally, questions."
- By early 1966, Joan said she "had become absolutely involved intellectually and spiritually with the Civil Rights movement and with the educational deficit that poverty created; I was not necessarily focused on young children, though."
- That moment came at a dinner party she held at her apartment in February 1966.
- For the next three years, she was involved in a swirl of activity that would bring together the educational experts, television artists and the money that would enable the launch of the first season of *Sesame Street* in 1969-70.

Life at Work

"Sunny day, keeping the clouds away
On my way to where the air is sweet.
Can you tell me how to get,
How to get to Sesame Street?"

—Opening lines of the Sesame Street theme song composed by Joe Raposo and Jeff Moss

- Many Americans were hoping for sunshine and sweetness as the 1969-70 television season opened, and what little there was came from an improbable source: a new television show for preschoolers called *Sesame Street*.
- The show first aired as the Vietnam War and protests against it were reaching a feverish pitch.
- Four protesters were shot and killed on the campus of Kent State University in Ohio in May 1970.
- It was also a time when interest in preschool education was high and disdain for popular television intense.
- "The timing was incredible," Joan said. "Every night the TV set brought you bad news. Finally, it was as if the public was saying 'So do something!' to the TV set, and one day they turned on the TV set and the TV set did something. And everyone understood that, for a change, TV was doing something.
- "There was huge idealism because we were trying to reach inner-city children as well as others."
- The way to *Sesame Street* had begun in the early 1960s when Joan met Lloyd N. Morrisett, who would become the show's co-creator.

Sesame Street's Big Bird *taught the alphabet to a pre-school audience.*

- Morrisett was a psychologist and executive at the Carnegie Corporation of New York, which was established by steel mill owner Andrew Carnegie in 1911 "to promote the advancement and diffusion of knowledge and understanding."
- Morrisett was about the same age as Joan.
- He moved to New York in 1959 to work for Carnegie, one of the nation's biggest private funders for educational and social improvement programs.
- He and Joan met a couple years later.
- In the early 1960s, Carnegie became increasingly interested in funding programs that would help children from poor households be successful in school.
- While several projects were funded, all were experiments involving only a few hundred children.
- Morrisett and his wife, Mary, were bemused and not a little worried when they woke up 6 a.m. on a Sunday morning in 1965 and found their three-year-old daughter, Sarah, had turned on the television herself and was intently watching.
- Even more concerning was that the only thing on the screen at that hour was what was a test pattern-a still image that was broadcast when the network was "off the air."
- For Morrisett, it helped reinforce his belief in the "the utter fascination that little kids had with television."
- He brought up the subject at a dinner party hosted by Joan and her husband in February 1966.
- As they chatted, Lloyd Morrisett asked: "Do you think television could be used to teach children?"
- "Lloyd talked about the possibility of Carnegie financing...A little three-month study," Joan said, "where [an] investigator would go around the country talking to various child development people.

- "I didn't know until that moment that I would be interested," Joan said. "I suddenly saw that this was a way of making television do something for the people that needed the help."
- With a $15,000 Carnegie grant to WNDT to cover Joan's salary and expenses, she traveled around the country from June to October 1966 talking with educators and child development psychologists.
- Joan left public television station WNDT in early 1967 and became an employee at Carnegie, where she would continue to shape the show.
- This was just a few years after the 1965 launch of Head Start, and in the peak of the "preschool moment."
- Educators, researchers and parents were keenly interested in early childhood education, not only as a way to help all children succeed in school, but especially to help children from impoverished backgrounds overcome their social obstacles.
- And the poor included a disproportionate number of black households.
- The preschool movement coincided with the Civil Rights movement.
- While Joan knew little about preschool educational theories, she, like many white liberals, supported the efforts of blacks to end segregation and gain equal footing in all spheres of life, from education to housing.
- But specifically targeting minority children had its own dangers.
- Louis Housman, a former commercial TV executive and a federal government advisor on the project, said a minority-oriented show would draw the ire of black parents who would consider it "demeaning" and "patronizing," while driving away the white, middle-class audience.
- Joan and Morrisett were continually asked by potential backers whether television could teach.
- She and Morrisett believed it could.
- After all, preschoolers were memorizing television commercials for products ranging from bread to beer.

Sesame Street *proved that television can be both educational and inspirational.*

- Joan decided that, while the creative people would be the final judges of what went on the air, they would work closely with educators and researchers to test and improve the show at every step.
- They enlisted funders to a show that would be an experiment.
- By early 1968, Joan and Morrisett had lined up $8 million in funding for a two-year experimental project that would produce six months of programs for the 1969-70 season.
- Half came from federal government sources, including $650,000 from Head Start.
- The rest came from Carnegie, the Ford Foundation, and other private sources; Carnegie's $1.5 million grant was one of its largest ever.
- With the funding in place, Carnegie announced in March 1968 the creation of the Children's Television Workshop with Joan as its executive director.
- Joan took to heart a key piece of advice from a public television executive: Keep the goals for the program simple and modest.
- "We would teach the alphabet, the recitation of the alphabet, recognition of letters, recognition of numbers when you see them, certain sounds of letters; because we were phonetic, we believed that phonics was the way to go, that learning the sounds of letters was useful."
- Joan had hired David D. Connell as executive producer.
- Connell had the same role for 12 years with the company that produced *Captain Kangaroo*, an hour-long children's television show on CBS since 1955.
- How would the show's producers know if they were truly engaging the preschoolers?
- The researchers would watch them.
- Young actor James Earl Jones caught the attention of the test audiences by reciting the alphabet slowly in his deep voice.
- Each letter appeared above his head a moment before Jones pronounced it, and researchers saw the value of repetition as the kids began to shout each letter before Jones said it.
- The insert made it into the show's second episode in 1969.
- The show's street scenes were originally filmed without any puppets—a move intended to clearly separate the show's "real" parts from "fantasy" ones.
- But researchers saw kids' attention fall away on the street scenes, and pick up only when the show switched to animation or puppets.
- "So it turned into a street where Oscar can come out of a trash can or Big Bird can come wandering by," Connell said.
- Jim Henson and his Muppets were hired for the project in 1968, and the Muppets multiplied with researchers' suggestions.
- Suggestion: Children ought to be taught that it's okay not to be happy all the time, and not to be pleasant all the time.
- Result: Oscar the Grouch.
- Suggestion: Show a child being smarter than the adults, so that you're modeling smart kids.
- Result: Bert and Ernie.
- Suggestion: Show a child as a child is—awkward and forever asking questions.
- Result: Big Bird.
- One of the last elements to fall into place was the show's name.
- The Muppets acted out the tortured naming process in a promotional video shown to potential funders in 1968.
- After a board of grousing Muppets came up with a name spanning a few dozen words, Kermit the Frog said, "Why don't you call your show 'Sesame Street.' You know, like 'open sesame.' It kind of gives the idea of a street where neat things happen."
- After the first season, the workshop released a study finding that 90 percent of preschoolers surveyed in a poor neighborhood in Brooklyn had seen *Sesame Street* in its first season.

- The 611 children surveyed lived in households with TV sets, and did not go off to daycare or nursery schools.
- Of them, 60 percent saw the show at least once a day.
- Separately, the independent Nielsen Rating Service estimated that half of the nation's 12 million children ages three to five had watched *Sesame Street* in its first season.
- Studies of 120 children in Maine, New York, and Tennessee showed thinking and reading skills improved more among preschoolers who watched the show compared with those who did not.
- The show won an Emmy award in 1970 for Outstanding Achievement in Children's Programming.
- And there were other signs of success.
- "Rubber Duckie," Ernie's signature tribute song to his beloved bathtub toy, reached No. 16 on *Billboard's* "Hot 100 Singles" chart in 1970.
- The song was nominated for a Grammy Award for Best Recording for Children, but it lost to *The Sesame Street Book & Record,* which included the song.
- And the weekly news magazine *Time* featured Sesame Street in its November 23, 1970, issue.
- "When Big Bird hit the cover of *Time,* I knew we had something that would last forever," Joan said.
- The Workshop didn't want to depend on government for funding.
- Most foundations like Carnegie made large grants to start up projects, expecting that recipients would find their own funds to continue the programs—usually government funds.
- The Workshop sought a new funding model for *Sesame Street.*
- By April 1970, Joan was talking about selling books and records to reinforce the show's lessons—and raise money.
- That month, the Children's Television Workshop broke away from its parent, National Educational Television, and became a non-profit company with Joan as its president.

Life in the Community: Racial Controversy

- While *Sesame Street* allowed the public to meet the Muppets, it also brought them into a world that was urban and integrated.
- A cast with educated black men and women in prominent roles might have escaped the notice of preschool viewers, but it was one of the most noticeable aspects of the show to older children and adults—both black and white—who had grown up with their own notions of racial identity.
- "It was the first show that really worked at integration—not only black and white men and women, but Muppets and human beings," Joan said.
- "It was a show that really taught kindness to one another."
- The racially mixed cast scared public officials in Mississippi.
- The state was one of the last to start an educational television network, and its first station in the state went on the air February 1, 1970, in Jackson, the state capital.
- Shortly afterward, the state legislature voted to spend $5.3 million to establish stations across the state.
- But the all-white state commission overseeing educational television voted to postpone showing *Sesame Street* even though it cost the state no money to air it.
- *The New York Times* carried a short news story noting that the commission chairman, Jackson banker James McKay, was the son-in-law of Jackson's former mayor, Allen Thompson.
- "Mr. Thompson is president and leading spokesman for FOCUS, a new group in Mississippi that is seeking to re-establish the principle of 'freedom of choice' in public schools."
- But the most telling aspect of the outcry was that some of the loudest voices were Mississippians.
- Newspaper editorials blasted the decision, and WDAM, a commercial station in Jackson, said it would offer airtime for *Sesame Street* if the commission didn't reverse its decision when it met again later that month.

- *The Delta Democratic-Times*, a family-owned newspaper in Greenville whose editor was Hodding Carter III, published two editorials languidly eviscerating the commission for the blocking of Big Bird.
- The May 5 editorial read: "We are penalized again, and our children more than adults, by the official determination to pretend that reality doesn't exist."
- On May 12, the Carters, who were longtime Democrats, took another tack: a tongue-in-cheek appeal to the Republican sensibilities of some of its readers.
- The editorial noted *Sesame Street* had the seal of approval from Republican Vice President Spiro Agnew.
- The editorial suggested, "white Mississippians, who like what he has to say about left-wing intellectuals, radical youths and school busing," should embrace the show and claim victory in the name of President Nixon's goal of bridging the generation gap.
- "We can't think of a bigger gap than between our three-year-olds' world and our own."
- And, by following Agnew, "radicals in the kindergarten would be thwarted."
- In late May, the commission met again and reversed its decision.

࿇࿇࿇࿇࿇࿇࿇࿇

Editorial: "No to Sesame Street,"
The Delta Democrat-Times, Greenville, Mississippi, May 5, 1970

It is not hard to sympathize with officials at Mississippi's educational television commission. They know the state's political and ideological realities, know that suspicious critics are closely examining everything they do and know that what the legislature gave this year it can take away next year. But when caution gives way to what appears to be panic at the first sign of possible controversy, a logical question arises. Exactly what is ETV supposed to be for?

The question must be asked because of the ETV commission's decision not to run *Sesame Street*, an educational show aimed at preschool children.

Sesame Street is an extraordinary venture in the use of television to do a serious job of educating young children rather than merely entertaining them, although it educates through a skillful blend of entertainment, psychology, color and sound teaching methods. Tests have repeatedly shown that the show, sponsored by several foundations through The Children's Television Workshop, does a successful job. One test suggested that children who had watched the show over a six-week period showed 2.5 times as much progress as children who had not.

But Mississippi's ETV commission won't be showing it for the time being because of one fatal defect, as measured by Mississippi's political leadership. *Sesame Street* is integrated. Some of its leading cast members are black, including the man who does much of the overt "teaching." The neighborhood of the "street" is a mixed one. And all that, of course, goes against the Mississippi grain.

It doesn't matter that integration in the schools is now a reality in Mississippi, and segregation is against the law of the land in virtually every field, including housing. Commercial television may portray this fact, but educational television, a state-controlled venture, may not. Thus, we are penalized again, and our children more than adults, by the official determination to pretend that reality doesn't exist.

There is no state which more desperately needs every educational tool it can find than Mississippi. There is no educational show on the market today better prepared than *Sesame Street* to teach preschool children what many cannot or do not learn in their homes. But "we decided it would be best to postpone it in the early days of ETV because some of the legislators might be offended," an ETV commission spokesman told *Democrat-Times Jackson* correspondent Ed Williams.

Mississippi ETV's officials maintain that *Sesame Street* is not being banned, but only postponed. Nevertheless, it is fairly apparent that those who run from anticipated pressure today are not very likely to show backbone when real pressure is applied. As in the case of the ETV decision not to show the award-winning documentary, Hospital, deciding against running *Sesame Street* seems to indicate that Mississippi ETV will settle for safe mediocrity every time. If that proves the case, there are strong reasons to ask whether the tax money which is being appropriated for educational television would not better be rediverted to the public schools. There, at least, the realities of 1970 cannot be avoided and the needs are immense.

∻∻∻∻∻∻∻∻

Editorial: "Agnew Likes It,"
The Delta Democrat-Times, Greenville, Mississippi, May 12, 1970

Vice President Spiro T. Agnew has a wide following among white Mississippians, who like what he has to say about left-wing intellectuals, radical youths and school busing.

Sesame Street does not have much following in Mississippi's educational television commission.

But the vice president thinks *Sesame Street,* the highly acclaimed educational television show for three- to five-year-olds, is one of the few examples of good television fare on the scene today.

Somehow there ought to be a way to get the vice president and the ETV commissioners together. The commissioners could reverse their earlier decision to reject showing *Sesame Street,* the vice president could laud their action, and his many followers would echo his support.

That way, everyone would win. The vice president, speaking for the "silent majority," would give a majority on the ETV commission enough nerve to risk displeasure from state politicians when they allow *Sesame Street* on the air. That would be a victory for our children and for common sense.

But it would also be a victory for the Nixon administration. Bridging the generation gap has suddenly become one of its major priorities, and we can't think of a bigger gap than between our three-year-olds' world and our own. Knowing that their vice president cares about the level of television they are offered would do wonders for the preschoolers' appreciation of this administration, and thus by indirection[,] of all authority. Radicals in the kindergarten would be thwarted. The American way would be upheld.

And all because the vice president likes *Sesame Street.*

1970: Earth Day Advocate

Miles Feimster didn't consider himself an environmentalist, but he did like the idea of honoring the natural world by setting aside one day in its honor.

Life at Home

- Miles Feimster was part of a furniture family from a furniture town in the heart of a furniture manufacturing region.
- He grew up in company-provided housing, substandard in many ways but extremely affordable: the rent was $8.00 a month.
- His father prided himself on being financially conservative; the family was permitted one window fan to battle the sometimes brutal summer heat of South-side Virginia.
- The monthly electric bill averaged $15.00 a month.
- Although the family was the proud owner of an electric range, the wood-burning "warm morning" cook stove was still used in the fall, winter and spring.
- Indoor plumbing had not yet arrived at the company housing in Martinsville, Virginia; therefore, the family outhouse was located on a hillside away from Indian Spring, the family's source of clean water for drinking, bathing and clothes washing.
- For washing clothes, the family relied upon a Maytag wringer washer.
- The water was heated in a galvanized steel tub placed over a fire pit; rinsing was done in the larger tub filled with cool, clean water.
- Both tubs were filled by carrying water from the spring in a 36-gallon aluminum bucket.
- The outhouse received a biannual Red Devil lye treatment to combat odor and disease.
- Every third year it was relocated, with precautions taken to integrate the abandoned latrine safely back into the landscape.
- Because the home was surrounded by streams on three sides, the family re-ditched every spring to insure proper drainage and reduce the mosquito breeding areas.
- To augment the family's food supply and hold down costs, Miles raised bantam chickens for meat and eggs.

Miles Feimster supported Earth Day.

Miles Feimster grew up in company-provided housing in the furniture manufacturing region of Martinsville, Virginia.

- Miles's young siblings, Allie, 14, and Hanson, 10, were entrusted with the job of selling surplus eggs to a neighbor.
- In addition, the family raised a Yorkshire hog each year that was located in a pen as far away from the house and water supply as possible.
- The family garden included tomatoes, corn, beans, potatoes, onions and greens.
- Miles's mother Addie's specialty was canning the crops at harvest; she also put up peaches, apples, jams and preserves for the coming winter.
- During the summer growing season, Addie Feimster enjoyed quilting, for which she had earned a highly esteemed reputation within the black and white communities of Martinsville.
- A Feimster quilt would fetch $30.00.
- Miles's favorite season was spring, which brought the opening of trout season on the Smith River.
- The rapidly moving river signaled new hope and opportunity.
- It was also the place where he began to understand the impact of man and his pollution on nature.
- At times, heavy industrial pollution gave the tender trout a metallic taste that diminished the joy of trout fishing and eating.
- But trout fishing was a cherished tradition in the Feimster household that improved the family table in all seasons.
- Miles Feimster's father, Nate, was a renowned local fisherman with many citation awards to prove his fish stories.
- He often credited his Cherokee heritage for his love of the wilds and his adeptness as a hunter.

Miles's mother and sister.

- Every year he took down at least two deer, which were usually given to the local needy.
- Addie Feimster would not touch her husband's deer kills.

Life at Work

- Eighteen-year-old Miles Feimster's participation in Earth Day, 1970, was ignited by a friend and classmate, Jan Lawless.
- Like Miles, she had grown up near the Smith River, playing along its banks and tributaries.
- It was she who had suggested that they participate in the Earth Day parade and teach-in at the local community college.
- Maybe this was a way to get people interested in the quality of the local air and water, Miles figured.
- He knew from experience that raw sewage was still pumped into the river in some places; on occasion the river changed color because of industrial discharges.
- And every teenager from the industrial areas of the town had seen the smokestack clouds rise and felt the resulting falling ash rainfall.
- Cleaning up the environment was not an abstract, theoretical concept for Miles.
- First, though, he would need approval to attend.
- Both his mother and grandmother wanted a promise that Earth Day was not going to be the type of protest in which a black teenager could be arrested, hosed or beaten.
- They had seen enough of that kind of protest.
- Miles's father and grandfather took for granted that something would go wrong.
- It was their nature to be cautious, especially with Miles pledging to ask hard questions about the very factories that supported the family.
- Pollution or not, the factories fed the community.
- Even though all wages were frozen by presidential mandate, to harness inflation, if a man could work 70 hours a week, that was prosperity.

Local schools held Earth Day programs.

Faculty from the community college coordinated local events.

- After Miles made the commitment to participate in the Earth Day environmental teach-in, he and his friend Jan were consumed by the possibilities.
- Most of their free time was spent in helping to prepare for the event scheduled for April 22, 1970.
- The date was part of a national campaign to raise awareness of environmental and conservationist issues.
- Significantly, the date was chosen by U.S. Senator Gaylord Nelson, a Democrat from Wisconsin, and Representative Paul R. McCloskey, a Republican from California.
- Environmental Teach-in Incorporated, a student-run organization, had been formed to coordinate the national campaign.
- Its goals and charter were clear and non-confrontational: organized by students with the approval of school authorities and political leaders, Earth Day sought to mobilize support for anti-pollution measures.
- Activities were created at more than 800 colleges and 2,000 high schools in every section of the nation.
- Even some of the nation's military bases, still on high alert because of the Vietnam War, elected to participate.
- In Martinsville, Virginia, biology instructor James M. McIntosh was named the local coordinator for Earth Day at Patrick Henry Community College.
- The announced topics for discussion included "What Is Pollution?," "What Is Being Done about It?," and "What Can the Individual Do to Help?"
- To kick off the teach-in, an Anti-Pollution Parade was scheduled for the afternoon of April 18, four days before Earth Day.
- Miles and Jan were eager to do their part.
- The parade was led by a hay wagon loaded with examples of pollutants, followed by students wearing gas masks and others carrying pollution protest signs.
- Jan and Miles both wore gas masks, which were hot.

- He was the only black teen in the parade and stayed toward the middle of the protest march in case the police decided to interrupt the proceedings.
- When the march ended, the 100 high school and college students who had participated were invigorated with the possibilities for change.
- To participate in the teach-in, which ran from 1:30 to 6:30 p.m. on Wednesday, April 22, Miles and Jan had to skip their afternoon high school classes—something they had never done before.
- The Earth Day protest had a high air of respectability—a far cry from the rag-tag anti-Vietnam War protests shown so prominently and so often on the nightly news.
- Virginia Assistant Attorney General, Gerald Bailes, was the keynote speaker, expounding on legal enforcement and pollution; local pediatrician Dr. John French spoke on the medical effects of pollution.

Miles' friend Jan encouraged him to participate in Earth Day.

- Also included were speakers from the state Air Pollution Board and the Bureau of Solid Waste and Vector Control.
- For Miles, the impact of the day of protest began to sink in when he realized that he and Jan were part of a national movement, aimed directly at the burgeoning environmental crisis in the United States.
- At Martinsville High School, two students condemned pollution by carrying signs and riding a tricycle before school to illustrate the effect of automobiles on the environment.
- As part of the Earth Day festivities at Patrick Henry Community College, an automobile engine was laid to rest before the start of the various antipollution seminars and speeches on the environment.
- Martinsville City Manager, Tom Noland, participated on a panel representing private citizens' groups, industry and government agencies, and others concerning the effect of pollution on the area.
- Miles and Jan stayed to the end, enthralled by the possibilities for change and the opportunities ahead.

Earth Day Around the United States

- To celebrate the kick-off of Earth Day, Virginia Governor Linwood Holton signed a statement designating a Virginia "Improved Environment Week."
- Senator William Spong, Jr., an early advocate of the anti-pollution cause, spoke at a program sponsored by the Department of Environmental Sciences at the University of Virginia in Charlottesville.
- At the College of William and Mary in Williamsburg, Virginia, Dr. William Sirl, a California research physicist and a member of the Sierra Club, spoke on the "value of the wilderness."
- Nationally, 10 million public school children participated in teach-in programs.
- In New York City, cars were banned on Fifth Avenue while a picnic was held.
- In Louisville, Kentucky, 1,500 students crowded into a concourse at Atherton High School to illustrate the problems of overpopulation.
- Nationwide, students rode horses, roller skates, and skateboards rather than cars or buses.

- While speaking at the University of California, Berkeley, Senator Gaylord Nelson, who had originated the Earth Day idea, proposed national policies on land use, herbicides and pesticides, national standards for air and water pollution, and a ban on oil drilling.
- New Jersey Governor William Cahill signed a bill creating a state Department of Environmental Protection.
- New York Governor Nelson Rockefeller signed a bill coordinating anti-pollution and conservation activities.
- Maryland Governor Marvin Mandel signed 21 bills and joint legislative resolutions dealing with the environment.
- During a speech in Philadelphia, Pennsylvania, Senator Edmond Muskie of Maine called for an environmental resolution against pollution.
- New York City Mayor John V. Lindsey rode an electric-powered car to his appointments that day, and told a Union Square rally, "There is a simple question: do we want to live or die?"
- In Washington, DC, Senator Bayh of Indiana called for a national environmental control agency to "conquer pollution as we have conquered space."
- Not all congressional speakers were received warmly: New York Senator Charles E. Goodell was greeted at a New York University by leaflets calling his speech "the biggest source of air pollution."
- Despite the participation of millions, arrests were few: in Boston a group protesting the air pollution of supersonic transport planes blocked the ticket counter at Logan International Airport, resulting in 13 arrests.
- While much of the nation observed Earth Day reverently, the Daughters of the American Revolution branded the environmental movement "distorted and exaggerated."

Environment Timeline

1898   Cornell became the first college to offer a program in forestry. The U.S. Rivers and Harbors Act banned the pollution of navigable waters.

1902   The U.S. Bureau of Reclamation was established.

1903   The nation's first wildlife refuge was formed when President Theodore Roosevelt protected Pelican Island, Florida, from hunters decimating the island's bird population.

1905   The United States Forest Service was established within the Department of Agriculture to manage forest reserves.

1908   The Grand Canyon in Arizona was set aside as a national monument. President Theodore Roosevelt hosted the first Governors' Conference on Conservation to inventory America's natural resources.

Chlorination was first used extensively at U.S. water treatment plants.

1911   Canada, Japan, Russia, and the United States signed a treaty to limit the annual harvest of northern fur seals. The Weeks Act appropriated $9 million to purchase six million acres of land in the eastern United States for the purpose of establishing national forests.

1913   President Woodrow Wilson approved a plan to dam the Hetch Hetchy Valley to serve as a reservoir for the city of San Francisco.

1914   Martha, the last passenger pigeon, died in the Cincinnati Zoo and became a symbol of species extinction.

1915   Dinosaur National Monument was established in Colorado.

1916   The National Park Service and the National Park System were established to conserve scenery, wildlife and "historic objects" for future generations.

1917   President Woodrow Wilson created Alaska's Mount McKinley National Park.

1918   The Save-the-Redwoods League was created. The hunting of migratory bird species was restricted by a treaty between the U.S. and Canada.

1919   Congress established the Grand Canyon National Park in Arizona.

1920   The U.S. Mineral Leasing Act regulated mining on federal lands.

1922   The Izaak Walton League was established as a nonprofit research and advocacy organization.

1924   Naturalist Aldo Leopold secured the designation of Gila National Forest in New Mexico as America's first extensive wilderness area.

1928   The Boulder Canyon Project (Hoover Dam) was authorized to bring irrigation, electric power and flood control systems to the Western United States.

1930   Chlorofluorocarbons (CFCs) were hailed as safe refrigerants because of their nontoxic and non-combustible properties.

1933   The Tennessee Valley Authority was created lo develop the Tennessee River for flood control, navigation, electric power, agriculture and forestry.

1935   Aldo Leopold, Robert Marshall, Benton MacKaye, Robert Sterling Yard and others joined to form the Wilderness Society.

1947 Everglades National Park was established in Florida. Effigy Mounds National Monument was established in Iowa.

1956 Congress passed the Colorado River Storage Project Bill halting dam construction within any national park or monument.

1961 Investigators in the U.S. Adirondacks confirmed that acid rain was killing some animal species living in and around the lakes.

1962 Silent Spring by Rachel Carson exposed the dangers of pesticides. The Padre Island National Seashore was established in Texas.

1963 Congress passed the first Clean Air Act.

1964 Congress passed the Wilderness Act, setting up the National Wilderness Preservation System.

1965 Congress passed the Solid Waste Disposal Act, the first major solid waste legislation.

1966 Congress passed the Rare and Endangered Species Act.

1967 Scientists predicted that increased amounts of carbon dioxide in the atmosphere would lead to global warming.

The bald eagle, California condor, whooping crane, gray wolf, and grizzly bear were placed on the Endangered Species List. Congress passed the Air Quality Act.

1968 Congress passed the Wild and Scenic Rivers Act, identifying areas of scenic beauty for preservation and recreation.

President Lyndon Johnson signed the Central Arizona Project into law, protecting the Colorado River from damming. North Cascades National Park was established in Washington State. Redwoods National Park was established in California.

1970 An estimated 20 million people participated in the first Earth Day demonstrations and activities across the country.

The National Environmental Policy Act was signed into law, which required an analysis of the environmental impacts of federal actions. The U.S. Environmental Protection Agency began operations. American and peregrine falcons were placed on the Endangered Species List.

1971: Vietnam Veteran

After two tours of duty in Vietnam, James Delucca joined Vietnam Veterans Against the War *to protest war crimes resulting from American policies and to assist Vietnam vets in gaining benefits.*

Life at Home

- James Delucca was conceived in a 1,200-square-foot home 30 miles north of Philadelphia, in a moment of enthusiasm shortly after World War II ended.
- The first-born son of a World War II veteran, James was often told how blessed he was to have clothes on his back and food on the table.
- His father worked as a warehouse manager for a company that manufactured air conditioner systems; James's mother was an elementary school teacher.
- The family was very patriotic and felt it was their duty to display an American flag on their front doorstep every day.
- When the forecast called for rain, James's father would make him take down and properly fold the flag with him.
- He was taught never to let the flag touch the ground or to show disrespect for the people who fought for the freedoms that they enjoyed.
- James was consumed with playing war with his friends, who pretended to be American heroes fighting against the evil Germans or the Japanese devils.
- All the while, James's father stayed on alert, positive that soon a nuclear attack would end the world as he knew it.
- He even worked with the neighbors to build a bomb shelter stocked with canned goods and water, just to be safe.
- The economy was growing rapidly in postwar America, with people buying automobiles, televisions and, of course, air conditioning systems.
- The gross national product grew from 200 million in 1940 to over 500 million by 1960, giving rise to an expanding middle class in America.
- As James got older, his father often said, "There is no greater honor than to die for your country."

Vietnam vet James Delucca was a vocal anti-war protester.

- James also learned about Communism and the devastating effect it could have if it spread throughout the world.
- His Catholic priest told the congregation it was a good thing to kill Communists.
- James wanted to be a hero like his father.
- In 1965, with high school winding down and the Vietnam War escalating, James enlisted in the army.
- Many of his friends did not believe that the United States belonged in the war, especially in a country no one could find on a map.
- James's father lectured him about weak, unpatriotic people; when America called, his father said, a patriot responded.
- James responded with two tours of duty in the jungles of Vietnam.

James was an infantry soldier.

Life at Work

- During his first tour, James Delucca was an infantry soldier.
- War was wet, bewildering, exciting, and depressing.
- Within weeks of arrival, he participated in a night-patrol firefight that haunted his dreams for months.
- Almost a third of the men in his unit had been killed or wounded within the first six months.
- James witnessed ambushes, torture and death until he was almost numb to its reality.
- There was no time to be a patriot; in Vietnam it was either fight or die.
- He could never explain why he signed up for a second tour; maybe fighting was all he knew.
- The second time he was in-country, sleeping was impossible, especially when it rained.
- By late 1967, the fighting grew more intense, the strategy of fighting more inexplicable, dissatisfaction with the war more pronounced.
- One day, he said out loud, "This is pointless."
- At that moment, he was ready to see the end of a war that turned kids into killers.

In Vietnam, it was either fight or die.

- James was shot twice in his left leg in March of 1968.
- He almost bled to death because both bullets hit his upper thigh.
- He was moved to a military hospital and sent back to the states after recovering from his injury.
- When he returned, he saw that there was almost as much conflict in the states as there had been in Vietnam; thousands of middle class Americans were demonstrating against the war he had been fighting.
- However, his father was still a proud patriot.

Protesting the war became a full-time job for James.

- Feeling nothing like the person who had left his family and friends after high school, James moved to New York City.
- He applied for and received a job with a furniture store in uptown Manhattan and became an assistant manager after only eight months.
- As he looked for a way to become involved in the peace movement, he saw anti-war demonstrators passing his store one day carrying a banner that read "Vietnam Veterans Against the War."
- James was intrigued.
- Over the next couple of months he followed the progress of these veterans from a distance as they participated in debates and attracted coverage in *The New York Times*.
- People were actually listening to what they had to say.
- Intrigued by their message, James officially joined the Vietnam Veterans Against the War in October of 1969 and was immediately asked to help active-duty soldiers understand their alternatives to war.
- But when he participated in his first full-scale demonstration behind the banner of VVAW, he was able to give full-throated expression to his frustration.
- James finally felt like he was part of something he could believe in.
- In September 1970, he was one of the first vets to sign up for a march that retraced the trip of George Washington's Revolutionary rag-tag army to reach Valley Forge.
- Dramatically enough, the march was called RAW for Rapid American Withdrawal.
- The purpose was to give Americans a feel for the types of conditions that their soldiers were experiencing.
- The Rapid American Withdrawal march had the potential to teach people—even his father—the absolute horrors of the war in Vietnam.
- For weeks James and other veterans posted flyers all over New York City designed to shock: "Help Us To End This War Before They Turn Your Son Into A Butcher!"
- The march was directed at middle America; the VVAW wanted President Nixon's "silent majority" to experience the war.

- In all, 150 veterans joined Operation RAW for the 86-mile march from Morristown, New Jersey, to Valley Forge State Park.
- Finally, veterans who had served in the jungles of Vietnam could expose the horrible conditions there as well as the war crimes.
- On the day of the march, all of the veterans dressed in army fatigue and those who received purple hearts wrapped a red-stained gauze armband around one of their arms.
- They all carried toy M16 rifles.
- Most had long hair, beards and a look of determination; James thought them a fearsome group.
- During the march the veterans acted out a number of powerful scenes, assisted by professional actors, who often portrayed captured Viet Cong soldiers or terrified civilians.

Many Vietnam veterans sought to expose war crimes as a way to help end the war.

- Whenever the march arrived at a town, the vets chained the terrified actors together as Vietnam hostages and screamed and pushed the actors to the ground.
- Protesting the war became a full time job for James.
- The marchers then fired their toy weapons at fleeing civilian actors or simulated the torture interrogation of a suspected Viet Cong prisoner.
- No ears were cut off during the brutal questioning, but they came close, James observed.
- At times, the veterans mixed the past and present so powerfully that the actors were truly terrified; Americans witnessing the guerilla theater were horrified and confused by what they saw.
- The press was mystified by the display of street theater.
- Some felt that these demonstrations were idiotic and pointless; others claimed they demonstrated how bad the conditions in Vietnam really were.
- Hundreds of people followed the march with cameras documenting the entire event; 1,500 greeted the VVAW when they reached Valley Forge Park.

"Are you hiding a Viet Cong in there?"

Anti-war propaganda.

- No matter how the public felt about the protest, James knew the VVAW was being heard and making a strong national impact.
- James then quit his job to help organize the Winter Soldier Investigation in 1971.
- His father was scandalized and told James he would not be welcome at the annual Thanksgiving gathering.
- The Winter Soldiers Investigation intended to gather testimonies of war crimes that were taking place as a result of American war policies.
- It was time to lay the blame for atrocities at the feet of those who made policy, not the soldiers who carried them out.

Life in the Community: New York City

- Vietnam Veterans Against the War was founded by six Vietnam war veterans after they marched together with over 400,000 other protesters in the April 15, 1967 Spring Mobilization to End the War anti-war demonstration.
- After talking to members of the Veterans for Peace group at that march, the veterans discovered there was no organization representing Vietnam veterans.
- Their purpose was to give voice to the growing opposition among returning servicemen to the decade-long war in Indochina.
- VVAW also took up the struggle for the rights and needs of veterans.
- In 1970, they started the first discussion groups to deal with traumatic after-effects of war.
- They were instrumental in exposing the harmful health effects of exposure to chemical defoliants such as Agent Orange.
- They also exposed the neglect of many disabled vets in VA hospitals and helped draft legislation to improve educational benefits and create job programs.

Anti-war veterans acted out powerful scenes, assisted by actors portraying captured Viet Cong soldiers or terrified civilians.

Vietnam War Timeline

1950 The United States sent the first shipload of arms aid to pro-French Vietnam.

1954 The Viet Minh overran the French fortress at Dien Bien Phu.

1955 The first U.S. advisers to South Vietnam were sent to train the South Vietnamese Army.

1956 President Dwight Eisenhower said the French were "involved in a hopelessly losing war in Indochina."

1961 President John Kennedy ordered 100 "special forces" troops to South Vietnam.

1962 President Kennedy ordered a build-up of American troops in Thailand to counter Communist attacks in Laos.

1963 South Vietnamese President Diem and his brother were assassinated outside of Saigon.

1964 The U.S. military contingent in Vietnam increased by 5,000 to total 21,000.

U.S. Navy destroyers Maddox and C. Turner Joy were reportedly attacked by North Vietnamese torpedo boats in the Gulf of Tonkin. Congress approved the Gulf of Tonkin resolution affirming "all necessary measures to repel any armed attack against the forces of the United States."

The U.S. declined an offer of secret peace talks with North Vietnam.

1965 A guerilla assault against the military barracks at Pleiku left eight Americans dead; President Johnson ordered a retaliatory air strike against North Vietnam known as Operation Rolling Thunder.

Alice Herz set herself on fire in Detroit shortly after President Johnson announced major troop increases and the bombing of North Vietnam. Hanoi restated a peace proposal. Quaker Norman Morrison set himself on fire and died outside Secretary of Defense Robert McNamara's Pentagon office. Congress appropriated $2.4 billion for the Vietnam war effort.

1966 The U.S. dropped 600,000 tons of bombs on North Vietnam. Bombing began around Haiphong and Hanoi, North Vietnam.

1967 Nguyen Van Thieu was elected president of South Vietnam. Congressman "Tip" O'Neill broke publicly with President Johnson and opposed continuation of the Vietnam War.

1968 The Communists launched the Tet Offensive, including attacks on nearly all 44 of the capitals of South Vietnam's provinces.

The My Lai Massacre occurred in Quang Ngai province. President Johnson announced he would not seek re-election and ordered a bombing halt. Draftees accounted for 38 percent of all American troops in Vietnam; over 12 percent of the draftees were college graduates.

1969 Expanded peace talks opened in Paris with representatives of the U.S., South Vietnam, North Vietnam, and the National Liberation Front (NLF).

President Richard Nixon proposed an "8-point Peace Plan."

President Nixon talked of a "Vietnamization" program to prepare the South Vietnamese to take over the U.S. combat role. An estimated one million

Americans across the United States participated in anti-war demonstrations, protest rallies and peace vigils.

President Nixon said he planned the withdrawal of all U.S. troops on a secret timetable. Congress gave the president the authority to institute the "draft lottery" system aimed at inducting 19-year-olds.

Chief U.S. negotiator Henry Cabot Lodge and his deputy resigned, expressing pessimism concerning the course of the negotiations. President Nixon announced the reduction of another 50,000 troops by mid-April 1970. A presidential commission recommended the institution of an all-volunteer army and elimination of the draft.

1970   News of increased U.S. involvement in Laos and Cambodia surfaced. President Nixon announced the withdrawal of another 150,000 troops over the next 12 months to lower troop strength to 284,000.

President Nixon issued an Executive Order that ended all occupational deferments and most paternity deferments.

U.S. forces invaded Cambodia, causing widespread war protests.

Four Kent State college students were shot to death by Ohio National Guardsmen during an anti-war protest, spawning protests nationwide. A peaceful anti-war rally held in Washington, DC, was attended by about 80,000 people including 10 members of Congress. The McGovern-Hatfield Amendment, providing for the withdrawal of all American troops by December 31, 1971, was defeated by the Senate.

President Nixon signed a bill repealing the Gulf of Tonkin resolution. The army began a campaign to intercept and confiscate personal mail containing anti-war material sent to soldiers in Vietnam. A two-year extension of the draft passed the Congress; 48 percent of manpower for the army were draftees or "draft motivated."

Vietnam Veterans Against the War, numbering 2,300, came to Washington, DC, to participate in Dewey Canyon III, "a military incursion into the country of Congress"; many threw away their military medals and ribbons at the foot of the statue of Chief Justice John Marshall.

Ten days of protests by a group calling themselves the "Mayday Tribe" included attempted work stoppages at several federal offices in Washington, DC. Approximately 10,000 anti-war protestors were arrested in Washington, DC. The Pentagon Papers were published.

U.S. troop levels dropped to 156,800. The U.S. heavily bombed military installations in North Vietnam.

1971: Life Insurance Agent

Just as Alex Haas's income as a life insurance agent in Omaha, Nebraska, began to take off, his wife suffered a debilitating brain aneurysm, placing his career—and their lives—on hold.

Life at Home

- Alex and Rebecca were living in their "dream home" in west Omaha.
- Their tri-level house, which cost $27,500, had three bedrooms, three baths, a living room, dining room, kitchen, and great room.
- Being the first owners allowed them to pick the wallpaper, the color of the kitchen cabinets, and other design features.
- Alex was proud of his home, but cautious about debt.
- His beliefs were heavily shaped by the Depression; he learned that when you lost your money, you had nothing.
- Born in 1915, his father was a district attorney; Alex wanted to be a farmer, but was advised by his grandmother to avoid farming and attend college instead.
- Reluctantly he agreed, after the experience of the Depression; he did not want to work his entire life only to become destitute because of an economic whim he could not control.
- Now the Haas family was experiencing a catastrophe that insurance cannot solve.
- Their lives had been reshaped by a brain aneurysm suffered by Rebecca, who was 44 years old.
- She was working as a receptionist at a plumbing and electrical engineering company in Omaha.
- She collapsed at work and was taken to the hospital.
- Following her surgery, she was provided intensive care in a private room for 10 days—the cost was $100 a day.
- Despite an eight-hour operation, she has lost the use of the left side of her body.
- Nearly four months were spent in physical therapy before coming home, and she was still

Insurance agent Alex Haas.

27

Rebecca and her daughters.

adjusting to the need to wear a brace and take her daily medication.

- She was now having grand mal seizures, which began a month after she finally arrived home.
- The family had hired an aide to assist Rebecca, but having someone else in the house had not worked well; she did not like having someone else in her home.
- Despite excellent medical insurance, the family owes $20,000 in medical fees—a staggering burden.
- The oldest daughter attended the University of Nebraska, while her younger sister attended an all-girls' Catholic high school run by the Sisters of the Sacred Heart.

Life at Work

- Alex had been an insurance agent for Equitable Life of New York for 21 years.
- Before his wife's illness, he began his day at 5:30 a.m., eating breakfast alone; he enjoyed his quiet time.
- After breakfast, he was joined by his younger daughter, who still lived at home, and his wife; he took them to school and work, respectively, in the family car.
- Rebecca never learned to drive.
- At the office, he reviewed the work prepared by his secretary; he was proud that his volume justifies an assistant, since not everyone had this type of help.
- He then spent the morning attempting to set up appointments with families, whom he liked to meet at their homes after dinner at about 7:00 or 7:30 p.m.

- In mid-afternoon, he normally picked up his daughter, then wents home to fix the evening meal before going to his first sales call.
- He enjoyed people and doing insurance interviews.
- Although a very fastidious man, he had the ability to make nearly everyone comfortable, even when talking about the need for life insurance.
- Before a call began, he is often served coffee and cake, which he must enjoy before discussing business, because to do otherwise would be considered rude.
- He never smoked or accepted an alcoholic drink while making a visit.
- Since Rebecca's illness, he spent more time at home caring for her.
- He also helped his younger daughter with her studies.
- Going to meet clients every night caused problems, so he thought about taking a supervisory job that required less selling, less night work, and probably less income overall.
- He put about 500 miles a week on his car, a red Dodge Charger with four-on-the-floor.
- He knows that people buy life insurance for a variety of reasons, but most want to provide financial protection for their families in case they die prematurely.
- Martin Luther King, Jr.'s, "I have a dream" speech several years ago turned a light on in his life as he realized that the blacks of northern Omaha had been denied the right to own homes and buy insurance.
- He decided to bring about a change, and began providing life insurance policies to African-Americans, despite some disapproving signals from his company.
- When he sold a policy to St. Louis Cardinal all-star pitcher Bob Gibson, the company was particularly cautious and required the professional athlete to undergo a complete physical examination before they would approve the $1 million coverage Gibson requested.
- Americans bought about three fourths of their new protection in 1971 on an individual basis, by personal decision, usually through a life insurance agent.
- Purchases of life insurance totaled $132 billion in 1971; group life insurance purchases were $49 billion.
- Part of his success grew from his extensive record keeping; he maintained detailed records of all the clients' children and regularly checked the newspapers for births and deaths.
- Families tended to buy life insurance while going through a life change, such as the birth of a child.
- In 1961, the average new policy was $6,300; by 1966, the average was $8,750, and by 1971, $11,670.
- Forty-three percent of adults who bought insurance had an income of less than $7,500.
- During the week, he attended mass on Wednesday and then again on Sunday; before his wife became ill, he was a member of the Catholic Men's Association and the men's choir.

Life in the Community: Omaha, Nebraska

- The river community of Omaha was known as the Gateway City.
- Founded in 1853 along the Missouri River, Omaha quickly became the cross point for rail traffic.
- With the resumption of regularly scheduled barge service in 1953, Omaha returned to its roots to become a river town again.
- Father Flanagan's Boys' Town, a famous refuge for homeless boys, sat on a hilltop 10 miles from the city.
- Omaha boasted three universities, three colleges, two schools of medicine, two pharmacy schools, one law school, eight nurses' training programs, 30 business and technical schools, and five Montessori preschools.
- Recently, just in time for the state's 100th anniversary, Omaha saw the resurgence of the Old Market into an artistic and cultural center.
- The dilapidated buildings were rescued by a combination of artists and businessmen; the Old Market had artist's lofts, restaurants, shops, and boutiques.

Nebraska's topography is mostly flat and well suited for agriculture.

- Although Nebraska was primarily an agricultural state, Omaha boasted more than 600 manufacturing concerns, which turn out everything from TV components to TV dinners.
- Statewide, 62 percent of Nebraska's 1.5 million people lived in urban areas and only 18 percent are engaged in farming.
- More than half of the industrial activity is devoted to the processing of food and food products; food processing is a $1 billion industry in Omaha alone.
- Omaha also became the meat packer of the world, taking the crown from Chicago; the city has 12 meat packing plants, including the major names in meat packing such as Swift's and Swanson's.
- The city was also known for Mutual of Omaha, an insurance company whose history, stability, and advertising campaigns had brought pride to Omaha.

The Insurance Industry

- Despite an uncertain economic climate, approximately 145 million people were insured by one or more life insurance policies; this equaled seven out of 10 people in the total population.
- The average ordinary life policy had a face value of $6,450 compared with $6,100 a year earlier.
- Purchases of new ordinary policies totalled $132 billion, an increase of $9.4 billion over 1970.
- The assets of legal reserve life insurance companies reached $222.1 billion, an increase of $14.8 billion over 1970; approximately $79 billion was in corporate bonds, $75 billion in mortgages, and only $20 billion in stocks.
- The new investments of life insurance companies during the year provided seven percent of the flow of financial capital from all investment sources in the nation that year.
- Nationwide, $789 billion in ordinary life insurance was in force; this represented a 7.9 percent increase over 1970 and a 116 percent increase during the past decade.
- Group life insurance represented another $581 billion, an increase of 202.5 percent over 1961.

- The average insured family nationwide had $25,700 in life insurance coverage; protection for all families was equivalent to 24 months of total disposable personal income per family.
- In Nebraska, the average amount of life insurance in force per family was $21,000.
- Approximately 86 percent of men and 74 percent of women had some type of life insurance protection.
- Ninety-two percent of men in the 45-54 age group had coverage.
- The western part of the United States had a lower incidence of life insurance ownership than did the rest of the nation.
- Benefit payments to beneficiaries and payments to policyholders passed $17 million in 1971—an increase of 94.9 percent during the past 10 years.
- That year, the industry was represented at the White House Conference on Aging, as it focused on retirement planning.

1972: Grateful Dead Fanatic

Even though Melissa Goldberg had grown up happy, she felt disenchanted by the "establishment's" hypocrisy, authoritarianism, and focus on capitalism and commercialism.

Life at Home

- Melissa Goldberg first fell under the spell of the Grateful Dead at the Monterey Pop Festival.
- Even though the Grateful Dead were sandwiched between the Who's Pete Townshend's guitar-smashing finale and Jimi Hendrix's electric guitar explosion, the Dead's long, intricate riffs captured Melissa's attention.
- Two months earlier she had abruptly left home and college behind in Madison, Wisconsin, to be part of the 1967 Summer of Love celebration well underway in San Francisco, California.
- Her father, a heart surgeon, and her mother, an English literature professor, had insisted that they knew what was best for their 19-year-old daughter.
- Melissa disagreed.
- She knew in her heart that now was the time to discover the rest of the world.
- She had grown up happy and well cared for in Madison; she even looked forward to the harsh winters when her snow-covered neighborhood felt at peace with itself.
- Then came the Vietnam War and America's invasion of that Asian country.
- Vietnam was but the first of many crimes that she had discovered during her freshman year: the virtual slavery of Negroes in Mississippi, the corruption of the industrial military complex, and the nation's materialistic obsession that robbed poor countries of opportunity.
- Melissa even came to realize that her parents—who had attended her every dance recital and piano performance—were part of the problem.
- She had been raised by the enemy.
- Even the cold winters seemed oppressive now.
- To prove her purity, she gave away all her possessions to the Salvation Army while home from college one weekend.
- Her father's response was swift and clear: He took away her car, further proving that

Melissa Goldberg became a full-fledged Deadhead at the Monterey Pop Festival.

America's ruling class was willing to do anything to crush rebellion.

- So initially, she let her parents catch her smoking marijuana.
- They first threatened to take her to the police: "I will not have illegal drugs in my house," her father had shouted as loudly as he could.
- Then they invited a friend for dinner, who turned out to be a psychiatrist intent on "letting her talk."
- She had no interest in discussing her internal hurts with a moldy old friend of her mother; besides her boyfriend was more than willing to share his stash of dope, drive her where she wanted to go, and even give her a place to stay if her parents threw her out of the house.
- The last major fight had been about the boy she was dating.
- They didn't think he was good enough for her.
- On that count, they were right.
- Although he had initially agreed—enthusiastically, in fact—to accompany her to the West Coast, when it came time to leave he proved to be as spineless and undependable as her parents had predicted he would be.
- Only one semester short of graduation from the University of Wisconsin in engineering, he elected to finish school, vowing all the while to join her the minute he got his degree.
- Melissa had no-zero-interest in waiting for a guy who could not be spontaneous and free.
- So she took to the road traveling by thumb-catching rides when she could and walking when she couldn't.

Melissa was convinced that her successful, materialistic parents were the enemy.

San Francisco's Haight-Ashbury district was ground zero for hippie culture.

- Melissa needed 13 days of hitchhiking to reach California, detouring at one point to New Mexico because the trucker was going that way, and then San Diego before reaching San Francisco.
- When she arrived, she was penniless, having given her money away to needy people along the way, and without a place to sleep.
- At the time, Melissa arrived in San Francisco's Haight-Ashbury district—Ground Zero for hippie culture—the Grateful Dead were a local phenomenon referenced often by TV commentators and bus operators ferrying middle-class tourists through Hippie City.
- The hippie hop tour through Haight-Ashbury was advertised as "The only foreign tour within the continental limits of the United States."
- The band was even photographed on their front porch for *Time* magazine's "Summer of Love" issue, making their abode a hippie White House of sorts.
- Melissa was quickly welcomed into a commune housed in a shabby chic Victorian that was exploring the emerging concepts of blending free love and free-form music.

Life on the Road

- To Melissa Goldberg, the Summer of Love in 1967 seemed to be one endless party.
- Everyone was either high on mescaline, grass or LSD; friends were living in tepees along the Big Sur, high school runaways were flocking to big harvest pot parties while she played bongos and drank red Mountain wine at all-night parties.
- As Melissa told friends back home, "it was the undressed rehearsal" for a changed world.
- When a British film crew from the BBC attempted to capture the essence of a "hippie party," they had to stop filming because there were too many naked party people.
- The footage was too risqué to be broadcast.
- Melissa had originally gone to the Monterey Pop Festival because the Jefferson Airplane and the Mamas & the Papas where there, but left in love with the Grateful Dead.
- The Grateful Dead, melded together in 1965, pioneered an eclectic style that fused elements of rock, folk, bluegrass, blues, reggae, country, jazz, psychedelia, and space rock.
- The Dead started their career as the Warlocks, a group formed in early 1965 from the remnants of a Palo Alto jug band called Mother McCree's Uptown Jug Champions.
- The first show under the new name Grateful Dead was in San Jose, California, in December 1965, at one of Ken Kesey's Acid Tests.
- In January, the Dead appeared at the Fillmore Auditorium in San Francisco and played at the Trips Festival, an early psychedelic rock show.
- Charter members of the Grateful Dead were: banjo and guitar player Jerry Garcia, guitarist Bob Weir, blues organist Ron "Pigpen" McKernan, the classically trained bassist Phil Lesh, and drummer Bill Kreutzmann.

Members of The Grateful Dead *rock and roll band.*

- The name "Grateful Dead" was chosen from an old dictionary, which defined "Grateful Dead" as "the soul of a dead person, or his angel, showing gratitude to someone who, as an act of charity, arranged his burial."
- The band's first LP, *The Grateful Dead*, was released on Warner Brothers Records in 1967.
- But their first live performance at the Monterey Pop Festival was unscheduled.
- Melissa awoke from sleep after midnight to discover an impromptu concert underway with Eric Burdon of the Animals singing "House of the Rising Sun" with Pete Townshend of The Who playing lead guitar.
- This was followed by jam sessions combining the talents of The Grateful Dead's Jerry Garcia, The Byrds, Jimi Hendrix, David Crosby, and the Jefferson Airplane.

The Grateful Dead *held a news conference after their drug bust.*

- Once the official festival began, Melissa got to hear Country Joe and the Fish sing antiwar ballads, Otis Redding mesmerizing with his energy, and Jimi Hendrix playing his Stratocaster with his teeth and then setting the guitar on fire.
- But Melissa's personal showstopper was Jerry Garcia and the Grateful Dead.
- Live performances featured long musical improvisations that made every concert unique; "Their music," wrote Lenny Kaye, "touches on ground that most other groups don't even know exists."
- She especially appreciated the Dead's decision to "borrow" nearly one million dollars' worth of Fender audio equipment to perform another free concert, this time in San Francisco.
- Even after the equipment was returned, the authorities failed to see the humor in the situation.
- Melissa desperately wanted be part of this world, where people threw off theories concerning music just as casually as her mother discussed Jewish holiday recipes.
- The idea of the moment was three-dimensional sound; the goal was for every instrument to be in stereo by fashioning every guitar and every drum set to have a right and left channel, so the audience could hear everything.
- Most bands thought this concept was technologically impossible.
- Melissa's chance to meet Jerry Garcia came because of a water balloon fight among several members of the band.
- Melissa took half a dozen blows—soaking her from head to toe—when Garcia rescued her and they started to hang out, even after the Dead were busted for pot possession and harder drugs began to circulate.
- And Melissa was unquestionably ready to join the caravan of fans when the Quick and the Dead Tour started in January 1968; the concept of the Dead spreading their vibe to the whole country was simply awesome.
- Melissa figured she was attached to the greatest show on Earth: a hippie Buffalo Bill show jammed with young, freaked-out American rock 'n' roll music.
- They took a song and turned it into a sound journey—one that sometimes had to be altered on the band's albums.

- The Grateful Dead's almost seamless, continuous soundtrack had to be cut into pieces because record companies paid royalties based on the number of tracks on an album, not the number of minutes recorded.
- Melissa trailed the Dead every step of the way; if they were playing, she was in the audience.
- She wasn't alone: One of the more unique customs of the Deadhead community was to go on tour with the band.
- Deadheads typically quit their jobs and left everything behind to follow the band from venue to venue, seeing as many shows as possible.
- The parking lot scene before and after a show resembled a street fair, complete with the sounds and smells one might expect.
- It was the "show before the show" and where friends met afterwards to exchange thoughts on the night's experience and to make plans to meet later on in the tour.
- Deadheads from around the country converged on what was known as "Shakedown Street," the main row of venders (Deadheads with goods to sell or barter with), which over the years reached mythical proportions.
- Melissa bought and sold homemade tie-dyed clothing and hemp jewelry.
- All the while, Deadheads sat around playing acoustic guitars, banging out deafening rhythms in drum circles, throwing Frisbees, or sleeping to recoup energy for that night's show.
- Different songs filled the air; once the gates opened, the experience simply moved inside.
- To keep track of her travels, Melissa kept a journal of the shows she attended, decorated with ticket stubs, pictures of friends at the shows, hand-drawn pictures, and most importantly, setlists!
- Melissa became fanatical about the setlist as a written record of the songs played (in order) during a show.
- Some Deadheads scribbled them on ticket stubs, matchboxes, or envelopes—usually in the dark—during the show.
- But Melissa was meticulous.
- She knew her setlists were part of the living legacy of the Grateful Dead and the Deadhead community.
- It wasn't always easy: Unlike most bands, the Dead didn't always end their songs.
- Often, she found, they simply segued into another song.
- Several times an entire set was nothing more than several songs played continuously.
- These song pairings encouraged a setlist shorthand that joined songs with an arrow.
- For this reason, some familiar song pairings were condensed: "China Cat Sunflower" followed by "I Know You Rider" would be written as "China/Rider," while "Scarlet Begonias" followed by "Fire on the Mountain" was recorded as "Scarlet/Fire."
- When she lost the bound notebook in a police raid, she took it as a sign that it was time to return home.
- Besides, the health of original band member Pigpen had deteriorated to the point that he

Deadheads typically quit their jobs to follow the band from venue to venue.

could no longer tour with the band; his final concert appearance was June 17, 1972, at the Hollywood Bowl.

• On June 18, 1972, Melissa made a long-distance phone call; she had not seen her parents in five years.

Life in the Community: San Francisco, California

• The flower child or hippie movement started around 1965 in San Francisco and spread across the United States, Canada, and parts of Europe.

• Inspired by the Beats of the fifties, who declared themselves independent from the "authoritarian order" of America, the Haight-Ashbury "anti-community" rested on a rejection of American commercialism.

• Haight residents eschewed the material benefits of modern life, encouraged by the distribution of free food and organized shelter by the Diggers, and the creation of institutions such as the Free Clinic for medical treatment.

• Psychedelic drug use became but one means to find a "new reality."

• According to Grateful Dead guitarist Bob Weir, "Haight-Ashbury was a ghetto of bohemians who wanted to do anything—and we did—but I don't think it has happened since. Yes, there was LSD. But Haight-Ashbury was not about drugs. It was about exploration, finding new ways of expression, being aware of one's existence."

During the "summer of love" hippies were a tourist attraction in San Francisco.

- An all-volunteer army of hippies flocked to San Francisco, congregating near the corner of Haight Street and Ashbury Street, where the world got its first view of this unique group.
- The place came to be known as the Haight-Ashbury district, where average Americans took bus tours to view the flower child phenomenon.
- Average Americans were shocked by their hair, clothing, drug experimentation and alternative lifestyles, even though most hippies were young people from prosperous middle-class homes.
- The Haight-Ashbury district was in the very center of San Francisco and incorporated Golden Gate Park.
- Musicians in the Jefferson Airplane, the Grateful Dead, and Janis Joplin's band Big Brother and the Holding Company all lived a short distance from the famous intersection.
- The prelude to the Summer of Love was the Human Be-In at Golden Gate Park on January 14, 1967, billed as a "gathering of tribes."
- Haight-Ashbury's own psychedelic newspaper, the San Francisco Oracle, commented: "A new concept of celebrations beneath the human underground must emerge, become conscious, and be shared, so a revolution can be formed with a renaissance of compassion, awareness, and love, and the revelation of unity for all mankind."
- The gathering of approximately 30,000 like-minded people made the Human Be-In the first event that confirmed there was a viable hippie scene.
- This was followed by the term "Summer of Love," when thousands of hippies gathered there, popularized by hit songs such as "San Francisco (Be Sure to Wear Some Flowers in Your Hair)" by Scott McKenzie.
- A July 7, 1967, *Time* magazine cover story on "The Hippies: Philosophy of a Subculture," and an August CBS News television report on "The Hippie Temptation" exposed the hippie subculture to

national attention and popularized the Flower Power movement across the country and around the world.
- The ever-increasing numbers of youth making a pilgrimage to the Haight-Ashbury district overwhelmed and alarmed the San Francisco authorities, whose public stance was that they would keep the hippies away.
- The mainstream media's coverage of hippie life in the Haight-Ashbury district drew youth from all over America, especially after writer Hunter S. Thompson labeled the district "Hashbury" in *The New York Times Magazine*.

The Touchhead's Guide to the Grateful Dead

The language of the Deadhead community is sometimes confusing and incomprehensible to the outsider or newbie (a Deadhead who has just "gotten on the bus"). Some language has evolved over the years through the use of mind-altering chemicals, through endless hours of conversations with other Deadheads in the parking lot before shows, and in the venues themselves. Some of the language has come about due to necessity, such as the need to alert others to the sudden appearance of law enforcement. Some of the more colorful dialect that is heard among Deadheads, especially at shows, includes:

- tripping on DNA: Going to a show with a member of your family.

- tour rats: Hardcore Deadheads who travel from show to show, live in the parking lot during a tour, earn money by selling homemade goods, or wait for a miracle ticket.

- miracle ticket: An extra ticket given to another Deadhead without a ticket free of charge.

- wooks: Hardcore backwoods hippies who attend shows wearing nothing but a pair of dirty shorts.

- ick: Tour slang to describe the common bacterial or viral infections resulting from undernourishment and overexposure while on tour.

- spin: To copy a tape.

- puddle: A larger-than-average-size dose of LSD.

- noodling: The description of the band's searching excursions during jams and solos.

- benji: A hundred-dollar bill used in case of emergencies. I think these exist in folklore alone.

- bugment: The music being so intense it makes your eyes bug out.

- crisp: A soundboard tape that has no saturation or hiss.

- the Pepto pink: Bob Weir's painfully pink guitar.

- teef: To steal something small and of no significance.

- de-reek: Getting rid of "truck mouth" with mouthwash or a breath mint.

- puppied: Being so relaxed that you want to snuggle with somebody.

- spinning madly: The copying of several tapes.

- biscuit shows: Good shows in out-of-the-way venues only the most hardcore Deadheads attend.

- family: Friends that are Deadheads.

- get on the bus: The moment people realize they are Grateful Dead fans.

As stated previously, Deadheads can often be found frantically writing down names of the songs during shows. Many years ago, Deadheads started using setlist shorthand in their setlists. Some examples of this setlist shorthand are found throughout the Deadhead community:

- BIODTL: Beat It On Down the Line

- FOTD: Friend of the Devil

- GDTRFB: Goin' Down the Road Feelin' Bad

- GDTS: Grateful Dead Ticket Sales

- NFA: Not Fade Away

- NSB: New Speedway Boogie

- TLEO: They Love Each Other

- WALSTIB: What a Long Strange Trip It's Been

- PITB: Playing in the Band

Line Donkeys, Deadheads that enter the venue with a backpack filled with food, books, clothing, etc., are a source of irritation at shows. Line Donkeys hold up the line, as all bags and purses are emptied, checked, and repacked before being admitted through the gates. Line Donkeys can easily add an extra 20 minutes to the entrance process if more than one are in line. Wedgers, the adult version of "budgers" found in elementary school, are also held in low regard. Lines will explode in choruses of displeasure when wedgers try and slime into the line.

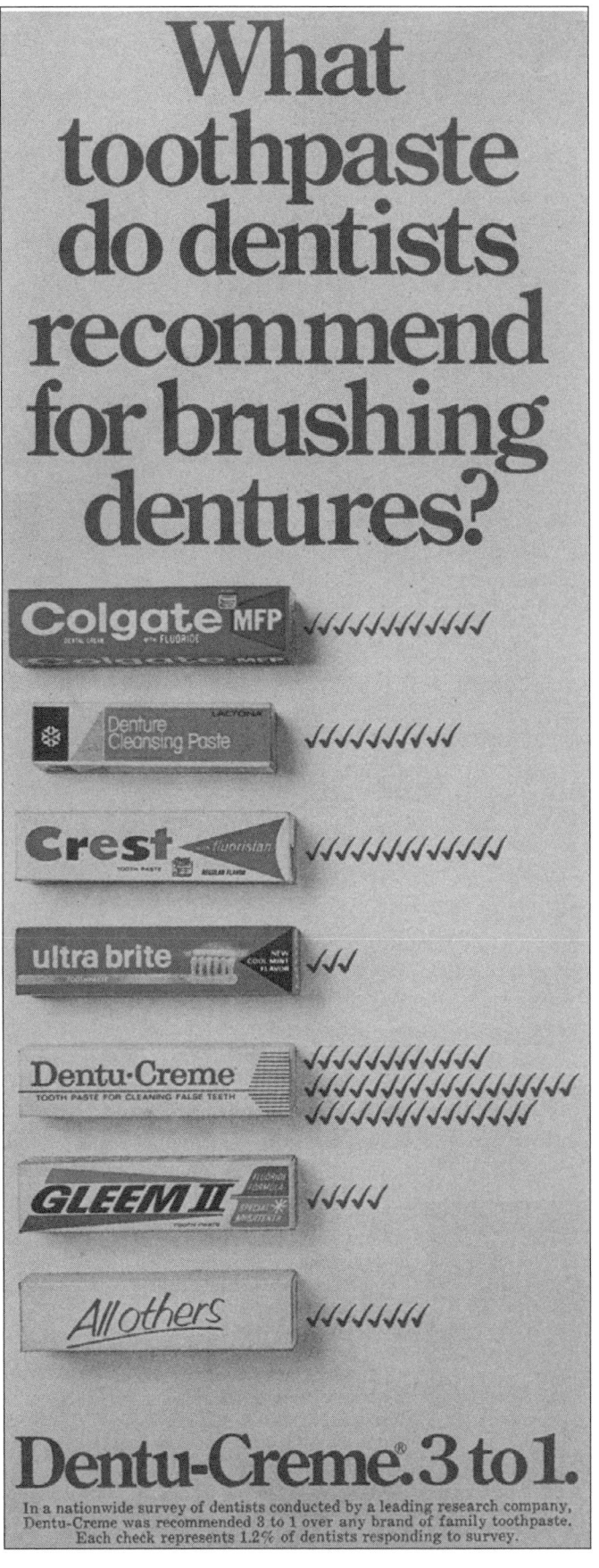

1972: Wrigly Family Engineer

Oliver Pitt, the 22-year-old grandnephew of the founder of Wrigley's Chewing Gum, worked for his family's company as a computer engineer.

Life at Home

- Oliver Pitt loved Chicago and couldn't wait to return after graduation from The Massachusetts Institute of Technology in Cambridge.
- He recently purchased—using some graduation money—an 1880s warehouse in Chicago's "near-Loop" area, planning to create loft apartments in the huge old building.
- The five-story brick building with broad windows was once used as a manufacturing facility; its hardwood floors, which he had refinished, show the ancient holes where machinery had been bolted to the floor.
- He especially loved the way the 12-foot ceilings create a liberating sense of spaciousness and independence.
- The building, like several on the block, had been used for warehousing since the 1950s, when manufacturing techniques began demanding more flexible space.
- Oliver believes the renovation of this building and the revitalization of the area will be an important contribution to the city.
- While New York City actively encouraged residential use of lofts, it was a brand-new concept in Chicago, where current zoning laws restrict residential use above the first floor of loft buildings.
- The city had nearly 300 commercial loft buildings containing 25 million square feet of space; the greatest concentration was just north of the Loop in a district loosely defined by the lake, the Chicago River, the North Branch and Chicago Avenue.
- Raw space, unimproved since it was built, rents for $0.90 to $1.50 per square foot; space with improvements goes for a maximum of $2.80.
- Oliver was engaged to a woman he met in college, Judy Kimbro, who worked on Wall Street in New York.
- She clearly and repeatedly stated her desire to have her own career and retain her maiden name after their marriage—an attitude that was causing considerable friction; he wanted a modern wife, but not too modern.

Oliver Pitt worked on the next generation of computers for Wrigley's Chewing Gum.

- To keep his relationship with Judy alive, he made frequent phone calls and writes letters, but felt a distance growing between them.
- He even experimented with sending little sketches and poems over fax machines he bought for each of them, but the transmission took 10 to 15 minutes a page, spoiling the spontaneity and fun of the pictures.
- He lived in an apartment purchased by his mother as an "investment" while he completed the renovations of the loft; the eight-room flat had double French doors that opened off his second-floor bedroom, allowing the sounds of the city to rush in.
- His mother furnished the apartment with Mission oak she found in a secondhand store; he supplemented her purchases with a large art deco armoire and two Tiffany lamps from the turn of the century.
- The apartment was close enough for him to hear jazz wafting from a nearby club where he loved to go at night.
- After four and a half years away at M.I.T., he was more than ready to return to the Midwest and his beloved Chicago.
- He was also happy to return to a city that understands the need for America to fight for its place in the world, including defeating the communists in Vietnam.
- Although he was number 10 in the draft board's lottery, he did not join the military because of his 4-F status, caused by arthritis.
- His family doctor provided the draft board with a letter saying he was unable to enter combat without taking his daily medication; the draft board provided him with a deferment without his having to participate in the induction process, where the normal military physical is given.

- In Chicago he felt at home, especially since he took a job with Wrigley.
- He grew up hearing tales about his famous granduncle, William Wrigley, who was known for his advertising audacity.
- Around the turn of the century, Wrigley obtained the number and address of every telephone subscriber in the United States and mailed each one a sample package of gum.
- A few years later, with a recession threatening, he increased his advertising, spending $250,000 in New York City alone, knowing his ads would have more impact during slow times.
- As important, he focused his advertising on a handful of flavors such as Juicy Fruit, Spearmint and Doublemint, dumping flavors such as peach, blood, banana and vanilla pepsin.

The Wrigley family was part of Chicago's growth.

- The company spent one seventh of its total income, or about $25 million, on advertising, most of it continuing to focus on a basic message: "Chewing gum is enjoyable and relaxing, a pleasant, inexpensive way of winding down that you can enjoy almost anywhere."
- In his household, which included 26 rooms on three stories near the lake, Uncle Wrigley was a legend.
- His mother, heiress to the Wrigley wealth through her mother, loved to tell stories around the dinner table, especially when Oliver's father was present; she didn't think her husband had as much get-up-and-go as her uncle had, and didn't mind if people knew it.

Life at Work

- Oliver's office was in downtown Chicago, only a few miles from where he grew up.
- Although officially a trainee, he reported each week to his cousin William Wrigley, the 39year-old grandson of founder William Wrigley, Jr.
- A third-generation, family-managed corporation, all Wrigley made, they liked to say, is "gum and money."
- Currently, 32 billion sticks of chewing gum disappear into American mouths each year.
- In 1970, Americans spent $272.8 million on chewing gum.
- Forty-five percent of the gum chewed in America came from Wrigley, which grossed $176 million last year, for satisfying America's "non-addictive habit."
- Ninety percent of the sugar content—and, as such, its taste—is gone in the first 10 minutes.
- Early on, Oliver decided that he was not interested in sales or management, but found his calling in college with the emergence of computers; he believed he could help turn Wrigley into a model of efficiency through the magic of computer technology.
- He even talked about the day all employees would have computers on their desks; some people at work, particularly those who don't type and don't care to learn, are convinced that this will not be necessary.
- The company used General Electric computers, which exited the data processing business, and most of the executives believe that now is the logical time to switch to IBM, which dominates the U.S. market.
- Oliver wanted to take another look at a small, $100 million sales company on the West Coast known as Intel.

- Unfortunately, Intel's earnings were suffering from too much growth and many in the Wrigley company were convinced that Intel would not be around in a decade, when they would need to update their equipment.
- Many believe Sperry-Rand or Control Data will be IBM's primary competitor in the future.
- Wrigley attempted to expand its product use into the workplace; a psychological study widely circulated within the company reported that a secretary who chewed gum was 19 percent more efficient than one who doesn't, and tends not to tap her feet or squirm in her chair while typing.
- Since Wrigley believed that gum belonged in the office, twice daily a woman walked through the Wrigley building with a tray of gum, encouraging everyone to take a stick or two; on Fridays, employees were permitted to take a couple of packs home for the weekend.
- Oliver appreciated the missionary zeal for gum chewing at Wrigley, but has banned gum from the processing room, fearing that a misplaced wad will gum up his always-temperamental computers.

Life in the Community: Chicago, Illinois

- Chicago was known for many things, but Oliver placed its pizza and jazz high on his list of favorites.
- A perfect night, especially when his fiancée visited, included a trip to Pizzeria Uno and a swing by a jazz club.
- At Pizzeria Uno's, the cradle of Chicago-style pizza, his favorite was a deep-dish cheese and sausage; another favorite restaurant for the couple was Chez Paul, where he asked Judy to marry him.
- Opened in 1969 by Bill Contos, Chez Paul offerd first-class service with Wedgwood china, Baccarat crystal, linens on the tables and food worthy of the setting.
- The night Judy was engaged, she had terrine of pheasant with pistachios, veal normande and asparagus hollandaise; neither of them can remember what he ate that night.
- When she was in town, the next stop after dinner was always music, often to a small jazz club that catered to Chicago natives who grew up enjoying the city's unique style of music.
- Chicago jazz grew out of the work of trumpeter Bix Beiderbecke, who was nurtured by an enthusiastic and understanding audience in the 1920s.
- Beiderbecke and his band, The Wolverines, started the white jazz movement, which blossomed in Chicago through other groups as well, such as The Austin High Gang.
- This was further enhanced by the work of Jelly Roll Morton, who played his piano in the city for nearly five years.
- Oliver went to a show at the club near his house several times a week after work, always limiting himself to two drinks before going home.
- His father used to take him there, and would often be asked to sit in with the band to play his smooth, sweet clarinet—one of Oliver's fondest memories of his dad.
- Two years ago, his father died; he had been drinking and drove his car into a tree while traveling at a very high rate of speed, leaving no skid marks on the road.

Chewing Gum through the Ages

- Humans have always compulsively chewed non-food items of some kind; down through history they have nibbled on their own fingers and, if agile enough, their toenails.
- Betel nut is a favorite in Asia, whale blubber is chewed in the Arctic and chicle in South America.
- The ancient Greeks, who were advanced in so many ways, favored sap from the mastic tree.
- American colonists munched on spruce tree resins, and later, on sweetened paraffin wax.
- H.L. Hollingsworth of Columbia University concluded in 1939 that gum chewing is a form of "retrogression to the entire erotic patterns of infancy" and a means of "suppressing the biting instincts" left over from prehistoric man.

Oliver's office was in downtown Chicago.

- Modern gum is a relatively recent product; according to one legend, General Santa Ana, conqueror of the Alamo, brought chicle to Manhattan in 1869.
- Then president-in-exile of Mexico, he was looking for ways to make money and happened to meet Thomas Adams, an American merchant and part-time inventor.
- Santa Ana showed Adams how to chew the dried sap of the sapodilla tree that grows in the jungles of the Mexican Yucatan peninsula.
- Adams's first efforts at transforming the sap into a useful rubber failed; then, with the help of his 12-year-old son, Adams boiled the chicle until it was soft, rolled it in sugar and thus created Adams New York Chewing Gum-Snapping and Stretching.

- Unfortunately, the sapodilla tree, the source of the sap, resists cultivation, preferring to flourish in the jungles of Mexico, Guatemala and British Honduras.
- To obtain the sap required climbing 70 feet in the air, where the sap flowed best, all the while avoiding poisonous snakes, malaria-bearing mosquitoes and the chicle fly, which can cause cancerous growths in the ears and nose.
- Today most gums have a synthetic base, eliminating the need to brave life-threatening dangers for a stick of gum.
- Chewing gum has appeared in a variety of forms through the years, including Love Gum, Fight the Red Menace Gum, Forbidden Fruit and Ox Heart Peppermint gums, and even Peerless Chips by the Texas Gum Company.
- Throughout history, the sale of chewing gum has increased when people were deprived or anxious; sales zoomed, for example, during Prohibition, World War II, and after the 1964 U.S. Surgeon General's report linking smoking to cancer.
- Today, advertising is being used to increase gum's popularity; Americans are urged to stretch their coffee breaks with gum, and some teachers even offer gum as a reward for good work.
- Wrigley prides itself on the fact that its gum has not changed size or shape; a stick of gum today is the same weight it was 70 years ago.
- However, the packaging has changed through the years; the air has been squeezed out of the package to get a tighter wrap, so the gum will have a longer shelf life-approximately six months.

Wrigley Advertising Letter to Merchants, May 20, 1907

"We want to HAND YOU fifty cents' worth of Wrigley Spearmint Gum, WITHOUT COST. Present this ticket at once to your jobber or wagon man and you WILL RECEIVE a box of Spearmint Gum containing 10 five-center packages ABSOLUTELY FREE.

We are starting in on a LARGE ADVERTISING CAMPAIGN and our object in GIVING YOU the half-box free is to have the goods in YOUR STORE when YOUR customers ask for it.

We know that SPEARMINT will be a big seller because our FLAVOR LASTS and the QUALITY IS IN THE GUM....

We have spent LARGE SUMS in the past two years advertising our WRIGLEY SPEARMINT GUM in the larger cities, primarily in streetcars and newspapers....Our goods have merit and when the CONSUMER once gets a chance to try OUR GUM, he forces the retail dealer to keep it in stock. Therefore, in order to get the FIRST box into 10 of the principal stores in your town, at the same time that the advertising posters are put up, we are making this OFFER TO YOU."

—William Wrigley

1973: Vietnam POW

Navy pilot Lieutenant Commander William Ellis spent nearly six years as a POW in a North Vietnam prison, dreaming of life back in the States with his wife and four children.

Life at Home

- On June 30, 1967, William Ellis carefully placed a letter from his wife in a box, the contents of which were carefully arranged by date and included a letter for each day of his absence.
- Twelve years of marriage had not dimmed their devotion.
- Besides, he needed to keep abreast of the activities of his four children.
- William, 10, wanted to spend the summer swimming and playing.
- Lucius, seven, was being tutored during the summer so he could catch up in school and calm down his temper.
- Elizabeth, four, loved horses and was pestering her grandparents to buy her a pony.
- Anne, two, was determined to be the center of attention.
- William's wife, Elizabeth, and the four children were spending the summer with her parents in the mountains of North Carolina.
- June 30, 1967, was also the day William flew his 200th combat mission.
- When William and his wingman took off from the USS Constellation in their A4-C Skyhawks, the mission was described as a routine armed reconnaissance over North Vietnam.
- The flight was uneventful, and the two pilots were returning when an explosion caused William to lose control of the plane.
- He pulled the ejector handle and was thrust from the craft as it plummeted into the jungle.
- Within moments of landing, he was assaulted by villagers who tore at his clothes while kicking and screaming at him.
- Six men and women dragged him, nearly naked, through the North Vietnamese village, hitting him for show and sport.
- Particular delight was taken in kicking his badly sprained and rapidly swelling ankle, while children were encouraged to throw rocks at him.

Navy Pilot William Ellis was a prisoner of war for six years.

William flew his 200ᵗʰ combat mission on June 30, 1967.

- When uniformed North Vietnamese soldiers arrived, the villagers were praised for their bravery.
- William was taken by truck to the "Hanoi Hilton," the central prisoner-of-war facility in North Vietnam.
- Immediately, a fierce interrogation began.
- Training told William to provide only his name, rank and serial number in accordance with the Geneva Convention.
- The North Vietnamese responded that Vietnam was not a declared war, and that he was a war criminal.
- Then he was beaten with hoses.
- His right arm was pulled behind his back so severely, his shoulder dislocated; the pain was excruciating.
- As long as he refused to talk or to denounce his country, the North Vietnamese withheld medical treatment.
- After four days of interrogation, he was placed in a cell measuring seven by nine feet and furnished with only a mat on the floor and a dented bucket for his waste.
- His ankle was broken, his many bruises were healing badly and his shoulder would not stop throbbing.
- For weeks, he was unable to sit and barely able to eat, while his body became covered with boils and sores.
- He was in solitary confinement—no talks with fellow fliers, no letters from home, no news of Elizabeth and the four children.
- For 18 months the days passed slowly, the loneliness was beyond words, and despair lingered constantly.
- Guards occasionally passed him food and allowed him out into the courtyard to empty his waste bucket; on seven occasions over 18 months he was allowed to take a cold bath from a sink.

- Quickly, he learned that whenever he encountered one of his keepers, he must bow; failure to show respect resulted in another beating.
- After the North Vietnamese attempted to set his broken ankle and failed, William rebroke the ankle and set it himself.
- Some prisoners were still on crutches months after being captured.
- Through trial and error, William learned that he could communicate with his neighboring cell by tapping out messages in code and writing notes using the rough toilet paper, ink made from cigarette ashes and a pen fashioned from bamboo.
- But most days were spent quietly, with nothing—absolutely nothing—to do.
- William passed the time thinking about how the children were growing up, what they might be doing and how they were coping without a father.
- He reassured himself that Elizabeth was a strong woman; in addition, his in-laws, Colonel and Mrs. DesChamps, were not people to be trifled with.
- He knew they were praying for him, and that his government was trying to gain his release.

After William's capture, children were assigned to guard him.

Life at Work

- Three years after his capture, conditions for William were improving at the Hanoi Hilton.
- He was moved out of solitary confinement and placed in a room with 55 other men—mostly pilots shot down on a mission.
- Food and baths were scheduled, he could occasionally shave, and was allowed to receive and send letters home—letters that tried to reassure his family that he was fine and would be home soon.
- All correspondence needed to be on a piece of paper no larger than a postcard.

American prisoner of war led by a Vietnamese soldier.

- He was told he could receive one postcard-sized letter a month, but received far, far fewer.
- He believed his captors must have been holding some mail, but there did not appear to be any pattern to it.
- Even with better conditions, he was periodically tortured on the flimsiest excuse—made to kneel on a small pebble for hours, bamboo slivers were inserted under his fingernails, and he was beaten with a strap.
- To maintain his health through the long ordeal, he exercised regularly, doing 100 pushups and sit-ups twice a day and running in place.
- On a diet of either pumpkin or cabbage soup, he lost 60 pounds.
- He knew from experience that if he did not eat his food quickly, it would be stolen by the rats infesting the prison.

- The prisoners exercised together, played games and "saw" movies through the eyes of a narrator.
- William's rendition of *To Kill a Mockingbird* was a particular favorite on movie night.
- Another favorite pastime was "grapevine"; when new prisoners were brought into any of the half-dozen POW camps in the area, they were exhaustively debriefed and the information passed from camp to camp.
- As a result, William knew about the navy's sweeping changes in hair regulations, the skin index of *Playboy* magazine, and how the World Series turned out.
- Letters from home indicated that his mother was doing well, his oldest son William started the prep school attended by Col. DesChamps, Lucius had been held back and was out of control, Elizabeth was quite the equestrian, and Anne loved to read.

New prisoners were exhaustively debriefed.

- Elizabeth spent her time calling and writing to the wives of the other POWs.
- As a result of her visits to Washington, dozens of congressmen knew her on a first-name basis.
- By the end of 1972, word was spreading at the prison camp that something was afoot.
- The loudspeaker in the dormitory still spewed English-language propaganda, but the guards had lost interest in the strict enforcement of prisoner routines.
- William was excited and scared; after more than five years, he might actually go home, but to what?
- Would he recognize his own children? Did his wife still love him? What would he do when he returned to the States? Certainly, he would never be able to fly again.
- The days went by faster, while the nights—when fears leapt up—dragged.
- In early 1973, the release of POWs was official; they were to be set free in stages during the next several months.
- The very ill were to go first, the remainder in order of their capture.
- William was able to say good-bye to several men who had been granted release.
- In March, he was on a truck to the Hanoi airport with no ceremony, no emotion, and many of his guards absent.

After their official release, POWs were set free in stages over several months.

- Yet, fear remained; the North Vietnamese could stop the release at any moment.
- All of the men were cautioned to act with reserve and decorum.
- It was not until William was aboard the Air Force C-141 and felt its wheels leave the ground that he could finally relax.
- Inside the plane, a cheer rang out.
- "Home, take me home," was all William could think.
- However, the first stop was Clark Air Force Base, Philippines, where the former POWs were admitted to the hospital for a checkup.
- For the first time in years, William put on a new navy uniform.

- He learned that, during his time as a POW, he had been promoted to commander.
- He now could look forward to quality food, rest in a real bed, and then a stopover in Hawaii.
- Ahead is Elizabeth, their children, and the future William thought he had lost.

Life in the Community: The Hanoi Hilton

- The Hanoi Hilton was named by the American fliers imprisoned there.
- Located on the outskirts of Hanoi, it was originally a French prison built shortly after World War II.
- It was surrounded by a red wall topped by several strands of barbed wire, with an entrance gate on a quiet street of the North Vietnamese capital.
- Inside was a large courtyard, and a long, low building that housed the camp and a special "interview room."
- In this room, the myriad of propaganda films were made that included interviews with communist journalists from Poland, East Germany and Cuba.
- North Vietnam was reportedly making money selling these films, along with pictures of downed pilots.
- Film footage of captured U.S. airmen, much of it obviously staged, was distributed widely in Iron Curtain countries and sold to Western outlets through East German and Japanese firms.
- In most of these films, the same prisoners were shown time after time being paraded through the streets, playing table tennis, carrying trays of food and attending church services.
- Inside the compound were clusters of buildings containing cells for one or two of the Americans.
- The crowded sleeping rooms were furnished with wooden pallets and straw mats.
- Every building had a loudspeaker that broadcast English-language news and propaganda.
- American prisoners were fed twice a day, and permitted to wash six times a week and shave twice a week.
- During the 1970s, a prisoner's day at the Hanoi Hilton started at 6 a.m.
- For the next four hours, the men washed, exercised and attended morning language classes.
- By 10 a.m., the first meal was served, eaten from porcelain-covered tin plates and cups.
- This was followed by more classes and exercise.
- At 3:30 p.m., prisoners listened to a news broadcast in English, a strong focus being the antiwar movement in America.
- The second and final meal of the day was brought at 4 p.m. And usually consisted of cabbage or pumpkin soup with bread or rice.
- The prisoners were not allowed access to the Red Cross parcels of concentrated food.
- Communist-style books translated into English were available.
- The first American shot down was captured in August 1964; by 1969, 200 Americans had been missing for more than three and a half years—longer than any U.S. serviceman was held prisoner in World War II.
- More than 1,600 Americans are listed as missing.

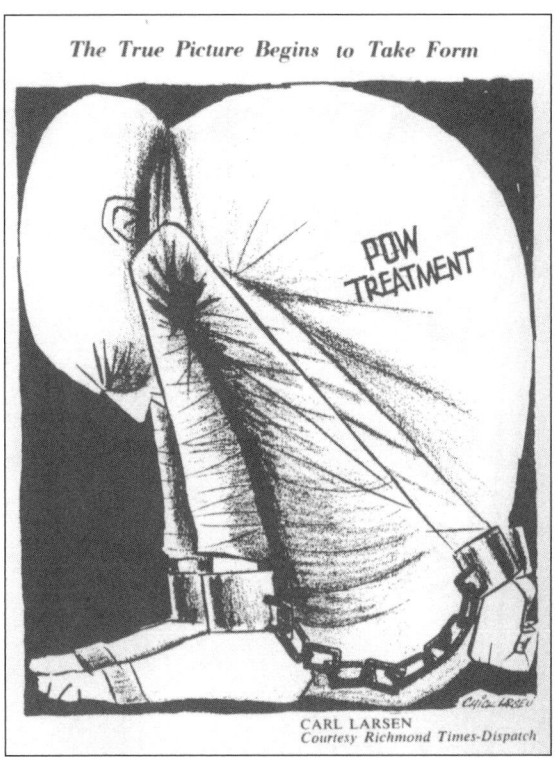

The True Picture Begins to Take Form

POW TREATMENT

CARL LARSEN
Courtesy Richmond Times-Dispatch

- The mass deaths of the Korean War, when 2,700 American prisoners died in captivity, have not been repeated in North Vietnam; currently, only 55 of the acknowledged POWs in Vietnam are reported to have died in captivity.

1973: Summer Intern at Family's Coal Company

At the end of the Woodberry Forest School year, Charles Ethridge returned home to work in the family coal business, while his friends and family spent the summer at the shore.

Life at Home

- Charles Ethridge was not happy.
- As school at Woodberry Forest in Virginia draws to a close, Charles was told he will be returning to Jasper, Alabama, despite his plans to visit friends this summer.
- After all his hard work at school, his father wanted him to learn the family coal business, while the rest of the family vacationed at Gulf Shores for three months.
- Not only that, classmate Punky Arthur invited him to spend a couple of weeks with his family in Maine, but his father was firm: This summer will be spent in Jasper working for the Cathcart Coal Company as the low man, assigned to work in the field.

- Worse yet, even the few people he knew in Jasper will be gone to the beach or the mountains.
- His father insisted that even if the family decided to sell the coal company, the Jasper community would continue to thrive on coal, and Charles needed to know coal.
- The only thing Charles knew is that Jasper is the last place he planned on settling when he finished prep school and college—the absolute last place.
- He believed his future was in Atlanta, Washington or New York; he had no desire to be a big fish in a pond of 12,000 people nestled in the Appalachian foothills northwest of Birmingham.
- But as the only son of Edward Ethridge and the heir apparent to the Cathcart fortune, he had little choice right now.
- After all, the Cathcarts were Jasper, having first arrived in 1893.
- Ancestors included several men who served in the United States Congress and Senate.

Charles Ethridge worked summers in the family business.

The Ethridge home

- Charles's great-grandfather was majority leader of the Senate, while his great-great-uncle was Speaker of the House of Representatives.
- Over the years, thanks to hard work, good politics and well-timed capital, the family had acquired major financial interests in Jasper's largest bank, the coal company, a land development company and Jasper's only radio station.
- Throughout history, Cathcart men have been raised to run one or another of the family businesses.
- Unfortunately for the family fortune, Charles's grandfather and grandmother produced only daughters.
- Marion, the eldest daughter, married Edward Ethridge, son of a local doctor and an honors graduate of the University of Alabama Law School; thus, the torch was passed to Edward, who now handles most of the family's affairs and was recently elected to the Board of Trustees of his alma mater.
- Charles loved and admired his family, but he simply wished to chart his own course.
- Since leaving Jasper to attend school in Virginia two years ago, his eyes have been opened to the possibilities of the wider world, leaving him little patience for the small, backward ideas of his former high school mates.
- Surrounded by bright students from throughout the South and Midwest, Charles was just beginning to grasp his potential when he was summoned home.
- Now, with the Arab oil embargo just under way and gas queues forming across the nation, a worldwide call has arisen for alternatives to foreign oil—including coal.
- Charles's father thought this could be a good—no, make that a great—year for domestic coal.
- After all, now that a cloud has formed around that darling of science, nuclear energy, and the Arabs have cut off America from its precious oil supplies, new life was being pumped into an old product—a great year indeed.
- The Ethridges' two-story home was about 110 years old, located on the finest street in town, and had six bedrooms, a large kitchen area, living room, den, a sewing room for Charles's mother and a small office for his father.
- The household was normally managed by a full-time maid/cook, who went to the Gulf Shores each summer with Charles's mother Anne, and his 16-year-old, wheelchair-bound sister Elizabeth, who

was in a serious automobile accident a year ago while returning from a school sporting event, where she was a cheerleader.
- She became a paraplegic and required around-the-clock care.
- The family insisted on only the safest vehicles for their children and often wondered what it would have taken to keep Elizabeth safe.

Life at Work and Prep School

- The 1,000-acre Woodberry Forest School, located in the foothills of central Virginia, was bounded on one side by the Rapidan River.
- The campus included hundreds of acres of woodlands, a working farm, a nine-hole golf course, and ample space for outdoor recreation such as hunting and fishing.
- Established in 1889, the school was well-known for offering the latest technology and superior athletic fields and facilities such as the Dick Gym.
- The enrollment at the time was 350 with 45 faculty members.
- Tuition for boarding students was $3,600 a year, with day students paying $1,800 annually.
- Charles lived in the Walker Building, the central school building and residential home to sophomores, juniors and seniors.
- He liked the rhythm of the school, including attending chapel services every Sunday after advisee dinner.
- A typical Monday, Wednesday or Thursday included breakfast from 7:15 to 7:50 a.m., morning classes, lunch at 1 p.m., athletics and extracurricular activities from 3:40 to 5:30 p.m., seated dinner with faculty from 7:45 to 8:45 p.m., followed by study periods running until 10 p.m.
- Woodberry has mandatory lights out for all students, generally at 10:30 p.m. During the week, 11 p.m. on Fridays and 1 a.m. on Saturday nights.
- The curriculum, the school liked to say, prepared students for not only the University of Virginia and the University of North Carolina, but also for colleges such as Davidson, Washington and Lee, Princeton and Yale.
- He had known since he was small that once he reached high school age he would be attending prep school at Woodberry.

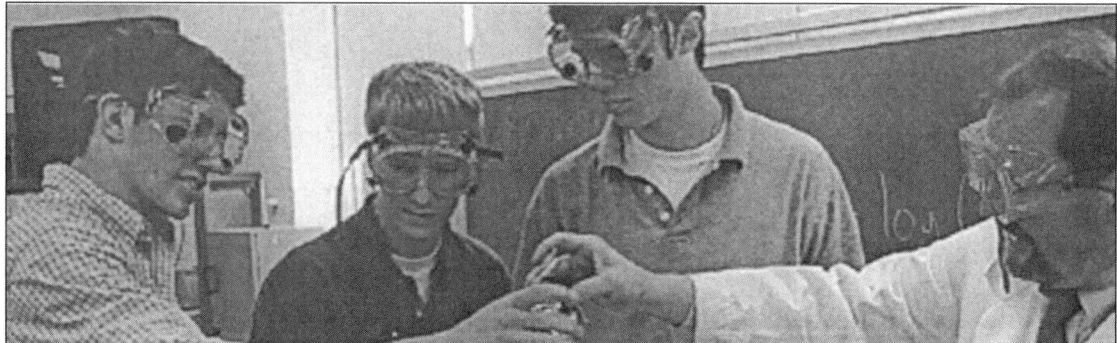

The Woodberry curriculum prepared students for the nation's finest colleges.

- After school desegregation began and the violence in schools rose, Charles was pleased that he had a place to which he could escape.
- The public high school he would have attended is integrated, but still self-segregated, with black and white students rarely mixing during classes or lunch breaks.
- On some days tensions were so high that changing classes in the hall could be dangerous if someone said the wrong thing at the wrong time.
- Woodberry was experiencing little of this trauma.

Life in the Community: Jasper, Alabama

- The city was named in honor of Sergeant William Jasper, a Revolutionary War soldier.
- Coal propelled its growth from a hamlet of only 200 people in 1886 to a town of more than 3,000 people just four years later.
- Most of the coal was shipped to Birmingham, 45 miles to the southeast, for the production of iron and steel.
- With a population of 12,000, Jasper's major customer for coal was the power industry.
- Alabama Power was the largest single buyer, replacing coal's traditional markets which formerly included the railroads and commercial heating.
- U.S. reliance on coal declined from nearly 50 percent of U.S. primary energy consumption at the end of World War II to about 18 percent today.
- Through the years, the industry had changed, too; with increased mechanization came fewer workers, most of whom at Cathcart Coal were over 40, with many of those approaching retirement.
- Cathcart Coal extracted the mineral from surface mines, using 100-foot-tall draglines to scoop up 15 cubic yards of topsoil at a time.
- Fifty years after the end of Prohibition, Jasper remains dry, with only private clubs such as the Walker County Country Club allowed to serve alcohol.

Changing America

- Heinz Kohut's book, *Analysis of the Self,* emphasized self-worth rather than instinctual drives, a challenge to current psychoanalytic theory.

The Woodberry campus included ample space for outdoor recreation.

- The United States Supreme Court ruled that employment advertisements could no longer specify gender.
- A cigarette-pack-size electronic brain-wave reader was developed that could detect and signal lapses in concentration.
- The median sales price of a single-family house was $28,900, up from $20,000 in 1968.
- Oregon became the first state to decriminalize marijuana.
- Cargo handling at most international airports was computerized; other everyday uses for the mechanical brain included "computer dating," a craze that swept the nation.
- More than 80 percent of General Motors cars were equipped with radial tires, up from 11 percent two years earlier.
- The percentage of foreign-born Americans fell to 4.7 percent.
- With one out of three meals eaten away from home, approximately one-quarter of the family food budget was spent in restaurants.

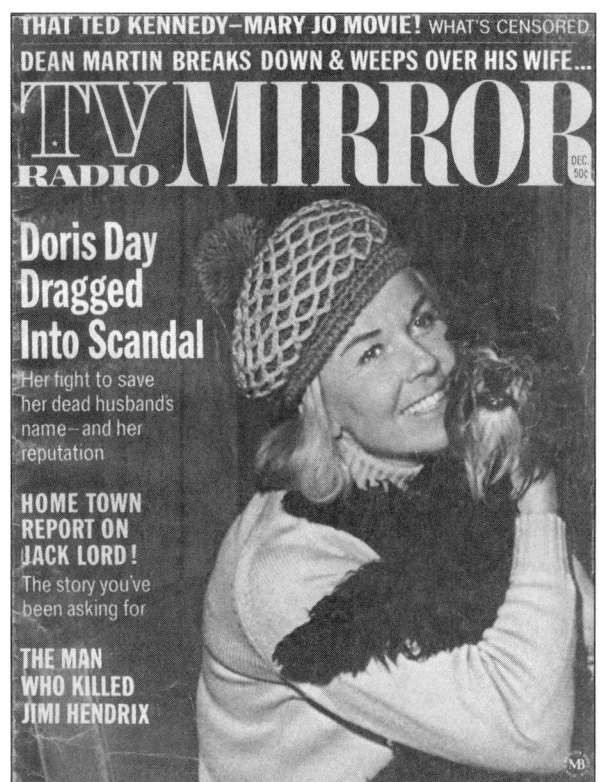

- Frederick Smith, son of the founder of Dixie Greyhound, invested $72 million in a mail service to deliver international packages within 24 hours; for $5 a package customers could buy Federal Express service.
- Fifty rock stars earned from $2 to $6 million a year.
- An estimated 600,000 people attended the Watkins Glen Rock Music Festival to hear the Grateful Dead and the Allman Brothers.
- The American Psychiatric Association revised its categorization of homosexuality, saying it was no longer considered a mental disorder.
- The Supreme Court allowed the use of local, not national standards to define when pornography is obscene.
- The University of Miami provided an athletic scholarship to a woman.
- Interest grew in Pentecostal and charismatic religions, as well as Eastern movements such as Hare Krishna, Zen and I Ching.

1973: Basketball Player & Coach

The day Reggie Earl Highlander was asked, as a student at one high school, to be an assistant coach at a rival school, was the day he became a real coach.

Life at Home

- In a hospital ward jammed with the latest crop of Baby Boomers, Reggie Earl Highlander looked diminutive to those who were polite, and downright scrawny to those who weren't.
- In 1948, the situation was the same in hospitals across America.
- Reggie's father was an auto mechanic with a wealth of experience keeping Government Issue machinery running down the muddy roads of Europe with a few tricks he had learned at his own father's knee.
- His mother was an English teacher who still believed—when no one else seemed to care—in using adverbs properly, when to use whom instead of who, and what a gerund might be.
- At age six, Reggie was small and skinny, and at 16, he was short and skinny.
- A mediocre but enthusiastic athlete, Reggie tried track, football and basketball.
- He liked basketball best, even though he lacked the proper body dynamics to hit a free throw, drive hard to the basket with his left hand or block out a really big opponent.
- His gift—and it was truly a gift—was the ability to anticipate his opponent's next move, predict where a teammate would be open, and analyze a player's tendencies.
- As a teen, Reggie could watch a pickup game for a few minutes and immediately know how to stop a player's jump shot or shut down his next drive.
- Or Reggie could tell his buddies how to set their shoulders, position their feet, or force the opposition to be unable to use his strengths.
- Reggie practiced much of his greatest athletic heroism in his head.
- Even when he was a little boy, everyone called him "Coach."
- Growing up in Grand Rapids, Michigan, Reggie worked just hard enough to avoid periodic "talks" with his parents concerning his "future."
- Reggie already knew his future—coach of the greatest basketball teams in the world.

Reggie Highlander became a basketball coach before graduating high school.

Reggie went to a school where football, and basketball, were very important.

- How many times had he changed the complexion of a game by crowding the center or forcing the point guard to hurry his passes?
- He would start coaching the mites and midgets in the YMCA, trek from gym to smelly gym in high school, and work his way toward college.
- That was the plan.
- First a small college—for a few years—where he could display his skills before moving into a Division I program eligible to play in the annual NCAA tournament.
- And best of all, UCLA coach John Wooden had demonstrated that a basketball coach can be both a gentleman and a winner.
- At college basketball tournament time, Reggie and the television set were inseparable.
- He watched every nuance and mentally recorded every gesture.
- Coaching at the college level was his destiny, even though he had stopped growing when he reached 5'6" and 148 pounds.
- Then, the unthinkable happened.
- The much-acclaimed and much-loved coach at a rival high school in the area was killed in an automobile crash.
- It was mid-season for a team with state championship potential.
- The team's assistant coach was fully capable of running the team, but he needed help.
- Reggie was flabbergasted when he was invited to a meeting in the boardroom of one of Grand Rapids' largest banks.
- There he was met by his principal, the rival school's principal, several coaches, and the Superintendent of Education.
- In what they admitted was an exceptionally unusual move, they were asking a student at one school to be an assistant coach at a rival school.
- The two teams had already met in league play—with each team winning once—and were unlikely to meet again.
- The delegation of adults reassured Reggie that he was not being disloyal to his school if he took the assignment.
- That was the day Reggie became a real coach.
- By the time Reggie Highlander entered college, he was well recognized in the coaching circles of the Midwest.
- The high school team he helped coach had not won the state championship, but the skills of three players had improved so markedly they were offered scholarships to play college ball.

Star players were slow to accept Reggie's advice.

- With more tools—especially scouting films of the opposing team—Reggie had proved himself to be a veritable genius at breaking down the tendencies of the opposition.
- At first, Reggie passed along all his advice to the head coach instead of talking with the players themselves.
- Quickly, his ideas paid dividends.
- Once his players knew that the opposing team's point guard always pointed his right foot in the direction he was going to pass, interceptions came more frequently.
- Knowing that a forward liked to dribble deep into the corner before passing made double teaming easier.
- So when Reggie turned his attention to the individuals on his team, they listened.
- One tall, gangly sophomore was taught how to leverage his size by pivoting off the hip of his opponent.
- Reggie taught the team's center that when he blocked out for a rebound, he could control more space if he set up a little farther away from the basket.
- At the annual athletic banquet, Reggie was singled out for his contributions; his future seemed assured.
- Then, at the University of Michigan, he was simply one anonymous freshman among thousands on the gigantic campus.
- His freshman year was spent surviving college in huge lecture halls, noisy dorms, and more free time than he had ever experienced.
- No one at the gym was interested in listening to ways they could be better; who did the short kid with no ball skills think he was, anyway?
- By his sophomore year, he was determined to learn everything about the emerging technology of video, and volunteered to scout games for a local high school.

- But instead of getting schooled in the new VCR format introduced by Phillips or the pioneering work of 3M, Reggie ran into a low-key, no-yelling coach who made it clear that Reggie's job was to teach, not simply to win games.
- His new mentor, Bob Summers, believed that high school was a formative time in the boys' lives.
- He understood how complicated life could be for a young man who looked big and strong, but was still wrestling with personal problems and pressures.
- The job of a coach was to encourage a boy's better self, to let his confidence grow.
- Coach Summers preached that every sport had its own special demand for courage—each demanded sacrifice and pain.
- If a player cut the wrong way on a play, it was an opportunity to get better, not humiliated with yelling in the huddle.
- Reggie had seen coaches run their teams until everyone had puked, athletes smacked with a wooden paddle for missing a layup in practice, and visited friends in the hospital after a coach had provoked a fistfight between two players he considered "weak."
- The world according to Coach Summers was not only different, but he also had a winning record that proved it worked.
- He emphasized the fundamentals, and demanded that each player remember he was part of a team and play tenacious defense.
- "No easy points," he would say at the break; "make them earn every point."
- Reggie spent so much time and ate so many meals at Coach Summers' house, the coach joked that Reggie should be a tax deduction.
- Reggie learned from Coach Summers that a coach's greatest reward was not the state championship trophy, but a "thank you" from a graduated player who understood the life lessons he had been taught.
- It was a winning season in many ways, and a home away from home for the next two years.
- When Reggie graduated, securely positioned in the vast middle of his class, he had three job offers.
- One suggested that he become the assistant to a soon-to-retire coach in Chicago; the second proposed that he take the head coaching slot at a small, rural high school; and a third outlined the joys of coaching junior high basketball in the inner city.

After graduation, Reggie received a job offer to coach at an inner city school.

- His father urged him to take the coaching job in Chicago, while his mother preferred the opportunities of being the boss in a rural school.
- Coach Summers said simply, "Follow your heart."
- Reggie took the position at a run-down school in Detroit.
- His motivation was simple: He needed to understand how to coach young black boys, who were starting to dominate the college ranks.
- His first practice was a total disaster; he was not ready for his new team of seventh- and eighth-grade kids to challenge his authority on the first day.
- They made jokes about his size, they didn't listen when he explained the schedule, and two players kept randomly running off and dribbling the ball.
- Reggie's greatest temptation was to yell and scream—maybe even toss a few players off the team for effect.
- Instead, he simply locked up the gym and asked the players to meet him on the city's most popular outdoor courts the next afternoon.
- When they all arrived the next day, he suggested they scrimmage any way they wished while he took notes.
- His first target was an immensely talented eighth-grader who was dominating the game.
- Five minutes into the game Reggie assigned a much smaller player to guard the star using specific instructions on where to stand, how to position his hands and when to jump.
- It worked like a charm.
- Reggie's target was thrown out of his rhythm and missed the next six shots in a row.
- Reggie then assigned an even smaller player to play defense.
- The new youngster certainly didn't dominate, but he held his own.
- For the rest of the afternoon, Reggie quietly taught his new team how to void an opponent's strengths; the kids said little to him, but they were clearly impressed.
- When he announced at the end of the day that tryouts would be held in the school gym the following day, all the players looked startled.
- Everyone has to earn his spot, he told the team.
- "I would rather have nine kids who want to be the best than 14 players who don't care to listen and be a part of a team."
- The challenge worked well, resulting in the school's first city championship in 12 years.
- Four of his best players stepped into starting roles at the high school level; suddenly, playing basketball for the white coach was a mark of excellence.
- At the end of his second year, Reggie was ready to move on and move up; a dozen offers flowed in.
- This time he selected a private high school outside Indianapolis, where the latest technology was a phone call away, and the students came from affluent families able to afford basketball camps in the summer and private tutors to hone the most skills.
- What they lacked was heart; no one played as though his life and happiness hung in the balance.
- Three weeks into the season, Reggie decided to promote two of the team's smallest players to the starting team; the two seniors they replaced were incredulous, but figured it was only temporary.
- Then, when they realized they were not starting at the Friday night game, they were furious and embarrassed.
- When Reggie substituted them back into the game, they played inconsistently, but with heart.
- For the remainder of the season, he jumbled the starting lineup.
- "Make them earn every point," he said repeatedly, and sensed a higher level of aggressiveness in their play.
- The team had made it to the state semi-finals before exiting the tournament in a one-point overtime loss.

- The experience had made it clear that young people needed to be challenged, and desired the same level of attention—black or white, rich or poor.
- Reggie's next challenge, he decided, needed to be a fully integrated team with championship potential.
- Just one more year and he would be ready for the next step.

Life in the Community: Grand Rapids, Michigan

- Grand Rapids, located on the Grand River about 25 miles east of Lake Michigan, was home to five of the world's leading office furniture companies and was nicknamed the "Furniture City."
- Over 2,000 years ago, people associated with the Hopewell culture occupied the Grand River Valley.
- Around A.D. 1700, the Ottawa Indians moved into the area and founded several villages along the Grand River.
- The Grand Rapids area was first settled by Europeans near the start of the nineteenth century by missionaries and fur traders, who traded their European metal and textile goods for fur pelts.
- In 1826, Detroit-born Louis Campau, the official founder of Grand Rapids, built his cabin, trading post, and blacksmith shop on the east bank of the Grand River near the rapids.
- Campau became perhaps the most important settler when, in 1831, he bought 72 acres of what is now the entire downtown business district of Grand Rapids.
- He purchased it from the federal government for $90 and named his tract Grand Rapids; immigrants from New York and New England began arriving in the 1830s.
- The first formal census occurred in 1845, which established a population of 1,510 and recorded an area of four square miles.
- During the second half of the nineteenth century, the city became a major lumbering center and the premier furniture manufacturing city of the United States.
- After an international exhibition in Philadelphia in 1876, Grand Rapids became recognized worldwide as a leader in the production of fine furniture.
- National home furnishing markets were held in Grand Rapids for about 75 years, concluding in the 1960s.
- The first improved road into the city was completed in 1855.
- This road was a private, toll plank road from Kalamazoo through Wayland, and a primary route for freight and passengers until about 1868.
- This road connected to the outside world via the Michigan Central Railroad at Kalamazoo.
- In 1880, the country's first hydroelectric generator was put to use on the city's west side.
- Michigan's economy underwent a transformation at the turn of the twentieth century.
- Many individuals, including Ransom E. Olds, John and Horace Dodge, Henry Leland, David Dunbar Buick, Henry Joy, Charles King, and Henry Ford, provided the concentration of engineering know-how and technological enthusiasm to start the birth of the automotive industry.
- Ford's development of the moving assembly line in Highland Park marked the beginning of a new era in transportation.
- More than other forms of public transportation, the automobile transformed people's private lives.
- It became the major industry of Detroit, and of Michigan in general, and permanently altered the socioeconomic life of the United States and much of the world.
- With the growth, the auto industry created jobs in Detroit that attracted immigrants from Europe and migrants from across the U.S., including those from the South.
- By 1920, Detroit was the fourth-largest city in the U.S.
- Residential housing was in short supply, and it took years for the market to catch up with the population boom.
- By the 1930s, so many immigrants had arrived that more than 30 languages were spoken in the public schools, and ethnic communities celebrated in annual heritage festivals.

The major industry in Michigan was automobile manufacturing.

- Grand Rapids was an early participant in the automobile industry, serving as home to the Austin Automobile Company from 1901 until 1921.
- Michigan held its first presidential primary election in 1910.
- With its rapid growth in industry, it was an important center of union industry-wide organizing, such as the rise of the United Auto Workers.
- In 1920, WWJ (AM) in Detroit became the first radio station in the U.S. to regularly broadcast commercial programs.
- Detroit continued to expand through the 1950s, at one point doubling its population in a decade.
- After World War II, housing was developed in suburban areas outside city cores; newly constructed Interstate Highways allowed commuters to navigate the region more easily.
- Modern advances in the auto industry resulted in increased automation, high-tech industry, and suburban growth since 1960.

ॐ ॐ ॐ ॐ ॐ ॐ ॐ

University of Michigan Timeline

1817   A legislative act established the Catholepistemiad, or University of Michigania; the Reverend John Monteith was appointed the first president of the Catholepistemiad. Fr. Gabriel Richard was appointed vice president and was the only other member of the faculty.

1821   The University adopted the official name "The University of Michigan" and reorganized to form a board of 21 trustees, including the governor.

1837 Michigan joined the Union as the twenty-sixth state on January 26. Ann Arbor was chosen as the permanent site for the University of Michigan (UM); 40 acres were given to the University by the Ann Arbor Land Company.

1838 The first book purchased by the UM library was a copy of J. J. Audubon's Birds of North America; the regents authorized $970 for its acquisition.

1840 Four identical houses were built for professors, the first buildings in Ann Arbor to have indoor plumbing.

1841 The University's first year of classes began for a student body consisting of six freshmen and one sophomore taught by two professors. Mason Hall, the first building, was completed.

1845 The first commencement, for 11 men, was held at the First Presbyterian Church.

1852 Henry Philip Tappan was inaugurated as the first president of the University. 1854 UM's first observatory opened; largely funded by subscriptions from Detroit, it was known as the Detroit Observatory.

1856 The first building designed and equipped solely as a chemical laboratory at a state university was built at UM.

1870 Michigan became the first American university to admit students upon graduation from approved high schools rather than by examination, and to institute a system of approval of high schools for purposes of regulating the privilege of such certification.

1890 The Michigan Daily began publication.

1894 Summer courses were given for the first time.

1897 Michiganensian (the UM yearbook) began publication.

1898 "The Victors" was composed by Louis Elbel, a senior music student.

1904 The Michigan Union was established for male students, alumni, faculty, and regents.

1911 "Varsity" was written by Earl Moore, Class of 1912, and J. Fred Lawton, Class of 1911.

1919 The Michigan Union building was opened as a gathering place for men only.

1923 The William L. Clements Library of American History was erected.

1925 The University Hospital, built by Albert Kahn, was dedicated.

1928 The University Museums building was completed.

1930 The University of Michigan Press was founded.

1933 The Law Quadrangle was completed.

1935 The University mandated the preservation of state and University history with the establishment of the Michigan Historical Collections.

1936 The Burton Memorial Tower was dedicated. The International Center was established with J. Raleigh Nelson as director.

1938 The Rackham Graduate School Building was completed by the architects Smith, Hinchman & Grylls.

1946 The Museum of Art was established in Alumni Memorial Hall. Willow Run Airport was acquired by the University.

1955 The North Campus was recognized as a campus geographic area.

1957 The Undergraduate Library (Shapiro) was built by Albert Kahn Associates.

1959 The Dearborn Center opened, headed by University Vice President William E. Stirton.

1960 On October 14, John F. Kennedy announced the concept of the Peace Corps during a presidential campaign stop on the steps of the Michigan Union.

1964 President Lyndon Johnson delivered his "Great Society" address to a crowd of more than 80,000 people gathered for spring commencement in Michigan Stadium on May 22.

1965 Astronaut Edward H. White (MSE AA 1959, Hon ScD 1965) became the first American to walk in space during the Gemini 4 mission commanded by James A. McDivitt (BSE AA 1959, Hon ScD 1965).

1971 Astronauts David R. Scott (1949-50), Alfred M. Worden (MA 1963), and James B. Irwin (M.S. 1957) traveled to the moon aboard Apollo 15.

1973 The Bentley Historical Library building, home of the Michigan Historical Collections, was completed.

1975: Antique Dealers

Roy and Dotty Eargle quickly learned the antique business: how to bid at auctions; where to make the best deals; and how to transform an abandoned Victorian house into a showplace.

Life at Home

- On a blistering hot morning in August 1973, the jet-lagged, exhausted Eargle family poured from a taxi onto the curb of a working-class neighborhood in Northern Virginia and stood silently appraising their new home, an aging 1950s cookie-cutter bungalow akin to all on the block.
- Tiredness was no match for the disappointment that clouded the faces of Roy and Dotty Eargle that day.
- A casual observer might well have dismissed the scene as that of just another down-and-out family migrating from Europe.
- Broke they were, yet flush with six successful years in Germany where Dotty was an understudy of Elizabeth Gruemer of the Berlin Opera and earned her degree in Concert Singing from the University of Heidelberg-Manheim.
- The bungalow was a world away from Germany where Dotty had sharpened her college-German to near fluency, performed her exceptional voice in a number of settings, and learned quickly to stand her ground in shopping and bus lines with strong, resolute German Putzfrauen.
- Roy got his foot in the door as a civilian employee of the Department of the Army, worked hard, and gained promotions to higher-level positions at the U.S. Army Headquarters, Berlin, and later at European Headquarters, Heidelberg.
- Roy's six-year tour of overseas Civil Service employment expired in August 1973.
- Fortunately, the Department offered to continue Roy's civilian employment upon his agreement to serve a minimum of one year at the Pentagon.
- They were also offered the incentive of expense-paid transportation home to America for the family, and temporary housing in the DC area: thus, arrival at the little bungalow in Virginia Hills.
- The move to DC proved to be its own nightmarish culture-shock.
- Without a single workday break from Germany to DC, Roy was initiated into the world's

Roy and Dotty Eargle created a successful antique business.

fastest-paced work environment, the Pentagon.

- He was thrown that first work day among the masses to negotiate the city's Great Bus and Transit Puzzle and, most traumatically, was awakened to the fact that survival in the world's second-most expensive city would require funds in excess of his meager Civil Service salary.
- Once again, necessity was the breeding ground of an entrepreneur.
- Since government apartments in Berlin and Heidelberg were completely furnished, the Eargles needed living room furniture, and Dotty decided that they should decorate with original Victorian wicker.
- The DC area was well populated with antique dealers who were in easy reach of abundant supplies of old furniture from New York and Pennsylvania.

The Eargles sold smaller items with a big mark up.

- With a ready local source from which to select, they began to acquire some beautiful pieces of wicker over the first several months.
- But the buying didn't seem to come to an end; on each new shopping trip, Dotty found a piece or two more desirable than the ones she had previously purchased.
- In this fashion, as the living room was filled, the less favored pieces were moved to the basement.
- By the end of the year, they both admitted that the buying had to cease, or there would be no money for food, rent or utility bills.
- Their small, two-line newspaper advertisement, "Original Victorian wicker for sale by private owner," in Sunday's *Washington Post* in late January 1974 drew over 60 telephone calls, and their unwanted inventory was gone within just a few days.
- Without further debate, they took up the initiative to become antique dealers.
- Dotty spent several weeks in March 1974 investigating the availability of rental spaces in various flea markets in the area before settling on an ancient brick and timber warehouse in Old Town Alexandria.
- Having developed a pleasant acquaintance with the manager during their wicker-buying days, Dotty was able to wheedle from him, outside the long waiting list, a coveted 10 foot by 10 foot space, albeit at the breathtaking rent of $20 per weekend.

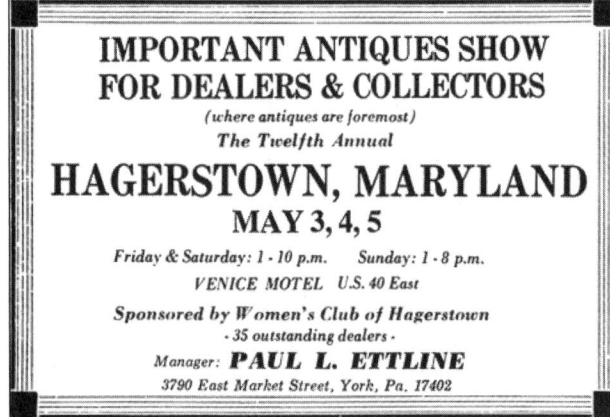

Dotty looked forward to their weekend "wicker hunts."

- In anticipation, Roy began to clean up the remaining pieces of unwanted wicker and sketching a layout of their meager inventory onto the 100 square foot plan of the flea market space.
- It quickly became painfully obvious that they didn't have nearly enough bait to go fishing and had to ask coworkers at the Pentagon to place antique items on consignment.
- Roy and Dotty then spent time pricing their goods and displaying them attractively so as to provide for convenient customer flow and inspection.

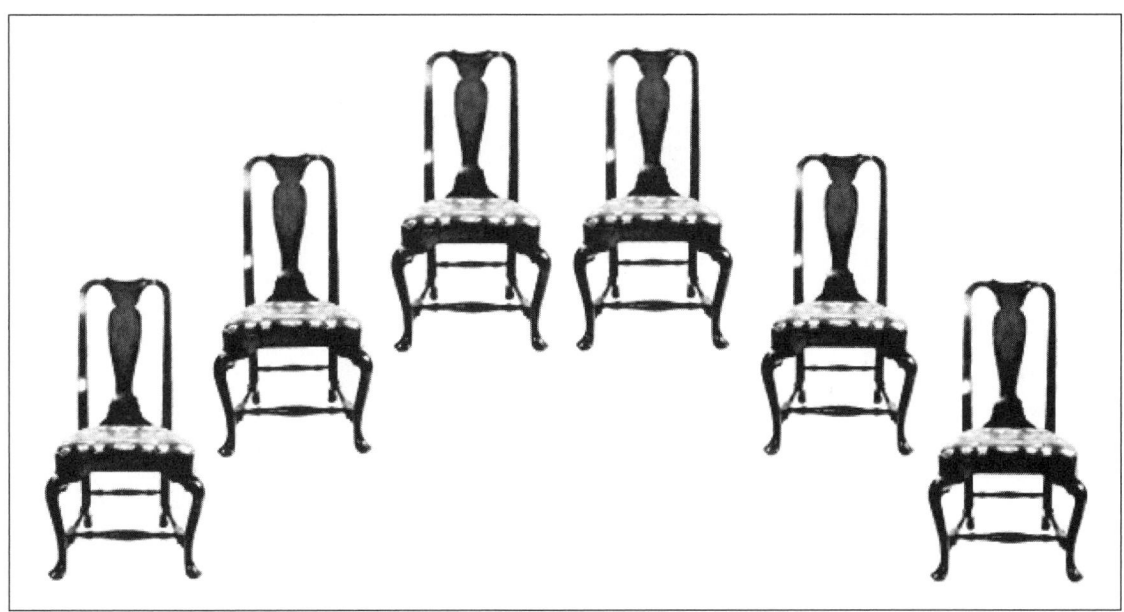

Roy and Dotty spent time displaying their goods in an appealing manner to attract customers' attention.

- They opened on the weekend of May 11, 1974, with glowing enthusiasm and smiley-faced sales tactics, but nothing helped to bring about the blow-out sales they had so naively hoped for.
- They settled for total weekend sales of $230.
- The letdown did, however, provide the self-examination they needed.
- Concluding that small, rustic items, both useful and decorative, were bestsellers, they realized that if they were to be successful, their inventory needed to change.
- That's when they discovered the world of auctioneering at Thorp's Country Auction on Routes 29 and 211, near Gainesville, Virginia.
- Old "Ed," the 1971 Volkswagen bus they brought back from Germany, became their "truck"; the rear seat folded down flat to make a fair-sized carrying space, although with only $150 seed money they didn't expect the need of a trailer.
- The low, squatty auction house, sided with split and knotted planks bleached white over the years by the hot Virginia sun, oozed from the dark soil just high enough to overshadow the tall, smothering hostas.
- When Roy and Dotty arrived, dozens of dusty pickups and vans were already squeezed into every available space.
- The large crowd was intimidating, adding to their already nervous concerns about the whole process of bidding.
- Roy signed in, obtained a bid card, and found seats to observe both the body language of the auctioneers and the bid-by-bid reactions of the audience.
- As the evening waned, they gingerly bid $5.00 on an old floor lamp, raised their bid to $7.00, and in doing so, had become antique dealers.

Life at Work
- Attempting to stay within their $150 "bank" that first night, Dotty and Roy Eargle bought a few lamps, old tools, and other small, rustic items believed to have crowd appeal.
- Their bidding system was elementary: Dotty nudged Roy lightly with her elbow when she thought they should bid or raise, and more forcefully when she thought they should quit or when she suspected that Roy was about to bid on something she didn't want.

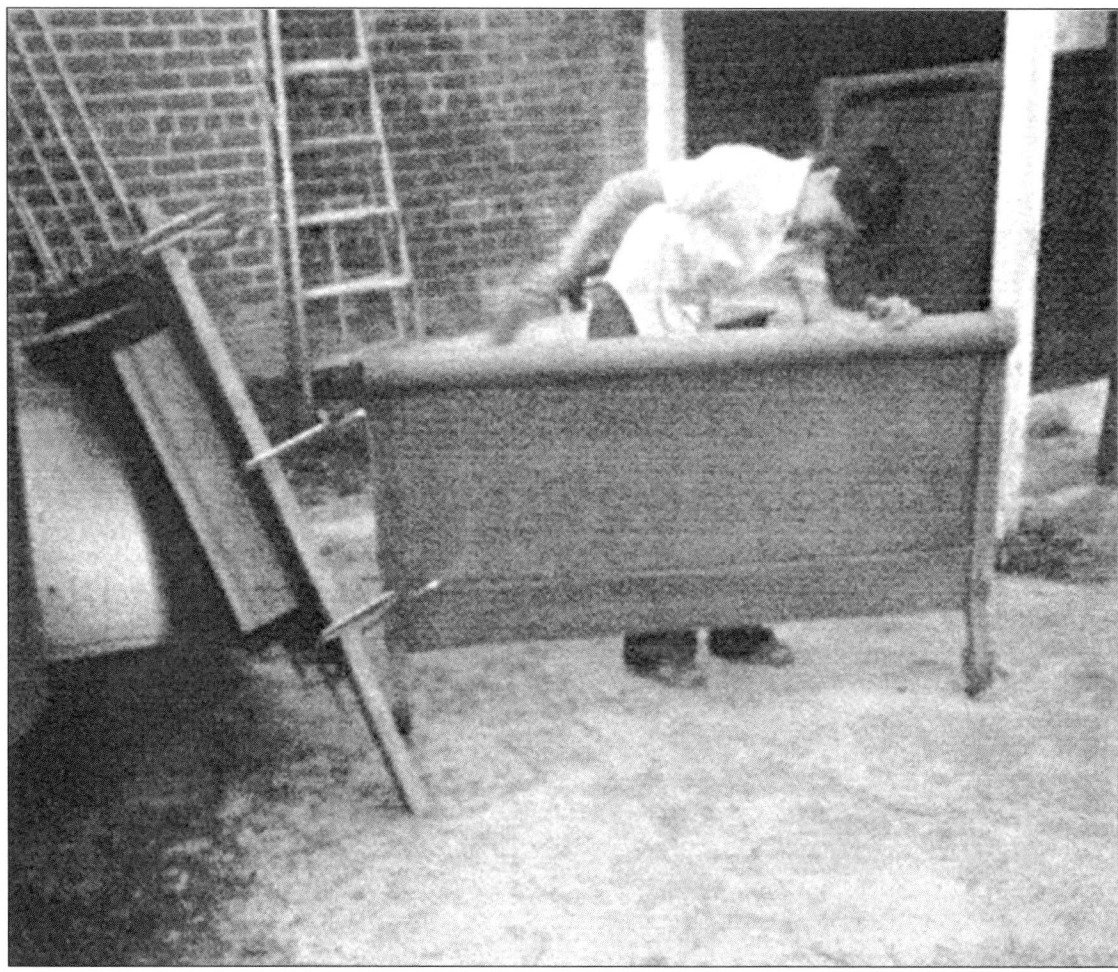

Dotty cleaned the furniture and Roy made necessary repairs.

- Afterwards, Dotty cleaned the purchases and Roy made any necessary repairs to get them ready for sale in the flea market booth—including the stated price.
- Competitive pricing was a challenge.
- They experimented in the beginning by marking items up 300 percent; that is, a 10-dollar cost on the stump, requiring only minor cleaning or repairs, became a 30-dollar sales item.
- The resulting end-prices seemed competitive and left the couple with room to bargain, as the public was certainly wont to do.
- They generally held to this method of pricing, even after refinishing high-quality golden oak became a major part of their business.
- As their little bank of seed money began to grow, they became experts at stuffing, cramming, and tying antique pieces on top of the bus until old Ed sometimes resembled a monster porcupine.
- This limited hauling capacity also taught Roy a lesson in both logistics and the sound intelligence that comes from the mouths of children.
- The Eargles were buying lots of oak "pressed back" chairs, which they refinished for resale by simply knocking them apart, cleaning the parts, and gluing them back together.
- Towards the end of an excellent buying night at Thorp's, when Roy suspected that Old Ed was already overloaded, a magnificent set of six carved oak chairs was brought out by the auctioneer.
- When Dotty whispered that they must get them, Roy whispered back that they had no room left in the bus.

- Their nine-year-old son elbowed Roy instantly and whispered, "Let's knock 'em apart, Dad. We gonna do it anyway to get 'em refinished."
- They never lost the purchase of a fine set of chairs after learning that closely held "corporate trade-secret."
- Buying was always a priority, so on the way back from his son's summer camp, Roy noticed a cluster of rundown, plank-sided farm buildings that seemed to reek of antiquity.
- After shooing aside a flock of Rhode Island Reds, several beagles, and a calico cat stretched across the freshly swept dirt pathway, Roy climbed a rickety pair of steps onto a wide front porch, slanting dangerously in several directions.

Handmade furniture delighted the Eargles.

- An old cow bell served as a doorknocker, the sound of which, after a long wait, brought to the door a thin, erect woman of indiscriminate age.
- A strong smell of shoe polish and the freshness of Octagon soap drifted from the doorway as clear, cloud-grey eyes searched Roy's face without speaking.
- Roy had struck the equivalent of an antique gold mine.
- The owner was a second-generation German who was born on the land and whose family had lost their wealth during the Great Depression.
- She was on her way to work in St. George's Kitchens as a dietician when Roy met her that Sunday.
- Roy learned that she was financially able to move to a little cottage in the town but was determined to save the land, which held a small tobacco allotment, for her children.
- Over the next few months, she led Roy into each snake-infested barn, from which he pulled handmade farm tables, jelly cupboards, linen presses, walnut and pine Empire-style pie safes, a wealth of *Gone With the Wind, Aladdin,* and other oil lamps, embroidery pieces and samplers, quilts, and boxes of Depression glass and old crockery.
- She explained that the stuff was moved from the original home place; intent on saving the furnishings for the children, her husband had stored them in the scattered barns around the compound.

Roy looked past the long grass and disrepair, and bought a Victorian building to live in and sell from.

- Now that her husband was dead, she had not known how to dispose of the large and diverse volume of furnishings.
- Because she was living in so remote an area, and since no previous inquiries presented themselves, she was eager to bargain with Roy, provided he bought everything.
- Their combined efforts during those long months in the summer of 1974 paid handsomely, and the Eargles quickly expanded at the Old Town Flea Market to several more sales spaces as they became available.
- Dotty refinished during the day, with Roy helping at night after his day job at the Pentagon.
- If necessary, Dotty would put in a full evening as well.
- Since further expansion space at the Old Town Market was severely limited, and the expiration of the lease on

their rental house in Virginia Hills was approaching, they needed to find new quarters for both the family and the growing business.

- Luckily, Roy had spotted an elegant three-story Victorian mansion in Old Alexandria that sat abandoned at the corner of Madison and North Washington streets.
- There were no signs on the property and the grass was always knee-high in the side yard.
- To the north of the mansion, with a narrow alley between, lay a modern motel and parking lot, and across the street stood an always-crowded Howard Johnson's restaurant.
- The property was strategically located on a major link between DC and Mount Vernon, making it a highly desirable spot for retail sales.
- Low-rent public housing occupied a number of city blocks to the west, which tended to detract from the property's comfortable and safe living accommodations.
- The mansion's location and potential as both living quarters and shop, however, outweighed the negative aspects of industry and public housing.

Life in the Community: Alexandria, Virginia

- Alexandria, Virginia, was shaped by its proximity to the nation's capital and was largely populated by civil servants and professional contractors.
- Major employers included the U.S. Department of Defense and the Center for Naval Analyses.
- In 1791, Alexandria was included in the area chosen by George Washington to become the District of Columbia.
- A portion of the City of Alexandria—known as "Old Town"—was originally in Virginia, ceded to the U.S. Government to form the District of Columbia, and later retro-ceded to Virginia by the federal government in 1846, when the District was reduced in size.

Alexandria's history and look made the building an ideal setting for an antique store.

- Its history and look made Alexandria the perfect place for an antique store.
- So Roy Eargle took the first opportunity in July 1974 to investigate the abandoned mansion he had spotted, stopping first at the adjoining motel where he learned that the house was part of the motel property held under lease by a property management firm in DC.
- With the manager's assistance, Roy contacted the senior partner of the family firm and they agreed to meet that afternoon.
- The senior partner explained that his family's interest was only in motel management, but that, under the terms of his lease, it had been necessary to take on the unwanted responsibility of the old home as well.
- The property, he informed Roy, was in an estate of 18 relatives who were unable to agree on any fair disposition of the property.
- Thus, it had lain dormant for over a decade.
- He told Roy quite frankly that he had never received much interest in the old house, and that the strict historical preservation ordinance in Old Alexandria prevented razing or altering the structure.
- The size, location and historic character of the property, however, was ideal for Roy and Dotty's antique business, and offered the interesting and efficient old-country custom of living over one's shop.
- The old gentlemen was delighted with their plans to restore the elegant rooms and architectural appurtenances of the home, and upgrade the infrastructure—all without violating the ordinances of the city.
- They negotiated a 10-year lease based on little more than the monthly pro rata share of the total property taxes and insurance that was favorably one-sided because it relieved that burden from the management company's master lease.
- The historic old mansion was an architectural gem, but basic care and maintenance had suffered greatly for two decades until the home was condemned by the city due to unsafe, out-of-date electrical and plumbing systems.
- The Eargles began their plans for restoration the minute they signed the long-term lease on September 15, 1974.
- They found the interior of the old home horribly defaced: the hardwood floors all were covered with sheet linoleum, and paneled heart pine doors and moldings lost their delicacy under multiple coats of cheap oil paint, as did the smoothly plastered walls, splattered with a plethora of garish colors.

"Antique Shops Report Booming Sales,"
Dan Gordon, *Nevada State Journal*, July 13, 1975

A washing machine that does not wash or a straight-back wooden bench do not sound like hot selling items in this world of plush sofas and rapid-action washers.

However, these items, if they happen to be antiques, not only sell, but are commanding high prices.

Antiques are not collecting dust in shops these days.

Instead, the demand for antique items has been steadily increasing, and one Reno dealer described the current interest among consumers as a "mania."

The Yankee Trader antique store on Highway 395 south of Reno has been in business for 23 years, and the owner Harold Andrews said the market has remained healthy throughout. However, in recent years, consumer interest has reached even greater heights.

Many of the items have lost their function in the modern world, but that has not diminished their value.

"The function of the furniture is secondary," Andrews said. "It's the appearance and the history that counts."

Andrews, himself, has a keen appreciation of the furniture he sells. While pointing to an ornate grandfather clock, he can rattle off who built the clock and when.

This type of knowledge is indispensable, because a dealer purchases the items for his store, and consequently must be able to spot quality goods.

Because these quality items are often hidden in remote places, like attics or under piles of used furniture, the dealer must have a sharp eye.

Andrews said there is a lively traffic for antique items in Nevada, but the strongest interest still exists in the East.

"Most antiques are back East," Andrews said.

The definition of an antique is an object of beauty or rarity that is at least 100 years old, and for that reason the East has a head start on the Western states as far as being a center for antiques.

Each year, to renew his supply of antiques, Andrews returns back to the East on a buying trip. He also buys locally and in California.

Andrews said through his 23 years in business in Nevada, he has developed a reputation that attracts many customers throughout the United States. He also said there is a healthy local trade.

Tastes differ across the country.

"This is Victorian country," Andrews said. "Most of the people are interested in Victorian furniture because that was the type used when the state was first settled."

Andrews himself is most interested in eighteenth-century American furniture....

Janet Thompson of the Old Timer store on West 2nd Street said both collectibles and antiques are good investments because they appreciate in value.

At the same time, consumers are increasingly attracted to antiques and collectibles because of the personal flavor of owning old furniture and decorations.

"When you buy an antique, it is something that no one else owns," Thompson said. "People can create their own personal atmosphere with antiques."

Selling antique or collectible items is not so difficult, she said. However, buying good furniture is becoming more and more difficult.

"It is becoming very hard to find good antiques," she said.

"'Ibis': Wading Through Antiques,"
The Pocono Record, June 7, 1975

Linda DeRussy and Paul Fuhrman, antique lovers both, sought to escape the urban pressures of New York City, so they found an apartment in Stroudsburg and began furnishing it with antiques that they found scouting auctions and flea markets.

Soon the apartment was cluttered and furniture items were piled on top of each other. The problem was solved when the two decided to open an antique store, though they never were in business before.

The store is unusual because it is stocked only with merchandise that the owners have had in their own home. It's not simply an antique store, either. Antiques are combined with clothing, jewelry, gifts, cosmetics, prints and toys.

"Ibis, a General Store and Antiques," is located on Main Street in Stroudsburg across from the Sherman theaters. It opened this spring, and the owners report that the idea of blending antiques with other types of merchandise was successful.

Antiques are acquired from rural areas in western Pennsylvania, and much of the other merchandise is imported from Europe, South America and Asia.

"So far, we are still buying from us," DeRussy said, though other local merchants warned them that the practice can be bad for business. Another unusual guideline is nothing made from plastic is sold.

The toys, many imported from the Soviet Union, are made from wood, which DeRussy prefers because they are attractive and fun to play with, but they are relatively indestructible.

History of Office Equipment
By 1900, nearly 100,000 people in the U.S. were working as secretaries, stenographers, and typists in an office. The average worker was employed for 60 hours per six-day work week. Specialized training was available for people who wished to study office skills.

Copiers
The mimeograph machine of the 1890s increased the number of copies that could be made from a few to a hundred, using a "master." But the only way to copy an original after it had been made was to retype, redraw, or re-photograph it. The first photostat machine was developed before World War I, but it was too expensive, too big, and required a trained operator.

After World War II, 3M and Eastman Kodak introduced the Thermo-Fax and Verifax copiers into the workplace. The office models were relatively inexpensive and easy to use, but their special paper was expensive and turned dark over time.

Chester Carlton's discovery of the effect of light in photoconductivity led to the success of the Haloid Xerox 914 machine in 1960.

Typewriters
The first typewriter to be commercially successful was invented in 1867 by C. Latham Sholes, Carlos Glidden, and Samuel W. Soule in Milwaukee, Wisconsin. The patent was sold for $12,000 to Densmore and Yost, who made an agreement with E. Remington and Sons to commercialize the machine as the Sholes and Glidden Type-Writer.

Remington began production of its first typewriter in 1873, in Ilion, New York, using the QWERTY keyboard layout, which was slowly adopted by other typewriter manufacturers.

Unfortunately, the typist could not see the characters as they were typed, giving life to the "visible typewriters" such as the Oliver typewriters, which were introduced in 1895.

By 1910, the manual typewriter had achieved a standardized design, including the invention of the Shift key, which reduced the number of required keys by half.

In 1941, IBM announced the Electromatic Model 04 electric typewriter, featuring the concept of proportional spacing. By assigning varied rather than uniform spacing to different-sized characters, the Type 04 recreated the appearance of a printed page, an effect that was further enhanced by a typewriter ribbon innovation that produced clearer, sharper characters on the page.

IBM introduced the IBM Selectric typewriter in 1961, which replaced the typebars with a spherical element (or typeball), slightly smaller than a golf ball, with reverse-image letters molded into its surface. The Selectric used a system of latches, metal tapes, and pulleys driven by an electric motor to rotate the ball into the correct position and then strike it against the ribbon and platen. The typeball moved laterally in front of the paper instead of the former platen-carrying carriage moving the paper across a stationary print position.

Dictating Equipment

Early attempts to transform Thomas Edison's early phonograph equipment into a dictation machine were a dismal failure in the late 1800s.

But practitioners of Scientific Management believed that dictating letters into a machine would cut the cost of producing a letter and make the executive more creative. Numerous attempts were made to popularize dictaphones, which were cumbersome to use.

It took magnetic tape in the 1950s to make dictating practical. Then letters, memos and bright ideas could be captured by tape recorders and played back easily.

Ballpoint Pen

The first patent on a ballpoint pen was issued on October 30, 1888, to John Loud, a leather tanner, who made a writing implement to write on the leather he tanned. Although the pen could be used to mark rough surfaces such as leather, it proved to be too coarse for letter writing and was not commercially exploited.

In the period between 1904 and 1946, there was intense interest in improving writing instruments. In the early inventions, the ink was placed in a thin tube whose end was blocked by a tiny revolving ball that did not always deliver the ink evenly and often smeared.

László Bíró, a Hungarian newspaper editor, frustrated by the amount of time wasted in filling up fountain pens and cleaning up smudged pages, designed in 1938 a new type of pen that used fast-drying printer's ink in a pressurized cartridge.

During World War II, U.S. businessman Milton Reynolds saw a Biro pen in a store in Buenos Aires and began producing the Biro design without a license as the Reynolds Rocket. The first ballpoint pens went on sale at Gimbels department store in New York City on October 29, 1945, for $12.50 each.

1975: Ear, Nose & Throat Doctor

Dr. Gerard Keshian moved to Fort Myers, Florida, to focus on bringing high-quality medicine to an underserved, small but rapidly-growing community in his native state.

Life at Home

- The Keshians lived in downtown Fort Myers, Florida, on the scenic Caloosahatchee River.
- Their home, built in the 1920s, was within blocks of Thomas Edison's winter home; a tourist attraction owned by the city.
- Both Gerard and Fay were native Floridians, a designation that was growing less common in this rapidly growing state.
- To help educate newcomers to the area, the couple actively raised money for a nature center, complete with an extensive boardwalk for viewing the flora and fauna of Florida.
- When they began last year, no money was available for a brochure, so Gerard made individual pictures of the plans, location, and plants and then pasted the pictures on paper to create individualized brochures; after Fay wrote the copy, they distributed each personalized presentation to key members of the community.
- Gerard did not like fundraising, but their efforts resulted in $85,000 being donated, and the boardwalk was now under way.
- As each stage of the boardwalk was completed, the Keshians went out to walk the new section; the children were less thrilled by this ritual than were their parents.
- The progress of the boardwalk was being charted by photographs from a helicopter provided by the publicly financed mosquito-control taxing district.
- Each May, Gerard and Fay took their three boys and one girl on a one-week driving tour of Florida.
- The parents were determined to teach the children about Florida before much of it disappears.
- The family often stayed in Howard Johnson Hotels, which always had swimming pools and television sets.

Energetic Dr. Keshian lived in downtown Fort Myers.

- Since Gerard and Fay refused to have a television set in their house, the children were often glued to the TV once they hit the motel room.
- Dr. Keshian believed that television was a poor influence and a time waster for all persons, particularly children.
- This year, the annual tour included a trip to Disney World, whose impact on tourism is tremendous.
- When Gerard was home, he and the children were often in his workshop making rockets, wooden boats, and electronic gadgets.
- The family also attached, from an Australian pine tree, a rope swing that attracted children—and sometimes adults—from miles around to the yard.
- Most weekends, the entire family travelled 18 miles outside the city to a 30-acre tract of land purchased in 1966 for $1,000 an acre.

Fay was a native Floridian.

- The use of drugs was on the rise in the community; in the country, Gerard kept the children away from their peers, many of whom he did not trust.
- There they have devised catapults made from surgical tubing, and pipe cannons loaded with palm seeds propelled by homemade gunpowder and fuses.
- Also, they worked as a family to identify most of the plants on the property, especially orchids and bromeliads, by common and Latin name.
- An out-of-state developer was digging canals near their property to create a housing development; the dredging was undercutting the water table and causing the land to dry up, so this family has formed a coalition of residents in the area to battle the company's expansion plans.
- Recently, Gerard acquired from a patient several used pinball machines, which he stripped and made into flashing, blinking, noise-making, scary objects for the annual Junior Welfare League Haunted House Fundraiser at Halloween.
- No Junior League existed when the Keshians moved to Fort Myers; Fay helped establish the organization and has served on many of its most critical boards.

The Keshians enjoyed everything Florida had to offer.

- Because of the various ages of the four children, their activities range from Cub Scouts to advanced ballet.
- Although most of the activities were near their home, Fay felt that she was constantly running a taxicab service for the children.
- The oldest child, the only girl, must be driven to school each morning; the other children were in private schools affiliated with either the Catholic Church or the Lutheran Church.
- Fay drove a five-year-old Oldsmobile, which her mother gave to her, while Gerard drove a Jeep Wagon with four-wheel drive.

- Both Gerard and Fay grew up in Tampa, Florida; after his father died in 1947, Gerard was determined to be a doctor despite the meager resources of the family.
- Fay also grew up without a father; she and her mother lived with her grandparents following her parents' divorce in the closing days of the Second World War.
- She attended Newcomb College in New Orleans, while Gerard attended nearby Tulane University in New Orleans, thanks to the generosity of a wealthy great-uncle who provided some tuition help; in addition, he had a work scholarship that required 20 hours of work a week in the physics lab.
- He graduated Phi Beta Kappa in 1956; they married that year and he began looking for a way to attend medical school.
- No money or scholarships were available for medical school and the rules forbade students from working.
- He eventually got $500 from his great-uncle, $500 from the Kiwanis Club, and a loan whose only guarantee was future earnings.

- After graduation from Tulane Medical, he served his internship in New Orleans, working 36 hours on and 12 hours off with a half-day off on either Saturday or Sunday.

Gerard and the children were often in the workshop.

- During this time, their first child was born, but with his work schedule, he participated little as a father in her early years.
- They next moved to Chicago to continue ear, nose, and throat specialty training, living in a garage apartment with a growing family, which then included two children.
- In 1963, he made $270 a month as a resident; the family attempted to get a Sears charge card that year and were denied.
- By 1964, they moved to Fort Myers, where he was required to practice for three years before taking exams to become Board qualified.
- The tests were so stressful he began smoking cigarettes again.

Life at Work

- With the area growing so rapidly, the demand for the services of an ear, nose, and throat specialist had skyrocketed.
- This was especially true since large numbers of families from the Midwest were retiring to the area, only to discover new allergies and ailments.
- Many lived in newly established residential developments literally dredged out of the wetlands to create overnight, canal communities.
- The canal-based development technique allowed the developer to use the dredged dirt to fill the land and make it higher above sea level; the residents who bought, as a result, had homes on a water-filled canal that connects to deeper water.
- Thousands of lots had been sold in this manner, waiting for the owner to retire; as a result, most of the lots were left barren to grow pollen-laden weeds and vegetation.
- Normally, he began work at 6:45 a.m., usually at one of the two hospitals in the area, where he performed surgery starting about 7:30 a.m.

Many Midwest families who retired to Florida lived in new residential developments dredged out of the wetlands.

- The most common surgeries were tonsillectomies, nose repair, cosmetic reconstruction, and occasionally the "pinning back" of obtrusive ears.
- Most days, surgery was completed by mid-morning, after which he saw patients until 6 p.m.; many nights he attended medical meetings or civic functions before returning home.
- The three doctors in the office each treated from 12 to 20 patients during the afternoon, sometimes doing minor surgery in the office and treating a variety of skin cancers common in the heat-soaked environment of Florida.
- During the summers, much time was spent treating swimmer's ear.
- A typical office visit costed $20; subsequent visits were $11 to $15 each.
- This office did not participate in Medicare assignments, and most of its clients did not have insurance; 20 percent did not pay their bills.
- Dr. Keshian often did not charge patients, particularly those with families, who he knows were unable to afford his services.
- He takes every Thursday off, working on Thursday mornings at the Senior Friendship Center treating approximately a dozen patients each week for free.
- He got interested in the Center through a presentation made to the Tuesday afternoon Rotary Club, of which he is a member.
- As a result of the cancers Gerard had seen, most commonly found in retirees who have been heavy drinkers and smokers their entire life, he did not hesitate to tell his patients about the consequences of prolonged use of alcohol and cigarettes.
- Personally, he and Fay occasionally had a glass of wine; rarely more than one.
- Dr. Keshian turned more of these cases over to his partner in order to focus on the delicate specialty of ear surgery.

- He treated a large number of male retirees who were experiencing hearing loss as a result of explosions and loud noises during their military service in World War II or the Korean War, since sound-protection was given little consideration in those days.
- Dinner was always at 7 p.m., prepared by Fay. The family rarely ate out; the fast food phenomenon sweeping the nation has been slow to reach this south Florida community.
- At work, he and his partners started a pension plan that forced him to save money; with four children it was not always easy to set aside funds for the future.
- To help fund the children's future, the sale of hearing aids has been established as a separate corporation owned by his children, with all revenues going to their college funds.
- The office was staffed by one nurse who assisted three doctors.
- Despite the conservative use of staff, the office overhead rose from 15 percent of total costs in 1964 to 25 percent.

Life in the Community: Fort Myers, Florida

- The rapid growth of southwest Florida, especially the sensitive wetland areas, was causing many natives to question the wisdom of growth.
- The area was ranked as one of the top five fastest growing areas in the nation; at its current rate of approximately 20 percent per year, the population will double every five years.
- Throughout most of the century, Fort Myers was untouched by growth; at the end of War World II, the town claimed only 10,600 residents.
- Mosquitoes, poor roads, heat, and the lack of an industrial base held down growth until the 1960s.
- Air conditioning, sophisticated telephone sales programs by developers, and the dream of a "Florida retirement" attracted millions.
- Nearly 500 new residents settled in the state each day since the mid-1960s.
- Almost overnight, a frontier-like state became the largest and most urban state in the region.
- Many of the new residents were retired, with approximately 25 percent of the population—the highest in the nation—over 65 years of age.
- The new residents, while bringing cash from years of working in Michigan, Ohio, and Indiana, were also impacting social programs and schools throughout the state.

Fort Myers was a popular, fast-growing area.

- The elderly consistently voted against new tax initiatives, including school construction, to protect their income, often stating publicly, "No new taxes; I have educated my children up North."
- Throughout the coastal communities and barrier islands of Florida, Georgia, and South Carolina, battles were raging between developers who promise change and environmentalists who wish to preserve.
- Greater affluence nationally and improved technology were allowing the islands and marshes to be developed.
- Conservationists in Fort Myers warned that the residential development was destroying the environmental characteristics people were flocking to see.
- The developers said that residents were simply trying to preserve the beauty for themselves and lock others out.
- Many communities, including nearby Sanibel Island, were attempting to control growth through comprehensive plans and tougher zoning laws.
- On the statewide level, environmental activism resulted in the Environmental Protection Act, the Land and Water Management Act, and the State Comprehensive Planning Act.
- Florida also began a land acquisition program to preserve the most sensitive and endangered lands, including Cayo Costa Island in southwest Florida.

Editorial, "Southerners Happiest about Their Lives," *Fort Myers News-Press,* November 24, 1975

"The research institute of a northern university recently announced it finds people in the South happiest of any region in the nation.

That may not be surprising to the 'Crackers' in our midst, or perhaps even to many transplanted Yankees who came to Dixie in search of happier (or cheaper) lives.

The study, undertaken by the Institute for Social Research of the University of Michigan, found that most Americans are satisfied with their lives, but that Southerners are more satisfied in almost every respect than their counterparts in the rest of the country.

This research, which is said to be the first scientific survey of how Americans evaluate their lives, might have a message for intellectual sociologists who have a tendency to put down the South.

For example, the South ranked at the bottom of the study of desirability done by the Environmental Protection Agency in 1973. That study, however, was based on data about socioeconomic factors, such as jobs, education, housing, and income. It didn't ask people how they felt about their lives, such as the Michigan study did.

Perhaps the sociologists assumed how people should feel about a region based on their own academically established criteria.

Interestingly, even Southern blacks are apparently more content than Northern blacks.

The report said 57 percent of Southern blacks said they were very well satisfied overall, compared with 43 percent of blacks in the rest of the nation.

Despite the griping that is heard and the negative outlook of many, the study found on a nationwide basis 63 percent of white Americans and 51 percent of blacks are generally 'very satisfied with their life as a whole.'

On a regional basis, the percentage of those satisfied with their lives broke down as follows: South, 67 percent; Central, 65 percent; East, 57 percent; West, 57 percent. It's a reminder that we live in a pretty fine area."

1975: Jamacian Immigrant & Caregiver

Jamaican Andrea Spencer emigrated to New York and, after seven years and several jobs, found an ideal position caring for two elderly sisters.

Life at Home

- Jamaica, the land of sunshine and laughter, had been hard on Andrea Spencer, even as a child.
- "All my years I been working, since I was 13."
- Seven years earlier, at age 38, she was ready for a change in a place called New York City.
- Her goal was not to leave Jamaica for America; rather, it was to exchange Jamaica for New York City where most Jamaican immigrants had settled.
- Friends who had worked there came back and said the same thing: "Twasn't bad; but 'twasn't good'; I knew it had to be better than Jamaica."
- While Andrea was still a small child, her mother died; her father left her in the care of her grandmother and disappeared.
- At 13 she left school to work as a domestic servant in a boarding school for boys.
- Her job was to clean up and feed the younger boys, some of whom were very young.
- She made $0.30 a week plus free room and board.
- Once a year she rode a bus for four hours each way to visit her grandmother in the country—"Once a year was all I could go."
- Her next job was decidedly a step up, working for "a nice, white woman" in Kingston, Jamaica.
- Next, she took a job at a wholesale dealer, where she cleaned the lobby and the shelves.
- "All my life I work for white folks and never had any trouble."
- By the time Andrea made the decision to leave, she had three children, two of whom were on their own; the youngest was left with an aunt.
- Andrea was determined to come alone: "No man come with me. I like being alone, choosing my own friends. Doing what I want. I'll never marry nobody again."
- Her ticket out was a scheme that involved New York housewives, Jamaican lawyers and women like herself.

Andrea Spencer left Jamaica for New York City when she was 38-years-old.

- The 1965 U.S. Immigration law included a work certificate provision that permitted individuals to enter the United States to take jobs that could not be filled from the resident workforce.
- The employer in each case had to provide evidence that he had unsuccessfully tried to find suitable workers from inside the country.
- Often employers did not try very hard, but most ran an advertisement in the local newspaper.
- Andrea paid 100 Jamaican dollars to a lawyer in Kingston; in exchange she received the work certification permit, a plane ticket, and placement as a live-in servant with a family in New York.
- She agreed to work one year at $55 per week plus room and board; the remainder of what she would have earned went to the officials who financed her trip and processed her papers.

- The agreement ended after 12 months, after which time she could negotiate her own working and living arrangements.
- The employment plan was similar to the managed service system used in the colonial era to bring employees to the Americas.
- The twentieth-century version was modified to bring a large number of domestic servants to wealthy U.S. homes in search of a maid or a cook.
- Jamaicans were particularly suited to this form of immigration; as native English speakers, they were attractive for families seeking domestic help.
- In 1968, the year Andrea emigrated, 17,000 Jamaicans entered the United States, 13,000 of whom were female; one in three of the women was a "private household worker." life at Work
- After seven years in New York, Andrea Spencer finally found the ideal job caring for two elderly sisters.
- The two women, both in their seventies, lived in a nice, overly decorated home, paid her well and, most important of all, treated her with respect.
- Her life in America had not begun that way.
- Andrea's first assignment upon arrival in America was caring for an upwardly mobile couple and their four children, who were accustomed to having their own way.

Top and above: Andrea's birthplace, Jamaica.

- The couple, who loved parties, dressing up and being seen, went out four to five times a week, leaving the children with babysitters or nannies.
- On the day Andrea arrived, the children were bold enough to lay bets in her presence on how long she would survive before quitting.
- Previously, the longest tenure of a nanny was 16 months; the shortest was 10 days.
- The two younger girls bet that Andrea would make it three to four months; the boys were determined to break their own record and see her gone in under 10 days.

- Quickly, it became clear they had overestimated the sweetness of her Jamaican accent and underestimated the strength of her Jamaican upbringing.
- When she hit the one-year mark and was free to seek other employment, the couple offered to double her pay and guaranteed one weekend a month off.
- Flattered, she accepted the raise and immediately regretted her decision; she lasted another seven months before moving on.
- Her next job was as a live-in maid to two wonderful children and their four horrid dogs.
- Every morning she awoke with eager anticipation of the children's new day and dreading the task of taking the four dogs for their walks.
- Invariably one of the little beasts would pee in the elevator on the way down from their ninth-floor apartment.
- Then at least two of the dogs would begin yapping as they walked through the marble lobby, attracting attention and humiliation.

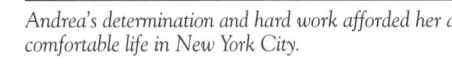

Andrea's determination and hard work afforded her a comfortable life in New York City.

- She tried taking the dogs out one at a time instead of as a group, but that took too much time away from the children, who were her primary responsibility.
- So she moved on and discovered that working with two elderly sisters reminded her of Jamaica, where she had spent so much time around her grandmother.
- Also, it was less painful; working with children sometimes reminded her of her own kids, whom she had not seen in years.

Bedford-Stuyvesant was home to a vast influx of West Indian immigrants, including Jamaicans.

- The women's Manhattan apartment was very Victorian in fashion, simply jammed tight with their travel memories; at every turn were souvenirs from their many trips abroad with their husbands when they were still alive.
- Every day was an education for an impoverished girl from Jamaica.
- In addition, the two women planned their day around the civilized habit of holding high tea most afternoons at 4 o'clock.
- This quaint habit also reminded her of Jamaica and the classic culture of the former British possession, where residents liked to believe that Bach lived in every Episcopal hymn and Shakespeare was still a living force.
- Another plus was the sisters' preference that she not live in-marking the first time since she'd come to America that she had her own place.
- Andrea proudly picked Bedford-Stuyvesant, which seemed to have attracted enough West Indians to be an inland Caribbean island all by itself.
- She arrived at 7 each morning, woke the sisters, prepared a light breakfast, and settled in for the first political argument of the day.

Women's roles evolved into less traditional paths.

- The older sister, Marlene, had once danced with Vice President Richard Nixon at the inaugural ball in 1957, believed that Watergate was "a big nothing," and that he was being hounded for political purposes.
- The younger sister, by two years and 11 months, was once married to a Cabinet undersecretary in the Kennedy Administration and vehemently believed that Nixon was only getting his "just desserts."
- From there the arguments would move to the cause of inflation, the impact of the Vietnam War and the role of women in tomorrow's America.
- Marlene was particularly proud of her granddaughters, who were focused on careers in law and medicine "if the men don't block their way."
- The younger one, Jill, would then talk about her grandchildren and how arts and motherhood were still a good combination in the twenty-first century.
- "In my day, home cooking is what kept the boys coming back," she would say and then laugh.
- Once a month the sisters hosted the Thursday Bridge Club, an event that included drinks, dinner, cigarette smoking, exuberant conversation, and cards.
- Andrea relished the exacting preparation, the elaborate meals and the carefree conversation.
- "Truly Americans have created Heaven on Earth and given it to themselves," she often thought.
- Life in Manhattan was quite a contrast to Bedford-Stuyvesant, where the music pulsed from every building, the food smells leapt from every kitchen and she thought of herself as a Jamaican.
- On any given Sunday afternoon, Jamaican teenage boys would be competing with the kids from Barbados on who could produce the best music.
- All the time the goal was to impress the girls.
- "In my day," Andrea thought to herself, "the goal was the same—to impress the girls—only I was too young to know and now I'm too old to care."

Life in the Community: New York City

- Andrea Spencer loved her apartment in the nation's second most populous black community, the Bedford-Stuyvesant section of New York City.
- Bedford-Stuyvesant was also home to the nation's largest concentration of voluntary black West Indian immigrants, a designation that included Jamaicans.
- For more than 35 years, Caribbean immigrants from Trinidad, Jamaica, Barbados, Granada, St. Vincent, and Montserrat had been congregating in Bedford-Stuyvesant's 653 square blocks.

- And for most of this time the cultural differences between West Indians and African Americans had been lost on outside observers.
- Inside Bedford-Stuyvesant, geographic distinctions and cultural habits were clearly defined and strictly noted, cultivated and respected.
- Four of the six elected officials from Bedford-Stuyvesant were West Indian, including Representative Shirley Chisholm.
- In the arts, every West Indian was openly proud of the national success of West Indian stars Harry Belafonte and Sidney Poitier.
- A quarter million Jamaicans inhabited New York City.
- Bedford-Stuyvesant was also the place to see the split between American blacks and West Indians.
- West Indians were said to work harder and succeed more than American blacks, who resented the comparisons.
- Mostly, the two groups stayed away from each other; mixing only brought trouble.

A quarter million Jamaicans lived in New York City.

࿐࿐࿐࿐࿐࿐࿐࿐

Jamaican Immigration Timeline

1619   Twenty indentured workers from the Caribbean islands arrived in Jamestown, Virginia, where they worked as free persons.

1850s   Large numbers of Jamaicans were recruited by American and European companies to harvest sugar in Panama and Costa Rica.

1869   Jamaican workers were imported as "swallow migrants" to harvest crops in the American South after the end of slavery; most returned home when the harvest was complete.

1881-1914   A total of 90,000 Jamaicans were recruited by the United States to work on the Panama Canal.

1930   The Census Bureau reported that 100,000 documented first-generation Caribbean immigrants and their children lived in the United States.

1965   Britain restricted the number of immigrants accepted from the newly independent black majority colonies, including Jamaica.

      The Immigration Reform Act opened the way for a new surge of immigrants from the Caribbean.

1966-1970   The United States legally admitted 62,700 Jamaicans.

1971-1975   The United States legally admitted 80,600 Jamaicans.

1976: Music Writer & Critic

Danny Goldberg started out as a low-paid writer at Billboard *magazine, and went on to become a rock 'n' roll insider and respected rock music critic.*

Life at Home

- Danny Goldberg's entry into the music business was completely practical; he needed a job and wanted to get his own apartment.
- According to the newspaper advertisement, *Billboard* magazine had an opening and Danny certainly had a need.
- After graduating from high school, Danny had enrolled at the University of California at Berkeley where he saw Janis Joplin's band Big Brother and the Holding Company, was introduced to LSD and spent five days at the Alameda County Juvenile Hall.
- Raised in New York by well-heeled liberals, Danny began his career at *Billboard* in 1968, where, as an 18-year-old college dropout, he took a job compiling chart data.
- Initially, his job entailed calling dozens of record stores around the country and asking them what was selling, thus providing the raw data for the *Billboard* sales charts, which influenced radio station airplay, TV bookings and orders from retailers.
- "I was at *Billboard* a few months and a promo guy from Capitol gave everybody a copy of (The Beatles') the White Album the day it came out. That was one hell of a perk," Danny said.
- It dawned on Danny that he could be part of the music business without being a musician; "After that I did the best I could to climb whatever ladders were in front of me."
- One of his first major writing assignments for *Billboard* was to cover a weekend event upstate that none of the regulars had any interest in attending: the Woodstock Festival.
- For this special assignment he was paid $0.30 a published inch.
- Along with his press pass to Woodstock, Danny got to ride to the festival in a stretch limousine, heard Santana and Jimi Hendrix for the first time, slept in a clean hotel room

Danny Goldberg worked at Billboard *and was a rock & roll insider.*

Danny's coverage of Woodstock led to his weekly column on rock music.

and was mesmerized by the performances of Joan Baez, Johnny Winter, and Janis Joplin.

- His front-page rhapsodic review landed him a full-time writer's job with Record World, to include a weekly column on rock music.
- That entry point would lead to friendships with Patti Smith, Stevie Nicks, and image management of the 1970s British supergroup, Led Zeppelin.
- Music and the music business were undergoing change, and Danny was determined to be in the epicenter.
- Two rock magazines, *Crawdaddy* and *Rolling Stone*, were applying serious critical intelligence to writing about rock 'n' roll; *Esquire, The Village Voice, The New York Times, The New Yorker* and *The New Republic* all had assigned talented writers to the rock 'n' roll beat.
- Underground rock radio was emerging as a rebellious reaction to the highly repetitive play lists of Top 40 stations—allowing extended cuts from albums to be played and non-traditional groups to receive airplay.
- Even the way the records were put together had changed—moving from a collection of songs to a conceptual, interconnected collection of songs that visited a single theme.
- No longer was the goal to release a record as a vehicle to sell singles, which sold for a dollar, but to construct a coherent, unified body of work that incorporated an overall artistic concept.
- At the same time, Jimi Hendrix and Eric Clapton were eliminating the boundaries of what a rock guitarist could express, and the technology of sound was expanding bands' options.
- By 1969, Danny had become a fixture at the legendary artists' hangout Max's Kansas City, where he would "worm my way" into a clique of influential rock critics.
- There he met future rocker and poet Patti Smith; "Everything about her exuded creativity. Every sentence she uttered. She had an intensity that just came out of her."

- By the early 1970s, Danny was no longer simply a writer—an observer—to the music scene; he was an insider.
- "The truth was that I revered rock musicians and felt guilty when I criticized them," he said.

Life at Work

- Danny Goldberg's first few forays into music public relations were forgettable.
- But that was before he was asked to fly to London and meet the super hot, bad boy band Led Zeppelin—they had a PR problem: they hated the media.
- In the spring of 1973, Led Zeppelin was the biggest band on the planet: their previous album—their fourth—had already sold eight million copies and included the song "Stairway to Heaven," the most played song on the album rock radio stations that year.
- Sales of the first four Zeppelin albums were so consistent that they represented more than one-fourth of the annual sales for the entire Atlantic Records catalogue.
- Formed in 1968, the English rock band Led Zeppelin was known for its heavy, guitar-driven blues-rock sound, also known as heavy metal, and their bad boy antics.
- The American press and Led Zeppelin were uncomfortable in each other's company; even Led Zeppelin's mammoth american tour in 1972 had not eased the problem.
- They wanted to hire Danny as their press agent, but it would not be an easy task.
- Hypersensitive to early bad reviews, members of the band had long demonized journalists; plus, they developed a reputation for throwing television sets out of hotel rooms, driving Harley-Davidsons down hotel hallways, and mistreating young groupies.
- Some members of Led Zeppelin had simply stopped doing interviews or were rude when they did.

Some touring bands were known for trashing the fancy hotels they stayed in.

- Television performances were avoided because the band's big sound did not translate well in the little box—further limiting the media exposure available.
- Before meeting the band the first time, danny had an audience with their legendary manager Peter Grant; who had "the ultimate chip on the ultimate shoulder."
- As one of the first managers to understand that the artists themselves had grown powerful enough to act independently, he had led Led Zeppelin away from the Premier Talent agency in 1971 and begun booking the band

Many popular bands thought that appearing on TV would diminish their fans' experience.

directly without an agent, thus saving 10 percent of the band's total cost, which did not endear him to the music establishment.
- Danny was 22, smart, innovative and possessed a long list of media contacts.
- Led Zeppelin, he was told, wanted the type of publicity that the Rolling Stones routinely received on tour; the former were selling out stadiums across the nation and felt they deserved better treatment from the press.
- Danny began his assault by creating a press release that demonstrated that Led Zeppelin's sold-out show in Tampa Stadium, with 56,800 seats, was larger than the Beatles' Shea Stadium show in 1965.
- Led Zeppelin tickets cost $5.50 each; the Tampa concert grossed $312,400.
- Newspapers across the country carried headlines proclaiming that Led Zeppelin had "broken the Beatles' record" even though the relative size of Tampa Stadium to Shea Stadium was not a true measure of popularity.
- A second series of stories featured the band's leased private plane, called the Starship, which boasted the band's name on the side, velvet couches and rock-star grandiosity.
- The airplane also had a fur-covered bed that was often used, but rarely for sleeping.
- Danny's PR philosophy emphasized the band's popularity and emphasized its role as the people's band despite what some rock critics might think.
- These stories and the momentum they created attracted increased attention of the powerhouse *Rolling Stone* magazine, which promised a major feature; owner Jann Wenner even pledged that the band could pick the writer of the article.
- Danny pleaded, but the band said no.
- Led Zeppelin was accustomed to going their own way—although they would eventually say yes.
- When they were first formed, they rarely got radio play until Boston's WBCN featured "Whole Lotta Love."

Some musicians preferred casual settings as opposed to formal venues.

- Boston had developed a reputation around the country of being reliable taste-makers, thanks to its concentration of trendsetting college students; Boston's acceptance of the band helped launch a national obsession.
- The band's first album and its blend of blues, folk and Eastern influences with distorted amplification made it one of the pivotal records in the creation of heavy metal music.
- In their first year, Led Zeppelin managed to complete four U.S. and four U.K. concert tours, and also released their second album, entitled Led Zeppelin II.
- Recorded almost entirely on the road at various North American recording studios, the second album was an even greater success and reached the number one chart position in the U.S. while establishing the blueprint for heavy metal bands that followed.
- Some early Led Zeppelin concerts lasted more than four hours, with expanded, improvised live versions of their songs.
- During this period of intensive concert touring, the band developed a reputation for off-stage excess.
- The group also increasingly resisted television appearances, enforcing their preference that their fans hear and see them in live concerts.
- Led Zeppelin were one of the most commercially successful and influential groups of the 1970s.
- By the mid-1970s, the symbols of success were everywhere: the band began to wear elaborate, flamboyant clothing, they traveled in a private jet airliner, rented out entire sections of hotels (including the Continental Hyatt House in Los Angeles, known colloquially as the "Riot House"), and became the subject of many of rock's most repeated stories of debauchery.
- Led Zeppelin's fourth album, released in November 1971, was a conspicuous display of fame: there was no indication of a title or a band name on the original cover.
- The cover displayed only symbols—no names or photographs—in response to being labeled as "hyped" and "overrated" by the music press.
- The band wanted to prove that the music could sell itself by giving no indication of who they were.

Led Zeppelin travelled in a private jet.

- *Led Zeppelin IV,* as it came to be called, was one of the bestselling albums in history, and its massive popularity cemented the band's superstardom in the 1970s.
- Zeppelin's next album, *Houses of the Holy,* was released in 1973. It featured further experimentation, with expanded use of synthesizers and mellotron orchestration.
- The orange album cover of *Houses of the Holy* depicted images of nude children climbing up the Giant's Causeway in Northern Ireland, causing controversy.
- In 1974, Led Zeppelin took a break from touring and launched their own record label, Swan Song, named after one of only five Led Zeppelin songs which the band never released commercially.
- In addition to using Swan Song as a vehicle to promote their own albums, the band expanded the label's roster, signing artists such as Bad Company, The Pretty Things, Maggie Bell, Detective, Dave Edmunds, Midnight Flyer, Sad Café and Wildlife.
- Led Zeppelin's double album, *Physical Graffiti,* was their first release on the Swan Song; a review in *Rolling Stone* referred to *Physical Graffiti* as Led Zeppelin's "bid for artistic respectability," adding that the only bands Led Zeppelin had to compete with for the title "The World's Best Rock Band" were The Rolling Stones and The Who.
- The album was a massive fiscal and critical success.

Life in the Community: Los Angeles, California
- Los Angeles, California, in the early 1960s was primed for a major musical innovation.
- With MGM musicals at their peak and film production a long-entrenched part of the scene, the city was filled with first-rate recording studios, orchestras, and session players.
- Initially, surf rock emerged as the southern California sound in the early 1960s, epitomized by the Beach Boys and their first single, "Surfin'," in 1961.

- By the middle of the decade, the tide had turned toward folk and psychedelic rock, and Hollywood clubs such as the Troubadour and the Whisky a Go Go propelled performers such as The Byrds, The Doors, Joni Mitchell, and Buffalo Springfield into the spotlight.
- Rock journalist Roy Trakin noted, "The summer of 1966 on L.A.'s Sunset Strip was a time when many young musicians thought anything was possible. A teenager from the San Fernando Valley might wind up jamming with Jimi Hendrix, while a 14-year-old hitchhiking on Sunset Boulevard could get picked up by Phil Spector's limousine."
- Folk and country rock dominated L.A.'s music scene in the early 1970s, best symbolized by the L.A.-based Eagles, whose *Hotel California* featured the Beverly Hills Hotel and Bungalows on the cover.
- The Rainbow Bar & Grill, which opened in 1972, emerged as a hot Sunset Strip hangout for rock stars.
- Los Angeles also enjoyed a very strong experimental rock scene in the early 1970s, centered around a club called the Rodney Bingenheimer's English Disco, run by Bingenheimer, who later, as a disc jockey for KROQ's "Rodney On The Roq," did much to promote L.A. punk bands.

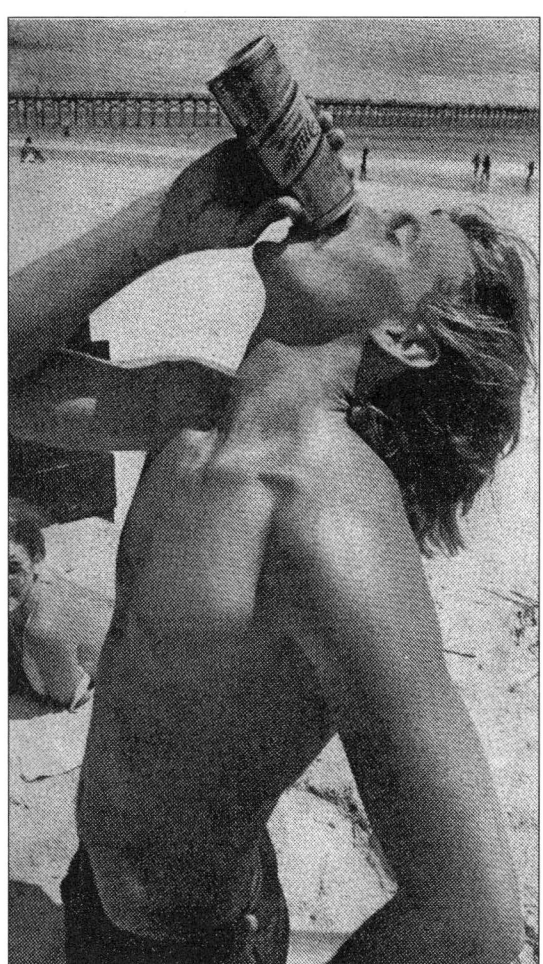

California was primed for a major musical revolution.

- In the mid-1970s, California punk arrived on the Sunset Strip and especially at Whisky a Go Go, which regularly hosted homegrown punk bands such as X, The Runaways and The Germs.

1976: Inventor of Liquid Paper

Bette Nesmith Graham's artistic bent came from her mother, while her entrepreneurial drive and her invention, Liquid Paper, *grew out of necessity.*

Life at Home

- Born in 1924 in Dallas, Texas, but raised in San Antonio, Bette Claire McMurray was strong willed, talkative and sometimes considered a discipline problem at school.
- Her artist mother owned a knitting shop and her father ran an auto parts store.
- When only 17 years old, she dropped out of Alamo Heights High School to marry her high school sweetheart, Warren Nesmith, just before he went off to war.
- Ten months later, their son Michael, who would be famous in the 1960s as a member of the music group The Monkees, was born in 1943.
- When her husband returned from war, their marriage rapidly fell apart, and by 1946 Bette found herself divorced and the single mother of a three-year-old.
- Putting aside her love of art, Bette talked her way into a job as a secretary even though she didn't know how to type.
- The firm liked her energetic spirit and agreed to send her to secretarial school to learn typing.
- By 1951, Bette had moved to Dallas and worked her way up to the role of executive secretary at Dallas Bank and Trust, when the company introduced new IBM electric typewriters.
- Bette, who still struggled to type an entire page without a single mistake, found that the new carbon film ribbons on the machines made matters worse; they did not erase well and corrections simply made a mess.
- Electric typewriters had come into widespread use after World War II, and even though the new machines made typing easier, making corrections with a pencil eraser was nearly impossible.
- Betty grew tired of having to retype the entire page because of a single error or typo.
- That's when she drew inspiration from the artists decorating the bank's front windows at Christmastime.
- To earn extra money, Bette was helping to dress the bank window when she noticed that the artists

Bette Nesmith Graham invented Liquid Paper out of necessity.

Bette was tired of retyping a whole page to fix one mistake.

painting the glass corrected their imperfections by painting another layer over them.
- If erasures were unnecessary on glass, why should they be required on paper?
- Bette then went home and attempted to mimic the artists' techniques by mixing up a white, water-based template paint which she applied with a thin paintbrush to cover her typing errors.
- It worked beautifully.
- Experimenting in her kitchen, she learned how to mix her special formula to match the exact shade of stationery.
- Her boss never noticed the correction paint on his documents, and for five years she kept her invention largely to herself.
- Eventually, word spread throughout the bank; other secretaries were willing to pay for a bottle of the mistake fixer.
- Working over her kitchen sink, Bette prepared the first batch of "Mistake Out" in 1956, which she had bottled with the help of her son and his friends.
- The reaction was enthusiastic, and the recipe for Bette Nesmith's Mistake Out continued to evolve; customers wanted the liquid to be thicker and dry faster.
- Unable to afford a chemist, she recruited a person who worked in the office supply store, her son's high school chemistry teacher, and a friend from a paint-manufacturing company to help her perfect her product.
- Experiments were conducted using an aging mixer on her kitchen counter.
- Nightly she mixed, bottled and shipped the product, now called Liquid Paper, after a full day at the office.
- She struggled to keep up with orders totaling hundreds of bottles per month from her garage.

Life at Work
- Being a full-time secretary and part-time entrepreneur was both exciting and exhausting for Bette Nesmith Graham.
- At one point, she attempted unsuccessfully to persuade IBM to market her invention.

- Knowing that women were not viewed as capable entrepreneurs, she signed her letters to the company "B. Nesmith" to disguise her gender.
- In her spare hours, she visited office supply stores to interest them in her correction fluid.
- Then, in 1958, Bette unexpectedly received an opportunity to market her product full-time after she had made a serious mistake on a letter she typed and sent out.
- She was fired on the spot.
- Suddenly, Liquid Paper was her only means of support; her $300-a-month salary, which had been used to support the family and develop the correction fluid, was gone.
- Luckily, a brief but glowing description of her product in an office trade magazine produced 500 orders from across the United States.
- The Secretary magazine followed up with a favorable report and more orders poured in.
- General Electric Company placed the first single large order for over 400 bottles in three colors—four times her monthly production.
- Despite these successes, in 1960 her company's expenses exceeded its income.
- But the increase in sales for IBM electric typewriters worldwide—and superb word of mouth advertising—were spurring the need for liquid paper correcting fluid.
- In 1961, a decade after she had invented liquid paper, Bette hired her first full-time employee.
- Help also came from a new husband, Robert Graham, who joined her in the business in 1962.
- Together they traveled throughout the South and West demonstrating their magic product.
- In 1963, Liquid Paper increased its weekly production tenfold from 500 to 5,000 bottles.

You no longer have to choose between tape dictation and belt dictation.

- Three years later, the company was selling 40,000 bottles per week, and moved its operations into a 10 by 26-foot metal shed Bette had built in her backyard.
- There the bottles were filled, labels attached and distribution handled.
- By 1968, the company was grossing $1 million annually and constructing its own automated factory.
- Bette's kitchen sink was no longer large enough to keep up with demand.
- The new factory, designed by Bette, included a daycare center for her employees to accommodate the needs of working mothers.
- Raised in the Methodist Church but having converted to Christian Science in 1942, Bette gave credit to her religion for her success.
- To that end, her corporate statement of policy emphasized egalitarian thinking and proclaimed that the company was built to foster the cultural,

educational and spiritual development of its employees.
- Company committees comprised a cross-section of employees.
- Every aspect of the new factory was designed to encourage communication between those who worked in the office complex and those in the plant.
- Her belief that women brought a more caring culture to the male-dominated business world was demonstrated by the fish pond included in the company greenway and the company library.
- In 1971, the number of bottles sold surpassed five million.
- By 1975, Liquid Paper Corporation had built an international headquarters in Dallas capable of producing 500 bottles a minute.
- But the sweet taste of success was tempered by her deteriorating relationship with her husband, Robert Graham.
- With their marriage ending and their messy divorce, Bette decided to retire in 1975, leaving her husband to run the company she had built.
- Shrewdly, Bette remained the majority stockholder.
- Almost immediately, she regretted her decision to retire.
- Her ex-husband eliminated the cherished Statement of Policy and changed the format for Liquid Paper to deprive her of many of her royalties.
- Bette then launched a fight for control of the company.
- A self-proclaimed feminist, Bette also established in 1976 a foundation designed to educate "mature" women in business practices.

Life in the Community: San Antonio, Texas
- San Antonio, the second-largest city in Texas, was famous for Spanish missions and the Alamo.
- San Antonio's economy depended upon attracting thousands of tourists annually and the strong military presence, including Fort Sam Houston, Lackland Air Force Base, and Randolph Air Force Base.
- Early Spanish settlement of San Antonio began as a means to reassert Spanish dominance over Texas from the nearby French in Louisiana.
- In 1719, the Marqués de San Miguel de Aguayo made a report to the king of Spain proposing that 400 families be transported from the Canary Islands, Galicia, or Havana to populate the province of Texas.
- San Antonio grew to become the largest Spanish settlement in Texas, and for most of its history, the capital of the Spanish—later Mexican—province of Tejas.
- The Battle of the Alamo took place from February 23 to March 6, 1836.
- The outnumbered Texian force was ultimately defeated, with all of the Alamo defenders seen as "martyrs" for the cause of Texas' freedom.
- "Remember the Alamo" became a rallying cry in the Texan Army's eventual success at defeating Santa Anna's army.

- In 1845, the United States annexed Texas and included it as a state in the Union, which led to the Mexican-American War.
- During the war, the population of San Antonio was reduced by almost two-thirds, or 800 inhabitants; by 1860, at the start of the Civil War, San Antonio had grown to a city of 15,000 people.
- In 1877, the first railroad reached San Antonio and the city was no longer on the frontier.
- At the beginning of the twentieth century, the streets of San Antonio's downtown section were widened to accommodate streetcars and modern traffic, with many historic buildings destroyed in the process.
- The city continued to experience steady population growth, and boasted a population of just over 650,000 in the 1970 Census.

1977: Daughter of Single Mother

Raised by a single mother, eight-year-old Maria Genovese enjoyed flying kites, washing dishes, and gossiping with her best friend, Barbara, in Buffalo, New York.

Life at Home

- Eight-year-old Maria Genovese and her mother Anne lived in an urban renewal housing project on the shores of Lake Erie, on the lower west side of Buffalo, New York.
- Maria attended a nearby elementary school and spent most afternoons at a daycare center organized by her mother, who was in her second year as an attorney for the Erie County Department of Social Services.
- Her specialty was child welfare; one of her most demanding tasks was determining which children should be removed from their homes because of abuse, neglect, or inadequate food.
- Maria never met her father, who was rarely mentioned, and she has learned not to ask too many questions.
- Shortly after they moved to the area, Maria's mother led a committee of parents to form an after-school daycare program at the housing complex.
- When school was over at 2 p.m., children from throughout the area were brought to the facility to study, play, watch TV or wrestle until their parents arrive.
- Like Maria, several of the children lived with only their mothers; most saw their fathers occasionally, some as often as weekly.
- Maria liked the center, especially since her mother was always busy and nearly always late getting home from court.
- She had dozens of friends at the center, and often they constructed intricate games or work on art projects together.
- Occasionally, with her mother's written permission, they went on field trips, which were tremendous fun as long as everyone behaved, held hands crossing the street, and kept quiet when the leader was talking.
- Maria hated for adults to get mad and scold the children.

Maria Genovese lived with her mother in Buffalo, New York.

- Maria's mother Anne grew up in a strong Catholic household in Queens.
- She attended parochial school, lived to watch American Bandstand with her friends, talked endlessly about guys and argued about what a boy was actually doing when he reached "second base"—and whether or not she would like that.
- In college she confronted a much wider—and wilder—world away from the protection of her home.
- She realized how sheltered she had been and concluded that she was letting down her country by not speaking out concerning the war in Vietnam.
- With some encouragement from her new friends, she felt it her duty to protest, often and loud.
- Quickly, she absorbed literature she had never seen in her home, regularly reading radical newspapers such as The Great Speckled Bird and discussing concepts of war and sacrifice well into the night—occasionally to the detriment of her studies.

Young Maria enjoyed Christmastime.

- She also fell in love with her soul mate, a man who shared her views and took her seriously.
- During the last days of her sophomore year, her boyfriend left the United States for Canada to escape the draft.
- Two weeks later she discovered she was pregnant with Maria.
- She wrote to her boyfriend repeatedly with the news, but never received a response.
- An abortion was unthinkable; her own father disowned her and forbade anyone in the family from speaking to her ever again.

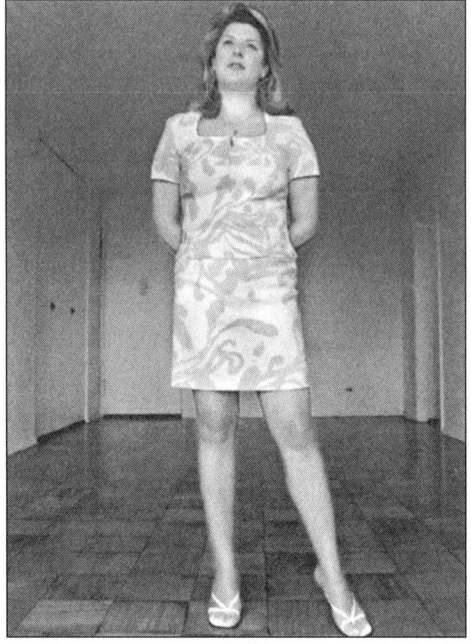

Maria's mother, Anne, worked her way through school.

- After the baby was born, Anne and little Maria attended college together, living on welfare, school loans, part-time jobs and a small trust fund set up two decades earlier by Anne's grandfather.
- Anne finished college with a degree in social work, a badly bruised ego, lots of student debt and a two-year-old child.
- Somehow, law school seemed the logical next step, so Anne and Maria went through it together, studying every minute of the day.
- Anne thought she could make a difference and make up for lost time with Maria.
- Poverty, unemployment, underemployment, rage and frustration were among the many issues Anne confronted each day on the job.
- Often after saving Buffalo's children, Anne had little time for her own, but pushed on.
- She worried a lot about whether she was a good parent, even while in the midst of organizing another project for the community.

- As a special treat, she and Maria stayed up night after night to watch every episode of the television miniseries Roots.
- Though Anne kept telling her what each scene meant, Maria didn't care about the history or who was wronged; she just loved the story and watching TV with her mom.

Life at School

- Most mornings, Maria walked to her second-grade class, only five blocks away.
- Even though the newspapers were filled with stories about the integration of schools, she saw little change; everyone in her class was white.
- Her mother said that will change soon; a judicial order handed down required that black children from the east side of Main Street be bussed into her school in the fall when she started the third grade.
- Maria had heard several of the mothers talk about moving to the suburbs where there were few blacks.
- Anne, on the other hand, was excited that the black children would have an opportunity to get a better education, and talked endlessly about what a great learning experience Maria would have going to school with black children.
- Maria didn't care as long as she gets to attend school; she loved learning and reading and being with her friends.
- Going to school was simply heaven, particularly her handwriting class, where the teacher consistently said her work was among the best.
- At night, when alone, Maria endlessly practiced her cursive strokes and prepared entire pages of script, simply for her own satisfaction.

Maria loved school and being with her friends.

- She also loved owning a calculator—a gift from her mother on her birthday in February.
- She was not allowed to use it at school, because calculators were banned there, and considered an inappropriate shortcut.
- But she used it at home to add up everything; last week she added up every telephone number on one page of the phone book, just for fun.
- When asked by her mother's friends, "Are you going to be a lawyer like your mother when you grow up?" she said she wanted to be a mathematician, which always drew praise.
- She was not really sure what a mathematician did all day except play with a calculator.
- Maria also loved to talk, especially with her friend Barbara who lived next door and was a year older.
- Barbara knew everything, even things about boys, because she had brothers.
- She also knew which songs were cool and had her own record player in her room.
- Thanks to Barbara, Maria learned that continuing to wear Mickey Mouse panties was baby stuff and should stop immediately.
- Just being around Barbara made Maria feel grown up.
- When they were together, Anne called them the "giggle girls."
- Several days this winter, school was cancelled because of snow.
- Buffalo experienced 47 consecutive days of snow, and not only was school cancelled, it was too cold even to go outside.
- For the past several months, Anne had been dating Joe Notvitski, a sociology professor who lived nearby.

Growing up in Buffalo meant lots of snow days!

- A native of Michigan and a Vietnam War veteran, he attended college on the G.I. Bill, and eventually earned a Ph.D.
- Maria loved having him around.
- Because of his flexible class schedule, he occasionally came by the daycare center around 4 p.m. And took Maria to the park and other places.
- With Anne's permission, the two explored the Buffalo Museum of Science, the Albright-Knox Art Gallery and her favorite, the Buffalo Zoo.
- Mr. Notvitski even promised to rent a boat and take her sailing on Lake Erie.
- Twice they flew kites together; Mr. Notvitski could make his kite dive like a rocket and then jump back into the sky at just the right moment.

- They also washed dishes together—Mr. Notvitski said he doesn't need a dishwashing machine as long as Maria was around—and sometimes they fix meals.
- Without being asked, he has took her to her favorite movie, Rocky, three times—more than any of her friends—and she hoped for a fourth showing.
- Maria was especially pleased that he ignored all the warnings from her mother about eating healthy, and snuck her a taco on the field trips and a pop tart for breakfast.
- It felt so deliciously wicked to eat a taco behind her mother's back.
- Maria spent even more time with Mr. Notvitski; her mother seemed to be called away almost nightly to handle emergencies, but she did not miss Maria's birthday party, which began at their apartment, but then shifted to his house.
- There she opened her presents, including a Bionic Woman doll, from her favorite television show, and a Beauty Salon and Repair Station.
- At Mr. Notvitski's, she also found a sign posted on the door of the spare bedroom where she often slept when her mother was away at night.
- Printed in green and white letters on computer paper were the words "Maria's Other Room."
- When she opened the door, she found that he had painted the room pink and hung frilly floral curtains just like in the magazines.

Life in the Community: Buffalo, New York

- The economic base of Buffalo was drying up due to the opening of the St. Lawrence Seaway, which ended the city's long run as a transportation center.
- The steel and automotive industries, which were a mainstay of the economy, began to contract.
- Buffalo's population was shrinking, its unemployment rate was rising, and the general age of the citizenry was getting older.
- At the same time, well-intentioned urban renewal projects and threats of desegregation were breaking apart many once-stable ethnic neighborhoods.
- Those who could afford to move into the suburbs were fleeing the city.
- Attempts to stem the tide with a new campus of the University of Buffalo on the lakefront ended with investments going to Amherst instead, making that community the fastest-growing in the state.

Changing America

- A Princeton University study showed that 6.8 million married couples had elected surgical contraception.
- The FDA banned Red Dye No. 2 as an additive in foods, drugs and cosmetics.
- The Supreme Court reversed a New York law that prohibited the distribution of contraceptives to minors.
- The Li'l Abner comic strip ceased publication.
- International tourism broke all records; popular destinations were Venice, London and Paris.

- America's infant mortality was 16.1 per 1,000 births; maternal mortality was 12.8 per 10,000 births.
- Fred M. Hechinger, editor of *The New York Times*, wrote, "The massive failure in basic skills—particularly reading and writing—is nothing short of scandalous."
- Charleston, South Carolina, hosted the new Spoleto Festival U.S.A., which opened with Tchaikovsky's Pique Dame.
- Van Gogh's painting "La Fin de la Journée" sold for $880,000.
- A study reported that alcohol consumed during pregnancy may injure the fetus.
- The Japanese car industry employed 7,000 robots for painting, welding and assembly.
- A study showed that only 21 percent of pregnant, unmarried teens chose to give birth, of whom 87 percent decided to keep their children.
- America imported 1.5 million foreign cars, breaking all previous records.
- The popularity of smoke detectors soared, with more than eight million sold.

1977: Professional Hockey Player

Sonny Howell credited hard work for his success in the National Hockey League, where only winning, beating a man to the puck, and having last-period stamina, mattered.

Life at Home

- One of seven children, Sonny Howell grew up playing basketball in Walpole, Massachusetts, where playing hockey was serious business.
- His three older brothers were basketball players, but most of Sonny's friends were obsessed with hockey.
- At first, Sonny followed his brothers' lead, and didn't play organized hockey until he was 13 years old.
- Then, almost overnight, he became fascinated by the angles and speed of the game.
- He skated on the bantam team as a high school freshman, followed by three years of varsity hockey.
- Never a great goal scorer, Sonny's size and versatility allowed the team to employ him in numerous positions—particularly on defense—to stop the competition's best player.
- It was a strategy that produced team wins, but did not endow Sonny with a total command of a single position.
- "They were always looking for someone who was big enough to play defense, so I was shifted from position to position; but I was sure I was still good enough to play at the college level."
- But it was football that brought Sonny to Colgate University in Hamilton, New York, on an athletic scholarship.
- Sonny was most interested in Colgate because of its academic standing, with athletics a means to an end.
- After a successful freshman year in football as a defensive halfback, Sonny was offered the chance to play hockey.
- The collegiate football and hockey seasons overlapped, so a choice had to be made: hockey defenseman or football defensive halfback.

Sonny Howell chose hockey over all other sports.

- Sonny chose hockey and developed into a spectacular player—the type that always hustled, always anticipated the next pass and never tired of being physical.
- Fortuitously, three Boston Bruins scouts were spectators at the Invitational Tournament during his senior year at Colgate.
- Sonny played well enough to get a tryout invitation with the Bruins.
- All he had to do was work hard and his career would be launched.

Life at Work

- Sonny Howell, at six foot two and 205 pounds, worked for months getting ready for the Boston Bruins training camp.
- "I ran, skated a couple of times a day, lifted weights—just everything I could think of from sun-up to sundown to get ready for the tryouts."
- Friends worked out with him in shifts—one in the morning, one in the afternoon and one in the early evening.
- Sonny's high energy and determination required three athletes to keep up with his training regimen.
- On the first day of training camp, Sonny was sure he was prepared.
- Within the first hour, he realized how much work he still had ahead if he wanted to be a professional.
- Camp was brutal.
- It seemed that everyone was faster and smarter.
- But no one worked harder.
- Time in the American Hockey League would be required before he was ready to handle the power moves and stick play of the National Hockey League.
- The American Hockey League was tough, populated by players desperate to move up to the NHL or terrified that they were about to be moved out of hockey altogether.
- Friendships were fluent and moods were mercurial.
- On the long bus rides from game to game, Sonny read history books—especially concerning World War I.
- His grandfather fought in the Great War and had returned from France with a limp, a souvenir rifle and an incurable wanderlust.
- After the war, the day-to-day duties on the farm paled beside the uncountable possibilities of travel and adventure.

Sonny was a versatile player and always hustled on the ice.

- Sonny's father grew up on the road, moving with his restless father every few years.
- The traveling stopped when the car his grandfather was driving through the mountains failed to make a turn and hurdled 1,200 feet to the canyon floor.
- Sonny believed that the secret to his grandfather's emotional life was concealed in the muddy trenches of WWI France.
- So before every away game, he checked another book out of the public library and studied his personal history.
- At the end of the first season with the Rochester Americans, Sonny had played well enough to earn the opportunity to make it in the big leagues.
- Sonny played 10 exhibition games with the pros, but lost his chance to move up on the last day.
- He was assigned to another season in the AHL.
- It was a huge disappointment.
- He had been so sure that he made the team that he told his father to buy season tickets to the big league club.
- So, based on his background, only one path was available: more hard work.
- His next opportunity came as a substitute for an injured player in the 1977 NHL playoffs.
- He played well and the team continued to win, so Sonny stayed and someone else moved down to the American Hockey League.
- With a reluctant nod from his pregnant wife, Sonny bought a house in Hamilton, New York, home of Colgate University.
- Even if his 30-year mortgage outlasted his career by 29 years, he and family would have a home.

Life in the Community: Hamilton, New York

- The village of Hamilton is about 10 miles from the geographic center of New York State, in the rolling hills of the Chenango Valley, approximately five hours from New York City.
- Hamilton was founded in 1795 by Elisha Payne and incorporated in 1816.
- By 1820, Hamilton was an active trading center for an extensive farming area and boasted two taverns, several stores, a schoolhouse, church, newspaper, grist mill and sawmill.

Hockey was a popular pastime in Hamilton, New York.

- For Sonny Howell and his family, the biggest attraction Hamilton had to offer was Colgate University.
- For many years, Hamilton's major industry had been the university.
- In addition, Hamilton was a charming and essentially rural community that had changed little in either size or character during the past 100 years.
- The college got its start in 1817, when 13 men—six clergy and seven laymen—had met with "13 dollars, 13 prayers, and 13 articles."
- In that meeting, the men founded the Baptist Education Society of the State of New York, the cornerstone in the foundation of what would become Colgate University.
- The state chartered the Baptist Education Society in 1819, choosing Hamilton as the location for its school.
- In 1823, Baptists in New York City—soapmaker William Colgate among them—consolidated their seminary with the Hamilton School to form the Hamilton Literary and Theological Institution.
- By 1846, the institution was renamed Madison University and, through a state charter, was given the right to grant degrees.
- Madison became Colgate in 1890, recognizing nearly 70 years of continuous involvement and service by the Colgate family.
- The Theological Division merged with the Rochester Theological Seminary in 1928 to become the Colgate Rochester Divinity School, and Colgate became nonsectarian.
- The university became coeducational in 1970.
- By 1977, Colgate was a highly selective, independent, coeducational liberal arts college enrolling approximately 2,700 undergraduates.
- With a population of 2,500, the village of Hamilton was roughly the size of the student body of Colgate.
- Approximately 85 percent of the university's faculty members lived within 10 minutes of its campus.

ふ今ふ今ふ今ふ今

Hockey Timeline

1877 The first known rules for hockey were published by the *Montréal Gazette*.

1888 The Amateur Hockey Association of Canada was formed, with four teams in Montréal, one in Ottawa and one in Quebec City.

Circa 1892 The first women's hockey game was played in Ottawa or Barrie, Ontario.

1893 Frederick Arthur (Lord Stanley of Preston and Governor-General of Canada) donated a trophy to be called the Dominion Hockey Challenge Cup, which later became known as the Stanley Cup.

1894 The first artificial ice rink opened in Baltimore.

1895 College athletes from the United States and Canada played the first international series of matches; the Canadians won all four games.

1896 The Winnipeg Victorias became the first team from Western Canada to win the Stanley Cup.

1900 The goal net was introduced.

1904 Five teams in the United States and Ontario formed the International Hockey League, the first league of professional teams; it lasted three seasons.

1910 The Montréal Canadiens played their first game after joining a new league called the National Hockey Association.

1911 Teams in Western Canada formed the Pacific Coast Hockey Association (PCHA) and introduced several innovations: blue lines were added to divide the ice into three zones, goaltenders were permitted to fall to the ice to make saves, forward passing was allowed in the neutral zone and the 60-minute game was divided into three 20-minute periods.

1912 The number of players allowed on the ice was reduced from seven to six per team.

1917 Four NHA teams reorganized to form the National Hockey League. The Seattle Metropolitans of the PCHA became the first American-based team to win the Stanley Cup.

1920 An ice hockey tournament was played at the Summer Olympics, with Canada winning.

1923 Foster Hewitt called the first hockey broadcast for radio, an intermediate game between teams from Kitchener and Toronto.

1924 The Boston Bruins defeated the Montréal Maroons 2-1 in the first NHL game played in the United States. The NHL increased the regular season schedule from 24 to 30 games; players on the first-place Hamilton Tigers refused to compete in the 1925 playoffs unless they were paid for the extra games played.

Ice hockey debuted at the Winter Olympics, with Canada winning the gold medal.

1926 The New York Rangers, Chicago Black Hawks and Detroit Cougars (later renamed the Red Wings) joined the NHL. The Western Hockey League disbanded and sold most of its players to the new NHL teams, leaving the NHL as the undisputed top hockey league in North America.

1929 The first offside rule was introduced.

1934 Ralph Bowman of the St. Louis Eagles scored the first penalty shot goal.

1936 The New York Americans defeated Toronto 3-2 in the first game to be broadcast coast-to-coast in Canada. Great Britain won the Olympic gold medal, marking Canada's first significant loss in international ice hockey.

1937 A rule to deal with icing was introduced.

1942 The Brooklyn Americans withdrew from the NHL, leaving the Canadiens, Maple Leafs, Red Wings, Bruins, Rangers and Black Hawks.

1945 The NHL season began in October for the first time.

1946 Babe Pratt became the first NHL player suspended for betting on games. Referees began using hand signals to indicate penalties and other rulings.

1947 Billy Reay of the Montréal Canadiens became the first NHL player to raise his arms and stick in celebration after scoring a goal.

1949 The center red line first appeared on the ice.

1952   Hockey Night in Canada made its television debut.

1955   NHL officials wore striped sweaters for the first time.

The Zamboni made its NHL debut when Montréal hosted Toronto.

1956   Jean Beliveau was the first hockey player to appear on the cover of Sports Illustrated. The USSR competed in Olympic ice hockey for the first time, winning the gold medal.

1957   The first NHL Player's Association was formed with Detroit's Ted Lindsay as president.

CBS became the first U.S. television network to carry NHL games.

1958   Willie O'Ree of the Boston Bruins became the first black player in the NHL.

1961   The Hockey Hall of Fame opened in Toronto.

1963   The first NHL amateur draft was held in Montréal, with 21 players selected.

1967   The NHL doubled in size, adding franchises in Pittsburgh, Los Angeles, Minnesota, Oakland, St. Louis and Philadelphia.

1970   The Buffalo Sabres and Vancouver Canucks joined the NHL.

1972   The World Hockey Association began play, outbidding NHL teams for several star players.

Star Bobby Hull became hockey's first million-dollar man when he left the Chicago Black Hawks and signed a 10-year, $2.75 million contract with the World Hockey Association (WHA) Winnipeg Jets.

The Atlanta Flames and New York Islanders joined the NHL.

1974   The Kansas City Scouts and Washington Capitals joined the NHL.

The USSR won the first World Junior Hockey Championship.

A second Canada-Soviet exhibition series took place, featuring Canadians from the WHA against the Soviet national team.

1975   Soviet club teams played in North America for the first time when the Central Red Army and Soviet Wings played a series of exhibition games against NHL teams.

1976   Two franchises moved: the California Seals became the Cleveland Barons and the Kansas City Scouts became the Colorado Rockies.

1977: American in China Helps Refugees

Born in Peking, China, to American parents running a YMCA, Harry Johnson made use of his government service experience to assist Vietnamese refugees arriving in Hong Kong.

Life at Home

- After a lifetime of government service, Harry Johnson was tackling a challenge he found impossible to resist: assisting refugees.
- At first, he provided aid to those fleeing the turbulent world of Communist China, but in 1977 the harbor of Hong Kong became a center for thousands of Vietnamese "boat people" seeking food, shelter and an opportunity to relocate to America.
- It was a consuming task, and Harry had never been happier.
- After three decades of managing information about the changing face of China, he was grappling daily with the economic realities of helping refugees.
- Harry was born in Peking, China, in 1919 while his parents were in language school in training for the job of running a YMCA in China.
- His father had been appointed general secretary for the YMCA in Nanchang, where Harry grew up.
- The first trip to the United States was a year-long sojourn in 1924 that included a coast-to-coast automobile trip.
- At age five, Harry was introduced to running water, flush toilets and electric lights aboard the ship that brought the family to Seattle.
- Following fad and fashion, the family camped their way across America, often following roads so rough they could barely claim that name.
- In China, the family lived in a two-story brick house in Nanchang that offered no plumbing and few amenities.
- Most of Harry's friends were American except for the children of servants.
- He spent little time at the YMCA, which served the Chinese with services such as English and Bible classes and vocational courses such as stone block lithography or complex wood chest carving.

Harry Johnson assisted Vietnamese refugees in Hong Kong.

- Summers in China were spent at the mountain resort of Kuling, an enclave of foreign residents of China, established by a New Zealand missionary and made available to Americans and others.
- School was provided by American missions and home schooling that followed the Calvert System in Baltimore, a program that was created for Americans living overseas, offering books, study guides and tests in a single package.
- The stock market crash of 1929 ultimately forced the reduction of the YMCA's support of its program in China.
- Most of the 150 American workers there had to be released; fortunately, the Chinese staff had been properly trained and continued the work.

Harry's family lived in a two-story brick house in Nanchang, China.

- Back in the U.S., when Harry entered the seventh grade in La Jolla, California, it was only his second year of formal education.
- When Harry's dad asked the boys if they wanted to return to China, both said yes, despite the conveniences of American life.
- They returned to China, and after high school, Harry entered college at Yenching University in Peking.
- His second year was spent at Occidental College in Los Angeles, California, where he felt like a misfit.
- His fellow students were so parochial that they rarely thought beyond, "Will I get a date on Saturday?" or "Will the Oxy team win this weekend?"
- His inability to acclimate drove him to transfer to the University of California at Berkeley.
- There he joined a co-op housing organization which controlled costs by doing much of their own work, such as waiting tables or policing the grounds.

Harry grew used to living in China.

- Room and board was $23.00 per month.
- This became his introduction to blue collar workers and people who promoted the concept of worker unionization.
- By his senior year, Harry was vice president of the house and head of entertainment.
- Discussion forums included a program on the war raging in Europe and America's role in early 1941.
- The panel included speakers from the American Legion, the Socialist Workers Party, and the local Communist Party, which initially refused to be on the same program with the Socialists and the Christian pacifists.
- In the discussion, the speaker from the American Legion nearly caused a riot by insisting, "We will soon get into this war and you will be the first to sign up."

- After the Japanese attack on Pearl Harbor, Harry enlisted in the Navy and was assigned to Japanese language school.
- In January 1943, he was assigned as a translator at the Pearl Harbor-based Joint Intelligence Center.
- There he translated captured Japanese documents, including soldiers' diaries and inscriptions on maps, and provided intelligence to the Pacific theater.
- He also organized the creation of a gazetteer of Japanese place names arranged by Chinese characters—much needed, as all Japanese gazetteers were arranged phonetically.
- After the war, Harry joined the Office of Naval Intelligence and 18 months later was assigned to the Naval Attaché's office at the American Embassy in Nanking, China.
- During that tour, Harry and his growing family were caught up in the Communist takeover of Nanking and for six months were their "guests" under constant threat of imprisonment.
- On their second daughter's first birthday, the family was allowed to board a ship to America.
- The next assignment was in the Pentagon.

Fishing was a big industry in Nanking.

Life at Work

- For some time, Harry understood that he was incompatible with the military mind.
- As early as the 1950s, Harry had been lambasted by his naval superiors at the Pentagon for suggesting that the Chinese Communists had viewed America's massing of troops along the Yalu River as an offensive act that helped trigger China's role in the Korean War.
- If only America had maintained communications, the always-wary and often-attacked Chinese might have responded to America's show of military might differently, he told them.
- The advice of the China expert was not well received; he was labeled a sympathizer and a Communist.
- Convinced by the experience that he was better suited to preserving world peace than planning the next war, Harry jumped at the opportunity to serve as a China expert at the State Department.
- From 1951 to 1974, he was with the State Department and served two four-year terms as a consul in Hong Kong while in the Foreign Service.
- At age 55 and retired from government service, Harry was ready for another challenge when he was asked to return to Hong Kong, this time for the International Rescue Committee, or IRC.
- He and his family had previously been stationed in Hong Kong from 1956 to 1961, then from 1965 to 1969.
- In 1974, Hong Kong felt like home.
- With headquarters 12,000 miles away, Harry enjoyed relative autonomy.
- His job, as IRC Hong Kong office director, was to run five-day nurseries and assist the Chinese nationals who had escaped the Communist mainland by fleeing to the island of Hong Kong, which had been a British colony since 1842.
- Then the Vietnam War officially ended in 1975, and the tide of refugees coming to Hong Kong began to change from predominately Chinese to Vietnamese.
- Within two years, what began as a trickle in 1975 became a flood, taxing the capacity of the available housing, sewage system and patience of the Hong Kong government.

- At first the refugees, many of whom had braved days at sea on rickety boats, were housed at warehouses at the docks while the governmental red tape was untangled.
- Then, practically overnight, Harry and the IRC were told to find housing for 800 desperate refugees, which quickly became 7,000 Vietnamese boat people.
- Quickly, the IRC transformed two buildings of 90 apartments each into dwellings for thousands.
- The apartments had been constructed as military officer housing before World War II and had been largely abandoned since then.
- Harry was consumed by the task of feeding, housing and processing the needy.
- Most had faced oppression for years and trusted few.
- The Hong Kong government supplied food; the Lutheran World Relief helped the people complete immigration applications, and the IRC attempted to keep pace with the boat people escaping Southeast Asia.
- In the aftermath of the Vietnam War, the homeless Vietnamese were people adrift, suffering through the trauma of war, the fall of South Vietnam, threats, relocations, re-education, escape, leaky ships, foreign languages, lots of paperwork, few personal documents, fewer connections to Hong Kong and strong desires to reach America.

Thousands of Vietnamese boat people arrived in Hong Kong in the 1970s.

- And in the center of the chaos was Harry, charged with untangling the bureaucracy, calming the people, securing aid, moving refugees in and out, dealing with the Hong Kong government, and paying a staff.

Life in the Community: Southeast Asia

- After the war in Vietnam ended on April 30, 1975, over 130,000 Vietnamese left the country in the final moments of that war.
- Of these, some 65,000 Vietnamese military and government officials and Vietnamese employees of the United States and their families were considered "at risk" and were evacuated directly by the U.S. military; another 65,000 got out on their own in military aircraft, ships and boats.
- Most were taken first to Guam and then resettled in the United States.
- The last two Americans to die in that war were lost late when their CH-46 evacuation helicopter crashed at sea near the USS Hancock, one of the navy ships receiving refugees; they were en route back to the mainland to collect more refugees.
- The United States thought that this initial wave would comprise all the Vietnamese war-related refugees needing sanctuary in the United States.
- In fact, this evacuation was merely the beginning.
- In the end, some three million people left their homes in the former French Indochinese colonies of Vietnam, Laos, and Cambodia, including 1.75 million Vietnamese land refugees and boat people.
- In the years immediately following 1975, only a small trickle of Vietnamese left on boats heading for destinations throughout the area: Malaysia, Thailand, Indonesia, Hong Kong, and the Philippines.
- But by 1977, the trickle had become a torrent.

- The exodus of those getting out of Vietnam was linked to the new policies pursued by Vietnam's unified revolutionary government.
- By the end of 1977, more than 15,600 Vietnamese had landed on the shores of Southeast Asian countries and Hong Kong.
- Refugee officials and diplomats commonly called them "the boat people."
- A few were indeed fishermen, but most were city folk who knew nothing of the ocean or its dangers.
- Nobody knew how many had drowned or been murdered by pirates.

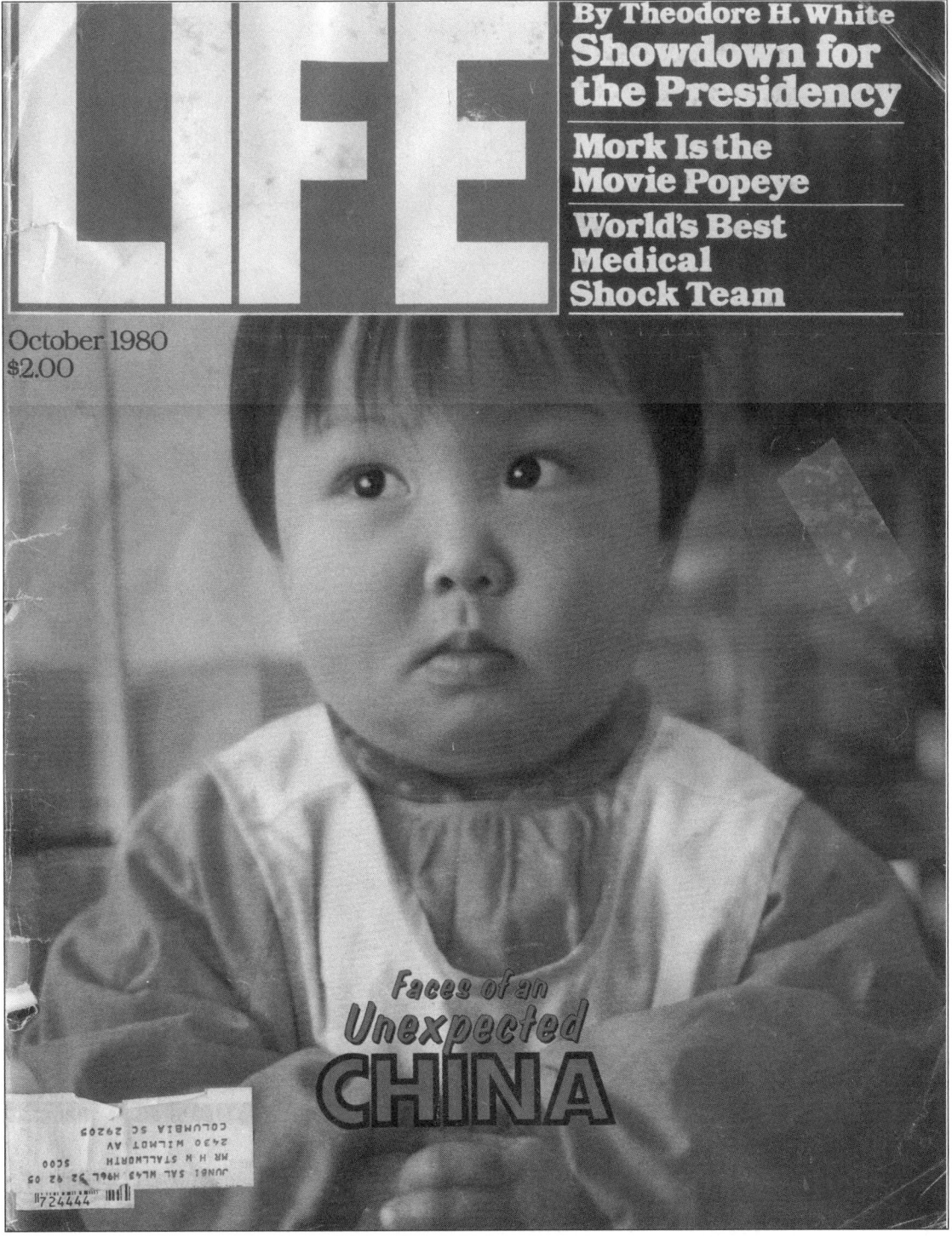

- But more than two years after the fall of Saigon, they kept coming, and in increasing numbers.
- Some ran the gauntlet of the pirates to the Thai coast where the Thais, their camps already full of Cambodians and Laotians, were beginning to turn them away.
- Some looked toward Singapore, which was not the refugee haven for which they had hoped.
- And some headed for the Philippines or Hong Kong.
- The refugees' stories had a sameness that could be summed up in the word "incompatibility," and reflected the Communists' demands that the South Vietnamese middle class learn to love their new role as agricultural laborers.
- Some spent months in detention camps, knowing that sooner or later they would be taken to a re-education camp.

- None of the Southeast Asian countries was prepared to let more than a handful stay permanently.
- And the American quota of 15,000 for Indochinese refugees fell far short of the total of 80,000 in camps in Thailand alone.
- Most governments felt that the continuing departure of refugees from Indochina was an American problem resulting from the Vietnam War, and did not want to consider letting these refugees stay in their countries.
- They didn't even want to call them "refugees," using instead the phrases "displaced persons" and "illegal immigrants."
- Most of the countries in the area had somewhat stable but historically delicate "balanced" multiethnic societies.
- They feared that the arrival and permanent resettlement of Vietnamese, especially ethnically Chinese Vietnamese, could upset that balance.
- The Hong Kong Chinese believed their British Crown colony to be a "three-legged stool," with one leg in Beijing, another in London, and the third in Hong Kong.
- This fragile tripod arrangement officially began on January 20, 1841, when Britain's China Trade Superintendent annexed Hong Kong Island on his own volition to obtain trade concessions, to recover compensation for thousands of chests of British opium confiscated earlier at Canton, and to redeem a bent British pride.
- Six days later, Commodore Sir J. Gordon Bremer led a British naval force onto Possession Point for the ritual planting of Her Majesty's flag.
- The annexation was instantly unpopular in both London and Beijing, but remained in place.

International Rescue Committee Timeline

1933 The American branch of the European-based International Relief Association (IRA) was founded at the suggestion of Albert Einstein to assist Germans suffering under Hitler; refugees from Mussolini's Italy and Franco's Spain were later assisted.

1940 The Emergency Rescue Committee (ERC) formed to aid European refugees trapped in Vichy France; over 2,000 political, cultural, union and academic leaders were rescued in 13 months.

1942 The IRA and ERC joined forces under the name International Relief and Rescue Committee, later shortened to the International Rescue Committee (IRC).

1946 The IRC, at the end of World War II, initiated emergency relief programs, established hospitals and children's centers, and started refugee resettlement efforts in Europe.

After the descent of the Iron Curtain in 1946, the IRC initiated a resettlement program for East European refugees, which continued until the end of the Cold War.

1950 The IRC intensified its aid in Europe with Project Berlin, providing food to the people of West Berlin amid increased Soviet oppression.

1954 In South Vietnam, the IRC began a program to aid one million refugees following defeat of the French by the North Vietnamese; the program was expanded to include resettlement for Indochinese refugees from Vietnam, Laos and Cambodia.

1956 The IRC began resettlement and relief programs for Hungarian refugees after the revolution was crushed by Soviet forces.

1960 An IRC resettlement program began for Cuban refugees fleeing the Castro dictatorship and for Haitian refugees escaping the Duvalier regime.

1962 IRC operations were extended to Africa when 200,000 Angolans fled to Zaire; the IRC also provided aid to Chinese fleeing to Hong Kong from the mainland.

1971 The IRC provided extensive support, especially medical, health, child care and schooling, for the 10 million East Pakistani refugees fleeing to India.

The IRC began the resettlement of Asian nationals persecuted and expelled from Uganda by dictator Idi Amin.

1975 Chilean refugees were assisted by the IRC in their efforts to win asylum in the U.S. President Gerald Ford signed the Indochina Migration and Refugee Act, which admitted 130,000 Southeast Asian refugees into the United States.

1976 The IRC began emergency relief, medical, educational and self-help programs for Indochinese refugees fleeing to Thailand, later to include thousands from Burma.

In Vietnam, the Fourth Party Congress began the mass relocation of people and forced collectivization of agriculture, creating economic chaos.

1977 The IRC organized the Citizens Commission on Indochinese Refugees and served as a leading advocate of people fleeing from Vietnam, Cambodia and Laos.

The "second wave" of Vietnamese refugees began with thousands fleeing the country every month.

1977: Elementary School Principal

Boyd Kesser was the principal of an elementary school just outside of Dallas during the controversial era of school desegregation.

Life at Home

- For Boyd Kesser, it was a dream come true—and a nightmare waiting to pounce.
- After 11 years as a schoolteacher, he had been named principal of a soon-to-be desegregated elementary school with the attendant increase in pay, prestige and recognition.
- He and his wife had recently had their third child and they needed a bigger house; now it was possible.
- The nightmare that hovered was not one of his doing; 23 years after the Supreme Court ruled in *Brown v. Board of Education*, Dallas elected to move ahead.
- His first year as principal would include the experience of managing a newly integrated school, including a government-ordered busing plan that had divided the community and spawned considerable bitterness.
- Boyd grew up in Minnesota, where issues of race rarely dominated the political scene.
- When he was 15, his father accepted a new position and moved the family to Dallas, Texas, which his younger sister pledged to hate "with every fiber in her body," but didn't.
- His mother, on the other hand, cheerfully closed her beauty salon, eagerly packed their possessions and pledged to love Texas as long as they both might live—but didn't.
- Seven months later she was gone, leaving behind a fluttering trail of accusations, apologies and demands.
- Boyd stayed with his dad in Texas; his mother and sister headed "home."
- Boyd buried his grief in learning Texas history and collecting bits and pieces of the state's glorious cowboy past.
- His collecting took him into remote areas of the state and taught him the exquisite diversity within its borders.
- High school graduation was followed by four years as a Marine, when he acquired even more skills—and love—for exploring remote locations.

Boyd Kesser loved to teach students of all ages and personalities.

- Shy and quiet, he was nicknamed "The Viper" by his buddies, in recognition of his ability to magically strike silently with lightning speed using deadly force.
- When he left military service, Rice University offered him a partial scholarship which, combined with his military benefits, made college expenses manageable.
- He told himself that coaching would be very fulfilling, especially football and baseball, but every time he entered a classroom his skin came alive, his senses were alert, and he felt the same adrenaline rush he had experienced as a trained sniper.
- He could not deny the truth; he loved teaching kids—no matter the age—and even enjoyed those who had grown a big mouth.

Kesser was popular with the students.

- So when he graduated, he cast his lot in with the schools, landing a math teaching position in a middle school outside Dallas.
- He stayed there for five years, then became an assistant principal/ disciplinarian for three years in a high school, followed by three years assisting at an elementary school.
- Finally, he was given opportunity to be a principal in a school constructed outside Dallas whose students had mixed ancestry and which experienced considerable busing.
- Previously, half the kids came from country folk who knew how to get things done with their hands; the other half were suburban kids who couldn't open an M&M candy bag without help, but had already been to Europe twice.
- Now the school's mix would include black youths from Dallas who were angry about the hour-long bus ride when there were schools closer to their homes.
- They were not happy about being taken from their schools and teachers, either.
- But Boyd was ready and determined to make it work.
- He understood that it had fallen to the schools—America's youth—to ameliorate and satisfy 200 years of race history.
- Separate housing, separate jobs, separate activities and separate attitudes for blacks and whites were all supposed to disappear through school desegregation.
- Problems that could not be addressed on the adult level were being handed to the children to smooth out.
- It was part of Boyd's job to bring everyone—including anxious parents—together after all of the social experiments within schools had been attempted for more than two decades.
- It was no accident that the pivotal Supreme Court decision launching the modern Civil Rights Movement was an education case: the 1954 *Brown v. Board of Education of Topeka, Kansas.*
- The drive to end segregated education and put African-American and white children in the same classrooms was the most radical and potentially far-reaching aspect of the Civil Rights Movement.
- That decision—intended to alter the racial attitudes and socialization of children from the youngest age—was necessary to end the inequality inherent in all "separate but equal" facilities, whether they were drinking fountains, public accommodations, or the schools.
- The Civil Rights struggle, Boyd understood, did not arise because someone believed that there was something magical about minority children sitting next to whites in a classroom, but instead was

based on a belief that the only way for minority children to get the full range of opportunities was to get access to those schools.

- Since 1954, the struggle for integrated schools had gone through a number of phases—especially as education became the focus of the South's "massive resistance" to the Court's rulings.
- This resistance was symbolized dramatically by Arkansas Governor Orval Faubus and his order that the state's national guard unit block the admission of nine African-American students to Little Rock's Central High School in 1957.
- The nearly month-long confrontation ended when President Eisenhower sent in U.S. troops to protect the students.
- Prince Edward County, Virginia, abandoned its entire public school system, leaving education to private interests that excluded African-American children from their schools.
- Many black children were essentially locked out of school for several years until the Supreme Court ruled Virginia's action unconstitutional.
- Most districts employed delaying tactics; 10 years after the courts called for racial integration of schools at "all deliberate speed," only 2.3 percent of black children in the Deep South attended desegregated schools.
- These tactics tried the patience of both African-Americans and the federal courts.
- In 1966, the Fifth Circuit Court, in United States v. Jefferson County Board of Education, ordered school districts not only to end segregation, but to "undo the harm" segregation had caused by racially balancing their schools under federal guidelines.
- A strong federal commitment to enforcement of the Civil Rights Act of 1964 proved critical; by 1968, the percentage of black children attending desegregated schools topped 32 percent.
- By 1976, the South had become the nation's most integrated region, with 55.1 percent of the South's African-American students attending majority white schools, compared with just 27.5 percent in the Northeast and 29.7 percent in the Midwest.

Armed guards on campus were not an uncommon sight as schools dealt with integration.

The consolidation of schools led to the loss of non-academic teaching positions.

- The first two weeks as principal were eventful for Boyd Kesser, starting with the mother of a first grader who was convinced her child was being ignored.
- Her first words, "Just because I'm black," told him where the conversation was going, so he went silent and listened to her complaint that her child's white teacher couldn't even pronounce her child's name.
- In the outer room was a white mother with a similar complaint; within minutes they joined together and told their stories, during which they admitted they were both frightened that their first graders would not be successful or happy.
- Boyd did little except allow the young mothers to talk; he pledged that the teachers would learn to pronounce the names properly and everyone agreed that first grade was a stressful time.
- After the first month passed, the protestors had stopped showing up, the teachers had settled down, and he could begin evaluating his teachers.
- In other school districts, the consolidation of schools had meant the loss of jobs—frequently those of black teachers—whose skills were prejudged.
- To Boyd's way of thinking, one of the most stabilizing forces in the community was being tossed aside during the consolidation process; in his experience, it was the veteran black teachers who had guided the peaceful desegregation of schools—often encouraging their own children to take a leadership role in integrating the classrooms.
- So he had been very intentional in his hiring of teachers—even when it meant white teachers he had known for years would not be offered contracts.
- This led to at least one embarrassing incident at the grocery store when a longtime teaching associate loudly dissected all the hiring mistakes he made as they both stood at the produce counter examining cantaloupes.
- The long history of the integration of Dallas' schools did not begin smoothly for those eager to see Brown brought to fruition; in a citywide election, Dallasites voted four to one against school integration.

- Powerful business interests then sought to stifle the various lawsuits that ensued.
- Until 1961, Dallas was the largest city in the South with a segregated school system, which drew this criticism from the courts: "Words without deeds are not enough."
- Consequently, in 1961, the Dallas School Board implemented a desegregation plan under the order of the Fifth Circuit Court.
- On September 6, 1961, 18 black children started first grade classes in what had been up until then segregated schools for whites only.
- But was only a token response.
- On October 6, 1970, *Tasby v. Estes* was filed in the U.S. District Court by Sam Tasby of Dallas on behalf of his two sons.
- The class-action lawsuit contended that the Dallas Independent School District was not racially integrated and white schools received more resources than black and "Chicano" schools.
- The greater Dallas community did not welcome this lawsuit, as many felt strongly that it had done its part to implement Brown.
- The judge disagreed.
- On July 16, 1971, District Judge William M. Taylor declared, "a dual system still exists," and ordered the Dallas School Board to come up with a plan for integration.
- Taylor's recommended plan included linking two majority-white classrooms with one minority classroom by television for at least one hour each day; less than a month later, the Fifth Circuit Court of Appeals threw out the TV plan.

"White flight" altered the racial makeup of schools.

- In 1971, busing to desegregate the schools began when several thousand black students were bused to predominantly white schools in North and East Dallas.
- Several hundred white students were reassigned to predominantly black schools, but the majority stayed home the first day.
- By 1975, the "white flight" out of the district had altered the racial makeup of the schools; white students were no longer in the majority, while black students became the dominant group.
- In March 1976, Taylor ordered the school district to implement a desegregation plan designed by a task force of the Dallas Alliance, an organization of political, civic and business leaders.
- The plan included establishing magnet schools, setting racial quotas for the district's administration, and busing about 20,000 students in grades four to eight.
- In August 1976, the schools opened without major incident under the desegregation plan.
- By the time the Christmas holidays arrived, Boyd knew every child by name and could count on hugs from at least a dozen students during the course of the day.
- The intensity of the joy he experienced was different now, but there was no question that working with young people was the greatest thrill a human could experience.
- These were his kids now, and he was eager to watch them grow.

Life in the Community: Dallas, Texas

- Dallas, Texas, was founded in 1841 and was formally incorporated as a city in February 1856.
- The city's prominence arose from its historical importance as a center for the oil and cotton industries, as well as its position along numerous railroad lines.
- With the advent of the Interstate Highway System in the 1950s and 1960s, Dallas became an east/west and north/south focal point of the interstate system with the convergence of four major highways in the city, along with a fifth interstate loop around the city.
- Dallas developed a strong industrial and financial sector, and a major inland port, due largely to the presence of Dallas/Fort Worth International Airport, one of the largest and busiest airports in the world.
- The city was the ninth most populous in the United States, and the third most populous in Texas.

1977: Real Estate Lawyer & Antique Store Owners

The Reynolds family lived outside Atlanta, where Martin Reynolds practiced real estate law and helped his wife Audrey manage a small antique store.

Life at Home

- The Reynolds family owned their own home in Smyrna, Georgia, a community north of rapidly expanding Atlanta.
- Martin and Audrey purchased the house five years after they were married, which was 10 years ago; they have talked about upgrading.
- Audrey thought the time to buy a bigger home was now because prices in the community were rising rapidly; Martin wanted to hold down his mortgage payments so he could invest in more land and take advantage of the growth coming their way.
- They owned two cars—Martin's brand-new one and Audrey's four-year-old station wagon, which she used to transport the children.
- The wagon was also used for "tailgating parties" when they attended football games at the University of Georgia, where they both graduated.
- They had season tickets to all the Georgia football games because, he said, entertaining at football games was good for business; actually, cheering for the Bulldogs is an obsession.
- The family recently purchased an English bulldog, the mascot of the University of Georgia, as a sign of their devotion to the team.
- At 38, Martin was beginning to feel that he understood how to make money, make connections, and be included in key real estate deals. He thought he is on the brink of a fortune and was convinced that Smyrna is about to explode with new growth, and he wanted to be one of those that profit.
- He and several friends formed an investment club to buy real estate, and for the past several years, they have been purchasing land—betting it would become valuable.
- They believed that by owning land, they could direct the growth of the town and earn substantial gains.
- None of the men were currently wealthy or is expecting his real estate investments to pay off

Martin Reynolds was a real estate lawyer.

Smyrna, Georgia

quickly; the monthly payments on raw land—which provided no income—were cutting down on each investor's cash flow.

- Yet all of the men, including another attorney, a doctor, and a banker, were optimistic that their investments would pay off big.
- Their wives were not so sure, but the women were not asked their opinion.
- Audrey believed the family was overextended, and was concerned about the number of empty office buildings in Atlanta, which was a good sign that growth was slowing and that the "pot of gold" her husband dreamed about was not around the corner as he claimed.
- She was worried that inflation would eat up their savings before the land deals were closed.
- The monthly electricity bill for 1,000 kilowatt hours was now around $60 a month, nearly double the rate of a few years ago.
- A private telephone line was $11.50 a month before long distance calls, while station-to-station calls cost $0.30 a minute; person-to-person calls were $1.75 for the first three minutes and $0.30 a minute thereafter.
- Some neighbors still had a two-party line costing $9.30 a month, but Martin's work was too confidential for that to be practical.
- The older black woman who helped clean the Reynolds' house was now demanding a raise to $3.00 an hour; babysitters for the youngest child want $1.00 an hour.
- Going out almost doesn't pay at those prices, Audrey had told her husband repeatedly; after all, regular gas had climbed to $0.64 per gallon and for the cars that need unleaded the price was even higher—$0.66 per gallon.
- President Carter announced plans for a five-cent increase in federal gasoline taxes, which would raise costs even more.
- Just last month, the charges for the children's visit to the dentist were $15.00 each for cleaning their teeth; a filling is now $12.00.
- Haircuts for men were $8.00-$10.00 in the city— and for women, a permanent was $35.00, a shampoo and set, $8.00, and a haircut, $10.00.

New homes like this one stopped being built as inflation threatened the financial stability of the community.

- To dry clean her husband's suits—and he always wore a suit—the dry cleaner charged $4.00 per suit, shirts were $1.50 each, and the dress she wore to a party last weekend ran $4.00.

Life at Work

- Up a flight of 29 wooden stairs in a bank building was Martin's office, where he and his two partners occupied half of the second floor.
- The bank, which occupied the first floor, was established at the turn of the century, and the building served as its headquarters.
- Thanks to restrictive banking laws, few competitors came into Cobb County, allowing the bank to grow quickly.
- Martin worked closely with the bank to close deals, perfect titles, and meet the difficult deadlines often demanded by customers.
- He spent so much time at the courthouse researching titles, often working on Saturdays and at night, he was given his own key to the building.
- Two days a week, he took coffee and biscuits to the women who worked in the records section of the courthouse.

Martin worked closely with bank officials and spent much of his time at the courthouse.

Smyrna was not far from the state capital in Atlanta.

- They called him the "Mayor of Smyrna" because he handled so many real estate transactions and loved to talk about how the town is going to grow.
- While travelling, he enjoyed buying antiques for his wife's business; he especially liked Southern furniture made prior to the Civil War.
- The family had three different wooden kitchen tables this year alone; after each new purchase, the earlier table goes to Audrey's antique store.
- Prices for quality furniture were rising quickly.
- He also collected Civil War bullets, belt buckles, and uniforms, and kept a metal detector in the trunk of the car so he could search sites for artifacts.
- Audrey kept her antique store open Tuesday through Friday from 10 a.m. to 3 p.m.; most of her business was by appointment only, and she never did business on Sundays.
- Twice a year, she sponsored a booth at the Atlanta Flea Market—an enormous, one-story building with 83,000 square feet of space.
- Some days she was unsure whether she wanted the antique store, or if Martin did.

Life in the Community: Smyrna, Georgia

- The rapid growth of Atlanta was remolding this Southern town into an international community, but the changes were not without their conflicts.
- Atlantans constantly debated the merits of imitating New York or forging their own image.
- Atlanta, the largest city between New Orleans and Washington, DC, was the financial, commercial, and cultural capital of the Southeast.
- Atlanta served as the headquarters for the Sixth Federal Reserve System, making the city the region's financial center; it was also the world headquarters of Coca-Cola.
- The city was proud of its 47 parks and three professional teams, covering baseball, football, and hockey.
- Atlanta's school system was the first in Georgia to integrate in the 1960s.
- In Atlanta, the price of a home sold through the Board of Realtors' Multiple Listing Service was $109,000; in Smyrna, the average is closer to $85,000.

Coca-Cola was important to industry in the Atlanta area.

- Condominiums were now being built and sold in Atlanta, costing an average of $66,000, though Martin did not believe his community is ready for "condos"; everyone in Smyrna took great pride in their yards.
- Many of his neighbors shared a "yard man" to help with the grass and leaves, since few could afford their own help as in the old days.
- Not everyone in the Smyrna community was interested in growth and change; many enjoyed the quiet pace of this Southern community.
- In Atlanta, foreclosures were rising; the Atlanta savings and loan associations reported that foreclosures doubled in the past year.
- The Georgia Railroad Bank and Trust Company of Augusta foreclosed on two pieces of property in the financially ailing Underground Atlanta.
- President Jimmy Carter declared 62 counties in the state eligible for federal assistance for farmers due to drought, making Georgia cattle farmers eligible for grants to feed their herds.
- According to the Tax Foundation, the average family paid about 40 percent of its family income in taxes, with about 29 percent of the family income expended for direct taxes such as property tax, auto and gas taxes, and Social Security, state, and federal taxes, and about 11 percent for indirect taxes.

The airport in Atlanta, Georgia

Life at Home

- The only child of farming parents, Andrei Dancescu was born in 1950 in a small village outside of Bucharest, Romania.
- Because Romania fell under the partial control of the Soviet Union after World War II, he grew up under Communist rule.
- From when he was very young, Andrei enjoyed drawing and sketching.
- Although it was difficult to purchase art supplies, his parents were supportive and helped him as much as they could.
- Times were hard in 1950s Romania.
- Soviet control was responsible for the exploitation of Romanian labor and resources.
- The so-called "SovRom" agreements created joint ventures between Romanian and Soviet firms that benefited the USSR almost exclusively.
- During this period, thousands of people were imprisoned by the government for political reasons.
- In 1957, when Andrei was only seven years old, his aunt (his father's sister) and her husband were among those arrested and sent to a prison camp.
- No one ever saw them again.
- Although he was young at the time, the event had a strong effect on Andrei.
- He soon began thinking about leaving the country once he got older.
- The Soviet control of Romania ended in 1958, but Communism remained in place under the rule of the new leader Nicolae Ceausescu.
- When he was 15, Andrei moved to Bucharest to attend an art institute and stayed with his mother's cousin, who lived in the city.
- In addition to studying art and design, he also began playing the guitar.
- He met a group of musicians his own age and formed a band; they became popular very quickly and wanted to play Beatles and Rolling Stones songs, but were afraid they would be considered rebellious in the eyes of the government.

Andrei Dancescu fled Communist Romania when he was 20-years-old.

137

Andrei left Romania in 1970 and moved to Rome, Italy.

- People were still afraid of the government; like many, Andrei vividly remembered the abrupt arrest of thousands, including his aunt and uncle.
- The band developed two distinct styles: traditional Romanian songs for public performances and British and American rock for underground clubs throughout the city.
- Their favorite song to play was "Twist and Shout."
- Andrei loved playing foreign rock music even though he couldn't understand the lyrics; only later in life, after he had learned English, did he fully understand the depth of his poor pronunciations.
- Andrei enjoyed city life more than his childhood in the country, but he still thought about leaving Romania; he wanted to be free to play the music he loved and not live in fear.
- Andrei left Romania in 1970, at the age of 20, and moved to Rome, Italy.
- He stayed with a family friend and enrolled in art school to sharpen his design skills; a music career seemed out of reach.
- While he developed his portfolio, he worked as a cook in a restaurant.
- There he met Samantha, the daughter of an American diplomat.
- She grew up in Rome and New York, but her father's position allowed her to travel the world.
- She had learned to speak Romanian from immigrant friends in Italy.
- Samantha and Andrei became very close and were married in Rome in 1972.
- Samantha's dream was to be a journalist in New York City; Andrei, too, secretly dreamed of living in the United States, but never thought it was possible, until he married Samantha.
- In 1973, Andrei and Samantha moved to Astoria, Queens, in New York, based on her American citizenship.
- When he first arrived in the United States, Andrei spoke practically no English; he and Samantha had always communicated in Romanian or Italian.
- Even though she was a native speaker, the only English he knew was "good day" and "thank you."

Life at Work

- Job opportunities were scarce for Andrei Dancescu because of the language barrier; his first job was as a line cook in a diner in Manhattan.
- Samantha got a job at *The New York Times for very little money, and Andrei felt pressure to get a better job.*
- Toward that end, Samantha began teaching him English after work.
- Each evening, they would read one complete page of *The New York Times* and work on the difficult parts.
- When their first child, Dan, was born, Andrei felt a deep need for his family in Romania, but couldn't afford to visit.

Working as a line cook was Andrei's first job in America.

- His growing family motivated Andrei to work harder to find a better job.
- He soon learned enough English to get a job as an assistant at a design firm.
- He applied for a designer position, but because his portfolio was lost in the move from Italy, he had no work to show, and was hired as a guy-Friday.
- His duties included running errands and answering the phone.
- Still not confident with his English-speaking skills, he dreaded answering the phone.
- One Friday afternoon, a client called to complain about not receiving a set of sketches.
- The client described the missing sketches, and Andrei said that he would drop them off Monday morning.
- Deciding to do the sketches himself, Andrei worked all weekend and delivered them Monday morning as promised.
- When his boss learned what he had done, he was angry until the client called to say how much he liked Andrei's work.
- Andrei was then promoted and asked to contribute design work for the firm, and given a substantial raise to $8,000 per year.
- Shortly after, Andrei and Samantha took their son on vacation to Puerto Rico.
- It was a special trip, because it was the first time since they had come to America that they could afford to go on vacation.

Andrei's sketches landed him a promotion.

- Andrei purchased a used Canon camera to document the trip, even though he had never seriously taken pictures before then.
- He photographed beaches, nature and the people of San Juan.
- When he got back to Queens and developed the pictures, he was so impressed and excited that he began considering a career in photography.
- Andrei started taking his camera with him everywhere.
- He walked all around the city, taking pictures of anything that caught his eye.

Taking his camera everywhere, Andrei quickly became a successful photojournalist.

- He began to read books on technique; his favorite was *The Negative by Ansel Adams*.
- In 1978, Samantha got Andrei his first freelance assignment as a photojournalist covering a student protest for *The New York Times*.
- He was paid $70 for the assignment.
- More importantly, the Times liked his work, and his reputation grew.
- His strategy was to accept as many assignments as he could, even from small newspapers and magazines, so that his name would be seen by more people.
- Remembering the tough economic times in Romania caused him to be assertive in pursuing new assignments.
- If he saw photographs in a newspaper or magazine that he thought were inferior to his own, he would call and tell the editor.
- Andrei would sometimes even offer to take assignments for little or no pay in order to establish a relationship with a client.
- His aggressiveness ruffled some feathers in the competitive world of professional photographers.
- His strategy worked, however, and soon he was making as much as $300 an assignment.
- He quickly became one of the most successful photojournalists in New York.
- Andrei was determined to make sure his son had the opportunities he himself had missed growing up in Romania, and education was the first step.
- As Andrei became more successful, feuds broke out between him and other photojournalists in the city.
- Some felt that he was not fair in how he pursued assignments, while others understood that it was the nature of the business.
- Andrei was deeply hurt by some of the things that were said about him and distanced himself more and more from the photojournalism community.

Life in the Community: Queens, New York

- Andrei Dancescu's work always kept him very busy, so he didn't have much free time to spend with neighbors and friends.
- He traveled on assignment as many as 20 weeks out of each year.
- One place he never accepted assignments from was Romania, because there were things of which he did not want to be reminded.
- He would visit his family every few years when he was on assignment at a neighboring country.
- Due to his constant traveling, he became friends with the owner of the car service company that transported him to and from nearby LaGuardia Airport.
- Because of the competitive, and sometimes hostile, nature of his work, Andrei was reluctant to socialize with his colleagues in the industry.
- He developed a love of cooking over the years and was able to find traditional Romanian ingredients in his multi-ethnic Queens neighborhood.

New York City was full of inspiration for photographers.

- He enjoyed cooking for family and close friends.
- Andrei avoided taking many pictures of friends and family, wanting to be seen with a personal, non-work side.
- He also did not want to be viewed as one of the paparazzi.
- One day, while walking around the city with his camera, he saw one of his childhood heroes, Mick Jagger.
- When Jagger saw Andrei's camera, he immediately turned and started walking in the other direction.
- The experience had a strong impact on Andrei, reminding him of the lack of personal freedom that existed in Romania when he was growing up.
- He vowed never to pry into people's lives with his photography.

∽∾∽∾∽∾∽∾

Romanian Immigration Timeline

1880s The first wave of Romanian immigration from what is now Romania began primarily from the agricultural provinces of Transylvania, Bukovina, and Banat, which were then part of the Austro-Hungarian Empire.

1900-1910 Thirty-seven thousand Romanians emigrated to the U.S. Overpopulation coupled with the steady consolidation of small, semi-feudal landholdings worked by peasants created a growing class of property-less laborers who sought opportunity in Europe and America.

At the height of emigration, around 94 percent of the emigrants were landless peasants and farmhands. Romanians who came to the U.S. nearly all found homes in the industrial Northeast and Midwest; New York, Pennsylvania and Ohio absorbed more than half of the total Romanian immigration.

1911-1914 Immigration continued at a rate of about 7,000 per year until World War I.

1924 U.S. immigration restrictions limited the number of Romanian entrants to 1,000 per year.

1930-1940 Immigration statistics showed a decrease of more than 30,000 Romanians in the U.S.

1970s Ninety percent of Romanian Americans continued to live in cities and tended to be employed as skilled factory workers and small-business entrepreneurs.

∽∾∽∾∽∾∽∾

"Rumanians Are Seeking Contacts with Lost 4 Million in the Soviet," by David Binder, *The New York Times*, October 10, 1976

The Rumanian Government has advised Western and independent powers with which it is friendly that it is seeking, for the first time in more than 30 years, to establish contacts with the four million ethnic Rumanians living in the Soviet Union.

American and Yugoslav officials said earlier this week that they had been told by high Rumanian authorities that this was the principal purpose of a visit last August by President Nicolae Ceausescu to the Soviet Republic of Moldavia, where most of the ethnic Rumanians live.

It was reported shortly after that visit that in talks with Leonid I. Brezhnev, the Soviet Communist Party chief, President Ceausescu had made some political concessions to the

Soviet Union mainly in ideological areas. But the Rumanian authorities told American and Yugoslav officials that these concessions carried little real substance.

More important, they said, was to make clear during Mr. Ceausescu's visit that neither Rumania nor the Soviet Union had territorial designs across the long frontier between the two countries.

Specifically, Mr. Ceausescu told Mr. Brezhnev that Rumania did not dispute the post-World War II frontiers that accorded the Soviet Union control over the regions of Northern Bukovina and Bessarabia, both of which were part of Rumania before the war.

The Soviet Union forced Rumania to cede both regions in 1940, but Rumania, joining the Axis powers in 1941 when it was still a monarchy, sent armored forces into Bukovina and Bessarabia to recapture the lost territories. The Soviet Army reconquered the regions in 1944.

Since then the Soviet leadership has asserted that Soviet Moldavia, the former Bessarabia, was inhabited not by ethnic Rumanians but by Moldavians, and that Northern Bukovina was mainly inhabited by Ukrainians. Since 1965, Rumania has claimed that most of these people are Rumanians.

After the war the Soviet Union also deported more than a million Rumanians to eastern Siberia, where they form an ethnic unit to this day.

1978: Champion Sailboat Crew Member

Jane Fisher crewed on a J24 sailboat that won the District D Championship, and then on a boat that won the 1978 World Championship in Annapolis, Maryland.

Life at Home

- Unlike most of her contemporaries and competitors, Jane Fisher had not been sailing since childhood.
- For most people, sailing was an obsession that captured them early in life, giving them plenty of time to gradually unravel the complicated beast known as wind.
- Growing up, Jane had pursued other sports and passions including soccer and rafting.
- Throughout college she'd worked as a raft guide on the Ocoee River in Tennessee and competed in raft races on the Gauley River in West Virginia.
- One year, her all-girl team qualified for the National Raft Race in Colorado.
- Rafting down treacherous rivers and choking on crashing whitewater demanded lightning quick decision-making and superior upper body strength.
- Lazy decisions, hidden rocks or obstreperous currents could send a rafting team into the water.
- At 26 years old, this veteran of numerous nasty, rock-laden swims—including two near drownings and dozens of stitches required for her head—Jane decided she'd had enough of whitewater.
- One evening while going to meet friends at a local Columbia, South Carolina bar, Jane met a man who asked if she'd like to go sailing.
- Blessed with a total ignorance of sailing, but a love of water, she agreed.
- The following Saturday she met up with the owner of the boat, Brad, and his Ranger 29.
- She and the rest of the crew were racing in the Saturday races held at Lake Murray, a 50,000 acre manmade lake near Lexington, South Carolina.
- Jane's first day of sailing was hectic-wind was blowing hard, people were yelling and she had no idea what was going on.
- She only knew that it was cold and she didn't want to fall into the water.
- After the race, she instinctively knew she'd found her new sport as she felt the familiar adrenaline and sported a huge grin.
- Jane spent the next couple of Saturdays with this crew, learning fundamentals

Jane Fisher traded whitewater rafting for sailboat racing.

of the sport, names of the boat parts, and trying not to get yelled at.

- Only after Jane went to the library and checked out several sailing books did the boat's many functions begin to make sense.

- Her research taught her the names of all the lines and why they were used.

- She also discovered that at five feet one inch tall and 105 pounds, she was very small for sailing, a sport that demands strength, endurance and quick decision-making under pressure.

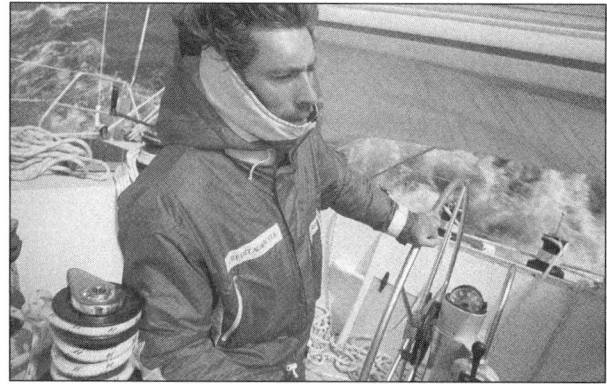

Brad introduced Jane to her new sport.

- At the gym, she focused on lifting weights to strengthen her shoulders, back, arms, abs, and legs so that all parts of her body could be utilized.

- She ran, rowed and pedaled a stationary bike to keep up her endurance.

- Jane also read voraciously—anything that she could find that contained tactical racing tips and quizzes that tested her knowledge.

- Finally, Jane sailed at every opportunity.

- By watching the water and reading the wind, figuring out how to set the sails to maximize boat speed became her new assignment.

- Jane sailed with Brad and his crew for almost a year.

- One spring day in 1975 a boat with two men in it sailed by and asked if Jane wanted to come aboard.

- Jane already knew that in this male-dominated sport, females had to be on their toes, but she was interested in talking to one of the men who spoke with reverence about sailing.

- These two men, Joe and Chip, were on Chip's J24 and looking to put together a group of five people who trained and raced together, traveling to different events.

- Jane literally jumped ship and began a new assignment on a J24.

Life at Work

- When Jane Fisher was asked to be part of the program as a J24 foredeck person, she had no idea what that job entailed.

- Joe and Chip said, "No problem, we'll teach you."

- Jane's weight of 105 pounds was perfect for the role: light crew were needed in the foredeck position so the bow of the boat did not dig into the water and slow the boat down.

Sailing was a male-dominated sport, but that didn't stop Jane from sailing at every opportunity that she had.

- On the day Jane came on board, two others were picked up: Steve as cockpit, and Mac as middle.

- Joe was to drive the boat, Chip was to trim the sails—both the genoa and the spinnaker.

- Steve balanced the boat, trim the tweens and help raise and lower the spinnaker.

- Mac kept the boom vang, outhaul, topping lift, cunningham and downhaul in check.

- Jane raised and lowered the genoa, adjust the genoa cunningham, put the

- pole up and down and raise and lower the spinnaker.
- Unfortunately for Jane, almost all of her work was required in the space of mere minutes.
- She called it the impossible dance because there were so many steps.
- Joe told her there was one way to do it right and a billion ways to mess it up.
- A "mess-up" slowed the boat down at crucial moments and the race could be lost.
- As the season progressed, Jane and Steve became fast friends, studying the mechanics and theories of sailing together and talking over all the nuances of the race.
- Steve got her a T-shirt that proclaimed her membership in the Foredeck Union with a rude graphic indicating when she would be getting around to their complaints on the back.
- Steve figured that since Jane was destined to be yelled at and expected to have six hands to do her job, she needed an outlet to vent.
- Jane soon learned that even though most of the problems occurred at the back of the boat, she would always be blamed in the heat of the moment.

Jane's team made it to four races.

- The team made it to four races, taking a third, second, first and second before the chemistry on the boat between Chip and Joe made the team fall apart.
- In the spring of 1976 Jane joined another team, one of whom was a former Olympic sailor from Russia, aboard a San Juan 31.
- She and Steve continued to be friends and hone their skills separately and apart.
- Jane had started to get noticed around the clubhouse and in the Southeastern circuit because of her size, skills and smile.
- Every year in the spring, the local yacht club held an Easter Regatta in which boats from as far away as Canada traveled to compete.
- Jane was asked to crew on a boat from Florida as their middle mast person because of her "local knowledge" of the lake.
- This was where she became fully aware of the sexism in this predominately male sport.
- In addition to her foredeck duties, it was assumed that she would make all of the lunches for the crew and do all of the shopping for the drinks and food.
- Her need to use the restroom—a bucket—while sailing for eight hours at a time was viewed with disgust.
- The more boats Jane sailed, the more she realized how personalities on shore would transform on the water in the midst of a heated race.
- She began to recognize those with whom she would enjoy sailing and those with whom she would not.
- Jane also discovered the joy of sailing at sunset and letting the wind purify her soul.
- But rough-water sailing was also inspirational.
- Once while Jane was sailing in Annapolis, Maryland, a tempestuous storm blew through and tore up the main sail, forcing her team to limp back into the harbor.
- No one was hurt, but the adrenaline rush was huge.
- Big wind or "Blowing Like Stink" was great fun, while one of the most challenging scenarios was sailing in light air.

- The entire crew must be spread out and balanced precisely to keep the boat flat or sometimes in a windward heel in order to keep the boat moving in light air.
- Typically in a sailboat race, since one cannot sail directly into the wind and must sail close to 45 degrees off the wind, the sailor is looking for the shortest course to the mark.
- When the wind is very light, one must sail for the wind and not to the shortest course.
- It is often slow and very hot when there is no breeze.
- Jane had many times walked off the boat with a concentration headache from peering so hard into the horizon for wind.
- Her reputation within the circuit continued to grow over the next two years, and Jane found herself sailing on a J24 whose owner lived in Wrightsville Beach, North Carolina.
- The trimmer lived in St. Augustine, Florida, the tactician in Jacksonville, Florida, the mast in Charlotte, North Carolina, and Jane in Columbia, South Carolina.
- Teams normally do better when they sail together all the time, but this team would only get together for big national regattas and when they could earn spots to bigger regattas.
- Somehow, after the first two races, the team gelled and worked together very well.
- Their first race was in 1978 at Oriental, North Carolina, a spot where the Neuse River and the ocean meet.
- With much laughter, combined with great finishes, the team finished first and earned a spot in the Nationals.
- The entire crew was aware that more work lay ahead if they were to compete against the "big boys" or professional sailors to win the Nationals.

Teamwork was critical to success and encouraged strong friendships.

- Throughout that spring, summer and fall they traveled all over the East Coast, competing in whatever regatta was open to J24s and fine tuning their movements and minds.
- In the process, Jane became fully cognizant of how beaten up she was getting on the bow of the boat.
- During one Saturday in Jacksonville, Florida, the bay was very choppy and the work difficult.
- During the first leg of the first race on a six-leg day, Jane lost her shoe.
- To try and balance on the bow of a boat with only one shoe was very difficult.
- Later that day Jane lost her balance and hit her temple very hard on the spinnaker ring, but managed to finish the race before making her way to the back of the boat.
- Since Jane rarely complained of her injuries, she was ignored until the skipper realized she was green and gritting her teeth.
- When asked what was the matter, Jane said she was trying not to throw up.
- The crew wanted to know why she hadn't said anything.
- When she said that she lost her shoe and then hit her head, they stared at her in amazement knowing they had also won the regatta.
- Next stop, the Nationals.
- Teams from all over the world would travel to see who could take home that year's world title in an event being held in Annapolis, Maryland, at a premier venue, the Chesapeake Bay.

Life in the Community: Lake Murray, South Carolina

- Lake Murray, where the Columbia Sailing Club was headquartered, was a 50,000-acre manmade lake in the Midlands of South Carolina.
- It covered approximately 78 square miles of land with 647 miles of shoreline, and provided electricity for South Carolina's entire Midlands region.

The Columbia Sailing Club was headquartered in Lake Murray.

- Lake Murray was completed in 1930 and gradually became renowned for striped bass fishing and summer water sports.
- In order to build Lake Murray, the Lexington Water Power Company relocated 5,000 citizens and removed three churches, six schools, and 2,000 graves.
- The first sailing club on Lake Murray was established in the 1930s, but dissolved when the winds of war blew across the world.
- The re-founding of the Columbia Sailing Club occurred in 1957; that year 19 members agreed to pay dues of $5 per quarter.
- The 1958 regatta resulted in strong media coverage, and the club was launched.
- Sailboat racing had arrived at Lake Murray.
- Columbia, located in the center of South Carolina, was that state's most populated city, the state capital, the home of the University of South Carolina's main campus, and the site of the South Carolina State Fair each October.
- Columbia was named for Christopher Columbus, and it was South Carolina's first planned city.
- Despite this, Columbia did not have a single paved street until Main Street was surfaced in 1908.

The first sailing club on Lake Murray was established in the 1930s.

"Sail Racing: A Gamble Against the Elements,"
Liz Larcom, *Del Rio News-Herald* (Texas), September 3, 1978

"We're gonna gamble," announced Mike Dungan, skipper of a Catalina 25 owned by Fred and Frankie Lee Harlow.

Still tied to the dock, he was already devising his tactics the fifth weekend of racing in Amistad Yacht Club's summer series.

His decision: to use the big 170 sail, gambling that the winds during the two-hour race would not come up so much that the big sail would not heel the boat over to an inefficient sailing angle.

His wife and sole crew member, C.J., dug out the big sail from the cabin of Lake Amistad's oldest sailboat (nine years), and soon the pair maneuvered the craft into the harbor of the Mexican marina.

"I had a cotton mouth on the start," confessed Mike.

With six sailboats circling the still harbor, stopwatches to check, and the signal flags of race official Jim Williams to watch, there was plenty to give a skipper cotton mouth.

Crossing the starting line early would draw a foul, but crossing even seconds late could cost a skipper the race in competition that is sometimes determined by split-seconds.

Today's course had been announced by Williams only 15 minutes earlier. Now he stood on the deck of his anchored sailboat, beside the starting (and finishing) line. At the sound of the horn the race was on.

"Fifteen seconds late!" exclaimed Mike, but as the boat headed out across the lake, five other sailboats trailed behind.

Mike had the helm while his only crew member C.J. trimmed the sails. Both watched the knot meter, wind direction, sails and other boats.

The course would cover only a corner of Lake Amistad's 85-mile length. With its broad expanses, varied destinations, and steady winds, uncrowded Amistad provides ideal sailing without the complication of tides....

"It's easy to get distracted," said Mike, eyes sweeping the knot meter as the boat skimmed along toward a distant buoy it must round. "You get busy watching the buoy and all the other boats and forget to watch your sails."

"Look at George come," said C.J., pointing at George Hall's Ericson 29 that was fast closing in behind. Soon the boats were dueling, the Ericson trying to pass on the upwind side. But the Catalina made the marker first and made a neat turn around it.

Next, the course headed for Chuy Island, back near the Mexican shore.

"We'll take it high," decided Mike. "I think there will be a good wind coming off the land just as we get there. If my theory is right I don't want to get caught too far downwind."

The boats spread out across the lake now, but the race outcome was far from evident. With the Portsmouth system, each model of boat had its handicap, so the boat out front would not necessarily be the winner.

"Sailing is relaxing," said C.J., who only minutes before had been using every ounce of muscle to pull on a rope. "It's work," she laughed. "But it's not like 'at work'." She paused, then added as she trimmed the sail a bit, "It's exciting!"

As Mike and C.J. approached Chuy Island, the breeze indeed picked up, but not much. It was clear the J24 owned by John Haire was reaching the island first.

As Mike and C.J. sought to keep Kaylea just far enough from Chuy Island to avoid running aground, the J24 maintained its lead and Woody, behind, took down the spare sail to ready for the last leg.

The wind was up as the helmsman aimed for the buoy that is Marker 7. Heeled over, Mike regretted the choice of the big sail as he watched John Haire's J24 sailing ahead of him.

The last buoy approached. "Now!" said the skipper, and the pair swung the sail around to the other side at the precise moment the boat rounded the buoy.

The finish line was next. Finishing with an unfavorable wind, the boats glided in. The race had taken about two hours.

Calculations the next day would determine the points winner, but first across the line was the only race-designed sailboat in the field, the J24. The Ericson 29 also preceded the Kaylea.

"The 170 didn't pay," said Mike, referring to his gamble with the big sail. But it hadn't lost him much either. Results the next day showed the Ericson 29 first, Mike and C.J. second, and the J24 third.

A pair of long sighs were heard as the Dungans stowed away the sails of the Kaylea. They nodded agreement when competitor Bonnie Chambers proclaimed from the dock, "I'm exhausted!"

Oliver Lorenz, skipper of a San Juan 21, said of sailing, "You're challenging other people, but you're challenging natural forces, too.

"You could go out on the lake and water ski, and you have done it all of five minutes. But a lot of tactics go into sailing a boat. I learn something new every time. You could sail forever and still learn something new every time."

1978: Founder of Sunshine Orange Juice Company

Seventy-seven year-old entrepreneurer Stefano Tornabene ran the orange juice empire he founded in the 1940s, while fending off lucrative merger offers from Fortune 500 companies.

Life at Home

- At 77, and well past retirement age, Stefano was still actively running the Sunshine Orange Juice Company he founded in 1947, playing golf when he wanted and living by his own rules.
- Considered an entrepreneur of the old school, he loved his company, his products and his employees, who had no doubts that he was firmly in control.
- He did not hesitate to use his elegant home by the water for company picnics, dinners or negotiating sessions, maintaining three servants year-round to assist in the necessary arrangements.
- He went to the office six days a week, working eight to nine hours before going home with additional paperwork.
- On Sundays, after church, he often played golf—his other all-consuming passion.
- Careful with his money in nearly every other aspect of his life, Stefano could not resist the urge to buy the latest golf innovations—especially new golf clubs.
- A stickler for detail but a strict manager of time, nevertheless he spent hours shopping for clubs styled specifically to his personal taste. StefanoTornabene was an entrepreneur of the old school.
- In the past 30 years, he has owned some 70 sets of clubs, and although he sold most of his clubs when he traded up, for sentimental reasons, he kept a set of Hogans custom-made for him a decade ago.
- He believed that the game of golf—like life—was determined by attitude: "If you are comfortable and confident in your clubs, that's always a positive."
- Fifteen major and 75 smaller manufacturers battled for a share of the $185 million in U.S. golf club sales.
- Modern clubs offered golfers a choice of grip, length, swing weight, flexibility of shaft and angles of loft and lie; "Technology is changing so fast, you have to work hard to keep up," Stefano warned.
- He came to the U.S. from Sicily more than half a century ago and founded Sunshine Orange Juice Company in 1947; a stern, powerfully built six-footer, he spoke fractured English with a thick accent.

Stefano Tornabene was an entrepreneur from the old school.

Stefano often hosted company events at his gulf-front home.

- Although his formal training ended in grade school, he had developed into a superb engineer with an innovative mind that is quick with numbers, and could rapidly spot minor errors on a profitability projection.
- For all his technical skills and head for math, he rarely remembered names, including those of associates with whom he had worked for years.
- None of his three grown children worked for the company; two were attorneys and one operated several shrimp boats out of the Gulf of Mexico.

Life at Work

- As founder and undisputed ruler of his orange juice empire, Stefano walked away from a merger with Kellogg, against the wishes of his board of directors.
- Even though the company went public a decade ago, he controlled more than 20 percent of the stock, giving him broad discretion over most decisions.
- He remained chairman and chief executive, but gave up the title of president last year after persistent prodding from the board.
- More than 40 people report directly to him, including the company's top financial, marketing and production heads, as well as plant managers, maintenance chiefs and even the head painter.
- On Saturdays, he held an open house to hear the problems of his subordinates who haven't been able to get his ear during the week; sitting in his large corner office on the second floor of the three-story headquarters building, he listened like a bona fide Wizard of Oz, pondered sagely and dispensed solutions.
- When a production executive complained that the bottle machine that picked up and packed orange juice bottles into cardboard cases was causing a bottleneck, Stefano redesigned the production flow; the cardboard case was lowered over the bottles themselves and then sealed from below-reducing breakage, improving speed and stopping the bottleneck.

- He loved handling the details of the company he created, and was preoccupied with the development of a new plastic cap for the orange juice bottles to replace the metal caps purchased from suppliers.
- He was also the company's official taster, personally sampling the company's beverages each morning while the quality-control team stood by nervously; he prided himself on having keen taste buds and a superb sense of when the product is right.
- His decision to tell the mighty marketing giant Kellogg "no" was the third time he has spurned their advances in the past five years.
- With revenues approaching $1.5 billion—about six times the size of Sunshine Orange Juice—Kellogg appeared to be a good partner, thanks to its $70 million marketing budget.
- By comparison, Sunshine spent $3 million on advertising last year.
- Both sides felt that this merger would allow advertisements not only to feature Kellogg's Special K, for example, but also a glass of orange juice without any increased costs.

Assembly line at Sunshine Orange Juice Company.

- Also, acceptance of the Kellogg offer would have pleased Wall Street analysts concerned about management succession at Sunshine; Kellogg viewed the merger as a way to move into the high-growth area of fruit juices.
- The Sunshine company earnings per share have risen an astounding 1,300 percent in the past decade, compared to slightly more than 200 percent for the larger Kellogg.
- The merger package Stefano eventually turned down was worth $382 million, which is $110 million more than the market value of his company's stock.
- He killed the deal, he says, because of a disagreement over a dividend for stockholders; in actuality, he was simply not ready to relinquish control of the company.
- He also believed many of his best executives who have worked with him in Florida for years would be asked to relocate to accommodate Kellogg, and was unsure whether they would survive the corporate environment of Kellogg.
- In addition, Kellogg made it clear during the negotiations that any significant new capital expenditures would have to be approved by the headquarters staff in Battle Creek, Michigan.
- Instead of selling, he wanted to grow the business even more by pushing its distribution beyond its traditional base on the eastern seaboard to markets in the Midwest and West.
- The company was also experimenting with an expanded product line, including a ground-up citrus-pulp fiber, which would be sold as a bulk additive for baked goods.
- Sunshine captured 40 percent of the orange juice market by pioneering the mass production of single-strength juice, a bottle of juice that comes ready to use and does not have to be reconstituted with water by the consumer; this "ready to use" approach had developed a large following among consumers willing to pay a few cents extra per quart to avoid adding water.
- Research indicated that the more educated people became, the more orange juice they consumed; doctors, dentists, lawyers and corporate executives were the nation's heaviest consumers.

Florida orange groves supplied most of the nation's orange juice.

- Since the Second World War, most of the nation's orange juice had been distributed as a concentrate, still an important part of the market.
- Minute Maid was the dominant player in orange juice concentrates; many believed that competing in the future against Minute Maid, owned by Coca-Cola, would require a merger.
- Thanks to years of high, consistent performance, Sunshine had no debt and little reason to bargain.
- Sunshine Orange Juice integrated its operations to the point where it made its own bottles, plastic containers and packing cases, builds its own production machinery, and even owned the 200 railroad cars that carried its products to market.
- The company relies heavily on independent Florida growers for its oranges and grapefruit, and was, therefore, considering whether to buy groves of its own.

Life in the Community: Bradenton, Florida
- Since the Second World War, when Americans think of Florida, they think of oranges.
- Florida lead the United States in producing more citrus fruit than any other nation, thanks to a warm climate and readily available water.
- In the spring, vast seas of rounded, dark-green trees laden with white blooms produced such an intense fragrance that ships' passengers off the Atlantic and Gulf coasts could smell it several miles out to sea.
- However, the size of the orange groves was shrinking in many areas as land was gobbled up for development.
- For most of the century, the state had been known for its hype and hustle, all designed to attract people to land deals, vacation homes or the next get-rich-quick scheme.

Florida lead the country in citrus fruit production, due to its warm climate and water supply.

- In 1940, Florida ranked twenty-seventh in population nationwide, boasting only two million people; the Sunshine State was ninth and growing, with many communities expanding at a pace of 10 percent or more each year.
- That population growth included thousands of Vietnamese refugees who came to the state in 1975 after the fall of South Vietnam.
- One of the fastest-growing areas was the southwest coast of Florida, including Bradenton.
- Stefano's business was one of the largest employers in the area; despite increasing tourism, especially in the winter months, he knew nearly everyone in town, and has used the same mechanic and barber for 30 years.
- During most of those years, Bradenton's pulse had been dictated by the nine-month growing season of oranges and the rush to process the delectable fruit into a concentrate for shipping.

The History of Oranges
- The first mention of oranges in literature appeared in the *Shu-ching*, a Chinese book compiled in the sixth century BC.
- Sanskrit literature of the eighth century BC mentioned mandarins, the orange fruit similar to tangerines.
- The earliest citrus fruit known in Europe was the citron, valued for its aromatic rind.
- Before the days of Alexander the Great, Greeks imported citrons from Persia.

- From Greece, citrons spread to Palestine, where one variety became a sacred food to be consumed during the Jewish Feast of Tabernacles.
- In the first century AD Romans ate sweet oranges they called "Indian fruit."
- In 1493, on a second voyage to Hispaniola, Columbus brought orange, lemon and citron seeds from the Canary Islands.
- Pedro Menendez de Aviles brought the sweet orange into Florida at St. Augustine in 1565, and by 1579, Menendez reported to Spain that oranges were flourishing in their new home.
- New Yorkers drank no orange juice until Spain ceded Florida to the British in 1763, when enterprising traders began shipping the fruit north.
- William Bartram, the great Philadelphia naturalist, found wild oranges in abundance in 1773.
- Oranges came into their own in 1821 when Spain ceded Florida to the United States.
- Between 1874 and 1877, the production of oranges in Florida exploded; the eastern United States was annually importing about 200 million oranges with a value of more than $2 million.
- Most oranges were from the Mediterranean, some from the West Indies and some from Florida.
- The crowning touch of Florida's citrus expansion came with the arrival in 1886 of a man named Lue Gim Gong, a Chinese man with tuberculosis, who came to Florida for its healthy climate.
- Lue Gim Gong then spent 39 years hybridizing new varieties of tomatoes, grapefruit and oranges.
- The Lue Gim Gong orange is still a factor in Florida's citrus industry.
- In 1935, the Florida Citrus Commission was established, through which 10 percent of each year's crop value is spent on advertising the health aspects of Florida lemons, grapefruits and oranges.
- In 1960, CBS-TV aired a program about Florida's widespread use of Caribbean migrant workers, whose low pay and poor housing were the norm; the show was entitled, Harvest of Shame.
- Food-processing plants dominated the 3,000-plus manufacturing establishments in the state, including packing houses, canneries and frozen concentrate plants that drew their raw material from the citrus and vegetable fields of Florida.
- Production was expected to exceed 202 million boxes of Florida citrus fruits.

1979: Boxing Cutman

Joe Austin dreamed of being the greatest lightweight boxer in the world, but settled on being a sought-after cutman for boxers when he realized that he lacked the power to become a real contender.

Life at Home

- Joe Austin grew up in an Ohio mill town, whose rhythms were dictated by the shift whistle's morning and afternoon calls to work.
- Invariably, the men of the town checked their pocket watches—to make sure they were correct—when the whistle blew for the second shift.
- It was a tough town, just outside of Cleveland, where every young boy had to prove himself with his fists.
- A child of the Great Depression, Joe had ample opportunities to fight simply to stay alive.
- He was better than most and gained a fierce reputation for fighting through pain even when he was losing—which wasn't often.
- When he was in junior high school and still weighed less than 100 pounds, the high school kids would organize fistfights just to see how much he could take.
- On more than one occasion, his father left work early so he could wager on his son.
- When Joe turned 16, he took his fighting skills to the Army, where he became an exhibition boxer, exempted from some of the more tedious drill exercises.
- Even when the Korean War broke out, he spent his time traveling from base to base putting on a lightweight boxing show.
- Often he was matched against the "girls" who had joined the "sissy" Air Force or the musclehead Marines.
- And when the fighting turned dirty, he knew those rules very well.
- In 1954 he turned pro.
- His first fight was in Spokane, Washington, where the liquor flowed freely and the rules were relaxed.
- His opponent was a tall, inexperienced country boy who was unaccustomed to being hit, but who had a powerful left hand.

Joe Austin was a successful boxing cutman.

- The fight lasted three rounds, and afterwards Joe had to help stop the bleeding he had caused.
- His next six fights were also victories.
- Then he met a true pro who pounded him unmercifully for four rounds before he was knocked out.
- Joe's hospital stay would have lasted two weeks, but he checked himself out so he could be in the ring the following Friday night.
- For the next decade, he was a fixture on fight cards throughout the Midwest—sometimes taking two fights a week.
- "I fought to eat," he recalled. "Fighting fed every part of me."
- Rarely did his bout receive—or deserve—top billing.
- Eventually, his sharp cheek bones that caused him to bleed easily, and a slow left hand that never delivered enough power, got in the way of his dream.
- So Joe, desperate to stay in the fight game, migrated to the role of cutman—an overlooked, but crucial assignment in the world of Blood Inc.

Life at Work

- For three decades, Joe Austin had made his living pressing his long thin fingers into the wounds of professional boxers—some great and some less than good.
- Through the years he had fought against having a nickname.
- While others loved to be called "Stitch" or "Doc," Joe wanted to remain invisible and not draw attention to himself.
- He cherished his privacy, and after a fight never hung out with the fight crowd or chased women.
- He had been married for 26 years.
- By nature most cutmen were vagabonds who rambled from fight to fight and arena to arena to earn two percent of the fighter's purse for the night.
- Some were clowns and some were brilliant, but for all, the job description was the same: perform miracles in an instant.
- Between rounds he had quickly and efficiently closed thousands of bloody cuts, gashes and noses.
- To learn his craft, he spent hours cutting himself and experimenting with different mixtures to close the wound.
- Some of his greatest discoveries became legend.
- In the early days, many of the best cutmen refused to share their secrets—even those who had enough work.
- But with experience and clever hands, Joe learned how to fix one brutal cut at a time, often working on a bleeding boxer between rounds and surrounded by a chorus of screaming fans.
- By definition, a cutman's job during a fight is to stop any bleeding from the face or nose and to reduce swelling around the boxer's eyes by applying cold pressure.
- The goal is to keep the boxer eligible and fighting.
- Blood flowing from the eyebrows must be kept out of the eyes if the fight is to continue.
- The tools of a cutman's trade vary from a lubricant like Vaseline, used to help keep facial

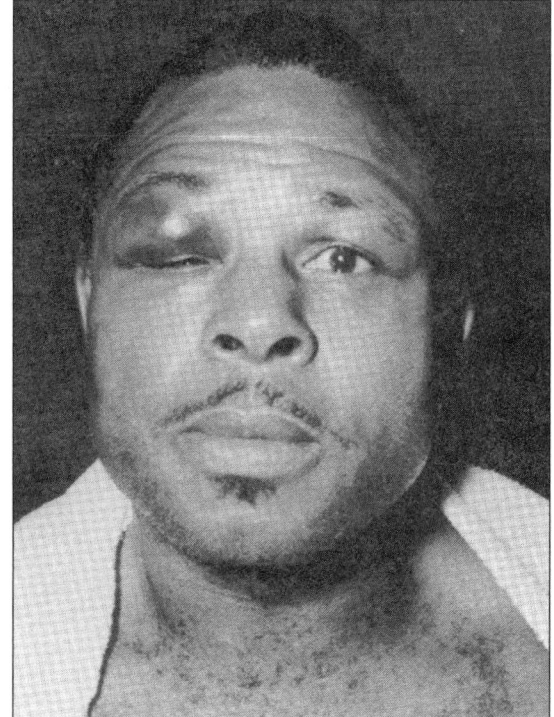

Cutmen had techniques to treat gashes and bruises.

skin elastic to avoid cuts, to more exotic chemicals that coagulate the blood quickly.

- Even the application of Vaseline requires skill.
- Just enough helps a boxer, but too much will get on the opponent's gloves, and then into the eyes of the cutman's fighter.
- Another tool of the trade is an endswell, a flat piece of steel, rounded at the edges, which is either kept on ice or filled with ice to keep it cold.
- Direct pressure with an endswell helps the cutman treat swelling, often called "a mouse."
- Chemicals such as epinephrine were used on cotton-tipped swabs to coagulate the blood and stop bleeding.
- After the bleeding is controlled, the cut is filled with Avitene, a powder that forms a sort of instant scab.

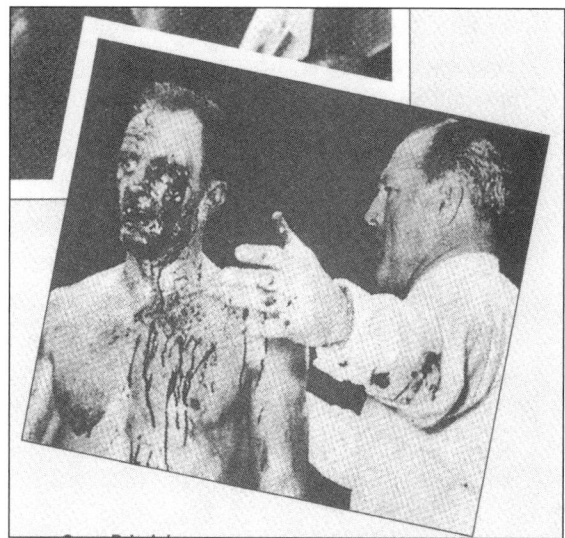

Sometimes not even Joe could stop the bleeding.

- Adrenaline hydrochloride on a cotton-tipped swab inserted into the nostrils stops the bleeding once the nose is pinched shut on it, thus saturating the area with the medicine.
- Joe was thrilled when he could stop nosebleeds so that the fight could continue.
- During one fight, he was working the corner of a promising middleweight contender who received a terrific gash above his left eye early in the first round.
- As the round ended, Joe immediately jumped into the ring and begin working on the cut, applying pressure over the wound between his fingers and palm.
- After he applied a special coagulant, the ringside physician was in his face and wanted to look at the cut.
- In the old days, Joe would have let him do so while also blocking the view.
- These days, blocking the physician's view is frowned on, and can get a cutman banned.
- The physician looked at the facial rip and said, "I'll give you another round to control the bleeding; if not, I'm going to stop the fight."
- The bleeding started to slow down between the second and third rounds, and by the fourth round Joe had the cut completely under control.
- His fighter won the bout and ended up receiving 40 stitches after the fight.
- It was a rough 32 minutes of extreme stress that drew a commendation from the New York State Athletic Commission doctors.
- But the praise must go to the fighter, also, Joe insisted.
- After all, his ringside handiwork would have been undone if the middleweight had not remembered to keep his hands up and protect his eye.
- To stop the fight, the ringside doctor must determine that the bleeding is uncontrollable.
- Joe believed it was important for the fighter's sake that the cutman had sufficient time to work on the cut—possibly one to three rounds, depending on the severity.
- In the end, it comes down to the cutman's skill.
- During one fight a cut was so bad it went in two different directions—across the eyebrow and down the side of the fighter's face.
- "He was so bad I had to pinch it with both hands; he literally had two flaps of skin hanging from his face," said Joe.
- Joe used Avitene, which he pushed into the cut.
- By the fifth round he had the cut under control, and his boxer got a split decision by the judges.
- Afterwards, the boxer was transported to the hospital, while Joe went to the airport and caught a flight home.

Life in the Community: St. Louis, Missouri

- During his travels as a cutman, Joe Austin had worked in a number of large American cities.
- Tampa, Florida, felt too transient, Chicago too cold, and Albuquerque, New Mexico, too foreign.
- For some reason, St. Louis, Missouri, the city struggling to regain its feet after 75 years of decline, felt just right.
- For most of the twentieth century, the rise and fall of St. Louis was inextricably linked to its role as a commercial center near the confluence of the Mississippi and Missouri rivers.
- Founded as a trading post in 1764 and named for King Louis IX of France, the city gained prominence in the 1800s as the capital of the Louisiana territory.
- St. Louis was a departure point for explorers Lewis and Clark, and as the community matured, it promoted itself as a gateway to the west.
- At the time of the 1904 World's Fair, which was visited by an astounding 20 million visitors in seven months, the city's total population topped 600,000.
- Then, in the 1950s, when postwar Americans wanted to live in their own homes, thousands fled to the suburbs.
- The metropolitan area grew to contain 2.4 million people, 12th largest in the nation, but the city itself was neglected.
- Downtown St. Louis became a shabby collection of old stores and offices; some homes had only dirt floors and no hot water.
- Revival began in the 1980s, when major corporations led by young executives from outside St. Louis decided to revitalize the once proud city.
- One of the first items on the agenda was construction on the waterfront of the towering stainless steel archway, rising 630 feet and becoming a major tourist attraction.
- Anheuser-Busch Brewery, which bought the Cardinals baseball team when its owner sought to move the franchise out of town, won support to build a new stadium.
- Private investment in condominiums and luxury homes followed.
- Joe Austin particularly enjoyed the ethnic ties that held many sections of the town together: the Italians in the Hill area of south St. Louis; the descendents of German and Dutch settlers who always kept their brick homes neat and clean; and the Jewish influence that led much of the renovation.

The World's Fair in St. Louis, Missouri, 1904

- Much of the change was fueled by federal redevelopment money—$34 million—which jumpstarted the main mall, the Midwest's biggest retail center under one roof, and the development of DeBaliviere Place for joining the cities near Forest Park, site of the World's Fair in 1904.
- It was there that Joe purchased for $60,000 a condominium that had been renovated from the shell of an abandoned apartment building.
- It gave him both the rustic old look he adored and the convenience of a modern home.
- A condominium demanded no attention to maintenance as he traveled the country attending to cutman chores.

"Will Destiny Match Leonard and Duran?"
The Indiana Gazette (Pennsylvania), November 28, 1979

The next big money bout in boxing likely will be Sugar Ray Leonard meeting Robert Duran and the clash of the most exciting personalities in the ring today—counting even the heavyweight division.

It's a fight that could be worth at least $2 million for each boxer, a miraculous purse for welterweights. And it signals the ultimate Renaissance of the little man in boxing, virtually shut out since the Mohammad Ali (aka Cassius Clay) era began 15 years ago.

Leonard, who emerged from the Montréal Olympics as a colorful reincarnation of the young Sugar Ray Robinson, has been groomed carefully for the welterweight championship since he turned pro on February 5, 1977.

Undefeated in 25 bouts—capped by a sensational one-round knockout of Andy (Hawk) Price here in late September—he has never been seriously pushed.

But Leonard must beat Wilfred Benitez for the World Boxing Council version of the welterweight title on November 30 before a Duran confrontation can be translated into millions of dollars.

Duran is a spectacular former lightweight champ who has lost only one bout in his 12-year career—and that was seven years ago. He graduated to the welterweight division because, at age 28, he could no longer make the 135-pound weight limit. In fact, he balloons so much between bouts, he may have trouble getting in under 147.

Their meeting, if destiny isn't detoured, promises the classic matchup of a flashy boxer (Sugar Ray) against the thunderous, aggressive clouter (Duran).

This is the kind of interest generated by John L. Sullivan versus Gentleman Jim Corbett, or Jack Dempsey versus Gene Tunney, or Joe Frazier versus Mohammad Ali.

Leonard, effusive and cocky, is a tribute to hype. He talks like Ali: "I've been ready for a championship fight from the time I turned pro. The time of reckoning is now.... When I start throwing punches, I hate to count. It's like counting money...I'll be glad to accommodate any champion as long as he's not a heavyweight."

But like Ali, Leonard backs it up with flashy ability. Astutely maneuvered by Angelo Dundee, who worked Ali's corner all those years, he ascended into the championship range under a bunch of setups, wearing them down more with a blizzard of punches than with devastating power.

1979: Hispanic Musician

Just when Eduardo "Lalo" Guerrero (Father of Chicano Music) thought his glory days had passed, his music was featureed in the Broadway play Zoot Suit.

Life at Home

- Billed as the "First Chicano Play on Broadway," *Zoot Suit* featured 1940s boogie woogie band music by Daniel Valdez and Eduardo "Lalo" Guerrero.

- The audiences loved the play and the music, breathing new life into Lalo's multi-decade career that encompassed 700 original songs, including "Canción Mexicana," the unofficial Mexican National Anthem.

- Fittingly, *Zoot Suit,* which hit Broadway in 1979, was a fictionalized version of the real-life Sleepy Lagoon murder trial, when a group of Chicano youths were charged with a murder that they did not commit, resulting in the Zoot Suit Riots.

- The play served as a modern-day symbol of the discrimination Chicanos often suffered in Anglo America, one of Lalo's many themes.

- During his career he recorded in virtually every genre of latin music, including salsa, norteña, banda, ranchera, bolero, corrido, cumbia, mambo, cha cha cha, socially relevant songs, swing, rock 'n' roll and blues.

- He also created children's music, comedy songs and parodies; generations of children in Mexico and the U.S. grew up with his "Ardillitas" (squirrels), and his parodies such as, "Tacos for Two," "Pancho Claus," "Elvis Perez" and "There's No Tortillas."

- In his songs about Cesar Chavez and the farm workers, martyred journalist Ruben Salazar, and the plight of illegal aliens, Lalo chronicled Chicano history.

- Lalo was born into a large family in Barrio Libre section of Tucson, arizona, on Christmas Eve 1916, four years after his parents immigrated to the United States from Mexico.

- His father worked for the Southern Pacific Railroad as a boilermaker; lalo gave credit for his musical skills to his mother and her philosophy of "embracing the spirit of being Chicano."

Eduardo "Lalo" Guerrero was known as the Father of Chicano Music.

- At 17, and influenced by the dire conditions of the Great Depression, he dropped out of high school and took to the road without the benefit of musical training.
- In Los Angeles, he was introduced to the Latin nightlife of the Anglo nightclubs El Trocadero, the Mocamba, and the Coconut Grove, just as Latin music was beginning to invade the United States in the form of the conga, rumba and other African-Caribbean rhythms.
- Some nightclubs even adapted a Latin decor complete with palm trees, coconuts and flamingoes, which opened the door to Latin orchestras and Mexican trios.
- Eighteen-year-old Lalo was initiated into the world of Hollywood entertainment as a trio singer; when the headliner orchestra took a break, the trio sang Mexican songs such as "Amapola," "Cuando Vuelva A Tu Lado," and "Munequita Linda," accompanied by three guitars.
- The story of Mexican-American music was indelibly written by wave after wave of immigrants who had spilled over the Mexican border throughout the twentieth century.
- When musicologist pioneer Charles Lummis went to California to record the fading remnants of the Spanish folk-song tradition in 1904, he had few hints that the popularity of Spanish-Mexican music was about to explode.
- Depressed conditions in Mexico in the first years of the century unleashed waves of opportunity-seeking immigrants into the Southwest.
- Many found middle-class prosperity by the 1940s, carving into society a gap between established Chicano families and impoverished newcomers; both groups thought about family, material wealth and music in different ways.

Life at Work

- Lalo Guerrero was performing on a Los Angeles street corner when producer Manuel Acuna heard him playing in 1939.
- He was in a recording studio the next day.

Lalo enjoyed Latin nightlife in Los Angeles.

- Later that year, Lalo's first trio, Los Carlistas, represented Arizona at the 1939 New York World's Fair, and while in New York, they were invited to perform on *The Major Bowes Amateur Hour on radio.*
- A fixture on radio since 1934, the *Major Bowes Amateur Hour* used a loud gong to dispatch acts that did not meet Major Bowes's standards; Lalo survived his appearance without a bell or gong.
- During the 1940s, Lalo would record 200 songs for Imperial Records, often under the Anglo name Don Edwards; the record

Lalo performed "Chicano Boogie" on The Major Bowes Amateur Hour.

company did not believe a singer with a Chicano name could sell records.

- He also appeared in several uncredited roles in movies, including *Boots and Saddles and His Kind of Woman.*
- During the Second World War, he held the only daytime job of his life, employed in an airline assembly line in San Diego where he also entertained at military camps and hospitals as part of a USO band.
- After the war ended, Lalo had returned to L.A. and was playing in a nightclub called "La Bamba," where the audience was largely Latin and he was forced to switch cultural gears; he was no longer performing to all-Anglo audiences.
- Mexican-Americans were emerging from their isolation, and Mexican nightclubs were proliferating.
- There, under the watchful attention of the audience, Lalo would compose and perform many of the songs that would be used in the Broadway play 30 years later.
- The rise of the Mexican-American middle class—and their appearance at his performances— encouraged him to focus more heavily on musical compositions for the Mexican market.
- Lalo quickly turned out hit after hit with Imperial Records, one of the most active labels on the West Coast; Lalo would compose the songs and Imperial's Acuna would write the arrangements.
- His first American hit was "Pancho López," a parody of the popular 1950s hit "The Ballad Of Davy Crockett."
- Lalo used the Davy Crockett melody and wrote his own lyrics, telling the story of a legendary Mexican character, winning acclaim in both the traditional American market and the Chicano world.
- Lalo went on to record several more parody songs, including "Pancho Claus," "Elvis Perez," "Tacos For Two" (to the tune of "Cocktails For Two"), and "There's No Tortillas" (to the tune of "O Sole Mio").
- Inspired by the success of Alvin and the Chipmunks, Lalo created a Latin chipmunk that became a child favorite and a magnet for lawsuits; Alvin creator David Seville sued for infringement, but the case was thrown out of court.

The profits from his novelty songs allowed Lalo to buy his own nightclub.

- Lalo used the profits from his novelty songs to buy a nightclub which he named Lalo.
- At the same time, Lalo understood the power his musical accomplishments allowed him to possess.
- So during the 1960s, he highlighted the discrimination suffered by the Chicano people and traveled to farming areas where he championed farm workers' causes, writing songs about Cesar Chavez and calling for the decent treatment of agricultural laborers.
- Then came the opportunities presented by the Broadway play *Zoot Suit*.
- The play was set in the barrios of Los Angeles, California, in the early 1940s against the backdrop of the Zoot Suit Riots and World War II.
- A Chicano, wearing his zoot suit on his last night of freedom before beginning his Naval service, was accused—along with his friends—of the murder of a rival "gangster" after a party.
- Unfairly prosecuted, the entire group was thrown in jail for a murder they did not commit.
- Narrated throughout, most of the songs were performed by El Pachuco, an idealized zootsuiter.
- The Broadway production debuted at the Winter Garden Theater on March 25, 1979, and closed on April 29 after 41 performances.

Life in the Community: East Los Angeles, California

- Hispanic East L.A. began life as a Spanish settlement, parceled out among the Pueblo of Los Angeles, the Mission San Gabriel Arcángel, and several ranchos.
- Large-scale development commenced with the arrival of the Southern Pacific Railroad in 1875, and expanded by numerous electric streetcar lines laid over the following three decades to connect the area to fast-growing Downtown Los Angeles.
- Areas along the Arroyo Seco such as Montecito Heights and Mt. Washington were once among the wealthiest neighborhoods in the region, their winding streets lined with finely detailed

Mediterranean villas and Craftsman frame houses and bungalows that enjoyed some of the finest views in Los Angeles.

- Meanwhile, Spanish Colonial bungalows and duplexes sprouted in working-class areas such as El Sereno and City Terrace.
- The East Los Angeles region had long had a very high concentration of Hispanic residents, primarily of Mexican descent.
- Since the early twentieth century, it had been the focus of the Hispanic population in Los Angeles County.
- And when the white population moved to segregated suburbs after World War II, Mexicans seized the opportunity to move into the region's housing at low prices.
- With the exception of a small but distinct Filipino population, the region was primarily Mexican-American by 1950.
- Many second- and third-generation Hispanics or Central Americans subsequently moved from East Los Angeles to other parts of southern California.
- From the 1970s onward, Orange County, the San Fernando Valley, the Inland Empire, and the Gateway Cities region of southeast Los Angeles County have also been major destinations for upwardly mobile Latino families.
- Meanwhile, recent immigrants from Mexico and Central America have continued to settle in the low-income parts of East Los Angeles where the parents of many U.S.-born Hispanics once lived.

A typical working class orchestra in East Los Angeles.

"Lulacs Dance to Have Guerrero Music Friday,"
Santa Fe New Mexican, June 15, 1951

Lalo Guerrero and his famed orchestra will play for a dance Friday night at Seth Hall under the sponsorship of the Lulacs.

Guerrero is the popular Latin-American singer, orchestra leader and prolific composer of Latin-American songs, as well as translator of American popular songs into Spanish. He is the composer of such songs as Prieta Linda, Tu Solo Tu, and wrote the Spanish lyrics to Mule Train. New releases such as "Dime Corazon" and "Lloro Por Te" are now being heard over the two local radio stations.

During the winter season, he plays in such nightspots as the Café Caliente, Olvera Street, Los Angeles, and the unique El Zarape nightclub in Hollywood. Most of his programs are televised nightly.

During the summer season, he tours the Southwestern states and sometimes travels down into Latin America.

&⤸&⤸&⤸&⤸&⤸&⤸&⤸

"High Hopes Held for Zoot Suit,"
by Jay Sharbutt, *Winnipeg Free Press,* March 12, 1979

It's an unlikely duo, the powerful Shubert Organization serving Broadway patrons and El Teatro Campesino, the "the peasant theater" originally formed in 1965 to serve striking farm workers in California.

But the two companies joined for Zoot Suit, a new play with music about pachucos, Mexican-American zootsuiters in Los Angeles during the Second World War, bigotry, hysteria and injustice.

To premiere in New York March 25, it's by an American born 38 years ago in Delano, California, one of 10 children of a migrant farm worker.

Valdez and Shubert president Bernard Jacobs have great hopes for Zoot Suit.

For Valdez, it's that this play he wrote and directed will pave the way for other Hispanic works in mainstream theater. For Jacob, it's that Zoot will prove you can develop a theater audience from New York's large Hispanic community that's never really been tapped.

Jacobs, 62, likens it to efforts to attract black audiences. They didn't succeed on a large scale until the all-black The Wiz clicked on Broadway in 1976, followed by Ain't Misbehaving and Eubie. Now, he says, "we're interested in developing a Hispanic audience. We think the time has come, and that this has unusual qualities.

Valdez isn't new to the theater. He got hooked on it under the worst circumstances as a child of six, stranded with his family on a cotton camp in California.

"We got stuck there because our truck broke down," he said. "We just stayed there, no money, the cotton season was over."

His father, he said, fished a lot in the San Joaquin River, not for fun, but to feed the family. A school bus passed by and the Valdez children hopped aboard to spend some of their time in school.

"It was haphazard," Valdez says. "We kind of went because there was nothing else to do during the day. I couldn't speak English so much of the time, I didn't know what was happening."

Then he saw a teacher taking masks out of paper lunch bags. "It really fascinated me," he said. "Someone was communicating the idea there was a play to be put on and parts were available. I got very excited and got a part in the play."

But the play was produced without Luis Valdez. "Just before I went on, my dad got the truck fixed and we split. I never got to the show.

"But ever since then, I've staged my own shows. That one stop was the turning point."

ॐ‑ॐ‑ॐ‑ॐ‑ॐ‑ॐ‑ॐ

Musical Events of 1979

- Stephen Stills became the first major rock artist to record digitally, laying down four songs at The Record Plant in Los Angeles.

- Rod Stewart's "Do Ya Think I'm Sexy" hit #1 on the *Billboard* charts and stayed there for four weeks.

- Forty-three million viewers watched Elvis! on ABC, a made-for-TV movie starring Kurt Russell as Elvis.

- The Bee Gees collected four Grammys for Saturday Night Fever.

- B.B. King became the first blues artist to tour the Soviet Union, kicking off a one-month tour there.

- Soul singer James Brown performed at the Grand Ole Opry.

- The Pretenders signed a contract with Sire Records.

- Singer Donny Hathaway died after falling 15 stories from his hotel room in New York City.

- MCA Records purchased ABC Records for a reported $20 million.

- Sex Pistols bassist Sid Vicious was found dead from an overdose, a day after being released on bail from Rikers Island prison.

- The Clash kicked off their first concert on their first American tour at the Berkeley Community Theatre outside San Francisco, California, with the song "I'm So Bored with the U.S.A."

- Van Halen released their second album, Van Halen II.

- Eric Clapton married Patti Boyd, ex-wife of Clapton's friend George Harrison.

- Kate Bush became the first artist to use a wireless microphone, enabling her to sing and dance at the same time.

- One hundred ten thousand people attended the California Music Festival at the L.A. Memorial Coliseum, where the performers included Aerosmith, The Boomtown Rats, Cheap Trick, Ted Nugent, and Van Halen.

- Ozzy Osbourne was fired as lead singer of Black Sabbath.

- Iron Maiden, Samson, and Angel Witch shared a bill at the Music Machine in Camden, London; critic Geoff Barton coined the term "New Wave of British Heavy Metal" in a review of the show for Sounds magazine.

- Three of the ex-Beatles performed on the same stage, as Paul McCartney, George Harrison, and Ringo Starr jammed with Eric Clapton, Ginger Baker, Mick Jagger, and others at a wedding reception for Clapton at his home.

- Elton John played eight concerts in the Soviet Union.

- Alternative Tentacles record label was established by Dead Kennedys frontman Jello Biafra.

- Bill Haley made his final studio recordings at Muscle Shoals, Alabama.

- The Bee Gees played to a sold-out crowd at Los Angeles Dodger Stadium as part of their Spirits Having Flown tour.

- Aerosmith and Ted Nugent headlined the World Series of Rock at Municipal Stadium in Cleveland, Ohio.

- Two hundred fifty thousand turned out in Central Park for a free concert by James Taylor in a campaign to restore Sheep Meadow, a 15-acre preserve in New York.

- "My Sharona" by The Knack hit #1 on the Billboard charts—the first time in over a year that a #1 song was not either a disco song or a ballad.

- Musicians United for Safe Energy (MUSE) staged a series of five "No Nukes" concerts at Madison Square Garden; Jackson Browne; Crosby, Stills and Nash; Bruce Springsteen and the E Street Band; Bonnie Raitt; Tom Petty; James Taylor; and Carly Simon were among the participants.

- The single "Rapper's Delight" by The Sugarhill Gang marked the commercial emergence of hip hop music.

- Stevie Wonder used digital audio recording technology on his album Journey through the Secret Life of Plants

1979: Vietnamese Immigrants

Vang Ghia and his family escaped from Laos into Thailand after the fall of Vietnam and emigrated to Fresno, California, where basketball became his greatest obsession.

Life at Home

- Vang Ghia was a 12-year-old Hmong boy living with his family in Fresno, California.
- He was the oldest child of the Vang family, a clan that followed a tradition of using the family name first, the given name second.
- His mother, who believed herself to be 37, has had eight other children, six of whom were still living.
- Ghia, his family and another family from the same subclan lived together in a two-bedroom apartment on the west side of Fresno.
- The eight members of the Vang family lived in one room, sleeping on pallets on the floor.
- The younger children, including their new-born brother, slept near the adults.
- The new baby was the first child in the family born in the United States, and the first born in a hospital.
- When he was born, the Vangs asked, through a cousin who could speak English, for the baby's placenta.
- The nurse relayed the request to the doctor, who, remembering stories he had heard of rural Asians eating their children's placentas, turned it down immediately.
- The Vangs were very upset at his refusal; in Hmong culture, the placenta of a newborn child is buried with the expectation that, after the child grows up and dies, it will retrace its life steps and then don the placenta—the baby's first jacket—in preparation for rejoining his ancestors and eventually be born again.
- Ghia's parents were afraid that because the placenta was sent away, their child would be forced to wander naked for all of eternity after his death.
- On the third day after the birth, the family held a soul-calling ceremony to name the child; friends were invited to the house and a pig was slaughtered—an invitation for an ancestor to inhabit the child's body.

Vang Ghia escaped from Laos with his family at 12-years-old.

The family slept on pallets on the floor in a Thai refugee camp.

- Eventually, the name Ger was bestowed upon the child; two chickens were then sacrificed, plucked, eviscerated and boiled.
- All in attendance were delighted to see that the chicken skulls were translucent and the tongues curled backward—signs that the soul of the ancestor is happy to reside in Ger's body and pleased with the name—even though the family has moved far away from its traditional territory and village in Laos.
- Ghia was born in the mountains of Laos where his family farmed, growing beans, melons, yams, corn and vegetables.
- Their most important cash crop was opium poppies.
- Forced to abandon their farm in 1976 because of the Hmong people's historic support of the United States during the Vietnam War, Ghia and his family fled Laos, crossing the Mekong River into Thailand to escape the wrath of the new communist government.
- Two of Ghia's siblings and several other family members died during the arduous trek.
- In Thailand, they lived in a refugee camp, barely able to survive on the meager food supplies, but grateful to be alive.
- There, they met American missionaries who taught Ghia and his other brothers and sisters to speak English.
- In appreciation for their support during the war, Laos Highland refugees, 90 percent of whom were Hmong, have been coming to the United States since 1975.
- Approximately 40,000 Hmong refugees have emigrated in the past four years.
- Three years after they left Laos, the family received permission to enter the United States.
- Their host family found them a place to live on the west side of Fresno, California, where a growing Hmong community was forming, including many members of the Vang clan.

Hmong refugees were not used to American homes.

- When they arrived in Fresno, Ghia's parents were not only unable to speak English, but were also labeled illiterate in their own language; the Hmong did not have an alphabet until the 1950s.
- Thanks to the missionaries in the refugee camps and hard work, the older children could read and write in English, and often served as translators for their parents during the early days in the United States.
- The family initially survived with the help of public assistance checks after Ghia's father was unable to find work.
- Ghia's mother joined with several of the other local Hmong women in sewing intricate story cloths, which told of life in their village and the exodus to Thailand.
- The ready market for story cloths was helping the family meet its needs, but finding work for Ghia's father has been more difficult.
- His skills as an Asian farmer did not transfer well into the highly mechanized agribusiness world of Fresno, where a good knowledge of machinery, chemicals and English was a necessity.
- He and several of the other Hmong men in the apartment complex started a large garden on nearby vacant land, growing a variety of fruits and vegetables for their families to eat.
- No one was certain to whom the land belongs; it was not a consideration, since the concept of private land ownership was rarely practiced by the Hmong people.

Life at School
- Ghia attended the seventh grade at a public school.
- When he first arrived, his skills, especially in conversational English, were far behind those of his American classmates.
- The two children from his American host family provided regular tutoring, and he has worked hard to catch up.

- He understood most of what was said in class, but confusion still arose.
- At first, when his new friends said things like, "See you later," he thought it was an invitation for another meeting.
- Some days, he hung around after school for several anxious hours attempting to fulfill his obligation to "see you later."
- His fellow classmates were a diverse group, including African-Americans, Mexicans, Chinese and a few whites.
- He encountered few problems and less prejudice than he had expected, although the majority of his time was spent with the other Hmong kids, who shared his language, problems and background.

Transition to American life was not easy and children studied hard.

- While still in Thailand, he learned about many aspects of American culture, including basketball, with which he has become obsessed.
- He played for the middle school B team.
- Even though he rarely got to play in a game, his family came to every home game and cheered wildly when he was on the court.
- The coach said he had natural talent and that with practice, he would catch up with the boys who have been playing the game their entire lives.
- Though Ghia adapted rapidly to American life, the transition for his parents continued to be more difficult.
- Issues such as cars, paved streets, neon signs, traffic lights and airplanes continually upset them.
- In Laos, his father possessed great instincts of where he was in the jungle and how to return home, no matter how dense the vegetation.
- In Fresno, he rarely went more than a few blocks from home without taking a child to guide him back.
- Once, the police brought him home after he had gotten lost and wandered the streets for hours.
- Afraid and unable to communicate with the policeman, Ghia's father showed the police the telephone number for their host family, who helped in the rescue mission.
- Afterward, he was withdrawn and declined to talk with his family for days.

Most of Ghia's time was spent with other Hmong children.

- He often sat in the community garden for hours, staring at the horizon; in Hmong culture, the man is always the leader, working and providing for his family.
- The Vang family contacted a local shaman to assist in the job search; thus far, several animals were sacrificed, with no result.
- The host family was concerned that he might be considering suicide.
- At Thanksgiving, when the host family held a traditional American dinner for the new Asian immigrants, everyone except Ghia's father piled into the host family's station wagon and headed across town.
- Upon entering the home, they were struck by the strange smells of turkey, cranberry sauce and cornbread, unknown in Laos.

Ghia worked hard to learn English so he could do well in school.

- The highlight of the meal was when Ghia's mother, who took English classes and gained confidence in her skills, told a story—all in English.
- She modestly described her latest sewing creation and the woman who bought it, and ended by saying how grateful she was to be in America and that the future will be bright.
- When she finished speaking, the host family was in tears.
- Ghia loved eating American food and asked for seconds of everything, especially the yams, which remind him of home.
- To accommodate both families, the adults and smallest children were seated at the dining room table, while Ghia and the other teens dined by themselves at fold-up card tables covered by a cloth.
- Ghia got so excited telling stories about his basketball team and his new friends that he knocked a small bowl of cranberry sauce off the table, embarrassing his mother.
- Afterward he apologized to his mother and to the host family for both his manners and his father's inability to attend this important family function.
- Before leaving, Ghia noticed that the house was filled with paintings of faraway cities or mountain ranges, or even drawings that had no point at all.
- His apartment was decorated by a line of 8"x10" photographs hung high on the living room wall of family members in Hmong costume and old images from Laos and the camps; pictures of parents and grandparents, enlarged from old snapshots, gaze out at their descendants all day long.
- In addition to practicing basketball, Ghia spent his spare time focused on learning to dance in time for his middle school's end-of-semester dance.
- Ghia had thought little about the event until Rosita, a cute Mexican girl in his class, asked him to go with her.
- Since then he has thought of little else.
- He asked numerous friends to teach him how to dance, got advice about what to wear, and even asked his sisters what girls like to talk about.

- His family had neither a radio nor a television, so he went to another friend's house just to know what music was popular.
- His mother was so excited about the dance she had set aside money to buy him a new shirt to wear.
- His father's concern was that his Hmong son was going out in public with a Mexican girl.

Life in the Community: Thailand and Fresno, California

- By the late 1970s in Thailand, 21 refugee camps had been established to receive hundreds of thousands of people fleeing Vietnam, Cambodia and Laos.
- The camps were supported by the United Nations High Commissioner for Refugees and staffed by volunteers, including many missionaries.
- The Thai government was instrumental in determining official and unofficial refugee camp policies; as a result, camps were opened and closed by Thai authorities, and refugees were shifted about abruptly.
- Ban Vinai became the largest Hmong settlement, both in Thailand and in the world, containing 40,000 people in an area of less than one square mile.
- There, many were taught English and Christianity by the missionaries.
- Fresno County was one of the largest counties in California, extending across the San Joaquin Valley from the Central Coast Ranges to the crest of the Sierra Nevada.
- With a population of more than 175,000, Fresno, which means "ash tree" in Spanish, was the ninth largest city in California; when the entire county was included, the population totalled nearly 500,000.
- Ninety percent of the west side housing in Fresno was occupied by Hispanics, blacks and Asians; because of recent immigration patterns, Fresno was considered the American Hmong capital.
- Canned, frozen and dehydrated fruit and vegetable processing lead all other industrial sectors in employment, accounting for one-third of all manufacturing activity.

Changing America

- Polls reported that 55 percent of the population, up from 23 percent in 1969, saw nothing wrong with premarital sex.
- The price of gold reached $524 per ounce, up from $223 in 1978.
- A public service advertisement read, "If 2,225,000 Americans were starving to death, this ad would be a lot bigger. Feed Cambodia."
- The tour of the Moscow Philharmonic in the United States was canceled after several Bolshoi Ballet stars defected.
- More than 100,000 attended a memorial concert in Boston for conductor Arthur Fiedler.

- Pioneer 11 reached Saturn and reported that its rings were composed of ice-covered rocks.
- Americans purchased 315,000 microcomputers, up from 172,000 in 1978.
- California was the first state to initiate gas rationing using a method of alternate-day purchasing.
- A study reported that T-shirts carrying slogans or mottoes expressed a wish for a connection with others.
- The sale of health foods topped $1.6 billion, up from $140 million in 1970.
- The U.S. Trust reported that 520,000 Americans were millionaires, or one in every 424.
- The federal government ordered the recall of numerous brands of hair dryers because of harmful amounts of asbestos.
- The divorce rate increased 69 percent in the past decade; the median duration of marriage stood at 6.6 years.

There was a growing Hmong community in Fresno.

1979: Family Business Owner

For seven generations, Blaine Maxwell's family operated the Maxwell Manufacturing Company, one of the oldest companies listed on the New York Stock Exchange.

Life at Home

- Blaine Maxwell's company, community and home were all intertwined; each had its beginnings more than 200 years ago in the small Connecticut village of Windsor Locks.
- Thanks to Blaine's energy and insight, Maxwell Manufacturing—for the first time in its 212-year history—joined the Forbes industry listing of the nation's largest companies.
- Blaine lived in a 199-year-old home built by an ancestor; a family member from every other generation has added a room or an addition to the building—and Blaine was no exception.
- Using lumber from a forest in Pennsylvania, Blaine and his wife Amy constructed an extensive library off the back to hold her books on architecture, Connecticut history and antiques.
- The entire room was built with traditional tools, and without nails or screws; the cost exceeded $500,000.
- His home and property sprawled over six acres.
- Founded in 1767, when the location of Maxwell Manufacturing's headquarters in Windsor Locks, Connecticut, was called Pine Meadow, the company remained largely unchanged from its colonial days—until two decades ago.
- At its origin, the company scoured wool sheared from local flocks and sold cattle feed to farmers.
- After 191 years, the company boasted sales of $9.5 million.
- Its transformation began after World War II, when Blaine returned from the war determined to change the family business.
- He said, "I saw what the modern world was going to be like and I wanted our company to be part of it."
- With his company now well-positioned for the future, Blaine spent most of his time working in his community and investing in energy.
- To pay tribute to Windsor Locks and the six generations that came before him, he and Amy personally paid to have the cemeteries in the community upgraded, cleaned and refurbished.

Blaine Maxwell guided his company through a period of rapid growth.

- He also established a fund at the public library to acquire books, papers, writings, pictures and etchings from the area.
- Cost had not been a factor; when an excellent example of local history was found at auction or through a New York book dealer, the Maxwells donated generously.
- Amy, whose Connecticut roots stretched back five generations, took a keen interest in preserving the past, and authored two local histories which were reviewed well and published by her family trust.
- On a statewide task force to save historic landmarks, bridges and homes, she travelled Connecticut, inspecting sites.

- On two occasions she used her own money to buy dilapidated buildings which were within days of meeting a wrecking ball.
- One building was completely renovated and sold—a process that took more than a year; the second was still awaiting word from the architect whether it could be saved at all.
- Through his company, Blaine annually funded scholarships for five students to attend college—provided they went into the sciences.
- Last year, the community did not produce enough high school graduates interested in both going to college and majoring in the sciences to use the generous grants, named after his great-great-great-great-grandfather, who started the company.
- The couple's other great joy was their Nantucket Island home, whose buildings and architecture wee little changed in more than 100 years.
- One of its greatest treasures was its isolation; they didn't even mind that the Sunday New York Times did not arrive there until Monday.
- Once described by Daniel Webster as a "city at sea," Nantucket was home to more than 125 whaling captains in the 1830s.
- Many traditions from the era were preserved; at 9 p.m. the old Lisbon bell at South Tower sounded a curfew, striking 52 times.
- Nantucket became the place where the couple's five children gathered in the summer with the 11 grandchildren, who learned to crab, fish and sail on the Island.
- Summer in Nantucket was particularly joyous with the return of their second son from the Peace Corps; he would enter law school in the fall.
- From a personal standpoint, Blaine was obsessed with being part of the solution to the energy crisis; natural gas, he told everyone, was the answer.

Top and above: Blaine's wife Amy worked to save historic landmarks and buildings.

- This unused resource, which was plentiful in the Western Hemisphere, could be the energy source of the future; he was determined that America should not become dependent on Arab oil, believing it would be the first step in eliminating American freedom.
- He was outraged recently when the Organization of the Petroleum Exporting Countries increased oil prices by 14.5 percent.
- *The New York Times* is reported that residential utility bills would be up an average of as much as $7.50 a month because of the rising price of oil.
- Even Saudi Arabia, a traditional friend of the United States, appeared unable to check OPEC's manipulation of oil production to control oil prices.
- To have an impact on America's energy future, he invested millions of dollars in Canada's Noranda Mines, which sat on one of the continent's richest natural gas deposits.
- Noranda's earnings doubled in four years, and the cheap Canadian dollar helped even more; because

Amy used her own money to save dilapidated buildings from destruction.

the company did about a quarter of its business abroad, mainly in the United States, it paid its miners and kept its books in Canadian dollars while receiving much of its income in foreign currencies.
- The resulting leverage effect on the company's earnings was enormous; for example, where U.S. producers of a product such as copper got $0.72 a pound, Noranda got $0.85 Canadian.
- In that way, a $0.01 decline in the value of the Canadian dollar meant an extra $5 million after taxes to the company; to Blaine, this meant Noranda would have the capital to continue exploration for natural gas and the building of pipelines.
- Noranda was the largest landowner in Canada, with 1.2 million of what may be the largest pool of natural gas yet discovered in North America.
- Potentially, the site could contain twice the gas reserves of those in New Mexico's prolific San Juan Basin, and double those in Alaska's Prudhoe Bay.
- More than $140 million was spent drilling 40 wells, most of them successful, with proven reserves of about one trillion cubic feet.
- As important, Noranda's fields were only 40 miles from an existing pipeline linking the Pacific Gas Transmission system at Kingsgate, British Columbia, with the lucrative markets in the United States.
- The stock of Noranda doubled in the past year, since Blaine began investing.

Life at Work
- During the past 20 years, Blaine Maxwell progressively transformed his family-owned company.
- Sales topped $350 million and net earnings were well over $20 million—both double—digit gains over the previous year.
- Thanks to his desire for change, the company made and sold hundreds of products—ranging from coatings for the inside of beer cans, adhesives for jet planes, cleaning systems for poultry processors and paper for tea bags—manufactured in 100 research and marketing facilities around the world.

- The headquarters were now in a modern concrete and glass building on the site of the company's original office, where from across the way, Blaine could keep an eye on the company's paper and non-woven fabric mill that was built along the Connecticut River in various stages over the past two centuries.
- The company concentrated on developing new specialty chemicals used by specific manufacturers such as Budweiser, Lear Siegler and Thomas J. Lipton; most of the company's growth has taken place through such innovations.
- One of its first acquisitions, Standard Insulation Company, signaled the company's determination to move away from its dependence on slow-growth, capital-intensive, nonwoven production into more research-intensive manufacturing businesses.
- If the company attempted to grow purely through non-wovens, they would not be in existence, Blaine believed; to grow, he preached, the company must be smart and responsive.
- He spent much of his time on the road meeting with customers—and training his staff; an ex-salesman himself, he insisted that his more than 700 salesmen be familiar enough with the customers' needs to actually run the machines on which the company's products were used.

The couple enjoyed spending time at their home on Nantucket Island.

- "When we go into the marketplace, we find out what a customer wants us to invent and then we come back to the lab and invent it," he said recently during a speech at a local Rotary Club meeting.
- Using this concept, the company developed a high-temperature exterior coating for cookware which was used to compete with DuPont's Teflon™.
- In order to expand its capacity, Maxwell Manufacturing made its first acquisition in five years—an Ohio manufacturer of water-treatment chemicals.
- Thanks to strategic positioning and planning, 22 of the 26 business segments within the company were either first or second in share for their market.
- In addition, Blaine believed his company was less affected by the soaring rate of inflation because of the industries to which he sold; 55 percent of the company's sales were in industries that traditionally resisted economic slumps, such as beer, soft drinks and medical supplies.

Life in the Community: Windsor Locks, Connecticut

- The pride of being from Connecticut extended to almost all of the state's three million-plus residents, including those who lived in speck-on-the-map villages.
- All of Connecticut could be contained 53 times within the borders of Texas; only two states were smaller—Rhode Island and Delaware.
- Connecticut's per capita income was the highest in the nation.

- The village of Windsor Locks, and the entire state, were been at the vanguard of preservation efforts; thousands of colonial homes were still actively used, thanks to this dedication.
- Blaine's 199-year-old home was surrounded by dozens of houses of similar age.
- During the American Revolution, the home was used for meetings to determine how cloth, firewood and ammunition would be distributed throughout New England.
- Blaine's ancestors fully realized that if the British won the war, the house would certainly be confiscated or burned.
- For a state known for its urbanization and industry, Connecticut was more than 60 percent wooded, with oak being the most common hardwood in the state.
- Salmon were restocked in Connecticut waters in hopes that sport and commercial fishing would be possible in the future.
- Like those of their neighbors, the Maxwells' home was furnished with antiques handed down through the family for generations.
- Amy was especially pleased to tell guests that her ancestors built the chairs they were sitting on and were probably the inventors of the roundabout chair.

Blaine believed his company escaped the affects of soaring inflation better than most.

1979: U.S. Marine

Leon Purvis joined the Marine Corps to escape both Mississippi and a drunken father, and was stationed in Guantanamo Bay, Cuba.

Life at Home

- The second time Leon Purvis journeyed outside his home of Tunicia, Mississippi, was to join the Marines at a recruiting station in Memphis.
- Even the poorest white families managed to send their children to a private academy to avoid court-ordered integration, but being one of six white kids in his senior class had its challenges.
- More than one black kid wanted to make his mark by whipping the white boy.
- Leon was not always the clear winner, but he did gain a measure of respect; by the time he was a senior, almost no one challenged him to meet after school by the football stadium.
- Leon's father spent some of his time doing odd farming jobs and the rest of the time drinking.
- His mother, who could not read, worked at the dry cleaner's pressing rich men's suits all day.
- Leon was the third of seven children, five of whom made it to adulthood.
- The family moved often, usually for nonpayment of rent, but never left the county.
- All Leon knew growing up was that he wanted to be somebody, somewhere else.
- At best an average-to-uninspired student, Leon began thinking in his sophomore year about the Marines.
- When a Marine recruiter visited the school, Leon learned about the places he would visit on active duty, the skills he could acquire, and the educational opportunities that awaited him.
- The next day, after his older brother got fired from the cotton mill and his father came home drunk, Leon cut school, borrowed a friend's car and drove to Memphis to enlist in the Marines following graduation.
- Three days after his father got arrested for public drunkenness at Leon's high school graduation, the boy was on his way to boot camp at Parris Island, South Carolina.
- There, his ideas about his toughness were immediately tested.
- After a particularly grueling march with full packs in the summer heat and humidity of coastal South Carolina, Leon asked his drill instructor if he could call home.
- Leon had never been away this long.
- The sergeant smiled reassuringly and said of course he could call home.
- Leon was told to meet the drill instructor after supper.

The Marines offered Leon Purvis an escape from Mississippi.

- Leon found himself in marsh water up to his neck, screaming "Home, Home!" as salt-water mosquitoes swarmed about his head in a dense cloud.
- After his voice gave out, he was made to continue calling home for what seemed like hours, his words coming out as a rasping noise.
- It was the last favor he asked anyone at Parris Island.
- At first, he was devastated by his failures at the rifle range and obstacle course, but slowly he started to feel like a Marine.
- He began to understand discipline, structure and being part of a team.
- It was impressed upon him that he was part of a noble effort, waged by only a qualified few, to defend America from communism and all the forces that were plotting to bring down the greatest country in the world.
- Therefore, he was pleased that, following basic and some additional training in California, he was assigned to help guard Guantanamo Bay, Cuba—the most dangerous communist threat in the Western Hemisphere.
- In his bunk, late at night, he envisioned himself standing between America and the godless hordes of communists in Cuba.

Leon's father spent some of his time doing odd farming jobs.

Life at Work

- When Leon Purvis arrived at Guantanamo Bay, his first reaction was joy—he was the first person in his family to leave the shores of America.
- His second reaction was discomfort at the oppressive heat and humidity.

Life at boot camp in Parris Island was a great challenge.

- While on the ferry crossing the bay to Gitmo, his base, Leon decided the weather was similar to Mississippi, but better than the hellhole of Parris Island.
- Seventeen miles of high, barbed-wire fence surrounded the entire base.
- In response, Cuba had constructed a barrier line approximately one mile from the American fence.
- Numerous watchtowers were erected on both sides of the line.
- Behind the American fence was the world's largest minefield, measuring 723 acres.
- Tooling down Sherman Avenue, the main street, Leon thought Guantanamo looked like most bases—littered with long metal Quonset huts, bowling alleys and government-designed parade fields.
- Gitmo was like a small city, containing 6,000 Americans, nearly 1,000 Jamaicans, several hundred Filipinos and about 400 Cubans, of whom 260 lived on base.

- The remaining 140 Cubans commuted each day, despite Castro's efforts to stop them.
- All worked at the base since before the revolution in 1959.
- Each day, they travelled to the Cuban line, removed their clothes, walked to a separate room to don their work clothes, and walked one mile to the American gate, where they were inspected, admitted and transported to their jobs.
- At the end of the day, the process was repeated in reverse.
- Of the Americans, most were civilian workers or dependents; the naval force totalled 1,800, while the Marines number 420.

Gitmo housed Americans, Jamaicans, Filipinos and Cubans.

- The navy operated a deep-water training base for 75 to 80 ships each year, while the Marines were responsible for guarding the 17mile fence and defending the base from attack, with patrols maintained along the fence itself.
- After a few weeks into the new duty, Leon's enthusiasm was waning.
- Guard duty on the communist front was not as dramatic as he had anticipated; he had not seen a Cuban who did not work at the base.
- Yet, he knew that without the Marines, the Cubans would have overrun Guantanamo years ago.

The Americans at the base were a combination of civilian workers, U.S. Navy and U.S. Marines.

- Just when he thought he was going to go crazy from boredom, word rocketed through the base that a Russian brigade had arrived in Cuba.
- Some speculated that this could be the first wave of Cossack attackers preparing to retake Guantanamo.
- World War III could start right here!
- Leon, now well-schooled in his role as a Marine, kept his mouth shut and did his job.
- If his superiors wanted him to know something or attack anything, he would be told.
- Then, the newspapers reported that President Jimmy Carter had ordered a mock landing of 1,800 Marines for October as a show of force for the Russians and Cubans.
- Leon wasn't sure that that many Marines were needed, but he grew excited to learn the invading American troops would remain on the base for a month to conduct joint exercises.
- The purpose, he was told, was to prove Guantanamo Bay's ground defense could be quickly reinforced.
- That would shake up the monotony of guarding Gitmo.
- Not that there wasn't a lot to do, especially for a poor boy from Mississippi.

- Because the base was located in a hostile country, soldiers were not allowed to leave the base; therefore, every luxury possible had been provided.
- Leon took a course in auto mechanics and learned to scuba dive, play golf and ride horses.
- The only animal he ever rode was a mean-as-a-snake mule who loved to bite.
- Through the post exchange, Leon bought a camera and regularly shot pictures of the horses he rode, the fish he caught and the boats he crewed on.
- He had choices he never had before: to reenlist, buy an auto repair garage back home, or even attend college.
- Imagine, a Purvis in college!
- He awaited the mock invasion while patrolling the fence dividing democracy from communism.

Life in the Community: Guantanamo Bay, Cuba

- Guantanamo Bay came under the control of the United States following the Spanish-American War in 1898; the first treaty was signed in 1903, leasing the bay to America for $2,000 a year.
- In 1934, the terms of the agreement were extended in perpetuity, and the annual rent for the 32 square miles of land doubled to $4,000.
- A check for the agreed-upon amount had been sent to the Cuban Government every year since then, though none have been cashed since the year after the Castro Government assumed power in 1959.
- The facility was divided into sections on either side of the bay, one containing the airfield and the other the naval station, with a ferry connecting the two.
- The base had facilities for docking, ship repair, ordnance, training, communications, supplies, and medical and administrative functions.

Guantanamo Bay came under the control of the United States following the Spanish-American War in 1898.

"On 'The Rock,' " *Newsweek*, October 15, 1979

When the Marines land on Windmill Beach on Guantanamo Bay next week, they will be staging an exercise at one of the oldest and most isolated U.S. bases in the world, and the only one on communist soil. *Newsweek's* David C. Martin flew to Guantanamo last week and filed this on-scene report:

Seventeen miles of fence, 420 Marines and the world's largest active minefield are all that stand between the Guantanamo naval base and the entire Cuban Army. But the reports of a Soviet combat brigade somewhere on the island caused less of a stir here than in Washington. Col. Mark Fennessy, commander of the Marine Corps detachment at Guantanamo, says the first he heard of the troops was when he read about them in the base newspaper, The Guantanamo Bay Gazette. Guantanamo's commanding officer, Navy Capt. John Fetterman, adds: "It's been business as usual down here."

Business is slow at "Gitmo." Christopher Columbus anchored here one day in 1494 to look for fresh water but left the next day, and many of Gitmo's 5,000 Americans wish they could do the same. "There are civilians as well as military people who are most unhappy here, who just can't stand the confinement," says Florence Franz, whose husband works for the U.S. Navy. More than 80 percent of the married personnel assigned to Guantanamo extend their tours. But with only 250 single women to go around, and with square dancing the principal action at the misnamed Gitmo Swingers Club, few bachelors volunteer to stay more than a year on "The Rock."

Despite its questionable charms, Guantanamo Bay is an important strategic asset for the U.S. The base serves as a beachhead on Castro's island. With its deep harbor and command of

14,000 square miles of open water, it also provides an ideal training area for the Navy's Atlantic fleet. Each year, about 75 U.S. naval vessels put into Gitmo for five to eight weeks of training in the Caribbean.

Next week's Marine exercise has both a political and military purpose. With the Cubans holding most of the high ground around the camp, the Marines could not withstand a major assault. "They say we're supposed to hold on for 48 hours before reinforcements arrive," says Steve Hesselgrave, a Navy technician. "But the Marines can't do it. The base is not defendable."

Guantanamo was captured by the Marines in 1898 during the Spanish-American War, and the U.S. held it ever since under a lease signed with Cuba in 1903. A second treaty, signed in 1934, made the lease perpetual and specified that it could be voided only by mutual consent or if the U.S. abandoned the base and its 45 square miles of Cuban territory. Fidel Castro likes to bluster about U.S. "imperialism" at Guantanamo Bay, but his troops have not tried to throw the Americans out. "We've had no trouble from them," says Marine Capt. Carlton Carter. "We carry out our duties and they carry out theirs."

"With U.S. Marines at Guantanamo,"
U.S. News & World Report, October 29, 1979

The 1,800 battle-clad Marines who swarmed ashore on the communist island of Cuba on October 17 signaled this message to Moscow and Havana:

The United States is ready and able to counter threatening adventures by the Soviet-Cuban alliance in the Western Hemisphere.

The landing at the U.S. naval base at Guantanamo was advertised as Jimmy Carter's response to the Kremlin's refusal to withdraw a Soviet combat brigade discovered in Cuba in August—in short, the president's way of altering what he called an "unacceptable status quo."

Military men monitoring the reinforcement exercise describe it as "technically flawless."

In a heavy squall, the Marines—together with their tanks and other heavy equipment—were lifted by amphibious craft and helicopter from the three warships that transported them from Camp Lejeune, NC.

Only minutes after the first troops landed, they were clambering into bunkers overlooking Cuban territory and patrolling the 17-mile perimeter fence, which is supported by a 723-acre minefield.

These troops reinforced the 420 Marines who comprise the permanent garrison in the 45-square mile American base on this communist island.

Besides the temporary beefing up of the Guantanamo garrison, its air defenses were reinforced by a squadron of Skyhawk attack warplanes that were flown in from North Carolina.

The whole operation was completed in only two hours, with the results summed up by one observer: "No mishaps, no casualties, no hitches."

As precise as this operation proved to be, the officers in charge emphasize this point: In a real crisis involving the Guantanamo base, the U.S. response would take a different form.

If the base were threatened, American troops would be airlifted directly from the U.S. mainland into Guantanamo. America's trump card, officials say, would be a naval blockade similar to the one clamped around the island by the U.S. in the 1962 missile crisis.

But the real purpose of the Marine operation was not to prove that the U.S. can hold Guantanamo against a 159,000-man army. Rather, the aim was to demonstrate that Cuban-Soviet adventurism in this region would face a powerful American challenge.

Despite the obvious vulnerability of their tight enclave, the 6,000 Americans in Guantanamo—sailors, civilian workers and dependents, as well as the Marine garrison—seem unflustered. Even while the well-publicized Marine reinforcement exercise was being organized, there were no threats from Cuba's President Fidel Castro.

There were reports, in the days before the landing, that the Cuban Army called up about 3,000 reservists near Guantanamo and increased its tank and antiaircraft deployments nearby. Cuban aerial surveillance was intensified, although no flights over the base were detected.

Marine detachments patrolling the perimeter began noticing increased numbers of Cubans from Havana's Frontier, a quasi-military unit.

Just before the first Marines disembarked, an unidentified vessel drew within 2,000 yards of the Nassau, one of the three American warships participating in the exercise. Presumably Cuban, it tracked the progress of the American naval vessels but disappeared into the mist when approached by an American destroyer that was leaving Guantanamo.

The Americans stationed at this base are not concerned with the danger from the Cubans so much as the disruption of their ordinary routine caused by the Marine reinforcements who are scheduled to remain here until mid-November. The mood was reflected in the comment of a Navy enlisted man, William Norton, who works at the base airfield. "Castro," he said, as the reinforcements moved in, "probably is sitting there on one of those mountains laughing about all of us crazy fools down here wasting our tax money by bringing in the Marines."

Laughing or not, Castro will have to get used to the presence of a more substantial American military presence at Guantanamo and in his neighborhood generally. Besides the Marine reinforcement exercise, the navy is planning other displays of military prowess in the region.

These moves are calculated by President Carter to demonstrate that the United States has the capacity—and the will—to bring its armed strength to bear in defense of its interests in the Western Hemisphere.

Is the message getting through to Castro and his Soviet patrons? Col. Mark Fennessy, the Marine commander at Guantanamo, has one answer: "We are not in an aggressive mode. But I'm sure they are showing a logical interest in what we're doing."

1979: Financial Whiz Kid

Born in rural Georgia, Hank Selman escaped the shadow of the neighborhood textile mill and became a financial junkie who lived for risk.

Life at Home

- As the 1970s came to an end, Hank Selman was making $600,000 a year and paying his 30-year-old wunderkinds at MVL, Inc. straight salaries of $100,000 each, plus stock plans worth nearly as much.
- A never-ending supply of Perrier in the corporate refrigerators was a company trademark.
- Sales were so spectacular in 1977 that MVL staged a seven-day extravaganza cruise to celebrate the previous year's sales, which cost the company $1.5 million.
- In 1978, the cost was even higher: 1,200 people earned the right to go to Acapulco, Mexico—all expenses paid.
- Although his San Francisco-based leasing company was only 12 years old, projections for the coming year, 1979, envisioned earnings of $61 million on $1.1 billion in revenue.
- Hank never dreamed MVL would come apart so quickly or crash so hard.
- Summers were spent at the country club in Dalton, Georgia, serving as a caddie for his father's bosses; winters, Hank worked part-time in Dalton's finest men's clothing store where he rubbed shoulders with the city's elite and bought the "right" clothing on discount.
- He attended Georgia Tech on a scholarship, and then fled to San Francisco the same night he received his degree in finance.
- First, he worked as an accountant and then as a business consultant, determined to be on an airplane two or three times a week.
- He regularly dropped a dozen picture postcards in the mail before boarding a return flight from London or Rome or Hong Kong.
- His high school friends thought he was a show-off, but his mother was very proud.
- Within a few years, he become very comfortable with complex, highly leveraged transactions that took advantage of federal tax laws to achieve higher-than-normal earnings.
- Making money was the point of every deal, of course, but Hank loved the high that resulted from looking over the "edge."
- Hank always thought of himself as the smartest person in the room and was rarely shy about proving this belief.

Hank Selman lived large and fell hard as a financial wheeler dealer.

- In fact, while matching wits with a recent Noble Prize winner in economics that Hank conceived the framework for his company MVL—named after his three daughters: Martha, Veronica and Lucy.
- Since IBM dominated the world of top-of-the-line mainframe computers, why not form a company to lease the giant mechanical brains to companies intimidated by the $100,000 to $1 million-plus price tag and the fear of the equipment becoming obsolete overnight?
- Hank decided that with a little creative financing, he could lease the System 370 Mainframe for less than IBM itself was charging, still take a substantial fee, and then make a killing on the residual value of the highly dependable computers at the back end of the lease.

Selman and his peers spent money without thinking, assuming it would last forever.

Life at Work

- MVL, Inc. was founded in 1967 by Hank Selman and Robert Crutz, a former IBM San Francisco branch manager.
- The two also shared a birthday, July 1, 1947, and a vision for making money—lots of money—leasing mainframe computers to businesses ready to join the computer age.
- Using only $72,000 of their own money, the two men raised $10 million in equity from the Fireman's Fund Insurance Company and $90 million in debt to buy IBM System/360 computers, which they put on lease.
- By the early 1970s, MVL became one of the first companies to write tax-leveraged leases for IBM System/370 computers.
- The entrepreneurial upstarts were able to cut the cost on their mainframe computer leases by reducing their effective cost of capital.
- MVL did this by offering investors willing to put up 20 percent of the cost of the computer as a tax advantage depreciation and investment tax credit, plus a share the computer residual value; lenders put up the rest.

Companies leased expensive IBM computers from Selman and MVL, Inc.

- As a result, the company leasing the computer got the needed equipment for prices below what they would have paid IBM for the same product.
- Adding a middleman who was armed with creative financing to the transaction actually reduced the cost of the product.
- MVL took a minimum risk; the leasing contract required lessees to pay lenders and equity investors for the machine, while MVL took a fee for putting the deal together and retained a financial interest in the residual value of the computer at the end of the lease.
- The idea was expanded in 1976 to include leasing bundles that comprised

IBM mainframe and compatible peripheral computers which MVL bought from independent manufacturers as a single package.

- Using aggressive selling strategies, MVL wrote $1.7 billion in leases on IBM equipment—second only to IBM—in the 1970s.
- And since Hank believed in an authoritarian top-down planning system, typically sales managers were told annually to achieve a 35 percent growth rate over the previous year.
- The original IBM System/360 family was announced in 1964, followed in the summer of 1970 by a family of machines called System/370.

MVL wrote expensive leases for IBM equipment.

- Big, fast disk drives were one of the strengths of IBM; in 1973, the big mainframe disk drive with 400 megabytes cost $111,600, or $279 per megabyte.
- With that leasing experience came further expansion: an airplane division was embraced by the market after it realized pretax profit of $13 million; another division handled less expensive types of equipment such as machine tools and microcomputers, and was grossing $80 million with wide profit margins.
- After that came the leasing of railroad cars and heavy equipment; anything seemed possible.
- As sales grew, so did MVL's flair for good living; Mercedes and Porsches filled the parking lot, Samadhi tanks large enough for floating meditation sessions became the rage.
- At the same time, stories about inflation and an unstable economy dominated the headlines of the business sections of the newspapers.
- Although the company was already heavily leveraged in 1979, MVL was still able to borrow $1.25 billion—a record for a company of its size in a single year—to expand into plug-compatible computers that used IBM software but cost less than IBM hardware.
- Hank remained convinced that 1979 was going to be another spectacular year, even when the sales started to slow.
- Most of the young staff had never experienced a downturn and could not imagine anything but growth.
- Then, within a six-month period, it all fell apart.
- The company reported losses of $60 million per quarter as its stock fell from a high of $28 to below $10; portfolio managers admitted for the first time "to my knowledge no analyst ever really knew what the company did."

Many executives at MVL never saw the downturn coming.

- What made the company so mysterious was MVL's team of young entrepreneurs, who had pioneered leasing methods complicated enough to produce huge profits.
- For years, Hank had made outrageous profit demands, and over time, the company had come to see itself as invincible.
- The downfall started in 1978 when the company gave its sales force permission to write leases for plug-compatible computers purchased from Hitachi and National Semiconductor Corp., both of which used IBM software but less expensive hardware.
- It was an immediate success, especially after IBM was unable to deliver some of its hottest new machines in quantity. In anticipation of an even bigger year in 1979, the company signed long-term
- That's when IBM announced it would launch a new line of aggressively priced machines in the first quarter of 1979; the

We challenge you to outgrow The Intelligent Typewriter.

IBM's new line of affordable computers threatened Selman's business.

market believed customers would hold off buying until the new machines became available.
- MVL plowed ahead.
- To compete with IBM's new pricing structure, Hank negotiated more favorable pricing from National Semiconductor, but in exchange had to buy more computers.
- In May, sales continued to be down, but the inventory of returned, obsolete IBM System/370s was growing rapidly; with IBM's new introduction, the old equipment had little to no residual value.
- Losses continued to grow while expenses continued unabated.
- By mid-summer, MVL withdrew a $50 million financing package when outside lenders, alarmed by the falling sales numbers, began to demand a premium interest rate for loans.
- By midyear, a showdown during a raucous board meeting resulted in changes in the corporate management structure, but left Hank still in charge.
- The computer group was cut back from 3,000 people to 2,000.
- When word spread throughout the industry that MVL's financial problems could impact its technical support going forward, buyers became wary of long-term leases.
- Fights developed with MVL's suppliers.
- Scrambling for cash, MVL grew desperate and again disposed of its assets: first a railcar manufacturing plant, then eight ships, and even the corporate airplane.
- That raised $175 million—not enough to meet severance payments to salespeople and to maintain the operation of the company.
- Retained earnings that had been built up over a decade fell from $107 million to $43 million within months.
- Major executives, in charge of the divisions still doing well, threatened to resign—further undercutting the profitability of the organization.
- Overnight, it seemed, the company lost a quarter of its 6,400 employees and 18 of its 32 divisions; its forays into manufacturing stopped and its highflying ways were cut back.
- In October, when Hank refused to resign, the Board of Directors summarily fired him.
- The next day, headlines speculated that the San Francisco-based leasing company could fail.

Life in the Community: San Francisco, California

- San Francisco was the fourth most populous city in California and the twelfth most populous city in the United States.
- As the only consolidated city-county in California, it encompassed a land area of 46.7 square miles and claimed the title of being the second-most densely populated large city in the United States.
- In 1776, the Spanish established a mission named for Francis of Assisi on the site, but it was the California Gold Rush in 1848 that propelled the city into a period of rapid growth. San Francisco increased its population in one year from 1,000 to 25,000,
- San Francisco entrepreneurs sought to capitalize on the Gold Rush, founding Wells Fargo in 1852 and the Bank of California in 1864.
- The development of the Port of San Francisco established the city as a center of trade; Levi Strauss opened a dry goods business and Domingo Ghirardelli began making chocolate.
- Immigrant laborers, including Chinese railroad workers who created the city's Chinatown quarter, made the city a polyglot culture.
- The first cable cars carried San Franciscans up Clay Street in 1873.
- By the turn of the twentieth century, San Francisco was known for its flamboyant style, stately hotels, ostentatious mansions on Nob Hill, and a thriving arts scene.
- On April 18, 1906, a major earthquake struck San Francisco and northern California; more than half the city's population of 400,000 were left homeless.
- Rejecting calls to completely remake the street grid, San Franciscans opted for speed, aided by loans from Amadeo Giannini's Bank of Italy, later to become Bank of America.
- In ensuing years, the city solidified its standing as a financial capital; during the Great Depression San Francisco undertook two great civil engineering projects, simultaneously constructing the San Francisco-Oakland Bay Bridge and the Golden Gate Bridge, completing them in 1936 and 1937, respectively.
- During World War II, the Hunters Point Naval Shipyard became a hub of activity, and Fort Mason became the primary port of embarkation for service members shipping out to the Pacific Theater of Operations.
- The U.N. Charter creating the United Nations was drafted and signed in San Francisco in 1945 and, in 1951, the Treaty of San Francisco officially ended the war with Japan.
- Urban planning projects in the 1950s and 1960s saw widespread destruction and redevelopment of west side neighborhoods and the construction of new freeways, of which only a series of short segments were built before being halted by citizen-led opposition.
- By the late 1970s, port activity moved to Oakland, San Francisco began to lose industrial jobs, and the city turned to tourism as the most important segment of its economy.

San Francisco, California in 1877

SECTION TWO: HISTORICAL SNAPSHOTS

The 1970s was a decade of great social, political, and economic change, including disbanding of the Beatles, the resignation of President Nixon, the expansion of women's roles, and the financial effects of inflation. Americans enjoyed the emergence of CB radio, heavy metal music, and the bittersweet return of American troops from the Vietnam War. These Historical Snapshots highlight hundreds of significant people, places, events, and things that dominated the 1970s.

Early 1970s

- A federal grand jury indicted Rev. Philip Berrigan and five others on charges of plotting to kidnap Henry Kissinger
- A jury found the Chicago Seven defendants not guilty of conspiring to incite a riot, in charges stemming from the violence at the 1968 Democratic National Convention; five of the defendants were found guilty on the lesser charge of crossing state lines to incite a riot
- A nuclear non-proliferation treaty went into effect, ratified by 43 nations
- A poll showed that 34 percent of the population believed marriage obsolete, up from 24 percent in 1969
- Acupuncture treatment centers, pocket calculators, the Polaroid SC-70, and electronic lock and key systems using plastic cards all made their first appearance
- After 3,242 performances, *Fiddler on the Roof* closed; it was the longest-running show in Broadway history
- Alvin Toffler published his book *Future Shock*
- *Apollo 13* was crippled on the way to the moon, preventing a planned moon landing
- *Apollo 17* landed on the moon, and Eugene Cernan became the last person to walk on the moon
- Black Sabbath's eponymous debut album, often regarded as the first heavy metal album, was released
- Casey Kasem's *American Top 40* debuted on Los Angeles radio
- Comedian George Carlin was arrested by Milwaukee police for public obscenity, for reciting his "Seven Words You Can Never Say on Television" at Summerfest
- Congress banned cigarette television advertisements, effective January 1, 1971
- Diana Ross and the Supremes performed their last concert together, at the Frontier Hotel in Las Vegas
- Direct dialing began between New York and London
- During a scientific meeting in Honolulu, Herbert Boyer and Stanley N. Cohen conceived the concept of recombinant DNA, which opened the door to genetically modified organisms
- Eleven Israeli athletes at the 1972 Summer Olympics in Munich were murdered after eight members of the Arab terrorist group Black September invaded the Olympic Village; five guerillas and one policeman were also killed in a failed hostage rescue
- First-class postal rates rose to $0.08 per ounce
- Five White House operatives were arrested for burglarizing the offices of the Democratic National Committee in the Watergate Complex in Washington, DC

- Garry Trudeau's comic strip *Doonesbury* debuted in approximately two dozen newspapers in the U.S.
- General Motors redesigned its automobiles to run on unleaded fuel
- *Gourmet* magazine circulation doubled to 550,000 in just four years; the fancy food industry continued to expand
- Guitarist Jimi Hendrix died in London of drug-related complications
- Heavyweight boxing champion Muhammed Ali's refusal of induction into the U.S. Army was heard by the Supreme Court
- *Hello, Dolly!* closed at the St. James Theater on Broadway after a run of 2,844 performances
- Hot pants in mini lengths filled the fashion scene
- "It's Too Late" by Carole King peaked at #1 on the pop singles chart and stayed there for five weeks
- Jane Fonda toured North Vietnam, during which she was photographed sitting on a North Vietnamese antiaircraft gun
- *Jonathan Livingston Seagull* by Richard Bach, *August 1914* by Alexander Solzhenitsyn and *I'm O.K., You're O.K.* by Thomas Harris were all bestsellers
- Kenneth A. Gibson of Newark, New Jersey, became the first black person to win a mayoral election in a major Northeast city
- *Life* magazine ceased publication
- *Look* magazine ceased publication
- *Mariner* 9 transmitted pictures from Mars
- Marlon Brando starred in *Last Tango in Paris*, the first graphically erotic movie featuring a major star
- *Masterpiece Theatre* premiered on PBS with host Alistair Cooke
- *Monday Night Football* debuted on ABC
- National Guardsmen fired at anti-war protestors at Kent State University, killing four and wounding 11 others, spawning campus protests nationwide
- One hundred thousand people demonstrated in New York's Wall Street district in support of U.S. policy in Vietnam and Cambodia
- Paul McCartney announced that the Beatles had disbanded as their twelfth album, *Let It Be*, was released
- Phonorecords were granted U.S. federal copyright protection for the first time
- Postal workers in a dozen cities went on strike for two weeks; President Richard Nixon assigned military units to New York City post offices
- President Nixon made an unprecedented eight-day visit to the People's Republic of China and met with Mao Zedong
- President Nixon ordered John Haldeman to do more wiretapping and political espionage against the Democrats
- President Nixon signed a measure banning cigarette advertising on radio and television
- President Richard Nixon ordered the development of a Space Shuttle program
- Sears reprinted its 1903, 1908 and 1927 catalogs after its 1902 edition sold 400,000 copies
- Shirley Chisholm, the first African-American congresswoman, announced her candidacy for president
- Singer Frank Sinatra was subpoenaed by a House committee on crime and denied all Mafia connections
- Snowmobiles, dune buggies, auto trains, and a law banning sex discrimination all make their first appearance
- Tennis player Billie Jean King became the first woman athlete to earn $100,000 in one year
- The *Pioneer 10* spacecraft became the first artificial satellite to leave the solar system

- The 1964 Gulf of Tonkin resolution, which amounted to a declaration of war against Vietnam, was repealed by Congress
- The 92nd U.S. Congress sent the proposed Equal Rights Amendment to the states for ratification
- The annual per capita consumption of beef reached 11 pounds
- The Beatles' film *Let It Be* premiered
- The Boeing 747 made its maiden voyage
- The Boston Marathon officially allowed women to compete for the first time
- The diamond-bladed scalpel was developed for eye microsurgery
- The Dow Jones Industrial Average closed above 1,000 (1,003.16) for the first time
- The federal government shut off power and fresh water supplies from the American Indians who had claimed Alcatraz Island
- The first Earth Day proclamation was issued by San Francisco Mayor Joseph Alioto
- The first financial derivatives exchange, the International Monetary Market (IMM), opened on the Chicago Mercantile Exchange
- The first New York City Marathon took place
- The fourth anniversary of the Broadway musical *Hair* was celebrated with a free concert in Central Park
- *The Godfather, Deliverance, Sounder* and *Deep Throat* all opened in movie theaters
- The HP-35, the first scientific handheld calculator, was introduced with a price of $395
- The Massachusetts Supreme Court ruled unconstitutional the law prohibiting the sale of contraceptives to single persons
- The Metropolitan Museum of Art paid a record $5.5 million for a Velásquez portrait
- The National Cancer Act was passed, providing $1.5 billion a year for research; the president urged an all-out attempt to find a cure
- *The New York Times* published the Pentagon Papers, leaked to it by Daniel Ellsberg
- The North Tower of the World Trade Center was topped out at 1,368 feet, making it the tallest building in the world
- The Nuclear Non-Proliferation Treaty went into effect, after ratification by 56 nations
- The number of fast food establishments increased from 1,120 in 1958 to 6,784 in 1972
- The phrases "think tank," "body language," "gross out," and "workaholic" all entered the language
- The situation comedy *All in the Family,* with Carroll O'Connor as Archie Bunker, began on CBS TV
- The Soviet Union landed *Lunokhod 1* on the moon-the first roving remote-controlled robot to land on a natural satellite
- The Soviet unmanned spaceship *Luna 20* landed on the moon and returned to Earth with 1.94 ounces of lunar soil
- The Supreme Court ruled that qualification for conscientious-objector status necessitated opposing all wars, not just the Vietnam War
- The Supreme Court ruled that the death penalty was "cruel and unusual punishment"
- The Twenty-sixth Amendment to the Constitution was ratified, lowering the minimum voting age from 21 to 18
- The U.N. General Assembly accepted membership of the People's Republic of China
- The U.S. ban on the pesticide DDT took effect
- The U.S. Occupational Safety and Health Administration (OSHA) was created
- The U.S. promoted its first female generals: Anna Mae Hays and Elizabeth P. Hoisington
- The U.S. Supreme Court ruled that companies may not refuse to hire women with small children if the same policy is not applied to men

- The U.S. Supreme Court upheld the use of busing to achieve racial desegregation in schools
- The United States and the Soviet Union joined some 70 nations in signing the Biological Weapons Convention, an agreement to ban biological warfare
- The United States launched *Landsat* 1, the first Earth-resources satellite
- The United States Public Health Service no longer advised children to have a smallpox vaccination
- The United States Supreme Court overturned the draft evasion conviction of boxer Muhammad Ali
- The Watergate burglary that would eventually lead to the resignation of President Richard Nixon occurred during the 1972 presidential campaign
- The Women's Strike for Equality took place down Fifth Avenue in New York City
- The World Trade Center Towers in New York City were completed
- Three fourths of all moviegoers were under age 30
- Two *Apollo 14* astronauts walked on the moon
- Two black students at Jackson State University in Mississippi were killed when police opened fire during student protests
- U.S. airlines began mandatory inspections of passengers and baggage
- *Venera 7* was launched and became the first spacecraft to successfully transmit data from the surface of another planet
- World War II Japanese soldier Shoichi Yokoi was discovered in Guam, where he had spent 28 years in the jungle
- Young women were appointed U.S. Senate pages for the first time

Mid 1970s

- A cigarette pack-size electronic brainwave reader was developed that could detect and signal lapses in concentration
- A computerized brain scanner known as CAT (computed axial tomography) was marketed
- A patent for the ATM was granted to Donald Wetzel, Tom Barnes, and George Chastain
- A record 120,000 Americans declared personal bankruptcy
- Actor Charlie Chaplin was knighted by Queen Elizabeth II
- Altair 8800 was released, sparking the era of the microcomputer
- An American *Apollo* and Soviet *Soyuz* spacecraft docked in orbit, marking the first such linkup between spacecraft from the two nations
- An endangered whooping crane was born in captivity
- An estimated 600,000 people attended the Watkins Glen Rock Music Festival to hear the Grateful Dead and the Allman Brothers
- Atari of Japan introduced the first low-priced integrated circuit for TV games
- Bantam books paid a record $1.8 million for the paperback rights to E. L. Doctorow's *Ragtime*
- Bestsellers included Jonathan Livingston Seagull by Richard Bach, Once Is Not Enough by Jacqueline Susann, Breakfast of Champions by Kurt Vonnegut, Jr. and I'm O.K., You're O.K. by Thomas Harris
- Bill Gates founded Microsoft in Albuquerque, New Mexico
- CBS sold the New York Yankees for $10 million to a 12-person syndicate led by George Steinbrenner, $3.2 million less than CBS paid
- Chrysler, followed by other auto companies, offered rebates to counter record low sales

- Clifford Alexander Jr. was confirmed as the first African-American Secretary of the United States Army
- Congress overrode President Nixon's veto of the War Powers Resolution, which limited presidential power to wage war without congressional approval
- Ella Grass o became Governor of Connecticut-the first female U.S. governor who did not succeed her husband
- Elvis Presley's concert from Hawaii was the first worldwide telecast by an entertainer and was watched by more people than had seen the Apollo moon landings
- Following President Nixon's visit to mainland China, the United States and the People's Republic of China agreed to establish liaison offices
- Former CIA Director Richard Helms divulged that the CIA had sponsored foreign assassinations, including a plan to kill Premier Fidel Castro of Cuba
- George Foreman defeated Joe Frazier to win the heavyweight world boxing championship
- Harvard changed its five-to-two male to female admissions policy to equal admissions
- Hit songs for the year were "Tie a Yellow Ribbon," "Delta Dawn," "Let's Get it On," "Me and Mrs. Jones," "Rocky Mountain High," "Could It Be I'm Falling in Love?"; Roberta Flack won the Grammy Award for best record with "Killing Me Softly with His Song"
- *Hotel California* by the Eagles was released
- *Humboldt's Gift* by Saul Bellow won the Pulitzer Prize for fiction, while *Why Survive? Being Old in America* by Robert N. Butler won for nonfiction
- In *Gregg v. Georgia*, the U.S. Supreme Court ruled that the death penalty was not inherently cruel or unusual and constitutionally acceptable
- In New York City, "Son of Sam" killed one person and seriously wounded another in the first of a series of attacks that terrorized the city for the next year
- In response to the energy crisis, daylight saving time commenced nearly two months early
- In Super Bowl IX, The Pittsburgh Steelers defeated the Minnesota Vikings 16-6 at Tulane Stadium in New Orleans, Louisiana
- In Super Bowl VII, the Miami Dolphins defeated the Washington Redskins 14-7, in front of 90,182 fans, to complete the NFL's first Perfect Season
- In the U.S. presidential election, Jimmy Carter defeated incumbent Gerald Ford, to become the first candidate from the Deep South to win since the Civil War
- *Live from Lincoln Center* debuted on PBS
- Many cities were hit by strikes, including a police strike in San Francisco, teachers' strikes in Chicago and Charleston, West Virginia, and strikes by sanitation workers in New York
- McDonald's opened its first drive-thru restaurant
- Minnesota became the first state to require businesses, restaurants, and institutions to establish no-smoking areas
- Movie premieres included *One Flew Over the Cuckoo's Nest, Dog Day Afternoon, Jaws, Nashville, Monty Python* and the *Holy Grail,* and *Three Days of the Condor*
- Muhammad Ali defeated Joe Frazier in a boxing match in Manila, The Philippines
- NBC aired the first episode of *Saturday Night Live* with George Carlin as the first host; Billy Preston and Janis Ian were the first musical guests
- New York City, under threat of default, was bailed out by union pension funds
- Nixon signed the Trans-Alaska Pipeline Authorization Act into law, allowing the construction of the Alaska Pipeline

- Nixon's attorney, J. Fred Buzhardt, revealed the existence of an 18 1/2-minute gap in one of the White House tape recordings related to the Watergate break-in
- Ohio became the first state to post distance on road signs in metric measurements
- Oregon became the first state to decriminalize marijuana
- "Pet Rocks" went on sale, featuring obedience, loyalty, and low maintenance costs
- Pink Floyd's *The Dark Side of the Moon*, one of rock's landmark albums, was released
- *Pioneer 10* sent back the first close-up images of Jupiter
- Popular movies included The Paper Chase, Scenes from a Marriage, The Last Detail, The Exorcist and American Graffiti
- Presiden t Gerald Ford posthumously pardoned Confederate General Robert E. Lee, restoring to him full rights of citizenship
- Rape laws were changed in nine states, narrowing the level of collaborative evidence necessary for conviction and restricting trial questions regarding the victim's past sex life
- Richard Nixon resigned the presidency of the United States; he was succeeded by his vice president, Gerald Ford
- Secretariat won the Belmont Stakes, becoming the first Triple Crown of Thoroughbred Racing winner since 1948
- Singer Bob Marley and his manager Don Taylor were shot in an assassination attempt in Kingston, Jamaica
- Skylab, juggernaut, biofeedback, ego trip, let it all hang out, and nouvelle cuisine entered the vernacular
- Space-exploring Pioneer Xproduced significant detail of Jupiter and its great red spot
- Spiro Agnew resigned as vice president, after which he pleaded no contest to charges of income tax evasion in federal court in Baltimore, Maryland
- Super Bowl X: The Pittsburgh Steelers defeated the Dallas Cowboys 21-17 at the Orange Bowl in Miami, Florida
- Teamsters Union president Jimmy Hoffa was reported missing and presumed dead
- Television premieres included *Baretta, The Jeffersons, Barney Miller, Starsky and Hutch, One Day at a Time, Welcome Back Kotter, Barnaby Jones, Police Story, The Young and the Restless* and *The Six-Million-Dollar Man*
- The *Viking 2* spacecraft landed at Utopia Planitia on Mars, taking the first close-up color photos of the planet's surface
- The 100 Club Punk Festival ignited the careers of several influential punk and post-punk bands, sparking the Punk Movement's introduction into mainstream culture
- The American Psychiatric Association revised its categorization of homosexuality, no longer declaring it a mental disorder
- The Atomic Energy Commission was dissolved
- The Boston Celtics defeated the Phoenix Suns 128-126 in triple overtime in the NBA Finals at the Boston Garden
- The Brewers' Society reported that Americans consumed an average of 151 pints of beer per year, 11.5 pints of wine, and 9.1 pints of spirits
- The Copyright Act of 1976 extended copyright duration for an additional 20 years in the U.S.
- The Cray-1, the first commercially developed supercomputer, was released by Seymour Cray's Cray Research.
- The Endangered Species Act was passed
- The first class of women was inducted at the United States Naval Academy in Annapolis, Maryland

- The first handheld cellular phone call was made by Martin Cooper in New York City
- The first laser printer was introduced by IBM, the IBM 3800
- The Heimlich maneuver, designed to assist people who choke on food, gained government approval
- The Irish rock band U2 was formed after drummer Larry Mullen Jr. posted a note seeking members for a band on the notice board of his Dublin school
- The Jovian-Plutonian gravitational effect was first reported by astronomer Patrick Moore
- The LexisNexis computerized legal research service began
- The median sale price of a single-family house was $28,900, up from $20,000 in 1968
- The New Jersey Supreme Court ruled that coma patient Karen Ann Quinlan could be disconnected from her ventilator; she remained comatose and died in 1985
- The Nobel Peace Prize was awarded to Henry Kissinger and North Vietnamese Le Duc Tho, who refused the honor because the war had not ended
- The punk rock group *The Ramones* released their first self-titled album
- The report, *Puerto Ricans in the Continental United States: An Uncertain Future*, documented that Puerto Ricans in the United States had a poverty rate of 33 percent in 1974, the highest of all major racial-ethnic groups in the country
- *The Rocky Horror Show* opened on Broadway in New York City
- The Rolling Stones concert tour grossed $13 million; singer Stevie Wonder signed a record contract for $13 million
- The Sears Tower in Chicago was finished, becoming the world's tallest building at 1,451 feet
- The so-called typical nuclear family, with working father, housewife, and two children, represented only seven percent of the population; average family size was 3.4, down from 4.3 in 1920
- *The Sting* with Paul Newman and Robert Redford captured the Academy Award for best picture; other popular movies included *The Paper Chase, Scenes from a Marriage, The Last Detail, The Exorcist* and *American Graffiti*
- The Suez Canal was reopened for the first time since the Six-Day War in 1967
- The Summer Jam at Watkins Glen, a massive rock festival featuring The Grateful Dead, The Allman Brothers Band, and The Band, attracted over 600,000 music fans
- The Supreme Court overturned state bans on abortion in its ruling on *Roe v. Wade*
- The U.S. Supreme Court ruled that employment advertisements could not longer specify gender
- The U.S. Treasury Department reintroduced the two-dollar bill as part of the Bicentennial celebration
- The United States vetoed a United Nations resolution that called for an independent Palestinian state
- The University of Miami provided an athletic scholarship to a woman
- The Vietnam War ended as North Vietnamese forces captured Saigon, resulting in mass evacuations of Americans and South Vietnamese
- The World Trade Center officially opened
- U.S. cities celebrated the 200th anniversary of the Declaration of Independence
- U.S. involvement in the Vietnam War ended with the signing of the Paris Peace Accords; the first American prisoners of war were released from Vietnam
- Unemployment reached 9.2 percent
- Vandalism and violence increased in public schools; homicides increased nearly 20 percent, rapes and robberies were up 40 percent since 1965

- Watergate burglar James W. McCord, Jr. admitted that he and other defendants had been pressured to remain silent, and named former Attorney General John Mitchell as "overall boss" of the operation
- *Wheel of Fortune* premiered on NBC
- Words and phrases entering popular usage were Skylab, juggernaut, biofeedback, egotrip, let it all hang out, and nouvelle cuisine
- Yankee Stadium, known as "The House That Ruth Built," closed for a two-year renovation at a cost of $160 million

Late 1970s

- 1.9 million women operated businesses
- 20,000 shopping malls generated 50 percent of total retail sales
- 45 million people watched the highest-rated TV interview in history, featuring former President Richard Nixon on the David Frost program; Nixon was paid $600,000, plus 10 percent of the show's profits
- A blowout at the Ixtoc I oil well in the southern Gulf of Mexico resulted in the worst oil spill in history
- A. J. Foyt became the first driver to win the Indianapolis 500 a record four times
- After campaigning by Anita Bryant and her anti-gay "Save Our Children" crusade, Miami-Dade County, Florida voters overwhelmingly voted to repeal the county's gay rights ordinance
- America's most serious nuclear power plant accident, at Three Mile Island, Pennsylvania, halted nuclear power expansion
- American Express became the first service company to top $1 billion in sales
- Americans purchased 315,000 microcomputers, up from 172,000 the previous year
- Americans with physical disabilities began staging protests at federal buildings in San Francisco, Los Angeles, and Washington, DC
- An estimated 20,000 to 30,000 American homes had computers
- An original Gutenberg Bible was sold for $2.2 million
- *Annie Hall* won Best Picture at the Academy Awards
- Anti-French demonstrations took place in Israel after Paris released Abu Daoud, responsible for the 1972 Munich massacre of Israeli athletes
- Attendance for the North American Soccer League rose 50 percent to 5.3 million fans
- Balloon angioplasty was developed for reopening diseased arteries of the heart
- Bestselling books included *The Complete Book of Running* by James Fixx, *Mommie Dearest* by Christina Crawford, *The Memoirs of Richard Nixon* by Richard Nixon, *War and Remembrance* by Herman Wouk and *Eye of the Needle* by Ken Follett
- California became the first state to initiate gas rationing, creating alternate-day purchasing
- California voters approved Proposition 13, which slashed property taxes nearly 60 percent
- California was the first state to initiate gas rationing using a method of alternate-day purchasing
- CB radios achieved cult status as 25 million Americans installed the devices in their cars
- CBS anchor Walter Cronkite acted as an intermediary between Anwar Sadat and Menachem Begin to arrange a meeting in Israel
- Charlie Chaplin's remains were stolen from Corsier-sur-Vevey, Switzerland
- Cheryl Tiegs, the world's highest-paid model, earned $1,000 a day

- Daniel Nathan and Hamilton Smith won the Nobel Prize for their work in restriction enzymes in molecular genetics
- Edith Bunker, a character on the television show *All in the Family*, said, "With credit, you can buy everything you can't afford"
- Egyptian President Anwar Sadat became the first Arab leader to officially visit Israel when he met with Israeli Prime Minister Menachem Begin to seek a permanent peace settlement
- Electrical workers in Mexico City discovered the remains of the Great Pyramid of Tenochtitlan in the middle of the city
- Electronic blackboards, nitrite-free hot dogs, Cracker Jack ice cream bars and the video digital sound disc all made their first appearance
- Elvis Presley died at Graceland Mansion in Memphis, Tennessee, and within a day of his death, two million of his records sold; his funeral cost $47,000
- Emmy Awards went to The Rockford Files for drama, All in the Family for comedy, The Muppet Show for variety and Hollywood Is Grinch Night for children
- Fashion for men saw a return to conservatism marked by narrow, silk challis ties with small patterns and Oxford and broadcloth shirts
- Films released included *Star Wars; Annie Hall; Saturday Night Fever; Close Encounters of the Third Kind; The Goodbye Girl; A Bridge Too Far; Exorcist II: The Heretic; The Turning Point; New York, New York;* and *Smokey and the Bandit*
- First Lady Betty Ford announced that she had entered a treatment program for alcohol and pill addiction
- Fleetwood Mac's Grammy-winning album *Rumours* was released
- Following her 1972 sex reassignment surgery, musician Wendy Carlos legally changed her name from Walter
- Ford Motor Company acquired 25 percent of Japan's Mazda Motor Company
- Former Attorney General John N. Mitchell was released on parole after 19 months at a federal prison in Alabama in connection with the Watergate scandal
- Giuseppe Verdi's opera *Otello* made its first appearance on *Live from the Met*
- Gold sold for $245 per ounce
- Grammy Awards were presented to the Eagles for "Hotel California" and to Fleetwood Mac for "Rumours"
- Hit songs included "I Will Survive," "Reunited," "Hot Stuff," "Too Much Heaven," "Mama Can't Buy You Love," "Tonight's the Night," "Nobody Does It Better," "Don'tLeave Me This Way," the "Theme from Rocky," "Torn between Two Lovers" and the title song of Star Wars
- In a ceremony at the White House, President Anwar Sadat of Egypt and Prime Minister Menachem Begin of Israel signed a peace treaty
- In response to the hostage crisis in Tehran, President Carter ordered a halt to all oil imports into the United States from Iran
- In Super Bowl XI, the Oakland Raiders defeated the Minnesota Vikings 32-14 at the Rose Bowl in Pasadena, California
- James Earl Ray, Martin Luther King's assassin, escaped from Brushy Mountain State Prison in Petros, Tennessee
- Jane Fonda and Tom Hayden toured 50 cities to speak out against nuclear power
- Jimmy Carter and Leonid Brezhnev signed the SALT II agreement in Vienna
- John Travolta's role in *Saturday Night Fever* inspired young Americans to wear flared jeans, an updated version of bellbottoms

- Judith Krantz received a record $3.2 million advance for the paperback rights to *Princess Daisy*
- Larry Ellison and Robert Miner founded Oracle Corporation in Belmont, California, after they persuaded the CIA to let them pick up a lapsed contract for a special database program
- Led Zeppelin played their last U.S. concert in Oakland, California, at the Oakland-Alameda County Coliseum
- Lockheed's top-secret stealth aircraft project, designated Have Blue, precursor to the U.S. F-117A Nighthawk, made its first flight
- Louise Brown, the first test tube baby, was born in Oldham, England, after a fertilized egg was implanted in her mother's womb
- *Marvel Comic, No. 1* was purchased for a record price of $43,000
- Mavis Hutchinson, 53, became the first woman to run across the United States; her trek took 69 days
- McDonald's introduced the Happy Meal
- Michael Jackson's breakthrough album *Off the Wall* sold seven million copies in the United States alone
- More than 315,000 microcomputers were sold
- More than 400,000 teenage abortions were performed, comprising one-third of all abortions in the United States
- Movie openings included *The Deer Hunter, Midnight Express, An Unmarried Woman, Superman, National Lampoon's Animal House, Annie Hall, The Goodbye Girl, Looking for Mr. Goodbar, Saturday Night Fever, Oh, God!, Pumping Iron, Kramer vs. Kramer, Apocalypse Now, Norma Rae, The China Syndrome, Star Trek: The Motion Picture,* and *10*
- Nine hundred American religious cult members, under the influence of Jim Jones, committed suicide in Guyana
- Norman Mailer's *The Executioner's Song* received the Pulitzer Prize for fiction, while Edmund Morris won the biography award for *The Rise of Theodore Roosevelt*
- Numerous brands of hair dryers were recalled because of suspected amounts of asbestos
- Ohio agreed to pay $675,000 to victim's families in the Kent State shootings
- Optical fiber was used to carry live telephone traffic for the first time
- Oracle was incorporated as Software Development Laboratories by Larry Ellison, Bob Miner, and Ed Oates
- Pelé played his final professional soccer game as a member of the New York Cosmos
- Pepsi topped Coca-Cola in sales for the first time
- Philips unveiled the compact disc
- *Pioneer 11* reached Saturn and showed that its rings were composed of ice-covered rocks and moonlets
- Pocket television, a woman referee for a heavyweight championship fight and the use of lethal drugs for capital punishment all made their first appearance
- Polls reported that 55 percent of the population saw nothing wrong with premarital sex, up from 23 percent in 1969
- President Jimmy Carter urged 65 degrees as the maximum thermostat temperature for heating homes to ease the energy crisis
- Record company EMI sacked the controversial U.K. punk rock band the Sex Pistols
- Resorts International opened the first legal casino in the eastern United States, in Atlantic City, New Jersey
- Robert Penn Warren won the Pulitzer Prize for poetry for his book *Now and Then*

- Saint Paul, Minnesota, became the second U.S. city to repeal its gay rights ordinance after Anita Bryant's successful 1977 anti-gay campaign in Dade County, Florida
- Senator Ted Kennedy announced that he would challenge President Jimmy Carter for the 1980 Democratic presidential nomination
- Seven states raised the legal drinking age from 18 to 20
- Sneakers comprised 50 percent of all shoe sales in America
- *Star Wars* became the highest grossing film up to that time
- Statewide limitations on indoor cigarette smoking were passed in Iowa and New Jersey
- Steven Jobs and Steve Wozniak founded the Apple Computer Company and produced the first pre-assembled, mass-produced personal computer
- Television premieres included *The Dukes of Hazzard, Archie Bunker's Place, Knot's Landing, Hart to Hart, The Incredible Hulk, Fantasy Island, Dallas, WKRP in Cincinnati, Diff'rent Strokes, Mork and Mindy,* and *Taxi*
- Television's late-night host, Johnny Carson, made $4 million, while *Happy Days'* Henry Winkler collected $990,000 for his acting talents
- Tenor Luciano Pavarotti and the PBS opera series *Live from the Met* both made their American television debuts
- The 2060 Chiron, the first of the outer solar system asteroids known as centaurs, was discovered by Charles Kowal
- The annual Mardi Gras celebration in New Orleans was canceled due to a strike called by the New Orleans Police Department
- The ban on women attending West Point was lifted
- The baseball commissioner's ban on female reporters in locker rooms was set aside by a federal judge
- The Bee Gees' album *Saturday Night Fever* sold a record 12 million copies
- The Big Ear, a radio telescope operated by Ohio State University, received a radio signal from deep space
- The Camp David Accords were signed between Israel and Egypt
- The CB radio fad resulted in record sales
- The comic strip *Garfield* made its debut
- The Copyright Act of 1976 took effect, making sweeping changes to United States copyright law
- The cost of a first-class postage stamp rose to $0.15 per ounce
- The Department of Energy was established
- The divorce rate increased 69 percent during the decade; the median duration of marriage stood at 6.6 years
- The Dow Jones Industrial Average peaked at 999 for the year, closing at 800 at year's end
- The Entertainment Sports Programming Network, known as ESPN, debuted
- The eradication of the smallpox virus was certified; it was the first human disease driven to extinction
- The FDA banned the use of the additive Red Dye # 2 in foods, drugs, and cosmetics
- The federal government approved a $1.5 billion bailout loan guarantee for the Chrysler Corporation
- The Federal Reserve System changed from an interest rate target policy to a money supply target policy, causing interest rate fluctuations and economic recession
- The first experiments of Use net, the precursor to Internet forums, were conducted by Tom Truscott and Jim Ellis of Duke University
- The first fusion reactions by laser were achieved
- The first Jiffy Lube fast oil-change automotive service center opened

- The first oil through the Trans-Alaska Pipeline System reached Valdez, Alaska
- The first U.S. Take Back the Night march occurred in San Francisco
- The first Usenet experiments were conducted by Tom Truscott and Jim Ellis of Duke University
- The first wave of Southeast Asian "boat people" arrived in San Francisco under a new U.S. resettlement program
- The Holy Crown of Hungary was returned to Hungary from the United States, where it had been held since World War II
- The inflation rate reached 12.4 percent, driving the prime rate to 12 percent
- The King Tutankhamen show touring America produced $5 million for the Cairo Museum
- The legal retirement age was raised to 70
- The modern Food Stamp Program began
- The Music for UNICEF Concert was held to promote the Year of the Child
- The musical play *Annie* opened on Broadway
- The near-meltdown of a nuclear power plant at Three Mile Island ignited anti-nuclear fears nationwide
- The New York Yankees clinched their 22nd Baseball World Series Championship, defeating the Los Angeles Dodgers 7-2 and winning the Series four games to two
- The One Child Policy was implemented in China
- The Pinwheel Network changed its name to Nickelodeon and began airing on various Warner Cable systems
- The Pittsburgh Pirates defeated the Baltimore Orioles in Game 7 of the World Series
- The play *Grease* passed *Fiddler on the Roof* as the longest-running Broadway show
- The price of gold reached $524 per ounce, up from $223 in 1978
- The prime lending rate at banks hit 14.5 percent
- The radio news program *Morning Edition* premiered on National Public Radio
- The rate of inflation reached 13.3 percent; the prime rate was 15.75 percent
- The sale of imported cars broke all records, passing 1.5 million
- The Seattle SuperSonics won the NBA Championship against the Washington Bullets
- The Sony Walkman, a portable cassette player with headphones, was introduced
- The space shuttle *Enterprise* test vehicle went on its maiden "flight" while sitting on top of a Boeing 747 at Edwards Air Force Base in California
- The Supreme Court reversed a New York law that prohibited the distribution of contraceptives to minors
- The Supreme Court ruled that "husbands only" alimony laws were unconstitutional
- The Susan B. Anthony dollar was introduced
- The Tandy Corporation TRS-80 Model I computer was introduced
- The tax code permitted 401(k) savings plans for the first time
- The television miniseries *Roots* drew 130 million viewers, the largest audience in TV history
- The trans-Alaska oil pipeline was completed after three years of work
- The two-year American tour of the King Tutankhamen show generated $5 million for the Cairo Museum
- The U.S. *Voyager I* space probe photos revealed Jupiter's rings
- The U.S. and Canada signed a pact to build a gas pipeline from Alaska to the Midwest
- The U.S. and the People's Republic of China established full diplomatic relations
- The U.S. Army announced that it had conducted 239 open-air tests of germ warfare

- The U.S. Senate followed the example of the House by adopting a stringent code of ethics requiring full financial disclosure and limits on outside income
- The U.S. Senate voted 68-32 to turn the Panama Canal over to Panamanian control on December 31, 1999
- The United States and the Soviet Union signed a Nuclear Non-Proliferation Act (NNPA), along with 15 other nations
- The United States established diplomatic relations with China and severed those with Taiwan
- The United States launched *Voyager 2*, an unmanned spacecraft carrying a 12-inch copper phonograph record containing greetings in dozens of languages, samples of music and sounds of nature
- The United States Supreme Court ruled that the spanking of school children by teachers was constitutional
- The USDA warned of the dangers of nitrites in processed and cured meat products, reporting that sodium nitrite may cause cancer
- The Vatican reaffirmed the Roman Catholic Church's ban on female priests
- The world premiere for *Star Trek: The Motion Picture* was held at the Smithsonian Institution in Washington, DC
- The world's first personal computer, the Commodore PET, was demonstrated at the Consumer Electronics Show in Chicago
- Three major networks controlled 91 percent of prime-time audiences
- Toni Morrison's Song of Solomon, Joan Didion's A Book of Common Prayer, John Cheever's Falconer and True Confessions by John Gregory Dunne were all published
- U.S. Trust reported that 520,000 Americans—one in every 424—*were millionaires*
- Video digital sound discs, electronic blackboards, throwaway toothbrushes, *Drabble* cartoons and Crackerjack ice cream bars all made their first appearance
- Volkswagen became the second non-American automobile manufacturer to open a plant in the United States; it produced the Rabbit in New Stanton, Pennsylvania

Despite a relatively steady increase in the annual income of Americans from 1970 to 1979, there was also a tremendous increase in the cost of basic utilities and consumer goods due to inflation. Economy of the Times illustrates three economic elements: Consumer Expenditures; Annual Income of Standard Jobs; and Selected Prices. We highlighted three years for each category—1972, 1977, and 1979. The Value of a Dollar chart, at the end of the section, shows the change in the value of $1.00 yearly, from 1860 to 2014.

Consumer Expenditures

The numbers below are per capita expenditures in the years 1972, 1977, 1979 for all employees nationwide.

Category	1972	1977	1979
Auto Parts	$38.11	$58.57	$63.98
Auto Usage	$460.70	$748.73	$885.12
Clothing	$225.83	$326.01	$377.68
Dentists	$26.68	$46.77	$54.65
Food	$755.11	$1,161.92	$1,390.33
Furniture	$45.55	$74.76	$90.20
Gas and Oil	$116.25	$212.95	$294.15
Health Insurance	$28.59	$42.68	$55.09
Housing	$534.07	$815.02	$1,006.86
Intercity Transport	$24.77	$44.95	$58.21
Local Transport	$16.19	$21.79	$21.33
New Auto Purchase	$150.55	$201.59	$219.06
Personal Business	$183.42	$300.13	$397.68
Personal Care	$61.46	$93.99	$111.53
Physicians	$79.09	$134.39	$163.52
Private Education and Research	$71.94	$108.97	$132.41
Recreation	$244.88	$392.30	$487.44
Religion/Welfare Activities	$72.42	$112.60	$148.85
Telephone and Telegraph	$59.08	$97.62	$114.19
Tobacco	$58.75	$77.19	$85.31
Utilities	$131.02	$251.54	$309.26
Per Capita Consumption	$3,658.00	$5,773.33	$7,036.95

Annual Income of Standard Jobs

The numbers below are annual income for standard jobs across America in the years 1972, 1977, and 1979.

Category	1972	1977	1979
Bituminous Coal Mining	$11,323.00	$18,292.00	$22,363.00
Building Trades	$10,747.00	$14,639.00	$16,785.00
Domestics	$4,478.00	$6,844.00	$7,912.00
Farm Labor	$3,900.00	$6,021.00	$7,154.00
Federal Civilian	$12,596.00	$17,488.00	$19,907.00
Federal Employees, Executive Departments	$10,331.00	$13,980.00	$15,961.00
Federal Military	$8,603.00	$10,854.00	$12,316.00
Finance, Insurance and Real Estate	$8,861.00	$12,184.00	$14,326.00
Gas and Electricity Workers	$11,420.00	$16,916.00	$19,697.00
Manufacturing, Durable Goods	$10,747.00	$14,730.00	$17,212.00
Manufacturing, Nondurable Goods	$8,636.00	$12,578.00	$14,738.00
Medical/Health Services Workers	$7,499.00	$11,248.00	$13,276.00
Miscellaneous Manufacturing	$7,800.00	$10,678.00	$12,563.00
Motion Picture Services	$8,882.00	$13,209.00	$16,821.00
Nonprofit Organization Workers	$6,088.00	$8,297.00	$9,564.00
Passenger Transportation Workers, Local and Highway	$7,496.00	$10,780.00	$12,266.00
Personal Services	$6,268.00	$8,322.00	$9,723.00
Private Industry, Including Farm Labor	$8,634.00	$12,222.00	$14,310.00
Public School Teachers	$9,284.00	$12,738.00	$14,306.00
Radio Broadcasting and Television Workers	$11,575.00	$15,708.00	$18,329.00
Railroad Workers	$11,991.00	$18,784.00	$23,021.00
State and Local Government Workers	$8,898.00	$12,359.00	$13,879.00
Telephone and Telegraph Workers	$10,518.00	$17,279.00	$20,646.00

Selected Prices

1972

Basketball	$4.98
Bathroom Scale	$17.99
Book, *The Joy of Sex*	$12.95
Cassette Tapes, 3-pack	$1.99
Coloring Book	$0.10
Cruise, Orient, 4 months	$3,105.00
Eggs, dozen	$0.39
Eye Drops, Visine	$0.99
Fabric Softener, Downy	$0.99
Food Processor	$39.99
Hair Dryer	$3.88
Home, Flushing, NY, 6 rooms	$48,500
Ice Bucket	$80.00
Jacket, Man's Leather	$80.00
Jeans, Woman's Corduroy	$4.88
Jewel Case, Gucci	$99.00
Life Vest	$20.59
Maternity Top	$8.00
Nonprescription Drug, Excedrin	$0.89
Pajamas, Child's	$5.49
Pepper Grinder, Cartier	$35.00
Radio, AM	$6.99
Soap, English Leather	$2.00
Stereo Cassette System	$400.00
Theatre Ticket, *Hair*	$12.00
Valise, Leather and Canvas	$175.00

Watch, Woman's Movado	$925.00
Wig, Human Hair	$29.99
Woman's Jumpsuit	$32.00

1977

Airfare, Round-Trip, NY to San Francisco	$252.00
Bean Bag Chair	$37.95
Bicycle	$64.99
Big Slider Gym	$64.99
Bikini Swimsuit	$13.00
Briefcase	$52.00
Calculator, Cannon Electric, 16 functions	$29.95
Casserole, Metal	$58.00
Catesbury Print	$150.00
CB Radio	$39.88
Chandis Lines Cruise, 8 days	$6.99
Cigarette Case	$34.95
Citizens Band Transceiver Car Stereo	$269.99
Coffee, per pound	$3.58
Computer, Apple II	$1,300.00
Cradle	$34.99
Drapes	$9.96
Elizabeth Arden Gown	$125.00
Firestone Forever Battery	$59.00
Fruit Cake	$6.00
Gamefisher Boat Motor	$119.00
Hotel Room, St. Moritz, New York	$31.00
Ice Bucket	$80.00

Ice Cream Machine. $24.95
Lawn Valet Sweeper and Bagger. $186.00
Makeup, Revlon Ultima II $8.50
Massage Shower Head $26.95
Maternity Top $9.00
Men's Jeans $13.00
Microwave Oven. $168.00
Motor Oil $0.39
Motorcycle Helmet $30.99
Movie Ticket. $1.00
Organic Roast Beef, half pound $1.99
Persian Baktiari Rug. $1,850.00
Portalign Drill Stand $19.99
Presto Pressure Cooker, 6-qt. $10.88
Saxon Plain Paper Copier $2,995.00
Seal-N-Save Food Sealer $16.49
Singapore by Croscill Bedspread. $39.00
Sno-Cone Maker. $5.66
Stereo Cassette System, Sony. $400.00
Stereo Wall System $199.00
Storm Windows, Triple Track $32.95
Stroller. $24.99
Sunglasses.. . . . .$7.99
Telescope $129.95
Theater Ticket, *A Chorus Line*, New York $17.50
Toughskin Jeans $6.39
Tricycle. $16.99

United Airlines Roundtrip Los Angeles to San Francisco $342.00

Viewmaster 3-D Viewer $17.44

Weebles, Horse and Wagon Toy $2.97

Women's "Earth" Shoes $23.50

1979

Airfare, Los Angeles to Boston $230.00

Alaskan King Crab, per pound $2.50

Automobile, Toyota Corolla $2,788.00

Baby Carrier, Pak-a-Poose $14.00

Baby Holder, Johnny Jump-Up $6.99

Bandages, Curad $0.69

Basketball Goal $49.99

Bicycle $64.99

Calculator, Texas Instruments, Pocket Size $74.95

Car Battery, Firestone Forever $59.00

Charcoal Starter, Gulf Lite $0.57

Cigarette Case $34.95

Circular Saw $22.88

Coatdress, Polyester $21.00

Collector's Case, Matchbox $6.97

Compact $4.50

Computer, Apple II $1,300.00

Diapers, Dozen $4.86

Donation, Save the Children Federation, per month $16.00

Dryer, Kenmore $149.00

Espresso Maker	$40.00
Figurine, Steuben Glass	$160.00
Floor Lamp	$78.50
Fruitcake, 3 loaves	$6.00
Golf School	$650.00
Guitar, Student	$19.95
Hair Dryer, Presto	$3.88
Hummingbird Feeder	$13.50
Ice Cream Machine	$24.95
Jeans, Men's	$13.00
Jumpsuit, Women's	$31.99

Massage Shower Head $26.95
Maternity Top $9.00
Microwave Oven. $168.00
Motor Oil, 10W30 . . . .$0.39
Motorcycle, Kawasaki $699.00
Perfume, Chanel No. 19 . . . .$9.50
Pressure Cooker, Presto. $10.88
Punch Bowl $35.00
Razor Blades $1.29
Shirt, Tie-dyed $5.99
Slow Cooker $13.79
Sno-Cone Maker. $5.66
Spinning Top $4.49
Stationery, 100 Sheets. $6.95
Stroller. $24.99
Sunglasses $7.99
Sweatercoat. $140.00
Theater Ticket, *A Chorus Line*, New York $17.50
Tie $10.00
Touring Cap, Man's L.L.Bean. $7.50
Tricycle $16.99
Turntable $199.95
Vacuum Cleaner, Eureka. $49.88
Viewer, Viewmaster 3-D $17.44
Vodka, 1.75 Liters $8.59
Vodka, Smirnoff $8.59
Weight Bench $35.87

The Value of a Dollar, 1860-2014

Composite Consumer Price Index; 1860=1

Year	Amount	Year	Amount	Year	Amount	Year	Amount
1860	$1.00	1899	$1.00	1938	$1.70	1977	$7.30
1861	$1.06	1900	$1.01	1939	$1.67	1978	$7.85
1862	$1.22	1901	$1.02	1940	$1.69	1979	$8.74
1863	$1.52	1902	$1.04	1941	$1.77	1980	$9.97
1864	$1.89	1903	$1.06	1942	$1.96	1981	$10.94
1865	$1.96	1904	$1.07	1943	$2.08	1982	$11.62
1866	$1.92	1905	$1.06	1944	$2.12	1983	$11.99
1867	$1.78	1906	$1.08	1945	$2.17	1984	$12.50
1868	$1.71	1907	$1.13	1946	$2.35	1985	$12.95
1869	$1.64	1908	$1.11	1947	$2.68	1986	$13.20
1870	$1.58	1909	$1.10	1948	$2.90	1987	$13.67
1871	$1.47	1910	$1.14	1949	$2.87	1988	$14.24
1872	$1.47	1911	$1.14	1950	$2.90	1989	$14.92
1873	$1.45	1912	$1.17	1951	$3.13	1990	$15.72
1874	$1.37	1913	$1.19	1952	$3.19	1991	$16.38
1875	$1.32	1914	$1.20	1953	$3.22	1992	$16.88
1876	$1.29	1915	$1.22	1954	$3.24	1993	$17.38
1877	$1.26	1916	$1.31	1955	$3.23	1994	$17.83
1878	$1.20	1917	$1.54	1956	$3.28	1995	$18.33
1879	$1.20	1918	$1.82	1957	$3.39	1996	$18.88
1880	$1.23	1919	$2.08	1958	$3.48	1997	$19.32
1881	$1.23	1920	$2.41	1959	$3.50	1998	$19.63
1882	$1.23	1921	$2.16	1960	$3.56	1999	$20.06
1883	$1.22	1922	$2.02	1961	$3.60	2000	$20.74
1884	$1.18	1923	$2.06	1962	$3.64	2001	$21.32
1885	$1.17	1924	$2.06	1963	$3.68	2002	$21.66
1886	$1.13	1925	$2.11	1964	$3.73	2003	$22.16
1887	$1.14	1926	$2.13	1965	$3.79	2004	$22.76
1888	$1.14	1927	$2.09	1966	$3.90	2005	$23.53
1889	$1.11	1928	$2.06	1967	$4.02	2006	$24.29
1890	$1.09	1929	$2.06	1968	$4.19	2007	$24.97
1891	$1.09	1930	$2.01	1969	$4.42	2008	$25.91
1892	$1.09	1931	$1.83	1970	$4.67	2009	$25.81
1893	$1.08	1932	$1.65	1971	$4.88	2010	$26.22
1894	$1.04	1933	$1.57	1972	$5.03	2011	$27.06
1895	$1.01	1934	$1.61	1973	$5.35	2012	$27.63
1896	$1.01	1935	$1.65	1974	$5.93	2013	$28.05
1897	$1.00	1936	$1.67	1975	$6.47	2014	$28.49
1898	$1.00	1937	$1.73	1976	$6.85		

221

SECTION FOUR: ALL AROUND US

This section offers a ringside seat to the issues and attitudes that were 1970s America. The 39 documents, listed in chronological order below, come from popular newspapers and magazines of the time, and are generally reprinted in their entirety. They show how Americans' changing ideas on music, education, movies, fashion, shopping, politics, and women's work were shaped.

"Organizing the High Schools,"
by Judy Penhiter, *WIN Magazine*, May 1970

Briefly, I'd like to say a few things about what we at War Resister's League/West in San Francisco are doing in relation to high school work. Over the past two years we have been gradually expanding our various projects concerning high schools. I hope that some of the ideas and techniques which we have implemented will be of help to others who are struggling to create a greater and all-encircling awareness among high school students.

In the beginning, we tried to establish contacts in all schools in the Bay Area. With the help of a few high school students that we knew, we began to compile a list of sympathetic teachers. In the private schools, we contacted principals. We talked to principals and teachers alike about some of our ideas concerning nonviolence, hopes for a better world, and our light/sound show (a show comprised of tapes, films and slides). Sometimes we went in with the approval of the administration and other times we were quietly whisked down the back stairs. It wasn't long before we no longer had to call teachers about the show; they called us. We usually tried not to take gigs if we would not be able to come back the following day to rap about the ideas presented in the films and tapes. The show, while stimulating, needs to be discussed because there are so many topics touched upon which can only be clarified and drawn together in discussions.

This year was barely in full swing when we felt the need to expand into doing more concentrated follow-up. It was hoped that if enough exposure to alternative lifestyles and beliefs could somehow be accomplished, some of them would begin to question their own lifestyles and beliefs which had formerly been taken for granted. Another hope was that people would become involved in working with us, Ecology Action, or similar groups. (This has been accomplished to some degree. Students do help us with some of our projects.) Two people who graduated last year have been with us for close to a year.

To accomplish these goals, we began having weekly high school potlucks where these kids could get together to rap about ideas, problems, future plans, and interesting subjects, and also be exposed to a growing and loving community. High school weekends were also planned to which someone would come to rap about their particular interests (ecology, etc.), or the kids would become involved in action projects such as beach clean-ups. After the lottery came into effect, we made six large posters which stand back to back on three display stands. The posters talk about the lottery, the draft, alternatives, non-registration and War Resisters League. Each day from 2 to 4 we take these displays to school and talk to students and provide relevant literature for them to read. We've just now moved to our second school after being in the first for well over a month. (It looks as though we may get a chance to test the anti-loitering act at the second school. We've been hassled but plan to exhaust all means of verbal communication before taking any further steps.) Day after day, the students saw us and began to identify with us. Now, with the groundwork in place, we are able to go into classes four, five or more times. And so, rather than just scratching the surface of nonviolence in our discussions, we are now able to cover both resistance activities and positive alternatives. Besides the light/sound show and follow-up raps, we have begun to do mock draft resistance trials, which seem to hold the interest of students who take the part of jurors. I think it is quite an informative experience for them, too. We've even ended up with a few acquittals.

In addition to the day-to-day activities, we have planned and carried out some one- to two-day special sessions. Recently, about 30 people got together to decide how to facilitate government operations, health and sanitation, education, postal system, food and water supplies, and so forth in a given situation in the year 1973. The students seem to enjoy it immensely and stated there were many subjects discussed about which they had not previously spent much time thinking. They felt we should plan together. We're in the process of doing just that, along with planning a weekend follow-up action project at a commune.

Another exercise in the middle stages is the peace games. About 30 people will take part in this exercise in mid-April. For those who know little about this particular topic, a peace game is a socio-drama in which a group of nonviolent people are invaded by a violent outside group and must determine means for coping with the situation. While it was originally planned to be practice in national defense through nonviolent means, I personally feel it is a help in everyday situations we face today in demonstrations, sit-ins, arrests, riots, and so forth. They do a tremendous job in helping a person to know how to best approach these tense situations.

Another thing which we are planning is a nonviolent fair. There will be displays on Gandhi, King, Dolci, the Czechoslovakian resistance, free schools, etc., free nonviolent food, bead making, god's eyes, bread baking, spinning, and the list continues. We held one last year which was well attended and well liked. This year, we hope to have it on the grounds of one of the two high schools here in San Francisco.

"March 14 Draft Card Turn-in in Chicago,"
WIN Peace and Freedom through Nonviolent Action, May 1, 1970

March 14, CADRE and War Tax Resistance prematurely ushered in Antidraft Week with a lively demonstration and draft card turn-in at the Fed. I Building. Twenty-three cards and 14 IRS forms were collected with the approval of some 200 people, mostly young men. It was like a resurgence of the Resistance movement, but with some differences. One sign read: "Give Peace a Chance/They Didn't Take It/ It's Rip-off Time." Another poster, headed "This Is A Low Sulfur Emission," showed a fellow burning a draft card with much black smoke. There were quite a few high school students so that even CADRE stalwarts began to look like the Old Guard.

One after the other, about a dozen young men gave their reasons before [throwing the] draft cards into a red can with the white omega:

"A draft card to me is the emblem the Jews had to wear in Germany....Right on to revolution!"

"I find freedom in subverting illegitimate authority."

"These laws are stupid. I'm just getting rid of it [draft card]."

"I'm free; I'm unhooked again."

Setting one afire with a lighter: "I hope this smoke goes toward Heaven."

"That little piece of paper, that means nothing. Just like a high school diploma."

Ripping up his 2-S: "It's a symbol of white middle class privilege. I don't dig it anymore."

"Students Strike Against Cambodia,"
Iconoclast, Reading, Pennsylvania, May 1970

On Thursday evening on May 1, President Nixon went on nationwide TV to announce the intervention of U.S. troops in Cambodia to attempt to drive Communist forces from their Cambodian sanctuaries. His pronouncement was steeped in terms of being a necessary concomitant to the Vietnamization, although he had not felt the move compulsory when he announced the projected withdrawal of 150,000 U.S. troops less than two weeks prior. This move came as somewhat of a surprise to most Americans, who merely expected Nixon to offer Cambodian Premier Lon Nol the logistical support he had requested. However, those Americans, particularly students, who knew that U.S. troops have functioned in Cambodia for several years with CIA fronts, were determined to coordinate a national strike to protest Nixon's deceptive maneuvering. The result: a national student strike against Cambodia.

The strike has already reached some 350 of the 1,500 colleges in the country, closing 225 of them, at least 80 of which will remain on strike for the current academic year. The strike has manifested itself in a variety of forms, both peaceful and violent, both legal and illegal, including teach-ins, picketing, mass rallies, petitions (to the legislators and other government officials), the burning of ROTC buildings and other conspicuous symbols of campus complicity with the War Machine. The most poignant example of the senseless provocation the "pig" presence has created from the student strike is, of course, the massacre of four students at Kent State in Ohio, where National Guardsmen, without an order from their commanding officer, spontaneously fired into a crowd of students that had already begun to disperse from a barrage of tear gas.

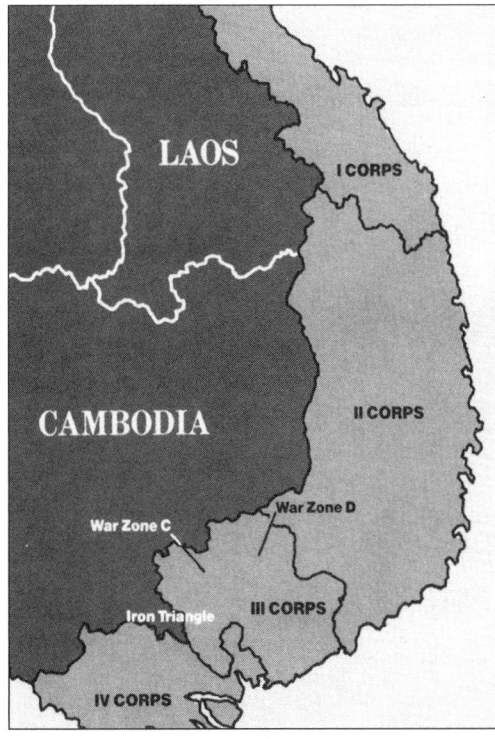

With four martyrs, the strike received a renewed impetus so that by Friday night, Nixon, after having consulted eight university presidents, was forced to call a press conference to explain his perspective on the student strike and its repercussions. While commending students who were employing the Constitutional right to express dissent to the extension of the Vietnam War into Cambodia, Nixon condemned any "violent" form of protest. But Nixon did not feel compelled to differentiate between violence toward property and violence to human life. He seemed oblivious to the fact that while the destruction of property has been perpetuated by the student demonstrators, loss of human life can be consistently attributed to the "pigs" at Kent State, on Wall Street, in New York City (where the "pigs" refused to respond to the attack on students by construction workers), and in Washington.

"What's Troubling High School Students?"
Today's Education, September 1970

Last spring, the editors of Today's Education invited seven secondary school students—six juniors and one senior—to come to our offices and discuss topics that trouble high school students today. The group—a cross-section of American youth—includes representatives from various racial groups, and urban, suburban and rural areas.

The seven are Jim Anderson, Falls Church, Virginia; Sue Arshack, Silver Spring, Maryland; Marsha Babcock, Omaha, Nebraska; Bob Dieterle, Nutley, New Jersey; Sandi Garcia, Nogales, Arizona; Tonya Kneece, Batesburg, South Carolina; and Eric Ward, Philadelphia, Pennsylvania.

Eric Ward: Basically, my school has the same problems that exist in all of our schools. There has to be a change in the traditional ways of education, and it has to come soon.

Students are being turned off. Young people today are not going to sit around and wait. They're going to make people pay attention even if it means tearing up books or setting buildings on fire.

Jim Anderson: Are you advocating violence to make the change?

Eric: No. I'm saying that this is what many of today's young cats have been doing in order to get what they want and that society must find some answers and listen to these cats, because things are not going to get any easier.

Bob Dieterle: You stress the need for change. That seems to be the trend today, that everything has to be changed, that everything has to be new. I don't quite understand why things have to be changed.

Eric: Well, probably if you came from a school like mine, you'd understand. If you went to school every morning and you walked into a dark building—I mean, totally dark—and you walked down a long hallway that looks like a subway, you'd understand. There's an atmosphere of unrest, dissent. Students are disgusted. They're frustrated.

When you're in a classroom with 50 other students, your teacher just cannot work with you individually. Then, at lunchtime, you go down to a lunchroom which is not a lunchroom. It's just some dingy place where they serve you food.

Is this fair to today's young people? I don't feel that students should have to come into what I call a subway system every morning. They should be able to come into a decent building.

But a new building isn't the answer to all educational problems. Teachers should be the kind of people who want to teach kids and really try to motivate them. And I think that teachers like that would turn the kids on.

Tonya Kneece: As Eric was saying, teachers have to try to relate to their students—and not only in class. If a teacher cares about his students, cares about their personal problems, kids go into his classroom knowing this and wanting to study under him.

But I think the bigger problem is the curriculum. We have teachers in my school who have been teaching the same thing for years and years.

Jim: High school prepares you for college. Right? Now, what type of course do you want?

Eric: I agree with you. The courses today do prepare you for college, but we need courses to teach you how to get along with each other. That's something that's got to be done, because people are not getting along. Let's face it. The conditions in this country are coming to a point where pretty soon things are going to blow. So, teaching people how to work with each other is important.

Not every kid in school is going to college. What about the kid who cannot read and cannot make it to college? We cannot forget them. I feel courses should be geared to relate to what all students need.

Sue Arshack: Saying that school is to prepare us for college is the biggest mistake we can possibly make. I think schools should also prepare us to live in the world rather than just prepare us for college.

Marsha Babcock: That's why I think the schools should offer more vocational courses than they do.

Jim: Do your schools have vocational courses?

Eric: Yeah. We have five vocational schools where students can go.

Marsha: In our city, they offer an electronics course. It's small; very few kids are in it. But I've gone down there and it's really neat.

Jim: Do you all know what an EFFE program is? EFFE means Experiment in Free Form Education. We're going to have one of these programs at my school. We'll drop all our old classes and set up experimental classes in anything we want.

Bob: We have something like that called May courses. Students suggest things they would like to study. Like, say, you wanted a subject on the stock market. You'd suggest it. Then, the subjects that get the most votes are put into the curriculum. Classes meet once a week. Kids can come out of the study halls or free periods and go to these classes. There's no homework, and kids get a pass or fail grade.

Jim: Are EFFE and May courses what you have in mind?

Eric: No. I think maybe you're missing what we're saying. We're not saying that we want to just drop everything that's been traditionally taught in school. But what we're saying—history, for example. We're taught what was done in the Civil War, what was done in the time of Columbus.

This is fine. We have to have a background. But what we're saying is: Why don't schools teach people what's happening in Vietnam? I mean, like why?

Sue: That kind of discussion makes people think, and who knows?

Eric: Amen.

Jim: Do you think schools are trying to be repressive? Stop you from thinking?

Sue: I don't know that they're trying to be repressive, but I think the whole system is set up in a way that leads to repression. Schools too often are not places for creative, expanded thinking, and one week of an EFFE program is tokenism—that's not what the whole year is about.

Sandi Garcia: I'm just noting the differences in our schools. Like my school is really bad. Have you ever seen army barracks? That's what we have for some of our classes. We don't have anything like some of the classes you've been talking about. We'll have four years of English and we'll have algebra, geometry, and that's it.

We don't have any protests or anything. But we're situated right on the border of Mexico, and we have a really big problem in drugs. Probably because of the big flow from Mexico. Parents don't even let their kids out anymore because of the drug scare.

"California Reservists Speak Out Against War,"
WIN Peace and Freedom through Nonviolent Action, December 15, 1970

In two separate actions, Northern California military Reservists recently demonstrated their opposition to the war.

On October 31, a contingent of Army, Marine and Coast Guard Reservists marched in a peace parade through downtown San Francisco.

The same week, 16 Marine Reservists in Marin County, just north of San Francisco, bought an advertisement in a local newspaper. Their ad supported a county ballot proposition calling for withdrawal of U.S. troops from all of Southeast Asia.

The Marines were all enlisted men of M Co., 23rd Marine Regiment, San Rafael. A Marine Corps spokesman made vague threats to the press that the men would be punished for their actions, but so far the Marine Corps has apparently been unable to find any regulation it can use against them.

"Sky Spies to Watch Pollution,"
Martinsville Bulletin (Virginia), March 3, 1970

Air and water pollution can be monitored effectively and traced to the source by survey satellites being developed by the United States, researchers reported today.

Two teams of researchers who are testing camera and sensor systems for the satellites, the first of which will be launched in March 1972, made their report to an Earth Conference....

The application with the broadest current user interest is detecting elements of water pollution, tracing them to their source, and measuring the dispersion and concentration of the pollutants.

To illustrate, the MIT-NASA team showed a picture of Massachusetts Bay, near Salem, and identified a plume-like image as the flow from a combined sanitary and storm sewer and a smaller plume as a surface slick created by a power plant coolant.

"Pollution Clean-up of Nation Will Take Time, Experts Warn,"
by Alton Blakeslee, *Martinsville Bulletin,* March 19, 1970

The galloping popular campaign to clean up the nation's polluted environment won't witness some magical quick fix.

And that is worrying some experts in pollution control.

They are concerned that enthusiasm will fade when the drive to clean up air, water and land runs into inevitable practical realities, even if given all the goodwill in the world to do the job.

Disappointment and fading interest could deflate the pressures to do what is really required—a continuing commitment and motivation to raise the money, to pass and enforce the laws, to develop technology and to do all the work first to halt and then correct manmade insults to the environment. And then to keep improving antipollution controls as population expands.

As one reality, take a river basin which is being polluted by raw sewage from a number of towns.

By popular demand, even law, all towns are asked to halt their pollution, right now. People along other rivers make similar demands.

But would there be enough engineers to make the essential surveys, then to plan and design the sewage treatment plants, or would there be enough skilled construction firms—given contracts for the lowest bid—to build all the plants for all the towns and cities at the same time?

The point is raised by Reinholt W. Thieme, a deputy assistant secretary of the Interior, not in terms of suggesting any slowdown, but merely to point out that some cities might have to wait their turn to complete the clean-up of the entire river.

&ᴥ&ᴥ&ᴥ&ᴥ&ᴥ

Seventy percent of the solid particles contaminating urban air have not been identified, and even if we had limitless resources we could not formulate really effective control programs because we know so little about the origin, nature and effects of most air pollutants.

—Dr. Rene Dubos of Rockefeller University

&ᴥ&ᴥ&ᴥ&ᴥ&ᴥ

"The Failures of Educational Reform," by Charles E. Silberman, *Crisis in the Classroom*, 1970

"The decade which began in 1955, and through which we are still churning," Professor Robert H. Anderson of Harvard predicted in the early '60s, "may come to be regarded as one of the major turning points in American public education." Anderson's optimism was widely shared: 1950s and '60s saw one of the largest and most sustained educational reform movements in American history, an effort that many observers, this writer included, thought would transform the schools.

Nothing of the sort happened; the reform movement has produced innumerable changes, and yet the schools themselves are largely unchanged. In one study, John I. Goodlad, dean of the UCLA Graduate School of Education, along with several colleagues, visited some 260 kindergarten-through-first grade classrooms in 100 schools in 13 states to determine the extent to which the reform movement had changed the schools. He found what this writer and his colleagues found: that things are much the same as they had been 20 years ago, and in some respects, not as good as they were 40 years ago, when the last great school reform movement was at its peak. "We were unable to discern much attention to pupil needs, attainments, or problems as a basis for individual opportunities to learn," he reports. "Teaching was predominantly telling and questioning by the teacher, with children responding one by one or occasionally in chorus. In all of this, the textbook was the most highly visible instrument of learning and teaching....Rarely did we find small groups intensely in pursuit of knowledge; rarely did we find individual pupils at work in self-sustaining inquiry...we are forced to conclude that much of the so-called educational reform movement has been blunted on the classroom door."

"Conservationists Disappointed,"
Martinsville Bulletin, April 2, 1970

Conservationists have expressed disappointment at President Nixon's failure to appoint a clearly qualified environmentalist as undersecretary of the Interior.

But they withheld judgment on Nixon's choice of multimillionaire Fred J. Russell, an unknown in the field of environment and resources, to succeed the highly respected Russell E. Train, the No. 2 job at Interior.

In a sense, some prominent conservation spokesmen said, the calm greeting of Russell amounts to a vote of confidence in Interior Secretary Hickel.

త్ళు-త్ళు-త్ళు-త్ళు-త్ళు

"Correpondence Between Nicholas Bageac and Henry W. Allen,"
Department of State, Washington, D.C.

April 22, 1971

Mr. Nicholas Bageac
87-30 Justice Avenue
Apartment 5F
Elmhurst, New York 11373

Dear Mr. Bageac:

Thank you for your letter of April 2 informing me that Mr. Baciu had arrived in the United States. I was very happy to learn that the family is now reunited and that your father-in-law-for all the trouble he has lived through—remains in good health. I am sure that you will find what you describe as "small" problems ahead. However, I am equally sure that you will meet them with the same vigor and determination which successfully brought your family back together in this country. While the arrival of the sixth member of your family needs neither the assistance nor approval of the State Department, may I wish him or her the best of starts in this world.

We appreciate your comments on immigration problems. As you are well aware, our immigration law was designed to facilitate the reunification of families, but it can be effective only in helping persons to get into the United States, not in getting them out of their own countries. Through the legal process, and where applicable with assistance from the United States Refugee Program, the U.S. Government does what it can to relieve the tribulations of the refugee. We know that it sometimes takes a long time, but we hope you will urge patience on friends of yours who may undertake to come to this country.

With greetings to Mrs. Bageac and all your family,

Sincerely,

Henry W. Allen
Refugee and Migration Officer
Office of Refugee and Migration Affairs

STATE ~ A.I.D. ~ USIA	DATE
ROUTING SLIP	April 22, 1971

TO:	Name or Title	Organ. Symbol	Room No.	Bldg.	Initials	Date
1.	Mr. Charles W. Schaller	EUR/BRY	5217	NS		
2.						
3.						
4.						
5.						

Approval	X	For Your Information		Note and Return	
As Requested		Initial for Clearance		Per Conversation	
Comment		Investigate		Prepare Reply	
File		Justify		See Me	
For Correction		Necessary Action		Signature	

REMARKS OR ADDITIONAL ROUTING

Attached is a letter from Romanian refugee
Nicholas Bageac of April 2, reporting the arrival
of his father-in-law, Victor Baciu, in the US.
This provides a happy ending to correspondence
between Mr. Bageac and the Department dating
back to December 1968.

FROM: (Name and Org. Symbol)		ROOM NO. & BLDG.		PHONE NO.
Henry W. Allen	S/R:ORM	2528	NS	28344

To DEPARTMENT OF STATE
WASHINGTON, D.C.

Nicholas Bageac
87-30 Justice Ave.
Elmhurst N Y 11373

August 20 1972

Dear Sir,

Due to the fact that I have legitimate desire and pride to vote in the presidential election this year I am asking your assistance to speed up my naturalization which has been slowly processing since March 1 when I had the first hearing with two witnesses.

The number of my file is 741768 Eastern District Brooklyn N.Y. The head of the department is Mr. Cohen and he answers at telephone no. (212) 596-3946 or 596-5165.

I called him a couple of times, and he said that more information about me is expected. I asked for an appointment offering my help to clarify any questions, but I was told that it cannot help and although I may take the trip, it is a waste of time.

Now with registration for voting closing at September 2 (yet I registered myself with the remark of naturalization underway) and the November election coming soon, I may remain out of voting if my naturalization process does not come to a conclusion. The usual time for the waiting period is three months and my case has already lapsed six months.

This is my first chance to vote freely, and besides that, being a U.S. citizen is an honor which I believe I deserve and I am deeply concerned with.

Sincerely yours,
Nicholas Bageac

———————————

August 21 1972

Dear Mr. Allen,

I would like to write to you in personal terms as a continuation of your assistance and encouragement when a problem with my wife's parents' immigration put us in contact last year. I am sure you have hundreds of cases every month and for a quick recollection I enclosed a copy of your last and so nice letter forwarded to me in April 1971.

Since then many things changed and mostly are good news. The expected baby was what I wished the most: a wonderful girl who brought our family a lot of joy and love. My 14-year-old son achieved beautiful results in school. My father-inlaw at 60 years of age got a job as a security guard in the first month he came and is extremely pleased in this country as he was born again. Me and my wife (both with degrees in engineering) we are working at the same company holding good positions. My mother-in-law takes care of the baby and household, a job for what always is hard to find labor.

We are a well-organized family, hard workers (everybody in his field), physically and morally healthy, and I see no reason why this country is not to be as pleased with us as we are (and thank God for that) with her.

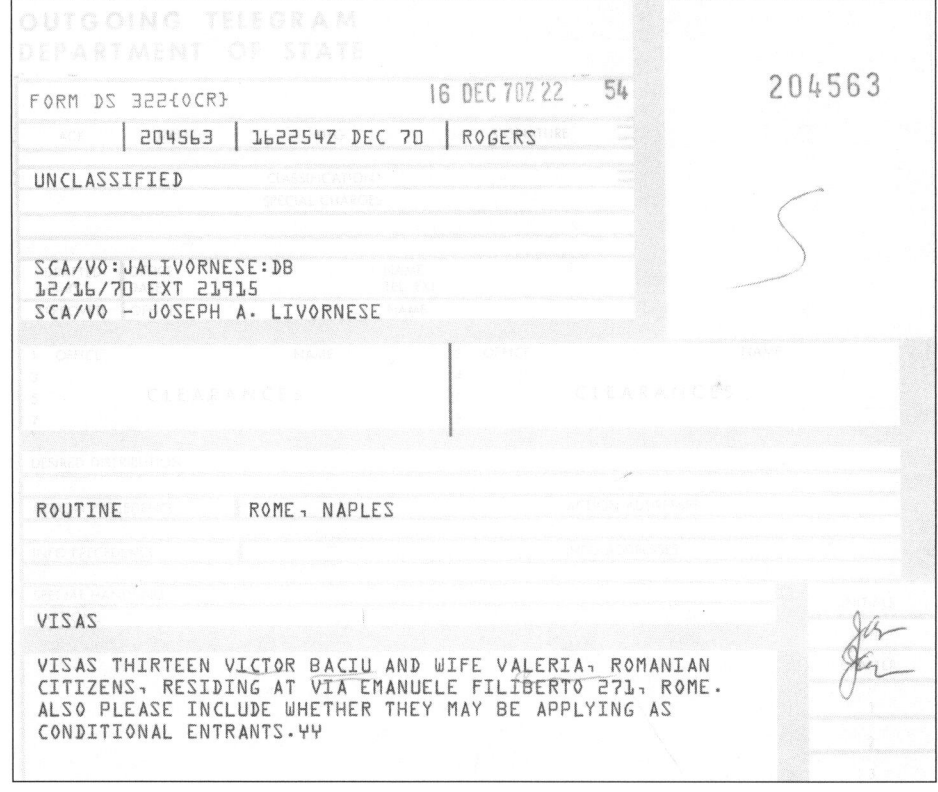

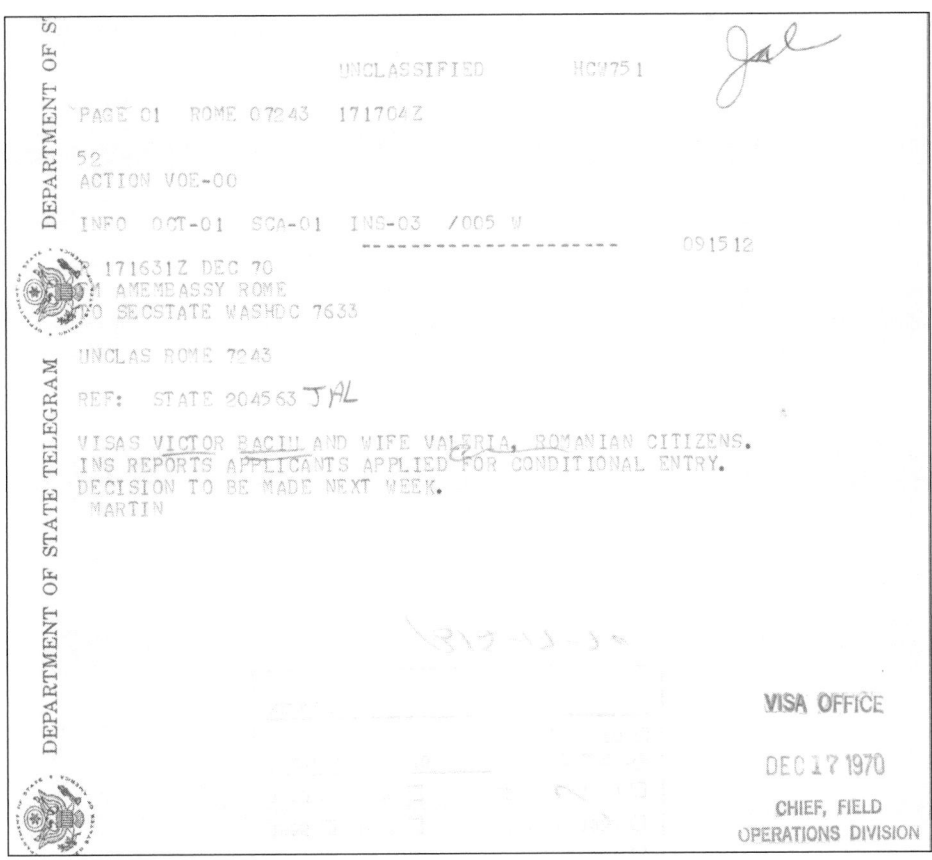

DEPARTMENT OF S

UNCLASSIFIED   HCM751

PAGE 01   ROME 07243   171704Z

52
ACTION VOE-00

INFO OCT-01 SCA-01 INS-03 /005 W
                                                                091512
R 171631Z DEC 70
M AMEMBASSY ROME
TO SECSTATE WASHDC 7633

UNCLAS ROME 7243

REF: STATE 204563 JAL

VISAS VICTOR BACIU AND WIFE VALERIA, ROMANIAN CITIZENS.
INS REPORTS APPLICANTS APPLIED FOR CONDITIONAL ENTRY.
DECISION TO BE MADE NEXT WEEK.
  MARTIN

VISA OFFICE

DEC 17 1970

CHIEF, FIELD
OPERATIONS DIVISION

DEPARTMENT OF STATE TELEGRAM

We have a high income per our family of six which enables us for more and more prosperity. Within some months we will move into a new $55,000 home in Westchester, N.Y., already bought on mortgage. So we could live as well as the president of the United States and even with less tensions and headaches.

The starting point of all these achievements and future chances was in October 1966 when, having gotten a passport for Yugoslavia, I swam from Koper (Yugoslavia) to Trieste (Italy). After four to five hours of swimming over the night I reached the other side of the Iron Curtain. That was the very starting point. I had only my wet, trembling and exhausted body still alive and a pair of bathing slips. At that time I couldn't say which one was worth more. It was cold, windy and terrible dark. I was alone and yet I had a long way to go up to the destination.

I did it, and now after six years, look at us: isn't this a great performance and a complete success? Thank God we are in this country and our children are on the safe side forever.

In addition to these things which make me a pleasure to let them be known, incidentally I have another problem for what I have to address myself to the Department of State: my naturalization processing is becoming much too slow just before the presidential election of November this year. It is easy to understand my anxiety to vote and to take part in the political life of this country. Nevertheless, being an American citizen at the time I am eligible to be is a great deal of concern for me.

I came to this country not to grab some money and go to enjoy it somewhere else, but to settle forever. It is this country where my children and grandchildren will live.

I am emotionally involved in any event internal and external related to this country, and I can no longer stay aside even without the right to cast my vote. My life and behavior are an open book and it speaks for itself. Furthermore, I am the father of an American citizen and I cannot realize what is wrong with me. Friends and acquaintances who had the first hearing after me have already gotten the citizenship.

A bureaucratic interpretation of my biographical statement could destroy my pride and ambition (a legitimate ambition) and strip me of all political rights.

These are my worries right now. I am afraid that people handling my file have little or no knowledge about the Communist regime. For instance: I was in UTM UNIUNEA TINERETULUI MUNCITOR WORKING YOUTH UNION. It was a youth organization run by the Communist party. That happened when I was attending the university and I was registered automatically. To refuse to join it was exactly to resign from attending university. I don't believe I was somebody to graduate without being a UTM member, at least at that time (1948-1953). Usually when somebody has been excluded from UTM (and I recall many cases), it was sure and well known that in a few weeks he had to be ousted from all universities. (I was lucky I kept my membership there.) Similar happened with SINDICAT (which is the Communist party-run-only UNION) for everybody who holds a job at a state company (and all are state companies). The difference is that if they fired you from the job, they didn't exclude you first from UNION (SINDICAT). Membership is automatic, and it is out of the question not to join it.

The ones who judge my statement (which was perfectly correct) could interpret that I was like a Communist party member, which is definitely something else.

So I have many reasons to worry about. Also, I feel some explanation is necessary, but nobody asks me anything while holding my file for six months with no answer so far. More than this, I offered my help to clarify some questions, but I was told that is a waste of time.

I enclosed a letter to the Department of State, and I would be very grateful to you to forward it to the right place or to suggest to me where I should send it.

With many thanks for your goodwill,

Sincerely,
Nicholas Bageac

––––––––––––––

March 13 1973

Dear Mr. Allen,

I received your letter at the end of January and I myself don't know how I was able not to answer you so far. You have been much too good to me and a simple apology is too little for my feeling of guilt. However, later is still better than never and once again I start my letter to thank you for all your efforts in assisting me to overcome some of my major difficulties. At the present time it looks to me there are no more problems of that kind which made me appeal to you. In an order to the

U.S. authority where you hold office, I believe my demands were legitimate, but I also know that it was your special attention and goodwill I have to consider and appreciate the most for the good and satisfactory results I have obtained.

Referring to the subject of my previous letter, the things went the way you supposed. Mr. Cohen of the INS office kept his promise toward you and solved my case faster than he was going to do it (but as I explained to you in my letter, still much slower than he was supposed to have it done). After you spoke to him (August 19, 1972) and at the very next ceremony of naturalization in Brooklyn Court of INS Office, on October 24, I was called and granted the American citizenship. That was my most important event in my lifetime. I have received the recognition of the U.S. and I know that I belong to the U.S. by all means. It is an honor, pride and responsibility. Of course, I'll never stop loving also my native country and its people. It was only the outside imposed and maintained regime which made my life miserable there. For my son's citizenship I have already applied and as soon as my wife will be eligible, she will send the petition. The immediate satisfaction of my naturalization came on September 2 when I voted in the presidential election: first time in my life to elect from more than one candidate. The vote was possible because I registered before though I did not have papers at that time.

All in all, I am a successful immigrant and proud of my achievements. Although my English has a clear foreign accent, I still feel like I was born here. Even I don't realize how I have been able to live for so long in another part of the world. My concern for this country is not less than that of any average American, and I believe more of our problems will be solved and drastically improved in the time to come. I hope that some of the unnecessary liberties have to be trimmed to preserve the true democracy, and I believe there is a solution for all evils of our society.

As far as my family is concerned, everything is fine. We keep the same team of three breadwinners: me, my wife and my father-in-law (who was just promoted as a supervisor at a security guard company). My mother-in-law is backing up the household, my 15-year-old son (who speaks far better English than Romanian) has good results in the ninth grade of high school, and finally my two-year-old daughter is the little terrorist of the whole family. We all are in good health and good spirits. What bothers us is that the house contractor who was supposed to have finished the house in the last months is further delaying the construction; he is building a development of about 75 houses including the roads in that area and we don't know for sure when it will be ready. We still hope that in August or September we will have been moved. The house we bought (with 80 percent in mortgage) has to be built in Westchester very close to Hastings and will fit our family number and requirements, putting an end to many inconveniences we have at this time. This house is our dream, and all our future satisfaction and pleasure are related to it. More and more, the anxiety is growing, but I hope one day the dream will come true, starting a much better life.

You were very kind writing to us about your family, and it was a nice thing learning from you in such a friendly manner.

We wish you and your family all good things and good health.

Thank you again, Mr. Allen, for all you have done for me, and for your kindness and goodwill, which made me fortunate to meet you.

Gratefully yours,
Nicholas Bageac

"Payroll Leadership the Key, UCAN Tries to Break Cycle," by Wes Iversen, *Omaha Sun*, April 1, 1971

"Most people don't realize it, black contractor Boyd V. Galloway claims, but contractors and builders are 'the basic people to any community.'

'A community can't pull itself up by its bootstraps,' he goes on, until some of its members can 'develop some payroll leadership.'

Galloway is president of the United Contractors Association of Nebraska, Inc. (UCAN), a group of about 40 black general contractors, specialty contractors, craftsmen, and construction workers. The development of that payroll leadership, through helping members secure bonding and thus to be able to bid on larger, more meaningful contracts, is an immediate goal.

While UCAN has been around since the fall of 1969, Galloway says there's been a new enthusiasm just in the past four months.

One reason is the hope of a $61,000 federal grant to set up a training program and facilities for minority contractors and workers. With the aid of Paul B. Allen, minority representative with the Mayor's Committee for Economic Development with the Small Business Administration (SBA) under Section 406 of the Economic Opportunity Act of 1964...under the UCAN proposal, the minority construction training program would be several-pronged. In addition to training the 'hard-core unemployed or underemployed,' the training encourages minority journeymen to set up their own contracting firms."

దొ≪దొ≪దొ≪దొ≪దొ≪దొ≪దొ≪

"'71 Year of the Ballot for Midlands' Youth," *Omaha World-Herald*, December 31, 1971

"It was a year of change for Midlands youth.

Mirrored in the pages of the 'Youth in the Midlands' section, young people moved into some areas that had been off-limits and began doing other things differently.

The vote for 18-year-olds probably will have the most lasting impact on teenagers.

Some Iowa and Nebraska youths already have voted, but only on local issues.

The arrival of the vote, however, brought the candidates' attention to young voters. Registration campaigns reached into the high schools for the first time....

And girls, through their own efforts and those of teachers, took a step toward a full share of school programs by participating in more sports. Although inter-school basketball, common in Iowa, still is not allowed in Nebraska, state championship contests in other sports were available to Cornhusker girls.

Midlands' student councils vowed to be 'relevant' to rid themselves of the school dance organizer image and to become the leaders their fellow students elected them to be.

Many students took a look at pollution and decided to do something. Some youths began to help each other out of the mire of drug abuse, replacing the escape into the chemical world with the message of Jesus, or by finding something else for drug users to do with their lives."

దొ≪దొ≪దొ≪దొ≪దొ≪దొ≪దొ≪

"Women Against Themselves," by Miriam Allen deFord, *The Humanist*, January/February 1971

"'Women were better off when the only taste they got of the competitive world was in cutting each other's throats over a cup of tea.'

'Women are already ahead, and the best they can get out of "liberation" is a setback.'

'Woman respects man for his strength...Should a wife become her husband's equal, she would lose some of that respect and he would lose his self-respect.'

'I don't care for women's liberation. I prefer the strong arms of my husband around me.'

'I would rather that my husband have more prestige at his career, and I be only the lady of the house.'

'Everything about us man has made—not woman. Women have got to be kidding when they say they want to help run the world. They are fighting a losing battle if they hope to equal men.'

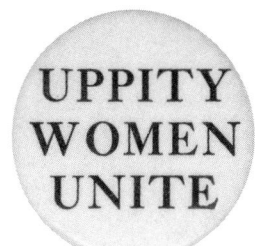

These are all actual quotations from women of our own time and place. One is from that sterling example of shrinking femininity: Shirley Temple Black.

When women marched for equal rights last August, a female group in New York gave 'Adam's Rib' awards to men 'for discriminating against women,' and a St. Louis dissident proposed that the semicentennial celebration of women's suffrage be transformed into 'be nice to a man day.'

Why? How do these women, who don't want to be considered fully responsible

human beings, with equal rights and opportunities in a democratic society, get that way? Why does a psychologist conclude from a study of college women that 'women are prejudiced against female professionals and...firmly refuse to recognize them as the equals of their male colleagues'? Why does Leslie

Ford remark that 'women would rather be taught by a third-rate man than a first-rate woman'?

It goes back a long, long way, and it's going to take more than demonstrations and conferences to undo it. And since in this country women make up 53 percent of the population, and most men are indifferent or opposed, we'd better try to understand those Women Against Themselves.

Theirs is the view of the female sex as secondary, ancillary, what Gillian Tindall calls 'the humble we-live-only-through-men attitude.' Woman to them is primarily sexual, a walking incubator, her true function to serve men and rear children. You can't call them Aunt Thomasinas, for (aside from the fact that people who think Uncle Tom liked being a slave have never read Uncle Tom's Cabin) I have never heard of a slave who approved of and advocated slavery. Nor were there any German Jews who thought the Nazis were right and that Jews deserved to be put in concentration camps and gas chambers. Nor, outside of mental hospitals, are there any destitute people who consider their poverty the proper order of society and who would rather be poor than prosperous.

Yet here we have a sizable proportion of articulate American women who honestly believe that they are inferior, that the male should be dominant, that the husband and father should be the family 'king,' that wives should obey their husbands, and that marriage should be a dictatorship instead of a partnership. They also believe that women ought to be paid less than men for the same work (otherwise they might pull all wages down, and then they themselves would have less to spend), that women ought not to aspire to administrative or executive jobs, and so on, through all the rest of the tenets of the patriarchal system."

"The Family Is out of Fashion," by Ann Richardson Roiphe, *The New York Times Magazine*, August 15, 1971

"Blood is thicker than water only in the sense of being the vitalizing stream of certain social stupidity," The Death of the Family, by David Cooper.

In a silent room on West 79th Street in New York City, 10 women rub their hands rhythmically over their large, pregnant bellies while their husbands stare at stopwatches, encouragingly giving hand signals. The couples are in training for natural childbirth with Mrs. Elizabeth Bing, who has spread the gospel in this country that male and female should share in the dramatic event of the birth of their child. Fifty to 60 new couples sign up for this course each month. What are they all doing? What are they doing several months later, walking around in their nursing bras, buying mobiles that swing from crib tops and potties with musical boxes and on and on to a future radically different from that of their childless past? Don't they know, this army of young people pushing strollers through the park, that they are behaving in a reactionary way? The nuclear family is not now a thing of fashion.

Weary from long discussion on economic theory and wasted by years of futile peace marches, bored by campaigns for compromise candidates and stunned by pollution and ecological reports, the intellectual community has turned with primal fury against a newly discovered evil: the family. Women's Liberation points out again and again how burdened, minimal and trivial is the life of the woman who tends the family. Books are appearing that attack the nuclear unit as the source of the alienated, bomb-throwing society we have come to know all too well. The call is out for new structures, babies brought up in daycare centers, new communes—or perhaps, as Germaine Greer proposes, let us do away with connected permanent relationships entirely. Let each man, woman and child shift for himself. Like the insects that fly singly throughout the ephemeral summer days.

One night my teenaged stepdaughter tearfully accused her father of being interested in her only if she was accepted into a good college so he could enjoy a little reflected status. My God, I thought, she's talking about the man who burped her, carried her to the zoo, played endless games of Monopoly and Clue, and stood in 100-degree heat to watch her ride dumb beasts in meaningless circles around a dusty ring. She's talking about the man who carried 10 bottles of ketchup all through Europe because she wouldn't eat anything without it. How did she miss the tenderness, despair, passion, pride and fear he feels for her? Of course, I knew the facts. She has to grow away, to tear apart the first love and start again—but how painful the ripping of the sinews, how wretched we all become in the process.

I looked at our new baby. "Da da," she says with joy, pulling off her father's glasses. He kisses her on the stomach. She laughs, comic, total, beautiful pleasure—but where is it going? Is it worth it? Sometimes it seems as if the tensions, the angers we have accumulated against each other will get together and flood out this family, each of us floating apart on a river of nightmares, to drown eventually.

The other day I looked at my 10-year-old. "Fix your hair," I said, "wash your face. You look like an orphan. Why won't you wear any of the dresses that hang neglected, wasted, in the closet?" Then I listened. It wasn't my voice speaking at all. It was my dead mother, out of my own body, screeching from the grave the very words I had so loathed. Within me the ghost of values past was possessing, displacing the present. Family of origin, family of procreation, tied together, despite my heroic efforts to separate them, to create a pure and different life. Patterns of the past, rejected or accepted, have a way of imposing themselves on the present. We all live with the dark designs of our early loves; our hates and our attractions are colored by the intense experience of family life. We cannot easily be freed. It is true as David Cooper in The Death of the Family says, "A thousand ghosts roam within us." They depersonalize, limit and bind us. We are like natives with large disks protruding from distorted lips, or like primitive tribes with earlobes stretched to elephantine proportions.

Most people suffer from anxieties, are neurosis-ridden, limited, uncreative, socially normal, but inwardly cut off from feelings of self. That is the usual result of our family system. No one I have ever known has made it through without scars on the psyche that became open wounds on the backs of the next generation, and yet I feel as I struggle over the bikes, sled and carriage that block access to our stairway that I and my contemporaries, male and female, are truly engaged in a revolutionary drama. We who live in families are the frontiersmen of a new world. That this was equally true of the generation before, and will apply to the generation after, is not discouraging, but from a certain distance, merely the stuff of history.

Margaret Mead, in writing a text to a photography book on the family, has said that "no society anywhere has ever sanctioned illegitimacy." This means that every society from Aborigine to Maoist China has structured some form of family life to raise, socialize and protect the children—to guarantee institutionally the social, sexual needs of the adults. Some of these systems have worked better than others; all of them have demanded a price from the participants—some personal freedoms and institutional pleasures must be abandoned when human groups are formed, and it is these very restrictions that enemies of the family are now calling abominations.

Germaine Greer would have us set no limit on sexual pleasure. Submit to no discipline of nursing schedules or possessive needs. She would have us abandon ugly security for free flight. David Cooper and R.D. Laing incriminate the family unit as the originator of all pathology, personal and political. They envision a utopia of people truly separate from one another, each self-realized and alive in his own present. David Cooper suggests that mothers should learn not to pick up babies when they wail in the first year of life, but allow them to experience the desolation and aloneness of their position. If we do this, he promises, we will create people who are not tied to others, not destroyed by family romance.

His method seems extreme, but the goals are unarguable. We all want better human beings. We want to create a society in which each man can live creatively and experience self-love and love of others. We want fewer divorces, fewer psychotics, no Lee Harvey Oswalds, and finally, in a wonderful new world, no Lyndon Johnsons, no George Wallaces, no bigots, no liars, no destroyers—the Pentagon turned into a botanical garden. But the question is, how do we make better people, how will we perfect, tame, simultaneously harness and free the conflicting forces of aggression and love that are an absolute part of every human child that opens its new eyes on the jaded world of its parents?

I cannot believe that further disconnection of child from parent, an atomization of each human unit into a single orbiting star, will achieve anything more than the certain death of the species. It seems self-evident that we are now stuck with one another, parent and child, male and female, and that the changes that must be made need to take into account the necessary balances we have to find in order to assume the separate dignity of each living soul. It is my baby's right to take her first steps away from me and my obligation to follow, not too close but not too far, for the next moment when she needs to be restrained from pulling the boiling soup down on her head.

As my husband and I go about our day, we are trying to form between us the shape of a family that will enable our children better to integrate the pressures on them from without and within, and to make them freer, their ghosts more benign than ours, their limitations less paralyzing. We try not to let our time go dead with security and wooden with known experiences. We attempt to do better than our parents—some days we succeed. Too often, we definitely don't. *Reprinted with permission.*

"For They Are All Honorable Men," by Jan Barry,
WIN Peace and Freedom through Nonviolent Action, March 15, 1971

They came from Texas and Alabama, New York and California, Kansas and Montana. They wore jeans and business suits, afros and crew cuts, field jackets and love beads. They were all Vietnam veterans who had come to Detroit, Michigan, to testify to first-hand knowledge of American crimes in Indochina.

These were the obverse of Tom Paine's "summer soldiers and sunshine patriots." In Vietnam, they had been sergeants, lance corporals, captains, and in at least two cases, majors. They were the true heirs of the men who endured the long, bitter winter at Valley Forge. These were the veterans of Vietnam who, in the face of public apathy and indifference, and official hostility and harassment, refused to forget.

Appropriately, the Detroit war crimes hearings, organized by the Vietnam Veterans Against the War, a national organization of 5,000 members, were called the Winter Soldier Investigation. For these were, truly, the "winter soldiers" of the war in Vietnam.

A dozen at a time, division after division, each group spanning the six years American combat forces have been in Vietnam, they walked onto the public stage hour after hour for three full days (January 31-February 2) and presented their eyewitness accounts of prisoners tortured and killed, civilians intimidated and shot, villages bombarded and burned, borders illegally and secretly crossed, indiscriminate defoliation and bombing and artillery daily and nightly used, massacres large and small....

Altogether, about 100 Vietnam veterans, from 1962 to the present, testified at the three-day hearings in Detroit's downtown Howard Johnson's Motor Lodge. Another 400-500 Vietnam veterans from all over the continental United States and Canada came and listened, added their support and conducted non-stop organizing meetings in the hallways and nearby rooms.

Much of the testimony was gruesomely familiar to even casual followers of the court-martial of Lt. William Calley. What was new was the evidence presented that the same grisly "incidents" permeated the experiences of men who had served in Vietnam in every year, in every major unit, in every region of Vietnam. One woman or child killed here, 30 killed there, a half-dozen somewhere else, 50 another day, in another place.

The pattern of daily, or near-daily American war atrocities year on end was too stark, and too thickly-woven, to be soon forgotten by those hundreds of Detroit and Canadian citizens who came to hear, 500 at a time, these men who so obviously had been there. Dozens of sober, concerned, middle-income and often middle-aged Detroiters had to be turned away for lack of room. The doubters were conspicuously hushed and few....

Yet it remained by and large a hostile press. The liberal, mostly Eastern-establishment papers imposed a near-blackout on the hearings, while the conservative, mostly Midwestern press reveled in retorts such as "alleged veterans," and "so-called hearings," and other hackneyed tricks of the put-down trade.

"The Crucial Math of Motherhood,"
Life, May 19, 1972

"This week there are two million more Americans than there were 12 months ago. In two huge metropolitan regions of the East and West, the population is shooting up even faster than it is in India. Although the national birthrate has actually been declining for the past decade, the inexorable mathematics of motherhood means that the U.S. is still growing by more than one percent a year. At this rate, there will be 280 million of us by the year 2000, enough to force a marked change in many of the ways we now live.

Both the Pill and easier abortion laws have helped lower the birthrate in recent years. So have inflation, job shortages, and the women's rights movement, all of which tend to encourage later marriages and fewer children. Last month, after an exhaustive two-year study, the Presidential Commission on Population Growth and the American Future recommended that we now seize the chance to stabilize our population. The commission, headed by John D. Rockefeller, III, favors abortion on request, free contraceptive information and supplies for all, including minors, and a national policy of zero population growth. Married couples would be encouraged to have an average of only two children (the present average is 2.3). President Nixon responded to his Commission's report by attacking both the legalization of abortion and the distribution of contraceptive supplies to minors....

No less than 15 percent of all babies born to married couples between 1966 and 1970 were unwanted, reported the Population Commission. 'The incidence of unwanted fertility,' declared the commissioners, 'in terms of ordinary medical health criteria would qualify as epidemic proportions. One third of all conceive their first child before they are married, and among couples who decide they have had enough children, a third still go on to have at least one more. If every family were able to have only the number of children it wanted,' the Commission concluded, 'the U.S. would have gone a long way toward solving its population problem.'"

"All about a Subject You Can Sink Your Teeth Into," by Norman Mark, *Today's Health,* November 1972

"It's harmless to your health, sloppy underfoot, ecologically neutral, popular through the ages when people feel deprived or anxious, and no longer a sign of vulgarity. It's...chewing gum, a welcome grind for the famous and unknown alike.

Phosphates are removed from laundry detergents and something else is put in that may be just as bad; small cars pollute less, but some studies find that people in them suffer more injuries in accidents; rats thrive on cereal boxes but grow thin on the cereal.

In such an improbable and dangerous world, fit more for machines than for humans, it's important to celebrate those rare occasions when we are greeted with pleasant surprises instead of nasty ones. So celebrate this: There is good news about chewing gum, that bane of parents and schoolteachers for the last generation or two. Both the gum manufacturers and a growing number of dental researchers agree that gum chewing is virtually harmless. Better yet, there is even evidence that chewing sugarless gum may be of some value in reducing cavities.

But before we get further into what gum does and does not do to your teeth, we have to admit that anywhere outside the mouth it is sticky stuff. It does no good for the soles of shoes and it looks ugly whenever it lands in public after it has been chewed. (Authorities on gum also point out that it doesn't retain much flavor if left on the bedpost overnight ...)

An average-sized stick of gum has only a little sugar and fewer than nine calories. But gum chewing increases the saliva in your mouth, which washes the sugar into your stomach along with many particles of food. So gum doesn't do much one way or another for your teeth.

But current studies offer preliminary indications that gum might someday benefit those who chew it. At the Eastman Dental Center in Rochester, New York, a team headed by Basil G. Bibby, D.M.D., Ph.D., is trying to learn which snack food causes the most decay. So far, Dr. Bibby says, the evidence shows that chewing gum does less harm to your teeth than hard and chewy candies, cookies, cakes and doughnuts.

'You hang on to that word moderation,' Dr. Bibby says. 'If you must have sugar, you might as well take it in gum as from a stick of candy or a cookie. A stick of gum is less destructive than a cookie, for instance. And the sugar in a carbonated beverage is less destructive than that in a candy bar ...'

If scientists could add some decay-fighting substance to gum, it could make a powerfully healthy habit. But saliva, which washes away the sugar in gum, also washes away almost everything else, including the dozens of additives scientists have been adding, unsuccessfully, to gum for decades. One new experiment in this area, however, does look promising.

Sidney B. Finn, D.D.S., professor of dentistry at the Dental Research Institute of the University of Alabama, is experimenting with a new phosphate—sodium trimetaphosphate—that has reduced tooth decay in test animals by about 60 percent. It has been added to gum chewed by 600 children in the Florida School for the Deaf and Blind in St. Augustine. We should know the results of Dr. Finn's research in about two years, after which we may have a chewing gum additive that can also cut down on decay."

ઠ∾ઠ∾ઠ∾ઠ∾ઠ∾ઠ∾ઠ∾ઠ∾

"Making Marines, Boot Camp Is Still the Meanest 11 Weeks of a Recruit's Life," by Richard Lawrence Stack, *Life,* November 24, 1972

These Marine recruits at Parris Island, SC, have just finished a four-hour "motivation" (read punishment) march, crawling the last 500 yards through mud and slime while trying to keep their mock weapons dry. One look at them and even the first-day rookie, rigid in his civvies, gets the message: Shape up or else.

While the other branches of the service woo volunteers by offering civilian comforts, the Marines are determined to stay "lean and mean" as ever. For the trainee, usually a teenager, that means surviving 11 weeks of relentlessly "hostile" environments in which he is pushed to the brink of physical and psychological endurance. What the Marines want is "a few good men." They don't get them; they make them.

The DI's Code: First humiliate, then motivate

Feared and hated, a consummate actor, the drill instructor plays angry god to his recruits. Even at mealtime he is there to harass—"Move your stupid butt"—as the recruit sidesteps down the chowline, trying to hold his tray at attention just below eye level. The DI's aim is absolute mental and physical domination over his men. First he humiliates, then he motivates. Since the

sorry night in 1956 when a DI marched his platoon into a swampy creek, drowning six of them, even DIs have had to live with certain restrictions. Physical training is more systematic now—the daily run in the Carolina sun is only three miles instead of open-ended. And a DI can no longer beat up a recruit—at least not in public.

Individuality is out—and so is hair

Shorn of their hair, and as much individuality as the Marines can drum out of them, the recruits pay avid attention as an instructor describes how to club an enemy from behind. Soon they will be practicing on each other. To make them think and act as a group, the recruits are isolated from the outside world of television, beer, phone calls and girlfriends. Often, they are punished

collectively for one man's mistake. They may speak only to their instructors—and then only when spoken to. If they blunder, they end up like the recruit in the mud, learning the hard way "to live to be an old man."

Breaking down a rookie with words alone

Physical abuse is forbidden, but the drill instructor can break a man with his tongue alone.... Three DIs take turns verbally slicing up a recruit guilty of poor marksmanship on the rifle range. "Get yourself together, dummy, or we'll send you to the 'motivation' platoon." The recruit's lip quavers. He'd already been there. "What do you want then, to go home to Mommy?" The recruit whimpers and the DIs zero in for the kill. "What's this? You're crying? The little girl is crying for Momma. Come on, girlie, let's have a big smile." But the recruit now is in tears.

"We call them names," explains a senior DI, "because if they ever become prisoners of war, they'll be called worse things than we call them. If they can't take it now, they won't be able to take it then."

෯෧෯෧෯෧෯෧෯෧

"Avery Repeats Stop Winter Olympics View,"
Pacific Stars and Stripes, **February 13, 1972**

SAPPORO, Japan—Avery Brundage, veteran president of the International Olympic Committee (IOC), said the Winter Olympic competition should be stopped because it is "not universal" and played with scandal.

In an exclusive interview with United Press International, the 84-year-old Chicago millionaire who has headed the IOC for 20 years took pains to praise the organization of the XI Winter Olympics at Sapporo.

At the same time, however, he repeated his contention that there should be no Winter Games at all.

"The Winter Games are not universal," he said. "There's also the problem of weather, location and ski scandals which have been with us for the last 10 years." Brundage often has said many top Alpine skiers are, in fact, professional, and as such should not be allowed to participate in the Olympics, which are for amateurs only.

He said, "The arrangements for the Sapporo Games are almost perfect. The facilities are excellent, while there is an abundance of snow, something we have not had in the past.

"Indeed, some of the sites are really beautiful. The biathlon course, for instance, is one of the prettiest I've seen. And, of course, events get off exactly as scheduled."

He said, "The Japanese deserve to be congratulated for the staging of a highly successful Games."

Brundage, an archrival of the Winter Games primarily because of the cost and commercialization of Alpine skiing, added: "But we must look at the Winter Games from the overall points of view.

"I understand the Japanese have spent nearly $600 million in these Games. Not all the money has gone to the Games sites, but a very substantial part of it has. This is excessive for 10 days of winter sports involving some 1,500 athletes, especially when you consider only 15 odd countries are represented in all the events. Two Filipino skiers can hardly be called a team, by way of example," he said.

Brundage, who has been president of the IOC since 1952, and plans to retire from the post at the conclusion of the Summer Games in Munich, took on the question of Austria's Karl Schranz, the 33-year-old superstar of the Alpine circuit who was booted out of the Games before he could compete for the Olympic gold medal that has eluded him in 18 years of competition.

Brundage said, "Mr. Schranz earned his living from skiing for 18 years. I believe that speaks for itself and proves my points.

"Mr. Schranz did not need to compete in the Games. He has capitalized on his Olympic fame. The reception he received on his return to Vienna from members of the Austrian government shows that sport has become a political factor in that country.

"We [IOC] do not like when an Austrian Minister contacts his counterparts in other countries in an effort to take over the Olympic Games. No sir, we do not like it."

Reminded that Schranz is not alone in violating Olympic rules, and that similar cases can be brought against those who compete in the Summer Games, Brundage said: "There may be isolated cases; we need proof of these, but none are so blatant."

Asked whether he thought the International Ski Federation (FIS) was trying to conform to IOC rules, now that it is investigating Annie Famose for doing a radio commentary on Alpine events for a European station, Brundage said: "It's a good sign, but a very mild one in view of the enormous violations over the years."

Brundage charged the FIS with being dishonest. "We are not through with the FIS. They allow athletes to violate the rules through the years and tell us unofficially the rules have been broken. Then they force athletes to sign entry forms claiming they have competed within the rules. We don't like it. I call that dishonest," he said.

Asked if he agreed with the charge that Denver, which hosts the 1976 Games, had been dishonest in its presentation when it won the right to play host at Amsterdam in 1970, Brundage said, "No."

"FIS has agreed to the change in Alpine and Nordic skiing sites. They should have looked at the possibilities before giving their sanction. Now we feel it's too late to take the Games away, especially after the expenditure the Denver people have been put to.

"They have guaranteed us the Games will be held under Olympic rules and we are satisfied on this point."

Looking back on his 20 years as president of the IOC, Brundage said: "Apart from the scandals in Alpine skiing, the Olympic movement is recognized as one of the great social forces in the world. It is not perfect but we do our best. I am proud of this fact."

Pressed about the fact that most Olympic medalists are not amateurs in the true sense of the word, Brundage said, "If a sport requires the training of athletes to the exclusion of their studies and their business, then it should be excluded from the Games."

Brundage rejected suggestions that some athletes train as many as eight hours a day. "Nobody needs to train for that time. I tried it when I was a competitor. The result was I became stale and my performance suffered."

⊱⊰⊱⊰⊱⊰⊱⊰

"IBM Feels Bite of Growing Computer Leasing Industry," *Lebanon Daily News* (Pennsylvania), August 14, 1972

The independent computer leasing industry is starting to bite the hand that feeds it.

Giant international Business Machines Corp., which has 70 percent of the world's computer business, owns the paw that's getting bit. Companies like Leasco Corp., IBM's biggest single customer, are doing the biting. Nor is IBM at all likely to retaliate. Any retaliatory measure might hurt IBM more than it would help.

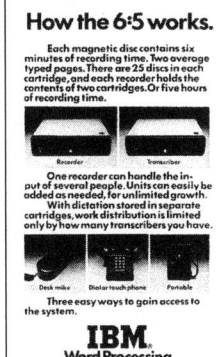

Asked about the matter, IBM said it doesn't care to comment.

To be specific, Leasco has taken some of the IBM 360 computers it owns and added more memory capacity so they compete rather well with the Model 150 series for the new IBM 370 computers. This is working out so well for Leasco that Executive Vice President Jack Leatham said he's not sure that Leasco will be interested in buying IBM's today's computers with "virtual storage" capacity just announced. Leasco rents these souped-up 360s for less than IBM charges for its 370s.

Of course, that's the essence of the independent computer leasing game—the ability to rent IBM's computers for less than IBM is willing to rent them.

"The reason we can do so is that all the IBM hardware will last much longer than IBM's depreciation policies prescribe," Leatham explained. Because it needs a high cash flow and because its global dominance of mainframe computer manufacturing industry enables it to do so, IBM sets its rental prices and comparatively short lifespans. Yet, said Leatham, one-third of IBM's 1401 computers, sold back in the late 1950s and early 1960s, are still in use.

ભ☜☜☜☜☜☜

"The 'Weaker Sex' Comes on Strong,"
Life, May 19, 1972

"Women," declares University of California physiologist Jack Wilmore, "have been pampered too long. Most of them would like to be stronger than they are." Wilmore, who teaches physical education at the Davis campus, believes there is no reason why women cannot be, pound for pound, just as strong as men. Nor need they fear any unsightly bulges. All they need to do is work out regularly with barbells, and depend on their naturally low level of the hormone testosterone to keep them from looking like Mr. America.

It wasn't all that easy getting girls to sign up for Weight Lifting I, so that Wilmore could test his theories. In fact, only four showed up for his first class last fall. But when he changed the name of the course to "Weight Training for Figure Control" and began spreading the word about how nicely his students were shaping up, candidates began flocking in. This term he has 200 co-eds grunting and groaning in the Davis Gym. Some of them have found that they doubled their strength in a single quarter. Meanwhile, Wilmore is keeping a close watch with his tape measures and calipers on the general distribution of adipose tissue and muscle.

Students choose Wilmore's weightlifting class for a variety of reasons. Some of the recruits obviously want to shed fat. A few say that their boyfriends urged them to try it. Others, like Natalie Nickerson, think, "It's neat to do something that girls aren't supposed to do."

ભ☜☜☜☜☜☜

"Going Home," January 19, 1973

At last the doors would open, at the Hanoi Hilton, the Zoo Annex, and all the other North Vietnamese prisons where American servicemen had endured as much as eight and a half years under sometimes brutal conditions. Two days earlier, in Paris, U.S. and North Vietnamese representatives had signed a peace agreement freeing the POWs. Now was a time for rejoicing.

At the Hanoi Hilton, however, there were no shouts of joy, no backslapping among the Americans as the hated commandant, nicknamed Weasel by the prisoners, impassively informed them that they were to be released. Many simply were numb and gaunt, having lost a third of their weight on the meager diet ordered by the North Vietnamese commandant.

Some had broken legs and arms that had not been set. Others did not want to be used in a propaganda event, fearing that communist cameras might be recording their emotions. Not a few remembered the hundreds of other Americans for whom there would be no homecoming, having died in captivity from lack of medical attention, starvation, and the brutality of the camps.

'Ten good men died in my arms, and I'm damned mad about that,' said Army Major Floyd Kushner, a physician who was a prisoner initially held in South Vietnam. 'It was all the result of maltreatment in South Vietnam. Our mortality rate in South Vietnam (among POWs) was 45 percent. I guess there was a parallel with Japanese treatment during World War II....'

In order to extract propaganda statements from Colonel Robinson Risner of Oklahoma City, North Vietnamese jailers attached 60-pound bars to his ankles and trussed him with ropes. As the iron bars pressed for hours against his ankles, the pain slowly rose until it reached an excruciating level. Risner agreed to make the statement. 'I made one more tape,' said the 48-year-old Risner. 'I wrote what they told me to write after a torture session. If I was told to say the war was wrong, I said the war was wrong....The pain became too severe. I myself have screamed all night. I have heard as many as four people holler at one time....'

Navy Lieutenant Commander John McCain II, 36, shot down and captured in October 1967, said the North Vietnamese both saved his life and tortured him after they learned his father was an admiral who would command the United States forces in the Pacific. 'My leg was broken, and I had other injuries when I was shot down,' he said. 'After four days with no medical treatment whatever...I realized I was dying...the Bug (the North Vietnamese jailer) came in and brought a doctor. I asked, "Are you going to take me to the hospital?" and they said, "Too late, too late." '

The Bug returned a short time later and told McCain, 'Your father is a big admiral.' McCain

was then sent to the hospital, where he was treated. 'In mid-1968, a man in charge of all the camps tried to get me to accept release,' McCain said. 'I didn't know at the time that it coincided with my father's appointment as commander in the Pacific. When I refused to take release ahead of Commander Everett Alvarez and the others who had been there longer, the treatment became very bad.' McCain's leg was re-broken, one arm was broken, his teeth were smashed, and other injuries were inflicted in torture sessions....

Navy Captain Jeremiah Denton, Jr., 48, of Virginia Beach, Virginia, said that beginning in October 1965, the North Vietnamese tried by torture and isolation to steamroller all of the POWs into tools of anti-Americanism and antiwar propaganda....

Of the more than seven and a half years Denton was held captive, four were spent in solitary confinement. As with many of the other prisoners, he found the isolation and loneliness as difficult to handle as any of the physical torture.

'A man does a lot of thinking during seven years, seven months in enemy prisons,' he said. 'Mental exercise...helped the mind escape the confines of tiny cells. But even more than thinking, a man does a lot of praying in an enemy prison. Prayer, even more than sheer thought, is the firmest anchor to windward.'

Many of the prisoners turned to prayer, even those who had strayed from the church over the years. Although the Weasel only allowed captives to use the Bible on special religious holidays, they managed to make it an integral part of their lives. Major Norman McDaniel of Greensboro, North Carolina, and other prisoners memorized as much of the book as possible during religious holidays, then wrote down what they remembered when they were allowed pencil and paper.

America rejoiced when the POWs returned home, beginning in February. Navy Commander Brian Woods of San Diego, California, and Air Force Major Glendon Perkins of Orlando, Florida, the first two of the returning prisoners, stepped onto their native soil in San Diego with a salute. 'This homecoming is not only for myself and Glendon Perkins, but for all the POWs,' Woods said. 'We are grateful and overwhelmed.'"

෴෴෴෴෴෴෴෴

"Length of Schoolboy's Hair Sharply Divides Community," Fort Myers News-Press, November 23, 1975

"Saguache, Colorado—Le Seaman studies his fifth-grade lessons at home because he can't go to school with his hair touching his collar. But if he decides to fight, the issue may go to court on grounds he is a victim of sexual discrimination.

Le began his first year at Mountain Valley Elementary School in September. Three weeks ago, the Saguache School Board suspended him for violating the school's dress code. The action has sharply divided this community in the San Luis Valley of central Colorado.

Even the five-member School Board, which met Friday night with its attorney, is at odds on the issue. Board member Patricia Hills said the vote to suspend 10-year-old Le was four to one, 'but I don't know where we stand right now.'

'You wonder what kind of people, what kind of sense...where's their common sense regarding education, making a hassle for this child?' said Norman Aaronson, an attorney for Colorado Rural Legal Services, which represents Le. 'It would be different if he was a high-school senior and a troublemaker, but he's a good student. His teacher wants him back; she told me yesterday that the kids keep asking, 'When's Le coming back?'"

"Critical Area Study of Charlotte Harbor Delayed," Fort Myers News-Press, October 22, 1975

"A lack of state staffing will delay study of the long-sought state critical area designation for the Charlotte Harbor Complex, state officials said Saturday in Fort Myers.

The Environmental Confederation of Southwest Florida struggled to organize its priorities and reasons for the protective state mandate, now in effect in Key West, the Green Swamp, and Big Cypress, but Eastern Tin, of the Division of State Planning, said more work is necessary.

The environmental group, composed of conservationists from about 40 organizations in five counties nominated a coastal stretch from Mantasota Key in Sarasota County to Wiggins Pass in Collier County last year. The proposal would include all barrier islands off the Lee County coast, but firm boundaries would not be drawn until after a nomination is accepted."

కావ్యావ్యావ్యావ్య

"Down and Out in America...,"
by members of the American Studies Program, SUNY at Buffalo,
***The New York Times Magazine*, February 9, 1975**

"I didn't realize it was this bad..." "Poor people are people that you didn't know..." "The government don't give a damn..." "Just a vicious circle of nothing..." "I had seven different jobs...every plant closed...that's it..." "And this country thinks it's so damn great..." The voices of those of the unemployed in Buffalo, NY. With the national unemployment rate at 7.1 percent, this city on Lake Erie epitomizes the special problems of the country's industrial urban areas. Buffalo's official unemployment in December was 10.3 percent, third-highest in the East.

Even 10.3 percent fails to suggest the full measure of unemployment. The official figure does not include many who, for bureaucratic reasons, are not counted in the eligible workforce. Nor does it include the great number of underemployed who work full-time but need another job to rise above the poverty level.

Further, the official figure is for the entire Standard Metropolitan Statistical Area—in Buffalo's case, a huge two-county tract that includes suburban, ex-urban and even rural areas. The overall figure thus hides the true rate of the heavily populated central city, with its many working class neighborhoods, including those of blacks, whose unemployment rate is double that of whites.

When these dimensions are added, one begins to see the extent of the problem. According to some government statistics, in the urban areas most heavily affected, actual unemployment and underemployment may total well over 60 percent of the labor force, broadly defined. Such a figure is probably closer to Buffalo's reality than the official 10.3 percent.

Buffalo's past prosperity stemmed from transportation advantages—the lake, the Erie Canal, the railroads—and the heavy industry they generated, especially grain milling, steel and automobiles. In recent years, however, these locational advantages have more or less evaporated, and many companies have moved. Buffalo's business leaders have sought to shift the city's base away from factories, but the decline in manufacturing has left a large pool of industrial workers whose skills are unsuited to what new jobs can be generated. *Reprinted with permission.*

కావ్యావ్యావ్యావ్య

"Paper Restoring: A Scary Business,"
***The New York Times*, May 3, 1975**

When Margo Feiden is scared, she shares her fears with her clients. As she talks, "somehow things come together," and, as in the fairytales, everything turns out happily in the end.

Well, you may ask, just what does Margo Feiden do that inspires such foreboding? Now that you've asked, here's the answer. She's a paper restorer and preserver, a profession not usually thought of as scary, probably because it's a profession not usually thought of it all.

The scary part of her work comes when it's necessary to reduce paper almost to its liquid state, and although the work isn't always suspenseful, it is frequently strange.

"Would you believe it is easier to fix something that's ripped than something that has been creased?" Miss Feiden asked somewhat rhetorically.

Miss Feiden, who is also Mrs. Stanley R. Goldmark, began her unusual work almost by accident. She was an art collector and art dealer (and still is), and noticed that, although age was being blamed for stains and discoloration, Rembrandt etchings were often in better condition than modern works.

"I began noticing that more drawing and etchings were stained when they were covered by a mat and framed, than those that remained unframed, and the theory that age was accountable for damage just didn't make sense to me," she said.

After reading everything available on the subject, experimenting and finally making her own paper in a bathtub, Feiden reached the conclusion that a hefty percentage of artwork requiring restoration had been damaged by improper framing. Now, with almost 12 years of experience behind her, her conclusions have solidified.

"Mats made of cardboard contain acids that attack paper," she said. "And some adhesives for holding mats or pictures in place promote the growth of damaging molds and fungi."

Feiden, who has done work for the graphics department of Sotheby Parke Bernet and a number of well-known collectors, restores documents, marriage licenses, works of art and books. She just finished working on a document (a receipt for their pay) signed by five of the men who signed the Declaration of Independence.

ᢂᢀᢂᢀᢂᢀᢂᢀᢂ

"Computer Feeds Crop of Chickens,"
Clovis News Journal (New Mexico), March 23, 1975

How would you like to prepare breakfast, lunch and dinner for a million plus egg-laying hens every day?

No big deal, right? All you have to do is take one ton of corn and blend in one ton of millet; add a combined ton of soybeans and meat by-products for body; stir well; and season to taste with a variety of vitamins and minerals. Blend well and pour into the troughs.

Wrong. Today preparing chicken feed requires all the nutritional expertise which goes into feeding an astronaut in space or a professional athlete in training.

"The nutritional value of eggs is a direct result of the hens' diet—the quality of the blends they receive," said John Prohoroff Jr., general manager of Prohoroff Poultry Farms, Santa Marcos, California.

Prohoroff Farms produces an average of one million marketable eggs a day on a 600-acre site north of San Diego.

To make sure the hens are receiving the most nutritious diet possible, two IBM computers were installed at the farm a year ago. An IBM 1130 computing system helps determine recipes used in blending feed for the firm's 1.2 million White Leghorn hens.

Another computer, an IBM System-7, controls the actual feed mixing operation to make sure the amounts of ingredients used correspond to the formulas prescribed by the first computer.

Prohoroff blends his own seed mixes and changes them frequently. Formulas are recalculated as often as six times a week for each flock of 70,000 hens.

The best diet for each flock varies constantly. As weather changes and the hens grow, their dietary needs change, Prohoroff explained.

കൈൾകൈൾകൈൾകൈ

"Housing for the Aged in Suburbia: Even the Affluent Find It Hard to Keep Up," by Wendy Schuman, *The New York Times*, April 18, 1976

"In Freeport, Long Island, an 80-year-old homeowner puts off insulating his freezing bathroom. 'I have to eat, I have to pay my taxes and oil bills,' he said. There is just no money left over for improvements, however necessary.

In White Plains, a widow of 68 sleeps on a fold-out sofa in her son's den. Living with five grandchildren is difficult, she says. 'I'm always in the way.' But with a $260-a-month income from Social Security, she simply cannot afford to move out.

Once a prosperous Manhattan couple with two boats and a weekend apartment on Long Island, Edward Futterer and his wife now live in a project for the low-income elderly in Islip. 'Our retirement money just went,' said Mr. Futterer, 78. 'I suppose we didn't expect to live so long.' There are 1,200 people on the waiting list for the 180 apartments in Mr. Futterer's project.

Many elderly residents of New York's suburbs—whatever their income level while they were working—have become poorer since retirement. A large number who live on fixed incomes, usually Social Security and pension payments, can barely make ends meet. Some have seen their savings depleted by high inflation. In the affluent suburbs of Long Island, Westchester and parts of Connecticut, old people frequently pay from half to three quarters of their income just for housing.

Indeed, no aspect of life in the suburbs is more difficult for the elderly than housing. Even those in higher income brackets are becoming more and more watchful of their savings. At Heritage Hills, a newly built adult community in Somers, New York, salesmen record more condominium buyers taking mortgages and using their capital for investment.

Both the Heritage group and another major builder of retirement communities, Leisure Technology, report that while condominium prices get higher, the age of purchasers is getting younger. At the new Heritage development, the minimum age requirement is 40, compared to 50 at the older Heritage Village in Southbury, Connecticut. Prices run about $8,000 higher at the newer project.

Among moderate and low-income senior citizens, the choices are more basic. 'We used to say that the elderly could only afford the essential trilogy—rent, food and clothing,' said John Nolon, executive director of Housing Action Council, which studies subsidized housing needs in Westchester. 'Now it seems that anything beyond rent is a luxury.'

Mr. Nolon ran a check of applicants for a new housing project in Peekskill and found that few had more than $1,000 a year left after paying for housing. In Westchester, there are 100,500 persons over 65, and 15 percent of them have incomes below the federal poverty level of $2,364.

The situation is not much better in Nassau County, where there are 128,000 persons over 65. In 1970, approximately 13 percent of them had below-poverty incomes. Fifteen years ago, there were only 80,000 elderly in the county. 'We're faced with a growing population that's getting poorer as it gets older,' said Adelaide Attard, executive director of the Nassau County Department of Senior Citizen Affairs. 'Since 80 percent of them still live in their own homes, they have the usual homeowners' problems, but are less able to cope than young working people.'

Those who opt to remain in their long-time homes complain most bitterly of property taxes. 'That's all they want to talk about at every meeting,' sighed Henry Doliner, president of Senior Forum, an organization of Nassau County senior citizen centers. 'More than Medicaid, it's property taxes.'

Currently, in New York State, elderly persons with annual incomes under $6,500 may be granted real-estate tax exemptions of up to 50 percent. But some are unaware of their eligibility. 'And what if you make $6,501?' noted Abe Seldin, chairman of the Nassau County Board of Assessors. 'I've seen cases where property taxes alone were 40 percent of the gross income.'

'It's a vicious cycle,' said Joseph Tortelli, director of the Westchester Office for the Aging. 'Apartments are so expensive that old people can't afford them. In their homes they can cut back on maintenance to cut costs. But the homes deteriorate and young people don't have the chance to move in.'

'We have a housing imbalance here,' agreed Mr. Nolon of Housing Action Council. 'Old people occupy large space because of high rents. Yet much of our housing stock is overcrowded.'

His agency surveyed thousands of one-bedroom rentals in Westchester and found that most cost between $200 and $300 a month, more than the average Social Security recipient collects each month.

Those who work with the elderly stress the need for many more units of publicly subsidized housing at low and moderate rents. Thousands of units have already been built in New York suburbs under a variety of government programs, but waiting lists of more than three years are common. Affluent suburban towns have not been quick to approve multi-family low-income dwellings, even for aged residents.

In Rockville Centre, a volunteer committee worked for five years to obtain a low-income project of 50 units that will finally open next month. More than 300 old people had applied for the apartments, which were funded under the federal 'Turnkey' program. One third were over the income level for eligibility, according to the committee's chairman, Ruth Ferman, but could not afford private rentals.

'They shouldn't have to uproot themselves in old age and move out of town,' Mrs. Ferman said. With an organization of social service and religious groups, she is exploring a plan for building moderately priced units under Section 8 of the 1974 federal Housing and Community Development Act.

Under Section 8, an elderly person may be eligible for a rent subsidy in existing apartments—if both his income and the apartment rent fall below prescribed levels for his region. Legislators are discussing various other programs of rent subsidy and tax abatement for landlords of elderly tenants.

Meanwhile, Mr. Nolon said, he was hoping for quick action by communities on allowing the sharing of large private homes. 'Old people do not have all the time in the world,' he observed." *Reprinted with permission.*

"It's 1986 and Every Student Has a Calculator,"
by George Immerzeel, *Instructor,* April 1976

(Pretend) The year is 1986. I have been using calculators in my classroom for some time now. I have had a few difficulties, but as I look back on my experiences, it has been fun and certainly worthwhile. All of my students are prepared for today's world because everyone in 1986 is using a calculator. Let me share some of these experiences with you.

Years ago I started with one calculator in the fifth- and sixth-grade math learning center. The students liked to play with the machine and soon learned to add, subtract, multiply and divide on it without help from me. Once in a while I took a few minutes to have the students share what they were learning using the calculator. When one of the students asked me how to find the square root of two, I knew it was time to use the machine in my teaching. I found if I gave the class a calculator problem-of-the-week, I stimulated a great deal of interest.

The students themselves began to bring in their own problems. One student asked how high the 17 billion hamburgers sold by a hamburger chain would be if they were piled on top of one another. Still another asked how many steers were required to provide the hamburgers. The students really took an interest in developing their own problems, and each problem had a way of leading to others.

I soon found that having one student at the calculator was an asset during our class discussions. That "machine student" could easily generate many examples when we wanted to learn to multiply by 10 or 100. The students soon learned that they could multiply by a power of 10 and it was easier to do without the calculator....

When I was correcting papers I found that using the calculator provided a handy answer key. It also helped me when students gave me fractional answers that were not in the lowest terms. The calculator made it easier for me to analyze student mistakes. I could quickly generate partial products for multiplication and compare them with the student computation. The calculator was also very useful to me when I was making up new worksheets for student activities with the calculator.

It must have been right after Christmas of 1975 when many students started bringing their own calculators to class. We found lots of new ways to use them. It was about then, too, that the PTA became interested in our "real" mathematics and bought us six more calculators, so we had one for each team of four students. These were a big help in extending our classroom activities.

❧❧❧❧❧❧❧❧

"Stanley Cup Well Running Dry for Flyers," by Paul Giordano,
Bucks County Courier Times (Pennsylvania), May 14, 1976

PHILADELPHIA—The Philadelphia Flyers had everything going for them last night, but the final score.

First off, the Montréal Canadiens were 0-5-1 at the Spectrum in their last six games.

Secondly, the Flyers, since the start of the 1974 playoffs, had won 22 of 24 playoff games at the Spectrum.

And last but by no means least, since she couldn't be there in person, Kate Smith's "God bless America" was played as her smiling picture, arm raised in salute, appeared on two gigantic projection screens hung from the rafters at each end of the ice.

The final score read: Montréal 3, Philadelphia 2. And the Canadiens were three up in the best-of-seven Stanley Cup finals.

It all started at 3:17 of the first period when Montréal's Steve Shutt curled what looked like a knuckleball by Wayne Stephenson from 70 feet out. The puck just hung in mid-air and then dropped in the net. A power play goal.

"Right at the end of the shot," Stephenson said, "it dropped. It hit the back of my glove and went in."

The Flyers, however, came on strong with a pair of goals by Reggie Leach, who had been shut out in the first two games. Leach scored on a power goal at 8:14 of the first, whipped the puck through goalie Dan Dryden's legs to give the Flyers a 2-1 lead as the first period ended.

"I'm the first one," Leach said. "He (Dryden) had his left side covered. He gave me about six inches of the net to shoot at and I kept it low."

The second?

"He (Bill Nyrop, Montréal defenseman) was trying to take a pass that wasn't too good. I took it from him and put it between Dryden's legs."

But it wasn't enough.

Gary Dornhoefer drew a two-minute penalty for elbowing with one second to play in the first period. Then, at 1:09 of the second, Shutt scored his second power play goal of the night and the game was knotted at 2-all.

It remained deadlocked until 9:16 into the third period when Pierre Bouchard tallied on a 50-footer.

"It either hit (Rick Chartraw, who was in the slot) who was screening," Stephenson said, "or something. It jumped to the right and changed direction."

"Just a routine shot," Fred Shero said. "We've scored a lot like that, too. Some may say the first and third Montréal goals were luck, but luck wasn't a factor. They just outplayed us."

"Inflation Still Potent, '78 Slump Inevitable," by James L. Green, Professor of Economics, University of Georgia, 1977

"Inflation-rising prices and surging costs—remains potent in today's uneasy business climate. Consumer prices moved up 0.8 percent in January, 1 percent in February, 0.6 percent in March, 0.8 percent in April, and 0.6 percent in May (an annual rate of 9.1 percent since the first of the year).

Since 1967, the consumer price index has risen an outrageous 80.7 percent. Your income gains are, as a result, almost worthless. For example, since May of last year, average weekly earnings have increased $13.97. But in terms of standard dollars, the real gain in purchasing power is only $0.69. More than half the price of inflation of the past 10 years has occurred since January 1, 1974, during a period of deep recession, high unemployment, and faltering economic recovery. Certainly, this reflects the new stagflation twist in economic affairs.

The Commerce Department reports that both personal income and consumer prices rose 0.6 percent in May. This would seem to leave consumers neither better nor worse off. Not so. The Commerce Department also advises that local units of government raised taxes some

12.1 percent on income, retail sales, and motor vehicles. Real estate taxes in 1976 were up 9.8 percent.

In fact, real discretionary incomes are lower.

As higher money incomes push us into higher marginal brackets of the tax schedule we pay more federal income taxes. Also, Social Security taxes are taking a larger bite, leaving us with less real discretionary income to spend as we choose as individuals.

Actually, one dollar in four flowing into federal coffers comes from Social Security contributions. In May, our spendable discretionary income was down 0.4 percent from a year earlier. This doesn't augur well for a sustained recovery."

"Does Atlanta Want Good Theater?" by Barbara Thomas, *The Atlanta Journal and Constitution*, July 17, 1977

"Atlantans who wring their hands and moan about the state of the arts here seem to have a terminal case of 'Why can't we be like New York?' If it can be done in a fashion not sounding like a Chamber of Commerce hype, I'd like to suggest that maybe many Atlantans don't want to be like Gotham, culturally or otherwise, and that if comparing ourselves to that urban center is our cultural yardstick, it's little wonder we're off the mark....

While Atlanta is constantly criticized for lack of good theater, good restaurants, and whatever has the populace irritated that week, the city does have a different set of 'plusses' that many urban areas do not have. The city is filled, either fortunately or unfortunately, depending on one's stance on a side of the fence, by leisure time activities that no other urban cultural center can claim.

Explains one native New Yorker transplanted to Atlanta, 'It's hard to imagine any excitement over the arts here at all, when 10 minutes away you have pools and tennis courts that are free, where you don't have to wait in line or pay $10 an hour to play on them. To expect Atlanta to have the same cultural dynamics as a city of glass and steel is like having your cake and eating it, too.'"

Editorial, "Economy and Energy," *The Atlanta Journal and Constitution*, July 18, 1977

"The headlines told good economic news. ' Building Boom to Hit 19 Percent,' said one; 'July Car Sales up 15 Percent,' said the other.

But is that good energy news?

The McGraw-Hill Information Systems Co. has reported that revenues in the U.S. construction industry will surge 19 percent over last year's total of $127.5 billion, with housing starts expected to total 1.75 million units in 1977. 'We expect a high plateau of housing activity for the remainder of 1977, and 1978 as well,' said a McGraw spokesman.

As for the automobiles, the four major U.S. auto makers reported combined new domestic car sales rose 15 percent during the first 10 days of July, compared with the same period in 1976. For the calendar year to date, new auto sales were up seven percent from a year ago.

There's no arguing that the new reports are good for the nation's economy and consumers. For now, at least. The boosts in housing starts and auto sales mean increased jobs and better payrolls, higher standards of living, reduced unemployment. The housing and auto industries are economic bellwethers, and when they are doing well, it indicates the rest of the economy is in fine health, also.

But—and this has become the important economic issue of all in the United States—how energy-efficient are these new cars being sold and new houses being built?

The energy crisis hasn't magically gone away. It's still with us and it's going to get worse. Our economy is rapidly moving into a new era—an era of energy shortage rather than energy abundance.

Historically, the U.S. economy has boomed, and Americans live the richest lives of any people of the world, in major part because of our energy abundance. But already, the growing shortages and higher prices and energy are forcing changes in our lifestyles, and much more drastic changes are ahead.

Surely today's new cars and new houses are more energy-efficient than they were just a couple of years ago, and further improvements are planned. But the improvements are coming too slowly; there's still too much emphasis on luxury rather than efficient use of energy. Meanwhile, Congress is too scared to take the strong action needed. While we mindlessly burn up energy, Congress fiddles."

International Rescue Committee, Hong Kong, Annual Report for 1977

The patterns for operations during 1976 of the International Rescue Committee in Hong Kong continued in 1977. Our immigration assistance caseload remained at about the same level, although we assisted over three times as many refugees from Vietnam as in the previous year. Relatively few came to be housed in our hostel or for financial assistance. Of the refugees who are getting into Hong Kong from China, many had relatives or friends who took them in and assisted them so that they did not need agency assistance. The plight of Chinese refugees in Hong Kong was made easier by a generally healthy economy which created a steady demand for unskilled labor....

The numbers of Vietnamese refugees getting to Hong Kong by boat increased from 191 in 1976 to 1,001 in 1977. IRC became further involved with assisting these refugees with their immigration to other countries, primarily to the United States, and also equipped with warm clothing some of those going to cold climates....

RESETTLEMENT ABROAD
IRC in Hong Kong helps refugees apply for immigration to the United States. Normally, refugees are assisted in applying under the seventh—or special refugee—preference of the Immigration and Nationality Act, which provides for "conditional entry" to the United States. After two years in this status, the refugee can become a permanent resident alien. If the refugee meets the requirements for immigration under the regular provisions of the Immigration and Nationality Act, rather than under the seventh preference, he is usually urged to apply this way, as he will thus become a permanent resident on arrival in the United States. An Indochina Parole Program was established before the end of the year, under which special numbers were allocated to Indochina refugees to permit them to enter the United States outside the regular visa process....

Our seventh preference caseload of 1,728 was slightly below our figures in 1976, possibly because we were devoting more time to Vietnamese refugees than before. We assisted 196 cases (342 persons) from Vietnam, of which 146 cases (265 persons) were boat people. We also helped about 50 percent more cases than in 1976 with applications for immigrant visas.

VIETNAMESE REFUGEES

During the year the pattern of Vietnamese refugees being picked up in the South China Sea and brought to Hong Kong in ships began to change as the refugees learned that they could make it all the way in their own boats, particularly if they departed from Danang, which is about the closest point. The numbers who started out and did not make it is unknown, but some observers believe that only about half survive. Many of the boats which successfully got to Hong Kong have not been very seaworthy and that they made it at all has been a miracle.

During the first three months of the year, no Vietnamese refugees got to Hong Kong by sea. After that there was an undulating flow, with no arrivals in November....

On arrival, immigration authorities sought a guarantee from the regional representative in Kuala Lumpur of the United Nations High Commissioner for Refugees (UNHCR) that he would care for the refugees and seek countries of ultimate asylum. With this assurance, the refugees were landed. ICEM [Inter-Governmental Committee for European Migration] then found hotel space for the refugees, interviewed them, and assigned them to one of four voluntary agencies who prepared immigration applications for them. In the case of those going to the United States, which was the destination for most of them, the applications were sent by the local agencies to corresponding agencies in New York to seek sponsorships. IRC accepted responsibility for resettlement of over half of the Vietnamese refugees who got to Hong Kong during 1977. After the application had been processed by the American Consulate General and INS [Immigration and Naturalization Service], and the refugees had been approved for immigration, ICEM arranged transportation. Where travel loans were required, which was so in most cases, the voluntary agencies prepared the loan documents. Refugees from Hong Kong were also accepted by France and Australia. A few were permitted to remain in Hong Kong.

IRC was able to purchase warm clothing for some of the refugees going to cold climates. Funds for these purchases were transmitted by the Hong Kong Christian Council from a fund sent by the Norwegian Churches. We also assisted a family to whom a baby was born in Hong Kong with money donated by the Ladies' Guild of St. Joseph's Church.

"CBS Inventor Recalled First Color Telecast,"
Naples Daily News, December 8, 1977

"Boy, they were good pictures," Dr. Peter C. Goldmark said, referring to photographs of the Jones Beach beauties he beamed from New York for man's first successful color telecast in 1940.

The pictures were taken at the Long Island resort and were transmitted from New York City's Chrysler Building.

Goldmark, 71, whose color television process began on Earth and soared to the moon, was killed in a Harrison, New York, automobile accident Wednesday. His many inventions did not bring him great wealth, however.

He was a "working man, a salaried employee," Leo Murray, a spokesman, said of Goldmark, a retired president of Columbia Broadcasting System Laboratories in Stamford, and vice president of CBS.

Almost as soon as the pictures of the girls were transmitted in 1940, the Radio Corporation of America locked legal horns with Goldmark's firm, CBS Laboratories, over the technological form of color.

RCA's chairman David Sarnoff rejected Goldmark's system, which was called the "field sequential system."

Sarnoff advocated an all-electric compatible system under which both black-and-white and color could be transmitted simultaneously. Such a system was adopted and is the one now in general use.

RCA in 1971 obtained the prestigious assignment of providing the National Aeronautics and Space Administration (NASA) with the camera to record the 12-day moon mission for Apollo 15.

But the only method that could have been used to relay the RCA pictures, due to the moon's low light levels, was Goldmark's, the same one RCA fought all the way to the Supreme Court in the 1960s.

The Hungarian-born Goldmark was asked how it felt to have his old corporate adversary use his system in its moon pictures.

"I watch television using their system, so they can use mine on the moon. It's a fair exchange. I think it was an engineering decision, really. I don't think the engineers gave the old fight any thought, "he said.

めゐめゐめゐめゐ

"Intrepid Joins Bich Team as French Hone for 1980," Newport Daily News, August 17, 1978

The note scribbled on the silver tape around France I's winch drum said in bold, black letters—"Ficker isn't quick as Bich."

Little did the crews on France I or Intrepid know how true it was. Baron Marcel Bich glanced at the wording as he climbed on board the 12-meter Sunday, laughed a little and that was that. Not a word.

Four hours later Bich was instructing the sailboat's tender, Nanny, to fetch Intrepid. "I suggest you pick up the Intrepid, which is approximately 1/2 hour behind France," Bich said in his decidedly French accent. The tickle in his voice was hard to disguise.

Bill Ficker, who etched his mark in America's Cup fame at the helm of Intrepid in 1970, was at the wheel again. But this time around, it was not a Cup summer, it was not a Cup race, the crew was not wearing Cup foul weather gear and their dreams were not silver lined. However can you explain the French beating the Americans? Un grand faux pas?

Baron Bich, the Bic pen and lighter entrepreneur, has returned to Newport this summer for four weeks of intensive crew and technical training. It is a means to an end. That end, of course, is winning the America's Cup in 1980.

All the stops have been pulled out of the French 12-meter hole. Bich failed in 1970 and 1974 with France I. He built a new France II for the 1977 skirmish, but ended up losing the challenge after substituting France I at the last minute.

He has another 12-meter on the drawing table for 1980—to be made this time out of aluminum instead of his traditional wood designs.

Bich usually sails his fleet of 12-meters, which now includes Intrepid, in Hyeres, along the southern coast of France. But his dream of winning the next America's Cup has closed the door on summers at home. Bich apparently has decided that the key to winning is practice on the other team's field.

"It's our only chance," Bruno Bich, the second-oldest Bich son, said this week. "The Americans fight so hard among themselves. For us, training here gives us the best chance to get used to the waters.

"This summer, we are enjoying ourselves sailing with Americans, but it is also giving us the chance to sail against another boat."

France I and Intrepid are towed out from the Newport Offshore Ltd. dock together each morning, but there the parallel ends. Intrepid is manned by Americans, many of whom are veterans of past America's Cup races. Lowell North, skipper of Enterprise during most of the last Cup defense competition, has taken a turn this summer at the helm of Intrepid. So has Gerry Driscoll, skipper of Intrepid in 1974 and scores of other veterans....

Bruno Bich described the daily races, divided into two 14-day sessions, as instructive for everyone. The plan is to give the French and Americans a chance to redefine 12-meter sailing in a non-Cup summer. "We have no intention of having any Americans sailing with us in the 1980s," he said. "In fact, I can tell you, we're planning not to do it."

Ficker looks at it as a learning session, too. "It's a chance to keep your hands in it," he said after Intrepid's epic loss to Bich Sunday. "It's a lot of fun to race hard for two weeks. The 12-meter world is very tight—the people in it are awfully well trained.

"It's also an opportunity for us to look at the fellows who might help us out in our 12-meter program. It gives us a chance to try different things."

"Nepal Is Nepal, New York Is 'Fat City,'"
by David Jarmul, *The New York Times*, June 9, 1979

"People wrote to me before I recently returned home to New York, after two years in the Peace Corps, about all the changes I'd find: disco, roller skating, a new mayor, a decent Rangers team.

But nobody warned me about what's remained the same: how rich and wasteful this city is.

New York's being rich sounds strange, I know. After all, the city was staving off bankruptcy when I left in 1977. And I hear similar sacrificial moans from New Yorkers now about gas prices and inflation.

But today, those cries ring hollow. After I've lived so long in a truly poor country, New York seems like Fat City. People here don't realize how lucky they have it.

My post was in Nepal. My first year was spent in a Himalayan hill bazaar, Ilam, the second in Katmandu, the capital. I taught English and writing, worked with blind students, set up several newspapers and organized a village literacy project.

The Peace Corps paid me $76 monthly, $92 in Katmandu. This was plenty. The per capita income in Nepal is less than $100 a year. Given the skewed distribution of wealth, many Nepalese live on less than $0.15 daily. Most children work. The literacy rate is below 20 percent.

One of my students in Ilam was Mardi Kumar, an untouchable. One week he didn't come to school. I went to his house to see why not. His father told me that Mardi's older brother was dying in the local hospital.

The doctor said Mardi's brother needed insulin. There was none to be had in eastern Nepal. The father pleaded with me. I was a foreigner; didn't I have some insulin? No, I didn't. A few days later his son died.

In Katmandu, I hired a cook, Harka Bahadur. I taught him to read Nepalese and gave him room, board and $1.75 weekly. The neighbors complained this was too much and would drive up local prices. I insisted. Harka supported his mother, wife and baby daughter on his salary. He had no money for eggs, fruit or medicines. In the winter I had to convince him to take a sweater I'd been given for the holidays.

Now I'm home. My first full day back, my folks took me to see the new shopping atrium at the Citicorp headquarters. I saw imported jams at $10 per bottle, exotic pastries, shiny furniture stores, a giant delicatessen, several chic cafes.

The following morning I had an argument with my father about Mother's Day. My father wanted me to buy my mother an azalea bush. As much as I love her, I couldn't bring myself to spend the money. My mother doesn't need an azalea bush, I told him. 'So why waste money that others need just to survive?'

My father told me that I was culture-shocked. I ought to stop converting New York prices into what they could buy abroad. Nepal was Nepal. This was New York, why take it out on my Mother....

The point is that right now I don't want to get back into a consumptive American life. I don't want to jump on the bottled water bandwagon when I can just as easily drink water out of the faucet like I did before I left and give the $0.70 per bottle to somebody who really needs it.

But, as I've learned quickly, to say these things out loud, even with the excuse of being just out of the Peace Corps, makes one come across like an Asianized Jeremiah. Friends ask me, quite rightly, just what it is that I expect them to do. Give up all of life's small luxuries until there are no more poor people? My instinctive reaction right now is to say yes.

That's idealistic and unworkable, I know, but I remember too vividly my Nepalese friends: Rudra Bahadur, the farmer across the street who thanked me profusely when I gave him my worn-out rugby shirt. Ram Prasad, a fellow teacher who almost burst into tears when I gave him the $7.00 calculator that I'd bought in Times Square. The brahmin village family—I don't even know their names—who shared with me their dinner of rice, lentils and dried yams when I appeared on their doorstep one evening while hiking.

Intellectually, I recognize that if a friend here spends $20 extra on a pair of blue jeans just to sport a designer label, it isn't going to make any difference in the lives of my Nepalese friends. Not unless the friend chooses to send the $20 to Nepal and just take a pair of Levi's.

But I can't choose for others. And I also know that I must fight off this moralism. I know there are many poor New Yorkers, poor Americans. Our country can't take upon itself all of the world's suffering. We shouldn't all go through life guilt-ridden. After all, that's Nepal; this is New York.

Still, as I face my new life ahead, I keep wondering: am I really as culture-shocked as people tell me, or is American society as profligate as it now seems to me? Will I be able to hold onto my new convictions about living modestly and helping others? Will I remember?" *Reprinted with permission.*

෯෩෯෩෯෩෯෩෯෩

"New Oxford's Powers Keeps Getting Better,"
by Jim Loose, *The Gettysburg Times*, February 1, 1979

For someone in her first year of playing basketball, Elecia Powers isn't having a bad season. In fact, the New Oxford center is having the kind of season that many experienced players envy.

Powers, a junior, is averaging 8.6 points per game and more than 12 rebounds per game. Within the Blue Mountain League, however, she has scored 119 points for an average 11.9 points per game. She has scored in double figures in eight of her last nine starts. Just the other day against Biglerville the 5-11 Powers scored 21 points and pulled down 18 rebounds. That was coming off a game against Littlestown in which she grabbed 19 rebounds.

"Yes, I was really surprised," said Powers when asked about her statistics. "I knew I could jump but I didn't know I could get all the rebounds. As far as the points, I wasn't really expecting as many as I have got this year."

Although Powers has played basketball since she was little, she has never competed on a cage team before this season. Her prior team competition was in volleyball, which she readily admits is her favorite sport.

"I was so used to playing volleyball I had to get everything together for basketball," she said. "It wasn't really hard. I just had to get adjusted to it."

One person who is glad she has made the adjustment is new Oxford coach Jeff Topper. Topper was more than pleased to have someone standing 5-11 around for the team, although he wasn't sure what to expect when Powers struggled through the first several games.

"I started to worry," Topper said. "It was kind of a letdown. But she started working at it hard and has now been a real pleasant surprise. She's helped us through this good streak we've been having (six straight wins)...."

One of Powers's biggest contributions this season, according to Topper, has been to take some of the pressure off the team's leading scorer, Theresa "Peep" Kuhn.

"Probably directly I would say rebounds [have been her greatest asset]," Topper said. "But her ability to score on some follow-up shots has helped. We weren't getting them early in the year; that was hard on Peep. With her [Powers] in there being big, it takes the pressure off the other inside people."

ॐ॰ॐ॰ॐ॰ॐ॰ॐ॰ॐ॰ॐ

"Rodgers Could Taste Third Boston Marathon Victory,"
Aiken Standard (South Carolina), April 17, 1979

BOSTON—Hometown boy Bill Rodgers, superstar marathoner with the fiery will to win, has renewed his claim to the elusive title as the world's top runner of the grueling road race.

"I could taste the third win," the 31-year-old former schoolteacher said Monday after wearing down Japan's Toshihiko Seko to set an American record in winning the 83rd Boston Marathon. "I don't want someone to take it away."

The five foot nine, 128-pounder from Melrose, Massachusetts, ran away from Seko on the famed "Heartbreak Hill" to win his third Boston event in two hours, nine minutes and 27 seconds. It broke the U.S. record he set in 1975.

The victory Monday, by 45 seconds over Seko, was a near breeze down the home stretch through cold rain. Rodgers won the 1978 race in 2:10:13 by only two seconds over Jeff Wells of Dallas in the closest 26-mile, 385-yard event on record.

Seko, 23-year-old college student in Japan, and the winner of the Fukuoka International Marathon in his homeland last December, ran with Rodgers for 20 miles before his legs went numb on the third of a brutal series of hills in Newton, Massachusetts.

Rodgers, who has won the Fukuoka race along with back-to-back victories in New York City's young but prestigious marathon, was beaten by Seko last December.

On the run from rustic Hopkinton to Boston, Rodgers said athletes tend to get overconfident, explaining, "You have to restrain yourself. Then you have to make your move at the right time."

For the victorious Connecticut native, now operator for a running store located along the Boston Marathon route, that charge came as Seko was struggling uphill.

Rodgers blasted 15 yards ahead in the big incline and widened his lead. Police escort motorcycles had to move quickly to stay ahead of the hard driving champion, whose goal is to win an Olympic gold medal at the Moscow Olympics.

SECTION FIVE: CENSUS DATA

This section begins with eighteen state-by-state ranking tables from the 1970, 1980, and 2010 Census, designed to help define the times during which the families profiled in Section One lived. Table topics are listed below. Following the state-by-state tables are reprints from the 1980 Census. This data is portrayed by maps, tables, graphs, charts and narrative, helping to visualize the environment at that time.

State-by-State Comparative Tables: 1970, 1980 and 2010

Note: When reviewing the ranking columns, be aware that the District of Columbia is included in the list of states.

Twentieth Decennial Census of the United States

1980 Census of Population

Volume 1: Characteristics of the Population

Part 1: United States Summary

Total Population

Area	Population			1970		1980		2010	
	1970	1980	2010	Area	Rank	Area	Rank	Area	Rank
Alabama	3,444,165	3,893,888	4,779,736	California	1	California	1	California	1
Alaska	300,382	401,851	710,231	New York	2	New York	2	Texas	2
Arizona	1,770,900	2,718,215	6,392,017	Pennsylvania	3	Texas	3	New York	3
Arkansas	1,923,295	2,286,435	2,915,918	Texas	4	Pennsylvania	4	Florida	4
California	19,953,134	23,667,902	37,253,956	Illinois	5	Illinois	5	Illinois	5
Colorado	2,207,259	2,889,964	5,029,196	Ohio	6	Ohio	6	Pennsylvania	6
Connecticut	3,031,709	3,107,576	3,574,097	Michigan	7	Florida	7	Ohio	7
Delaware	548,104	594,338	897,934	New Jersey	8	Michigan	8	Michigan	8
D.C.	756,510	638,333	601,723	Florida	9	New Jersey	9	Georgia	9
Florida	6,789,443	9,746,324	18,801,310	Massachusetts	10	North Carolina	10	North Carolina	10
Georgia	4,589,575	5,463,105	9,687,653	Indiana	11	Massachusetts	11	New Jersey	11
Hawaii	768,561	964,691	1,360,301	North Carolina	12	Indiana	12	Virginia	12
Idaho	712,567	943,935	1,567,582	Missouri	13	Georgia	13	Washington	13
Illinois	11,113,976	11,426,518	12,830,632	Virginia	14	Virginia	14	Massachusetts	14
Indiana	5,193,669	5,490,224	6,483,802	Georgia	15	Missouri	15	Indiana	15
Iowa	2,824,376	2,913,808	3,046,355	Wisconsin	16	Wisconsin	16	Arizona	16
Kansas	2,246,578	2,363,679	2,853,118	Tennessee	17	Tennessee	17	Tennessee	17
Kentucky	3,218,706	3,660,777	4,339,367	Maryland	18	Maryland	18	Missouri	18
Louisiana	3,641,306	4,205,900	4,533,372	Minnesota	19	Louisiana	19	Maryland	19
Maine	992,048	1,124,660	1,328,361	Louisiana	20	Washington	20	Wisconsin	20
Maryland	3,922,399	4,216,975	5,773,552	Alabama	21	Minnesota	21	Minnesota	21
Massachusetts	5,689,170	5,737,037	6,547,629	Washington	22	Alabama	22	Colorado	22
Michigan	8,875,083	9,262,078	9,883,640	Kentucky	23	Kentucky	23	Alabama	23
Minnesota	3,804,971	4,075,970	5,303,925	Connecticut	24	South Carolina	24	South Carolina	24
Mississippi	2,216,912	2,520,638	2,967,297	Iowa	25	Connecticut	25	Louisiana	25
Missouri	4,676,501	4,916,686	5,988,927	South Carolina	26	Oklahoma	26	Kentucky	26
Montana	694,409	786,690	989,415	Oklahoma	27	Iowa	27	Oregon	27
Nebraska	1,483,493	1,569,825	1,826,341	Kansas	28	Colorado	28	Oklahoma	28
Nevada	488,738	800,493	2,700,551	Mississippi	29	Arizona	29	Connecticut	29
New Hampshire	737,681	920,610	1,316,470	Colorado	30	Oregon	30	Iowa	30
New Jersey	7,168,164	7,364,823	8,791,894	Oregon	31	Mississippi	31	Mississippi	31
New Mexico	1,016,000	1,302,894	2,059,179	Arkansas	32	Kansas	32	Arkansas	32
New York	18,236,967	17,558,072	19,378,102	Arizona	33	Arkansas	33	Kansas	33
North Carolina	5,082,059	5,881,766	9,535,483	West Virginia	34	West Virginia	34	Utah	34
North Dakota	617,761	652,717	672,591	Nebraska	35	Nebraska	35	Nevada	35
Ohio	10,652,017	10,797,630	11,536,504	Utah	36	Utah	36	New Mexico	36
Oklahoma	2,559,229	3,025,290	3,751,351	New Mexico	37	New Mexico	37	West Virginia	37
Oregon	2,091,385	2,633,105	3,831,074	Maine	38	Maine	38	Nebraska	38
Pennsylvania	11,793,909	11,863,895	12,702,379	Rhode Island	39	Hawaii	39	Idaho	39
Rhode Island	946,725	947,154	1,052,567	Hawaii	40	Rhode Island	40	Hawaii	40
South Carolina	2,590,516	3,121,820	4,625,364	D.C.	41	Idaho	41	Maine	41
South Dakota	665,507	690,768	814,180	New Hampshire	42	New Hampshire	42	New Hampshire	42
Tennessee	3,923,687	4,591,120	6,346,105	Idaho	43	Nevada	43	Rhode Island	43
Texas	11,196,730	14,229,191	25,145,561	Montana	44	Montana	44	Montana	44
Utah	1,059,273	1,461,037	2,763,885	South Dakota	45	South Dakota	45	Delaware	45
Vermont	444,330	511,456	625,741	North Dakota	46	North Dakota	46	South Dakota	46
Virginia	4,648,494	5,346,818	8,001,024	Delaware	47	D.C.	47	Alaska	47
Washington	3,409,169	4,132,156	6,724,540	Nevada	48	Delaware	48	North Dakota	48
West Virginia	1,744,237	1,949,644	1,852,994	Vermont	49	Vermont	49	Vermont	49
Wisconsin	4,417,731	4,705,767	5,686,986	Wyoming	50	Wyoming	50	D.C.	50
Wyoming	332,416	469,557	563,626	Alaska	51	Alaska	51	Wyoming	51
United States	203,211,926	226,545,805	308,745,538	United States	–	United States	–	United States	–

Source: U.S. Census Bureau, 1970 Census of Population; U.S. Census Bureau, 1980 Census of Population; U.S. Census Bureau, Census 2010

White Population

Area	Percent of Population			1970		1980		2010	
	1970	1980	2010	Area	Rank	Area	Rank	Area	Rank
Alabama	73.5	73.7	68.5	Vermont	1	Vermont	1	Vermont	1
Alaska	78.8	77.0	66.6	New Hampshire	2	New Hampshire	2	Maine	2
Arizona	90.6	82.4	73.0	Maine	3	Maine	3	West Virginia	3
Arkansas	81.4	82.6	77.0	Iowa	4	Iowa	4	New Hampshire	4
California	89.0	76.1	57.5	Minnesota	5	Minnesota	5	Iowa	5
Colorado	95.7	88.9	81.3	Idaho	6	West Virginia	6	Wyoming	6
Connecticut	93.5	90.0	77.5	Utah	7	North Dakota	7	North Dakota	7
Delaware	85.1	82.0	68.8	Wyoming	8	Idaho	8	Montana	8
D.C.	27.6	26.9	38.4	Oregon	9	Wyoming	9	Idaho	9
Florida	84.2	83.9	75.0	North Dakota	10	Nebraska	10	Kentucky	10
Georgia	73.8	72.2	59.7	Rhode Island	11	Rhode Island	11	Wisconsin	11
Hawaii	38.7	33.0	24.7	Nebraska	12	Utah	12	Nebraska	12
Idaho	98.0	95.5	89.0	Wisconsin	13	Oregon	13	Utah	13
Illinois	86.3	80.8	71.5	Massachusetts	14	Wisconsin	14	South Dakota	14
Indiana	92.8	91.1	84.3	West Virginia	15	Montana	15	Minnesota	15
Iowa	98.5	97.4	91.3	Colorado	16	Massachusetts	16	Indiana	16
Kansas	94.4	91.7	83.8	Montana	17	South Dakota	17	Kansas	17
Kentucky	92.6	92.3	87.7	Washington	18	Kentucky	18	Oregon	18
Louisiana	69.8	69.2	62.5	South Dakota	19	Kansas	19	Missouri	19
Maine	99.3	98.6	95.2	Kansas	20	Washington	20	Ohio	20
Maryland	81.4	74.9	58.1	Connecticut	21	Indiana	21	Pennsylvania	21
Massachusetts	96.2	93.4	80.4	Indiana	22	Connecticut	22	Rhode Island	22
Michigan	88.2	84.9	78.9	Kentucky	23	Pennsylvania	23	Colorado	23
Minnesota	98.1	96.5	85.3	Nevada	24	Colorado	24	Massachusetts	24
Mississippi	62.8	64.0	59.1	Pennsylvania	25	Ohio	25	Michigan	25
Missouri	89.3	88.3	82.8	Arizona	26	Missouri	26	Connecticut	26
Montana	95.4	94.0	89.4	Ohio	27	Nevada	27	Tennessee	27
Nebraska	96.5	94.9	86.1	New Mexico	28	Oklahoma	28	Washington	28
Nevada	91.7	87.4	66.1	Missouri	29	Michigan	29	Arkansas	29
New Hampshire	99.3	98.8	93.8	Oklahoma	30	Florida	30	Florida	30
New Jersey	88.5	83.2	68.5	California	31	Tennessee	31	Arizona	31
New Mexico	90.1	75.0	68.3	New Jersey	32	New Jersey	32	Oklahoma	32
New York	86.8	79.5	65.7	Michigan	33	Arkansas	33	Illinois	33
North Carolina	76.7	75.7	68.4	New York	34	Arizona	34	Texas	34
North Dakota	97.0	95.8	90.0	Texas	35	Delaware	35	Delaware	35
Ohio	90.5	88.8	82.6	Illinois	36	Illinois	36	New Jersey	36
Oklahoma	89.1	85.8	72.1	Delaware	37	New York	37	Virginia	36
Oregon	97.1	94.5	83.6	Florida	38	Virginia	38	Alabama	38
Pennsylvania	91.0	89.7	81.9	Tennessee	39	Texas	39	North Carolina	39
Rhode Island	96.6	94.6	81.4	Maryland	40	Alaska	40	New Mexico	40
South Carolina	69.2	68.7	66.1	Arkansas	41	California	41	Alaska	41
South Dakota	94.7	92.6	85.9	Virginia	42	North Carolina	42	Nevada	42
Tennessee	83.9	83.5	77.5	Alaska	43	New Mexico	43	South Carolina	42
Texas	86.7	78.7	70.4	North Carolina	44	Maryland	44	New York	44
Utah	97.4	94.6	86.0	Georgia	45	Alabama	45	Louisiana	45
Vermont	99.6	99.0	95.2	Alabama	46	Georgia	46	Georgia	46
Virginia	80.9	79.1	68.5	Louisiana	47	Louisiana	47	Mississippi	47
Washington	95.3	91.4	77.2	South Carolina	48	South Carolina	48	Maryland	48
West Virginia	95.9	96.1	93.9	Mississippi	49	Mississippi	49	California	49
Wisconsin	96.4	94.4	86.2	Hawaii	50	Hawaii	50	D.C.	50
Wyoming	97.1	95.0	90.7	D.C.	51	D.C.	51	Hawaii	51
United States	87.4	83.2	72.4	United States	–	United States	–	United States	–

Source: U.S. Census Bureau, 1970 Census of Population; U.S. Census Bureau, 1980 Census of Population; U.S. Census Bureau, Census 2010

Black Population

Area	Percent of Population 1970	Percent of Population 1980	Percent of Population 2010	1970 Area	1970 Rank	1980 Area	1980 Rank	2010 Area	2010 Rank
Alabama	26.2	25.5	26.1	D.C.	1	D.C.	1	D.C.	1
Alaska	2.9	3.4	3.2	Mississippi	2	Mississippi	2	Mississippi	2
Arizona	3.0	2.7	4.0	South Carolina	3	South Carolina	3	Louisiana	3
Arkansas	18.3	16.3	15.4	Louisiana	4	Louisiana	4	Georgia	4
California	7.0	7.6	6.1	Alabama	5	Georgia	5	Maryland	5
Colorado	3.0	3.5	4.0	Georgia	6	Alabama	6	South Carolina	6
Connecticut	5.9	7.0	10.1	North Carolina	7	Maryland	7	Alabama	7
Delaware	14.2	16.1	21.3	Virginia	8	North Carolina	8	North Carolina	8
D.C.	71.0	70.3	50.7	Arkansas	9	Virginia	9	Delaware	9
Florida	15.3	13.7	15.9	Maryland	10	Arkansas	10	Virginia	10
Georgia	25.8	26.8	30.4	Tennessee	11	Delaware	11	Tennessee	11
Hawaii	0.9	1.8	1.5	Florida	12	Tennessee	12	Florida	12
Idaho	0.3	0.2	0.6	Delaware	13	Illinois	13	New York	13
Illinois	12.8	14.6	14.5	Illinois	14	Florida	14	Arkansas	14
Indiana	6.8	7.5	9.1	Texas	15	New York	15	Illinois	15
Iowa	1.1	1.4	2.9	New York	16	Michigan	16	Michigan	16
Kansas	4.7	5.3	5.8	Michigan	17	New Jersey	17	New Jersey	17
Kentucky	7.1	7.0	7.7	New Jersey	18	Texas	18	Ohio	18
Louisiana	29.8	29.4	32.0	Missouri	19	Missouri	19	Texas	19
Maine	0.2	0.2	1.1	Ohio	20	Ohio	20	Missouri	20
Maryland	17.8	22.7	29.4	Pennsylvania	21	Pennsylvania	21	Pennsylvania	21
Massachusetts	3.0	3.8	6.6	Kentucky	22	California	22	Connecticut	22
Michigan	11.1	12.9	14.1	California	23	Indiana	23	Indiana	23
Minnesota	0.9	1.3	5.1	Indiana	24	Kentucky	24	Nevada	24
Mississippi	36.8	35.2	37.0	Oklahoma	25	Connecticut	25	Kentucky	25
Missouri	10.2	10.4	11.5	Connecticut	26	Oklahoma	26	Oklahoma	26
Montana	0.2	0.2	0.4	Nevada	27	Nevada	27	Massachusetts	27
Nebraska	2.6	3.0	4.5	Kansas	28	Kansas	28	Wisconsin	28
Nevada	5.6	6.3	8.1	West Virginia	29	Wisconsin	29	California	29
New Hampshire	0.3	0.4	1.1	Massachusetts	30	Massachusetts	30	Kansas	30
New Jersey	10.7	12.5	13.7	Arizona	31	Colorado	31	Rhode Island	31
New Mexico	1.9	1.8	2.0	Colorado	31	Alaska	32	Minnesota	32
New York	11.8	13.6	15.8	Alaska	33	West Virginia	33	Nebraska	33
North Carolina	22.1	22.4	21.4	Wisconsin	34	Nebraska	34	Arizona	34
North Dakota	0.4	0.3	1.1	Nebraska	35	Rhode Island	35	Colorado	35
Ohio	9.1	9.9	12.2	Rhode Island	36	Arizona	36	Washington	36
Oklahoma	6.7	6.7	7.4	Washington	37	Washington	37	West Virginia	37
Oregon	1.2	1.4	1.8	New Mexico	38	New Mexico	38	Alaska	38
Pennsylvania	8.6	8.8	10.8	Oregon	39	Hawaii	39	Iowa	39
Rhode Island	2.6	2.9	5.7	Iowa	40	Iowa	40	New Mexico	40
South Carolina	30.4	30.3	27.9	Hawaii	41	Oregon	41	Oregon	41
South Dakota	0.2	0.3	1.2	Minnesota	42	Minnesota	42	Hawaii	42
Tennessee	15.8	15.8	16.6	Wyoming	43	Wyoming	43	South Dakota	43
Texas	12.4	12.0	11.8	Utah	44	Utah	44	Maine	44
Utah	0.6	0.6	1.0	North Dakota	45	New Hampshire	45	North Dakota	44
Vermont	0.1	0.2	1.0	New Hampshire	46	North Dakota	46	New Hampshire	46
Virginia	18.5	18.8	19.3	Idaho	47	South Dakota	47	Utah	47
Washington	2.0	2.5	3.5	Montana	48	Idaho	48	Vermont	48
West Virginia	3.8	3.3	3.4	Maine	49	Maine	49	Wyoming	49
Wisconsin	2.9	3.8	6.3	South Dakota	50	Montana	50	Idaho	50
Wyoming	0.7	0.7	0.8	Vermont	51	Vermont	51	Montana	51
United States	11.1	11.7	12.6	United States	–	United States	–	United States	–

Source: U.S. Census Bureau, 1970 Census of Population; U.S. Census Bureau, 1980 Census of Population; U.S. Census Bureau, Census 2010

American Indian/Alaska Native Population

Area	Percent of Population			1970		1980		2010	
	1970	1980	2010	Area	Rank	Area	Rank	Area	Rank
Alabama	0.0	0.1	0.5	New Mexico	1	Alaska	1	Alaska	1
Alaska	5.4	15.9	14.7	Alaska	2	New Mexico	2	New Mexico	2
Arizona	5.4	5.6	4.6	Arizona	3	South Dakota	3	South Dakota	3
Arkansas	0.1	0.4	0.7	South Dakota	4	Arizona	4	Oklahoma	4
California	0.4	0.8	0.9	Montana	5	Oklahoma	5	Montana	5
Colorado	0.4	0.6	1.1	Oklahoma	6	Montana	6	North Dakota	6
Connecticut	0.0	0.1	0.3	North Dakota	7	North Dakota	7	Arizona	7
Delaware	0.1	0.2	0.4	Nevada	8	Nevada	8	Wyoming	8
D.C.	0.1	0.1	0.3	Wyoming	9	Wyoming	9	Washington	9
Florida	0.1	0.2	0.3	Utah	10	Washington	10	Oregon	10
Georgia	0.0	0.1	0.3	Washington	11	Utah	11	Idaho	11
Hawaii	0.1	0.2	0.3	Idaho	12	Idaho	12	North Carolina	12
Idaho	0.9	1.1	1.3	North Carolina	13	North Carolina	13	Nevada	13
Illinois	0.1	0.1	0.3	Oregon	14	Oregon	14	Utah	13
Indiana	0.0	0.1	0.2	Minnesota	15	Minnesota	15	Minnesota	15
Iowa	0.1	0.1	0.3	California	16	California	16	Colorado	16
Kansas	0.3	0.6	0.9	Nebraska	17	Kansas	17	Nebraska	17
Kentucky	0.0	0.1	0.2	Wisconsin	18	Colorado	18	Kansas	18
Louisiana	0.1	0.2	0.6	Colorado	19	Wisconsin	18	California	19
Maine	0.2	0.3	0.6	Kansas	20	Nebraska	20	Wisconsin	20
Maryland	0.1	0.1	0.3	Maine	21	Michigan	21	Arkansas	21
Massachusetts	0.0	0.1	0.2	Michigan	22	Arkansas	22	Texas	22
Michigan	0.1	0.4	0.6	Mississippi	22	Maine	23	Louisiana	23
Minnesota	0.6	0.8	1.1	Texas	24	Rhode Island	24	Maine	24
Mississippi	0.1	0.2	0.5	New York	24	Hawaii	25	Michigan	25
Missouri	0.1	0.2	0.4	Hawaii	26	Louisiana	25	Alabama	26
Montana	3.9	4.7	6.3	Louisiana	26	Texas	27	Rhode Island	27
Nebraska	0.4	0.5	1.0	Rhode Island	26	Missouri	28	New York	28
Nevada	1.6	1.6	1.1	D.C.	29	Mississippi	28	Mississippi	29
New Hampshire	0.0	0.1	0.2	Delaware	30	New York	30	Delaware	30
New Jersey	0.0	0.1	0.3	Missouri	30	Delaware	31	Missouri	31
New Mexico	7.1	8.1	9.3	Maryland	32	Florida	32	South Carolina	32
New York	0.1	0.2	0.5	Iowa	32	Maryland	33	Florida	33
North Carolina	0.8	1.1	1.2	Florida	34	Iowa	33	Virginia	34
North Dakota	2.3	3.0	5.4	Illinois	34	Alabama	33	Iowa	35
Ohio	0.0	0.1	0.2	Virginia	34	Vermont	33	D.C.	36
Oklahoma	3.8	5.6	8.5	Arkansas	34	Virginia	37	Maryland	36
Oregon	0.6	1.0	1.3	South Carolina	38	South Carolina	37	Vermont	36
Pennsylvania	0.0	0.0	0.2	Massachusetts	39	D.C.	39	Illinois	39
Rhode Island	0.1	0.3	0.5	Connecticut	40	Connecticut	40	Georgia	40
South Carolina	0.0	0.1	0.4	New Jersey	40	New Hampshire	40	New Jersey	40
South Dakota	4.8	6.5	8.8	Indiana	40	Illinois	42	Tennessee	42
Tennessee	0.0	0.1	0.3	Alabama	40	Indiana	42	Connecticut	43
Texas	0.1	0.2	0.6	Ohio	44	Georgia	42	Hawaii	43
Utah	1.0	1.3	1.1	Tennessee	44	Massachusetts	45	Massachusetts	45
Vermont	0.0	0.1	0.3	Georgia	46	New Jersey	46	Indiana	46
Virginia	0.1	0.1	0.3	Vermont	46	Ohio	46	New Hampshire	47
Washington	0.9	1.4	1.5	Pennsylvania	46	Tennessee	46	Kentucky	48
West Virginia	0.0	0.0	0.2	New Hampshire	46	Kentucky	49	Ohio	49
Wisconsin	0.4	0.6	0.9	Kentucky	46	Pennsylvania	50	Pennsylvania	50
Wyoming	1.5	1.5	2.3	West Virginia	51	West Virginia	50	West Virginia	51
United States	0.3	0.6	0.9	United States	–	United States	–	United States	–

Source: U.S. Census Bureau, 1970 Census of Population; U.S. Census Bureau, 1980 Census of Population; U.S. Census Bureau, Census 2010

Asian Population

Area	Percent of Population			1970		1980		2010	
	1970	1980	2010	Area	Rank	Area	Rank	Area	Rank
Alabama	0.0	0.2	1.1	Hawaii	1	Hawaii	1	Hawaii	1
Alaska	0.8	2.0	5.3	California	2	California	2	California	2
Arizona	0.4	0.8	2.7	Washington	3	Washington	3	New Jersey	3
Arkansas	0.0	0.2	1.2	Alaska	4	Alaska	4	New York	4
California	2.6	5.3	13.0	D.C.	5	New York	5	Nevada	5
Colorado	0.4	1.0	2.7	New York	6	Nevada	5	Washington	6
Connecticut	0.2	0.6	3.7	Oregon	6	Maryland	7	Maryland	7
Delaware	0.2	0.6	3.1	Utah	8	New Jersey	8	Virginia	8
D.C.	0.6	1.0	3.5	Nevada	9	Illinois	9	Alaska	9
Florida	0.1	0.5	2.4	Colorado	10	Oregon	10	Massachusetts	10
Georgia	0.1	0.4	3.2	Arizona	11	Virginia	11	Illinois	11
Hawaii	47.2	60.4	38.6	Idaho	11	Colorado	12	Minnesota	12
Idaho	0.4	0.6	1.2	Illinois	13	D.C.	12	Texas	13
Illinois	0.4	1.4	4.5	Maryland	14	Utah	14	Connecticut	14
Indiana	0.1	0.3	1.5	Massachusetts	15	Massachusetts	15	Oregon	15
Iowa	0.0	0.4	1.7	Rhode Island	15	Texas	16	D.C.	16
Kansas	0.1	0.6	2.3	Virginia	17	Arizona	17	Georgia	17
Kentucky	0.0	0.2	1.1	Wyoming	18	Delaware	18	Delaware	18
Louisiana	0.1	0.5	1.5	New Jersey	18	Minnesota	19	Rhode Island	19
Maine	0.1	0.2	1.0	Delaware	20	Kansas	20	Arizona	20
Maryland	0.3	1.5	5.5	Connecticut	21	Idaho	21	Colorado	20
Massachusetts	0.3	0.8	5.3	New Mexico	22	Connecticut	22	Pennsylvania	22
Michigan	0.1	0.6	2.4	Florida	23	Michigan	22	Florida	23
Minnesota	0.1	0.6	4.0	Michigan	24	Florida	24	Michigan	24
Mississippi	0.1	0.2	0.8	Minnesota	24	Louisiana	25	Kansas	25
Missouri	0.1	0.4	1.6	Texas	26	Oklahoma	25	Wisconsin	26
Montana	0.1	0.3	0.6	Kansas	26	Rhode Island	27	North Carolina	27
Nebraska	0.1	0.4	1.7	Montana	26	Pennsylvania	28	New Hampshire	28
Nevada	0.5	1.7	7.2	Nebraska	29	New Mexico	29	Utah	29
New Hampshire	0.1	0.3	2.1	Wisconsin	29	Missouri	30	Nebraska	30
New Jersey	0.2	1.4	8.2	Missouri	29	Nebraska	31	Iowa	31
New Mexico	0.1	0.5	1.3	Pennsylvania	32	Georgia	31	Oklahoma	32
New York	0.6	1.7	7.3	Ohio	33	Ohio	33	Ohio	33
North Carolina	0.0	0.3	2.1	New Hampshire	33	Wyoming	34	Missouri	34
North Dakota	0.1	0.3	1.0	Oklahoma	35	Iowa	35	Indiana	35
Ohio	0.1	0.4	1.6	Indiana	36	Wisconsin	36	Louisiana	36
Oklahoma	0.1	0.5	1.7	Mississippi	36	South Carolina	37	Tennessee	37
Oregon	0.6	1.3	3.6	Louisiana	38	Indiana	38	New Mexico	38
Pennsylvania	0.1	0.5	2.7	Georgia	38	North Carolina	39	South Carolina	39
Rhode Island	0.3	0.5	2.8	South Carolina	38	Montana	40	Vermont	40
South Carolina	0.1	0.3	1.2	Maine	38	New Hampshire	40	Arkansas	41
South Dakota	0.0	0.2	0.9	North Dakota	38	Tennessee	42	Idaho	42
Tennessee	0.0	0.3	1.4	Iowa	43	North Dakota	42	Kentucky	43
Texas	0.1	0.8	3.8	Tennessee	43	Mississippi	44	Alabama	44
Utah	0.6	1.0	2.0	Vermont	45	Arkansas	44	North Dakota	45
Vermont	0.0	0.2	1.2	Arkansas	45	Kentucky	46	Maine	46
Virginia	0.3	1.2	5.5	North Carolina	45	West Virginia	46	South Dakota	47
Washington	1.2	2.4	7.1	West Virginia	45	Vermont	48	Mississippi	48
West Virginia	0.0	0.2	0.6	South Dakota	49	Maine	48	Wyoming	49
Wisconsin	0.1	0.3	2.2	Alabama	49	Alabama	50	West Virginia	50
Wyoming	0.2	0.4	0.7	Kentucky	49	South Dakota	50	Montana	51
United States	0.6	1.5	4.7	United States	–	United States	–	United States	–

Source: U.S. Census Bureau, 1970 Census of Population; U.S. Census Bureau, 1980 Census of Population; U.S. Census Bureau, Census 2010

271

Hispanic Population

Area	Percent of Population			1970		1980		2010	
	1970	1980	2010	Area	Rank	Area	Rank	Area	Rank
Alabama	0.3	0.8	3.8	New Mexico	1	New Mexico	1	New Mexico	1
Alaska	1.4	2.2	5.5	Arizona	2	Texas	2	California	2
Arizona	18.8	16.3	29.6	Texas	3	California	3	Texas	2
Arkansas	0.4	0.7	6.3	California	4	Arizona	4	Arizona	4
California	15.5	19.1	37.6	Colorado	5	Colorado	5	Nevada	5
Colorado	12.9	11.8	20.6	Florida	6	New York	6	Florida	6
Connecticut	2.4	4.0	13.4	Wyoming	7	Florida	7	Colorado	7
Delaware	1.1	1.6	8.1	Nevada	8	Hawaii	8	New Jersey	8
D.C.	2.0	2.7	9.1	New York	9	Nevada	9	New York	9
Florida	6.6	8.8	22.4	Utah	10	New Jersey	10	Illinois	10
Georgia	0.6	1.1	8.8	Illinois	11	Illinois	11	Connecticut	11
Hawaii	3.0	7.4	8.8	Hawaii	12	Wyoming	12	Utah	12
Idaho	2.5	3.8	11.2	Idaho	13	Utah	13	Rhode Island	13
Illinois	3.2	5.5	15.8	Connecticut	14	Connecticut	14	Oregon	14
Indiana	1.2	1.5	6.0	Kansas	15	Idaho	15	Washington	15
Iowa	0.6	0.9	4.9	Washington	16	Washington	16	Idaho	16
Kansas	2.0	2.6	10.5	D.C.	17	D.C.	17	Kansas	17
Kentucky	0.3	0.7	3.0	New Jersey	18	Kansas	18	Massachusetts	18
Louisiana	1.3	2.3	4.2	Oregon	19	Oregon	19	Nebraska	19
Maine	0.3	0.4	1.2	Nebraska	20	Massachusetts	20	D.C.	20
Maryland	1.3	1.5	8.1	Alaska	20	Louisiana	21	Wyoming	21
Massachusetts	1.1	2.4	9.5	Michigan	22	Alaska	22	Hawaii	22
Michigan	1.3	1.7	4.4	Louisiana	22	Rhode Island	23	Oklahoma	23
Minnesota	0.6	0.7	4.7	Maryland	24	Oklahoma	24	Georgia	24
Mississippi	0.3	0.9	2.7	Oklahoma	25	Nebraska	25	North Carolina	25
Missouri	0.8	1.0	3.5	Indiana	26	Michigan	26	Delaware	26
Montana	1.1	1.2	2.8	Massachusetts	27	Delaware	27	Maryland	26
Nebraska	1.4	1.8	9.1	Delaware	27	Indiana	28	Virginia	28
Nevada	5.5	6.7	26.5	Montana	29	Maryland	29	Arkansas	29
New Hampshire	0.3	0.5	2.7	Virginia	30	Virginia	30	Indiana	30
New Jersey	1.8	6.7	17.6	Wisconsin	31	Wisconsin	31	Wisconsin	31
New Mexico	40.0	36.6	46.3	Ohio	32	Pennsylvania	32	Pennsylvania	32
New York	4.7	9.4	17.6	Missouri	33	Montana	33	Alaska	33
North Carolina	0.4	0.9	8.3	Rhode Island	34	Georgia	34	South Carolina	34
North Dakota	0.3	0.5	2.0	Georgia	35	Ohio	35	Iowa	35
Ohio	0.8	1.1	3.0	Iowa	36	South Carolina	36	Minnesota	36
Oklahoma	1.3	1.9	8.8	Minnesota	37	Missouri	37	Tennessee	37
Oregon	1.6	2.5	11.7	Vermont	38	Mississippi	38	Michigan	38
Pennsylvania	0.3	1.2	5.6	Arkansas	39	North Carolina	39	Louisiana	39
Rhode Island	0.7	2.0	12.4	South Dakota	40	Iowa	40	Alabama	40
South Carolina	0.4	1.0	5.1	North Carolina	40	Alabama	41	Missouri	41
South Dakota	0.4	0.5	2.7	South Carolina	42	Minnesota	42	Ohio	42
Tennessee	0.3	0.7	4.5	Alabama	43	Arkansas	43	Kentucky	43
Texas	18.3	20.9	37.6	Pennsylvania	44	Tennessee	43	Montana	44
Utah	4.1	4.1	12.9	Maine	44	Kentucky	43	New Hampshire	45
Vermont	0.5	0.6	1.4	Mississippi	46	West Virginia	46	Mississippi	46
Virginia	1.0	1.4	7.9	West Virginia	47	Vermont	47	South Dakota	47
Washington	2.0	2.9	11.2	New Hampshire	47	New Hampshire	48	North Dakota	48
West Virginia	0.3	0.6	1.2	Tennessee	49	South Dakota	49	Vermont	49
Wisconsin	0.9	1.3	5.9	Kentucky	49	North Dakota	50	Maine	50
Wyoming	5.5	5.2	8.9	North Dakota	51	Maine	51	West Virginia	51
United States	4.5	6.4	16.3	United States	–	United States	–	United States	–

Source: U.S. Census Bureau, 1970 Census of Population; U.S. Census Bureau, 1980 Census of Population; U.S. Census Bureau, Census 2010

Foreign-Born Population

Area	Percent of Population			1970		1980		2010	
	1970	1980	2010	Area	Rank	Area	Rank	Area	Rank
Alabama	0.5	1.0	3.4	New York	1	California	1	California	1
Alaska	2.6	4.0	7.2	Hawaii	2	Hawaii	2	New York	2
Arizona	4.3	6.0	14.2	New Jersey	3	New York	3	New Jersey	3
Arkansas	0.4	1.0	4.3	California	4	Florida	4	Nevada	4
California	8.8	15.1	27.2	Massachusetts	5	New Jersey	5	Florida	5
Colorado	2.7	3.9	9.8	Connecticut	6	Rhode Island	6	Hawaii	6
Connecticut	8.6	8.6	13.2	Florida	7	Massachusetts	7	Texas	7
Delaware	2.9	3.2	8.2	Rhode Island	8	Connecticut	8	Massachusetts	8
D.C.	4.4	6.4	13.0	Illinois	9	Illinois	9	Arizona	9
Florida	8.0	10.9	19.2	New Hampshire	10	Nevada	10	Illinois	10
Georgia	0.7	1.7	9.6	Michigan	11	D.C.	11	Connecticut	11
Hawaii	9.8	14.2	17.7	Washington	12	Texas	12	Maryland	11
Idaho	1.8	2.5	5.9	D.C.	13	Arizona	12	D.C.	13
Illinois	5.7	7.2	13.6	Arizona	14	Washington	14	Washington	14
Indiana	1.6	1.9	4.4	Maine	14	Maryland	15	Rhode Island	15
Iowa	1.4	1.6	4.1	Vermont	16	Michigan	16	Virginia	16
Kansas	1.2	2.0	6.3	Pennsylvania	17	New Hampshire	17	Colorado	17
Kentucky	0.5	0.9	3.1	Nevada	18	Oregon	18	New Mexico	18
Louisiana	1.1	2.0	3.6	Oregon	19	Vermont	18	Oregon	18
Maine	4.3	3.9	3.3	Maryland	19	New Mexico	20	Georgia	20
Maryland	3.2	4.6	13.2	Wisconsin	21	Alaska	20	Delaware	21
Massachusetts	8.7	8.7	14.5	Ohio	21	Colorado	22	Utah	21
Michigan	4.8	4.5	5.9	North Dakota	21	Maine	22	North Carolina	23
Minnesota	2.6	2.6	7.0	Delaware	24	Utah	24	Alaska	24
Mississippi	0.4	0.9	2.2	Texas	25	Pennsylvania	25	Minnesota	25
Missouri	1.4	1.7	3.7	Utah	25	Virginia	26	Kansas	26
Montana	2.8	2.3	2.0	Montana	25	Delaware	27	Idaho	27
Nebraska	1.9	2.0	5.9	Colorado	28	Ohio	28	Michigan	27
Nevada	3.7	6.7	19.3	Alaska	29	Wisconsin	29	Nebraska	27
New Hampshire	5.0	4.4	5.3	Minnesota	29	Minnesota	30	Pennsylvania	30
New Jersey	8.9	10.3	20.3	New Mexico	31	Idaho	31	New Hampshire	31
New Mexico	2.2	4.0	9.7	Wyoming	32	Montana	32	Oklahoma	32
New York	11.6	13.6	21.7	Nebraska	33	North Dakota	32	South Carolina	33
North Carolina	0.6	1.3	7.4	Idaho	34	Wyoming	34	Wisconsin	34
North Dakota	3.0	2.3	2.4	Indiana	35	Kansas	34	Indiana	35
Ohio	3.0	2.8	3.8	Virginia	35	Louisiana	34	Tennessee	35
Oklahoma	0.8	1.9	5.2	South Dakota	35	Nebraska	34	Arkansas	37
Oregon	3.2	4.1	9.7	Missouri	38	Oklahoma	38	Iowa	38
Pennsylvania	3.8	3.4	5.6	Iowa	38	Indiana	38	Vermont	39
Rhode Island	7.8	8.9	12.6	Kansas	40	Georgia	40	Ohio	40
South Carolina	0.6	1.5	4.7	Louisiana	41	Missouri	40	Missouri	41
South Dakota	1.6	1.4	2.3	West Virginia	42	Iowa	42	Louisiana	42
Tennessee	0.5	1.1	4.4	Oklahoma	43	South Carolina	43	Alabama	43
Texas	2.8	6.0	16.1	Georgia	44	South Dakota	44	Maine	44
Utah	2.8	3.5	8.2	North Carolina	45	North Carolina	45	Kentucky	45
Vermont	4.2	4.1	4.0	South Carolina	45	Tennessee	46	Wyoming	45
Virginia	1.6	3.3	10.8	Alabama	47	West Virginia	46	North Dakota	47
Washington	4.6	5.8	12.7	Tennessee	47	Alabama	48	South Dakota	48
West Virginia	1.0	1.1	1.3	Kentucky	47	Arkansas	48	Mississippi	49
Wisconsin	3.0	2.7	4.6	Arkansas	50	Mississippi	50	Montana	50
Wyoming	2.1	2.0	3.1	Mississippi	50	Kentucky	50	West Virginia	51
United States	4.7	6.2	12.7	United States	–	United States	–	United States	–

Source: U.S. Census Bureau, 1970 Census of Population; U.S. Census Bureau, 1980 Census of Population; U.S. Census Bureau, Census 2010

Urban Population

Area	Percent of Population			1970		1980		2010	
	1970	1980	2010	Area	Rank	Area	Rank	Area	Rank
Alabama	58.6	60.0	55.0	D.C.	1	D.C.	1	D.C.	1
Alaska	56.9	64.3	60.5	California	2	California	2	New Jersey	2
Arizona	79.6	83.8	86.7	New Jersey	3	New Jersey	3	California	3
Arkansas	50.0	51.6	52.0	Rhode Island	4	Rhode Island	4	Massachusetts	4
California	90.9	91.3	93.2	New York	5	Hawaii	5	Rhode Island	5
Colorado	78.5	80.6	82.0	Massachusetts	6	Nevada	6	Nevada	6
Connecticut	78.4	78.8	87.9	Illinois	7	New York	7	Hawaii	7
Delaware	72.2	70.6	80.1	Hawaii	8	Utah	8	Florida	8
D.C.	100.0	100.0	100.0	Florida	9	Florida	9	Connecticut	9
Florida	81.7	84.3	89.3	Nevada	10	Arizona	10	Illinois	10
Georgia	60.3	62.4	70.7	Utah	11	Massachusetts	10	Arizona	11
Hawaii	83.1	86.5	90.0	Texas	12	Illinois	12	Maryland	12
Idaho	54.1	54.0	63.8	Arizona	13	Colorado	13	New York	13
Illinois	83.2	83.3	87.3	Colorado	14	Maryland	14	Utah	14
Indiana	64.9	64.2	72.1	Connecticut	15	Texas	15	Colorado	15
Iowa	57.2	58.6	61.4	Maryland	16	Connecticut	16	Washington	16
Kansas	66.1	66.7	71.1	Ohio	17	Washington	17	Texas	17
Kentucky	52.3	50.9	55.9	Michigan	18	Ohio	18	Delaware	18
Louisiana	66.5	68.6	72.1	Washington	19	New Mexico	19	Ohio	19
Maine	50.8	47.5	36.6	Delaware	20	Michigan	20	Oregon	20
Maryland	76.6	80.3	86.4	Pennsylvania	21	Delaware	21	Pennsylvania	21
Massachusetts	84.6	83.8	91.1	Missouri	22	Pennsylvania	22	New Mexico	22
Michigan	74.0	70.7	72.2	New Mexico	23	Louisiana	23	Michigan	23
Minnesota	66.5	66.9	68.3	Oklahoma	24	Missouri	24	Indiana	24
Mississippi	44.5	47.3	48.7	Oregon	25	Oregon	25	Louisiana	24
Missouri	70.1	68.1	68.3	Louisiana	26	Oklahoma	26	Virginia	26
Montana	53.4	52.9	52.0	Minnesota	26	Minnesota	27	Kansas	27
Nebraska	61.5	62.9	68.4	Kansas	28	Kansas	28	Georgia	28
Nevada	80.9	85.3	90.6	Wisconsin	29	Virginia	29	Nebraska	29
New Hampshire	56.4	52.2	55.6	Indiana	30	Alaska	30	Minnesota	30
New Jersey	88.9	89.0	94.7	Virginia	31	Indiana	31	Missouri	30
New Mexico	69.8	72.1	73.7	Nebraska	32	Wisconsin	31	Wisconsin	32
New York	85.7	84.6	85.6	Wyoming	33	Nebraska	33	Oklahoma	33
North Carolina	45.5	48.0	59.1	Georgia	34	Wyoming	34	Idaho	34
North Dakota	44.3	48.8	54.0	Tennessee	35	Georgia	35	Tennessee	35
Ohio	75.3	73.3	78.9	Alabama	36	Tennessee	36	Wyoming	36
Oklahoma	68.0	67.3	65.1	Iowa	37	Alabama	37	Iowa	37
Oregon	67.1	67.9	77.9	Alaska	38	Iowa	38	South Carolina	38
Pennsylvania	71.5	69.3	76.4	New Hampshire	39	South Carolina	39	Alaska	39
Rhode Island	87.1	87.0	90.9	Idaho	40	Idaho	40	North Carolina	40
South Carolina	48.3	54.1	61.2	Montana	41	Montana	41	Kentucky	41
South Dakota	44.6	46.4	51.6	Kentucky	42	New Hampshire	42	New Hampshire	42
Tennessee	59.1	60.4	63.6	Maine	43	Arkansas	43	Alabama	43
Texas	79.7	79.6	80.7	Arkansas	44	Kentucky	44	North Carolina	44
Utah	80.4	84.4	85.4	South Carolina	45	North Dakota	45	Arkansas	45
Vermont	32.2	33.8	33.6	North Carolina	46	North Carolina	46	Montana	45
Virginia	63.2	66.0	71.4	South Dakota	47	Maine	47	South Dakota	47
Washington	73.4	73.5	81.3	Mississippi	48	Mississippi	48	Mississippi	48
West Virginia	39.1	36.2	46.4	North Dakota	49	South Dakota	49	West Virginia	49
Wisconsin	65.9	64.2	65.8	West Virginia	50	West Virginia	50	Maine	50
Wyoming	60.5	62.7	62.4	Vermont	51	Vermont	51	Vermont	51
United States	73.6	73.7	77.6	United States	–	United States	–	United States	–

Source: U.S. Census Bureau, 1970 Census of Population; U.S. Census Bureau, 1980 Census of Population; U.S. Census Bureau, Census 2010

Rural Population

Area	Percent of Population 1970	Percent of Population 1980	Percent of Population 2010	1970 Area	Rank	1980 Area	Rank	2010 Area	Rank
Alabama	41.4	40.0	45.0	Vermont	1	Vermont	1	Vermont	1
Alaska	43.1	35.7	39.5	West Virginia	2	West Virginia	2	Maine	2
Arizona	20.4	16.2	13.3	North Dakota	3	South Dakota	3	West Virginia	3
Arkansas	50.0	48.4	48.0	Mississippi	4	Mississippi	4	Mississippi	4
California	9.1	8.7	6.8	South Dakota	5	Maine	5	South Dakota	5
Colorado	21.5	19.4	18.0	North Carolina	6	North Carolina	6	Arkansas	6
Connecticut	21.6	21.2	12.1	South Carolina	7	North Dakota	7	Montana	6
Delaware	27.8	29.4	19.9	Arkansas	8	Kentucky	8	North Dakota	8
D.C.	0.0	0.0	0.0	Maine	9	Arkansas	9	Alabama	9
Florida	18.3	15.7	10.7	Kentucky	10	New Hampshire	10	New Hampshire	10
Georgia	39.7	37.6	29.3	Montana	11	Montana	11	Kentucky	11
Hawaii	16.9	13.5	10.0	Idaho	12	Idaho	12	North Carolina	12
Idaho	45.9	46.0	36.2	New Hampshire	13	South Carolina	13	Alaska	13
Illinois	16.8	16.7	12.7	Alaska	14	Iowa	14	South Carolina	14
Indiana	35.1	35.8	27.9	Iowa	15	Alabama	15	Iowa	15
Iowa	42.8	41.4	38.6	Alabama	16	Tennessee	16	Wyoming	16
Kansas	33.9	33.3	28.9	Tennessee	17	Georgia	17	Tennessee	17
Kentucky	47.7	49.1	44.1	Georgia	18	Wyoming	18	Idaho	18
Louisiana	33.5	31.4	27.9	Wyoming	19	Nebraska	19	Oklahoma	19
Maine	49.2	52.5	63.4	Nebraska	20	Indiana	20	Wisconsin	20
Maryland	23.4	19.7	13.6	Virginia	21	Wisconsin	20	Minnesota	21
Massachusetts	15.4	16.2	8.9	Indiana	22	Alaska	22	Missouri	21
Michigan	26.0	29.3	27.8	Wisconsin	23	Virginia	23	Nebraska	23
Minnesota	33.5	33.1	31.7	Kansas	24	Kansas	24	Georgia	24
Mississippi	55.5	52.7	51.3	Louisiana	25	Minnesota	25	Kansas	25
Missouri	29.9	31.9	31.7	Minnesota	25	Oklahoma	26	Virginia	26
Montana	46.6	47.1	48.0	Oregon	27	Oregon	27	Indiana	27
Nebraska	38.5	37.1	31.6	Oklahoma	28	Missouri	28	Louisiana	27
Nevada	19.1	14.7	9.4	New Mexico	29	Louisiana	29	Michigan	29
New Hampshire	43.6	47.8	44.4	Missouri	30	Pennsylvania	30	New Mexico	30
New Jersey	11.1	11.0	5.3	Pennsylvania	31	Delaware	31	Pennsylvania	31
New Mexico	30.2	27.9	26.3	Delaware	32	Michigan	32	Oregon	32
New York	14.3	15.4	14.4	Washington	33	New Mexico	33	Ohio	33
North Carolina	54.5	52.0	40.9	Michigan	34	Ohio	34	Delaware	34
North Dakota	55.7	51.2	46.0	Ohio	35	Washington	35	Texas	35
Ohio	24.7	26.7	21.1	Maryland	36	Connecticut	36	Washington	36
Oklahoma	32.0	32.7	34.9	Connecticut	37	Texas	37	Colorado	37
Oregon	32.9	32.1	22.1	Colorado	38	Maryland	38	Utah	38
Pennsylvania	28.5	30.7	23.6	Arizona	39	Colorado	39	New York	39
Rhode Island	12.9	13.0	9.1	Texas	40	Illinois	40	Maryland	40
South Carolina	51.7	45.9	38.8	Utah	41	Arizona	41	Arizona	41
South Dakota	55.4	53.6	48.4	Nevada	42	Massachusetts	41	Illinois	42
Tennessee	40.9	39.6	36.4	Florida	43	Florida	43	Connecticut	43
Texas	20.3	20.4	19.3	Hawaii	44	Utah	44	Florida	44
Utah	19.6	15.6	14.6	Illinois	45	New York	45	Hawaii	45
Vermont	67.8	66.2	66.4	Massachusetts	46	Nevada	46	Nevada	46
Virginia	36.8	34.0	28.6	New York	47	Hawaii	47	Rhode Island	47
Washington	26.6	26.5	18.7	Rhode Island	48	Rhode Island	48	Massachusetts	48
West Virginia	60.9	63.8	53.6	New Jersey	49	New Jersey	49	California	49
Wisconsin	34.1	35.8	34.2	California	50	California	50	New Jersey	50
Wyoming	39.5	37.3	37.6	D.C.	51	D.C.	51	D.C.	51
United States	26.4	26.3	22.4	United States	–	United States	–	United States	–

Source: U.S. Census Bureau, 1970 Census of Population; U.S. Census Bureau, 1980 Census of Population; U.S. Census Bureau, Census 2010

Males per 100 Females

Area	Males per 100 Females 1970	1980	2010	1970 Area	Rank	1980 Area	Rank	2010 Area	Rank
Alabama	93.3	92.5	94.3	Alaska	1	Alaska	1	Alaska	1
Alaska	119.1	112.8	108.5	Hawaii	2	Hawaii	2	Wyoming	2
Arizona	96.8	96.9	98.7	Nevada	3	Wyoming	3	North Dakota	3
Arkansas	94.1	93.5	96.5	North Dakota	4	Nevada	4	Nevada	4
California	96.8	97.2	98.8	Wyoming	5	North Dakota	5	Utah	5
Colorado	97.5	98.5	100.5	Montana	6	Idaho	6	Montana	6
Connecticut	94.2	93.1	94.8	Idaho	7	Montana	7	Colorado	7
Delaware	95.2	93.1	93.9	Washington	8	Washington	8	Idaho	8
D.C.	86.8	86.1	89.5	South Dakota	9	Colorado	9	Hawaii	9
Florida	93.2	92.2	95.6	Virginia	10	Utah	10	South Dakota	10
Georgia	94.6	93.5	95.4	Utah	11	South Dakota	11	Washington	11
Hawaii	108.1	105.2	100.3	Colorado	12	New Mexico	12	California	12
Idaho	99.7	99.7	100.4	New Mexico	13	California	12	Arizona	13
Illinois	94.2	94.0	96.2	Arizona	14	Oregon	14	Minnesota	14
Indiana	95.1	94.4	96.8	California	14	Arizona	15	Nebraska	14
Iowa	94.6	94.6	98.1	South Carolina	16	Texas	16	Wisconsin	14
Kansas	96.2	95.9	98.4	Wisconsin	17	Minnesota	17	Kansas	17
Kentucky	96.3	95.6	96.8	Kentucky	17	Virginia	18	Texas	17
Louisiana	94.7	94.2	95.9	Kansas	19	Wisconsin	18	Iowa	19
Maine	94.8	94.4	95.8	Rhode Island	19	Kansas	20	Oklahoma	20
Maryland	95.5	94.0	93.6	Michigan	21	Kentucky	21	Oregon	20
Massachusetts	91.6	90.8	93.7	Minnesota	22	Oklahoma	22	New Mexico	22
Michigan	96.1	95.2	96.3	Texas	23	Nebraska	23	New Hampshire	23
Minnesota	96.0	96.1	98.5	Oregon	23	Michigan	24	West Virginia	23
Mississippi	94.0	92.9	94.4	North Carolina	23	New Hampshire	25	Vermont	25
Missouri	93.2	92.7	96.0	New Hampshire	26	Vermont	26	Indiana	26
Montana	99.9	99.6	100.8	Vermont	27	South Carolina	27	Kentucky	26
Nebraska	95.4	95.3	98.5	Maryland	28	Iowa	28	Arkansas	28
Nevada	102.8	102.4	102.0	Nebraska	29	Indiana	29	Michigan	29
New Hampshire	95.7	95.0	97.3	Delaware	30	Maine	29	Virginia	29
New Jersey	93.7	92.2	94.8	Indiana	31	North Carolina	31	Illinois	31
New Mexico	97.2	97.2	97.7	Oklahoma	32	Louisiana	32	Missouri	32
New York	91.5	90.5	93.8	Maine	33	West Virginia	33	Louisiana	33
North Carolina	95.9	94.3	95.0	Louisiana	34	Illinois	34	Maine	34
North Dakota	101.8	101.3	102.1	Georgia	35	Maryland	34	Florida	35
Ohio	94.1	93.5	95.4	Iowa	35	Georgia	36	Georgia	36
Oklahoma	94.9	95.4	98.0	Illinois	37	Ohio	36	Ohio	36
Oregon	95.9	97.0	98.0	Connecticut	37	Arkansas	36	Pennsylvania	38
Pennsylvania	92.4	91.9	95.1	Ohio	39	Tennessee	39	Tennessee	38
Rhode Island	96.2	91.0	93.4	Arkansas	39	Connecticut	40	North Carolina	40
South Carolina	96.5	94.7	94.7	Mississippi	41	Delaware	40	Connecticut	41
South Dakota	98.4	97.3	100.1	West Virginia	42	Mississippi	42	New Jersey	41
Tennessee	93.7	93.3	95.1	New Jersey	43	Missouri	43	South Carolina	43
Texas	95.9	96.8	98.4	Tennessee	43	Alabama	44	Mississippi	44
Utah	97.6	98.4	100.9	Alabama	45	Florida	45	Alabama	45
Vermont	95.6	94.9	97.1	Florida	46	New Jersey	45	Delaware	46
Virginia	97.7	96.0	96.3	Missouri	46	Pennsylvania	47	New York	47
Washington	98.7	98.7	99.3	Pennsylvania	48	Rhode Island	48	Massachusetts	48
West Virginia	93.9	94.1	97.3	Massachusetts	49	Massachusetts	49	Maryland	49
Wisconsin	96.3	96.0	98.5	New York	50	New York	50	Rhode Island	50
Wyoming	100.7	105.0	104.1	D.C.	51	D.C.	51	D.C.	51
United States	94.8	94.5	96.7	United States	–	United States	–	United States	–

Source: U.S. Census Bureau, 1970 Census of Population; U.S. Census Bureau, 1980 Census of Population; U.S. Census Bureau, Census 2010

Median Age

Area	Years 1970	Years 1980	Years 2010	1970 Area	1970 Rank	1980 Area	1980 Rank	2010 Area	2010 Rank
Alabama	27.0	29.2	37.9	Alaska	1	Alaska	1	Alaska	1
Alaska	22.9	26.0	33.8	Hawaii	2	Hawaii	2	Wyoming	2
Arizona	26.3	29.2	35.9	Nevada	3	Wyoming	3	North Dakota	3
Arkansas	29.1	30.6	37.4	North Dakota	4	Nevada	4	Nevada	4
California	28.1	29.9	35.2	Wyoming	5	North Dakota	5	Utah	5
Colorado	26.2	28.6	36.1	Montana	6	Idaho	6	Montana	6
Connecticut	29.1	32.0	40.0	Idaho	7	Montana	7	Colorado	7
Delaware	26.8	29.7	38.8	Washington	8	Washington	8	Idaho	8
D.C.	28.4	31.0	33.8	South Dakota	9	Colorado	9	Hawaii	9
Florida	32.3	34.7	40.7	Virginia	10	Utah	10	South Dakota	10
Georgia	25.9	28.6	35.3	Utah	11	South Dakota	11	Washington	11
Hawaii	25.0	28.3	38.6	Colorado	12	New Mexico	12	California	12
Idaho	26.4	27.5	34.6	New Mexico	13	California	12	Arizona	13
Illinois	28.6	29.9	36.6	Arizona	14	Oregon	14	Minnesota	14
Indiana	27.2	29.2	37.0	California	14	Arizona	15	Nebraska	14
Iowa	28.8	30.0	38.1	South Carolina	16	Texas	16	Wisconsin	14
Kansas	28.7	30.1	36.0	Wisconsin	17	Minnesota	17	Kansas	17
Kentucky	27.5	29.1	38.1	Kentucky	17	Virginia	18	Texas	17
Louisiana	24.8	27.3	35.8	Kansas	19	Wisconsin	18	Iowa	19
Maine	28.6	30.4	42.7	Rhode Island	19	Kansas	20	Oklahoma	20
Maryland	27.1	30.3	38.0	Michigan	21	Kentucky	21	Oregon	20
Massachusetts	29.0	31.1	39.1	Minnesota	22	Oklahoma	22	New Mexico	22
Michigan	26.3	28.8	38.9	Texas	23	Nebraska	23	New Hampshire	23
Minnesota	26.8	29.2	37.4	Oregon	23	Michigan	24	West Virginia	23
Mississippi	25.1	27.6	36.0	North Carolina	23	New Hampshire	25	Vermont	25
Missouri	29.4	30.8	37.9	New Hampshire	26	Vermont	26	Indiana	26
Montana	27.1	29.0	39.8	Vermont	27	South Carolina	27	Kentucky	26
Nebraska	28.6	29.7	36.2	Maryland	28	Iowa	28	Arkansas	28
Nevada	27.8	30.2	36.3	Nebraska	29	Indiana	29	Michigan	29
New Hampshire	28.0	30.1	41.1	Delaware	30	Maine	29	Virginia	29
New Jersey	30.1	32.2	39.0	Indiana	31	North Carolina	31	Illinois	31
New Mexico	23.9	27.3	36.7	Oklahoma	32	Louisiana	32	Missouri	32
New York	30.3	31.8	38.0	Maine	33	West Virginia	33	Louisiana	33
North Carolina	26.5	29.6	37.4	Louisiana	34	Illinois	34	Maine	34
North Dakota	26.4	28.1	37.0	Georgia	35	Maryland	34	Florida	35
Ohio	27.7	29.9	38.8	Iowa	35	Georgia	36	Georgia	36
Oklahoma	29.4	30.1	36.2	Illinois	37	Ohio	36	Ohio	36
Oregon	29.0	30.2	38.4	Connecticut	37	Arkansas	36	Pennsylvania	38
Pennsylvania	30.7	32.1	40.1	Ohio	39	Tennessee	39	Tennessee	38
Rhode Island	29.2	31.7	39.4	Arkansas	39	Connecticut	40	North Carolina	40
South Carolina	24.8	28.0	37.9	Mississippi	41	Delaware	40	Connecticut	41
South Dakota	27.4	28.8	36.9	West Virginia	42	Mississippi	42	New Jersey	41
Tennessee	28.1	30.1	38.0	New Jersey	43	Missouri	43	South Carolina	43
Texas	26.4	28.0	33.6	Tennessee	43	Alabama	44	Mississippi	44
Utah	23.1	24.2	29.2	Alabama	45	Florida	45	Alabama	45
Vermont	26.8	29.4	41.5	Florida	46	New Jersey	45	Delaware	46
Virginia	26.8	29.8	37.5	Missouri	46	Pennsylvania	47	New York	47
Washington	27.5	29.8	37.3	Pennsylvania	48	Rhode Island	48	Massachusetts	48
West Virginia	30.0	30.4	41.3	Massachusetts	49	Massachusetts	49	Maryland	49
Wisconsin	27.2	29.4	38.5	New York	50	New York	50	Rhode Island	50
Wyoming	27.2	27.0	36.8	D.C.	51	D.C.	51	D.C.	51
United States	28.1	30.0	37.2	United States	–	United States	–	United States	–

Source: U.S. Census Bureau, 1970 Census of Population; U.S. Census Bureau, 1980 Census of Population; U.S. Census Bureau, Census 2010

High School Graduates

Area	Percent of Population			1970		1980		2010	
	1970	1980	2010	Area	Rank	Area	Rank	Area	Rank
Alabama	41.3	56.5	82.1	Utah	1	Alaska	1	Wyoming	1
Alaska	66.7	82.5	91.0	Alaska	2	Utah	2	Minnesota	2
Arizona	58.1	72.4	85.6	Nevada	3	Colorado	3	Montana	3
Arkansas	39.9	55.5	82.9	Colorado	4	Wyoming	4	New Hampshire	4
California	62.6	73.5	80.7	Washington	5	Washington	5	Alaska	5
Colorado	63.9	78.6	89.7	Wyoming	6	Oregon	6	Vermont	5
Connecticut	56.0	70.3	88.6	California	7	Nevada	7	Iowa	7
Delaware	54.6	68.6	87.7	Hawaii	8	Montana	8	Utah	7
D.C.	55.2	67.1	87.4	Oregon	9	Hawaii	9	Nebraska	9
Florida	52.6	66.7	85.5	Kansas	10	Idaho	10	Maine	10
Georgia	40.6	56.4	84.3	Idaho	11	California	11	North Dakota	10
Hawaii	61.9	73.8	89.9	Nebraska	12	Nebraska	12	Wisconsin	12
Idaho	59.5	73.7	88.3	Montana	13	Kansas	13	Hawaii	13
Illinois	52.6	66.5	86.9	Iowa	14	Minnesota	14	Washington	14
Indiana	52.9	66.4	87.0	Massachusetts	15	Arizona	15	Colorado	15
Iowa	59.0	71.5	90.6	Arizona	16	New Hampshire	16	South Dakota	16
Kansas	59.9	73.3	89.2	Minnesota	17	Massachusetts	17	Kansas	17
Kentucky	38.5	53.1	81.9	New Hampshire	17	Iowa	18	Massachusetts	18
Louisiana	42.2	57.7	81.9	Vermont	19	Vermont	19	Oregon	19
Maine	54.7	68.7	90.3	Connecticut	20	Connecticut	20	Michigan	20
Maryland	52.3	67.4	88.1	New Mexico	21	Wisconsin	21	Connecticut	21
Massachusetts	58.5	72.2	89.1	D.C.	21	New Mexico	22	Pennsylvania	22
Michigan	52.8	68.0	88.7	Maine	23	Maine	23	Idaho	23
Minnesota	57.6	73.1	91.8	Delaware	24	Delaware	24	Maryland	24
Mississippi	41.0	54.8	81.0	Wisconsin	25	Michigan	25	Ohio	24
Missouri	48.8	63.5	86.9	South Dakota	26	South Dakota	26	New Jersey	26
Montana	59.2	74.4	91.7	Ohio	27	New Jersey	27	Delaware	27
Nebraska	59.3	73.4	90.4	Indiana	28	Maryland	27	D.C.	28
Nevada	65.2	75.5	84.7	Michigan	29	D.C.	29	Indiana	29
New Hampshire	57.6	72.3	91.5	New York	30	Ohio	30	Illinois	30
New Jersey	52.5	67.4	88.0	Florida	31	Florida	31	Missouri	30
New Mexico	55.2	68.9	83.3	Illinois	31	Illinois	32	Virginia	32
New York	52.7	66.3	84.9	New Jersey	33	Indiana	33	Oklahoma	33
North Carolina	38.5	54.8	84.7	Maryland	34	North Dakota	33	Arizona	34
North Dakota	50.3	66.4	90.3	Oklahoma	35	New York	35	Florida	35
Ohio	53.2	67.0	88.1	North Dakota	36	Oklahoma	36	New York	36
Oklahoma	51.6	66.0	86.2	Pennsylvania	37	Pennsylvania	37	Nevada	37
Oregon	60.0	75.6	88.8	Missouri	38	Missouri	38	North Carolina	37
Pennsylvania	50.2	64.7	88.4	Virginia	39	Texas	39	Georgia	39
Rhode Island	46.4	61.1	83.5	Texas	40	Virginia	40	South Carolina	40
South Carolina	37.8	53.7	84.1	Rhode Island	41	Rhode Island	41	Tennessee	41
South Dakota	53.3	67.9	89.6	Louisiana	42	Louisiana	42	Rhode Island	42
Tennessee	41.8	56.2	83.6	Tennessee	43	Alabama	43	New Mexico	43
Texas	47.4	62.6	80.7	West Virginia	44	Georgia	44	West Virginia	44
Utah	67.3	80.0	90.6	Alabama	45	Tennessee	45	Arkansas	45
Vermont	57.1	71.0	91.0	Mississippi	46	West Virginia	46	Alabama	46
Virginia	47.8	62.4	86.5	Georgia	47	Arkansas	47	Kentucky	47
Washington	63.5	77.6	89.8	Arkansas	48	Mississippi	48	Louisiana	47
West Virginia	41.6	56.0	83.2	North Carolina	49	North Carolina	48	Mississippi	49
Wisconsin	54.5	69.6	90.1	Kentucky	49	South Carolina	50	California	50
Wyoming	62.9	77.9	92.3	South Carolina	51	Kentucky	51	Texas	50
United States	52.3	66.5	85.6	United States	–	United States	–	United States	–

Source: U.S. Census Bureau, 1970 Census of Population; U.S. Census Bureau, 1980 Census of Population; U.S. Census Bureau, Census 2010

College Graduates

Area	Percent of Population			1970		1980		2010	
	1970	1980	2010	Area	Rank	Area	Rank	Area	Rank
Alabama	7.8	12.2	21.9	D.C.	1	D.C.	1	D.C.	1
Alaska	14.1	21.1	27.9	Colorado	2	Colorado	2	Massachusetts	2
Arizona	12.6	17.4	25.9	Alaska	3	Alaska	3	Colorado	3
Arkansas	6.7	10.8	19.5	Utah	4	Connecticut	4	Maryland	4
California	13.4	19.6	30.1	Hawaii	4	Maryland	5	Connecticut	5
Colorado	14.9	23.0	36.4	Maryland	6	Hawaii	6	New Jersey	6
Connecticut	13.7	20.7	35.5	Connecticut	7	Massachusetts	7	Virginia	7
Delaware	13.1	17.5	27.8	California	8	Utah	8	Vermont	8
D.C.	17.8	27.5	50.1	Delaware	9	California	9	New Hampshire	9
Florida	10.3	14.9	25.8	New Mexico	10	Virginia	10	New York	10
Georgia	9.2	14.6	27.3	Washington	10	Washington	11	Minnesota	11
Hawaii	14.0	20.3	29.5	Arizona	12	Vermont	11	Washington	12
Idaho	10.0	15.8	24.4	Massachusetts	12	New Jersey	13	Illinois	13
Illinois	10.3	16.2	30.8	Virginia	14	New Hampshire	14	Rhode Island	14
Indiana	8.3	12.5	22.7	New York	15	New York	15	California	15
Iowa	9.1	13.9	24.9	Wyoming	16	Oregon	15	Kansas	16
Kansas	11.4	17.0	29.8	New Jersey	16	New Mexico	17	Hawaii	17
Kentucky	7.2	11.1	20.5	Oregon	16	Delaware	18	Utah	18
Louisiana	9.0	13.9	21.4	Vermont	19	Montana	18	Montana	19
Maine	8.4	14.4	26.8	Kansas	20	Arizona	20	Oregon	19
Maryland	13.9	20.4	36.1	Minnesota	21	Minnesota	20	Nebraska	21
Massachusetts	12.6	20.0	39.0	Montana	22	Wyoming	22	Alaska	22
Michigan	9.4	14.3	25.2	Texas	23	Kansas	23	Delaware	23
Minnesota	11.1	17.4	31.8	New Hampshire	23	Texas	24	North Dakota	24
Mississippi	8.1	12.3	19.5	Nevada	25	Illinois	25	Georgia	25
Missouri	9.0	13.9	25.6	Florida	26	Idaho	26	Pennsylvania	26
Montana	11.0	17.5	28.8	Illinois	26	Nebraska	27	Maine	27
Nebraska	9.6	15.5	28.6	Idaho	28	Rhode Island	28	North Carolina	28
Nevada	10.8	14.4	21.7	Oklahoma	28	Oklahoma	29	South Dakota	29
New Hampshire	10.9	18.2	32.8	Wisconsin	30	Florida	30	Wisconsin	29
New Jersey	11.8	18.3	35.4	Nebraska	31	Wisconsin	31	Arizona	31
New Mexico	12.7	17.6	25.0	Michigan	32	North Dakota	31	Texas	31
New York	11.9	17.9	32.5	Rhode Island	32	Georgia	33	Florida	33
North Carolina	8.5	13.2	26.5	Ohio	34	Nevada	34	Missouri	34
North Dakota	8.4	14.8	27.6	Georgia	35	Maine	34	Michigan	35
Ohio	9.3	13.7	24.6	Iowa	36	Michigan	36	New Mexico	36
Oklahoma	10.0	15.1	22.9	Louisiana	37	South Dakota	37	Iowa	37
Oregon	11.8	17.9	28.8	Missouri	37	Louisiana	38	Ohio	38
Pennsylvania	8.7	13.6	27.1	South Carolina	37	Missouri	38	South Carolina	39
Rhode Island	9.4	15.4	30.2	Pennsylvania	40	Iowa	38	Idaho	40
South Carolina	9.0	13.4	24.5	South Dakota	41	Ohio	41	Wyoming	41
South Dakota	8.6	14.0	26.3	North Carolina	42	Pennsylvania	42	Tennessee	42
Tennessee	7.9	12.6	23.1	Maine	43	South Carolina	43	Oklahoma	43
Texas	10.9	16.9	25.9	North Dakota	43	North Carolina	44	Indiana	44
Utah	14.0	19.9	29.3	Indiana	45	Tennessee	45	Alabama	45
Vermont	11.5	19.0	33.6	Mississippi	46	Indiana	46	Nevada	46
Virginia	12.3	19.1	34.2	Tennessee	47	Mississippi	47	Louisiana	47
Washington	12.7	19.0	31.1	Alabama	48	Alabama	48	Kentucky	48
West Virginia	6.8	10.4	17.5	Kentucky	49	Kentucky	49	Arkansas	49
Wisconsin	9.8	14.8	26.3	West Virginia	50	Arkansas	50	Mississippi	49
Wyoming	11.8	17.2	24.1	Arkansas	51	West Virginia	51	West Virginia	51
United States	10.7	16.2	28.2	United States	–	United States	–	United States	–

Source: U.S. Census Bureau, 1970 Census of Population; U.S. Census Bureau, 1980 Census of Population; U.S. Census Bureau, Census 2010

One-Person Households

Area	Percent of Population			1970		1980		2010	
	1970	1980	2010	Area	Rank	Area	Rank	Area	Rank
Alabama	14.6	20.4	27.4	D.C.	1	D.C.	1	D.C.	1
Alaska	13.7	20.1	25.6	California	2	New York	2	North Dakota	2
Arizona	16.5	20.9	26.1	New York	3	California	3	Montana	3
Arkansas	17.2	21.3	27.1	Montana	4	Nevada	4	Rhode Island	4
California	21.0	24.7	23.3	Washington	5	Massachusetts	5	South Dakota	5
Colorado	18.0	23.5	27.9	Nevada	6	Nebraska	6	New York	6
Connecticut	16.0	21.6	27.3	Nebraska	7	Washington	7	Ohio	7
Delaware	15.3	20.9	25.6	Missouri	7	Illinois	8	Massachusetts	8
D.C.	32.1	39.5	44.0	Oregon	9	Rhode Island	8	Nebraska	8
Florida	18.7	23.6	27.2	Oklahoma	10	Kansas	10	Maine	10
Georgia	14.4	20.5	25.4	Massachusetts	11	Missouri	10	Pennsylvania	10
Hawaii	12.8	17.1	23.3	Florida	12	Florida	12	Iowa	12
Idaho	16.5	19.9	23.8	Illinois	13	Colorado	13	West Virginia	12
Illinois	18.5	24.0	27.8	Iowa	13	Oregon	13	Missouri	14
Indiana	16.5	21.4	26.9	Kansas	15	South Dakota	13	Vermont	15
Iowa	18.5	23.4	28.4	Rhode Island	16	Oklahoma	16	Wisconsin	15
Kansas	18.4	23.8	27.8	South Dakota	17	Montana	16	Minnesota	17
Kentucky	15.2	20.0	27.5	Colorado	18	Iowa	16	New Mexico	17
Louisiana	16.0	21.3	26.9	Wyoming	18	Minnesota	19	Wyoming	17
Maine	16.8	21.3	28.6	Minnesota	20	North Dakota	20	Colorado	20
Maryland	14.9	20.8	26.1	Pennsylvania	21	Pennsylvania	21	Michigan	20
Massachusetts	18.8	24.4	28.7	Arkansas	22	Wisconsin	22	Illinois	22
Michigan	15.5	21.1	27.9	New Hampshire	23	Ohio	23	Kansas	22
Minnesota	17.7	23.2	28.0	North Dakota	23	Vermont	24	Kentucky	24
Mississippi	15.4	20.4	26.3	Wisconsin	25	Texas	25	Oklahoma	24
Missouri	19.3	23.8	28.3	Vermont	26	Connecticut	26	Alabama	26
Montana	19.8	23.4	29.7	Maine	26	Indiana	27	Oregon	26
Nebraska	19.3	24.3	28.7	Ohio	28	Wyoming	28	Connecticut	28
Nevada	19.4	24.6	25.7	Arizona	29	Louisiana	28	Florida	29
New Hampshire	17.0	21.2	25.6	Idaho	29	Arkansas	28	Washington	29
New Jersey	15.8	21.1	25.2	Indiana	29	Maine	28	Arkansas	31
New Mexico	14.9	21.0	28.0	Texas	32	New Hampshire	32	North Carolina	32
New York	20.2	26.0	29.1	Connecticut	33	New Jersey	33	Indiana	33
North Carolina	13.3	20.0	27.0	Louisiana	33	Michigan	33	Louisiana	33
North Dakota	17.0	22.9	31.5	West Virginia	33	New Mexico	35	Tennessee	33
Ohio	16.6	22.4	28.9	New Jersey	36	Arizona	36	South Carolina	36
Oklahoma	19.1	23.4	27.5	Michigan	37	Delaware	36	Mississippi	37
Oregon	19.2	23.5	27.4	Mississippi	38	Maryland	38	Arizona	38
Pennsylvania	17.3	22.7	28.6	Delaware	39	West Virginia	39	Maryland	38
Rhode Island	18.2	24.0	29.6	Kentucky	40	Virginia	40	Virginia	40
South Carolina	13.8	19.2	26.5	New Mexico	41	Georgia	40	Nevada	41
South Dakota	18.1	23.5	29.4	Maryland	41	Mississippi	42	Alaska	42
Tennessee	14.4	20.4	26.9	Alabama	43	Alabama	42	Delaware	42
Texas	16.3	21.7	24.2	Utah	44	Tennessee	42	New Hampshire	42
Utah	14.4	17.2	18.7	Virginia	44	Alaska	45	Georgia	45
Vermont	16.8	22.0	28.2	Georgia	44	North Carolina	46	New Jersey	46
Virginia	14.4	20.5	26.0	Tennessee	44	Kentucky	46	Texas	47
Washington	19.6	24.2	27.2	South Carolina	48	Idaho	48	Idaho	48
West Virginia	16.0	20.7	28.4	Alaska	49	South Carolina	49	California	49
Wisconsin	16.9	22.5	28.2	North Carolina	50	Utah	50	Hawaii	49
Wyoming	18.0	21.3	28.0	Hawaii	51	Hawaii	51	Utah	51
United States	17.6	22.7	26.7	United States	–	United States	–	United States	–

Source: U.S. Census Bureau, 1970 Census of Population; U.S. Census Bureau, 1980 Census of Population; U.S. Census Bureau, Census 2010

Homeownership

Area	Percent of Population			1970		1980		2010	
	1970	1980	2010	Area	Rank	Area	Rank	Area	Rank
Alabama	66.7	70.1	69.7	Michigan	1	West Virginia	1	West Virginia	1
Alaska	50.3	58.3	63.1	Indiana	2	Michigan	2	Minnesota	2
Arizona	65.3	68.3	66.0	Iowa	2	Idaho	3	Iowa	3
Arkansas	66.7	70.5	66.9	Minnesota	4	Iowa	4	Michigan	3
California	54.9	55.9	56.0	Idaho	5	Indiana	5	Delaware	5
Colorado	63.4	64.5	65.5	Maine	5	Minnesota	5	Maine	6
Connecticut	62.5	63.9	67.5	South Dakota	7	Mississippi	7	New Hampshire	7
Delaware	68.0	69.1	72.0	Utah	8	Maine	8	Vermont	8
D.C.	28.2	35.5	42.0	Oklahoma	9	Utah	9	Utah	9
Florida	68.6	68.3	67.3	Kansas	10	Oklahoma	9	Idaho	10
Georgia	61.1	65.0	65.7	Wisconsin	10	Arkansas	11	Indiana	11
Hawaii	46.9	51.7	57.7	Vermont	10	Kansas	12	Alabama	12
Idaho	70.1	72.0	69.9	West Virginia	13	South Carolina	12	Mississippi	13
Illinois	59.4	62.6	67.4	Pennsylvania	14	Alabama	14	Pennsylvania	13
Indiana	71.7	71.7	69.8	Florida	15	Kentucky	15	South Carolina	15
Iowa	71.7	71.8	72.1	North Dakota	16	Pennsylvania	16	Wyoming	15
Kansas	69.1	70.2	67.7	New Hampshire	17	Missouri	17	Missouri	17
Kentucky	66.9	70.0	68.7	Delaware	18	South Dakota	18	Kentucky	18
Louisiana	63.1	65.5	67.3	Ohio	19	Wyoming	19	New Mexico	19
Maine	70.1	70.9	71.3	Missouri	20	Delaware	20	Tennessee	20
Maryland	58.8	62.0	67.5	Kentucky	21	Vermont	21	South Dakota	21
Massachusetts	57.5	57.5	62.3	Washington	22	North Dakota	21	Wisconsin	21
Michigan	74.4	72.7	72.1	Arkansas	23	Montana	23	Montana	23
Minnesota	71.5	71.7	73.1	Alabama	23	Tennessee	23	Kansas	24
Mississippi	66.3	71.0	69.6	Tennessee	23	Nebraska	25	Ohio	25
Missouri	67.2	69.6	68.8	New Mexico	26	Ohio	25	Connecticut	26
Montana	65.7	68.6	68.0	Wyoming	26	North Carolina	25	Maryland	26
Nebraska	66.4	68.4	67.2	Nebraska	26	Arizona	28	Illinois	28
Nevada	58.5	59.6	58.8	Mississippi	29	Florida	28	Florida	29
New Hampshire	68.2	67.6	70.9	Oregon	30	Wisconsin	30	Louisiana	29
New Jersey	60.9	62.0	65.4	South Carolina	30	New Mexico	31	Oklahoma	29
New Mexico	66.4	68.1	68.5	Montana	32	New Hampshire	32	Nebraska	32
New York	47.3	48.6	53.3	North Carolina	33	Washington	33	Virginia	32
North Carolina	65.4	68.4	66.7	Arizona	34	Virginia	33	Arkansas	34
North Dakota	68.4	68.7	65.4	Texas	35	Louisiana	35	North Carolina	35
Ohio	67.7	68.4	67.6	Colorado	36	Oregon	36	Arizona	36
Oklahoma	69.2	70.7	67.3	Louisiana	37	Georgia	37	Georgia	37
Oregon	66.1	65.1	62.1	Connecticut	38	Colorado	38	Colorado	38
Pennsylvania	68.8	69.9	69.6	Virginia	39	Texas	39	New Jersey	39
Rhode Island	57.9	58.8	60.7	Georgia	40	Connecticut	40	North Dakota	39
South Carolina	66.1	70.2	69.3	New Jersey	41	Illinois	41	Washington	41
South Dakota	69.6	69.3	68.1	Illinois	42	New Jersey	42	Texas	42
Tennessee	66.7	68.6	68.2	Maryland	43	Maryland	42	Alaska	43
Texas	64.7	64.3	63.7	Nevada	44	Nevada	44	Massachusetts	44
Utah	69.3	70.7	70.5	Rhode Island	45	Rhode Island	45	Oregon	45
Vermont	69.1	68.7	70.7	Massachusetts	46	Alaska	46	Rhode Island	46
Virginia	62.0	65.6	67.2	California	47	Massachusetts	47	Nevada	47
Washington	66.8	65.6	63.9	Alaska	48	California	48	Hawaii	48
West Virginia	68.9	73.6	73.4	New York	49	Hawaii	49	California	49
Wisconsin	69.1	68.2	68.1	Hawaii	50	New York	50	New York	50
Wyoming	66.4	69.2	69.3	D.C.	51	D.C.	51	D.C.	51
United States	62.9	64.4	65.1	United States	–	United States	–	United States	–

Source: U.S. Census Bureau, 1970 Census of Population; U.S. Census Bureau, 1980 Census of Population; U.S. Census Bureau, Census 2010

Median Home Value

Area	Median Home Value ($) 1970	1980	2010	1970 Area	Rank	1980 Area	Rank	2010 Area	Rank
Alabama	12,200	33,900	123,900	Hawaii	1	Hawaii	1	Hawaii	1
Alaska	22,700	76,300	241,400	Connecticut	2	California	2	D.C.	2
Arizona	16,300	54,800	168,800	New Jersey	3	Alaska	3	California	3
Arkansas	10,500	31,100	106,300	California	4	D.C.	4	New Jersey	4
California	23,100	84,500	370,900	Alaska	5	Nevada	5	Massachusetts	5
Colorado	17,300	64,100	236,600	New York	6	Connecticut	6	Maryland	6
Connecticut	25,500	65,600	288,800	Nevada	7	Colorado	7	New York	7
Delaware	17,100	44,400	243,600	D.C.	8	New Jersey	8	Connecticut	8
D.C.	21,300	68,800	426,900	Massachusetts	9	Washington	9	Washington	9
Florida	15,000	45,100	164,200	Illinois	10	Wyoming	10	Rhode Island	10
Georgia	14,600	36,900	156,200	Maryland	11	Maryland	11	Virginia	11
Hawaii	35,100	118,100	525,400	Washington	12	Utah	12	Oregon	12
Idaho	14,100	45,600	165,100	Rhode Island	13	Oregon	13	Delaware	13
Illinois	19,800	52,800	191,800	Minnesota	14	Arizona	14	New Hampshire	14
Indiana	13,800	37,200	123,300	Ohio	15	Minnesota	15	Alaska	15
Iowa	13,900	40,600	123,400	Michigan	16	Illinois	16	Colorado	16
Kansas	12,100	37,800	127,300	Colorado	17	Wisconsin	17	Utah	17
Kentucky	12,600	34,200	121,600	Wisconsin	17	Massachusetts	18	Vermont	18
Louisiana	14,600	43,000	137,500	Delaware	19	Virginia	19	Minnesota	19
Maine	12,800	37,900	179,100	Virginia	19	New Hampshire	19	Illinois	20
Maryland	18,700	58,300	301,400	Utah	21	Rhode Island	21	Montana	21
Massachusetts	20,600	48,400	334,100	Vermont	22	Montana	22	Wyoming	22
Michigan	17,500	39,000	123,300	New Hampshire	22	New York	23	Maine	23
Minnesota	18,000	53,100	194,300	Arizona	24	Idaho	23	Nevada	24
Mississippi	11,200	31,400	100,100	Oregon	25	New Mexico	25	Wisconsin	25
Missouri	14,400	36,700	139,000	Wyoming	26	Florida	26	Arizona	26
Montana	14,000	46,500	181,200	Florida	27	Ohio	27	Pennsylvania	27
Nebraska	12,400	38,000	127,600	Louisiana	28	Delaware	28	Idaho	28
Nevada	22,400	68,700	174,800	Georgia	28	North Dakota	29	Florida	29
New Hampshire	16,400	48,000	243,000	Missouri	30	Louisiana	30	New Mexico	30
New Jersey	23,400	60,200	339,200	Idaho	31	Vermont	31	Georgia	31
New Mexico	13,000	45,300	161,200	Montana	32	Iowa	32	North Carolina	32
New York	22,500	45,600	296,500	Iowa	33	Texas	33	Missouri	33
North Carolina	12,800	36,000	154,200	Indiana	34	Pennsylvania	33	Tennessee	33
North Dakota	13,000	43,900	123,000	Pennsylvania	35	Michigan	35	South Carolina	35
Ohio	17,600	44,900	134,400	New Mexico	36	West Virginia	36	Louisiana	36
Oklahoma	11,100	35,600	111,400	South Carolina	36	Nebraska	37	Ohio	37
Oregon	15,400	56,900	244,500	North Dakota	36	Maine	38	South Dakota	38
Pennsylvania	13,600	39,100	165,500	North Carolina	39	Kansas	39	Texas	39
Rhode Island	18,200	46,800	254,500	Maine	39	Indiana	40	Nebraska	40
South Carolina	13,000	35,100	138,100	Kentucky	41	Georgia	41	Kansas	41
South Dakota	11,400	36,600	129,700	Tennessee	42	Missouri	42	Alabama	42
Tennessee	12,500	35,600	139,000	Nebraska	43	South Dakota	43	Iowa	43
Texas	12,000	39,100	128,100	Alabama	44	North Carolina	44	Indiana	44
Utah	16,800	57,300	217,200	Kansas	45	Oklahoma	45	Michigan	44
Vermont	16,400	42,200	216,800	Texas	46	Tennessee	45	North Dakota	46
Virginia	17,100	48,000	249,100	South Dakota	47	South Carolina	47	Kentucky	47
Washington	18,500	59,900	271,800	West Virginia	48	Kentucky	48	Oklahoma	48
West Virginia	11,300	38,500	95,100	Mississippi	49	Alabama	49	Arkansas	49
Wisconsin	17,300	48,600	169,400	Oklahoma	50	Mississippi	50	Mississippi	50
Wyoming	15,300	59,800	180,100	Arkansas	51	Arkansas	51	West Virginia	51
United States	17,000	47,200	179,900	United States	–	United States	–	United States	–

Source: U.S. Census Bureau, 1970 Census of Population; U.S. Census Bureau, 1980 Census of Population; U.S. Census Bureau, Census 2010

Median Gross Rent

Area	Median Gross Rent ($/month)			1970		1980		2010	
	1970	1980	2010	Area	Rank	Area	Rank	Area	Rank
Alabama	69	188	667	Alaska	1	Alaska	1	Hawaii	1
Alaska	189	368	981	Nevada	2	Hawaii	2	D.C.	2
Arizona	109	264	844	Hawaii	3	Nevada	3	California	3
Arkansas	71	185	638	Connecticut	4	California	4	Maryland	4
California	126	283	1,163	Maryland	4	New Jersey	5	New Jersey	5
Colorado	110	252	863	California	6	Maryland	6	New York	6
Connecticut	127	260	992	New Jersey	6	Arizona	7	Virginia	7
Delaware	111	247	952	Illinois	8	Connecticut	8	Massachusetts	8
D.C.	119	224	1,198	D.C.	9	Virginia	9	Connecticut	9
Florida	112	255	947	Massachusetts	10	Oregon	10	Alaska	10
Georgia	86	211	819	Minnesota	10	Florida	11	Delaware	11
Hawaii	132	311	1,291	Michigan	12	Massachusetts	11	Nevada	11
Idaho	92	218	683	Virginia	12	Washington	13	New Hampshire	13
Illinois	124	246	848	Washington	14	Colorado	14	Florida	14
Indiana	105	218	683	Wisconsin	14	Wyoming	14	Washington	15
Iowa	99	226	629	Florida	16	New Hampshire	16	Rhode Island	16
Kansas	94	218	682	New York	17	Michigan	17	Colorado	17
Kentucky	83	198	613	Delaware	17	New York	18	Illinois	18
Louisiana	81	214	736	Colorado	19	Delaware	19	Arizona	19
Maine	90	216	707	Arizona	20	Texas	20	Vermont	20
Maryland	127	266	1,131	Oregon	21	Illinois	20	Georgia	21
Massachusetts	117	255	1,009	Indiana	22	Minnesota	22	Oregon	22
Michigan	115	250	730	Ohio	22	Utah	23	Texas	23
Minnesota	117	236	764	Iowa	24	Wisconsin	24	Utah	24
Mississippi	65	180	672	New Hampshire	24	Iowa	25	Minnesota	25
Missouri	96	211	682	Vermont	26	Ohio	26	Pennsylvania	26
Montana	89	200	642	Utah	27	D.C.	27	Louisiana	27
Nebraska	95	213	669	North Dakota	27	Pennsylvania	27	North Carolina	28
Nevada	141	310	952	Missouri	29	Vermont	27	Michigan	29
New Hampshire	99	251	951	Texas	30	Rhode Island	30	South Carolina	30
New Jersey	126	270	1,114	Nebraska	30	Idaho	31	Wisconsin	31
New Mexico	88	215	699	Kansas	32	Kansas	31	Maine	32
New York	111	249	1,020	Rhode Island	33	Indiana	31	New Mexico	33
North Carolina	86	205	731	Pennsylvania	33	Maine	34	Tennessee	34
North Dakota	97	206	583	Idaho	35	New Mexico	35	Wyoming	35
Ohio	105	225	685	Maine	36	Oklahoma	35	Ohio	36
Oklahoma	82	215	659	Montana	37	Louisiana	37	Idaho	37
Oregon	107	257	816	New Mexico	38	Nebraska	38	Indiana	37
Pennsylvania	93	224	763	South Dakota	38	Georgia	39	Kansas	39
Rhode Island	93	222	868	Wyoming	40	Missouri	39	Missouri	39
South Carolina	77	206	728	Georgia	41	South Carolina	41	Mississippi	41
South Dakota	88	188	591	North Carolina	41	North Dakota	41	Nebraska	42
Tennessee	82	203	697	Kentucky	43	North Carolina	43	Alabama	43
Texas	95	246	801	Oklahoma	44	Tennessee	44	Oklahoma	44
Utah	97	235	796	Tennessee	44	Montana	45	Montana	45
Vermont	98	224	823	Louisiana	46	Kentucky	46	Arkansas	46
Virginia	115	259	1,019	South Carolina	47	West Virginia	47	Iowa	47
Washington	113	254	908	West Virginia	48	Alabama	48	Kentucky	48
West Virginia	72	195	571	Arkansas	49	South Dakota	48	South Dakota	49
Wisconsin	113	234	715	Alabama	50	Arkansas	50	North Dakota	50
Wyoming	87	252	693	Mississippi	51	Mississippi	51	West Virginia	51
United States	108	243	855	United States	–	United States	–	United States	–

Source: U.S. Census Bureau, 1970 Census of Population; U.S. Census Bureau, 1980 Census of Population; U.S. Census Bureau, Census 2010

Households Lacking Complete Plumbing

Area	Percent of Households			1970		1980		2010	
	1970	1980	2010	Area	Rank	Area	Rank	Area	Rank
Alabama	16.9	5.2	3.6	Mississippi	1	Alaska	1	Alaska	1
Alaska	17.2	12.2	11.9	Kentucky	2	Kentucky	2	West Virginia	2
Arizona	5.2	2.6	2.3	South Carolina	3	Mississippi	3	Maine	3
Arkansas	18.4	5.3	4.3	Arkansas	4	West Virginia	4	New Mexico	4
California	2.1	1.4	1.1	West Virginia	5	Maine	5	Arkansas	5
Colorado	5.0	1.8	1.3	Alaska	6	Arkansas	6	Mississippi	5
Connecticut	2.7	1.4	1.1	Alabama	7	North Carolina	7	Montana	7
Delaware	5.1	2.0	1.6	North Carolina	8	Alabama	7	Louisiana	8
D.C.	2.3	2.4	2.2	Maine	9	Virginia	9	Alabama	9
Florida	5.1	1.2	1.4	Tennessee	10	South Carolina	9	Kentucky	10
Georgia	13.2	3.8	2.2	North Dakota	11	New Mexico	11	Oklahoma	11
Hawaii	5.6	2.3	1.5	South Dakota	12	Tennessee	12	Indiana	12
Idaho	5.3	2.0	1.6	Virginia	13	South Dakota	13	Michigan	12
Illinois	4.8	2.0	2.1	Georgia	14	North Dakota	14	Missouri	12
Indiana	6.5	2.1	3.1	Louisiana	15	Georgia	15	South Dakota	12
Iowa	7.5	2.4	1.7	New Mexico	16	Montana	16	Pennsylvania	16
Kansas	5.6	2.0	2.3	Missouri	17	Vermont	17	South Carolina	17
Kentucky	20.8	7.5	3.5	Montana	18	Louisiana	18	Texas	17
Louisiana	11.5	3.1	3.9	Vermont	19	Missouri	19	Vermont	17
Maine	15.4	5.8	4.7	Minnesota	20	New York	20	North Carolina	20
Maryland	4.4	2.1	1.5	Texas	21	New Hampshire	20	North Dakota	21
Massachusetts	3.6	1.7	1.0	Iowa	22	Minnesota	22	Tennessee	21
Michigan	4.4	1.8	3.1	Wisconsin	23	Texas	23	Arizona	23
Minnesota	8.2	2.8	2.1	Oklahoma	24	Arizona	23	Kansas	23
Mississippi	24.3	7.2	4.3	New Hampshire	25	Wisconsin	25	Ohio	23
Missouri	9.7	3.0	3.1	Indiana	26	Pennsylvania	25	D.C.	26
Montana	9.0	3.4	4.1	Nebraska	27	D.C.	27	Georgia	26
Nebraska	6.1	1.9	2.2	Wyoming	28	Iowa	27	Nebraska	26
Nevada	3.2	1.4	1.2	Hawaii	29	Hawaii	29	Illinois	29
New Hampshire	7.0	2.9	1.6	Kansas	29	Wyoming	29	Minnesota	29
New Jersey	2.5	1.7	1.2	Idaho	31	Indiana	31	Virginia	31
New Mexico	10.6	4.8	4.6	Arizona	32	Maryland	31	Rhode Island	32
New York	3.2	2.9	1.6	Ohio	32	Illinois	33	Wyoming	32
North Carolina	15.6	5.2	2.5	Florida	34	Idaho	33	Wisconsin	34
North Dakota	13.8	4.2	2.4	Delaware	34	Kansas	33	Iowa	35
Ohio	5.2	2.0	2.3	Pennsylvania	34	Oklahoma	33	Delaware	36
Oklahoma	7.1	2.0	3.2	Colorado	37	Delaware	33	Idaho	36
Oregon	3.6	1.8	1.3	Illinois	38	Ohio	33	New Hampshire	36
Pennsylvania	5.1	2.5	2.7	Michigan	39	Rhode Island	39	New York	36
Rhode Island	3.1	1.9	1.9	Maryland	39	Nebraska	39	Hawaii	40
South Carolina	18.6	5.1	2.6	Oregon	41	Colorado	41	Maryland	40
South Dakota	13.6	4.3	3.1	Massachusetts	41	Oregon	41	Washington	40
Tennessee	14.8	4.6	2.4	Washington	43	Michigan	41	Florida	43
Texas	7.7	2.6	2.6	Nevada	44	New Jersey	44	Colorado	44
Utah	2.7	1.1	1.2	New York	44	Washington	44	Oregon	44
Vermont	8.4	3.3	2.6	Rhode Island	46	Massachusetts	44	Nevada	46
Virginia	13.4	5.1	2.0	Utah	47	California	47	New Jersey	46
Washington	3.4	1.7	1.5	Connecticut	47	Nevada	47	Utah	46
West Virginia	18.3	6.9	5.2	New Jersey	49	Connecticut	47	California	49
Wisconsin	7.2	2.5	1.8	D.C.	50	Florida	50	Connecticut	49
Wyoming	5.9	2.3	1.9	California	51	Utah	51	Massachusetts	51
United States	6.9	2.7	2.2	United States	–	United States	–	United States	–

Source: U.S. Census Bureau, 1970 Census of Population; U.S. Census Bureau, 1980 Census of Population; U.S. Census Bureau, Census 2010

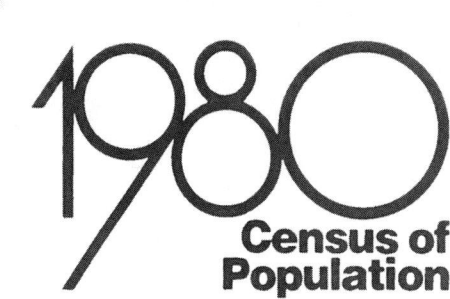

VOLUME 1
CHARACTERISTICS OF THE POPULATION

CHAPTER B

General Population Characteristics

PART1

UNITED STATES SUMMARY

PC80-1-B1

Issued May 1983

U.S. Department of Commerce
Malcolm Baldrige, Secretary
Robert G. Dederick,
Under Secretary for
Economic Affairs

BUREAU OF THE CENSUS
Bruce Chapman, Director

For sale by the Superintendent of Documents, U.S. Government Printing Office Washington, D.C. 20402

FIGURE 1. **Regions and Census Divisions of the United States**

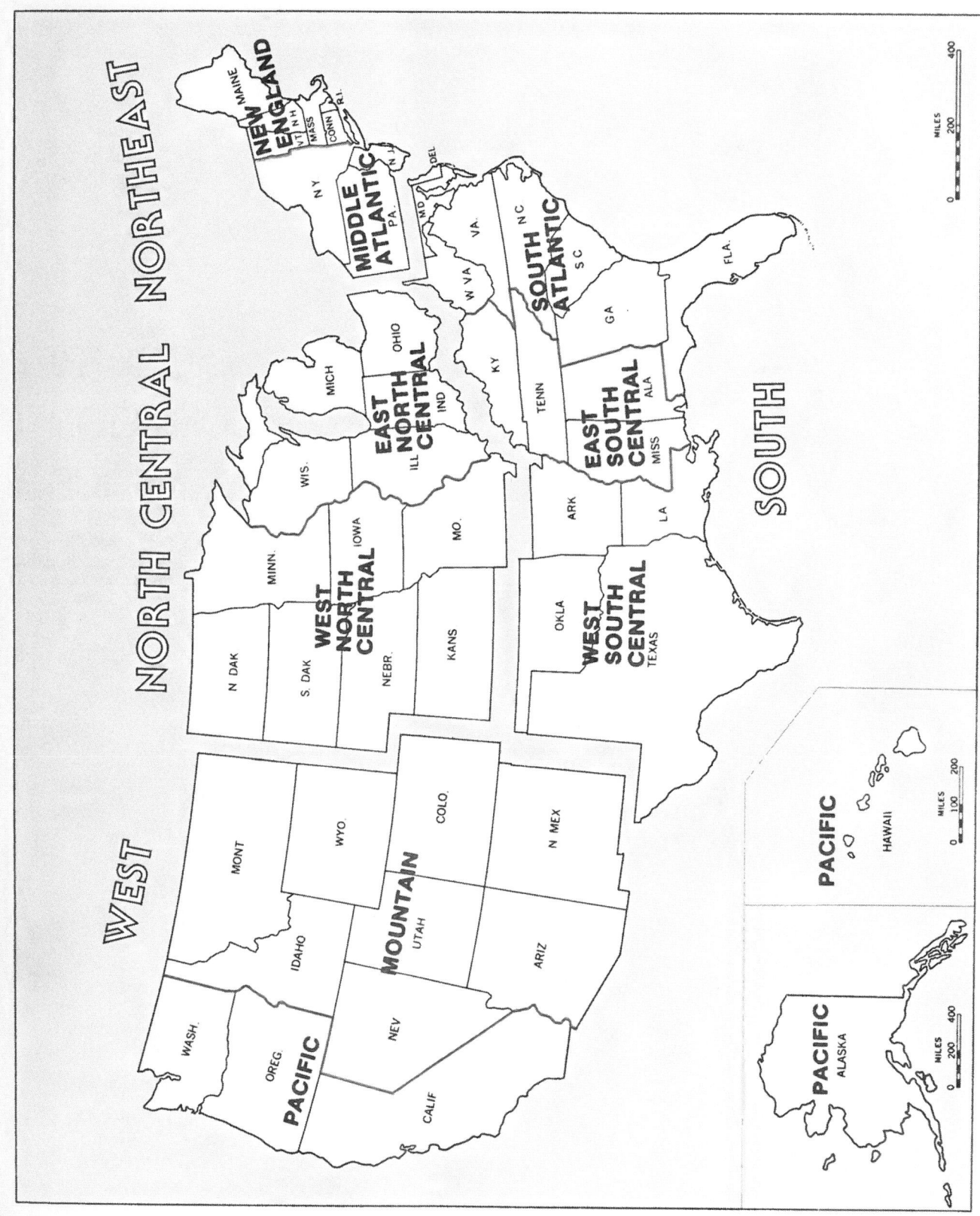

FIGURE 2. **Standard Consolidated Statistical Areas and Standard Metropolitan Statistical Areas of the United States: 1980**

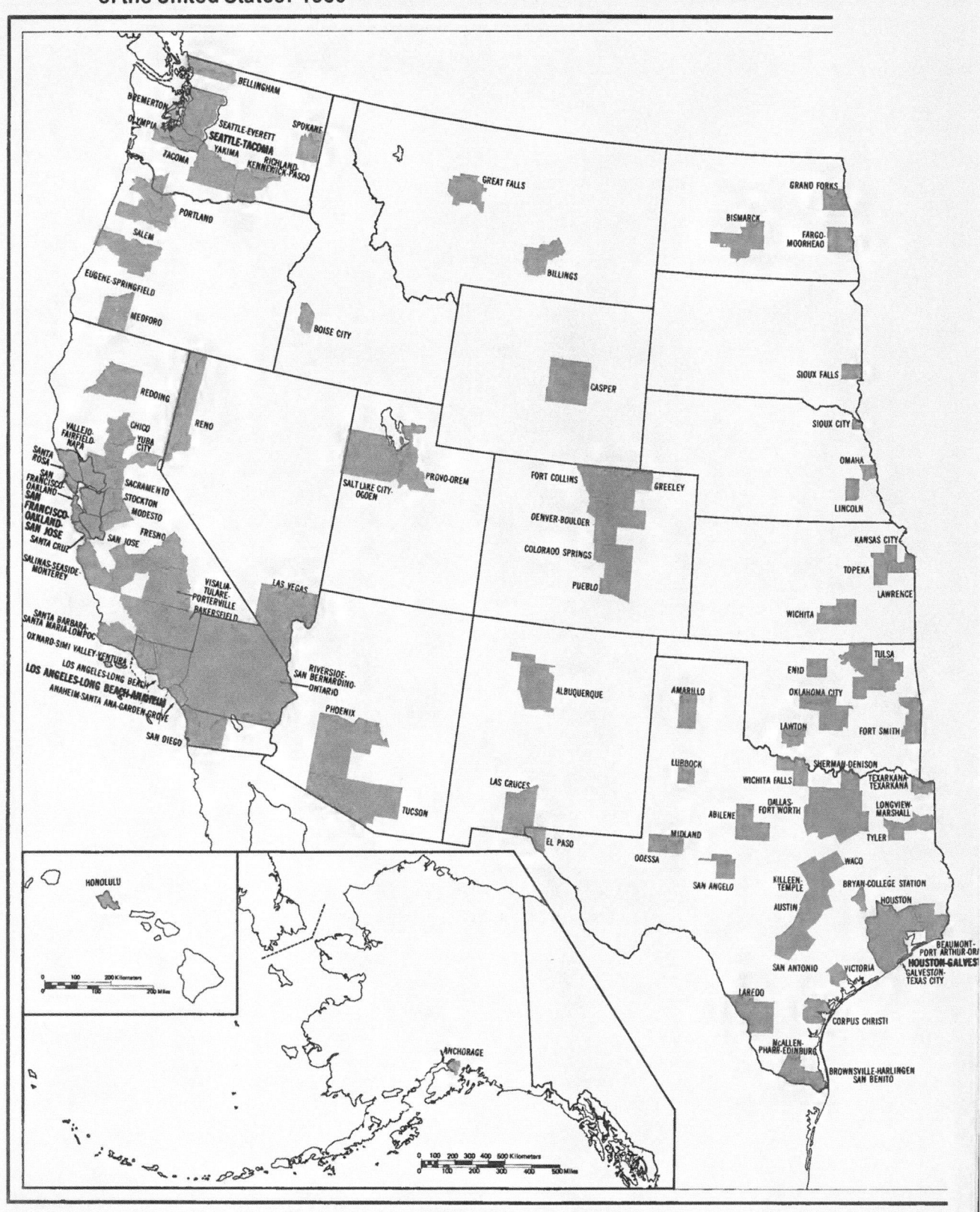

FIGURE 2.

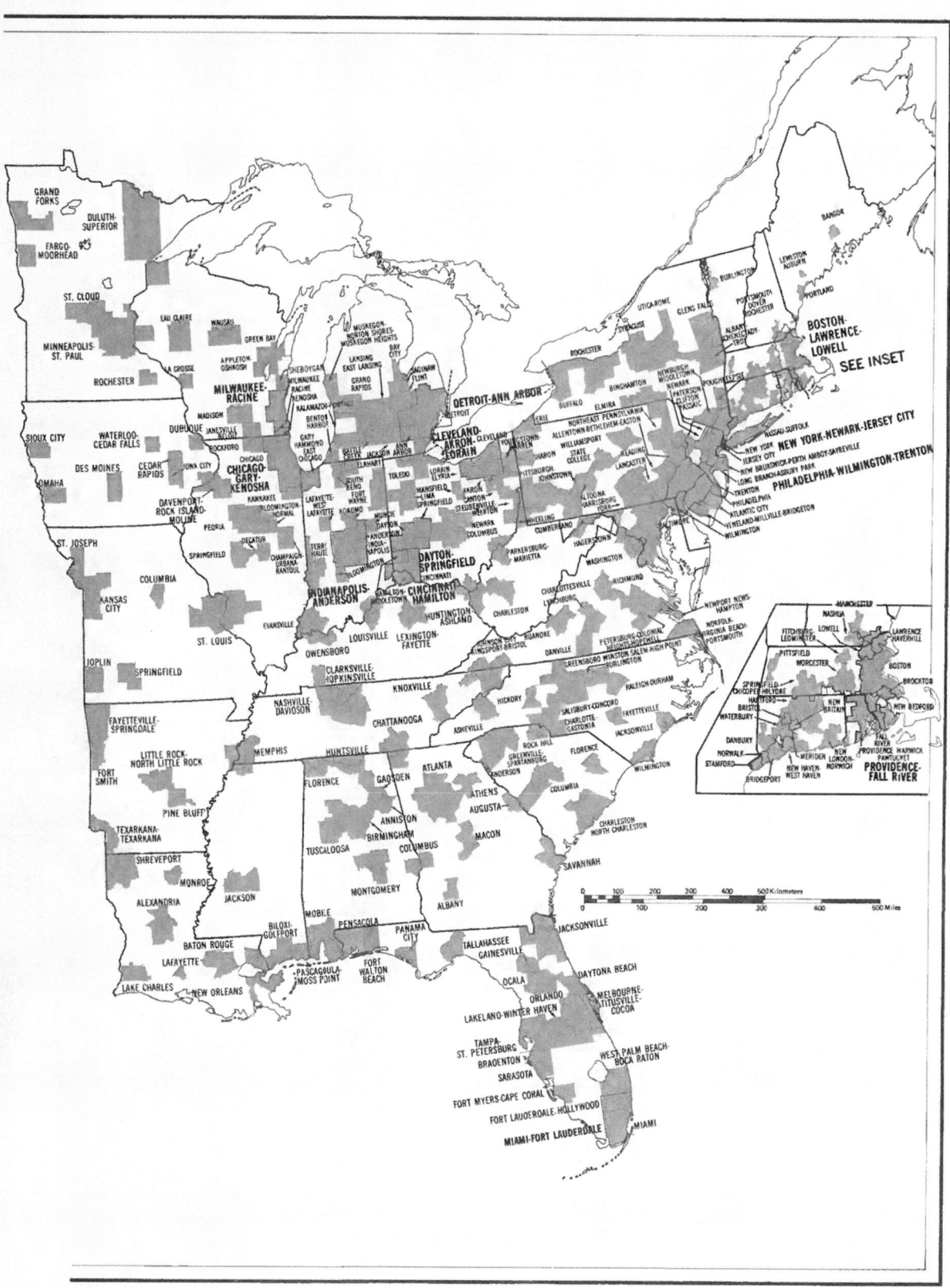

FIGURE 3. **Urbanized Areas of the United States: 1980**

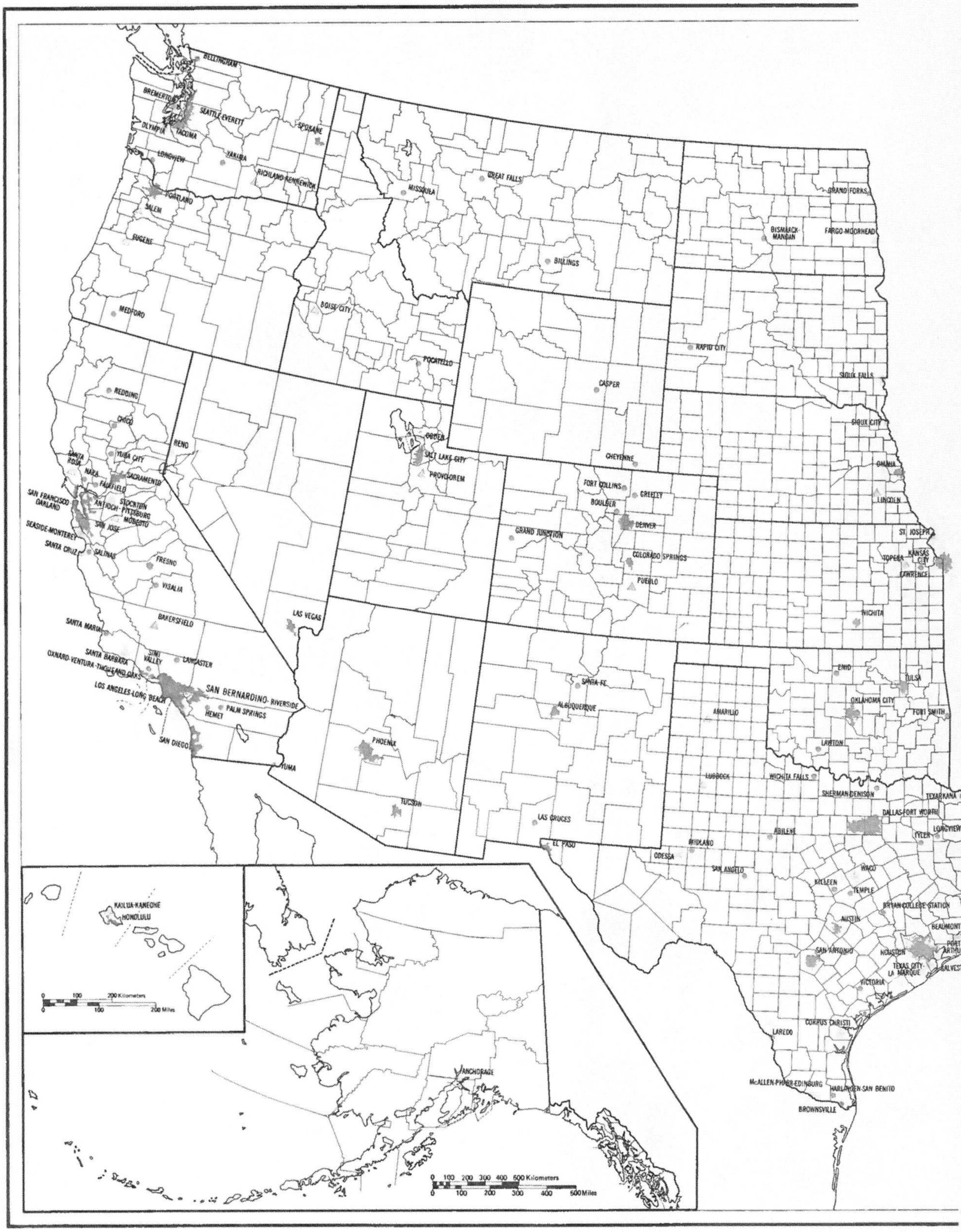

U.S. Department of Commerce

1–8 UNITED STATES SUMMARY

Bureau of the Census

GENERAL POPULATION CHARACTERISTICS

FIGURE 3.

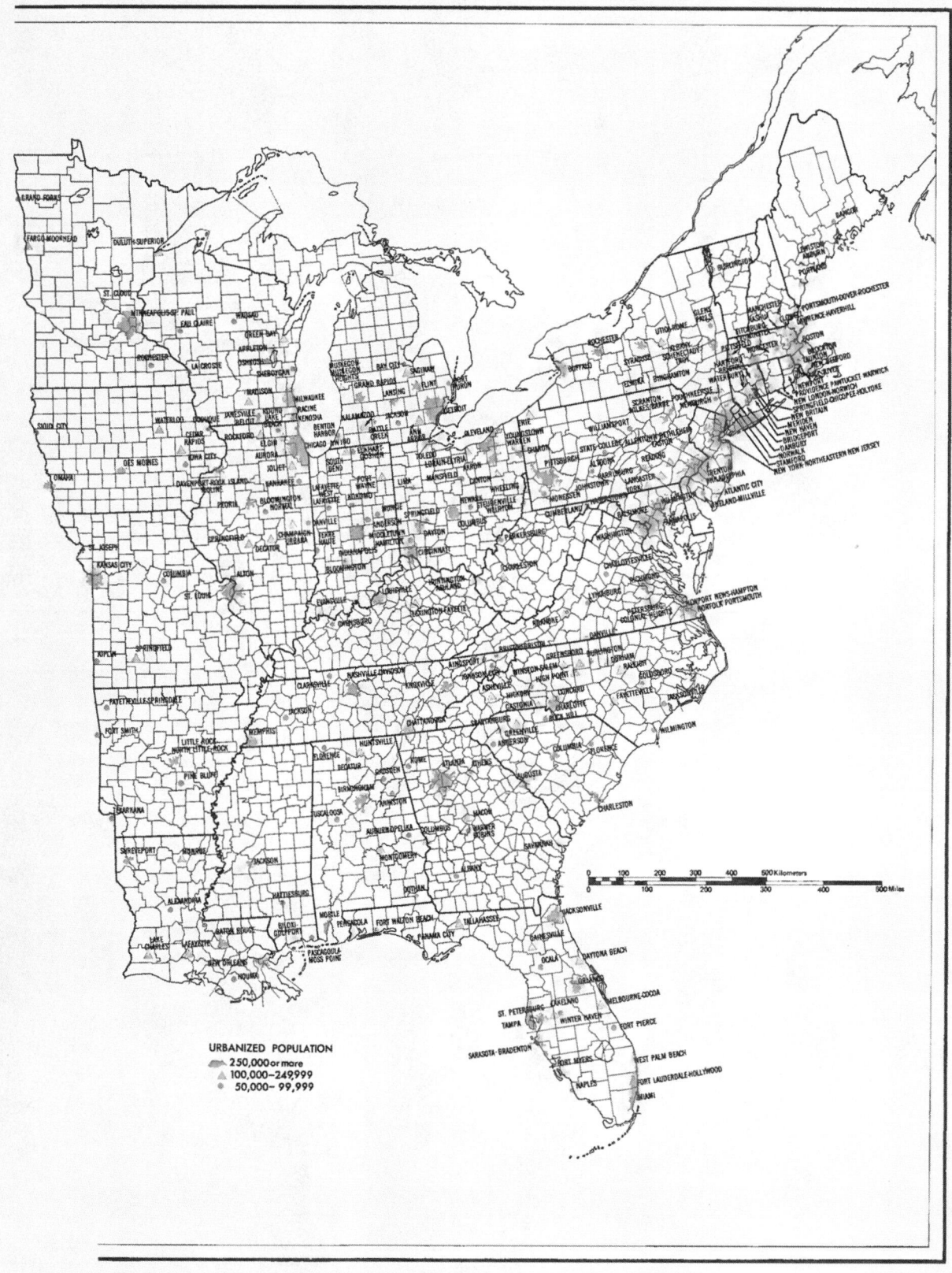

URBANIZED POPULATION

250,000 or more
100,000-249,999
50,000- 99,999

FIGURE 4. **Types of County Subdivisions for the 1980 Census**

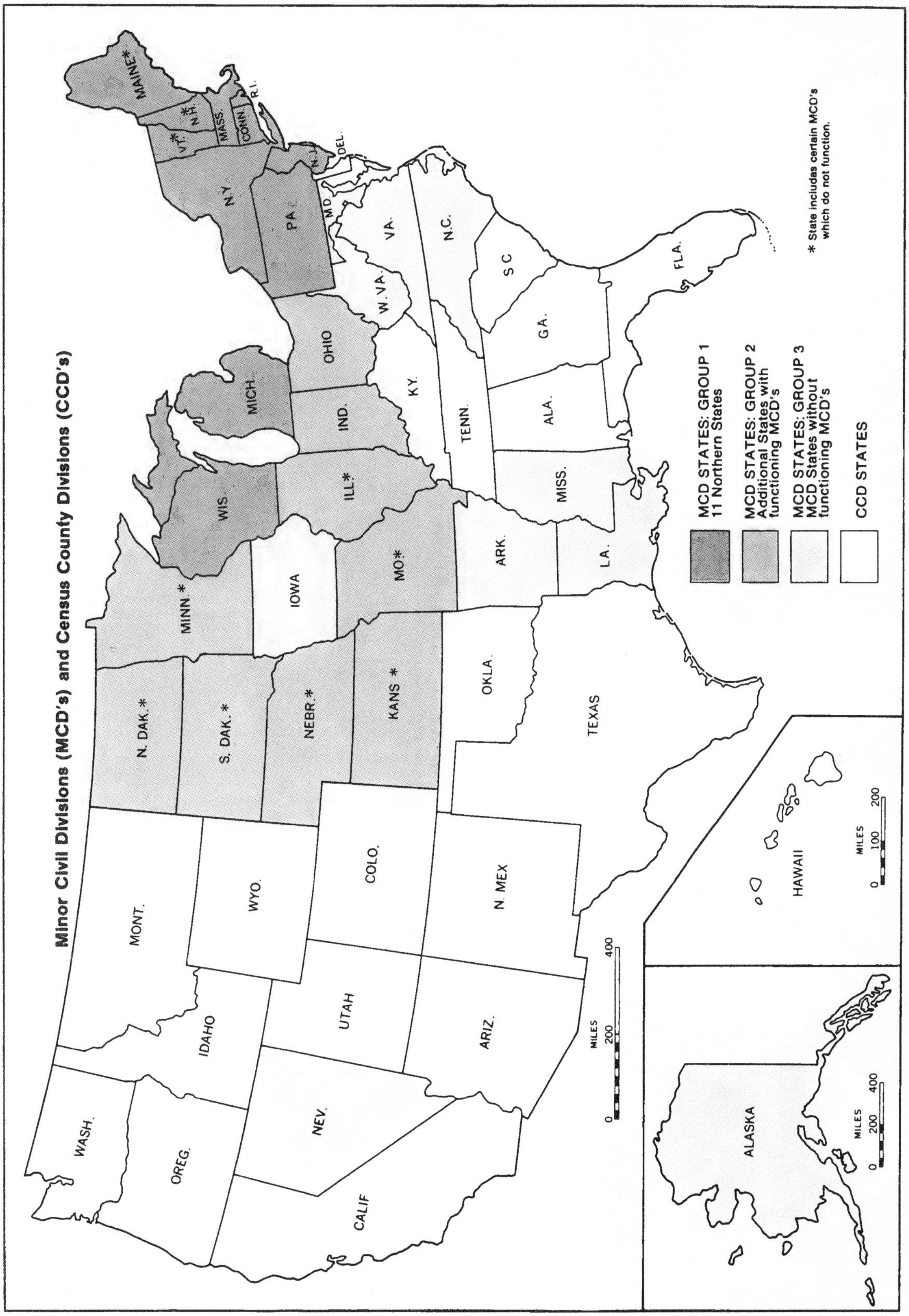

Minor Civil Divisions (MCD's) and Census County Divisions (CCD's)

* State includes certain MCD's which do not function.

MAINE*

VT.* N.H.* MASS. CONN. R.I.

N.Y. N.J. DEL.

PA. MD.

VA. N.C.

W. VA.

OHIO

MICH. IND. KY. S.C.

WIS. ILL.* TENN. GA.

MINN.* IOWA MO.* ALA.

N. DAK.* S. DAK.* NEBR.* KANS.* ARK. MISS. LA.

MONT. WYO. COLO. OKLA. FLA.

IDAHO UTAH N. MEX TEXAS

WASH. NEV. ARIZ.

OREG. CALIF

HAWAII

MILES 0 100 200

ALASKA

MILES 0 200 400

MILES 0 200 400

MCD STATES: GROUP 1
11 Northern States

MCD STATES: GROUP 2
Additional States with functioning MCD's

MCD STATES: GROUP 3
MCD States without functioning MCD's

CCD STATES

FIGURE 5. **Total Population and Percent Change From Preceding Census for the United States: 1790 to 1980**

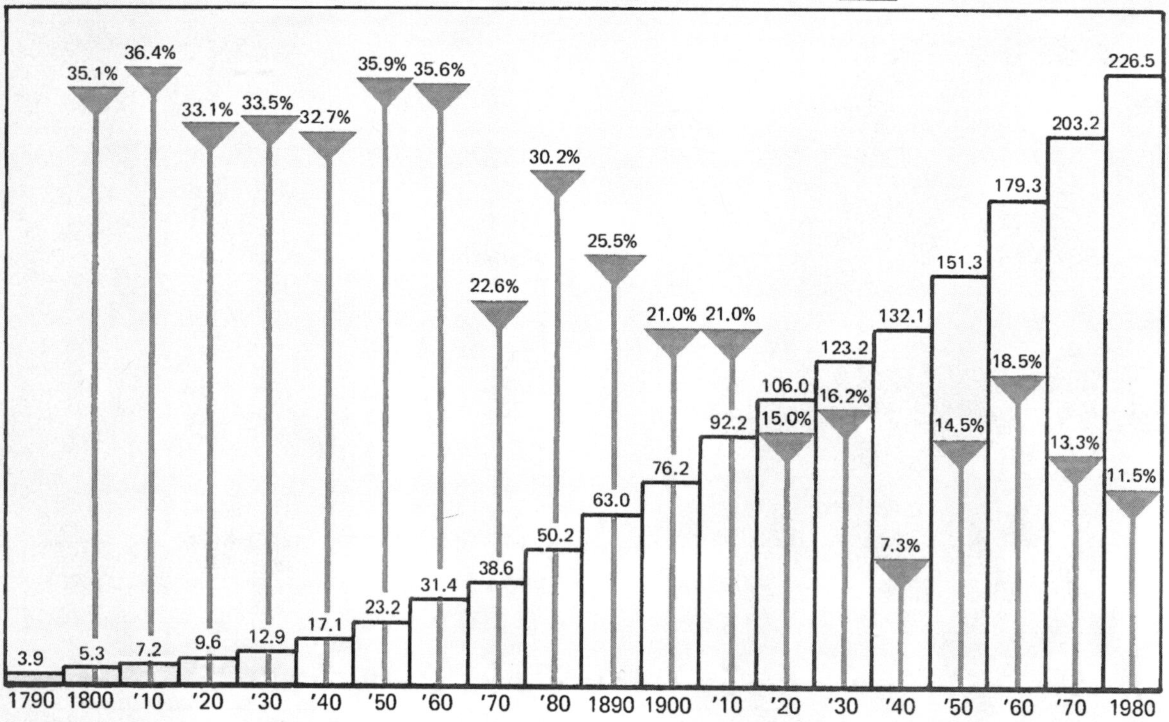

Percent change

Population in millions

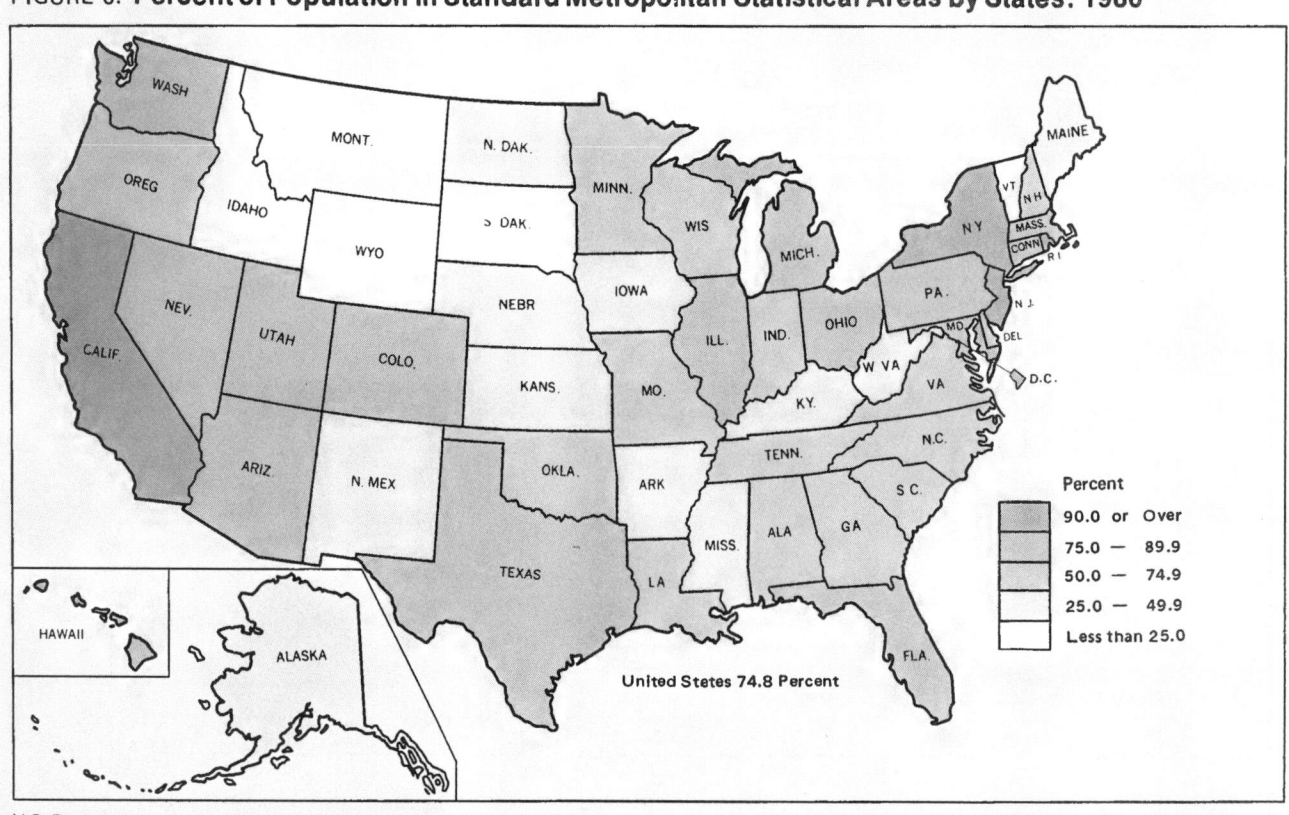

FIGURE 6. **Percent of Population in Standard Metropolitan Statistical Areas by States: 1980**

Percent
90.0 or Over
75.0 — 89.9
50.0 — 74.9
25.0 — 49.9
Less than 25.0

United States 74.8 Percent

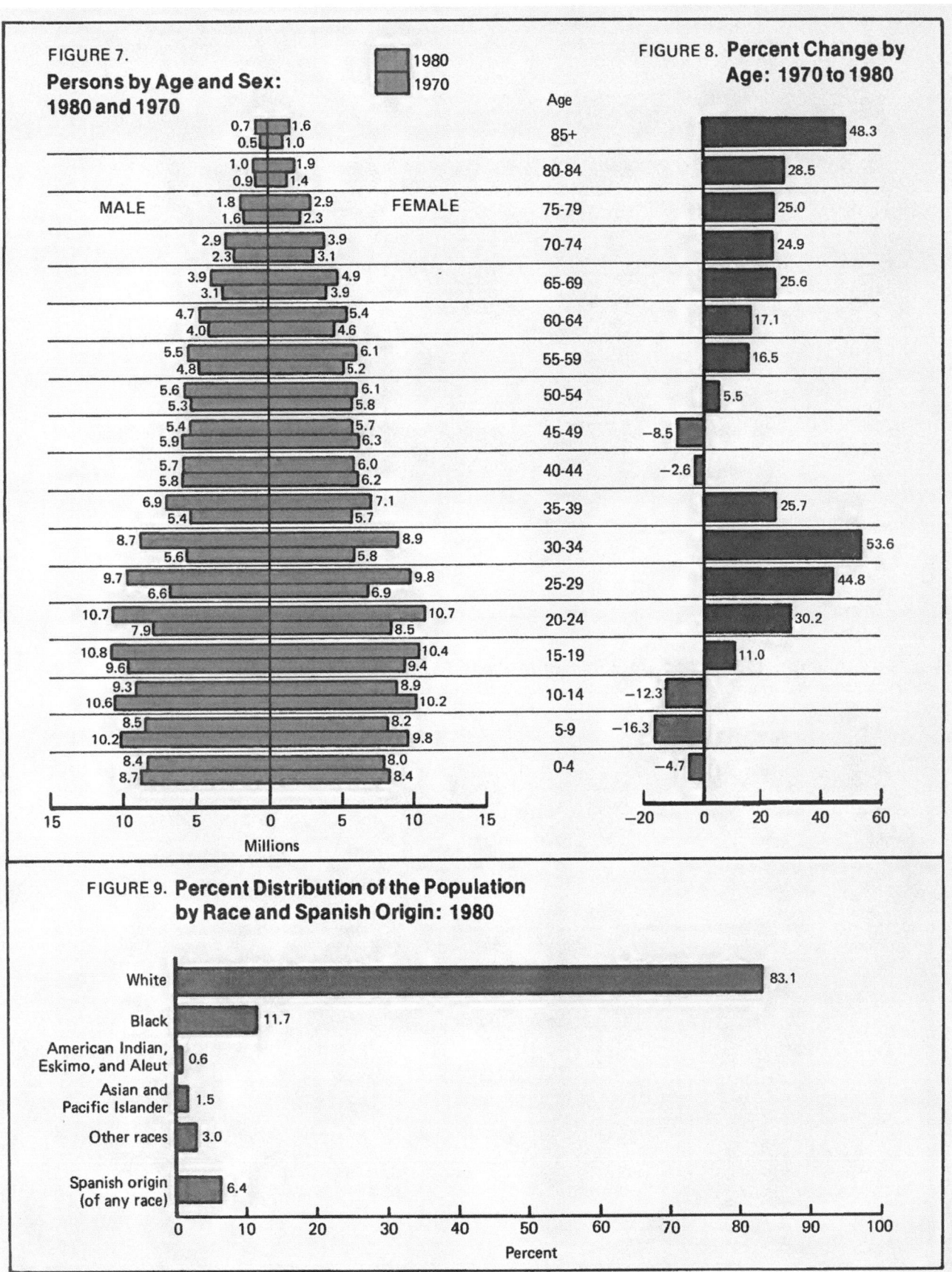

FIGURE 7.
Persons by Age and Sex: 1980 and 1970

1980
1970

Age

FIGURE 8. **Percent Change by Age: 1970 to 1980**

MALE   FEMALE

Age	Male 1980	Male 1970	Female 1980	Female 1970	Percent Change
85+	0.7	0.5	1.6	1.0	48.3
80-84	1.0	0.9	1.9	1.4	28.5
75-79	1.8	1.6	2.9	2.3	25.0
70-74	2.9	2.3	3.9	3.1	24.9
65-69	3.9	3.1	4.9	3.9	25.6
60-64	4.7	4.0	5.4	4.6	17.1
55-59	5.5	4.8	6.1	5.2	16.5
50-54	5.6	5.3	6.1	5.8	5.5
45-49	5.4	5.9	5.7	6.3	−8.5
40-44	5.7	5.8	6.0	6.2	−2.6
35-39	6.9	5.4	7.1	5.7	25.7
30-34	8.7	5.6	8.9	5.8	53.6
25-29	9.7	6.6	9.8	6.9	44.8
20-24	10.7	7.9	10.7	8.5	30.2
15-19	10.8	9.6	10.4	9.4	11.0
10-14	9.3	10.6	8.9	10.2	−12.3
5-9	8.5	10.2	8.2	9.8	−16.3
0-4	8.4	8.7	8.0	8.4	−4.7

15   10   5   0   5   10   15
Millions

−20   0   20   40   60

FIGURE 9. **Percent Distribution of the Population by Race and Spanish Origin: 1980**

	Percent
White	83.1
Black	11.7
American Indian, Eskimo, and Aleut	0.6
Asian and Pacific Islander	1.5
Other races	3.0
Spanish origin (of any race)	6.4

0   10   20   30   40   50   60   70   80   90   100
Percent

U.S. Department of Commerce   Bureau of the Census

1–12   UNITED STATES SUMMARY   GENERAL POPULATION CHARACTERISTICS

FIGURE 10. **Number of Black Persons by State: 1980**

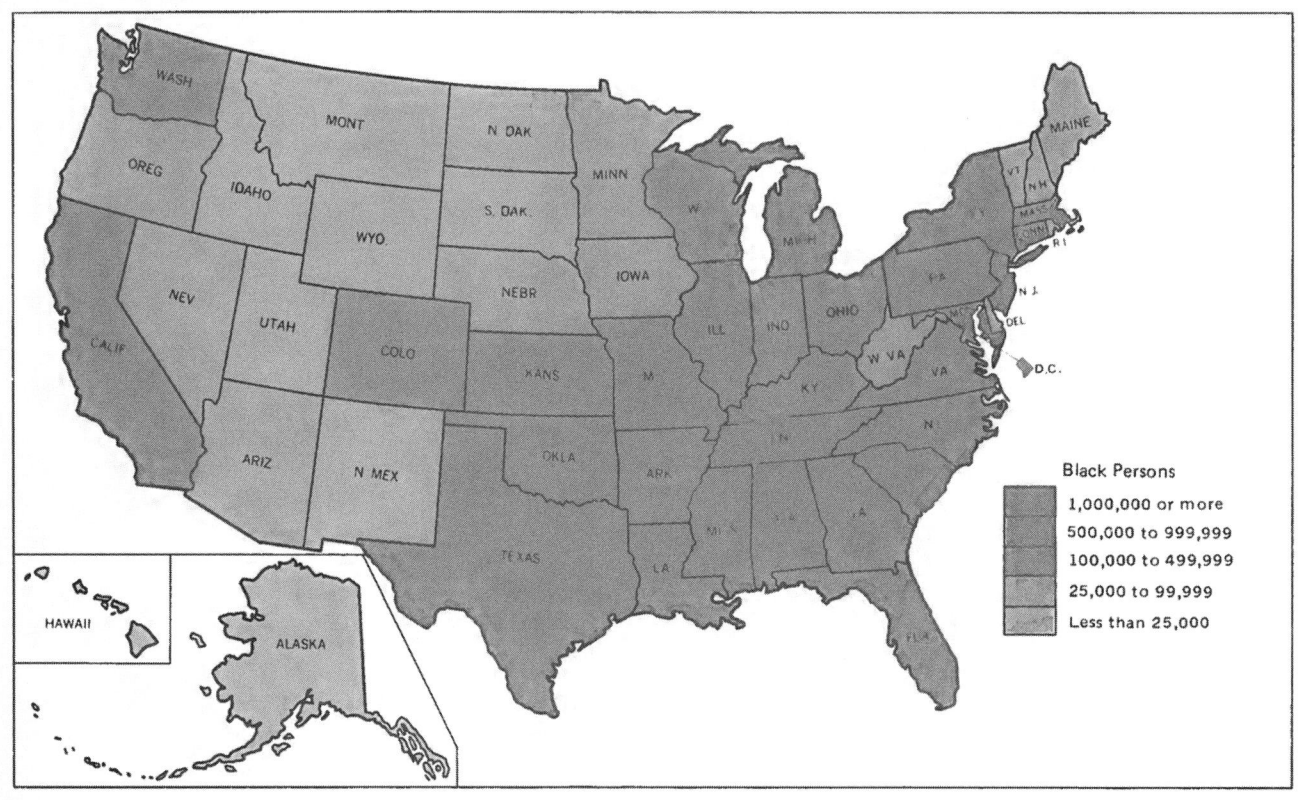

Black Persons

- 1,000,000 or more
- 500,000 to 999,999
- 100,000 to 499,999
- 25,000 to 99,999
- Less than 25,000

FIGURE 11. **Number of American Indian, Eskimo, and Aleut Persons by State: 1980**

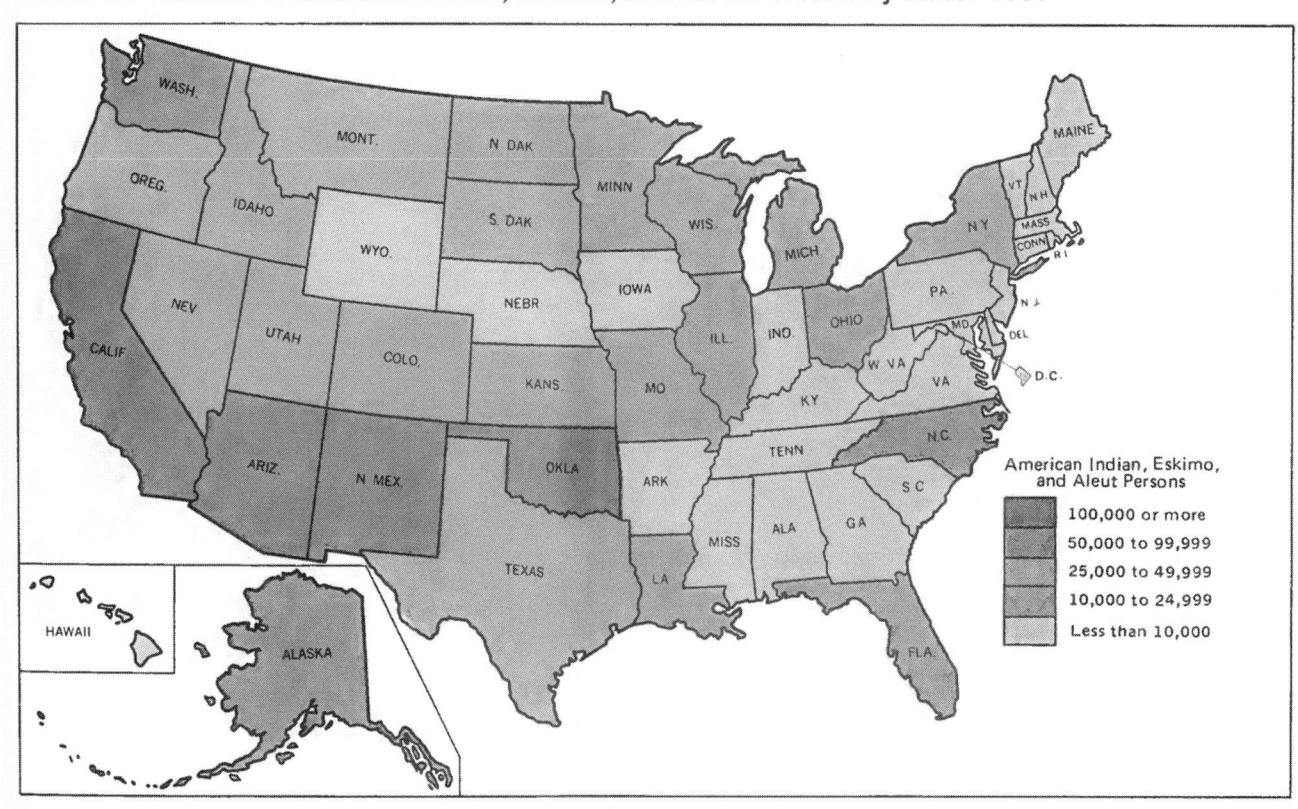

American Indian, Eskimo, and Aleut Persons

- 100,000 or more
- 50,000 to 99,999
- 25,000 to 49,999
- 10,000 to 24,999
- Less than 10,000

FIGURE 12. **Number of Asian and Pacific Islander Persons by State: 1980**

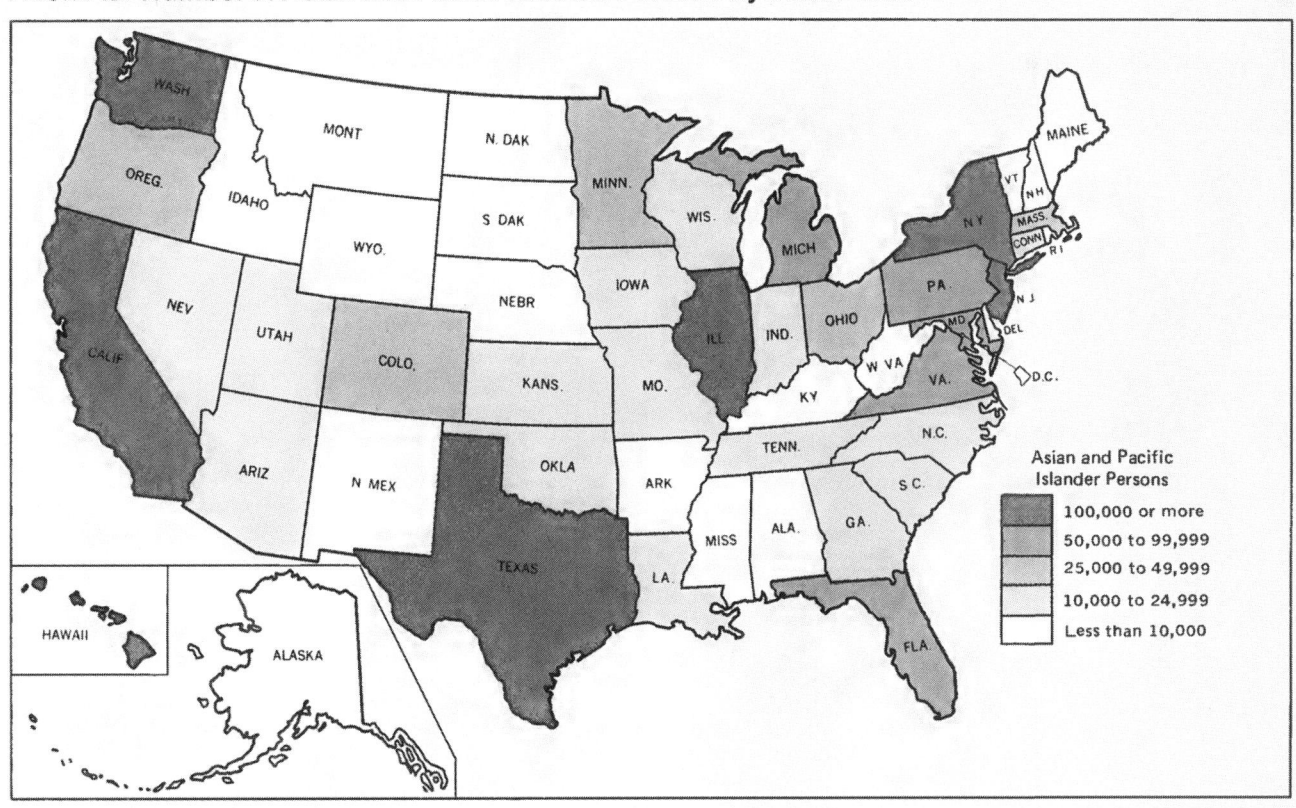

FIGURE 13.
Percent Distribution of Persons of Spanish Origin by Type of Spanish Origin: 1980

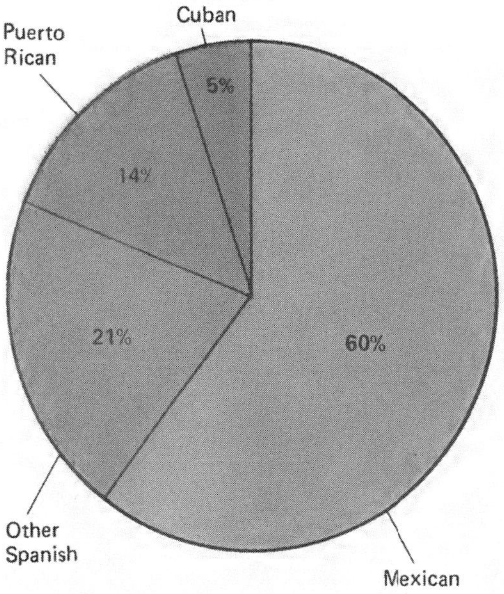

- Cuban 5%
- Puerto Rican 14%
- Other Spanish 21%
- Mexican 60%

FIGURE 14.
Percent Distribution of Persons of Spanish Origin by Residence in Selected States: 1980

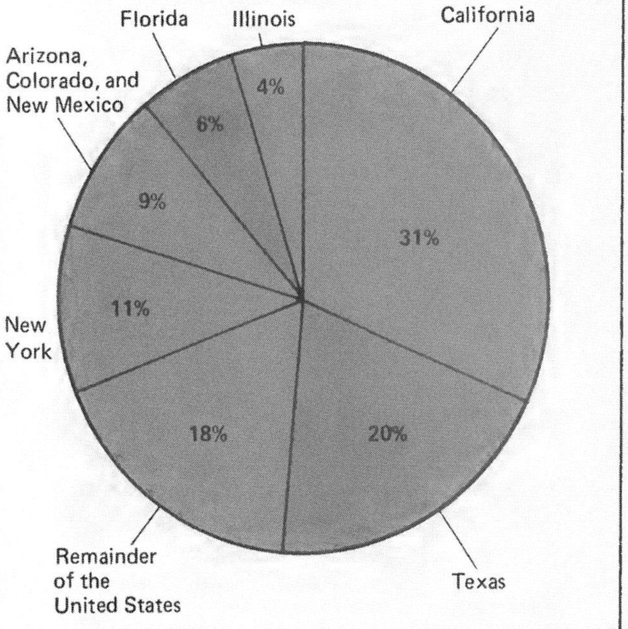

- Florida 6%
- Illinois 4%
- California 31%
- Arizona, Colorado, and New Mexico 9%
- New York 11%
- Remainder of the United States 18%
- Texas 20%

U.S. Department of Commerce

Bureau of the Census

1–14   UNITED STATES SUMMARY

GENERAL POPULATION CHARACTERISTICS

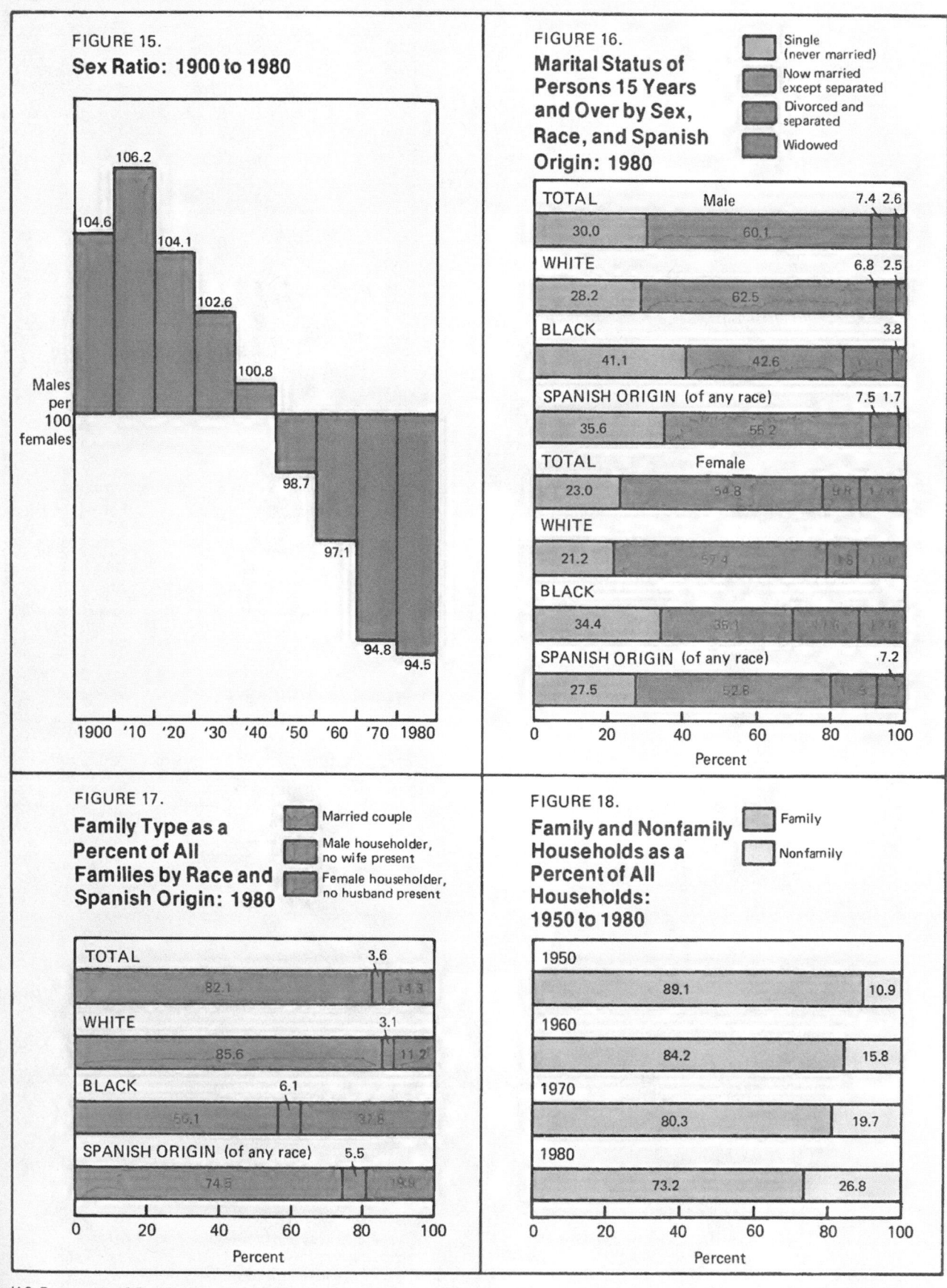

FIGURE 15.
Sex Ratio: 1900 to 1980

Males per 100 females

106.2
104.6
104.1
102.6
100.8
98.7
97.1
94.8
94.5

1900 '10 '20 '30 '40 '50 '60 '70 1980

FIGURE 16.
Marital Status of Persons 15 Years and Over by Sex, Race, and Spanish Origin: 1980

- Single (never married)
- Now married except separated
- Divorced and separated
- Widowed

	Male		
TOTAL	30.0	60.1	7.4 2.6
WHITE	28.2	62.5	6.8 2.5
BLACK	41.1	42.6	3.8
SPANISH ORIGIN (of any race)	35.6	55.2	7.5 1.7

	Female		
TOTAL	23.0	54.8	
WHITE	21.2	57.4	
BLACK	34.4	36.1	
SPANISH ORIGIN (of any race)	27.5	52.8	7.2

Percent
0 20 40 60 80 100

FIGURE 17.
Family Type as a Percent of All Families by Race and Spanish Origin: 1980

- Married couple
- Male householder, no wife present
- Female householder, no husband present

TOTAL	82.1	3.6	14.3
WHITE	85.6	3.1	11.2
BLACK	56.1	6.1	37.8
SPANISH ORIGIN (of any race)	74.6	5.5	19.9

Percent
0 20 40 60 80 100

FIGURE 18.
Family and Nonfamily Households as a Percent of All Households: 1950 to 1980

- Family
- Nonfamily

1950	89.1	10.9
1960	84.2	15.8
1970	80.3	19.7
1980	73.2	26.8

Percent
0 20 40 60 80 100

CORRECTION NOTE

Shown below are corrections to the 1980 census counts of the total population for States, places and towns or townships of 50,000 or more, central cities of SMSA's, American Indian reservations, and Alaska Native villages. Some corrections in this note may be in addition to or supersede those in the correction notes in the PC80-1-B State reports, which also show corrections for places of 1,000 or more population, counties, and county subdivisions. The tables of this report have not been revised to reflect any of these corrections.

Any additional corrections made after this report is printed are available by writing to Data User Services Division, Customer Services (Corrections), Bureau of the Census, Washington, D.C. 20233.

Corrections for the total and American Indian populations on American Indian reservations will be published in the 1980 census Supplementary Reports, PC80-S1 series, "Population and Housing Unit Counts for American Indian Areas and Alaska Native Villages: 1980."

	1980 population As shown in the table	Corrected		1980 population As shown in the table	Corrected
United States.............	226 545 805	226 548 632	Connecticut:		
			New Haven city..................	126 109	126 101
Alabama.......................	3 893 888	3 893 978	Stamford city..................	102 453	102 466
			Greenwich town..................	59 578	59 565
Alaska:			New Haven town..................	126 109	126 101
			Stamford town..................	102 453	102 466
Saxman Alaska Native Village......	434	273			
Selawik Alaska Native Village.....	361	535	District of Columbia..........	638 333	638 432
			Washington city................	638 333	638 432
Arizona......................	2 718 215	2 718 425			
			Florida......................	9 746 324	9 746 421
Scottsdale city.................	88 412	88 622	Bradenton city.................	30 170	30 228
Tempe city......................	106 743	106 920			
Hopi Reservation, Ariz..........	6 906	6 896	Georgia......................	5 463 105	5 463 087
Navajo Reservation, Ariz.-N.Mex.-			Albany city....................	74 059	74 425
Utah.......................	110 433	110 443	Savannah city..................	141 390	141 651
Arkansas.....................	2 286 435	2 286 419			
			Idaho......................	943 935	944 038
Little Rock city................	158 461	158 915	Boise City city................	102 451	102 160
North Little Rock city..........	64 288	64 388	Kootenai Reservation, Idaho.......	-	40
California..................	23 667 902	23 667 837			
			Illinois...................	11 426 518	11 427 414
Anaheim city....................	219 311	219 494	Champaign city.................	58 133	58 267
Chico city......................	26 603	26 716	Decatur city...................	94 081	93 896
Compton city....................	81 286	81 347	Elgin city.....................	63 798	63 668
Concord city....................	103 255	103 763	Moline city....................	45 709	46 278
Daly City city.................	78 519	78 427	Rock Island city...............	47 036	46 928
Fresno city....................	218 202	217 129	Springfield city...............	99 637	100 054
Hayward city...................	94 167	94 342			
Long Beach city................	361 334	361 355	Indiana.....................	5 490 224	5 490 260
Los Angeles city...............	2 966 850	2 968 579	Fort Wayne city................	172 196	172 349
Orange city....................	91 788	91 450			
Pasadena city..................	118 550	118 072	Kansas.....................	2 363 679	2 364 236
Pico Rivera city...............	53 459	53 387			
Riverside city.................	170 876	170 591	Kentucky...................	3 660 777	3 660 257
San Bernardino city............	117 490	118 794	Louisville city................	298 451	298 694
San Jose city..................	629 442	629 531			
San Mateo city.................	77 561	77 640	Louisiana...................	4 205 900	4 206 098
Santa Ana city.................	203 713	204 023	Baton Rouge city...............	219 419	219 844
Santa Clara city...............	87 746	87 700	New Orleans city...............	557 515	557 927
Tulare city....................	22 526	22 530			
Walnut Creek city..............	53 643	53 490			
West Covina city...............	80 291	81 292			
Whittier city..................	69 717	68 558			
Colorado....................	2 889 964	2 889 735			
Colorado Springs city..........	215 150	214 821			
Lakewood city..................	112 860	113 808			

	1980 population			1980 population	
	As shown in the table	Corrected		As shown in the table	Corrected
Maine....................	1 124 660	1 125 030	Oklahoma.....................	3 025 290	3 025 495
			Oklahoma City city..............	403 213	403 484
Maryland.................	4 216 975	4 216 941			
			Oregon...................	2 633 105	2 633 149
Baltimore city..................	786 755	786 741			
Bethesda (CDP)..................	62 736	63 022	Pennsylvania..................	11 863 895	11 864 751
			Pittsburgh city.................	423 938	423 959
Massachusetts.............	5 737 037	5 737 081	Abington township, Montgomery		
			County..........................	59 084	58 836
Michigan..................	9 262 078	9 262 070	Haverford township............	52 349	52 371
			Lower Merion township............	59 651	59 629
Ann Arbor city..................	107 966	107 969			
Isabella Reservation, Mich.......	23 020	23 373	South Carolina..............	3 121 820	3 122 814
			Anderson city..................	27 313	27 638
Minnesota:			Columbia city..................	101 208	101 229
			Florence city..................	30 062	29 842
Rochester city..................	57 890	57 906	North Charleston city..........	62 534	62 562
Mille Lacs Reservation,			Rock Hill city.................	35 344	35 327
Minn............................	37	17	Spartanburg city...............	43 968	43 826
Vermillion Lake Reservation,					
Minn............................	116	110	Tennessee:		
White Earth Reservation,					
Minn............................	9 505	9 486	Chattanooga city..................	169 565	169 728
			Knoxville city.................	175 030	175 045
Mississippi..............	2 520 638	2 520 631	Memphis city...................	646 356	646 174
Missouri.................	4 916 686	4 916 759	Texas...................	14 229 191	14 227 574
Joplin city....................	38 893	39 023	Austin city....................	345 496	345 890
Kansas City city................	448 159	448 033	Corpus Christi city............	231 999	231 134
			San Antonio city..............	785 880	786 023
Montana:			Temple city....................	42 483	42 354
			Texas City city................	41 403	41 201
Billings city....................	66 798	66 842			
			Utah:		
Nebraska:					
			Salt Lake City city.............	163 033	163 034
Omaha city......................	314 255	313 939	Sandy City city................	50 546	52 210
			West Valley (COP).............	72 378	72 433
New Jersey...................	7 364 823	7 365 011			
			Virginia....................	5 346 818	5 346 797
East Orange city..................	77 690	77 878			
Middletown (COP)..................	61 615	62 298	Washington.................	4 132 156	4 132 204
			Pasco city.....................	17 944	18 425
New Mexico..................	1 302 894	1 303 046	Lower Elwah Reservation, Wash....	67	64
Albuquerque city..................	331 767	332 239	West Virginia..............	1 949 644	1 950 258
Nambe Pueblo, N. Mex............	386	1 097	Parkersburg city...............	39 967	39 946
Picuris Pueblo, N. Mex..........	337	1 539	Weirton city...................	24 736	25 371
Pojoaque Pueblo, N. Mex.........	1 191	1 143			
Sandia Pueblo, N. Mex...........	683	2 692	Wisconsin....................	4 705 767	4 705 642
San Juan Pueblo, N. Mex.........	4 365	4 090			
Santa Clara Pueblo, N. Mex......	6 740	8 222	Appleton city..................	59 032	58 913
Taos Pueblo, N. Mex............	1 421	4 693	Milwaukee city.................	636 212	636 297
Tesuque Pueblo, N. Mex..........	252	369	Waukesha city..................	50 319	50 365
			Wisconsin Winnebago Reservation..	658	416
New York:					
Brooklyn borough................	2 230 936	2 230 844			
Staten Island borough...........	352 121	352 213			
North Carolina..............	5 881 766	5 881 385			
Charlotte city..................	314 447	315 473			
Durham city....................	100 831	100 538			
Jacksonville city..............	17 056	18 259			
Ohio....................	10 797 630	10 797 624			
Canton city....................	94 730	93 077			
Columbus city..................	564 871	565 032			
Dayton city....................	203 371	193 536			
Lima city.....................	47 381	47 827			

Table 37. Summary of General Characteristics: 1980

[For meaning of symbols, see Introduction. For definitions of terms, see appendixes A and B]

United States Urban and Rural and Size of Place Inside and Outside SMSA's	Persons													Households		
		Percent								15 years and over—Percent now married, including separated		In group quarters				
	Total	Change 1970–80	Black	Spanish origin	Under 18 years	18 to 64 years	65 years and over	Median age	Fertility ratio	Male	Female	Total	Percent of total persons	Total	Percent change 1970–80	Persons per household
United States	226 545 805	11.5	11.7	6.4	28.1	60.6	11.3	30.0	279	62.0	57.4	5 749 648	2.5	80 389 673	26.7	2.75
URBAN AND RURAL AND SIZE OF PLACE																
Urban	167 050 992	11.9	13.5	7.9	27.1	61.5	11.4	29.9	268	60.0	54.5	4 820 287	2.9	60 551 717	27.3	2.68
Inside urbanized areas	139 170 683	17.5	14.4	8 3	27.0	62.0	10.9	30.0	262	59.5	54.3	3 492 839	2.5	50 541 185	33.7	2.68
Central cities	67 035 302	4.9	22.6	10.6	26.3	61.8	12.0	29.6	269	55.2	49.5	2 046 072	3.1	25 275 501	18.1	2.57
Urban fringe	72 135 381	32.3	6.9	6.1	27.7	62.3	10.0	30.4	255	63.4	58.8	1 446 767	2.0	25 265 684	54.0	2.80
Outside urbanized areas	27 880 309	–9.7	8 9	5.7	27.6	58.6	13.8	29.6	302	62.6	55.6	1 327 448	4 8	10 010 532	2.7	2.65
Places of 10,000 or more	13 481 787	–18.9	9.7	6.1	26.9	60.2	12.9	28.7	288	60.4	53.9	778 598	5.8	4 838 838	–7.3	2.63
Places of 2,500 to 10,000	14 398 522	1.0	8.2	5.3	28.3	57.0	14.7	30.5	316	64 6	57.2	548 850	3.8	5 171 694	14.2	2.68
Rural	59 494 813	10.4	6.6	2.5	31.0	58.1	10.9	30.1	313	67.7	66.4	929 361	1.6	19 837 956	24.9	2.95
Places of 1,000 to 2,500	7 037 840	5.7	6.1	3.5	28.7	55.9	15.4	31.7	323	66.9	59.6	161 645	2.3	2 550 142	17.9	2.70
Other rural	52 456 973	11.1	6.6	2.3	31.3	58.4	10.3	30.0	312	67.8	67.4	767 716	1.5	17 287 814	26.0	2.99
INSIDE AND OUTSIDE SMSA's																
Inside SMSA's	169 430 623	10.3	12.7	7.6	27.7	61.6	10.7	29.9	268	60.9	56.1	4 147 742	2.4	60 497 718	25.6	2.73
Urban	145 442 528	(NA)	14.0	8.3	27.1	61.9	11.0	30.0	264	59.7	54.5	3 743 381	2.6	52 705 003	(NA)	2.69
Central cities	67 854 344	(NA)	22.5	10.8	26.3	61.8	11.9	29.5	270	55.2	49.6	2 089 631	3.1	25 526 162	(NA)	2.58
Not in central cities	77 588 184	(NA)	6.6	6.1	27.9	62.0	10.2	30.4	259	63.6	58.9	1 653 750	2.1	27 178 841	(NA)	2.79
Rural	23 988 095	(NA)	4 5	3 0	31.3	59.6	9.0	29 8	293	67 8	67.3	404 361	1.7	7 792 715	(NA)	3.03
Outside SMSA's	57 115 182	15.2	8.8	3.2	29.4	57.6	13.0	30.1	317	65.5	61.4	1 601 906	2.8	19 891 955	30.3	2.79
Urban	21 608 464	(NA)	10.1	4 9	27.1	58.6	14.3	29 7	299	61.9	54.7	1 076 906	5.0	7 846 714	(NA)	2.62
Rural	35 506 718	(NA)	8.0	2.2	30.7	57.1	12 2	30.4	328	67.7	65.8	525 000	1.5	12 045 241	(NA)	2.90

Table 38. Persons by Race and Sex: 1980

[For meaning of symbols, see Introduction. For definitions of terms, see appendixes A and B]

United States Urban and Rural and Size of Place Inside and Outside SMSA's	Total persons	White	Black	American Indian	Eskimo	Aleut	Japanese	Chinese	Filipino	Korean	Asian Indian	Vietnamese	Hawaiian	Guamanian	Samoan	Other
United States	226 545 805	188 371 622	26 495 025	1 364 033	42 162	14 205	700 974	806 040	774 652	354 593	361 531	261 729	166 814	32 158	41 948	6 758 319
Male	110 053 161	91 685 333	12 519 189	673 517	21 525	7 186	320 941	407 544	374 191	147 825	187 083	135 640	82 256	16 583	21 249	3 453 099
Female	116 492 644	96 686 289	13 975 836	690 516	20 637	7 019	380 033	398 496	400 461	206 768	174 448	126 089	84 558	15 575	20 699	3 305 220
URBAN AND RURAL AND SIZE OF PLACE																
Urban	167 050 992	134 321 744	22 594 016	719 047	13 650	7 525	643 081	781 798	716 128	329 746	334 683	249 674	136 915	29 653	40 305	6 133 027
Male	80 292 291	64 638 068	10 596 862	351 472	6 675	3 707	295 674	395 619	344 709	139 824	174 977	129 812	67 473	15 386	20 375	3 111 658
Female	86 758 701	69 683 676	11 997 154	367 575	6 975	3 818	347 407	386 179	371 419	189 922	159 706	119 862	69 442	14 267	19 930	3 021 369
Inside urbanized areas	139 170 683	110 148 772	20 106 051	507 941	9 263	5 887	583 113	750 424	655 309	308 150	311 910	231 886	101 177	26 953	36 475	5 387 372
Male	66 975 219	53 114 020	9 420 120	248 892	4 549	2 885	268 487	379 491	314 306	132 814	163 679	120 625	49 907	13 943	18 405	2 723 096
Female	72 195 464	57 034 752	10 685 931	259 049	4 714	3 002	314 626	370 933	341 003	175 336	148 231	111 261	51 270	13 010	18 070	2 664 276
Central cities	67 035 302	46 408 745	15 143 702	286 201	6 702	3 913	309 630	468 430	336 492	143 543	137 038	127 920	56 854	12 106	18 147	3 575 879
Male	31 899 486	22 152 755	7 022 482	138 659	3 215	1 910	143 557	237 842	162 135	62 213	72 681	68 010	27 762	6 184	9 084	1 790 997
Female	35 135 816	24 255 990	8 121 220	147 542	3 487	2 003	166 073	230 588	174 357	81 330	64 357	59 910	29 092	5 922	9 063	1 784 882
Urban fringe	72 135 381	63 740 027	4 962 349	221 740	2 561	1 974	273 483	281 994	318 817	164 607	174 872	103 966	44 323	14 847	18 328	1 811 493
Male	35 075 733	30 961 265	2 397 638	110 233	1 334	975	124 930	141 649	152 171	70 601	90 998	52 615	22 145	7 759	9 321	932 099
Female	37 059 648	32 778 762	2 564 711	111 507	1 227	999	148 553	140 345	166 646	94 006	83 874	51 351	22 178	7 088	9 007	879 394
Outside urbanized areas	27 880 309	24 172 972	2 487 965	211 106	4 387	1 638	59 968	31 374	60 819	21 596	22 773	17 788	35 738	2 700	3 830	745 655
Male	13 317 072	11 524 048	1 176 742	102 580	2 126	822	27 187	16 128	30 403	7 010	11 298	9 187	17 566	1 443	1 970	388 562
Female	14 563 237	12 648 924	1 311 223	108 526	2 261	816	32 781	15 246	30 416	14 586	11 475	8 601	18 172	1 257	1 860	357 093
Places of 10,000 or more	13 481 787	11 555 904	1 307 678	87 554	1 211	468	38 176	20 187	26 788	12 857	13 040	10 622	12 996	1 595	709	392 002
Male	6 450 320	5 515 138	620 883	42 653	583	235	17 528	10 558	13 312	4 288	6 836	5 576	6 519	863	409	204 939
Female	7 031 467	6 040 766	686 795	44 901	628	233	20 648	9 629	13 476	8 569	6 204	5 046	6 477	732	300	187 063
Places of 2,500 to 10,000	14 398 522	12 617 068	1 180 287	123 552	3 176	1 170	21 792	11 187	34 031	8 739	9 733	7 166	22 742	1 105	3 121	353 653
Male	6 866 752	6 008 910	555 859	59 927	1 543	587	9 659	5 570	17 091	2 722	4 462	3 611	11 047	580	1 561	183 623
Female	7 531 770	6 608 158	624 428	63 625	1 633	583	12 133	5 617	16 940	6 017	5 271	3 555	11 695	525	1 560	170 030
Rural	59 494 813	54 049 878	3 901 009	644 986	28 512	6 680	57 893	24 242	58 524	24 847	26 848	12 055	29 899	2 505	1 643	625 292
Male	29 760 870	27 047 265	1 922 327	322 045	14 850	3 479	25 267	11 925	29 482	8 001	12 106	5 828	14 783	1 197	874	341 441
Female	29 733 943	27 002 613	1 978 682	322 941	13 662	3 201	32 626	12 317	29 042	16 846	14 742	6 227	15 116	1 308	769	283 851
Places of 1,000 to 2,500	7 037 840	6 379 516	427 467	70 805	5 457	1 121	11 265	2 952	11 908	3 050	3 535	2 248	5 501	345	232	112 438
Male	3 369 682	3 053 753	200 230	34 660	2 764	570	5 172	1 430	6 076	939	1 448	1 150	2 704	165	128	58 493
Female	3 668 158	3 325 763	227 237	36 145	2 693	551	6 093	1 522	5 832	2 111	2 087	1 098	2 797	180	104	53 945
Other rural	52 456 973	47 670 362	3 473 542	574 181	23 055	5 559	46 628	21 290	46 616	21 797	23 313	9 807	24 398	2 160	1 411	512 854
Male	26 391 188	23 993 512	1 722 097	287 385	12 086	2 909	20 095	10 495	23 406	7 062	10 658	4 678	12 079	1 032	746	282 948
Female	26 065 785	23 676 850	1 751 445	286 796	10 969	2 650	26 533	10 795	23 210	14 735	12 655	5 129	12 319	1 128	665	229 906
INSIDE AND OUTSIDE SMSA's																
Inside SMSA's	169 430 623	138 064 178	21 477 741	679 227	10 307	6 590	621 844	774 569	704 451	327 873	333 088	241 752	125 100	29 435	40 363	5 994 105
Male	82 071 794	67 014 038	10 113 127	335 689	5 072	3 199	284 970	391 430	339 495	139 396	174 028	125 458	61 653	15 177	20 359	3 048 703
Female	87 358 829	71 050 140	11 364 614	343 538	5 235	3 391	336 874	383 139	364 956	188 477	159 060	116 294	63 447	14 258	20 004	2 945 402
Urban	145 442 528	115 719 395	20 404 523	542 244	9 518	6 057	597 024	759 419	678 084	314 463	317 396	236 188	117 267	28 006	39 366	5 673 578
Male	70 006 334	55 792 276	9 567 897	265 895	4 666	2 955	274 505	383 954	326 229	134 826	166 367	122 830	57 742	14 492	19 825	2 871 875
Female	75 436 194	59 927 119	10 836 626	276 349	4 852	3 102	322 519	375 465	351 855	179 637	151 029	113 358	59 525	13 514	19 541	2 801 703
Central cities	67 854 344	46 946 692	15 297 000	286 266	6 719	3 928	299 301	468 376	348 482	146 698	139 895	136 104	48 403	13 117	19 149	3 694 214
Male	32 313 824	22 427 712	7 095 432	138 846	3 236	1 914	138 398	237 801	167 975	63 666	74 309	72 441	23 539	6 692	9 577	1 852 286
Female	35 540 520	24 518 980	8 201 568	147 420	3 483	2 014	160 903	230 575	180 507	83 032	65 586	63 663	24 864	6 425	9 572	1 841 928
Not in central cities	77 588 184	68 772 703	5 107 523	255 978	2 799	2 129	297 723	291 043	329 602	167 765	177 501	100 084	68 864	14 889	20 217	1 979 364
Male	37 692 510	33 364 564	2 472 465	127 049	1 430	1 041	136 107	146 153	158 254	71 160	92 058	50 389	34 203	7 800	10 248	1 019 589
Female	39 895 674	35 408 139	2 635 058	128 929	1 369	1 088	161 616	144 890	171 348	96 605	85 443	49 695	34 661	7 089	9 969	959 775
Rural	23 988 095	22 344 783	1 073 218	136 983	789	533	24 820	15 150	26 367	13 410	15 692	5 564	7 833	1 429	997	320 527
Male	12 065 460	11 221 762	545 230	69 794	406	244	10 465	7 476	13 266	4 570	7 661	2 628	3 911	685	534	176 828
Female	11 922 635	11 123 021	527 988	67 189	383	289	14 355	7 674	13 101	8 840	8 031	2 936	3 922	744	463	143 699
Outside SMSA's	57 115 182	50 307 444	5 017 284	684 806	31 855	7 615	79 130	31 471	70 201	26 720	28 443	19 977	41 714	2 723	1 585	764 214
Male	27 981 367	24 671 295	2 406 062	337 828	16 453	3 987	35 971	16 114	34 696	8 429	13 055	10 182	20 603	1 406	890	404 396
Female	29 133 815	25 636 149	2 611 222	346 978	15 402	3 628	43 159	15 357	35 505	18 291	15 388	9 795	21 111	1 317	695	359 819
Urban	21 608 464	18 602 349	2 189 493	176 803	4 132	1 468	46 057	22 379	38 044	15 283	17 287	13 486	19 648	1 647	939	459 449
Male	10 285 957	8 845 792	1 028 965	85 577	2 009	752	21 169	11 665	18 480	4 998	8 610	6 982	9 731	894	550	239 783
Female	11 322 507	9 756 557	1 160 528	91 226	2 123	716	24 888	10 714	19 564	10 285	8 677	6 504	9 917	753	389	219 666
Rural	35 506 718	31 705 095	2 827 791	508 003	27 723	6 147	33 073	9 092	32 157	11 437	11 156	6 491	22 066	1 076	646	304 765
Male	17 695 410	15 825 503	1 377 097	252 251	14 444	3 235	14 802	4 449	16 216	3 431	4 445	3 200	10 872	512	340	164 613
Female	17 811 308	15 879 592	1 450 694	255 752	13 279	2 912	18 271	4 643	15 941	8 006	6 711	3 291	11 194	564	306	140 152

Table 39. Total Persons and Spanish Origin Persons by Type of Spanish Origin, Race, and Sex: 1980

[For meaning of symbols, see Introduction. For definitions of terms, see appendixes A and B]

United States Urban and Rural and Size of Place Inside and Outside SMSA's	Total persons	Spanish origin								Not of Spanish origin			
		Total	Type				Race			Total	White	Black	Other races
			Mexican	Puerto Rican	Cuban	Other Spanish	White	Black	Other races				
United States	226 545 805	14 608 673	8 740 439	2 013 945	803 226	3 051 063	8 115 256	390 852	6 102 565	211 937 132	180 256 366	26 104 173	5 576 593
Male	110 053 161	7 279 831	4 442 641	982 320	382 320	1 472 550	3 993 786	187 229	3 098 816	102 773 330	87 691 547	12 331 960	2 749 823
Female	116 492 644	7 328 842	4 297 798	1 031 625	420 906	1 578 513	4 121 470	203 623	3 003 749	109 163 802	92 564 819	13 772 213	2 826 770
URBAN AND RURAL AND SIZE OF PLACE													
Urban	167 050 992	13 133 865	7 659 041	1 954 524	785 323	2 734 977	7 266 377	336 571	5 530 917	153 917 127	127 055 367	22 257 445	4 604 315
Male	80 292 291	6 506 905	3 871 779	948 502	372 992	1 313 632	3 560 031	160 595	2 786 279	73 785 386	61 078 037	10 436 267	2 271 082
Female	86 758 701	6 626 960	3 787 262	1 006 022	412 331	1 421 345	3 706 346	175 976	2 744 638	80 131 741	65 977 330	11 821 178	2 333 233
Inside urbanized areas	139 170 683	11 552 502	6 400 599	1 897 213	768 443	2 486 247	6 409 468	304 362	4 838 672	127 618 181	103 739 304	19 801 689	4 077 188
Male	66 975 219	5 709 283	3 236 716	916 662	364 239	1 191 666	3 136 378	145 098	2 427 807	61 265 936	49 977 642	9 275 022	2 013 272
Female	72 195 464	5 843 219	3 163 883	980 551	404 204	1 294 581	3 273 090	159 264	2 410 865	66 352 245	53 761 662	10 526 667	2 063 916
Central cities	67 035 302	7 134 392	3 910 156	1 454 875	316 154	1 453 207	3 655 829	234 192	3 244 371	59 900 910	42 752 916	14 909 510	2 238 484
Male	31 899 486	3 505 516	1 969 904	695 421	148 184	692 007	1 782 719	110 720	1 612 077	28 393 970	20 370 036	6 911 762	1 112 172
Female	35 135 816	3 628 876	1 940 252	759 454	167 970	761 200	1 873 110	123 472	1 632 294	31 506 940	22 382 880	7 997 748	1 126 312
Urban fringe	72 135 381	4 418 110	2 490 443	442 338	452 289	1 033 040	2 753 639	70 170	1 594 301	67 717 271	60 986 388	4 892 179	1 838 704
Male	35 075 733	2 203 767	1 266 812	221 241	216 055	499 659	1 353 659	34 378	815 730	32 871 966	29 607 606	2 363 260	901 100
Female	37 059 648	2 214 343	1 223 631	221 097	236 234	533 381	1 399 980	35 792	778 571	34 845 305	31 378 782	2 528 919	937 604
Outside urbanized areas	27 880 309	1 581 363	1 258 442	57 311	16 880	248 730	856 909	32 209	692 245	26 298 946	23 316 063	2 455 756	527 127
Male	13 317 072	797 622	635 063	31 840	8 753	121 966	423 653	15 497	358 472	12 519 450	11 100 395	1 161 245	257 810
Female	14 563 237	783 741	623 379	25 471	8 127	126 764	433 256	16 712	333 773	13 779 496	12 215 668	1 294 511	269 317
Places of 10,000 or more	13 481 787	816 018	651 078	32 551	9 757	122 632	441 251	16 108	358 659	12 665 769	11 114 653	1 291 570	259 546
Male	6 450 320	411 217	327 753	18 029	5 056	60 379	217 822	7 784	185 611	6 039 103	5 297 316	613 099	128 688
Female	7 031 467	404 801	323 325	14 522	4 701	62 253	223 429	8 324	173 048	6 626 666	5 817 337	678 471	130 858
Places of 2,500 to 10,000	14 398 522	765 345	607 364	24 760	7 123	126 098	415 658	16 101	333 586	13 633 177	12 201 410	1 164 186	267 581
Male	6 866 752	386 405	307 310	13 811	3 697	61 587	205 831	7 713	172 861	6 480 347	5 803 079	548 146	129 122
Female	7 531 770	378 940	300 054	10 949	3 426	64 511	209 827	8 388	160 725	7 152 830	6 398 331	616 040	138 459
Rural	59 494 813	1 474 808	1 081 398	59 421	17 903	316 086	848 879	54 281	571 648	58 020 005	53 200 999	3 846 728	972 278
Male	29 760 870	772 926	570 862	33 818	9 328	158 918	433 755	26 634	312 537	28 987 944	26 613 510	1 895 693	478 741
Female	29 733 943	701 882	510 536	25 603	8 575	157 168	415 124	27 647	259 111	29 032 061	26 587 489	1 951 035	493 537
Places of 1,000 to 2,500	7 037 840	243 550	190 115	7 844	1 713	43 878	132 186	5 495	105 869	6 794 290	6 247 330	421 972	124 988
Male	3 369 682	123 729	97 109	4 152	882	21 586	66 092	2 531	55 106	3 245 953	2 987 661	197 699	60 593
Female	3 668 158	119 821	93 006	3 692	831	22 292	66 094	2 964	50 763	3 548 337	3 259 669	224 273	64 395
Other rural	52 456 973	1 231 258	891 283	51 577	16 190	272 208	716 693	48 786	465 779	51 225 715	46 953 669	3 424 756	847 290
Male	26 391 188	649 197	473 753	29 666	8 446	137 332	367 663	24 103	257 431	25 741 991	23 625 849	1 697 994	418 148
Female	26 065 785	582 061	417 530	21 911	7 744	134 876	349 030	24 683	208 348	25 483 724	23 327 820	1 726 762	429 142
INSIDE AND OUTSIDE SMSA's													
Inside SMSA's	169 430 623	12 794 946	7 423 500	1 948 704	781 353	2 641 389	7 067 825	322 476	5 404 645	156 635 677	130 996 353	21 155 265	4 484 059
Male	82 071 794	6 356 371	3 769 506	946 095	370 963	1 269 807	3 470 980	154 419	2 730 972	75 715 423	63 543 058	9 958 708	2 213 657
Female	87 358 829	6 438 575	3 653 994	1 002 609	410 390	1 371 582	3 596 845	168 057	2 673 673	80 920 254	67 453 295	11 196 557	2 270 402
Urban	145 442 528	12 083 778	6 875 778	1 914 920	771 703	2 521 377	6 661 952	308 984	5 112 842	133 358 750	109 057 443	20 095 539	4 205 768
Male	70 006 334	5 980 091	3 478 359	926 408	365 893	1 209 431	3 262 596	147 450	2 570 045	64 026 243	52 529 680	9 420 447	2 076 116
Female	75 436 194	6 103 687	3 397 419	988 512	405 810	1 311 946	3 399 356	161 534	2 542 797	69 332 507	56 527 763	10 675 092	2 129 652
Central cities	67 854 344	7 348 909	4 040 905	1 515 621	323 109	1 469 274	3 753 961	237 679	3 357 269	60 505 435	43 192 731	15 059 321	2 253 383
Male	32 313 824	3 615 927	2 039 010	724 953	151 524	700 440	1 833 145	112 417	1 670 365	28 697 897	20 594 567	6 983 015	1 120 315
Female	35 540 520	3 732 982	2 001 895	790 668	171 585	768 834	1 920 816	125 262	1 686 904	31 807 538	22 598 164	8 076 306	1 133 068
Not in central cities	77 588 184	4 734 869	2 834 873	399 299	448 594	1 052 103	2 907 991	71 305	1 755 573	72 853 315	65 864 712	5 036 218	1 952 385
Male	37 692 510	2 364 164	1 439 349	201 455	214 369	508 991	1 429 451	35 033	899 680	35 328 346	31 935 113	2 437 432	955 801
Female	39 895 674	2 370 705	1 395 524	197 844	234 225	543 112	1 478 540	36 272	855 893	37 524 969	33 929 599	2 598 786	996 584
Rural	23 988 095	711 168	547 722	33 784	9 650	120 012	405 873	13 492	291 803	23 276 927	21 938 910	1 059 726	278 291
Male	12 065 460	376 280	291 147	19 687	5 070	60 376	208 384	6 969	160 927	11 689 180	11 013 378	538 261	137 541
Female	11 922 635	334 888	256 575	14 097	4 580	59 636	197 489	6 523	130 876	11 587 747	10 925 532	521 465	140 750
Outside SMSA's	57 115 182	1 813 727	1 316 939	65 241	21 873	409 674	1 047 431	68 376	697 920	55 301 455	49 260 013	4 948 908	1 092 534
Male	27 981 367	923 460	673 135	36 225	11 357	202 743	522 806	32 810	367 844	27 057 907	24 148 489	2 373 252	536 166
Female	29 133 815	890 267	643 804	29 016	10 516	206 931	524 625	35 566	330 076	28 243 548	25 111 524	2 575 656	556 368
Urban	21 608 464	1 050 087	783 263	39 604	13 620	213 600	604 425	27 587	418 075	20 558 377	17 997 924	2 161 906	398 547
Male	10 285 957	526 814	393 420	22 094	7 099	104 201	297 435	13 145	216 234	9 759 143	8 548 357	1 015 820	194 966
Female	11 322 507	523 273	389 843	17 510	6 521	109 399	306 990	14 442	201 841	10 799 234	9 449 567	1 146 086	203 581
Rural	35 506 718	763 640	533 676	25 637	8 253	196 074	443 006	40 789	279 845	34 743 078	31 262 089	2 787 002	693 987
Male	17 695 410	396 646	279 715	14 131	4 258	98 542	225 371	19 665	151 610	17 298 764	15 600 132	1 357 432	341 200
Female	17 811 308	366 994	253 961	11 506	3 995	97 532	217 635	21 124	128 235	17 444 314	15 661 957	1 429 570	352 787

Table 44. Persons by Age, Race, and Sex: 1980 and 1970

[For meaning of symbols, see introduction. For definitions of terms, see appendixes A and B]

United States / Urban / Rural / Inside SMSA's / Outside SMSA's	1980 Number: Total	1980 Number: Urban	1980 Number: Rural	1980 Number: Inside SMSA's	1980 Number: Outside SMSA's	1980 Percent distribution: Urban	1980 Percent distribution: Rural	1980 Percent distribution: Inside SMSA's	1980 Percent distribution: Outside SMSA's	1970: Total	1970: Urban	1970: Rural	1970: Inside SMSA's	1970: Outside SMSA's
TOTAL														
Both sexes	**226 545 805**	**167 050 992**	**59 494 813**	**169 430 623**	**57 115 182**	**100.0**	**100.0**	**100.0**	**100.0**	**203 211 926**	**149 324 930**	**53 886 996**	**153 624 018**	**49 587 908**
Under 5 years	16 348 254	11 785 180	4 563 074	11 974 963	4 373 291	7.1	7.7	7.1	7.7	17 154 337	12 492 437	4 661 900	13 035 956	4 118 381
Under 1 year	3 533 692	2 574 428	959 264	2 596 282	937 410	1.5	1.6	1.5	1.6	3 485 277	2 567 332	917 945	2 651 677	833 600
1 year	3 269 557	2 361 564	907 993	2 392 697	876 860	1.4	1.5	1.4	1.5	3 377 502	2 469 246	908 256	2 566 649	810 853
2 years	3 223 816	2 317 416	906 400	2 357 151	866 665	1.4	1.5	1.4	1.5	3 290 419	2 396 176	894 243	2 502 482	787 937
3 years	3 179 441	2 281 332	898 109	2 326 633	852 808	1.4	1.5	1.4	1.5	3 418 679	2 474 480	944 199	2 595 218	823 461
4 years	3 141 748	2 250 440	891 308	2 302 200	839 548	1.3	1.5	1.4	1.5	3 582 460	2 585 203	997 257	2 719 930	862 530
5 to 9 years	16 699 956	11 844 261	4 855 695	12 275 926	4 424 030	7.1	8.2	7.2	7.7	19 956 247	14 255 635	5 700 612	15 073 283	4 882 964
5 years	3 162 691	2 253 298	909 393	2 315 667	847 024	1.3	1.5	1.4	1.5	3 811 077	2 734 761	1 076 316	2 884 844	926 233
6 years	3 109 095	2 208 324	900 771	2 276 004	833 091	1.3	1.5	1.3	1.5	3 952 146	2 828 927	1 123 219	2 988 097	964 049
7 years	3 273 052	2 317 853	955 199	2 400 709	872 343	1.4	1.6	1.4	1.5	4 012 474	2 862 855	1 149 619	3 026 969	985 505
8 years	3 394 998	2 399 844	995 154	2 497 020	897 978	1.4	1.7	1.5	1.6	4 052 265	2 888 913	1 163 352	3 057 339	994 926
9 years	3 760 120	2 664 942	1 095 178	2 786 526	973 594	1.6	1.8	1.6	1.7	4 128 285	2 940 179	1 188 106	3 116 034	1 012 251
10 to 14 years	18 242 129	12 866 013	5 376 116	13 516 797	4 725 332	7.7	9.0	8.0	8.3	20 789 468	14 739 966	6 049 502	15 577 023	5 212 445
10 years	3 716 530	2 632 011	1 084 519	2 759 468	957 062	1.6	1.8	1.6	1.7	4 282 106	3 042 050	1 240 056	3 215 789	1 066 317
11 years	3 580 644	2 525 371	1 055 273	2 654 511	926 133	1.5	1.8	1.6	1.6	4 126 685	2 932 802	1 193 883	3 106 352	1 020 333
12 years	3 518 982	2 479 728	1 039 254	2 607 844	911 138	1.5	1.7	1.5	1.6	4 183 341	2 967 866	1 215 475	3 140 175	1 043 166
13 years	3 643 189	2 563 521	1 079 668	2 696 534	946 655	1.5	1.8	1.6	1.7	4 101 977	2 903 787	1 198 190	3 067 159	1 034 818
14 years	3 782 784	2 665 382	1 117 402	2 798 440	984 344	1.6	1.9	1.7	1.7	4 095 359	2 893 461	1 201 898	3 047 548	1 047 811
15 to 19 years	21 168 124	15 503 316	5 664 808	15 709 062	5 459 062	9.3	9.5	9.3	9.6	19 070 348	13 941 281	5 129 067	14 174 378	4 895 970
15 years	4 059 898	2 860 257	1 199 641	2 998 498	1 061 400	1.7	2.0	1.8	1.9	4 029 034	2 843 974	1 185 060	2 991 098	1 037 936
16 years	4 180 875	2 958 012	1 222 863	3 091 325	1 089 550	1.8	2.1	1.8	1.9	3 889 652	2 745 965	1 143 687	2 876 213	1 013 439
17 years	4 223 848	3 015 023	1 208 825	3 126 568	1 097 280	1.8	2.0	1.8	1.9	3 825 343	2 720 905	1 104 438	2 828 383	996 960
18 years	4 251 779	3 195 956	1 055 823	3 157 404	1 094 375	1.9	1.8	1.9	1.9	3 766 102	2 832 288	933 814	2 794 434	971 668
19 years	4 451 724	3 474 068	977 656	3 335 267	1 116 457	2.1	1.6	2.0	2.0	3 560 217	2 798 149	762 068	2 684 250	875 967
20 to 24 years	21 318 704	16 770 023	4 548 681	16 329 371	4 989 333	10.0	7.6	9.6	8.7	16 371 021	12 896 364	3 474 657	12 745 058	3 625 963
20 years	4 387 100	3 454 635	932 465	3 313 467	1 073 633	2.1	1.6	2.0	1.9	3 490 530	2 773 463	717 067	2 668 638	821 892
21 years	4 285 763	3 393 571	892 192	3 262 979	1 022 784	2.0	1.5	1.9	1.8	3 328 238	(NA)	(NA)	2 571 875	756 363
25 to 29 years	19 520 919	14 920 255	4 600 664	15 061 376	4 459 543	8.9	7.7	8.9	7.8	13 476 993	10 202 031	3 274 962	10 597 484	2 879 509
30 to 34 years	17 560 920	13 007 733	4 553 187	13 531 637	4 029 283	7.8	7.7	8.0	7.1	11 430 436	8 390 225	3 040 211	8 866 218	2 564 218
35 to 39 years	13 965 302	10 069 592	3 895 710	10 680 145	3 285 157	6.0	6.5	6.3	5.8	11 106 851	8 134 561	2 972 290	8 590 158	2 516 693
40 to 44 years	11 669 408	8 390 402	3 279 006	8 839 745	2 829 663	5.0	5.5	5.2	5.0	11 980 954	8 875 423	3 105 531	9 266 036	2 714 918
45 to 49 years	11 089 755	8 083 037	3 006 718	8 405 054	2 684 701	4.8	5.1	5.0	4.7	12 115 939	9 047 116	3 068 823	9 354 170	2 761 769
50 to 54 years	11 710 032	8 680 125	3 029 907	8 872 065	2 837 967	5.2	5.1	5.2	5.0	11 104 018	8 201 416	2 902 602	8 405 365	2 698 653
55 to 59 years	11 615 254	8 661 706	2 953 548	8 734 370	2 880 884	5.2	5.0	5.2	5.0	9 973 028	7 278 846	2 694 182	7 393 459	2 579 569
60 to 64 years	10 087 621	7 423 145	2 664 476	7 375 436	2 712 185	4.4	4.5	4.4	4.7	8 616 784	6 238 514	2 378 270	6 269 410	2 347 374
65 to 69 years	8 782 481	6 423 647	2 358 834	6 259 715	2 522 766	3.8	4.0	3.7	4.4	6 991 625	5 054 537	1 937 088	5 018 451	1 973 174
70 to 74 years	6 798 124	5 032 521	1 765 603	4 805 404	1 992 720	3.0	3.0	2.8	3.5	5 443 831	3 981 347	1 462 484	3 900 581	1 543 250
75 to 79 years	4 793 722	3 613 862	1 179 860	3 397 012	1 396 710	2.2	2.0	2.0	2.4	3 834 834	2 813 214	1 021 620	2 715 475	1 119 359
80 to 84 years	2 935 033	2 249 374	685 659	2 087 878	847 155	1.3	1.2	1.2	1.5	2 284 311	1 676 365	607 946	1 597 069	687 242
85 years and over	2 240 067	1 726 800	513 267	1 574 667	665 400	1.0	0.9	0.9	1.2	1 510 901	1 105 652	405 249	1 044 444	466 457
18 years and over	162 790 845	121 722 246	41 068 599	122 446 546	40 344 299	72.9	69.0	72.3	70.6	133 567 845	99 526 048	34 041 797	101 242 062	32 325 783
62 years and over	31 402 347	23 341 519	8 060 828	22 378 576	9 023 771	14.0	13.5	13.2	15.8	25 000 504	18 196 902	6 803 602	17 852 317	7 148 187
65 years and over	25 549 427	19 046 204	6 503 223	18 124 676	7 424 751	11.4	10.9	10.7	13.0	20 065 502	14 631 115	5 434 387	14 276 020	5 789 482
Median	30.0	29.9	30.1	29.9	30.1	...	...	...	...	28.1	28.1	27.9	27.9	28.6
Male	**110 053 161**	**80 292 291**	**29 760 870**	**82 071 794**	**27 981 367**	**100.0**	**100.0**	**100.0**	**100.0**	**98 912 192**	**71 958 564**	**26 953 628**	**74 537 467**	**24 374 725**
Under 5 years	8 362 009	6 021 583	2 340 426	6 123 306	2 238 703	7.5	7.9	7.5	8.0	8 745 499	6 362 797	2 382 702	6 645 199	2 100 300
Under 1 year	1 806 338	1 314 579	491 759	1 326 518	479 820	1.6	1.7	1.6	1.7	1 777 915	1 309 654	468 261	1 352 928	424 987
1 year	1 674 095	1 208 658	465 437	1 224 802	449 293	1.5	1.6	1.5	1.6	1 721 763	1 257 653	464 110	1 308 087	413 676
2 years	1 648 044	1 183 496	464 548	1 204 554	443 490	1.5	1.6	1.5	1.6	1 678 842	1 221 303	457 539	1 276 843	401 999
3 years	1 625 693	1 164 931	460 762	1 189 445	436 248	1.5	1.5	1.4	1.6	1 740 906	1 258 269	482 637	1 321 594	419 312
4 years	1 607 839	1 149 919	457 920	1 177 987	429 852	1.4	1.5	1.4	1.5	1 826 073	1 315 918	510 155	1 385 747	440 326
5 to 9 years	8 539 080	6 041 357	2 497 723	6 272 193	2 266 887	7.5	8 4	7.6	8.1	10 168 496	7 248 492	2 920 004	7 678 441	2 490 055
5 years	1 618 300	1 150 451	467 849	1 183 323	434 977	1.4	1.6	1.4	1.6	1 941 004	1 390 041	550 963	1 468 838	472 166
6 years	1 589 501	1 127 068	462 433	1 163 404	426 097	1.4	1.6	1.4	1.5	2 012 834	1 438 090	574 744	1 521 401	491 433
7 years	1 672 647	1 181 898	490 749	1 225 898	446 749	1.5	1.6	1.5	1.6	2 043 834	1 455 141	588 693	1 541 448	502 386
8 years	1 735 956	1 223 961	511 995	1 275 953	460 003	1.5	1.7	1.6	1.6	2 065 571	1 469 300	596 271	1 557 646	507 925
9 years	1 922 676	1 357 979	564 697	1 423 615	499 061	1.7	1.9	1.7	1.8	2 105 253	1 495 920	609 333	1 589 108	516 145
10 to 14 years	9 316 221	6 544 347	2 771 874	6 893 378	2 422 843	8.2	9.3	8.4	8.7	10 590 737	7 476 619	3 114 118	7 926 005	2 664 732
10 years	1 901 610	1 342 399	559 211	1 409 675	491 935	1.7	1.9	1.7	1.8	2 183 371	1 545 263	638 108	1 638 235	545 136
11 years	1 828 934	1 285 536	543 398	1 354 406	474 528	1.6	1.8	1.7	1.7	2 100 739	1 487 249	613 490	1 579 663	521 076
12 years	1 796 333	1 260 226	536 107	1 329 828	466 505	1.6	1.8	1.6	1.7	2 132 903	1 507 417	625 486	1 599 088	533 815
13 years	1 856 566	1 300 767	555 799	1 372 819	483 747	1.6	1.9	1.7	1.7	2 088 820	1 471 580	617 240	1 559 323	529 497
14 years	1 932 778	1 355 419	577 359	1 426 650	506 128	1.7	1.9	1.7	1.8	2 084 904	1 465 110	619 794	1 549 696	535 208
15 to 19 years	10 755 409	7 803 186	2 952 223	7 959 708	2 795 701	9.7	9.9	9.7	10.0	9 633 847	6 972 189	2 661 658	7 124 634	2 509 213
15 years	2 069 726	1 449 164	620 562	1 525 789	543 937	1.8	2.1	1.9	1.9	2 053 643	1 439 779	613 864	1 521 142	532 501
16 years	2 135 125	1 499 664	635 461	1 574 575	560 550	1.9	2.1	1.9	2 0	1 979 619	1 385 652	593 967	1 459 621	519 998
17 years	2 160 114	1 530 350	629 764	1 594 637	565 477	1.9	2.1	1.9	2.0	1 944 907	1 372 681	572 226	1 433 112	511 795
18 years	2 153 292	1 599 203	554 089	1 594 511	558 781	2.0	1.9	1.9	2.0	1 893 207	1 402 076	491 131	1 394 552	498 655
19 years	2 237 152	1 724 805	512 347	1 670 196	566 956	2.1	1.7	2.0	2.0	1 762 471	1 372 001	390 470	1 316 207	446 264
20 to 24 years	10 663 231	8 335 189	2 328 042	8 132 315	2 530 916	10.4	7.8	9.9	9.0	7 917 269	6 218 656	1 698 613	6 108 926	1 808 343
20 years	2 200 363	1 714 338	486 025	1 655 424	544 939	2.1	1.6	2.0	1.9	1 680 817	1 330 155	350 662	1 274 347	406 470
21 years	2 144 501	1 685 132	459 369	1 625 474	519 027	2.1	1.5	2.0	1.9	1 585 637	(NA)	(NA)	1 212 305	373 332
25 to 29 years	9 705 107	7 395 948	2 309 159	7 456 434	2 248 673	9.2	7.8	9.1	8.0	6 621 567	5 011 979	1 609 568	5 191 702	1 429 865
30 to 34 years	8 676 796	6 404 844	2 271 952	6 655 708	2 021 088	8.0	7.6	8.1	7.2	5 595 790	4 095 546	1 500 244	4 335 978	1 259 812
35 to 39 years	6 861 509	4 909 764	1 951 745	5 231 839	1 629 670	6.1	6.6	6.4	5.8	5 412 423	3 946 755	1 465 668	4 193 130	1 219 293
40 to 44 years	5 708 210	4 052 389	1 655 821	4 308 637	1 399 573	5.0	5.6	5.2	5.0	5 818 813	4 268 895	1 549 918	4 494 057	1 324 756
45 to 49 years	5 388 249	3 882 533	1 505 716	4 083 020	1 305 229	4.8	5.1	5.0	4.7	5 851 334	4 329 795	1 521 539	4 511 624	1 339 710
50 to 54 years	5 620 670	4 113 307	1 507 363	4 252 371	1 368 299	5.1	5.1	5.2	4 9	5 347 916	3 907 222	1 440 694	4 043 329	1 304 587
55 to 59 years	5 481 863	4 042 082	1 439 781	4 120 777	1 361 086	5.0	4.8	5.0	4.9	4 765 821	3 417 226	1 348 595	3 516 603	1 249 218
60 to 64 years	4 669 892	3 381 825	1 288 067	3 409 197	1 260 695	4.2	4 3	4.2	4.5	4 026 972	2 842 921	1 184 051	2 904 369	1 122 603
65 to 69 years	3 902 955	2 766 122	1 136 833	2 747 017	1 155 938	3.4	3 8	3.3	4.1	3 122 084	2 170 584	951 500	2 204 162	917 922
70 to 74 years	2 853 547	2 027 634	825 913	1 976 342	877 205	2.5	2.8	2.4	3.1	2 315 000	1 614 884	700 116	1 622 434	692 566
75 to 79 years	1 847 661	1 327 980	519 681	1 277 486	570 175	1.7	1.7	1.6	2.0	1 560 661	1 089 317	471 344	1 078 570	482 091
80 to 84 years	1 019 227	742 589	276 638	705 399	313 828	0.9	0.9	0.9	1.1	875 584	608 715	266 869	594 069	281 515
85 years and over	681 525	499 612	181 913	466 667	214 858	0.6	0.6	0.6	0.8	542 379	375 972	166 407	364 235	178 144
18 years and over	77 470 886	57 205 826	20 265 060	58 087 916	19 382 970	71.2	68 1	70.8	69.3	63 429 291	46 672 544	16 756 747	47 873 947	15 555 344
62 years and over	13 001 054	9 305 845	3 695 209	9 125 291	3 875 763	11.6	12 4	11.1	13.9	10 708 654	7 471 184	3 237 470	7 508 883	3 199 771
65 years and over	10 304 915	7 363 937	2 940 978	7 172 911	3 132 004	9.2	9.9	8.7	11.2	8 415 708	5 859 472	2 556 236	5 863 470	2 552 238
Median	28.8	28.6	29.3	28.7	28.8	...	...	...	...	26.8	26.7	27.2	26.7	27.1

Table 44. **Persons by Age, Race, and Sex: 1980 and 1970**—Con.

[For meaning of symbols, see introduction. For definitions of terms, see appendixes A and B]

United States Urban Rural Inside SMSA's Outside SMSA's	1980 Total	1980 Number Urban	1980 Number Rural	1980 Number Inside SMSA's	1980 Number Outside SMSA's	1980 Percent distribution Urban	1980 Percent distribution Rural	1980 Percent distribution Inside SMSA's	1980 Percent distribution Outside SMSA's	1970 Total	1970 Urban	1970 Rural	1970 Inside SMSA's	1970 Outside SMSA's
TOTAL—Con.														
Female	**116 492 644**	**86 758 701**	**29 733 943**	**87 358 829**	**29 133 815**	**100.0**	**100.0**	**100.0**	**100.0**	**104 299 734**	**77 366 366**	**26 933 368**	**79 086 551**	**25 213 183**
Under 5 years	7 986 245	5 763 597	2 222 648	5 851 657	2 134 588	6.6	7.5	6.7	7.3	8 408 838	6 129 640	2 279 198	6 390 757	2 018 081
Under 1 year	1 727 354	1 259 849	467 505	1 269 764	457 590	1.5	1.6	1.5	1.6	1 707 362	1 257 678	449 684	1 298 749	408 613
1 year	1 595 462	1 152 906	442 556	1 167 895	427 567	1.3	1.5	1.3	1.5	1 655 739	1 211 593	444 146	1 258 562	397 177
2 years	1 575 772	1 133 920	441 852	1 152 597	423 175	1.3	1.5	1.3	1.5	1 611 577	1 174 873	436 704	1 225 639	385 938
3 years	1 553 748	1 116 401	437 347	1 137 188	416 560	1.3	1.5	1.3	1.4	1 677 773	1 216 211	461 562	1 273 624	404 149
4 years	1 533 909	1 100 521	433 388	1 124 213	409 696	1.3	1.5	1.3	1.4	1 756 387	1 269 285	487 102	1 334 183	422 204
5 to 9 years	8 160 876	5 802 904	2 357 972	6 003 733	2 157 143	6.7	7.9	6.9	7.4	9 787 751	7 007 143	2 780 608	7 394 842	2 392 909
5 years	1 544 391	1 102 847	441 544	1 132 344	412 047	1.3	1.5	1.3	1.4	1 870 073	1 344 720	525 353	1 416 006	454 067
6 years	1 519 594	1 081 256	438 338	1 112 600	406 994	1.2	1.5	1.3	1.4	1 939 312	1 390 837	548 475	1 466 696	472 616
7 years	1 600 405	1 135 955	464 450	1 174 811	425 594	1.3	1.6	1.3	1.5	1 968 640	1 407 714	560 926	1 485 521	483 119
8 years	1 659 042	1 175 883	483 159	1 221 067	437 975	1.4	1.6	1.4	1.5	1 986 694	1 419 613	567 081	1 499 693	487 001
9 years	1 837 444	1 306 963	530 481	1 362 911	474 533	1.5	1.8	1.6	1.6	2 023 032	1 444 259	578 773	1 526 926	496 106
10 to 14 years	8 925 908	6 321 666	2 604 242	6 623 419	2 302 489	7.3	8.8	7.6	7.9	10 198 731	7 263 347	2 935 384	7 651 018	2 547 713
10 years	1 814 920	1 289 612	525 308	1 349 793	465 127	1.5	1.8	1.5	1.6	2 098 735	1 496 787	601 948	1 577 554	521 181
11 years	1 751 710	1 239 835	511 875	1 300 105	451 605	1.4	1.7	1.5	1.6	2 025 946	1 445 553	580 393	1 526 689	499 257
12 years	1 722 649	1 219 502	503 147	1 278 016	444 633	1.4	1.7	1.5	1.5	2 050 438	1 460 449	589 989	1 541 087	509 351
13 years	1 786 623	1 262 754	523 869	1 323 715	462 908	1.5	1.8	1.5	1.6	2 013 157	1 432 207	580 950	1 507 836	505 321
14 years	1 850 006	1 309 963	540 043	1 371 790	478 216	1.5	1.8	1.6	1.6	2 010 455	1 428 351	582 104	1 497 852	512 603
15 to 19 years	10 412 715	7 700 130	2 712 585	7 749 354	2 663 361	8.9	9.1	8.9	9.1	9 436 501	6 969 092	2 467 409	7 049 744	2 386 757
15 years	1 990 172	1 411 093	579 079	1 472 709	517 463	1.6	1.9	1.7	1.8	1 975 391	1 404 195	571 196	1 469 956	505 435
16 years	2 045 750	1 458 348	587 402	1 516 750	529 000	1.7	2.0	1.7	1.8	1 910 033	1 360 313	549 720	1 416 592	493 441
17 years	2 063 734	1 484 673	579 061	1 531 931	531 803	1.7	1.9	1.8	1.8	1 880 436	1 348 224	532 212	1 395 271	485 165
18 years	2 098 487	1 596 753	501 734	1 562 893	535 594	1.8	1.7	1.8	1.8	1 872 895	1 430 212	442 683	1 399 882	473 013
19 years	2 214 572	1 749 263	465 309	1 665 071	549 501	2.0	1.6	1.9	1.9	1 797 746	1 426 148	371 598	1 368 043	429 703
20 to 24 years	10 655 473	8 434 834	2 220 639	8 197 056	2 458 417	9.7	7.5	9.4	8.4	8 453 752	6 677 708	1 776 044	6 636 132	1 817 620
20 years	2 186 737	1 740 297	446 440	1 658 043	528 694	2.0	1.5	1.9	1.8	1 809 713	1 443 308	366 405	1 394 291	415 422
21 years	2 141 262	1 708 439	432 823	1 637 505	503 757	2.0	1.5	1.9	1.7	1 742 601	(NA)	(NA)	1 359 570	383 031
25 to 29 years	9 815 812	7 524 307	2 291 505	7 604 942	2 210 870	8.7	7.7	8.7	7.6	6 855 426	5 190 052	1 665 374	5 405 782	1 449 644
30 to 34 years	8 884 124	6 602 889	2 281 235	6 875 929	2 008 195	7.6	7.7	7.9	6.9	5 834 646	4 294 679	1 539 967	4 530 240	1 304 406
35 to 39 years	7 103 793	5 159 828	1 943 965	5 448 306	1 655 487	5.9	6.5	6.2	5.7	5 694 428	4 187 806	1 506 622	4 397 028	1 297 400
40 to 44 years	5 961 198	4 338 013	1 623 185	4 531 108	1 430 090	5.0	5.5	5.2	4.9	6 162 141	4 606 528	1 555 613	4 771 979	1 390 162
45 to 49 years	5 701 506	4 200 504	1 501 002	4 322 034	1 379 472	4.8	5.0	4.9	4.7	6 264 605	4 717 321	1 547 284	4 842 546	1 422 059
50 to 54 years	6 089 362	4 566 818	1 522 544	4 619 694	1 469 668	5.3	5.1	5.3	5.0	5 756 102	4 294 194	1 461 908	4 362 036	1 394 066
55 to 59 years	6 133 391	4 619 624	1 513 767	4 613 593	1 519 798	5.3	5.1	5.3	5.2	5 207 207	3 861 620	1 345 587	3 876 856	1 330 351
60 to 64 years	5 417 729	4 041 320	1 376 409	3 966 239	1 451 490	4.7	4.6	4.5	5.0	4 589 812	3 395 593	1 194 219	3 365 041	1 224 771
65 to 69 years	4 879 526	3 657 525	1 222 001	3 512 698	1 366 828	4.2	4.1	4.0	4.7	3 869 541	2 883 953	985 588	2 814 289	1 055 252
70 to 74 years	3 944 577	3 004 887	939 690	2 829 062	1 115 515	3.5	3.2	3.2	3.8	3 128 831	2 366 463	762 368	2 278 147	850 684
75 to 79 years	2 946 061	2 285 882	660 179	2 119 526	826 535	2.6	2.2	2.4	2.8	2 274 173	1 723 897	550 276	1 636 905	637 268
80 to 84 years	1 915 806	1 506 785	409 021	1 382 479	533 327	1.7	1.4	1.6	1.8	1 408 727	1 067 650	341 077	1 003 000	405 727
85 years and over	1 558 542	1 227 188	331 354	1 108 000	450 542	1.4	1.1	1.3	1.5	968 522	729 680	238 842	680 209	288 313
18 years and over	85 319 959	64 516 420	20 803 539	64 358 630	20 961 329	74.4	70.0	73.7	71.9	70 138 554	52 853 504	17 285 050	53 368 115	16 770 439
62 years and over	18 401 293	14 035 674	4 365 619	13 253 285	5 148 008	16.2	14.7	15.2	17.7	14 291 850	10 725 718	3 566 132	10 343 434	3 948 416
65 years and over	15 244 512	11 682 267	3 562 245	10 951 765	4 292 747	13.5	12.0	12.5	14.7	11 649 794	8 771 643	2 878 151	8 412 550	3 237 244
Median	31.2	31.3	31.0	31.1	31.5	...	...	...	...	29.3	29.5	28.7	29.1	30.0
WHITE														
Both sexes	**188 371 622**	**134 321 744**	**54 049 878**	**138 064 178**	**50 307 444**	**100.0**	**100.0**	**100.0**	**100.0**	**177 748 975**	**128 773 240**	**48 975 735**	**133 573 871**	**44 175 104**
Under 5 years	12 634 075	8 595 363	4 038 712	8 950 933	3 683 142	6.4	7.5	6.5	7.3	14 423 140	10 294 343	4 128 797	10 898 051	3 525 089
Under 1 year	2 719 445	1 872 443	847 002	1 932 292	787 153	1.4	1.6	1.4	1.6	2 935 089	2 121 732	813 357	2 219 936	715 153
1 year	2 528 598	1 724 402	804 196	1 789 647	738 951	1.3	1.5	1.3	1.5	2 851 928	2 045 337	806 591	2 154 996	696 932
2 years	2 497 249	1 694 019	803 230	1 765 938	731 311	1.3	1.5	1.3	1.5	2 762 530	1 971 617	790 913	2 089 485	673 045
3 years	2 460 551	1 665 141	795 410	1 741 472	719 079	1.2	1.5	1.3	1.4	2 872 719	2 036 570	836 149	2 168 594	704 125
4 years	2 428 232	1 639 358	788 874	1 721 584	706 648	1.2	1.5	1.2	1.4	3 000 874	2 119 087	881 787	2 265 040	735 834
5 to 9 years	13 032 966	8 716 294	4 316 672	9 292 465	3 740 501	6.5	8.0	6.7	7.4	16 897 426	11 824 507	5 072 919	12 693 460	4 203 966
5 years	2 456 167	1 650 249	805 918	1 742 047	714 120	1.2	1.5	1.3	1.4	3 208 463	2 254 526	953 937	2 415 400	793 063
6 years	2 410 344	1 611 956	798 388	1 708 727	701 617	1.2	1.5	1.2	1.4	3 338 213	2 340 574	997 639	2 510 329	827 884
7 years	2 539 701	1 692 945	846 756	1 805 127	734 574	1.3	1.6	1.3	1.5	3 394 875	2 372 178	1 022 697	2 546 837	848 038
8 years	2 658 627	1 771 713	886 914	1 897 245	761 382	1.3	1.6	1.4	1.5	3 444 037	2 405 701	1 038 336	2 584 204	859 833
9 years	2 968 127	1 989 431	978 696	2 139 319	828 808	1.5	1.8	1.5	1.6	3 511 838	2 451 528	1 060 310	2 636 690	875 148
10 to 14 years	14 460 922	9 680 510	4 780 412	10 456 528	4 004 394	7.2	8.8	7.6	8.0	17 681 117	12 309 578	5 371 539	13 191 740	4 489 377
10 years	2 946 378	1 977 424	968 954	2 131 985	814 393	1.5	1.8	1.5	1.6	3 624 787	2 523 564	1 101 223	2 707 989	916 798
11 years	2 846 168	1 904 441	941 727	2 058 497	787 671	1.4	1.7	1.5	1.6	3 512 236	2 449 019	1 063 217	2 631 609	880 627
12 years	2 786 155	1 862 520	923 635	2 014 676	771 479	1.4	1.7	1.5	1.5	3 563 400	2 483 078	1 080 322	2 663 782	899 618
13 years	2 889 432	1 931 155	958 277	2 088 619	800 813	1.4	1.8	1.5	1.6	3 495 074	2 431 521	1 063 553	2 603 526	891 548
14 years	2 992 789	2 004 970	987 819	2 162 751	830 038	1.5	1.8	1.6	1.6	3 485 620	2 422 396	1 063 224	2 584 834	900 786
15 to 19 years	16 962 102	11 964 956	4 997 146	12 323 391	4 638 711	8.9	9.2	8.9	9.2	16 370 360	11 850 356	4 520 004	12 128 976	4 241 384
15 years	3 232 449	2 170 806	1 061 643	2 334 375	898 074	1.6	2.0	1.7	1.8	3 440 465	2 392 780	1 047 685	2 546 836	893 629
16 years	3 343 837	2 260 719	1 083 118	2 419 071	924 766	1.7	2.0	1.8	1.8	3 332 604	2 322 800	1 009 804	2 459 503	873 101
17 years	3 380 772	2 312 704	1 068 068	2 450 652	930 120	1.7	2.0	1.8	1.8	3 287 148	2 311 325	975 823	2 426 237	860 911
18 years	3 417 053	2 489 359	927 694	2 485 521	931 532	1.9	1.7	1.8	1.9	3 247 187	2 426 718	820 469	2 400 211	846 976
19 years	3 587 991	2 731 368	856 623	2 633 772	954 219	2.0	1.6	1.9	1.9	3 062 956	2 396 733	666 223	2 296 189	766 767
20 to 24 years	17 288 774	13 253 751	4 035 023	12 987 465	4 301 309	9.9	7.5	9.4	8.6	14 281 827	11 154 543	3 127 284	11 047 755	3 234 072
20 years	3 539 235	2 721 110	818 125	2 619 783	919 452	2.0	1.5	1.9	1.8	3 006 088	2 375 826	630 262	2 283 856	722 232
21 years	3 473 418	2 685 946	787 472	2 592 704	880 714	2.0	1.5	1.9	1.8	2 886 947	(NA)	(NA)	2 215 222	671 725
25 to 29 years	15 984 830	11 811 037	4 173 793	12 075 379	3 909 451	8.8	7.7	8.7	7.8	11 811 914	8 785 164	3 026 750	9 204 105	2 607 809
30 to 34 years	14 644 799	10 445 606	4 199 193	11 042 561	3 602 238	7.8	7.8	8.0	7.2	9 967 437	7 150 792	2 816 645	7 643 075	2 324 362
35 to 39 years	11 761 107	8 141 815	3 619 292	8 797 490	2 963 617	6.1	6.7	6.4	5.9	9 720 869	6 964 948	2 755 921	7 437 957	2 282 912
40 to 44 years	9 825 833	6 786 402	3 039 431	7 274 525	2 551 308	5.1	5.6	5.3	5.1	10 606 832	7 725 377	2 881 455	8 136 548	2 470 284
45 to 49 years	9 456 991	6 669 634	2 787 357	7 030 078	2 426 913	5.0	5.2	5.1	4.8	10 844 642	7 990 624	2 854 018	8 320 138	2 524 504
50 to 54 years	10 157 561	7 344 641	2 812 920	7 581 835	2 575 726	5.5	5.2	5.5	5.1	10 001 857	7 303 839	2 698 018	7 532 292	2 469 565
55 to 59 years	10 237 758	7 486 095	2 751 663	7 603 373	2 634 385	5.6	5.1	5.5	5.2	9 006 502	6 508 793	2 497 709	6 650 282	2 356 220
60 to 64 years	8 975 711	6 492 774	2 482 937	6 489 459	2 486 252	4.8	4.6	4.7	4.9	7 804 710	5 601 032	2 203 678	5 658 771	2 145 939
65 to 69 years	7 812 247	5 628 525	2 183 722	5 512 848	2 299 399	4.2	4.0	4.0	4.6	6 299 054	4 519 584	1 779 470	4 511 943	1 787 111
70 to 74 years	6 095 352	4 461 014	1 634 338	4 273 203	1 822 149	3.3	3.0	3.1	3.6	4 982 083	3 627 023	1 355 060	3 565 975	1 416 108
75 to 79 years	4 310 284	3 222 856	1 087 428	3 035 574	1 274 710	2.4	2.0	2.2	2.5	3 552 571	2 601 761	950 810	2 517 304	1 035 267
80 to 84 years	2 685 349	2 048 128	637 221	1 902 825	782 524	1.5	1.2	1.4	1.6	2 119 822	1 554 198	565 624	1 483 230	636 592
85 years and over	2 044 961	1 572 343	472 618	1 434 246	610 715	1.2	0.9	1.0	1.2	1 376 812	1 006 778	370 034	952 269	424 543
18 years and over	138 286 601	100 585 348	37 701 253	102 160 154	36 126 447	74.9	69.8	74.0	71.8	118 687 075	87 317 907	31 369 168	89 358 044	29 329 031
62 years and over	28 177 572	20 708 340	7 469 232	19 918 451	8 259 121	15.4	13.8	14.4	16.4	22 800 190	16 511 541	6 288 649	16 259 393	6 540 797
65 years and over	22 948 193	16 932 866	6 015 327	16 158 696	6 789 497	12.6	11.1	11.7	13.5	18 330 342	13 309 344	5 020 998	13 030 721	5 299 621
Median	31.3	31.4	30.8	31.3	31.2	...	...	...	...	28.9	29.0	28.7	28.7	29.6

Table 44. **Persons by Age, Race, and Sex: 1980 and 1970**—Con.

[For meaning of symbols, see Introduction. For definitions of terms, see appendixes A and B]

United States Urban Rural Inside SMSA's Outside SMSA's	1980									1970				
		Number				Percent distribution								
	Total	Urban	Rural	Inside SMSA's	Outside SMSA's	Urban	Rural	Inside SMSA's	Outside SMSA's	Total	Urban	Rural	Inside SMSA's	Outside SMSA's
WHITE—Con.														
Male	**91 685 333**	**64 638 068**	**27 047 265**	**67 014 038**	**24 671 295**	**100.0**	**100.0**	**100.0**	**100.0**	**86 720 987**	**62 210 243**	**24 510 744**	**64 974 616**	**21 746 371**
Under 5 years	6 484 021	4 408 385	2 075 636	4 593 458	1 890 563	6.8	7.7	6.9	7.7	7 374 333	5 259 385	2 114 948	5 571 305	1 803 028
Under 1 year	1 395 560	960 329	435 231	991 207	404 353	1.5	1.6	1.5	1.6	1 501 250	1 085 438	415 812	1 135 769	365 481
1 year	1 299 045	885 859	413 186	919 383	379 662	1.4	1.5	1.4	1.5	1 458 143	1 045 135	413 008	1 101 443	356 700
2 years	1 280 931	868 584	412 347	905 915	375 016	1.3	1.5	1.4	1.5	1 414 274	1 008 585	405 689	1 069 645	344 629
3 years	1 261 857	853 069	408 788	893 131	368 726	1.3	1.5	1.3	1.5	1 466 847	1 038 489	428 358	1 107 339	359 508
4 years	1 246 628	840 544	406 084	883 822	362 806	1.3	1.5	1.3	1.5	1 533 819	1 081 738	452 081	1 157 109	376 710
5 to 9 years	6 685 142	4 459 996	2 225 146	4 763 194	1 921 948	6.9	8.2	7.1	7.8	8 633 093	6 029 317	2 603 776	6 484 529	2 148 564
5 years	1 260 475	844 911	415 564	892 832	367 643	1.3	1.5	1.3	1.5	1 638 441	1 149 075	489 366	1 233 299	405 142
6 years	1 236 396	825 781	410 615	876 642	359 754	1.3	1.5	1.3	1.5	1 704 717	1 193 234	511 483	1 281 675	423 042
7 years	1 301 581	865 403	436 178	924 195	377 386	1.3	1.6	1.4	1.5	1 734 099	1 209 290	524 809	1 300 702	433 397
8 years	1 364 028	906 891	457 137	973 051	390 977	1.4	1.7	1.5	1.6	1 760 037	1 226 857	533 180	1 320 324	439 713
9 years	1 522 662	1 017 010	505 652	1 096 474	426 188	1.6	1.9	1.6	1.7	1 795 799	1 250 861	544 938	1 348 529	447 270
10 to 14 years	7 408 443	4 939 181	2 469 262	5 349 345	2 059 098	7.6	9.1	8.0	8.3	9 033 725	6 263 521	2 770 204	6 732 902	2 300 823
10 years	1 511 857	1 011 303	500 554	1 092 110	419 747	1.6	1.9	1.6	1.7	1 853 786	1 285 714	568 072	1 383 755	470 031
11 years	1 457 937	972 302	485 635	1 053 370	404 567	1.5	1.8	1.6	1.6	1 793 731	1 246 256	547 475	1 342 730	451 001
12 years	1 427 928	950 087	477 841	1 031 331	396 597	1.5	1.8	1.5	1.6	1 821 354	1 264 665	556 689	1 360 182	461 172
13 years	1 477 087	983 043	494 044	1 066 808	410 279	1.5	1.8	1.6	1.7	1 785 238	1 236 275	548 963	1 327 773	457 465
14 years	1 533 634	1 022 446	511 188	1 105 726	427 908	1.6	1.9	1.6	1.7	1 779 616	1 230 611	549 005	1 318 462	461 154
15 to 19 years	8 634 142	6 030 965	2 603 177	6 258 771	2 375 371	9.3	9.6	9.3	9.6	8 291 270	5 946 591	2 344 679	6 115 872	2 175 398
15 years	1 652 399	1 102 796	549 603	1 191 341	461 058	1.7	2.0	1.8	1.9	1 758 578	1 215 283	543 295	1 299 051	459 527
16 years	1 710 931	1 148 197	562 734	1 234 771	476 160	1.8	2.1	1.8	1.9	1 700 014	1 175 888	524 126	1 251 401	448 613
17 years	1 731 264	1 175 722	555 542	1 252 227	479 037	1.8	2.1	1.9	1.9	1 675 393	1 170 303	505 090	1 233 117	442 276
18 years	1 733 097	1 246 349	486 748	1 257 995	475 102	1.9	1.8	1.9	1.9	1 636 643	1 205 078	431 565	1 201 946	434 697
19 years	1 806 451	1 357 901	448 550	1 322 437	484 014	2.1	1.7	2.0	2.0	1 520 642	1 180 039	340 603	1 130 357	390 285
20 to 24 years	8 683 292	6 625 042	2 058 250	6 502 340	2 180 952	10.2	7.6	9.7	8.8	6 940 820	5 419 236	1 521 584	5 327 793	1 613 027
20 years	1 779 255	1 353 607	425 648	1 312 934	466 321	2.1	1.6	2.0	1.9	1 451 545	1 144 986	306 559	1 095 154	356 391
21 years	1 743 560	1 339 319	404 241	1 297 041	446 519	2.1	1.5	1.9	1.8	1 380 527	(NA)	(NA)	1 049 623	330 904
25 to 29 years	8 005 295	5 915 412	2 089 883	6 030 976	1 974 319	9.2	7.7	9.0	8.0	5 849 792	4 364 070	1 485 722	4 550 992	1 298 800
30 to 34 years	7 299 659	5 205 175	2 094 484	5 487 477	1 812 182	8.1	7.7	8.2	7.3	4 925 069	3 532 476	1 392 593	3 776 929	1 148 140
35 to 39 years	5 831 107	4 015 642	1 815 465	4 354 489	1 476 618	6.2	6.7	6.5	6.0	4 784 375	3 420 126	1 364 249	3 670 878	1 113 497
40 to 44 years	4 849 516	3 309 287	1 540 229	3 579 479	1 270 037	5.1	5.7	5.3	5.1	5 194 497	3 749 500	1 444 997	3 979 703	1 214 794
45 to 49 years	4 638 737	3 236 363	1 402 374	3 449 804	1 188 933	5.0	5.2	5.1	4.8	5 257 619	3 838 501	1 419 118	4 027 075	1 230 544
50 to 54 years	4 918 060	3 511 585	1 406 475	3 666 611	1 251 449	5.4	5.2	5.5	5.1	4 832 555	3 490 890	1 341 665	3 634 802	1 197 753
55 to 59 years	4 852 744	3 507 615	1 345 129	3 602 398	1 250 346	5.4	5.0	5.4	5.1	4 310 921	3 059 691	1 251 230	3 167 201	1 143 720
60 to 64 years	4 173 113	2 970 209	1 202 904	3 013 430	1 159 683	4.6	4.4	4.5	4.7	3 647 243	2 549 784	1 097 459	2 619 410	1 027 833
65 to 69 years	3 481 640	2 426 646	1 054 994	2 424 573	1 057 067	3.8	3.9	3.6	4.3	2 807 974	1 932 881	875 093	1 974 918	833 056
70 to 74 years	2 552 321	1 788 084	764 237	1 750 672	801 649	2.8	2.8	2.6	3.2	2 107 552	1 459 349	648 203	1 473 256	634 296
75 to 79 years	1 650 386	1 172 675	477 711	1 131 962	518 424	1.8	1.8	1.7	2.1	1 437 628	1 000 033	437 595	993 746	443 882
80 to 84 years	923 308	667 394	255 914	635 545	287 763	1.0	0.9	0.9	1.2	805 564	558 290	247 274	546 385	259 179
85 years and over	614 407	448 412	165 995	419 514	194 893	0.7	0.6	0.6	0.8	486 957	336 602	150 355	326 920	160 037
18 years and over	66 013 133	47 403 791	18 609 342	48 629 702	17 383 431	73.3	68.8	72.6	70.5	56 545 851	41 096 546	15 449 305	42 402 311	14 143 540
62 years and over	11 641 812	8 217 277	3 424 535	8 095 896	3 545 916	12.7	12.7	12.1	14.4	9 722 155	6 732 682	2 989 473	6 799 204	2 922 951
65 years and over	9 222 062	6 503 211	2 718 851	6 362 266	2 859 796	10.1	10.1	9.5	11.6	7 645 675	5 287 155	2 358 520	5 315 225	2 330 450
Median	30.0	29.9	30.0	30.0	29.8	...	...	...	...	27.6	27.5	28.0	27.5	28.2
Female	**96 686 289**	**69 683 676**	**27 002 613**	**71 050 140**	**25 636 149**	**100.0**	**100.0**	**100.0**	**100.0**	**91 027 988**	**66 562 997**	**24 464 991**	**68 599 255**	**22 428 733**
Under 5 years	6 150 054	4 186 978	1 963 076	4 357 475	1 792 579	6.0	7.3	6.1	7.0	7 048 807	5 034 958	2 013 849	5 326 746	1 722 061
Under 1 year	1 323 885	912 114	411 771	941 085	382 800	1.3	1.5	1.3	1.5	1 433 839	1 036 294	397 545	1 084 167	349 672
1 year	1 229 553	838 543	391 010	870 264	359 289	1.2	1.4	1.2	1.4	1 393 785	1 000 202	393 583	1 053 553	340 232
2 years	1 216 318	825 435	390 883	860 023	356 295	1.2	1.4	1.2	1.4	1 348 256	963 032	385 224	1 019 840	328 416
3 years	1 198 694	812 072	386 622	848 341	350 353	1.2	1.4	1.2	1.4	1 405 872	998 081	407 791	1 061 255	344 617
4 years	1 181 604	798 814	382 790	837 762	343 842	1.1	1.4	1.2	1.3	1 467 055	1 037 349	429 706	1 107 931	359 124
5 to 9 years	6 347 824	4 256 298	2 091 526	4 529 271	1 818 553	6.1	7.7	6.4	7.1	8 264 333	5 795 190	2 469 143	6 208 931	2 055 402
5 years	1 195 692	805 338	390 354	849 215	346 477	1.2	1.4	1.2	1.4	1 570 022	1 105 451	464 571	1 182 101	387 921
6 years	1 173 948	786 175	387 773	832 085	341 863	1.1	1.4	1.2	1.3	1 633 496	1 147 340	486 156	1 228 654	404 842
7 years	1 238 120	827 542	410 578	880 932	357 188	1.2	1.5	1.2	1.4	1 660 776	1 162 888	497 888	1 246 135	414 641
8 years	1 294 599	864 822	429 777	924 194	370 405	1.2	1.6	1.3	1.4	1 684 000	1 178 844	505 156	1 263 880	420 120
9 years	1 445 465	972 421	473 044	1 042 845	402 620	1.4	1.8	1.5	1.6	1 716 039	1 200 667	515 372	1 288 161	427 878
10 to 14 years	7 052 479	4 741 329	2 311 150	5 107 183	1 945 296	6.8	8.6	7.2	7.6	8 647 392	6 046 057	2 601 335	6 458 838	2 188 554
10 years	1 434 521	966 121	468 400	1 039 875	394 646	1.4	1.7	1.5	1.5	1 771 001	1 237 850	533 151	1 324 234	446 767
11 years	1 388 231	932 139	456 092	1 005 127	383 104	1.3	1.7	1.4	1.5	1 718 505	1 202 763	515 742	1 288 879	429 626
12 years	1 358 227	912 433	445 794	983 345	374 882	1.3	1.7	1.4	1.5	1 742 046	1 218 413	523 633	1 303 600	438 446
13 years	1 412 345	948 112	464 233	1 021 811	390 534	1.4	1.7	1.4	1.5	1 709 836	1 195 246	514 590	1 275 753	434 083
14 years	1 459 155	982 524	476 631	1 057 025	402 130	1.4	1.8	1.5	1.6	1 706 004	1 191 785	514 219	1 266 372	439 632
15 to 19 years	8 327 960	5 933 991	2 393 969	6 064 620	2 263 340	8.5	8.9	8.5	8.8	8 079 090	5 903 765	2 175 325	6 013 104	2 065 986
15 years	1 580 050	1 068 010	512 040	1 143 034	437 016	1.5	1.9	1.6	1.7	1 681 887	1 177 497	504 390	1 247 785	434 102
16 years	1 632 906	1 112 522	520 384	1 184 300	448 606	1.6	1.9	1.7	1.7	1 632 590	1 146 912	485 678	1 208 102	424 488
17 years	1 649 508	1 136 982	512 526	1 198 425	451 083	1.6	1.9	1.7	1.8	1 611 755	1 141 022	470 733	1 193 120	418 635
18 years	1 683 956	1 243 010	440 946	1 227 526	456 430	1.8	1.6	1.7	1.8	1 610 544	1 221 640	388 904	1 198 265	412 279
19 years	1 781 540	1 373 467	408 073	1 311 335	470 205	2.0	1.5	1.8	1.8	1 542 314	1 216 694	325 620	1 165 832	376 482
20 to 24 years	8 605 482	6 628 709	1 976 773	6 485 125	2 120 357	9.5	7.3	9.1	8.3	7 341 007	5 735 307	1 605 700	5 719 962	1 621 045
20 years	1 759 980	1 367 503	392 477	1 306 849	453 131	2.0	1.5	1.8	1.8	1 554 543	1 230 840	323 703	1 188 702	365 841
21 years	1 729 858	1 346 627	383 231	1 295 663	434 195	1.9	1.4	1.8	1.7	1 506 420	(NA)	(NA)	1 165 599	340 821
25 to 29 years	7 979 535	5 895 625	2 083 910	6 044 403	1 935 132	8.5	7.7	8.5	7.5	5 962 122	4 421 094	1 541 028	4 653 113	1 309 009
30 to 34 years	7 345 140	5 240 431	2 104 709	5 555 084	1 790 056	7.5	7.8	7.8	7.0	5 042 368	3 618 316	1 424 052	3 866 146	1 176 222
35 to 39 years	5 930 000	4 126 173	1 803 827	4 443 001	1 486 999	5.9	6.7	6.3	5.8	4 936 494	3 544 822	1 391 672	3 767 079	1 169 415
40 to 44 years	4 976 317	3 477 115	1 499 202	3 695 046	1 281 271	5.0	5.6	5.2	5.0	5 412 335	3 975 877	1 436 458	4 156 845	1 255 490
45 to 49 years	4 818 254	3 433 271	1 384 983	3 580 274	1 237 980	4.9	5.1	5.0	4.8	5 587 023	4 152 123	1 434 900	4 293 063	1 293 960
50 to 54 years	5 239 501	3 833 056	1 406 445	3 915 224	1 324 277	5.5	5.2	5.5	5.2	5 169 302	3 812 949	1 356 353	3 897 490	1 271 812
55 to 59 years	5 385 014	3 978 480	1 406 534	4 000 975	1 384 039	5.7	5.2	5.6	5.4	4 695 581	3 449 102	1 246 479	3 483 081	1 212 500
60 to 64 years	4 802 598	3 522 565	1 280 033	3 476 029	1 326 569	5.1	4.7	4.9	5.2	4 157 467	3 051 248	1 106 219	3 039 361	1 118 106
65 to 69 years	4 330 607	3 201 879	1 128 728	3 088 275	1 242 332	4.6	4.2	4.3	4.8	3 491 080	2 586 703	904 377	2 537 025	954 055
70 to 74 years	3 543 031	2 672 930	870 101	2 522 531	1 020 500	3.8	3.2	3.6	4.0	2 874 531	2 167 674	706 857	2 092 719	781 812
75 to 79 years	2 659 898	2 050 181	609 717	1 903 612	756 286	2.9	2.3	2.7	3.0	2 114 943	1 601 728	513 215	1 523 558	591 385
80 to 84 years	1 762 041	1 380 734	381 307	1 267 280	494 761	2.0	1.4	1.8	1.9	1 314 258	995 908	318 350	936 845	377 413
85 years and over	1 430 554	1 123 931	306 623	1 014 732	415 822	1.6	1.1	1.4	1.6	889 855	670 176	219 679	625 349	264 506
18 years and over	72 273 468	53 181 557	19 091 911	53 530 452	18 743 016	76.3	70.7	75.3	73.1	62 141 224	46 221 361	15 919 863	46 955 733	15 185 491
62 years and over	16 535 760	12 491 063	4 044 697	11 822 555	4 713 205	17.9	15.0	16.6	18.4	13 078 035	9 778 859	3 299 176	9 460 189	3 617 846
65 years and over	13 726 131	10 429 655	3 296 476	9 796 430	3 929 701	15.0	12.2	13.8	15.3	10 684 667	8 022 189	2 662 478	7 715 496	2 969 171
Median	32.5	32.9	31.6	32.5	32.5	...	...	...	...	30.2	30.5	29.4	29.9	31.1

GENERAL POPULATION CHARACTERISTICS

UNITED STATES SUMMARY 1—39

304

Table 44. Persons by Age, Race, and Sex: 1980 and 1970—Con.

[For meaning of symbols, see Introduction. For definitions of terms, see appendixes A and B]

United States Urban Rural Inside SMSA's Outside SMSA's	1980									1970				
	Total	Number				Percent distribution								
		Urban	Rural	Inside SMSA's	Outside SMSA's	Urban	Rural	Inside SMSA's	Outside SMSA's	Total	Urban	Rural	Inside SMSA's	Outside SMSA's
BLACK														
Both sexes	**26 495 025**	**22 594 016**	**3 901 009**	**21 477 741**	**5 017 284**	**100.0**	**100.0**	**100.0**	**100.0**	**22 580 289**	**18 367 318**	**4 212 971**	**17 872 116**	**4 708 173**
Under 5 years	2 436 169	2 085 178	350 991	1 955 212	480 957	9.2	9.0	9.1	9.6	2 432 638	1 980 375	452 263	1 922 005	510 633
Under 1 year	530 964	456 191	74 773	427 016	103 948	2.0	1.9	2.0	2.1	487 199	398 555	88 644	385 331	101 868
1 year	486 890	417 193	69 697	390 854	96 036	1.8	1.8	1.8	1.9	466 446	380 151	86 295	368 355	98 091
2 years	477 708	408 122	69 586	382 829	94 879	1.8	1.8	1.8	1.9	469 964	382 425	87 539	371 182	98 782
3 years	470 660	402 088	68 572	377 265	93 395	1.8	1.8	1.8	1.9	487 809	396 131	91 678	385 112	102 697
4 years	469 947	401 584	68 363	377 248	92 699	1.8	1.8	1.8	1.8	521 220	423 113	98 107	412 025	109 195
5 to 9 years	2 490 717	2 121 996	368 721	2 003 137	487 580	9.4	9.5	9.3	9.7	2 747 428	2 213 254	534 174	2 161 293	586 135
5 years	468 080	398 369	69 711	374 324	93 756	1.8	1.8	1.7	1.9	540 061	436 183	103 878	425 313	114 748
6 years	467 645	398 329	69 316	374 607	93 038	1.8	1.8	1.7	1.9	550 724	443 889	106 835	433 242	117 482
7 years	498 320	423 912	74 408	399 736	98 584	1.9	1.9	1.9	2.0	555 169	447 021	108 148	436 408	118 761
8 years	506 709	432 060	74 649	408 654	98 055	1.9	1.9	1.9	2.0	546 786	440 243	106 543	430 136	116 650
9 years	549 963	469 326	80 637	445 816	104 147	2.1	2.1	2.1	2.1	554 688	445 918	108 770	436 194	118 494
10 to 14 years	2 673 272	2 249 634	423 638	2 142 622	530 650	10.0	10.9	10.0	10.6	2 809 869	2 224 392	585 477	2 177 127	632 742
10 years	536 456	455 713	80 743	432 628	103 828	2.0	2.1	2.0	2.1	593 719	474 382	119 337	463 391	130 328
11 years	513 788	433 934	79 854	412 796	100 992	1.9	2.0	1.9	2.0	554 764	442 508	112 256	433 036	121 728
12 years	517 587	435 382	82 205	414 937	102 650	1.9	2.1	1.9	2.0	560 273	443 907	116 366	434 931	125 342
13 years	537 569	450 640	86 929	429 605	107 964	2.0	2.2	2.0	2.2	548 936	432 213	116 723	423 151	125 785
14 years	567 872	473 965	93 907	452 656	115 216	2.1	2.4	2.1	2.3	552 177	431 382	120 795	422 618	129 559
15 to 19 years	2 984 863	2 498 790	486 073	2 374 056	610 807	11.1	12.5	11.1	12.2	2 423 045	1 890 608	532 437	1 846 127	576 918
15 years	595 146	494 874	100 272	473 488	121 658	2.2	2.6	2.2	2.4	531 985	412 430	119 555	405 003	126 982
16 years	600 439	498 683	101 756	477 322	123 117	2.2	2.6	2.2	2.5	502 731	385 696	117 035	378 855	123 876
17 years	600 169	497 627	102 542	475 678	124 491	2.2	2.6	2.2	2.5	483 695	371 360	112 335	363 662	120 033
18 years	589 101	495 337	93 764	467 257	121 844	2.2	2.4	2.2	2.4	463 572	364 105	99 467	353 384	110 188
19 years	600 008	512 269	87 739	480 311	119 697	2.3	2.2	2.2	2.4	441 062	357 017	84 045	345 223	95 839
20 to 24 years	2 724 806	2 358 102	366 704	2 226 884	497 922	10.4	9.4	10.4	9.9	1 814 220	1 517 210	297 010	1 478 838	335 382
20 years	582 281	499 663	82 618	469 236	113 045	2.2	2.1	2.2	2.3	424 258	348 833	75 425	337 482	86 776
21 years	553 644	478 488	75 156	450 274	103 370	2.1	1.9	2.1	2.1	383 456	(NA)	(NA)	310 656	72 800
25 to 29 years	2 321 319	2 024 868	296 451	1 932 738	388 581	9.0	7.6	9.0	7.7	1 428 257	1 221 719	206 538	1 201 431	226 826
30 to 34 years	1 888 713	1 649 894	238 819	1 592 458	296 255	7.3	6.1	7.4	5.9	1 252 935	1 068 931	184 004	1 053 197	199 738
35 to 39 years	1 457 747	1 272 064	185 683	1 233 727	224 020	5.6	4.8	5.7	4.5	1 195 727	1 017 004	178 723	999 115	196 612
40 to 44 years	1 251 067	1 086 369	164 698	1 053 003	198 064	4.8	4.2	4.9	3.9	1 197 865	1 009 661	188 204	988 582	209 283
45 to 49 years	1 142 948	988 141	154 807	954 248	188 700	4.4	4.0	4.4	3.8	1 122 779	939 708	183 071	916 546	206 233
50 to 54 years	1 128 926	968 797	160 129	929 240	199 686	4.3	4.1	4.3	4.0	989 467	811 164	178 303	786 510	202 957
55 to 59 years	1 036 784	882 815	153 969	843 720	193 064	3.9	3.9	3.9	3.8	873 528	701 278	172 250	673 884	199 644
60 to 64 years	870 836	725 392	145 444	685 890	184 946	3.2	3.7	3.2	3.7	733 777	580 088	153 689	552 514	181 263
65 to 69 years	776 997	632 341	144 656	589 091	187 906	2.8	3.7	2.7	3.7	626 917	487 005	139 912	457 847	169 070
70 to 74 years	563 567	454 709	108 858	419 647	143 920	2.0	2.8	2.0	2.9	415 903	320 100	95 803	300 410	115 493
75 to 79 years	387 399	310 703	76 696	284 450	102 949	1.4	2.0	1.3	2.1	254 487	191 150	63 337	177 936	76 551
80 to 84 years	199 975	159 517	40 458	145 379	54 596	0.7	1.0	0.7	1.1	144 063	106 650	37 413	98 417	45 646
85 years and over	158 920	124 706	34 214	112 239	46 681	0.6	0.9	0.5	0.9	117 384	87 021	30 363	80 337	37 047
18 years and over	17 099 113	14 646 024	2 453 089	13 950 282	3 148 831	64.8	62.9	65.0	62.8	13 071 943	10 779 811	2 292 132	10 464 171	2 607 772
62 years and over	2 576 394	2 088 013	488 381	1 934 141	642 253	9.2	12.5	9.0	12.8	1 978 925	1 522 550	456 375	1 429 137	549 788
65 years and over	2 086 858	1 681 976	404 882	1 550 806	536 052	7.4	10.4	7.2	10.7	1 558 754	1 191 926	366 828	1 114 947	443 807
Median	24.9	25.0	24.3	25.1	23.9	...	...	...	...	22.2	22.9	20.0	22.7	20.5
Male	**12 519 189**	**10 596 862**	**1 922 327**	**10 113 127**	**2 406 062**	**100.0**	**100.0**	**100.0**	**100.0**	**10 748 316**	**8 657 231**	**2 091 085**	**8 472 314**	**2 276 002**
Under 5 years	1 227 900	1 050 998	176 902	985 841	242 059	9.9	9.2	9.7	10.1	1 219 567	992 519	227 048	963 849	255 718
Under 1 year	267 044	229 461	37 583	214 972	52 072	2.2	2.0	2.1	2.2	244 504	199 944	44 560	193 250	51 254
1 year	245 307	210 489	34 818	197 129	48 178	2.0	1.8	1.9	2.0	233 632	190 249	43 383	184 546	49 086
2 years	240 629	205 345	35 284	192 763	47 866	1.9	1.8	1.9	2.0	235 078	191 319	43 759	185 853	49 225
3 years	237 612	202 949	34 663	190 512	47 100	1.9	1.8	1.9	2.0	244 653	198 587	46 066	193 190	51 463
4 years	237 308	202 754	34 554	190 465	46 843	1.9	1.8	1.9	1.9	261 700	212 420	49 280	207 010	54 690
5 to 9 years	1 255 253	1 068 977	186 276	1 009 217	246 036	10.1	9.7	10.0	10.2	1 377 355	1 108 378	268 977	1 082 870	294 485
5 years	236 209	200 929	35 280	188 629	47 580	1.9	1.8	1.9	2.0	270 724	218 513	52 211	213 052	57 672
6 years	235 737	200 639	35 098	188 770	46 967	1.9	1.8	1.9	2.0	276 000	222 202	53 798	217 096	58 904
7 years	251 220	213 937	37 283	201 749	49 471	2.0	1.9	2.0	2.1	278 026	223 664	54 362	218 540	59 486
8 years	255 098	217 298	37 800	205 534	49 564	2.1	2.0	2.0	2.1	274 276	220 487	53 789	215 483	58 793
9 years	276 989	236 174	40 815	224 535	52 454	2.2	2.1	2.2	2.2	278 329	223 512	54 817	218 699	59 630
10 to 14 years	1 344 324	1 129 639	214 685	1 077 072	267 252	10.7	11.2	10.7	11.1	1 406 715	1 109 327	297 388	1 087 936	318 779
10 years	270 689	229 793	40 896	218 084	52 605	2.2	2.1	2.2	2.2	297 458	237 260	60 198	231 988	65 470
11 years	258 838	218 278	40 560	207 955	50 883	2.1	2.1	2.1	2.1	277 098	220 340	56 758	216 000	61 098
12 years	259 055	217 789	41 266	207 729	51 326	2.1	2.1	2.1	2.1	281 327	221 993	59 334	217 810	63 517
13 years	270 002	225 772	44 230	215 646	54 356	2.1	2.3	2.1	2.3	274 426	215 118	59 308	211 055	63 371
14 years	285 740	238 007	47 733	227 658	58 082	2.2	2.5	2.3	2.4	276 406	214 616	61 790	211 083	65 323
15 to 19 years	1 489 065	1 237 345	251 720	1 178 818	310 247	11.7	13.1	11.7	12.9	1 201 605	923 773	277 832	907 281	294 324
15 years	299 219	247 815	51 404	237 551	61 668	2.3	2.7	2.3	2.6	266 309	204 775	61 534	202 116	64 193
16 years	302 757	250 055	52 702	239 911	62 846	2.4	2.7	2.4	2.6	252 145	190 885	61 260	189 054	63 091
17 years	302 629	248 956	53 673	238 780	63 849	2.3	2.8	2.4	2.7	241 838	183 063	58 775	180 486	61 352
18 years	291 685	243 146	48 539	229 899	61 786	2.3	2.5	2.3	2.6	228 318	175 915	52 403	171 791	56 527
19 years	292 775	247 373	45 402	232 677	60 098	2.3	2.4	2.3	2.5	212 995	169 135	43 860	163 834	49 161
20 to 24 years	1 300 253	1 110 808	189 445	1 051 971	248 282	10.5	9.9	10.4	10.3	839 848	687 984	151 864	673 158	166 690
20 years	281 531	238 833	42 698	225 191	56 340	2.3	2.2	2.2	2.3	198 565	160 218	38 347	155 064	43 501
21 years	265 062	226 275	38 787	213 429	51 633	2.1	2.0	2.1	2.1	175 755	(NA)	(NA)	139 493	36 262
25 to 29 years	1 084 442	932 893	151 549	892 958	191 484	8.8	7.9	8.8	8.0	657 544	553 589	103 955	548 396	109 148
30 to 34 years	870 997	751 181	119 816	727 158	143 839	7.1	6.2	7.2	6.0	568 086	479 157	88 929	475 556	92 530
35 to 39 years	662 338	571 845	90 493	557 373	104 965	5.4	4.7	5.5	4.4	540 539	456 266	84 273	451 648	88 891
40 to 44 years	566 539	488 594	77 945	476 551	89 988	4.6	4.1	4.7	3.7	543 737	455 776	87 961	450 224	93 513
45 to 49 years	515 277	443 403	71 874	431 733	83 544	4.2	3.7	4.3	3.5	520 095	433 506	86 589	426 206	93 889
50 to 54 years	504 531	431 359	73 172	417 369	87 162	4.1	3.8	4.1	3.6	458 526	372 862	85 664	364 670	93 856
55 to 59 years	466 506	395 874	70 632	381 551	84 955	3.7	3.7	3.8	3.5	404 704	320 617	84 087	311 602	93 102
60 to 64 years	385 052	317 857	67 195	303 682	81 370	3.0	3.5	3.0	3.4	334 425	260 028	74 397	250 827	83 598
65 to 69 years	331 725	265 205	66 520	249 948	81 777	2.5	3.5	2.5	3.4	277 117	210 837	66 280	201 450	75 667
70 to 74 years	234 315	184 322	49 993	172 063	62 252	1.7	2.6	1.7	2.6	183 822	138 170	45 652	131 639	52 183
75 to 79 years	152 755	118 780	33 975	110 128	42 627	1.1	1.8	1.1	1.8	109 959	79 979	29 980	75 424	34 535
80 to 84 years	74 951	57 901	17 050	53 324	21 627	0.5	0.9	0.5	0.9	58 674	41 691	16 983	38 948	19 726
85 years and over	52 966	39 881	13 085	36 370	16 596	0.4	0.7	0.4	0.7	45 998	32 772	13 226	30 630	15 368
18 years and over	7 787 107	6 600 422	1 186 685	6 324 755	1 462 352	62.3	61.7	62.5	60.8	5 984 387	4 868 284	1 116 103	4 766 003	1 218 384
62 years and over	1 061 352	842 181	219 171	789 925	271 427	7.9	11.4	7.8	11.3	865 860	650 531	215 329	619 771	246 089
65 years and over	846 712	666 089	180 623	621 833	224 879	6.3	9.4	6.1	9.3	675 570	503 449	172 121	478 091	197 479
Median	23.5	23.6	23.3	23.8	22.6	...	...	...	...	20.9	21.4	19.5	21.3	19.5

Table 44. Persons by Age, Race, and Sex: 1980 and 1970—Con.

[For meaning of symbols, see Introduction. For definitions of terms, see appendixes A and B]

United States Urban Rural Inside SMSA's Outside SMSA's	1980									1970				
		Number				Percent distribution								
	Total	Urban	Rural	Inside SMSA's	Outside SMSA's	Urban	Rural	Inside SMSA's	Outside SMSA's	Total	Urban	Rural	Inside SMSA's	Outside SMSA's
BLACK—Con.														
Female	13 975 836	11 997 154	1 978 682	11 364 614	2 611 222	100.0	100.0	100.0	100.0	11 831 973	9 710 087	2 121 886	9 399 802	2 432 171
Under 5 years	1 208 269	1 034 180	174 089	969 371	238 898	8.6	8.8	8.5	9.1	1 213 071	987 856	225 215	958 156	254 915
Under 1 year	263 920	226 730	37 190	212 044	51 876	1.9	1.9	1.9	2.0	242 695	198 611	44 084	192 081	50 614
1 year	241 583	206 704	34 879	193 725	47 858	1.7	1.8	1.7	1.8	232 814	189 902	42 912	183 809	49 005
2 years	237 079	202 777	34 302	190 066	47 013	1.7	1.7	1.7	1.8	234 886	191 106	43 780	185 329	49 557
3 years	233 048	199 139	33 909	186 753	46 295	1.7	1.7	1.6	1.8	243 156	197 544	45 612	191 922	51 234
4 years	232 639	198 830	33 809	186 783	45 856	1.7	1.7	1.6	1.8	259 520	210 693	48 827	205 015	54 505
5 to 9 years	1 235 464	1 053 019	182 445	993 920	241 544	8.8	9.2	8.7	9.3	1 370 073	1 104 876	265 197	1 078 423	291 650
5 years	231 871	197 440	34 431	185 695	46 176	1.6	1.7	1.6	1.8	269 337	217 670	51 667	212 261	57 076
6 years	231 908	197 690	34 218	185 837	46 071	1.6	1.7	1.6	1.8	274 724	221 687	53 037	216 146	58 578
7 years	247 100	209 975	37 125	197 987	49 113	1.8	1.9	1.7	1.9	277 143	223 357	53 786	217 868	59 275
8 years	251 611	214 762	36 849	203 120	48 491	1.8	1.9	1.8	1.9	272 510	219 756	52 754	214 653	57 857
9 years	272 974	233 152	39 822	221 281	51 693	1.9	2.0	1.9	2.0	276 359	222 406	53 953	217 495	58 864
10 to 14 years	1 328 948	1 119 995	208 953	1 065 550	263 398	9.3	10.6	9.4	10.1	1 403 154	1 115 065	288 089	1 089 191	313 963
10 years	265 767	225 920	39 847	214 544	51 223	1.9	2.0	1.9	2.0	296 261	237 122	59 139	231 403	64 858
11 years	254 950	215 656	39 294	204 841	50 109	1.8	2.0	1.8	1.9	277 666	222 168	55 498	217 036	60 630
12 years	258 532	217 593	40 939	207 208	51 324	1.8	2.1	1.8	2.0	278 946	221 914	57 032	217 121	61 825
13 years	267 567	224 868	42 699	213 959	53 608	1.9	2.2	1.9	2.1	274 510	217 095	57 415	212 096	62 414
14 years	282 132	235 958	46 174	224 998	57 134	2.0	2.3	2.0	2.2	275 771	216 766	59 005	211 535	64 236
15 to 19 years	1 495 798	1 261 445	234 353	1 195 238	300 560	10.5	11.8	10.5	11.5	1 221 440	966 835	254 605	938 846	282 594
15 years	295 927	247 059	48 868	235 937	59 990	2.1	2.5	2.1	2.3	265 676	207 655	58 021	202 887	62 789
16 years	297 682	248 628	49 054	237 411	60 271	2.1	2.5	2.1	2.3	250 586	194 811	55 775	189 801	60 785
17 years	297 540	248 671	48 869	236 898	60 642	2.1	2.5	2.1	2.3	241 857	188 297	53 560	183 176	58 681
18 years	297 416	252 191	45 225	237 358	60 058	2.1	2.3	2.1	2.3	235 254	188 190	47 064	181 593	53 661
19 years	307 233	264 896	42 337	247 634	59 599	2.2	2.1	2.2	2.3	228 067	187 882	40 185	181 389	46 678
20 to 24 years	1 424 553	1 247 294	177 259	1 174 913	249 640	10.4	9.0	10.3	9.6	974 372	829 226	145 146	805 680	168 692
20 years	300 750	260 830	39 920	244 045	56 705	2.2	2.0	2.1	2.2	225 693	188 615	37 078	182 418	43 275
21 years	288 582	252 213	36 369	236 845	51 737	2.1	1.8	2.1	2.0	207 701	(NA)	(NA)	171 163	36 538
25 to 29 years	1 236 877	1 091 975	144 902	1 039 780	197 097	9.1	7.3	9.1	7.5	770 713	668 130	102 583	653 035	117 678
30 to 34 years	1 017 716	898 713	119 003	865 300	152 416	7.5	6.0	7.6	5.8	684 849	589 774	95 075	577 641	107 208
35 to 39 years	795 409	700 219	95 190	676 354	119 055	5.8	4.8	6.0	4.6	655 188	560 738	94 450	547 467	107 721
40 to 44 years	684 528	597 775	86 753	576 452	108 076	5.0	4.4	5.1	4.1	654 128	553 885	100 243	538 358	115 770
45 to 49 years	627 671	544 738	82 933	522 515	105 156	4.5	4.2	4.6	4.0	602 684	506 202	96 482	490 340	112 344
50 to 54 years	624 395	537 438	86 957	511 871	112 524	4.5	4.4	4.5	4.3	530 941	438 302	92 639	421 840	109 101
55 to 59 years	570 278	486 941	83 337	462 169	108 109	4.1	4.2	4.1	4.1	468 824	380 661	88 163	362 282	106 542
60 to 64 years	485 784	407 535	78 249	382 208	103 576	3.4	4.0	3.4	4.0	399 352	320 060	79 292	301 687	97 665
65 to 69 years	445 272	367 136	78 136	339 143	106 129	3.1	3.9	3.0	4.1	349 800	276 168	73 532	256 397	93 403
70 to 74 years	329 252	270 387	58 865	247 584	81 668	2.3	3.0	2.2	3.1	232 081	181 930	50 151	168 771	63 310
75 to 79 years	234 644	191 923	42 721	174 322	60 322	1.6	2.2	1.5	2.3	144 528	111 171	33 357	102 512	42 016
80 to 84 years	125 024	101 616	23 408	92 055	32 969	0.8	1.2	0.8	1.3	85 389	64 959	20 430	59 469	25 920
85 years and over	105 954	84 825	21 129	75 869	30 085	0.7	1.1	0.7	1.2	71 386	54 249	17 137	49 707	21 679
18 years and over	9 312 006	8 045 602	1 266 404	7 625 527	1 686 479	67.1	64.0	67.1	64.6	7 087 556	5 911 527	1 176 029	5 698 168	1 389 388
62 years and over	1 515 042	1 245 832	269 210	1 144 216	370 826	10.4	13.6	10.1	14.2	1 113 065	872 019	241 046	809 366	303 699
65 years and over	1 240 146	1 015 887	224 259	928 973	311 173	8.5	11.3	8.2	11.9	883 184	688 477	194 707	636 856	246 328
Median	26.1	26.2	25.4	26.3	25.3	...	...	...	...	23.5	24.1	21.0	23.9	21.8

Table 67. Persons by Age, Race, Spanish Origin, and Sex, for States: 1980

[For meaning of symbols, see Introduction. For definitions of terms, see appendixes A and B]

States	Race Total Both sexes	Total Male	Total Female	Race White Both sexes	White Male	White Female	Race Black Both sexes	Black Male	Black Female	Spanish origin[1] Both sexes	Spanish Male	Spanish Female
ALABAMA												
Total persons	3 893 888	1 871 534	2 022 354	2 872 621	1 396 508	1 476 113	996 335	462 865	533 470	33 299	16 188	17 111
Under 5 years	296 412	150 350	146 062	195 900	100 000	95 900	98 118	49 176	48 942	3 045	1 516	1 529
Under 1 year	62 806	31 888	30 918	41 022	21 042	19 980	21 295	10 596	10 699	661	315	346
1 year	58 922	29 869	29 053	38 908	19 800	19 108	19 545	9 845	9 700	604	299	305
2 years	58 720	29 734	28 986	38 961	19 882	19 079	19 269	9 613	9 656	596	316	280
3 years	58 169	29 522	28 647	38 676	19 721	18 955	18 996	9 560	9 436	593	293	300
4 years	57 795	29 337	28 458	38 333	19 555	18 778	19 013	9 562	9 451	591	293	298
5 to 9 years	314 150	160 615	153 535	212 100	108 938	103 162	99 781	50 545	49 236	3 091	1 583	1 508
5 years	59 135	30 145	28 990	39 452	20 219	19 233	19 211	9 696	9 515	606	319	287
6 years	59 457	30 280	29 177	39 787	20 470	19 317	19 220	9 585	9 635	560	264	296
7 years	62 608	31 974	30 634	41 707	21 280	20 427	20 464	10 475	9 989	648	352	296
8 years	64 068	32 805	31 263	43 637	22 464	21 173	19 982	10 115	9 867	585	317	268
9 years	68 882	35 411	33 471	47 517	24 505	23 012	20 904	10 674	10 230	692	331	361
10 to 14 years	328 096	167 885	160 211	224 636	115 805	108 831	101 429	51 049	50 380	3 232	1 617	1 615
10 years	67 155	34 287	32 868	46 451	23 928	22 523	20 259	10 142	10 117	634	298	336
11 years	64 241	32 968	31 273	44 359	23 055	21 304	19 458	9 697	9 761	621	315	306
12 years	62 840	32 022	30 818	42 955	22 066	20 889	19 500	9 766	9 734	617	292	325
13 years	65 125	33 339	31 786	44 316	22 788	21 528	20 441	10 355	10 086	677	340	337
14 years	68 735	35 269	33 466	46 555	23 968	22 587	21 771	11 089	10 682	683	372	311
15 to 19 years	377 406	190 792	186 614	259 511	132 546	126 965	115 603	56 948	58 655	3 867	2 055	1 812
15 years	73 816	37 549	36 267	50 293	25 689	24 604	23 156	11 655	11 501	711	344	367
16 years	74 787	38 292	36 495	50 993	26 295	24 698	23 410	11 821	11 589	717	375	342
17 years	74 987	38 193	36 794	50 973	26 060	24 913	23 583	11 882	11 701	796	433	363
18 years	75 939	38 311	37 628	52 469	26 847	25 622	22 945	11 155	11 790	851	480	371
19 years	77 877	38 447	39 430	54 783	27 655	27 128	22 509	10 435	12 074	792	423	369
20 to 24 years	361 187	177 550	183 637	258 516	130 089	128 427	99 587	45 789	53 798	3 656	1 954	1 702
20 years	76 093	37 598	38 495	53 911	27 303	26 608	21 577	9 962	11 615	826	436	390
21 years	73 269	35 473	37 796	52 400	26 128	26 272	20 212	8 995	11 217	767	432	335
25 to 29 years	315 460	154 658	160 802	232 027	115 906	116 121	80 330	37 189	43 141	2 719	1 344	1 375
30 to 34 years	283 292	138 949	144 343	220 103	109 648	110 455	60 531	28 080	32 451	2 141	1 016	1 125
35 to 39 years	228 920	111 298	117 622	183 496	90 884	92 612	43 591	19 529	24 062	1 699	779	920
40 to 44 years	200 794	95 998	104 796	160 204	78 440	81 764	39 307	16 975	22 332	1 505	664	841
45 to 49 years	191 929	91 518	100 411	152 963	74 938	78 025	37 901	16 127	21 774	1 400	654	746
50 to 54 years	197 066	92 262	104 804	156 034	75 097	80 937	40 219	16 858	23 361	1 371	625	746
55 to 59 years	190 062	87 747	102 315	151 310	71 082	80 228	38 188	16 421	21 767	1 261	591	670
60 to 64 years	169 099	76 539	92 560	132 914	61 062	71 852	35 754	15 284	20 470	1 121	507	614
65 to 69 years	156 295	67 931	88 364	118 630	52 014	66 616	37 270	15 765	21 505	1 085	442	643
70 to 74 years	122 087	50 261	71 826	92 736	38 027	54 709	29 035	12 114	16 921	949	401	548
75 to 79 years	82 626	31 608	51 018	61 863	23 235	38 628	20 536	8 296	12 240	629	250	379
80 to 84 years	44 988	15 594	29 394	34 450	11 628	22 822	10 438	3 934	6 504	315	109	206
85 years and over	34 019	9 979	24 040	25 228	7 169	18 059	8 717	2 786	5 931	213	81	132
18 years and over	2 731 640	1 278 650	1 452 990	2 087 726	993 721	1 094 005	626 858	276 737	350 121	21 707	10 320	11 387
62 years and over	536 759	218 803	317 756	408 996	166 771	242 225	126 427	51 533	74 894	3 825	1 568	2 257
65 years and over	440 015	175 373	264 642	332 907	132 073	200 834	105 996	42 895	63 101	3 191	1 283	1 908
Median	29.2	27.8	30.7	31.2	29.8	32 6	24.1	22.5	25.6	24.6	23.2	26.3
ALASKA												
Total persons	401 851	213 041	188 810	309 728	165 589	144 139	13 643	7 678	5 965	9 507	5 054	4 453
Under 5 years	38 949	20 040	18 909	28 216	14 530	13 686	1 591	806	785	1 291	677	614
Under 1 year	8 753	4 452	4 301	6 402	3 251	3 151	366	186	180	308	143	165
1 year	8 084	4 189	3 895	5 802	3 004	2 798	374	184	190	271	150	121
2 years	7 624	3 959	3 665	5 547	2 896	2 651	308	165	143	243	138	105
3 years	7 377	3 756	3 621	5 399	2 731	2 668	274	139	135	265	135	130
4 years	7 111	3 684	3 427	5 066	2 648	2 418	269	132	137	204	111	93
5 to 9 years	35 043	17 943	17 100	25 373	13 046	12 327	1 319	665	654	1 099	561	538
5 years	6 956	3 610	3 346	5 000	2 620	2 380	275	142	133	236	136	100
6 years	6 670	3 356	3 314	4 742	2 422	2 320	244	113	131	228	118	110
7 years	7 014	3 556	3 458	5 088	2 567	2 521	303	147	156	198	92	106
8 years	6 887	3 545	3 342	5 039	2 594	2 445	244	138	106	228	109	119
9 years	7 516	3 876	3 640	5 504	2 843	2 661	253	125	128	209	106	103
10 to 14 years	34 282	17 720	16 562	24 662	12 798	11 864	1 019	510	509	807	418	389
10 years	7 332	3 736	3 596	5 474	2 833	2 641	225	97	128	189	99	90
11 years	6 748	3 485	3 263	4 945	2 546	2 399	197	107	90	162	83	79
12 years	6 530	3 327	3 203	4 734	2 433	2 301	209	99	110	153	71	82
13 years	6 710	3 479	3 231	4 704	2 446	2 258	184	92	92	141	72	69
14 years	6 962	3 693	3 269	4 805	2 540	2 265	204	115	89	162	93	69
15 to 19 years	37 154	19 819	17 335	26 453	14 270	12 183	1 192	658	534	900	486	414
15 years	7 380	3 824	3 556	5 181	2 687	2 494	216	107	109	162	67	95
16 years	7 503	3 982	3 521	5 349	2 863	2 486	193	101	92	177	89	88
17 years	7 588	4 008	3 580	5 397	2 881	2 516	198	108	90	180	101	79
18 years	6 962	3 729	3 233	5 005	2 737	2 268	255	139	116	157	84	73
19 years	7 721	4 276	3 445	5 521	3 102	2 419	330	203	127	224	145	79
20 to 24 years	45 090	24 186	20 904	34 170	18 317	15 853	2 406	1 509	897	1 374	805	569
20 years	8 404	4 677	3 727	6 184	3 466	2 718	487	335	152	279	167	112
21 years	8 728	4 823	3 905	6 481	3 590	2 891	483	325	158	273	169	104
25 to 29 years	48 645	25 564	23 081	39 000	20 534	18 466	2 144	1 268	876	1 229	669	560
30 to 34 years	42 163	22 676	19 487	34 879	18 966	15 913	1 185	732	453	991	466	525
35 to 39 years	31 316	17 077	14 239	25 993	14 359	11 634	745	424	321	596	312	284
40 to 44 years	22 706	12 484	10 222	18 470	10 304	8 166	592	331	261	449	239	210
45 to 49 years	18 404	9 982	8 422	14 793	8 154	6 639	459	256	203	296	160	136
50 to 54 years	15 839	8 711	7 128	12 903	7 247	5 656	346	186	160	192	106	86
55 to 59 years	12 617	6 777	5 840	10 237	5 534	4 703	266	138	128	133	74	59
60 to 64 years	8 096	4 303	3 793	6 442	3 510	2 932	165	86	79	64	37	27
65 to 69 years	5 206	2 740	2 466	3 773	2 008	1 765	102	56	46	47	23	24
70 to 74 years	3 106	1 538	1 568	2 187	1 057	1 130	64	32	32	17	9	8
75 to 79 years	1 845	883	962	1 241	573	668	32	18	14	13	6	7
80 to 84 years	771	351	420	525	236	289	9	2	7	8	5	3
85 years and over	619	247	372	411	146	265	7	1	6	1	1	—
18 years and over	271 106	145 524	125 582	215 550	116 784	98 766	9 107	5 381	3 726	5 791	3 141	2 650
62 years and over	15 971	8 128	7 843	11 627	5 939	5 688	301	150	151	128	71	57
65 years and over	11 547	5 759	5 788	8 137	4 020	4 117	214	109	105	86	44	42
Median	26 0	26.3	25.7	27.0	27 4	26 6	23 5	23.8	23.0	22.4	22.3	22.5

[1]Persons of Spanish origin may be of any race

Table 67. Persons by Age, Race, Spanish Origin, and Sex, for States: 1980—Con.

[For meaning of symbols, see Introduction. For definitions of terms, see appendixes A and B]

States	Race Total Both sexes	Total Male	Total Female	White Both sexes	White Male	White Female	Black Both sexes	Black Male	Black Female	Spanish origin[1] Both sexes	Male	Female
ARIZONA												
Total persons	2 718 215	1 337 942	1 380 273	2 240 761	1 098 982	1 141 779	74 977	38 894	36 083	440 701	220 246	220 455
Under 5 years	213 883	109 075	104 808	155 559	79 351	76 208	7 389	3 825	3 564	54 763	27 940	26 823
Under 1 year	47 545	24 340	23 205	34 430	17 730	16 700	1 670	875	795	12 241	6 205	6 036
1 year	42 638	21 692	20 946	30 983	15 741	15 242	1 507	771	736	10 902	5 601	5 301
2 years	41 777	21 082	20 695	30 491	15 359	15 132	1 373	722	651	10 765	5 387	5 378
3 years	41 305	21 302	20 003	30 089	15 472	14 617	1 403	726	677	10 490	5 419	5 071
4 years	40 618	20 659	19 959	29 566	15 049	14 517	1 436	731	705	10 365	5 328	5 037
5 to 9 years	211 067	107 650	103 417	156 993	80 415	76 578	7 198	3 656	3 542	50 731	25 652	25 079
5 years	40 975	20 990	19 985	29 993	15 413	14 580	1 389	719	670	10 464	5 348	5 116
6 years	39 779	20 133	19 646	29 099	14 819	14 280	1 380	684	696	9 885	4 913	4 972
7 years	41 692	21 481	20 211	30 820	15 928	14 892	1 519	763	756	10 058	5 146	4 912
8 years	42 014	21 410	20 604	31 577	16 181	15 396	1 409	735	674	9 941	5 028	4 913
9 years	46 607	23 636	22 971	35 504	18 074	17 430	1 501	755	746	10 383	5 217	5 166
10 to 14 years	219 573	111 583	107 990	167 338	85 306	82 032	7 277	3 644	3 633	47 772	24 234	23 538
10 years	45 531	23 156	22 375	34 984	17 802	17 182	1 560	785	775	9 848	5 065	4 783
11 years	43 325	22 040	21 285	33 245	16 934	16 311	1 411	698	713	9 320	4 743	4 577
12 years	42 548	21 599	20 949	32 275	16 541	15 734	1 384	680	704	9 349	4 660	4 689
13 years	43 494	22 038	21 456	32 972	16 764	16 208	1 405	708	697	9 504	4 764	4 740
14 years	44 675	22 750	21 925	33 862	17 265	16 597	1 517	773	744	9 751	5 002	4 749
15 to 19 years	252 017	128 283	123 734	194 925	99 026	95 899	8 729	4 678	4 051	50 905	26 081	24 824
15 years	47 962	24 340	23 622	36 709	18 628	18 081	1 614	845	769	10 180	5 240	4 940
16 years	49 303	25 128	24 175	37 914	19 287	18 627	1 615	836	779	10 249	5 220	5 029
17 years	49 699	25 305	24 394	38 333	19 572	18 761	1 638	861	777	10 318	5 248	5 070
18 years	50 798	25 923	24 875	39 682	20 203	19 479	1 814	955	859	9 882	5 117	4 765
19 years	54 255	27 587	26 668	42 287	21 336	20 951	2 048	1 181	867	10 276	5 256	5 020
20 to 24 years	263 783	133 486	130 297	210 452	106 315	104 137	9 082	5 006	4 076	45 814	23 080	22 734
20 years	54 602	27 747	26 855	43 157	21 833	21 324	1 984	1 143	841	9 790	4 928	4 862
21 years	53 076	26 900	26 176	42 124	21 304	20 820	1 906	1 045	861	9 320	4 722	4 598
25 to 29 years	236 051	119 140	116 911	191 675	96 311	95 364	7 191	3 931	3 260	39 366	20 171	19 195
30 to 34 years	207 764	104 855	102 909	173 363	87 382	85 981	5 390	2 977	2 413	31 669	15 889	15 780
35 to 39 years	162 873	80 333	82 540	137 921	68 203	69 718	3 898	1 976	1 922	23 909	11 668	12 241
40 to 44 years	135 115	66 836	68 279	113 887	56 493	57 394	3 463	1 802	1 661	19 861	9 644	10 217
45 to 49 years	125 071	61 538	63 533	106 975	52 916	54 059	3 118	1 594	1 524	17 395	8 380	9 015
50 to 54 years	126 749	60 295	66 454	111 222	53 052	58 170	2 698	1 330	1 368	15 898	7 608	8 290
55 to 59 years	132 507	61 155	71 352	119 876	55 155	64 721	2 345	1 124	1 221	13 076	6 317	6 759
60 to 64 years	124 400	57 682	66 718	114 911	53 162	61 749	2 112	1 043	1 069	9 745	4 672	5 073
65 to 69 years	114 844	53 009	61 835	106 810	49 283	57 527	1 897	868	1 029	7 511	3 525	3 986
70 to 74 years	87 276	39 867	47 409	81 401	37 022	44 379	1 373	658	715	5 483	2 545	2 938
75 to 79 years	55 485	24 236	31 249	51 408	22 310	29 098	980	437	543	3 605	1 585	2 020
80 to 84 years	29 879	11 889	17 990	27 913	11 005	16 908	477	196	281	1 842	730	1 112
85 years and over	19 878	7 030	12 848	18 132	6 275	11 857	360	149	211	1 356	525	831
18 years and over	1 926 728	934 861	991 867	1 647 915	796 423	851 492	48 246	25 227	23 019	256 688	126 712	129 976
62 years and over	381 583	170 650	210 933	354 441	157 897	196 544	6 323	2 927	3 396	25 267	11 544	13 723
65 years and over	307 362	136 031	171 331	285 664	125 895	159 769	5 087	2 308	2 779	19 797	8 910	10 887
Median	29.2	28.2	30.1	31.2	30.1	32.3	23.7	23.5	24.0	21.7	21.3	22.1
ARKANSAS												
Total persons	2 286 435	1 104 688	1 181 747	1 890 322	919 191	971 131	373 768	174 668	199 100	17 904	8 742	9 162
Under 5 years	175 592	90 138	85 454	132 128	68 195	63 933	41 275	20 853	20 422	2 063	1 054	1 009
Under 1 year	37 546	19 298	18 248	27 984	14 523	13 461	9 096	4 534	4 562	444	225	219
1 year	34 660	17 683	16 977	25 994	13 324	12 670	8 237	4 146	4 091	441	228	213
2 years	34 653	17 736	16 917	26 133	13 431	12 702	8 091	4 107	3 984	390	194	196
3 years	34 443	17 740	16 703	26 035	13 447	12 588	7 989	4 067	3 922	394	203	191
4 years	34 290	17 681	16 609	25 982	13 470	12 512	7 862	3 999	3 863	394	204	190
5 to 9 years	180 365	92 287	88 078	139 324	71 630	67 694	38 910	19 538	19 372	1 811	952	859
5 years	34 935	17 880	17 055	26 674	13 809	12 865	7 840	3 846	3 994	372	190	182
6 years	34 330	17 673	16 657	26 288	13 570	12 718	7 615	3 881	3 734	367	201	166
7 years	35 589	18 136	17 453	27 319	14 014	13 305	7 850	3 900	3 950	352	187	165
8 years	36 410	18 533	17 877	28 478	14 530	13 948	7 506	3 775	3 731	332	180	152
9 years	39 101	20 065	19 036	30 565	15 707	14 858	8 099	4 136	3 963	388	194	194
10 to 14 years	185 491	94 932	90 559	144 323	74 286	70 037	39 235	19 683	19 552	1 844	950	894
10 years	38 033	19 489	18 544	29 810	15 282	14 528	7 811	4 000	3 811	380	186	194
11 years	36 507	18 665	17 842	28 781	14 829	13 952	7 343	3 657	3 686	387	207	180
12 years	35 764	18 333	17 431	27 632	14 316	13 316	7 737	3 824	3 913	349	167	182
13 years	36 676	18 701	17 975	28 409	14 593	13 816	7 900	3 923	3 977	362	185	177
14 years	38 511	19 744	18 767	29 691	15 266	14 425	8 444	4 279	4 165	366	205	161
15 to 19 years	214 322	108 641	105 681	168 030	85 550	82 480	44 094	21 870	22 224	2 030	1 052	978
15 years	42 655	21 793	20 862	33 201	17 015	16 186	9 059	4 570	4 489	379	195	184
16 years	43 677	22 212	21 465	34 219	17 427	16 792	9 054	4 548	4 506	389	216	173
17 years	43 594	22 262	21 332	34 015	17 405	16 610	9 142	4 639	4 503	425	211	214
18 years	41 939	21 244	20 695	32 954	16 821	16 133	8 515	4 155	4 360	401	207	194
19 years	42 457	21 130	21 327	33 641	16 882	16 759	8 324	3 958	4 366	436	223	213
20 to 24 years	193 769	95 013	98 756	156 326	77 804	78 522	34 884	15 836	19 048	1 918	983	935
20 years	40 940	20 088	20 852	32 514	16 217	16 297	7 883	3 579	4 304	444	234	210
21 years	39 250	19 408	19 842	31 637	15 892	15 745	7 084	3 223	3 861	379	196	183
25 to 29 years	174 313	85 136	89 177	143 656	70 968	72 688	28 228	13 000	15 228	1 506	745	761
30 to 34 years	161 024	78 989	82 035	138 529	68 581	69 948	20 491	9 538	10 953	1 257	574	683
35 to 39 years	133 636	64 914	68 722	117 598	57 739	59 859	14 628	6 548	8 080	852	395	457
40 to 44 years	113 779	55 535	58 244	99 715	49 434	50 281	12 998	5 545	7 383	729	337	392
45 to 49 years	107 324	51 379	55 945	93 997	45 673	48 324	12 370	5 282	7 088	649	293	356
50 to 54 years	110 435	51 978	58 457	96 199	46 109	50 090	13 396	5 522	7 874	628	266	362
55 to 59 years	113 577	52 325	61 252	99 640	46 406	53 234	13 243	5 585	7 658	609	279	330
60 to 64 years	110 331	50 680	59 651	96 119	44 565	51 554	13 701	5 913	7 788	516	236	280
65 to 69 years	106 299	48 578	57 721	91 229	41 978	49 251	14 585	6 399	8 186	494	216	278
70 to 74 years	86 148	37 625	48 523	73 612	32 149	41 463	12 178	5 331	6 847	432	179	253
75 to 79 years	60 428	24 701	35 727	50 514	20 519	29 995	9 624	4 068	5 556	310	122	188
80 to 84 years	33 248	12 705	20 543	27 881	10 424	17 457	5 231	2 235	2 996	158	76	82
85 years and over	26 354	9 132	17 222	21 502	7 181	14 321	4 767	1 922	2 845	98	33	65
18 years and over	1 615 061	761 064	853 997	1 373 112	653 233	719 879	227 093	100 837	126 256	10 993	5 164	5 829
62 years and over	377 218	162 334	214 884	321 214	138 346	182 868	54 355	23 337	31 018	1 793	759	1 034
65 years and over	312 477	132 741	179 736	264 738	112 251	152 487	46 385	19 955	26 430	1 492	626	866
Median	30.6	29.2	31.9	32.2	30.8	33.4	23.2	21.6	24.7	23.0	21.7	24.4

[1]Persons of Spanish origin may be of any race.

GENERAL POPULATION CHARACTERISTICS

Table 67. Persons by Age, Race, Spanish Origin, and Sex, for States: 1980—Con.

[For meaning of symbols, see Introduction. For definitions of terms, see appendixes A and B]

States	Race — Total			Race — White			Race — Black			Spanish origin[1]		
	Both sexes	Male	Female	Both sexes	Male	Female	Both sexes	Male	Female	Both sexes	Male	Female
CALIFORNIA												
Total persons	23 667 902	11 666 485	12 001 417	18 030 893	8 843 872	9 187 021	1 819 281	890 178	929 103	4 544 331	2 299 114	2 245 217
Under 5 years	1 708 400	873 639	834 761	1 145 003	586 494	558 509	155 965	78 975	76 990	547 386	278 903	268 483
Under 1 year	377 712	193 310	184 402	252 944	129 602	123 342	33 893	17 191	16 702	121 718	62 177	59 541
1 year	341 475	174 827	166 648	229 273	117 753	111 520	31 400	15 797	15 603	107 607	54 919	52 688
2 years	334 406	171 188	163 218	224 203	115 003	109 200	30 628	15 561	15 067	106 968	54 571	52 397
3 years	331 405	169 135	162 270	222 063	113 314	108 749	29 901	15 123	14 778	103 977	52 798	51 179
4 years	323 402	165 179	158 223	216 520	110 822	105 698	30 143	15 303	14 840	107 116	54 438	52 678
5 to 9 years	1 650 348	843 750	806 598	1 130 892	578 964	551 928	152 707	77 256	75 451	484 659	246 440	238 219
5 years	320 673	163 663	157 010	216 349	110 548	105 801	29 164	14 695	14 469	101 220	51 396	49 824
6 years	309 167	158 123	151 044	208 487	106 857	101 630	28 589	14 521	14 068	95 184	48 227	46 957
7 years	321 800	164 959	156 841	219 034	112 184	106 850	29 599	15 153	14 446	96 273	49 305	46 968
8 years	328 374	168 122	160 252	226 833	116 423	110 410	30 595	15 444	15 151	93 028	47 192	45 836
9 years	370 334	188 883	181 451	260 189	132 952	127 237	34 760	17 443	17 317	98 954	50 320	48 634
10 to 14 years	1 796 019	915 240	880 779	1 273 925	649 693	624 232	174 368	88 333	86 035	447 725	226 040	221 685
10 years	372 037	189 801	182 236	263 182	134 266	128 916	35 516	18 069	17 447	95 695	48 536	47 159
11 years	356 234	181 497	174 737	253 061	128 938	124 123	33 688	17 176	16 512	90 180	45 518	44 662
12 years	345 433	176 569	168 864	245 174	125 502	119 672	33 117	16 758	16 359	86 289	43 709	42 580
13 years	354 690	180 076	174 614	251 864	128 212	123 652	34 886	17 507	17 379	86 743	43 422	43 321
14 years	367 625	187 297	180 328	260 644	132 775	127 869	37 161	18 823	18 338	88 818	44 855	43 963
15 to 19 years	2 130 465	1 091 684	1 038 781	1 533 704	783 516	750 188	199 712	101 910	97 802	495 457	256 991	238 466
15 years	394 656	200 403	194 253	282 722	143 600	139 122	38 490	19 480	19 010	92 870	46 955	45 915
16 years	413 416	210 884	202 532	298 158	151 840	146 318	39 227	19 927	19 300	96 576	49 653	46 923
17 years	426 119	218 898	207 221	307 528	157 365	150 163	39 650	20 159	19 491	99 945	52 205	47 740
18 years	432 864	222 428	210 436	311 858	159 476	152 382	39 859	20 384	19 475	99 931	52 548	47 383
19 years	463 410	239 071	224 339	333 438	171 235	162 203	42 486	21 960	20 526	106 135	55 630	50 505
20 to 24 years	2 355 965	1 213 068	1 142 897	1 703 336	873 394	829 942	201 226	101 728	99 498	533 611	281 540	252 071
20 years	468 066	243 276	224 790	335 995	173 682	162 313	42 102	21 840	20 262	107 746	57 287	50 459
21 years	464 384	240 503	223 881	335 365	172 656	162 709	40 070	20 536	19 534	105 759	56 009	49 750
25 to 29 years	2 232 964	1 132 811	1 100 153	1 641 294	831 146	810 148	176 819	86 823	89 996	463 714	241 318	222 396
30 to 34 years	2 010 051	1 008 606	1 001 445	1 526 540	768 890	757 650	145 888	70 069	75 819	359 493	183 343	176 150
35 to 39 years	1 552 444	776 545	775 899	1 199 120	602 632	596 488	113 798	54 463	59 335	261 935	131 400	130 535
40 to 44 years	1 262 494	629 452	633 042	971 520	485 838	485 682	98 219	48 355	49 864	209 438	104 039	105 399
45 to 49 years	1 164 130	578 420	585 714	917 012	458 326	458 686	83 504	40 711	42 793	179 988	88 904	91 084
50 to 54 years	1 195 800	578 795	617 005	976 446	475 320	501 126	75 709	35 947	39 762	164 344	79 533	84 811
55 to 59 years	1 202 140	573 119	629 021	1 018 300	485 447	532 853	70 132	32 921	37 211	130 296	63 467	66 829
60 to 64 years	992 428	467 607	524 821	858 518	405 652	452 866	55 883	25 590	30 293	86 778	40 134	46 644
65 to 69 years	839 247	378 259	460 988	731 614	328 971	402 643	45 965	20 116	25 849	66 814	29 142	37 672
70 to 74 years	631 731	269 849	361 882	555 541	234 083	321 458	31 176	12 971	18 205	48 598	21 254	27 344
75 to 79 years	448 406	175 580	272 826	397 301	152 529	244 772	20 143	7 858	12 285	34 930	15 008	19 922
80 to 84 years	276 849	95 767	181 082	251 335	85 329	166 006	10 046	3 623	6 423	17 103	7 065	10 038
85 years and over	218 017	64 294	153 723	199 492	57 648	141 844	8 021	2 529	5 492	12 062	4 593	7 469
18 years and over	17 278 944	8 403 671	8 875 273	13 592 665	6 575 916	7 016 749	1 218 874	586 048	632 826	2 775 170	1 398 918	1 376 252
62 years and over	2 984 610	1 251 251	1 733 359	2 631 257	1 091 846	1 539 411	146 469	61 266	85 203	226 957	98 717	128 240
65 years and over	2 414 250	983 749	1 430 501	2 135 283	858 560	1 276 723	115 351	47 097	68 254	179 507	77 062	102 445
Median	29.9	28.9	30.9	31.9	30.7	33.0	25.7	24.8	26.5	22.8	22.5	23.1
COLORADO												
Total persons	2 889 964	1 434 293	1 455 671	2 571 498	1 273 291	1 298 207	101 703	52 111	49 592	339 717	170 412	169 305
Under 5 years	216 495	110 954	105 541	182 501	93 546	88 955	9 153	4 674	4 479	38 730	19 657	19 073
Under 1 year	48 034	24 577	23 457	40 430	20 677	19 753	2 014	989	1 025	8 747	4 423	4 324
1 year	43 542	22 385	21 157	36 737	18 897	17 840	1 814	914	900	7 697	3 975	3 722
2 years	42 433	21 578	20 855	35 965	18 346	17 619	1 733	869	864	7 465	3 711	3 754
3 years	41 746	21 428	20 318	35 122	17 988	17 134	1 814	986	828	7 458	3 746	3 712
4 years	40 740	20 986	19 754	34 247	17 638	16 609	1 778	916	862	7 363	3 802	3 561
5 to 9 years	213 135	108 961	104 174	180 897	92 759	88 138	9 261	4 566	4 695	36 618	18 588	18 030
5 years	40 892	20 948	19 944	34 601	17 749	16 852	1 757	899	858	7 178	3 618	3 560
6 years	39 767	20 308	19 459	33 410	17 078	16 332	1 728	861	867	7 110	3 593	3 517
7 years	41 437	21 181	20 256	35 000	17 999	17 001	1 824	878	946	7 281	3 653	3 628
8 years	42 999	22 016	20 983	36 676	18 807	17 869	1 861	924	937	7 275	3 786	3 489
9 years	48 040	24 508	23 532	41 210	21 126	20 084	2 091	1 004	1 087	7 774	3 938	3 836
10 to 14 years	226 147	115 145	111 002	195 332	99 667	95 665	9 402	4 788	4 614	36 014	17 952	18 062
10 years	47 577	24 371	23 206	41 051	21 065	19 986	1 963	976	987	7 538	3 848	3 690
11 years	45 791	23 337	22 454	39 672	20 269	19 403	1 853	950	903	7 121	3 561	3 560
12 years	43 541	22 078	21 463	37 606	19 176	18 430	1 824	923	901	6 949	3 392	3 557
13 years	44 142	22 360	21 782	38 241	19 405	18 836	1 813	899	914	7 039	3 484	3 555
14 years	45 096	22 999	22 097	38 762	19 752	19 010	1 949	1 040	909	7 367	3 667	3 700
15 to 19 years	268 588	137 609	130 979	232 902	119 211	113 691	11 427	5 998	5 429	39 895	20 246	19 649
15 years	49 353	25 283	24 070	42 618	21 841	20 777	2 125	1 074	1 051	7 886	4 030	3 856
16 years	51 254	26 171	25 083	44 504	22 735	21 769	2 091	1 052	1 039	8 064	4 117	3 947
17 years	52 429	26 756	25 673	45 672	23 286	22 386	2 060	1 083	977	8 104	4 140	3 964
18 years	55 690	28 581	27 109	48 358	24 748	23 610	2 358	1 259	1 099	7 885	3 944	3 941
19 years	59 862	30 818	29 044	51 750	26 601	25 149	2 793	1 530	1 263	7 956	4 015	3 941
20 to 24 years	302 606	154 319	148 287	263 281	133 577	129 704	13 190	7 365	5 825	36 295	18 355	17 940
20 years	60 376	30 958	29 418	52 154	26 625	25 529	2 805	1 589	1 216	7 853	3 954	3 899
21 years	59 490	30 726	28 764	51 638	26 522	25 116	2 648	1 500	1 148	7 178	3 702	3 476
25 to 29 years	302 601	153 566	149 035	267 638	135 400	132 238	11 048	5 888	5 160	32 451	16 700	15 751
30 to 34 years	266 944	136 128	130 816	239 887	122 319	117 568	8 239	4 339	3 900	26 778	13 552	13 226
35 to 39 years	193 509	97 252	96 257	174 637	87 710	86 927	6 173	3 184	2 989	19 223	9 573	9 650
40 to 44 years	153 444	76 653	76 791	138 427	69 177	69 250	5 220	2 606	2 614	15 701	7 891	7 810
45 to 49 years	137 882	69 013	68 869	125 217	62 713	62 504	4 825	2 511	2 314	13 267	6 528	6 739
50 to 54 years	132 978	64 918	68 060	122 518	59 833	62 685	3 801	1 921	1 880	11 870	5 843	6 027
55 to 59 years	125 711	60 307	65 404	117 347	56 399	60 948	2 995	1 408	1 587	9 640	4 576	5 064
60 to 64 years	102 599	48 894	53 705	96 587	46 084	50 503	2 214	1 032	1 182	7 054	3 317	3 737
65 to 69 years	84 108	37 868	46 240	79 519	35 837	43 682	1 782	750	1 032	5 714	2 618	3 096
70 to 74 years	64 558	27 687	36 871	61 158	26 128	35 030	1 236	495	741	4 331	2 049	2 282
75 to 79 years	44 924	17 641	27 283	42 510	16 573	25 937	812	291	521	3 070	1 496	1 574
80 to 84 years	29 372	10 054	19 318	27 947	9 483	18 464	500	160	340	1 692	817	875
85 years and over	24 363	7 324	17 039	23 193	6 875	16 318	425	135	290	1 374	634	740
18 years and over	2 081 151	1 021 023	1 060 128	1 879 974	919 457	960 517	67 611	34 874	32 737	204 301	101 928	102 373
62 years and over	306 234	128 410	177 824	289 920	121 193	168 727	5 940	2 381	3 559	20 197	9 491	10 706
65 years and over	247 325	100 574	146 751	234 327	94 896	139 431	4 755	1 831	2 924	16 181	7 614	8 567
Median	28.6	27.9	29.3	29.3	28.6	30.0	24.4	24.0	24.8	22.5	22.3	22.7

[1] Persons of Spanish origin may be of any race.

Table 67. Persons by Age, Race, Spanish Origin, and Sex, for States: 1980—Con.

[For meaning of symbols, see Introduction. For definitions of terms, see appendixes A and B]

States	Total Both sexes	Total Male	Total Female	White Both sexes	White Male	White Female	Black Both sexes	Black Male	Black Female	Spanish origin[1] Both sexes	Spanish origin[1] Male	Spanish origin[1] Female
CONNECTICUT												
Total persons	3 107 576	1 498 005	1 609 571	2 799 420	1 351 586	1 447 834	217 433	102 128	115 305	124 499	60 576	63 923
Under 5 years	185 188	94 479	90 709	154 556	79 036	75 520	19 635	9 931	9 704	15 631	7 999	7 632
Under 1 year	39 161	20 172	18 989	32 571	16 829	15 742	4 223	2 164	2 059	3 387	1 724	1 663
1 year	36 803	18 743	18 060	30 537	15 554	14 983	4 089	2 080	2 009	3 136	1 593	1 543
2 years	36 520	18 560	17 960	30 609	15 587	15 022	3 816	1 923	1 893	3 038	1 564	1 474
3 years	36 133	18 303	17 830	30 117	15 334	14 783	3 738	1 850	1 888	3 139	1 613	1 526
4 years	36 571	18 701	17 870	30 722	15 732	14 990	3 769	1 914	1 855	2 931	1 505	1 426
5 to 9 years	205 758	105 508	100 250	175 035	90 008	85 027	20 409	10 350	10 059	14 555	7 510	7 045
5 years	37 239	19 222	18 017	31 475	16 314	15 161	3 669	1 893	1 776	2 867	1 478	1 389
6 years	36 846	18 975	17 871	31 281	16 149	15 132	3 601	1 810	1 791	2 804	1 463	1 341
7 years	39 590	20 060	19 530	33 601	17 085	16 516	3 969	1 972	1 997	2 826	1 420	1 406
8 years	42 753	21 828	20 925	36 452	18 668	17 784	4 228	2 123	2 105	2 905	1 533	1 372
9 years	49 330	25 423	23 907	42 226	21 792	20 434	4 942	2 552	2 390	3 153	1 616	1 537
10 to 14 years	256 283	130 582	125 701	221 242	113 147	108 095	24 667	12 247	12 420	14 837	7 477	7 360
10 years	50 803	25 759	25 044	43 761	22 286	21 475	4 823	2 373	2 450	3 071	1 527	1 544
11 years	49 294	25 102	24 192	42 493	21 759	20 734	4 713	2 325	2 388	2 997	1 474	1 523
12 years	49 274	25 158	24 116	42 632	21 817	20 815	4 649	2 338	2 311	2 897	1 448	1 449
13 years	51 790	26 448	25 342	44 692	22 911	21 781	5 051	2 523	2 528	2 907	1 491	1 416
14 years	55 122	28 115	27 007	47 664	24 374	23 290	5 431	2 688	2 743	2 965	1 537	1 428
15 to 19 years	288 383	146 275	142 108	252 135	128 277	123 858	26 020	12 886	13 134	14 385	7 224	7 161
15 years	58 080	29 497	28 583	50 624	25 779	24 845	5 475	2 727	2 748	2 914	1 462	1 452
16 years	59 199	30 154	29 045	51 511	26 291	25 220	5 629	2 793	2 836	2 921	1 468	1 453
17 years	58 411	29 729	28 682	51 111	26 024	25 087	5 259	2 697	2 562	2 875	1 456	1 419
18 years	55 852	28 428	27 424	48 956	25 076	23 880	4 958	2 412	2 546	2 694	1 348	1 346
19 years	56 841	28 467	28 374	49 933	25 107	24 826	4 699	2 257	2 442	2 981	1 490	1 491
20 to 24 years	272 382	135 362	137 020	242 003	120 945	121 058	21 125	9 857	11 268	12 504	5 957	6 547
20 years	55 230	27 411	27 819	48 720	24 197	24 523	4 573	2 210	2 363	2 635	1 315	1 320
21 years	55 542	27 470	28 072	49 327	24 532	24 795	4 312	2 022	2 290	2 495	1 176	1 319
25 to 29 years	249 260	123 182	126 078	222 739	110 966	111 773	18 019	8 120	9 899	10 923	5 150	5 773
30 to 34 years	241 873	117 419	124 454	216 652	105 910	110 742	17 291	7 736	9 555	9 948	4 648	5 300
35 to 39 years	204 479	99 619	104 860	184 150	90 442	93 708	14 129	6 280	7 849	7 791	3 576	4 215
40 to 44 years	164 823	79 838	84 985	148 189	72 265	75 924	11 901	5 239	6 662	6 117	2 825	3 292
45 to 49 years	161 649	78 231	83 418	148 069	71 979	76 090	10 019	4 552	5 467	4 803	2 291	2 512
50 to 54 years	177 252	85 632	91 620	165 508	80 127	85 381	9 167	4 256	4 911	3 884	1 854	2 030
55 to 59 years	178 712	85 285	93 427	168 729	80 603	88 126	8 005	3 730	4 275	3 007	1 407	1 600
60 to 64 years	156 670	73 078	83 592	149 372	69 806	79 566	5 908	2 632	3 276	2 154	997	1 157
65 to 69 years	126 415	56 435	69 980	120 791	54 054	66 737	4 561	1 926	2 635	1 536	659	877
70 to 74 years	93 302	38 383	54 919	89 638	36 894	52 744	2 966	1 180	1 786	1 034	421	613
75 to 79 years	66 081	24 333	41 748	63 651	23 468	40 183	1 953	686	1 267	721	309	412
80 to 84 years	43 337	14 051	29 286	42 146	13 636	28 510	953	308	645	369	156	213
85 years and over	35 729	10 313	25 416	34 815	10 023	24 792	705	212	493	300	116	184
18 years and over	2 284 657	1 078 056	1 206 601	2 095 341	991 301	1 104 040	136 359	61 383	74 976	70 766	33 204	37 562
62 years and over	455 545	185 531	270 014	437 761	178 313	259 448	14 321	5 727	8 594	5 116	2 188	2 928
65 years and over	364 864	143 515	221 349	351 041	138 075	212 966	11 138	4 312	6 826	3 960	1 661	2 299
Median	32.0	30.6	33.3	33.0	31.6	34 4	24 2	22.7	25.5	21 1	20.1	22.1
DELAWARE												
Total persons	594 338	286 599	307 739	487 817	236 317	251 500	95 845	44 999	50 846	9 661	4 834	4 827
Under 5 years	41 151	20 984	20 167	30 934	15 877	15 057	9 026	4 495	4 531	1 246	635	611
Under 1 year	8 951	4 632	4 319	6 680	3 488	3 192	2 004	1 006	998	278	145	133
1 year	8 413	4 266	4 147	6 304	3 230	3 074	1 888	917	971	267	138	129
2 years	8 136	4 126	4 010	6 128	3 129	2 999	1 780	881	899	229	106	123
3 years	7 874	4 028	3 846	5 949	3 042	2 907	1 685	859	826	257	144	113
4 years	7 777	3 932	3 845	5 873	2 988	2 885	1 669	832	837	215	102	113
5 to 9 years	42 076	21 441	20 635	32 086	16 374	15 712	8 787	4 427	4 360	1 088	557	531
5 years	7 829	3 955	3 874	5 944	2 957	2 987	1 669	877	792	204	109	95
6 years	7 544	3 852	3 692	5 718	2 938	2 780	1 578	779	799	210	115	95
7 years	8 225	4 142	4 083	6 330	3 205	3 125	1 664	813	851	214	119	95
8 years	8 747	4 465	4 282	6 728	3 462	3 266	1 782	880	902	215	103	112
9 years	9 731	5 027	4 704	7 366	3 812	3 554	2 094	1 078	1 016	245	111	134
10 to 14 years	48 870	24 895	23 975	37 249	19 141	18 108	10 544	5 212	5 332	1 066	539	527
10 years	9 719	4 934	4 785	7 385	3 742	3 643	2 079	1 049	1 030	238	133	105
11 years	9 262	4 784	4 478	7 074	3 699	3 375	1 978	985	993	199	86	113
12 years	9 318	4 660	4 658	7 037	3 563	3 474	2 069	990	1 079	239	106	103
13 years	10 046	5 078	4 968	7 697	3 897	3 800	2 144	1 078	1 066	219	116	103
14 years	10 525	5 439	5 086	8 056	4 240	3 816	2 274	1 110	1 164	201	98	103
15 to 19 years	59 748	29 572	30 176	47 342	23 467	23 875	11 364	5 565	5 799	1 097	528	569
15 years	11 162	5 652	5 510	8 634	4 416	4 218	2 310	1 128	1 182	232	111	121
16 years	11 661	5 920	5 741	9 092	4 607	4 485	2 359	1 203	1 156	223	114	109
17 years	11 675	5 854	5 821	9 191	4 625	4 566	2 293	1 121	1 172	223	111	112
18 years	12 344	6 015	6 329	9 908	4 822	5 086	2 210	1 078	1 132	203	98	105
19 years	12 906	6 131	6 775	10 517	4 997	5 520	2 192	1 035	1 157	216	94	122
20 to 24 years	58 123	28 339	29 784	47 435	23 451	23 984	9 677	4 359	5 318	1 022	524	498
20 years	12 452	5 977	6 475	10 150	4 965	5 185	2 082	904	1 178	231	126	105
21 years	12 274	5 897	6 377	10 004	4 861	5 143	2 037	916	1 121	227	126	101
25 to 29 years	49 622	24 242	25 380	40 506	20 190	20 316	8 130	3 587	4 543	859	426	433
30 to 34 years	45 414	22 144	23 270	37 432	18 562	18 870	7 008	3 164	3 844	688	339	349
35 to 39 years	37 100	18 029	19 071	30 913	15 180	15 733	5 354	2 469	2 885	594	293	301
40 to 44 years	31 168	15 199	15 969	25 973	12 740	13 233	4 477	2 076	2 401	458	237	221
45 to 49 years	30 959	15 099	15 860	26 262	12 909	13 353	4 190	1 950	2 240	383	203	180
50 to 54 years	32 251	15 547	16 704	28 010	13 544	14 466	3 907	1 830	2 077	333	168	165
55 to 59 years	31 847	15 051	16 796	27 909	13 230	14 679	3 708	1 699	2 009	246	126	120
60 to 64 years	26 830	12 741	14 089	23 712	11 267	12 445	2 954	1 396	1 558	183	95	88
65 to 69 years	21 218	9 495	11 723	18 460	8 299	10 161	2 606	1 132	1 474	168	79	89
70 to 74 years	15 412	6 294	9 118	13 560	5 489	8 071	1 739	758	981	99	29	70
75 to 79 years	10 507	3 922	6 585	9 198	3 396	5 802	1 234	499	735	62	30	32
80 to 84 years	6 773	2 176	4 597	6 080	1 940	4 140	661	226	435	37	15	22
85 years and over	5 269	1 429	3 840	4 756	1 261	3 495	479	155	324	32	11	21
18 years and over	427 743	201 853	225 890	360 631	171 277	189 354	60 526	27 413	33 113	5 583	2 767	2 816
62 years and over	74 453	30 532	43 921	65 603	26 815	38 788	8 347	3 512	4 835	497	210	287
65 years and over	59 179	23 316	35 863	52 054	20 385	31 669	6 719	2 770	3 949	398	164	234
Median	29.7	28.7	30 8	31.1	29 9	32.3	24 2	23 1	25 1	21 5	21 3	21 7

[1] Persons of Spanish origin may be of any race.

Table 67. Persons by Age, Race, Spanish Origin, and Sex, for States: 1980—Con.

[For meaning of symbols, see Introduction. For definitions of terms, see appendixes A and B]

States	Race									Spanish origin[1]		
	Total			White			Block					
	Both sexes	Male	Female	Both sexes	Male	Female	Both sexes	Male	Female	Both sexes	Male	Female
DISTRICT OF COLUMBIA												
Total persons	638 333	295 417	342 916	171 768	80 104	91 664	448 906	206 814	242 092	17 679	7 984	9 695
Under 5 years	34 365	17 285	17 080	4 563	2 345	2 218	28 684	14 370	14 314	1 150	587	563
Under 1 year	7 472	3 779	3 693	1 106	578	528	6 098	3 059	3 039	294	150	144
1 year	6 934	3 469	3 465	944	486	458	5 761	2 877	2 884	220	104	116
2 years	6 807	3 455	3 352	882	436	446	5 706	2 906	2 800	240	130	110
3 years	6 655	3 294	3 361	871	451	420	5 575	2 731	2 844	207	117	90
4 years	6 497	3 288	3 209	760	394	366	5 544	2 797	2 747	189	86	103
5 to 9 years	36 618	18 685	17 933	4 379	2 314	2 065	31 244	15 861	15 383	976	483	493
5 years	6 588	3 338	3 250	778	383	395	5 632	2 873	2 759	193	97	96
6 years	6 572	3 402	3 170	836	454	382	5 527	2 836	2 691	183	87	96
7 years	7 113	3 627	3 486	891	463	428	6 016	3 049	2 967	193	102	91
8 years	7 742	3 917	3 825	861	467	394	6 681	3 356	3 325	200	95	105
9 years	8 603	4 401	4 202	1 013	547	466	7 388	3 747	3 641	207	102	105
10 to 14 years	42 133	21 139	20 994	4 664	2 383	2 281	36 683	18 324	18 359	924	493	431
10 years	8 444	4 230	4 214	1 085	533	552	7 204	3 618	3 586	185	96	89
11 years	7 961	4 041	3 920	909	463	446	6 886	3 489	3 397	170	89	81
12 years	8 074	3 980	4 094	918	476	442	7 014	3 422	3 592	184	102	82
13 years	8 585	4 283	4 302	934	480	454	7 496	3 727	3 769	204	111	93
14 years	9 069	4 605	4 464	818	431	387	8 083	4 068	4 015	181	95	86
15 to 19 years	57 624	27 964	29 660	10 265	4 948	5 317	46 078	22 361	23 717	1 549	759	790
15 years	9 593	4 732	4 861	927	486	441	8 512	4 175	4 337	204	91	113
16 years	10 274	5 136	5 138	1 049	509	540	9 042	4 530	4 512	223	104	119
17 years	10 508	5 233	5 275	1 054	564	490	9 223	4 546	4 677	238	132	106
18 years	12 648	6 102	6 546	3 052	1 463	1 589	9 294	4 484	4 810	398	193	205
19 years	14 601	6 761	7 840	4 183	1 926	2 257	10 007	4 626	5 381	486	239	247
20 to 24 years	69 563	32 278	37 285	20 936	9 893	11 043	46 411	21 265	25 146	2 386	1 211	1 175
20 years	13 938	6 643	7 295	3 996	1 889	2 107	9 535	4 545	4 990	487	268	219
21 years	13 997	6 489	7 508	4 171	1 967	2 204	9 388	4 303	5 085	482	251	231
25 to 29 years	66 343	31 205	35 138	22 224	10 832	11 392	41 528	19 084	22 444	2 263	1 074	1 189
30 to 34 years	56 209	26 805	29 404	19 984	10 027	9 957	34 036	15 658	18 378	1 903	860	1 043
35 to 39 years	41 450	19 932	21 518	13 806	7 326	6 480	26 256	11 959	14 297	1 393	598	795
40 to 44 years	32 815	15 763	17 052	8 364	4 512	3 852	23 358	10 768	12 590	1 144	477	667
45 to 49 years	30 204	14 122	16 082	7 097	3 754	3 343	22 265	10 005	12 260	903	348	555
50 to 54 years	33 137	15 148	17 989	7 826	3 829	3 997	24 504	11 006	13 498	856	302	554
55 to 59 years	34 093	15 209	18 884	8 830	4 026	4 804	24 548	10 877	13 671	762	296	466
60 to 64 years	29 492	12 651	16 841	8 416	3 697	4 719	20 546	8 750	11 796	507	174	333
65 to 69 years	26 382	10 769	15 613	8 627	3 382	5 245	17 372	7 228	10 144	414	134	280
70 to 74 years	19 848	7 592	12 256	7 825	2 827	4 998	11 731	4 632	7 099	243	94	149
75 to 79 years	13 436	4 664	8 772	6 018	1 971	4 047	7 217	2 596	4 621	169	64	105
80 to 84 years	8 236	2 505	5 731	4 503	1 203	3 300	3 603	1 245	2 358	83	18	65
85 years and over	6 385	1 701	4 684	3 441	835	2 606	2 842	825	2 017	54	12	42
18 years and over	494 842	223 207	271 635	155 132	71 503	83 629	325 518	145 008	180 510	13 964	6 094	7 870
62 years and over	91 242	34 285	56 957	35 465	12 368	23 097	54 370	21 314	33 056	1 245	410	835
65 years and over	74 287	27 231	47 056	30 414	10 218	20 196	42 765	16 526	26 239	963	322	641
Median	31.0	29.9	32.1	34.6	33.5	36.0	29.2	27.9	30.4	29.0	27.1	30.9
FLORIDA												
Total persons	9 746 324	4 675 626	5 070 698	8 184 513	3 928 309	4 256 204	1 342 688	636 961	705 727	858 158	413 671	444 487
Under 5 years	570 224	291 286	278 938	418 330	214 377	203 953	133 876	67 576	66 300	54 251	27 864	26 387
Under 1 year	123 569	63 355	60 214	90 645	46 605	44 040	29 126	14 745	14 381	11 449	5 896	5 553
1 year	113 123	57 642	55 481	83 039	42 375	40 664	26 543	13 434	13 109	10 442	5 350	5 092
2 years	111 864	57 095	54 769	81 717	41 775	39 942	26 563	13 434	13 129	10 819	5 521	5 298
3 years	111 381	56 767	54 614	81 976	42 017	39 959	25 845	12 952	12 893	10 883	5 582	5 301
4 years	110 287	56 427	53 860	80 953	41 605	39 348	25 799	13 011	12 788	10 658	5 515	5 143
5 to 9 years	621 534	317 254	304 280	466 210	238 886	227 324	137 140	69 036	68 104	58 418	30 136	28 282
5 years	114 045	58 468	55 577	84 234	43 396	40 838	26 257	13 269	12 988	11 079	5 755	5 324
6 years	114 022	58 334	55 688	84 500	43 356	41 144	25 967	13 131	12 836	11 203	5 779	5 424
7 years	123 000	62 602	60 398	91 480	46 808	44 672	27 786	13 916	13 870	11 710	6 055	5 655
8 years	129 121	65 882	63 239	97 392	49 759	47 633	28 213	14 299	13 914	11 876	6 090	5 786
9 years	141 346	71 968	69 378	108 604	55 567	53 037	28 917	14 421	14 496	12 550	6 457	6 093
10 to 14 years	685 016	349 914	335 102	527 431	270 373	257 058	139 931	70 674	69 257	65 205	33 075	32 130
10 years	138 809	71 051	67 758	107 432	55 117	52 315	27 720	14 082	13 638	12 679	6 421	6 258
11 years	132 979	67 843	65 136	102 861	52 691	50 170	26 705	13 443	13 262	11 980	6 076	5 904
12 years	130 951	66 834	64 117	100 670	51 599	49 071	26 914	13 571	13 343	12 311	6 246	6 065
13 years	137 837	70 272	67 565	105 545	53 942	51 603	28 754	14 531	14 223	13 573	6 836	6 737
14 years	144 440	73 914	70 526	110 923	57 024	53 899	29 838	15 047	14 791	14 662	7 496	7 166
15 to 19 years	811 340	411 458	399 882	637 333	324 674	312 659	151 762	74 752	77 010	85 141	43 949	41 192
15 years	157 415	80 377	77 038	122 088	62 528	59 560	31 245	15 697	15 548	16 089	8 260	7 829
16 years	162 169	82 593	79 576	126 912	64 764	62 148	31 066	15 596	15 470	16 977	8 664	8 313
17 years	163 278	83 506	79 772	127 699	65 401	62 298	31 163	15 766	15 397	17 926	9 277	8 649
18 years	160 614	81 092	79 522	127 032	64 631	62 401	29 032	13 955	15 077	16 846	8 777	8 069
19 years	167 864	83 890	83 974	133 602	67 350	66 252	29 256	13 738	15 518	17 303	8 971	8 332
20 to 24 years	811 427	404 245	407 182	653 187	328 660	324 527	134 424	62 434	71 990	76 140	39 504	36 636
20 years	165 674	82 328	83 346	132 387	66 531	65 856	28 286	13 015	15 271	16 476	8 560	7 916
21 years	161 056	80 297	80 759	129 253	65 018	64 235	27 098	12 618	14 480	15 541	8 066	7 475
25 to 29 years	739 848	366 758	373 090	603 259	301 937	301 322	114 082	53 158	60 924	64 237	31 416	32 821
30 to 34 years	671 563	329 786	341 777	561 321	278 198	283 123	90 918	42 112	48 806	55 628	25 851	29 777
35 to 39 years	554 240	269 171	285 069	466 033	228 220	237 813	72 329	33 169	39 160	54 313	24 749	29 564
40 to 44 years	484 538	234 788	249 750	405 197	197 629	207 568	65 427	30 205	35 222	58 398	27 696	30 702
45 to 49 years	471 279	227 935	243 344	401 984	195 705	206 279	57 564	26 598	30 966	55 523	26 613	28 910
50 to 54 years	517 881	242 231	275 650	453 841	212 948	240 893	54 489	24 657	29 832	54 280	26 275	28 005
55 to 59 years	555 209	250 526	304 683	500 306	225 460	274 846	47 687	21 685	26 002	44 255	20 650	23 605
60 to 64 years	564 652	251 914	312 738	517 195	230 681	286 514	42 067	18 778	23 289	36 773	16 201	20 572
65 to 69 years	579 012	258 435	320 577	535 403	239 373	296 030	38 947	17 073	21 874	34 582	14 559	20 023
70 to 74 years	480 141	212 018	268 123	448 481	198 415	250 066	27 845	11 980	15 865	27 124	11 556	15 568
75 to 79 years	329 211	141 044	188 167	307 652	132 285	175 367	18 753	7 612	11 141	19 215	8 128	11 087
80 to 84 years	181 867	73 874	107 993	171 833	70 051	101 782	8 660	3 294	5 366	8 029	3 144	4 885
85 years and over	117 342	42 989	74 353	109 517	40 437	69 080	6 787	2 168	4 619	6 646	2 305	4 341
18 years and over	7 386 688	3 470 696	3 915 992	6 395 843	3 011 980	3 383 863	838 267	382 616	455 651	629 292	296 395	332 897
62 years and over	2 028 861	880 845	1 148 016	1 887 386	821 007	1 066 379	124 713	52 762	71 951	116 667	48 770	67 897
65 years and over	1 687 573	728 360	959 213	1 572 886	680 561	892 325	100 992	42 127	58 865	95 596	39 692	55 904
Median	34.7	32.9	36.6	37.3	35.1	39.6	24.0	22.9	25.0	32.2	30.2	34.1

[1]Persons of Spanish origin may be of any race.

Table 67. **Persons by Age, Race, Spanish Origin, and Sex, for States: 1980**—Con.

[For meaning of symbols, see Introduction. For definitions of terms, see appendixes A and B]

States	Total			White			Black			Spanish origin[1]		
	Both sexes	Male	Female	Both sexes	Male	Female	Both sexes	Male	Female	Both sexes	Male	Female
GEORGIA												
Total persons	5 463 105	2 640 445	2 822 660	3 947 135	1 928 589	2 018 546	1 465 181	686 341	778 840	61 260	31 205	30 055
Under 5 years	414 935	212 098	202 837	268 190	138 311	129 879	141 662	71 275	70 387	5 802	2 902	2 900
Under 1 year	89 197	45 510	43 687	57 102	29 467	27 635	30 982	15 466	15 516	1 325	665	660
1 year	83 024	42 404	40 620	53 408	27 564	25 844	28 574	14 323	14 251	1 140	589	551
2 years	81 901	41 816	40 085	52 969	27 270	25 699	27 885	14 034	13 851	1 170	568	602
3 years	80 541	41 169	39 372	52 675	27 227	25 448	26 887	13 487	13 400	1 115	555	560
4 years	80 272	41 199	39 073	52 036	26 783	25 253	27 334	13 965	13 369	1 052	525	527
5 to 9 years	446 831	228 195	218 636	297 104	152 648	144 456	145 083	73 178	71 905	5 562	2 807	2 755
5 years	83 224	42 467	40 757	54 478	28 032	26 446	27 768	13 945	13 823	1 080	551	529
6 years	83 804	42 823	40 981	55 058	28 262	26 796	27 824	14 083	13 741	1 062	539	523
7 years	89 281	45 634	43 647	58 883	30 288	28 595	29 497	14 877	14 620	1 146	569	577
8 years	91 237	46 372	44 865	60 933	31 225	29 708	29 415	14 702	14 713	1 040	516	524
9 years	99 285	50 899	48 386	67 752	34 841	32 911	30 579	15 571	15 008	1 234	632	602
10 to 14 years	469 598	239 230	230 368	315 065	161 574	153 491	150 945	75 806	75 139	5 559	2 752	2 807
10 years	96 169	49 198	46 971	65 594	33 719	31 875	29 738	15 054	14 684	1 118	555	563
11 years	92 504	46 838	45 666	63 020	32 203	30 817	28 721	14 244	14 477	1 088	515	573
12 years	89 803	45 626	44 177	60 294	30 841	29 453	28 811	14 429	14 382	1 067	544	523
13 years	93 720	47 858	45 862	62 246	31 984	30 262	30 828	15 526	15 302	1 116	574	542
14 years	97 402	49 710	47 692	63 911	32 827	31 084	32 847	16 553	16 294	1 170	564	606
15 to 19 years	530 773	272 746	258 027	357 566	185 364	172 202	168 035	84 204	83 831	7 506	4 461	3 045
15 years	103 911	53 078	50 833	69 372	35 641	33 731	33 834	17 087	16 747	1 274	683	591
16 years	105 046	53 670	51 376	70 553	36 177	34 376	33 804	17 147	16 657	1 162	598	564
17 years	105 809	54 980	50 829	71 315	37 287	34 028	33 556	17 098	16 458	1 463	881	582
18 years	106 188	54 930	51 258	71 735	37 617	34 118	33 098	16 377	16 721	1 767	1 142	625
19 years	109 819	56 088	53 731	74 591	38 642	35 949	33 743	16 495	17 248	1 840	1 157	683
20 to 24 years	516 084	256 138	259 946	358 007	180 375	177 632	151 187	71 770	79 417	7 899	4 595	3 304
20 years	106 612	53 409	53 203	73 246	37 199	36 047	31 947	15 307	16 640	1 715	1 023	692
21 years	102 653	51 445	51 208	71 043	36 061	34 982	30 230	14 556	15 674	1 686	983	703
25 to 29 years	481 276	234 385	246 891	340 448	169 338	171 110	134 149	61 855	72 294	5 914	3 120	2 794
30 to 34 years	448 765	218 987	229 778	334 829	166 219	168 610	108 211	50 201	58 010	4 547	2 179	2 368
35 to 39 years	356 263	174 635	181 628	274 817	137 349	137 468	77 637	35 486	42 151	3 611	1 722	1 889
40 to 44 years	291 069	141 615	149 454	224 682	111 690	112 992	63 551	28 545	35 006	2 866	1 319	1 547
45 to 49 years	266 793	128 881	137 912	208 536	103 203	105 333	56 208	24 762	31 446	2 530	1 249	1 281
50 to 54 years	261 211	123 677	137 534	205 901	99 884	106 017	53 887	23 153	30 734	2 229	1 034	1 195
55 to 59 years	246 907	114 405	132 502	196 929	92 856	104 073	49 117	21 168	27 949	1 909	901	1 008
60 to 64 years	215 869	97 800	118 069	168 949	78 033	90 916	46 272	19 508	26 764	1 559	670	889
65 to 69 years	188 897	80 736	108 161	143 107	61 939	81 168	45 285	18 604	26 681	1 442	633	809
70 to 74 years	141 977	56 629	85 348	109 043	43 553	65 490	32 558	12 950	19 608	1 060	406	654
75 to 79 years	93 763	33 178	60 585	72 127	25 380	46 747	21 383	7 724	13 659	664	260	404
80 to 84 years	52 660	16 463	36 197	41 686	12 832	28 854	10 831	3 579	7 252	332	112	220
85 years and over	39 434	10 647	28 787	30 149	8 041	22 108	9 180	2 573	6 607	269	83	186
18 years and over	3 816 975	1 799 194	2 017 781	2 855 536	1 366 951	1 488 585	926 297	414 750	511 547	40 438	20 582	19 856
62 years and over	639 245	252 817	386 428	492 121	195 849	296 272	145 387	56 353	89 034	4 594	1 834	2 760
65 years and over	516 731	197 653	319 078	396 112	151 745	244 367	119 237	45 430	73 807	3 767	1 494	2 273
Median	28.6	27.3	29.9	30.5	29.3	31.8	24.2	22.6	25.6	23.8	22.7	25.3
HAWAII												
Total persons	964 691	494 683	470 008	318 770	171 064	147 706	17 364	11 804	5 560	71 263	36 605	34 658
Under 5 years	77 848	40 004	37 844	24 783	12 785	11 998	1 988	1 000	988	9 733	5 009	4 724
Under 1 year	17 229	8 856	8 373	5 656	2 944	2 712	461	230	231	2 194	1 123	1 071
1 year	15 650	8 173	7 477	5 073	2 679	2 394	445	222	223	1 955	1 021	934
2 years	15 270	7 871	7 399	4 837	2 464	2 373	402	208	194	1 901	1 004	897
3 years	15 079	7 675	7 404	4 771	2 448	2 323	383	191	192	1 844	940	904
4 years	14 620	7 429	7 191	4 446	2 250	2 196	297	149	148	1 839	921	918
5 to 9 years	73 057	37 555	35 502	22 095	11 346	10 749	1 252	640	612	8 018	4 088	3 930
5 years	14 237	7 378	6 859	4 320	2 205	2 115	277	143	134	1 667	879	788
6 years	14 056	7 068	6 988	4 228	2 080	2 148	269	136	133	1 571	799	772
7 years	14 329	7 370	6 959	4 293	2 197	2 096	261	144	117	1 523	769	754
8 years	14 650	7 579	7 071	4 386	2 315	2 071	217	109	108	1 576	790	786
9 years	15 785	8 160	7 625	4 868	2 549	2 319	228	108	120	1 681	851	830
10 to 14 years	74 870	38 459	36 411	21 300	10 988	10 312	846	434	412	7 372	3 745	3 627
10 years	15 874	8 236	7 638	4 862	2 499	2 363	197	101	96	1 637	847	790
11 years	14 513	7 436	7 077	4 336	2 242	2 094	175	95	80	1 397	706	691
12 years	14 334	7 382	6 952	4 014	2 092	1 922	140	69	71	1 401	701	700
13 years	14 718	7 573	7 145	4 047	2 103	1 944	182	86	96	1 459	754	705
14 years	15 431	7 832	7 599	4 041	2 052	1 989	152	83	69	1 478	737	741
15 to 19 years	86 446	45 673	40 773	25 864	14 552	11 312	1 671	1 241	430	7 927	3 961	3 966
15 years	16 251	8 368	7 883	4 344	2 241	2 103	143	77	66	1 494	749	745
16 years	16 606	8 524	8 082	4 386	2 278	2 108	114	67	47	1 626	769	857
17 years	16 951	8 606	8 345	4 530	2 334	2 196	150	84	66	1 610	774	836
18 years	17 033	9 246	7 787	5 213	3 055	2 158	432	338	94	1 548	824	724
19 years	19 605	10 929	8 676	7 391	4 644	2 747	832	675	157	1 649	845	804
20 to 24 years	105 682	59 070	46 612	42 576	26 086	16 490	5 439	4 320	1 119	8 734	4 831	3 903
20 years	21 909	12 870	9 039	8 988	5 957	3 031	1 284	1 085	199	1 837	1 056	781
21 years	21 796	12 814	8 982	9 113	5 995	3 118	1 344	1 120	224	1 825	1 064	761
25 to 29 years	95 287	48 864	46 423	37 092	19 635	17 457	2 661	1 822	839	7 012	3 518	3 494
30 to 34 years	84 314	42 990	41 324	33 039	18 075	15 564	1 380	919	461	5 257	2 652	2 605
35 to 39 years	63 948	32 684	31 264	24 026	13 037	10 989	732	505	227	3 764	1 884	1 880
40 to 44 years	47 468	23 765	23 703	15 792	8 666	7 126	445	317	128	2 797	1 386	1 411
45 to 49 years	45 240	21 589	23 651	12 862	6 881	5 981	291	194	97	2 460	1 175	1 285
50 to 54 years	49 204	23 298	25 906	13 003	6 675	6 328	206	124	82	2 212	1 053	1 159
55 to 59 years	47 383	23 502	23 881	13 107	6 748	6 359	178	123	55	1 770	917	853
60 to 64 years	37 794	18 871	18 923	11 089	5 783	5 306	125	85	40	1 244	628	616
65 to 69 years	29 153	15 384	13 769	8 498	4 298	4 200	64	37	27	1 178	699	479
70 to 74 years	20 222	10 991	9 231	5 952	2 787	3 165	45	26	19	880	539	341
75 to 79 years	13 673	6 796	6 877	3 570	1 550	2 020	25	9	16	528	304	224
80 to 84 years	7 541	3 177	4 364	2 076	743	1 333	8	4	4	228	138	90
85 years and over	5 561	2 011	3 550	1 446	429	1 017	8	4	4	149	78	71
18 years and over	689 108	353 167	335 941	237 332	129 092	108 240	12 871	9 502	3 369	41 410	21 471	19 939
62 years and over	97 582	48 960	48 622	27 904	13 037	14 867	211	113	98	3 687	2 127	1 560
65 years and over	76 150	38 359	37 791	21 542	9 807	11 735	150	80	70	2 963	1 758	1 205
Median	28.3	27.6	29.1	28.0	27.4	28.7	22.3	22.4	21.6	21.4	21.4	21.4

[1] Persons of Spanish origin may be of any race.

GENERAL POPULATION CHARACTERISTICS

UNITED STATES SUMMARY 1—163

Table 67. Persons by Age, Race, Spanish Origin, and Sex, for States: 1980—Con.

[For meaning of symbols, see Introduction. For definitions of terms, see appendixes A and B]

States	Total			White			Black			Spanish origin[1]		
	Both sexes	Male	Female	Both sexes	Male	Female	Both sexes	Male	Female	Both sexes	Male	Female
IDAHO												
Total persons	943 935	471 155	472 780	901 641	448 320	453 321	2 716	1 646	1 070	36 615	20 137	16 478
Under 5 years	93 531	48 073	45 458	88 178	45 380	42 798	295	151	144	5 411	2 750	2 661
Under 1 year	20 341	10 418	9 923	19 051	9 766	9 285	76	45	31	1 320	681	639
1 year	19 256	9 749	9 507	18 135	9 184	8 951	67	35	32	1 132	565	567
2 years	18 435	9 598	8 837	17 417	9 088	8 329	55	21	34	1 039	538	501
3 years	18 278	9 366	8 912	17 338	8 885	8 453	41	25	16	984	485	499
4 years	17 221	8 942	8 279	16 237	8 457	7 780	56	25	31	936	481	455
5 to 9 years	82 734	42 392	40 342	77 991	40 024	37 967	254	130	124	4 399	2 182	2 217
5 years	16 945	8 650	8 295	15 972	8 153	7 819	51	28	23	956	471	485
6 years	16 131	8 203	7 928	15 213	7 769	7 444	60	32	28	867	421	446
7 years	16 152	8 362	7 790	15 216	7 885	7 331	40	20	20	844	439	405
8 years	16 090	8 199	7 891	15 170	7 727	7 443	46	22	24	881	442	439
9 years	17 416	8 978	8 438	16 420	8 490	7 930	57	28	29	851	409	442
10 to 14 years	79 218	40 501	38 717	74 944	38 395	36 549	193	97	96	3 849	1 951	1 898
10 years	16 567	8 481	8 086	15 683	8 040	7 643	43	18	25	801	411	390
11 years	15 955	8 099	7 856	15 114	7 688	7 426	32	14	18	762	393	369
12 years	15 382	7 906	7 476	14 546	7 500	7 046	38	24	14	782	389	393
13 years	15 595	7 946	7 649	14 749	7 525	7 224	38	20	18	733	375	358
14 years	15 719	8 069	7 650	14 852	7 642	7 210	42	21	21	771	383	388
15 to 19 years	87 982	44 000	43 982	82 987	41 150	41 837	292	190	102	4 503	2 542	1 961
15 years	16 432	8 298	8 134	15 533	7 820	7 713	30	14	16	826	427	399
16 years	17 130	8 668	8 462	16 195	8 180	8 015	43	28	15	874	455	419
17 years	17 620	9 078	8 542	16 622	8 507	8 115	53	39	14	916	545	371
18 years	18 209	9 063	9 146	17 180	8 450	8 730	69	42	27	886	522	364
19 years	18 591	8 893	9 698	17 457	8 193	9 264	97	67	30	1 001	593	408
20 to 24 years	86 234	43 487	42 747	80 750	40 170	40 580	496	336	160	4 553	2 794	1 759
20 years	17 685	8 845	8 840	16 500	8 100	8 400	111	82	29	1 010	653	357
21 years	17 202	8 766	8 436	16 061	8 068	7 993	106	68	38	904	580	324
25 to 29 years	82 461	41 803	40 658	78 062	39 340	38 722	379	255	124	3 547	2 052	1 495
30 to 34 years	72 941	37 079	35 862	69 630	35 267	34 363	223	154	69	2 666	1 501	1 165
35 to 39 years	57 644	29 156	28 488	55 411	27 954	27 457	111	70	41	1 918	1 092	826
40 to 44 years	46 682	23 720	22 962	44 989	22 804	22 185	104	60	44	1 359	779	580
45 to 49 years	40 973	20 467	20 506	39 554	19 734	19 820	83	52	31	1 145	633	512
50 to 54 years	40 476	20 061	20 415	39 297	19 437	19 860	62	36	26	907	541	366
55 to 59 years	41 182	19 934	21 248	40 215	19 392	20 823	61	34	27	750	412	338
60 to 64 years	38 197	18 444	19 753	37 448	18 021	19 427	48	24	24	564	332	232
65 to 69 years	33 040	16 118	16 922	32 515	15 832	16 683	39	19	20	374	173	201
70 to 74 years	25 252	11 819	13 433	24 882	11 626	13 256	34	14	20	261	155	106
75 to 79 years	16 664	7 271	9 393	16 363	7 098	9 265	24	13	11	218	146	72
80 to 84 years	10 248	3 930	6 318	10 107	3 869	6 238	6	4	2	118	60	58
85 years and over	8 476	2 900	5 576	8 318	2 827	5 491	13	7	5	73	42	31
18 years and over	637 270	314 145	323 125	612 178	300 014	312 164	1 848	1 187	661	20 340	11 827	8 513
62 years and over	116 057	52 901	63 156	114 169	51 900	62 269	140	72	68	1 353	750	603
65 years and over	93 680	42 038	51 642	92 185	41 252	50 933	115	57	58	1 044	576	468
Median	27.5	27.0	28.0	27.9	27.4	28.4	23.3	23.7	22.1	20.1	21.0	18.8
ILLINOIS												
Total persons	11 426 518	5 537 537	5 888 981	9 233 327	4 488 136	4 745 191	1 675 398	782 455	892 943	635 602	331 608	303 994
Under 5 years	842 241	430 469	411 772	616 480	316 109	300 371	162 770	82 245	80 525	83 505	42 377	41 128
Under 1 year	184 025	93 846	90 179	133 451	68 348	65 103	36 329	18 355	17 974	18 901	9 579	9 322
1 year	167 177	85 264	81 913	122 918	62 940	59 978	31 915	16 085	15 830	16 234	8 111	8 123
2 years	165 352	84 633	80 719	121 986	62 685	59 301	31 104	15 625	15 479	16 199	8 309	7 890
3 years	163 623	83 626	79 997	119 698	61 349	58 349	31 683	16 033	15 650	16 276	8 246	8 030
4 years	162 064	83 100	78 964	118 427	60 787	57 640	31 739	16 147	15 592	15 895	8 132	7 763
5 to 9 years	849 613	434 098	415 515	624 467	320 410	304 057	170 168	85 482	84 686	72 446	37 161	35 285
5 years	161 446	82 660	78 786	118 782	60 898	57 884	31 142	15 775	15 367	15 376	7 904	7 472
6 years	157 479	80 458	77 021	114 788	58 861	55 927	31 732	15 977	15 755	14 283	7 325	6 958
7 years	166 909	85 171	81 738	121 118	62 047	59 071	34 622	17 380	17 242	14 611	7 528	7 083
8 years	173 563	88 661	84 902	127 434	65 620	61 814	35 449	17 594	17 855	14 108	7 185	6 923
9 years	190 216	97 148	93 068	142 345	72 984	69 361	37 223	18 756	18 467	14 068	7 219	6 849
10 to 14 years	919 385	469 422	449 963	700 979	359 467	341 512	172 888	86 602	86 286	61 680	31 321	30 359
10 years	186 351	95 450	90 901	140 868	72 506	68 362	35 247	17 705	17 542	13 563	6 833	6 730
11 years	179 471	91 596	87 875	136 953	70 160	66 793	33 268	16 776	16 492	12 452	6 253	6 199
12 years	177 849	90 602	87 247	135 276	69 268	66 008	33 693	16 747	16 946	11 884	6 079	5 805
13 years	184 723	94 183	90 540	141 285	72 319	68 966	34 935	17 458	17 477	11 650	5 923	5 727
14 years	190 991	97 591	93 400	146 597	75 214	71 383	35 745	17 916	17 829	12 131	6 233	5 898
15 to 19 years	1 066 995	543 725	523 270	832 023	425 807	406 216	186 264	92 286	93 978	68 001	35 667	32 334
15 years	205 698	104 701	100 997	159 650	81 478	78 172	37 251	18 784	18 467	12 586	6 356	6 230
16 years	210 909	107 796	103 113	164 563	84 365	80 198	37 305	18 777	18 528	12 738	6 575	6 163
17 years	215 191	110 147	105 044	167 738	86 324	81 414	37 887	18 788	19 099	13 439	7 004	6 435
18 years	213 991	109 013	104 978	166 927	85 363	81 564	36 940	18 217	18 723	14 049	7 613	6 436
19 years	221 206	112 068	109 138	173 145	88 277	84 868	36 881	17 720	19 161	15 189	8 119	7 070
20 to 24 years	1 073 008	533 097	539 911	845 134	424 077	421 057	170 046	77 798	92 248	76 238	41 439	34 799
20 years	218 741	108 785	109 956	171 214	85 699	85 515	36 187	16 912	19 275	15 591	8 518	7 073
21 years	213 348	105 935	107 413	167 746	84 063	83 683	34 572	15 786	18 786	14 970	8 098	6 872
25 to 29 years	985 619	488 484	497 135	781 992	393 473	388 519	144 587	64 557	80 030	66 453	35 884	30 569
30 to 34 years	869 244	427 350	441 894	700 156	349 148	351 008	118 239	52 106	66 133	51 872	27 518	24 354
35 to 39 years	700 599	342 300	358 299	568 885	281 553	287 332	94 520	41 521	52 999	37 101	19 398	17 703
40 to 44 years	593 096	289 497	303 599	481 984	238 044	243 940	83 410	36 733	46 677	30 245	15 789	14 456
45 to 49 years	559 129	272 240	286 889	463 602	227 951	235 651	75 174	33 748	41 426	25 380	13 354	12 026
50 to 54 years	602 312	291 318	310 994	512 788	250 106	262 682	73 485	33 117	40 368	21 106	11 266	9 840
55 to 59 years	593 160	283 082	310 078	516 032	247 414	268 618	64 506	29 246	35 260	15 432	8 324	7 108
60 to 64 years	510 232	236 521	273 711	452 150	210 234	241 916	49 864	22 427	27 437	9 170	4 574	4 596
65 to 69 years	432 764	189 786	242 978	385 610	169 328	216 282	40 998	17 699	23 299	6 500	2 891	3 609
70 to 74 years	328 719	134 564	194 155	294 386	120 268	174 118	30 059	12 323	17 736	4 464	2 012	2 452
75 to 79 years	236 701	88 236	148 465	213 625	79 047	134 578	20 247	7 890	12 357	3 242	1 454	1 788
80 to 84 years	149 019	49 669	99 350	137 038	45 093	91 945	10 492	3 986	6 506	1 616	690	926
85 years and over	114 682	33 679	81 003	105 996	30 607	75 389	7 681	2 689	4 992	1 151	489	662
18 years and over	8 183 481	3 880 904	4 302 577	6 799 450	3 239 983	3 559 467	1 057 129	471 777	585 352	379 208	200 814	178 394
62 years and over	1 557 748	632 466	925 282	1 400 689	566 588	834 101	136 855	56 823	80 032	21 796	9 891	11 905
65 years and over	1 261 885	495 934	765 951	1 136 655	444 343	692 312	109 477	44 587	64 890	16 973	7 536	9 437
Median	29.9	28 6	31.1	31.5	30.1	32.9	24.3	22.8	25.5	22.1	22.3	21.8

[1]Persons of Spanish origin may be of any race.

Table 67. Persons by Age, Race, Spanish Origin, and Sex, for States: 1980—Con.

[For meaning of symbols, see Introduction. For definitions of terms, see appendixes A and B]

States	Total			White			Black			Spanish origin[1]		
	Both sexes	Male	Female	Both sexes	Male	Female	Both sexes	Male	Female	Both sexes	Male	Female
INDIANA												
Total persons	5 490 224	2 665 825	2 824 399	5 004 394	2 433 638	2 570 756	414 785	196 534	218 251	87 047	44 123	42 924
Under 5 years	418 764	214 955	203 809	368 577	189 494	179 083	41 633	21 130	20 503	11 199	5 669	5 530
Under 1 year	89 205	45 834	43 371	78 206	40 274	37 932	9 171	4 609	4 562	2 448	1 227	1 221
1 year	83 567	42 857	40 710	73 718	37 778	35 940	8 119	4 200	3 919	2 204	1 143	1 061
2 years	82 875	42 584	40 291	73 080	37 637	35 443	8 108	4 102	4 006	2 200	1 119	1 081
3 years	81 889	42 010	39 879	72 256	37 148	35 108	8 011	4 051	3 960	2 178	1 098	1 080
4 years	81 228	41 670	39 558	71 317	36 657	34 660	8 224	4 168	4 056	2 169	1 082	1 087
5 to 9 years	433 053	221 919	211 134	383 669	197 085	186 584	41 670	20 854	20 816	9 921	4 970	4 951
5 years	82 355	41 902	40 453	72 737	37 069	35 668	8 008	3 999	4 009	2 058	1 034	1 024
6 years	80 967	41 700	39 267	71 483	36 890	34 593	7 983	4 033	3 950	1 955	960	995
7 years	85 077	43 492	41 585	75 079	38 521	36 558	8 385	4 142	4 243	1 981	970	1 011
8 years	88 357	45 372	42 985	78 519	40 425	38 094	8 332	4 168	4 164	1 919	994	925
9 years	96 297	49 453	46 844	85 851	44 180	41 671	8 962	4 512	4 450	2 008	1 012	996
10 to 14 years	454 828	232 327	222 501	406 841	208 431	198 410	41 530	20 612	20 918	8 870	4 545	4 325
10 years	92 989	47 547	45 442	83 096	42 681	40 415	8 393	4 112	4 281	1 919	971	948
11 years	89 068	45 653	43 415	79 740	40 992	38 748	8 072	4 029	4 043	1 699	874	825
12 years	87 615	44 956	42 659	78 205	40 230	37 975	8 144	4 083	4 061	1 760	901	859
13 years	91 403	46 466	44 937	81 819	41 749	40 070	8 352	4 110	4 242	1 715	877	838
14 years	93 753	47 705	46 048	83 981	42 779	41 202	8 569	4 278	4 291	1 777	922	855
15 to 19 years	529 628	266 689	262 939	475 374	239 850	235 524	46 854	23 068	23 786	9 749	4 888	4 861
15 years	101 857	51 890	49 967	91 322	46 650	44 672	9 178	4 564	4 614	1 887	952	935
16 years	105 262	53 761	51 501	94 365	48 262	46 103	9 592	4 815	4 777	1 851	961	890
17 years	104 554	53 043	51 511	93 792	47 600	46 192	9 362	4 734	4 628	1 982	987	995
18 years	106 419	53 044	53 375	95 579	47 782	47 797	9 211	4 463	4 748	1 969	949	1 020
19 years	111 536	54 951	56 585	100 316	49 556	50 760	9 511	4 492	5 019	2 060	1 039	1 021
20 to 24 years	518 661	256 924	261 737	467 526	232 725	234 801	42 693	19 741	22 952	9 737	5 019	4 718
20 years	108 520	53 650	54 870	97 739	48 502	49 237	9 025	4 231	4 794	2 062	1 063	999
21 years	106 682	52 642	54 040	96 303	47 680	48 623	8 643	4 012	4 631	1 958	1 012	946
25 to 29 years	462 851	229 755	233 096	418 752	209 039	209 713	36 160	16 746	19 414	8 076	4 189	3 887
30 to 34 years	411 557	202 401	209 156	377 023	186 167	190 856	28 023	13 026	14 997	6 225	3 232	2 993
35 to 39 years	332 036	163 201	168 835	305 933	151 130	154 803	21 814	9 977	11 837	4 455	2 200	2 255
40 to 44 years	281 547	138 100	143 447	259 609	128 006	131 603	18 548	8 477	10 071	3 612	1 677	1 935
45 to 49 years	266 812	129 714	137 098	245 918	120 115	125 803	18 093	8 247	9 846	3 597	1 839	1 758
50 to 54 years	283 300	136 906	146 394	262 579	127 303	135 276	18 289	8 404	9 885	3 568	1 900	1 668
55 to 59 years	278 021	131 999	146 022	259 727	123 301	136 426	16 612	7 834	8 778	2 704	1 442	1 262
60 to 64 years	233 782	108 167	125 615	219 886	101 786	118 100	12 782	5 833	6 949	1 695	891	804
65 to 69 years	197 805	88 209	109 596	185 896	82 946	102 950	11 126	4 913	6 213	1 285	614	671
70 to 74 years	152 654	63 503	89 151	144 013	59 768	84 245	8 014	3 447	4 567	983	471	512
75 to 79 years	110 419	41 533	68 886	104 390	39 132	65 258	5 542	2 210	3 332	728	347	381
80 to 84 years	70 096	23 638	46 458	66 777	22 351	44 426	3 068	1 207	1 861	382	146	236
85 years and over	54 410	15 885	38 525	51 904	15 009	36 895	2 334	808	1 526	261	84	177
18 years and over	3 871 906	1 837 930	2 033 976	3 565 828	1 696 116	1 869 712	261 820	119 825	141 995	51 337	26 039	25 298
62 years and over	721 241	295 356	425 885	681 032	278 211	402 821	37 291	15 884	21 407	4 562	2 138	2 424
65 years and over	585 384	232 768	352 616	552 980	219 206	333 774	30 084	12 585	17 499	3 639	1 662	1 977
Median	29.2	28.0	30.4	29.8	28.5	31.0	24.1	23.1	25.0	21.9	21.9	21.8
IOWA												
Total persons	2 913 808	1 416 390	1 497 418	2 839 225	1 378 981	1 460 244	41 700	20 842	20 858	25 536	12 848	12 688
Under 5 years	221 628	113 305	108 323	212 781	108 814	103 967	4 544	2 348	2 196	3 395	1 727	1 668
Under 1 year	48 309	24 736	23 573	46 355	23 715	22 640	1 041	563	478	731	377	354
1 year	44 615	22 974	21 641	42 816	22 047	20 769	936	488	448	717	366	351
2 years	44 210	22 511	21 699	42 493	21 631	20 862	888	440	448	689	367	322
3 years	42 852	21 826	21 026	41 135	20 969	20 166	857	438	419	658	346	312
4 years	41 642	21 258	20 384	39 982	20 452	19 530	822	419	403	600	271	329
5 to 9 years	211 041	107 877	103 164	202 794	103 671	99 123	4 219	2 167	2 052	2 965	1 523	1 442
5 years	41 200	21 198	20 002	39 561	20 346	19 215	775	409	366	621	329	292
6 years	39 274	19 991	19 283	37 621	19 155	18 466	888	439	449	597	325	272
7 years	40 455	20 754	19 701	38 786	19 895	18 891	836	439	397	563	285	278
8 years	42 890	21 917	20 973	41 268	21 093	20 175	843	448	395	603	282	321
9 years	47 222	24 017	23 205	45 558	23 182	22 376	877	432	445	581	302	279
10 to 14 years	231 700	118 841	112 859	224 140	114 961	109 179	4 210	2 176	2 034	2 688	1 349	1 339
10 years	47 174	24 280	22 894	45 567	23 460	22 107	916	471	445	568	295	273
11 years	45 340	23 253	22 087	43 786	22 440	21 346	824	430	394	528	253	275
12 years	44 535	22 740	21 795	43 145	21 986	21 159	753	412	341	526	274	252
13 years	46 340	23 726	22 614	44 850	22 977	21 873	844	425	419	524	257	267
14 years	48 311	24 842	23 469	46 792	24 098	22 694	873	438	435	542	270	272
15 to 19 years	277 633	140 188	137 445	269 160	135 841	133 319	5 034	2 581	2 453	2 837	1 394	1 443
15 years	51 934	26 753	25 181	50 399	25 991	24 408	894	435	459	557	283	274
16 years	54 449	27 900	26 549	52 869	27 094	25 775	940	506	434	578	287	291
17 years	55 121	27 908	27 213	53 508	27 104	26 404	943	456	487	539	263	276
18 years	56 874	28 217	28 657	55 060	27 292	27 768	1 092	551	541	596	292	304
19 years	59 255	29 410	29 845	57 324	28 360	28 964	1 165	633	532	567	269	298
20 to 24 years	272 024	135 749	136 275	263 240	131 148	132 092	4 880	2 479	2 401	2 806	1 489	1 317
20 years	57 650	28 456	29 194	55 696	27 391	28 305	1 134	600	534	639	338	301
21 years	55 065	27 342	27 723	53 288	26 415	26 873	1 005	515	490	536	272	264
25 to 29 years	243 200	123 366	119 834	235 671	119 458	116 213	3 896	2 009	1 887	2 334	1 260	1 124
30 to 34 years	205 954	103 613	102 341	200 193	100 694	99 499	2 920	1 482	1 438	1 812	940	872
35 to 39 years	161 246	79 979	81 267	157 396	78 088	79 308	1 961	959	1 002	1 192	547	645
40 to 44 years	141 451	69 655	71 796	138 339	68 085	70 254	1 769	886	883	959	481	478
45 to 49 years	135 520	65 675	69 845	132 849	64 422	68 427	1 608	754	854	870	420	450
50 to 54 years	145 902	71 343	74 559	143 374	70 129	73 245	1 583	774	809	894	439	455
55 to 59 years	145 854	69 954	75 900	143 898	69 026	74 872	1 338	627	711	768	391	377
60 to 64 years	133 071	62 177	70 894	131 580	61 512	70 068	1 050	475	575	498	250	248
65 to 69 years	117 905	53 196	64 709	116 601	52 628	63 973	971	444	527	427	192	235
70 to 74 years	96 949	41 052	55 897	95 999	40 661	55 338	665	269	396	354	159	195
75 to 79 years	75 104	28 875	46 229	74 422	28 599	45 823	471	203	268	337	146	191
80 to 84 years	52 686	18 160	34 526	52 232	18 001	34 231	313	113	200	189	75	114
85 years and over	44 940	13 385	31 555	44 556	13 243	31 313	268	96	172	151	66	95
18 years and over	2 087 935	993 806	1 094 129	2 042 734	971 346	1 071 388	25 950	12 754	13 196	14 814	7 416	7 398
62 years and over	465 740	191 088	274 652	461 117	189 168	271 949	3 293	1 398	1 895	1 744	775	969
65 years and over	387 584	154 668	232 916	383 810	153 132	230 678	2 688	1 125	1 563	1 458	638	830
Median	30.0	28.7	31.4	30.3	28.9	31.7	22.7	22.1	23.5	21.5	21.3	21.6

[1] Persons of Spanish origin may be of any race.

Table 67. Persons by Age, Race, Spanish Origin, and Sex, for States: 1980—Con.

[For meaning of symbols, see Introduction. For definitions of terms, see appendixes A and B]

States	Total Both sexes	Total Male	Total Female	White Both sexes	White Male	White Female	Black Both sexes	Black Male	Black Female	Spanish origin¹ Both sexes	Spanish origin¹ Male	Spanish origin¹ Female
KANSAS												
Total persons	2 363 679	1 156 941	1 206 738	2 168 221	1 058 004	1 110 217	126 127	63 179	62 948	63 339	32 941	30 398
Under 5 years	180 877	92 984	87 893	159 900	82 235	77 665	12 541	6 359	6 182	8 504	4 382	4 122
Under 1 year	39 814	20 521	19 293	34 987	18 069	16 918	2 855	1 457	1 398	1 913	958	955
1 year	36 434	18 779	17 655	32 175	16 570	15 605	2 547	1 286	1 261	1 739	915	824
2 years	35 644	18 279	17 365	31 513	16 141	15 372	2 497	1 279	1 218	1 703	904	799
3 years	34 947	17 955	16 992	31 050	15 968	15 082	2 293	1 153	1 140	1 632	847	785
4 years	34 038	17 450	16 588	30 175	15 487	14 688	2 349	1 184	1 165	1 517	758	759
5 to 9 years	169 015	86 823	82 192	150 301	77 442	72 859	11 513	5 756	5 757	7 117	3 619	3 498
5 years	33 585	17 247	16 338	29 825	15 364	14 461	2 216	1 125	1 091	1 515	736	779
6 years	31 955	16 294	15 661	28 415	14 522	13 893	2 139	1 059	1 080	1 329	667	662
7 years	33 061	16 977	16 084	29 289	15 065	14 224	2 323	1 153	1 170	1 445	778	667
8 years	33 233	17 258	15 975	29 587	15 430	14 157	2 277	1 145	1 132	1 324	674	650
9 years	37 181	19 047	18 134	33 185	17 061	16 124	2 558	1 274	1 284	1 504	764	740
10 to 14 years	175 363	89 670	85 693	157 253	80 467	76 786	11 882	5 991	5 891	6 326	3 231	3 095
10 years	36 398	18 655	17 743	32 651	16 726	15 925	2 402	1 235	1 167	1 385	706	679
11 years	34 754	17 755	16 999	31 129	15 876	15 253	2 309	1 167	1 142	1 297	694	603
12 years	33 408	17 109	16 299	29 967	15 383	14 584	2 270	1 136	1 134	1 171	583	588
13 years	34 527	17 522	17 005	30 974	15 762	15 212	2 348	1 153	1 195	1 190	585	605
14 years	36 276	18 629	17 647	32 532	16 720	15 812	2 553	1 300	1 253	1 283	663	620
15 to 19 years	217 721	111 484	106 237	195 139	99 540	95 599	15 259	8 050	7 209	7 161	3 794	3 367
15 years	39 323	20 261	19 062	35 291	18 145	17 146	2 754	1 457	1 297	1 312	669	643
16 years	41 661	21 151	20 510	37 633	19 124	18 509	2 737	1 350	1 387	1 394	705	689
17 years	42 796	21 762	21 034	38 622	19 639	18 983	2 886	1 445	1 441	1 337	724	613
18 years	44 837	22 956	21 881	40 057	20 428	19 629	3 196	1 684	1 512	1 446	776	670
19 years	49 104	25 354	23 750	43 536	22 204	21 332	3 686	2 114	1 572	1 672	920	752
20 to 24 years	232 788	119 895	112 893	206 303	104 810	101 493	16 917	9 696	7 221	7 987	4 566	3 421
20 years	49 149	25 495	23 654	43 112	21 930	21 182	3 967	2 364	1 603	1 703	981	722
21 years	46 962	24 240	22 722	41 323	20 943	20 380	3 600	2 126	1 474	1 706	1 006	700
25 to 29 years	202 671	103 213	99 458	183 638	93 223	90 415	11 245	5 857	5 388	6 085	3 298	2 787
30 to 34 years	171 947	86 831	85 116	157 786	79 662	78 124	8 245	4 111	4 134	4 591	2 397	2 194
35 to 39 years	135 209	67 276	67 933	125 206	62 439	62 767	6 103	2 855	3 248	3 136	1 601	1 535
40 to 44 years	114 431	56 367	58 064	106 386	52 533	53 853	5 079	2 359	2 720	2 450	1 237	1 213
45 to 49 years	112 515	54 817	57 698	105 315	51 448	53 867	4 762	2 223	2 539	2 279	1 136	1 143
50 to 54 years	118 914	58 057	60 857	112 083	54 905	57 178	4 676	2 159	2 517	2 152	1 022	1 130
55 to 59 years	119 932	57 852	62 080	113 948	55 079	58 869	4 234	1 949	2 285	1 807	880	927
60 to 64 years	106 033	49 421	56 612	101 319	47 235	54 084	3 612	1 659	1 953	1 127	545	582
65 to 69 years	94 208	42 230	51 978	90 061	40 396	49 665	3 288	1 468	1 820	835	388	447
70 to 74 years	79 203	33 338	45 865	76 036	32 013	44 023	2 557	1 052	1 505	642	299	343
75 to 79 years	59 399	22 630	36 769	56 927	21 629	35 298	1 994	781	1 213	533	267	266
80 to 84 years	39 998	13 857	26 141	38 512	13 269	25 243	1 168	462	706	341	151	190
85 years and over	33 455	10 196	23 259	32 108	9 679	22 429	1 052	392	660	266	128	138
18 years and over	1 714 644	824 290	890 354	1 589 221	760 952	828 269	81 814	40 821	40 993	37 349	19 611	17 738
62 years and over	368 088	150 912	217 176	352 795	144 401	208 394	12 135	5 104	7 031	3 222	1 535	1 687
65 years and over	306 263	122 251	184 012	293 644	116 986	176 658	10 059	4 155	5 904	2 617	1 233	1 384
Median	30.1	28.7	31.6	30.9	29.5	32.5	23.3	22.5	24.4	21.5	21.5	21.6
KENTUCKY												
Total persons	3 660 777	1 789 039	1 871 738	3 379 006	1 651 422	1 727 584	259 477	126 159	133 318	27 406	14 457	12 949
Under 5 years	282 731	144 779	137 952	256 274	131 500	124 774	23 986	12 025	11 961	2 485	1 297	1 188
Under 1 year	59 679	30 424	29 255	53 860	27 509	26 351	5 239	2 632	2 607	552	267	285
1 year	56 511	29 130	27 381	50 985	26 360	24 625	5 028	2 509	2 519	504	266	238
2 years	55 962	28 741	27 221	50 941	26 265	24 676	4 562	2 238	2 324	451	235	216
3 years	55 764	28 563	27 201	50 635	25 970	24 665	4 660	2 352	2 308	505	291	214
4 years	54 815	27 921	26 894	49 853	25 396	24 457	4 497	2 294	2 203	473	238	235
5 to 9 years	289 411	148 353	141 058	264 012	135 558	128 454	23 395	11 792	11 603	2 306	1 176	1 130
5 years	55 006	28 142	26 864	50 135	25 705	24 430	4 425	2 216	2 209	434	218	216
6 years	54 336	27 796	26 540	49 541	25 399	24 142	4 378	2 190	2 188	444	226	218
7 years	57 214	29 343	27 871	52 083	26 756	25 327	4 757	2 409	2 348	460	237	223
8 years	59 396	30 561	28 835	54 186	27 923	26 263	4 816	2 431	2 385	489	249	240
9 years	63 459	32 511	30 948	58 067	29 775	28 292	5 019	2 546	2 473	479	246	233
10 to 14 years	301 745	154 689	147 056	277 186	142 275	134 911	23 061	11 650	11 411	2 427	1 243	1 184
10 years	61 200	31 527	29 673	56 110	28 912	27 198	4 747	2 444	2 303	508	254	254
11 years	59 261	30 217	29 044	54 399	27 743	26 656	4 526	2 308	2 218	467	235	232
12 years	58 230	29 713	28 517	53 475	27 416	26 059	4 447	2 135	2 312	450	236	214
13 years	60 389	31 003	29 386	55 607	28 523	27 084	4 528	2 344	2 184	470	245	225
14 years	62 665	32 229	30 436	57 595	29 681	27 914	4 813	2 419	2 394	532	273	259
15 to 19 years	354 439	183 893	170 546	320 869	165 304	155 565	31 212	17 024	14 188	3 414	2 096	1 318
15 years	68 339	34 972	33 367	62 862	32 221	30 641	5 216	2 631	2 585	552	294	258
16 years	69 454	35 646	33 808	63 464	32 499	30 965	5 686	2 978	2 708	548	281	267
17 years	71 050	37 670	33 380	64 334	33 926	30 408	6 247	3 421	2 826	691	418	273
18 years	71 432	37 206	34 226	63 931	32 799	31 132	6 865	3 931	2 934	799	544	255
19 years	74 164	38 399	35 765	66 278	33 859	32 419	7 198	4 063	3 135	824	559	265
20 to 24 years	346 119	174 464	171 655	312 032	155 912	156 120	30 724	16 438	14 286	3 383	2 123	1 260
20 years	72 837	37 358	35 479	65 031	32 916	32 115	7 140	3 973	3 167	740	473	267
21 years	70 178	35 276	34 902	62 781	31 135	31 646	6 703	3 686	3 017	741	480	261
25 to 29 years	309 338	153 713	155 625	284 110	141 480	142 630	22 354	10 789	11 565	2 231	1 247	984
30 to 34 years	276 288	136 724	139 564	257 847	128 051	129 796	16 261	7 703	8 558	1 781	898	883
35 to 39 years	217 968	107 429	110 539	204 656	101 295	103 361	11 814	5 422	6 392	1 376	669	707
40 to 44 years	186 552	91 098	95 454	175 112	85 981	89 131	10 348	4 585	5 763	1 330	630	700
45 to 49 years	174 422	84 730	89 692	163 556	79 867	83 689	10 092	4 557	5 535	1 157	572	585
50 to 54 years	179 830	86 160	93 670	168 639	81 189	87 450	10 606	4 744	5 862	1 102	536	566
55 to 59 years	178 333	84 360	93 973	167 342	79 440	87 902	10 564	4 750	5 814	1 031	478	553
60 to 64 years	153 773	71 009	82 764	144 262	66 791	77 471	9 202	4 114	5 088	891	411	480
65 to 69 years	138 938	61 836	77 102	129 962	57 989	71 973	8 679	3 746	4 933	898	420	478
70 to 74 years	110 050	46 561	63 489	102 886	43 586	59 300	6 940	2 895	4 045	654	295	359
75 to 79 years	78 771	30 844	47 927	73 559	28 758	44 801	5 037	2 023	3 014	501	198	303
80 to 84 years	47 033	17 071	29 962	44 082	15 949	28 133	2 863	1 095	1 768	255	102	153
85 years and over	35 036	11 326	23 710	32 620	10 497	22 123	2 339	807	1 532	184	66	118
18 years and over	2 578 047	1 232 930	1 345 117	2 390 874	1 143 443	1 247 431	171 886	81 662	90 224	18 397	9 748	8 649
62 years and over	499 392	208 826	290 566	467 260	195 562	271 698	31 104	12 918	18 186	3 010	1 312	1 698
65 years and over	409 828	167 638	242 190	383 109	156 779	226 330	25 858	10 566	15 292	2 492	1 081	1 411
Median	29.1	27.8	30.4	29.5	28.3	30.8	24.5	22.9	26.3	24.5	23.1	26.8

¹Persons of Spanish origin may be of any race

Table 67. Persons by Age, Race, Spanish Origin, and Sex, for States: 1980—Con.

[For meaning of symbols, see Introduction. For definitions of terms, see appendixes A and B]

States	Total Both sexes	Total Male	Total Female	White Both sexes	White Male	White Female	Black Both sexes	Black Male	Black Female	Spanish origin[1] Both sexes	Spanish origin[1] Male	Spanish origin[1] Female
LOUISIANA												
Total persons	4 205 900	2 039 894	2 166 006	2 912 172	1 430 724	1 481 448	1 238 241	580 656	657 585	99 134	49 081	50 053
Under 5 years	361 533	183 668	177 865	225 238	115 545	109 693	130 198	65 039	65 159	9 231	4 721	4 510
Under 1 year	79 642	40 422	39 220	49 507	25 311	24 196	28 802	14 443	14 359	2 166	1 109	1 057
1 year	72 312	37 000	35 312	45 161	23 398	21 763	25 955	12 991	12 964	1 866	945	921
2 years	71 159	36 163	34 996	44 250	22 729	21 521	25 720	12 850	12 870	1 687	879	808
3 years	70 162	35 555	34 607	43 839	22 416	21 423	25 109	12 508	12 601	1 812	909	903
4 years	68 258	34 528	33 730	42 481	21 691	20 790	24 612	12 247	12 365	1 700	879	821
5 to 9 years	345 966	175 871	170 095	218 729	111 882	106 847	121 861	61 201	60 660	8 699	4 489	4 210
5 years	67 143	34 189	32 954	42 111	21 683	20 428	23 950	11 939	12 011	1 594	881	813
6 years	66 138	33 598	32 540	41 338	21 121	20 217	23 793	11 963	11 830	1 664	870	794
7 years	68 230	34 761	33 469	42 567	21 719	20 848	24 573	12 469	12 104	1 752	897	855
8 years	69 886	35 521	34 365	44 709	22 891	21 818	24 104	12 076	12 028	1 728	888	840
9 years	74 569	37 802	36 767	48 004	24 468	23 536	25 441	12 754	12 687	1 861	953	908
10 to 14 years	371 795	188 922	182 873	234 510	119 782	114 728	132 179	66 517	65 662	9 470	4 814	4 656
10 years	75 042	37 867	37 175	48 496	24 608	23 888	25 453	12 700	12 753	1 867	935	932
11 years	72 719	37 340	35 379	46 507	23 971	22 536	25 214	12 846	12 368	1 772	893	879
12 years	71 940	36 296	35 644	44 819	22 760	22 059	26 167	13 053	13 114	1 831	909	922
13 years	74 813	37 970	36 843	46 801	23 875	22 926	26 943	13 572	13 371	1 950	1 009	941
14 years	77 281	39 449	37 832	47 887	24 568	23 319	28 402	14 346	14 056	2 050	1 068	982
15 to 19 years	426 511	213 774	212 383	274 748	139 023	135 725	145 865	71 727	74 138	11 139	5 660	5 479
15 years	83 477	42 448	41 029	52 858	27 133	25 725	29 638	14 809	14 829	2 134	1 052	1 082
16 years	83 922	42 553	41 369	53 672	27 380	26 292	29 183	14 605	14 578	2 137	1 099	1 038
17 years	83 775	42 077	41 698	53 740	27 169	26 571	28 995	14 355	14 640	2 190	1 111	1 079
18 years	85 659	42 443	43 216	55 503	27 744	27 759	29 029	14 075	14 954	2 247	1 136	1 111
19 years	89 324	44 253	45 071	58 975	29 597	29 378	29 020	13 883	15 137	2 431	1 262	1 169
20 to 24 years	420 276	209 838	210 438	287 518	146 299	141 219	125 799	59 536	66 263	11 091	5 972	5 119
20 years	88 826	43 886	44 940	59 617	29 992	29 625	27 838	13 104	14 734	2 463	1 314	1 149
21 years	84 875	42 328	42 547	57 618	29 320	28 298	25 856	12 205	13 651	2 311	1 252	1 059
25 to 29 years	368 732	182 871	185 861	258 883	131 769	127 069	103 663	47 795	55 868	8 576	4 277	4 299
30 to 34 years	312 027	153 772	158 255	226 839	114 741	112 098	80 054	36 531	43 523	7 032	3 548	3 484
35 to 39 years	244 245	118 909	125 336	180 573	90 396	90 177	60 167	26 794	33 373	5 895	2 818	3 077
40 to 44 years	205 974	99 613	106 361	151 364	75 513	75 851	51 847	22 722	29 125	5 232	2 495	2 737
45 to 49 years	193 171	92 251	100 920	143 374	70 351	73 023	47 572	20 852	26 720	4 551	2 155	2 396
50 to 54 years	200 735	95 246	105 489	151 060	73 711	77 349	47 849	20 680	27 169	4 453	2 112	2 341
55 to 59 years	189 278	88 440	100 838	143 647	68 452	75 195	44 282	19 369	24 913	3 793	1 801	1 992
60 to 64 years	161 732	74 116	87 616	121 467	56 448	65 019	39 282	17 195	22 087	2 999	1 394	1 605
65 to 69 years	143 592	63 174	80 418	105 273	46 631	58 642	37 419	16 133	21 286	2 528	1 095	1 433
70 to 74 years	111 309	46 295	65 014	81 158	33 400	47 758	29 502	12 630	16 872	1 918	760	1 158
75 to 79 years	76 653	29 138	47 515	55 431	20 383	35 048	20 784	8 535	12 249	1 337	518	819
80 to 84 years	42 190	14 697	27 493	31 096	10 350	20 746	10 870	4 237	6 633	670	268	402
85 years and over	30 535	9 299	21 236	21 309	6 048	15 261	9 048	3 163	5 885	520	184	336
18 years and over	2 875 432	1 364 355	1 511 077	2 073 425	1 001 833	1 071 592	766 187	344 130	422 057	65 273	31 795	33 478
62 years and over	496 412	204 534	291 878	363 559	148 697	214 862	129 934	54 495	75 439	8 627	3 579	5 048
65 years and over	404 279	162 603	241 676	294 267	116 812	177 455	107 623	44 698	62 925	6 973	2 825	4 148
Median	27.3	26.2	28.4	29.1	28.0	30.2	23.4	22.0	24.8	25.0	23.9	26.1
MAINE												
Total persons	1 124 660	546 235	578 425	1 109 850	538 588	571 262	3 128	1 906	1 222	5 005	2 606	2 399
Under 5 years	78 514	40 177	38 337	76 995	39 392	37 603	336	160	176	579	311	268
Under 1 year	16 646	8 556	8 090	16 302	8 372	7 930	79	38	41	136	70	66
1 year	15 669	8 009	7 660	15 352	7 845	7 507	83	41	42	117	59	58
2 years	15 661	8 044	7 617	15 342	7 874	7 468	63	29	34	123	67	56
3 years	15 300	7 864	7 436	15 023	7 724	7 299	60	31	29	104	62	42
4 years	15 238	7 704	7 534	14 976	7 577	7 399	51	21	30	99	53	46
5 to 9 years	84 179	43 264	40 915	82 670	42 494	40 176	285	168	117	496	257	239
5 years	15 362	7 920	7 442	15 077	7 781	7 296	58	36	22	85	46	39
6 years	15 820	8 114	7 706	15 512	7 954	7 558	58	39	19	88	42	46
7 years	16 557	8 489	8 068	16 280	8 363	7 917	56	28	28	93	50	43
8 years	17 537	8 973	8 564	17 217	8 805	8 412	57	29	28	109	52	57
9 years	18 903	9 768	9 135	18 584	9 591	8 993	56	36	20	121	67	54
10 to 14 years	94 277	48 258	46 019	92 728	47 491	45 237	255	120	135	513	303	210
10 years	18 869	9 614	9 255	18 533	9 439	9 094	56	27	29	97	63	34
11 years	18 138	9 432	8 706	17 834	9 276	8 558	56	23	33	102	60	42
12 years	18 350	9 320	9 030	18 043	9 185	8 858	47	20	27	96	61	35
13 years	19 150	9 725	9 425	18 850	9 573	9 277	47	26	21	111	65	46
14 years	19 770	10 167	9 603	19 468	10 018	9 450	49	24	25	107	54	53
15 to 19 years	107 412	54 741	52 671	105 735	53 831	51 904	373	233	140	590	333	257
15 years	21 001	10 653	10 348	20 685	10 499	10 186	47	26	21	116	70	46
16 years	21 521	11 124	10 397	21 202	10 956	10 246	71	38	33	126	71	55
17 years	21 895	11 191	10 704	21 568	11 023	10 545	44	26	18	106	62	44
18 years	21 428	10 919	10 509	21 069	10 723	10 346	80	54	26	125	69	56
19 years	21 567	10 854	10 713	21 211	10 630	10 581	131	89	42	117	61	56
20 to 24 years	98 438	48 900	49 538	96 703	47 877	48 826	526	371	155	588	331	257
20 years	20 785	10 442	10 343	20 421	10 230	10 191	107	76	31	138	86	52
21 years	20 187	10 173	10 014	19 784	9 922	9 862	138	98	40	132	82	50
25 to 29 years	92 242	45 334	46 908	90 755	44 522	46 233	355	235	120	466	238	228
30 to 34 years	86 557	43 356	43 201	85 359	42 741	42 618	243	167	76	357	175	182
35 to 39 years	66 954	33 518	33 436	66 044	33 070	32 974	172	120	52	263	124	139
40 to 44 years	55 771	27 624	28 147	55 053	27 284	27 769	112	70	42	208	92	116
45 to 49 years	54 724	26 787	27 937	54 105	26 479	27 626	100	68	32	212	96	116
50 to 54 years	57 297	27 618	29 679	56 812	27 380	29 432	91	56	35	159	75	84
55 to 59 years	56 566	26 716	29 850	56 192	26 556	29 636	69	33	36	165	81	84
60 to 64 years	50 811	23 708	27 103	50 511	23 555	26 956	62	38	24	107	53	54
65 to 69 years	45 122	20 335	24 787	44 863	20 206	24 657	47	27	20	120	52	68
70 to 74 years	37 166	15 581	21 585	36 970	15 499	21 471	39	17	22	69	33	36
75 to 79 years	26 956	10 402	16 554	26 815	10 344	16 471	23	10	13	55	30	25
80 to 84 years	17 575	5 957	11 618	17 486	5 928	11 558	25	6	19	35	13	22
85 years and over	14 099	3 959	10 140	14 054	3 939	10 115	15	7	8	23	9	14
18 years and over	803 273	381 568	421 705	794 002	376 733	417 269	2 090	1 368	722	3 069	1 532	1 537
62 years and over	170 782	70 071	100 711	169 871	69 665	100 206	187	87	100	365	165	200
65 years and over	140 918	56 234	84 684	140 188	55 916	84 272	149	67	82	302	137	165
Median	30.4	29.2	31.6	30.5	29.3	31.7	22.7	23.5	21.3	22.5	21.2	24.4

[1] Persons of Spanish origin may be of any race.

GENERAL POPULATION CHARACTERISTICS

UNITED STATES SUMMARY 1—167

Table 67. Persons by Age, Race, Spanish Origin, and Sex, for States: 1980—Con.

[For meaning of symbols, see Introduction. For definitions of terms, see appendixes A and B]

States	Total Both sexes	Total Male	Total Female	White Both sexes	White Male	White Female	Black Both sexes	Black Male	Black Female	Spanish origin[1] Both sexes	Spanish origin[1] Male	Spanish origin[1] Female
MARYLAND												
Total persons	4 216 975	2 042 810	2 174 165	3 158 838	1 539 765	1 619 073	958 150	453 983	504 167	64 746	31 521	33 225
Under 5 years	272 274	139 363	132 911	185 822	95 607	90 215	76 910	38 925	37 985	5 768	2 969	2 799
Under 1 year	58 743	29 989	28 754	39 967	20 433	19 534	16 732	8 492	8 240	1 294	668	626
1 year	54 282	27 761	26 521	36 915	18 951	17 964	15 507	7 910	7 597	1 110	559	551
2 years	54 200	27 721	26 479	37 087	19 140	17 947	15 299	7 663	7 636	1 125	597	528
3 years	52 573	26 844	25 729	35 910	18 489	17 421	14 816	7 425	7 391	1 136	589	547
4 years	52 476	27 048	25 428	35 943	18 594	17 349	14 556	7 435	7 121	1 103	556	547
5 to 9 years	292 916	149 606	143 310	202 406	103 635	98 771	80 930	41 102	39 828	5 504	2 905	2 599
5 years	52 878	27 070	25 808	36 677	18 832	17 845	14 339	7 256	7 083	1 003	526	477
6 years	52 290	26 690	25 600	36 055	18 369	17 686	14 411	7 403	7 008	1 020	534	486
7 years	57 132	29 228	27 904	39 448	20 250	19 198	15 761	8 004	7 757	1 076	552	524
8 years	61 836	31 599	30 237	42 540	21 864	20 676	17 300	8 717	8 583	1 138	610	528
9 years	68 780	35 019	33 761	47 686	24 320	23 366	19 119	9 722	9 397	1 267	683	584
10 to 14 years	356 578	181 707	174 871	248 747	127 306	121 441	98 692	49 741	48 951	6 027	3 091	2 936
10 years	69 863	35 783	34 080	48 482	24 952	23 530	19 303	9 759	9 544	1 183	616	567
11 years	68 890	35 080	33 810	48 242	24 722	23 520	18 826	9 435	9 391	1 176	610	566
12 years	69 535	35 357	34 178	48 177	24 732	23 445	19 516	9 710	9 806	1 177	595	582
13 years	72 435	36 971	35 464	50 833	25 974	24 859	19 921	10 131	9 790	1 261	639	622
14 years	75 855	38 516	37 339	53 013	26 926	26 087	21 126	10 706	10 420	1 230	631	599
15 to 19 years	405 011	205 244	199 767	287 959	146 915	141 044	108 407	53 839	54 568	6 879	3 597	3 282
15 years	81 212	41 464	39 748	57 088	29 313	27 775	22 411	11 276	11 135	1 380	718	662
16 years	82 928	42 473	40 455	58 762	30 130	28 632	22 477	11 466	11 011	1 307	670	637
17 years	81 622	41 408	40 214	57 887	29 402	28 485	22 032	11 120	10 912	1 372	721	651
18 years	78 820	39 477	39 343	56 306	28 537	27 769	20 746	10 024	10 722	1 401	743	658
19 years	80 429	40 422	40 007	57 916	29 533	28 383	20 741	9 953	10 788	1 419	745	674
20 to 24 years	392 391	193 252	199 139	285 287	143 112	142 175	98 104	45 622	52 482	6 772	3 447	3 325
20 years	80 108	39 789	40 319	58 003	29 274	28 729	20 351	9 596	10 755	1 422	735	687
21 years	78 717	38 874	39 843	57 075	28 680	28 395	19 817	9 261	10 556	1 372	718	654
25 to 29 years	371 136	180 711	190 425	269 365	134 533	134 832	91 716	41 483	50 233	6 313	3 113	3 200
30 to 34 years	354 443	172 115	182 328	261 109	129 926	131 183	82 405	37 189	45 216	5 666	2 595	3 071
35 to 39 years	291 194	141 427	149 767	218 785	107 978	110 807	63 297	29 060	34 237	4 789	2 154	2 635
40 to 44 years	235 873	116 118	119 755	177 275	88 421	88 854	51 217	23 942	27 275	4 044	1 832	2 212
45 to 49 years	218 899	107 307	111 592	169 335	83 869	85 466	44 337	20 811	23 526	3 324	1 547	1 777
50 to 54 years	227 589	110 853	116 736	183 171	89 884	93 287	40 631	19 141	21 490	2 938	1 383	1 555
55 to 59 years	222 682	104 727	117 955	184 355	87 014	97 341	35 766	16 464	19 302	2 144	991	1 153
60 to 64 years	180 380	84 809	95 571	150 781	71 220	79 561	27 857	12 821	15 036	1 484	696	788
65 to 69 years	142 288	62 872	79 416	118 322	52 560	65 762	22 588	9 737	12 851	1 209	498	711
70 to 74 years	104 921	43 036	61 885	88 521	36 027	52 494	15 539	6 622	8 917	769	305	464
75 to 79 years	71 837	26 405	45 432	60 942	22 031	38 911	10 328	4 143	6 185	553	205	348
80 to 84 years	43 898	14 285	29 613	38 273	12 156	26 117	5 313	2 004	3 309	323	125	198
85 years and over	32 665	8 973	23 692	28 383	7 571	20 812	4 113	1 337	2 776	240	68	172
18 years and over	3 049 445	1 446 789	1 602 656	2 348 126	1 124 372	1 223 754	634 698	290 353	344 345	43 388	20 447	22 941
62 years and over	497 920	203 473	294 447	420 175	170 704	249 471	73 463	30 937	42 526	3 916	1 603	2 313
65 years and over	395 609	155 571	240 038	334 441	130 345	204 096	57 881	23 843	34 038	3 094	1 201	1 893
Median	30.3	29.2	31.2	31.9	30.7	33.0	25.8	24.7	26.8	26.1	24.6	27.6
MASSACHUSETTS												
Total persons	5 737 037	2 730 893	3 006 144	5 362 836	2 551 151	2 811 685	221 279	105 050	116 229	141 043	68 386	72 657
Under 5 years	337 215	173 029	164 186	301 519	154 905	146 614	18 658	9 530	9 128	17 900	9 212	8 688
Under 1 year	71 730	36 771	34 959	63 996	32 822	31 174	4 014	2 076	1 938	3 846	1 951	1 895
1 year	67 612	34 641	32 971	60 612	31 088	29 524	3 606	1 825	1 781	3 541	1 827	1 714
2 years	66 659	34 248	32 411	59 592	30 657	28 935	3 755	1 927	1 828	3 505	1 818	1 687
3 years	65 206	33 448	31 758	58 276	29 928	28 348	3 570	1 809	1 761	3 495	1 825	1 670
4 years	66 008	33 921	32 087	59 043	30 410	28 633	3 713	1 893	1 820	3 513	1 791	1 722
5 to 9 years	374 734	191 602	183 132	338 842	173 505	165 337	19 685	9 866	9 819	16 679	8 500	8 179
5 years	67 549	34 378	33 171	60 650	30 907	29 743	3 589	1 797	1 792	3 448	1 756	1 692
6 years	67 826	34 900	32 926	61 107	31 425	29 682	3 500	1 800	1 700	3 234	1 666	1 568
7 years	73 204	37 313	35 891	65 984	33 673	32 311	3 964	1 977	1 987	3 336	1 693	1 643
8 years	77 685	39 644	38 041	70 398	36 007	34 391	4 115	2 052	2 063	3 269	1 690	1 579
9 years	88 470	45 367	43 103	80 703	41 493	39 210	4 517	2 240	2 277	3 392	1 695	1 697
10 to 14 years	461 332	235 669	225 663	423 276	216 445	206 831	23 065	11 636	11 429	15 721	7 999	7 722
10 years	90 309	46 211	44 098	82 689	42 402	40 287	4 492	2 226	2 266	3 304	1 702	1 602
11 years	88 852	45 486	43 366	81 504	41 766	39 738	4 400	2 231	2 169	3 045	1 550	1 495
12 years	90 209	46 091	44 118	82 655	42 281	40 374	4 614	2 309	2 305	3 071	1 582	1 489
13 years	93 814	47 770	46 044	86 204	43 953	42 251	4 634	2 356	2 278	3 161	1 562	1 599
14 years	98 148	50 111	48 037	90 224	46 043	44 181	4 925	2 514	2 411	3 140	1 603	1 537
15 to 19 years	548 239	274 859	273 380	505 884	253 767	252 117	26 040	12 934	13 106	16 089	8 042	8 047
15 years	103 889	53 151	50 738	95 793	49 027	46 766	5 023	2 585	2 438	3 203	1 667	1 536
16 years	106 454	53 928	52 526	98 308	49 841	48 467	5 088	2 556	2 532	3 169	1 561	1 608
17 years	106 765	54 696	52 069	98 637	50 648	47 989	5 087	2 560	2 527	3 043	1 508	1 535
18 years	112 457	55 503	56 954	103 722	51 175	52 547	5 268	2 561	2 707	3 231	1 624	1 607
19 years	118 674	57 581	61 093	109 424	53 076	56 348	5 574	2 672	2 902	3 443	1 682	1 761
20 to 24 years	552 902	270 713	282 189	511 228	250 616	260 612	24 367	11 558	12 809	15 591	7 426	8 165
20 years	115 453	55 888	59 565	106 272	51 455	54 817	5 443	2 569	2 874	3 426	1 728	1 698
21 years	113 319	55 389	57 930	104 959	51 361	53 598	4 964	2 351	2 613	3 109	1 487	1 622
25 to 29 years	489 175	239 341	249 834	452 140	221 554	230 586	20 983	9 952	11 031	13 419	6 390	7 029
30 to 34 years	446 395	217 649	228 746	414 583	202 785	211 798	17 940	8 306	9 634	11 236	5 220	6 016
35 to 39 years	348 552	169 502	179 050	324 489	158 362	166 127	14 533	6 577	7 956	8 437	3 901	4 536
40 to 44 years	278 748	134 925	143 823	260 514	126 332	134 182	10 879	5 013	5 866	6 094	2 786	3 308
45 to 49 years	278 261	134 444	143 817	263 030	127 300	135 730	9 359	4 329	5 030	4 830	2 281	2 549
50 to 54 years	306 574	146 211	160 363	292 745	139 828	152 917	8 850	4 057	4 793	3 979	1 836	2 143
55 to 59 years	310 995	145 603	165 392	299 137	140 132	159 005	7 891	3 587	4 304	3 225	1 471	1 754
60 to 64 years	277 384	126 323	151 061	268 019	122 160	145 859	6 313	2 803	3 510	2 690	1 189	1 501
65 to 69 years	235 574	101 023	134 551	228 474	98 076	130 398	4 763	1 953	2 810	2 010	863	1 147
70 to 74 years	187 041	73 235	113 806	182 235	71 293	110 942	3 177	1 285	1 892	1 305	564	741
75 to 79 years	137 828	48 145	89 683	134 432	46 859	87 573	2 251	810	1 441	941	373	568
80 to 84 years	92 180	28 513	63 667	90 098	27 747	62 351	1 379	480	899	500	191	309
85 years and over	73 908	20 107	53 801	72 191	19 485	52 706	1 146	374	772	397	142	255
18 years and over	4 246 648	1 968 818	2 277 830	4 006 461	1 856 780	2 149 681	144 673	66 317	78 356	81 328	37 939	43 389
62 years and over	888 064	343 822	544 242	863 691	333 966	529 725	16 240	6 419	9 821	6 723	2 831	3 892
65 years and over	726 531	271 023	455 508	707 430	263 460	443 970	12 716	4 902	7 814	5 153	2 133	3 020
Median	31.1	29.6	32.6	31.7	30.1	33.3	24.7	23.6	25.8	21.2	20.3	22.2

[1]Persons of Spanish origin may be of any race.

Table 67. Persons by Age, Race, Spanish Origin, and Sex, for States: 1980—Con.

[For meaning of symbols, see Introduction. For definitions of terms, see appendixes A and B]

States	Race									Spanish origin[1]		
	Total			White			Black					
	Both sexes	Male	Female	Both sexes	Male	Female	Both sexes	Male	Female	Both sexes	Male	Female
MICHIGAN												
Total persons	9 262 078	4 516 189	4 745 889	7 872 241	3 851 504	4 020 737	1 199 023	568 933	630 090	162 440	81 853	80 587
Under 5 years	685 113	350 158	334 955	552 415	283 406	269 009	110 550	55 822	54 728	19 844	10 055	9 789
Under 1 year	146 176	74 504	71 672	118 389	60 598	57 791	23 133	11 614	11 519	4 400	2 225	2 175
1 year	137 879	70 577	67 302	111 823	57 399	54 424	21 558	10 949	10 609	4 037	2 032	2 005
2 years	135 894	69 491	66 403	109 764	56 372	53 392	21 813	10 988	10 825	3 877	1 944	1 933
3 years	132 398	67 789	64 609	106 521	54 753	51 768	21 593	10 937	10 656	3 772	1 927	1 845
4 years	132 766	67 797	64 969	105 918	54 284	51 634	22 453	11 334	11 119	3 758	1 927	1 831
5 to 9 years	727 120	372 134	354 986	579 689	298 046	281 643	125 717	63 153	62 564	19 267	9 835	9 432
5 years	134 302	68 824	65 478	107 526	55 327	52 199	22 442	11 271	11 171	3 628	1 831	1 797
6 years	135 064	68 862	66 202	107 063	54 871	52 192	23 799	11 869	11 930	3 722	1 932	1 790
7 years	142 170	72 902	69 268	111 780	57 630	54 150	25 925	13 058	12 867	3 801	1 953	1 848
8 years	149 098	76 313	72 785	119 038	61 180	57 858	25 820	12 999	12 821	3 889	1 972	1 917
9 years	166 486	85 233	81 253	134 282	69 038	65 244	27 731	13 956	13 775	4 227	2 147	2 080
10 to 14 years	801 874	409 805	392 069	657 606	337 126	320 480	124 845	62 724	62 121	18 730	9 605	9 125
10 years	163 521	83 815	79 706	133 025	68 402	64 623	26 233	13 262	12 971	3 977	2 066	1 911
11 years	157 200	80 335	76 865	128 565	66 012	62 553	24 727	12 332	12 395	3 819	1 924	1 895
12 years	155 671	79 542	76 129	127 205	65 195	62 010	24 618	12 345	12 273	3 643	1 901	1 742
13 years	160 697	81 761	78 936	132 527	67 587	64 940	24 436	12 239	12 197	3 650	1 866	1 794
14 years	164 785	84 352	80 433	136 284	69 930	66 354	24 831	12 546	12 285	3 631	1 848	1 783
15 to 19 years	901 277	455 211	446 066	759 726	385 037	374 689	122 723	60 400	62 323	18 682	9 478	9 204
15 years	175 948	89 757	86 191	147 030	75 207	71 823	25 135	12 581	12 554	3 797	1 932	1 865
16 years	181 652	93 066	88 586	152 598	78 427	74 171	25 323	12 704	12 619	3 796	1 881	1 915
17 years	180 279	91 578	88 701	152 085	77 364	74 721	24 491	12 263	12 228	3 751	1 967	1 784
18 years	178 645	89 804	88 841	151 370	76 478	74 892	23 599	11 458	12 141	3 704	1 900	1 804
19 years	184 753	91 006	93 747	156 643	77 561	79 082	24 175	11 394	12 781	3 634	1 798	1 836
20 to 24 years	894 430	441 426	453 004	755 808	375 784	380 024	118 959	55 503	63 456	17 250	8 639	8 611
20 years	182 845	90 090	92 755	155 124	76 967	78 157	23 849	11 132	12 717	3 544	1 752	1 792
21 years	180 689	89 137	91 552	153 075	76 011	77 064	23 684	11 081	12 603	3 543	1 785	1 758
25 to 29 years	806 918	399 270	407 648	678 249	339 588	338 661	108 840	49 651	59 189	14 630	7 325	7 305
30 to 34 years	708 369	348 315	360 054	599 021	297 810	301 211	91 171	41 692	49 479	12 126	6 098	6 028
35 to 39 years	564 427	277 801	286 626	485 095	240 410	244 685	66 441	30 869	35 572	8 422	4 190	4 232
40 to 44 years	464 572	226 920	237 652	403 071	198 487	204 584	52 148	23 540	28 608	6 761	3 347	3 414
45 to 49 years	445 514	215 594	229 920	386 944	188 820	198 124	51 206	23 136	28 070	6 314	3 101	3 213
50 to 54 years	485 417	236 446	248 971	425 488	208 429	217 059	53 697	24 965	28 732	6 153	3 203	2 960
55 to 59 years	471 411	225 704	245 707	416 501	199 514	216 987	50 010	23 767	26 243	4 717	2 442	2 275
60 to 64 years	393 378	183 822	209 556	350 436	163 997	186 439	39 800	18 396	21 404	2 972	1 462	1 510
65 to 69 years	319 381	144 113	175 268	284 124	128 310	155 814	32 655	14 632	18 023	2 250	1 062	1 188
70 to 74 years	237 129	100 502	136 627	213 062	89 929	123 133	22 136	9 665	12 471	1 787	832	955
75 to 79 years	169 213	66 767	102 446	153 145	59 986	93 159	14 728	6 168	8 560	1 349	642	707
80 to 84 years	104 882	36 894	67 988	96 353	33 571	62 782	7 772	3 022	4 750	708	329	379
85 years and over	81 653	25 307	56 346	75 508	23 254	52 254	5 625	1 828	3 797	468	208	260
18 years and over	6 510 092	3 109 691	3 400 401	5 630 818	2 701 928	2 928 890	762 962	349 686	413 276	93 255	46 578	46 677
62 years and over	1 140 398	479 922	660 476	1 026 409	430 346	596 063	105 091	45 574	59 517	8 206	3 872	4 334
65 years and over	912 258	373 583	538 675	822 192	335 050	487 142	82 916	35 315	47 601	6 562	3 073	3 489
Median	28 8	27.8	29.8	29 6	28.6	30.7	24 9	23 8	25.8	21.3	21.1	21.5
MINNESOTA												
Total persons	4 075 970	1 997 826	2 078 144	3 935 770	1 927 503	2 008 267	53 344	27 256	26 088	32 123	16 228	15 895
Under 5 years	307 249	157 312	149 937	289 006	148 385	140 621	5 927	2 973	2 954	4 514	2 299	2 215
Under 1 year	67 423	34 622	32 801	63 510	32 687	30 823	1 289	615	674	989	524	465
1 year	63 362	32 546	30 816	59 575	30 696	28 879	1 256	643	613	919	482	437
2 years	60 667	30 821	29 846	57 104	29 090	28 014	1 141	563	578	923	461	462
3 years	58 309	29 926	28 383	54 756	28 201	26 555	1 126	583	543	861	428	433
4 years	57 488	29 397	28 091	54 061	27 711	26 350	1 115	569	546	822	404	418
5 to 9 years	296 295	151 556	144 739	278 945	142 970	135 975	5 934	3 022	2 912	3 799	1 953	1 846
5 years	57 162	29 137	28 025	53 589	27 340	26 249	1 105	573	532	748	388	360
6 years	54 959	28 058	26 901	51 663	26 414	25 249	1 065	545	520	755	379	376
7 years	56 770	28 990	27 780	53 290	27 306	25 984	1 209	626	583	760	395	365
8 years	59 675	30 552	29 123	56 240	28 855	27 385	1 256	626	630	723	365	358
9 years	67 729	34 819	32 910	64 163	33 055	31 108	1 299	652	647	813	426	387
10 to 14 years	333 378	170 607	162 771	318 499	163 111	155 388	5 438	2 776	2 662	3 484	1 784	1 700
10 years	67 415	34 504	32 911	64 046	32 818	31 228	1 261	651	610	773	404	369
11 years	65 754	33 827	31 927	62 774	32 377	30 397	1 050	509	541	692	343	349
12 years	64 214	33 040	31 174	61 327	31 604	29 723	1 056	544	512	674	346	328
13 years	66 030	33 642	32 388	63 229	32 181	31 048	1 016	527	489	675	351	324
14 years	69 965	35 594	34 371	67 123	34 131	32 992	1 055	545	510	670	340	330
15 to 19 years	399 818	202 254	197 564	385 171	194 788	190 383	5 374	2 666	2 708	3 550	1 781	1 769
15 years	74 950	38 420	36 530	72 041	36 941	35 100	1 045	516	529	702	363	339
16 years	78 782	40 538	38 244	75 872	39 065	36 807	1 069	531	538	664	324	340
17 years	81 154	41 497	39 657	78 269	39 990	38 279	1 075	544	531	684	345	339
18 years	80 514	40 043	40 471	77 627	38 587	39 040	1 034	501	533	739	392	347
19 years	84 418	41 756	42 662	81 362	40 205	41 157	1 151	574	577	761	357	404
20 to 24 years	393 566	194 835	198 731	378 358	186 961	191 397	6 056	3 118	2 938	3 448	1 755	1 693
20 years	82 283	40 455	41 828	79 200	38 916	40 284	1 187	590	597	722	363	359
21 years	78 800	38 539	40 261	75 862	37 024	38 838	1 164	600	564	692	361	331
25 to 29 years	363 435	182 607	180 828	348 971	175 040	173 931	5 823	3 144	2 679	3 217	1 678	1 539
30 to 34 years	313 104	156 565	156 539	301 669	150 713	150 956	4 393	2 349	2 044	2 412	1 255	1 157
35 to 39 years	246 356	123 094	123 262	238 466	119 110	119 356	3 060	1 626	1 434	1 695	835	860
40 to 44 years	202 860	101 011	101 849	196 963	97 987	98 976	2 245	1 194	1 051	1 294	632	662
45 to 49 years	187 051	92 929	94 122	182 329	90 658	91 671	1 959	951	1 008	1 090	525	565
50 to 54 years	193 199	95 107	98 092	189 224	93 142	96 082	1 789	903	886	868	433	435
55 to 59 years	189 457	92 356	97 101	186 057	90 669	95 388	1 616	821	795	740	393	347
60 to 64 years	170 638	80 521	90 117	168 123	79 354	88 769	1 171	588	583	514	241	273
65 to 69 years	149 114	67 914	81 200	147 040	66 928	80 112	933	442	491	463	218	245
70 to 74 years	121 034	52 201	68 833	119 559	51 529	68 030	698	305	393	378	187	191
75 to 79 years	92 738	36 637	56 101	91 769	36 245	55 524	435	179	256	326	124	202
80 to 84 years	63 889	23 337	40 552	63 301	23 106	40 195	268	110	158	201	81	120
85 years and over	52 789	16 983	35 806	52 320	16 807	35 513	225	89	136	130	54	76
18 years and over	2 904 162	1 397 896	1 506 266	2 823 138	1 357 041	1 466 097	32 856	16 894	15 962	18 276	9 160	9 116
62 years and over	580 333	244 497	335 836	573 330	241 373	331 957	3 209	1 449	1 760	1 784	791	993
65 years and over	479 564	197 072	282 492	473 989	194 615	279 374	2 559	1 125	1 434	1 498	664	834
Median	29 2	28.3	30.1	29.5	28 6	30.5	23 4	23.6	23.1	21.0	20.8	21.2

[1] Persons of Spanish origin may be of any race.

Table 67. Persons by Age, Race, Spanish Origin, and Sex, for States: 1980—Con.

[For meaning of symbols, see Introduction. For definitions of terms, see appendixes A and B]

States	Race — Total — Both sexes	Male	Female	White — Both sexes	Male	Female	Black — Both sexes	Male	Female	Spanish origin[1] — Both sexes	Male	Female
MISSISSIPPI												
Total persons	2 520 638	1 213 878	1 306 760	1 615 190	788 620	826 570	887 206	416 392	470 814	24 731	12 007	12 724
Under 5 years	215 279	109 699	105 580	115 955	59 782	56 173	97 384	48 975	48 409	2 410	1 220	1 190
Under 1 year	46 210	23 588	22 622	24 583	12 615	11 968	21 227	10 787	10 440	554	280	274
1 year	42 951	21 789	21 162	23 077	11 894	11 183	19 509	9 710	9 799	429	216	213
2 years	42 429	21 659	20 770	22 934	11 838	11 096	19 094	9 634	9 460	458	220	238
3 years	41 993	21 419	20 574	22 868	11 824	11 044	18 754	9 425	9 329	468	244	224
4 years	41 696	21 244	20 452	22 493	11 611	10 882	18 800	9 419	9 381	501	260	241
5 to 9 years	219 048	111 432	107 616	121 223	62 296	58 927	96 010	48 177	47 833	2 489	1 252	1 237
5 years	42 052	21 497	20 555	23 034	11 960	11 074	18 671	9 346	9 325	461	233	228
6 years	41 479	21 026	20 453	22 695	11 567	11 128	18 418	9 249	9 169	468	223	245
7 years	43 839	22 278	21 561	23 920	12 272	11 648	19 551	9 819	9 732	509	268	241
8 years	44 430	22 636	21 794	24 889	12 816	12 073	19 188	9 647	9 541	515	254	261
9 years	47 248	23 995	23 253	26 685	13 681	13 004	20 182	10 116	10 066	536	274	262
10 to 14 years	226 276	115 552	110 724	126 412	65 232	61 180	98 205	49 500	48 705	2 647	1 289	1 358
10 years	46 925	24 011	22 914	26 586	13 686	12 900	20 004	10 174	9 830	513	246	267
11 years	44 483	22 739	21 744	24 980	12 953	12 027	19 127	9 590	9 537	529	267	262
12 years	43 571	22 268	21 303	24 285	12 560	11 725	18 962	9 550	9 412	526	258	268
13 years	44 845	22 784	22 061	24 825	12 696	12 129	19 729	9 949	9 780	527	247	280
14 years	46 452	23 750	22 702	25 736	13 337	12 399	20 383	10 237	10 146	552	271	281
15 to 19 years	258 878	130 990	127 888	148 869	76 414	72 455	108 100	53 549	54 551	3 054	1 615	1 439
15 years	50 789	25 825	24 964	28 338	14 490	13 848	22 094	11 160	10 934	564	288	276
16 years	50 934	25 941	24 993	28 959	14 735	14 224	21 639	11 033	10 606	546	284	262
17 years	51 871	26 570	25 301	29 445	15 291	14 154	22 054	11 076	10 978	609	317	292
18 years	52 358	26 501	25 857	30 515	15 764	14 751	21 443	10 517	10 926	659	367	292
19 years	52 926	26 153	26 773	31 612	16 134	15 478	20 870	9 763	11 107	676	359	317
20 to 24 years	233 505	115 488	118 017	144 093	73 557	70 536	87 223	40 705	46 518	2 690	1 430	1 260
20 years	51 191	25 294	25 897	30 669	15 719	14 950	20 052	9 308	10 744	616	331	285
21 years	47 670	23 578	24 092	29 421	15 039	14 382	17 851	8 316	9 535	539	297	242
25 to 29 years	197 129	96 364	100 765	128 117	64 158	63 959	67 025	31 270	35 755	1 987	965	1 022
30 to 34 years	172 410	84 132	88 278	121 264	60 664	60 600	49 475	22 707	26 768	1 536	702	834
35 to 39 years	138 089	66 611	71 478	100 707	49 774	50 933	36 195	16 302	19 893	1 240	586	654
40 to 44 years	122 416	58 655	63 761	88 975	44 254	44 721	32 506	13 956	18 550	1 079	504	575
45 to 49 years	113 662	53 565	60 097	83 288	40 813	42 475	29 638	12 444	17 194	962	450	512
50 to 54 years	118 157	54 881	63 276	86 048	41 599	44 449	31 495	13 025	18 470	925	414	511
55 to 59 years	112 768	51 548	61 220	82 602	38 917	43 685	29 740	12 440	17 300	797	353	444
60 to 64 years	103 664	46 974	56 690	73 445	33 794	39 651	29 882	13 018	16 864	788	335	453
65 to 69 years	99 536	43 446	56 090	67 382	29 519	37 863	31 865	13 820	18 045	775	321	454
70 to 74 years	80 413	34 210	46 203	54 235	22 585	31 650	25 936	11 530	14 406	612	269	343
75 to 79 years	55 281	21 726	33 555	36 539	13 800	22 739	18 598	7 880	10 718	374	158	216
80 to 84 years	30 618	11 021	19 597	20 863	7 014	13 849	9 661	3 985	5 676	215	87	128
85 years and over	23 509	7 584	15 925	15 173	4 448	10 725	8 268	3 109	5 159	151	57	94
18 years and over	1 706 441	798 859	907 582	1 164 858	556 794	608 064	529 820	236 471	293 349	15 466	7 357	8 109
62 years and over	348 505	144 384	204 121	236 005	96 278	139 727	111 466	47 712	63 754	2 584	1 095	1 489
65 years and over	289 357	117 987	171 370	194 192	77 366	116 826	94 328	40 324	54 004	2 127	892	1 235
Median	27.6	26.1	29.1	30.9	29.4	32.4	22.3	20.9	23.7	23.2	22.0	24.5
MISSOURI												
Total persons	4 916 686	2 365 487	2 551 199	4 345 521	2 096 742	2 248 779	514 276	240 721	273 555	51 653	25 886	25 767
Under 5 years	354 144	181 697	172 447	300 678	154 672	146 006	47 648	24 069	23 579	5 443	2 751	2 692
Under 1 year	76 885	39 217	37 668	65 247	33 398	31 849	10 395	5 194	5 201	1 196	570	626
1 year	71 361	37 010	34 351	60 420	31 393	29 027	9 747	4 992	4 755	1 109	566	543
2 years	70 252	35 943	34 309	59 789	30 680	29 109	9 275	4 666	4 609	1 100	578	522
3 years	68 459	35 070	33 389	58 239	29 926	28 313	9 085	4 575	4 510	1 073	539	534
4 years	67 187	34 457	32 730	56 983	29 275	27 708	9 146	4 642	4 504	965	498	467
5 to 9 years	355 426	181 730	173 696	300 911	154 363	146 548	48 967	24 632	24 335	4 967	2 564	2 403
5 years	67 732	34 607	33 125	57 307	29 379	27 928	9 255	4 661	4 594	1 020	509	511
6 years	65 822	33 770	32 052	55 610	28 652	26 958	9 102	4 561	4 541	913	495	418
7 years	69 966	35 694	34 272	58 929	30 115	28 814	9 972	5 053	4 919	998	516	482
8 years	72 489	36 855	35 634	61 395	31 348	30 047	10 002	4 980	5 022	987	501	486
9 years	79 417	40 804	38 613	67 670	34 869	32 801	10 636	5 377	5 259	1 049	543	506
10 to 14 years	382 168	195 538	186 630	326 014	167 453	158 561	51 493	25 772	25 721	4 903	2 523	2 380
10 years	78 240	40 249	37 991	66 766	34 506	32 260	10 428	5 218	5 210	1 022	518	504
11 years	74 366	38 267	36 099	63 734	32 851	30 883	9 681	4 943	4 738	935	504	431
12 years	73 116	37 062	36 054	62 330	31 695	30 635	9 886	4 915	4 971	920	456	464
13 years	76 813	39 225	37 588	65 467	33 541	31 926	10 473	5 272	5 201	981	509	472
14 years	79 633	40 735	38 898	67 717	34 860	32 857	11 025	5 424	5 601	1 045	536	509
15 to 19 years	461 336	234 870	226 466	397 604	202 569	195 035	58 015	29 141	28 874	6 370	3 465	2 905
15 years	87 538	44 975	42 563	74 913	38 639	36 274	11 690	5 852	5 838	1 054	563	491
16 years	90 408	46 279	44 129	78 102	40 026	38 076	11 320	5 752	5 568	1 152	573	579
17 years	92 799	47 851	44 948	79 849	41 266	38 583	11 855	5 970	5 885	1 281	708	573
18 years	94 012	47 994	46 018	81 229	41 410	39 819	11 491	5 827	5 664	1 413	817	596
19 years	96 579	47 771	48 808	83 511	41 228	42 283	11 659	5 740	5 919	1 470	804	666
20 to 24 years	445 442	219 935	225 507	386 365	191 583	194 782	52 590	24 875	27 715	5 701	3 001	2 700
20 years	93 478	46 252	47 226	80 847	40 046	40 801	11 291	5 476	5 815	1 290	698	592
21 years	89 370	44 205	45 165	77 303	38 367	38 936	10 773	5 136	5 637	1 185	620	565
25 to 29 years	398 398	196 248	202 150	349 396	173 480	175 916	42 576	19 626	22 950	4 613	2 329	2 284
30 to 34 years	354 339	173 204	181 135	314 217	155 221	158 996	34 529	15 308	19 221	3 691	1 805	1 886
35 to 39 years	291 743	141 811	149 932	260 555	127 608	132 947	27 234	12 278	14 956	2 710	1 291	1 419
40 to 44 years	248 823	120 901	127 922	222 503	109 138	113 365	23 330	10 337	12 993	2 349	1 094	1 255
45 to 49 years	242 875	117 508	125 367	218 258	106 639	111 619	22 280	9 788	12 492	2 169	1 086	1 083
50 to 54 years	253 677	121 583	132 094	229 515	110 941	118 574	22 081	9 716	12 365	2 136	1 030	1 106
55 to 59 years	254 957	120 188	134 769	233 004	110 455	122 549	20 445	9 028	11 417	1 805	895	910
60 to 64 years	225 232	103 253	121 979	206 980	95 328	111 652	17 220	7 452	9 768	1 284	583	701
65 to 69 years	207 946	91 914	116 032	191 256	84 811	106 445	15 831	6 786	9 045	1 099	474	625
70 to 74 years	173 114	71 771	101 343	160 146	66 352	93 794	12 256	5 137	7 119	958	384	574
75 to 79 years	127 288	47 976	79 312	117 554	44 182	73 372	9 154	3 569	5 585	755	332	423
80 to 84 years	78 706	27 202	51 504	73 563	25 195	48 368	4 794	1 888	2 906	420	171	249
85 years and over	61 072	18 158	42 914	57 002	16 752	40 250	3 833	1 319	2 514	280	108	172
18 years and over	3 554 203	1 667 417	1 886 786	3 185 054	1 500 323	1 684 731	331 303	148 674	182 629	32 853	16 204	16 649
62 years and over	779 898	317 122	462 776	720 952	292 967	427 985	55 636	22 865	32 771	4 245	1 786	2 459
65 years and over	648 126	257 021	391 105	599 521	237 292	362 229	45 868	18 699	27 169	3 512	1 469	2 043
Median	30.8	29.3	32.3	31.7	30.1	33.2	24.8	23.3	26.3	23.6	22.5	24.7

[1] Persons of Spanish origin may be of any race.

Table 67. Persons by Age, Race, Spanish Origin, and Sex, for States: 1980—Con.

[For meaning of symbols, see Introduction. For definitions of terms, see appendixes A and B]

States	Total			White			Black			Spanish origin[1]		
	Both sexes	Male	Female	Both sexes	Male	Female	Both sexes	Male	Female	Both sexes	Male	Female
MONTANA												
Total persons	786 690	392 625	394 065	740 148	369 314	370 834	1 786	1 139	647	9 974	5 119	4 855
Under 5 years	64 455	33 092	31 363	58 474	30 075	28 399	189	105	84	1 414	709	705
Under 1 year	14 146	7 246	6 900	12 794	6 612	6 182	41	17	24	309	153	156
1 year	13 155	6 746	6 409	11 905	6 120	5 785	48	34	14	297	129	168
2 years	12 619	6 495	6 124	11 543	5 937	5 606	25	12	13	262	141	121
3 years	12 394	6 371	6 023	11 197	5 752	5 445	31	17	14	297	161	136
4 years	12 141	6 234	5 907	11 035	5 654	5 381	44	25	19	249	125	124
5 to 9 years	60 238	30 872	29 366	54 926	28 131	26 795	163	98	65	1 194	647	547
5 years	11 961	6 171	5 790	10 878	5 621	5 257	34	23	11	234	132	102
6 years	11 433	5 973	5 460	10 413	5 441	4 972	26	14	12	239	132	107
7 years	11 549	5 885	5 664	10 482	5 350	5 132	29	15	14	215	104	111
8 years	11 978	6 132	5 846	10 949	5 609	5 340	35	18	17	261	141	120
9 years	13 317	6 711	6 606	12 204	6 110	6 094	39	28	11	245	138	107
10 to 14 years	62 539	31 882	30 657	57 391	29 301	28 090	149	75	74	1 089	529	560
10 years	12 854	6 493	6 361	11 815	5 983	5 832	33	17	16	225	110	115
11 years	12 499	6 324	6 175	11 502	5 841	5 661	20	10	10	229	105	124
12 years	11 895	6 076	5 819	10 901	5 550	5 351	31	15	16	193	103	90
13 years	12 477	6 358	6 119	11 454	5 859	5 595	33	18	15	221	104	117
14 years	12 814	6 631	6 183	11 719	6 068	5 651	32	15	17	221	107	114
15 to 19 years	74 622	38 568	36 054	68 840	35 531	33 309	181	130	51	1 192	633	559
15 years	14 185	7 367	6 818	13 013	6 763	6 250	25	10	15	228	123	105
16 years	15 037	7 791	7 246	13 850	7 172	6 678	29	15	14	252	135	117
17 years	15 441	8 063	7 378	14 263	7 423	6 840	16	11	5	249	140	109
18 years	14 854	7 743	7 111	13 763	7 124	6 639	44	38	6	256	133	123
19 years	15 105	7 604	7 501	13 951	7 049	6 902	67	56	11	207	102	105
20 to 24 years	74 018	37 197	36 821	68 939	34 595	34 344	353	253	100	1 106	560	546
20 years	15 151	7 637	7 514	14 040	7 026	7 014	70	57	13	215	98	117
21 years	14 768	7 391	7 377	13 696	6 851	6 845	78	56	22	242	123	119
25 to 29 years	71 516	36 022	35 494	67 270	33 915	33 355	213	148	65	935	463	472
30 to 34 years	61 409	31 558	29 851	58 092	29 931	28 161	144	93	51	763	405	358
35 to 39 years	48 045	24 392	23 653	45 671	23 226	22 445	91	70	21	439	223	216
40 to 44 years	40 374	20 244	20 130	38 309	19 260	19 049	71	47	24	414	200	214
45 to 49 years	36 314	18 205	18 109	34 672	17 456	17 216	52	28	24	346	178	168
50 to 54 years	37 363	18 536	18 827	35 977	17 872	18 105	42	27	15	283	141	142
55 to 59 years	36 557	18 060	18 497	35 413	17 477	17 936	24	16	8	237	129	108
60 to 64 years	34 681	16 946	17 735	33 714	16 493	17 221	34	12	22	160	82	78
65 to 69 years	29 609	14 110	15 499	28 798	13 705	15 093	26	14	12	124	64	60
70 to 74 years	21 919	10 165	11 754	21 405	9 919	11 486	19	9	10	116	63	53
75 to 79 years	14 922	6 374	8 548	14 546	6 186	8 360	21	10	11	85	49	36
80 to 84 years	9 272	3 426	5 846	9 039	3 330	5 709	11	3	8	42	24	18
85 years and over	8 837	2 976	5 861	8 672	2 911	5 761	3	1	2	35	20	15
18 years and over	554 795	273 558	281 237	528 231	260 449	267 782	1 215	825	390	5 548	2 836	2 712
62 years and over	104 915	47 029	57 886	102 277	45 766	56 511	97	42	55	491	262	229
65 years and over	84 559	37 051	47 508	82 460	36 051	46 409	80	37	43	402	220	182
Median	29.0	28.4	29.6	29.6	29.0	30.2	22.9	22.9	22.9	20.5	20.4	20.5
NEBRASKA												
Total persons	1 569 825	765 894	803 931	1 490 381	726 796	763 585	48 390	23 478	24 912	28 025	14 263	13 762
Under 5 years	122 946	62 703	60 243	113 747	58 000	55 747	5 216	2 702	2 514	3 922	1 944	1 978
Under 1 year	26 899	13 791	13 108	24 838	12 708	12 130	1 173	608	565	923	486	437
1 year	24 668	12 623	12 045	22 776	11 660	11 116	1 097	562	535	756	357	399
2 years	24 285	12 331	11 954	22 505	11 408	11 097	996	537	459	760	375	385
3 years	23 737	12 027	11 710	21 993	11 141	10 852	978	506	472	751	371	380
4 years	23 357	11 931	11 426	21 635	11 083	10 552	972	489	483	732	355	377
5 to 9 years	118 045	60 399	57 646	109 524	56 075	53 449	5 006	2 506	2 500	3 343	1 666	1 677
5 years	23 473	12 052	11 421	21 868	11 200	10 668	893	469	424	704	356	348
6 years	22 365	11 360	11 005	20 653	10 553	10 100	1 004	448	556	676	336	340
7 years	22 936	11 793	11 143	21 242	10 903	10 339	994	527	467	660	310	350
8 years	23 672	12 061	11 611	21 907	11 187	10 720	1 046	517	529	651	332	319
9 years	25 599	13 133	12 466	23 854	12 232	11 622	1 069	545	524	652	332	320
10 to 14 years	120 907	61 803	59 104	112 627	57 606	55 021	5 059	2 539	2 520	3 029	1 592	1 437
10 years	24 827	12 587	12 240	23 140	11 790	11 350	1 029	485	544	647	334	313
11 years	23 819	12 186	11 633	22 230	11 377	10 853	961	485	476	623	323	300
12 years	23 233	11 839	11 394	21 634	11 016	10 618	934	478	456	545	287	258
13 years	23 931	12 293	11 638	22 251	11 414	10 837	1 044	537	507	574	301	273
14 years	25 097	12 898	12 199	23 372	12 009	11 363	1 091	554	537	640	347	293
15 to 19 years	147 249	74 437	72 812	137 969	69 710	68 259	5 927	3 036	2 891	3 166	1 594	1 572
15 years	27 192	13 836	13 356	25 369	12 930	12 439	1 168	588	580	637	303	334
16 years	28 792	14 760	14 032	26 910	13 794	13 116	1 203	626	577	602	315	287
17 years	29 288	14 949	14 339	27 470	14 001	13 469	1 190	634	556	619	302	317
18 years	30 111	15 016	15 095	28 292	14 102	14 190	1 162	581	581	636	328	291
19 years	31 866	15 876	15 990	29 928	14 883	15 045	1 204	607	597	671	328	343
20 to 24 years	148 734	74 697	74 037	139 603	70 056	69 547	5 309	2 566	2 743	3 258	1 746	1 512
20 years	31 100	15 445	15 655	29 216	14 477	14 739	1 109	560	549	663	337	326
21 years	29 747	14 963	14 784	27 859	13 964	13 895	1 131	558	573	618	346	272
25 to 29 years	134 794	67 366	67 428	127 174	63 560	63 614	4 327	2 099	2 228	2 682	1 406	1 276
30 to 34 years	114 407	57 398	57 009	108 602	54 620	53 982	3 308	1 563	1 745	1 992	1 014	978
35 to 39 years	88 424	44 229	44 195	84 204	42 246	41 958	2 563	1 183	1 380	1 329	678	651
40 to 44 years	75 350	37 445	37 905	71 794	35 755	36 039	2 234	1 047	1 187	1 099	551	548
45 to 49 years	73 797	36 065	37 732	70 721	34 597	36 124	1 988	978	1 010	1 017	503	514
50 to 54 years	76 856	37 910	38 946	74 131	36 682	37 449	1 825	811	1 014	915	455	460
55 to 59 years	75 104	36 566	38 538	72 845	35 528	37 317	1 515	685	830	716	351	365
60 to 64 years	67 528	31 490	36 038	65 790	30 714	35 076	1 200	534	666	456	219	237
65 to 69 years	61 481	27 847	33 634	60 049	27 202	32 847	1 047	462	585	357	162	195
70 to 74 years	52 540	22 608	29 932	51 513	22 138	29 375	762	338	424	276	150	126
75 to 79 years	39 987	15 678	24 309	39 199	15 353	23 846	558	235	323	224	103	121
80 to 84 years	27 932	9 836	18 096	27 487	9 659	17 828	316	124	192	120	64	56
85 years and over	23 744	7 417	16 327	23 402	7 295	16 107	230	70	160	124	65	59
18 years and over	1 122 655	537 444	585 211	1 074 734	514 390	560 344	29 548	13 883	15 665	15 855	8 123	7 732
62 years and over	245 233	101 768	143 465	240 196	99 603	140 593	3 622	1 526	2 096	1 341	663	678
65 years and over	205 684	83 386	122 298	201 650	81 647	120 003	2 913	1 229	1 684	1 101	544	557
Median	29.7	28.6	30.9	30.2	29.1	31.4	22.7	21.7	23.7	20.8	21.0	20.7

[1] Persons of Spanish origin may be of any race.

GENERAL POPULATION CHARACTERISTICS

UNITED STATES SUMMARY 1—171

Table 67. Persons by Age, Race, Spanish Origin, and Sex, for States: 1980—Con.

[For meaning of symbols, see Introduction. For definitions of terms, see appendixes A and B]

States	Total Both sexes	Total Male	Total Female	White Both sexes	White Male	White Female	Black Both sexes	Black Male	Black Female	Spanish origin[1] Both sexes	Spanish origin[1] Male	Spanish origin[1] Female
NEVADA												
Total persons	800 493	405 060	395 433	700 345	354 833	345 512	50 999	25 593	25 406	53 879	28 048	25 831
Under 5 years	56 132	28 657	27 475	46 236	23 639	22 597	5 165	2 603	2 562	5 930	2 995	2 935
Under 1 year	12 762	6 627	6 135	10 520	5 465	5 055	1 210	628	582	1 354	665	689
1 year	11 404	5 813	5 591	9 361	4 784	4 577	1 079	526	553	1 173	599	574
2 years	10 659	5 408	5 251	8 768	4 442	4 326	981	502	479	1 092	568	524
3 years	10 843	5 540	5 303	8 988	4 597	4 391	930	471	459	1 166	597	569
4 years	10 464	5 269	5 195	8 599	4 351	4 248	965	476	489	1 145	566	579
5 to 9 years	55 689	28 498	27 191	45 925	23 597	22 328	5 412	2 732	2 680	5 266	2 673	2 593
5 years	10 260	5 251	5 009	8 484	4 351	4 133	960	479	481	1 055	551	504
6 years	10 247	5 319	4 928	8 292	4 359	3 933	1 082	518	564	1 009	520	489
7 years	10 994	5 622	5 372	9 017	4 630	4 387	1 109	576	533	1 063	522	541
8 years	11 458	5 863	5 595	9 484	4 833	4 651	1 126	597	529	1 008	519	489
9 years	12 730	6 443	6 287	10 648	5 424	5 224	1 135	562	573	1 131	561	570
10 to 14 years	61 744	31 580	30 164	51 803	26 477	25 326	5 605	2 907	2 698	5 099	2 585	2 514
10 years	12 692	6 552	6 140	10 661	5 510	5 151	1 150	581	569	1 057	562	495
11 years	11 968	6 109	5 859	10 029	5 142	4 887	1 052	544	508	989	480	509
12 years	11 862	6 062	5 800	9 966	5 108	4 858	1 059	532	527	1 003	518	485
13 years	12 373	6 344	6 029	10 340	5 271	5 069	1 173	632	541	997	517	480
14 years	12 849	6 513	6 336	10 807	5 446	5 361	1 171	618	553	1 053	508	545
15 to 19 years	70 162	35 867	34 295	59 107	30 180	28 927	5 800	2 892	2 908	5 880	3 088	2 792
15 years	13 648	6 989	6 659	11 412	5 825	5 587	1 180	593	587	1 126	550	576
16 years	14 251	7 221	7 030	12 032	6 079	5 953	1 169	578	591	1 186	625	561
17 years	14 335	7 463	6 872	11 987	6 211	5 776	1 225	628	597	1 251	692	559
18 years	13 427	6 889	6 538	11 352	5 843	5 509	1 082	526	556	1 125	584	541
19 years	14 501	7 305	7 196	12 324	6 222	6 102	1 144	567	577	1 192	637	555
20 to 24 years	77 442	39 336	38 106	65 873	33 374	32 499	6 037	3 049	2 988	6 121	3 354	2 767
20 years	14 761	7 650	7 111	12 376	6 387	5 989	1 251	647	604	1 223	697	526
21 years	14 866	7 616	7 250	12 630	6 435	6 195	1 152	606	546	1 234	694	540
25 to 29 years	75 951	38 632	37 319	65 213	33 198	32 015	5 128	2 580	2 548	5 489	3 015	2 474
30 to 34 years	69 197	35 089	34 108	60 608	30 961	29 647	3 972	1 910	2 062	4 268	2 221	2 047
35 to 39 years	57 116	29 276	27 840	50 551	26 075	24 476	3 159	1 544	1 615	3 555	1 776	1 779
40 to 44 years	48 195	25 068	23 127	42 649	22 309	20 340	2 737	1 403	1 334	2 942	1 545	1 397
45 to 49 years	42 852	22 109	20 743	38 317	19 943	18 374	2 141	1 083	1 058	2 443	1 271	1 172
50 to 54 years	42 558	21 594	20 964	38 973	19 834	19 139	1 659	848	811	2 141	1 155	986
55 to 59 years	42 116	21 208	20 908	39 480	19 902	19 578	1 269	631	638	1 605	847	758
60 to 64 years	35 583	17 870	17 713	33 544	16 850	16 694	1 059	523	536	1 140	569	571
65 to 69 years	27 980	13 705	14 275	26 438	12 965	13 473	833	406	427	782	382	400
70 to 74 years	18 018	8 541	9 477	16 961	8 001	8 960	524	268	256	518	232	286
75 to 79 years	10 776	4 709	6 067	10 168	4 423	5 745	307	139	168	380	184	196
80 to 84 years	5 342	2 117	3 225	5 048	1 977	3 071	124	53	71	190	101	89
85 years and over	3 640	1 204	2 436	3 451	1 128	2 323	68	22	46	130	55	75
18 years and over	584 694	294 652	290 042	520 950	263 005	257 945	31 243	15 552	15 691	34 021	17 928	16 093
62 years and over	86 345	40 698	45 647	81 596	38 382	43 214	2 396	1 155	1 241	2 612	1 263	1 349
65 years and over	65 756	30 276	35 480	62 066	28 494	33 572	1 856	888	968	2 000	954	1 046
Median	30.2	30.0	30.4	31.3	31.1	31.5	22.9	22.7	23.2	23.8	23.9	23.7
NEW HAMPSHIRE												
Total persons	920 610	448 462	472 148	910 099	443 057	467 042	3 990	2 275	1 715	5 587	2 806	2 781
Under 5 years	62 512	31 883	30 629	61 441	31 348	30 093	382	193	189	605	303	302
Under 1 year	13 300	6 818	6 482	13 076	6 700	6 376	81	36	45	125	62	63
1 year	12 519	6 384	6 135	12 323	6 281	6 042	64	36	28	120	68	52
2 years	12 517	6 309	6 208	12 303	6 217	6 086	76	30	46	126	58	68
3 years	12 146	6 260	5 886	11 920	6 127	5 793	87	54	33	121	65	56
4 years	12 030	6 112	5 918	11 819	6 023	5 796	74	37	37	113	50	63
5 to 9 years	67 997	34 800	33 197	66 962	34 276	32 686	386	187	199	577	301	276
5 years	12 479	6 355	6 124	12 266	6 228	6 038	83	51	32	126	67	59
6 years	12 372	6 439	5 933	12 167	6 338	5 829	67	30	37	115	62	53
7 years	13 208	6 692	6 516	13 006	6 592	6 414	75	36	39	105	50	55
8 years	14 151	7 182	6 969	13 947	7 071	6 876	70	38	32	117	69	48
9 years	15 787	8 132	7 655	15 576	8 047	7 529	91	32	59	114	53	61
10 to 14 years	76 763	39 684	37 079	75 861	39 189	36 672	359	195	164	589	303	286
10 years	15 332	7 940	7 392	15 133	7 833	7 300	80	44	36	122	55	67
11 years	15 025	7 735	7 290	14 857	7 640	7 217	64	33	31	114	56	58
12 years	14 949	7 755	7 194	14 777	7 651	7 126	66	44	22	125	64	61
13 years	15 464	8 025	7 439	15 283	7 937	7 346	72	31	41	113	64	49
14 years	15 993	8 229	7 764	15 811	8 128	7 683	77	43	34	115	64	51
15 to 19 years	87 776	44 217	43 559	86 701	43 631	43 070	482	266	216	646	353	293
15 years	16 934	8 621	8 313	16 784	8 547	8 237	56	25	31	113	57	56
16 years	17 085	8 748	8 337	16 890	8 637	8 253	69	43	26	127	66	61
17 years	16 791	8 545	8 246	16 621	8 471	8 150	69	29	40	96	54	42
18 years	17 915	8 883	9 032	17 644	8 729	8 915	138	74	64	159	88	71
19 years	19 051	9 420	9 631	18 762	9 247	9 515	150	95	55	151	88	63
20 to 24 years	83 624	41 075	42 549	82 267	40 307	41 960	629	394	235	594	285	309
20 years	17 966	8 849	9 117	17 649	8 650	8 999	159	106	53	148	72	76
21 years	17 178	8 403	8 775	16 898	8 245	8 653	142	81	61	116	62	54
25 to 29 years	79 468	39 156	40 312	78 369	38 617	39 752	393	242	151	504	248	256
30 to 34 years	77 928	38 683	39 245	76 871	38 177	38 694	324	188	136	448	221	227
35 to 39 years	60 091	30 379	29 712	59 304	29 973	29 331	238	146	92	324	158	166
40 to 44 years	46 937	23 549	23 388	46 409	23 259	23 150	212	131	81	288	150	138
45 to 49 years	44 295	22 175	22 120	43 842	21 955	21 887	150	91	59	231	104	127
50 to 54 years	45 826	22 345	23 481	45 498	22 181	23 317	132	82	50	181	103	78
55 to 59 years	44 749	21 366	23 383	44 492	21 240	23 252	91	52	39	158	83	75
60 to 64 years	39 677	18 600	21 077	39 507	18 507	21 000	66	42	24	141	76	65
65 to 69 years	34 366	15 364	19 002	34 231	15 307	18 924	51	25	26	114	48	66
70 to 74 years	27 422	11 291	16 131	27 318	11 251	16 067	40	17	23	78	33	45
75 to 79 years	19 241	7 227	12 014	19 166	7 203	11 963	24	7	17	56	20	36
80 to 84 years	12 288	4 031	8 257	12 243	4 012	8 231	14	9	5	32	10	22
85 years and over	9 650	2 637	7 013	9 617	2 624	6 993	17	8	9	21	7	14
18 years and over	662 528	316 181	346 347	655 540	312 589	342 951	2 669	1 603	1 066	3 480	1 722	1 758
62 years and over	126 206	51 369	74 837	125 718	51 163	74 555	184	90	94	388	164	224
65 years and over	102 967	40 550	62 417	102 575	40 397	62 178	146	66	80	301	118	183
Median	30.1	29.2	31.1	30.2	29.3	31.2	22.7	23.4	21.6	23.0	22.2	23.6

[1]Persons of Spanish origin may be of any race

Table 67. Persons by Age, Race, Spanish Origin, and Sex, for States: 1980—Con.

[For meaning of symbols, see Introduction. For definitions of terms, see appendixes A and B]

States	Race									Spanish origin[1]		
	Total			White			Black					
	Both sexes	Male	Female	Both sexes	Male	Female	Both sexes	Male	Female	Both sexes	Male	Female
NEW JERSEY												
Total persons	7 364 823	3 533 012	3 831 811	6 127 467	2 949 619	3 177 848	925 066	430 806	494 260	491 883	238 915	252 968
Under 5 years	463 289	237 346	225 943	347 771	178 818	168 953	79 900	40 484	39 416	51 428	26 491	24 937
Under 1 year	97 359	49 938	47 421	72 359	37 203	35 156	17 292	8 798	8 494	11 084	5 653	5 431
1 year	91 585	46 742	44 843	58 581	35 265	33 316	16 127	8 004	8 123	10 122	5 310	4 812
2 years	91 355	47 028	44 327	58 968	35 697	33 271	15 499	7 903	7 596	10 124	5 200	4 924
3 years	91 278	46 578	44 700	58 707	35 106	33 601	15 596	7 942	7 654	9 999	5 100	4 899
4 years	91 712	47 060	44 652	59 156	35 547	33 609	15 386	7 837	7 549	10 099	5 228	4 871
5 to 9 years	508 447	259 606	248 841	387 481	198 357	189 124	86 569	43 656	42 913	50 685	25 915	24 770
5 years	93 362	47 746	45 616	70 942	36 349	34 593	15 479	7 817	7 662	10 032	5 182	4 850
6 years	93 266	47 727	45 539	70 778	36 301	34 477	15 694	7 886	7 808	9 902	5 148	4 754
7 years	98 701	50 284	48 417	74 674	38 190	36 484	17 113	8 560	8 553	10 037	5 172	4 865
8 years	104 106	53 082	51 024	79 597	40 656	38 941	17 820	9 057	8 763	9 931	4 981	4 950
9 years	119 012	60 767	58 245	91 490	46 861	44 629	20 463	10 336	10 127	10 783	5 432	5 351
10 to 14 years	605 841	308 725	297 116	474 446	242 621	231 825	100 223	50 158	50 065	50 520	25 742	24 778
10 years	120 198	61 419	58 779	93 499	47 912	45 587	20 116	10 160	9 956	10 353	5 343	5 010
11 years	116 997	59 667	57 330	91 457	46 778	44 679	19 251	9 696	9 555	9 765	4 921	4 844
12 years	117 364	59 843	57 521	91 665	46 843	44 822	19 542	9 775	9 767	9 848	5 042	4 806
13 years	122 748	62 404	60 344	96 749	49 318	47 431	20 029	10 008	10 021	10 183	5 200	4 983
14 years	128 534	65 392	63 142	101 076	51 770	49 306	21 285	10 519	10 766	10 371	5 236	5 135
15 to 19 years	670 665	341 153	329 512	536 125	274 066	262 059	104 742	51 941	52 801	52 366	26 555	25 831
15 years	135 636	69 066	66 570	107 815	54 988	52 827	21 695	10 970	10 725	10 625	5 366	5 259
16 years	139 053	70 613	68 440	111 040	56 642	54 398	21 939	10 890	11 049	10 612	5 400	5 212
17 years	138 595	71 222	67 373	111 076	57 268	53 808	21 533	10 870	10 663	10 692	5 436	5 256
18 years	128 908	66 006	62 902	103 085	53 175	49 910	20 133	9 952	10 181	10 179	5 160	5 019
19 years	128 473	64 246	64 227	103 109	51 993	51 116	19 442	9 259	10 183	10 278	5 193	5 085
20 to 24 years	614 828	301 855	312 973	501 138	249 248	251 890	85 709	39 247	46 462	46 716	22 495	24 221
20 years	124 854	61 757	63 097	100 778	50 434	50 344	18 249	8 524	9 725	9 876	4 831	5 045
21 years	122 729	60 091	62 638	99 900	49 538	50 362	17 426	7 941	9 485	9 372	4 574	4 798
25 to 29 years	574 135	278 848	295 287	468 708	231 723	236 985	75 745	33 554	42 191	42 764	19 868	22 896
30 to 34 years	563 758	270 274	293 484	452 710	225 481	237 229	69 161	30 169	38 992	40 434	18 603	21 831
35 to 39 years	479 749	230 157	249 592	393 855	191 557	202 298	60 153	26 012	34 141	33 966	15 621	18 345
40 to 44 years	400 074	193 465	206 609	328 039	159 940	168 099	52 291	23 412	28 879	30 058	14 297	15 761
45 to 49 years	394 038	189 797	204 241	334 174	162 062	172 112	46 101	20 903	25 198	25 367	12 263	13 104
50 to 54 years	432 520	207 573	224 947	380 351	183 395	196 956	42 077	19 318	22 759	20 997	10 332	10 665
55 to 59 years	430 048	203 380	226 668	386 356	183 258	203 098	36 335	16 639	19 696	15 266	7 443	7 823
60 to 64 years	367 660	170 391	197 269	334 366	155 704	178 662	28 034	12 418	15 616	10 697	4 831	5 866
65 to 69 years	303 670	133 579	170 091	277 131	122 440	154 691	22 550	9 403	13 147	8 037	3 424	4 613
70 to 74 years	227 037	93 464	133 573	208 688	86 016	122 672	15 676	6 298	9 378	5 478	2 199	3 279
75 to 79 years	157 921	59 268	98 653	145 736	54 551	91 185	10 543	4 023	6 520	3 939	1 640	2 299
80 to 84 years	98 912	32 881	66 031	92 711	30 603	62 108	5 320	1 931	3 389	1 849	744	1 105
85 years and over	72 231	21 250	50 981	67 681	19 779	47 902	3 937	1 240	2 697	1 296	452	844
18 years and over	5 373 962	2 516 434	2 857 528	4 587 838	2 160 925	2 426 913	593 207	263 778	329 429	307 321	144 565	162 756
62 years and over	1 071 871	437 904	633 967	985 751	402 926	582 825	73 405	29 610	43 795	26 462	11 070	15 392
65 years and over	859 771	340 442	519 329	791 947	313 389	478 558	58 026	22 895	35 131	20 599	8 459	12 140
Median	32.2	30.7	33.4	33.6	32.2	35.3	25.3	23.7	26.8	24.4	23.2	25.4
NEW MEXICO												
Total persons	1 302 894	642 157	660 737	977 587	481 738	495 849	24 020	12 550	11 470	477 222	235 881	241 341
Under 5 years	114 731	58 537	56 194	75 939	38 987	36 952	2 488	1 305	1 183	51 222	25 892	25 330
Under 1 year	25 903	13 145	12 758	16 923	8 660	8 263	566	283	283	11 608	5 863	5 745
1 year	23 197	11 905	11 292	15 393	7 907	7 486	498	255	243	10 411	5 308	5 103
2 years	22 073	11 249	10 824	14 736	7 573	7 163	475	249	226	9 816	4 925	4 891
3 years	22 054	11 345	10 709	14 613	7 578	7 035	470	252	218	9 861	5 038	4 823
4 years	21 504	10 893	10 611	14 274	7 269	7 005	479	266	213	9 526	4 758	4 768
5 to 9 years	109 615	55 704	53 911	74 766	38 124	36 642	2 246	1 156	1 090	48 564	24 779	23 785
5 years	21 293	10 693	10 600	14 313	7 210	7 103	408	215	193	9 533	4 813	4 720
6 years	20 954	10 715	10 239	13 950	7 170	6 780	447	229	218	9 303	4 842	4 461
7 years	21 795	10 983	10 812	14 826	7 489	7 337	447	230	217	9 707	4 898	4 809
8 years	21 860	11 143	10 717	15 195	7 787	7 408	428	214	214	9 700	4 876	4 824
9 years	23 713	12 170	11 543	16 482	8 468	8 014	516	268	248	10 321	5 350	4 971
10 to 14 years	114 101	58 030	56 071	80 067	40 838	39 229	2 309	1 169	1 140	50 045	25 319	24 726
10 years	23 668	12 121	11 547	16 731	8 571	8 160	483	252	231	10 136	5 127	5 009
11 years	22 472	11 499	10 973	15 823	8 152	7 671	412	195	217	9 713	4 941	4 772
12 years	21 825	11 058	10 767	15 271	7 745	7 526	476	259	217	9 663	4 915	4 748
13 years	22 526	11 459	11 067	15 730	8 090	7 640	436	210	226	10 105	5 128	4 977
14 years	23 610	11 893	11 717	16 512	8 280	8 232	502	253	249	10 428	5 208	5 220
15 to 19 years	132 306	66 969	65 337	93 313	47 579	45 734	2 871	1 549	1 322	56 567	28 534	28 033
15 years	25 722	12 980	12 742	18 052	9 162	8 890	540	260	280	11 283	5 729	5 554
16 years	26 562	13 482	13 080	18 808	9 618	9 190	548	288	260	11 542	5 898	5 644
17 years	27 176	13 893	13 283	19 395	9 904	9 491	515	285	230	11 852	6 086	5 766
18 years	25 858	13 116	12 742	18 213	9 327	8 886	577	305	272	10 828	5 440	5 388
19 years	26 988	13 498	13 490	18 845	9 568	9 277	691	411	280	11 062	5 381	5 681
20 to 24 years	125 428	62 568	62 860	88 417	44 374	44 043	3 034	1 693	1 341	48 845	24 170	24 675
20 years	26 024	12 861	13 163	18 230	9 055	9 175	649	338	311	10 523	5 096	5 427
21 years	25 009	12 443	12 566	17 637	8 907	8 730	572	321	251	9 949	4 818	5 131
25 to 29 years	115 344	57 567	57 777	84 224	41 891	42 333	2 347	1 325	1 022	41 012	20 440	20 572
30 to 34 years	101 303	50 658	50 645	77 120	38 673	38 447	1 668	910	758	34 785	17 117	17 668
35 to 39 years	78 236	38 499	39 737	61 366	30 310	31 056	1 158	587	571	26 021	12 714	13 307
40 to 44 years	66 702	32 627	34 075	52 498	25 857	26 641	1 033	544	489	22 708	10 875	11 833
45 to 49 years	61 811	30 229	31 582	49 588	24 472	25 116	1 061	544	517	20 234	9 725	10 509
50 to 54 years	60 232	29 018	31 214	49 640	24 116	25 524	953	439	514	18 685	8 885	9 800
55 to 59 years	58 424	27 812	30 612	49 741	23 749	25 992	757	379	378	16 334	7 864	8 470
60 to 64 years	48 755	23 390	25 365	42 008	20 194	21 814	625	298	327	12 114	5 742	6 372
65 to 69 years	43 075	19 887	23 188	36 941	17 075	19 866	591	237	354	10 878	5 046	5 832
70 to 74 years	31 657	14 332	17 325	27 108	12 198	14 910	391	196	195	8 050	3 713	4 337
75 to 79 years	20 921	8 753	12 168	17 689	7 190	10 499	262	116	146	5 673	2 562	3 111
80 to 84 years	11 470	4 395	7 075	9 845	3 586	6 259	122	61	61	3 004	1 396	1 608
85 years and over	8 783	3 182	5 601	7 317	2 525	4 792	104	42	62	2 481	1 108	1 373
18 years and over	884 987	429 531	455 456	690 560	335 105	355 455	15 374	8 087	7 287	292 714	142 178	150 536
62 years and over	144 469	64 215	80 254	123 620	54 397	69 223	1 847	832	1 015	37 071	17 105	19 966
65 years and over	115 906	50 549	65 357	98 900	42 574	56 326	1 470	652	818	30 086	13 825	16 261
Median	27.3	26.6	28.0	29.5	28.7	30.4	23.4	23.2	23.6	23.2	22.7	23.7

[1] Persons of Spanish origin may be of any race.

Table 67. Persons by Age, Race, Spanish Origin, and Sex, for States: 1980—Con.

[For meaning of symbols, see Introduction. For definitions of terms, see appendixes A and B]

States	Race									Spanish origin[1]		
	Total			White			Black					
	Both sexes	Male	Female	Both sexes	Male	Female	Both sexes	Male	Female	Both sexes	Male	Female
NEW YORK												
Total persons	17 558 072	8 339 422	9 218 650	13 960 868	6 671 300	7 289 568	2 402 006	1 094 310	1 307 696	1 659 300	782 875	876 425
Under 5 years	1 135 925	580 389	555 536	808 874	415 362	393 512	203 994	102 428	101 566	169 747	86 864	82 883
Under 1 year	240 554	122 502	118 052	169 470	86 941	82 529	44 185	22 129	22 056	36 710	18 539	18 171
1 year	224 407	115 187	109 220	159 953	82 402	77 551	39 742	20 042	19 700	33 866	17 439	16 427
2 years	225 626	115 117	110 509	160 409	82 187	78 222	40 831	20 437	20 394	33 821	17 331	16 490
3 years	223 568	114 179	109 389	159 680	81 915	77 765	40 006	20 173	19 833	33 158	16 979	16 179
4 years	221 770	113 404	108 366	159 362	81 917	77 445	39 230	19 647	19 583	32 192	16 576	15 616
5 to 9 years	1 184 879	605 546	579 333	872 826	447 848	424 978	201 277	101 108	100 169	156 462	79 807	76 655
5 years	221 874	113 693	108 181	161 108	82 920	78 188	38 535	19 414	19 121	30 954	15 726	15 228
6 years	217 071	110 553	106 518	158 602	81 180	77 422	37 065	18 595	18 470	29 562	14 978	14 584
7 years	229 232	117 094	112 138	168 827	86 625	82 202	38 787	19 432	19 355	30 272	15 545	14 727
8 years	239 568	122 433	117 135	178 284	91 460	86 824	39 618	19 899	19 719	30 817	15 752	15 065
9 years	277 134	141 773	135 361	206 005	105 663	100 342	47 272	23 768	23 504	34 857	17 806	17 051
10 to 14 years	1 406 060	717 004	689 056	1 056 245	541 086	515 159	237 417	118 890	118 527	165 841	83 954	81 887
10 years	278 522	142 607	135 915	208 949	107 277	101 672	46 596	23 516	23 080	34 045	17 233	16 812
11 years	270 997	138 444	132 553	204 124	104 601	99 523	44 855	22 571	22 284	32 206	16 425	15 781
12 years	271 542	138 305	133 237	203 647	104 312	99 335	45 800	22 808	22 992	32 428	16 412	16 016
13 years	285 231	145 300	139 931	214 868	110 131	104 737	48 200	24 131	24 069	33 037	16 601	16 436
14 years	299 768	152 348	147 420	224 657	114 765	109 892	51 966	25 864	26 102	34 125	17 283	16 842
15 to 19 years	1 598 571	803 639	794 932	1 217 487	615 957	601 530	260 464	127 882	132 582	172 614	85 507	87 107
15 years	315 775	160 721	155 054	237 453	121 329	116 124	54 503	27 387	27 116	34 839	17 709	17 130
16 years	323 055	164 079	158 976	243 736	124 354	119 382	54 805	27 416	27 389	35 352	17 746	17 606
17 years	322 169	163 299	158 870	244 235	124 642	119 593	53 412	26 505	26 907	35 207	17 312	17 895
18 years	314 983	157 062	157 921	242 049	121 461	120 588	49 397	24 000	25 397	33 390	16 368	17 022
19 years	322 589	158 478	164 111	250 014	124 171	125 843	48 347	22 574	25 773	33 826	16 372	17 454
20 to 24 years	1 519 946	737 556	782 390	1 183 713	584 005	599 708	217 586	97 961	119 625	160 303	74 173	86 130
20 years	314 719	153 957	160 762	244 271	121 137	123 134	46 434	21 485	24 949	32 932	15 427	17 505
21 years	307 969	149 822	158 147	240 639	118 946	121 693	44 178	19 948	24 230	31 608	14 714	16 894
25 to 29 years	1 428 376	690 997	737 379	1 112 117	547 523	564 594	197 955	87 940	110 015	151 255	69 441	81 814
30 to 34 years	1 351 839	649 344	702 495	1 054 915	515 657	539 258	184 187	80 624	103 563	140 303	64 020	76 283
35 to 39 years	1 106 907	526 286	580 621	855 006	414 496	440 510	165 468	70 890	94 578	114 843	52 667	62 176
40 to 44 years	936 312	446 856	489 456	721 214	349 519	371 695	143 124	63 014	80 110	98 148	45 079	53 069
45 to 49 years	911 511	433 243	478 268	731 673	352 710	378 963	122 335	53 484	68 851	84 209	38 086	46 123
50 to 54 years	996 602	469 110	527 492	832 059	397 490	434 569	117 458	50 391	67 067	71 812	31 930	39 882
55 to 59 years	979 370	456 018	523 352	836 978	393 751	443 227	105 437	45 504	59 933	56 332	24 897	31 435
60 to 64 years	841 007	382 502	458 505	732 319	336 977	395 342	81 763	33 739	48 024	40 469	16 996	23 473
65 to 69 years	724 522	312 502	412 020	638 467	278 204	360 263	65 137	25 396	39 741	31 097	12 226	18 871
70 to 74 years	567 906	229 349	338 557	509 680	206 823	302 857	44 198	16 563	27 635	20 668	7 978	12 690
75 to 79 years	413 557	153 100	260 457	375 232	138 946	236 286	29 277	10 363	18 914	13 731	5 349	8 382
80 to 84 years	261 799	88 035	173 764	242 565	81 226	161 339	14 637	4 998	9 639	6 671	2 436	4 235
85 years and over	192 983	57 946	135 037	179 498	53 720	125 778	10 292	3 135	7 157	4 795	1 465	3 330
18 years and over	12 870 209	5 948 384	6 921 825	10 497 499	4 896 679	5 600 820	1 596 598	690 576	906 022	1 061 852	479 483	582 369
62 years and over	2 646 909	1 060 549	1 586 360	2 371 498	953 688	1 417 810	208 768	78 940	129 828	99 355	38 677	60 678
65 years and over	2 160 767	840 932	1 319 835	1 945 442	758 919	1 186 523	163 541	60 455	103 086	76 962	29 454	47 508
Median	31.8	30.3	33.2	33.3	31.7	35.1	27.0	24.9	28.7	25.1	23.7	26.4
NORTH CAROLINA												
Total persons	5 881 766	2 855 385	3 026 381	4 457 507	2 176 628	2 280 879	1 318 857	626 026	692 831	56 667	29 748	26 919
Under 5 years	404 076	206 283	197 793	278 979	143 412	135 567	113 921	57 171	56 750	5 444	2 822	2 622
Under 1 year	84 760	43 216	41 544	58 557	30 277	28 280	23 877	11 769	12 108	1 317	688	629
1 year	80 196	40 931	39 265	55 191	28 326	26 865	22 745	11 479	11 266	1 154	600	554
2 years	80 815	41 538	39 277	56 008	28 897	27 111	22 551	11 459	11 092	1 089	581	508
3 years	79 278	40 384	38 894	54 935	28 047	26 888	22 217	11 262	10 955	945	484	461
4 years	79 027	40 214	38 813	54 288	27 865	26 423	22 531	11 202	11 329	939	469	470
5 to 9 years	447 688	229 002	218 686	312 409	160 797	151 612	124 431	62 729	61 702	4 906	2 536	2 370
5 years	82 872	42 446	40 426	57 234	29 414	27 820	23 451	11 924	11 527	991	520	471
6 years	83 023	42 465	40 558	57 326	29 557	27 769	23 574	11 849	11 725	963	486	477
7 years	88 499	45 478	43 021	61 348	31 706	29 642	24 865	12 552	12 313	944	511	433
8 years	92 132	47 090	45 042	64 649	33 174	31 475	25 376	12 862	12 514	982	498	484
9 years	101 162	51 523	49 639	71 852	36 946	34 906	27 165	13 542	13 623	1 026	521	505
10 to 14 years	482 228	246 258	235 970	339 349	174 339	165 010	133 217	67 039	66 178	4 757	2 429	2 328
10 years	99 011	50 552	48 459	70 078	35 915	34 163	26 844	13 611	13 233	944	449	495
11 years	95 454	48 785	46 669	67 782	34 826	32 956	25 716	12 964	12 752	951	483	468
12 years	93 707	47 898	45 809	65 812	33 849	31 963	26 025	13 088	12 937	946	476	470
13 years	95 773	48 591	47 182	67 529	34 367	33 162	26 380	13 301	13 079	952	494	458
14 years	98 283	50 432	47 851	68 148	35 382	32 766	28 252	14 075	14 177	964	527	437
15 to 19 years	566 322	291 140	275 182	401 636	207 587	194 049	153 287	77 318	75 969	6 798	3 917	2 881
15 years	105 675	53 881	51 794	74 107	38 091	36 016	29 549	14 771	14 778	1 054	550	504
16 years	108 615	55 272	53 343	76 412	39 129	37 283	30 241	15 115	15 126	1 028	542	486
17 years	109 453	55 808	53 645	77 091	39 325	37 766	30 257	15 387	14 870	1 114	582	532
18 years	116 680	60 357	56 323	83 208	43 261	39 947	31 035	15 690	15 345	1 533	943	590
19 years	125 899	65 822	60 077	90 818	47 781	43 037	32 205	16 355	15 850	2 069	1 300	769
20 to 24 years	579 512	298 630	280 882	422 695	220 015	202 680	143 012	70 670	72 342	8 873	5 677	3 196
20 years	125 275	65 917	59 358	90 841	48 328	42 513	31 287	15 662	15 625	2 192	1 493	699
21 years	120 396	63 116	57 280	87 747	46 428	41 319	29 737	14 909	14 828	2 074	1 358	716
25 to 29 years	502 579	249 262	253 317	375 136	188 413	186 723	116 514	55 459	61 055	5 220	2 817	2 403
30 to 34 years	461 169	226 948	234 221	360 329	179 407	180 922	91 377	43 094	48 283	3 924	1 941	1 983
35 to 39 years	368 492	180 562	187 930	295 763	146 693	149 070	66 082	30 696	35 386	2 819	1 327	1 492
40 to 44 years	314 142	152 028	162 114	252 652	123 875	128 777	56 283	25 703	30 580	2 604	1 214	1 390
45 to 49 years	296 939	141 985	154 954	241 048	117 369	123 679	51 987	22 860	29 127	2 257	1 089	1 168
50 to 54 years	304 396	143 788	160 608	246 128	118 503	127 625	55 155	23 963	31 192	1 988	930	1 058
55 to 59 years	295 910	137 794	158 116	240 713	113 355	127 358	52 450	23 238	29 212	1 841	848	993
60 to 64 years	255 132	115 455	139 677	205 824	93 869	111 955	47 166	20 641	26 525	1 579	705	874
65 to 69 years	222 696	95 855	126 841	176 921	76 465	100 456	44 069	18 692	25 377	1 443	623	820
70 to 74 years	164 891	66 274	98 617	133 036	53 343	79 693	30 620	12 413	18 207	1 009	416	593
75 to 79 years	109 126	40 271	68 855	87 728	31 980	55 748	20 645	7 951	12 694	633	252	381
80 to 84 years	61 265	20 435	40 830	50 682	16 627	34 055	10 199	3 661	6 538	312	113	199
85 years and over	45 203	13 415	31 788	36 479	10 579	25 900	8 442	2 728	5 714	260	92	168
18 years and over	4 224 031	2 008 881	2 215 150	3 299 160	1 581 535	1 717 625	857 241	393 814	463 427	38 364	20 287	18 077
62 years and over	750 037	302 357	447 680	603 558	242 936	360 622	140 928	57 112	83 816	4 544	1 888	2 656
65 years and over	603 181	236 250	366 931	484 846	188 994	295 852	113 975	45 445	68 530	3 657	1 496	2 161
Median	29.6	28.1	31.1	31.4	29.8	32.8	24.7	23.3	26.0	23.3	22.3	25.1

[1]Persons of Spanish origin may be of any race.

Table 67. Persons by Age, Race, Spanish Origin, and Sex, for States: 1980—Con.

[For meaning of symbols, see Introduction. For definitions of terms, see appendixes A and B]

States	Total			White			Black			Spanish origin[1]		
	Both sexes	Male	Female	Both sexes	Male	Female	Both sexes	Male	Female	Both sexes	Male	Female
NORTH DAKOTA												
Total persons	652 717	328 426	324 291	625 557	314 594	310 963	2 568	1 670	898	3 902	2 031	1 871
Under 5 years	54 752	28 210	26 542	50 882	26 270	24 612	344	182	162	662	327	335
Under 1 year	12 019	6 177	5 842	11 137	5 747	5 390	88	46	42	131	64	67
1 year	11 156	5 699	5 457	10 403	5 325	5 078	73	39	34	157	73	84
2 years	10 988	5 679	5 309	10 254	5 310	4 944	67	35	32	134	65	69
3 years	10 398	5 343	5 055	9 637	4 956	4 681	64	30	34	115	51	64
4 years	10 191	5 312	4 879	9 451	4 932	4 519	52	32	20	125	74	51
5 to 9 years	49 016	25 079	23 937	45 712	23 357	22 355	257	138	119	488	258	230
5 years	9 859	5 019	4 840	9 187	4 689	4 498	53	20	33	116	61	55
6 years	9 451	4 834	4 617	8 798	4 487	4 311	55	34	21	105	60	45
7 years	9 754	5 032	4 722	9 076	4 666	4 410	61	31	30	94	47	47
8 years	9 661	4 916	4 745	8 996	4 555	4 441	42	25	17	94	48	46
9 years	10 291	5 278	5 013	9 655	4 960	4 695	46	28	18	79	42	37
10 to 14 years	51 043	26 328	24 715	47 991	24 750	23 241	131	74	57	364	182	182
10 years	10 597	5 473	5 124	9 948	5 140	4 808	28	19	9	77	34	43
11 years	9 890	5 104	4 786	9 321	4 802	4 519	24	14	10	68	29	39
12 years	9 643	4 949	4 694	9 020	4 642	4 378	22	15	7	70	43	27
13 years	10 281	5 313	4 968	9 699	5 019	4 680	24	10	14	71	38	33
14 years	10 632	5 489	5 143	10 003	5 147	4 856	33	16	17	78	38	40
15 to 19 years	63 977	32 920	31 057	60 636	31 134	29 502	282	203	79	464	256	208
15 years	11 562	5 833	5 729	10 885	5 488	5 397	21	12	9	83	44	39
16 years	12 011	6 245	5 766	11 400	5 932	5 468	15	8	7	71	40	31
17 years	12 607	6 361	6 246	11 927	5 998	5 929	32	16	16	82	38	44
18 years	13 170	6 813	6 357	12 510	6 466	6 044	87	70	17	100	51	49
19 years	14 627	7 668	6 959	13 914	7 250	6 664	127	97	30	128	83	45
20 to 24 years	69 393	35 889	33 504	66 023	34 005	32 018	672	488	184	588	338	250
20 years	14 705	7 664	7 041	13 962	7 206	6 756	145	115	30	130	84	46
21 years	14 218	7 369	6 849	13 520	6 966	6 554	150	115	35	109	61	48
25 to 29 years	58 470	30 691	27 779	56 017	29 473	26 544	381	259	122	376	198	178
30 to 34 years	45 687	23 969	21 718	43 818	23 070	20 748	201	133	68	283	135	148
35 to 39 years	34 248	17 568	16 680	32 899	16 883	16 016	141	95	46	181	91	90
40 to 44 years	29 398	14 711	14 687	28 278	14 166	14 112	84	57	27	130	59	71
45 to 49 years	28 631	14 065	14 566	27 831	13 713	14 118	29	17	12	88	43	45
50 to 54 years	30 497	15 279	15 218	29 816	14 947	14 869	14	8	6	78	41	37
55 to 59 years	29 218	14 543	14 675	28 698	14 299	14 399	3	–	3	62	30	32
60 to 64 years	27 942	13 691	14 251	27 493	13 482	14 011	7	4	3	41	22	19
65 to 69 years	25 930	12 315	13 615	25 593	12 157	13 436	5	3	2	27	13	14
70 to 74 years	21 217	9 715	11 502	20 958	9 581	11 377	8	5	3	30	16	14
75 to 79 years	15 301	6 635	8 666	15 117	6 553	8 564	4	1	3	24	13	11
80 to 84 years	9 857	3 924	5 933	9 741	3 889	5 852	2	1	1	10	6	4
85 years and over	8 140	2 894	5 246	8 054	2 865	5 189	3	2	1	6	3	3
18 years and over	461 726	230 370	231 356	446 760	222 799	223 961	1 768	1 240	528	2 152	1 142	1 010
62 years and over	97 301	43 692	53 609	96 052	43 133	52 919	25	14	11	119	60	59
65 years and over	80 445	35 483	44 962	79 463	35 045	44 418	22	12	10	97	51	46
Median	28.1	27.5	29.0	28.6	27.9	29 4	21.8	22.1	21.1	19.8	19.9	19.6
OHIO												
Total persons	10 797 630	5 217 137	5 580 493	9 597 458	4 649 831	4 947 627	1 076 748	505 987	570 761	119 883	60 018	59 865
Under 5 years	787 150	402 970	384 180	675 545	346 531	329 014	96 525	48 809	47 716	14 302	7 299	7 003
Under 1 year	168 692	86 390	82 302	144 103	74 076	70 027	21 290	10 661	10 629	3 184	1 630	1 554
1 year	158 444	81 159	77 285	135 618	69 638	65 980	19 871	9 995	9 876	2 850	1 466	1 384
2 years	155 126	79 247	75 879	133 527	68 289	65 238	18 629	9 468	9 161	2 792	1 426	1 366
3 years	152 624	78 371	74 253	131 386	67 582	63 804	18 255	9 262	8 993	2 762	1 379	1 383
4 years	152 264	77 803	74 461	130 911	66 946	63 965	18 480	9 423	9 057	2 714	1 398	1 316
5 to 9 years	821 480	420 944	400 536	707 920	363 532	344 388	99 945	50 489	49 456	13 137	6 759	6 378
5 years	154 477	79 420	75 057	133 136	68 602	64 534	18 500	9 400	9 100	2 705	1 392	1 313
6 years	151 395	77 612	73 783	130 386	67 085	63 301	18 286	9 170	9 116	2 423	1 232	1 191
7 years	160 334	82 005	78 329	137 678	70 440	67 238	19 974	10 197	9 777	2 642	1 376	1 266
8 years	168 830	86 581	82 249	145 428	74 731	70 697	20 746	10 453	10 293	2 629	1 350	1 279
9 years	186 444	95 326	91 118	161 292	82 674	78 618	22 439	11 269	11 170	2 738	1 409	1 329
10 to 14 years	886 625	453 689	432 936	772 414	395 910	376 504	102 940	52 147	50 793	12 500	6 265	6 235
10 years	180 831	92 518	88 313	156 816	80 387	76 429	21 522	10 907	10 615	2 640	1 316	1 324
11 years	175 346	89 649	85 697	152 493	78 159	74 334	20 449	10 295	10 154	2 531	1 303	1 228
12 years	170 590	87 336	83 254	148 878	76 308	72 570	19 587	9 961	9 626	2 352	1 166	1 186
13 years	177 278	90 682	86 596	154 901	79 398	75 503	20 255	10 200	10 055	2 417	1 216	1 201
14 years	182 580	93 504	89 076	159 326	81 658	77 668	21 127	10 784	10 343	2 560	1 264	1 296
15 to 19 years	1 007 679	507 990	499 689	882 329	446 339	435 990	114 390	56 095	58 295	13 318	6 719	6 599
15 years	195 654	99 604	96 050	171 041	87 411	83 630	22 536	11 175	11 361	2 608	1 336	1 272
16 years	201 383	103 490	97 893	176 116	90 652	85 464	23 044	11 690	11 354	2 723	1 425	1 298
17 years	202 028	102 793	99 235	176 727	90 157	86 570	23 166	11 546	11 620	2 669	1 333	1 336
18 years	201 130	100 161	100 969	176 148	88 013	88 135	22 889	11 062	11 827	2 647	1 325	1 322
19 years	207 484	101 942	105 542	182 297	90 106	92 191	22 755	10 622	12 133	2 671	1 300	1 371
20 to 24 years	1 004 919	494 190	510 729	884 100	438 124	445 976	108 133	49 501	58 632	12 894	6 465	6 429
20 years	204 093	99 985	104 108	179 320	88 447	90 873	22 408	10 312	12 096	2 641	1 296	1 345
21 years	202 141	98 784	103 357	177 963	87 615	90 348	21 703	9 904	11 799	2 595	1 312	1 283
25 to 29 years	907 679	448 273	459 406	801 675	398 974	402 701	92 643	42 597	50 046	10 579	5 367	5 212
30 to 34 years	815 697	399 928	415 769	728 504	360 221	368 283	75 072	33 910	41 162	8 963	4 471	4 492
35 to 39 years	640 594	311 241	329 353	574 810	281 375	293 435	57 082	25 526	31 556	6 319	3 060	3 259
40 to 44 years	559 229	269 713	289 516	500 493	243 180	257 313	52 123	23 105	29 018	5 440	2 623	2 817
45 to 49 years	538 718	260 370	278 348	481 469	234 440	247 029	52 225	23 510	28 715	5 104	2 542	2 562
50 to 54 years	587 889	283 276	304 613	529 608	256 495	273 113	54 173	24 821	29 352	4 851	2 478	2 373
55 to 59 years	581 948	275 126	306 822	529 855	250 760	279 095	48 967	22 850	26 117	3 878	1 964	1 914
60 to 64 years	488 563	227 180	261 383	448 339	208 638	239 701	38 104	17 571	20 533	2 669	1 324	1 345
65 to 69 years	400 761	176 850	223 911	367 396	162 172	205 224	31 664	13 929	17 735	2 114	961	1 153
70 to 74 years	305 793	125 787	180 006	282 081	115 799	166 282	22 544	9 499	13 045	1 548	700	848
75 to 79 years	216 318	80 584	135 734	199 852	74 003	125 849	15 610	6 265	9 345	1 204	561	643
80 to 84 years	138 162	46 598	91 564	129 287	43 200	86 087	8 348	3 214	5 134	632	273	359
85 years and over	108 426	32 428	75 998	101 781	30 138	71 643	6 260	2 149	4 111	431	187	244
18 years and over	7 703 310	3 633 647	4 069 663	6 917 695	3 275 638	3 642 057	708 592	320 131	388 461	71 944	35 601	36 343
62 years and over	1 452 308	592 832	859 476	1 340 906	545 713	795 193	105 593	44 695	60 898	7 389	3 384	4 005
65 years and over	1 169 460	462 247	707 213	1 080 397	425 312	655 085	84 426	35 056	49 370	5 929	2 682	3 247
Median	29.9	28.6	31.2	30.5	29.2	31.8	25 8	24 6	26.9	22.5	22.3	22.8

[1]Persons of Spanish origin may be of any race.

Table 67. Persons by Age, Race, Spanish Origin, and Sex, for States: 1980—Con.

[For meaning of symbols, see Introduction. For definitions of terms, see appendixes A and B]

States	Race — Total			Race — White			Race — Black			Spanish origin[1]		
	Both sexes	Male	Female	Both sexes	Male	Female	Both sexes	Male	Female	Both sexes	Male	Female
OKLAHOMA												
Total persons	3 025 290	1 476 705	1 548 585	2 597 791	1 266 336	1 331 455	204 674	99 411	105 263	57 419	29 895	27 524
Under 5 years	233 307	119 624	113 683	188 817	97 180	91 637	20 882	10 444	10 438	7 708	3 853	3 855
Under 1 year	50 774	25 721	25 053	40 906	20 858	20 048	4 720	2 303	2 417	1 772	860	912
1 year	46 601	23 842	22 759	37 522	19 200	18 322	4 245	2 148	2 097	1 568	800	768
2 years	45 359	23 322	22 037	36 977	19 074	17 903	3 889	1 926	1 963	1 532	781	751
3 years	45 585	23 309	22 276	36 961	19 005	17 956	3 978	1 998	1 980	1 477	708	769
4 years	44 988	23 430	21 558	36 451	19 043	17 408	4 050	2 069	1 981	1 359	704	655
5 to 9 years	229 573	117 801	111 772	186 723	95 978	90 745	19 926	10 165	9 761	6 412	3 282	3 130
5 years	45 011	23 324	21 687	36 621	19 039	17 582	3 902	1 982	1 920	1 330	700	630
6 years	43 296	22 201	21 095	35 116	17 969	17 147	3 804	1 964	1 840	1 251	668	583
7 years	45 189	23 054	22 135	36 700	18 766	17 934	3 919	1 969	1 950	1 230	597	633
8 years	46 343	23 609	22 734	37 685	19 219	18 466	4 001	2 067	1 934	1 297	636	661
9 years	49 734	25 613	24 121	40 601	20 985	19 616	4 300	2 183	2 117	1 304	681	623
10 to 14 years	230 675	118 628	112 047	188 163	96 838	91 325	19 537	9 897	9 640	5 835	2 956	2 879
10 years	48 366	24 971	23 395	39 706	20 502	19 204	3 988	2 068	1 920	1 268	629	639
11 years	46 298	23 743	22 555	37 796	19 328	18 468	3 853	1 979	1 874	1 137	567	570
12 years	44 366	22 752	21 614	36 197	18 538	17 659	3 672	1 823	1 849	1 121	562	559
13 years	44 848	22 903	21 945	36 558	18 719	17 839	3 845	1 933	1 912	1 137	595	542
14 years	46 797	24 259	22 538	37 906	19 751	18 155	4 179	2 094	2 085	1 172	603	569
15 to 19 years	278 987	144 127	134 860	228 759	117 702	111 057	24 450	12 854	11 596	6 829	3 761	3 068
15 years	51 607	26 600	25 007	41 898	21 593	20 305	4 539	2 304	2 235	1 257	654	603
16 years	53 862	27 649	26 213	44 096	22 600	21 496	4 543	2 314	2 229	1 243	652	591
17 years	55 860	29 120	26 740	45 904	23 921	21 983	4 754	2 490	2 264	1 378	744	634
18 years	56 990	29 399	27 591	46 872	23 984	22 888	5 103	2 775	2 328	1 409	833	576
19 years	60 668	31 359	29 309	49 989	25 604	24 385	5 511	2 971	2 540	1 542	878	664
20 to 24 years	284 242	144 884	139 358	237 589	119 981	117 608	23 338	12 306	11 032	7 313	4 167	3 146
20 years	59 643	30 845	28 798	49 356	25 273	24 083	5 271	2 843	2 428	1 564	894	670
21 years	57 117	28 942	28 175	47 366	23 688	23 678	4 981	2 679	2 302	1 519	870	649
25 to 29 years	252 745	127 185	125 560	216 022	108 676	107 346	17 396	8 622	8 774	5 635	3 083	2 552
30 to 34 years	222 829	110 659	112 170	193 691	96 557	97 134	13 088	6 281	6 807	4 193	2 140	2 053
35 to 39 years	182 315	89 761	92 554	160 546	79 321	81 225	9 551	4 398	5 153	3 057	1 585	1 472
40 to 44 years	154 905	76 010	78 895	136 855	67 527	69 328	8 191	3 781	4 410	2 194	1 088	1 106
45 to 49 years	148 544	72 138	76 406	132 086	64 617	67 469	7 701	3 418	4 283	1 865	954	911
50 to 54 years	150 186	72 247	77 939	134 645	65 205	69 440	7 419	3 229	4 190	1 660	806	854
55 to 59 years	150 228	71 471	78 757	135 450	64 762	70 688	7 057	3 135	3 922	1 372	658	714
60 to 64 years	130 628	60 557	70 071	118 301	55 110	63 191	6 258	2 719	3 539	1 006	504	502
65 to 69 years	122 727	54 179	68 548	110 595	48 975	61 620	6 341	2 697	3 644	782	380	402
70 to 74 years	102 006	42 904	59 102	92 448	38 927	53 521	5 252	2 186	3 066	654	279	375
75 to 79 years	73 625	28 637	44 988	66 341	25 671	40 670	4 155	1 700	2 455	478	206	272
80 to 84 years	43 787	15 605	28 182	39 832	14 100	25 732	2 270	882	1 388	261	114	147
85 years and over	33 981	10 288	23 693	30 928	9 209	21 719	1 862	697	1 165	165	79	86
18 years and over	2 170 406	1 037 283	1 133 123	1 902 190	908 226	993 964	130 493	61 797	68 696	33 586	17 754	15 832
62 years and over	451 249	186 328	264 921	408 288	168 543	239 745	23 470	9 721	13 749	2 873	1 317	1 556
65 years and over	376 126	151 613	224 513	340 144	136 882	203 262	19 880	8 162	11 718	2 340	1 058	1 282
Median	30.1	28.6	31.6	31.3	29.8	32.8	23.6	22.3	25.1	21.2	21.2	21.2
OREGON												
Total persons	2 633 105	1 296 566	1 336 539	2 490 610	1 222 845	1 267 765	37 060	19 136	17 924	65 847	35 453	30 394
Under 5 years	198 046	101 867	96 179	182 172	93 718	88 454	3 802	1 926	1 876	8 931	4 672	4 259
Under 1 year	43 082	22 001	21 081	39 519	20 167	19 352	844	413	431	2 098	1 079	1 019
1 year	39 945	20 559	19 386	36 689	18 881	17 808	763	377	386	1 843	976	867
2 years	38 905	20 018	18 887	35 785	18 382	17 403	807	446	361	1 748	915	833
3 years	38 664	20 108	18 556	35 718	18 604	17 114	677	347	330	1 667	894	773
4 years	37 450	19 181	18 269	34 461	17 684	16 777	711	343	368	1 575	808	767
5 to 9 years	189 329	96 981	92 348	175 116	89 809	85 307	3 513	1 792	1 721	7 219	3 682	3 537
5 years	36 845	18 914	17 931	33 960	17 470	16 490	702	342	360	1 493	794	699
6 years	35 613	18 167	17 446	32 747	16 682	16 065	676	346	330	1 432	725	707
7 years	36 875	18 708	18 167	34 050	17 331	16 719	690	331	359	1 395	670	725
8 years	37 686	19 381	18 305	34 891	17 932	16 959	690	365	325	1 409	728	681
9 years	42 310	21 811	20 499	39 468	20 394	19 074	755	408	347	1 490	765	725
10 to 14 years	202 503	103 554	98 949	189 206	96 744	92 462	3 586	1 851	1 735	6 727	3 450	3 277
10 years	42 855	21 954	20 901	39 929	20 481	19 448	779	400	379	1 440	733	707
11 years	40 399	20 581	19 818	37 780	19 249	18 531	673	360	313	1 362	712	650
12 years	38 887	19 857	19 030	36 316	18 546	17 770	669	340	329	1 344	682	662
13 years	39 680	20 460	19 220	37 130	19 138	17 992	704	345	359	1 271	662	609
14 years	40 682	20 702	19 980	38 051	19 330	18 721	761	406	355	1 310	661	649
15 to 19 years	225 868	114 745	111 123	210 431	106 610	103 821	3 992	2 059	1 933	7 696	4 262	3 434
15 years	42 448	21 848	20 600	39 703	20 439	19 264	726	370	356	1 379	715	664
16 years	44 544	22 858	21 686	41 659	21 405	20 254	778	386	392	1 468	778	690
17 years	46 187	23 686	22 501	43 080	22 023	21 057	833	410	423	1 587	909	678
18 years	45 582	22 954	22 628	42 488	21 308	21 180	772	403	369	1 552	867	685
19 years	47 107	23 399	23 708	43 501	21 435	22 066	883	490	393	1 710	993	717
20 to 24 years	237 860	117 847	120 013	220 408	108 301	112 107	4 119	2 242	1 877	7 914	4 589	3 325
20 years	46 124	22 804	23 320	42 620	20 885	21 735	855	458	397	1 591	956	635
21 years	45 697	22 493	23 204	42 197	20 592	21 605	817	435	382	1 547	883	664
25 to 29 years	253 530	126 883	126 647	237 238	118 119	119 119	3 821	2 073	1 748	7 314	4 144	3 170
30 to 34 years	227 623	115 103	112 520	214 980	108 384	106 596	3 004	1 641	1 363	5 754	3 126	2 628
35 to 39 years	170 660	86 031	84 629	162 466	81 797	80 669	1 985	1 048	937	3 695	2 010	1 685
40 to 44 years	133 136	67 083	66 053	126 939	63 891	63 048	1 624	842	782	2 572	1 421	1 151
45 to 49 years	119 286	58 959	60 327	114 115	56 418	57 697	1 383	702	681	1 984	1 005	979
50 to 54 years	124 319	60 354	63 965	119 718	58 171	61 547	1 345	650	695	1 779	924	855
55 to 59 years	129 919	61 999	67 920	125 820	59 993	65 827	1 357	658	699	1 403	755	648
60 to 64 years	117 690	56 047	61 643	114 706	54 578	60 128	1 142	556	586	979	492	487
65 to 69 years	105 183	49 289	55 894	102 859	48 143	54 716	956	475	481	703	351	352
70 to 74 years	79 371	35 402	43 969	77 685	34 594	43 091	724	340	384	512	251	261
75 to 79 years	55 342	22 759	32 583	54 301	22 293	32 008	391	177	214	347	174	173
80 to 84 years	35 009	12 805	22 204	34 459	12 585	21 874	165	64	101	192	84	108
85 years and over	28 431	8 858	19 573	27 991	8 697	19 294	151	40	111	126	61	65
18 years and over	1 910 048	925 772	984 276	1 819 674	878 707	940 967	23 822	12 401	11 421	38 536	21 247	17 289
62 years and over	372 577	162 140	210 437	364 911	158 542	206 369	3 012	1 386	1 626	2 400	1 165	1 235
65 years and over	303 336	129 113	174 223	297 295	126 312	170 983	2 387	1 096	1 291	1 880	921	959
Median	30.2	29.5	30.9	30.7	29.9	31.4	24.4	24.3	24.5	21.5	21.8	21.1

[1]Persons of Spanish origin may be of any race.

Table 67. Persons by Age, Race, Spanish Origin, and Sex, for States: 1980—Con.

[For meaning of symbols, see Introduction. For definitions of terms, see appendixes A and B]

States	Race — Total Both sexes	Male	Female	White Both sexes	Male	Female	Black Both sexes	Male	Female	Spanish origin¹ Both sexes	Male	Female
PENNSYLVANIA												
Total persons	11 863 895	5 682 590	6 181 305	10 652 320	5 116 879	5 535 441	1 046 810	483 860	562 950	153 961	76 530	77 431
Under 5 years	747 458	382 271	365 187	645 498	331 037	314 461	82 292	41 265	41 027	18 138	9 211	8 927
Under 1 year	158 327	80 893	77 434	136 394	69 821	66 573	17 698	8 957	8 741	3 894	1 910	1 984
1 year	149 281	76 495	72 786	129 226	66 413	62 813	16 219	8 118	8 101	3 580	1 857	1 723
2 years	148 147	75 794	72 353	128 178	65 800	62 378	16 133	8 095	8 038	3 639	1 856	1 783
3 years	145 787	74 468	71 319	125 671	64 380	61 291	16 240	8 119	8 121	3 497	1 764	1 733
4 years	145 916	74 621	71 295	126 029	64 623	61 406	16 002	7 976	8 026	3 528	1 824	1 704
5 to 9 years	805 151	412 460	392 691	693 694	358 515	340 179	87 479	44 174	43 305	17 376	8 888	8 488
5 years	147 886	75 735	72 151	129 321	65 798	62 523	15 737	7 945	7 792	3 399	1 753	1 646
6 years	147 603	75 262	72 341	123 013	65 394	62 619	15 872	7 956	7 916	3 353	1 662	1 691
7 years	157 625	80 801	76 824	136 533	70 138	66 395	17 365	8 742	8 623	3 359	1 741	1 618
8 years	166 280	85 297	80 983	144 473	74 181	70 292	18 078	9 200	8 878	3 507	1 801	1 706
9 years	185 757	95 365	90 392	161 354	83 004	78 350	20 427	10 331	10 096	3 758	1 931	1 827
10 to 14 years	931 891	476 210	455 681	813 315	416 321	396 994	101 507	51 229	50 278	17 338	8 815	8 523
10 years	183 596	93 953	89 643	159 806	81 962	77 844	20 085	10 115	9 970	3 511	1 802	1 709
11 years	181 485	92 407	89 078	158 563	80 741	77 822	19 460	9 889	9 571	3 456	1 755	1 701
12 years	181 133	92 650	88 483	157 939	81 002	76 937	19 830	9 932	9 898	3 479	1 785	1 694
13 years	188 859	96 281	92 578	165 051	84 375	80 676	20 570	10 251	10 319	3 379	1 696	1 683
14 years	196 818	100 919	95 899	171 956	88 241	83 715	21 562	11 042	10 520	3 513	1 777	1 736
15 to 19 years	1 080 610	545 210	535 400	951 349	481 094	470 255	113 188	55 924	57 264	17 279	8 689	8 590
15 years	209 999	107 428	102 571	183 887	94 224	89 663	22 909	11 589	11 320	3 434	1 708	1 726
16 years	215 188	110 076	105 112	183 764	96 707	92 057	23 283	11 787	11 496	3 434	1 758	1 676
17 years	213 609	109 234	104 375	187 040	95 928	91 112	23 417	11 675	11 742	3 458	1 731	1 727
18 years	216 129	107 026	109 103	191 212	94 949	96 263	21 759	10 453	11 306	3 406	1 718	1 688
19 years	225 685	111 446	114 239	204 446	99 286	101 160	21 820	10 420	11 400	3 547	1 774	1 773
20 to 24 years	1 059 815	522 900	536 915	942 427	468 190	474 237	101 185	46 397	54 788	15 946	8 119	7 827
20 years	221 397	108 904	112 493	196 562	97 181	99 381	21 450	9 950	11 500	3 452	1 786	1 666
21 years	218 843	107 312	111 531	194 917	96 334	98 583	20 612	9 246	11 366	3 280	1 685	1 595
25 to 29 years	945 051	468 512	476 539	842 273	420 637	421 636	86 383	39 768	46 615	13 506	6 671	6 835
30 to 34 years	847 847	416 215	431 632	759 695	376 023	383 672	72 531	32 761	39 770	11 808	5 666	6 142
35 to 39 years	682 283	330 811	351 472	613 488	300 182	313 306	57 088	24 888	32 200	8 760	4 179	4 581
40 to 44 years	591 789	284 324	307 465	531 884	257 699	274 185	51 151	22 162	28 989	7 140	3 471	3 669
45 to 49 years	600 257	286 858	313 399	542 899	261 546	281 353	50 930	22 177	28 753	6 030	3 021	3 009
50 to 54 years	695 755	329 850	365 905	636 816	303 722	333 094	53 892	23 706	30 186	5 371	2 716	2 655
55 to 59 years	712 074	332 033	380 041	655 147	306 906	349 241	52 100	23 331	28 769	4 386	2 100	2 286
60 to 64 years	632 981	289 152	343 829	583 839	269 814	319 025	41 424	18 105	23 319	3 369	1 564	1 805
65 to 69 years	537 045	235 802	301 243	499 524	220 229	279 295	35 230	14 596	20 634	2 654	1 194	1 460
70 to 74 years	407 020	166 668	240 352	379 701	155 627	224 074	25 680	10 372	15 308	1 954	891	1 063
75 to 79 years	282 000	104 968	177 032	262 477	97 382	165 095	18 310	7 101	11 209	1 520	763	757
80 to 84 years	174 908	59 328	115 580	164 617	55 351	109 266	9 620	3 679	5 941	815	367	448
85 years and over	129 960	39 018	90 942	122 677	36 604	86 073	6 820	2 225	4 595	571	205	366
18 years and over	8 740 599	4 084 911	4 655 688	7 935 122	3 724 147	4 210 975	705 923	312 141	393 782	90 783	44 419	46 364
62 years and over	1 900 484	774 023	1 126 461	1 773 960	722 734	1 051 226	118 761	47 992	70 769	9 458	4 331	5 127
65 years and over	1 530 933	605 784	925 149	1 428 996	565 193	863 803	95 660	37 973	57 687	7 514	3 420	4 094
Median	32.1	30.4	33.6	32.7	31.1	34.4	27.1	25.3	28.7	22.0	21.5	22.6
RHODE ISLAND												
Total persons	947 154	451 251	495 903	895 692	426 601	470 091	27 584	13 351	14 233	19 707	9 678	10 029
Under 5 years	56 692	28 887	27 805	51 354	26 188	25 166	2 803	1 424	1 379	2 212	1 107	1 105
Under 1 year	12 075	6 215	5 860	10 917	5 627	5 290	600	307	293	521	259	262
1 year	11 471	5 756	5 715	10 365	5 199	5 166	574	294	280	449	218	231
2 years	11 335	5 771	5 564	10 279	5 227	5 052	565	287	278	431	209	222
3 years	11 017	5 648	5 369	9 951	5 109	4 842	546	279	267	422	217	205
4 years	10 794	5 497	5 297	9 842	5 026	4 816	518	257	261	389	204	185
5 to 9 years	61 465	31 458	30 007	55 514	28 914	27 600	2 693	1 348	1 345	1 966	1 013	953
5 years	11 135	5 692	5 443	10 202	5 223	4 979	484	244	240	404	203	201
6 years	11 276	5 837	5 439	10 353	5 357	4 996	489	236	253	389	203	186
7 years	11 916	6 106	5 810	10 926	5 600	5 326	544	261	283	379	199	180
8 years	12 708	6 497	6 211	11 691	5 963	5 728	556	289	267	371	191	180
9 years	14 430	7 326	7 104	13 342	6 771	6 571	620	318	302	423	217	206
10 to 14 years	74 170	37 965	36 205	69 118	35 362	33 756	2 806	1 424	1 382	1 933	988	945
10 years	14 520	7 380	7 140	13 452	6 847	6 605	583	303	280	405	194	211
11 years	14 075	7 143	6 932	13 102	6 646	6 456	539	263	276	375	170	205
12 years	14 634	7 614	7 020	13 666	7 086	6 580	535	295	240	391	210	181
13 years	15 158	7 706	7 452	14 142	7 190	6 952	567	273	294	398	228	170
14 years	15 783	8 122	7 661	14 756	7 593	7 163	582	290	292	364	186	178
15 to 19 years	89 773	44 771	45 002	84 003	41 902	42 101	3 265	1 614	1 651	2 026	1 002	1 024
15 years	16 810	8 541	8 269	15 729	7 992	7 737	626	316	310	389	194	195
16 years	16 878	8 611	8 267	15 789	8 057	7 732	616	305	311	380	181	199
17 years	16 836	8 474	8 362	15 770	7 958	7 812	592	285	307	368	193	175
18 years	18 747	9 181	9 566	17 564	8 580	8 984	657	338	319	448	221	227
19 years	20 502	9 964	10 538	19 151	9 315	9 836	774	370	404	441	213	228
20 to 24 years	90 231	44 292	45 939	84 547	41 536	43 011	3 150	1 513	1 637	2 186	1 117	1 069
20 years	19 617	9 583	10 034	18 378	8 993	9 385	642	313	329	437	218	219
21 years	19 114	9 259	9 855	17 942	8 712	9 230	662	311	351	432	221	211
25 to 29 years	76 215	37 646	38 569	71 473	35 225	36 248	2 539	1 287	1 252	1 835	888	947
30 to 34 years	69 820	34 583	35 237	66 030	32 688	33 342	2 008	1 001	1 007	1 657	823	834
35 to 39 years	54 393	26 577	27 816	51 658	25 270	26 388	1 391	645	746	1 189	568	621
40 to 44 years	44 470	21 513	22 957	41 939	20 333	21 606	1 318	594	724	942	457	485
45 to 49 years	44 708	21 438	23 270	42 607	20 467	22 140	1 161	526	635	806	390	416
50 to 54 years	53 096	25 210	27 886	51 070	24 229	26 841	1 195	587	608	777	363	414
55 to 59 years	55 748	26 182	29 566	54 105	25 416	28 689	944	451	493	614	309	305
60 to 64 years	49 451	22 460	26 991	48 137	21 926	26 211	741	305	436	525	225	300
65 to 69 years	42 414	18 346	24 068	41 409	17 914	23 495	559	246	313	394	177	217
70 to 74 years	33 148	12 994	20 154	32 450	12 716	19 734	408	156	252	271	121	150
75 to 79 years	23 891	8 619	15 272	23 404	8 429	14 975	283	110	173	174	62	112
80 to 84 years	15 491	4 947	10 544	15 170	4 819	10 351	174	67	107	111	39	72
85 years and over	11 978	3 363	8 615	11 704	3 267	8 437	146	53	93	89	29	60
18 years and over	704 303	327 315	376 988	672 418	312 130	360 288	17 448	8 249	9 199	12 459	6 002	6 457
62 years and over	155 637	61 202	94 435	152 126	59 782	92 344	1 979	800	1 179	1 328	549	779
65 years and over	126 922	48 269	78 653	124 137	47 145	76 992	1 570	632	938	1 039	428	611
Median	31.7	30.1	33.3	32.3	30.6	33.9	23.5	22.9	24.1	23.9	23.3	24.6

¹Persons of Spanish origin may be of any race.

Table 67. Persons by Age, Race, Spanish Origin, and Sex, for States: 1980—Con.

[For meaning of symbols, see Introduction. For definitions of terms, see appendixes A and B]

States	Race									Spanish origin[1]		
	Total			White			Black					
	Both sexes	Male	Female	Both sexes	Male	Female	Both sexes	Male	Female	Both sexes	Male	Female
SOUTH CAROLINA												
Total persons	3 121 820	1 518 013	1 603 807	2 147 224	1 057 161	1 090 063	948 623	447 793	500 830	33 426	17 002	16 424
Under 5 years	238 516	121 766	116 750	145 614	74 850	70 764	90 218	45 523	44 695	3 116	1 581	1 535
Under 1 year	50 686	25 913	24 773	30 839	15 878	14 961	19 272	9 727	9 545	672	336	336
1 year	47 466	24 334	23 132	28 897	15 016	13 881	18 046	9 062	8 984	619	304	315
2 years	47 504	24 188	23 316	29 156	14 879	14 277	17 839	9 042	8 797	588	307	281
3 years	47 130	24 082	23 048	28 827	14 821	14 006	17 770	8 989	8 781	620	315	305
4 years	45 730	23 249	22 481	27 895	14 256	13 639	17 291	8 703	8 588	617	319	298
5 to 9 years	253 643	129 490	124 153	157 514	81 134	76 380	93 533	47 049	46 484	2 992	1 571	1 421
5 years	47 533	24 121	23 412	29 292	15 026	14 266	17 727	8 854	8 873	593	317	276
6 years	47 763	24 517	23 246	29 298	15 136	14 162	17 972	9 128	8 844	562	293	269
7 years	50 790	25 888	24 902	31 387	16 149	15 238	18 826	9 429	9 397	630	329	301
8 years	51 848	26 450	25 398	32 293	16 598	15 695	19 079	9 610	9 469	557	311	246
9 years	55 709	28 514	27 195	35 244	18 225	17 019	19 929	10 028	9 901	650	321	329
10 to 14 years	266 179	135 477	130 702	164 458	84 483	79 975	99 601	49 911	49 690	3 194	1 560	1 634
10 years	54 100	27 657	26 443	34 041	17 589	16 452	19 567	9 824	9 743	614	324	290
11 years	52 690	26 882	25 808	33 172	16 981	16 191	19 074	9 663	9 411	627	313	314
12 years	51 244	26 216	25 028	31 571	16 320	15 251	19 230	9 660	9 570	623	286	337
13 years	52 749	26 714	26 035	32 337	16 567	15 770	20 039	9 951	10 088	656	317	339
14 years	55 396	28 008	27 388	33 337	17 026	16 311	21 691	10 813	10 878	674	320	354
15 to 19 years	317 234	163 108	154 126	200 069	104 360	95 709	114 518	57 174	57 344	4 418	2 564	1 854
15 years	59 621	30 263	29 358	36 475	18 600	17 875	22 762	11 445	11 317	713	349	364
16 years	61 682	31 324	30 358	38 051	19 446	18 605	23 295	11 706	11 589	746	402	344
17 years	62 325	32 396	29 929	38 751	20 372	18 379	23 092	11 748	11 344	828	487	341
18 years	65 052	33 620	31 432	41 626	21 950	19 676	22 791	11 280	11 511	1 034	629	405
19 years	68 554	35 505	33 049	45 166	23 992	21 174	22 578	10 995	11 583	1 097	697	400
20 to 24 years	313 738	159 883	153 855	211 194	110 804	100 390	99 012	46 972	52 040	4 446	2 652	1 794
20 years	67 365	34 674	32 691	44 916	23 926	20 990	21 688	10 272	11 416	1 075	650	425
21 years	64 313	33 130	31 183	43 507	23 247	20 260	20 037	9 420	10 617	950	583	367
25 to 29 years	273 131	135 275	137 862	186 268	94 106	92 162	83 893	39 766	44 127	3 066	1 552	1 514
30 to 34 years	243 604	120 580	123 024	175 026	88 118	86 908	65 737	31 176	34 561	2 392	1 157	1 235
35 to 39 years	192 166	94 996	97 170	143 339	72 292	71 047	46 906	21 789	25 117	1 789	852	937
40 to 44 years	158 339	76 628	81 711	118 450	58 537	59 913	38 482	17 418	21 064	1 495	666	829
45 to 49 years	150 057	71 739	78 318	113 323	55 520	57 803	35 766	15 826	19 940	1 272	570	702
50 to 54 years	149 126	70 040	79 086	112 117	54 065	58 052	36 330	15 689	20 641	1 144	531	613
55 to 59 years	149 937	69 431	80 506	114 323	53 963	60 360	35 141	15 259	19 882	1 137	532	605
60 to 64 years	128 816	58 324	70 492	95 574	43 833	51 741	32 869	14 345	18 524	965	426	539
65 to 69 years	110 235	47 436	62 799	79 405	34 569	44 836	30 534	12 742	17 792	767	327	440
70 to 74 years	79 292	31 574	47 718	58 668	23 282	35 386	20 380	8 199	12 181	570	228	342
75 to 79 years	50 457	18 156	32 301	36 942	13 101	23 841	13 389	5 014	8 375	348	134	214
80 to 84 years	27 340	8 699	18 641	20 631	6 435	14 196	6 659	2 252	4 407	164	52	112
85 years and over	20 004	5 411	14 593	14 309	3 709	10 600	5 655	1 689	3 966	151	47	104
18 years and over	2 179 854	1 037 297	1 142 557	1 566 361	758 276	808 085	596 122	270 411	325 711	21 837	11 052	10 785
62 years and over	360 872	144 347	216 525	264 566	105 939	158 627	95 344	38 033	57 311	2 560	1 049	1 511
65 years and over	287 328	111 276	176 052	209 955	81 096	128 859	76 617	29 896	46 721	2 000	788	1 212
Median	28.0	26.7	29 4	30.2	28.8	31.7	23.8	22.5	25.0	23.1	22.0	24.9
SOUTH DAKOTA												
Total persons	690 768	340 683	350 085	639 669	315 343	324 326	2 144	1 407	737	4 023	2 091	1 932
Under 5 years	58 446	29 770	28 676	51 002	26 094	24 908	283	145	138	621	309	312
Under 1 year	13 157	6 628	6 529	11 455	5 788	5 667	55	23	32	158	86	72
1 year	11 857	5 973	5 884	10 445	5 291	5 154	61	33	28	141	68	73
2 years	11 335	5 761	5 574	9 932	5 106	4 826	63	32	31	104	47	57
3 years	11 175	5 769	5 406	9 722	4 990	4 732	53	29	24	117	59	58
4 years	10 922	5 639	5 283	9 448	4 919	4 529	51	28	23	101	49	52
5 to 9 years	52 871	26 810	26 061	46 278	23 510	22 768	187	103	84	475	242	233
5 years	10 547	5 404	5 143	9 227	4 730	4 497	52	35	17	102	51	51
6 years	10 251	5 114	5 137	8 962	4 489	4 473	33	18	15	90	51	39
7 years	10 262	5 230	5 032	8 927	4 579	4 348	30	11	19	90	45	45
8 years	10 439	5 297	5 142	9 149	4 633	4 516	36	15	21	93	54	39
9 years	11 372	5 765	5 607	10 013	5 079	4 934	36	24	12	100	41	59
10 to 14 years	54 400	27 743	26 657	48 116	24 552	23 564	125	74	51	429	227	202
10 years	11 077	5 765	5 312	9 806	5 106	4 700	35	18	17	97	51	46
11 years	10 653	5 439	5 214	9 407	4 819	4 588	14	6	8	79	50	29
12 years	10 422	5 281	5 141	9 198	4 682	4 516	28	21	7	93	50	43
13 years	10 756	5 423	5 333	9 540	4 790	4 750	22	15	7	79	38	41
14 years	11 492	5 835	5 657	10 165	5 155	5 010	26	14	12	81	38	43
15 to 19 years	68 641	34 616	34 025	62 326	31 349	30 977	250	175	75	508	280	228
15 years	12 616	6 336	6 280	11 276	5 666	5 610	22	10	12	91	51	40
16 years	13 522	6 867	6 655	12 247	6 201	6 046	24	14	10	113	55	58
17 years	13 751	7 065	6 686	12 473	6 377	6 096	23	13	10	97	51	46
18 years	13 843	6 934	6 909	12 666	6 325	6 341	68	55	13	98	59	39
19 years	14 909	7 414	7 495	13 664	6 780	6 884	113	83	30	109	64	45
20 to 24 years	66 553	33 789	32 764	61 418	31 117	30 301	474	349	125	503	278	225
20 years	14 559	7 303	7 256	13 359	6 663	6 696	126	95	31	109	65	44
21 years	13 548	6 838	6 710	12 456	6 256	6 200	116	87	29	109	54	55
25 to 29 years	56 868	29 122	27 746	52 685	27 046	25 639	340	243	97	356	206	150
30 to 34 years	45 959	23 739	22 220	42 786	22 191	20 595	138	106	32	304	146	158
35 to 39 years	35 251	17 522	17 729	32 951	16 436	16 515	106	68	38	177	80	97
40 to 44 years	31 181	15 263	15 918	29 275	14 345	14 930	68	42	26	137	62	75
45 to 49 years	31 399	15 295	16 104	29 650	14 495	15 155	42	26	16	121	60	61
50 to 54 years	33 569	16 693	16 876	32 145	16 037	16 108	28	19	9	112	62	50
55 to 59 years	33 567	16 782	16 785	32 285	16 158	16 127	23	14	9	90	49	41
60 to 64 years	31 044	15 074	15 970	30 016	14 580	15 436	24	14	10	59	29	30
65 to 69 years	27 640	12 900	14 740	26 806	12 508	14 298	20	9	11	46	20	26
70 to 74 years	22 875	10 138	12 737	22 280	9 872	12 408	12	6	6	29	20	9
75 to 79 years	17 699	7 288	10 411	17 267	7 092	10 175	12	6	6	24	7	17
80 to 84 years	12 378	4 708	7 670	12 142	4 612	7 530	8	6	2	15	6	9
85 years and over	10 427	3 431	6 996	10 241	3 349	6 892	4	2	2	17	8	9
18 years and over	485 162	236 092	249 070	458 277	222 943	235 334	1 480	1 048	432	2 197	1 156	1 041
62 years and over	109 281	47 230	62 051	106 407	45 920	60 487	69	35	34	164	75	89
65 years and over	91 019	38 465	52 554	88 736	37 433	51 303	56	29	27	131	61	70
Median	28.8	27.9	29 8	29.8	28.8	30.9	21.9	22.5	20.7	19.8	19.8	19.8

[1] Persons of Spanish origin may be of any race.

Table 67. Persons by Age, Race, Spanish Origin, and Sex, for States: 1980—Con.

[For meaning of symbols, see Introduction. For definitions of terms, see appendixes A and B]

States	Race Total Both sexes	Male	Female	White Both sexes	Male	Female	Black Both sexes	Male	Female	Spanish origin[1] Both sexes	Male	Female
TENNESSEE												
Total persons	4 591 120	2 216 600	2 374 520	3 835 452	1 862 465	1 972 987	725 942	339 168	386 774	34 077	16 880	17 197
Under 5 years	326 088	167 368	158 720	256 082	131 846	124 236	66 967	33 962	33 005	2 945	1 575	1 370
Under 1 year	69 334	35 577	33 757	53 843	27 782	26 061	14 811	7 460	7 351	659	370	289
1 year	65 440	33 599	31 841	51 188	26 309	24 879	13 687	7 003	6 684	585	311	274
2 years	64 526	33 101	31 425	50 955	26 252	24 703	12 991	6 558	6 433	577	301	276
3 years	63 782	32 684	31 098	50 395	25 841	24 554	12 769	6 509	6 260	567	293	274
4 years	63 006	32 407	30 599	49 701	25 662	24 039	12 709	6 432	6 277	557	300	257
5 to 9 years	349 928	179 209	170 719	278 417	142 948	135 469	68 852	34 955	33 897	2 857	1 358	1 499
5 years	65 387	33 401	31 986	51 865	26 542	25 323	12 974	6 604	6 370	568	269	299
6 years	65 680	33 800	31 880	52 008	26 759	25 249	13 177	6 790	6 387	525	264	261
7 years	69 105	35 336	33 769	54 832	28 059	26 773	13 733	7 021	6 712	607	282	325
8 years	71 635	36 673	34 962	57 255	29 473	27 782	13 854	6 927	6 927	556	254	302
9 years	78 121	39 999	38 122	62 457	32 115	30 342	15 114	7 613	7 501	601	289	312
10 to 14 years	369 940	189 403	180 537	296 208	152 427	143 781	71 570	35 867	35 703	2 969	1 518	1 451
10 years	76 368	39 232	37 136	61 272	31 548	29 724	14 598	7 420	7 178	610	327	283
11 years	72 478	36 924	35 554	58 232	29 758	28 474	13 820	6 949	6 871	573	278	295
12 years	70 769	36 324	34 445	56 662	29 319	27 343	13 682	6 787	6 895	545	267	278
13 years	73 431	37 489	35 942	58 930	30 230	28 700	14 081	7 040	7 041	583	294	289
14 years	76 894	39 434	37 460	61 112	31 572	29 540	15 389	7 671	7 718	658	352	306
15 to 19 years	430 253	219 497	210 756	344 189	176 592	167 597	83 276	41 288	41 988	4 033	2 256	1 777
15 years	83 159	42 233	40 926	66 622	33 947	32 675	16 126	8 079	8 047	672	351	321
16 years	84 900	43 580	41 320	67 837	34 985	32 852	16 650	8 378	8 272	710	374	336
17 years	84 545	43 371	41 174	67 312	34 604	32 708	16 762	8 508	8 254	779	425	354
18 years	87 012	44 558	42 454	69 633	35 990	33 643	16 669	8 143	8 526	914	532	382
19 years	90 637	45 755	44 882	72 785	37 066	35 719	17 069	8 180	8 889	958	574	384
20 to 24 years	423 413	209 291	214 122	342 693	171 073	171 620	76 705	35 843	40 862	3 971	2 224	1 747
20 years	88 513	44 090	44 423	71 120	35 773	35 347	16 570	7 813	8 757	915	533	382
21 years	84 813	41 649	43 164	68 590	34 076	34 514	15 441	7 098	8 343	806	430	376
25 to 29 years	387 987	190 309	197 678	319 961	158 631	161 330	64 290	29 804	34 486	2 876	1 454	1 422
30 to 34 years	356 636	175 239	181 397	304 637	151 250	153 387	48 772	22 499	26 273	2 236	1 065	1 171
35 to 39 years	287 670	140 666	147 004	251 174	124 376	126 798	34 221	15 155	19 066	1 858	841	1 017
40 to 44 years	246 171	119 172	126 999	214 692	105 565	109 127	29 908	12 822	17 086	1 608	714	894
45 to 49 years	231 276	110 242	121 034	201 457	97 474	103 983	28 590	12 229	16 361	1 558	732	826
50 to 54 years	234 090	110 846	123 244	204 259	97 963	106 296	28 983	12 500	16 483	1 408	679	729
55 to 59 years	230 307	106 819	123 488	202 176	94 506	107 670	27 552	12 071	15 481	1 294	554	740
60 to 64 years	199 773	90 901	108 872	174 345	79 795	94 550	24 979	10 920	14 059	1 274	589	685
65 to 69 years	180 932	79 489	101 443	155 496	68 683	86 813	25 042	10 663	14 379	1 133	491	642
70 to 74 years	142 095	59 030	83 065	122 279	50 684	71 595	19 484	8 242	11 242	886	372	514
75 to 79 years	97 293	37 063	60 230	83 564	31 534	52 030	13 512	5 459	8 053	642	255	387
80 to 84 years	55 825	19 426	36 399	48 433	16 570	31 863	7 272	2 825	4 447	296	112	184
85 years and over	41 443	12 630	28 813	35 390	10 548	24 842	5 967	2 064	3 903	233	91	142
18 years and over	3 292 560	1 551 436	1 741 124	2 802 974	1 331 708	1 471 266	469 015	209 419	259 596	23 145	11 279	11 866
62 years and over	633 222	260 023	373 199	546 126	224 097	322 029	85 686	35 460	50 226	3 914	1 649	2 265
65 years and over	517 588	207 638	309 950	445 162	178 019	267 143	71 277	29 253	42 024	3 190	1 321	1 869
Median	30.1	28.7	31.4	31.3	29.9	32.6	24.7	23.2	26.0	25.4	23.7	27.5
TEXAS												
Total persons	14 229 191	6 998 723	7 230 468	11 198 441	5 505 355	5 693 086	1 710 175	822 917	887 258	2 985 824	1 486 944	1 498 880
Under 5 years	1 169 061	597 435	571 626	855 726	438 715	417 011	160 354	80 681	79 673	352 359	179 553	172 806
Under 1 year	256 701	130 688	126 013	187 040	95 577	91 463	35 513	17 766	17 747	77 282	39 234	38 048
1 year	232 008	118 906	113 102	169 970	87 426	82 544	32 094	16 131	15 963	68 552	35 390	33 162
2 years	227 491	116 258	111 233	167 203	85 739	81 464	30 912	15 480	15 432	67 983	34 685	33 298
3 years	227 103	116 133	110 970	166 343	85 254	81 089	30 934	15 707	15 227	69 015	35 021	33 994
4 years	225 758	115 450	110 308	165 170	84 719	80 451	30 901	15 597	15 304	69 527	35 223	34 304
5 to 9 years	1 169 889	596 734	573 155	859 433	439 632	419 801	163 782	82 782	81 000	346 310	175 958	170 352
5 years	224 021	114 188	109 833	164 184	83 740	80 444	30 428	15 426	15 002	68 408	34 887	33 721
6 years	222 436	113 515	108 921	162 122	83 068	79 054	31 254	15 779	15 475	67 963	34 373	33 590
7 years	231 939	118 502	113 437	169 429	86 947	82 482	33 030	16 669	16 361	69 649	35 612	34 037
8 years	235 922	120 364	115 558	173 761	88 911	84 850	33 391	16 869	16 522	68 763	34 998	33 765
9 years	255 571	130 165	125 406	189 937	96 966	92 971	35 679	18 039	17 640	71 327	36 088	35 239
10 to 14 years	1 179 988	602 487	577 501	875 515	448 766	426 749	168 051	84 437	83 614	326 438	165 585	160 853
10 years	249 151	127 181	121 970	186 201	95 506	90 695	34 125	17 060	17 065	69 111	35 028	34 083
11 years	235 813	120 349	115 464	176 054	90 131	85 923	32 427	16 329	16 098	65 305	33 176	32 129
12 years	227 489	116 278	111 211	168 438	86 537	81 901	32 526	16 315	16 211	63 442	32 053	31 389
13 years	230 855	117 688	113 167	170 441	87 220	83 221	33 778	17 027	16 751	63 742	32 216	31 526
14 years	236 680	120 991	115 689	174 381	89 372	85 009	35 195	17 706	17 489	64 838	33 112	31 726
15 to 19 years	1 352 533	691 034	661 321	1 013 523	517 035	496 488	191 606	96 869	94 737	337 270	173 110	164 160
15 years	256 119	130 043	126 076	190 422	96 908	93 514	37 022	18 576	18 446	68 252	34 461	33 791
16 years	262 483	134 147	128 336	196 803	100 674	96 129	37 270	18 773	18 497	67 230	34 530	32 700
17 years	268 566	137 581	130 985	201 774	102 956	98 818	37 460	19 145	18 315	68 264	35 236	33 028
18 years	273 322	140 058	133 264	205 625	105 102	100 523	38 446	19 441	19 005	65 882	34 119	31 763
19 years	291 865	149 205	142 660	218 899	111 395	107 504	41 408	20 934	20 474	67 642	34 764	32 878
20 to 24 years	1 420 358	721 080	699 278	1 081 253	546 253	535 000	186 534	93 484	93 050	311 146	159 558	151 588
20 years	288 527	147 407	141 120	217 228	110 283	106 945	39 858	20 282	19 576	65 789	33 796	31 993
21 years	278 789	141 438	137 351	211 180	106 494	104 686	37 619	19 008	18 611	61 620	31 501	30 119
25 to 29 years	1 302 054	657 264	644 790	1 008 762	509 856	498 906	156 093	75 493	80 600	269 764	136 954	132 810
30 to 34 years	1 124 483	562 178	562 305	895 143	449 835	445 308	120 681	56 940	63 741	221 970	110 041	111 929
35 to 39 years	880 229	437 868	442 361	713 727	357 240	356 487	90 486	42 301	48 185	161 016	78 745	82 271
40 to 44 years	723 002	355 987	367 015	589 209	292 449	296 760	75 568	34 691	40 877	129 909	62 135	67 774
45 to 49 years	681 391	333 884	347 507	560 354	277 250	283 104	71 731	32 971	38 760	116 129	55 015	61 114
50 to 54 years	680 275	328 145	352 130	567 168	276 093	291 075	69 258	31 416	37 842	109 183	50 832	58 351
55 to 59 years	643 396	306 388	337 008	546 627	261 629	284 998	61 457	27 997	33 460	91 621	43 243	48 378
60 to 64 years	531 549	249 336	282 213	456 722	215 369	241 353	51 700	23 048	28 652	62 360	29 066	33 294
65 to 69 years	476 110	212 743	263 367	407 439	182 400	225 039	49 131	21 417	27 714	55 253	25 222	30 031
70 to 74 years	371 155	158 024	213 131	317 776	134 638	183 138	38 721	16 610	22 111	41 663	19 087	22 576
75 to 79 years	261 280	101 748	159 532	222 963	85 610	137 353	28 051	11 583	16 468	29 146	12 923	16 223
80 to 84 years	150 594	52 225	98 369	130 872	44 359	86 513	14 799	5 753	9 046	14 233	5 935	8 298
85 years and over	112 022	34 163	77 859	96 229	28 226	68 003	12 172	4 444	7 728	10 054	3 982	6 072
18 years and over	9 923 085	4 800 296	5 122 789	8 018 768	3 877 704	4 141 064	1 106 236	518 523	587 713	1 756 971	861 621	895 350
62 years and over	1 675 372	700 417	974 955	1 437 576	597 826	839 750	172 124	72 722	99 402	184 703	83 168	101 535
65 years and over	1 371 161	558 903	812 258	1 175 279	475 233	700 046	142 874	59 807	83 067	150 349	67 149	83 200
Median	28.0	27.1	29.1	29.5	28.5	30.6	24.6	23.5	25.7	22.1	21.5	22.6

[1]Persons of Spanish origin may be of any race.

GENERAL POPULATION CHARACTERISTICS

UNITED STATES SUMMARY 1—179

Table 67. Persons by Age, Race, Spanish Origin, and Sex, for States: 1980—Con.

[For meaning of symbols, see Introduction. For definitions of terms, see appendixes A and B]

States	Total Both sexes	Total Male	Total Female	White Both sexes	White Male	White Female	Black Both sexes	Black Male	Black Female	Spanish origin[1] Both sexes	Spanish Male	Spanish Female
UTAH												
Total persons	1 461 037	724 501	736 536	1 382 550	684 092	698 458	9 225	5 382	3 843	60 302	30 785	29 517
Under 5 years	189 962	97 310	92 652	179 243	91 942	87 301	959	475	484	9 200	4 722	4 478
Under 1 year	42 233	21 662	20 571	39 777	20 438	19 339	216	102	114	2 117	1 085	1 032
1 year	39 408	20 177	19 231	37 220	19 080	18 140	210	118	92	1 912	964	948
2 years	38 240	19 546	18 694	36 107	18 500	17 607	165	73	92	1 854	919	935
3 years	36 447	18 643	17 804	34 424	17 614	16 810	197	96	101	1 685	894	791
4 years	33 634	17 282	16 352	31 715	16 310	15 405	171	86	85	1 632	860	772
5 to 9 years	146 187	74 483	71 704	137 575	70 197	67 378	764	383	381	7 250	3 633	3 617
5 years	31 471	15 945	15 526	29 695	15 062	14 633	155	75	80	1 527	775	752
6 years	29 198	14 970	14 228	27 448	14 094	13 354	147	66	81	1 403	694	709
7 years	28 650	14 614	14 036	26 950	13 748	13 202	159	87	72	1 429	735	694
8 years	27 665	14 164	13 501	26 011	13 333	12 678	146	77	69	1 388	689	699
9 years	29 203	14 790	14 413	27 471	13 960	13 511	157	78	79	1 503	740	763
10 to 14 years	125 681	64 228	61 453	117 952	60 331	57 621	659	327	332	6 401	3 234	3 167
10 years	27 394	14 031	13 363	25 766	13 226	12 540	149	77	72	1 367	677	690
11 years	25 509	13 038	12 471	24 014	12 273	11 741	119	56	63	1 274	640	634
12 years	24 324	12 381	11 943	22 829	11 621	11 208	132	67	65	1 222	610	612
13 years	24 560	12 564	11 996	22 971	11 771	11 200	136	66	70	1 298	664	634
14 years	23 894	12 214	11 680	22 372	11 440	10 932	123	61	62	1 240	643	597
15 to 19 years	138 903	69 021	69 882	128 710	63 538	65 172	1 497	986	511	7 069	3 662	3 407
15 years	24 998	12 658	12 340	23 223	11 759	11 464	162	92	70	1 314	653	661
16 years	26 092	13 215	12 877	24 198	12 223	11 975	237	138	99	1 424	731	693
17 years	27 185	13 955	13 230	25 061	12 776	12 285	343	227	116	1 430	796	634
18 years	29 809	14 920	14 889	27 695	13 727	13 968	363	263	100	1 398	731	667
19 years	30 819	14 273	16 546	28 533	13 053	15 480	392	266	126	1 503	751	752
20 to 24 years	155 676	75 915	79 761	145 541	70 409	75 132	1 455	972	483	6 876	3 622	3 254
20 years	28 716	11 995	16 721	26 616	10 838	15 778	334	250	84	1 414	731	683
21 years	31 158	14 724	16 434	29 017	13 565	15 452	349	238	111	1 406	704	702
25 to 29 years	135 087	68 860	66 227	126 517	64 327	62 190	989	629	360	5 855	3 048	2 807
30 to 34 years	105 688	53 430	52 258	99 828	50 386	49 442	674	407	267	4 294	2 152	2 142
35 to 39 years	79 178	39 561	39 617	75 352	37 604	37 748	413	237	176	2 948	1 468	1 480
40 to 44 years	63 628	31 574	32 054	60 749	30 115	30 634	337	188	149	2 309	1 196	1 113
45 to 49 years	57 021	28 201	28 820	54 737	27 074	27 663	266	150	116	1 965	990	975
50 to 54 years	55 845	27 594	28 251	53 659	26 503	27 156	279	152	127	1 788	936	852
55 to 59 years	52 701	25 604	27 097	50 966	24 711	26 255	288	153	135	1 377	702	675
60 to 64 years	46 260	22 152	24 108	44 968	21 553	23 415	215	114	101	978	455	523
65 to 69 years	38 183	17 636	20 547	37 274	17 201	20 073	163	91	72	735	326	409
70 to 74 years	29 637	13 031	16 606	28 988	12 694	16 294	123	50	73	591	299	292
75 to 79 years	20 242	8 263	11 979	19 813	8 056	11 757	77	40	37	348	172	176
80 to 84 years	12 306	4 627	7 679	12 039	4 527	7 512	34	17	17	181	96	85
85 years and over	8 852	3 011	5 841	8 639	2 924	5 715	33	11	22	137	72	65
18 years and over	920 932	448 652	472 280	875 298	424 864	450 434	6 101	3 740	2 361	33 283	17 016	16 267
62 years and over	135 978	59 359	76 619	132 826	57 884	74 942	545	266	279	2 516	1 212	1 304
65 years and over	109 220	46 568	62 652	106 753	45 402	61 351	430	209	221	1 992	965	1 027
Median	24.2	23.8	24.5	24.4	24.0	24.8	22.2	22.2	22.2	20.2	20.2	20.1
VERMONT												
Total persons	511 456	249 080	262 376	506 736	246 670	260 066	1 135	645	490	3 304	1 634	1 670
Under 5 years	35 998	18 480	17 518	35 541	18 245	17 296	94	54	40	256	122	134
Under 1 year	7 682	3 978	3 704	7 597	3 934	3 663	17	9	8	43	19	24
1 year	7 249	3 703	3 546	7 152	3 653	3 499	24	16	8	53	26	27
2 years	7 046	3 594	3 452	6 950	3 546	3 404	19	8	11	58	29	29
3 years	7 102	3 629	3 473	7 016	3 586	3 430	18	13	5	55	25	30
4 years	6 919	3 576	3 343	6 826	3 526	3 300	16	8	8	47	23	24
5 to 9 years	37 855	19 507	18 348	37 323	19 243	18 080	104	51	53	255	141	114
5 years	7 013	3 660	3 353	6 914	3 609	3 305	18	8	10	46	28	18
6 years	6 769	3 465	3 304	6 671	3 418	3 253	19	10	9	38	21	17
7 years	7 501	3 837	3 664	7 384	3 778	3 606	19	8	11	52	28	24
8 years	7 788	4 014	3 774	7 675	3 953	3 722	19	12	7	59	28	31
9 years	8 784	4 531	4 253	8 679	4 485	4 194	29	13	16	60	36	24
10 to 14 years	42 650	21 930	20 720	42 214	21 712	20 502	121	72	49	292	140	152
10 years	8 717	4 540	4 177	8 615	4 486	4 129	21	12	9	65	36	29
11 years	8 430	4 240	4 190	8 328	4 186	4 142	27	18	9	61	27	34
12 years	8 189	4 246	3 943	8 111	4 210	3 901	23	13	10	54	23	31
13 years	8 470	4 340	4 130	8 395	4 301	4 094	23	14	9	56	28	28
14 years	8 844	4 564	4 280	8 765	4 529	4 236	27	15	12	56	26	30
15 to 19 years	51 287	25 552	25 735	50 774	25 276	25 498	157	81	76	416	202	214
15 years	9 382	4 847	4 535	9 309	4 813	4 496	17	7	10	53	19	34
16 years	9 686	4 971	4 715	9 614	4 937	4 677	18	10	8	59	29	30
17 years	9 747	4 965	4 782	9 674	4 925	4 749	16	12	4	69	33	36
18 years	10 797	5 227	5 570	10 665	5 152	5 513	45	21	24	109	58	51
19 years	11 675	5 542	6 133	11 512	5 449	6 063	61	31	30	126	63	63
20 to 24 years	48 637	23 975	24 662	47 918	23 575	24 343	196	106	90	463	254	209
20 years	10 665	5 232	5 433	10 491	5 132	5 359	51	28	23	129	62	67
21 years	10 512	5 240	5 272	10 344	5 143	5 201	50	26	24	100	63	37
25 to 29 years	44 845	21 997	22 848	44 365	21 764	22 601	107	66	41	284	140	144
30 to 34 years	42 325	21 186	21 139	41 880	20 963	20 917	84	55	29	260	113	147
35 to 39 years	32 371	16 283	16 088	32 065	16 122	15 943	73	47	26	195	106	89
40 to 44 years	25 023	12 511	12 512	24 817	12 385	12 432	48	32	16	118	60	58
45 to 49 years	23 618	11 769	11 849	23 465	11 689	11 776	30	20	10	125	61	64
50 to 54 years	24 156	11 788	12 368	24 047	11 743	12 304	23	10	13	133	71	62
55 to 59 years	23 502	11 143	12 359	23 404	11 098	12 306	26	15	11	115	57	58
60 to 64 years	21 023	9 803	11 220	20 952	9 771	11 181	19	11	8	120	53	67
65 to 69 years	18 580	8 499	10 081	18 511	8 470	10 041	19	9	10	102	53	49
70 to 74 years	15 193	6 342	8 851	15 150	6 326	8 824	11	6	5	61	25	36
75 to 79 years	11 212	4 351	6 861	11 167	4 335	6 832	13	6	7	51	20	31
80 to 84 years	7 174	2 372	4 802	7 152	2 366	4 786	5	2	3	27	9	18
85 years and over	6 007	1 592	4 415	5 991	1 587	4 404	5	2	3	31	7	24
18 years and over	366 138	174 380	191 758	363 061	172 795	190 266	765	439	326	2 320	1 150	1 170
62 years and over	70 589	28 931	41 658	70 347	28 836	41 511	65	32	33	351	153	198
65 years and over	58 166	23 156	35 010	57 971	23 084	34 887	53	25	28	272	114	158
Median	29.4	28.4	30.3	29.5	28.5	30.4	21.8	22.5	21.2	24.6	24.0	25.4

[1]Persons of Spanish origin may be of any race.

Table 67. Persons by Age, Race, Spanish Origin, and Sex, for States: 1980—Con.

[For meaning of symbols, see Introduction. For definitions of terms, see appendixes A and B]

States	Race									Spanish origin[1]		
	Total			White			Black					
	Both sexes	Male	Female	Both sexes	Male	Female	Both sexes	Male	Female	Both sexes	Male	Female
VIRGINIA												
Total persons	5 346 818	2 618 310	2 728 508	4 229 798	2 080 189	2 149 609	1 008 668	484 406	524 262	79 868	39 769	40 099
Under 5 years	360 686	184 738	175 948	268 499	138 150	130 349	81 572	41 195	40 377	7 442	3 814	3 628
Under 1 year	77 346	39 582	37 764	57 178	29 386	27 792	17 828	8 963	8 865	1 675	890	785
1 year	72 259	37 054	35 205	53 807	27 746	26 061	16 306	8 213	8 093	1 532	783	749
2 years	71 697	36 656	35 041	53 348	27 483	25 865	16 332	8 165	8 167	1 458	731	727
3 years	69 895	35 744	34 151	52 360	26 850	25 510	15 526	7 891	7 635	1 396	679	717
4 years	69 489	35 702	33 787	51 806	26 685	25 121	15 580	7 963	7 617	1 381	731	650
5 to 9 years	387 524	198 256	189 268	292 409	150 550	141 859	84 256	42 254	42 002	6 871	3 465	3 406
5 years	71 637	36 712	34 925	53 843	27 774	26 069	15 681	7 912	7 769	1 356	700	656
6 years	70 909	36 184	34 725	53 524	27 467	26 057	15 293	7 699	7 594	1 289	651	638
7 years	76 057	38 741	37 316	57 170	29 340	27 830	16 660	8 275	8 385	1 327	664	663
8 years	80 281	41 188	39 093	60 552	31 237	29 315	17 539	8 835	8 704	1 388	684	704
9 years	88 640	45 431	43 209	67 320	34 732	32 588	19 083	9 533	9 550	1 511	766	745
10 to 14 years	431 051	219 464	211 587	324 294	165 837	158 457	97 469	48 857	48 612	7 015	3 649	3 366
10 years	87 701	44 782	42 919	66 795	34 205	32 590	18 799	9 485	9 314	1 465	778	687
11 years	84 818	43 292	41 526	64 330	32 964	31 366	18 565	9 377	9 188	1 380	725	655
12 years	83 307	42 385	40 922	62 569	32 131	30 438	18 883	9 313	9 570	1 375	710	665
13 years	85 831	43 562	42 269	64 344	32 750	31 594	19 752	9 873	9 879	1 380	723	657
14 years	89 394	45 443	43 951	66 256	33 787	32 469	21 470	10 809	10 661	1 415	713	702
15 to 19 years	505 674	259 129	246 545	382 231	196 924	185 307	114 382	57 256	57 126	8 193	4 361	3 832
15 years	96 593	49 037	47 556	72 117	36 657	35 460	22 813	11 524	11 289	1 476	716	760
16 years	98 788	50 633	48 155	74 302	38 192	36 110	22 830	11 559	11 271	1 472	747	725
17 years	99 692	50 787	48 905	75 424	38 600	36 824	22 581	11 325	11 256	1 555	805	750
18 years	101 648	52 174	49 474	77 043	39 793	37 250	22 789	11 345	11 444	1 702	949	753
19 years	108 953	56 498	52 455	83 345	43 682	39 663	23 369	11 503	11 866	1 988	1 144	844
20 to 24 years	530 968	272 928	258 040	411 272	213 314	197 958	107 950	53 003	54 947	10 043	5 754	4 289
20 years	109 646	57 253	52 393	84 622	44 631	39 991	22 645	11 186	11 459	2 070	1 243	827
21 years	108 248	56 284	51 964	83 599	43 927	39 672	22 261	10 981	11 280	2 141	1 258	883
25 to 29 years	477 912	236 875	241 037	374 394	186 912	187 482	91 093	44 013	47 080	8 330	4 165	4 165
30 to 34 years	449 952	221 884	228 068	365 764	181 959	183 805	71 580	34 201	37 379	7 308	3 398	3 910
35 to 39 years	366 110	181 620	184 490	301 869	151 321	150 548	54 490	25 678	28 812	5 841	2 640	3 201
40 to 44 years	296 775	147 602	149 173	242 843	122 322	120 521	46 775	21 642	25 133	4 468	2 078	2 390
45 to 49 years	271 560	133 359	138 201	221 870	110 220	111 650	44 853	20 874	23 979	3 572	1 677	1 895
50 to 54 years	274 347	132 543	141 804	225 625	110 182	115 443	45 461	20 901	24 560	2 929	1 375	1 554
55 to 59 years	267 889	126 807	141 082	221 434	105 025	116 409	44 229	20 733	23 496	2 400	1 116	1 284
60 to 64 years	221 066	103 377	117 689	181 564	85 072	96 492	37 972	17 662	20 310	1 802	821	981
65 to 69 years	182 975	81 048	101 927	148 419	65 687	82 732	33 321	14 854	18 467	1 424	586	838
70 to 74 years	135 321	55 486	79 835	111 905	45 463	66 442	22 592	9 697	12 895	919	368	551
75 to 79 years	91 476	33 751	57 725	75 354	27 276	48 078	15 614	6 274	9 340	685	273	412
80 to 84 years	54 401	17 830	36 571	45 894	14 666	31 228	8 252	3 064	5 188	361	141	220
85 years and over	41 131	11 613	29 518	34 158	9 309	24 849	6 807	2 248	4 559	265	88	177
18 years and over	3 872 484	1 865 395	2 007 089	3 122 753	1 512 203	1 610 550	677 147	317 692	359 455	54 037	26 573	27 464
62 years and over	630 856	258 123	372 733	518 947	210 542	308 405	108 040	46 027	62 013	4 660	1 912	2 748
65 years and over	505 304	199 728	305 576	415 730	162 401	253 329	86 586	36 137	50 449	3 654	1 456	2 198
Median	29.8	28.6	30.9	30.8	29.7	32.0	25.9	25.0	26.9	25.2	23.8	26 8
WASHINGTON												
Total persons	4 132 156	2 052 307	2 079 849	3 779 170	1 870 620	1 908 550	105 574	57 135	48 439	120 016	63 516	56 500
Under 5 years	306 123	156 679	149 444	268 633	137 799	130 834	10 153	5 104	5 049	16 729	8 564	8 165
Under 1 year	67 354	34 538	32 816	58 850	30 304	28 546	2 257	1 135	1 122	3 917	1 937	1 980
1 year	61 810	31 726	30 084	54 264	27 910	26 354	2 090	1 033	1 057	3 313	1 697	1 616
2 years	60 175	30 538	29 637	52 830	26 912	25 918	1 997	986	1 011	3 366	1 679	1 687
3 years	59 233	30 386	28 847	52 163	26 768	25 395	1 902	965	937	3 120	1 661	1 459
4 years	57 551	29 491	28 060	50 526	25 905	24 621	1 907	985	922	3 013	1 590	1 423
5 to 9 years	296 011	151 442	144 569	262 058	134 268	127 790	9 219	4 605	4 614	13 488	6 883	6 605
5 years	56 689	29 116	27 573	49 933	25 641	24 292	1 781	905	876	2 801	1 410	1 391
6 years	55 137	28 347	26 790	48 610	25 053	23 557	1 709	875	834	2 659	1 357	1 302
7 years	56 716	28 747	27 969	50 045	25 406	24 639	1 699	820	879	2 653	1 342	1 311
8 years	59 731	30 658	29 073	52 985	27 252	25 733	1 848	924	924	2 624	1 341	1 283
9 years	67 738	34 574	33 164	60 485	30 916	29 569	2 182	1 081	1 101	2 751	1 433	1 318
10 to 14 years	321 995	165 160	156 835	289 326	148 549	140 777	9 463	4 762	4 701	12 380	6 265	6 115
10 years	67 730	34 907	32 823	60 525	31 201	29 324	2 115	1 096	1 019	2 690	1 337	1 353
11 years	65 119	33 518	31 601	58 534	30 197	28 337	1 855	928	927	2 543	1 273	1 270
12 years	62 237	31 779	30 458	55 993	28 665	27 328	1 823	897	926	2 400	1 215	1 185
13 years	62 604	32 002	30 602	56 359	28 826	27 533	1 806	902	904	2 344	1 218	1 126
14 years	64 305	32 954	31 351	57 915	29 660	28 255	1 864	939	925	2 403	1 222	1 181
15 to 19 years	369 023	189 332	179 691	331 101	169 022	162 079	11 634	6 409	5 225	13 867	7 550	6 317
15 years	68 562	35 154	33 498	61 757	31 664	30 093	2 061	1 050	1 011	2 523	1 303	1 220
16 years	72 283	37 107	35 176	65 264	33 512	31 752	2 056	1 033	1 023	2 564	1 331	1 233
17 years	74 296	38 037	36 259	66 987	34 183	32 804	2 165	1 117	1 048	2 739	1 484	1 255
18 years	74 244	38 144	36 100	66 444	33 907	32 537	2 465	1 391	1 074	2 869	1 605	1 264
19 years	79 548	40 890	38 658	70 649	35 756	34 893	2 887	1 818	1 069	3 172	1 827	1 345
20 to 24 years	400 542	206 258	194 284	355 424	180 637	174 787	15 126	9 310	5 816	15 176	8 699	6 477
20 years	79 452	41 225	38 227	70 246	35 925	34 321	3 156	1 988	1 168	3 163	1 823	1 340
21 years	79 060	40 765	38 295	69 698	35 341	34 357	3 208	1 999	1 209	3 140	1 861	1 279
25 to 29 years	389 997	197 253	192 744	352 032	177 257	174 775	11 451	6 503	4 948	12 489	6 804	5 685
30 to 34 years	354 645	178 753	175 892	324 474	163 525	160 949	8 592	4 647	3 945	9 616	5 022	4 594
35 to 39 years	273 382	138 715	134 667	252 292	127 972	124 320	5 820	3 287	2 533	6 499	3 469	3 030
40 to 44 years	213 832	108 450	105 382	197 414	100 228	97 186	4 496	2 485	2 011	4 882	2 588	2 294
45 to 49 years	193 473	97 405	96 068	179 529	90 752	88 777	3 991	2 226	1 765	3 839	2 045	1 794
50 to 54 years	198 548	97 453	101 095	186 025	91 696	94 329	3 977	2 035	1 942	3 355	1 720	1 635
55 to 59 years	203 986	98 323	105 663	193 037	93 036	100 001	3 821	1 935	1 886	2 594	1 345	1 249
60 to 64 years	179 037	86 540	92 497	171 392	82 762	88 630	2 853	1 519	1 334	1 645	853	792
65 to 69 years	151 324	70 295	81 029	145 438	67 329	78 109	2 072	1 005	1 067	1 348	675	673
70 to 74 years	112 023	49 475	62 548	107 846	47 244	60 602	1 361	666	695	956	494	462
75 to 79 years	77 409	30 999	46 410	74 825	29 682	45 143	791	366	425	585	286	299
80 to 84 years	49 330	17 106	32 224	47 907	16 586	31 321	435	155	280	318	140	178
85 years and over	41 476	12 669	28 807	40 417	12 276	28 141	319	116	203	250	114	136
18 years and over	2 992 796	1 468 728	1 524 068	2 765 145	1 350 645	1 414 500	70 457	39 464	30 993	69 593	37 686	31 907
62 years and over	535 534	230 619	304 570	515 885	221 152	294 733	6 534	3 128	3 406	4 326	2 158	2 168
65 years and over	431 562	180 544	251 018	416 433	173 117	243 316	4 978	2 308	2 670	3 457	1 709	1 748
Median	29.8	29.0	30.6	30.5	29.6	31.3	24.0	24.0	24.0	21.1	21.4	20.8

[1] Persons of Spanish origin may be of any race.

GENERAL POPULATION CHARACTERISTICS

UNITED STATES SUMMARY 1—181

Table 67. Persons by Age, Race, Spanish Origin, and Sex, for States: 1980—Con.

[For meaning of symbols, see Introduction. For definitions of terms, see appendixes A and B]

States	Race — Total			Race — White			Race — Black			Spanish origin[1]		
	Both sexes	Male	Female	Both sexes	Male	Female	Both sexes	Male	Female	Both sexes	Male	Female
WEST VIRGINIA												
Total persons	1 949 644	945 408	1 004 236	1 874 751	910 221	964 530	65 051	30 421	34 630	12 707	6 278	6 429
Under 5 years	145 583	74 737	70 846	139 351	71 589	67 762	5 155	2 634	2 521	1 082	529	553
Under 1 year	30 297	15 628	14 669	29 017	14 950	14 067	1 072	571	501	232	115	117
1 year	28 708	14 686	14 022	27 395	14 026	13 369	1 080	542	538	216	98	118
2 years	29 085	14 890	14 195	27 897	14 296	13 601	972	500	472	213	107	106
3 years	28 854	14 678	14 176	27 618	14 081	13 537	1 024	508	516	222	109	113
4 years	28 639	14 855	13 784	27 424	14 236	13 188	1 007	513	494	199	100	99
5 to 9 years	152 802	78 350	74 452	146 614	75 251	71 363	5 197	2 600	2 597	1 072	562	510
5 years	29 360	15 056	14 304	28 116	14 428	13 688	1 043	534	509	201	93	108
6 years	28 462	14 680	13 782	27 371	14 124	13 247	900	451	449	215	120	95
7 years	30 839	15 798	15 041	29 557	15 153	14 404	1 073	545	528	219	106	113
8 years	31 181	15 925	15 256	29 942	15 326	14 616	1 035	506	529	223	127	96
9 years	32 960	16 891	16 069	31 628	16 220	15 408	1 146	564	582	214	116	98
10 to 14 years	157 489	81 004	76 485	151 092	77 638	73 454	5 602	2 970	2 632	1 175	610	565
10 years	32 115	16 685	15 430	30 868	16 041	14 827	1 069	568	501	209	108	101
11 years	31 547	16 206	15 341	30 242	15 525	14 717	1 125	582	543	237	133	104
12 years	30 627	15 643	14 984	29 411	15 016	14 395	1 064	548	516	248	116	132
13 years	31 064	15 866	15 198	29 781	15 195	14 586	1 124	590	534	223	117	106
14 years	32 136	16 604	15 532	30 790	15 861	14 929	1 220	682	538	258	136	122
15 to 19 years	174 204	88 174	86 030	166 313	84 185	82 128	7 171	3 633	3 538	1 273	676	597
15 years	34 665	17 852	16 813	33 198	17 109	16 089	1 338	679	659	238	125	113
16 years	34 742	17 742	17 000	33 258	17 004	16 254	1 342	674	668	295	154	141
17 years	34 355	17 499	16 856	32 810	16 742	16 068	1 427	703	724	226	124	102
18 years	34 444	17 290	17 154	32 802	16 425	16 377	1 478	775	703	258	136	122
19 years	35 998	17 791	18 207	34 245	16 905	17 340	1 586	802	784	256	137	119
20 to 24 years	172 688	85 141	87 547	165 020	81 271	83 749	6 672	3 324	3 348	1 145	600	545
20 years	35 408	17 350	18 058	33 687	16 478	17 209	1 510	753	757	255	135	120
21 years	35 170	17 207	17 963	33 595	16 368	17 227	1 396	729	667	232	124	108
25 to 29 years	160 954	80 019	80 935	154 368	76 856	77 512	5 465	2 605	2 860	1 022	479	543
30 to 34 years	144 649	72 479	72 170	140 046	70 245	69 801	3 595	1 793	1 802	840	409	431
35 to 39 years	109 878	54 825	55 053	106 523	53 322	53 201	2 484	1 076	1 408	682	324	358
40 to 44 years	97 541	47 757	49 784	94 758	46 500	48 258	2 191	935	1 256	598	285	313
45 to 49 years	93 307	44 093	49 214	90 627	42 974	47 653	2 260	912	1 348	585	284	301
50 to 54 years	104 805	49 542	55 263	101 419	48 196	53 223	3 099	1 231	1 868	670	318	352
55 to 59 years	105 219	49 342	55 877	101 732	47 829	53 903	3 252	1 412	1 840	591	267	324
60 to 64 years	92 657	42 084	50 573	89 409	40 720	48 689	3 068	1 287	1 781	569	261	308
65 to 69 years	82 953	37 071	45 882	79 576	35 677	43 899	3 208	1 322	1 886	511	248	263
70 to 74 years	64 345	27 104	37 241	61 546	25 967	35 579	2 645	1 090	1 555	344	162	182
75 to 79 years	44 272	17 276	26 996	42 167	16 424	25 743	1 995	813	1 182	290	143	147
80 to 84 years	26 889	9 929	16 960	25 658	9 414	16 244	1 160	484	676	165	84	81
85 years and over	19 409	6 481	12 928	18 532	6 163	12 369	832	300	532	93	37	56
18 years and over	1 390 008	658 224	731 784	1 338 428	634 888	703 540	44 990	20 161	24 829	8 619	4 174	4 445
62 years and over	292 117	122 388	169 729	279 885	117 398	162 487	11 576	4 741	6 835	1 744	832	912
65 years and over	237 868	97 861	140 007	227 479	93 645	133 834	9 840	4 009	5 831	1 403	674	729
Median	30.4	29.1	31.7	30.5	29.2	31.8	27.4	25.1	29.7	27.9	26.6	29.0
WISCONSIN												
Total persons	4 705 767	2 305 427	2 400 340	4 443 035	2 177 806	2 265 229	182 592	87 288	95 304	62 972	32 510	30 462
Under 5 years	346 940	178 111	168 829	316 240	162 719	153 521	20 409	10 201	10 208	9 109	4 612	4 497
Under 1 year	75 319	38 690	36 629	68 489	35 193	33 296	4 558	2 328	2 230	2 011	1 049	962
1 year	69 787	35 979	33 808	63 605	32 847	30 758	4 068	2 043	2 025	1 884	983	901
2 years	68 703	35 100	33 603	62 725	32 152	30 573	3 904	1 922	1 982	1 830	892	938
3 years	67 005	34 293	32 712	61 121	31 377	29 744	3 934	1 954	1 980	1 708	863	845
4 years	66 126	34 049	32 077	60 300	31 150	29 150	3 945	1 954	1 991	1 676	825	851
5 to 9 years	344 804	176 843	167 961	313 835	161 331	152 504	21 530	10 820	10 710	7 487	3 755	3 732
5 years	66 716	34 563	32 153	60 719	31 527	29 192	4 018	2 074	1 944	1 554	767	787
6 years	64 011	32 735	31 276	58 139	29 829	28 310	4 070	2 032	2 038	1 504	762	742
7 years	66 448	33 997	32 451	60 190	30 792	29 398	4 327	2 205	2 122	1 481	771	710
8 years	69 187	35 423	33 764	62 976	32 324	30 652	4 338	2 157	2 181	1 423	698	725
9 years	78 442	40 125	38 317	71 811	36 859	34 952	4 777	2 352	2 425	1 525	757	768
10 to 14 years	392 247	200 634	191 613	362 555	185 652	176 903	21 218	10 697	10 521	6 783	3 449	3 334
10 years	78 002	39 941	38 061	71 650	36 729	34 921	4 540	2 279	2 261	1 474	781	693
11 years	75 747	38 730	37 017	69 955	35 775	34 180	4 130	2 104	2 026	1 360	691	669
12 years	75 554	38 547	37 007	69 565	35 539	34 026	4 321	2 189	2 132	1 327	649	678
13 years	79 977	40 918	39 059	74 230	37 991	36 239	4 084	2 072	2 012	1 306	665	641
14 years	82 967	42 498	40 469	77 155	39 618	37 537	4 143	2 053	2 090	1 316	663	653
15 to 19 years	466 612	235 736	230 876	436 852	220 906	215 946	21 150	10 447	10 703	7 105	3 670	3 435
15 years	88 839	45 431	43 408	83 049	42 529	40 520	4 098	2 043	2 055	1 323	673	650
16 years	91 856	47 063	44 793	85 861	43 973	41 888	4 300	2 222	2 078	1 422	739	683
17 years	93 134	47 414	45 720	87 152	44 354	42 798	4 295	2 186	2 109	1 397	746	651
18 years	93 902	47 029	46 873	87 977	44 133	43 844	4 223	2 047	2 176	1 383	721	662
19 years	98 881	48 799	50 082	92 813	45 917	46 896	4 234	1 949	2 285	1 580	791	789
20 to 24 years	450 026	224 250	225 776	421 067	210 121	210 946	19 841	9 240	10 601	7 447	4 000	3 447
20 years	95 169	47 076	48 093	89 292	44 233	45 059	4 012	1 881	2 131	1 559	797	762
21 years	92 035	45 502	46 533	86 251	42 651	43 600	4 012	1 883	2 129	1 531	800	731
25 to 29 years	401 915	202 273	199 642	376 189	189 933	186 256	17 495	8 037	9 458	6 066	3 273	2 793
30 to 34 years	348 115	174 497	173 618	327 841	164 994	162 847	13 878	6 384	7 494	4 558	2 437	2 121
35 to 39 years	271 661	134 821	136 840	257 318	128 037	129 281	9 762	4 466	5 296	3 129	1 591	1 538
40 to 44 years	230 312	114 330	115 982	218 574	108 799	109 775	8 140	3 718	4 422	2 547	1 288	1 259
45 to 49 years	219 866	108 401	111 465	209 858	103 827	106 031	7 068	3 155	3 913	2 131	1 106	1 025
50 to 54 years	233 079	114 761	118 318	224 205	110 552	113 653	6 534	3 073	3 461	1 920	1 018	902
55 to 59 years	229 046	110 278	118 768	222 159	106 884	115 275	5 066	2 485	2 581	1 466	767	699
60 to 64 years	206 947	96 830	110 117	202 048	94 534	107 514	3 579	1 687	1 892	945	465	500
65 to 69 years	184 722	84 318	100 404	180 912	82 632	98 280	2 733	1 228	1 505	743	369	374
70 to 74 years	145 693	62 950	82 743	143 054	61 846	81 208	1 856	753	1 103	634	311	323
75 to 79 years	107 568	43 289	64 279	105 806	42 584	63 222	1 211	474	737	475	219	256
80 to 84 years	70 577	25 539	45 038	69 629	25 165	44 464	604	234	370	263	121	142
85 years and over	55 637	17 566	38 071	54 893	17 290	37 603	518	189	329	144	59	85
18 years and over	3 347 947	1 609 931	1 738 016	3 194 343	1 537 248	1 657 095	106 742	49 119	57 623	35 451	18 536	16 915
62 years and over	687 248	291 071	396 177	674 642	285 693	388 949	8 895	3 781	5 114	2 788	1 341	1 447
65 years and over	564 197	233 662	330 535	554 294	229 517	324 777	6 922	2 878	4 044	2 259	1 079	1 180
Median	29.4	28.3	30.4	29.9	28.9	31.0	21.7	20.8	22.6	20.6	21.0	20.3

[1]Persons of Spanish origin may be of any race.

Table 67. Persons by Age, Race, Spanish Origin, and Sex, for States: 1980—Con.

[For meaning of symbols, see Introduction. For definitions of terms, see appendixes A and B]

States	Race									Spanish origin[1]		
	Total			White			Black					
	Both sexes	Male	Female	Both sexes	Male	Female	Both sexes	Male	Female	Both sexes	Male	Female
WYOMING												
Total persons	469 557	240 560	228 997	446 488	228 540	217 948	3 364	1 882	1 482	24 499	12 849	11 650
Under 5 years	44 845	22 896	21 949	41 934	21 434	20 500	360	178	182	3 370	1 690	1 680
Under 1 year	10 128	5 157	4 971	9 464	4 815	4 649	90	44	46	757	378	379
1 year	9 280	4 689	4 591	8 665	4 390	4 275	69	30	39	723	365	358
2 years	8 695	4 470	4 225	8 172	4 221	3 951	62	29	33	650	325	325
3 years	8 481	4 341	4 140	7 918	4 034	3 884	68	43	25	608	313	295
4 years	8 261	4 239	4 022	7 715	3 974	3 741	71	32	39	632	309	323
5 to 9 years	39 297	20 305	18 992	36 875	19 059	17 816	291	153	138	2 849	1 438	1 411
5 years	8 085	4 138	3 947	7 578	3 893	3 685	48	29	19	611	300	311
6 years	7 560	3 923	3 637	7 059	3 662	3 397	62	35	27	523	262	261
7 years	7 724	3 944	3 780	7 230	3 689	3 541	66	27	39	602	298	304
8 years	7 721	3 998	3 723	7 270	3 751	3 519	54	31	23	567	281	286
9 years	8 207	4 302	3 905	7 738	4 064	3 674	61	31	30	546	297	249
10 to 14 years	37 124	19 119	18 005	34 894	18 011	16 883	266	138	128	2 564	1 289	1 275
10 years	7 960	4 127	3 833	7 507	3 900	3 607	49	24	25	560	278	282
11 years	7 506	3 825	3 681	7 024	3 591	3 433	63	29	34	517	266	251
12 years	7 155	3 689	3 466	6 723	3 475	3 248	48	28	20	511	254	257
13 years	7 158	3 682	3 476	6 732	3 460	3 272	64	35	29	481	245	236
14 years	7 345	3 796	3 549	6 908	3 585	3 323	42	22	20	495	246	249
15 to 19 years	42 579	22 019	20 560	40 051	20 696	19 355	402	225	177	2 638	1 379	1 259
15 years	7 786	4 093	3 693	7 337	3 860	3 477	67	32	35	502	266	236
16 years	8 164	4 091	4 073	7 696	3 849	3 847	58	29	29	503	267	236
17 years	8 337	4 328	4 009	7 854	4 088	3 766	68	33	35	518	272	246
18 years	8 696	4 520	4 176	8 180	4 243	3 937	96	61	35	497	252	245
19 years	9 596	4 987	4 609	8 984	4 656	4 328	113	70	43	618	322	296
20 to 24 years	50 668	26 748	23 920	47 665	25 070	22 595	557	356	201	2 802	1 523	1 279
20 years	9 804	5 233	4 571	9 212	4 893	4 319	125	86	39	539	293	246
21 years	9 746	5 051	4 695	9 115	4 717	4 398	126	83	43	579	307	272
25 to 29 years	49 335	26 229	23 106	46 766	24 843	21 923	387	236	151	2 510	1 351	1 159
30 to 34 years	39 400	20 982	18 418	37 555	19 976	17 579	248	155	93	1 889	1 055	834
35 to 39 years	29 413	15 360	14 053	28 199	14 733	13 466	144	84	60	1 278	674	604
40 to 44 years	23 582	12 170	11 412	22 543	11 644	10 899	148	86	62	1 042	559	483
45 to 49 years	20 690	10 490	10 200	19 855	10 080	9 775	130	65	65	834	433	401
50 to 54 years	20 915	10 893	10 022	20 228	10 540	9 688	102	58	44	769	412	357
55 to 59 years	18 930	9 517	9 413	18 345	9 202	9 143	77	35	42	637	328	309
60 to 64 years	15 604	7 715	7 889	15 203	7 531	7 672	89	38	51	406	210	196
65 to 69 years	13 079	6 085	6 994	12 779	5 935	6 844	57	31	26	357	190	167
70 to 74 years	9 788	4 497	5 291	9 606	4 405	5 201	38	18	20	244	139	105
75 to 79 years	6 649	2 724	3 925	6 494	2 647	3 847	36	14	22	163	96	67
80 to 84 years	4 186	1 566	2 620	4 110	1 535	2 575	16	7	9	73	40	33
85 years and over	3 473	1 245	2 228	3 386	1 199	2 187	16	5	11	74	43	31
18 years and over	324 004	165 728	158 276	309 898	158 239	151 659	2 254	1 319	935	14 193	7 627	6 566
62 years and over	46 201	20 520	25 681	45 159	20 010	25 149	221	100	121	1 158	644	514
65 years and over	37 175	16 117	21 058	36 375	15 721	20 654	163	75	88	911	508	403
Median	27.0	26.7	27.3	27.2	26.9	27.6	23.0	23.2	22.8	21.5	22.1	20.8

[1]Persons of Spanish origin may be of any race.

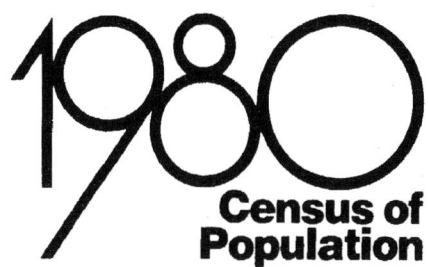

VOLUME 1
CHARACTERISTICS OF THE POPULATION

CHAPTER C

General Social and Economic Characteristics

PART 1

UNITED STATES SUMMARY

PC80-1-C1

Issued December 1983

U.S. Department of Commerce
Malcolm Baldrige, Secretary
Clarence J. Brown,
Deputy Secretary

BUREAU OF THE CENSUS
C.L. Kincannon, Deputy Director

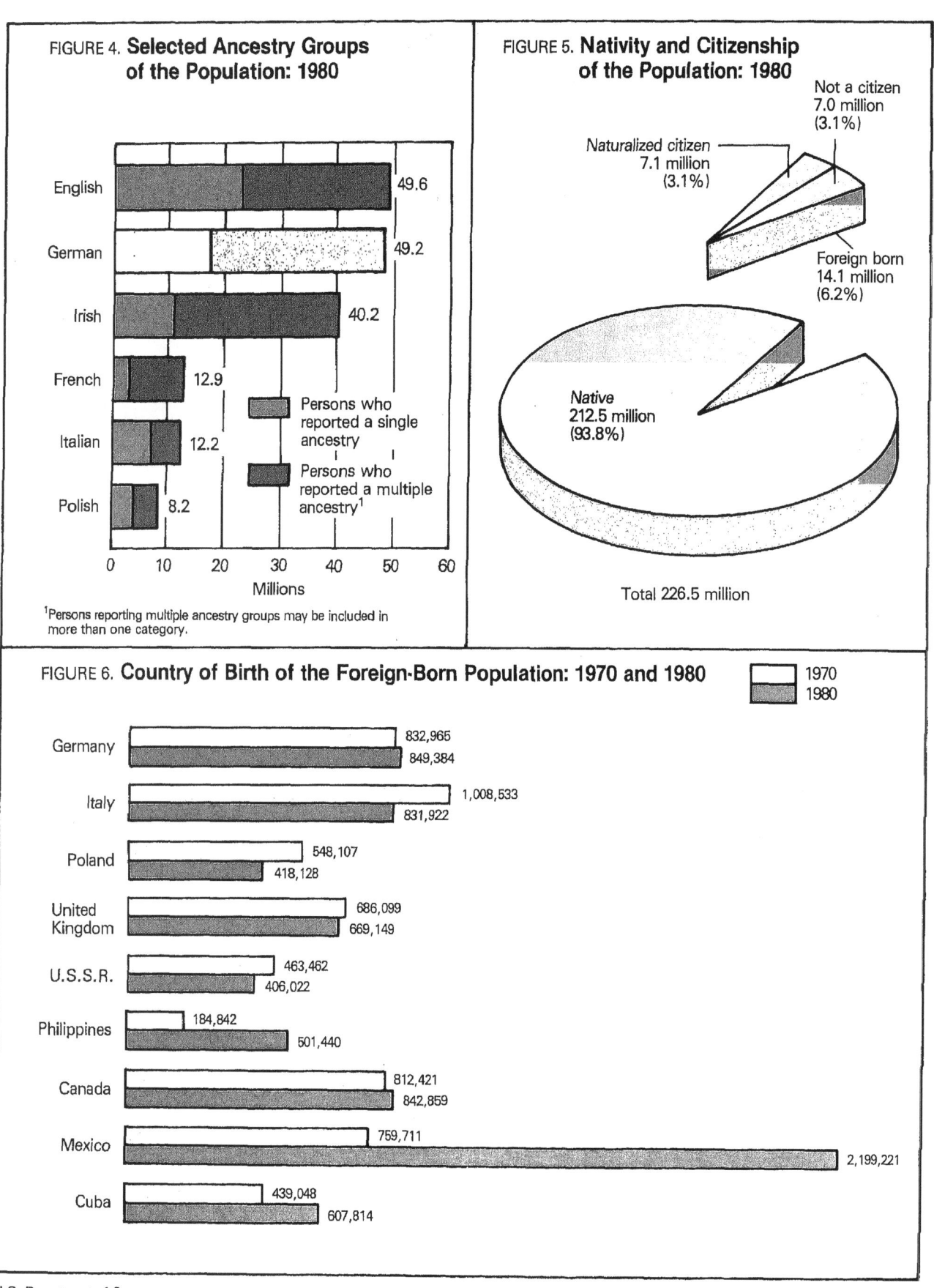

FIGURE 4. **Selected Ancestry Groups of the Population: 1980**

English 49.6
German 49.2
Irish 40.2
French 12.9
Italian 12.2
Polish 8.2

Persons who reported a single ancestry

Persons who reported a multiple ancestry[1]

0   10   20   30   40   50   60
Millions

[1]Persons reporting multiple ancestry groups may be included in more than one category.

FIGURE 5. **Nativity and Citizenship of the Population: 1980**

Not a citizen
7.0 million
(3.1%)

Naturalized citizen
7.1 million
(3.1%)

Foreign born
14.1 million
(6.2%)

Native
212.5 million
(93.8%)

Total 226.5 million

FIGURE 6. **Country of Birth of the Foreign-Born Population: 1970 and 1980**

1970
1980

Germany 832,965 / 849,384
Italy 1,008,533 / 831,922
Poland 548,107 / 418,128
United Kingdom 686,099 / 669,149
U.S.S.R. 463,462 / 406,022
Philippines 184,842 / 501,440
Canada 812,421 / 842,859
Mexico 759,711 / 2,199,221
Cuba 439,048 / 607,814

FIGURE 7. **Percent of the Population 5 to 17 Years Old Who Speak a Language Other Than English at Home by States: 1980**

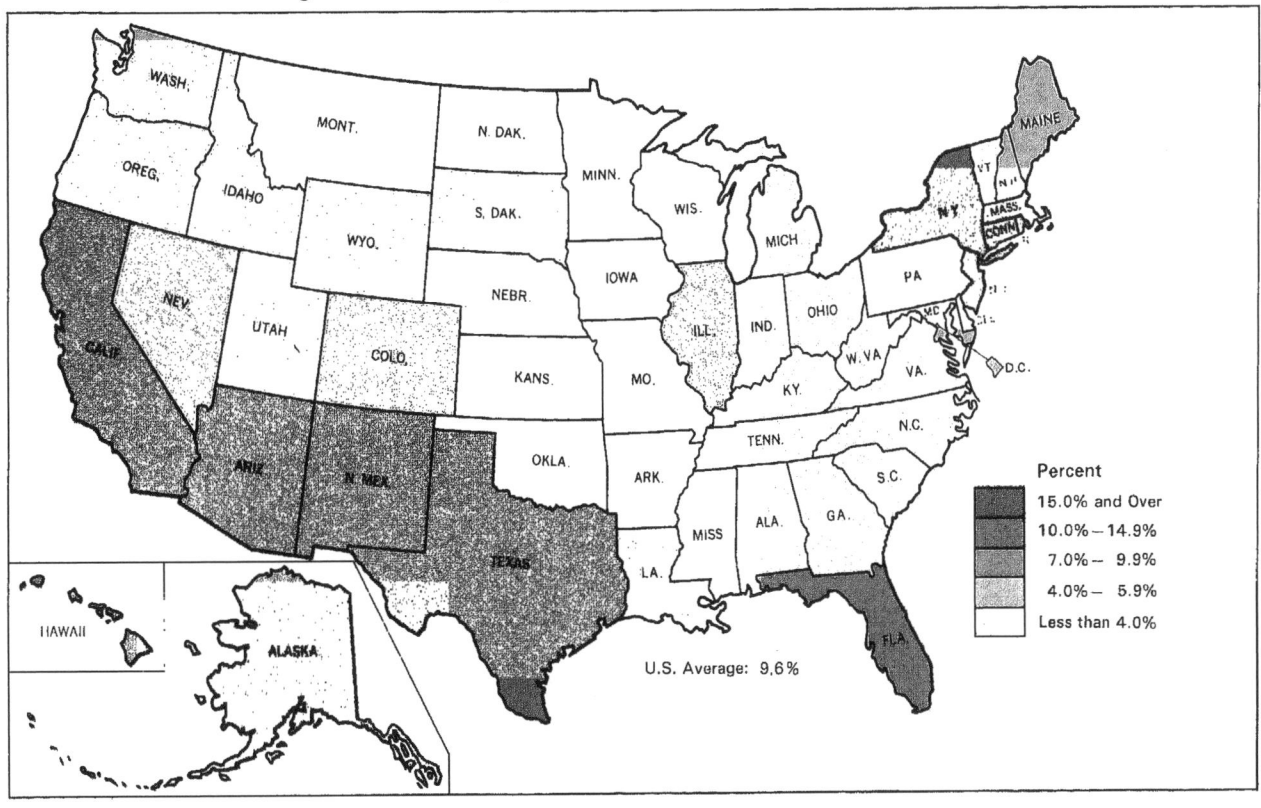

Percent

	15.0% and Over
	10.0% – 14.9%
	7.0% – 9.9%
	4.0% – 5.9%
	Less than 4.0%

U.S. Average: 9.6%

FIGURE 8. **Children Ever Born Per 1,000 Women 15 to 44 Years by States: 1980**

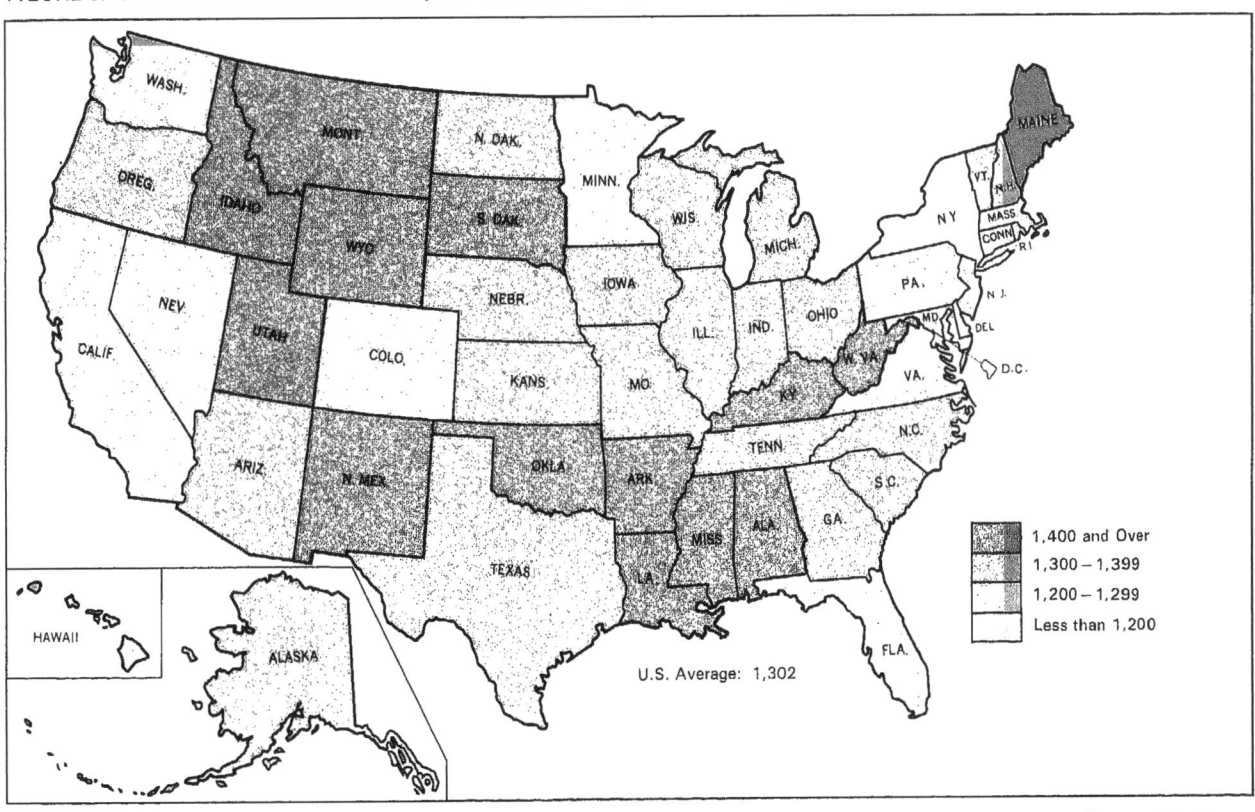

	1,400 and Over
	1,300 – 1,399
	1,200 – 1,299
	Less than 1,200

U.S. Average: 1,302

U.S. Department of Commerce

GENERAL SOCIAL AND ECONOMIC CHARACTERISTICS

Bureau of the Census

UNITED STATES SUMMARY   1–10g

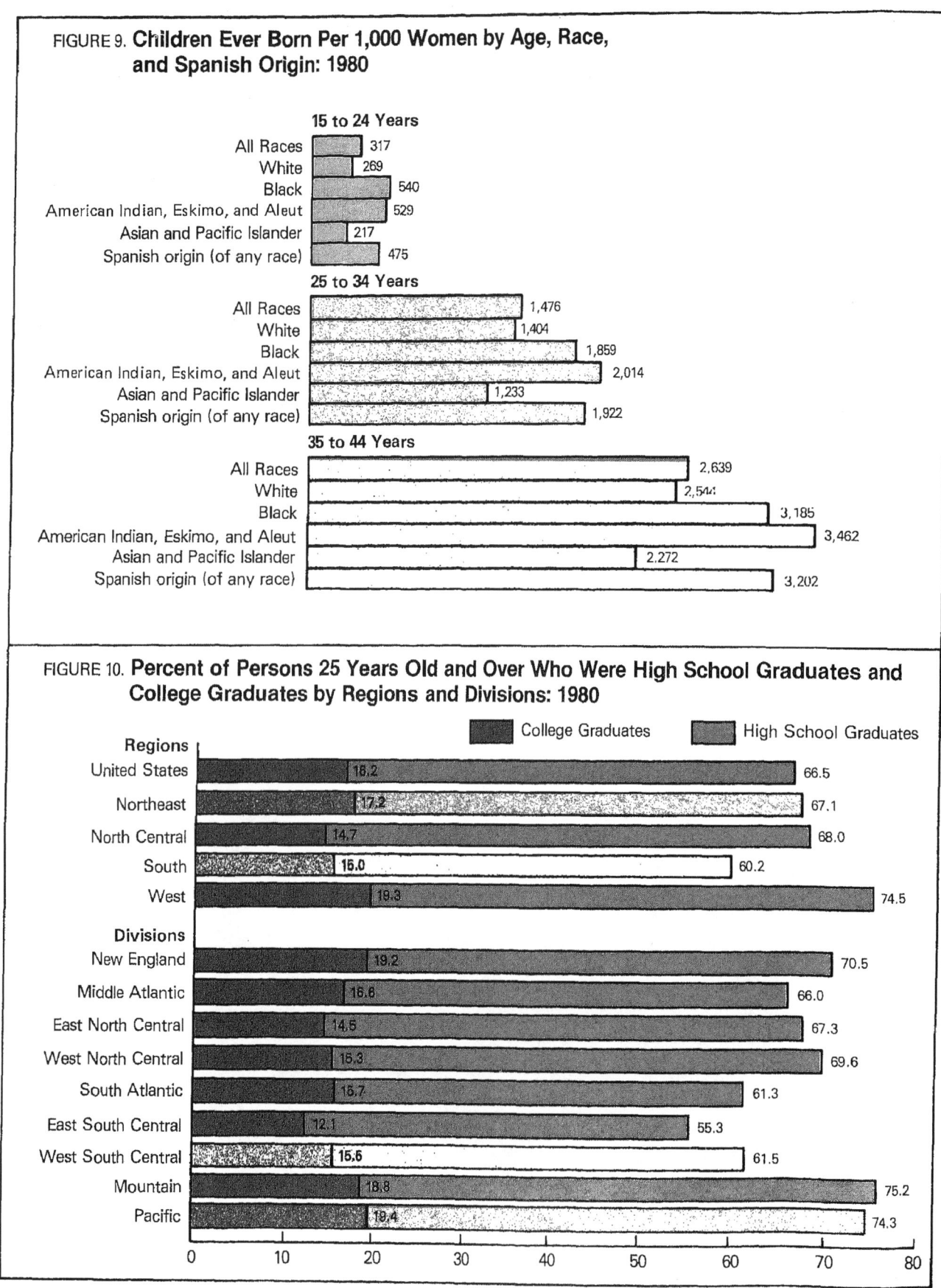

FIGURE 9. **Children Ever Born Per 1,000 Women by Age, Race, and Spanish Origin: 1980**

15 to 24 Years

All Races	317
White	269
Black	540
American Indian, Eskimo, and Aleut	529
Asian and Pacific Islander	217
Spanish origin (of any race)	475

25 to 34 Years

All Races	1,476
White	1,404
Black	1,859
American Indian, Eskimo, and Aleut	2,014
Asian and Pacific Islander	1,233
Spanish origin (of any race)	1,922

35 to 44 Years

All Races	2,639
White	2,544
Black	3,185
American Indian, Eskimo, and Aleut	3,462
Asian and Pacific Islander	2,272
Spanish origin (of any race)	3,202

FIGURE 10. **Percent of Persons 25 Years Old and Over Who Were High School Graduates and College Graduates by Regions and Divisions: 1980**

College Graduates   High School Graduates

Regions

	College Graduates	High School Graduates
United States	16.2	66.5
Northeast	17.2	67.1
North Central	14.7	68.0
South	15.0	60.2
West	19.3	74.5

Divisions

	College Graduates	High School Graduates
New England	19.2	70.5
Middle Atlantic	16.6	66.0
East North Central	14.5	67.3
West North Central	15.3	69.6
South Atlantic	15.7	61.3
East South Central	12.1	55.3
West South Central	15.6	61.5
Mountain	18.8	75.2
Pacific	19.4	74.3

FIGURE 11. **Percent of Persons 25 Years Old and Over Who Were High School Graduates and College Graduates by Race: 1940—1980**

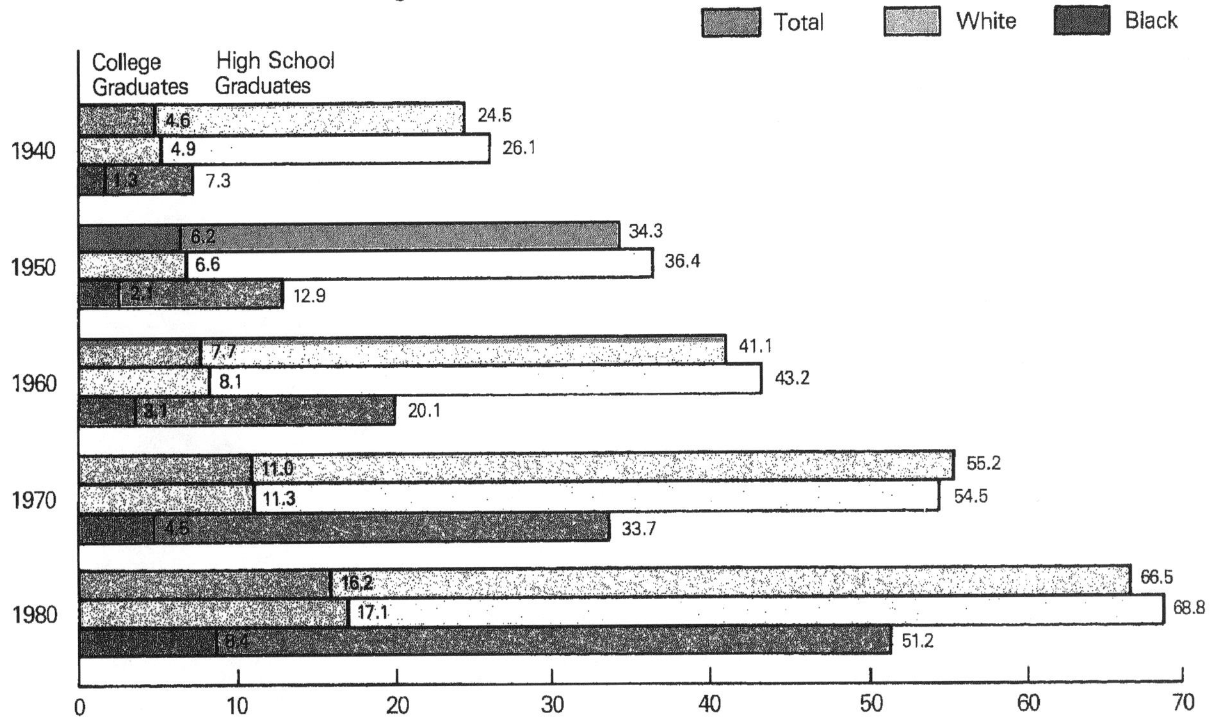

Total
White
Black
College Graduates
High School Graduates
1940
4.6
24.5
4.9
26.1
1.3
7.3
1950
6.2
34.3
6.6
36.4
2.1
12.9
1960
7.7
41.1
8.1
43.2
3.1
20.1
1970
11.0
55.2
11.3
54.5
4.5
33.7
1980
16.2
66.5
17.1
68.8
8.4
51.2
0
10
20
30
40
50
60
70

FIGURE 12. **Percent of Elementary School Children Enrolled in Private Schools by States: 1980**

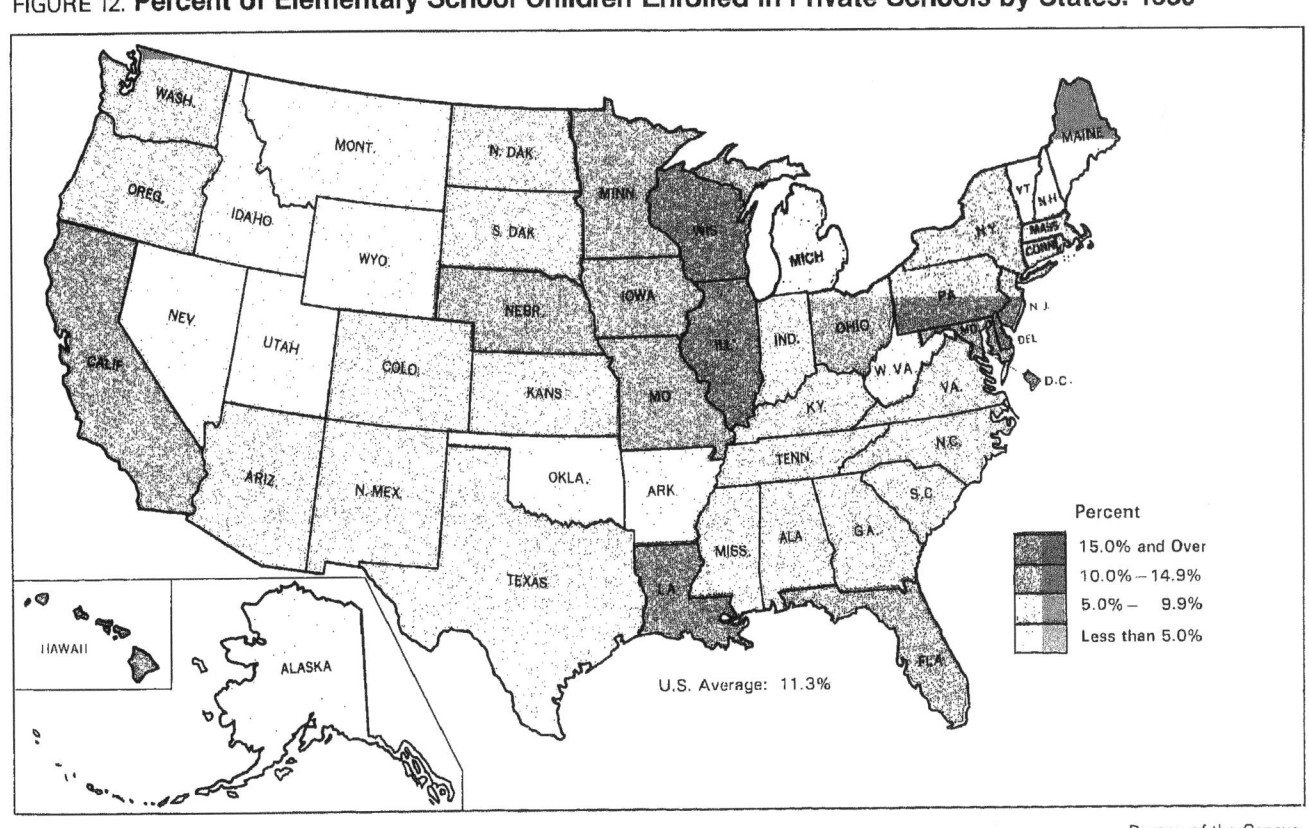

WASH.
MONT.
N. DAK.
MAINE
OREG.
IDAHO
MINN.
S. DAK.
WYO.
WIS.
MICH
VT
NH
N.Y.
MASS
CONN
NEV.
UTAH
NEBR.
IOWA
PA
N.J.
CALIF.
COLO.
ILL.
IND.
OHIO
MD.
DEL
KANS.
MO.
W.VA
D.C.
VA.
KY.
N.C.
TENN.
ARIZ.
N. MEX.
OKLA.
ARK.
S.C.
MISS.
ALA.
GA.
TEXAS
LA.
FLA.
HAWAII
ALASKA
Percent
15.0% and Over
10.0% – 14.9%
5.0% – 9.9%
Less than 5.0%
U.S. Average: 11.3%

FIGURE 13. **Percent Enrolled in School by Age: 1910—1980**

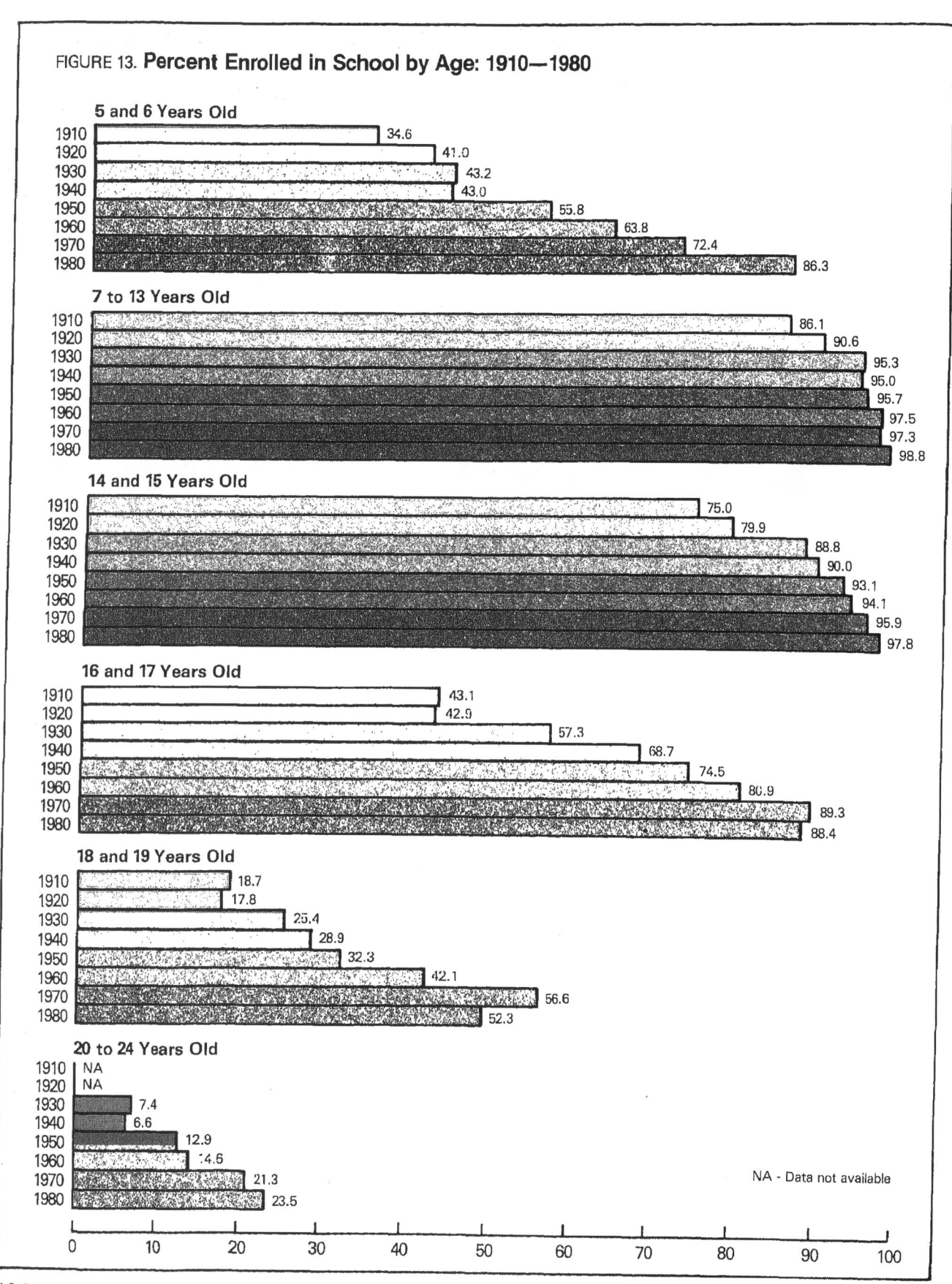

5 and 6 Years Old

Year	Percent
1910	34.6
1920	41.0
1930	43.2
1940	43.0
1950	55.8
1960	63.8
1970	72.4
1980	86.3

7 to 13 Years Old

Year	Percent
1910	86.1
1920	90.6
1930	95.3
1940	95.0
1950	95.7
1960	97.5
1970	97.3
1980	98.8

14 and 15 Years Old

Year	Percent
1910	75.0
1920	79.9
1930	88.8
1940	90.0
1950	93.1
1960	94.1
1970	95.9
1980	97.8

16 and 17 Years Old

Year	Percent
1910	43.1
1920	42.9
1930	57.3
1940	68.7
1950	74.5
1960	80.9
1970	89.3
1980	88.4

18 and 19 Years Old

Year	Percent
1910	18.7
1920	17.8
1930	25.4
1940	28.9
1950	32.3
1960	42.1
1970	56.6
1980	52.3

20 to 24 Years Old

Year	Percent
1910	NA
1920	NA
1930	7.4
1940	6.6
1950	12.9
1960	14.6
1970	21.3
1980	23.5

NA - Data not available

0   10   20   30   40   50   60   70   80   90   100

U.S. Department of Commerce

1—10j **UNITED STATES SUMMARY**

Bureau of the Census

GENERAL SOCIAL AND ECONOMIC CHARACTERISTICS

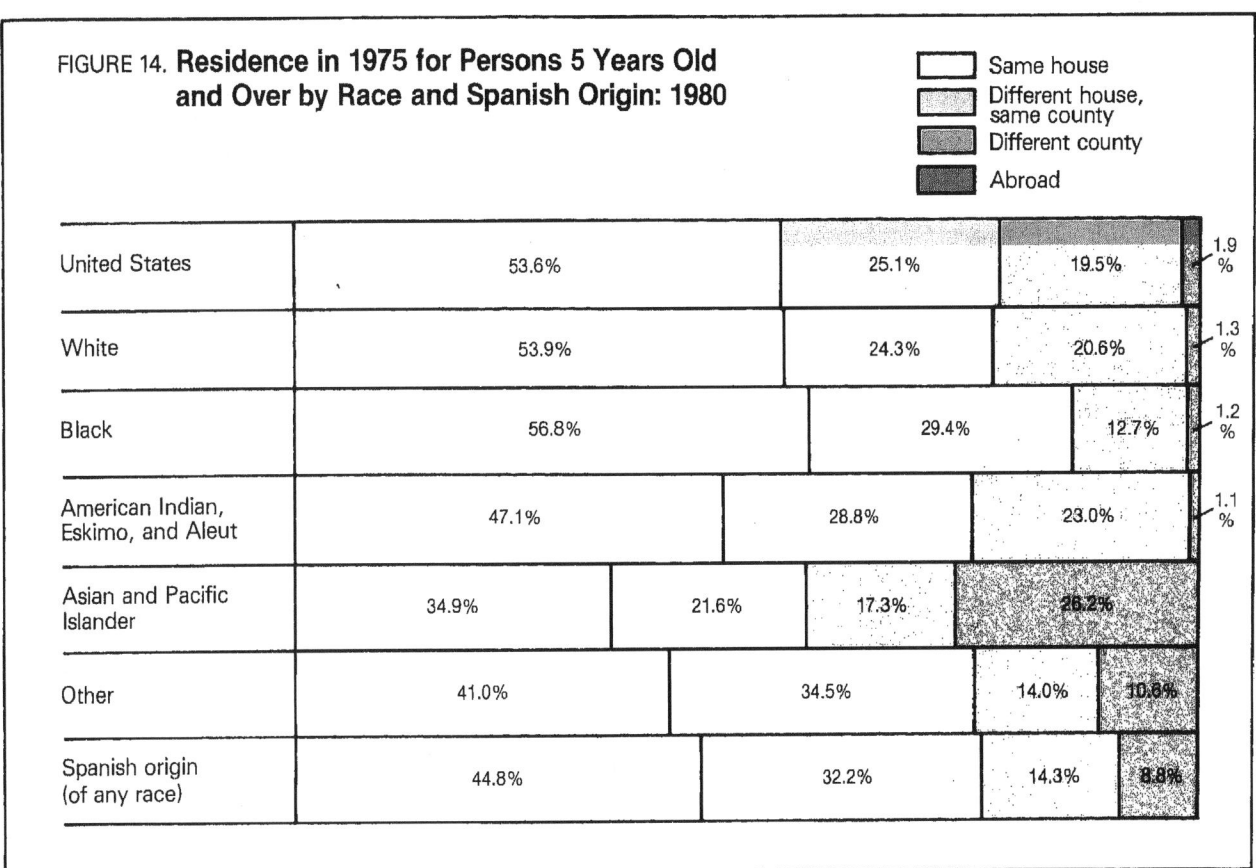

FIGURE 14. **Residence in 1975 for Persons 5 Years Old and Over by Race and Spanish Origin: 1980**

Legend:
- Same house
- Different house, same county
- Different county
- Abroad

	Same house	Different house, same county	Different county	Abroad
United States	53.6%	25.1%	19.5%	1.9%
White	53.9%	24.3%	20.6%	1.3%
Black	56.8%	29.4%	12.7%	1.2%
American Indian, Eskimo, and Aleut	47.1%	28.8%	23.0%	1.1%
Asian and Pacific Islander	34.9%	21.6%	17.3%	26.2%
Other	41.0%	34.5%	14.0%	10.8%
Spanish origin (of any race)	44.8%	32.2%	14.3%	8.8%

FIGURE 15. **Movers, 1975-1980 by States: 1980**

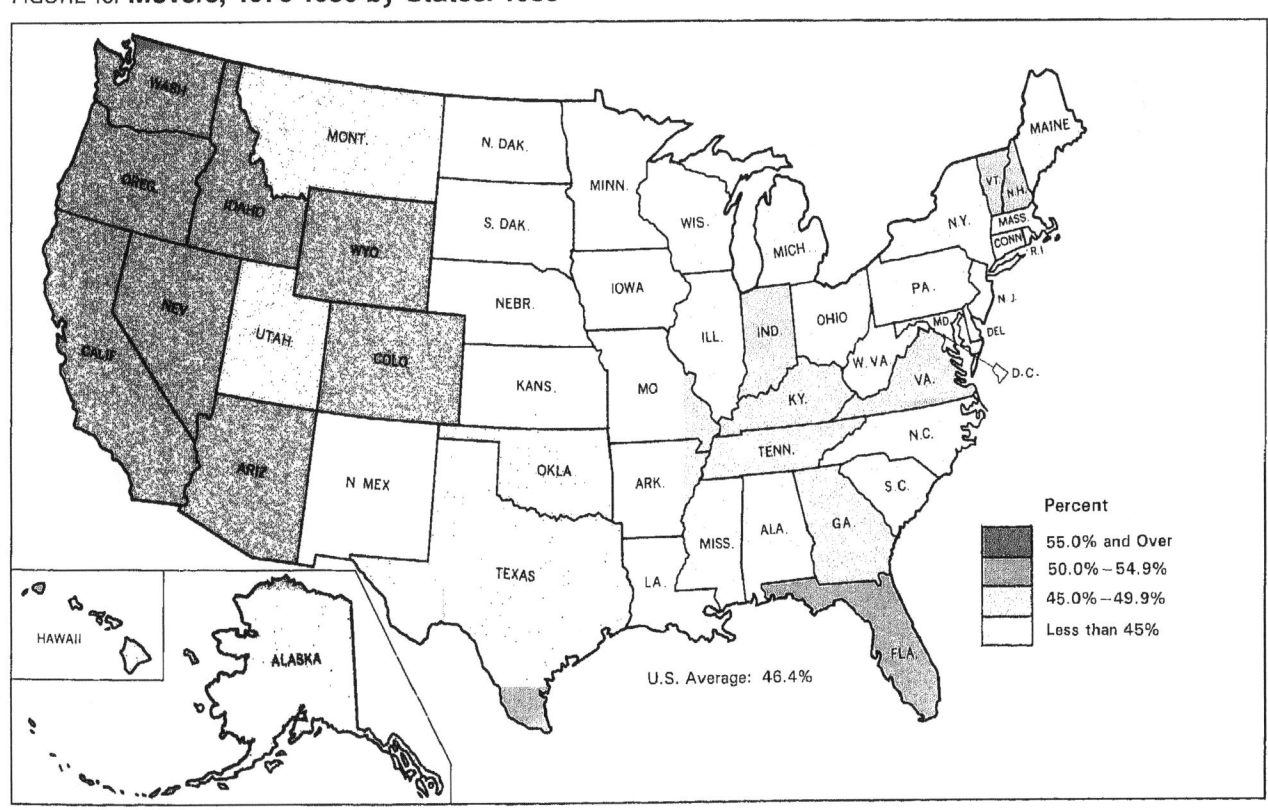

Percent
- 55.0% and Over
- 50.0% – 54.9%
- 45.0% – 49.9%
- Less than 45%

U.S. Average: 46.4%

U.S. Department of Commerce　　　　　　　　　　　　　　　　　　Bureau of the Census
GENERAL SOCIAL AND ECONOMIC CHARACTERISTICS　　　　UNITED STATES SUMMARY　1–10k

339

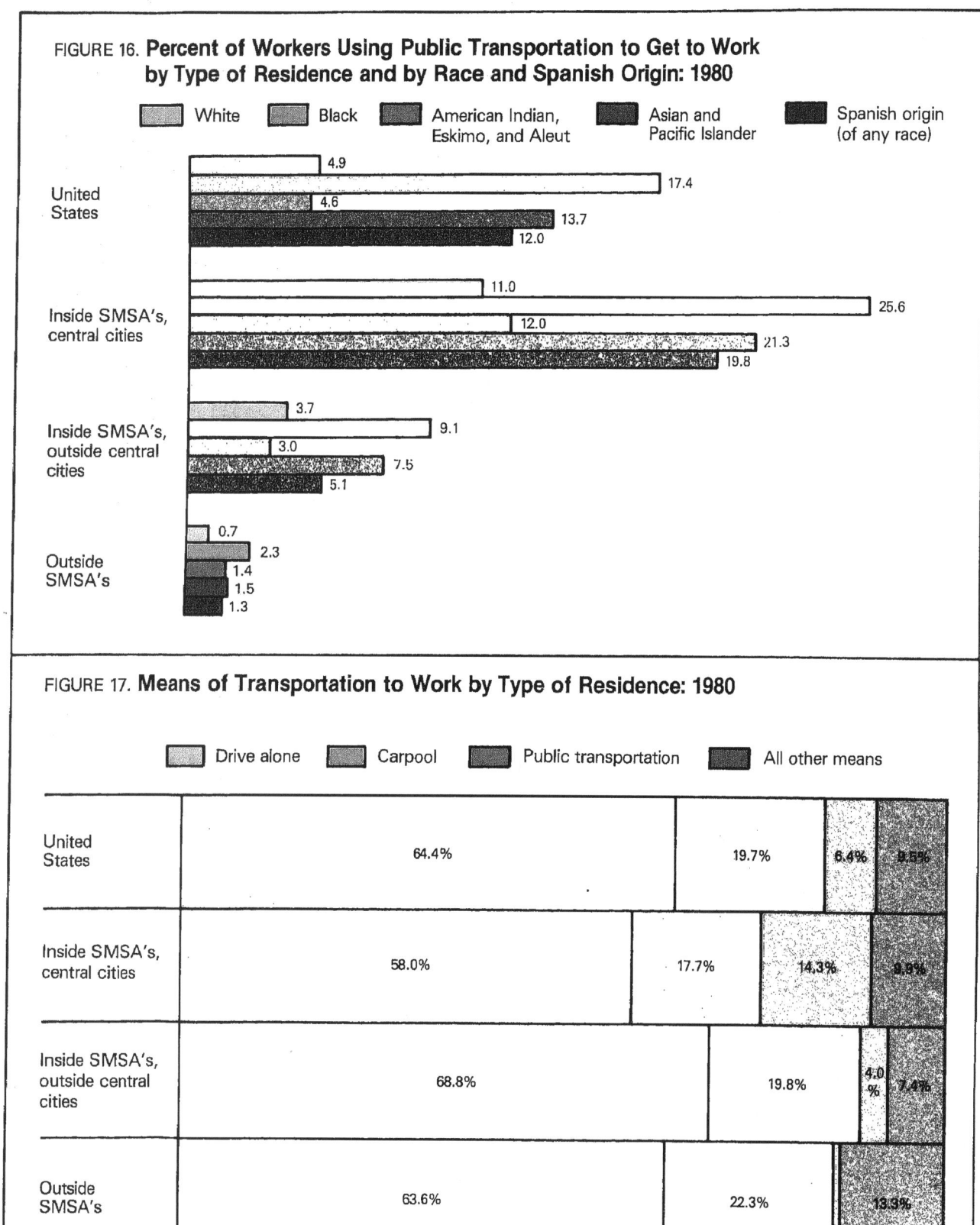

FIGURE 16. **Percent of Workers Using Public Transportation to Get to Work by Type of Residence and by Race and Spanish Origin: 1980**

White   Black   American Indian, Eskimo, and Aleut   Asian and Pacific Islander   Spanish origin (of any race)

United States
4.9
17.4
4.6
13.7
12.0

Inside SMSA's, central cities
11.0
25.6
12.0
21.3
19.8

Inside SMSA's, outside central cities
3.7
9.1
3.0
7.5
5.1

Outside SMSA's
0.7
2.3
1.4
1.5
1.3

FIGURE 17. **Means of Transportation to Work by Type of Residence: 1980**

Drive alone   Carpool   Public transportation   All other means

	Drive alone	Carpool	Public transportation	All other means
United States	64.4%	19.7%	6.4%	9.5%
Inside SMSA's, central cities	58.0%	17.7%	14.3%	9.9%
Inside SMSA's, outside central cities	68.8%	19.8%	4.0%	7.4%
Outside SMSA's	63.6%	22.3%	13.3%	0.8%

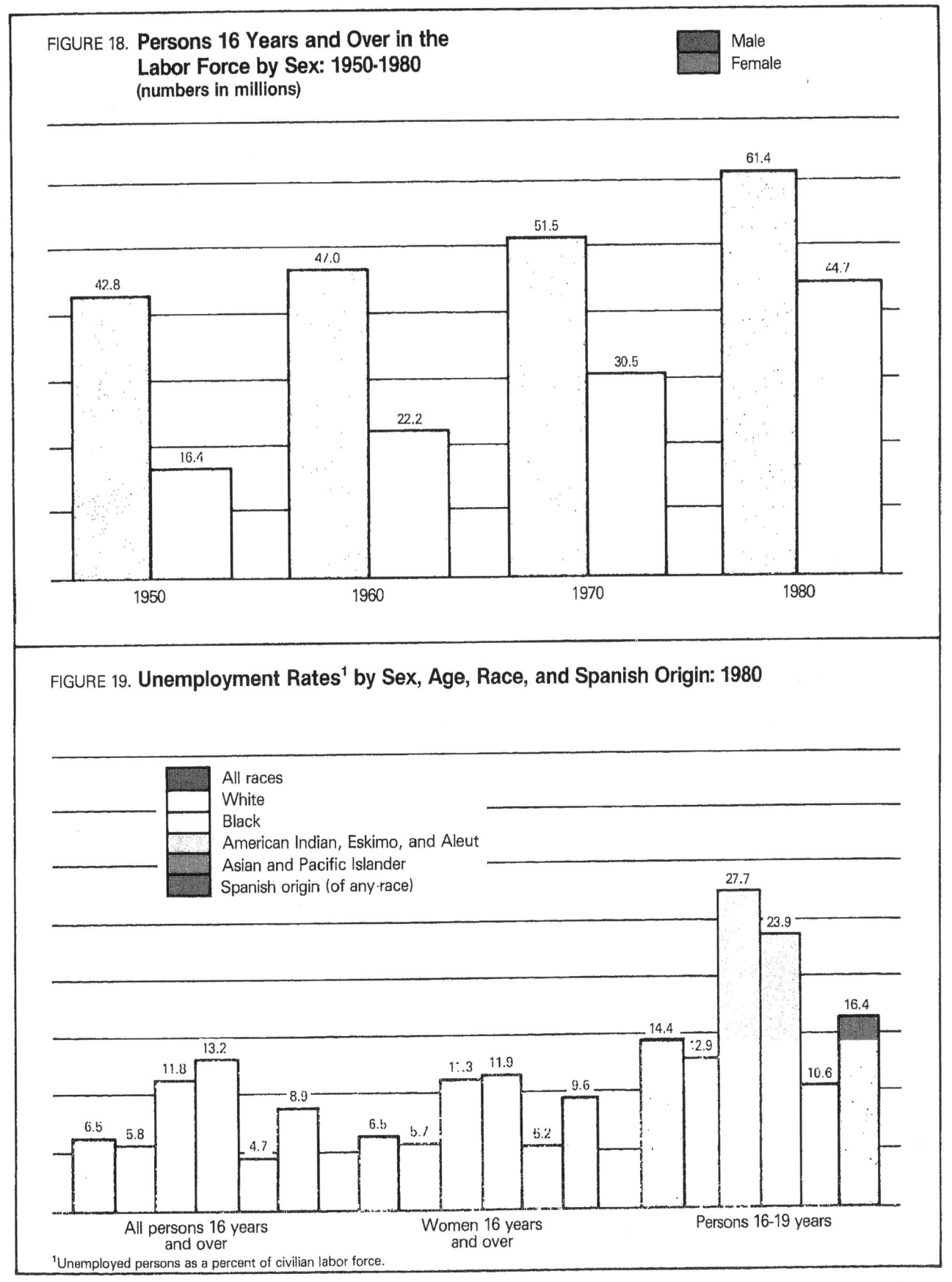

FIGURE 18. **Persons 16 Years and Over in the Labor Force by Sex: 1950-1980**
(numbers in millions)

Male
Female

61.4

51.5

47.0

44.7

42.8

30.5

22.2

16.4

1950   1960   1970   1980

FIGURE 19. **Unemployment Rates[1] by Sex, Age, Race, and Spanish Origin: 1980**

All races
White
Black
American Indian, Eskimo, and Aleut
Asian and Pacific Islander
Spanish origin (of any race)

27.7

23.9

16.4

14.4

13.2

12.9

11.8

11.3   11.9

10.6

9.6

8.9

6.5   5.8

6.5   5.7

5.2

4.7

All persons 16 years
and over

Women 16 years
and over

Persons 16-19 years

[1]Unemployed persons as a percent of civilian labor force.

U.S. Department of Commerce

Bureau of the Census

GENERAL SOCIAL AND ECONOMIC CHARACTERISTICS

UNITED STATES SUMMARY 1—10m

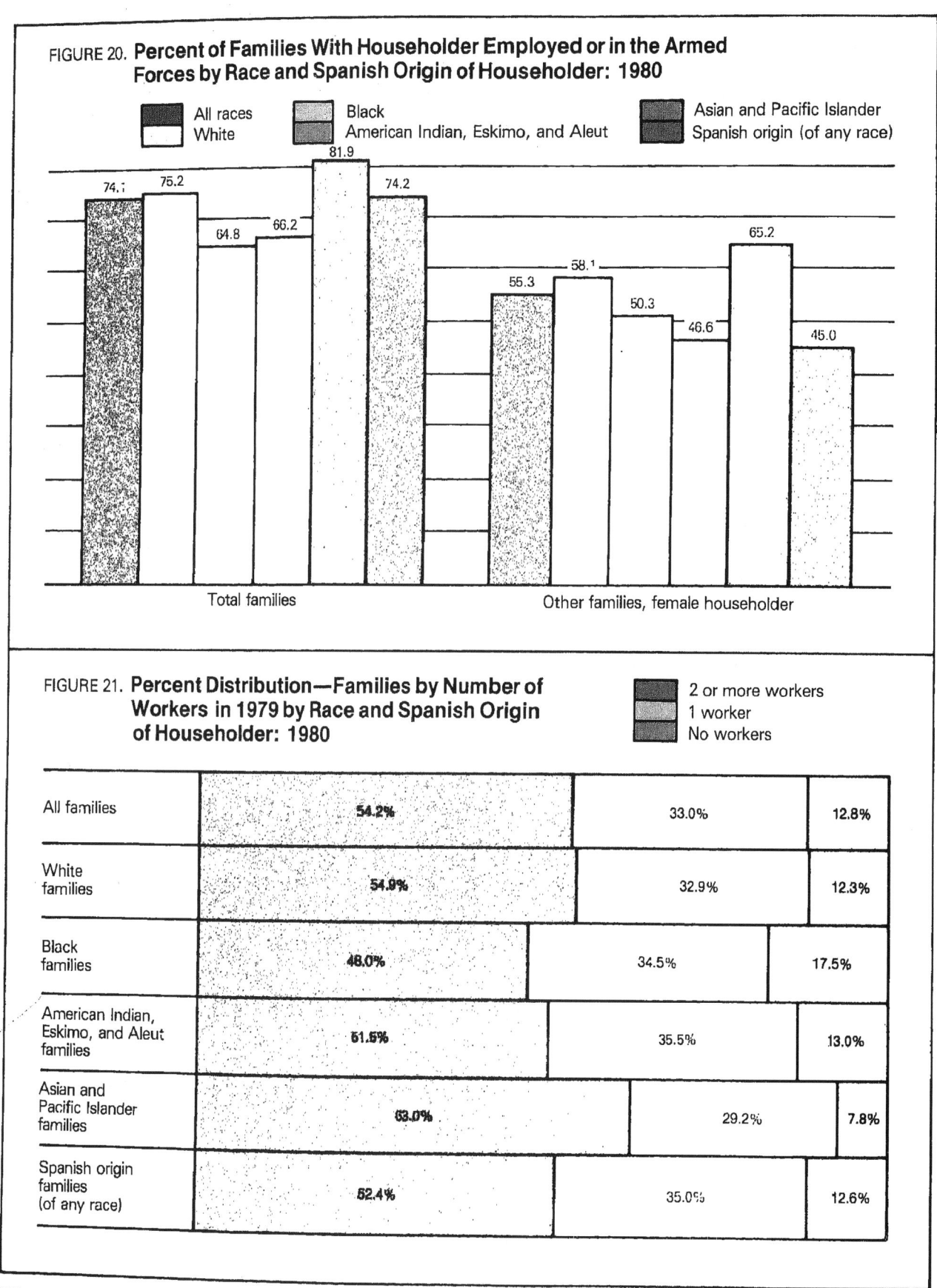

FIGURE 20. **Percent of Families With Householder Employed or in the Armed Forces by Race and Spanish Origin of Householder: 1980**

All races
White

Black
American Indian, Eskimo, and Aleut

Asian and Pacific Islander
Spanish origin (of any race)

81.9

74.7 75.2

64.8 66.2

74.2

55.3 58.1

50.3

46.6

65.2

45.0

Total families

Other families, female householder

FIGURE 21. **Percent Distribution—Families by Number of Workers in 1979 by Race and Spanish Origin of Householder: 1980**

2 or more workers
1 worker
No workers

	2 or more workers	1 worker	No workers
All families	54.2%	33.0%	12.8%
White families	54.9%	32.9%	12.3%
Black families	48.0%	34.5%	17.5%
American Indian, Eskimo, and Aleut families	51.5%	35.5%	13.0%
Asian and Pacific Islander families	63.0%	29.2%	7.8%
Spanish origin families (of any race)	52.4%	35.0%	12.6%

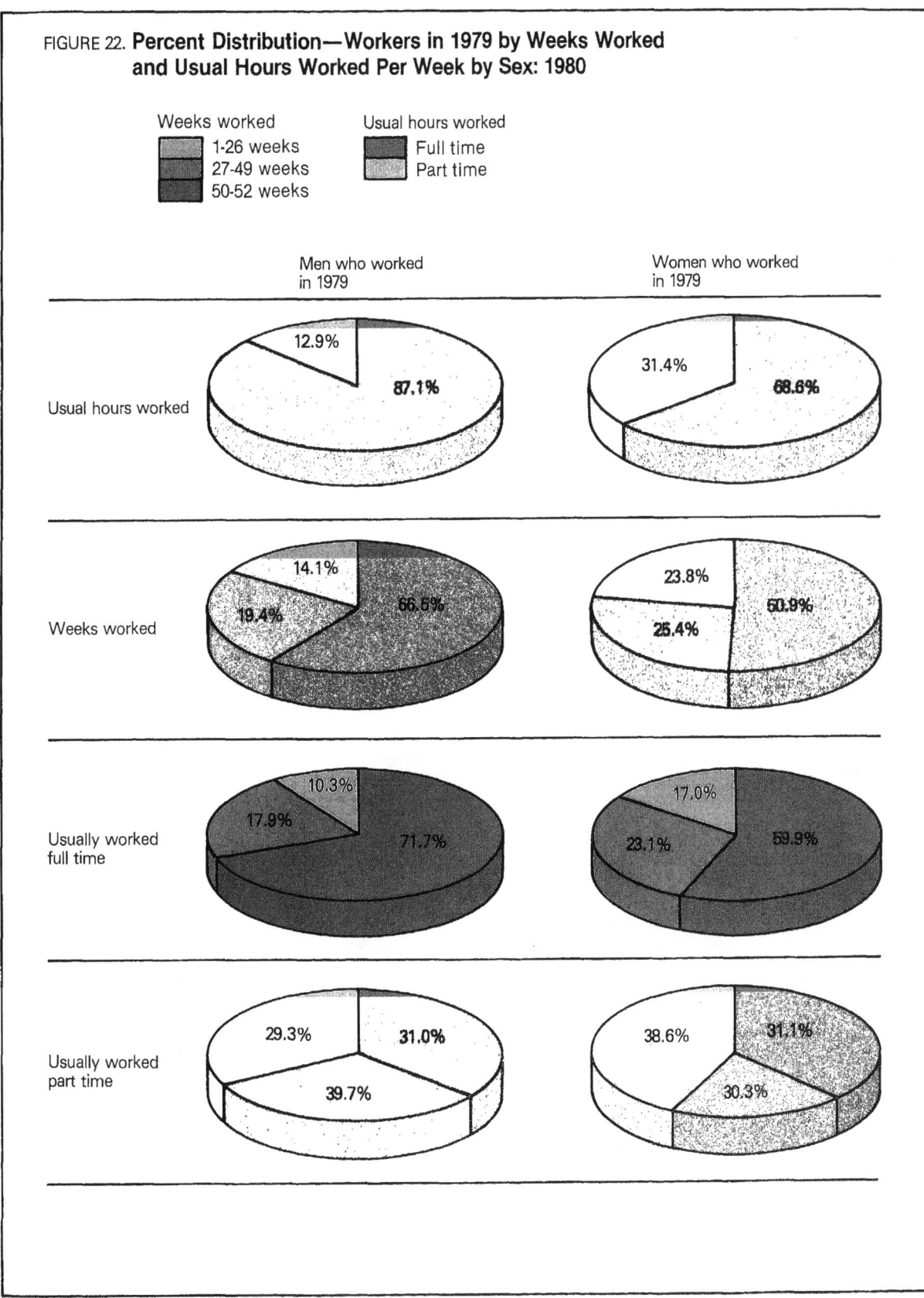

FIGURE 22. **Percent Distribution—Workers in 1979 by Weeks Worked
and Usual Hours Worked Per Week by Sex: 1980**

Weeks worked
- 1-26 weeks
- 27-49 weeks
- 50-52 weeks

Usual hours worked
- Full time
- Part time

Men who worked in 1979

Women who worked in 1979

Usual hours worked
- 12.9%
- 87.1%
- 31.4%
- 68.6%

Weeks worked
- 14.1%
- 19.4%
- 66.5%
- 23.8%
- 25.4%
- 50.9%

Usually worked full time
- 10.3%
- 17.9%
- 71.7%
- 17.0%
- 23.1%
- 59.9%

Usually worked part time
- 29.3%
- 31.0%
- 39.7%
- 38.6%
- 31.1%
- 30.3%

U.S. Department of Commerce
GENERAL SOCIAL AND ECONOMIC CHARACTERISTICS

Bureau of the Census
UNITED STATES SUMMARY 1—10o

FIGURE 23. **Percent Noninstitutional Population 16 to 64 Years Old With a Work Disability by States: 1980**

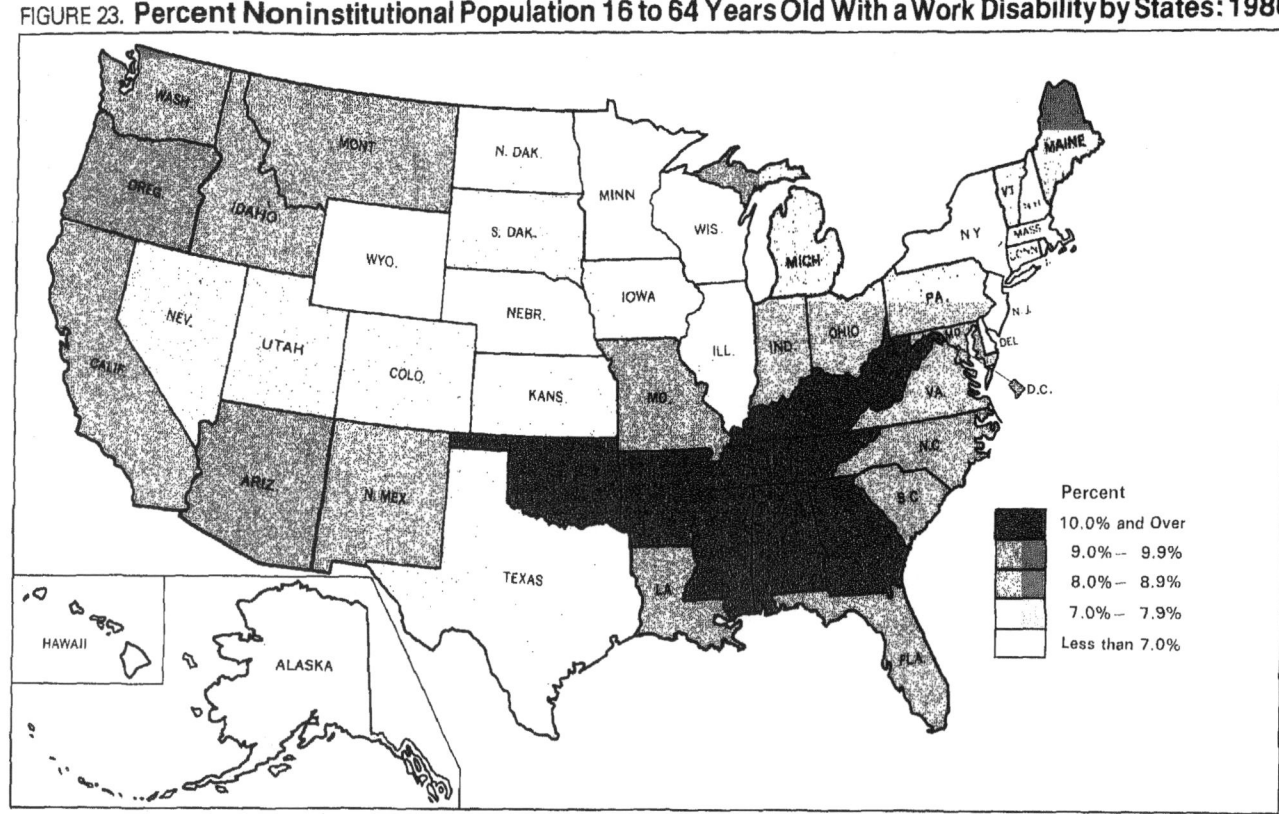

Percent	
	10.0% and Over
	9.0% — 9.9%
	8.0% — 8.9%
	7.0% — 7.9%
	Less than 7.0%

FIGURE 24. **Class of Worker by Sex for Employed Persons: 1940—1980**

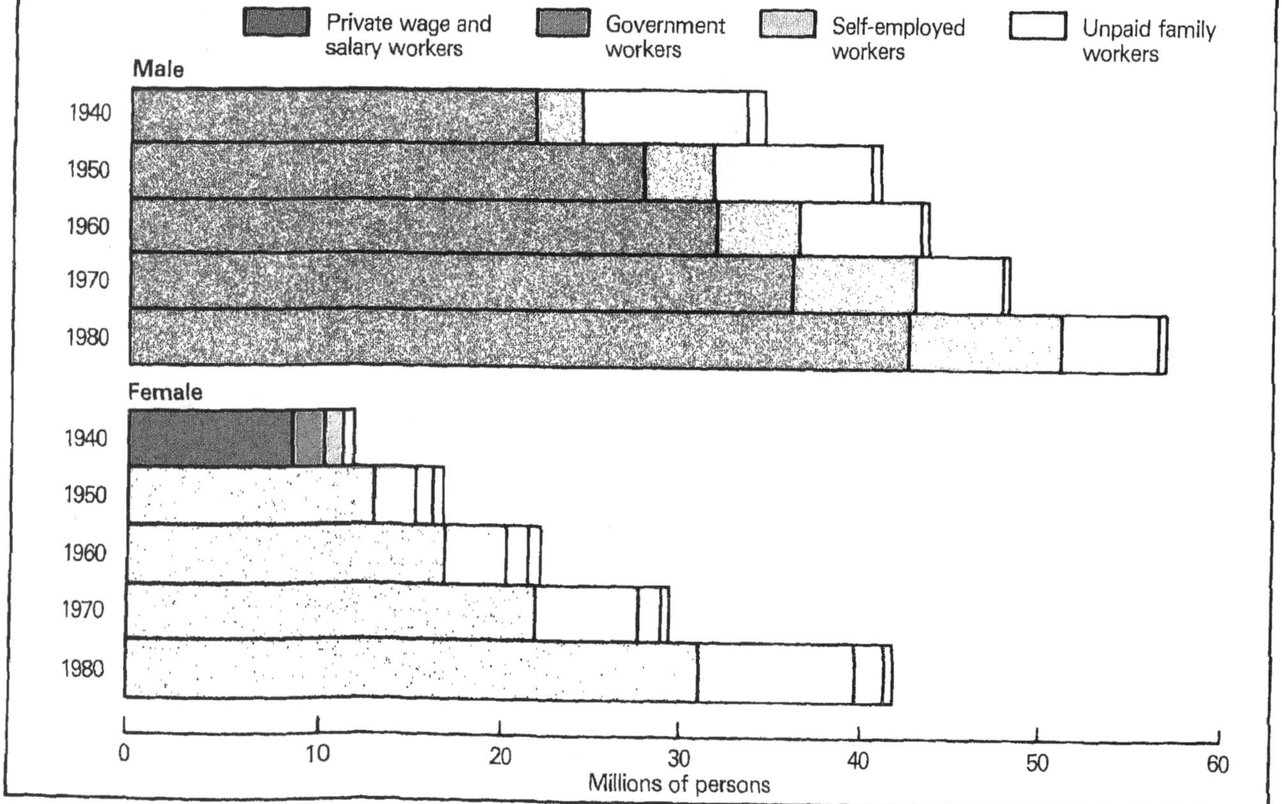

Private wage and salary workers   Government workers   Self-employed workers   Unpaid family workers

Male
1940
1950
1960
1970
1980

Female
1940
1950
1960
1970
1980

0   10   20   30   40   50   60
Millions of persons

FIGURE 25. **Major Occupation of Employed Persons by Sex: 1980 and 1970**

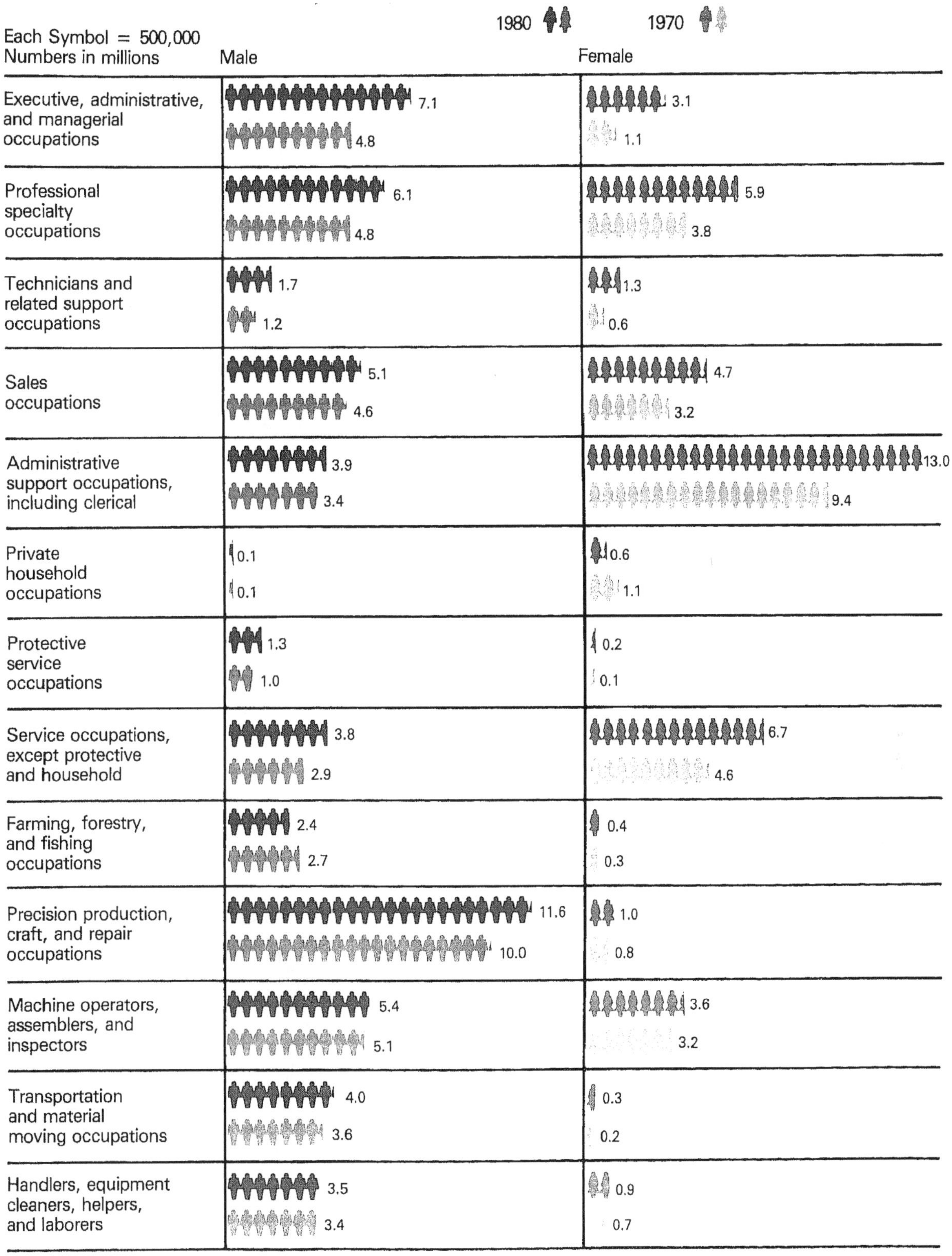

Each Symbol = 500,000
Numbers in millions   Male   Female

Occupation	1980 Male	1970 Male	1980 Female	1970 Female
Executive, administrative, and managerial occupations	7.1	4.8	3.1	1.1
Professional specialty occupations	6.1	4.8	5.9	3.8
Technicians and related support occupations	1.7	1.2	1.3	0.6
Sales occupations	5.1	4.6	4.7	3.2
Administrative support occupations, including clerical	3.9	3.4	13.0	9.4
Private household occupations	0.1	0.1	0.6	1.1
Protective service occupations	1.3	1.0	0.2	0.1
Service occupations, except protective and household	3.8	2.9	6.7	4.6
Farming, forestry, and fishing occupations	2.4	2.7	0.4	0.3
Precision production, craft, and repair occupations	11.6	10.0	1.0	0.8
Machine operators, assemblers, and inspectors	5.4	5.1	3.6	3.2
Transportation and material moving occupations	4.0	3.6	0.3	0.2
Handlers, equipment cleaners, helpers, and laborers	3.5	3.4	0.9	0.7

FIGURE 26. **Median Household Income in 1979 by States: 1980**

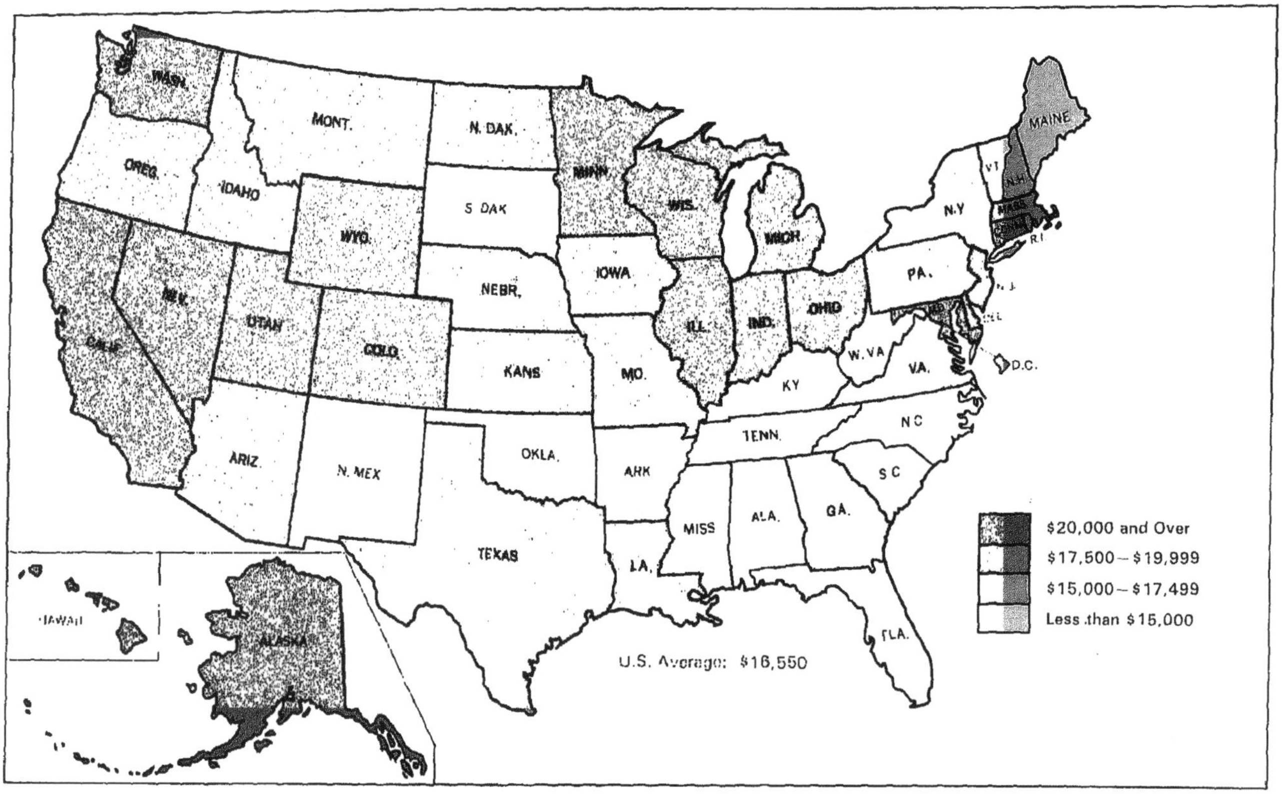

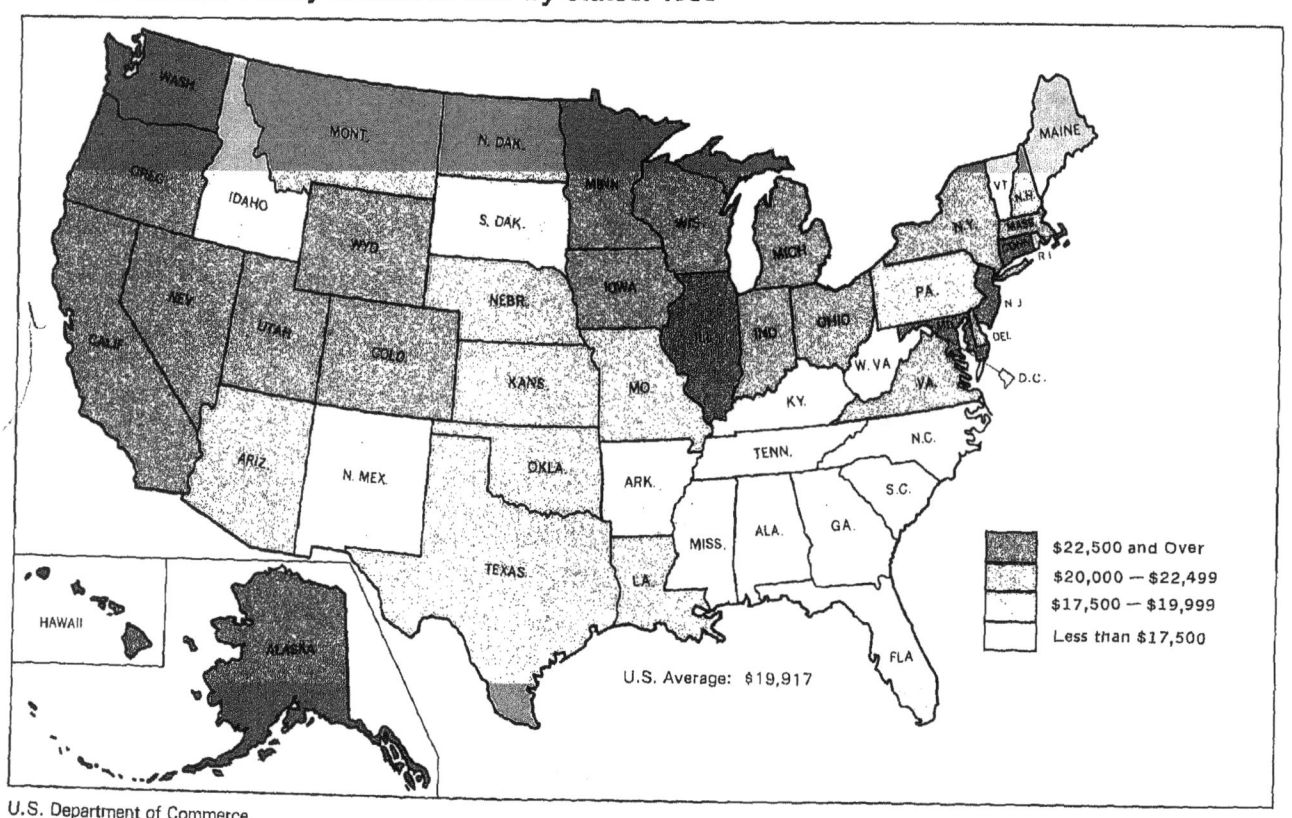

FIGURE 27. **Median Family Income in 1979 by States: 1980**

U.S. Department of Commerce
1–10r UNITED STATES SUMMARY

Bureau of the Census
GENERAL SOCIAL AND ECONOMIC CHARACTERISTICS

FIGURE 28. **Household and Family Income in 1979 by States: 1980**

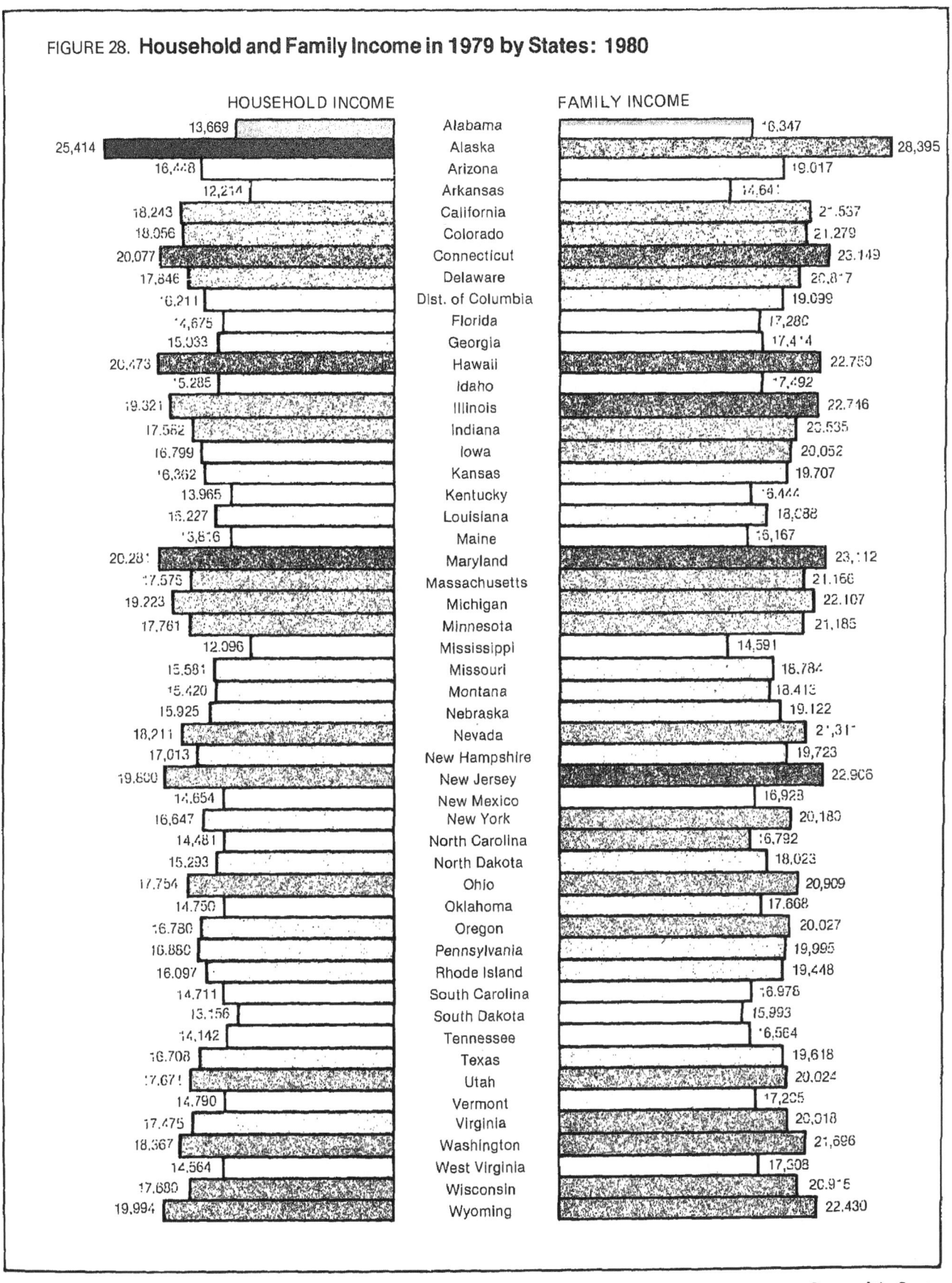

HOUSEHOLD INCOME

FAMILY INCOME

State	Household Income	Family Income
Alabama	13,669	16,347
Alaska	25,414	28,395
Arizona	16,448	19,017
Arkansas	12,214	14,641
California	18,243	21,537
Colorado	18,056	21,279
Connecticut	20,077	23,149
Delaware	17,846	20,817
Dist. of Columbia	16,211	19,099
Florida	14,675	17,280
Georgia	15,033	17,414
Hawaii	20,473	22,750
Idaho	15,285	17,492
Illinois	19,321	22,746
Indiana	17,562	20,535
Iowa	16,799	20,052
Kansas	16,362	19,707
Kentucky	13,965	16,444
Louisiana	15,227	18,088
Maine	13,816	16,167
Maryland	20,281	23,112
Massachusetts	17,575	21,166
Michigan	19,223	22,107
Minnesota	17,761	21,185
Mississippi	12,096	14,591
Missouri	15,581	18,784
Montana	15,420	18,413
Nebraska	15,925	19,122
Nevada	18,211	21,311
New Hampshire	17,013	19,723
New Jersey	19,800	22,906
New Mexico	14,654	16,928
New York	16,647	20,180
North Carolina	14,481	16,792
North Dakota	15,293	18,023
Ohio	17,754	20,909
Oklahoma	14,750	17,668
Oregon	16,780	20,027
Pennsylvania	16,880	19,995
Rhode Island	16,097	19,448
South Carolina	14,711	16,978
South Dakota	13,156	15,993
Tennessee	14,142	16,564
Texas	16,708	19,618
Utah	17,671	20,024
Vermont	14,790	17,205
Virginia	17,475	20,018
Washington	18,367	21,696
West Virginia	14,564	17,308
Wisconsin	17,680	20,915
Wyoming	19,994	22,430

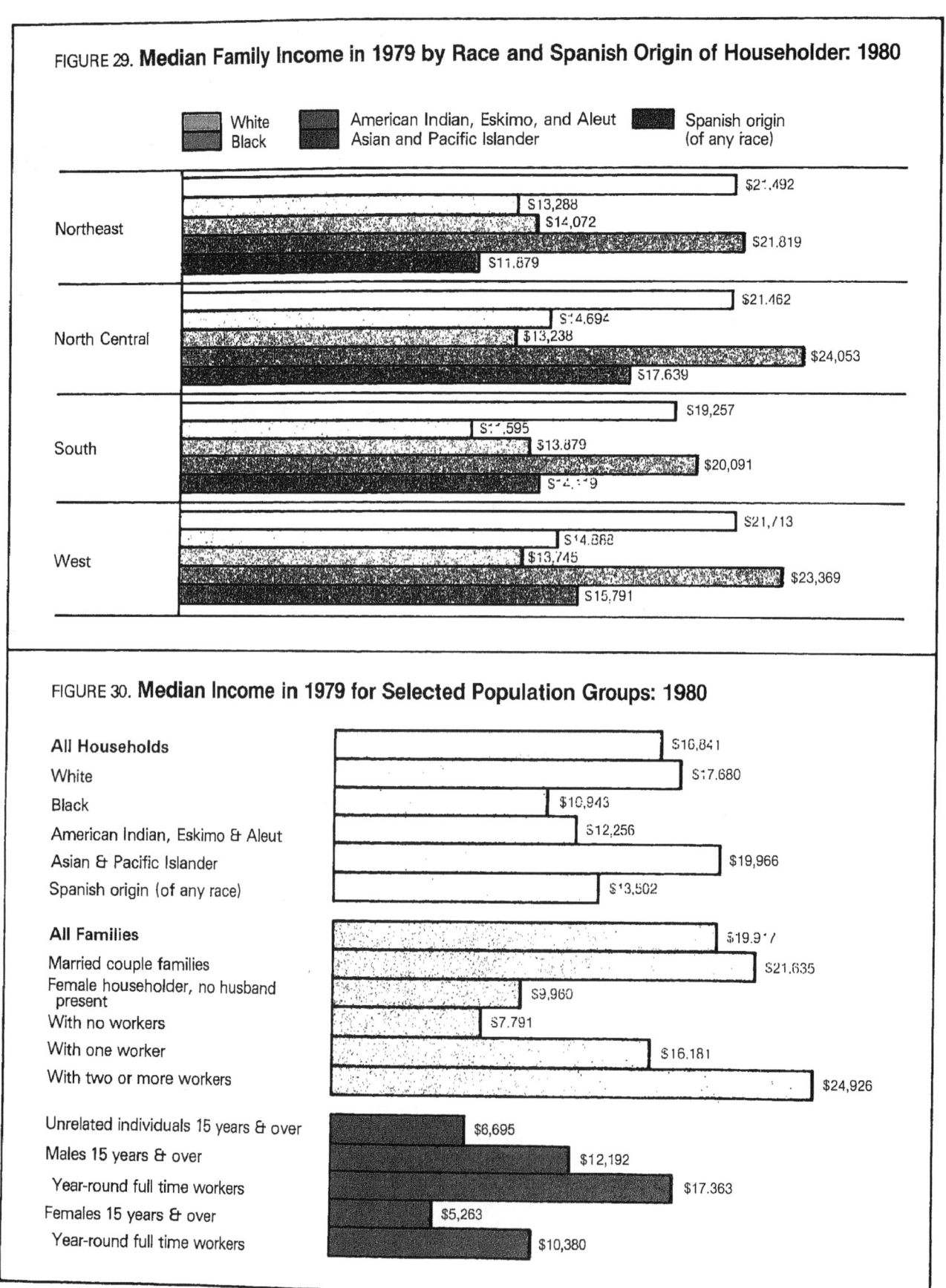

FIGURE 29. **Median Family Income in 1979 by Race and Spanish Origin of Householder: 1980**

White
Black
American Indian, Eskimo, and Aleut
Asian and Pacific Islander
Spanish origin
(of any race)

Northeast
$21,492
$13,288
$14,072
$21,819
$11,879

North Central
$21,462
$14,694
$13,238
$24,053
$17,639

South
$19,257
$11,595
$13,879
$20,091
$12,119

West
$21,713
$14,368
$13,745
$23,369
$15,791

FIGURE 30. **Median Income in 1979 for Selected Population Groups: 1980**

All Households — $16,841
White — $17,680
Black — $10,943
American Indian, Eskimo & Aleut — $12,256
Asian & Pacific Islander — $19,966
Spanish origin (of any race) — $13,502

All Families — $19,917
Married couple families — $21,635
Female householder, no husband present — $9,960
With no workers — $7,791
With one worker — $16,181
With two or more workers — $24,926

Unrelated individuals 15 years & over — $6,695
Males 15 years & over — $12,192
Year-round full time workers — $17,363
Females 15 years & over — $5,263
Year-round full time workers — $10,380

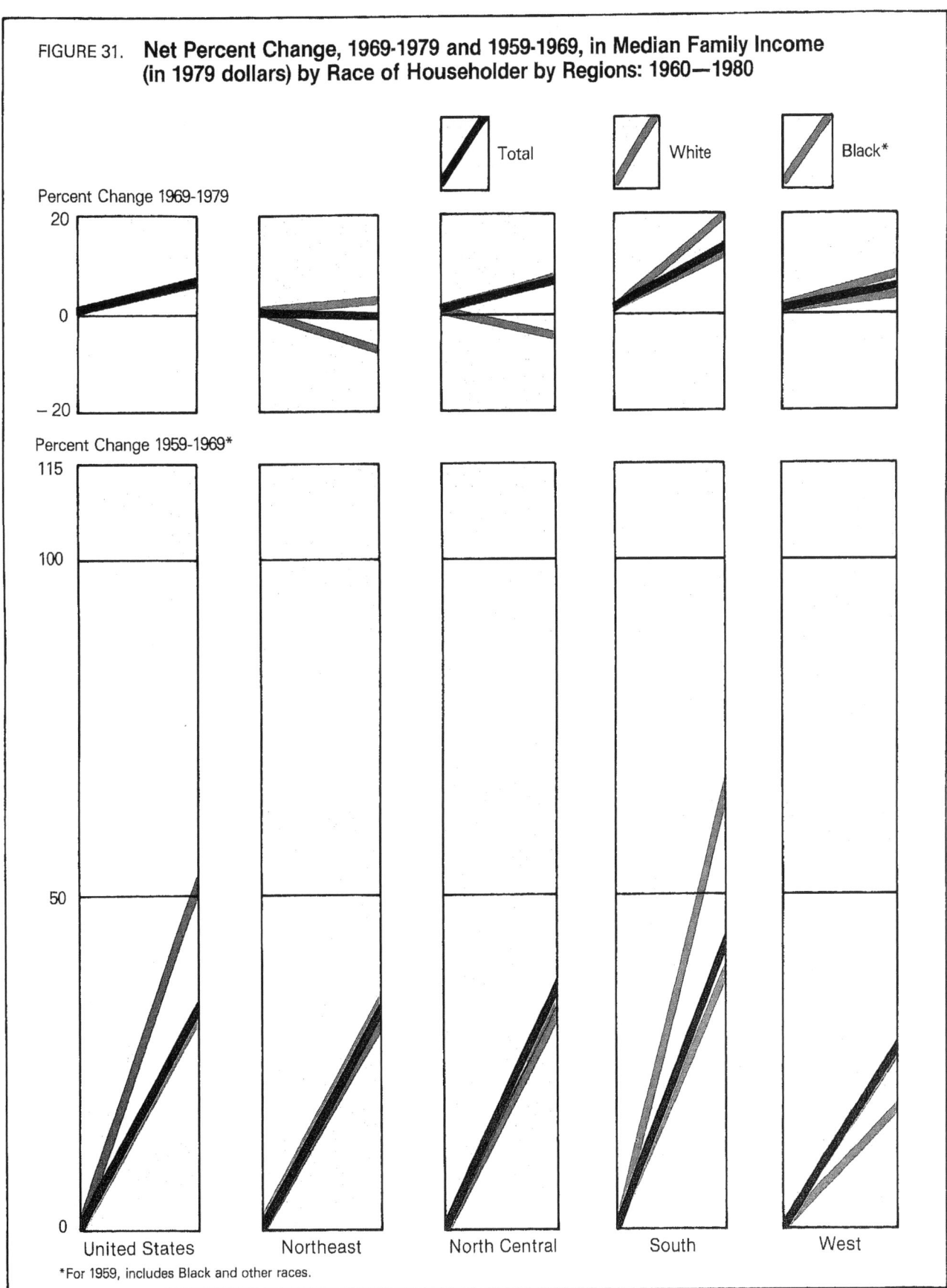

FIGURE 31. **Net Percent Change, 1969-1979 and 1959-1969, in Median Family Income (in 1979 dollars) by Race of Householder by Regions: 1960—1980**

*For 1959, includes Black and other races.

U.S. Department of Commerce   Bureau of the Census
GENERAL SOCIAL AND ECONOMIC CHARACTERISTICS   UNITED STATES SUMMARY 1—10u

FIGURE 32. **Percent of Persons With Income in 1979 Below the Poverty Level by States: 1980**

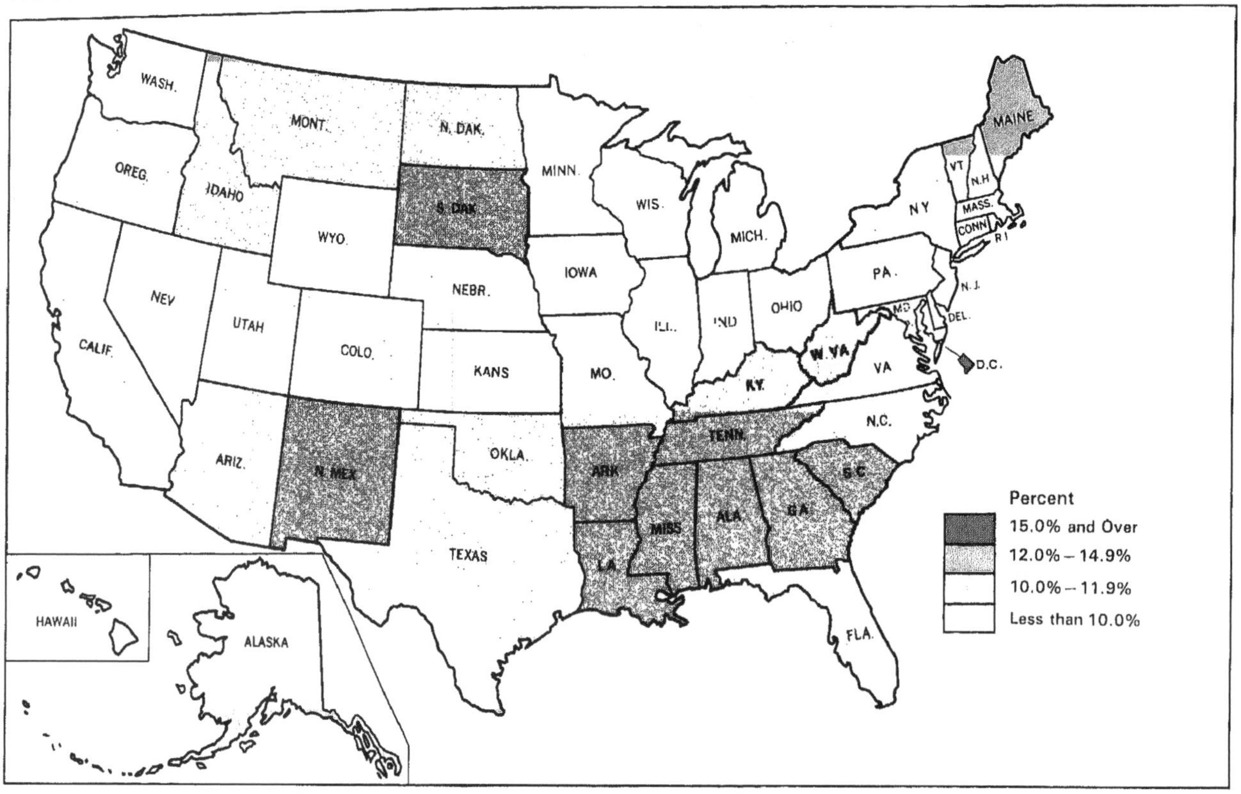

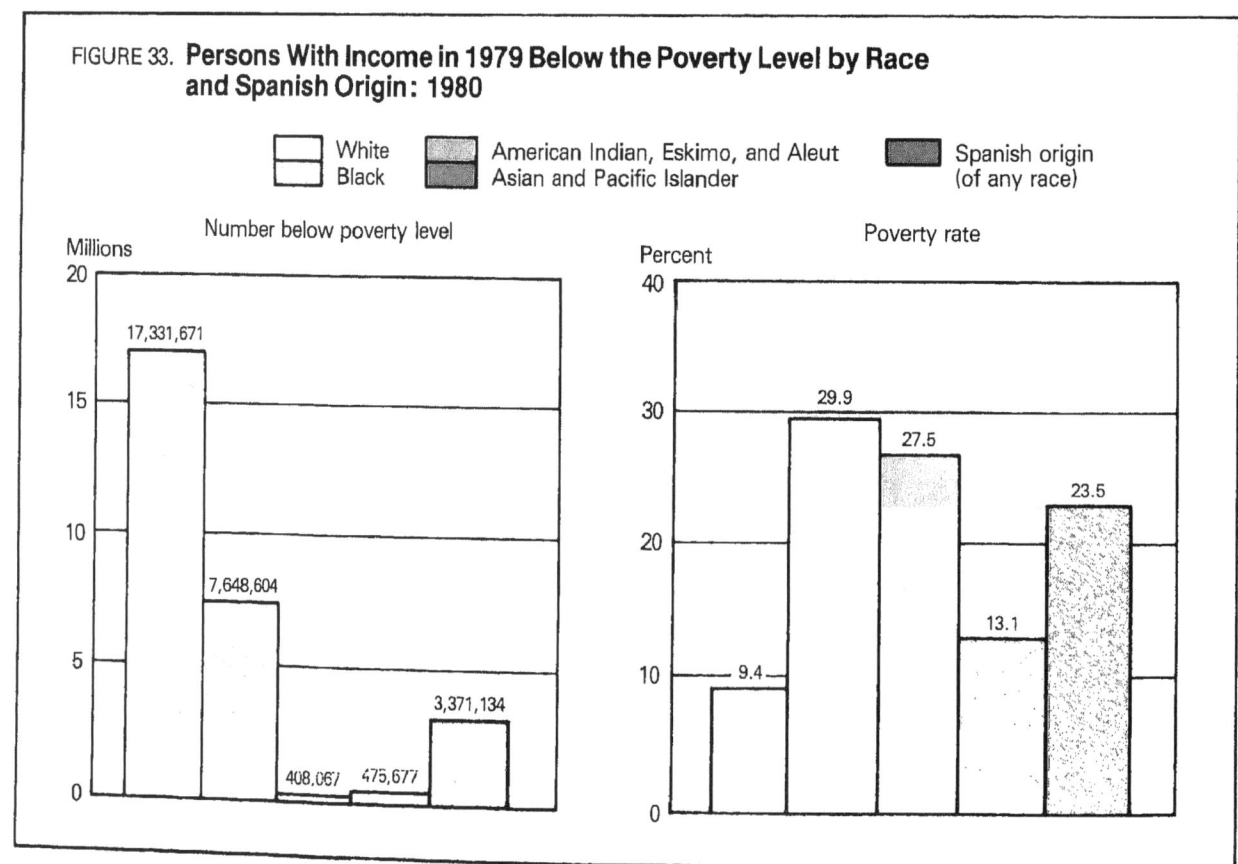

FIGURE 33. **Persons With Income in 1979 Below the Poverty Level by Race and Spanish Origin: 1980**

U.S. Department of Commerce
1–10v UNITED STATES SUMMARY

Bureau of the Census
GENERAL SOCIAL AND ECONOMIC CHARACTERISTICS

FIGURE 34. **Families With Income in 1969 and 1979 Below the Poverty Level by Family Type : 1970 and 1980**

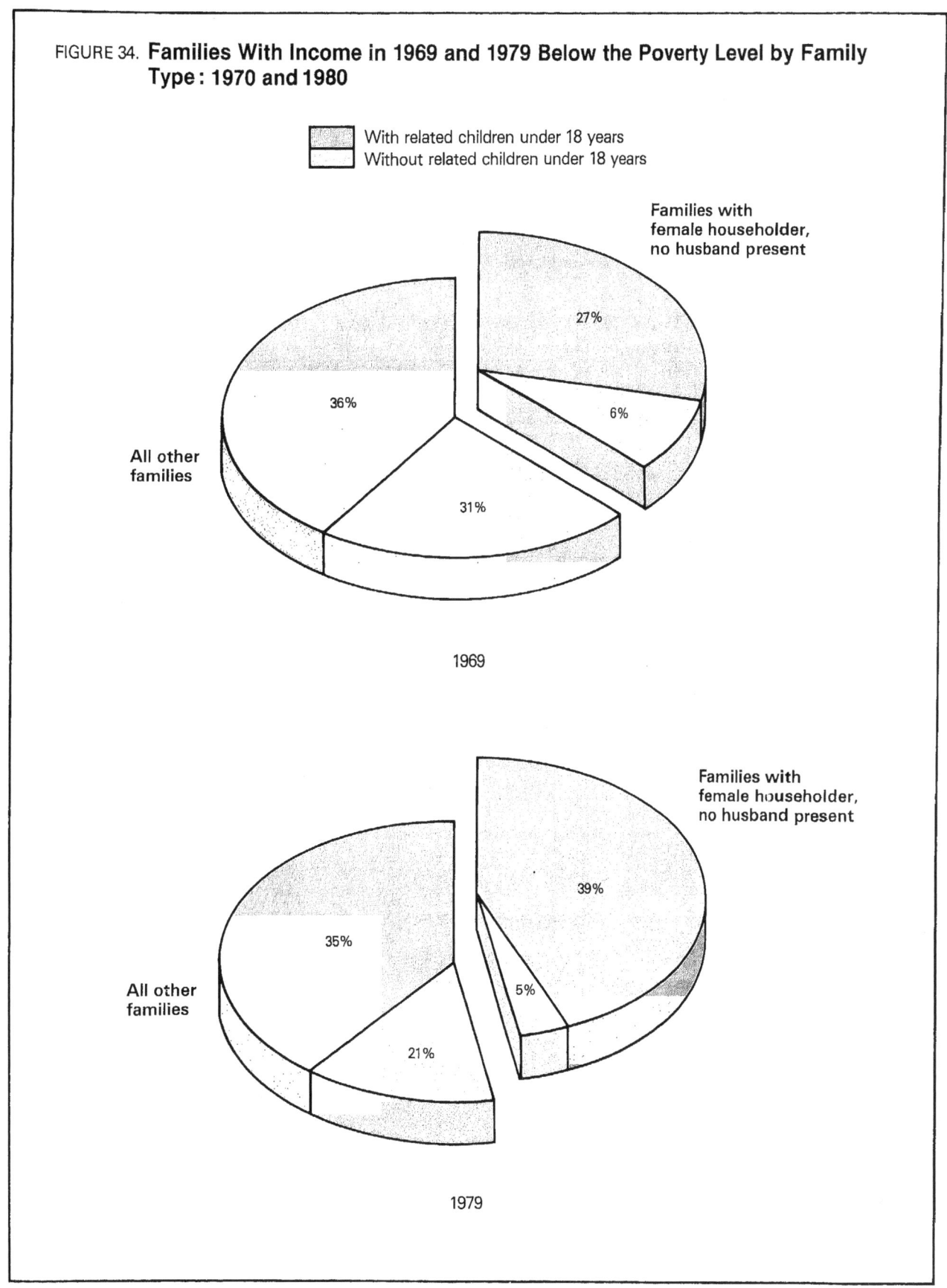

With related children under 18 years
Without related children under 18 years

Families with
female householder,
no husband present

27%

6%

36%

All other
families

31%

1969

Families with
female householder,
no husband present

39%

5%

35%

All other
families

21%

1979

CORRECTION NOTE

Corrections to the 1980 census counts of the total population have been made to some of the areas shown in this report. These corrections can be found in the correction note in PC80-1-A1, Number of Inhabitants, United States Summary, or PC80-1-B, General Population Characteristics, individual State reports and United States Summary. Any additional corrections made after these reports were printed are available by writing to Data User Services Division, Customer Services (Corrections), Bureau of the Census, Washington, D.C. 20233.

Shown below are corrections to the population characteristics shown in the tables(s) of this report.

In table 80 the 1960 data shown for "Black" persons actually is for "Black and other races."

OCCUPATION AND INDUSTRY

The 1970 data on occupation and industry have been redistributed according to the 1980 classification system; these redistributed data may not sum to the 1970 total "Employed persons 16 years and over" because a few employed cases allocated to "unemployed, last job armed forces" in 1970 have been excluded from the adjusted data.

In table 95, numbers and percent distributions have been corrected for the category $10,000 to $24,999, as follows:

Table 95. **Income in 1979, 1969, and 1959 of Persons by Sex and Race: 1960 to 1980**

[In 1979 dollars. Data are estimates based on a sample; see Introduction. For meaning of symbols, see Introduction. For definitions of terms, see appendixes A and B]

United States Regions	Number					Percent distribution				
	United States	Northeast	North Central	South	West	United States	Northeast	North Central	South	West
TOTAL										
1980										
Persons 15 years and over	175 307 629	38 765 075	45 260 854	57 933 216	33 348 484	100.0	100.0	100.0	100.0	100.0
* * *	*	*	*	*	*	*	*	*	*	*
$9,000 to $9,999	5 780 732	1 270 969	1 425 149	1 997 253	1 087 361	3.3	3.3	3.1	3.4	3.3
$10,000 to $24,999	48 805 353	11 056 181	13 259 999	14 833 223	9 655 950	27.8	28.5	29.3	25.6	29.0
$10,000 to $14,999	23 508 570	5 327 284	6 043 694	7 673 881	4 463 711	13.4	13.7	13.4	13.2	13.4
* * *	*	*	*	*	*	*	*	*	*	*
Males 15 years and over	83 824 951	18 170 740	21 647 802	27 664 163	16 342 246	100.0	100.0	100.0	100.0	100.0
* * *	*	*	*	*	*	*	*	*	*	*
$9,000 to $9,999	2 780 801	591 320	645 523	1 022 276	521 682	3.3	3.3	3.0	3.7	3.2
$10,000 to $24,999	33 208 794	7 402 698	9 181 716	10 277 923	6 346 457	39.6	40.7	42.4	37.2	38.8
$10,000 to $14 999	13 411 030	2 983 910	3 408 424	4 583 322	2 435 374	16.0	16.4	15.7	16.6	14.9
* * *	*	*	*	*	*	*	*	*	*	*
Females 15 years and over	91 482 678	20 594 335	23 613 052	30 269 053	17 006 238	100.0	100.0	100.0	100.0	100.0
* * *	*	*	*	*	*	*	*	*	*	*
$9,000 to $9,999	2 999 931	679 649	779 626	974 977	565 679	3.3	3.3	3.3	3.2	3.3
$10,000 to $24,999	15 596 559	3 653 483	4 078 283	4 555 300	3 309 493	17.0	17.7	17.3	15.0	19.5
$10,000 to $14,999	10 097 540	2 343 374	2 635 270	3 090 559	2 028 337	11.0	11.4	11.2	10.2	11.9
* * *	*	*	*	*	*	*	*	*	*	*
WHITE										
1980										
Persons 15 years and over	148 694 602	33 965 054	40 667 346	46 420 379	27 641 823	100.0	100.0	100.0	100.0	100.0
* * *	*	*	*	*	*	*	*	*	*	*
$9,000 to $9,999	4 868 573	1 099 861	1 278 883	1 604 181	885 648	3.3	3.2	3.1	3.5	3.2
$10,000 to $24,999	42 916 994	9 913 639	12 071 039	12 725 662	8 206 658	28.9	29.2	29.7	27.4	29.7
$10,000 to $14,999	20 298 238	4 689 003	5 476 276	6 417 813	3 715 146	13.7	13.8	13.5	13.8	13.4
* * *	*	*	*	*	*	*	*	*	*	*
Males 15 years and over	71 348 399	16 009 326	19 509 992	22 321 935	13 507 146	100.0	100.0	100.0	100.0	100.0
* * *	*	*	*	*	*	*	*	*	*	*
$9,000 to $9,999	2 312 165	510 489	582 647	802 900	416 129	3.2	3.2	3.0	3.6	3.1
$10,000 to $24,999	29 459 541	6 727 817	8 453 335	8 880 527	5 397 802	41.3	42.0	43.3	39.8	40.0
$10,000 to $14,999	11 592 083	2 650 360	3 117 572	3 818 763	2 005 388	16.2	16.6	16.0	17.1	14.8
* * *	*	*	*	*	*	*	*	*	*	*
Females 15 years and over	77 346 203	17 955 728	21 157 354	24 098 444	14 134 677	100.0	100.0	100.0	100.0	100.0
* * *	*	*	*	*	*	*	*	*	*	*
$9,000 to $9,999	2 556 408	589 372	696 236	801 281	469 519	3.3	3.3	3.3	3.3	3.3
$10,000 to $24,999	13 457 457	3 185 762	3 617 704	3 845 135	2 808 856	17.4	17.7	17.1	16.0	19.9
$10,000 to $14,999	8 706 155	2 038 643	2 358 704	2 599 050	1 709 758	11.3	11.4	11.1	10.8	12.1
* * *	*	*	*	*	*	*	*	*	*	*
BLACK										
1980										
Persons 15 years and over	18 897 157	3 534 576	3 750 143	9 959 435	1 653 003	100.0	100.0	100.0	100.0	100.0
* * *	*	*	*	*	*	*	*	*	*	*
$9,000 to $9,999	648 951	130 193	119 491	340 388	58 879	3.4	3.7	3.2	3.4	3.6
$10,000 to $24,999	4 090 577	888 876	974 712	1 787 111	439 878	21.6	25.1	26.0	17.9	26.6
$10,000 to $14,999	2 253 734	493 491	461 732	1 074 658	223 853	11.9	14.0	12.3	10.8	13.5
* * *	*	*	*	*	*	*	*	*	*	*
Males 15 years and over	8 677 940	1 570 228	1 718 370	4 572 463	816 879	100.0	100.0	100.0	100.0	100.0
* * *	*	*	*	*	*	*	*	*	*	*
$9,000 to $9,999	320 967	57 331	48 830	186 424	28 382	3.7	3.7	2.8	4.1	3.5
$10,000 to $24,999	2 505 500	505 694	580 014	1 158 254	261 538	28.9	32.2	33.8	25.3	32.0
$10,000 to $14,999	1 220 091	241 257	226 064	639 208	113 562	14.1	15.4	13.2	14.0	13.9
* * *	*	*	*	*	*	*	*	*	*	*
Females 15 years and over	10 219 217	1 964 348	2 031 773	5 386 972	836 124	100.0	100.0	100.0	100.0	100.0
* * *	*	*	*	*	*	*	*	*	*	*
$9,000 to $9,999	327 984	72 862	70 661	153 964	30 497	3.2	3.7	3.5	2.9	3.6
$10,000 to $24,999	1 585 077	383 182	394 698	628 857	178 340	15.5	19.5	19.4	11.7	21.3
$10,000 to $14,999	1 033 643	252 234	235 668	435 450	110 291	10.1	12.8	11.6	8.1	13.2

Table 72. Summary of Social Characteristics: 1980

[Data are estimates based on a sample; see Introduction. For meaning of symbols, see Introduction. For definitions of terms, see appendixes A and B]

United States — Urban and Rural and Size of Place — Inside and Outside SMSA's	Total persons — Number	Percent foreign born	Native persons—Percent born in State of residence	Persons 5 years and over — Percent living in different house in 1975	Percent who speak a language other than English at home	Persons 3 years old and over enrolled in kindergarten or elementary school—Percent in private school	Civilian persons 16 to 19 years old—Percent not enrolled in school, not high school graduates	Persons 18 to 24 years old—Percent enrolled in school	Persons 25 years old and over — Percent high school graduates	Percent completed 4 or more years of college	Persons 60 years and over—Percent living alone	Families—Percent with no own children under 6 years	Persons under 18—Percent living with two parents	Children ever born per 1,000 women 35 to 44 years
United States	226 545 805	6.2	68.2	46.4	11.0	11.8	13.4	31.8	66.5	16.2	24.2	22.3	76.7	2 639
URBAN AND RURAL AND SIZE OF PLACE														
Urban	167 054 638	7.7	65.2	48.0	13.0	13.8	13.1	34.5	68.6	18.1	25.3	22.1	73.7	2 561
Inside urbanized areas	139 182 696	8.6	64.0	47.7	13.9	15.1	12.9	34.1	69.7	18.8	24.8	21.9	73.2	2 522
Central cities	67 035 742	9.6	65.3	48.2	16.6	16.8	15.5	35.8	64.9	17.3	28.2	22.6	64.9	2 565
Urban fringe	72 146 954	7.8	62.9	47.2	11.3	13.5	10.5	32.2	74.1	20.2	21.2	21.2	80.4	2 488
Outside urbanized areas	27 871 942	3.2	70.6	49.6	8.4	7.9	13.6	36.7	63.0	14.1	27.4	23.3	76.2	2 780
Places of 10,000 or more	13 480 685	3.5	69.4	51.9	8.7	8.8	12.8	42.6	64.6	15.6	27.7	23.6	75.0	2 740
Places of 2,500 to 10,000	14 391 257	3.0	71.7	47.4	8.0	7.0	14.3	29.7	61.5	12.8	27.2	23.1	77.2	2 817
Rural	59 491 167	2.0	76.1	41.9	5.3	6.8	14.2	22.0	60.4	11.0	20.8	22.8	84.0	2 849
Places of 1,000 to 2,500	7 034 378	2.3	75.4	42.9	6.5	5.4	13.8	22.2	60.0	11.3	27.0	22.3	79.6	2 865
Other rural	52 456 789	1.9	76.2	41.8	5.2	6.9	14.3	22.0	60.5	11.0	19.7	22.9	84.6	2 847
Rural farm	5 617 903	1.3	84.4	23.0	5.6	10.5	8.2	26.0	62.0	9.6	12.8	16.7	92.8	3 021
INSIDE AND OUTSIDE SMSA's														
Inside SMSA's	169 430 577	7.6	65.6	47.3	12.6	13.6	12.9	32.8	69.0	17.9	24.1	22.1	75.4	2 563
Urban	145 451 315	8.5	64.2	47.9	13.7	14.7	13.0	34.0	69.5	18.6	24.9	22.0	73.5	2 531
Central cities	67 854 918	9.7	65.0	48.3	16.8	16.8	15.6	35.7	64.8	17.2	28.1	22.6	64.9	2 566
Not in central cities	77 596 397	7.3	63.6	47.5	11.0	13.0	10.7	32.2	73.6	19.8	21.7	21.5	80.5	2 505
Rural	23 979 262	2.6	73.6	44.1	5.7	8.3	12.5	24.1	65.7	13.4	18.9	22.8	85.8	2 732
Outside SMSA's	57 115 228	2.0	75.3	43.7	6.2	6.5	14.7	28.5	59.0	11.2	24.3	22.9	80.1	2 887
Urban	21 603 323	2.9	71.3	49.0	7.9	8.1	13.6	37.9	62.4	14.1	27.9	23.0	75.0	2 789
Rural	35 511 905	1.5	77.7	40.4	5.1	5.7	15.4	20.6	56.9	9.4	21.8	22.9	82.8	2 940

Table 73. Summary of Economic Characteristics: 1980

[Data are estimates based on a sample; see Introduction. For meaning of symbols, see Introduction. For definitions of terms, see appendixes A and B]

United States — Urban and Rural and Size of Place — Inside and Outside SMSA's	Percent in labor force — Male, 16 years and over	Female, 16 years and over — Total	With own children under 6 years	Nonworkers per 100 workers	Civilian labor force—Percent unemployed	Employed persons 16 years and over—Percent in manufacturing industries	Workers 16 years and over — Percent worked outside area of residence	Percent in carpools	Percent using public transportation	Families—Percent with no workers in 1979	Median income in 1979 (dollars) — Households	Families	Per capita income in 1979 (dollars)	Income in 1979 below poverty level — Percent of persons for whom poverty status is determined	Percent of families
United States	75.1	49.9	45.7	114	6.5	22.4	...	19.7	6.4	12.8	16 841	19 917	7 298	12.4	9.6
URBAN AND RURAL AND SIZE OF PLACE															
Urban	75.7	51.4	46.5	108	6.4	21.5	...	18.7	8.2	12.8	17 159	20 653	7 645	12.1	9.2
Inside urbanized areas	76.4	52.1	45.9	105	6.3	21.3	...	18.3	9.5	12.6	17 738	21 243	7 887	11.8	9.0
Central cities	73.2	51.2	47.4	111	7.3	19.7	...	17.7	14.5	15.1	14 914	18 379	7 166	16.5	12.9
Urban fringe	79.2	53.0	44.6	101	5.4	22.7	...	18.8	5.2	10.5	20 790	23 639	8 557	7.4	5.7
Outside urbanized areas	72.1	47.6	49.1	123	6.9	22.5	...	21.2	1.1	13.9	14 501	17 791	6 439	14.0	10.2
Places of 10,000 or more	72.4	49.0	50.1	118	6.8	21.7	...	20.2	1.3	13.1	14 608	18 118	6 527	14.3	10.2
Places of 2,500 to 10,000	71.9	46.3	48.1	128	7.0	23.2	...	22.2	0.9	14.6	14 402	17 501	6 356	13.6	10.2
Rural	73.7	45.4	43.6	130	7.0	25.4	...	22.8	0.8	12.6	15 954	17 995	6 322	13.2	10.6
Places of 1,000 to 2,500	71.3	44.9	46.5	133	7.0	24.5	...	23.3	0.8	15.1	14 220	17 205	6 227	13.2	10.0
Other rural	74.0	45.5	43.3	130	7.0	25.5	...	22.8	0.8	12.2	16 202	18 110	6 335	13.2	10.6
Rural farm	78.1	40.3	37.9	119	3.6	13.4	...	13.3	0.4	8.1	16 498	17 730	6 851	14.7	12.5
INSIDE AND OUTSIDE SMSA's															
Inside SMSA's	76.4	51.5	45.5	108	6.3	22.1	...	19.0	8.1	12.3	17 880	21 128	7 743	11.4	8.7
Urban	76.3	52.0	46.0	106	6.3	21.5	...	18.5	9.2	12.6	17 683	21 165	7 838	11.7	9.0
Central cities	73.3	51.2	47.3	111	7.3	20.0	...	17.7	14.3	15.1	14 955	18 398	7 158	16.5	12.9
Not in central cities	78.9	52.6	44.8	102	5.5	22.7	...	19.1	4.9	10.6	20 488	23 303	8 433	7.6	5.8
Rural	77.0	48.2	42.8	119	6.3	26.2	...	22.0	1.0	10.3	19 088	20 940	7 165	9.3	7.4
Outside SMSA's	71.3	45.1	46.2	132	7.2	23.5	...	22.3	0.8	14.1	14 040	16 592	5 977	15.4	12.0
Urban	71.2	47.4	49.8	124	6.9	21.6	...	20.5	1.1	14.2	13 937	17 302	6 346	14.8	10.8
Rural	71.4	43.6	44.2	138	7.5	24.8	...	23.4	0.6	14.1	14 104	16 204	5 753	15.8	12.7

Table 74. Race by Sex: 1980

United States
Urban and Rural and Size of Place
Inside and Outside SMSA's

[Data are estimates based on a sample; see Introduction. For meaning of symbols, see Introduction. For definitions of terms, see appendixes A and B]

Columns "Japanese" through "Samoan" fall under the spanning heading "Asian and Pacific Islander."

	White	Black	American Indian	Eskimo	Aleut	Japanese	Chinese	Filipino	Korean	Asian Indian	Vietnamese	Hawaiian	Guamanian	Samoan	Other	Race, n.e.c.
URBAN AND RURAL AND SIZE OF PLACE																
United States	189 035 012	26 482 349	1 478 523	42 098	13 715	716 331	812 178	781 894	357 393	387 223	245 025	172 346	30 695	39 520	183 835	5 767 668
Male	92 050 198	12 508 991	729 538	21 242	6 938	328 703	410 936	377 172	149 954	193 463	127 484	83 984	15 540	20 089	93 232	2 930 049
Female	96 984 814	13 973 358	748 985	20 856	6 777	387 628	401 242	404 722	207 439	193 760	117 541	88 362	15 155	19 431	90 603	2 837 619
Urban	134 948 026	22 583 845	806 590	13 210	7 275	656 234	787 548	722 586	332 137	357 085	233 418	141 808	28 135	37 920	173 933	5 224 888
Male	64 979 736	10 585 378	393 899	6 172	3 555	302 286	398 794	347 339	141 630	180 938	121 931	68 965	14 358	19 284	88 564	2 634 414
Female	69 968 290	11 998 467	412 691	7 038	3 720	353 948	388 754	375 247	190 507	176 147	111 487	72 843	13 777	18 636	85 369	2 590 474
Inside urbanized areas	110 735 104	20 096 606	578 865	8 966	5 786	594 976	755 479	661 722	310 331	331 256	217 338	105 326	25 772	34 132	156 617	4 564 420
Male	53 431 091	9 411 217	283 443	4 236	2 780	274 234	382 241	316 775	134 611	168 959	113 525	51 064	13 131	17 320	79 823	2 291 795
Female	57 304 013	10 685 389	295 422	4 730	3 006	320 742	373 238	344 947	175 720	162 297	103 813	54 262	12 641	16 812	76 794	2 272 625
Central cities	46 374 448	15 142 971	321 429	6 174	3 778	315 076	469 604	341 693	167 047	162 558	118 981	60 018	12 391	16 820	91 172	3 068 558
Male	22 351 623	7 124 113	155 845	2 880	1 935	146 009	238 361	164 805	72 019	82 957	63 704	28 513	6 348	8 758	47 704	1 524 148
Female	24 022 825	8 018 858	165 584	3 294	1 843	169 067	231 243	176 888	95 028	79 601	55 277	31 505	6 043	8 062	43 468	1 544 410
Urban fringe	64 360 656	4 953 635	257 436	2 792	2 008	279 900	285 875	320 029	143 284	168 698	98 357	45 308	13 381	17 312	65 445	1 495 862
Male	31 079 468	2 287 104	127 598	1 356	845	128 225	143 880	151 970	62 592	86 002	49 821	22 551	6 783	8 562	32 119	767 647
Female	33 281 188	2 666 531	129 838	1 436	1 163	151 675	141 995	168 059	80 692	82 696	48 536	22 757	6 598	8 750	33 326	728 215
Outside urbanized areas	24 212 922	2 487 239	227 725	4 244	1 489	61 258	32 069	60 864	21 806	25 829	16 080	36 482	2 363	3 788	17 316	660 468
Male	11 548 645	1 174 161	110 456	1 936	775	28 052	16 553	30 564	7 019	11 979	8 406	17 901	1 227	1 964	8 741	342 619
Female	12 664 277	1 313 078	117 269	2 308	714	33 206	15 516	30 300	14 787	13 850	7 674	18 581	1 136	1 824	8 575	317 849
Places of 10,000 or more	11 585 754	1 307 050	95 537	1 134	378	38 711	20 608	34 306	12 837	14 596	9 340	23 575	1 426	3 175	10 099	343 181
Male	5 532 728	619 706	46 814	474	173	18 327	10 867	17 164	4 262	7 247	4 933	11 403	732	1 618	5 313	178 323
Female	6 053 026	687 344	48 723	660	205	20 384	9 741	17 142	8 575	7 349	4 407	12 172	694	1 557	4 786	164 858
Places of 2,500 to 10,000	12 627 168	1 180 189	132 188	3 110	1 111	22 547	11 461	26 558	8 969	11 233	6 740	12 907	937	613	7 217	317 287
Male	6 015 911	554 455	63 642	1 462	602	9 725	5 686	13 400	2 757	4 732	3 473	6 498	495	346	3 428	164 296
Female	6 611 257	625 734	68 546	1 648	509	12 822	5 775	13 158	6 212	6 501	3 267	6 409	442	267	3 789	152 991
Rural	54 086 986	3 898 504	671 933	28 888	6 440	60 097	24 630	59 308	25 256	30 138	11 607	30 538	2 560	1 600	9 902	542 780
Male	27 070 462	1 923 613	335 639	15 070	3 383	26 417	12 142	29 833	8 324	12 525	5 553	15 019	1 182	805	4 668	295 635
Female	27 016 524	1 974 891	336 294	13 818	3 057	33 680	12 488	29 475	16 932	17 613	6 054	15 519	1 378	795	5 234	247 145
Places of 1,000 to 2,500	6 382 081	427 261	73 855	540	1 102	11 446	3 421	12 077	2 988	4 043	2 243	5 510	284	286	1 714	100 527
Male	3 054 999	201 112	36 479	296	555	5 326	1 728	6 100	1 041	1 488	1 161	2 725	143	141	795	52 116
Female	3 327 082	226 149	37 376	244	547	6 120	1 693	5 977	1 947	2 555	1 082	2 785	141	145	919	48 411
Other rural	47 704 905	3 471 243	598 078	28 348	5 338	48 651	21 209	47 231	22 268	26 095	9 364	25 028	2 276	1 314	8 188	442 253
Male	24 015 463	1 722 501	299 160	14 774	2 828	21 091	10 414	23 733	7 283	11 037	4 392	12 294	1 039	664	3 873	243 519
Female	23 689 442	1 748 742	298 918	13 574	2 510	27 560	10 795	23 498	14 985	15 058	4 972	12 734	1 237	650	4 315	198 734
Rural farm	5 432 353	111 107	26 627	147	28	8 922	605	2 078	525	898	504	691	136	26	517	30 333
Male	2 822 918	56 763	13 599	76	11	4 608	230	1 038	401	406	231	378	95	14	270	16 689
Female	2 609 435	54 344	13 028	71	17	4 314	375	1 040	124	492	273	313	41	12	247	13 644
INSIDE AND OUTSIDE SMSA's																
Inside SMSA's	138 678 083	21 465 642	768 085	9 848	6 383	636 621	780 833	710 881	330 463	355 244	227 044	129 550	28 203	38 014	166 166	5 099 517
Male	67 346 777	10 103 279	378 868	4 715	3 061	292 276	394 687	341 970	141 262	179 790	118 336	62 829	14 253	19 289	84 418	2 579 321
Female	71 331 306	11 362 363	389 217	5 133	3 322	344 345	386 146	368 911	189 201	175 454	108 708	66 721	13 950	18 725	81 748	2 520 196
Urban	116 319 324	20 395 613	618 183	9 140	5 882	610 244	765 070	683 487	316 913	338 057	221 680	121 632	26 714	37 016	161 541	4 820 819
Male	56 115 264	9 558 381	302 606	4 331	2 853	280 965	386 987	328 316	136 614	172 058	115 846	58 998	13 584	18 783	82 181	2 444 010
Female	60 204 060	10 837 232	315 577	4 809	3 029	329 279	378 083	355 171	180 299	165 999	105 834	62 634	13 130	18 233	79 360	2 376 809
Central cities	47 323 238	15 295 838	323 324	6 215	4 147	304 816	468 973	354 251	146 338	151 230	126 510	51 443	13 321	18 198	94 334	3 172 742
Male	22 632 362	7 090 376	156 942	2 893	1 948	140 871	238 203	170 940	64 044	77 926	67 695	24 278	6 564	8 989	49 430	1 595 427
Female	24 690 876	8 205 462	166 382	3 322	2 199	163 945	230 770	183 311	82 294	73 304	58 815	27 165	6 757	9 209	44 904	1 577 315
Not in central cities	68 996 086	5 099 775	294 859	2 925	1 735	305 428	296 097	329 236	170 575	186 827	95 170	70 189	13 393	18 818	67 207	1 648 077
Male	33 482 902	2 468 005	145 664	1 438	905	140 094	148 784	157 376	72 570	94 132	48 151	34 720	7 020	9 794	32 751	848 583
Female	35 513 184	2 631 770	149 195	1 487	830	165 334	147 313	171 860	98 005	92 695	47 019	35 469	6 373	9 024	34 456	799 494
Rural	22 358 759	1 070 029	149 902	708	501	26 377	15 763	27 394	13 550	17 187	5 364	7 918	1 489	998	4 625	278 698
Male	11 231 513	544 898	76 262	384	208	11 311	7 700	13 654	4 648	7 732	2 490	3 831	669	506	2 237	153 423
Female	11 127 246	525 131	73 640	324	293	15 066	8 063	13 740	8 902	9 455	2 874	4 087	820	492	2 388	125 275
Outside SMSA's	50 356 929	5 016 707	710 438	32 250	7 332	79 710	31 345	71 013	26 930	31 979	17 981	42 796	2 492	1 506	17 669	668 151
Male	24 703 421	2 405 712	350 670	16 527	3 877	36 427	16 249	35 202	8 692	13 673	9 148	21 155	1 287	800	8 814	350 728
Female	25 653 508	2 610 995	359 768	15 723	3 455	43 283	15 096	35 811	18 238	18 306	8 833	21 641	1 205	706	8 855	317 423
Urban	18 628 702	2 188 232	188 407	4 070	1 393	45 990	22 478	39 099	15 224	19 028	11 738	20 176	1 421	904	12 392	404 069
Male	8 864 472	1 026 997	91 293	1 841	702	21 321	11 807	19 023	5 016	8 880	6 085	9 967	774	501	6 383	208 516
Female	9 764 230	1 161 235	97 114	2 229	691	24 669	10 671	20 076	10 208	10 148	5 653	10 209	647	403	6 009	195 553
Rural	31 728 227	2 828 475	522 031	28 180	5 939	33 720	8 867	31 914	11 706	12 951	6 243	22 620	1 071	602	5 277	264 082
Male	15 838 949	1 378 715	259 377	14 686	3 175	15 106	4 442	16 179	3 676	4 793	3 063	11 188	513	299	2 431	142 212
Female	15 889 278	1 449 760	262 654	13 494	2 764	18 614	4 425	15 735	8 030	8 158	3 180	11 432	558	303	2 846	121 870

1—12   **UNITED STATES SUMMARY**

GENERAL SOCIAL AND ECONOMIC CHARACTERISTI

Table 75. Persons by Spanish Origin, Race, and Sex: 1980

[Data are estimates based on a sample; see Introduction. For meaning of symbols, see Introduction. For definitions of terms, see appendixes A and B]

United States Urban and Rural and Size of Place Inside and Outside SMSA's	Spanish origin										Not of Spanish origin				
		Type				Race									
	Total	Mexican	Puerto Rican	Cuban	Other Spanish	White	Black	American Indian, Eskimo, and Aleut	Asian and Pacific Islander	Race, n.e.c.	White	Black	American Indian, Eskimo, and Aleut	Asian and Pacific Islander	Race, n.e.c.
United States	**14 603 683**	**8 678 632**	**2 004 961**	**806 223**	**3 113 867**	**8 432 174**	**390 492**	**101 529**	**175 835**	**5 503 653**	**180 602 838**	**26 091 857**	**1 432 807**	**3 550 605**	**264 015**
Male	7 274 333	4 410 299	976 724	385 491	1 501 819	4 154 920	187 736	50 800	85 889	2 794 988	87 895 278	12 321 255	706 918	1 714 668	135 061
Female	7 329 350	4 268 333	1 028 237	420 732	1 612 048	4 277 254	202 756	50 729	89 946	2 708 665	92 707 560	13 770 602	725 889	1 835 937	128 954
URBAN AND RURAL AND SIZE OF PLACE															
Urban	**13 132 385**	**7 613 150**	**1 944 761**	**790 353**	**2 784 121**	**7 558 994**	**338 639**	**82 814**	**160 907**	**4 991 031**	**127 389 032**	**22 245 206**	**744 261**	**3 309 897**	**233 857**
Male	6 503 864	3 848 310	942 345	376 842	1 336 367	3 708 182	161 266	40 937	78 508	2 514 971	61 271 554	10 424 112	362 689	1 605 581	119 443
Female	6 628 521	3 764 840	1 002 416	413 511	1 447 754	3 850 812	177 373	41 877	82 399	2 476 060	66 117 478	11 821 094	381 572	1 704 316	114 414
Inside urbanized areas	11 551 015	6 362 221	1 887 175	774 651	2 526 968	6 674 811	307 977	70 908	142 991	4 354 328	104 060 293	19 788 629	522 709	3 049 958	210 092
Male	5 705 599	3 217 011	910 042	368 760	1 209 786	3 269 771	146 382	35 063	69 666	2 184 717	50 161 320	9 264 835	255 396	1 482 017	107 078
Female	5 845 416	3 145 210	977 133	405 891	1 317 182	3 405 040	161 595	35 845	73 325	2 169 611	53 898 973	10 523 794	267 313	1 567 941	103 014
Central cities	7 133 085	3 888 839	1 446 995	319 709	1 477 542	3 835 707	238 123	39 811	74 148	2 945 296	42 938 741	14 904 648	291 925	1 644 081	123 262
Male	3 502 417	1 958 474	690 397	151 191	702 355	1 872 208	112 310	19 818	36 144	1 461 937	20 479 415	6 905 548	140 842	807 261	62 211
Female	3 630 668	1 930 365	756 598	168 518	775 187	1 963 499	125 813	19 993	38 004	1 483 359	22 459 326	7 999 100	151 083	836 820	61 051
Urban fringe	4 417 930	2 473 382	440 180	454 942	1 049 426	2 839 104	69 854	31 097	68 843	1 409 032	61 121 552	4 883 981	230 784	1 405 877	86 830
Male	2 203 182	1 258 537	219 645	217 569	507 431	1 397 563	34 072	15 245	33 522	722 780	29 681 905	2 359 287	114 554	674 756	44 867
Female	2 214 748	1 214 845	220 535	237 373	541 995	1 441 541	35 782	15 852	35 321	686 252	31 439 647	2 524 694	116 230	731 121	41 963
Outside urbanized areas	1 581 370	1 250 929	57 586	15 702	257 153	884 183	30 662	11 906	17 916	636 703	23 328 739	2 456 577	221 552	259 939	23 765
Male	798 265	631 299	32 303	8 082	126 581	438 411	14 884	5 874	8 842	330 254	11 110 234	1 159 277	107 293	123 564	12 365
Female	783 105	619 630	25 283	7 620	130 572	445 772	15 778	6 032	9 074	306 449	12 218 505	1 297 300	114 259	136 375	11 400
Places of 10,000 or more	814 439	644 989	33 303	9 157	126 990	455 267	15 712	5 841	7 870	329 749	11 130 487	1 291 338	91 208	139 781	13 432
Male	411 405	324 828	18 719	4 640	63 218	225 824	7 522	2 910	4 013	171 136	5 306 910	612 184	44 551	67 434	7 187
Female	403 034	320 161	14 584	4 517	63 772	229 443	8 190	2 931	3 857	158 613	5 823 577	679 154	46 657	72 347	6 245
Places of 2,500 to 10,000	766 931	605 940	24 283	6 545	130 163	428 916	14 950	6 065	10 046	306 954	12 198 252	1 165 239	130 344	120 158	10 333
Male	386 860	306 471	13 584	3 442	63 363	212 587	7 362	2 964	4 829	159 118	5 803 324	547 093	62 742	56 130	5 178
Female	380 071	299 469	10 699	3 103	66 800	216 329	7 588	3 101	5 217	147 836	6 394 928	618 146	67 602	64 028	5 155
Rural	**1 471 298**	**1 065 482**	**60 200**	**15 870**	**329 746**	**873 180**	**51 853**	**18 715**	**14 928**	**512 622**	**53 213 806**	**3 846 651**	**688 546**	**240 708**	**30 158**
Male	770 469	561 989	34 379	8 649	165 452	446 738	26 470	9 863	7 381	280 017	26 623 724	1 897 143	344 229	109 087	15 618
Female	700 829	503 493	25 821	7 221	164 294	426 442	25 383	8 852	7 547	232 605	26 590 082	1 949 508	344 317	131 621	14 540
Places of 1,000 to 2,500	244 000	189 640	7 777	1 504	45 079	138 036	4 929	2 208	2 384	96 443	6 244 045	422 332	78 289	41 628	4 084
Male	123 644	96 648	4 053	733	22 210	68 830	2 413	1 215	1 214	49 972	2 986 169	198 699	38 615	19 434	2 144
Female	120 356	92 992	3 724	771	22 869	69 206	2 516	993	1 170	46 471	3 257 876	223 633	39 674	22 194	1 940
Other rural	1 227 298	875 842	52 423	14 366	284 667	735 144	46 924	16 507	12 544	416 179	46 969 761	3 424 319	610 257	199 080	26 074
Male	646 825	465 341	30 326	7 916	143 242	377 908	24 057	8 648	6 167	230 045	23 637 555	1 698 444	305 614	89 653	13 474
Female	580 473	410 501	22 097	6 450	141 425	357 236	22 867	7 859	6 377	186 134	23 332 206	1 725 875	304 643	109 427	12 600
Rural farm	79 753	61 379	1 500	419	16 455	48 716	1 138	663	587	28 649	5 383 637	109 969	26 139	16 721	1 684
Male	42 815	33 297	787	281	8 450	25 784	572	322	285	15 852	2 797 134	56 191	13 364	7 878	837
Female	36 938	28 082	713	138	8 005	22 932	566	341	302	12 797	2 586 503	53 778	12 775	8 843	847
INSIDE AND OUTSIDE SMSA's															
Inside SMSA's	**12 793 162**	**7 377 293**	**1 940 742**	**787 507**	**2 687 620**	**7 358 255**	**326 360**	**81 352**	**156 907**	**4 870 288**	**131 319 828**	**21 139 282**	**702 964**	**3 246 112**	**229 229**
Male	6 351 922	3 745 249	940 610	375 708	1 290 355	3 617 243	156 022	40 346	76 445	2 461 866	63 729 534	9 947 257	346 298	1 572 665	117 455
Female	6 441 240	3 632 044	1 000 132	411 799	1 397 265	3 741 012	170 338	41 006	80 462	2 408 422	67 590 294	11 192 025	356 666	1 673 447	111 774
Urban	12 080 573	6 835 343	1 905 981	778 080	2 561 169	6 938 478	312 918	74 048	149 975	4 605 154	109 380 846	20 082 695	559 157	3 132 379	215 665
Male	5 975 455	3 457 830	920 252	370 536	1 226 837	3 401 206	148 875	36 587	73 107	2 315 680	52 714 058	9 409 506	273 203	1 521 225	110 218
Female	6 105 118	3 377 513	985 729	407 544	1 334 332	3 537 272	164 043	37 461	76 868	2 289 474	56 666 788	10 673 189	285 954	1 611 154	105 447
Central cities	7 347 019	4 020 000	1 507 175	326 667	1 493 177	3 941 351	241 111	41 074	75 215	3 048 268	43 381 887	15 054 727	292 612	1 654 199	124 474
Male	3 612 930	2 028 107	719 549	154 583	710 691	1 927 449	113 706	20 485	36 866	1 514 424	20 704 913	6 976 670	141 298	812 487	62 891
Female	3 734 089	1 991 893	787 626	172 084	782 486	2 013 902	127 405	20 589	38 349	1 533 844	22 676 974	8 078 057	151 314	841 712	61 583
Not in central cities	4 733 554	2 815 343	398 806	451 413	1 067 992	2 997 127	71 807	32 974	74 760	1 556 886	65 998 959	5 027 968	266 545	1 478 180	91 191
Male	2 362 525	1 429 723	200 703	215 953	516 146	1 473 757	35 169	16 102	36 241	801 256	32 009 145	2 432 836	131 905	708 738	47 327
Female	2 371 029	1 385 620	198 103	235 460	551 846	1 523 370	36 638	16 872	38 519	755 630	33 989 814	2 595 132	134 640	769 442	43 864
Rural	712 589	541 950	34 761	9 427	126 451	419 777	13 442	7 304	6 932	265 134	21 938 982	1 056 587	143 807	113 733	13 564
Male	376 467	287 419	20 358	5 172	63 518	216 037	7 147	3 759	3 338	146 186	11 015 476	537 751	73 095	51 440	7 237
Female	336 122	254 531	14 403	4 255	62 933	203 740	6 295	3 545	3 594	118 948	10 923 506	518 836	70 712	62 293	6 327
Outside SMSA's	**1 810 521**	**1 301 339**	**64 219**	**18 716**	**426 247**	**1 073 919**	**64 132**	**20 177**	**18 928**	**633 365**	**49 283 010**	**4 952 575**	**729 843**	**304 493**	**34 786**
Male	922 411	665 050	36 114	9 783	211 464	537 677	31 714	10 454	9 444	333 122	24 165 744	2 373 998	360 620	142 003	17 606
Female	888 110	636 289	28 105	8 933	214 783	536 242	32 418	9 723	9 484	300 243	25 117 266	2 578 577	369 223	162 490	17 180
Urban	1 051 812	777 807	38 780	12 273	222 952	620 516	25 721	8 766	10 932	385 877	18 008 186	2 162 511	185 104	177 518	18 192
Male	528 409	390 480	22 093	6 306	109 530	306 976	12 391	4 350	5 401	199 291	8 557 496	1 014 606	89 486	84 356	9 225
Female	523 403	387 327	16 687	5 967	113 422	313 540	13 330	4 416	5 531	186 586	9 450 690	1 147 905	95 618	93 162	8 967
Rural	758 709	523 532	25 439	6 443	203 295	453 403	38 411	11 411	7 996	247 488	31 274 824	2 790 064	544 739	126 975	16 594
Male	394 002	274 570	14 021	3 477	101 934	230 701	19 323	6 104	4 043	133 831	15 608 248	1 359 392	271 134	57 647	8 381
Female	364 707	248 962	11 418	2 966	101 361	222 702	19 088	5 307	3 953	113 657	15 666 576	1 430 672	273 605	69 328	8 213

Table 76. **Selected Ancestry Groups: 1980**

[Data are estimates based on a sample; see Introduction. For meaning of symbols, see Introduction. For definitions of terms, see appendixes A and B]

United States Urban and Rural and Size of Place Inside and Outside SMSA's	Total persons	Single ancestry group											
		Dutch	English	French	German	Greek	Hungarian	Irish	Italian	Norwegian	Polish	Portuguese	Russian
United States -----------------	226 545 805	1 404 794	23 748 772	3 068 907	17 943 485	615 882	727 223	10 337 353	6 883 320	1 260 997	3 805 740	616 362	1 378 446
URBAN AND RURAL AND SIZE OF PLACE													
Urban ---------------	167 054 638	898 672	14 821 079	2 158 382	11 765 333	573 343	620 638	7 604 752	6 196 952	820 687	3 229 267	527 560	1 298 733
Inside urbanized areas ----------------	139 182 696	686 928	11 165 005	1 667 449	9 118 932	540 630	578 451	6 337 290	5 777 006	606 312	2 980 093	476 971	1 258 423
Central cities ------------------	67 035 742	263 600	5 009 745	776 080	3 803 798	263 725	232 010	2 693 407	2 279 976	291 415	1 259 062	235 210	575 643
Urban fringe ------------------	72 146 954	423 328	6 155 260	891 369	5 315 134	276 905	346 441	3 643 883	3 497 030	314 897	1 721 031	241 761	682 780
Outside urbanized areas -------------	27 871 942	211 744	3 656 074	490 933	2 646 401	32 713	42 187	1 267 462	419 946	214 375	249 174	50 589	40 310
Places of 10,000 or more ------------	13 480 685	93 903	1 711 845	236 632	1 260 539	18 583	18 980	609 620	217 727	102 250	117 544	25 093	20 512
Places of 2,500 to 10,000 ------------	14 391 257	117 841	1 944 229	254 301	1 385 862	14 130	23 207	657 842	202 219	112 125	131 630	25 496	19 798
Rural ---------------	59 491 167	506 122	8 927 693	910 525	6 178 152	42 539	106 585	2 732 601	686 368	440 310	576 473	88 802	79 713
Places of 1,000 to 2,500 ------------	7 034 378	57 764	978 692	111 729	764 544	4 623	13 436	327 794	92 164	70 717	70 113	8 307	8 884
Other rural -------------	52 456 789	448 358	7 949 001	798 796	5 413 608	37 916	93 149	2 404 807	594 204	369 593	506 360	80 495	70 829
Rural farm -------------	5 617 903	74 239	836 970	56 049	1 056 489	1 772	4 976	228 033	24 705	94 963	42 001	13 762	4 792
INSIDE AND OUTSIDE SMSA's													
Inside SMSA's -------------	169 430 577	964 972	14 957 497	2 058 614	12 334 621	573 096	653 670	7 648 352	6 274 178	745 606	3 353 407	524 893	1 315 764
Urban ---------------	145 451 315	742 954	11 884 651	1 725 495	9 758 996	547 484	590 423	6 582 046	5 869 057	632 195	3 041 797	475 043	1 267 707
Central cities ------------------	67 854 918	274 527	5 023 872	772 259	3 808 434	268 073	242 305	2 710 102	2 353 792	287 645	1 301 317	223 669	583 594
Not in central cities ------------------	77 596 397	468 427	6 860 779	953 236	5 950 562	279 411	348 118	3 871 944	3 515 265	344 550	1 740 480	251 374	684 113
Rural ---------------	23 979 262	222 018	3 072 846	333 119	2 575 625	25 612	63 247	1 066 306	405 121	113 411	311 610	49 850	48 057
Outside SMSA's -------------	57 115 228	439 822	8 791 275	1 010 293	5 608 864	42 786	73 553	2 689 001	609 142	515 391	452 333	91 469	62 682
Urban ---------------	21 603 323	155 718	2 936 428	432 887	2 006 337	25 859	30 215	1 022 706	327 895	188 492	187 470	52 517	31 026
Rural ---------------	35 511 905	284 104	5 854 847	577 406	3 602 527	16 927	43 338	1 666 295	281 247	326 899	264 863	38 952	31 656

Table 76. **Selected Ancestry Groups: 1980**—Con.

[Data are estimates based on a sample; see Introduction. For meaning of symbols, see Introduction. For definitions of terms, see appendixes A and B]

United States Urban and Rural and Size of Place Inside and Outside SMSA's	Single ancestry group—Con.				Multiple ancestry group	Ancestry not specified		Selected multiple ancestry groups					
	Scottish	Swedish	Ukrainian	Other		Total	Not reported	English and other group(s)	French and other group(s)	German and other group(s)	Irish and other group(s)	Italian and other group(s)	Polish and other group(s)
United States -----------------	1 172 904	1 288 341	381 084	43 931 068	69 737 760	38 243 367	23 182 019	25 849 263	9 835 259	31 280 661	29 828 349	5 300 372	4 422 297
URBAN AND RURAL AND SIZE OF PLACE													
Urban ---------------	866 893	930 241	327 950	37 600 621	51 534 459	25 279 076	15 938 878	18 770 756	7 210 642	22 513 983	21 840 479	4 429 044	3 573 772
Inside urbanized areas ----------------	711 914	735 632	304 748	33 202 474	42 951 783	20 082 655	12 818 320	15 458 779	5 957 426	18 529 696	18 050 336	3 996 394	3 222 406
Central cities ------------------	284 201	312 368	122 535	21 735 069	16 847 004	10 050 894	6 621 709	5 992 568	2 394 265	7 105 801	7 140 744	1 301 329	1 124 125
Urban fringe ------------------	427 713	423 264	182 213	11 467 405	26 104 779	10 031 761	6 196 611	9 466 211	3 563 161	11 423 895	10 909 592	2 695 065	2 098 281
Outside urbanized areas -------------	154 979	194 609	23 202	4 398 147	8 582 676	5 196 421	3 120 558	3 311 977	1 253 216	3 984 287	3 790 143	432 650	351 366
Places of 10,000 or more ------------	74 731	96 365	9 822	2 265 718	4 165 906	2 434 915	1 486 054	1 612 343	607 628	1 934 953	1 846 006	213 008	166 024
Places of 2,500 to 10,000 ------------	80 248	98 244	13 380	2 132 429	4 416 770	2 761 506	1 634 504	1 699 634	645 588	2 049 334	1 944 137	219 642	185 342
Rural ---------------	306 011	358 100	53 134	6 330 447	18 203 301	12 964 291	7 243 141	7 078 507	2 624 617	8 766 678	7 987 870	871 328	848 525
Places of 1,000 to 2,500 ------------	37 967	53 105	6 852	822 685	2 199 549	1 405 453	795 479	846 171	311 632	1 048 454	966 631	103 610	96 143
Other rural -------------	268 044	304 995	46 282	5 507 762	16 003 752	11 558 838	6 447 662	6 232 336	2 312 985	7 718 224	7 021 239	767 718	752 382
Rural farm -------------	25 751	51 036	3 014	343 838	1 700 432	1 055 081	578 356	660 339	201 881	964 567	682 922	33 278	54 178
INSIDE AND OUTSIDE SMSA's													
Inside SMSA's -------------	865 726	891 356	342 099	36 317 580	53 557 500	26 051 646	16 376 017	19 601 884	7 475 064	23 687 380	22 597 530	4 624 576	3 800 409
Urban ---------------	741 310	768 426	311 045	34 133 021	45 145 984	21 233 681	13 548 431	16 320 281	6 256 836	19 602 677	18 992 360	4 111 325	3 317 140
Central cities ------------------	286 073	310 507	128 091	22 092 957	17 051 235	10 136 466	6 688 430	6 058 345	2 416 656	7 186 721	7 223 553	1 337 497	1 154 517
Not in central cities ------------------	455 237	457 919	182 954	12 040 064	28 094 749	11 097 215	6 860 001	10 261 936	3 840 180	12 415 956	11 768 807	2 773 828	2 162 623
Rural ---------------	124 416	122 930	31 054	2 184 559	8 411 516	4 817 965	2 827 586	3 281 603	1 218 228	4 084 703	3 605 170	513 251	483 269
Outside SMSA's -------------	307 178	396 985	38 985	7 613 488	16 180 260	12 191 721	6 806 002	6 247 379	2 360 195	7 593 281	7 230 819	675 796	621 888
Urban ---------------	125 583	161 815	16 905	3 467 600	6 388 475	4 045 395	2 390 447	2 450 475	953 806	2 911 306	2 848 119	317 719	256 632
Rural ---------------	181 595	235 170	22 080	4 145 888	9 791 785	8 146 326	4 415 555	3 796 904	1 406 389	4 681 975	4 382 700	358 077	365 256

Table 77. Nativity by Race: 1900 to 1980

[For years prior to 1960, excludes data for Alaska and Hawaii. Data are estimates based on a sample; see Introduction. For meaning of symbols, see Introduction. For definitions of terms, see appendixes A and B]

United States Regions Urban and Rural	Total			White			Black		
	Total	Native	Foreign born	Total	Native	Foreign born	Total	Native	Foreign born
NUMBER									
1980	226 545 805	212 465 899	14 079 906	189 035 012	179 711 066	9 323 946	26 482 349	25 666 629	815 720
Urban	167 054 638	154 139 673	12 914 965	134 948 026	126 503 117	8 444 909	22 583 845	21 799 964	783 881
Rural	59 491 167	58 326 226	1 164 941	54 086 986	53 207 949	879 037	3 898 504	3 866 665	31 839
Northeast	49 135 283	44 629 360	4 505 923	42 477 376	39 178 990	3 298 386	4 849 969	4 358 047	491 922
Urban	38 908 074	34 718 500	4 189 574	32 446 658	29 432 178	3 014 480	4 735 606	4 248 200	487 406
Rural	10 227 209	9 910 860	316 349	10 030 718	9 746 812	283 906	114 363	109 847	4 516
North Central	58 865 670	56 751 480	2 114 190	52 283 150	50 713 136	1 570 014	5 332 907	5 270 280	62 627
Urban	41 518 921	39 626 173	1 892 748	35 250 950	33 869 592	1 381 358	5 216 121	5 155 498	60 623
Rural	17 346 749	17 125 307	221 442	17 032 200	16 843 544	188 656	116 786	114 782	2 004
South	75 372 362	72 477 605	2 894 757	59 101 152	57 127 089	1 974 063	14 038 782	13 834 724	204 058
Urban	50 413 049	47 812 071	2 600 978	38 172 833	36 404 888	1 767 945	10 426 653	10 246 604	180 049
Rural	24 959 313	24 665 534	293 779	20 928 319	20 722 201	206 118	3 612 129	3 588 120	24 009
West	43 172 490	38 607 454	4 565 036	35 173 334	32 691 851	2 481 483	2 260 691	2 203 578	57 113
Urban	36 214 594	31 982 929	4 231 665	29 077 585	26 796 459	2 281 126	2 205 465	2 149 662	55 803
Rural	6 957 896	6 624 525	333 371	6 095 749	5 895 392	200 357	55 226	53 916	1 310
1970	203 210 158	193 590 856	9 619 302	178 119 221	169 385 451	8 733 770	22 539 362	22 285 904	253 458
Urban	149 332 119	140 611 792	8 720 327	129 077 211	121 187 106	7 890 105	18 331 549	18 082 864	248 685
Rural	53 878 039	52 979 064	898 975	49 042 010	48 198 345	843 665	4 207 813	4 203 040	4 773
Northeast	49 044 015	44 924 334	4 119 681	44 401 708	40 623 920	3 777 788	4 332 990	4 134 290	198 700
Urban	39 450 971	35 654 689	3 796 282	34 964 544	31 501 007	3 463 537	(NA)	(NA)	(NA)
Rural	9 593 044	9 269 645	323 399	9 437 164	9 122 913	314 251	(NA)	(NA)	(NA)
North Central	56 564 917	54 691 356	1 873 561	51 699 213	49 918 782	1 780 431	4 563 020	4 547 819	15 201
Urban	40 463 674	38 807 030	1 656 644	35 805 238	34 236 101	1 569 137	(NA)	(NA)	(NA)
Rural	16 101 243	15 884 326	216 917	15 893 975	15 682 681	211 294	(NA)	(NA)	(NA)
South	62 792 882	61 476 677	1 316 205	50 501 725	49 281 547	1 220 178	11 954 149	11 927 608	26 541
Urban	40 550 757	39 368 237	1 182 520	32 287 549	31 192 958	1 094 591	(NA)	(NA)	(NA)
Rural	22 242 125	22 108 440	133 685	18 214 176	18 088 589	125 587	(NA)	(NA)	(NA)
West	34 808 344	32 498 489	2 309 855	31 516 575	29 561 202	1 955 373	1 689 203	1 676 187	13 016
Urban	28 866 717	26 781 836	2 084 881	26 019 880	24 257 040	1 762 840	(NA)	(NA)	(NA)
Rural	5 941 627	5 716 653	224 974	5 496 695	5 304 162	192 533	(NA)	(NA)	(NA)
1960	179 325 671	169 587 528	9 738 143	158 837 671	149 543 638	9 294 033	18 848 619	18 723 297	125 322
1950	150 844 547	140 413 454	10 431 093	134 478 365	124 382 950	10 095 415	15 044 598	14 930 756	113 842
1940	132 165 129	120 508 488	11 656 641	118 701 558	107 282 420	11 419 138	12 865 518	12 781 577	83 941
1930	123 202 660	108 919 405	14 283 255	110 286 740	96 303 335	13 983 405	11 891 143	11 792 523	98 620
1920	106 021 568	92 001 365	14 020 203	94 820 915	81 108 161	13 712 754	10 463 131	10 389 328	73 803
1910	92 228 531	78 598 458	13 630 073	81 731 957	68 386 412	13 345 545	9 827 763	9 787 424	40 339
1900	76 212 168	65 767 451	10 444 717	66 809 196	56 595 379	10 213 817	8 833 994	8 813 658	20 336
PERCENT DISTRIBUTION									
1980	100.0	93.8	6.2	100.0	95.1	4.9	100.0	96.9	3.1
Urban	100.0	92.3	7.7	100.0	93.7	6.3	100.0	96.5	3.5
Rural	100.0	98.0	2.0	100.0	98.4	1.6	100.0	99.2	0.8
Northeast	100.0	90.8	9.2	100.0	92.2	7.8	100.0	89.9	10.1
Urban	100.0	89.2	10.8	100.0	90.7	9.3	100.0	89.7	10.3
Rural	100.0	96.9	3.1	100.0	97.2	2.8	100.0	96.1	3.9
North Central	100.0	96.4	3.6	100.0	97.0	3.0	100.0	98.8	1.2
Urban	100.0	95.4	4.6	100.0	96.1	3.9	100.0	98.8	1.2
Rural	100.0	98.7	1.3	100.0	98.9	1.1	100.0	98.3	1.7
South	100.0	96.2	3.8	100.0	96.7	3.3	100.0	98.5	1.5
Urban	100.0	94.8	5.2	100.0	95.4	4.6	100.0	98.3	1.7
Rural	100.0	98.8	1.2	100.0	99.0	1.0	100.0	99.3	0.7
West	100.0	89.4	10.6	100.0	92.9	7.1	100.0	97.5	2.5
Urban	100.0	88.3	11.7	100.0	92.2	7.8	100.0	97.5	2.5
Rural	100.0	95.2	4.8	100.0	96.7	3.3	100.0	97.6	2.4
1970	100.0	95.3	4.7	100.0	95.1	4.9	100.0	98.9	1.1
Urban	100.0	94.2	5.8	100.0	93.9	6.1	100.0	98.6	1.4
Rural	100.0	98.3	1.7	100.0	98.3	1.7	100.0	99.9	0.1
Northeast	100.0	91.6	8.4	100.0	91.5	8.5	100.0	95.4	4.6
Urban	100.0	90.4	9.6	100.0	90.1	9.9	100.0	(NA)	(NA)
Rural	100.0	96.6	3.4	100.0	96.7	3.3	100.0	(NA)	(NA)
North Central	100.0	96.7	3.3	100.0	96.6	3.4	100.0	99.7	0.3
Urban	100.0	95.9	4.1	100.0	95.6	4.4	100.0	(NA)	(NA)
Rural	100.0	98.7	1.3	100.0	98.7	1.3	100.0	(NA)	(NA)
South	100.0	97.9	2.1	100.0	97.6	2.4	100.0	99.8	0.2
Urban	100.0	97.1	2.9	100.0	96.6	3.4	100.0	(NA)	(NA)
Rural	100.0	99.4	0.6	100.0	99.3	0.7	100.0	(NA)	(NA)
West	100.0	93.4	6.6	100.0	93.8	6.2	100.0	99.2	0.8
Urban	100.0	92.8	7.2	100.0	93.2	6.8	100.0	(NA)	(NA)
Rural	100.0	96.2	3.8	100.0	96.5	3.5	100.0	(NA)	(NA)
1960	100.0	94.6	5.4	100.0	94.1	5.9	100.0	99.3	0.7
1950	100.0	93.1	6.9	100.0	92.5	7.5	100.0	99.2	0.8
1940	100.0	91.2	8.8	100.0	90.4	9.6	100.0	99.3	0.7
1930	100.0	88.4	11.6	100.0	87.3	12.7	100.0	99.2	0.8
1920	100.0	86.8	13.2	100.0	85.5	14.5	100.0	99.3	0.7
1910	100.0	85.2	14.8	100.0	83.7	16.3	100.0	99.6	0.4
1900	100.0	86.3	13.7	100.0	84.7	15.3	100.0	99.8	0.2

Table 78. Place of Birth of Native Persons by Race: 1900 to 1980

[For years prior to 1960, excludes data for Alaska and Hawaii. Data are estimates based on a sample; see Introduction. For meaning of symbols, see Introduction. For definitions of terms, see appendixes A and B]

United States Regions	Number					Percent distribution				
	Total	Born in State of residence	Born in different State	Born abroad, at sea, etc.¹	State of birth not reported	Total	Born in State of residence	Born in different State	Born abroad, at sea, etc.¹	State of birth not reported
TOTAL										
1980	212 465 899	144 871 155	65 451 542	2 143 202	...	100.0	68.2	30.8	1.0	...
Northeast	44 629 360	34 138 646	9 540 380	950 334	...	100.0	76.5	21.4	2.1	...
North Central	56 751 480	42 242 508	14 227 525	281 447	...	100.0	74.4	25.1	0.5	...
South	72 477 605	48 912 283	23 058 425	506 897	...	100.0	67.5	31.8	0.7	...
West	38 607 454	19 577 718	18 625 212	404 524	...	100.0	50.7	48.2	1.0	...
1970	193 590 856	131 717 862	50 638 986	2 261 367	8 972 641	100.0	68.0	26.2	1.2	4.6
Northeast	44 924 334	33 717 004	7 949 200	1 019 571	2 238 559	100.0	75.1	17.7	2.3	5.0
North Central	54 691 356	39 742 616	12 355 440	344 558	2 248 742	100.0	72.7	22.6	0.6	4.1
South	61 476 677	42 586 278	15 611 575	440 522	2 838 302	100.0	69.3	25.4	0.7	4.6
West	32 498 489	15 671 964	14 722 771	456 716	1 647 038	100.0	48.2	45.3	1.4	5.1
1960	169 587 528	119 293 444	44 691 064	1 061 890	4 541 130	100.0	70.3	26.4	0.6	2.7
1950	139 868 715	102 788 395	35 284 210	426 325	1 369 785	100.0	73.5	25.2	0.3	1.0
1940	120 074 379	92 609 754	26 905 986	279 125	279 514	100.0	77.1	22.4	0.2	0.2
1930	108 570 897	82 677 619	25 388 100	266 709	238 469	100.0	76.2	23.4	0.2	0.2
1920	91 789 928	71 071 013	20 274 450	130 883	313 582	100.0	77.4	22.1	0.1	0.3
1910	78 456 380	61 185 305	16 910 114	75 276	285 685	100.0	78.0	21.6	0.1	0.4
1900	65 653 299	51 901 722	13 501 045	70 074	180 458	100.0	79.1	20.6	0.1	0.3
WHITE										
1980	179 711 066	122 113 771	56 194 867	1 402 428	...	100.0	68.0	31.3	0.8	...
Northeast	39 178 990	30 928 455	7 751 736	498 799	...	100.0	78.9	19.8	1.3	...
North Central	50 713 136	38 686 105	11 820 315	206 716	...	100.0	76.3	23.3	0.4	...
South	57 127 089	36 651 676	20 065 661	409 752	...	100.0	64.2	35.1	0.7	...
West	32 691 851	15 847 535	16 557 155	287 161	...	100.0	48.5	50.6	0.9	...
1970	169 385 451	115 397 413	44 856 968	2 055 444	7 075 626	100.0	68.1	26.5	1.2	4.2
Northeast	(NA)	(NA)	(NA)	(NA)	(NA)	(NA)	(NA)	(NA)	(NA)	(NA)
North Central	(NA)	(NA)	(NA)	(NA)	(NA)	(NA)	(NA)	(NA)	(NA)	(NA)
South	(NA)	(NA)	(NA)	(NA)	(NA)	(NA)	(NA)	(NA)	(NA)	(NA)
West	(NA)	(NA)	(NA)	(NA)	(NA)	(NA)	(NA)	(NA)	(NA)	(NA)
1960	149 543 638	105 655 812	39 245 099	999 119	3 643 608	100.0	70.7	26.2	0.7	2.4
1950	124 382 950	91 984 045	30 824 650	377 500	1 196 755	100.0	74.0	24.8	0.3	1.0
1940	106 795 732	82 533 805	23 791 540	217 103	253 284	100.0	77.3	22.3	0.2	0.2
1930	96 303 335	(NA)	(NA)	(NA)	(NA)	100.0	(NA)	(NA)	(NA)	(NA)
1920	81 108 161	62 524 789	18 196 836	115 314	271 222	100.0	77.1	22.4	0.1	0.3
1910	68 386 412	52 806 091	15 264 203	70 769	245 349	100.0	77.2	22.3	0.1	0.4
1900	56 595 379	44 278 021	12 097 790	65 929	153 639	100.0	78.2	21.4	0.1	0.3
BLACK²										
1980	25 666 629	17 748 030	7 798 529	120 070	...	100.0	69.1	30.4	0.5	...
Northeast	4 358 047	2 636 239	1 671 763	50 045	...	100.0	60.5	38.4	1.1	...
North Central	5 270 280	3 067 300	2 191 310	11 670	...	100.0	58.2	41.6	0.2	...
South	13 834 724	11 114 267	2 677 892	42 565	...	100.0	80.3	19.4	0.3	...
West	2 203 578	930 224	1 257 564	15 790	...	100.0	42.2	57.1	0.7	...
1970	22 285 904	14 955 417	5 434 752	125 927	1 769 808	100.0	67.1	24.4	0.6	7.9
Northeast	4 134 290	2 297 599	1 314 935	72 926	448 830	100.0	55.6	31.8	1.8	10.9
North Central	4 547 819	2 424 297	1 690 794	14 021	418 707	100.0	53.3	37.2	0.3	9.2
South	11 927 608	9 579 841	1 572 459	24 858	750 450	100.0	80.3	13.2	0.2	6.3
West	1 676 187	653 680	856 564	14 122	151 821	100.0	39.0	51.1	0.8	9.1
1960	20 043 890	13 637 632	5 445 965	62 771	897 522	100.0	68.0	27.2	0.3	4.5
1950	15 485 765	10 804 350	4 459 560	48 825	173 030	100.0	69.8	28.8	0.3	1.1
1940	13 278 647	10 075 949	3 114 446	62 022	26 230	100.0	75.9	23.5	0.5	0.2
1930	12 267 562	(NA)	(NA)	(NA)	(NA)	100.0	(NA)	(NA)	(NA)	(NA)
1920	10 681 767	8 546 224	2 077 614	15 569	42 360	100.0	80.0	19.5	0.1	0.4
1910	10 069 968	8 379 214	1 645 911	4 507	40 336	100.0	83.2	16.3	–	0.4
1900	9 057 920	7 623 701	1 403 255	4 145	26 819	100.0	84.2	15.5	–	0.3

¹For years prior to 1960, includes persons born in Alaska and Hawaii.   ²For years prior to 1970, includes Black and other races.

Table 79. Country of Birth of Foreign Born Persons: 1980 and 1970

[Data are estimates based on a sample; see Introduction. For meaning of symbols, see Introduction. For definitions of terms, see appendixes A and B]

United States Regions	1980					1970				
	United States	Northeast	North Central	South	West	United States	Northeast	North Central	South	West
NUMBER										
Foreign born persons	14 079 906	4 505 923	2 114 190	2 894 757	4 565 036	9 619 302	4 119 681	1 873 561	1 316 205	2 309 855
Europe	4 743 550	2 148 364	989 959	693 598	911 629	5 248 564	2 599 214	1 270 408	506 146	872 796
Austria	145 607	67 136	32 299	21 802	24 370	214 014	113 792	51 132	20 571	28 519
Czechoslovakia	112 707	47 776	33 383	15 138	16 410	160 899	70 480	58 404	14 490	17 525
France	120 215	40 218	15 955	30 511	33 531	105 385	43 675	16 092	17 539	28 079
Germany	849 384	270 509	194 961	194 709	189 205	832 965	332 058	225 221	120 121	155 565
Greece	210 998	106 266	50 305	29 526	24 901	177 275	87 832	47 318	20 708	21 417
Hungary	144 368	61 926	36 615	19 273	26 554	183 236	86 224	54 122	16 121	26 769
Ireland	197 817	127 273	27 825	17 105	25 614	251 375	174 797	35 214	15 168	26 196
Italy	831 922	567 612	120 212	60 456	83 642	1 008 533	706 940	150 873	53 501	97 219
Netherlands	103 136	21 797	25 355	15 350	40 634	110 570	26 156	34 317	10 687	39 410
Poland	418 128	215 001	124 119	43 276	35 732	548 107	309 846	163 781	35 192	39 288
Portugal	177 437	140 124	1 398	4 770	31 145	91 034	69 789	903	1 802	18 540
Sweden	77 157	19 963	23 529	10 331	23 334	127 070	34 679	47 708	10 771	33 912
United Kingdom	669 149	219 121	113 422	143 112	193 494	686 099	275 522	131 815	101 912	176 850
England	442 499	132 032	73 394	99 972	137 101	458 114	167 505	86 052	75 324	129 233
Northern Ireland	19 831	8 515	3 017	3 720	4 579	40 837	24 721	5 599	3 712	6 805
Scotland	142 001	57 187	26 745	24 898	33 171	170 134	76 925	36 385	20 351	36 473
Wales	13 528	4 441	2 818	2 467	3 802	17 014	6 371	3 779	2 525	4 339
Yugoslavia	152 967	48 247	70 674	8 449	25 597	153 745	44 267	77 880	5 822	25 776
U.S.S.R.	406 022	192 895	74 245	62 581	76 301	463 462	255 573	88 479	46 073	73 337
Asia	2 539 777	528 307	396 347	448 354	1 166 769	824 887	219 604	120 807	100 219	384 257
China	286 120	94 202	24 367	30 095	137 456	172 132	57 172	18 715	15 474	80 771
India	206 087	71 326	51 097	47 324	36 340	51 000	17 003	14 286	9 107	10 604
Japan	221 794	33 540	24 974	37 934	125 346	120 235	18 101	12 889	13 578	75 667
Korea	289 885	56 221	52 915	60 079	120 670	38 711	8 409	8 164	7 514	14 624
Philippines	501 440	57 024	60 198	59 233	324 985	184 842	21 897	19 334	18 953	124 658
Vietnam	231 120	21 741	30 945	68 425	110 009	(NA)	(NA)	(NA)	(NA)	(NA)
North and Central America	4 664 903	1 020 399	439 674	1 243 063	1 961 767	2 361 153	722 089	283 323	556 641	799 100
Canada	842 859	274 871	156 185	134 091	277 712	812 421	333 415	164 485	82 714	231 807
Mexico	2 199 221	18 126	215 247	527 795	1 438 053	759 711	8 860	76 660	202 950	471 241
West Indies	1 258 363	635 866	44 655	504 723	73 119	675 108	344 152	33 867	248 694	48 395
Cuba	607 814	138 235	21 995	395 351	52 233	439 048	144 479	24 126	230 697	39 746
Dominican Republic	169 147	154 333	1 967	10 380	2 467	61 228	56 525	1 257	2 397	1 049
Jamaica	196 811	138 468	10 048	40 511	7 784	68 576	54 823	4 199	6 361	3 193
South America	561 011	279 389	42 683	125 866	113 073	255 238	124 025	25 716	43 465	62 032
North Africa	71 450	26 263	9 778	14 635	20 774	32 396	15 303	4 430	4 582	8 081
Other Africa	128 273	41 708	23 025	38 048	25 492	29 067	11 147	5 440	5 685	6 795
All other countries	78 896	10 185	8 194	12 057	48 460	88 803	31 412	7 029	13 655	36 707
Country not reported	886 024	258 413	130 285	256 555	240 771	315 732	141 314	67 929	39 739	66 750
PERCENT DISTRIBUTION										
Foreign born persons	100.0	100.0	100.0	100.0	100.0	100.0	100.0	100.0	100.0	100.0
Europe	33.7	47.7	46.8	24.0	20.0	54.6	63.1	67.8	38.5	37.8
Austria	1.0	1.5	1.5	0.8	0.5	2.2	2.8	2.7	1.6	1.2
Czechoslovakia	0.8	1.1	1.6	0.5	0.4	1.7	1.7	3.1	1.1	0.8
France	0.9	0.9	0.8	1.1	0.7	1.1	1.1	0.9	1.3	1.2
Germany	6.0	6.0	9.2	6.7	4.1	8.7	8.1	12.0	9.1	6.7
Greece	1.5	2.4	2.4	1.0	0.5	1.8	2.1	2.5	1.6	0.9
Hungary	1.0	1.4	1.7	0.7	0.6	1.9	2.1	2.9	1.2	1.2
Ireland	1.4	2.8	1.3	0.6	0.6	2.6	4.2	1.9	1.2	1.1
Italy	5.9	12.6	5.7	2.1	1.8	10.5	17.2	8.1	4.1	4.2
Netherlands	0.7	0.5	1.2	0.5	0.9	1.1	0.6	1.8	0.8	1.7
Poland	3.0	4.8	5.9	1.5	0.8	5.7	7.5	8.7	2.7	1.7
Portugal	1.3	3.1	0.1	0.2	0.7	0.9	1.7	–	0.1	0.8
Sweden	0.5	0.4	1.1	0.4	0.5	1.3	0.8	2.5	0.8	1.5
United Kingdom	4.8	4.9	5.4	4.9	4.2	7.1	6.7	7.0	7.7	7.7
England	3.1	2.9	3.5	3.5	3.0	4.8	4.1	4.6	5.7	5.6
Northern Ireland	0.1	0.2	0.1	0.1	0.1	0.4	0.6	0.3	0.3	0.3
Scotland	1.0	1.3	1.3	0.9	0.7	1.8	1.9	1.9	1.5	1.6
Wales	0.1	0.1	0.1	0.1	0.1	0.2	0.2	0.2	0.2	0.2
Yugoslavia	1.1	1.1	3.3	0.3	0.6	1.6	1.1	4.2	0.4	1.1
U.S.S.R.	2.9	4.3	3.5	2.2	1.7	4.8	6.2	4.7	3.5	3.2
Asia	18.0	11.7	18.7	15.5	25.6	8.6	5.3	6.4	7.6	16.6
China	2.0	2.1	1.2	1.0	3.0	1.8	1.4	1.0	1.2	3.5
India	1.5	1.6	2.4	1.6	0.8	0.5	0.4	0.8	0.7	0.5
Japan	1.6	0.7	1.2	1.3	2.7	1.2	0.4	0.7	1.0	3.3
Korea	2.1	1.2	2.5	2.1	2.6	0.4	0.2	0.4	0.6	0.6
Philippines	3.6	1.3	2.8	2.0	7.1	1.9	0.5	1.0	1.4	5.4
Vietnam	1.6	0.5	1.5	2.4	2.4	(NA)	(NA)	(NA)	(NA)	(NA)
North and Central America	33.1	22.6	20.8	42.9	43.0	24.5	17.5	15.1	42.3	34.6
Canada	6.0	6.1	7.4	4.6	6.1	8.4	8.1	8.8	6.3	10.0
Mexico	15.6	0.4	10.2	18.2	31.5	7.9	0.2	4.1	15.4	20.4
West Indies	8.9	14.1	2.1	17.4	1.6	7.0	8.4	1.8	18.9	2.1
Cuba	4.3	3.1	1.0	13.7	1.1	4.6	3.5	1.3	17.5	1.7
Dominican Republic	1.2	3.4	0.1	0.4	0.1	0.6	1.4	0.1	0.2	–
Jamaica	1.4	3.1	0.5	1.4	0.2	0.7	1.3	0.2	0.5	0.1
South America	4.0	6.2	2.0	4.3	2.5	2.7	3.0	1.4	3.3	2.7
North Africa	0.5	0.6	0.5	0.5	0.5	0.3	0.4	0.2	0.3	0.3
Other Africa	0.9	0.9	1.1	1.3	0.6	0.3	0.3	0.3	0.4	0.3
All other countries	0.6	0.2	0.4	0.4	1.1	0.9	0.8	0.4	1.0	1.6
Country not reported	6.3	5.7	6.2	8.9	5.3	3.3	3.4	3.6	3.0	2.9

Table 80. **Residence 5 Years Ago by Race: 1960 to 1980**

[Data are estimates based on a sample; see Introduction. For meaning of symbols, see Introduction. For definitions of terms, see appendixes A and B]

United States Regions	Persons 5 years and over	Same house	Different house in United States									Abroad	Moved, residence not reported
			Total	Same county	Different county								
					Total	Same State	Different State						
							Total	Northeast	North Central	South	West		
NUMBER													
Total													
1980	**210 323 291**	**112 695 416**	**93 696 039**	**52 749 574**	**40 946 465**	**20 588 011**	**20 358 454**	**4 585 180**	**5 198 334**	**6 394 116**	**4 180 824**	**3 931 836**	...
Northeast	46 051 696	28 435 785	16 751 470	10 267 371	6 484 099	3 683 614	2 800 485	1 525 689	359 631	654 153	261 012	864 441	...
North Central	54 512 659	30 197 695	23 777 261	14 397 648	9 379 613	5 561 204	3 818 409	465 393	1 693 604	1 029 329	630 083	537 703	...
South	69 880 051	36 590 971	32 168 841	16 812 783	15 356 058	6 975 945	8 380 113	1 816 719	1 877 780	3 641 696	1 043 918	1 120 239	...
West	39 878 885	17 470 965	20 998 467	11 271 772	9 726 695	4 367 248	5 359 447	777 379	1 267 319	1 068 938	2 245 811	1 409 453	...
1970	**186 094 822**	**98 563 661**	**75 093 663**	**43 356 797**	**31 736 866**	**15 656 054**	**16 080 812**	**3 345 495**	**4 280 744**	**5 269 769**	**3 184 804**	**2 696 618**	**9 740 880**
Northeast	45 056 836	27 012 861	15 069 656	9 142 425	5 927 231	3 296 764	2 630 467	1 357 768	396 587	626 013	250 099	820 519	2 153 800
North Central	51 733 976	28 325 262	20 494 874	12 491 919	8 002 955	4 358 969	3 643 986	449 833	1 620 232	1 007 058	566 863	439 512	2 474 328
South	57 426 841	29 153 085	24 307 553	13 510 217	10 797 336	4 870 872	5 926 464	1 063 799	1 282 091	2 784 119	796 455	739 737	3 226 466
West	31 877 169	14 072 453	15 221 580	8 212 236	7 009 344	3 129 449	3 879 895	474 095	981 834	852 579	1 571 387	696 850	1 886 286
1960	**159 003 793**	**79 331 018**	**75 196 460**	**47 387 163**	**27 809 297**	**13 667 810**	**14 141 487**	**2 841 619**	**3 987 115**	**4 946 463**	**2 366 290**	**2 002 822**	**2 473 493**
Northeast	40 024 689	22 854 218	15 921 421	10 697 081	5 224 340	3 021 812	2 202 528	1 158 424	314 030	568 877	161 197	592 201	656 849
North Central	45 613 695	23 556 699	21 004 211	14 079 747	6 924 464	3 779 295	3 145 169	353 818	1 442 884	966 659	381 808	361 122	691 663
South	48 548 666	23 100 318	24 251 674	14 952 510	9 299 164	4 297 113	5 002 051	882 783	1 088 395	2 511 750	519 123	504 761	691 913
West	24 816 743	9 819 783	14 019 154	7 657 825	6 361 329	2 569 590	3 791 739	446 594	1 141 806	899 177	1 304 162	544 738	433 068
White													
1980	**176 526 656**	**95 181 085**	**79 132 354**	**42 833 520**	**36 298 834**	**18 414 818**	**17 884 016**	**4 049 835**	**4 728 180**	**5 382 439**	**3 723 562**	**2 213 217**	...
Northeast	39 997 528	25 280 420	14 240 674	8 481 329	5 759 345	3 261 215	2 498 130	1 383 088	327 107	552 554	235 381	476 434	...
North Central	48 612 375	27 173 894	21 113 513	12 397 043	8 716 470	5 291 646	3 424 824	417 081	1 564 687	869 910	573 146	324 968	...
South	55 201 392	28 334 238	26 145 753	12 887 424	13 258 329	6 036 912	7 221 417	1 559 355	1 688 985	3 081 482	891 595	721 401	...
West	32 715 361	14 392 533	17 632 414	9 067 724	8 564 690	3 825 045	4 739 645	690 311	1 147 401	878 493	2 023 440	690 414	...
1970	**163 672 885**	**87 190 498**	**66 318 035**	**36 828 871**	**29 489 164**	**14 656 282**	**14 832 882**	**3 164 381**	**4 068 747**	**4 585 437**	**3 014 317**	**2 257 887**	**7 906 465**
Northeast	(NA)	(NA)	(NA)	(NA)	(NA)	(NA)	(NA)	(NA)	(NA)	(NA)	(NA)	(NA)	(NA)
North Central	(NA)	(NA)	(NA)	(NA)	(NA)	(NA)	(NA)	(NA)	(NA)	(NA)	(NA)	(NA)	(NA)
South	(NA)	(NA)	(NA)	(NA)	(NA)	(NA)	(NA)	(NA)	(NA)	(NA)	(NA)	(NA)	(NA)
West	(NA)	(NA)	(NA)	(NA)	(NA)	(NA)	(NA)	(NA)	(NA)	(NA)	(NA)	(NA)	(NA)
1960	**141 472 121**	**70 912 792**	**66 712 441**	**40 790 334**	**25 922 107**	**12 843 941**	**13 078 166**	**2 721 840**	**3 816 222**	**4 277 586**	**2 262 518**	**1 834 950**	**2 011 938**
Northeast	37 288 031	21 582 490	14 604 675	9 746 214	4 858 461	2 870 439	1 988 022	1 116 591	297 884	419 116	154 431	548 881	551 985
North Central	42 537 882	22 359 756	19 282 062	12 672 344	6 609 718	3 706 598	2 903 120	339 444	1 380 893	815 410	367 373	339 254	556 810
South	38 728 501	17 924 257	19 815 852	11 401 639	8 414 213	3 802 227	4 611 986	835 066	1 037 934	2 244 670	494 316	464 675	523 717
West	22 917 707	9 046 289	13 009 852	6 970 137	6 039 715	2 464 677	3 575 038	430 739	1 099 511	798 390	1 246 398	482 140	379 426
Black													
1980	**24 000 883**	**13 623 592**	**10 096 880**	**7 052 928**	**3 043 952**	**1 356 523**	**1 687 429**	**370 713**	**333 829**	**810 978**	**171 909**	**280 411**	...
Northeast	4 437 022	2 536 371	1 789 683	1 312 706	476 977	276 630	200 347	83 123	20 903	83 656	12 665	110 968	...
North Central	4 818 129	2 657 833	2 133 687	1 661 215	472 472	186 213	286 259	32 105	96 221	129 908	28 025	26 609	...
South	12 691 791	7 486 653	5 096 110	3 420 854	1 675 256	755 400	919 856	208 241	144 314	480 489	86 812	109 028	...
West	2 053 941	942 735	1 077 400	658 153	419 247	138 280	280 967	47 244	72 391	116 925	44 407	33 806	...
1970	**20 129 816**	**10 346 841**	**7 917 838**	**5 995 972**	**1 921 866**	**849 985**	**1 071 881**	**158 891**	**179 548**	**646 544**	**86 898**	**186 930**	**1 678 207**
Northeast	3 864 524	1 937 814	1 451 627	1 036 313	415 314	220 843	194 471	48 454	16 648	120 544	8 825	98 332	376 751
North Central	4 070 124	1 879 186	1 780 197	1 413 058	367 139	95 041	272 098	22 628	68 919	163 642	16 909	20 162	390 579
South	10 685 885	5 937 903	3 934 938	3 038 596	896 342	466 252	430 090	69 417	56 686	268 387	35 600	46 087	766 957
West	1 509 283	591 938	751 076	508 005	243 071	67 849	175 222	18 392	37 295	93 971	25 564	22 349	143 920
1960	**17 531 672**	**8 418 226**	**8 484 019**	**6 596 829**	**1 887 190**	**823 869**	**1 063 321**	**119 779**	**170 893**	**668 877**	**103 772**	**167 872**	**461 555**
Northeast	2 736 658	1 271 728	1 316 746	950 867	365 879	151 373	214 506	41 833	16 146	149 761	6 766	43 320	104 864
North Central	3 075 813	1 196 943	1 722 149	1 407 403	314 746	72 697	242 049	14 374	61 991	151 249	14 435	21 868	134 853
South	9 820 165	5 176 061	4 435 822	3 550 871	884 951	494 886	390 065	47 717	50 461	267 080	24 807	40 086	168 196
West	1 899 036	773 494	1 009 302	687 688	321 614	104 913	216 701	15 855	42 295	100 787	57 764	62 598	53 642
PERCENT DISTRIBUTION													
Total													
1980	100.0	**53.6**	**44.5**	**25.1**	**19.5**	**9.8**	**9.7**	**2.2**	**2.5**	**3.0**	**2.0**	**1.9**	...
Northeast	100.0	61.7	36.4	22.3	14.1	8.0	6.1	3.3	0.8	1.4	0.6	1.9	...
North Central	100.0	55.4	43.6	26.4	17.2	10.2	7.0	0.9	3.1	1.9	1.2	1.0	...
South	100.0	52.4	46.0	24.1	22.0	10.0	12.0	2.6	2.7	5.2	1.5	1.6	...
West	100.0	43.8	52.7	28.3	24.4	11.0	13.4	1.9	3.2	2.7	5.6	3.5	...
1970	**100.0**	**53.0**	**40.4**	**23.3**	**17.1**	**8.4**	**8.6**	**1.8**	**2.3**	**2.8**	**1.7**	**1.4**	**5.2**
Northeast	100.0	60.0	33.4	20.3	13.2	7.3	5.8	3.0	0.9	1.4	0.6	1.8	4.8
North Central	100.0	54.8	39.6	24.1	15.5	8.4	7.0	0.9	3.1	1.9	1.1	0.8	4.8
South	100.0	50.8	42.3	23.5	18.8	8.5	10.3	1.9	2.2	4.8	1.4	1.3	5.6
West	100.0	44.1	47.8	25.8	22.0	9.8	12.2	1.5	3.1	2.7	4.9	2.2	5.9
1960	**100.0**	**49.9**	**47.3**	**29.8**	**17.5**	**8.6**	**8.9**	**1.8**	**2.5**	**3.1**	**1.5**	**1.3**	**1.6**
Northeast	100.0	57.1	39.8	26.7	13.1	7.5	5.5	2.9	0.8	1.4	0.4	1.5	1.6
North Central	100.0	51.6	46.0	30.9	15.2	8.3	6.9	0.8	3.2	2.1	0.8	0.8	1.5
South	100.0	47.6	50.0	30.8	19.2	8.9	10.3	1.8	2.2	5.2	1.1	1.0	1.4
West	100.0	39.6	56.5	30.9	25.6	10.4	15.3	1.8	4.6	3.6	5.3	2.2	1.7
White													
1980	**100.0**	**53.9**	**44.8**	**24.3**	**20.6**	**10.4**	**10.1**	**2.3**	**2.7**	**3.0**	**2.1**	**1.3**	...
Northeast	100.0	63.2	35.6	21.2	14.4	8.2	6.2	3.5	0.8	1.4	0.6	1.2	...
North Central	100.0	55.9	43.4	25.5	17.9	10.9	7.0	0.9	3.2	1.8	1.2	0.7	...
South	100.0	51.3	47.4	23.3	24.0	10.9	13.1	2.8	3.1	5.6	1.6	1.3	...
West	100.0	44.0	53.9	27.7	26.2	11.7	14.5	2.1	3.5	2.7	6.2	2.1	...
1970	**100.0**	**53.3**	**40.5**	**22.5**	**18.0**	**9.0**	**9.1**	**1.9**	**2.5**	**2.8**	**1.8**	**1.4**	**4.8**
Northeast	(NA)	(NA)	(NA)	(NA)	(NA)	(NA)	(NA)	(NA)	(NA)	(NA)	(NA)	(NA)	(NA)
North Central	(NA)	(NA)	(NA)	(NA)	(NA)	(NA)	(NA)	(NA)	(NA)	(NA)	(NA)	(NA)	(NA)
South	(NA)	(NA)	(NA)	(NA)	(NA)	(NA)	(NA)	(NA)	(NA)	(NA)	(NA)	(NA)	(NA)
West	(NA)	(NA)	(NA)	(NA)	(NA)	(NA)	(NA)	(NA)	(NA)	(NA)	(NA)	(NA)	(NA)
1960	**100.0**	**50.1**	**47.2**	**28.8**	**18.3**	**9.1**	**9.2**	**1.9**	**2.7**	**3.0**	**1.6**	**1.3**	**1.4**
Northeast	100.0	57.9	39.2	26.1	13.0	7.7	5.3	3.0	0.8	1.1	0.4	1.5	1.5
North Central	100.0	52.6	45.3	29.8	15.5	8.7	6.8	0.8	3.2	1.9	0.9	0.8	1.3
South	100.0	46.3	51.2	29.4	21.7	9.8	11.9	2.2	2.7	5.8	1.3	1.2	1.4
West	100.0	39.5	56.8	30.4	26.4	10.8	15.6	1.9	4.8	3.5	5.4	2.1	1.7
Black													
1980	**100.0**	**56.8**	**42.1**	**29.4**	**12.7**	**5.7**	**7.0**	**1.5**	**1.4**	**3.4**	**0.7**	**1.2**	...
Northeast	100.0	57.2	40.3	29.6	10.7	6.2	4.5	1.9	0.5	1.9	0.3	2.5	...
North Central	100.0	55.2	44.3	34.5	9.8	3.9	5.9	0.7	2.0	2.7	0.6	0.6	...
South	100.0	59.0	40.2	27.0	13.2	6.0	7.2	1.6	1.1	3.8	0.7	0.9	...
West	100.0	45.9	52.5	32.0	20.4	6.7	13.7	2.3	3.5	5.7	2.2	1.6	...
1970	**100.0**	**51.4**	**39.3**	**29.8**	**9.5**	**4.2**	**5.3**	**0.8**	**0.9**	**3.2**	**0.4**	**0.9**	**8.3**
Northeast	100.0	50.1	37.6	26.8	10.7	5.7	5.0	1.3	0.4	3.1	0.2	2.5	9.7
North Central	100.0	46.2	43.7	34.7	9.0	2.3	6.7	0.6	1.7	4.0	0.4	0.5	9.6
South	100.0	55.6	36.8	28.4	8.4	4.4	4.0	0.6	0.5	2.5	0.3	0.4	7.2
West	100.0	39.2	49.8	33.7	16.1	4.5	11.6	1.2	2.5	6.2	1.7	1.5	9.5
1960	**100.0**	**48.0**	**48.4**	**37.6**	**10.8**	**4.7**	**6.1**	**0.7**	**1.0**	**3.8**	**0.6**	**1.0**	**2.6**
Northeast	100.0	46.5	48.1	34.7	13.4	5.5	7.8	1.5	0.6	5.5	0.2	1.6	3.8
North Central	100.0	38.9	56.0	45.8	10.2	2.4	7.9	0.5	2.0	4.9	0.5	0.7	4.4
South	100.0	52.7	45.2	36.2	9.0	5.0	4.0	0.5	0.5	2.7	0.3	0.4	1.7
West	100.0	40.7	53.1	36.2	16.9	5.5	11.4	0.8	2.2	5.3	3.0	3.3	2.8

1—18 UNITED STATES SUMMARY

GENERAL SOCIAL AND ECONOMIC CHARACTERISTICS

360

Table 81. School Enrollment by Age: 1910 to 1980

[Data for persons enrolled in school include persons in nursery school and above in 1970 and 1980, and in kindergarten and above for earlier years. For years prior to 1960, excludes data for Alaska and Hawaii. Data are estimates based on a sample; see Introduction. For meaning of symbols, see Introduction. For definitions of terms, see appendixes A and B]

United States Regions	Persons 5 to 34 years old¹	5 and 6	7 to 13	14 and 15	16 and 17	18 and 19	20 and 21	22 to 24	25 to 34
1980									
United States	114 593 142	6 250 345	24 867 527	7 915 325	8 460 778	8 623 979	8 659 136	12 634 678	37 181 374
Enrolled in school	57 961 496	5 392 483	24 570 506	7 739 575	7 478 643	4 514 290	2 808 724	2 186 802	3 270 473
Percent enrolled	50.6	86.3	98.8	97.8	88.4	52.3	32.4	17.3	8.8
Northeast	23 862 432	1 213 381	5 216 175	1 745 486	1 826 069	1 804 558	1 784 053	2 551 127	7 721 583
Enrolled in school	12 495 416	1 090 732	5 162 819	1 718 396	1 662 568	1 038 568	674 084	462 005	686 244
Percent enrolled	52.4	89.9	99.0	98.4	91.0	57.6	37.8	18.1	8.9
North Central	29 848 712	1 667 950	6 562 058	2 083 217	2 245 844	2 282 016	2 271 508	3 294 193	9 441 926
Enrolled in school	15 292 635	1 428 123	6 502 015	2 050 238	2 033 711	1 222 331	735 149	548 284	772 784
Percent enrolled	51.2	85.6	99.1	98.4	90.6	53.6	32.4	16.6	8.2
South	38 412 384	2 159 216	8 473 536	2 663 506	2 835 091	2 912 689	2 909 306	4 204 931	12 254 109
Enrolled in school	19 108 269	1 819 660	8 350 441	2 585 383	2 421 985	1 440 816	868 858	664 435	956 691
Percent enrolled	49.7	84.3	98.5	97.1	85.4	49.5	29.9	15.8	7.8
West	22 469 614	1 209 798	4 615 758	1 423 116	1 553 774	1 624 716	1 694 269	2 584 427	7 763 756
Enrolled in school	11 065 176	1 053 968	4 555 231	1 385 558	1 360 379	812 575	530 633	512 078	854 754
Percent enrolled	49.2	87.1	98.7	97.4	87.6	50.0	31.3	19.8	11.0
1970									
United States	101 060 548	7 781 512	28 912 225	8 311 326	7 807 477	7 274 046	6 656 594	9 463 339	24 854 029
Enrolled in school	57 752 854	5 630 803	28 120 929	7 972 677	6 971 172	4 117 197	2 043 405	1 382 082	1 514 589
Percent enrolled	57.1	72.4	97.3	95.9	89.3	56.6	30.7	14.6	6.1
Northeast	23 195 844	1 809 062	6 624 790	1 892 463	1 778 389	1 638 167	1 476 368	2 156 938	5 819 667
Enrolled in school	13 527 991	1 452 677	6 472 420	1 831 904	1 623 669	981 262	501 965	314 913	349 180
Percent enrolled	58.3	80.3	97.7	96.8	91.3	59.9	34.0	14.6	6.0
North Central	28 177 284	2 210 838	8 289 973	2 368 254	2 213 542	2 044 904	1 780 175	2 543 230	6 726 368
Enrolled in school	16 627 718	1 682 448	8 099 304	2 292 470	2 014 323	1 190 134	589 238	376 398	383 403
Percent enrolled	59.0	76.1	97.7	96.8	91.0	58.2	33.1	14.8	5.7
South	31 850 068	2 439 960	9 022 590	2 639 841	2 469 445	2 333 525	2 172 279	3 017 345	7 755 083
Enrolled in school	17 251 770	1 454 216	8 688 754	2 484 090	2 101 498	1 222 767	569 137	359 064	372 244
Percent enrolled	54.2	59.6	96.3	94.1	85.1	52.4	26.2	11.9	4.8
West	17 837 352	1 321 652	4 974 872	1 410 768	1 346 101	1 257 450	1 227 772	1 745 826	4 552 911
Enrolled in school	10 345 375	1 041 462	4 860 450	1 364 213	1 231 682	723 034	383 065	331 707	409 762
Percent enrolled	58.0	78.8	97.7	96.7	91.5	57.5	31.2	19.0	9.0
1960									
United States	82 387 814	7 792 226	24 935 029	5 550 090	5 710 672	4 774 537	4 393 246	6 409 923	22 822 091
Enrolled in school	43 769 592	4 971 868	24 324 115	5 222 690	4 621 507	2 009 441	926 051	651 960	1 041 960
Percent enrolled	53.1	63.8	97.5	94.1	80.9	42.1	21.1	10.2	4.6
1950									
United States	46 532 055	5 502 810	16 801 950	4 267 680	4 175 195	4 344 325	11 440 095	(²)	(NA)
Enrolled in school	29 085 685	3 059 130	16 077 270	3 963 575	3 104 265	1 400 700	1 480 745	(²)	(NA)
Percent enrolled	62.5	55.6	95.7	92.9	74.4	32.2	12.9	(²)	(NA)
1940									
United States	46 351 915	4 196 792	15 828 035	4 828 249	4 892 170	5 018 834	11 587 835	(²)	(NA)
Enrolled in school	26 759 099	1 805 211	15 034 695	4 347 665	3 361 206	1 449 485	760 837	(²)	(NA)
Percent enrolled	57.7	43.0	95.0	90.0	68.7	28.9	6.6	(²)	(NA)
1930									
United States	47 034 979	5 020 535	17 209 566	4 678 084	4 663 137	4 593 279	10 870 378	(²)	(NA)
Enrolled in school	27 359 490	2 168 220	16 398 400	4 156 378	2 669 857	1 165 338	801 297	(²)	(NA)
Percent enrolled	58.2	43.2	95.3	88.8	57.3	25.4	7.4	(²)	(NA)
1920									
United States	40 746 789	4 686 154	15 306 793	3 907 710	3 828 131	3 740 980	9 277 021	(²)	(NA)
Enrolled in school	(NA)	1 922 125	13 869 010	3 124 129	1 644 061	666 299	(NA)	(²)	(NA)
Percent enrolled	(NA)	41.0	90.6	79.9	42.9	17.8	(NA)	(²)	(NA)
1910									
United States	36 988 359	4 069 232	12 950 418	3 569 347	3 650 951	3 691 427	9 056 984	(²)	(NA)
Enrolled in school	(NA)	1 406 026	11 146 173	2 676 465	1 573 377	689 285	(NA)	(²)	(NA)
Percent enrolled	(NA)	34.6	86.1	75.0	43.1	18.7	(NA)	(²)	(NA)

¹For years 1930, 1940, and 1950, includes persons 5 to 24 years old; for years 1910 and 1920, includes persons 5 to 19 years old.   ²Included in preceding category.

Table 82. School Enrollment and Type of School by Race: 1960 to 1980

[Data are estimates based on a sample; see Introduction. For meaning of symbols, see Introduction. For definitions of terms, see appendixes A and B]

United States Regions	Persons 3 years old and over enrolled in school	Kindergarten			Elementary (1 to 8 years)			High school (1 to 4 years)			College		
		Total	Private Number	Private Percent	Total	Private Number	Private Percent	Total	Private Number	Private Percent	Total	Private Number	Private Percent
TOTAL													
1980[1]	62 054 304	3 210 098	513 031	16.0	28 775 352	3 252 115	11.3	15 260 109	1 358 577	8.9	12 379 094	2 419 919	19.5
Northeast	13 361 436	613 933	104 706	17.1	6 023 342	942 030	15.6	3 421 177	433 853	12.7	2 794 895	891 115	31.9
North Central	16 207 717	842 122	97 918	11.6	7 563 935	986 549	13.0	4 120 261	377 709	9.2	3 041 431	579 382	19.0
South	20 410 941	1 136 135	227 178	20.0	9 891 733	840 176	8.5	4 930 012	354 187	7.2	3 696 194	579 224	15.7
West	12 074 210	617 908	83 229	13.5	5 296 342	483 360	9.1	2 788 659	192 828	6.9	2 846 574	370 198	13.0
1970[1 2]	58 634 996	3 024 398	479 989	15.9	33 210 219	3 835 041	11.5	14 480 634	1 417 169	9.8	6 966 033	2 339 980	33.6
Northeast	13 756 373	787 222	93 084	11.8	7 615 607	1 420 700	18.7	3 410 105	550 825	16.2	1 702 339	944 817	55.5
North Central	16 826 188	998 616	61 790	6.2	9 434 109	1 367 721	14.5	4 190 267	460 157	11.0	1 966 593	585 835	29.8
South	17 505 253	657 121	267 394	40.7	10 497 636	621 974	5.9	4 305 769	241 736	5.6	1 798 907	555 303	30.9
West	10 547 182	581 439	57 721	9.9	5 662 867	424 646	7.5	2 574 493	164 451	6.4	1 498 194	254 025	17.0
1960[3]	43 769 583	2 150 521	304 147	14.1	28 987 577	4 167 304	14.4	9 696 039	1 080 595	11.1	2 935 446	1 207 657	41.1
Northeast	10 281 546	619 052	94 194	15.2	6 560 784	1 518 054	23.1	2 338 740	421 606	18.0	762 970	(NA)	(NA)
North Central	12 709 112	821 345	81 245	9.9	8 261 249	1 604 007	19.4	2 785 988	360 849	13.0	840 530	(NA)	(NA)
South	13 585 798	265 582	93 126	35.1	9 609 150	598 474	6.2	2 942 987	171 745	5.8	768 079	(NA)	(NA)
West	7 193 136	444 542	35 582	8.0	4 556 399	446 765	9.8	1 628 328	126 395	7.8	563 867	(NA)	(NA)
WHITE													
1980[1]	49 614 028	2 486 636	421 465	16.9	22 705 073	2 821 583	12.4	12 209 926	1 187 502	9.7	10 295 430	2 093 307	20.3
Northeast	11 130 430	502 991	87 684	17.4	4 961 904	819 071	16.5	2 854 386	386 163	13.5	2 395 908	795 916	33.2
North Central	13 954 434	712 057	81 650	11.5	6 456 295	883 840	13.7	3 583 932	340 530	9.5	2 669 017	516 487	19.4
South	15 091 419	806 599	187 383	23.2	7 201 462	738 684	10.3	3 592 893	310 105	8.6	2 932 263	475 653	16.2
West	9 437 745	464 989	64 748	13.9	4 085 412	379 988	9.3	2 178 715	150 704	6.9	2 298 242	305 251	13.3
1970[1 2]	50 504 385	2 621 049	435 383	16.6	28 160 356	3 633 136	12.9	12 524 745	1 334 475	10.7	6 393 230	2 159 288	33.8
Northeast	12 341 908	695 983	87 354	12.6	6 754 262	1 362 913	20.2	3 078 862	529 436	17.2	1 605 346	896 846	55.9
North Central	15 215 249	899 181	56 967	6.3	8 451 476	1 316 277	15.6	3 807 166	439 828	11.6	1 853 858	551 264	29.7
South	13 514 324	510 815	238 569	46.7	7 905 482	568 688	7.2	3 326 622	217 315	6.5	1 578 624	480 753	30.5
West	9 432 904	515 070	52 493	10.2	5 049 136	385 258	7.6	2 312 095	147 896	6.4	1 355 402	230 425	17.0
1960[3]	38 323 913	1 927 100	287 199	14.9	25 016 064	4 028 099	16.1	8 637 647	1 038 032	12.0	2 743 102	1 142 236	41.6
Northeast	9 557 823	570 763	92 419	16.2	6 056 255	1 488 678	24.6	2 191 408	412 514	18.8	739 397	(NA)	(NA)
North Central	11 780 614	746 245	78 698	10.5	7 611 626	1 572 527	20.7	2 616 686	352 108	13.5	806 057	(NA)	(NA)
South	10 409 721	208 710	83 322	39.9	7 192 861	549 669	7.6	2 332 686	156 988	6.7	675 464	(NA)	(NA)
West	6 575 755	401 382	32 760	8.2	4 155 318	417 221	10.0	1 496 871	116 422	7.8	522 184	(NA)	(NA)
BLACK[4]													
1980[1]	8 830 803	498 281	62 156	12.5	4 316 697	263 372	6.1	2 272 877	109 629	4.8	1 376 829	200 893	14.6
Northeast	1 628 334	75 934	11 502	15.1	765 251	81 933	10.7	434 222	33 587	7.7	284 191	56 110	19.7
North Central	1 825 140	101 744	12 041	11.8	898 339	73 892	8.2	454 634	28 456	6.3	284 460	43 038	15.1
South	4 598 509	282 747	32 796	11.6	2 322 118	78 222	3.4	1 190 302	35 190	3.0	631 364	83 258	13.2
West	778 820	37 856	5 817	15.4	330 989	29 325	8.9	193 719	12 396	6.4	176 814	18 487	10.5
1970[1 2]	7 303 289	356 115	39 338	11.0	4 615 623	165 741	3.6	1 772 979	66 789	3.8	430 747	142 497	33.1
Northeast	1 326 547	85 785	5 078	5.9	819 720	52 794	6.4	313 270	19 274	6.2	76 816	36 191	47.1
North Central	1 510 571	93 202	4 393	4.7	930 491	45 431	4.9	364 121	18 352	5.0	92 865	27 882	30.0
South	3 892 787	142 142	27 614	19.4	2 535 122	50 734	2.0	958 214	22 943	2.4	205 732	69 696	33.9
West	573 384	34 986	2 253	6.4	330 290	16 782	5.1	137 374	6 220	4.5	55 334	8 728	15.8
1960[3]	5 445 670	223 421	16 948	7.6	3 971 513	139 205	3.5	1 058 392	42 563	4.0	192 344	65 421	34.0
Northeast	723 723	48 289	1 775	3.7	504 529	29 376	5.8	147 332	9 092	6.2	23 573	(NA)	(NA)
North Central	928 498	75 100	2 547	3.4	649 623	31 480	4.8	169 302	8 741	5.2	34 473	(NA)	(NA)
South	3 176 077	56 872	9 804	17.2	2 416 289	48 805	2.0	610 301	14 757	2.4	92 615	(NA)	(NA)
West	617 381	43 160	2 822	6.5	401 081	29 544	7.4	131 457	9 973	7.6	41 683	(NA)	(NA)

[1]Total includes nursery school, not shown separately. [2]includes persons 3 to 34 years old. [3]includes persons 5 to 34 years old. [4]for 1960, includes Black and other races.

Table 83. Years of School Completed by Race and Sex: 1940 to 1980

[Data for race groups in 1950 and all data for 1940 exclude Alaska and Hawaii. Data are estimates based on a sample; see Introduction. For meaning of symbols, see Introduction. For definitions of terms, see appendixes A and B]

United States Regions	Persons 25 years old and over	Elementary			High school		College			Percent high school graduates	Median years of school completed
		0 to 4 years	5 to 7 years	8 years	1 to 3 years	4 years	1 to 3 years	4 years	5 or more years		
TOTAL											
1980	132 835 687	4 755 239	8 837 241	10 665 203	20 277 514	45 947 035	20 794 975	11 420 499	10 137 981	66.5	12.5
Male	62 416 454	2 407 672	4 267 377	4 892 529	8 862 989	19 422 198	10 038 976	6 123 449	6 401 264	67.3	12.6
Female	70 419 233	2 347 567	4 569 864	5 772 674	11 414 525	26 524 837	10 755 999	5 297 050	3 736 717	65.8	12.4
Northeast	29 903 010	859 695	1 852 769	2 543 972	4 578 823	10 864 233	4 047 401	2 663 136	2 492 981	67.1	12.5
Male	13 766 122	364 520	858 446	1 122 303	2 060 222	4 460 835	1 913 738	1 441 026	1 545 032	68.0	12.6
Female	16 136 888	495 175	994 323	1 421 669	2 518 601	6 403 398	2 133 663	1 222 110	947 949	66.4	12.4
North Central	34 084 932	693 069	1 631 896	3 501 594	5 088 118	13 154 118	4 995 550	2 734 966	2 285 621	68.0	12.5
Male	16 044 579	354 062	828 498	1 646 290	2 271 867	5 649 411	2 385 293	1 438 670	1 470 488	68.2	12.5
Female	18 040 353	339 007	803 398	1 855 304	2 816 251	7 504 707	2 610 257	1 296 296	815 133	67.8	12.4
South	43 690 800	2 389 139	4 218 191	3 246 220	7 523 582	13 480 807	6 295 367	3 610 221	2 927 273	60.2	12.3
Male	20 458 000	1 289 547	2 022 644	1 470 716	3 150 635	5 709 993	3 060 868	1 907 494	1 846 103	61.2	12.4
Female	23 232 800	1 099 592	2 195 547	1 775 504	4 372 947	7 770 814	3 234 499	1 702 727	1 081 170	59.4	12.3
West	25 156 945	813 336	1 134 385	1 373 417	3 086 991	8 447 877	5 456 657	2 412 176	2 432 106	74.5	12.7
Male	12 147 753	399 543	557 789	653 220	1 380 265	3 601 959	2 679 077	1 336 259	1 539 641	75.4	12.9
Female	13 009 192	413 793	576 596	720 197	1 706 726	4 845 918	2 777 580	1 075 917	892 465	73.7	12.6
1970	109 899 359	6 039 314	11 032 712	14 015 364	21 285 922	34 158 051	11 650 730	6 657 604	5 059 662	52.3	12.1
Male	51 869 770	3 152 174	5 475 479	6 708 041	9 633 537	14 365 218	5 526 759	3 518 159	3 490 403	51.9	12.1
Female	58 029 589	2 887 140	5 557 233	7 307 323	11 652 385	19 792 833	6 123 971	3 139 445	1 569 259	52.8	12.1
Northeast	27 685 389	1 280 487	2 673 924	3 646 313	5 425 917	9 033 583	2 532 381	1 719 256	1 373 526	52.9	12.1
Male	12 868 055	582 004	1 293 680	1 684 798	2 537 046	3 677 846	1 205 161	937 441	950 079	52.6	12.1
Female	14 817 334	698 483	1 380 244	1 961 517	2 888 871	5 355 737	1 327 220	781 815	423 447	53.2	12.1
North Central	30 291 997	1 041 180	2 375 380	4 931 967	5 676 358	10 318 166	3 035 618	1 668 458	1 244 870	53.7	12.1
Male	14 376 881	545 022	1 228 182	2 422 401	2 628 142	4 403 977	1 409 413	866 917	872 827	52.5	12.1
Female	15 915 116	496 158	1 147 198	2 509 566	3 048 216	5 914 189	1 626 205	801 541	372 043	54.8	12.1
South	33 331 294	2 965 072	4 788 716	3 614 552	6 938 891	8 560 066	3 199 093	1 972 175	1 292 729	45.1	11.3
Male	15 660 500	1 634 929	2 340 696	1 691 497	2 967 402	3 619 359	1 502 174	1 011 828	892 615	44.9	11.2
Female	17 670 794	1 330 143	2 448 020	1 923 055	3 971 489	4 940 707	1 696 919	960 347	400 114	45.3	11.4
West	18 590 679	752 575	1 194 692	1 822 530	3 244 756	6 246 236	2 883 638	1 297 715	1 148 537	62.3	12.4
Male	8 964 334	390 219	612 921	909 345	1 500 947	2 664 036	1 410 011	701 973	774 882	61.9	12.4
Female	9 626 345	362 356	581 771	913 185	1 743 809	3 582 200	1 473 627	595 742	373 655	62.6	12.3
1960	99 438 084	8 302 582	13 753 827	17 442 933	19 115 915	24 455 484	8 742 070	4 613 367	3 011 906	41.1	10.5
Male	47 930 513	4 506 179	7 019 007	8 516 320	8 973 036	10 154 325	4 122 689	2 510 097	2 128 863	39.5	10.3
Female	51 507 571	3 796 403	6 734 820	8 926 613	10 142 879	14 301 159	4 619 381	2 103 270	883 043	42.5	10.7
Northeast	26 412 632	1 847 548	3 370 899	4 994 566	5 367 973	6 662 082	2 031 723	1 265 682	872 159	41.0	10.7
Male	12 542 479	896 817	1 707 550	2 353 398	2 577 183	2 680 114	982 268	721 402	623 747	39.9	10.4
Female	13 870 153	950 731	1 663 349	2 641 168	2 790 790	3 981 968	1 049 455	544 280	248 412	42.0	10.7
North Central	28 697 480	1 544 495	3 395 200	6 329 459	5 457 288	7 539 653	2 457 913	1 192 868	780 604	41.7	10.7
Male	13 937 880	849 910	1 815 500	3 160 848	2 587 339	3 185 283	1 127 310	650 650	561 040	39.6	10.3
Female	14 759 600	694 585	1 579 700	3 168 611	2 869 949	4 354 370	1 330 603	542 218	219 564	43.7	10.8
South	28 975 516	4 049 171	5 613 073	3 839 530	5 255 971	5 868 817	2 303 258	1 299 004	746 696	35.3	9.6
Male	13 872 499	2 272 571	2 752 395	1 822 426	2 348 903	2 413 409	1 073 961	668 032	520 802	33.7	9.1
Female	15 103 021	1 776 600	2 860 678	2 017 104	2 907 068	3 455 408	1 229 297	630 972	225 894	36.7	9.9
West	15 352 456	861 368	1 374 655	2 279 378	3 034 683	4 384 936	1 949 176	855 813	612 447	50.8	12.0
Male	7 577 711	486 881	743 583	1 179 656	1 459 619	1 875 531	939 154	470 013	423 274	48.9	11.8
Female	7 774 745	374 487	631 072	1 099 722	1 575 064	2 509 405	1 010 022	385 800	189 173	52.7	12.1
1950¹	87 483 480	9 445 870	13 910 700	17 706 275	14 800 555	17 663 545	6 258 775	5 284 580	(²)	34.3	9.3
Male	42 628 350	5 052 975	6 994 125	8 822 375	6 976 480	7 510 770	2 902 820	3 026 825	(²)	32.6	9.0
Female	44 855 130	4 392 895	6 916 575	8 883 900	7 824 075	10 152 775	3 355 955	2 257 755	(²)	36.0	9.6
Northeast	24 439 755	2 217 715	3 488 630	5 281 315	4 224 385	5 405 150	1 415 060	1 617 145	(²)	35.7	9.6
Male	11 695 835	1 075 725	1 703 825	2 557 050	2 017 710	2 277 625	681 845	963 610	(²)	34.8	9.4
Female	12 743 920	1 141 990	1 784 805	2 724 265	2 206 675	3 127 525	733 215	653 535	(²)	36.5	9.7
North Central	26 324 060	1 829 010	3 480 945	6 893 455	4 355 500	5 719 310	1 923 330	1 443 390	(²)	35.4	9.4
Male	12 909 280	992 615	1 823 680	3 482 505	2 066 955	2 448 395	874 470	838 545	(²)	33.2	9.0
Female	13 414 780	836 395	1 657 265	3 410 950	2 288 545	3 270 915	1 048 860	604 845	(²)	37.5	9.9
South	25 123 045	4 613 720	5 732 930	3 458 265	4 166 935	3 558 365	1 652 030	1 334 970	(²)	26.7	8.6
Male	12 222 550	2 541 425	2 805 870	1 676 570	1 896 525	1 487 525	745 795	725 070	(²)	24.9	8.4
Female	12 900 495	2 072 295	2 927 060	1 781 695	2 270 410	2 070 840	906 235	609 900	(²)	28.4	8.7
West	11 596 620	785 425	1 208 195	2 073 240	2 053 735	2 980 720	1 268 355	889 075	(²)	45.6	11.2
Male	5 800 685	443 210	660 750	1 106 250	995 290	1 297 225	600 710	499 600	(²)	42.8	10.7
Female	5 795 935	342 215	547 445	966 900	1 058 445	1 683 495	667 645	389 475	(²)	48.5	11.7
1940¹	74 775 836	10 104 612	13 656 146	20 756 918	11 181 995	10 551 680	4 075 184	2 513 900	893 431	24.5	8.6
Male	37 463 087	5 550 390	7 007 812	10 631 478	5 332 803	4 507 244	1 823 981	1 374 647	646 581	22.7	8.6
Female	37 312 749	4 554 222	6 648 334	10 125 440	5 849 192	6 044 436	2 251 203	1 139 253	246 850	26.3	8.7
Northeast	21 658 029	2 530 870	3 372 549	7 006 929	3 235 089	3 103 749	910 050	802 353	269 681	24.0	8.7
Male	10 674 592	1 304 663	1 700 156	3 487 338	1 553 953	1 303 588	423 075	472 790	202 587	23.0	8.6
Female	10 983 437	1 226 207	1 672 393	3 519 591	1 681 136	1 800 161	486 975	329 563	67 094	24.9	8.7
North Central	23 555 758	2 017 851	3 632 378	8 318 322	3 523 231	3 495 048	1 335 899	697 135	288 768	25.0	8.7
Male	11 902 877	1 134 864	1 934 671	4 322 634	1 688 272	1 498 783	586 781	381 915	209 806	22.8	8.6
Female	11 652 881	882 987	1 697 707	3 995 688	1 834 959	1 996 265	749 118	315 220	78 962	27.2	8.8
South	21 191 471	4 857 289	5 696 722	3 130 879	2 981 549	2 283 025	1 127 050	642 840	195 135	20.3	7.9
Male	10 547 425	2 697 662	2 824 467	1 561 765	1 386 719	970 466	486 935	319 586	140 832	18.5	7.7
Female	10 644 046	2 159 627	2 872 255	1 569 114	1 594 830	1 312 559	640 115	323 254	54 303	22.1	8.1
West	8 370 578	698 602	954 497	2 300 788	1 442 126	1 669 858	702 185	371 572	139 847	34.8	9.4
Male	4 338 193	413 201	548 518	1 259 741	703 859	734 407	327 190	200 356	93 356	31.7	8.9
Female	4 032 385	285 401	405 969	1 041 047	738 267	935 451	374 995	171 216	46 491	38.2	10.1

¹Totals include persons with years of school completed not reported. ²Included in preceding category.

Table 83. Years of School Completed by Race and Sex: 1940 to 1980—Con.

[Data for race groups in 1950 and all data for 1940 exclude Alaska and Hawaii. Data are estimates based on a sample; see Introduction. For meaning of symbols, see Introduction. For definitions of terms, see appendixes A and B]

United States Regions	Persons 25 years old and over	Elementary			High school		College			Percent high school graduates	Median years of school completed
		0 to 4 years	5 to 7 years	8 years	1 to 3 years	4 years	1 to 3 years	4 years	5 or more years		
WHITE											
1980	114 290 384	2 997 005	6 631 933	9 391 468	16 663 849	40 784 148	18 263 953	10 422 559	9 135 469	68.8	12.5
Male	53 941 163	1 507 020	3 257 197	4 339 723	7 315 405	17 174 006	8 831 698	5 660 839	5 855 275	69.6	12.6
Female	60 349 221	1 489 985	3 374 736	5 051 745	9 348 444	23 610 142	9 432 255	4 761 720	3 280 194	68.1	12.5
Northeast	26 453 660	633 348	1 494 918	2 305 214	3 854 418	9 793 114	3 611 175	2 477 792	2 283 681	68.7	12.5
Male	12 250 484	264 777	700 551	1 017 865	1 753 047	4 016 996	1 715 586	1 354 467	1 427 195	69.5	12.6
Female	14 203 176	368 571	794 367	1 287 349	2 101 371	5 776 118	1 895 589	1 123 325	856 486	68.0	12.4
North Central	30 877 020	505 404	1 342 796	3 258 835	4 381 844	12 196 850	4 511 060	2 576 309	2 103 922	69.3	12.5
Male	14 582 709	254 381	687 977	1 535 806	1 964 572	5 237 093	2 166 958	1 366 171	1 369 751	69.5	12.5
Female	16 294 311	251 023	654 819	1 723 029	2 417 272	6 959 757	2 344 102	1 210 138	734 171	69.0	12.4
South	35 741 721	1 434 944	3 054 041	2 666 514	5 904 309	11 441 349	5 417 286	3 238 441	2 584 837	63.5	12.4
Male	16 879 814	777 567	1 499 062	1 228 909	2 477 628	4 821 795	2 644 736	1 752 650	1 677 467	64.6	12.5
Female	18 861 907	657 377	1 554 979	1 437 605	3 426 681	6 619 554	2 772 550	1 485 791	907 370	62.5	12.4
West	21 217 983	423 309	740 178	1 160 905	2 523 278	7 352 835	4 724 432	2 130 017	2 163 029	77.2	12.8
Male	10 228 156	210 295	369 607	557 143	1 120 158	3 098 122	2 304 418	1 187 551	1 380 862	77.9	12.9
Female	10 989 827	213 014	370 571	603 762	1 403 120	4 254 713	2 420 014	942 466	782 167	76.4	12.7
1970	98 245 635	4 376 311	8 953 261	12 814 399	18 517 629	31 617 691	10 903 616	6 295 963	4 766 765	54.5	12.1
Male	46 527 222	2 242 281	4 503 036	6 175 370	8 462 196	13 272 817	5 174 668	3 367 827	3 329 027	54.0	12.1
Female	51 718 413	2 134 030	4 450 225	6 639 029	10 055 433	18 344 874	5 728 948	2 928 136	1 437 738	55.0	12.1
Northeast	25 399 527	1 090 957	2 322 089	3 403 561	4 814 913	8 411 402	2 392 854	1 653 095	1 310 656	54.2	12.1
Male	11 846 854	485 066	1 129 476	1 576 548	2 275 373	3 421 459	1 139 078	907 374	912 480	53.9	12.1
Female	13 552 673	605 891	1 192 613	1 827 013	2 539 540	4 989 943	1 253 776	745 721	398 176	54.5	12.1
North Central	28 038 658	846 773	2 055 685	4 663 218	5 054 440	9 753 006	2 869 810	1 607 967	1 187 759	55.0	12.1
Male	13 335 046	436 244	1 070 460	2 296 009	2 355 301	4 162 895	1 332 800	841 333	840 004	53.8	12.1
Female	14 703 612	410 529	985 225	2 367 209	2 699 139	5 590 111	1 537 010	766 634	347 755	56.1	12.2
South	27 789 419	1 839 965	3 552 152	3 055 416	5 708 957	7 673 975	2 957 231	1 814 302	1 187 421	49.1	11.8
Male	13 152 115	1 012 447	1 776 207	1 457 057	2 473 961	3 241 348	1 392 082	957 220	841 793	48.9	11.8
Female	14 637 304	827 518	1 775 945	1 598 359	3 234 996	4 432 627	1 565 149	857 082	345 628	49.2	11.9
West	17 018 031	598 616	1 023 335	1 692 204	2 939 319	5 779 308	2 683 721	1 220 599	1 080 929	63.3	12.4
Male	8 193 207	308 524	526 893	845 756	1 357 561	2 447 115	1 310 708	661 900	734 750	62.9	12.4
Female	8 824 824	290 092	496 442	846 448	1 581 758	3 332 193	1 373 013	558 699	346 179	63.6	12.4
1960	89 581 174	5 988 729	11 450 906	16 179 146	17 273 976	23 099 636	8 310 937	4 401 669	2 876 175	43.2	10.9
Male	43 258 756	3 212 461	5 945 544	7 941 872	8 177 224	9 587 939	3 918 069	2 422 493	2 053 157	41.6	10.7
Female	46 322 418	2 776 268	5 505 362	8 237 274	9 096 752	13 511 697	4 392 868	1 979 176	823 018	44.7	11.2
Northeast	24 724 629	1 629 508	3 033 311	4 727 800	4 967 746	6 338 541	1 950 703	1 232 152	844 868	41.9	10.8
Male	11 756 608	778 542	1 544 175	2 228 600	2 399 760	2 549 578	942 861	705 933	607 159	40.9	10.7
Female	12 968 021	850 966	1 489 136	2 499 200	2 567 986	3 788 963	1 007 842	526 219	237 709	42.9	10.9
North Central	26 878 070	1 290 883	3 035 060	6 030 890	5 024 479	7 232 096	2 352 341	1 158 554	753 767	42.8	10.8
Male	13 059 534	703 181	1 633 260	3 016 791	2 391 290	3 056 624	1 078 486	635 061	544 841	40.7	10.5
Female	13 818 536	587 702	1 401 800	3 014 099	2 633 189	4 175 472	1 273 855	523 493	208 926	44.7	11.2
South	23 714 470	2 380 220	4 170 638	3 276 795	4 458 880	5 398 460	2 150 197	1 189 388	689 900	39.8	10.4
Male	11 429 908	1 345 115	2 110 859	1 586 481	2 032 928	2 225 807	1 004 800	630 464	493 454	38.1	10.0
Female	12 284 570	1 035 105	2 059 779	1 690 314	2 425 952	3 172 653	1 145 397	558 924	196 446	41.3	10.7
West	14 264 005	688 118	1 211 901	2 143 661	2 822 871	4 130 543	1 857 696	821 575	587 640	51.9	12.1
Male	7 012 755	385 623	657 268	1 110 008	1 353 250	1 755 942	891 026	451 035	407 703	50.0	12.0
Female	7 251 250	302 495	554 633	1 033 653	1 469 621	2 374 601	965 770	370 540	179 937	53.7	12.1
1950[1]	79 338 785	6 884 250	11 692 065	16 769 940	13 738 320	17 004 570	6 019 935	5 107 960	(2)	36.4	9.8
Male	38 683 835	3 659 275	5 970 040	8 396 060	6 518 915	7 226 740	2 792 970	2 946 275	(2)	34.6	9.3
Female	40 654 950	3 224 975	5 722 025	8 373 880	7 219 405	9 777 830	3 226 965	2 161 685	(2)	38.2	10.0
Northeast	23 219 995	2 013 905	3 189 900	5 085 610	5 004 815	5 236 705	1 375 295	1 587 240	(2)	36.7	9.7
Male	11 117 045	968 845	1 562 525	2 466 265	1 921 420	2 204 770	661 865	948 465	(2)	35.8	9.5
Female	12 102 950	1 045 060	1 627 375	2 619 345	2 083 395	3 031 935	713 430	638 775	(2)	37.5	9.8
North Central	24 977 005	1 593 740	3 162 380	6 669 300	4 105 195	5 549 355	1 866 390	1 410 640	(2)	36.4	9.5
Male	12 241 065	859 910	1 663 310	3 373 820	1 953 995	2 375 140	847 105	822 005	(2)	34.2	9.0
Female	12 735 940	733 830	1 499 070	3 295 480	2 151 200	3 174 215	1 019 285	588 635	(2)	38.5	9.9
South	20 086 930	2 594 495	4 235 155	3 016 085	3 666 775	3 332 905	1 541 285	1 238 105	(2)	31.6	8.9
Male	9 822 100	1 449 540	2 141 430	1 490 595	1 694 705	1 396 395	700 125	685 650	(2)	29.6	8.7
Female	10 264 830	1 144 955	2 093 725	1 525 490	1 972 070	1 936 510	841 160	552 455	(2)	33.5	9.3
West	11 054 855	682 110	1 104 630	1 998 945	1 961 535	2 885 605	1 236 965	871 975	(2)	46.7	11.4
Male	5 503 625	380 980	602 775	1 065 380	948 795	1 250 435	583 875	490 155	(2)	43.9	10.9
Female	5 551 230	301 130	501 855	933 565	1 012 740	1 635 170	653 090	381 820	(2)	49.4	11.9
1940[1]	67 999 523	7 322 114	11 662 366	19 966 742	10 603 592	10 255 333	3 948 681	2 442 380	877 405	26.1	8.7
Male	34 113 972	4 034 706	6 085 911	10 258 382	5 089 656	4 381 386	1 769 814	1 339 794	635 501	24.2	8.7
Female	33 885 551	3 287 408	5 576 455	9 708 380	5 513 936	5 873 947	2 178 867	1 102 586	241 904	28.1	8.8
Northeast	20 824 487	2 346 586	3 138 565	6 814 181	3 128 727	3 041 913	891 050	791 509	266 401	24.4	8.7
Male	10 268 932	1 204 394	1 587 661	3 396 385	1 508 070	1 277 474	413 484	466 722	200 152	23.5	8.7
Female	10 555 555	1 142 192	1 550 904	3 417 796	1 620 657	1 764 439	477 566	324 787	66 249	25.4	8.7
North Central	22 662 048	1 812 853	3 391 064	8 121 457	3 395 810	3 426 544	1 309 560	684 950	284 730	25.4	9.0
Male	11 453 286	1 020 100	1 812 688	4 224 230	1 632 710	1 469 057	574 112	375 717	207 062	23.2	8.7
Female	11 208 762	792 753	1 578 376	3 897 227	1 763 100	1 957 487	735 448	309 233	77 668	27.7	8.8
South	16 432 037	2 548 145	4 233 345	2 785 883	2 673 827	2 152 750	1 055 938	599 576	187 743	24.6	8.5
Male	8 229 270	1 448 993	2 171 969	1 411 459	1 266 107	920 303	461 136	300 414	135 976	22.4	8.4
Female	8 202 767	1 099 152	2 061 376	1 374 424	1 407 720	1 232 447	594 802	299 162	51 767	26.8	8.7
West	8 080 951	614 530	899 392	2 245 241	1 405 228	1 634 126	692 133	366 345	138 531	35.4	9.5
Male	4 162 484	361 219	513 593	1 226 308	682 769	714 552	321 082	196 941	92 311	32.2	9.0
Female	3 918 467	253 311	385 799	1 018 933	722 459	919 574	371 051	169 404	46 220	38.8	10.2

[1]Totals include persons with years of school completed not reported. [2]Included in preceding category.

Table 83. **Years of School Completed by Race and Sex: 1940 to 1980**—Con.

[Data for race groups in 1950 and all data for 1940 exclude Alaska and Hawaii. Data are estimates based on a sample; see Introduction. For meaning of symbols, see Introduction. For definitions of terms, see appendixes A and B]

United States Regions	Persons 25 years old and over	Elementary			High school		College			Percent high school graduates	Median years of school completed
		0 to 4 years	5 to 7 years	8 years	1 to 3 years	4 years	1 to 3 years	4 years	5 or more years		
BLACK³											
1980	**13 195 318**	1 083 778	1 550 293	933 110	2 876 194	3 861 896	1 785 985	584 710	519 352	**51.2**	**12.0**
Male	5 895 269	591 035	706 244	397 886	1 207 618	1 670 806	823 774	254 523	243 383	50.8	12.0
Female	7 300 049	492 743	844 049	535 224	1 668 576	2 191 090	962 211	330 187	275 969	51.5	12.0
Northeast	2 545 375	117 027	239 191	168 937	583 450	880 608	342 627	110 290	103 245	56.4	12.2
Male	1 099 279	59 109	107 539	72 598	242 626	361 949	153 707	50 663	51 088	56.2	12.2
Female	1 446 096	57 918	131 652	96 339	340 824	518 659	188 920	59 627	52 157	56.7	12.2
North Central	2 623 881	133 541	225 183	199 503	624 399	824 321	410 141	107 013	99 780	54.9	12.2
Male	1 176 761	74 351	108 961	89 853	269 790	355 138	181 897	48 768	48 003	53.9	12.1
Female	1 447 120	59 190	116 222	109 650	354 609	469 183	228 244	58 245	51 777	55.8	12.2
South	6 883 424	789 369	1 014 965	513 345	1 477 109	1 790 179	744 779	302 813	250 865	44.9	11.3
Male	3 068 489	433 696	455 922	212 293	609 847	781 641	344 886	120 854	109 350	44.2	11.1
Female	3 814 935	355 673	559 043	301 052	867 262	1 008 538	399 893	181 959	141 515	45.4	11.4
West	1 142 638	43 841	70 954	51 325	191 236	366 788	288 438	64 594	65 462	68.7	12.6
Male	550 740	23 879	33 822	23 142	85 355	172 078	143 284	34 238	34 942	69.8	12.6
Female	591 898	19 962	37 132	28 183	105 881	194 710	145 154	30 356	30 520	67.7	12.5
1970	**10 375 093**	1 513 154	1 939 650	1 089 211	2 571 500	2 196 611	609 008	269 971	185 988	**31.4**	**9.8**
Male	4 713 703	833 731	902 602	478 444	1 078 331	941 409	283 422	103 756	92 008	30.1	9.4
Female	5 661 390	679 423	1 037 048	610 767	1 493 169	1 255 202	325 586	166 215	93 980	32.5	10.1
Northeast	2 114 133	169 417	330 368	228 384	586 516	588 135	125 026	49 140	37 147	37.8	10.7
Male	936 164	87 682	153 273	101 318	249 708	242 412	59 485	21 906	20 380	36.8	10.5
Female	1 177 969	81 735	177 095	127 066	336 808	345 723	65 541	27 234	16 767	38.6	10.8
North Central	2 106 069	185 146	304 895	251 414	596 105	531 962	151 712	48 702	36 133	36.5	10.6
Male	972 273	104 265	150 454	118 080	261 553	228 387	70 167	20 395	18 972	34.8	10.4
Female	1 133 796	80 881	154 441	133 334	334 552	303 575	81 545	28 307	17 161	38.0	10.8
South	5 376 248	1 105 194	1 214 214	544 507	1 199 230	848 034	226 160	147 527	91 382	24.4	8.7
Male	2 431 270	611 915	553 855	227 871	481 059	362 930	102 260	50 121	41 259	22.9	8.2
Female	2 944 978	493 279	660 359	316 636	718 171	485 104	123 900	97 406	50 123	25.7	9.0
West	778 643	53 397	90 173	64 906	189 648	228 480	106 110	24 602	21 326	48.9	11.9
Male	373 996	29 869	45 020	31 175	86 011	107 680	51 510	11 334	11 397	48.6	11.8
Female	404 647	23 528	45 153	33 731	103 638	120 800	54 600	13 268	9 929	49.1	11.9
1960	**9 053 945**	2 153 765	2 193 536	1 166 103	1 722 251	1 168 842	371 577	277 871	(²)	**20.1**	**8.2**
Male	4 240 021	1 199 506	1 013 996	523 302	733 169	480 213	172 058	117 777	(²)	18.2	7.7
Female	4 813 924	954 259	1 179 540	642 801	989 082	688 629	199 519	160 094	(²)	21.8	8.4
Northeast	1 609 439	202 418	327 272	256 969	390 301	310 270	74 956	47 253	(²)	26.9	9.1
Male	740 935	107 851	157 246	119 310	172 218	125 041	36 207	23 062	(²)	24.9	8.9
Female	868 504	94 567	170 026	137 659	218 083	185 229	38 749	24 191	(²)	28.6	9.4
North Central	1 734 701	244 853	346 957	284 567	418 725	291 350	98 631	49 618	(²)	25.3	9.0
Male	833 756	141 673	175 284	136 976	189 069	121 942	45 064	23 748	(²)	22.9	8.7
Female	900 945	103 180	171 673	147 591	229 656	169 408	53 567	25 870	(²)	27.6	9.4
South	5 174 164	1 649 207	1 426 347	552 814	783 410	456 257	147 050	159 079	(²)	14.7	7.0
Male	2 400 655	916 900	633 975	231 330	310 118	182 158	66 027	60 147	(²)	12.8	6.3
Female	2 773 509	732 307	792 372	321 484	473 292	274 099	81 023	98 932	(²)	16.4	7.5
West	535 641	57 287	92 960	71 753	129 815	110 965	50 940	21 921	(²)	34.3	10.1
Male	264 675	33 082	47 491	35 686	61 764	51 072	24 760	10 820	(²)	32.7	9.8
Female	270 966	24 205	45 469	36 067	68 051	59 893	26 180	11 101	(²)	35.9	10.3
1950¹	**7 795 380**	2 467 895	2 161 145	890 885	1 021 740	599 590	221 030	160 050	(²)	**13.0**	**6.8**
Male	3 729 785	1 334 925	988 940	398 795	432 905	251 610	98 330	69 170	(²)	11.7	6.4
Female	4 065 595	1 132 970	1 172 205	492 090	588 835	347 980	122 700	90 880	(²)	14.2	7.2
Northeast	1 183 085	193 810	293 270	190 825	215 720	163 955	38 120	26 270	(²)	20.4	8.4
Male	552 580	98 945	137 370	87 525	93 600	70 225	18 910	12 670	(²)	19.6	8.3
Female	630 505	94 865	155 900	103 300	122 120	93 730	19 210	13 600	(²)	21.0	8.5
North Central	1 295 275	226 330	308 860	215 380	243 370	161 330	53 565	29 380	(²)	19.7	8.4
Male	638 240	127 220	155 040	103 820	109 205	68 790	25 095	14 200	(²)	17.9	8.2
Female	657 035	99 110	153 820	111 560	134 165	92 540	28 470	15 180	(²)	21.5	8.6
South	4 983 200	2 001 905	1 485 685	436 310	493 285	220 670	108 625	94 815	(²)	8.8	5.8
Male	2 371 645	1 082 455	658 290	182 645	198 075	88 545	44 475	38 120	(²)	7.5	5.3
Female	2 611 555	919 450	827 395	253 665	295 210	132 125	64 150	56 695	(²)	9.9	6.3
West	333 820	45 850	73 330	48 370	69 365	53 635	20 720	9 585	(²)	26.2	8.9
Male	167 320	26 305	38 240	24 805	32 025	24 050	9 850	4 180	(²)	23.9	8.6
Female	166 500	19 545	35 090	23 565	37 340	29 585	10 870	5 405	(²)	28.4	9.2
1940¹	**6 776 313**	2 782 408	1 993 780	790 158	578 403	296 347	126 503	71 520	16 026	**7.7**	**5.8**
Male	3 349 115	1 515 684	921 901	373 096	243 147	125 858	54 167	34 853	11 080	6.9	5.4
Female	3 427 198	1 266 814	1 071 879	417 060	335 256	170 489	72 336	36 667	4 946	8.4	6.2
Northeast	833 542	184 284	233 984	192 748	106 362	61 836	19 000	10 844	3 280	11.7	7.8
Male	405 660	100 269	112 495	90 953	45 883	26 114	9 591	6 068	2 435	11.2	7.6
Female	427 882	84 015	121 489	101 795	60 479	35 722	9 409	4 776	845	12.1	8.1
North Central	893 710	204 998	241 314	196 865	127 421	68 504	26 339	12 185	4 038	12.6	7.9
Male	449 591	114 764	121 983	98 404	55 562	29 726	12 669	6 198	2 744	11.6	7.6
Female	444 119	90 234	119 331	98 461	71 859	38 778	13 670	5 987	1 294	13.6	8.1
South	4 759 434	2 309 144	1 463 377	344 996	307 722	130 275	71 112	43 264	7 392	5.4	5.1
Male	2 318 155	1 248 669	652 498	150 306	120 612	50 163	25 799	19 172	4 856	4.4	4.5
Female	2 441 279	1 060 475	810 879	194 690	187 110	80 112	45 313	24 092	2 536	6.3	5.5
West	289 627	84 072	55 105	55 547	36 898	35 732	10 052	5 227	1 316	18.4	8.1
Male	175 709	51 982	34 925	33 433	21 090	19 855	6 108	3 415	1 045	17.7	7.9
Female	113 918	32 090	20 180	22 114	15 808	15 877	3 944	1 812	271	19.5	8.2

¹Totals include persons with years of school completed not reported. ²Included in preceding category. ³For 1940, includes Black and other races.

Table 84. Children Ever Born by Age and Race of Women: 1910 and 1940 to 1980

[For years prior to 1960, excludes data for Alaska and Hawaii. Data are estimates based on a sample; see Introduction. For meaning of symbols, see Introduction. For definitions of terms, see appendixes A and B]

United States Urban and Rural	1980			1970			1960	1950	1940[1]	1910[1]
	Total	Urban	Rural	Total	Urban	Rural				
TOTAL										
Women 15 to 24 years	21 063 445	16 130 042	4 933 403	17 831 849	13 601 461	4 230 388	12 108 547	11 292 210	12 035 000	8 987 694
Children ever born[2]	6 670 367	4 836 249	1 834 118	6 422 530	4 588 275	1 834 255	6 536 181	4 950 750	3 478 000	3 452 000
Per 1,000 women	317	300	372	360	337	434	540	438	289	384
Women ever married	6 123 373	4 386 408	1 736 965	6 453 186	4 819 875	1 633 311	5 012 172	4 984 290	3 850 200	2 841 264
Percent ever married	29.1	27.2	35.2	36.2	35.4	38.6	41.4	44.1	32.0	31.6
Children ever born	5 238 234	3 633 994	1 604 240	6 422 530	4 588 275	1 834 255	6 536 181	4 950 750	3 478 000	3 452 000
Per 1,000 women ever married	855	828	924	995	952	1 123	1 304	993	903	1 215
Women 25 to 34 years	18 747 239	14 170 611	4 576 628	12 678 144	9 464 794	3 213 350	11 648 537	12 221 730	10 752 880	7 237 914
Children ever born[2]	27 676 463	19 714 387	7 962 076	27 108 281	19 260 633	7 847 648	26 047 951	20 117 778	14 934 000	14 395 000
Per 1,000 women	1 476	1 391	1 740	2 138	2 035	2 442	2 236	1 646	1 389	1 989
Women ever married	15 684 467	11 493 435	4 191 032	11 416 701	8 412 464	3 004 237	10 643 493	10 851 390	8 737 220	5 713 048
Percent ever married	83.7	81.1	91.6	90.1	88.9	93.5	91.4	88.8	81.3	78.9
Children ever born	26 480 573	18 662 577	7 817 996	27 108 281	19 260 633	7 847 648	26 047 951	20 117 778	14 934 000	14 395 000
Per 1,000 women ever married	1 688	1 624	1 865	2 374	2 290	2 612	2 447	1 854	1 709	2 520
Women 35 to 44 years	13 067 348	9 501 489	3 565 859	11 864 123	8 811 506	3 052 617	12 336 352	10 754 460	9 096 120	5 515 856
Children ever born[2]	34 490 834	24 331 014	10 159 820	35 069 769	25 022 899	10 046 870	30 445 230	22 719 054	20 973 000	19 613 000
Per 1,000 women	2 639	2 561	2 849	2 956	2 840	3 291	2 468	2 113	2 306	3 556
Women ever married	12 273 301	8 825 944	3 447 357	11 197 317	8 266 027	2 931 290	11 587 575	9 868 080	8 151 240	4 879 893
Percent ever married	93.9	92.9	96.7	94.4	93.8	96.0	93.9	91.8	89.6	88.5
Children ever born	33 962 228	23 876 000	10 086 228	35 069 769	25 022 899	10 046 870	30 445 230	22 719 054	20 973 000	19 613 000
Per 1,000 women ever married	2 767	2 705	2 926	3 132	3 027	3 427	2 627	2 302	2 573	4 019
WHITE										
Women 15 to 24 years	16 996 982	12 622 303	4 374 679	15 416 111	11 638 340	3 777 771	10 594 302	9 918 930	10 679 020	7 854 824
Children ever born[2]	4 575 856	3 050 369	1 525 487	5 322 406	3 691 870	1 630 536	5 474 740	4 101 450	2 865 000	2 759 000
Per 1,000 women	269	242	349	345	317	432	517	413	268	351
Women ever married	5 214 476	3 606 720	1 607 756	5 703 925	4 191 442	1 512 483	4 428 905	4 354 560	3 302 220	2 369 159
Percent ever married	30.7	28.6	36.8	37.0	36.0	40.0	41.8	43.9	30.9	30.2
Children ever born	4 134 129	2 707 370	1 426 759	5 322 406	3 691 870	1 630 536	5 474 740	4 101 450	2 865 000	2 759 000
Per 1,000 women ever married	793	751	887	933	881	1 078	1 236	942	868	1 165
Women 25 to 34 years	15 394 841	11 203 435	4 191 406	11 024 757	8 045 428	2 979 329	10 219 625	10 902 120	9 597 980	6 419 314
Children ever born[2]	21 610 109	14 483 629	7 126 480	23 138 370	16 014 965	7 123 405	22 346 471	17 673 174	12 974 000	12 280 000
Per 1,000 women	1 404	1 293	1 700	2 099	1 991	2 391	2 187	1 621	1 352	1 913
Women ever married	13 194 208	9 308 057	3 886 151	10 035 723	7 226 414	2 809 309	9 394 319	9 685 320	7 765 020	5 016 869
Percent ever married	85.7	83.1	92.7	91.0	89.8	94.3	91.9	88.8	80.9	78.2
Children ever born	21 332 376	14 252 833	7 079 543	23 138 370	16 014 965	7 123 405	22 346 471	17 673 174	12 974 000	12 280 000
Per 1,000 women ever married	1 617	1 531	1 822	2 306	2 216	2 536	2 379	1 825	1 671	2 448
Women 35 to 44 years	10 930 907	7 628 604	3 302 303	10 371 427	7 551 483	2 819 944	11 007 183	9 619 710	8 143 920	4 957 514
Children ever born[2]	27 811 816	18 667 953	9 143 863	29 953 211	20 993 190	8 960 021	26 654 388	19 995 060	18 450 000	17 066 000
Per 1,000 women	2 544	2 447	2 769	2 888	2 780	3 177	2 422	2 079	2 265	3 442
Women ever married	10 374 601	7 165 126	3 209 475	9 828 988	7 110 907	2 718 081	10 351 697	8 804 040	7 269 620	4 360 176
Percent ever married	94.9	93.9	97.2	94.8	94.2	96.4	94.0	91.5	89.3	88.0
Children ever born	27 711 238	18 584 853	9 126 385	29 953 211	20 993 190	8 960 021	26 654 388	19 995 060	18 450 000	17 066 000
Per 1,000 women ever married	2 671	2 594	2 844	3 047	2 952	3 296	2 575	2 271	2 538	3 914
BLACK										
Women 15 to 24 years	2 919 168	2 508 892	410 276	2 175 224	1 778 709	396 515	1 411 869	1 312 320	1 304 500	1 103 864
Children ever born[2]	1 576 309	1 346 604	229 705	1 018 068	839 624	178 444	996 798	820 325	591 000	655 000
Per 1,000 women	540	537	560	468	472	450	706	625	453	593
Women ever married	535 200	454 920	80 280	676 450	572 998	103 452	538 593	607 950	531 600	458 919
Percent ever married	18.3	18.1	19.6	31.1	32.2	26.1	38.1	46.3	40.8	41.6
Children ever born	691 951	577 137	114 814	1 018 068	839 624	178 444	996 798	820 325	591 000	655 000
Per 1,000 women ever married	1 293	1 269	1 430	1 505	1 465	1 725	1 851	1 349	1 112	1 427
Women 25 to 34 years	2 267 364	2 001 572	265 792	1 448 007	1 252 662	195 345	1 298 102	1 266 180	1 123 380	796 830
Children ever born[2]	4 214 490	3 635 396	579 094	3 576 256	2 962 203	614 053	3 422 776	2 338 367	1 883 000	2 004 000
Per 1,000 women	1 859	1 816	2 179	2 470	2 365	3 143	2 637	1 847	1 676	2 515
Women ever married	1 588 563	1 388 812	199 751	1 206 325	1 045 776	160 549	1 132 490	1 121 490	945 000	676 559
Percent ever married	70.1	69.4	75.2	83.3	83.5	82.2	87.2	88.6	84.1	84.9
Children ever born	3 393 628	2 901 392	492 236	3 576 256	2 962 203	614 053	3 422 776	2 338 367	1 883 000	2 004 000
Per 1,000 women ever married	2 136	2 089	2 464	2 965	2 833	3 825	3 022	2 085	1 993	2 962
Women 35 to 44 years	1 480 456	1 298 722	181 734	1 311 907	1 114 431	197 476	1 224 071	1 105 500	926 080	542 290
Children ever born[2]	4 714 649	3 996 486	718 163	4 577 690	3 638 331	939 359	3 470 843	2 619 585	2 416 000	2 446 000
Per 1,000 women	3 185	3 077	3 952	3 489	3 265	4 757	2 835	2 370	2 609	4 511
Women ever married	1 291 955	1 131 828	160 127	1 199 257	1 019 275	179 982	1 138 425	1 036 710	856 520	504 352
Percent ever married	87.3	87.1	88.1	91.4	91.5	91.1	93.0	93.8	92.5	93.0
Children ever born	4 334 478	3 668 378	666 100	4 577 690	3 638 331	939 359	3 470 843	2 619 585	2 416 000	2 446 000
Per 1,000 women ever married	3 355	3 241	4 160	3 817	3 570	5 219	3 049	2 527	2 821	4 850

[1]Data shown for 1940 and 1910 include estimates of children for women with no report on children ever born and therefore differ from the data in the fertility reports of the 1940 census. [2]For years prior to 1980, single (never-married) women were counted as childless.

Table 85. Veteran Status by Race: 1980, 1970, and 1960

[Data are estimates based on a sample; see Introduction. For meaning of symbols, see Introduction. For definitions of terms, see appendixes A and B]

United States	Civilian males 16 years and over	Veterans		Period of service							Nonveterans
		Total	Percent of civilian males 16 years and over	May 1975 or later only	Vietnam era, Vietnam era and Korean conflict	Korean conflict	Korean conflict and World War II	World War II	World War I	Other service	
TOTAL											
1980	80 242 375	27 406 299	34.2	854 100	7 784 811	3 872 931	772 229	10 319 940	476 290	3 325 998	52 836 076
1970	65 286 205	28 112 495	43.1	...	4 503 798	4 702 306	863 123	12 461 635	1 587 598	3 994 035	37 173 710
1960	56 773 447	23 103 249	40.7	...	...	4 051 288	803 287	13 042 489	2 608 189	2 597 996	33 670 198
Percent Distribution											
1980	...	100.0	...	3.1	28.4	14.1	2.8	37.7	1.7	12.1	...
1970	...	100.0	...	...	16.0	16.7	3.1	44.3	5.6	14.2	...
1960	...	100.0	...	...	...	17.5	3.5	56.5	11.3	11.2	...
WHITE											
1980	68 534 491	24 685 299	36.0	628 667	6 805 695	3 502 851	729 914	9 534 996	448 302	3 034 874	43 849 192
1970	58 216 824	25 828 431	44.4	...	4 110 757	4 223 677	817 571	11 442 987	1 465 824	3 767 615	32 388 393
1960	50 987 463	21 327 599	41.8	...	...	3 677 015	758 569	12 031 908	2 421 000	2 439 107	29 659 864
Percent Distribution											
1980	...	100.0	...	2.5	27.6	14.2	3.0	38.6	1.8	12.3	...
1970	...	100.0	...	...	15.9	16.4	3.2	44.3	5.7	14.6	...
1960	...	100.0	...	...	...	17.2	3.6	56.4	11.4	11.4	...
BLACK[1]											
1980	8 121 981	2 076 714	25.6	175 616	707 830	286 766	30 980	638 780	24 511	212 231	6 045 267
1970	6 271 848	2 029 775	32.4	...	345 159	426 746	38 497	917 837	113 192	188 344	4 242 073
1960	5 785 984	1 775 650	30.7	...	...	374 273	44 718	1 010 581	187 189	158 889	4 010 334
Percent Distribution											
1980	...	100.0	...	8.5	34.1	13.8	1.5	30.8	1.2	10.2	...
1970	...	100.0	...	...	17.0	21.0	1.9	45.2	5.6	9.3	...
1960	...	100.0	...	...	...	21.1	2.5	56.9	10.5	8.9	...
BLACK AS PERCENT OF ALL RACES[1]											
1980	10.1	7.6	...	20.6	9.1	7.4	4.0	6.2	5.1	6.4	11.4
1970	9.6	7.2	...	...	7.7	9.1	4.5	7.4	7.1	4.7	11.4
1960	10.2	7.7	...	...	...	9.2	5.6	7.7	7.2	6.1	11.9

[1]For 1960, includes Black and other races.

Table 86. Labor Force Status by Sex and Race: 1940 to 1980

[Data are estimates based on a sample; see Introduction. For meaning of symbols, see Introduction. For definitions of terms, see appendixes A and B]

United States Regions	16 years and over				14 years and over			
	1980	1970	1960	1950¹	1970	1960	1950¹	1940¹
UNITED STATES								
Total								
Total	171 214 258	141 087 270	120 726 426	107 436 005	149 398 189	126 276 548	112 354 034	101 102 924
Labor force	106 084 668	82 048 781	69 234 105	59 198 160	82 897 433	69 877 481	60 053 968	52 789 499
Percent of total	62.0	58.2	57.3	55.1	55.5	55.3	53.5	52.2
Armed Forces	1 634 851	1 997 735	1 732 280	996 975	1 999 088	1 733 402	982 313	278 000
Civilian labor force	104 449 817	80 051 046	67 501 825	58 201 185	80 898 345	68 144 079	59 071 655	52 511 499
Employed	97 639 355	76 553 599	64 046 657	55 373 580	77 308 792	64 639 252	56 239 449	44 888 083
Unemployed	6 810 462	3 497 447	3 455 168	2 827 605	3 589 553	3 504 827	2 832 206	7 623 416
Percent of civilian labor force	6.5	4.4	5.1	4.9	4.4	5.1	4.8	14.5
Not in labor force	65 129 590	59 038 489	51 492 321	48 237 845	66 500 756	56 399 067	52 300 066	48 313 425
Inmate of institution	2 389 482	1 956 822	(NA)	(NA)	1 759 910	1 444 136	(NA)	(NA)
Male								
Total	81 732 090	67 235 510	58 477 442	52 432 575	71 481 904	61 315 294	55 311 617	50 553 748
Labor force	61 416 203	51 502 114	47 012 517	42 754 130	52 076 663	47 467 721	43 553 386	39 944 240
Percent of male	75.1	76.6	80.4	81.5	72.9	77.4	78.7	79.0
Armed Forces	1 489 715	1 952 875	1 703 995	964 675	1 954 134	1 705 052	954 619	278 000
Civilian labor force	59 926 488	49 549 239	45 308 522	41 789 455	50 122 529	45 762 669	42 598 767	39 666 240
Employed	56 004 690	47 623 754	43 045 658	39 719 910	48 138 665	43 466 951	40 519 462	33 749 905
Unemployed	3 921 798	1 925 485	2 262 864	2 069 545	1 983 864	2 295 718	2 079 305	5 916 335
Percent of civilian labor force	6.5	3.9	5.0	5.0	4.0	5.0	4.9	14.9
Not in labor force	20 315 887	15 733 396	11 464 925	9 678 445	19 405 241	13 847 573	11 758 231	10 609 508
Inmate of institution	1 162 833	1 017 734	(NA)	(NA)		1 040 875	878 905	(NA)
Female								
Total	89 482 168	73 851 760	62 248 984	55 003 430	77 916 285	64 961 254	57 042 417	50 549 176
Labor force	44 668 465	30 546 667	22 221 588	16 444 030	30 820 770	22 409 760	16 500 582	12 845 259
Percent of female	49.9	41.4	35.7	29.9	39.6	34.5	28.9	25.4
Armed Forces	145 136	44 860	28 285	32 300	44 954	28 350	27 694	--
Civilian labor force	44 523 329	30 501 807	22 193 303	16 411 730	30 775 816	22 381 410	16 472 888	12 845 259
Employed	41 634 665	28 929 845	21 000 999	15 653 670	29 170 127	21 172 301	15 719 987	11 138 178
Unemployed	2 888 664	1 571 962	1 192 304	758 060	1 605 689	1 209 109	752 901	1 707 081
Percent of civilian labor force	6.5	5.2	5.4	4.6	5.2	5.4	4.6	13.3
Not in labor force	44 813 703	43 305 093	40 027 396	38 559 400	47 095 515	42 551 494	40 541 835	37 703 917
Inmate of institution	1 226 649	939 088	(NA)	(NA)	(NA)	719 035	565 231	(NA)
White								
Total								
Total	145 425 287	125 367 127	108 280 139	96 968 030	132 459 533	113 122 890	101 333 125	91 428 165
Labor force	90 434 967	72 954 518	61 898 066	53 103 450	73 720 097	62 478 134	53 908 723	47 169 389
Percent of total	62.2	58.2	57.2	54.8	55.7	55.2	53.2	51.6
Armed Forces	1 243 072	1 777 465	1 591 772	928 745	1 778 631	1 592 711	915 206	270 500
Civilian labor force	89 191 895	71 177 053	60 306 294	52 174 705	71 941 466	60 885 423	52 993 517	46 898 889
Employed	84 027 375	68 282 503	57 472 291	49 822 855	68 971 782	58 010 262	50 637 186	40 224 589
Unemployed	5 164 520	2 894 550	2 834 003	2 351 850	2 969 684	2 875 161	2 356 331	6 674 300
Percent of civilian labor force	5.8	4.1	4.7	4.5	4.1	4.7	4.4	14.2
Not in labor force	54 990 320	52 412 609	46 382 073	43 864 580	58 739 436	50 644 756	47 424 402	44 258 776
Inmate of institution	1 944 671	1 653 971	(NA)	(NA)	(NA)	1 473 242	1 237 919	(NA)
Male								
Total	69 672 383	59 946 581	52 553 757	47 394 425	63 578 712	55 036 120	49 979 010	45 823 031
Labor force	53 022 518	46 388 804	42 528 974	38 751 140	46 909 412	42 939 884	39 496 968	36 167 566
Percent of male	76.1	77.4	80.9	81.8	73.8	78.0	79.0	78.9
Armed Forces	1 137 892	1 738 702	1 566 294	899 760	1 739 796	1 567 168	890 010	270 500
Civilian labor force	51 884 626	44 650 102	40 962 680	37 851 380	45 169 616	41 372 716	38 606 958	35 897 066
Employed	48 843 987	43 029 769	39 079 244	36 090 675	43 501 103	39 461 685	36 837 888	30 661 006
Unemployed	3 040 639	1 620 333	1 883 436	1 760 705	1 668 513	1 911 031	1 769 070	5 236 060
Percent of civilian labor force	5.9	3.6	4.6	4.7	3.7	4.6	4.6	14.6
Not in labor force	16 649 865	13 557 777	10 024 783	8 643 285	16 669 300	12 096 236	10 482 042	9 655 465
Inmate of institution	825 821	788 919	(NA)	(NA)	824 560	726 178	(NA)	
Female								
Total	75 752 904	65 420 546	55 726 382	49 573 605	68 880 821	58 086 770	51 354 115	45 605 134
Labor force	37 412 449	26 565 714	19 369 092	14 352 310	26 810 685	19 538 250	14 411 755	11 001 823
Percent of female	49.4	40.6	34.8	29.0	38.9	33.6	28.1	24.1
Armed Forces	105 180	38 763	25 478	28 985	38 835	25 543	25 196	--
Civilian labor force	37 307 269	26 526 951	19 343 614	14 323 325	26 771 850	19 512 707	14 386 559	11 001 823
Employed	35 183 388	25 252 734	18 393 047	13 732 180	25 470 679	18 548 577	13 799 298	9 563 583
Unemployed	2 123 881	1 274 217	950 567	591 145	1 301 171	964 130	587 261	1 438 240
Percent of civilian labor force	5.7	4.8	4.9	4.1	4.9	4.9	4.1	13.1
Not in labor force	38 340 455	38 854 832	36 357 290	35 221 295	42 070 136	38 548 520	36 942 360	34 603 311
Inmate of institution	1 118 850	865 052	(NA)	(NA)	648 682	511 741	(NA)	
Black²								
Total								
Total	18 294 925	14 015 283	12 446 287	10 467 975	15 129 883	13 153 658	11 020 909	9 674 759
Labor force	10 866 343	8 092 391	7 336 039	6 094 710	8 167 657	7 399 347	6 145 245	5 620 110
Percent of total	59.4	57.7	58.9	58.2	54.0	56.3	55.8	58.1
Armed Forces	283 907	180 813	140 508	68 230	180 989	140 691	67 107	7 500
Civilian labor force	10 582 436	7 911 578	7 195 531	6 026 480	7 986 668	7 258 656	6 078 138	5 612 610
Employed	9 334 048	7 361 143	6 574 366	5 550 725	7 420 346	6 628 990	5 602 263	4 663 494
Unemployed	1 248 388	550 435	621 165	475 755	566 322	629 666	475 875	949 116
Percent of civilian labor force	11.8	7.0	8.6	7.9	7.1	8.7	7.8	16.9
Not in labor force	7 428 582	5 922 892	5 110 248	4 373 265	6 962 226	5 754 311	4 875 664	4 054 649
Inmate of institution	367 906	283 344	(NA)	(NA)	(NA)	286 668	206 217	(NA)
Male								
Total	8 374 051	6 449 469	5 923 685	5 038 150	7 010 499	6 279 174	5 332 607	4 730 717
Labor force	5 582 862	4 501 560	4 483 543	4 002 990	4 550 486	4 527 837	4 056 418	3 776 674
Percent of male	66.7	69.8	75.7	79.5	64.9	72.1	76.1	79.8
Armed Forces	252 070	175 525	137 701	64 915	175 679	137 884	64 609	7 500
Civilian labor force	5 330 792	4 326 035	4 345 842	3 938 075	4 374 807	4 389 953	3 991 809	3 769 174
Employed	4 674 871	4 052 063	3 966 414	3 629 235	4 091 390	4 005 266	3 681 574	3 088 899
Unemployed	655 921	273 972	379 428	308 840	283 417	384 687	310 235	680 275
Percent of civilian labor force	12.3	6.3	8.7	7.8	6.5	8.8	7.8	18.0
Not in labor force	2 791 189	1 947 909	1 440 142	1 035 160	2 460 013	1 751 337	1 276 189	954 043
Inmate of institution	277 251	214 691	(NA)	(NA)	216 315	152 727	(NA)	
Female								
Total	9 920 874	7 565 814	6 522 602	5 429 825	8 119 384	6 874 484	5 688 302	4 944 042
Labor force	5 283 481	3 590 831	2 852 496	2 091 720	3 617 171	2 871 510	2 088 827	1 843 436
Percent of female	53.3	47.5	43.7	38.5	44.5	41.8	36.7	37.3
Armed Forces	31 837	5 288	2 807	3 315	5 310	2 807	2 498	--
Civilian labor force	5 251 644	3 585 543	2 849 689	2 088 405	3 611 861	2 868 703	2 086 329	1 843 436
Employed	4 659 177	3 309 080	2 607 952	1 921 490	3 328 956	2 623 724	1 920 689	1 574 595
Unemployed	592 467	276 463	241 737	166 915	282 905	244 979	165 640	268 841
Percent of civilian labor force	11.3	7.7	8.5	8.0	7.8	8.5	7.9	14.6
Not in labor force	4 637 393	3 974 983	3 670 106	3 338 105	4 502 213	4 002 974	3 599 475	3 100 606
Inmate of institution	90 655	68 653	(NA)	(NA)	(NA)	70 353	53 490	(NA)

¹Excludes data for Alaska and Hawaii. ²for years prior to 1970, includes Black and other races.

Table 86. Labor Force Status by Sex and Race: 1940 to 1980—Con.

[Data are estimates based on a sample; see Introduction. For meaning of symbols, see Introduction. For definitions of terms, see appendixes A and B]

United States Regions	16 years and over				14 years and over			
	1980	1970	1960	1950¹	1970	1960	1950¹	1940¹
NORTHEAST								
Total								
Total	37 868 817	34 730 504	31 289 629	29 419 505	(NA)	32 561 165	30 405 105	(NA)
Labor force	23 036 729	20 238 081	18 144 466	16 335 725	(NA)	18 260 059	16 383 740	(NA)
Percent of total	60.8	58.3	58.0	55.5	(NA)	56.1	53.9	(NA)
Armed Forces	117 424	194 505	213 840	131 865	(NA)	213 927	131 865	(NA)
Civilian labor force	22 919 305	20 043 576	17 930 626	16 203 860	(NA)	18 046 132	16 251 875	(NA)
Employed	21 393 306	19 270 843	16 999 181	15 251 475	(NA)	17 106 813	15 295 015	(NA)
Unemployed	1 525 999	772 733	931 445	952 385	(NA)	939 319	956 860	(NA)
Percent of civilian labor force	6.7	4.0	5.2	5.9	(NA)	5.2	5.9	(NA)
Not in labor force	14 832 088	14 492 423	13 145 163	13 083 780	(NA)	14 301 106	14 021 365	(NA)
Inmate of institution	555 584	(NA)	(NA)	(NA)	(NA)	516 683	(NA)	(NA)
Male	17 712 800	16 260 439	14 897 083	14 099 315	(NA)	15 547 371	14 600 740	(NA)
Labor force	13 147 006	12 509 058	12 040 089	11 406 175	(NA)	12 122 080	11 442 150	(NA)
Percent of male	74.2	76.9	80.8	80.9	(NA)	78.0	78.4	(NA)
Armed Forces	107 691	190 180	210 284	126 540	(NA)	210 353	126 540	(NA)
Civilian labor force	13 039 315	12 318 878	11 829 805	11 279 635	(NA)	11 911 727	11 315 610	(NA)
Employed	12 166 857	11 890 009	11 232 146	10 563 355	(NA)	11 308 811	10 596 590	(NA)
Unemployed	872 458	428 869	597 659	716 280	(NA)	602 916	719 020	(NA)
Percent of civilian labor force	6.7	3.5	5.1	6.4	(NA)	5.1	6.4	(NA)
Not in labor force	4 565 794	3 751 381	2 856 994	2 693 140	(NA)	3 425 291	3 158 590	(NA)
Inmate of institution	248 787	(NA)	(NA)	(NA)	(NA)	276 658	(NA)	(NA)
Female	20 156 017	18 470 065	16 392 546	15 320 190	(NA)	17 013 794	15 804 365	(NA)
Labor force	9 889 723	7 729 023	6 104 377	4 929 550	(NA)	6 137 979	4 941 590	(NA)
Percent of female	49.1	41.8	37.2	32.2	(NA)	36.1	31.3	(NA)
Armed Forces	9 733	4 325	3 556	5 325	(NA)	3 574	5 325	(NA)
Civilian labor force	9 879 990	7 724 698	6 100 821	4 924 225	(NA)	6 134 405	4 936 265	(NA)
Employed	9 226 449	7 380 834	5 767 035	4 688 120	(NA)	5 798 002	4 698 425	(NA)
Unemployed	653 541	343 864	333 786	236 105	(NA)	336 403	237 840	(NA)
Percent of civilian labor force	6.6	4.5	5.5	4.8	(NA)	5.5	4.8	(NA)
Not in labor force	10 266 294	10 741 042	10 288 169	10 390 640	(NA)	10 875 815	10 862 775	(NA)
Inmate of institution	306 797	(NA)	(NA)	(NA)	(NA)	240 025	(NA)	(NA)
White								
Total	33 218 009	(NA)	29 213 982	27 901 470	(NA)	30 398 397	28 831 635	(NA)
Labor force	20 325 442	(NA)	16 838 206	15 426 105	(NA)	16 948 478	15 472 430	(NA)
Percent of total	61.2	(NA)	57.6	55.3	(NA)	55.7	53.7	(NA)
Armed Forces	96 791	(NA)	195 876	123 170	(NA)	195 956	123 170	(NA)
Civilian labor force	20 228 651	(NA)	16 642 330	15 302 935	(NA)	16 752 522	15 349 260	(NA)
Employed	19 010 511	(NA)	15 824 623	14 448 995	(NA)	15 928 005	14 491 385	(NA)
Unemployed	1 218 140	(NA)	817 707	853 940	(NA)	824 517	857 875	(NA)
Percent of civilian labor force	6.0	(NA)	4.9	5.6	(NA)	4.9	5.6	(NA)
Not in labor force	12 892 567	(NA)	12 375 776	12 475 365	(NA)	13 449 919	13 359 205	(NA)
Inmate of institution	474 132	(NA)	(NA)	(NA)	(NA)	433 898	(NA)	(NA)
Male	15 626 311	(NA)	13 934 927	13 385 095	(NA)	14 541 635	13 859 290	(NA)
Labor force	11 744 350	(NA)	11 281 349	10 856 030	(NA)	11 359 779	10 890 860	(NA)
Percent of male	75.2	(NA)	81.0	81.1	(NA)	78.1	78.6	(NA)
Armed Forces	89 703	(NA)	192 733	118 250	(NA)	192 795	118 250	(NA)
Civilian labor force	11 654 647	(NA)	11 088 616	10 737 780	(NA)	11 166 984	10 772 610	(NA)
Employed	10 949 203	(NA)	10 558 810	10 088 245	(NA)	10 632 589	10 120 615	(NA)
Unemployed	705 444	(NA)	529 806	649 535	(NA)	534 395	651 995	(NA)
Percent of civilian labor force	6.1	(NA)	4.8	6.0	(NA)	4.8	6.1	(NA)
Not in labor force	3 881 961	(NA)	2 653 578	2 529 065	(NA)	3 181 856	2 968 430	(NA)
Inmate of institution	185 952	(NA)	(NA)	(NA)	(NA)	231 237	(NA)	(NA)
Female	17 591 698	(NA)	15 279 055	14 516 375	(NA)	15 856 762	14 972 345	(NA)
Labor force	8 581 092	(NA)	5 556 857	4 570 075	(NA)	5 588 699	4 581 570	(NA)
Percent of female	48.8	(NA)	36.4	31.5	(NA)	35.2	30.6	(NA)
Armed Forces	7 088	(NA)	3 143	4 920	(NA)	3 161	4 920	(NA)
Civilian labor force	8 574 004	(NA)	5 553 714	4 565 155	(NA)	5 585 538	4 576 650	(NA)
Employed	8 061 308	(NA)	5 265 813	4 360 750	(NA)	5 295 416	4 370 770	(NA)
Unemployed	512 696	(NA)	287 901	204 405	(NA)	290 122	205 880	(NA)
Percent of civilian labor force	6.0	(NA)	5.2	4.5	(NA)	5.2	4.5	(NA)
Not in labor force	9 010 606	(NA)	9 722 198	9 946 300	(NA)	10 268 063	10 390 775	(NA)
Inmate of institution	288 180	(NA)	(NA)	(NA)	(NA)	222 661	(NA)	(NA)
Black²								
Total	3 422 855	2 767 665	2 075 647	1 518 035	(NA)	2 162 768	1 573 470	(NA)
Labor force	1 998 691	1 624 049	1 306 260	909 620	(NA)	1 311 581	911 310	(NA)
Percent of total	58.4	58.7	62.9	59.9	(NA)	60.6	57.9	(NA)
Armed Forces	15 270	17 559	17 964	8 695	(NA)	17 971	8 695	(NA)
Civilian labor force	1 983 421	1 606 490	1 288 296	900 925	(NA)	1 293 610	902 615	(NA)
Employed	1 742 419	1 510 424	1 174 558	802 480	(NA)	1 178 808	803 630	(NA)
Unemployed	241 002	96 066	113 738	98 445	(NA)	114 802	98 985	(NA)
Percent of civilian labor force	12.2	6.0	8.8	10.9	(NA)	8.9	11.0	(NA)
Not in labor force	1 424 164	1 143 616	769 387	608 415	(NA)	851 187	662 160	(NA)
Inmate of institution	69 609	(NA)	(NA)	(NA)	(NA)	62 785	(NA)	(NA)
Male	1 513 987	1 233 753	962 156	714 220	(NA)	1 005 736	741 450	(NA)
Labor force	991 699	884 112	758 740	550 145	(NA)	762 301	551 290	(NA)
Percent of male	65.5	71.7	78.9	77.0	(NA)	75.8	74.4	(NA)
Armed Forces	13 037	16 837	17 551	8 290	(NA)	17 558	8 290	(NA)
Civilian labor force	978 662	867 275	741 189	541 855	(NA)	744 743	543 000	(NA)
Employed	848 306	815 272	673 336	475 110	(NA)	676 222	475 975	(NA)
Unemployed	130 356	52 003	67 853	66 745	(NA)	68 521	67 025	(NA)
Percent of civilian labor force	13.3	6.0	9.2	12.3	(NA)	9.2	12.3	(NA)
Not in labor force	522 288	349 641	203 416	164 075	(NA)	243 435	190 160	(NA)
Inmate of institution	52 823	(NA)	(NA)	(NA)	(NA)	45 421	(NA)	(NA)
Female	1 908 868	1 533 912	1 113 491	803 815	(NA)	1 157 032	832 020	(NA)
Labor force	1 006 992	739 937	547 520	359 475	(NA)	549 280	360 020	(NA)
Percent of female	52.8	48.2	49.2	44.7	(NA)	47.5	43.3	(NA)
Armed Forces	2 233	722	413	405	(NA)	413	405	(NA)
Civilian labor force	1 004 759	739 215	547 107	359 070	(NA)	548 867	359 615	(NA)
Employed	894 113	695 152	501 222	327 370	(NA)	502 586	327 655	(NA)
Unemployed	110 646	44 063	45 885	31 700	(NA)	46 281	31 960	(NA)
Percent of civilian labor force	11.0	6.0	8.4	8.8	(NA)	8.4	8.9	(NA)
Not in labor force	901 876	793 975	565 971	444 340	(NA)	607 752	472 000	(NA)
Inmate of institution	16 786	(NA)	(NA)	(NA)	(NA)	17 364	(NA)	(NA)

¹Excludes data for Alaska and Hawaii. ²For years prior to 1970, includes Black and other races.

GENERAL SOCIAL AND ECONOMIC CHARACTERISTICS **UNITED STATES SUMMARY 1—27**

Table 86. Labor Force Status by Sex and Race: 1940 to 1980—Con.

[Data are estimates based on a sample; see Introduction. For meaning of symbols, see Introduction. For definitions of terms, see appendixes A and B]

United States Regions	16 years and over				14 years and over			
	1980	1970	1960	1950[1]	1970	1960	1950[1]	1940[1]
NORTH CENTRAL								
Total								
Total	44 178 493	38 868 154	34 626 721	31 992 650	(NA)	36 157 249	33 211 680	(NA)
Labor force	27 705 296	22 813 413	19 829 454	17 650 995	(NA)	20 047 265	17 800 060	(NA)
Percent of total	62.7	58.7	57.3	55.2	(NA)	55.4	53.6	(NA)
Armed Forces	156 239	210 792	183 525	89 935	(NA)	183 690	89 935	(NA)
Civilian labor force	27 549 057	22 602 621	19 645 929	17 561 060	(NA)	19 863 575	17 710 125	(NA)
Employed	25 517 077	21 649 502	18 698 558	16 893 565	(NA)	18 903 043	17 033 400	(NA)
Unemployed	2 031 980	953 119	947 371	667 495	(NA)	960 532	676 725	(NA)
Percent of civilian labor force	7.4	4.2	4.8	3.8	(NA)	4.8	3.8	(NA)
Not in labor force	16 473 197	16 054 741	14 797 267	14 341 655	(NA)	16 109 984	15 411 620	(NA)
Inmate of institution	695 008	(NA)	(NA)	(NA)	(NA)	518 788	(NA)	(NA)
Male								
Male	21 093 150	18 530 003	16 804 932	15 674 335	(NA)	17 588 420	16 295 805	(NA)
Labor force	16 101 306	14 394 838	13 633 455	12 915 030	(NA)	13 786 118	13 025 755	(NA)
Percent of male	76.3	77.7	81.1	82.4	(NA)	78.4	79.9	(NA)
Armed Forces	140 991	205 591	180 593	84 380	(NA)	180 754	84 380	(NA)
Civilian labor force	15 960 315	14 189 247	13 452 862	12 830 650	(NA)	13 605 364	12 941 375	(NA)
Employed	14 712 806	13 657 860	12 810 927	12 335 460	(NA)	12 954 908	12 440 275	(NA)
Unemployed	1 247 509	531 387	641 935	495 190	(NA)	650 456	501 100	(NA)
Percent of civilian labor force	7.8	3.7	4.8	3.9	(NA)	4.8	3.9	(NA)
Not in labor force	4 991 844	4 135 165	3 171 477	2 759 305	(NA)	3 802 302	3 270 050	(NA)
Inmate of institution	313 193	(NA)	(NA)	(NA)	(NA)	297 926	(NA)	(NA)
Female								
Female	23 085 343	20 338 151	17 821 789	16 318 315	(NA)	18 568 829	16 915 875	(NA)
Labor force	11 603 990	8 418 575	6 195 999	4 735 965	(NA)	6 261 147	4 774 305	(NA)
Percent of female	50.3	41.4	34.8	29.0	(NA)	33.7	28.2	(NA)
Armed Forces	15 248	5 201	2 932	5 555	(NA)	2 936	5 555	(NA)
Civilian labor force	11 588 742	8 413 374	6 193 067	4 730 410	(NA)	6 258 211	4 768 750	(NA)
Employed	10 804 271	7 991 642	5 887 631	4 558 105	(NA)	5 948 135	4 593 125	(NA)
Unemployed	784 471	421 732	305 436	172 305	(NA)	310 076	175 625	(NA)
Percent of civilian labor force	6.8	5.0	4.9	3.6	(NA)	5.0	3.7	(NA)
Not in labor force	11 481 353	11 919 576	11 625 790	11 582 350	(NA)	12 307 682	12 141 570	(NA)
Inmate of institution	381 815	(NA)	(NA)	(NA)	(NA)	220 862	(NA)	(NA)
White								
Total	39 727 216	(NA)	32 389 325	30 319 515	(NA)	33 816 919	31 474 800	(NA)
Labor force	25 032 367	(NA)	18 526 689	16 697 675	(NA)	18 737 755	16 843 405	(NA)
Percent of total	63.0	(NA)	57.2	55.1	(NA)	55.4	53.5	(NA)
Armed Forces	125 873	(NA)	169 845	84 835	(NA)	169 975	84 835	(NA)
Civilian labor force	24 906 494	(NA)	18 356 844	16 612 840	(NA)	18 567 780	16 758 570	(NA)
Employed	23 274 239	(NA)	17 562 953	16 049 860	(NA)	17 762 080	16 187 095	(NA)
Unemployed	1 632 255	(NA)	793 891	562 980	(NA)	805 700	571 475	(NA)
Percent of civilian labor force	6.6	(NA)	4.3	3.4	(NA)	4.3	3.4	(NA)
Not in labor force	14 694 849	(NA)	13 862 636	13 621 840	(NA)	15 079 164	14 631 395	(NA)
Inmate of institution	606 202	(NA)	(NA)	(NA)	(NA)	460 224	(NA)	(NA)
Male								
Male	19 027 004	(NA)	15 733 199	14 853 530	(NA)	16 465 496	15 444 230	(NA)
Labor force	14 686 734	(NA)	12 814 630	12 274 055	(NA)	12 962 472	12 382 445	(NA)
Percent of male	77.2	(NA)	81.4	82.6	(NA)	78.7	80.2	(NA)
Armed Forces	114 510	(NA)	167 286	79 630	(NA)	167 412	79 630	(NA)
Civilian labor force	14 572 224	(NA)	12 647 344	12 194 425	(NA)	12 795 060	12 302 815	(NA)
Employed	13 553 482	(NA)	12 103 568	11 769 290	(NA)	12 243 631	11 872 220	(NA)
Unemployed	1 018 742	(NA)	543 776	425 135	(NA)	551 429	430 595	(NA)
Percent of civilian labor force	7.0	(NA)	4.3	3.5	(NA)	4.3	3.5	(NA)
Not in labor force	4 340 270	(NA)	2 918 569	2 579 475	(NA)	3 503 024	3 061 785	(NA)
Inmate of institution	245 957	(NA)	(NA)	(NA)	(NA)	252 496	(NA)	(NA)
Female								
Female	20 700 212	(NA)	16 656 126	15 465 985	(NA)	17 351 423	16 030 570	(NA)
Labor force	10 345 633	(NA)	5 712 059	4 423 620	(NA)	5 775 283	4 460 960	(NA)
Percent of female	50.0	(NA)	34.3	28.6	(NA)	33.3	27.8	(NA)
Armed Forces	11 363	(NA)	2 559	5 205	(NA)	2 563	5 205	(NA)
Civilian labor force	10 334 270	(NA)	5 709 500	4 418 415	(NA)	5 772 720	4 455 755	(NA)
Employed	9 720 757	(NA)	5 459 385	4 280 570	(NA)	5 518 449	4 314 875	(NA)
Unemployed	613 513	(NA)	250 115	137 845	(NA)	254 271	140 880	(NA)
Percent of civilian labor force	5.9	(NA)	4.4	3.1	(NA)	4.4	3.2	(NA)
Not in labor force	10 354 579	(NA)	10 944 067	11 042 365	(NA)	11 576 140	11 569 610	(NA)
Inmate of institution	360 245	(NA)	(NA)	(NA)	(NA)	207 728	(NA)	(NA)
Black[2]								
Total	3 631 904	2 832 063	2 237 396	1 673 135	(NA)	2 340 330	1 736 880	(NA)
Labor force	2 142 992	1 667 772	1 302 765	953 320	(NA)	1 309 510	956 655	(NA)
Percent of total	59.0	58.9	58.2	57.0	(NA)	56.0	55.0	(NA)
Armed Forces	23 596	18 717	13 680	5 100	(NA)	13 715	5 100	(NA)
Civilian labor force	2 119 396	1 649 055	1 289 085	948 220	(NA)	1 295 795	951 555	(NA)
Employed	1 776 892	1 514 209	1 135 605	843 705	(NA)	1 140 963	846 305	(NA)
Unemployed	342 504	134 846	153 480	104 515	(NA)	154 832	105 250	(NA)
Percent of civilian labor force	16.2	8.2	11.9	11.0	(NA)	11.9	11.1	(NA)
Not in labor force	1 488 912	1 164 291	934 631	719 815	(NA)	1 030 820	780 225	(NA)
Inmate of institution	79 770	(NA)	(NA)	(NA)	(NA)	58 564	(NA)	(NA)
Male								
Male	1 658 801	1 312 039	1 071 733	820 805	(NA)	1 122 924	851 575	(NA)
Labor force	1 100 098	938 342	818 825	640 975	(NA)	823 646	643 310	(NA)
Percent of male	66.3	71.5	76.4	78.1	(NA)	73.3	75.5	(NA)
Armed Forces	20 371	18 225	13 307	4 750	(NA)	13 342	4 750	(NA)
Civilian labor force	1 079 727	920 117	805 518	636 225	(NA)	810 304	638 560	(NA)
Employed	884 383	848 370	707 359	566 170	(NA)	711 277	568 055	(NA)
Unemployed	195 344	71 747	98 159	70 055	(NA)	99 027	70 505	(NA)
Percent of civilian labor force	18.1	7.8	12.2	11.0	(NA)	12.2	11.0	(NA)
Not in labor force	558 703	373 697	252 908	179 830	(NA)	299 278	208 265	(NA)
Inmate of institution	60 024	(NA)	(NA)	(NA)	(NA)	45 430	(NA)	(NA)
Female								
Female	1 973 103	1 520 024	1 165 663	852 330	(NA)	1 217 406	885 305	(NA)
Labor force	1 042 894	729 430	483 940	312 345	(NA)	485 864	313 345	(NA)
Percent of female	52.9	48.0	41.5	36.6	(NA)	39.9	35.4	(NA)
Armed Forces	3 225	492	373	350	(NA)	373	350	(NA)
Civilian labor force	1 039 669	728 938	483 567	311 995	(NA)	485 491	312 995	(NA)
Employed	892 509	665 839	428 246	277 535	(NA)	429 686	278 250	(NA)
Unemployed	147 160	63 099	55 321	34 460	(NA)	55 805	34 745	(NA)
Percent of civilian labor force	14.2	8.7	11.4	11.0	(NA)	11.5	11.1	(NA)
Not in labor force	930 209	790 594	681 723	539 985	(NA)	731 542	571 960	(NA)
Inmate of institution	19 746	(NA)	(NA)	(NA)	(NA)	13 134	(NA)	(NA)

[1]Excludes data for Alaska and Hawaii. [2]for years prior to 1970, includes Black and other races.

Table 86. Labor Force Status by Sex and Race: 1940 to 1980—Con.

[Data are estimates based on a sample; see Introduction. For meaning of symbols, see Introduction. For definitions of terms, see appendixes A and B]

United States Regions	16 years and over				14 years and over			
	1980	1970	1960	1950¹	1970	1960	1950¹	1940¹

SOUTH

Total

Total	56 552 817	43 320 525	36 064 431	31 966 590	(NA)	37 948 263	33 524 525	(NA)
Labor force	34 433 990	24 711 178	20 215 258	17 400 275	(NA)	20 398 374	17 588 740	(NA)
Percent of total	60.9	57.0	56.1	54.4	(NA)	53.8	52.5	(NA)
Armed Forces	848 271	982 451	806 136	491 995	(NA)	806 776	491 995	(NA)
Civilian labor force	33 585 719	23 728 727	19 409 122	16 908 280	(NA)	19 591 598	17 096 745	(NA)
Employed	31 678 379	22 797 477	18 449 010	16 234 190	(NA)	18 615 539	16 411 950	(NA)
Unemployed	1 907 340	931 250	960 112	674 090	(NA)	976 059	684 795	(NA)
Percent of civilian labor force	5.7	3.9	4.9	4.0	(NA)	5.0	4.0	(NA)
Not in labor force	22 118 827	18 609 347	15 849 173	14 566 315	(NA)	17 549 889	15 935 785	(NA)
Inmate of institution	740 421	(NA)	(NA)	(NA)	(NA)	458 702	(NA)	(NA)
Male	26 959 721	20 666 324	17 455 395	15 603 415	(NA)	18 417 937	16 392 850	(NA)
Labor force	19 916 740	15 483 150	13 717 224	12 729 025	(NA)	13 851 958	12 876 045	(NA)
Percent of male	73.9	74.9	78.6	81.6	(NA)	75.2	78.5	(NA)
Armed Forces	768 259	958 704	790 976	476 900	(NA)	791 585	476 900	(NA)
Civilian labor force	19 148 481	14 524 446	12 926 248	12 252 125	(NA)	13 060 373	12 399 145	(NA)
Employed	18 135 224	14 051 822	12 303 361	11 777 135	(NA)	12 426 784	11 917 325	(NA)
Unemployed	1 013 257	472 624	622 887	474 990	(NA)	633 589	481 820	(NA)
Percent of civilian labor force	5.3	3.3	4.8	3.9	(NA)	4.9	3.9	(NA)
Not in labor force	7 042 981	5 183 174	3 738 171	2 874 390	(NA)	4 565 979	3 516 805	(NA)
Inmate of institution	396 019	(NA)	(NA)	(NA)	(NA)	298 711	(NA)	(NA)
Female	29 593 096	22 654 201	18 609 036	16 363 175	(NA)	19 530 326	17 131 675	(NA)
Labor force	14 517 250	9 228 028	6 498 034	4 671 250	(NA)	6 546 416	4 712 695	(NA)
Percent of female	49.1	40.7	34.9	28.5	(NA)	33.5	27.5	(NA)
Armed Forces	80 012	23 747	15 160	15 095	(NA)	15 191	15 095	(NA)
Civilian labor force	14 437 238	9 204 281	6 482 874	4 656 155	(NA)	6 531 225	4 697 600	(NA)
Employed	13 543 155	8 745 655	6 145 649	4 457 055	(NA)	6 188 755	4 494 625	(NA)
Unemployed	894 083	458 626	337 225	199 100	(NA)	342 470	202 975	(NA)
Percent of civilian labor force	6.2	5.0	5.2	4.3	(NA)	5.2	4.3	(NA)
Not in labor force	15 075 846	13 426 173	12 111 002	11 691 925	(NA)	12 983 910	12 418 980	(NA)
Inmate of institution	344 402	(NA)	(NA)	(NA)	(NA)	159 991	(NA)	(NA)

White

Total	45 409 181	(NA)	29 302 281	25 375 435	(NA)	30 739 565	26 550 150	(NA)
Labor force	27 759 270	(NA)	16 332 984	13 584 885	(NA)	16 470 400	13 708 405	(NA)
Percent of total	61.1	(NA)	55.8	53.5	(NA)	53.6	51.6	(NA)
Armed Forces	627 997	(NA)	744 120	454 870	(NA)	744 669	454 870	(NA)
Civilian labor force	27 131 273	(NA)	15 588 864	13 130 015	(NA)	15 725 731	13 253 535	(NA)
Employed	25 844 773	(NA)	14 909 351	12 675 465	(NA)	15 035 385	12 791 580	(NA)
Unemployed	1 286 500	(NA)	679 513	454 550	(NA)	690 346	461 955	(NA)
Percent of civilian labor force	4.7	(NA)	4.4	3.5	(NA)	4.4	3.5	(NA)
Not in labor force	17 649 911	(NA)	12 969 297	11 790 550	(NA)	14 269 165	12 841 745	(NA)
Inmate of institution	539 036	(NA)	(NA)	(NA)	(NA)	324 685	(NA)	(NA)
Male	21 804 166	(NA)	14 274 593	12 469 900	(NA)	15 012 372	13 069 595	(NA)
Labor force	16 397 645	(NA)	11 368 919	10 208 420	(NA)	11 471 728	10 307 625	(NA)
Percent of male	75.2	(NA)	79.6	81.9	(NA)	76.4	78.9	(NA)
Armed Forces	571 958	(NA)	730 304	441 860	(NA)	730 822	441 860	(NA)
Civilian labor force	15 825 687	(NA)	10 638 615	9 766 560	(NA)	10 740 906	9 865 765	(NA)
Employed	15 115 338	(NA)	10 181 576	9 426 525	(NA)	10 276 218	9 520 730	(NA)
Unemployed	710 349	(NA)	457 039	340 035	(NA)	464 688	345 035	(NA)
Percent of civilian labor force	4.5	(NA)	4.3	3.5	(NA)	4.3	3.5	(NA)
Not in labor force	5 406 521	(NA)	2 905 674	2 261 480	(NA)	3 540 644	2 761 970	(NA)
Inmate of institution	246 007	(NA)	(NA)	(NA)	(NA)	198 184	(NA)	(NA)
Female	23 605 015	(NA)	15 027 688	12 905 535	(NA)	15 727 193	13 480 555	(NA)
Labor force	11 361 625	(NA)	4 964 065	3 376 465	(NA)	4 998 672	3 400 780	(NA)
Percent of female	48.1	(NA)	33.0	26.2	(NA)	31.8	25.2	(NA)
Armed Forces	56 039	(NA)	13 816	13 010	(NA)	13 847	13 010	(NA)
Civilian labor force	11 305 586	(NA)	4 950 249	3 363 455	(NA)	4 984 825	3 387 770	(NA)
Employed	10 729 435	(NA)	4 727 775	3 248 940	(NA)	4 759 167	3 270 850	(NA)
Unemployed	576 151	(NA)	222 474	114 515	(NA)	225 658	116 920	(NA)
Percent of civilian labor force	5.1	(NA)	4.5	3.4	(NA)	4.5	3.5	(NA)
Not in labor force	12 243 390	(NA)	10 063 623	9 529 070	(NA)	10 728 521	10 079 775	(NA)
Inmate of institution	293 029	(NA)	(NA)	(NA)	(NA)	126 501	(NA)	(NA)

Black²

Total	9 635 585	7 354 582	6 762 150	6 591 155	(NA)	7 208 698	6 974 375	(NA)
Labor force	5 711 113	4 157 260	3 882 274	3 815 390	(NA)	3 927 974	3 880 335	(NA)
Percent of total	59.3	56.5	57.4	57.9	(NA)	54.5	55.6	(NA)
Armed Forces	174 161	98 414	62 016	37 125	(NA)	62 107	37 125	(NA)
Civilian labor force	5 536 952	4 058 846	3 820 258	3 778 265	(NA)	3 865 867	3 843 210	(NA)
Employed	4 976 037	3 799 112	3 539 659	3 558 725	(NA)	3 580 154	3 620 370	(NA)
Unemployed	560 915	259 734	280 599	219 540	(NA)	285 713	222 840	(NA)
Percent of civilian labor force	10.1	6.4	7.3	5.8	(NA)	7.4	5.8	(NA)
Not in labor force	3 924 472	3 197 322	2 879 876	2 775 765	(NA)	3 280 724	3 094 040	(NA)
Inmate of institution	183 279	(NA)	(NA)	(NA)	(NA)	134 017	(NA)	(NA)
Male	4 409 163	3 384 672	3 180 802	3 133 515	(NA)	3 405 565	3 323 255	(NA)
Labor force	2 935 642	2 303 658	2 348 305	2 520 605	(NA)	2 380 230	2 568 420	(NA)
Percent of male	66.6	68.1	73.8	80.4	(NA)	69.9	77.3	(NA)
Armed Forces	154 067	95 430	60 672	35 040	(NA)	60 763	35 040	(NA)
Civilian labor force	2 781 575	2 208 228	2 287 633	2 485 565	(NA)	2 319 467	2 533 380	(NA)
Employed	2 510 513	2 092 096	2 121 785	2 350 610	(NA)	2 150 566	2 396 595	(NA)
Unemployed	271 062	116 132	165 848	134 955	(NA)	168 901	136 785	(NA)
Percent of civilian labor force	9.7	5.3	7.2	5.4	(NA)	7.3	5.4	(NA)
Not in labor force	1 473 521	1 081 014	832 497	612 910	(NA)	1 025 335	754 835	(NA)
Inmate of institution	136 422	(NA)	(NA)	(NA)	(NA)	100 527	(NA)	(NA)
Female	5 226 422	3 969 910	3 581 348	3 457 640	(NA)	3 803 133	3 651 120	(NA)
Labor force	2 775 471	1 853 602	1 533 969	1 294 785	(NA)	1 547 744	1 311 950	(NA)
Percent of female	53.1	46.7	42.8	37.4	(NA)	40.7	35.9	(NA)
Armed Forces	20 094	2 984	1 344	2 085	(NA)	1 344	2 085	(NA)
Civilian labor force	2 755 377	1 850 618	1 532 625	1 292 700	(NA)	1 546 400	1 309 830	(NA)
Employed	2 465 524	1 707 016	1 417 874	1 208 115	(NA)	1 429 588	1 223 775	(NA)
Unemployed	289 853	143 602	114 751	84 585	(NA)	116 812	86 055	(NA)
Percent of civilian labor force	10.5	7.8	7.5	6.5	(NA)	7.6	6.6	(NA)
Not in labor force	2 450 951	2 116 308	2 047 379	2 162 855	(NA)	2 255 389	2 339 205	(NA)
Inmate of institution	46 857	(NA)	(NA)	(NA)	(NA)	33 490	(NA)	(NA)

¹Excludes data for Alaska and Hawaii. ²For years prior to 1970, includes Black and other races.

Table 86. Labor Force Status by Sex and Race: 1940 to 1980—Con.

[Data are estimates based on a sample; see Introduction. For meaning of symbols, see Introduction. For definitions of terms, see appendixes A and B]

United States Regions	16 years and over				14 years and over			
	1980	1970	1960	1950¹	1970	1960	1950¹	1940¹
WEST								
Total								
Total	32 614 131	24 168 087	18 745 645	14 057 260	(NA)	19 609 839	14 562 090	(NA)
Labor force	20 908 653	14 286 109	11 044 927	7 811 165	(NA)	11 171 778	7 870 450	(NA)
Percent of total	64.1	59.1	58.9	55.6	(NA)	57.0	54.0	(NA)
Armed Forces	512 917	609 987	528 779	283 180	(NA)	529 009	283 180	(NA)
Civilian labor force	20 395 736	13 676 122	10 516 148	7 527 985	(NA)	10 642 769	7 587 270	(NA)
Employed	19 050 593	12 835 777	9 899 908	6 994 350	(NA)	10 013 852	7 047 785	(NA)
Unemployed	1 345 143	840 345	616 240	533 635	(NA)	628 917	539 485	(NA)
Percent of civilian labor force	6.6	6.1	5.9	7.1	(NA)	5.9	7.1	(NA)
Not in labor force	11 705 478	9 881 978	7 700 718	6 246 095	(NA)	8 438 061	6 691 640	(NA)
Inmate of institution	398 469	(NA)	(NA)	(NA)	(NA)	265 737	(NA)	(NA)
Male								
Male	15 966 419	11 778 744	9 320 032	7 055 510	(NA)	9 761 625	7 311 710	(NA)
Labor force	12 251 151	9 115 068	7 621 749	5 703 900	(NA)	7 707 564	5 747 050	(NA)
Percent of male	76.7	77.4	81.8	80.8	(NA)	79.0	78.6	(NA)
Armed Forces	472 774	598 400	522 142	276 855	(NA)	522 360	276 855	(NA)
Civilian labor force	11 778 377	8 516 668	7 099 607	5 427 045	(NA)	7 185 204	5 470 195	(NA)
Employed	10 989 803	8 024 063	6 699 224	5 043 960	(NA)	6 776 443	5 083 300	(NA)
Unemployed	788 574	492 605	400 383	383 085	(NA)	408 761	386 895	(NA)
Percent of civilian labor force	6.7	5.8	5.6	7.1	(NA)	5.7	7.1	(NA)
Not in labor force	3 715 268	2 663 676	1 698 283	1 351 610	(NA)	2 054 061	1 564 660	(NA)
Inmate of institution	204 834	(NA)	(NA)	(NA)	(NA)	167 636	(NA)	(NA)
Female								
Female	16 647 712	12 389 343	9 425 613	7 001 750	(NA)	9 848 214	7 250 380	(NA)
Labor force	8 657 502	5 171 041	3 423 178	2 107 265	(NA)	3 464 214	2 123 400	(NA)
Percent of female	52.0	41.7	36.3	30.1	(NA)	35.2	29.3	(NA)
Armed Forces	40 143	11 587	6 637	6 325	(NA)	6 649	6 325	(NA)
Civilian labor force	8 617 359	5 159 454	3 416 541	2 100 940	(NA)	3 457 565	2 117 075	(NA)
Employed	8 060 790	4 811 714	3 200 684	1 950 390	(NA)	3 237 409	1 964 485	(NA)
Unemployed	556 569	347 740	215 857	150 550	(NA)	220 156	152 590	(NA)
Percent of civilian labor force	6.5	6.7	6.3	7.2	(NA)	6.4	7.2	(NA)
Not in labor force	7 990 210	7 218 302	6 002 435	4 894 485	(NA)	6 384 000	5 126 980	(NA)
Inmate of institution	193 635	(NA)	(NA)	(NA)	(NA)	98 101	(NA)	(NA)
White								
Total	27 070 881	(NA)	17 374 551	13 371 610	(NA)	18 167 990	13 849 260	(NA)
Labor force	17 317 888	(NA)	10 200 187	7 394 785	(NA)	10 321 504	7 451 855	(NA)
Percent of total	64.0	(NA)	58.7	55.3	(NA)	56.8	53.8	(NA)
Armed Forces	392 411	(NA)	481 931	265 870	(NA)	482 111	265 870	(NA)
Civilian labor force	16 925 477	(NA)	9 718 256	7 128 915	(NA)	9 839 393	7 185 985	(NA)
Employed	15 897 852	(NA)	9 175 364	6 648 535	(NA)	9 284 791	6 700 045	(NA)
Unemployed	1 027 625	(NA)	542 892	480 380	(NA)	554 602	485 940	(NA)
Percent of civilian labor force	6.1	(NA)	5.6	6.7	(NA)	5.6	6.8	(NA)
Not in labor force	9 752 993	(NA)	7 174 364	5 976 825	(NA)	7 846 486	6 397 405	(NA)
Inmate of institution	325 301	(NA)	(NA)	(NA)	(NA)	234 435	(NA)	(NA)
Male								
Male	13 214 902	(NA)	8 611 038	6 685 900	(NA)	9 016 669	6 928 710	(NA)
Labor force	10 193 789	(NA)	7 064 076	5 412 635	(NA)	7 145 908	5 454 265	(NA)
Percent of male	77.1	(NA)	82.0	81.0	(NA)	79.3	78.7	(NA)
Armed Forces	361 721	(NA)	475 971	260 020	(NA)	476 139	260 020	(NA)
Civilian labor force	9 832 068	(NA)	6 588 105	5 152 615	(NA)	6 669 769	5 194 245	(NA)
Employed	9 225 964	(NA)	6 235 290	4 806 615	(NA)	6 309 246	4 844 645	(NA)
Unemployed	606 104	(NA)	352 815	346 000	(NA)	360 523	349 600	(NA)
Percent of civilian labor force	6.2	(NA)	5.4	6.7	(NA)	5.4	6.7	(NA)
Not in labor force	3 021 113	(NA)	1 546 962	1 273 265	(NA)	1 870 761	1 474 445	(NA)
Inmate of institution	147 905	(NA)	(NA)	(NA)	(NA)	142 688	(NA)	(NA)
Female								
Female	13 855 979	(NA)	8 763 513	6 685 710	(NA)	9 151 321	6 920 550	(NA)
Labor force	7 124 099	(NA)	3 136 111	1 982 150	(NA)	3 175 596	1 997 590	(NA)
Percent of female	51.4	(NA)	35.8	29.6	(NA)	34.7	28.9	(NA)
Armed Forces	30 690	(NA)	5 960	5 850	(NA)	5 972	5 850	(NA)
Civilian labor force	7 093 409	(NA)	3 130 151	1 976 300	(NA)	3 169 624	1 991 740	(NA)
Employed	6 671 888	(NA)	2 940 074	1 841 920	(NA)	2 975 545	1 855 400	(NA)
Unemployed	421 521	(NA)	190 077	134 380	(NA)	194 079	136 340	(NA)
Percent of civilian labor force	5.9	(NA)	6.1	6.8	(NA)	6.1	6.8	(NA)
Not in labor force	6 731 880	(NA)	5 627 402	4 703 560	(NA)	5 975 725	4 922 960	(NA)
Inmate of institution	177 396	(NA)	(NA)	(NA)	(NA)	91 747	(NA)	(NA)
Black²								
Total	1 604 581	1 060 973	1 371 094	685 650	(NA)	1 441 849	712 830	(NA)
Labor force	1 013 547	643 310	844 740	416 380	(NA)	850 274	418 595	(NA)
Percent of total	63.2	60.6	61.6	60.7	(NA)	59.0	58.7	(NA)
Armed Forces	70 880	46 123	46 848	17 310	(NA)	46 898	17 310	(NA)
Civilian labor force	942 667	597 187	797 892	399 070	(NA)	803 376	401 285	(NA)
Employed	838 700	537 398	724 544	345 815	(NA)	729 061	347 740	(NA)
Unemployed	103 967	59 789	73 348	53 255	(NA)	74 315	53 545	(NA)
Percent of civilian labor force	11.0	10.0	9.2	13.3	(NA)	9.3	13.3	(NA)
Not in labor force	591 034	417 663	526 354	269 270	(NA)	591 575	294 235	(NA)
Inmate of institution	35 248	(NA)	(NA)	(NA)	(NA)	31 302	(NA)	(NA)
Male								
Male	792 100	519 005	708 994	369 610	(NA)	744 956	383 000	(NA)
Labor force	555 423	375 448	557 673	291 265	(NA)	561 656	292 785	(NA)
Percent of male	70.1	72.3	78.7	78.8	(NA)	75.4	76.4	(NA)
Armed Forces	64 595	45 033	46 171	16 835	(NA)	46 221	16 835	(NA)
Civilian labor force	490 828	330 415	511 502	274 430	(NA)	515 435	275 950	(NA)
Employed	431 669	296 325	463 934	237 345	(NA)	467 197	238 655	(NA)
Unemployed	59 159	34 090	47 568	37 085	(NA)	48 238	37 295	(NA)
Percent of civilian labor force	12.1	10.3	9.3	13.5	(NA)	9.4	13.5	(NA)
Not in labor force	236 677	143 557	151 321	78 345	(NA)	183 300	90 215	(NA)
Inmate of institution	27 982	(NA)	(NA)	(NA)	(NA)	24 948	(NA)	(NA)
Female								
Female	812 481	541 968	662 100	316 040	(NA)	696 893	329 830	(NA)
Labor force	458 124	267 862	287 067	125 115	(NA)	288 618	125 810	(NA)
Percent of female	56.4	49.4	43.4	39.6	(NA)	41.4	38.1	(NA)
Armed Forces	6 285	1 090	677	475	(NA)	677	475	(NA)
Civilian labor force	451 839	266 772	286 390	124 640	(NA)	287 941	125 335	(NA)
Employed	407 031	241 073	260 610	108 470	(NA)	261 864	109 085	(NA)
Unemployed	44 808	25 699	25 780	16 170	(NA)	26 077	16 250	(NA)
Percent of civilian labor force	9.9	9.6	9.0	13.0	(NA)	9.1	13.0	(NA)
Not in labor force	354 357	274 106	375 033	190 925	(NA)	408 275	204 020	(NA)
Inmate of institution	7 266	(NA)	(NA)	(NA)	(NA)	6 354	(NA)	(NA)

¹Excludes data for Alaska and Hawaii. ²For years prior to 1970, includes Black and other races.

Table 87. Labor Force Status by Age, Race, and Sex: 1940 to 1980

[For years prior to 1960, excludes data for Alaska and Hawaii. Data are estimates based on a sample; see Introduction. For meaning of symbols, see Introduction. For definitions of terms, see appendixes A and B]

United States Regions	Persons 14 years and over	14 and 15 years	Persons 16 years and over — Total	16 to 19	20 to 24	25 to 34	35 to 44	45 to 54	55 to 64	65 and over
UNITED STATES										
Total										
1980										
Total	(NA)	(NA)	171 214 258	17 084 757	21 293 814	37 181 374	25 637 555	22 732 301	21 786 071	25 498 386
Labor force	(NA)	(NA)	106 084 668	8 396 936	16 016 658	29 265 325	20 286 987	16 804 478	12 091 450	3 222 834
Percent of total	(NA)	(NA)	62.0	49.1	75.2	78.7	79.1	73.9	55.5	12.6
Male	(NA)	(NA)	81 732 090	8 676 324	10 639 312	18 434 135	12 570 207	10 957 148	10 192 396	10 262 568
Labor force	(NA)	(NA)	61 416 203	4 548 799	8 795 366	17 111 419	11 832 701	9 883 776	7 265 081	1 979 061
Percent of male	(NA)	(NA)	75.1	52.4	82.7	92.8	94.1	90.2	71.3	19.3
Female	(NA)	(NA)	89 482 168	8 408 433	10 654 502	18 747 239	13 067 348	11 775 153	11 593 675	15 235 818
Labor force	(NA)	(NA)	44 668 465	3 848 137	7 221 292	12 153 906	8 454 286	6 920 702	4 826 369	1 243 773
Percent of female	(NA)	(NA)	49.9	45.8	67.8	64.8	64.7	58.8	41.6	8.2
1970										
Total	149 398 189	8 310 919	141 087 270	15 083 042	16 104 869	24 845 947	23 132 821	23 158 493	18 660 224	20 101 874
Labor force	82 897 433	848 652	82 048 781	6 201 662	10 953 861	17 110 928	16 652 683	16 625 482	11 240 391	3 263 774
Percent of total	55.5	10.2	58.2	41.1	68.0	68.9	72.0	71.8	60.2	16.2
Male	71 481 904	4 246 394	67 235 510	7 611 877	7 753 863	12 167 803	11 268 698	11 172 259	8 823 380	8 437 630
Labor force	52 076 663	574 549	51 502 114	3 592 922	6 271 281	11 423 663	10 687 668	10 334 053	7 100 031	2 092 496
Percent of male	72.9	13.5	76.6	47.2	80.9	93.9	94.8	92.5	80.5	24.8
Female	77 916 285	4 064 525	73 851 760	7 471 165	8 351 006	12 678 144	11 864 123	11 986 234	9 836 844	11 664 244
Labor force	30 820 770	274 103	30 546 667	2 608 740	4 682 580	5 687 265	5 965 015	6 291 429	4 140 360	1 171 278
Percent of female	39.6	6.7	41.4	34.9	56.1	44.9	50.3	52.5	42.1	10.0
1960										
Total	126 276 516	5 550 090	120 726 426	10 485 178	10 803 165	22 822 095	24 075 532	20 625 375	15 707 844	16 207 237
Labor force	69 877 476	643 371	69 234 105	4 336 674	7 029 053	14 720 901	16 490 421	14 361 866	9 145 638	3 149 552
Percent of total	55.3	11.6	57.3	41.4	65.1	64.5	68.5	69.6	58.2	19.4
Male	61 315 353	2 837 911	58 477 442	5 263 650	5 283 228	11 173 569	11 739 191	10 139 666	7 569 153	7 308 985
Labor force	47 467 720	455 203	47 012 517	2 633 574	4 554 010	10 604 072	11 224 835	9 467 557	6 297 735	2 230 734
Percent of male	77.4	16.0	80.4	50.0	86.2	94.9	95.6	93.4	83.2	30.5
Female	64 961 163	2 712 179	62 248 984	5 221 528	5 519 937	11 648 526	12 336 341	10 485 709	8 138 691	8 898 252
Labor force	22 409 756	188 168	22 221 588	1 703 100	2 475 043	4 116 829	5 265 586	4 894 309	2 847 903	918 818
Percent of female	34.5	6.9	35.7	32.6	44.8	35.3	42.7	46.7	35.0	10.3
1950										
Total	111 693 240	4 268 610	107 424 630	8 543 760	11 410 380	23 612 220	21 246 210	17 183 940	13 183 410	12 244 710
Labor force	59 670 540	447 900	59 222 640	3 535 800	7 057 980	14 419 980	13 635 210	10 672 050	7 019 310	2 882 310
Percent of total	53.4	10.5	55.1	41.4	61.9	61.1	64.2	62.1	53.2	23.5
Male	54 610 050	2 176 830	52 433 220	4 266 210	5 540 520	11 454 180	10 398 720	8 496 120	6 547 260	5 730 210
Labor force	43 117 500	338 220	42 779 280	2 204 430	4 537 140	10 552 680	9 836 490	7 813 320	5 462 010	2 373 210
Percent of male	79.0	15.5	81.6	51.7	81.9	92.1	94.6	92.0	83.4	41.4
Female	57 083 190	2 091 780	54 991 410	4 277 550	5 869 860	12 158 040	10 847 490	8 687 820	6 636 150	6 514 500
Labor force	16 553 040	109 680	16 443 360	1 331 370	2 520 840	3 867 300	3 798 720	2 858 730	1 557 300	509 100
Percent of female	29.0	5.2	29.9	31.1	42.9	31.8	35.0	32.9	23.5	7.8
1940										
Total	101 015 740	4 847 840	96 167 900	9 929 120	11 587 660	21 311 660	18 350 580	15 464 900	10 548 800	8 975 180
Labor force	52 966 280	254 660	52 711 620	3 705 820	7 690 820	13 592 780	11 193 200	9 009 640	5 402 760	2 116 600
Percent of total	52.4	5.3	54.8	37.3	66.4	63.8	61.0	58.3	51.2	23.6
Male	50 543 840	2 442 320	48 101 520	4 953 480	5 667 300	10 515 500	9 201 680	7 958 040	5 407 780	4 397 740
Labor force	39 958 800	198 520	39 760 280	2 366 220	4 992 600	9 999 740	8 705 540	7 320 420	4 538 160	1 837 600
Percent of male	79.1	8.1	82.7	47.8	88.1	95.1	94.6	92.0	83.9	41.8
Female	50 471 900	2 405 520	48 066 380	4 975 640	5 920 360	10 796 160	9 148 900	7 506 860	5 141 020	4 577 440
Labor force	13 007 480	56 140	12 951 340	1 339 600	2 698 220	3 593 040	2 487 660	1 689 220	864 600	279 000
Percent of female	25.8	2.3	26.9	26.9	45.6	33.3	27.2	22.5	16.8	6.1
White										
1980										
Total	(NA)	(NA)	145 425 287	13 770 657	17 364 246	30 795 002	21 642 271	19 598 737	19 312 804	22 941 570
Labor force	(NA)	(NA)	90 434 967	7 204 975	13 360 657	24 404 170	17 197 024	14 598 440	10 789 311	2 880 390
Percent of total	(NA)	(NA)	62.2	52.3	76.9	79.2	79.5	74.5	55.9	12.6
Male	(NA)	(NA)	69 672 383	7 004 345	8 726 875	15 400 161	10 711 364	9 541 836	9 077 081	9 210 721
Labor force	(NA)	(NA)	53 022 518	3 887 607	7 358 985	14 526 921	10 199 286	8 712 547	6 549 492	1 787 680
Percent of male	(NA)	(NA)	76.1	55.5	84.3	94.3	95.2	91.3	72.2	19.4
Female	(NA)	(NA)	75 752 904	6 766 312	8 637 371	15 394 841	10 930 907	10 056 901	10 235 723	13 730 849
Labor force	(NA)	(NA)	37 412 449	3 317 368	6 001 672	9 877 249	6 997 738	5 885 893	4 239 819	1 092 710
Percent of female	(NA)	(NA)	49.4	49.0	69.5	64.2	64.0	58.5	41.4	8.0
1970										
Total	132 459 533	7 092 406	125 367 127	13 004 565	14 116 927	21 796 048	20 398 583	20 814 320	16 876 408	18 360 276
Labor force	73 720 097	765 579	72 954 518	5 561 426	9 661 298	14 936 592	14 666 667	14 967 384	10 206 432	2 954 719
Percent of total	55.7	10.8	58.2	42.8	68.4	68.5	71.9	71.9	60.5	16.1
Male	63 578 712	3 632 131	59 946 581	6 582 928	6 836 431	10 771 291	10 027 156	10 077 615	7 987 036	7 664 124
Labor force	46 909 412	520 608	46 388 804	3 222 309	5 577 473	10 201 833	9 589 644	9 398 759	6 489 687	1 909 099
Percent of male	73.8	14.3	77.4	48.9	81.6	94.7	95.6	93.3	81.3	24.9
Female	68 880 821	3 460 275	65 420 546	6 421 637	7 280 496	11 024 757	10 371 427	10 736 705	8 889 372	10 696 152
Labor force	26 810 685	244 971	26 565 714	2 339 117	4 083 825	4 734 759	5 077 023	5 568 625	3 716 745	1 045 620
Percent of female	38.9	7.1	40.6	36.4	56.1	42.9	49.0	51.9	41.8	9.8
1960										
Total	113 122 871	4 842 732	108 280 139	9 219 115	9 479 847	20 161 526	21 563 524	18 616 098	14 281 082	14 958 947
Labor force	62 478 137	580 071	61 898 066	3 918 732	6 198 569	12 936 804	14 686 474	12 942 428	8 323 533	2 891 526
Percent of total	55.2	12.0	57.2	42.5	65.4	64.2	68.1	69.5	58.3	19.3
Male	55 036 172	2 482 415	52 553 757	4 637 487	4 657 470	9 941 904	10 556 349	9 165 457	6 874 668	6 720 422
Labor force	42 939 887	410 913	42 528 974	2 368 376	4 040 870	9 514 079	10 162 841	8 614 270	5 770 622	2 057 916
Percent of male	78.0	16.6	80.9	51.1	86.8	95.7	96.3	94.0	83.9	30.6
Female	58 086 699	2 360 317	55 726 382	4 581 628	4 822 377	10 219 622	11 007 175	9 450 641	7 406 414	8 238 525
Labor force	19 538 250	169 158	19 369 092	1 550 356	2 157 699	3 422 725	4 523 633	4 328 158	2 552 911	833 610
Percent of female	33.6	7.2	34.8	33.8	44.7	33.5	41.1	45.8	34.5	10.1

Table 87. Labor Force Status by Age, Race, and Sex: 1940 to 1980—Con.

[For years prior to 1960, excludes data for Alaska and Hawaii. Data are estimates based on a sample; see Introduction. For meaning of symbols, see Introduction. For definitions of terms, see appendixes A and B]

United States Regions	Persons 14 years and over	14 and 15 years	Persons 16 years and over Total	16 to 19	20 to 24	25 to 34	35 to 44	45 to 54	55 to 64	65 and over
UNITED STATES—Con.										
White—Con.										
1950										
Total	100 701 990	3 741 270	96 960 720	7 521 240	10 113 570	21 152 460	19 048 230	15 546 330	12 235 800	11 343 090
Labor force	53 502 180	375 630	53 126 550	3 132 750	6 300 450	12 850 470	12 126 030	9 593 460	6 483 030	2 640 360
Percent of total	53.1	10.0	54.8	41.7	62.3	60.8	63.7	61.7	53.0	23.3
Male	49 312 050	1 915 530	47 396 520	3 770 220	4 941 120	10 308 720	9 345 870	7 681 320	6 058 020	5 291 250
Labor force	39 059 100	284 820	38 774 280	1 927 620	4 054 980	9 565 560	8 882 250	7 092 960	5 069 700	2 181 210
Percent of male	79.2	14.9	81.8	51.1	82.1	92.8	95.0	92.3	83.7	41.2
Female	51 389 940	1 825 740	49 564 200	3 751 020	5 172 450	10 843 740	9 702 360	7 865 010	6 177 780	6 051 840
Labor force	14 443 080	90 810	14 352 270	1 205 130	2 245 470	3 284 910	3 243 780	2 500 500	1 413 330	459 150
Percent of female	28.1	5.0	29.0	32.1	43.4	30.3	33.4	31.8	22.9	7.6
1940										
Total	91 433 500	4 298 260	87 135 240	8 841 360	10 350 020	19 107 100	16 487 260	14 182 660	9 825 660	8 341 180
Labor force	47 374 720	180 560	47 194 160	3 233 300	6 884 680	12 093 020	9 924 860	8 167 760	4 970 740	1 919 800
Percent of total	51.8	4.2	54.2	36.6	66.5	63.3	60.2	57.6	50.6	23.0
Male	45 856 580	2 171 360	43 685 220	4 429 900	5 092 860	9 471 680	8 295 760	7 298 580	5 020 960	4 075 480
Labor force	36 207 940	146 160	36 061 780	2 054 860	4 483 980	9 035 660	7 868 800	6 727 840	4 210 880	1 679 760
Percent of male	79.0	6.7	82.5	46.4	88.0	95.4	94.9	92.2	83.9	41.2
Female	45 576 920	2 126 900	43 450 020	4 411 460	5 257 160	9 635 420	8 191 500	6 884 080	4 804 700	4 265 700
Labor force	11 166 780	34 400	11 132 380	1 178 440	2 400 700	3 057 360	2 056 060	1 439 920	759 860	240 040
Percent of female	24.5	1.6	25.6	26.7	45.7	31.7	25.1	20.9	15.8	5.6
Black[1]										
1980										
Total	(NA)	(NA)	18 294 925	2 391 456	2 708 151	4 238 855	2 709 414	2 265 603	1 914 575	2 066 871
Labor force	(NA)	(NA)	10 866 343	798 961	1 817 545	3 270 374	2 111 907	1 593 445	999 073	275 038
Percent of total	(NA)	(NA)	59.4	33.4	67.1	77.2	77.9	70.3	52.2	13.3
Male	(NA)	(NA)	8 374 051	1 194 703	1 284 079	1 971 491	1 228 958	1 010 018	854 001	830 801
Labor force	(NA)	(NA)	5 582 862	435 802	943 549	1 646 198	1 060 544	818 129	531 676	146 964
Percent of male	(NA)	(NA)	66.7	36.5	73.5	83.5	86.3	81.0	62.3	17.7
Female	(NA)	(NA)	9 920 874	1 196 753	1 424 072	2 267 364	1 480 456	1 255 585	1 060 574	1 236 070
Labor force	(NA)	(NA)	5 283 481	363 159	873 996	1 624 176	1 051 363	775 316	467 397	128 074
Percent of female	(NA)	(NA)	53.3	30.3	61.4	71.6	71.0	61.7	44.1	10.4
1970										
Total	15 129 883	1 114 600	14 015 283	1 885 166	1 755 024	2 658 155	2 402 679	2 104 181	1 624 081	1 585 997
Labor force	8 167 657	75 266	8 092 391	576 138	1 150 354	1 913 578	1 753 614	1 482 946	935 169	280 592
Percent of total	54.0	6.8	57.7	30.6	65.5	72.0	73.0	70.5	57.6	17.7
Male	7 010 499	561 030	6 449 469	931 353	804 413	1 210 148	1 090 772	974 645	746 414	691 724
Labor force	4 550 486	48 926	4 501 560	333 886	614 858	1 060 464	960 587	828 211	540 739	162 815
Percent of male	64.9	8.7	69.8	35.8	76.4	87.6	88.1	85.0	72.4	23.5
Female	8 119 384	553 570	7 565 814	953 813	950 611	1 448 007	1 311 907	1 129 536	877 667	894 273
Labor force	3 617 171	26 340	3 590 831	242 252	535 496	853 114	793 027	654 735	394 430	117 777
Percent of female	44.5	4.8	47.5	25.4	56.3	58.9	60.4	58.0	44.9	13.2
1960										
Total	13 153 645	707 358	12 446 287	1 266 063	1 323 318	2 660 569	2 512 008	2 009 277	1 426 762	1 248 290
Labor force	7 399 339	63 300	7 336 039	417 942	830 484	1 784 097	1 803 947	1 419 438	822 105	258 026
Percent of total	56.3	8.9	58.9	33.0	62.8	67.1	71.8	70.6	57.6	20.7
Male	6 279 181	355 496	5 923 685	626 163	625 758	1 231 665	1 182 842	974 209	694 485	588 563
Labor force	4 527 833	44 290	4 483 543	265 198	513 140	1 089 993	1 061 994	853 287	527 113	172 818
Percent of male	72.1	12.5	75.7	42.4	82.0	88.5	89.8	87.6	75.9	29.4
Female	6 874 464	351 862	6 522 602	639 900	697 560	1 428 904	1 329 166	1 035 068	732 277	659 727
Labor force	2 871 506	19 010	2 852 496	152 744	317 344	694 104	741 953	566 151	294 992	85 208
Percent of female	41.8	5.4	43.7	23.9	45.5	48.6	55.8	54.7	40.3	12.9
1950										
Total	10 991 250	527 340	10 463 910	1 022 520	1 296 810	2 459 760	2 197 980	1 637 610	947 610	901 620
Labor force	6 168 360	72 270	6 096 090	403 050	757 530	1 569 510	1 509 180	1 078 590	536 280	241 950
Percent of total	56.1	13.7	58.3	39.4	58.4	63.8	68.7	65.9	56.6	26.8
Male	5 298 000	261 300	5 036 700	495 990	599 400	1 145 460	1 052 850	814 800	489 240	438 960
Labor force	4 058 400	53 400	4 005 000	276 810	482 160	987 120	954 240	720 360	392 310	192 000
Percent of male	76.6	20.4	79.5	55.8	80.4	86.2	90.6	88.4	80.2	43.7
Female	5 693 250	266 040	5 427 210	526 530	697 410	1 314 300	1 145 130	822 810	458 370	462 660
Labor force	2 109 960	18 870	2 091 090	126 240	275 370	582 390	554 940	358 230	143 970	49 950
Percent of female	37.1	7.1	38.5	24.0	39.5	44.3	48.5	43.5	31.4	10.8
1940										
Total	9 582 240	549 580	9 032 660	1 087 760	1 237 640	2 204 560	1 863 320	1 282 240	723 140	634 000
Labor force	5 591 560	74 100	5 517 460	472 520	806 140	1 499 760	1 268 340	841 880	432 020	196 800
Percent of total	58.4	13.5	61.1	43.4	65.1	68.0	68.1	65.7	59.7	31.0
Male	4 687 260	270 960	4 416 300	523 580	574 440	1 043 820	905 920	659 460	386 820	322 260
Labor force	3 750 860	52 360	3 698 500	311 360	508 620	964 080	836 740	592 580	327 280	157 840
Percent of male	80.0	19.3	83.7	59.5	88.5	92.4	92.4	89.9	84.6	49.0
Female	4 894 980	278 620	4 616 360	564 180	663 200	1 160 740	957 400	622 780	336 320	311 740
Labor force	1 840 700	21 740	1 818 960	161 160	297 520	535 680	431 600	249 300	104 740	38 960
Percent of female	37.6	7.8	39.4	28.6	44.9	46.1	45.1	40.0	31.1	12.5

[1]For years prior to 1970, includes Black and other races.

Table 87. Labor Force Status by Age, Race, and Sex: 1940 to 1980—Con.

[For years prior to 1960, excludes data for Alaska and Hawaii. Data are estimates based on a sample; see Introduction. For meaning of symbols, see Introduction. For definitions of terms, see appendixes A and B]

United States Regions	Persons 14 years and over	14 and 15 years	Persons 16 years and over							
			Total	16 to 19	20 to 24	25 to 34	35 to 44	45 to 54	55 to 64	65 and over
NORTHEAST										
Total										
1980										
Total	(NA)	(NA)	37 868 817	3 630 627	4 335 180	7 721 583	5 583 289	5 281 819	5 254 088	6 062 231
Labor force	(NA)	(NA)	23 036 729	1 654 449	3 200 270	5 963 721	4 365 307	3 986 569	3 094 792	771 621
Percent of total	(NA)	(NA)	60.8	45.6	73.8	77.2	78.2	75.5	58.9	12.7
Male	(NA)	(NA)	17 712 800	1 825 999	2 120 679	3 760 644	2 689 855	2 515 970	2 435 931	2 363 722
Labor force	(NA)	(NA)	13 147 006	857 995	1 684 264	3 474 286	2 532 949	2 301 008	1 827 020	469 484
Percent of male	(NA)	(NA)	74.2	47.0	79.4	92.4	94.2	91.5	75.0	19.9
Female	(NA)	(NA)	20 156 017	1 804 628	2 214 501	3 960 939	2 893 434	2 765 849	2 818 157	3 698 509
Labor force	(NA)	(NA)	9 889 723	796 454	1 516 006	2 489 435	1 832 358	1 685 561	1 267 772	302 137
Percent of female	(NA)	(NA)	49.1	44.1	68.5	62.8	63.3	60.9	45.0	8.2
1970										
Total	36 622 743	1 892 239	34 730 504	3 416 739	3 628 376	5 829 379	5 737 104	6 025 094	4 883 717	5 210 095
Labor force	20 414 352	176 271	20 238 081	1 396 811	2 430 176	3 902 167	4 091 279	4 420 313	3 099 904	897 431
Percent of total	55.7	9.3	58.3	40.9	67.0	66.9	71.3	73.4	63.5	17.2
Male	17 226 642	966 203	16 260 439	1 704 614	1 687 770	2 814 414	2 773 958	2 867 906	2 284 795	2 126 982
Labor force	12 626 635	117 577	12 509 058	747 189	1 307 995	2 641 069	2 641 303	2 691 538	1 914 473	565 493
Percent of male	73.3	12.2	76.9	43.8	77.5	93.8	95.2	93.9	83.8	26.6
Female	19 396 101	926 036	18 470 065	1 712 125	1 940 606	3 014 965	2 963 146	3 157 188	2 598 922	3 083 113
Labor force	7 787 717	58 694	7 729 023	649 624	1 122 181	1 261 098	1 449 976	1 728 775	1 185 431	331 938
Percent of female	40.2	6.3	41.8	37.9	57.8	41.8	48.9	54.8	45.6	10.8
1960										
Total	32 561 165	1 271 536	31 289 629	2 409 555	2 467 447	5 691 686	6 339 857	5 574 736	4 399 350	4 406 998
Labor force	18 260 059	115 593	18 144 466	1 010 319	1 648 642	3 660 664	4 339 452	3 950 720	2 645 355	889 314
Percent of total	56.1	9.1	58.0	41.9	66.8	64.3	68.4	70.9	60.1	20.2
Male	15 547 371	650 288	14 897 083	1 182 619	1 171 990	2 760 722	3 050 515	2 697 646	2 095 786	1 937 805
Labor force	12 122 080	81 991	12 040 089	544 942	989 224	2 624 808	2 930 687	2 543 956	1 790 824	615 648
Percent of male	78.0	12.6	80.8	46.1	84.4	95.1	96.1	94.3	85.4	31.8
Female	17 013 794	621 248	16 392 546	1 226 936	1 295 457	2 930 964	3 289 342	2 877 090	2 303 564	2 469 193
Labor force	6 137 979	33 602	6 104 377	465 377	659 418	1 035 856	1 408 765	1 406 764	854 531	273 666
Percent of female	36.1	5.4	37.2	37.9	50.9	35.3	42.8	48.9	37.1	11.1
1950										
Total	30 405 105	985 600	29 419 505	2 053 745	2 926 005	6 332 300	5 831 565	4 946 730	3 875 900	3 453 260
Labor force	16 383 740	48 015	16 335 725	822 355	1 905 585	3 904 195	3 735 320	3 085 440	2 074 415	808 415
Percent of total	53.9	4.9	55.5	40.0	65.1	61.7	64.1	62.4	53.5	23.4
Male	14 600 740	501 425	14 099 315	1 007 135	1 396 345	3 020 915	2 810 250	2 409 110	1 896 045	1 559 515
Labor force	11 442 150	35 975	11 406 175	425 240	1 090 590	2 771 550	2 653 780	2 220 205	1 596 685	648 125
Percent of male	78.4	7.2	80.9	42.2	78.1	91.7	94.4	92.2	84.2	41.6
Female	15 804 365	484 175	15 320 190	1 046 610	1 529 660	3 311 385	3 021 315	2 537 620	1 979 855	1 893 745
Labor force	4 941 590	12 040	4 929 550	397 115	814 995	1 132 645	1 081 540	865 235	477 730	160 290
Percent of female	31.3	2.5	32.2	37.9	53.3	34.2	35.8	34.1	24.1	8.5
1940										
Total	28 645 620	1 247 820	27 397 800	2 607 360	3 164 620	5 926 040	5 356 060	4 631 600	3 126 820	2 585 300
Labor force	15 488 320	16 980	15 471 340	1 031 340	2 317 500	3 946 340	3 318 860	2 709 560	1 571 640	576 100
Percent of total	54.1	1.4	56.5	39.6	73.2	66.6	62.0	58.5	50.3	22.3
Male	14 143 840	628 580	13 515 260	1 302 020	1 529 340	2 885 420	2 669 820	2 363 540	1 565 300	1 199 820
Labor force	11 163 160	11 420	11 151 740	572 760	1 348 160	2 746 160	2 526 200	2 175 520	1 296 620	486 320
Percent of male	78.9	1.8	82.5	44.0	88.2	95.2	94.6	92.0	82.8	40.5
Female	14 501 780	619 240	13 882 540	1 305 340	1 635 280	3 040 620	2 686 240	2 268 060	1 561 520	1 385 480
Labor force	4 325 160	5 560	4 319 600	458 580	969 340	1 200 180	792 660	534 040	275 020	89 780
Percent of female	29.8	0.9	31.1	35.1	59.3	39.5	29.5	23.5	17.6	6.5
White										
1980										
Total	(NA)	(NA)	33 218 009	3 056 979	3 707 370	6 596 523	4 753 141	4 667 396	4 784 184	5 652 416
Labor force	(NA)	(NA)	20 325 442	1 490 505	2 827 345	5 168 213	3 742 041	3 549 384	2 833 866	714 088
Percent of total	(NA)	(NA)	61.2	48.8	76.3	78.3	78.7	76.0	59.2	12.6
Male	(NA)	(NA)	15 626 311	1 542 008	1 833 819	3 252 682	2 316 619	2 243 231	2 231 524	2 206 428
Labor force	(NA)	(NA)	11 744 350	770 780	1 492 799	3 061 724	2 211 164	2 076 307	1 691 457	440 119
Percent of male	(NA)	(NA)	75.2	50.0	81.4	94.1	95.4	92.6	75.8	19.9
Female	(NA)	(NA)	17 591 698	1 514 971	1 873 551	3 343 841	2 436 522	2 424 165	2 552 660	3 445 988
Labor force	(NA)	(NA)	8 581 092	719 725	1 334 546	2 106 489	1 530 877	1 473 077	1 142 409	273 969
Percent of female	(NA)	(NA)	48.8	47.5	71.2	63.0	62.8	60.8	44.8	8.0
1970										
Total	(NA)	(NA)	(NA)	(NA)	(NA)	(NA)	(NA)	(NA)	(NA)	(NA)
Labor force	(NA)	(NA)	(NA)	(NA)	(NA)	(NA)	(NA)	(NA)	(NA)	(NA)
Percent of total	(NA)	(NA)	(NA)	(NA)	(NA)	(NA)	(NA)	(NA)	(NA)	(NA)
Male	(NA)	(NA)	(NA)	(NA)	(NA)	(NA)	(NA)	(NA)	(NA)	(NA)
Labor force	(NA)	(NA)	(NA)	(NA)	(NA)	(NA)	(NA)	(NA)	(NA)	(NA)
Percent of male	(NA)	(NA)	(NA)	(NA)	(NA)	(NA)	(NA)	(NA)	(NA)	(NA)
Female	(NA)	(NA)	(NA)	(NA)	(NA)	(NA)	(NA)	(NA)	(NA)	(NA)
Labor force	(NA)	(NA)	(NA)	(NA)	(NA)	(NA)	(NA)	(NA)	(NA)	(NA)
Percent of female	(NA)	(NA)	(NA)	(NA)	(NA)	(NA)	(NA)	(NA)	(NA)	(NA)
1960										
Total	30 398 397	1 184 415	29 213 982	2 244 628	2 244 730	5 194 929	5 877 997	5 242 963	4 165 005	4 243 730
Labor force	16 948 478	110 272	16 838 206	948 660	1 499 932	3 324 293	4 003 009	3 710 454	2 503 272	848 586
Percent of total	55.8	9.3	57.6	42.3	66.8	64.0	68.1	70.8	60.1	20.0
Male	14 541 635	606 708	13 934 927	1 104 958	1 073 366	2 533 720	2 835 316	2 542 290	1 983 116	1 862 161
Labor force	11 359 779	78 430	11 281 349	511 647	906 686	2 424 970	2 736 970	2 407 533	1 703 134	590 628
Percent of male	78.1	12.9	81.0	46.3	84.5	95.7	96.5	94.7	85.9	31.7
Female	15 856 762	577 707	15 279 055	1 139 670	1 171 364	2 661 209	3 042 681	2 700 673	2 181 889	2 381 569
Labor force	5 588 699	31 842	5 556 857	437 013	593 047	899 741	1 266 039	1 302 921	800 138	257 958
Percent of female	35.2	5.5	36.4	38.3	50.6	33.8	41.6	48.2	36.7	10.8

Table 87. Labor Force Status by Age, Race, and Sex: 1940 to 1980—Con.

[For years prior to 1960, excludes data for Alaska and Hawaii. Data are estimates based on a sample; see Introduction. For meaning of symbols, see Introduction. For definitions of terms, see appendixes A and B]

United States Regions	Persons 14 years and over	14 and 15 years	Persons 16 years and over							
			Total	16 to 19	20 to 24	25 to 34	35 to 44	45 to 54	55 to 64	65 and over
NORTHEAST—Con.										
White—Con.										
1950										
Total	28 831 635	930 140	27 901 470	1 940 215	2 741 260	5 929 930	5 491 335	4 694 235	3 745 115	3 359 380
Labor force	15 472 430	46 325	15 426 105	785 110	1 794 825	3 642 335	3 501 230	2 917 205	2 000 650	784 750
Percent of total	53.7	5.0	55.3	40.5	65.5	61.4	63.8	62.1	53.4	23.4
Male	13 859 290	474 170	13 385 095	953 345	1 314 705	2 838 105	2 651 775	2 281 255	1 829 020	1 516 890
Labor force	10 890 860	34 830	10 856 030	404 455	1 030 070	2 618 690	2 515 840	2 111 000	1 544 900	631 075
Percent of male	78.6	7.3	81.1	42.4	78.3	92.3	94.9	92.5	84.5	41.6
Female	14 972 345	455 970	14 516 375	986 870	1 426 555	3 091 825	2 839 560	2 412 980	1 916 095	1 842 490
Labor force	4 581 570	11 495	4 570 075	380 655	764 755	1 023 645	985 390	806 205	455 750	153 675
Percent of female	30.6	2.5	31.5	38.6	53.6	33.1	34.7	33.4	23.8	8.3
1940										
Total	27 572 480	1 199 480	26 373 000	2 514 160	3 045 720	5 662 680	5 100 300	4 472 700	3 044 420	2 533 020
Labor force	14 840 100	16 480	14 823 620	996 520	2 234 020	3 761 000	3 139 500	2 603 880	1 524 900	563 800
Percent of total	53.8	1.4	56.2	39.6	73.3	66.4	61.6	58.2	50.1	22.3
Male	13 633 680	604 840	13 028 840	1 258 480	1 480 720	2 768 980	2 542 780	2 279 900	1 522 820	1 175 160
Labor force	10 765 700	11 120	10 754 580	554 260	1 306 320	2 640 940	2 410 740	2 102 560	1 263 080	476 680
Percent of male	79.0	1.8	82.5	44.0	88.2	95.4	94.8	92.2	82.9	40.6
Female	13 938 800	594 640	13 344 160	1 255 680	1 565 000	2 893 700	2 557 520	2 192 800	1 521 600	1 357 860
Labor force	4 074 400	5 360	4 069 040	442 260	927 700	1 120 060	728 760	501 320	261 820	87 120
Percent of female	29.2	0.9	30.5	35.2	59.3	38.7	28.5	22.9	17.2	6.4
Black[1]										
1980										
Total	(NA)	(NA)	3 422 855	426 488	450 992	770 240	587 841	466 333	382 681	338 280
Labor force	(NA)	(NA)	1 998 691	120 089	271 070	557 392	450 700	336 257	215 283	47 900
Percent of total	(NA)	(NA)	58.4	28.2	60.1	72.4	76.7	72.1	56.3	14.2
Male	(NA)	(NA)	1 513 987	210 715	203 993	343 624	257 197	204 158	165 764	128 535
Labor force	(NA)	(NA)	991 699	63 741	135 294	274 173	219 014	166 626	108 835	24 016
Percent of male	(NA)	(NA)	65.5	30.2	66.3	79.8	85.2	81.6	65.7	18.7
Female	(NA)	(NA)	1 908 868	215 773	246 999	426 616	330 643	262 175	216 917	209 745
Labor force	(NA)	(NA)	1 006 992	56 348	135 776	283 219	231 686	169 631	106 448	23 884
Percent of female	(NA)	(NA)	52.8	26.1	55.0	66.4	70.1	64.7	49.1	11.4
1970										
Total	2 954 754	187 089	2 767 665	316 691	336 841	605 767	527 754	430 481	292 318	257 813
Labor force	1 636 530	12 481	1 624 049	98 493	210 076	406 669	373 781	307 480	174 789	52 761
Percent of total	55.4	6.7	58.7	31.1	62.4	67.1	70.8	71.4	59.8	20.5
Male	1 328 235	94 482	1 233 753	153 227	144 362	264 980	237 316	195 914	128 536	109 418
Labor force	891 620	7 508	884 112	51 449	105 021	227 693	207 180	168 358	95 558	28 853
Percent of male	67.1	7.9	71.7	33.6	72.7	85.9	87.3	85.9	74.3	26.4
Female	1 626 519	92 607	1 533 912	163 464	192 479	340 787	290 438	234 567	163 782	148 395
Labor force	744 910	4 973	739 937	47 044	105 055	178 976	166 601	139 122	79 231	23 908
Percent of female	45.8	5.4	48.2	28.8	54.6	52.5	57.4	59.3	48.4	16.1
1960										
Total	2 162 768	87 121	2 075 647	164 927	222 717	496 757	461 860	331 773	234 345	163 268
Labor force	1 311 840	5 321	1 306 260	61 659	148 710	336 371	336 443	240 266	142 083	40 728
Percent of total	60.6	6.1	62.9	37.4	66.8	67.7	72.8	72.4	60.6	24.9
Male	1 005 736	43 580	962 156	77 661	98 624	227 002	215 199	155 356	112 670	75 644
Labor force	762 301	3 561	758 740	33 295	82 339	200 256	193 717	136 423	87 690	25 020
Percent of male	75.8	8.2	78.9	42.9	83.5	88.2	90.0	87.8	77.8	33.1
Female	1 157 032	43 541	1 113 491	87 266	124 093	269 755	246 661	176 417	121 675	87 624
Labor force	549 280	1 760	547 520	28 364	66 371	136 115	142 726	103 843	54 393	15 708
Percent of female	47.5	4.0	49.2	32.5	53.5	50.5	57.9	58.9	44.7	17.9
1950										
Total	1 573 470	55 435	1 518 035	113 530	184 745	402 370	340 230	252 495	130 785	93 880
Labor force	911 310	1 690	909 620	37 245	110 760	261 860	234 090	168 235	73 765	23 665
Percent of total	57.9	3.0	59.9	32.8	60.0	65.1	68.8	66.6	56.4	25.2
Male	741 450	27 230	714 220	53 790	81 640	182 810	158 475	127 855	67 025	42 625
Labor force	551 290	1 145	550 145	20 785	60 520	152 860	137 940	109 205	51 785	17 050
Percent of male	74.4	4.2	77.0	38.6	74.1	83.6	87.0	85.4	77.3	40.0
Female	832 020	28 205	803 815	59 740	103 105	219 560	181 755	124 640	63 760	51 255
Labor force	360 020	545	359 475	16 460	50 240	109 000	96 150	59 030	21 980	6 615
Percent of female	43.3	1.9	44.7	27.6	48.7	49.6	52.9	47.4	34.5	12.9
1940										
Total	1 073 140	48 340	1 024 800	93 200	118 900	263 360	255 760	158 900	82 400	52 280
Labor force	648 220	500	647 720	34 820	83 480	185 340	179 360	105 680	46 740	12 300
Percent of total	60.4	1.0	63.2	37.4	70.2	70.4	70.1	66.5	56.7	23.5
Male	510 160	23 740	486 420	43 540	48 620	116 440	127 040	83 640	42 480	24 660
Labor force	397 460	300	397 160	18 500	41 840	105 220	115 460	72 960	33 540	9 640
Percent of male	77.9	1.3	81.6	42.5	86.1	90.4	90.9	87.2	79.0	39.1
Female	562 980	24 600	538 380	49 660	70 280	146 920	128 720	75 260	39 920	27 620
Labor force	250 760	200	250 560	16 320	41 640	80 120	63 900	32 720	13 200	2 660
Percent of female	44.5	0.8	46.5	32.9	59.2	54.5	49.6	43.5	33.1	9.6

[1]For years prior to 1970, includes Black and other races.

Table 87. **Labor Force Status by Age, Race, and Sex: 1940 to 1980**—Con.

[For years prior to 1960, excludes data for Alaska and Hawaii. Data are estimates based on a sample; see Introduction. For meaning of symbols, see Introduction. For definitions of terms, see appendixes A and B]

United States Regions	Persons 14 years and over	14 and 15 years	Persons 16 years and over							
			Total	16 to 19	20 to 24	25 to 34	35 to 44	45 to 54	55 to 64	65 and over

NORTH CENTRAL

Total

1980

Total	(NA)	(NA)	44 178 493	4 527 860	5 565 701	9 441 926	6 472 602	5 873 718	5 610 835	6 685 851
Labor force	(NA)	(NA)	27 705 296	2 379 736	4 256 020	7 437 706	5 149 076	4 396 916	3 238 507	847 335
Percent of total	(NA)	(NA)	62.7	52.6	76.5	78.8	79.6	74.9	57.7	12.7
Male	(NA)	(NA)	21 093 150	2 287 496	2 761 075	4 686 698	3 173 982	2 854 555	2 648 717	2 680 627
Labor force	(NA)	(NA)	16 101 306	1 258 532	2 312 827	4 396 802	3 020 407	2 622 846	1 971 979	517 913
Percent of male	(NA)	(NA)	76.3	55.0	83.8	93.8	95.2	91.9	74.5	19.3
Female	(NA)	(NA)	23 085 343	2 240 364	2 804 626	4 755 228	3 298 620	3 019 163	2 962 118	4 005 224
Labor force	(NA)	(NA)	11 603 990	1 121 204	1 943 193	3 040 904	2 128 669	1 774 070	1 266 528	329 422
Percent of female	(NA)	(NA)	50.3	50.0	69.3	63.9	64.5	58.8	42.8	8.2

1970

Total	41 236 848	2 368 694	38 868 154	4 259 127	4 317 030	6 766 429	6 297 461	6 347 595	5 145 818	5 734 694
Labor force	23 102 920	289 507	22 813 413	1 922 090	2 953 610	4 641 724	4 539 046	4 599 774	3 191 302	965 867
Percent of total	56.0	12.2	58.7	45.1	68.4	68.6	72.1	72.5	62.0	16.8
Male	19 742 895	1 212 892	18 530 003	2 136 089	2 017 033	3 323 535	3 087 508	3 081 959	2 462 069	2 421 810
Labor force	14 587 355	192 517	14 394 838	1 076 234	1 642 409	3 154 958	2 959 679	2 898 367	2 043 590	619 601
Percent of male	73.9	15.9	77.7	50.4	81.4	94.9	95.9	94.0	83.0	25.6
Female	21 493 953	1 155 802	20 338 151	2 123 038	2 299 997	3 442 894	3 209 953	3 265 636	2 683 749	3 312 884
Labor force	8 515 565	96 990	8 418 575	845 856	1 311 201	1 486 766	1 579 367	1 701 407	1 147 712	346 266
Percent of female	39.6	8.4	41.4	39.8	57.0	43.2	49.2	52.1	42.8	10.5

1960

Total	36 157 249	1 530 528	34 626 721	2 921 846	3 007 395	6 455 798	6 765 751	5 874 172	4 643 571	4 958 188
Labor force	20 047 265	217 811	19 829 454	1 296 456	1 941 161	4 101 583	4 597 353	4 105 903	2 783 101	1 003 897
Percent of total	55.4	14.2	57.3	44.4	64.5	63.5	68.0	69.9	59.9	20.2
Male	17 588 420	783 488	16 804 932	1 440 958	1 426 094	3 177 694	3 321 910	2 907 757	2 267 783	2 262 736
Labor force	13 786 118	152 663	13 633 455	750 265	1 240 813	3 037 693	3 198 378	2 746 409	1 947 480	712 417
Percent of male	78.4	19.5	81.1	52.1	87.0	95.6	96.3	94.5	85.9	31.5
Female	18 568 829	747 040	17 821 789	1 480 888	1 581 301	3 278 104	3 443 841	2 966 415	2 375 788	2 695 452
Labor force	6 261 147	65 148	6 195 999	546 191	700 348	1 063 890	1 398 975	1 359 494	835 621	291 480
Percent of female	33.7	8.7	34.8	36.9	44.3	32.5	40.6	45.8	35.2	10.8

1950

Total	33 211 680	1 219 030	31 992 650	2 392 320	3 276 270	6 836 885	6 137 330	5 184 280	4 209 800	3 955 765
Labor force	17 800 060	149 065	17 650 995	1 045 655	2 057 300	4 156 970	3 909 700	3 222 285	2 284 365	974 720
Percent of total	53.6	12.2	55.2	43.7	62.8	60.8	63.7	62.2	54.3	24.6
Male	16 295 805	621 470	15 674 335	1 177 430	1 587 625	3 329 190	3 013 115	2 575 465	2 110 875	1 880 635
Labor force	13 025 755	110 725	12 915 030	616 365	1 321 440	3 103 595	2 866 365	2 394 995	1 801 380	810 890
Percent of male	79.9	17.8	82.4	52.3	83.2	93.2	95.1	93.0	85.3	43.1
Female	16 915 875	597 560	16 318 315	1 214 890	1 688 645	3 507 695	3 124 215	2 608 815	2 098 925	2 075 130
Labor force	4 774 305	38 340	4 735 965	429 290	735 860	1 053 375	1 043 335	827 290	482 985	163 830
Percent of female	28.2	6.4	29.0	35.3	43.6	30.0	33.4	31.7	23.0	7.9

1940

Total	31 277 340	1 424 460	29 852 880	2 906 380	3 423 120	6 326 860	5 652 040	5 012 660	3 464 660	3 067 160
Labor force	16 089 420	54 980	16 034 440	1 061 440	2 286 640	3 958 760	3 374 780	2 883 300	1 772 360	697 160
Percent of total	51.4	3.9	53.7	36.5	66.8	62.6	59.7	57.5	51.2	22.7
Male	15 762 580	719 620	15 042 960	1 453 960	1 683 000	3 131 960	2 845 800	2 602 580	1 795 640	1 530 020
Labor force	12 452 600	44 400	12 408 200	662 280	1 486 160	2 991 200	2 710 160	2 413 200	1 526 520	618 680
Percent of male	79.0	6.2	82.5	45.6	88.3	95.5	95.2	92.7	85.0	40.4
Female	15 514 760	704 840	14 809 920	1 452 420	1 740 120	3 194 900	2 806 240	2 410 080	1 669 020	1 537 140
Labor force	3 636 820	10 580	3 626 240	399 160	800 480	967 560	664 620	470 100	245 840	78 480
Percent of female	23.4	1.5	24.5	27.5	46.0	30.3	23.7	19.5	14.7	5.1

White

1980

Total	(NA)	(NA)	39 727 216	3 965 508	4 884 688	8 333 974	5 785 682	5 313 030	5 176 915	6 267 419
Labor force	(NA)	(NA)	25 032 367	2 176 655	3 810 556	6 618 507	4 620 195	4 003 521	3 006 381	794 552
Percent of total	(NA)	(NA)	63.0	54.9	78.0	79.4	79.9	75.4	58.1	12.7
Male	(NA)	(NA)	19 027 004	2 007 230	2 437 065	4 170 856	2 856 562	2 598 644	2 448 816	2 507 831
Labor force	(NA)	(NA)	14 686 734	1 151 745	2 078 294	3 967 836	2 743 542	2 412 876	1 843 701	488 740
Percent of male	(NA)	(NA)	77.2	57.4	85.3	95.1	96.0	92.9	75.3	19.5
Female	(NA)	(NA)	20 700 212	1 958 278	2 447 623	4 163 118	2 929 120	2 714 386	2 728 099	3 759 588
Labor force	(NA)	(NA)	10 345 633	1 024 910	1 732 262	2 650 671	1 876 653	1 590 645	1 164 680	305 812
Percent of female	(NA)	(NA)	50.0	52.3	70.8	63.7	64.1	58.6	42.7	8.1

1970

Total	(NA)	(NA)	(NA)	(NA)	(NA)	(NA)	(NA)	(NA)	(NA)	(NA)
Labor force	(NA)	(NA)	(NA)	(NA)	(NA)	(NA)	(NA)	(NA)	(NA)	(NA)
Percent of total	(NA)	(NA)	(NA)	(NA)	(NA)	(NA)	(NA)	(NA)	(NA)	(NA)
Male	(NA)	(NA)	(NA)	(NA)	(NA)	(NA)	(NA)	(NA)	(NA)	(NA)
Labor force	(NA)	(NA)	(NA)	(NA)	(NA)	(NA)	(NA)	(NA)	(NA)	(NA)
Percent of male	(NA)	(NA)	(NA)	(NA)	(NA)	(NA)	(NA)	(NA)	(NA)	(NA)
Female	(NA)	(NA)	(NA)	(NA)	(NA)	(NA)	(NA)	(NA)	(NA)	(NA)
Labor force	(NA)	(NA)	(NA)	(NA)	(NA)	(NA)	(NA)	(NA)	(NA)	(NA)
Percent of female	(NA)	(NA)	(NA)	(NA)	(NA)	(NA)	(NA)	(NA)	(NA)	(NA)

1960

Total	33 816 919	1 427 594	32 389 325	2 731 712	2 779 543	5 931 467	6 283 540	5 518 003	4 385 411	4 759 649
Labor force	18 737 755	211 066	18 526 689	1 238 027	1 802 812	3 762 763	4 259 311	3 860 989	2 638 255	964 532
Percent of total	55.4	14.8	57.2	45.3	64.9	63.4	67.8	70.0	60.2	20.3
Male	16 465 496	732 297	15 733 199	1 350 450	1 323 215	2 933 024	3 088 596	2 731 883	2 138 427	2 167 604
Labor force	12 962 472	147 842	12 814 630	716 269	1 157 850	2 823 017	2 989 503	2 592 682	1 849 219	686 090
Percent of male	78.7	20.2	81.4	53.0	87.5	96.2	96.8	94.9	86.5	31.7
Female	17 351 423	695 297	16 656 126	1 381 262	1 456 328	2 998 443	3 194 944	2 786 120	2 246 984	2 592 045
Labor force	5 775 283	63 224	5 712 059	521 758	644 962	939 746	1 269 808	1 268 307	789 036	278 442
Percent of female	33.3	9.1	34.3	37.8	44.3	31.3	39.7	45.5	35.1	10.7

Table 87. Labor Force Status by Age, Race, and Sex: 1940 to 1980—Con.

[For years prior to 1960, excludes data for Alaska and Hawaii. Data are estimates based on a sample; see Introduction. For meaning of symbols, see Introduction. For definitions of terms, see appendixes A and B]

United States Regions	Persons 14 years and over	14 and 15 years	Persons 16 years and over							
			Total	16 to 19	20 to 24	25 to 34	35 to 44	45 to 54	55 to 64	65 and over
NORTH CENTRAL—Con.										
White—Con.										
1950										
Total	31 474 800	1 155 285	30 319 515	2 267 515	3 074 995	6 413 270	5 774 675	4 904 245	4 050 965	3 833 850
Labor force	16 843 405	145 730	16 697 675	1 006 985	1 942 960	3 889 860	3 668 450	3 044 645	2 197 885	946 890
Percent of total	53.5	12.6	55.1	44.4	63.2	60.7	63.5	62.1	54.3	24.7
Male	15 444 230	590 700	14 853 530	1 118 620	1 493 845	3 127 330	2 835 750	2 430 510	2 025 970	1 821 505
Labor force	12 382 445	108 390	12 274 055	591 890	1 249 325	2 930 955	2 708 985	2 269 205	1 735 120	788 575
Percent of male	80.2	18.3	82.6	52.9	83.6	93.7	95.5	93.4	85.6	43.3
Female	16 030 570	564 585	15 465 985	1 148 895	1 581 150	3 285 940	2 938 925	2 473 735	2 024 995	2 012 345
Labor force	4 460 960	37 340	4 423 620	415 095	693 635	958 905	959 465	775 440	462 765	158 315
Percent of female	27.8	6.6	28.6	36.1	43.9	29.2	32.6	31.3	22.9	7.9
1940										
Total	30 131 720	1 373 400	28 758 320	2 807 100	3 304 800	6 067 460	5 388 640	4 827 120	3 370 000	2 993 200
Labor force	15 465 380	53 600	15 411 780	1 027 780	2 213 660	3 793 080	3 206 980	2 768 500	1 719 660	682 120
Percent of total	51.3	3.9	53.6	36.6	67.0	62.5	59.5	57.4	51.0	22.8
Male	15 197 120	694 980	14 502 140	1 406 220	1 628 120	3 012 620	2 715 840	2 502 860	1 743 440	1 493 040
Labor force	12 020 200	43 500	11 976 700	641 360	1 439 960	2 884 280	2 593 560	2 326 620	1 484 560	606 360
Percent of male	79.1	6.3	82.6	45.6	88.4	95.7	95.5	93.0	85.2	40.6
Female	14 934 600	678 420	14 256 180	1 400 880	1 676 680	3 054 840	2 672 800	2 324 260	1 626 560	1 500 160
Labor force	3 445 180	10 100	3 435 080	386 420	773 700	908 800	613 420	441 880	235 100	75 760
Percent of female	23.1	1.5	24.1	27.6	46.1	29.7	23.0	19.0	14.5	5.1
Black[1]										
1980										
Total	(NA)	(NA)	3 631 904	464 026	543 997	853 322	539 268	473 474	383 527	374 290
Labor force	(NA)	(NA)	2 142 992	159 914	353 397	634 755	414 565	330 910	202 619	46 832
Percent of total	(NA)	(NA)	59.0	34.5	65.0	74.4	76.9	69.9	52.8	12.5
Male	(NA)	(NA)	1 658 801	229 611	252 429	389 794	242 781	213 573	176 201	154 412
Labor force	(NA)	(NA)	1 100 098	82 576	179 907	319 300	208 568	172 840	111 477	25 430
Percent of male	(NA)	(NA)	66.3	36.0	71.3	85.9	81.9	80.9	63.3	16.5
Female	(NA)	(NA)	1 973 103	234 415	291 568	463 528	296 487	259 901	207 326	219 878
Labor force	(NA)	(NA)	1 042 894	77 338	173 490	315 455	205 997	158 070	91 142	21 402
Percent of female	(NA)	(NA)	52.9	33.0	59.5	68.1	69.5	60.8	44.0	9.7
1970										
Total	3 056 447	224 384	2 832 063	369 920	356 074	555 106	517 965	433 575	309 770	289 653
Labor force	1 685 025	17 253	1 667 772	125 156	235 279	399 258	376 555	306 054	177 459	48 011
Percent of total	55.1	7.7	58.9	33.8	66.1	71.9	72.7	70.6	57.3	16.6
Male	1 425 060	113 021	1 312 039	180 753	159 013	251 825	237 311	205 636	146 832	130 669
Labor force	949 319	10 977	938 342	67 979	121 730	221 976	211 358	177 872	108 654	28 773
Percent of male	66.6	9.7	71.5	37.6	76.6	88.1	89.1	86.5	74.0	22.0
Female	1 631 387	111 363	1 520 024	189 167	197 061	303 281	280 654	227 939	162 938	158 984
Labor force	735 706	6 276	729 430	57 177	113 549	177 282	165 197	128 182	68 805	19 238
Percent of female	45.1	5.6	48.0	30.2	57.6	58.5	58.9	56.2	42.2	12.1
1960										
Total	2 340 330	102 934	2 237 396	190 134	227 852	524 331	482 211	356 169	258 160	198 539
Labor force	1 309 510	6 745	1 302 765	58 429	138 349	338 820	338 042	244 914	144 846	39 365
Percent of total	56.0	6.6	58.2	30.7	60.7	64.6	70.1	68.8	56.1	19.8
Male	1 122 924	51 191	1 071 733	90 508	102 879	244 670	233 314	175 874	129 356	95 132
Labor force	823 646	4 821	818 825	33 996	82 963	214 676	208 875	153 727	98 261	26 327
Percent of male	73.3	9.4	76.4	37.6	80.6	87.7	89.5	87.4	76.0	27.7
Female	1 217 406	51 743	1 165 663	99 626	124 973	279 661	248 897	180 295	128 804	103 407
Labor force	485 864	1 924	483 940	24 433	55 386	124 144	129 167	91 187	46 585	13 038
Percent of female	39.9	3.7	41.5	24.5	44.3	44.4	51.9	50.6	36.2	12.6
1950										
Total	1 736 880	63 745	1 673 135	124 805	201 275	423 615	362 655	280 035	158 835	121 915
Labor force	956 655	3 335	953 320	38 670	114 340	267 110	241 250	177 640	86 480	27 830
Percent of total	55.1	5.2	57.0	31.0	56.8	63.1	66.5	63.4	54.4	22.8
Male	851 575	30 770	820 805	58 810	93 780	201 860	177 365	144 955	84 905	59 130
Labor force	643 310	2 335	640 975	24 475	72 115	172 640	157 380	125 790	66 260	22 315
Percent of male	75.5	7.6	78.1	41.6	76.9	85.5	88.7	86.8	78.0	37.7
Female	885 305	32 975	852 330	65 995	107 495	221 755	185 290	135 080	73 930	62 785
Labor force	313 345	1 000	312 345	14 195	42 225	94 470	83 870	51 850	20 220	5 515
Percent of female	35.4	3.0	36.6	21.5	39.3	42.6	45.3	38.4	27.4	8.8
1940										
Total	1 145 620	51 060	1 094 560	99 280	118 320	259 400	263 400	185 540	94 660	73 960
Labor force	624 040	1 380	622 660	33 660	72 980	165 680	167 800	114 800	52 700	15 040
Percent of total	54.5	2.7	56.9	33.9	61.7	63.9	63.7	61.9	55.7	20.3
Male	565 460	24 640	540 820	47 740	54 880	119 340	129 960	99 720	52 200	36 980
Labor force	432 400	900	431 500	20 920	46 200	106 920	116 600	86 580	41 960	12 320
Percent of male	76.5	3.7	79.8	43.8	84.2	89.6	89.7	86.8	80.4	33.3
Female	580 160	26 420	553 740	51 540	63 440	140 060	133 440	85 820	42 460	36 980
Labor force	191 640	480	191 160	12 740	26 780	58 760	51 200	28 220	10 740	2 720
Percent of female	33.0	1.8	34.5	24.7	42.2	42.0	38.4	32.9	25.3	7.4

[1]For years prior to 1970, includes Black and other races.

Table 87. Labor Force Status by Age, Race, and Sex: 1940 to 1980—Con.

[For years prior to 1960, excludes data for Alaska and Hawaii. Data are estimates based on a sample; see Introduction. For meaning of symbols, see Introduction. For definitions of terms, see appendixes A and B]

United States Regions	Persons 14 years and over	14 and 15 years	Persons 16 years and over							
			Total	16 to 19	20 to 24	25 to 34	35 to 44	45 to 54	55 to 64	65 and over
SOUTH										
Total										
1980										
Total	(NA)	(NA)	56 552 817	5 747 780	7 114 237	12 254 109	8 522 860	7 426 441	7 017 900	8 469 470
Labor force	(NA)	(NA)	34 433 990	2 685 752	5 303 179	9 708 612	6 715 431	5 331 469	3 623 634	1 065 913
Percent of total	(NA)	(NA)	60.9	46.7	74.5	79.2	78.8	71.8	51.6	12.6
Male	(NA)	(NA)	26 959 721	2 934 324	3 567 397	6 059 346	4 169 535	3 551 806	3 244 036	3 433 277
Labor force	(NA)	(NA)	19 916 740	1 520 734	2 957 624	5 608 582	3 892 214	3 120 533	2 161 212	655 841
Percent of male	(NA)	(NA)	73.9	51.8	82.9	92.6	93.3	87.9	66.6	19.1
Female	(NA)	(NA)	29 593 096	2 813 456	3 546 840	6 194 763	4 353 345	3 874 635	3 773 864	5 036 193
Labor force	(NA)	(NA)	14 517 250	1 165 018	2 345 555	4 100 030	2 823 217	2 210 936	1 462 422	410 072
Percent of female	(NA)	(NA)	49.1	41.4	66.1	66.2	64.9	57.1	38.8	8.1
1970										
Total	45 959 312	2 638 787	43 320 525	4 804 097	5 185 134	7 709 399	7 067 818	6 841 739	5 658 776	6 053 562
Labor force	24 931 452	220 274	24 711 178	1 776 760	3 529 944	5 422 468	5 102 610	4 767 770	3 172 413	939 213
Percent of total	54.2	8.3	57.0	37.0	68.1	70.3	72.2	69.7	56.1	15.5
Male	22 012 438	1 346 114	20 666 324	2 445 940	2 559 884	3 766 699	3 408 687	3 286 649	2 636 474	2 561 991
Labor force	15 637 243	154 093	15 483 150	1 104 734	2 104 492	3 525 047	3 192 979	2 952 411	1 995 054	608 433
Percent of male	71.0	11.4	74.9	45.2	82.2	93.6	93.7	89.8	75.7	23.7
Female	23 946 874	1 292 673	22 654 201	2 358 157	2 625 250	3 942 700	3 659 131	3 555 090	3 022 302	3 491 571
Labor force	9 294 209	66 181	9 228 028	672 026	1 425 452	1 897 421	1 909 631	1 815 359	1 177 359	330 780
Percent of female	38.8	5.1	40.7	28.5	54.3	48.1	52.2	51.1	39.0	9.5
1960										
Total	37 948 263	1 883 832	36 064 431	3 537 269	3 551 642	6 967 789	7 065 981	6 042 141	4 416 426	4 483 183
Labor force	20 398 374	183 116	20 215 258	1 317 908	2 269 192	4 538 984	4 825 392	4 071 366	2 380 045	812 371
Percent of total	53.8	9.7	56.1	37.3	63.9	65.1	68.3	67.4	53.9	18.1
Male	18 417 937	962 542	17 455 395	1 806 032	1 776 864	3 374 136	3 424 919	2 948 410	2 095 778	2 029 256
Labor force	13 851 958	134 734	13 717 224	874 094	1 521 079	3 171 089	3 228 134	2 689 920	1 642 129	590 779
Percent of male	75.2	14.0	78.6	48.4	85.6	94.0	94.3	91.2	78.4	29.1
Female	19 530 326	921 290	18 609 036	1 731 237	1 774 778	3 593 653	3 641 062	3 093 731	2 320 648	2 453 927
Labor force	6 546 416	48 382	6 498 034	443 814	748 113	1 367 895	1 597 258	1 381 446	737 916	221 592
Percent of female	33.5	5.3	34.9	25.6	42.2	38.1	43.9	44.7	31.8	9.0
1950										
Total	33 524 525	1 557 935	31 966 590	3 049 950	3 793 595	7 260 120	6 422 475	4 826 405	3 361 945	3 252 100
Labor force	17 588 740	188 465	17 400 275	1 237 215	2 250 200	4 392 075	4 103 735	2 934 390	1 716 370	766 290
Percent of total	52.5	12.1	54.4	40.6	59.3	60.5	63.9	60.8	51.1	23.6
Male	16 392 850	789 435	15 603 415	1 534 060	1 846 805	3 528 045	3 139 405	2 367 015	1 657 975	1 530 110
Labor force	12 876 045	147 020	12 729 025	868 080	1 540 740	3 217 650	2 949 020	2 155 830	1 350 185	647 520
Percent of male	78.5	18.6	81.6	56.6	83.4	91.2	93.9	91.1	81.4	42.3
Female	17 131 675	768 500	16 363 175	1 515 890	1 946 790	3 732 075	3 283 070	2 459 390	1 703 970	1 721 990
Labor force	4 712 695	41 445	4 671 250	369 135	709 460	1 174 425	1 154 715	778 560	366 185	118 770
Percent of female	27.5	5.4	28.5	24.4	36.4	31.5	35.2	31.7	21.5	6.9
1940										
Total	30 157 500	1 722 860	28 434 640	3 449 920	3 817 900	6 765 060	5 347 580	4 065 780	2 697 280	2 291 120
Labor force	15 727 580	168 820	15 558 760	1 324 000	2 353 820	4 239 440	3 259 820	2 365 180	1 393 840	622 660
Percent of total	52.2	9.8	54.7	38.4	61.7	62.7	61.0	58.2	51.7	27.2
Male	14 989 920	865 440	14 124 480	1 709 340	1 858 620	3 317 680	2 649 960	2 063 360	1 378 140	1 147 380
Labor force	11 964 240	131 680	11 832 560	939 320	1 647 420	3 144 780	2 495 860	1 890 680	1 169 680	544 820
Percent of male	79.8	15.2	83.8	55.0	88.6	94.8	94.2	91.6	84.9	47.5
Female	15 167 580	857 420	14 310 160	1 740 580	1 959 280	3 447 380	2 697 620	2 002 420	1 319 140	1 143 740
Labor force	3 763 340	37 140	3 726 200	384 680	706 400	1 094 660	763 960	474 500	224 160	77 840
Percent of female	24.8	4.3	26.0	22.1	36.1	31.8	28.3	23.7	17.0	6.8
White										
1980										
Total	(NA)	(NA)	45 409 181	4 258 325	5 409 135	9 612 082	6 939 195	6 126 528	5 916 218	7 147 698
Labor force	(NA)	(NA)	27 759 270	2 155 626	4 118 590	7 625 486	5 476 620	4 428 750	3 065 287	888 911
Percent of total	(NA)	(NA)	61.1	50.6	76.1	79.3	78.9	72.3	51.8	12.4
Male	(NA)	(NA)	21 804 166	2 183 260	2 741 092	4 810 387	3 440 532	2 975 104	2 755 330	2 898 461
Labor force	(NA)	(NA)	16 397 645	1 220 050	2 326 007	4 534 325	3 251 397	2 648 578	1 858 746	558 542
Percent of male	(NA)	(NA)	75.2	55.9	84.9	94.3	94.5	89.0	67.5	19.3
Female	(NA)	(NA)	23 605 015	2 075 065	2 668 043	4 801 695	3 498 663	3 151 424	3 160 888	4 249 237
Labor force	(NA)	(NA)	11 361 625	935 576	1 792 583	3 091 161	2 225 223	1 780 172	1 206 541	330 369
Percent of female	(NA)	(NA)	48.1	45.1	67.2	64.4	63.6	56.5	38.2	7.8
1970										
Total	(NA)	(NA)	(NA)	(NA)	(NA)	(NA)	(NA)	(NA)	(NA)	(NA)
Labor force	(NA)	(NA)	(NA)	(NA)	(NA)	(NA)	(NA)	(NA)	(NA)	(NA)
Percent of total	(NA)	(NA)	(NA)	(NA)	(NA)	(NA)	(NA)	(NA)	(NA)	(NA)
Male	(NA)	(NA)	(NA)	(NA)	(NA)	(NA)	(NA)	(NA)	(NA)	(NA)
Labor force	(NA)	(NA)	(NA)	(NA)	(NA)	(NA)	(NA)	(NA)	(NA)	(NA)
Percent of male	(NA)	(NA)	(NA)	(NA)	(NA)	(NA)	(NA)	(NA)	(NA)	(NA)
Female	(NA)	(NA)	(NA)	(NA)	(NA)	(NA)	(NA)	(NA)	(NA)	(NA)
Labor force	(NA)	(NA)	(NA)	(NA)	(NA)	(NA)	(NA)	(NA)	(NA)	(NA)
Percent of female	(NA)	(NA)	(NA)	(NA)	(NA)	(NA)	(NA)	(NA)	(NA)	(NA)
1960										
Total	30 739 565	1 437 284	29 302 281	2 752 866	2 834 937	5 665 004	5 801 964	4 930 033	3 619 398	3 698 079
Labor force	16 470 400	137 416	16 332 984	1 060 861	1 824 967	3 652 368	3 917 349	3 291 863	1 929 983	655 593
Percent of total	53.6	9.6	55.7	38.5	64.4	64.5	67.5	66.8	53.3	17.7
Male	15 012 372	737 779	14 274 593	1 412 686	1 431 999	2 778 389	2 844 119	2 422 118	1 719 763	1 665 519
Labor force	11 471 728	102 809	11 368 919	702 461	1 238 024	2 642 284	2 708 715	2 230 789	1 361 679	484 967
Percent of male	76.4	13.9	-79.6	49.7	86.5	95.1	95.2	92.1	79.2	29.1
Female	15 727 193	699 505	15 027 688	1 340 180	1 402 938	2 886 615	2 957 845	2 507 915	1 899 635	2 032 560
Labor force	4 998 672	34 607	4 964 065	358 400	586 943	1 010 084	1 208 634	1 061 074	568 304	170 626
Percent of female	31.8	4.9	33.0	26.7	41.8	35.0	40.9	42.3	29.9	8.4

GENERAL SOCIAL AND ECONOMIC CHARACTERISTICS

UNITED STATES SUMMARY 1—37

Table 87. Labor Force Status by Age, Race, and Sex: 1940 to 1980—Con.

[For years prior to 1960, excludes data for Alaska and Hawaii. Data are estimates based on a sample; see Introduction. For meaning of symbols, see Introduction. For definitions of terms, see appendixes A and B]

United States Regions	Persons 14 years and over	14 and 15 years	Persons 16 years and over							
			Total	16 to 19	20 to 24	25 to 34	35 to 44	45 to 54	55 to 64	65 and over
SOUTH—Con.										
White—Con.										
1950										
Total	26 550 150	1 174 715	25 375 435	2 320 255	2 968 250	5 811 195	5 078 945	3 824 030	2 762 545	2 610 215
Labor force	13 708 405	123 520	13 584 885	930 905	1 768 805	3 468 515	3 181 390	2 273 450	1 372 915	588 905
Percent of total	51.6	10.5	53.5	40.1	59.6	59.7	62.6	59.5	49.7	22.6
Male	13 069 595	599 695	12 469 900	1 180 880	1 466 920	2 857 165	2 505 815	1 883 800	1 353 810	1 221 510
Labor force	10 307 625	99 205	10 208 420	650 710	1 226 315	2 633 180	2 367 010	1 721 560	1 102 515	507 040
Percent of male	78.9	16.5	81.9	55.1	83.6	92.2	94.5	91.4	81.4	41.5
Female	13 480 555	575 020	12 905 535	1 139 375	1 501 330	2 954 030	2 573 130	1 940 230	1 408 735	1 388 705
Labor force	3 400 780	24 315	3 376 465	280 195	542 490	835 335	814 290	551 890	270 400	81 865
Percent of female	25.2	4.2	26.2	24.6	36.1	28.3	31.6	28.4	19.2	5.9
1940										
Total	23 178 840	1 292 940	21 885 900	2 595 860	2 864 640	5 169 680	4 079 100	3 182 700	2 186 600	1 807 320
Labor force	11 635 620	97 720	11 537 900	931 280	1 733 420	3 153 320	2 393 420	1 781 520	1 084 220	460 720
Percent of total	50.2	7.6	52.7	35.9	60.5	61.0	58.7	56.0	49.6	25.5
Male	11 602 060	653 200	10 948 860	1 298 380	1 412 640	2 562 040	2 045 680	1 619 720	1 109 680	900 720
Labor force	9 216 420	81 320	9 135 100	674 820	1 246 780	2 441 120	1 932 540	1 486 760	937 700	415 380
Percent of male	79.4	12.4	83.4	52.0	88.3	95.3	94.5	91.8	84.5	46.1
Female	11 576 780	639 740	10 937 040	1 297 480	1 452 000	2 607 640	2 033 420	1 562 980	1 076 920	906 600
Labor force	2 419 200	16 400	2 402 800	256 460	486 640	712 200	460 880	294 760	146 520	45 340
Percent of female	20.9	2.6	22.0	19.8	33.5	27.3	22.7	18.9	13.6	5.0
Black[1]										
1980										
Total	(NA)	(NA)	9 635 585	1 299 353	1 452 808	2 208 838	1 325 565	1 133 447	996 743	1 218 831
Labor force	(NA)	(NA)	5 711 113	440 773	1 006 955	1 761 288	1 042 779	790 432	505 010	163 876
Percent of total	(NA)	(NA)	59.3	33.9	69.3	79.7	78.7	69.7	50.7	13.4
Male	(NA)	(NA)	4 409 163	649 293	691 381	1 034 381	602 424	499 133	440 285	492 266
Labor force	(NA)	(NA)	2 935 642	245 492	522 272	882 183	524 017	404 181	268 918	88 579
Percent of male	(NA)	(NA)	66.6	37.8	75.5	85.3	87.0	81.0	61.1	18.0
Female	(NA)	(NA)	5 226 422	650 060	761 427	1 174 457	723 141	634 314	556 458	726 565
Labor force	(NA)	(NA)	2 775 471	195 281	484 683	879 105	518 762	386 251	236 092	75 297
Percent of female	(NA)	(NA)	53.1	30.0	63.7	74.9	71.7	60.9	42.4	10.4
1970										
Total	7 981 485	626 903	7 354 582	1 065 793	912 541	1 264 153	1 163 793	1 080 160	915 306	952 836
Labor force	4 198 069	40 809	4 157 260	308 081	602 342	939 093	862 017	757 473	522 067	166 187
Percent of total	52.6	6.5	56.5	28.9	66.0	74.3	74.1	70.1	57.0	17.4
Male	3 700 025	315 353	3 384 672	527 979	425 423	580 420	521 037	495 922	420 159	413 732
Labor force	2 330 941	27 283	2 303 658	187 227	328 579	513 213	459 407	417 555	300 509	97 168
Percent of male	63.0	8.7	68.1	35.5	77.2	88.4	88.2	84.2	71.5	23.5
Female	4 281 460	311 550	3 969 910	537 814	487 118	683 733	642 756	584 238	495 147	539 104
Labor force	1 867 128	13 526	1 853 602	120 854	273 763	425 880	402 610	339 918	221 558	69 019
Percent of female	43.6	4.3	46.7	22.5	56.2	62.3	62.6	58.2	44.7	12.8
1960										
Total	7 208 698	446 548	6 762 150	784 403	716 705	1 302 785	1 264 017	1 112 108	797 028	785 104
Labor force	3 927 974	45 700	3 882 274	257 047	444 225	886 616	908 043	779 503	450 062	156 778
Percent of total	54.5	10.2	57.4	32.8	62.0	68.1	71.8	70.1	56.5	20.0
Male	3 405 565	224 763	3 180 802	393 346	344 865	595 747	580 800	526 292	376 015	363 737
Labor force	2 380 230	31 925	2 348 305	171 633	283 055	528 805	519 419	459 131	280 450	105 812
Percent of male	69.9	14.2	73.8	43.6	82.1	88.8	89.4	87.2	74.6	29.1
Female	3 803 133	221 785	3 581 348	391 057	371 840	707 038	683 217	585 816	421 013	421 367
Labor force	1 547 744	13 775	1 533 969	85 414	161 170	357 811	388 624	320 372	169 612	50 966
Percent of female	40.7	6.2	42.8	21.8	43.3	50.6	56.9	54.7	40.3	12.1
1950										
Total	6 974 375	383 220	6 591 155	729 695	825 345	1 448 925	1 343 530	1 002 375	599 400	641 885
Labor force	3 880 335	64 945	3 815 390	306 310	481 395	923 160	922 345	660 940	343 455	177 385
Percent of total	55.6	16.9	57.9	42.0	58.3	63.7	68.7	65.9	57.3	27.6
Male	3 323 255	189 740	3 133 515	353 180	379 885	670 880	633 590	483 215	304 165	308 600
Labor force	2 568 420	47 815	2 520 605	217 370	314 425	584 470	581 920	434 270	247 670	140 480
Percent of male	77.3	25.2	80.4	61.5	82.8	87.1	91.8	89.9	81.4	45.5
Female	3 651 120	193 480	3 457 640	376 515	445 460	778 045	709 940	519 160	295 235	333 285
Labor force	1 311 915	17 130	1 294 785	88 940	166 970	339 090	340 425	226 670	95 785	36 905
Percent of female	35.9	8.9	37.4	23.6	37.5	43.6	48.0	43.7	32.4	11.1
1940										
Total	6 978 660	429 920	6 548 740	854 060	953 260	1 595 380	1 268 480	883 080	510 680	483 800
Labor force	4 091 960	71 100	4 020 860	392 720	620 400	1 086 120	866 400	583 660	309 620	161 940
Percent of total	58.6	16.5	61.4	46.0	65.1	68.1	68.3	66.1	60.6	33.5
Male	3 387 560	212 240	3 175 620	410 960	445 980	755 640	604 280	443 640	268 460	246 660
Labor force	2 747 820	50 360	2 697 460	264 500	400 640	703 660	563 320	403 920	231 980	129 440
Percent of male	81.1	23.7	84.9	64.4	89.8	93.1	93.2	91.0	86.4	52.5
Female	3 590 800	217 680	3 373 120	443 100	507 280	839 740	664 200	439 440	242 220	237 140
Labor force	1 344 140	20 740	1 323 400	128 220	219 760	382 460	303 080	179 740	77 640	32 500
Percent of female	37.4	9.5	39.2	28.9	43.3	45.5	45.6	40.9	32.1	13.7

[1]For years prior to 1970, includes Black and other races.

Table 87. Labor Force Status by Age, Race, and Sex: 1940 to 1980—Con.

[For years prior to 1960, excludes data for Alaska and Hawaii. Data are estimates based on a sample; see Introduction. For meaning of symbols, see Introduction. For definitions of terms, see appendixes A and B]

United States Regions	Persons 14 years and over	14 and 15 years	Persons 16 years and over							
			Total	16 to 19	20 to 24	25 to 34	35 to 44	45 to 54	55 to 64	65 and over
WEST										
Total										
1980										
Total	(NA)	(NA)	32 614 131	3 178 490	4 278 696	7 763 756	5 058 784	4 150 323	3 903 248	4 280 834
Labor force	(NA)	(NA)	20 908 653	1 676 999	3 257 189	6 155 286	4 057 173	3 089 524	2 134 517	537 965
Percent of total	(NA)	(NA)	64.1	52.8	76.1	79.3	80.2	74.4	54.7	12.6
Male	(NA)	(NA)	15 966 419	1 628 505	2 190 161	3 927 447	2 536 835	2 034 817	1 863 712	1 784 942
Labor force	(NA)	(NA)	12 251 151	911 538	1 840 651	3 631 749	2 387 131	1 839 389	1 304 870	335 823
Percent of male	(NA)	(NA)	76.7	56.0	84.0	92.5	94.1	90.4	70.0	18.8
Female	(NA)	(NA)	16 647 712	1 549 985	2 088 535	3 836 309	2 521 949	2 115 506	2 039 536	2 495 892
Labor force	(NA)	(NA)	8 657 502	765 461	1 416 538	2 523 537	1 670 042	1 250 135	829 647	202 142
Percent of female	(NA)	(NA)	52.0	49.4	67.8	65.8	66.2	59.1	40.7	8.1
1970										
Total	25 579 286	1 411 199	24 168 087	2 603 079	2 974 329	4 540 740	4 030 438	3 944 065	2 971 913	3 103 523
Labor force	14 448 709	162 600	14 286 109	1 106 001	2 040 131	3 144 569	2 919 748	2 837 625	1 776 772	461 263
Percent of total	56.5	11.5	59.1	42.5	68.6	69.3	72.4	71.9	59.8	14.9
Male	12 499 929	721 185	11 778 744	1 325 234	1 489 176	2 263 155	1 998 545	1 935 745	1 440 042	1 326 847
Labor force	9 225 430	110 362	9 115 068	664 767	1 216 385	2 102 589	1 893 707	1 791 737	1 146 914	298 969
Percent of male	73.8	15.3	77.4	50.2	81.7	92.9	94.8	92.6	79.6	22.5
Female	13 079 357	690 014	12 389 343	1 277 845	1 485 153	2 277 585	2 031 893	2 008 320	1 531 871	1 776 676
Labor force	5 223 279	52 238	5 171 041	441 234	823 746	1 041 980	1 026 041	1 045 888	629 858	162 294
Percent of female	39.9	7.6	41.7	34.5	55.5	45.7	50.5	52.1	41.1	9.1
1960										
Total	19 609 839	864 194	18 745 645	1 616 508	1 776 681	3 706 822	3 903 943	3 134 326	2 248 497	2 358 868
Labor force	11 171 778	126 851	11 044 927	711 991	1 170 058	2 419 670	2 728 224	2 233 877	1 337 137	443 970
Percent of total	57.0	14.7	58.9	44.0	65.9	65.3	69.9	71.3	59.5	18.8
Male	9 761 625	441 593	9 320 032	834 041	908 280	1 861 017	1 941 847	1 585 853	1 109 806	1 079 188
Labor force	7 707 564	85 815	7 621 749	464 273	802 894	1 770 482	1 867 636	1 487 272	917 302	311 890
Percent of male	79.0	19.4	81.8	55.7	88.4	95.1	96.2	93.8	82.7	28.9
Female	9 848 214	422 601	9 425 613	782 467	868 401	1 845 805	1 962 096	1 548 473	1 138 691	1 279 680
Labor force	3 464 214	41 036	3 423 178	247 718	367 164	649 188	860 588	746 605	419 835	132 080
Percent of female	35.2	9.7	36.3	31.7	42.3	35.2	43.9	48.2	36.9	10.3
1950										
Total	14 562 090	504 830	14 057 260	1 019 205	1 441 435	3 212 090	2 848 475	2 214 705	1 725 625	1 595 725
Labor force	7 870 450	59 285	7 811 165	410 420	876 375	1 968 765	1 871 655	1 416 755	929 730	337 465
Percent of total	54.0	11.7	55.6	40.3	60.8	61.3	65.7	64.0	53.9	21.1
Male	7 311 710	256 200	7 055 510	526 335	728 490	1 589 140	1 439 425	1 132 925	875 205	763 990
Labor force	5 747 050	43 150	5 703 900	273 575	600 295	1 463 130	1 359 130	1 030 875	703 885	273 010
Percent of male	78.6	16.8	80.8	52.0	82.4	92.1	94.4	91.0	80.4	35.7
Female	7 250 380	248 630	7 001 750	492 870	712 945	1 622 950	1 409 050	1 081 780	850 420	831 735
Labor force	2 123 400	16 135	2 107 265	136 845	276 080	505 635	512 525	385 880	225 845	64 455
Percent of female	29.3	6.5	30.1	27.8	38.7	31.2	36.4	35.7	26.6	7.7
1940										
Total	10 935 280	452 700	10 482 580	965 460	1 182 020	2 293 700	1 994 900	1 754 860	1 260 040	1 031 600
Labor force	5 660 960	13 880	5 647 080	289 040	732 860	1 448 240	1 239 740	1 051 600	664 920	220 680
Percent of total	51.8	3.1	53.9	29.9	62.0	63.1	62.1	59.9	52.8	21.4
Male	5 647 500	228 680	5 418 820	488 160	596 340	1 180 440	1 036 100	928 560	668 700	520 520
Labor force	4 378 800	11 020	4 367 780	191 860	510 860	1 117 600	973 320	841 020	545 340	187 780
Percent of male	77.5	4.8	80.6	39.3	85.7	94.7	93.9	90.6	81.6	36.1
Female	5 287 780	224 020	5 063 760	477 300	585 680	1 113 260	958 800	826 300	591 340	511 080
Labor force	1 282 160	2 860	1 279 300	97 180	222 000	330 640	266 420	210 580	119 580	32 900
Percent of female	24.2	1.3	25.3	20.4	37.9	29.7	27.8	25.5	20.2	6.4
White										
1980										
Total	(NA)	(NA)	27 070 881	2 489 845	3 363 053	6 252 423	4 164 253	3 491 783	3 435 487	3 874 037
Labor force	(NA)	(NA)	17 317 888	1 382 189	2 604 166	4 991 964	3 358 168	2 616 785	1 881 777	482 839
Percent of total	(NA)	(NA)	64.0	55.5	77.4	79.8	80.6	74.9	54.8	12.5
Male	(NA)	(NA)	13 214 902	1 271 847	1 714 899	3 166 236	2 097 651	1 724 857	1 641 411	1 598 001
Labor force	(NA)	(NA)	10 193 789	745 032	1 461 885	2 963 036	1 993 183	1 574 786	1 155 588	300 279
Percent of male	(NA)	(NA)	77.1	58.6	85.2	93.6	95.0	91.3	70.4	18.8
Female	(NA)	(NA)	13 855 979	1 217 998	1 648 154	3 086 187	2 066 602	1 766 926	1 794 076	2 276 036
Labor force	(NA)	(NA)	7 124 099	637 157	1 142 281	2 028 928	1 364 985	1 041 999	726 189	182 560
Percent of female	(NA)	(NA)	51.4	52.3	69.3	65.7	66.0	59.0	40.5	8.0
1970										
Total	(NA)	(NA)	(NA)	(NA)	(NA)	(NA)	(NA)	(NA)	(NA)	(NA)
Labor force	(NA)	(NA)	(NA)	(NA)	(NA)	(NA)	(NA)	(NA)	(NA)	(NA)
Percent of total	(NA)	(NA)	(NA)	(NA)	(NA)	(NA)	(NA)	(NA)	(NA)	(NA)
Male	(NA)	(NA)	(NA)	(NA)	(NA)	(NA)	(NA)	(NA)	(NA)	(NA)
Labor force	(NA)	(NA)	(NA)	(NA)	(NA)	(NA)	(NA)	(NA)	(NA)	(NA)
Percent of male	(NA)	(NA)	(NA)	(NA)	(NA)	(NA)	(NA)	(NA)	(NA)	(NA)
Female	(NA)	(NA)	(NA)	(NA)	(NA)	(NA)	(NA)	(NA)	(NA)	(NA)
Labor force	(NA)	(NA)	(NA)	(NA)	(NA)	(NA)	(NA)	(NA)	(NA)	(NA)
Percent of female	(NA)	(NA)	(NA)	(NA)	(NA)	(NA)	(NA)	(NA)	(NA)	(NA)
1960										
Total	18 167 990	793 439	17 374 551	1 489 909	1 620 637	3 370 126	3 600 023	2 925 099	2 111 268	2 257 489
Labor force	10 321 504	121 317	10 200 187	671 184	1 070 858	2 197 380	2 506 805	2 079 122	1 252 023	422 815
Percent of total	56.8	15.3	58.7	45.0	66.1	65.2	69.6	71.1	59.3	18.7
Male	9 016 669	405 631	8 611 038	769 393	828 890	1 696 771	1 788 318	1 469 166	1 033 362	1 025 138
Labor force	7 145 908	81 832	7 064 076	437 999	738 111	1 624 226	1 727 653	1 383 266	856 590	296 231
Percent of male	79.3	20.2	82.0	56.9	89.0	95.7	96.6	94.2	82.9	28.9
Female	9 151 321	387 808	8 763 513	720 516	791 747	1 673 355	1 811 705	1 455 933	1 077 906	1 232 351
Labor force	3 175 596	39 485	3 136 111	233 185	332 747	573 154	779 152	695 856	395 433	126 584
Percent of female	34.7	10.2	35.8	32.4	42.0	34.3	43.0	47.8	36.7	10.3

Table 87. Labor Force Status by Age, Race, and Sex: 1940 to 1980—Con.

[For years prior to 1960, excludes data for Alaska and Hawaii. Data are estimates based on a sample; see Introduction. For meaning of symbols, see Introduction. For definitions of terms, see appendixes A and B]

United States Regions	Persons 14 years and over	14 and 15 years	Persons 16 years and over							
			Total	16 to 19	20 to 24	25 to 34	35 to 44	45 to 54	55 to 64	65 and over
WEST—Con.										
White—Con.										
1950										
Total	13 849 260	477 650	13 371 610	963 380	1 353 375	3 022 650	2 697 875	2 114 725	1 670 160	1 549 445
Labor force	7 451 855	57 070	7 394 785	392 825	824 365	1 844 175	1 762 615	1 347 285	898 120	325 400
Percent of total	53.8	11.9	55.3	40.8	60.9	61.0	65.3	63.8	53.8	21.0
Male	6 928 710	242 810	6 685 900	498 140	684 135	1 493 165	1 355 595	1 074 335	843 095	737 435
Labor force	5 454 265	41 630	5 412 635	262 000	565 965	1 380 230	1 283 010	979 540	679 240	262 650
Percent of male	78.7	17.1	81.0	52.6	82.7	92.4	94.6	91.2	80.6	35.6
Female	6 920 550	234 840	6 685 710	465 240	669 240	1 529 485	1 342 280	1 040 390	827 065	812 010
Labor force	1 997 590	15 440	1 982 150	130 825	258 400	463 945	479 605	367 745	218 880	62 750
Percent of female	28.9	6.6	29.6	28.1	38.6	30.3	35.7	35.3	26.5	7.7
1940										
Total	10 550 460	432 440	10 118 020	924 240	1 134 860	2 207 280	1 919 220	1 700 140	1 224 640	1 007 640
Labor force	5 433 620	12 760	5 420 860	277 720	703 580	1 385 620	1 184 960	1 013 860	641 960	213 160
Percent of total	51.5	3.0	53.6	30.0	62.0	62.8	61.7	59.6	52.4	21.2
Male	5 423 720	218 340	5 205 380	466 820	571 380	1 128 040	991 460	896 100	645 020	506 560
Labor force	4 205 620	10 220	4 195 400	184 420	490 920	1 069 320	931 960	811 900	525 540	181 340
Percent of male	77.5	4.7	80.6	39.5	85.9	94.8	94.0	90.6	81.5	35.8
Female	5 126 740	214 100	4 912 640	457 420	563 480	1 079 240	927 760	804 040	579 620	501 080
Labor force	1 228 000	2 540	1 225 460	93 300	212 660	316 300	253 000	201 960	116 420	31 820
Percent of female	24.0	1.2	24.9	20.4	37.7	29.3	27.3	25.1	20.1	6.4
Black¹										
1980										
Total	(NA)	(NA)	1 604 581	201 589	260 354	406 455	256 740	192 349	151 624	135 470
Labor force	(NA)	(NA)	1 013 547	78 185	186 123	316 939	203 863	135 846	76 161	16 430
Percent of total	(NA)	(NA)	63.2	38.8	71.5	78.0	79.4	70.6	50.2	12.1
Male	(NA)	(NA)	792 100	105 084	136 276	203 692	126 555	93 154	71 751	55 588
Labor force	(NA)	(NA)	555 423	43 993	106 076	170 542	108 945	74 482	42 446	8 939
Percent of male	(NA)	(NA)	70.1	41.9	77.8	83.7	86.1	80.0	59.2	16.1
Female	(NA)	(NA)	812 481	96 505	124 078	202 763	130 185	99 195	79 873	79 882
Labor force	(NA)	(NA)	458 124	34 192	80 047	146 397	94 918	61 364	33 715	7 491
Percent of female	(NA)	(NA)	56.4	35.4	64.5	72.2	72.9	61.9	42.2	9.4
1970										
Total	1 137 197	76 224	1 060 973	132 762	149 568	233 129	193 167	159 965	106 687	85 695
Labor force	648 033	4 723	643 310	44 408	102 657	168 558	141 261	111 939	60 854	13 633
Percent of total	57.0	6.2	60.6	33.4	68.6	72.3	73.1	70.0	57.0	15.9
Male	557 179	38 174	519 005	69 394	75 615	112 923	95 108	77 173	50 887	37 905
Labor force	378 606	3 158	375 448	27 231	59 528	97 582	82 642	64 426	36 018	8 021
Percent of male	68.0	8.3	72.3	39.2	78.7	86.4	86.9	83.5	70.8	21.2
Female	580 018	38 050	541 968	63 368	73 953	120 206	98 059	82 792	55 800	47 790
Labor force	269 427	1 565	267 862	17 177	43 129	70 976	58 619	47 513	24 836	5 612
Percent of female	46.5	4.1	49.4	27.1	58.3	59.0	59.8	57.4	44.5	11.7
1960										
Total	1 441 849	70 755	1 371 094	126 599	156 044	336 696	303 920	209 227	137 229	101 379
Labor force	850 274	5 534	844 740	40 807	99 200	222 290	221 419	154 755	85 114	21 155
Percent of total	59.0	7.8	61.6	32.2	63.6	66.0	72.9	74.0	62.0	20.9
Male	744 956	35 962	708 994	64 648	79 390	164 246	153 529	116 687	76 444	54 050
Labor force	561 656	3 983	557 673	26 274	64 783	146 256	139 983	104 006	60 712	15 659
Percent of male	75.4	11.1	78.7	40.6	81.6	89.0	91.2	89.1	79.4	29.0
Female	696 893	34 793	662 100	61 951	76 654	172 450	150 391	92 540	60 785	47 329
Labor force	288 618	1 551	287 067	14 533	34 417	76 034	81 436	50 749	24 402	5 496
Percent of female	41.4	4.5	43.4	23.5	44.9	44.1	54.1	54.8	40.1	11.6
1950										
Total	712 830	27 180	685 650	55 825	88 060	189 440	150 600	99 980	55 465	46 280
Labor force	418 595	2 215	416 380	17 595	52 010	124 590	109 040	69 470	31 610	12 065
Percent of total	58.7	8.1	60.7	31.5	59.1	65.8	72.4	69.5	57.0	26.1
Male	383 000	13 390	369 610	28 195	44 355	95 975	83 830	58 590	32 110	26 555
Labor force	292 785	1 520	291 265	11 575	34 330	82 900	76 120	51 335	24 645	10 360
Percent of male	76.4	11.4	78.8	41.1	77.4	86.4	90.8	87.6	76.8	39.0
Female	329 830	13 790	316 040	27 630	43 705	93 465	66 770	41 390	23 355	19 725
Labor force	125 810	695	125 115	6 020	17 680	41 690	32 920	18 135	6 965	1 705
Percent of female	38.1	5.0	39.6	21.8	40.5	44.6	49.3	43.8	29.8	8.6
1940										
Total	384 820	20 260	364 560	41 220	47 160	86 420	75 680	54 720	35 400	23 960
Labor force	227 340	1 120	226 220	11 320	29 280	62 620	54 780	37 740	22 960	7 520
Percent of total	59.1	5.5	62.1	27.5	62.1	72.5	72.4	69.0	64.9	31.4
Male	223 780	10 340	213 440	21 340	24 960	52 400	44 640	32 460	23 680	13 960
Labor force	173 180	800	172 380	7 440	19 940	48 280	41 360	29 120	19 800	6 440
Percent of male	77.4	7.7	80.8	34.9	79.9	92.1	92.7	89.7	83.6	46.1
Female	161 040	9 920	151 120	19 880	22 200	34 020	31 040	22 260	11 720	10 000
Labor force	54 160	320	53 840	3 880	9 340	14 340	13 420	8 620	3 160	1 080
Percent of female	33.6	3.2	35.6	19.5	42.1	42.2	43.2	38.7	27.0	10.8

¹For years prior to 1970, includes Black and other races.

Table 88. Weeks Worked in Previous Year by Race and Sex: 1950 to 1980

[For 1950, excludes data for Alaska and Hawaii. Data are estimates based on a sample; see Introduction. For meaning of symbols, see Introduction. For definitions of terms, see appendixes A and B]

United States Regions	Total	Worked in previous year							Did not work in previous year
		Total	50 to 52 weeks	48 and 49 weeks	40 to 47 weeks	27 to 39 weeks	14 to 26 weeks	1 to 13 weeks	
UNITED STATES									
Both Sexes									
Total, 16 years and over[1]									
1980	171 214 258	114 477 241	68 342 458	4 945 172	10 542 967	9 684 038	10 728 356	10 234 250	56 737 017
1970	141 087 270	92 410 059	53 661 993	5 396 953	7 877 725	7 851 116	7 709 409	9 912 863	48 677 211
1960	126 276 556	77 368 085	43 972 721	4 329 913	6 899 064	7 189 760	6 498 414	8 478 213	48 908 471
1950[4]	111 693 240	60 531 450	36 026 820	7 602 120	(2)	5 299 340	6 027 140	5 576 030	51 161 790
White, 16 years and over[1]									
1980	145 425 287	98 220 741	59 569 175	3 968 979	8 983 769	8 191 047	9 082 322	8 425 449	47 204 546
1970	125 367 127	82 266 718	48 458 223	4 573 050	6 775 026	6 870 118	6 853 942	8 736 359	43 100 409
1960	113 122 902	69 183 482	40 203 802	3 763 330	5 984 987	6 204 171	5 627 516	7 399 676	43 939 420
1950[4]	100 701 990	54 215 840	32 944 410	6 671 280	(2)	4 582 240	5 129 060	4 888 850	46 486 150
Black, 16 years and over[13]									
1980	18 294 925	11 238 447	6 119 244	631 925	1 078 615	1 028 810	1 108 168	1 271 685	7 056 478
1970	14 015 283	9 006 130	4 597 379	744 821	1 003 299	881 409	749 478	1 029 744	5 009 153
1960	13 153 654	8 184 603	3 768 919	566 583	914 077	985 589	870 898	1 078 537	4 969 051
1950[4]	10 991 250	6 315 610	3 082 410	930 840	(2)	717 100	898 080	687 180	4 675 640
Male									
Total, 16 years and over[1]									
1980	81 732 090	64 867 639	43 113 565	2 855 305	5 356 939	4 376 379	4 804 802	4 360 649	16 864 451
1970	67 235 510	55 786 915	37 608 767	3 362 001	4 157 826	3 416 927	3 227 270	4 014 124	11 448 595
1960	61 315 362	50 301 864	32 666 364	2 941 460	4 297 265	3 890 819	3 034 008	3 471 948	11 013 498
1950[4]	54 610 050	41 780 010	27 283 440	5 436 990	(2)	3 242 180	3 325 190	2 492 210	12 830 040
White, 16 years and over[1]									
1980	69 672 383	56 223 063	38 099 231	2 310 772	4 577 906	3 680 059	4 021 671	3 533 424	13 449 320
1970	59 946 581	50 227 551	34 358 631	2 885 483	3 585 392	2 990 727	2 874 488	3 532 830	9 719 030
1960	55 036 177	45 504 253	30 165 320	2 577 861	3 734 918	3 354 516	2 629 711	3 041 927	9 531 924
1950[4]	49 312 050	37 914 570	25 146 430	4 794 420	(2)	2 835 670	2 900 360	2 237 690	11 397 480
Black, 16 years and over[13]									
1980	8 374 051	5 753 283	3 338 741	332 867	514 999	459 329	523 778	583 569	2 620 768
1970	6 449 469	4 883 375	2 843 207	427 763	518 953	377 684	302 277	413 491	1 566 094
1960	6 279 185	4 797 611	2 501 044	363 599	562 347	536 303	404 297	430 021	1 481 574
1950[4]	5 298 000	3 865 440	2 137 010	642 570	(2)	406 510	424 830	254 520	1 432 560
Female									
Total, 16 years and over[1]									
1980	89 482 168	49 609 602	25 228 893	2 089 867	5 186 028	5 307 659	5 923 554	5 873 601	39 872 566
1970	73 851 760	36 623 144	16 053 226	2 034 952	3 719 899	4 434 189	4 482 139	5 898 739	37 228 616
1960	64 961 194	27 066 221	11 306 357	1 388 453	2 601 799	3 298 941	3 464 406	5 006 265	37 894 973
1950[4]	57 083 190	18 751 440	8 743 380	2 165 130	(2)	2 057 160	2 701 950	3 083 820	38 331 750
White, 16 years and over[1]									
1980	75 752 904	41 997 678	21 469 944	1 658 207	4 405 863	4 510 988	5 060 651	4 892 025	33 755 226
1970	65 420 546	32 039 167	14 099 592	1 687 567	3 189 634	3 879 391	3 979 454	5 203 529	33 381 379
1960	58 086 725	23 679 229	10 038 482	1 185 469	2 250 069	2 849 655	2 997 805	4 357 749	34 407 496
1950[4]	51 389 940	16 301 270	7 797 980	1 876 860	(2)	1 746 570	2 228 700	2 651 160	35 088 670
Black, 16 years and over[13]									
1980	9 920 874	5 485 164	2 780 503	299 058	563 616	569 481	584 390	688 116	4 435 710
1970	7 565 814	4 122 755	1 754 172	317 058	484 346	503 725	447 201	616 253	3 443 059
1960	6 874 469	3 386 992	1 267 875	202 984	351 730	449 286	466 601	648 516	3 487 477
1950[4]	5 693 250	2 450 170	945 400	288 270	(2)	310 590	473 250	432 660	3 243 080
NORTHEAST									
Both Sexes									
Total, 16 years and over[1]									
1980	37 868 817	24 537 667	15 197 317	921 265	2 201 032	1 882 753	2 234 707	2 100 593	13 331 150
1970	34 730 504	22 607 961	13 320 505	1 387 077		1 752 110	1 775 333	2 302 099	12 122 543
1960	32 561 170	19 876 577	11 792 435	1 095 662	1 827 833	1 728 742	1 548 122	1 883 783	12 684 593
1950[4]	(NA)	(NA)	(NA)	(NA)	(NA)	(NA)	(NA)	(NA)	(NA)
White, 16 years and over[1]									
1980	33 218 009	21 787 696	13 604 603	771 370	1 956 385	1 672 528	1 972 874	1 809 936	●11 430 313
1970	(NA)	(NA)	(NA)	(NA)	(NA)	(NA)	(NA)	(NA)	(NA)
1960	30 398 402	18 500 102	11 069 889	996 575	1 672 508	1 579 380	1 421 574	1 760 176	11 898 300
1950[4]	(NA)	(NA)	(NA)	(NA)	(NA)	(NA)	(NA)	(NA)	(NA)
Black, 16 years and over[13]									
1980	3 422 855	2 024 655	1 185 400	106 861	178 260	149 673	186 411	218 050	1 398 200
1970	2 767 665	1 788 549	955 188	165 715	210 492	153 139	134 704	169 311	979 116
1960	2 162 768	1 376 475	722 546	99 087	155 325	149 362	126 548	123 607	786 293
1950[4]	(NA)	(NA)	(NA)	(NA)	(NA)	(NA)	(NA)	(NA)	(NA)

[1]14 years and over in 1960 and in 1950. [2]Included in preceding category. [3]For years prior to 1970, includes Black and other races. [4]"Did not work in previous year" includes "Work in 1949 not reported."

Table 88. Weeks Worked in Previous Year by Race and Sex: 1950 to 1980—Con.

[For 1950, excludes data for Alaska and Hawaii. Data are estimates based on a sample; see Introduction. For meaning of symbols, see Introduction. For definitions of terms, see appendixes A and B]

United States Regions	Total	Worked in previous year							Did not work in previous year
		Total	50 to 52 weeks	48 and 49 weeks	40 to 47 weeks	27 to 39 weeks	14 to 26 weeks	1 to 13 weeks	
NORTHEAST—Con.									
Male									
Total, 16 years and over[1]									
1980	17 712 800	13 777 950	9 432 346	510 755	1 053 458	861 595	1 004 079	915 717	3 934 850
1970	16 260 439	13 482 592	9 196 718	834 278	1 031 697	749 782	725 493	944 624	2 777 847
1960	15 547 376	12 722 566	8 565 834	703 113	1 044 446	934 348	700 843	773 982	2 824 810
1950	(NA)	(NA)	(NA)	(NA)	(NA)	(NA)	(NA)	(NA)	(NA)
White, 16 years and over[1]									
1980	15 626 311	12 362 831	8 565 425	433 147	940 620	762 560	879 865	781 214	3 263 480
1970	(NA)	(NA)	(NA)	(NA)	(NA)	(NA)	(NA)	(NA)	(NA)
1960	14 541 640	11 940 302	8 106 937	646 964	961 341	856 787	643 696	724 577	2 601 338
1950	(NA)	(NA)	(NA)	(NA)	(NA)	(NA)	(NA)	(NA)	(NA)
Black, 16 years and over[1][3]									
1980	1 513 987	1 001 095	611 443	52 461	79 069	68 994	88 743	100 385	512 892
1970	1 233 753	946 554	570 013	90 442	103 841	62 354	51 316	68 588	287 199
1960	1 005 736	782 264	458 897	56 149	83 105	77 561	57 147	49 405	223 472
1950	(NA)	(NA)	(NA)	(NA)	(NA)	(NA)	(NA)	(NA)	(NA)
Female									
Total, 16 years and over[1]									
1980	20 156 017	10 759 717	5 764 971	410 510	1 147 574	1 021 158	1 230 628	1 184 876	9 396 300
1970	18 470 065	9 125 369	4 123 787	552 779	1 039 140	1 002 328	1 049 840	1 357 475	9 344 696
1960	17 013 794	7 154 011	3 226 601	392 549	783 387	794 394	847 279	1 109 801	9 859 783
1950	(NA)	(NA)	(NA)	(NA)	(NA)	(NA)	(NA)	(NA)	(NA)
White, 16 years and over[1]									
1980	17 591 698	9 424 865	5 039 178	338 223	1 015 765	909 968	1 093 009	1 028 722	8 166 833
1970	(NA)	(NA)	(NA)	(NA)	(NA)	(NA)	(NA)	(NA)	(NA)
1960	15 856 762	6 559 800	2 962 952	349 611	711 167	722 593	777 878	1 035 599	9 296 962
1950	(NA)	(NA)	(NA)	(NA)	(NA)	(NA)	(NA)	(NA)	(NA)
Black, 16 years and over[1][3]									
1980	1 908 868	1 023 560	573 957	54 400	99 191	80 679	97 668	117 665	885 308
1970	1 533 912	841 995	385 175	75 273	106 651	90 785	83 388	100 723	691 917
1960	1 157 032	594 211	263 649	42 938	72 220	71 801	69 401	74 202	562 821
1950	(NA)	(NA)	(NA)	(NA)	(NA)	(NA)	(NA)	(NA)	(NA)
NORTH CENTRAL									
Both Sexes									
Total, 16 years and over[1]									
1980	44 178 493	30 173 706	17 987 686	1 260 033	2 773 972	2 692 206	2 811 978	2 647 831	14 004 787
1970	38 868 154	25 809 073	15 025 328	1 509 277	2 131 242	2 208 592	2 200 623	2 734 011	13 059 081
1960	36 157 258	22 239 377	12 788 662	1 250 521	1 939 344	2 038 092	1 820 184	2 402 574	13 917 881
1950	(NA)	(NA)	(NA)	(NA)	(NA)	(NA)	(NA)	(NA)	(NA)
White, 16 years and over[1]									
1980	39 727 216	27 410 910	16 554 103	1 093 880	2 490 353	2 422 723	2 520 094	2 329 757	12 316 306
1970	(NA)	(NA)	(NA)	(NA)	(NA)	(NA)	(NA)	(NA)	(NA)
1960	33 816 919	20 867 628	12 139 486	1 149 501	1 783 778	1 878 252	1 679 607	2 237 004	12 949 291
1950	(NA)	(NA)	(NA)	(NA)	(NA)	(NA)	(NA)	(NA)	(NA)
Black, 16 years and over[1][3]									
1980	3 631 904	2 204 256	1 141 899	131 022	229 457	215 944	229 620	256 314	1 427 648
1970	2 832 063	1 837 274	940 435	169 638	219 083	165 385	149 461	193 272	994 789
1960	2 340 339	1 371 749	649 176	101 020	155 566	159 840	140 577	165 570	968 590
1950	(NA)	(NA)	(NA)	(NA)	(NA)	(NA)	(NA)	(NA)	(NA)
Male									
Total, 16 years and over[1]									
1980	21 093 150	17 141 511	11 391 171	730 356	1 458 772	1 202 519	1 241 995	1 116 698	3 951 639
1970	18 530 003	15 644 513	10 658 522	948 787	1 126 612	924 059	906 380	1 080 153	2 885 490
1960	17 588 424	14 642 512	9 620 034	858 340	1 238 807	1 101 916	845 793	977 622	2 945 912
1950	(NA)	(NA)	(NA)	(NA)	(NA)	(NA)	(NA)	(NA)	(NA)
White, 16 years and over[1]									
1980	19 027 004	15 692 582	10 591 391	638 939	1 313 425	1 077 068	1 101 751	970 008	3 334 422
1970	(NA)	(NA)	(NA)	(NA)	(NA)	(NA)	(NA)	(NA)	(NA)
1960	16 465 496	13 798 851	9 185 722	793 093	1 140 535	1 002 591	772 606	904 304	2 666 645
1950	(NA)	(NA)	(NA)	(NA)	(NA)	(NA)	(NA)	(NA)	(NA)
Black, 16 years and over[1][3]									
1980	1 658 801	1 123 664	613 732	69 540	114 885	97 802	109 608	118 097	535 137
1970	1 312 039	1 007 846	588 119	100 797	112 787	70 385	58 707	77 051	304 193
1960	1 122 928	843 661	434 312	65 247	98 272	99 325	73 187	73 318	279 267
1950	(NA)	(NA)	(NA)	(NA)	(NA)	(NA)	(NA)	(NA)	(NA)

[1]14 years and over in 1960 and in 1950. [2]Included in preceding category. [3]For years prior to 1970, includes Black and other races. [4]"Did not work in previous year" includes "Work in 1949 not reported."

Table 88. **Weeks Worked in Previous Year by Race and Sex: 1950 to 1980**—Con.

[For 1950, excludes data for Alaska and Hawaii. Data are estimates based on a sample; see Introduction. For meaning of symbols, see Introduction. For definitions of terms, see appendixes A and B]

United States Regions	Total	Worked in previous year							Did not work in previous year
		Total	50 to 52 weeks	48 and 49 weeks	40 to 47 weeks	27 to 39 weeks	14 to 26 weeks	1 to 13 weeks	

NORTH CENTRAL—Con.

Female

Total, 16 years and over[1]
1980	23 085 343	13 032 195	6 596 515	529 677	1 315 200	1 489 687	1 569 983	1 531 133	10 053 148
1970	20 338 151	10 164 560	4 366 806	560 490	1 004 630	1 284 533	1 294 243	1 653 858	10 173 591
1960	18 568 834	7 596 865	3 168 628	392 181	700 537	936 176	974 391	1 424 952	10 971 969
1950[4]	(NA)	(NA)	(NA)	(NA)	(NA)	(NA)	(NA)	(NA)	(NA)

White, 16 years and over[1]
1980	20 700 212	11 718 328	5 962 712	454 941	1 176 928	1 345 655	1 418 343	1 359 749	8 981 884
1970	(NA)	(NA)	(NA)	(NA)	(NA)	(NA)	(NA)	(NA)	(NA)
1960	17 351 423	7 068 777	2 953 764	356 408	643 243	875 661	907 001	1 332 700	10 282 646
1950[4]	(NA)	(NA)	(NA)	(NA)	(NA)	(NA)	(NA)	(NA)	(NA)

Black, 16 years and over[1][3]
1980	1 973 103	1 080 592	528 167	61 482	114 572	118 142	120 012	138 217	892 511
1970	1 520 024	829 428	352 316	68 841	106 296	95 000	90 754	116 221	690 596
1960	1 217 411	528 088	214 864	35 773	57 294	60 515	67 390	92 252	689 323
1950[4]	(NA)	(NA)	(NA)	(NA)	(NA)	(NA)	(NA)	(NA)	(NA)

SOUTH

Both Sexes

Total, 16 years and over[1]
1980	56 552 817	37 173 880	22 359 782	1 587 617	3 306 269	3 096 208	3 439 995	3 384 009	19 378 937
1970	43 320 525	27 780 298	16 322 780	1 533 860	2 251 674	2 434 927	2 267 563	2 969 495	15 540 227
1960	37 948 263	22 741 581	12 426 413	1 272 667	2 045 069	2 294 839	2 034 173	2 668 420	15 206 682
1950[4]	(NA)	(NA)	(NA)	(NA)	(NA)	(NA)	(NA)	(NA)	(NA)

White, 16 years and over[1]
1980	45 409 181	30 201 000	18 590 482	1 193 976	2 642 698	2 432 705	2 747 945	2 593 194	15 208 181
1970	(NA)	(NA)	(NA)	(NA)	(NA)	(NA)	(NA)	(NA)	(NA)
1960	30 739 565	18 236 147	10 519 602	964 971	1 525 232	1 706 247	1 520 547	1 999 548	12 503 418
1950[4]	(NA)	(NA)	(NA)	(NA)	(NA)	(NA)	(NA)	(NA)	(NA)

Black, 16 years and over[1][3]
1980	9 635 585	5 957 991	3 221 853	326 860	568 393	570 574	585 679	684 632	3 677 594
1970	7 354 582	4 666 577	2 337 511	351 289	498 269	493 966	401 803	583 739	2 688 005
1960	7 208 698	4 505 434	1 906 811	307 696	519 837	588 592	513 626	668 872	2 703 264
1950[4]	(NA)	(NA)	(NA)	(NA)	(NA)	(NA)	(NA)	(NA)	(NA)

Male

Total, 16 years and over[1]
1980	26 959 721	21 036 934	14 135 507	916 107	1 648 351	1 364 757	1 538 332	1 433 880	5 922 787
1970	20 666 324	16 769 068	11 365 054	956 717	1 206 635	1 061 525	959 379	1 219 758	3 897 256
1960	18 417 937	14 742 085	9 199 482	876 861	1 323 827	1 236 154	983 049	1 122 712	3 675 852
1950[4]	(NA)	(NA)	(NA)	(NA)	(NA)	(NA)	(NA)	(NA)	(NA)

White, 16 years and over[1]
1980	21 804 166	17 381 086	11 993 684	699 838	1 324 225	1 069 781	1 215 355	1 078 203	4 423 080
1970	(NA)	(NA)	(NA)	(NA)	(NA)	(NA)	(NA)	(NA)	(NA)
1960	15 012 372	12 167 665	7 947 338	674 045	993 491	927 136	755 316	870 339	2 844 707
1950[4]	(NA)	(NA)	(NA)	(NA)	(NA)	(NA)	(NA)	(NA)	(NA)

Black, 16 years and over[1][3]
1980	4 409 163	3 057 140	1 782 851	174 003	270 576	248 156	272 107	309 447	1 352 023
1970	3 384 672	2 523 028	1 448 669	203 079	263 159	213 301	163 978	230 842	861 644
1960	3 405 565	2 574 420	1 252 144	202 816	330 336	309 018	227 733	252 373	831 145
1950[4]	(NA)	(NA)	(NA)	(NA)	(NA)	(NA)	(NA)	(NA)	(NA)

Female

Total, 16 years and over[1]
1980	29 593 096	16 136 946	8 224 275	671 510	1 657 918	1 731 451	1 901 663	1 950 129	13 456 150
1970	22 654 201	11 011 230	4 957 726	577 143	1 045 039	1 373 402	1 308 184	1 749 736	11 642 971
1960	19 530 326	7 999 496	3 226 931	395 806	721 242	1 058 685	1 051 124	1 545 708	11 530 830
1950[4]	(NA)	(NA)	(NA)	(NA)	(NA)	(NA)	(NA)	(NA)	(NA)

White, 16 years and over[1]
1980	23 605 015	12 819 914	6 596 798	494 138	1 318 473	1 362 924	1 532 590	1 514 991	10 785 101
1970	(NA)	(NA)	(NA)	(NA)	(NA)	(NA)	(NA)	(NA)	(NA)
1960	15 727 193	6 068 482	2 572 264	290 926	531 741	779 111	765 231	1 129 209	9 658 711
1950[4]	(NA)	(NA)	(NA)	(NA)	(NA)	(NA)	(NA)	(NA)	(NA)

Black, 16 years and over[1][3]
1980	5 226 422	2 900 851	1 439 002	152 857	297 817	322 418	313 572	375 185	2 325 571
1970	3 969 910	2 143 549	888 842	148 210	235 110	280 665	237 825	352 897	1 826 361
1960	3 803 133	1 931 014	654 667	104 880	189 501	279 574	285 893	416 499	1 872 119
1950[4]	(NA)	(NA)	(NA)	(NA)	(NA)	(NA)	(NA)	(NA)	(NA)

[1]14 years and over in 1960 and in 1950. [2]Included in preceding category. [3]For years prior to 1970, includes Black and other races. [4]"Did not work in previous year" includes "Work in 1949 not reported."

Table 88. Weeks Worked in Previous Year by Race and Sex: 1950 to 1980—Con.

[For 1950, excludes data for Alaska and Hawaii. Data are estimates based on a sample; see Introduction. For meaning of symbols, see Introduction. For definitions of terms, see appendixes A and B]

United States Regions	Total	Worked in previous year							Did not work in previous year
		Total	50 to 52 weeks	48 and 49 weeks	40 to 47 weeks	27 to 39 weeks	14 to 26 weeks	1 to 13 weeks	
WEST									
Both Sexes									
Total, 16 years and over[1]									
1980	32 614 131	22 591 988	12 797 673	1 176 257	2 261 694	2 012 871	2 241 676	2 101 817	10 022 143
1970	24 168 087	16 212 727	8 993 380	966 739	1 423 972	1 455 487	1 465 890	1 907 259	7 955 360
1960	19 609 865	12 510 550	6 965 211	711 063	1 086 818	1 128 087	1 095 935	1 523 436	7 099 315
1950[4]	(NA)	(NA)	(NA)	(NA)	(NA)	(NA)	(NA)	(NA)	(NA)
White, 16 years and over[1]									
1980	27 070 881	18 821 135	10 819 987	909 753	1 894 333	1 663 091	1 841 409	1 692 562	8 249 746
1970	(NA)	(NA)	(NA)	(NA)	(NA)	(NA)	(NA)	(NA)	(NA)
1960	18 168 016	11 579 605	6 474 825	652 283	1 003 469	1 040 292	1 005 788	1 402 948	6 588 411
1950[4]	(NA)	(NA)	(NA)	(NA)	(NA)	(NA)	(NA)	(NA)	(NA)
Black, 16 years and over[1][3]									
1980	1 604 581	1 051 545	570 092	67 182	102 505	92 619	106 458	112 689	553 036
1970	1 060 973	713 730	364 245	58 179	75 455	68 919	63 510	83 422	347 243
1960	1 441 849	930 945	490 386	58 780	83 349	87 795	90 147	120 488	510 904
1950[4]	(NA)	(NA)	(NA)	(NA)	(NA)	(NA)	(NA)	(NA)	(NA)
Male									
Total, 16 years and over[1]									
1980	15 966 419	12 911 244	8 154 541	698 087	1 196 358	947 508	1 020 396	894 354	3 055 175
1970	11 778 744	9 890 742	6 388 473	622 219	792 882	681 561	636 018	769 589	1 888 002
1960	9 761 625	8 194 701	5 281 014	503 146	690 185	618 401	504 323	597 632	1 566 924
1950[4]	(NA)	(NA)	(NA)	(NA)	(NA)	(NA)	(NA)	(NA)	(NA)
White, 16 years and over[1]									
1980	13 214 902	10 786 564	6 948 731	538 848	999 636	770 650	824 700	703 999	2 428 338
1970	(NA)	(NA)	(NA)	(NA)	(NA)	(NA)	(NA)	(NA)	(NA)
1960	9 016 669	7 597 435	4 925 323	463 759	639 551	568 002	458 093	542 707	1 419 234
1950[4]	(NA)	(NA)	(NA)	(NA)	(NA)	(NA)	(NA)	(NA)	(NA)
Black, 16 years and over[1][3]									
1980	792 100	571 384	330 715	36 863	50 469	44 377	53 320	55 640	220 716
1970	519 005	405 947	236 406	33 445	39 166	31 644	28 276	37 010	113 058
1960	744 956	597 266	355 691	39 387	50 634	50 399	46 230	54 925	147 690
1950[4]	(NA)	(NA)	(NA)	(NA)	(NA)	(NA)	(NA)	(NA)	(NA)
Female									
Total, 16 years and over[1]									
1980	16 647 712	9 680 744	4 643 132	478 170	1 065 336	1 065 363	1 221 280	1 207 463	6 966 968
1970	12 389 343	6 321 985	2 604 907	344 520	631 090	773 926	829 872	1 137 670	6 067 358
1960	9 848 240	4 315 849	1 684 197	207 917	396 633	509 686	591 612	925 804	5 532 391
1950[4]	(NA)	(NA)	(NA)	(NA)	(NA)	(NA)	(NA)	(NA)	(NA)
White, 16 years and over[1]									
1980	13 855 979	8 034 571	3 871 256	370 905	894 697	892 441	1 016 709	988 563	5 821 408
1970	(NA)	(NA)	(NA)	(NA)	(NA)	(NA)	(NA)	(NA)	(NA)
1960	9 151 347	3 982 170	1 549 502	188 524	363 918	472 290	547 695	860 241	5 169 177
1950[4]	(NA)	(NA)	(NA)	(NA)	(NA)	(NA)	(NA)	(NA)	(NA)
Black, 16 years and over[1][3]									
1980	812 481	480 161	239 377	30 319	52 036	48 242	53 138	57 049	332 320
1970	541 968	307 783	127 839	24 734	36 289	37 275	35 234	46 412	234 185
1960	696 893	333 679	134 695	19 393	32 715	37 396	43 917	65 563	363 214
1950[4]	(NA)	(NA)	(NA)	(NA)	(NA)	(NA)	(NA)	(NA)	(NA)

[1]14 years and over in 1960 and in 1950. [2]included in preceding category. [3]for years prior to 1970, includes Black and other races. [4]"Did not work in previous year" includes "Work in 1949 not reported."

Table 89. **Occupation of Employed Persons by Race and Sex: 1980 and 1970**

[Data are estimates based on a sample; see Introduction. For meaning of symbols, see Introduction. For definitions of terms, see appendixes A and B]

United States Regions	1980 Total	1980 White	1980 Black	1980 Percent Total	1980 Percent White	1980 Percent Black	1970 Total	1970 White	1970 Black	1970 Percent Total	1970 Percent White	1970 Percent Black
UNITED STATES												
Employed persons 16 years and over	**97 639 355**	**84 027 375**	**9 334 048**	**100.0**	**100.0**	**100.0**	**76 553 161**	**68 282 104**	**7 361 105**	**100.0**	**100.0**	**100.0**
Managerial and professional specialty occupations	22 151 648	20 067 464	1 317 080	22.7	23.9	14.1	14 529 543	13 670 182	672 796	19.0	20.0	9.1
Executive, administrative, and managerial occupations	10 133 551	9 336 266	487 432	10.4	11.1	5.2	5 882 313	5 649 388	173 701	7.7	8.3	2.4
Professional specialty occupations	12 018 097	10 731 198	829 648	12.3	12.8	8.9	8 647 230	8 020 794	499 095	11.3	11.7	6.8
Technical, sales, and administrative support occupations	29 593 506	26 150 562	2 352 079	30.3	31.1	25.2	22 346 736	20 768 058	1 340 100	29.2	30.4	18.2
Technicians and related support occupations	2 981 951	2 590 639	247 834	3.1	3.1	2.7	1 776 529	1 618 801	128 997	2.3	2.4	1.8
Sales occupations	9 760 157	8 998 463	468 364	10.0	10.7	5.0	7 770 844	7 442 011	262 101	10.2	10.9	3.6
Administrative support occupations, including clerical	16 851 398	14 561 460	1 635 881	17.3	17.3	17.5	12 799 363	11 707 246	949 002	16.7	17.1	12.9
Service occupations	12 629 425	9 765 973	2 156 194	12.9	11.6	23.1	9 707 741	7 503 289	2 043 573	12.7	11.0	27.8
Private household occupations	589 352	312 472	241 717	0.6	0.4	2.6	1 151 937	526 155	609 574	1.5	0.8	8.3
Protective service occupations	1 475 315	1 253 799	176 304	1.5	1.5	1.9	1 036 869	944 545	79 779	1.4	1.4	1.1
Service occupations, except protective and household	10 564 758	8 199 702	1 738 173	10.8	9.8	18.6	7 518 935	6 032 589	1 354 220	9.8	8.8	18.4
Farming, forestry, and fishing occupations	2 811 258	2 437 307	182 190	2.9	2.9	2.0	2 906 172	2 544 096	309 859	3.8	3.7	4.2
Precision production, craft, and repair occupations	12 594 175	11 249 214	834 947	12.9	13.4	8.9	10 800 039	9 985 635	710 263	14.1	14.6	9.6
Operators, fabricators, and laborers	17 859 343	14 356 855	2 491 558	18.3	17.1	26.7	16 262 930	13 810 844	2 284 514	21.2	20.2	31.0
Machine operators, assemblers, and inspectors	9 084 988	7 242 863	1 256 932	9.3	8.6	13.5	8 376 549	7 220 826	1 067 860	10.9	10.6	14.5
Transportation and material moving occupations	4 389 412	3 665 245	563 210	4.5	4.4	6.0	3 738 884	3 223 141	486 088	4.9	4.7	6.6
Handlers, equipment cleaners, helpers, and laborers	4 384 943	3 448 747	671 416	4.5	4.1	7.2	4 147 497	3 366 877	730 566	5.4	4.9	9.9
Employed females 16 years and over	**41 634 665**	**35 183 388**	**4 659 177**	**100.0**	**100.0**	**100.0**	**28 929 776**	**25 252 676**	**3 309 069**	**100.0**	**100.0**	**100.0**
Managerial and professional specialty occupations	8 954 843	7 876 425	770 809	21.5	22.4	16.5	4 904 666	4 459 637	379 862	17.0	17.7	11.5
Executive, administrative, and managerial occupations	3 070 247	2 746 156	219 108	7.4	7.8	4.7	1 077 753	1 007 875	55 592	3.7	4.0	1.7
Professional specialty occupations	5 884 596	5 130 269	551 701	14.1	14.6	11.8	3 826 913	3 451 762	324 270	13.2	13.7	9.8
Technical, sales, and administrative support occupations	18 971 458	16 646 739	1 639 737	45.6	47.3	35.2	13 116 176	12 110 736	862 529	45.3	48.0	26.1
Technicians and related support occupations	1 302 889	1 089 273	155 450	3.1	3.1	3.3	611 246	517 740	83 934	2.1	2.1	2.5
Sales occupations	4 671 493	4 231 750	283 771	11.2	12.0	6.1	3 154 074	2 978 801	144 387	10.9	11.8	4.4
Administrative support occupations, including clerical	12 997 076	11 325 716	1 200 516	31.2	32.2	25.8	9 350 856	8 614 195	634 208	32.3	34.1	19.2
Service occupations	7 451 845	5 725 271	1 363 664	17.9	16.3	29.3	5 783 653	4 312 271	1 386 774	20.0	17.1	41.9
Private household occupations	562 886	297 021	233 024	1.4	0.8	5.0	1 109 855	504 589	590 547	3.8	2.0	17.8
Protective service occupations	168 861	132 677	30 648	0.4	0.4	0.7	67 300	57 079	9 135	0.2	0.2	0.3
Service occupations, except protective and household	6 720 098	5 295 573	1 099 992	16.1	15.1	23.6	4 606 498	3 750 603	787 092	15.9	14.9	23.8
Farming, forestry, and fishing occupations	404 269	347 744	25 368	1.0	1.0	0.5	254 171	203 610	43 582	0.9	0.8	1.3
Precision production, craft, and repair occupations	977 950	802 126	108 755	2.3	2.3	2.3	764 525	673 005	80 799	2.6	2.7	2.4
Operators, fabricators, and laborers	4 874 300	3 785 083	750 844	11.7	10.8	16.1	4 106 585	3 493 417	555 523	14.2	13.8	16.8
Machine operators, assemblers, and inspectors	3 646 237	2 803 586	571 893	8.8	8.0	12.3	3 237 399	2 756 454	433 926	11.2	10.9	13.1
Transportation and material moving occupations	347 880	293 092	44 147	0.8	0.8	0.9	155 415	137 832	16 543	0.5	0.5	0.5
Handlers, equipment cleaners, helpers, and laborers	880 183	688 405	134 804	2.1	2.0	2.9	713 771	599 131	105 054	2.5	2.4	3.2
NORTHEAST												
Employed persons 16 years and over	**21 393 306**	**19 010 511**	**1 742 419**	**100.0**	**100.0**	**100.0**	**19 270 754**	**17 636 460**	**1 510 414**	**100.0**	**100.0**	**100.0**
Managerial and professional specialty occupations	5 224 287	4 809 810	273 012	24.4	25.3	15.7	3 864 572	3 679 922	149 367	20.1	20.9	9.9
Executive, administrative, and managerial occupations	2 286 556	2 130 860	104 406	10.7	11.2	6.0	1 535 624	1 480 348	45 645	8.0	8.4	3.0
Professional specialty occupations	2 937 731	2 678 950	168 606	13.7	14.1	9.7	2 328 948	2 199 574	103 722	12.1	12.5	6.9
Technical, sales, and administrative support occupations	6 764 667	6 056 275	543 125	31.6	31.9	31.2	6 008 730	5 583 243	396 100	31.2	31.7	26.2
Technicians and related support occupations	658 999	584 697	51 347	3.1	3.1	2.9	467 459	427 362	36 217	2.4	2.4	2.4
Sales occupations	2 030 673	1 904 304	85 552	9.5	10.0	4.9	1 925 414	1 851 327	65 943	10.0	10.5	4.4
Administrative support occupations, including clerical	4 074 995	3 567 274	406 226	19.0	18.8	23.3	3 615 857	3 304 554	293 940	18.8	18.7	19.5
Service occupations	2 760 450	2 252 173	404 121	12.9	11.8	23.2	2 328 450	1 938 996	366 145	12.1	11.0	24.2
Private household occupations	109 972	68 119	37 148	0.5	0.4	2.1	197 681	113 052	82 338	1.0	0.6	5.5
Protective service occupations	397 367	340 612	49 151	1.9	1.8	2.8	327 273	296 500	28 533	1.7	1.7	1.9
Service occupations, except protective and household	2 253 111	1 843 442	317 822	10.5	9.7	18.2	1 803 496	1 529 444	255 274	9.4	8.7	16.9
Farming, forestry, and fishing occupations	276 946	265 614	7 061	1.3	1.4	0.4	289 901	273 151	14 633	1.5	1.5	1.0
Precision production, craft, and repair occupations	2 530 320	2 337 741	138 459	11.8	12.3	7.9	2 624 426	2 467 866	146 887	13.6	14.0	9.7
Operators, fabricators, and laborers	3 836 636	3 288 898	376 641	17.9	17.3	21.6	4 154 675	3 693 282	437 282	21.6	20.9	29.0
Machine operators, assemblers, and inspectors	2 117 367	1 795 575	199 675	9.9	9.4	11.5	2 320 096	2 076 838	225 063	12.0	11.8	14.9
Transportation and material moving occupations	857 005	751 081	87 093	4.0	4.0	5.0	865 081	771 092	91 344	4.5	4.4	6.0
Handlers, equipment cleaners, helpers, and laborers	862 264	742 242	89 873	4.0	3.9	5.2	969 498	845 352	120 875	5.0	4.8	8.0
Employed females 16 years and over	**9 226 449**	**8 061 308**	**894 113**	**100.0**	**100.0**	**100.0**	**7 380 815**	**6 635 998**	**695 147**	**100.0**	**100.0**	**100.0**
Managerial and professional specialty occupations	2 058 773	1 852 679	153 248	22.3	23.0	17.1	1 245 207	1 157 249	76 708	16.9	17.4	11.0
Executive, administrative, and managerial occupations	637 192	578 096	44 852	6.9	7.2	5.0	248 698	233 026	13 584	3.4	3.5	2.0
Professional specialty occupations	1 421 581	1 274 583	108 396	15.4	15.8	12.1	996 509	924 223	63 124	13.5	13.9	9.1
Technical, sales, and administrative support occupations	4 288 423	3 823 958	371 055	46.5	47.4	41.5	3 492 717	3 222 510	254 039	47.3	48.6	36.5
Technicians and related support occupations	285 016	244 716	30 775	3.1	3.0	3.4	159 127	135 368	22 285	2.2	2.0	3.2
Sales occupations	949 324	882 849	47 566	10.3	11.0	5.3	761 902	725 797	32 803	10.3	10.9	4.7
Administrative support occupations, including clerical	3 054 083	2 696 393	292 714	33.1	33.4	32.7	2 571 688	2 361 345	198 951	34.8	35.6	28.6
Service occupations	1 485 917	1 210 956	237 934	16.1	15.0	26.6	1 209 436	982 698	218 144	16.4	14.8	31.4
Private household occupations	104 246	64 188	35 813	1.1	0.8	4.0	188 763	107 299	79 433	2.6	1.6	11.4
Protective service occupations	44 823	36 471	7 430	0.5	0.5	0.8	25 015	21 446	3 230	0.3	0.3	0.5
Service occupations, except protective and household	1 336 848	1 110 297	194 691	14.5	13.8	21.8	995 658	853 953	135 481	13.5	12.9	19.5
Farming, forestry, and fishing occupations	44 461	43 277	682	0.5	0.5	0.1	30 505	27 144	3 115	0.4	0.4	0.4
Precision production, craft, and repair occupations	193 692	166 649	17 666	2.1	2.1	2.0	191 479	172 263	18 043	2.6	2.6	2.6
Operators, fabricators, and laborers	1 155 183	963 789	113 528	12.5	12.0	12.7	1 211 471	1 074 134	125 098	16.4	16.2	18.0
Machine operators, assemblers, and inspectors	895 454	739 442	88 844	9.7	9.2	9.9	980 164	867 492	101 598	13.3	13.1	14.6
Transportation and material moving occupations	68 661	62 154	4 701	0.7	0.8	0.5	33 887	31 368	2 418	0.5	0.5	0.3
Handlers, equipment cleaners, helpers, and laborers	191 068	162 193	19 983	2.1	2.0	2.2	197 420	175 274	21 082	2.7	2.6	3.0
NORTH CENTRAL												
Employed persons 16 years and over	**25 517 077**	**23 274 239**	**1 776 892**	**100.0**	**100.0**	**100.0**	**21 649 366**	**20 032 516**	**1 514 198**	**100.0**	**100.0**	**100.0**
Managerial and professional specialty occupations	5 426 412	5 061 928	261 782	21.3	21.7	14.7	3 832 421	3 666 967	137 033	17.7	18.3	9.0
Executive, administrative, and managerial occupations	2 451 428	2 322 490	99 392	9.6	10.0	5.6	1 548 248	1 503 188	39 320	7.2	7.5	2.6
Professional specialty occupations	2 974 984	2 739 438	162 390	11.7	11.8	9.1	2 284 173	2 163 779	97 713	10.6	10.8	6.5
Technical, sales, and administrative support occupations	7 457 483	6 852 124	499 556	29.2	29.4	28.1	6 090 544	5 734 525	333 688	28.1	28.6	22.0
Technicians and related support occupations	731 176	660 697	50 751	2.9	2.8	2.9	468 168	433 201	31 205	2.2	2.2	2.1
Sales occupations	2 467 210	2 349 826	93 831	9.7	10.1	5.3	2 130 061	2 060 712	64 305	9.8	10.3	4.2
Administrative support occupations, including clerical	4 259 097	3 841 601	354 974	16.7	16.5	20.0	3 492 315	3 240 612	238 178	16.1	16.2	15.7
Service occupations	3 393 136	2 939 243	379 262	13.3	12.6	21.3	2 711 725	2 334 296	358 971	12.5	11.7	23.7
Private household occupations	112 073	88 272	22 052	0.4	0.4	1.2	231 660	166 823	63 080	1.1	0.8	4.2
Protective service occupations	334 907	291 961	38 432	1.3	1.3	2.2	249 663	228 977	18 865	1.2	1.1	1.2
Service occupations, except protective and household	2 946 156	2 559 010	318 778	11.5	11.0	17.9	2 230 402	1 938 496	277 026	10.3	9.7	18.3
Farming, forestry, and fishing occupations	982 202	968 048	7 416	3.8	4.2	0.4	1 040 819	1 022 631	14 399	4.8	5.1	1.0
Precision production, craft, and repair occupations	3 212 426	3 020 677	145 853	12.6	13.0	8.2	3 106 457	2 943 582	151 895	14.3	14.7	10.0
Operators, fabricators, and laborers	5 045 418	4 432 219	483 023	19.8	19.0	27.2	4 867 400	4 330 515	518 212	22.5	21.6	34.2
Machine operators, assemblers, and inspectors	2 700 632	2 340 126	278 498	10.6	10.1	15.7	2 608 138	2 311 083	286 491	12.0	11.5	18.9
Transportation and material moving occupations	1 187 383	1 075 867	95 250	4.7	4.6	5.4	1 065 809	973 220	89 933	4.9	4.9	5.9
Handlers, equipment cleaners, helpers, and laborers	1 157 403	1 016 226	109 275	4.5	4.4	6.1	1 193 453	1 046 212	141 788	5.5	5.2	9.4

Table 89. **Occupation of Employed Persons by Race and Sex: 1980 and 1970**—Con.

[Data are estimates based on a sample; see Introduction. For meaning of symbols, see Introduction. For definitions of terms, see appendixes A and B]

United States Regions	1980						1970					
				Percent						Percent		
	Total	White	Black	Total	White	Black	Total	White	Black	Total	White	Black
NORTH CENTRAL—Con.												
Employed females 16 years and over	**10 804 271**	**9 720 757**	**892 509**	**100.0**	**100.0**	**100.0**	**7 991 626**	**7 282 944**	**665 839**	**100.0**	**100.0**	**100.0**
Managerial and professional specialty occupations	2 190 652	1 997 536	152 784	20.3	20.5	17.1	1 298 468	1 213 128	74 990	16.2	16.7	11.3
Executive, administrative, and managerial occupations	703 001	647 548	45 872	6.5	6.7	5.1	270 095	255 356	13 284	3.4	3.5	2.0
Professional specialty occupations	1 487 651	1 349 988	106 912	13.8	13.9	12.0	1 028 373	957 772	61 706	12.9	13.2	9.3
Technical, sales, and administrative support occupations	4 878 869	4 454 089	359 247	45.2	45.8	40.3	3 649 343	3 408 522	227 096	45.7	46.8	34.1
Technicians and related support occupations	340 325	299 071	33 112	3.1	3.1	3.7	167 527	144 587	21 336	2.1	2.0	3.2
Sales occupations	1 215 754	1 145 273	57 599	11.3	11.8	6.5	912 522	872 088	38 045	11.4	12.0	5.7
Administrative support occupations, including clerical	3 322 790	3 009 745	268 536	30.8	31.0	30.1	2 569 294	2 391 847	167 715	32.1	32.8	25.2
Service occupations	2 109 217	1 844 578	225 658	19.5	19.0	25.3	1 680 420	1 441 836	227 652	21.0	19.8	34.2
Private household occupations	107 856	85 176	21 080	1.0	0.9	2.4	224 286	161 832	60 814	2.8	2.2	9.1
Protective service occupations	40 409	32 417	7 406	0.4	0.3	0.8	15 784	13 532	2 113	0.2	0.2	0.3
Service occupations, except protective and household	1 960 952	1 726 985	197 172	18.1	17.8	22.1	1 440 350	1 266 472	164 725	18.0	17.4	24.7
Farming, forestry, and fishing occupations	138 801	136 469	1 225	1.3	1.4	0.1	73 404	69 764	3 133	0.9	1.0	0.5
Precision production, craft, and repair occupations	236 737	212 393	18 364	2.2	2.2	2.1	228 778	208 816	18 639	2.9	2.9	2.8
Operators, fabricators, and laborers	1 249 995	1 075 692	135 231	11.6	11.1	15.2	1 061 213	940 878	114 329	13.3	12.9	17.2
Machine operators, assemblers, and inspectors	907 025	775 596	101 562	8.4	8.0	11.4	801 713	711 416	85 511	10.0	9.8	12.8
Transportation and material moving occupations	96 641	86 918	8 603	0.9	0.9	1.0	46 710	43 317	3 266	0.6	0.6	0.5
Handlers, equipment cleaners, helpers, and laborers	246 329	213 178	25 066	2.3	2.2	2.8	212 790	186 145	25 552	2.7	2.6	3.8
SOUTH												
Employed persons 16 years and over	**31 678 379**	**25 844 773**	**4 976 037**	**100.0**	**100.0**	**100.0**	**22 797 365**	**18 895 925**	**3 799 101**	**100.0**	**100.0**	**100.0**
Managerial and professional specialty occupations	6 814 143	6 039 771	632 612	21.5	23.4	12.7	4 052 129	3 709 621	321 493	17.8	19.6	8.5
Executive, administrative, and managerial occupations	3 179 365	2 907 127	217 466	10.0	11.2	4.4	1 668 141	1 592 483	69 597	7.3	8.4	1.8
Professional specialty occupations	3 634 778	3 132 644	415 146	11.5	12.1	8.3	2 383 988	2 117 138	251 896	10.5	11.2	6.6
Technical, sales, and administrative support occupations	9 351 578	8 123 053	1 024 229	29.5	31.4	20.6	6 286 621	5 796 298	468 629	27.6	30.7	12.3
Technicians and related support occupations	965 368	820 123	116 949	3.0	3.2	2.4	498 438	449 277	46 031	2.2	2.4	1.2
Sales occupations	3 209 180	2 913 489	231 061	10.1	11.3	4.6	2 328 778	2 215 889	105 977	10.2	11.7	2.8
Administrative support occupations, including clerical	5 177 030	4 389 441	676 219	16.3	17.0	13.6	3 459 405	3 131 132	316 621	15.2	16.6	8.3
Service occupations	3 958 538	2 617 397	1 200 650	12.5	10.1	24.1	2 974 293	1 776 242	1 180 842	13.0	9.4	31.1
Private household occupations	265 624	85 245	172 090	0.8	0.3	3.5	571 647	132 550	436 482	2.5	0.7	11.5
Protective service occupations	464 008	386 488	69 247	1.5	1.5	1.4	283 256	254 853	25 653	1.2	1.3	0.7
Service occupations, except protective and household	3 228 906	2 145 664	959 313	10.2	8.3	19.3	2 119 390	1 388 839	718 707	9.3	7.3	18.9
Farming, forestry, and fishing occupations	933 277	740 543	158 566	2.9	2.9	3.2	1 053 333	775 931	270 779	4.6	4.1	7.1
Precision production, craft, and repair occupations	4 399 634	3 800 629	472 595	13.9	14.7	9.5	3 335 861	2 966 896	355 512	14.6	15.7	9.4
Operators, fabricators, and laborers	6 221 209	4 523 380	1 487 385	19.6	17.5	29.9	5 095 128	3 870 937	1 201 846	22.3	20.5	31.6
Machine operators, assemblers, and inspectors	3 051 863	2 226 013	717 672	9.6	8.6	14.4	2 530 476	2 019 113	499 337	11.1	10.7	13.1
Transportation and material moving occupations	1 571 128	1 193 245	338 217	5.0	4.6	6.8	1 219 943	937 747	278 166	5.4	5.0	7.3
Handlers, equipment cleaners, helpers, and laborers	1 598 218	1 104 122	431 496	5.0	4.3	8.7	1 344 709	914 077	424 343	5.9	4.8	11.2
Employed females 16 years and over	**13 543 155**	**10 729 435**	**2 465 524**	**100.0**	**100.0**	**100.0**	**8 745 633**	**6 997 858**	**1 707 016**	**100.0**	**100.0**	**100.0**
Managerial and professional specialty occupations	2 862 202	2 419 306	387 181	21.1	22.5	15.7	1 452 304	1 249 818	195 254	16.6	17.9	11.4
Executive, administrative, and managerial occupations	989 805	873 260	98 644	7.3	8.1	4.0	323 142	299 065	22 525	3.7	4.3	1.3
Professional specialty occupations	1 872 397	1 546 046	288 537	13.8	14.4	11.7	1 129 162	950 753	172 729	12.9	13.6	10.1
Technical, sales, and administrative support occupations	5 980 289	5 133 723	717 756	44.2	47.8	29.1	3 630 634	3 328 993	288 779	41.5	47.6	16.9
Technicians and related support occupations	434 207	346 434	76 082	3.2	3.2	3.1	178 032	146 082	30 644	2.0	2.1	1.8
Sales occupations	1 539 486	1 355 412	148 059	11.4	12.6	6.0	929 941	866 174	60 724	10.6	12.4	3.6
Administrative support occupations, including clerical	4 006 596	3 431 877	493 615	29.6	32.0	20.0	2 522 661	2 316 737	197 411	28.8	33.1	11.6
Service occupations	2 428 167	1 537 299	807 208	17.9	14.3	32.7	1 929 949	1 058 290	860 931	22.1	15.1	50.4
Private household occupations	255 322	81 058	166 341	1.9	0.8	6.7	552 612	126 524	423 636	6.3	1.8	24.8
Protective service occupations	51 387	37 793	12 615	0.4	0.4	0.5	16 505	13 190	3 165	0.2	0.2	0.2
Service occupations, except protective and household	2 121 458	1 418 448	628 252	15.7	13.2	25.5	1 360 832	918 576	434 130	15.6	13.1	25.4
Farming, forestry, and fishing occupations	125 589	98 505	22 324	0.9	0.9	0.9	98 604	61 460	36 215	1.1	0.9	2.1
Precision production, craft, and repair occupations	331 892	257 549	62 430	2.5	2.4	2.5	231 805	192 340	38 126	2.7	2.7	2.2
Operators, fabricators, and laborers	1 815 016	1 283 053	468 625	13.4	12.0	19.0	1 402 337	1 106 957	287 711	16.0	15.8	16.9
Machine operators, assemblers, and inspectors	1 397 922	988 470	358 773	10.3	9.2	14.6	1 141 998	911 408	224 155	13.1	13.0	13.1
Transportation and material moving occupations	119 107	90 359	26 684	0.9	0.8	1.1	50 835	40 459	10 203	0.6	0.6	0.6
Handlers, equipment cleaners, helpers, and laborers	297 987	204 224	83 168	2.2	1.9	3.4	209 504	155 090	53 353	2.4	2.2	3.1
WEST												
Employed persons 16 years and over	**19 050 593**	**15 897 852**	**838 700**	**100.0**	**100.0**	**100.0**	**12 835 676**	**11 717 203**	**537 392**	**100.0**	**100.0**	**100.0**
Managerial and professional specialty occupations	4 686 806	4 155 955	149 674	24.6	26.1	17.8	2 780 421	2 613 672	64 903	21.7	22.3	12.1
Executive, administrative, and managerial occupations	2 216 202	1 975 789	66 168	11.6	12.4	7.9	1 130 300	1 073 369	19 139	8.8	9.2	3.6
Professional specialty occupations	2 470 604	2 180 166	83 506	13.0	13.7	10.0	1 650 121	1 540 303	45 764	12.9	13.1	8.5
Technical, sales, and administrative support occupations	6 019 778	5 119 110	285 169	31.6	32.2	34.0	3 960 841	3 653 992	141 683	30.9	31.2	26.4
Technicians and related support occupations	626 408	525 122	28 787	3.3	3.3	3.4	342 464	308 961	15 544	2.7	2.6	2.9
Sales occupations	2 053 094	1 830 844	57 920	10.8	11.5	6.9	1 386 591	1 314 083	25 876	10.8	11.2	4.8
Administrative support occupations, including clerical	3 340 276	2 763 144	198 462	17.5	17.4	23.7	2 231 786	2 030 948	100 263	17.4	17.3	18.7
Service occupations	2 517 301	1 957 160	172 161	13.2	12.3	20.5	1 693 273	1 453 755	137 615	13.2	12.4	25.6
Private household occupations	101 683	70 836	10 427	0.5	0.4	1.2	150 949	113 730	27 674	1.2	1.0	5.1
Protective service occupations	279 033	234 738	19 474	1.5	1.5	2.3	176 677	164 215	6 728	1.4	1.4	1.3
Service occupations, except protective and household	2 136 585	1 651 586	142 260	11.2	10.4	17.0	1 365 647	1 175 810	103 213	10.6	10.0	19.2
Farming, forestry, and fishing occupations	618 833	463 102	9 147	3.2	2.9	1.1	522 119	472 383	10 048	4.1	4.0	1.9
Precision production, craft, and repair occupations	2 451 795	2 090 167	78 040	12.9	13.1	9.3	1 733 295	1 607 291	55 969	13.5	13.7	10.4
Operators, fabricators, and laborers	2 756 080	2 112 358	144 509	14.5	13.3	17.2	2 145 727	1 916 110	127 174	16.7	16.4	23.7
Machine operators, assemblers, and inspectors	1 215 126	881 149	61 087	6.4	5.5	7.3	917 839	813 792	56 969	7.2	6.9	10.6
Transportation and material moving occupations	773 896	645 052	42 650	4.1	4.1	5.1	588 051	541 082	26 645	4.6	4.6	5.0
Handlers, equipment cleaners, helpers, and laborers	767 058	586 157	40 772	4.0	3.7	4.9	639 837	561 236	43 560	5.0	4.8	8.1
Employed females 16 years and over	**8 060 790**	**6 671 888**	**407 031**	**100.0**	**100.0**	**100.0**	**4 811 702**	**4 335 876**	**241 067**	**100.0**	**100.0**	**100.0**
Managerial and professional specialty occupations	1 843 216	1 606 904	77 596	22.9	24.1	19.1	908 687	839 442	32 910	18.9	19.4	13.7
Executive, administrative, and managerial occupations	740 249	647 252	29 740	9.2	9.7	7.3	235 818	220 428	6 199	4.9	5.1	2.6
Professional specialty occupations	1 102 967	959 652	47 856	13.7	14.4	11.8	672 869	619 014	26 711	14.0	14.3	11.1
Technical, sales, and administrative support occupations	3 823 877	3 234 969	191 679	47.4	48.5	47.1	2 343 482	2 150 711	92 615	48.7	49.6	38.4
Technicians and related support occupations	243 341	199 052	15 481	3.0	3.0	3.8	106 560	91 703	9 669	2.2	2.1	4.0
Sales occupations	966 929	848 216	30 547	12.0	12.7	7.5	549 709	514 742	12 815	11.4	11.9	5.3
Administrative support occupations, including clerical	2 613 607	2 187 701	145 651	32.4	32.8	35.8	1 687 213	1 544 266	70 131	35.1	35.6	29.1
Service occupations	1 428 544	1 132 438	92 864	17.7	17.0	22.8	963 848	829 447	80 047	20.0	19.1	33.2
Private household occupations	95 462	66 599	9 790	1.2	1.0	2.4	144 194	108 934	26 664	3.0	2.5	11.1
Protective service occupations	32 242	25 996	3 197	0.4	0.4	0.8	9 996	8 911	627	0.2	0.2	0.3
Service occupations, except protective and household	1 300 840	1 039 843	79 877	16.1	15.6	19.6	809 658	711 602	52 756	16.8	16.4	21.9
Farming, forestry, and fishing occupations	95 418	69 493	1 137	1.2	1.0	0.3	51 658	45 242	1 119	1.1	1.0	0.5
Precision production, craft, and repair occupations	215 629	165 535	10 295	2.7	2.5	2.5	112 463	99 586	5 991	2.3	2.3	2.5
Operators, fabricators, and laborers	654 106	462 549	33 460	8.1	6.9	8.2	431 564	371 448	28 385	9.0	8.6	11.8
Machine operators, assemblers, and inspectors	445 836	300 078	22 714	5.5	4.5	5.6	313 524	266 138	22 662	6.5	6.1	9.4
Transportation and material moving occupations	63 471	53 661	4 159	0.8	0.8	1.0	23 983	22 688	656	0.5	0.5	0.3
Handlers, equipment cleaners, helpers, and laborers	144 799	108 810	6 587	1.8	1.6	1.6	94 057	82 622	5 067	2.0	1.9	2.1

Table 90. Industry and Class of Worker of Employed Persons by Race and Sex: 1980 and 1970

[Data are estimates based on a sample; see Introduction. For meaning of symbols, see Introduction. For definitions of terms, see appendixes A and B]

United States

	1980 Total	1980 White	1980 Black	1980 Percent Total	1980 Percent White	1980 Percent Black	1970 Total	1970 White	1970 Black	1970 Percent Total	1970 Percent White	1970 Percent Black
INDUSTRY												
Employed persons 16 years and over	97 639 355	84 027 375	9 334 048	100.0	100.0	100.0	76 553 161	68 282 104	7 361 105	100.0	100.0	100.0
Agriculture, forestry, and fisheries	2 913 589	2 554 976	161 065	3.0	3.0	1.7	2 837 048	2 523 559	262 739	3.7	3.7	3.6
Mining	1 028 178	948 911	42 029	1.1	1.1	0.5	603 645	577 465	22 020	0.8	0.8	0.3
Construction	5 739 598	5 105 836	403 992	5.9	6.1	4.3	4 572 226	4 132 992	392 658	6.0	6.1	5.3
Manufacturing	21 914 754	18 705 053	2 163 603	22.4	22.3	23.2	19 866 351	17 905 394	1 791 429	26.0	26.2	24.3
Nondurable goods	8 435 543	7 063 668	940 224	8.6	8.4	10.1	7 990 580	7 166 605	743 651	10.4	10.5	10.1
Durable goods	13 479 211	11 641 385	1 223 379	13.8	13.9	13.1	11 875 771	10 738 789	1 047 778	15.5	15.7	14.2
Transportation, communications, and other public utilities	7 087 455	6 003 704	827 283	7.3	7.1	8.9	5 930 826	5 231 725	642 509	7.7	7.7	8.7
Wholesale and retail trade	19 933 926	17 788 047	1 295 626	20.4	21.2	13.9	15 376 323	14 167 905	1 017 212	20.1	20.7	13.8
Wholesale trade	4 217 232	3 796 001	259 997	4.3	4.5	2.8	3 389 995	(NA)	(NA)	4.4	(NA)	(NA)
Retail trade	15 716 694	13 992 046	1 035 629	16.1	16.7	11.1	11 986 328	(NA)	(NA)	15.7	(NA)	(NA)
Finance, insurance, and real estate	5 898 059	5 231 499	449 853	6.0	6.2	4.8	3 847 030	3 583 974	223 302	5.0	5.2	3.0
Business and repair services	4 081 677	3 564 988	340 054	4.2	4.2	3.6	2 496 760	2 269 980	197 486	3.3	3.3	2.7
Personal services	3 075 764	2 312 315	571 224	3.2	2.8	6.1	3 467 006	2 428 191	978 421	4.5	3.6	13.3
Entertainment and recreation services	1 007 070	889 144	76 419	1.0	1.1	0.8	631 789	570 471	52 494	0.8	0.8	0.7
Professional and related services	19 811 819	16 719 601	2 300 399	20.3	19.9	24.6	13 334 141	11 727 674	1 418 112	17.4	17.2	19.3
Public administration	5 147 466	4 203 301	702 501	5.3	5.0	7.5	3 590 016	3 162 774	362 723	4.7	4.6	4.9
Employed females 16 years and over	41 634 665	35 183 388	4 659 177	100.0	100.0	100.0	28 929 776	(NA)	(NA)	100.0	(NA)	(NA)
Agriculture, forestry, and fisheries	522 050	456 765	29 342	1.3	1.3	0.6	318 069	(NA)	(NA)	1.1	(NA)	(NA)
Mining	124 173	110 782	8 536	0.3	0.3	0.2	50 331	(NA)	(NA)	0.2	(NA)	(NA)
Construction	479 766	438 746	26 234	1.2	1.2	0.6	267 236	(NA)	(NA)	0.9	(NA)	(NA)
Manufacturing	6 995 805	5 781 947	810 178	16.8	16.4	17.4	5 663 651	(NA)	(NA)	19.6	(NA)	(NA)
Nondurable goods	3 493 250	2 839 365	437 426	8.4	8.1	9.4	3 126 690	(NA)	(NA)	10.8	(NA)	(NA)
Durable goods	3 502 555	2 942 582	372 752	8.4	8.4	8.0	2 536 961	(NA)	(NA)	8.8	(NA)	(NA)
Transportation, communications, and other public utilities	1 752 965	1 446 084	239 996	4.2	4.1	5.2	1 264 207	(NA)	(NA)	4.4	(NA)	(NA)
Wholesale and retail trade	9 138 160	8 201 124	588 278	21.9	23.3	12.6	6 335 015	(NA)	(NA)	21.9	(NA)	(NA)
Wholesale trade	1 133 761	1 018 060	67 617	2.7	2.9	1.5	777 109	(NA)	(NA)	2.7	(NA)	(NA)
Retail trade	8 004 399	7 183 064	520 661	19.2	20.4	11.2	5 557 906	(NA)	(NA)	19.2	(NA)	(NA)
Finance, insurance, and real estate	3 421 717	3 005 386	286 904	8.2	8.5	6.2	1 922 147	(NA)	(NA)	6.6	(NA)	(NA)
Business and repair services	1 380 020	1 195 014	130 241	3.3	3.4	2.8	707 515	(NA)	(NA)	2.4	(NA)	(NA)
Personal services	2 165 306	1 583 521	456 693	5.2	4.5	9.8	2 502 240	(NA)	(NA)	8.6	(NA)	(NA)
Entertainment and recreation services	407 324	365 735	27 058	1.0	1.0	0.6	224 607	(NA)	(NA)	0.8	(NA)	(NA)
Professional and related services	13 144 812	10 974 426	1 682 576	31.6	31.2	36.1	8 467 364	(NA)	(NA)	29.3	(NA)	(NA)
Public administration	2 102 567	1 623 858	373 141	5.1	4.6	8.0	1 207 394	(NA)	(NA)	4.2	(NA)	(NA)
CLASS OF WORKER												
Employed persons 16 years and over	97 639 355	84 027 375	9 334 048	100.0	100.0	100.0	76 553 599	68 282 503	7 361 143	100.0	100.0	100.0
Private wage and salary workers	73 772 204	63 875 106	6 565 487	75.6	76.0	70.3	57 917 538	51 720 701	5 545 534	75.7	75.7	75.3
Federal government workers	3 762 008	2 856 457	693 500	3.9	3.4	7.4	3 284 241	2 680 273	529 866	4.3	3.9	7.2
State government workers	4 473 825	3 645 982	617 821	4.6	4.3	6.6	3 016 396	2 652 115	305 850	3.9	3.9	4.2
Local government workers	8 453 968	6 915 895	1 221 081	8.7	8.2	13.1	6 020 000	5 240 348	724 304	7.9	7.7	9.8
Self-employed workers	6 677 871	6 264 520	223 808	6.8	7.5	2.4	5 911 204	5 603 809	243 460	7.7	8.2	3.3
In agriculture	1 284 649	1 236 803	23 831	1.3	1.5	0.3	1 452 776	1 385 272	50 985	1.9	2.0	0.7
Unpaid family workers	499 479	469 415	12 351	0.5	0.6	0.1	404 220	385 257	12 129	0.5	0.6	0.2
In agriculture	139 760	135 065	2 483	0.1	0.2	–	107 833	101 800	4 413	0.1	0.1	0.1
Employed females 16 years and over	41 634 665	35 183 388	4 659 177	100.0	100.0	100.0	28 929 845	25 252 734	3 309 080	100.0	100.0	100.0
Private wage and salary workers	31 219 189	26 722 785	3 132 298	75.0	76.0	67.2	21 948 403	19 247 485	2 434 441	75.9	76.2	73.6
Federal government workers	1 484 036	1 038 226	356 032	3.6	3.0	7.6	1 087 744	832 584	229 231	3.8	3.3	6.9
State government workers	2 363 754	1 859 088	394 681	5.7	5.3	8.5	1 418 753	1 207 077	182 377	4.9	4.8	5.5
Local government workers	4 695 676	3 817 753	712 254	11.3	10.9	15.3	3 128 349	2 706 631	395 066	10.8	10.7	11.9
Self-employed workers	1 529 190	1 420 135	57 899	3.7	4.0	1.2	1 061 210	985 146	61 197	3.7	3.9	1.8
In agriculture	135 929	131 861	1 709	0.3	0.4	–	77 056	70 068	5 292	0.3	0.3	0.2
Unpaid family workers	342 820	325 401	6 013	0.8	0.9	0.1	285 386	273 811	6 768	1.0	1.1	0.2
In agriculture	69 113	67 623	623	0.2	0.2	–	46 283	43 672	1 674	0.2	0.2	0.1

Table 91. Class of Worker of Employed Persons by Industry and Sex: 1940 to 1980

[Data are estimates based on a sample; see Introduction. For meaning of symbols, see Introduction. For definitions of terms, see appendixes A and B]

United States	Male					Female				
	Total	Private wage and salary workers	Government workers	Self-employed workers	Unpaid family workers	Total	Private wage and salary workers	Government workers	Self-employed workers	Unpaid family workers
NUMBER										
1980										
Employed persons 16 years and over	56 004 690	42 553 015	8 146 335	5 148 681	156 659	41 634 665	31 219 189	8 543 466	1 529 190	342 820
Agriculture	2 266 555	1 018 891	28 297	1 148 720	70 647	493 658	278 369	10 247	135 929	69 113
Nonagriculture industries	53 738 135	41 534 124	8 118 038	3 999 961	86 012	41 141 007	30 940 820	8 533 219	1 393 261	273 707
1970										
Employed persons 16 years and over	47 623 754	35 969 135	6 685 791	4 849 994	118 834	28 929 845	21 948 403	5 634 846	1 061 210	285 386
Agriculture	2 441 811	973 693	30 848	1 375 720	61 550	308 131	178 970	5 822	77 056	46 283
Nonagriculture industries	45 181 943	34 995 442	6 654 943	3 474 274	57 284	28 621 714	21 769 433	5 629 024	984 154	239 103
1960										
Employed persons 14 years and over	43 466 946	31 743 386	4 681 582	6 834 343	207 635	21 172 301	16 459 533	3 178 415	1 067 749	466 604
Agriculture	3 846 314	1 232 355	18 580	2 437 673	157 706	410 420	157 910	1 908	122 000	128 602
Nonagriculture industries[1]	39 620 632	30 511 031	4 663 002	4 396 670	49 929	20 761 881	16 301 623	3 176 507	945 749	338 002
1950										
Employed persons 14 years and over	40 662 374	27 885 243	3 510 786	8 629 582	636 763	15 772 899	12 279 035	2 043 211	971 253	479 400
Agriculture	6 321 559	1 497 326	19 392	4 210 334	594 507	587 088	149 134	1 621	116 710	319 623
Nonagriculture industries[1]	34 340 815	26 387 917	3 491 394	4 419 248	42 256	15 185 811	12 129 901	2 041 590	854 543	159 777
1940										
Employed persons 14 years and over	33 892 239	21 758 357	2 275 343	8 837 804	1 020 735	11 178 076	8 488 173	1 317 609	944 000	428 294
Agriculture	7 957 759	1 999 655	19 938	4 993 271	944 895	491 704	111 394	812	153 021	226 477
Nonagriculture industries[1]	25 934 480	19 758 702	2 255 405	3 844 533	75 840	10 686 372	8 376 779	1 316 797	790 979	201 817
PERCENT DISTRIBUTION										
1980										
Employed persons 16 years and over	100.0	76.0	14.5	9.2	0.3	100.0	75.0	20.5	3.7	0.8
Agriculture	100.0	45.0	1.2	50.7	3.1	100.0	56.4	2.1	27.5	14.0
Nonagriculture industries	100.0	77.3	15.1	7.4	0.2	100.0	75.2	20.7	3.4	0.7
1970										
Employed persons 16 years and over	100.0	75.5	14.0	10.2	0.2	100.0	75.9	19.5	3.7	1.0
Agriculture	100.0	39.9	1.3	56.3	2.5	100.0	58.1	1.9	25.0	15.0
Nonagriculture industries	100.0	77.5	14.7	7.7	0.1	100.0	76.1	19.7	3.4	0.8
1960										
Employed persons 14 years and over	100.0	73.0	10.8	15.7	0.5	100.0	77.7	15.0	5.0	2.2
Agriculture	100.0	32.0	0.5	63.4	4.1	100.0	38.5	0.5	29.7	31.3
Nonagriculture industries[1]	100.0	77.0	11.8	11.1	0.1	100.0	78.5	15.3	4.6	1.6
1950										
Employed persons 14 years and over	100.0	68.6	8.6	21.2	1.6	100.0	77.8	13.0	6.2	3.0
Agriculture	100.0	23.7	0.3	66.6	9.4	100.0	25.4	0.3	19.9	54.4
Nonagriculture industries[1]	100.0	76.8	10.2	12.9	0.1	100.0	79.9	13.4	5.6	1.1
1940										
Employed persons 14 years and over	100.0	64.2	6.7	26.1	3.0	100.0	75.9	11.8	8.4	3.8
Agriculture	100.0	25.1	0.3	62.7	11.9	100.0	22.7	0.2	31.1	46.1
Nonagriculture industries[1]	100.0	76.2	8.7	14.8	0.3	100.0	78.4	12.3	7.4	1.9

[1]Includes persons with industry not reported.

Table 92. Household Income in 1979 and 1969 by Race: 1980 and 1970

[In 1979 dollars. Data are estimates based on a sample; see Introduction. For meaning of symbols, see Introduction. For definitions of terms, see appendixes A and B]

United States Regions	Number					Percent distribution				
	United States	Northeast	North Central	South	West	United States	Northeast	North Central	South	West
TOTAL										
1980										
Households	80 467 427	17 479 448	20 877 402	26 506 599	15 603 978	100.0	100.0	100.0	100.0	100.0
Less than $5,000	10 663 441	2 254 198	2 542 525	4 074 723	1 791 995	13.3	12.9	12.2	15.4	11.5
Less than $2,500	3 739 237	695 671	836 638	1 577 879	629 049	4.6	4.0	4.0	6.0	4.0
$2,500 to $4,999	6 924 204	1 558 527	1 705 887	2 496 844	1 162 946	8.6	8.9	8.2	9.4	7.5
$5,000 to $9,999	12 772 409	2 678 053	3 133 715	4 596 850	2 363 791	15.9	15.3	15.0	17.3	15.1
$5,000 to $7,499	6 439 024	1 370 727	1 590 985	2 316 727	1 160 585	8.0	7.8	7.6	8.7	7.4
$7,500 to $9,999	6 333 385	1 307 326	1 542 730	2 280 123	1 203 206	7.9	7.5	7.4	8.6	7.7
$10,000 to $14,999	12 342 073	2 594 754	3 058 376	4 323 578	2 365 365	15.3	14.8	14.6	16.3	15.2
$10,000 to $12,499	6 689 434	1 391 199	1 634 241	2 365 831	1 298 163	8.3	8.0	7.8	8.9	8.3
$12,500 to $14,999	5 652 639	1 203 555	1 424 135	1 957 747	1 067 202	7.0	6.9	6.8	7.4	6.8
$15,000 to $24,999	21 383 458	4 683 167	5 744 380	6 860 986	4 094 925	26.6	26.8	27.5	25.9	26.2
$15,000 to $17,499	6 050 963	1 312 201	1 559 339	2 030 942	1 148 481	7.5	7.5	7.5	7.7	7.4
$17,500 to $19,999	5 328 086	1 169 748	1 429 155	1 729 042	1 000 141	6.6	6.7	6.8	6.5	6.4
$20,000 to $22,499	5 610 405	1 235 395	1 528 964	1 754 983	1 091 063	7.0	7.1	7.3	6.6	7.0
$22,500 to $24,999	4 394 004	965 823	1 226 922	1 346 019	855 240	5.5	5.5	5.9	5.1	5.5
$25,000 or more	23 306 046	5 269 276	6 398 406	6 650 462	4 987 902	29.0	30.1	30.6	25.1	32.0
$25,000 to $34,999	12 659 261	2 816 833	3 576 136	3 700 389	2 565 903	15.7	16.1	17.1	14.0	16.4
$35,000 to $49,999	6 954 720	1 589 447	1 907 085	1 907 936	1 550 252	8.6	9.1	9.1	7.2	9.9
$50,000 to $74,999	2 574 043	606 984	653 612	705 329	608 118	3.2	3.5	3.1	2.7	3.9
$75,000 or more	1 118 022	256 012	261 573	336 808	263 629	1.4	1.5	1.3	1.3	1.7
Median	$16 841	$17 310	$17 753	$15 318	$17 831	...	...	...	...	...
Mean	$20 306	$20 781	$20 715	$18 883	$21 646	...	...	...	...	...
1970										
Households	63 637 721	15 530 192	17 581 814	19 328 655	11 197 060	100.0	100.0	100.0	100.0	100.0
Less than $5,000	9 256 070	1 883 512	2 363 254	3 559 683	1 449 621	14.5	12.1	13.4	18.4	12.9
Less than $1,000	1 549 775	317 801	369 769	631 077	231 128	2.4	2.0	2.1	3.3	2.1
$1,000 to $1,999	1 563 569	320 403	374 291	635 553	233 322	2.5	2.1	2.1	3.3	2.1
$2,000 to $2,999	2 133 817	426 784	567 687	814 615	324 731	3.4	2.7	3.2	4.2	2.9
$3,000 to $3,999	2 123 616	425 402	564 381	808 669	325 164	3.3	2.7	3.2	4.2	2.9
$4,000 to $4,999	1 885 293	393 122	487 126	669 769	335 276	3.0	2.5	2.8	3.5	3.0
$5,000 to $9,999	9 048 805	1 923 412	2 284 376	3 298 865	1 542 152	14.2	12.4	13.0	17.1	13.8
$5,000 to $5,999	1 881 013	392 469	485 385	669 639	333 520	3.0	2.5	2.8	3.5	3.0
$6,000 to $6,999	1 815 230	382 441	458 623	667 647	306 519	2.9	2.5	2.6	3.5	2.7
$7,000 to $7,999	1 811 090	382 292	457 094	665 932	305 772	2.8	2.5	2.6	3.4	2.7
$8,000 to $8,999	3 541 472	766 210	883 274	1 295 647	596 341	5.6	4.9	5.0	6.7	5.3
$9,000 to $9,999	(¹)	(¹)	(¹)	(¹)	(¹)	(¹)	(¹)	(¹)	(¹)	(¹)
$10,000 to $14,999	9 775 098	2 279 328	2 529 693	3 314 559	1 651 518	15.4	14.7	14.4	17.1	14.7
$15,000 to $24,999	19 578 391	4 960 476	5 752 665	5 434 603	3 430 647	30.8	31.9	32.7	28.1	30.6
$25,000 or more	15 979 357	4 483 464	4 651 826	3 720 945	3 123 122	25.1	28.9	26.5	19.3	27.9
Median	$16 802	$18 321	$17 764	$14 222	$17 699	...	...	...	...	...
Mean	$19 435	$21 211	$19 956	$16 943	$20 455	...	...	...	...	...
WHITE										
1980										
Households	68 991 307	15 304 847	18 811 065	21 623 541	13 251 854	100.0	100.0	100.0	100.0	100.0
Less than $5,000	7 994 898	1 724 826	2 072 749	2 785 457	1 411 866	11.6	11.3	11.0	12.9	10.7
Less than $2,500	2 588 920	489 292	644 468	990 671	464 489	3.8	3.2	3.4	4.6	3.5
$2,500 to $4,999	5 405 978	1 235 534	1 428 281	1 794 786	947 377	7.8	8.1	7.6	8.3	7.1
$5,000 to $9,999	10 463 284	2 239 296	2 764 855	3 514 776	1 944 357	15.2	14.6	14.7	16.3	14.7
$5,000 to $7,499	5 222 867	1 136 816	1 392 536	1 743 537	949 978	7.6	7.4	7.4	8.1	7.2
$7,500 to $9,999	5 240 417	1 102 480	1 372 319	1 771 239	994 379	7.6	7.2	7.3	8.2	7.5
$10,000 to $14,999	10 459 843	2 233 782	2 753 853	3 493 494	1 978 714	15.2	14.6	14.6	16.2	14.9
$10,000 to $12,499	5 626 168	1 184 879	1 464 638	1 895 949	1 080 702	8.2	7.7	7.8	8.8	8.2
$12,500 to $14,999	4 833 675	1 048 903	1 289 215	1 597 545	898 012	7.0	6.9	6.9	7.4	6.8
$15,000 to $24,999	18 824 882	4 214 356	5 264 521	5 840 319	3 505 686	27.3	27.5	28.0	27.0	26.5
$15,000 to $17,499	5 240 484	1 160 977	1 417 451	1 691 224	970 832	7.6	7.6	7.5	7.8	7.3
$17,500 to $19,999	4 671 184	1 050 208	1 304 644	1 462 812	853 520	6.8	6.9	6.9	6.8	6.4
$20,000 to $22,499	4 981 811	1 121 548	1 406 998	1 512 979	940 286	7.2	7.3	7.5	7.0	7.1
$22,500 to $24,999	3 931 403	881 623	1 135 428	1 173 304	741 048	5.7	5.8	6.0	5.4	5.6
$25,000 or more	21 248 400	4 892 587	5 955 087	5 989 495	4 411 231	30.8	32.0	31.7	27.7	33.3
$25,000 to $34,999	11 436 698	2 592 077	3 319 243	3 278 746	2 246 632	16.6	16.9	17.6	15.2	17.0
$35,000 to $49,999	6 355 489	1 479 813	1 770 249	1 734 367	1 371 060	9.2	9.7	9.4	8.0	10.3
$50,000 to $74,999	2 396 521	574 131	615 726	658 160	548 504	3.5	3.8	3.3	3.0	4.1
$75,000 or more	1 059 692	246 566	249 869	318 222	245 035	1.5	1.6	1.3	1.5	1.8
Median	$17 680	$18 199	$18 260	$16 505	$18 438	...	...	...	...	...
Mean	$21 173	$21 644	$21 206	$20 130	$22 281	...	...	...	...	...

¹Included in preceding category.

Table 92. Household Income in 1979 and 1969 by Race: 1980 and 1970—Con.

[In 1979 dollars. Data are estimates based on a sample; see Introduction. For meaning of symbols, see Introduction. For definitions of terms, see appendixes A and B]

United States Regions	Number					Percent distribution				
	United States	Northeast	North Central	South	West	United States	Northeast	North Central	South	West
WHITE—Con.										
1970										
Households	56 733 436	14 145 788	16 212 018	16 100 334	10 275 286	100.0	100.0	100.0	100.0	100.0
Less than $5,000	7 518 182	(NA)	(NA)	(NA)	(NA)	13.3	(NA)	(NA)	(NA)	(NA)
Less than $1,000	1 211 877	(NA)	(NA)	(NA)	(NA)	2.1	(NA)	(NA)	(NA)	(NA)
$1,000 to $1,999	1 224 602	(NA)	(NA)	(NA)	(NA)	2.2	(NA)	(NA)	(NA)	(NA)
$2,000 to $2,999	1 760 841	(NA)	(NA)	(NA)	(NA)	3.1	(NA)	(NA)	(NA)	(NA)
$3,000 to $3,999	1 752 921	(NA)	(NA)	(NA)	(NA)	3.1	(NA)	(NA)	(NA)	(NA)
$4,000 to $4,999	1 567 941	(NA)	(NA)	(NA)	(NA)	2.8	(NA)	(NA)	(NA)	(NA)
$5,000 to $9,999	7 579 445	(NA)	(NA)	(NA)	(NA)	13.4	(NA)	(NA)	(NA)	(NA)
$5,000 to $5,999	1 564 551	(NA)	(NA)	(NA)	(NA)	2.8	(NA)	(NA)	(NA)	(NA)
$6,000 to $6,999	1 512 454	(NA)	(NA)	(NA)	(NA)	2.7	(NA)	(NA)	(NA)	(NA)
$7,000 to $7,999	1 510 550	(NA)	(NA)	(NA)	(NA)	2.7	(NA)	(NA)	(NA)	(NA)
$8,000 to $8,999	2 991 890	(NA)	(NA)	(NA)	(NA)	5.3	(NA)	(NA)	(NA)	(NA)
$9,000 to $9,999	(¹)	(NA)	(NA)	(NA)	(NA)	(¹)	(NA)	(NA)	(NA)	(NA)
$10,000 to $14,999	8 522 503	(NA)	(NA)	(NA)	(NA)	15.0	(NA)	(NA)	(NA)	(NA)
$15,000 to $24,999	17 975 387	(NA)	(NA)	(NA)	(NA)	31.7	(NA)	(NA)	(NA)	(NA)
$25,000 or more	15 137 919	(NA)	(NA)	(NA)	(NA)	26.7	(NA)	(NA)	(NA)	(NA)
Median	$17 535	(NA)	(NA)	(NA)	(NA)	...	...	...	...	...
Mean	$20 194	(NA)	(NA)	(NA)	(NA)	...	...	...	...	...
BLACK										
1980										
Households	8 413 161	1 631 847	1 724 196	4 273 977	783 141	100.0	100.0	100.0	100.0	100.0
Less than $5,000	2 151 976	397 929	413 939	1 180 359	159 749	25.6	24.4	24.0	27.6	20.4
Less than $2,500	915 907	152 904	165 979	533 554	63 470	10.9	9.4	9.6	12.5	8.1
$2,500 to $4,999	1 236 069	245 025	247 960	646 805	96 279	14.7	15.0	14.4	15.1	12.3
$5,000 to $9,999	1 760 698	327 674	314 944	961 937	156 143	20.9	20.1	18.3	22.5	19.9
$5,000 to $7,499	937 691	173 238	170 546	513 043	80 864	11.1	10.6	9.9	12.0	10.3
$7,500 to $9,999	823 007	154 436	144 398	448 894	75 279	9.8	9.5	8.4	10.5	9.6
$10,000 to $14,999	1 374 866	273 099	252 643	719 780	129 344	16.3	16.7	14.7	16.8	16.5
$10,000 to $12,499	779 338	156 041	141 019	407 770	74 508	9.3	9.6	8.2	9.5	9.5
$12,500 to $14,999	595 528	117 058	111 624	312 010	54 836	7.1	7.2	6.5	7.3	7.0
$15,000 to $24,999	1 793 612	356 018	390 947	867 103	179 544	21.3	21.8	22.7	20.3	22.9
$15,000 to $17,499	577 739	114 311	115 965	290 819	56 644	6.9	7.0	6.7	6.8	7.2
$17,500 to $19,999	464 335	89 949	102 002	227 134	45 250	5.5	5.5	5.9	5.3	5.8
$20,000 to $22,499	435 068	87 007	99 027	204 166	44 868	5.2	5.3	5.7	4.8	5.7
$22,500 to $24,999	316 470	64 751	73 953	144 984	32 782	3.8	4.0	4.3	3.4	4.2
$25,000 or more	1 332 009	277 127	351 723	544 798	158 361	15.8	17.0	20.4	12.7	20.2
$25,000 to $34,999	824 754	171 926	207 569	353 216	92 043	9.8	10.5	12.0	8.3	11.8
$35,000 to $49,999	381 991	80 483	110 476	142 030	49 002	4.5	4.9	6.4	3.3	6.3
$50,000 to $74,999	98 560	20 822	27 925	36 119	13 694	1.2	1.3	1.6	0.8	1.7
$75,000 or more	26 704	3 896	5 753	13 433	3 622	0.3	0.2	0.3	0.3	0.5
Median	$10 943	$11 447	$12 362	$9 970	$12 553	...	...	...	...	...
Mean	$14 051	$14 427	$15 586	$12 928	$16 012	...	...	...	...	...
1970										
Households	6 235 714	1 293 056	1 292 731	3 141 047	508 880	100.0	100.0	100.0	100.0	100.0
Less than $5,000	1 627 848	243 458	267 080	1 014 155	103 155	26.1	18.8	20.7	32.3	20.3
Less than $1,000	314 997	49 302	52 335	194 883	18 477	5.1	3.8	4.0	6.2	3.6
$1,000 to $1,999	316 066	49 312	52 488	195 713	18 553	5.1	3.8	4.1	6.2	3.6
$2,000 to $2,999	351 170	47 489	57 185	225 280	21 216	5.6	3.7	4.4	7.2	4.2
$3,000 to $3,999	348 933	47 583	56 818	223 219	21 313	5.6	3.7	4.4	7.1	4.2
$4,000 to $4,999	296 682	49 772	48 254	175 060	23 596	4.8	3.8	3.7	5.6	4.6
$5,000 to $9,999	1 366 574	254 263	221 957	789 301	101 053	21.9	19.7	17.2	25.1	19.9
$5,000 to $5,999	295 782	49 881	48 043	174 485	23 373	4.7	3.9	3.7	5.6	4.6
$6,000 to $6,999	281 954	51 551	44 801	165 648	19 954	4.5	4.0	3.5	5.3	3.9
$7,000 to $7,999	279 768	51 468	44 586	163 844	19 870	4.5	4.0	3.4	5.2	3.9
$8,000 to $8,999	509 070	101 363	84 527	285 324	37 856	8.2	7.8	6.5	9.1	7.4
$9,000 to $9,999	(¹)	(¹)		(¹)	(¹)	(¹)	(¹)	(¹)	(¹)	(¹)
$10,000 to $14,999	1 147 558	257 626	226 440	568 027	95 465	18.4	19.9	17.5	18.1	18.8
$15,000 to $24,999	1 423 548	351 627	371 406	564 200	136 315	22.8	27.2	28.7	18.0	26.8
$25,000 or more	670 186	186 082	205 848	205 364	72 892	10.7	14.4	15.9	6.5	14.3
Median	$10 504	$12 804	$13 505	$8 365	$12 604	...	...	...	...	...
Mean	$12 612	$14 648	$15 071	$10 460	$14 474	...	...	...	...	...

¹Included in preceding category.

Table 93. **Family Income in 1979, 1969, and 1959 by Race: 1960 to 1980**

[In 1979 dollars. Data are estimates based on a sample; see Introduction. For meaning of symbols, see Introduction. For definitions of terms, see appendixes A and B]

United States Regions	Number					Percent distribution				
	United States	Northeast	North Central	South	West	United States	Northeast	North Central	South	West
TOTAL										
1980										
Families	59 190 133	12 731 633	15 424 495	20 009 695	11 024 310	100.0	100.0	100.0	100.0	100.0
Less than $5,000	4 344 476	851 230	963 325	1 835 312	694 609	7.3	6.7	6.2	9.2	6.3
Less than $2,500	1 759 207	322 680	377 027	757 341	302 159	3.0	2.5	2.4	3.8	2.7
$2,500 to $4,999	2 585 269	528 550	586 298	1 077 971	392 450	4.4	4.2	3.8	5.4	3.6
$5,000 to $9,999	7 746 464	1 535 362	1 791 011	3 063 352	1 356 739	13.1	12.1	11.6	15.3	12.3
$5,000 to $7,499	3 681 759	732 636	847 522	1 478 787	622 814	6.2	5.8	5.5	7.4	5.6
$7,500 to $9,999	4 064 705	802 726	943 489	1 584 565	733 925	6.9	6.3	6.1	7.9	6.7
$10,000 to $14,999	8 709 248	1 780 985	2 107 129	3 260 771	1 560 363	14.7	14.0	13.7	16.3	14.2
$10,000 to $12,499	4 558 332	915 761	1 079 825	1 735 550	827 196	7.7	7.2	7.0	8.7	7.5
$12,500 to $14,999	4 150 916	865 224	1 027 304	1 525 221	733 167	7.0	6.8	6.7	7.6	6.7
$15,000 to $24,999	17 423 535	3 801 911	4 704 876	5 801 708	3 115 040	29.4	29.9	30.5	29.0	28.3
$15,000 to $17,499	4 633 192	989 876	1 187 215	1 637 451	818 650	7.8	7.8	7.7	8.2	7.4
$17,500 to $19,999	4 304 511	939 755	1 154 917	1 457 794	752 045	7.3	7.4	7.5	7.3	6.8
$20,000 to $22,499	4 676 793	1 031 212	1 286 735	1 512 611	846 235	7.9	8.1	8.3	7.6	7.7
$22,500 to $24,999	3 809 039	841 068	1 076 009	1 193 852	698 110	6.4	6.6	7.0	6.0	6.3
$25,000 or more	20 966 410	4 762 145	5 858 154	6 048 552	4 297 559	35.4	37.4	38.0	30.2	39.0
$25,000 to $34,999	11 301 814	2 523 609	3 244 536	3 351 561	2 182 108	19.1	19.8	21.0	16.7	19.8
$35,000 to $49,999	6 332 965	1 456 945	1 768 313	1 750 141	1 357 566	10.7	11.4	11.5	8.7	12.3
$50,000 to $74,999	2 326 739	550 766	604 697	641 662	529 614	3.9	4.3	3.9	3.2	4.8
$75,000 or more	1 004 892	230 825	240 608	305 188	228 271	1.7	1.8	1.6	1.5	2.1
Median	$19 917	$20 651	$20 988	$17 857	$20 974	...	...	...	...	...
Mean	$23 092	$23 877	$23 732	$21 294	$24 553	...	...	...	...	...
1970										
Families	51 168 599	12 394 267	14 184 786	15 907 699	8 681 847	100.0	100.0	100.0	100.0	100.0
Less than $5,000	4 198 808	732 909	963 280	1 910 492	592 126	8.2	5.9	6.8	12.0	6.8
Less than $1,000	644 965	125 209	137 615	283 557	98 584	1.3	1.0	1.0	1.8	1.1
$1,000 to $1,999	650 438	125 511	139 072	286 881	98 974	1.3	1.0	1.0	1.8	1.1
$2,000 to $2,999	875 372	133 738	200 551	428 525	112 558	1.7	1.1	1.4	2.7	1.3
$3,000 to $3,999	886 306	136 931	203 900	430 673	114 802	1.7	1.1	1.4	2.7	1.3
$4,000 to $4,999	1 141 727	211 520	282 142	480 856	167 208	2.2	1.7	2.0	3.0	1.9
$5,000 to $9,999	6 323 719	1 224 105	1 533 752	2 585 181	980 682	12.4	9.9	10.8	16.3	11.3
$5,000 to $5,999	1 149 113	213 337	283 560	483 147	169 069	2.2	1.7	2.0	3.0	1.9
$6,000 to $6,999	1 262 622	241 251	305 340	518 346	197 685	2.5	1.9	2.2	3.3	2.3
$7,000 to $7,999	1 266 798	242 824	306 270	519 293	198 411	2.5	2.0	2.2	3.3	2.3
$8,000 to $8,999	2 645 186	526 692	638 582	1 064 395	415 517	5.2	4.2	4.5	6.7	4.8
$9,000 to $9,999	(¹)	(¹)	(¹)	(¹)	(¹)	(¹)	(¹)	(¹)	(²)	(¹)
$10,000 to $14,999	7 920 203	1 764 635	2 025 992	2 880 143	1 249 433	15.5	14.2	14.3	18.1	14.4
$15,000 to $24,999	17 731 653	4 462 753	5 252 759	5 025 911	2 990 229	34.7	36.0	37.0	31.6	34.4
$25,000 or more	14 994 216	4 209 865	4 409 003	3 505 972	2 869 376	29.3	34.0	31.1	22.0	33.1
Median	$18 988	$20 699	$20 027	$15 996	$20 251	...	...	...	...	...
Mean	$21 778	$23 944	$22 463	$18 782	$23 061	...	...	...	...	...
1960										
Families	45 128 393	11 473 669	13 118 834	13 512 034	7 023 860	100.0	100.0	100.0	100.0	100.0
Less than $5,000	5 918 163	913 510	1 478 172	2 899 650	626 831	13.1	8.0	11.3	21.5	8.9
Less than $1,000	1 008 996	146 626	239 131	523 030	100 209	2.2	1.3	1.8	3.9	1.4
$1,000 to $1,999	1 010 007	146 773	239 371	523 554	100 309	2.2	1.3	1.8	3.9	1.4
$2,000 to $2,999	1 186 275	183 065	296 506	581 044	125 660	2.6	1.6	2.3	4.3	1.8
$3,000 to $3,999	1 354 802	217 763	351 132	636 009	149 898	3.0	1.9	2.7	4.7	2.1
$4,000 to $4,999	1 358 083	219 283	352 032	636 013	150 755	3.0	1.9	2.7	4.7	2.1
$5,000 to $9,999	8 095 516	1 727 437	2 138 739	3 176 930	1 052 413	17.9	15.1	16.3	23.5	15.0
$5,000 to $5,999	1 511 390	290 291	394 081	636 229	190 789	3.3	2.5	3.0	4.7	2.7
$6,000 to $6,999	1 511 390	290 291	394 081	636 229	190 789	3.3	2.5	3.0	4.7	2.7
$7,000 to $7,999	1 622 033	1 146 855	1 350 577	1 904 472	670 835	3.6	10.0	10.3	14.1	9.6
$8,000 to $8,999	1 719 874	(¹)	(¹)	(¹)	(¹)	3.8	(¹)	(¹)	(¹)	(¹)
$9,000 to $9,999	1 730 829	(¹)	(¹)	(¹)	(¹)	3.8	(¹)	(¹)	(¹)	(¹)
$10,000 to $14,999	10 556 666	2 869 468	3 164 249	2 954 863	1 568 086	23.4	25.0	24.1	21.9	22.3
$15,000 to $24,999	13 842 243	5 963 255	6 337 674	4 480 591	3 776 527	30.7	52.0	48.3	33.2	53.8
$25,000 or more	6 715 804	(¹)	(¹)	(¹)	(¹)	14.9	(¹)	(¹)	(¹)	(¹)
Median	$14 095	$15 417	$14 673	$11 119	$15 808	...	...	...	...	...
WHITE										
1980										
Families	50 644 862	11 167 719	13 921 135	16 318 126	9 237 882	100.0	100.0	100.0	100.0	100.0
Less than $5,000	2 841 388	548 257	704 626	1 104 017	484 488	5.6	4.9	5.1	6.8	5.2
Less than $2,500	1 107 735	202 119	275 025	426 288	204 303	2.2	1.8	2.0	2.6	2.2
$2,500 to $4,999	1 733 653	346 138	429 601	677 729	280 185	3.4	3.1	3.1	4.2	3.0
$5,000 to $9,999	6 048 636	1 226 715	1 530 493	2 238 746	1 052 682	11.9	11.0	11.0	13.7	11.4
$5,000 to $7,499	2 798 904	567 530	708 033	1 049 119	474 222	5.5	5.1	5.1	6.4	5.1
$7,500 to $9,999	3 249 732	659 185	822 460	1 189 627	578 460	6.4	5.9	5.9	7.3	6.3
$10,000 to $14,999	7 272 157	1 521 731	1 886 682	2 594 124	1 269 620	14.4	13.6	13.6	15.9	13.7
$10,000 to $12,499	3 759 529	770 627	958 812	1 363 771	666 319	7.4	6.9	6.9	8.4	7.2
$12,500 to $14,999	3 512 628	751 104	927 870	1 230 353	603 301	6.9	6.7	6.7	7.5	6.5
$15,000 to $24,999	15 344 097	3 436 987	4 333 532	4 931 525	2 642 053	30.3	30.8	31.1	30.2	28.6
$15,000 to $17,499	3 998 149	877 505	1 082 252	1 357 375	681 017	7.9	7.9	7.8	8.3	7.4
$17,500 to $19,999	3 773 601	848 007	1 060 072	1 230 304	635 218	7.5	7.6	7.6	7.5	6.9
$20,000 to $22,499	4 159 015	940 952	1 191 145	1 303 139	723 779	8.2	8.4	8.6	8.0	7.8
$22,500 to $24,999	3 413 332	770 523	1 000 063	1 040 707	602 039	6.7	6.9	7.2	6.4	6.5
$25,000 or more	19 138 584	4 434 029	5 465 802	5 449 714	3 789 039	37.8	39.7	39.3	33.4	41.0
$25,000 to $34,999	10 225 115	2 329 723	3 021 010	2 970 598	1 903 784	20.2	20.9	21.7	18.2	20.6
$35,000 to $49,999	5 791 725	1 359 598	1 644 013	1 591 176	1 196 938	11.4	12.2	11.8	9.8	13.0
$50,000 to $74,999	2 168 387	522 161	570 724	599 170	476 332	4.3	4.7	4.1	3.7	5.2
$75,000 or more	953 357	222 547	230 055	288 770	211 985	1.9	2.0	1.7	1.8	2.3
Median	$20 835	$21 492	$21 462	$19 257	$21 713	...	...	...	...	...
Mean	$24 166	$24 939	$24 332	$22 747	$25 487	...	...	...	...	...
1970										
Families	45 770 351	11 342 807	13 120 526	13 335 846	7 971 172	100.0	100.0	100.0	100.0	100.0
Less than $5,000	3 197 715	597 837	812 898	1 279 664	507 316	7.0	5.3	6.2	9.6	6.4
Less than $1,000	470 711	96 534	109 300	182 662	82 215	1.0	0.9	0.8	1.4	1.0
$1,000 to $1,999	475 287	96 954	110 715	185 013	82 605	1.0	0.9	0.8	1.4	1.0
$2,000 to $2,999	666 515	111 990	171 519	286 030	96 976	1.5	1.0	1.3	2.1	1.2
$3,000 to $3,999	676 459	114 687	174 607	288 155	99 010	1.5	1.0	1.3	2.2	1.2
$4,000 to $4,999	908 743	177 672	246 757	337 804	146 510	2.0	1.6	1.9	2.5	1.8

¹Included in preceding category. ²for 1960, includes Black and other races.

Table 93. Family Income in 1979, 1969, and 1959 by Race: 1960 to 1980—Con.

[In 1979 dollars. Data are estimates based on a sample; see Introduction. For meaning of symbols, see Introduction. For definitions of terms, see appendixes A and B]

United States Regions	Number					Percent distribution				
	United States	Northeast	North Central	South	West	United States	Northeast	North Central	South	West
WHITE—Con.										
1970—Con.										
Families—Con.										
$5,000 to $9,999	5 166 143	1 032 786	1 359 353	1 901 912	872 092	11.3	9.1	10.4	14.3	10.9
$5,000 to $5,999	915 759	179 180	248 174	340 099	148 306	2.0	1.6	1.9	2.6	1.9
$6,000 to $6,999	1 023 580	202 352	269 958	375 364	175 906	2.2	1.8	2.1	2.8	2.2
$7,000 to $7,999	1 028 987	203 878	270 996	377 503	176 610	2.2	1.8	2.1	2.8	2.2
$8,000 to $8,999	1 090 233	447 376	570 225	808 946	371 270	2.4	3.9	4.3	6.1	4.7
$9,000 to $9,999	1 107 584	(¹)	(¹)	(¹)	(¹)	2.4	(¹)	(¹)	(¹)	(¹)
$10,000 to $14,999	6 875 303	1 551 766	1 835 811	2 359 480	1 128 246	15.0	13.7	14.0	17.7	14.2
$15,000 to $24,999	16 312 647	4 138 472	4 908 393	4 494 321	2 771 461	35.6	36.5	37.4	33.7	34.8
$25,000 or more	14 218 543	4 021 947	4 204 070	3 300 467	2 692 059	31.1	35.5	32.0	24.7	33.8
Median	$19 722	$21 227	$20 390	$17 267	$20 540	...	...	...	...	...
Mean	$22 607	$24 621	$22 904	$20 120	$23 413	...	...	...	...	...
1960										
Families	40 872 873	10 779 937	12 338 795	11 189 296	6 564 848	100.0	100.0	100.0	100.0	100.0
Less than $5,000	4 536 753	798 165	1 310 710	1 875 310	552 563	11.1	7.4	10.6	16.8	8.4
Less than $1,000	746 346	126 499	209 368	324 453	86 021	1.8	1.2	1.7	2.9	1.3
$1,000 to $1,999	747 090	126 626	209 578	324 778	86 108	1.8	1.2	1.7	2.9	1.3
$2,000 to $2,999	909 593	159 977	262 937	375 874	110 805	2.2	1.5	2.1	3.4	1.7
$3,000 to $3,999	1 064 957	191 862	313 953	424 725	134 417	2.6	1.8	2.5	3.8	2.0
$4,000 to $4,999	1 068 767	193 201	314 874	425 480	135 212	2.6	1.8	2.6	3.8	2.1
$5,000 to $9,999	6 859 019	1 532 761	1 950 380	2 425 433	950 450	16.8	14.2	15.8	21.7	14.5
$5,000 to $5,999	1 246 615	255 710	357 870	460 707	172 328	3.0	2.4	2.9	4.1	2.6
$6,000 to $6,999	1 246 614	255 710	357 870	460 707	172 327	3.0	2.4	2.9	4.1	2.6
$7,000 to $7,999	1 375 276	1 021 341	1 234 640	1 504 019	605 795	3.4	9.5	10.0	13.4	9.2
$8,000 to $8,999	1 489 051	(¹)	(¹)	(¹)	(¹)	3.6	(¹)	(¹)	(¹)	(¹)
$9,000 to $9,999	1 501 463	(¹)	(¹)	(¹)	(¹)	3.7	(¹)	(¹)	(¹)	(¹)
$10,000 to $14,999	9 706 531	2 679 486	2 952 751	2 619 240	1 455 054	23.7	24.9	23.9	23.4	22.2
$15,000 to $24,999	13 231 180	5 769 523	6 124 952	4 269 313	3 606 782	32.4	53.5	49.6	38.2	54.9
$25,000 or more	6 539 390	(¹)	(¹)	(¹)	(¹)	16.0	(¹)	(¹)	(¹)	(¹)
Median	$14 675	$15 733	$14 927	$12 474	$16 047	...	...	...	...	...
BLACK²										
1980										
Families	6 105 698	1 136 825	1 234 909	3 201 003	532 961	100.0	100.0	100.0	100.0	100.0
Less than $5,000	1 181 543	213 158	224 932	665 283	78 170	19.4	18.8	18.2	20.8	14.7
Less than $2,500	500 941	83 722	86 427	297 855	32 937	8.2	7.4	7.0	9.3	6.2
$2,500 to $4,999	680 602	129 436	138 505	367 428	45 233	11.1	11.4	11.2	11.5	8.5
$5,000 to $9,999	1 277 106	222 426	221 315	730 677	102 688	20.9	19.6	17.9	22.8	19.3
$5,000 to $7,499	673 002	117 531	119 433	384 105	51 933	11.0	10.3	9.7	12.0	9.7
$7,500 to $9,999	604 104	104 895	101 882	346 572	50 755	9.9	9.2	8.3	10.8	9.5
$10,000 to $14,999	1 033 321	190 128	181 161	574 713	87 319	16.9	16.7	14.7	18.0	16.4
$10,000 to $12,499	576 259	106 444	99 721	320 632	49 462	9.4	9.4	8.1	10.0	9.3
$12,500 to $14,999	457 062	83 684	81 440	254 081	37 857	7.5	7.4	6.6	7.9	7.1
$15,000 to $24,999	1 436 928	271 568	297 806	736 205	131 349	23.5	23.9	24.1	23.0	24.6
$15,000 to $17,499	444 786	82 919	84 281	238 229	39 357	7.3	7.3	6.8	7.4	7.4
$17,500 to $19,999	370 253	67 386	76 241	193 785	32 841	6.1	5.9	6.2	6.1	6.2
$20,000 to $22,499	353 647	67 675	76 540	175 919	33 513	5.8	6.0	6.2	5.5	6.3
$22,500 to $24,999	268 242	53 588	60 744	128 272	25 638	4.4	4.7	4.9	4.0	4.8
$25,000 or more	1 176 800	239 545	309 695	494 125	133 435	19.3	21.1	25.1	15.4	25.0
$25,000 to $34,999	722 661	147 260	179 639	319 496	76 266	11.8	13.0	14.5	10.0	14.3
$35,000 to $49,999	344 477	71 271	100 175	130 592	42 439	5.6	6.3	8.1	4.1	8.0
$50,000 to $74,999	86 869	17 779	24 943	32 365	11 782	1.4	1.6	2.0	1.0	2.2
$75,000 or more	22 793	3 235	4 938	11 672	2 948	0.4	0.3	0.4	0.4	0.6
Median	$12 598	$13 288	$14 694	$11 595	$14 888	...	...	...	...	...
Mean	$15 684	$16 146	$17 477	$14 445	$17 989	...	...	...	...	...
1970										
Families	4 863 401	982 633	1 004 412	2 501 211	375 145	100.0	100.0	100.0	100.0	100.0
Less than $5,000	941 486	128 759	143 010	1 275 532	50 860	19.4	13.1	14.2	51.0	13.6
Less than $1,000	162 158	27 336	26 970	98 643	9 209	3.3	2.8	2.7	3.9	2.5
$1,000 to $1,999	163 066	27 223	27 009	99 613	9 221	3.4	2.8	2.7	4.0	2.5
$2,000 to $2,999	197 796	20 651	27 588	140 194	9 363	4.1	2.1	2.7	5.6	2.5
$3,000 to $3,999	198 698	21 134	27 835	140 195	9 534	4.1	2.2	2.8	5.6	2.5
$4,000 to $4,999	219 768	32 415	33 608	140 212	13 533	4.5	3.3	3.3	5.6	3.6
$5,000 to $9,999	1 082 953	181 129	164 455	834 774	69 137	22.3	18.4	16.4	33.4	18.4
$5,000 to $5,999	220 022	32 684	33 588	140 774	13 137	4.5	3.3	3.3	5.6	3.6
$6,000 to $6,999	223 932	36 829	33 280	140 189	13 561	4.6	3.7	3.3	5.6	3.7
$7,000 to $7,999	222 674	36 861	33 183	139 835	13 988	4.6	3.7	3.3	5.6	3.7
$8,000 to $8,999	208 416	74 755	64 404	138 659	13 971	4.3	7.6	6.4	5.5	3.7
$9,000 to $9,999	207 909	(¹)	(¹)	245 527	27 617	4.3	(¹)	(¹)	9.8	7.4
$10,000 to $14,999	960 322	200 288	180 504	506 337	73 193	19.7	20.4	18.0	20.2	19.5
$15,000 to $24,999	1 265 536	305 184	327 542	516 925	115 886	26.0	31.1	32.6	20.7	30.9
$25,000 or more	613 104	167 273	188 902	190 861	66 069	12.6	17.0	18.8	7.6	17.6
Median	$12 012	$14 507	$15 372	$9 702	$14 610	...	...	...	...	...
Mean	$14 085	$16 356	$16 873	$11 725	$16 414	...	...	...	...	...
1960										
Families	4 255 521	693 732	780 039	2 322 738	459 012	100.0	100.0	100.0	100.0	100.0
Less than $5,000	1 381 417	115 343	167 463	1 024 340	74 271	32.5	16.6	21.5	44.1	16.2
Less than $1,000	262 684	20 126	29 763	198 577	14 218	6.2	2.9	3.8	8.5	3.1
$1,000 to $1,999	262 918	20 147	29 793	198 776	14 202	6.2	2.9	3.8	8.6	3.1
$2,000 to $2,999	276 677	23 088	33 569	205 170	14 850	6.5	3.3	4.3	8.8	3.2
$3,000 to $3,999	289 831	25 900	37 179	211 283	15 469	6.8	3.7	4.8	9.1	3.4
$4,000 to $4,999	289 307	26 082	37 159	210 534	15 532	6.8	3.8	4.8	9.1	3.4
$5,000 to $9,999	1 236 493	194 674	188 359	751 495	101 965	29.1	28.1	24.1	32.4	22.2
$5,000 to $5,999	264 774	34 580	36 211	175 521	18 462	6.2	5.0	4.6	7.6	4.0
$6,000 to $6,999	264 774	34 580	36 211	175 521	18 462	6.2	5.0	4.6	7.6	4.0
$7,000 to $7,999	246 756	125 514	115 937	400 453	65 041	5.8	18.1	14.9	17.2	14.2
$8,000 to $8,999	230 823	(¹)	(¹)	(¹)	(¹)	5.4	(¹)	(¹)	(¹)	(¹)
$9,000 to $9,999	229 366	(¹)	(¹)	(¹)	(¹)	5.4	(¹)	(¹)	(¹)	(¹)
$10,000 to $14,999	850 134	189 982	211 497	335 623	113 032	20.0	27.4	27.1	14.4	24.6
$15,000 to $24,999	611 227	193 732	212 721	211 278	169 745	14.4	27.9	27.3	9.1	37.0
$25,000 or more	176 250	(¹)	(¹)	(¹)	(¹)	4.1	(¹)	(¹)	(¹)	(¹)
Median	$7 872	$10 885	$10 758	$5 782	$12 294	...	...	...	...	...

¹Included in preceding category. ²For 1960, includes Black and other races.

GENERAL SOCIAL AND ECONOMIC CHARACTERISTICS

Table 94. Income in 1979, 1969, and 1959 of Unrelated Individuals by Race: 1960 to 1980

[In 1979 dollars. Data are estimates based on a sample; see Introduction. For meaning of symbols, see Introduction. For definitions of terms, see appendixes A and B]

United States Regions	Number					Percent distribution				
	United States	Northeast	North Central	South	West	United States	Northeast	North Central	South	West
TOTAL										
1980										
Unrelated individuals 15 years and over	30 041 869	6 600 618	7 491 906	9 143 746	6 805 599	100.0	100.0	100.0	100.0	100.0
Less than $1,000	2 516 424	567 218	545 804	880 288	523 114	8.4	8.6	7.3	9.6	7.7
$1,000 to $1,999	1 749 263	382 451	449 167	611 989	305 656	5.8	5.8	6.0	6.7	4.5
$2,000 to $2,999	2 575 125	479 503	669 151	1 025 840	400 631	8.6	7.3	8.9	11.2	5.9
$3,000 to $3,999	2 858 088	713 430	750 511	850 608	543 539	9.5	10.8	10.0	9.3	8.0
$4,000 to $4,999	2 283 751	526 528	568 816	609 414	578 993	7.6	8.0	7.6	6.7	8.5
$5,000 to $5,999	1 842 912	397 109	459 692	555 593	430 518	6.1	6.0	6.1	6.1	6.3
$6,000 to $6,999	1 719 645	353 650	407 396	546 752	411 847	5.7	5.4	5.4	6.0	6.1
$7,000 to $9,999	4 083 398	867 557	1 010 088	1 245 218	960 535	13.6	13.1	13.5	13.6	14.1
$7,000 to $7,999	1 469 812	312 818	360 871	454 351	341 772	4.9	4.7	4.8	5.0	5.0
$8,000 to $8,999	1 393 443	292 306	345 486	424 243	331 408	4.6	4.4	4.6	4.6	4.9
$9,000 to $9,999	1 220 143	262 433	303 731	366 624	287 355	4.1	4.0	4.1	4.0	4.2
$10,000 to $14,999	4 753 467	1 051 773	1 205 880	1 353 345	1 142 469	15.8	15.9	16.1	14.8	16.8
$10,000 to $11,999	2 235 328	494 705	557 764	647 952	534 907	7.4	7.5	7.4	7.1	7.9
$12,000 to $14,999	2 518 139	557 068	648 116	705 393	607 562	8.4	8.4	8.7	7.7	8.9
$15,000 to $24,999	4 134 492	921 268	1 086 027	1 055 948	1 071 249	13.8	14.0	14.5	11.5	15.7
$25,000 or more	1 525 304	340 131	339 374	408 751	437 048	5.1	5.2	4.5	4.5	6.4
$25,000 to $49,999	1 292 046	287 584	294 753	340 489	369 220	4.3	4.4	3.9	3.7	5.4
$50,000 or more	233 258	52 547	44 621	68 262	67 828	0.8	0.8	0.6	0.7	1.0
Median	$6 695	$6 662	$6 743	$6 070	$7 610	...	...	...	...	...
Mean	$9 282	$9 307	$9 186	$8 595	$10 285	...	...	...	...	...
1970										
Unrelated individuals 14 years and over	18 696 505	4 519 920	4 995 752	5 375 235	3 805 598	100.0	100.0	100.0	100.0	100.0
Less than $1,000	2 098 936	459 942	546 396	755 163	337 435	11.2	10.2	10.9	14.0	8.9
$1,000 to $1,999	2 099 892	460 532	547 838	752 994	338 530	11.2	10.2	11.0	14.0	8.9
$2,000 to $2,999	2 046 632	466 580	589 529	616 731	373 792	10.9	10.3	11.8	11.5	9.8
$3,000 to $3,999	2 011 091	458 312	578 207	604 739	369 833	10.8	10.1	11.6	11.3	9.7
$4,000 to $4,999	1 180 905	265 198	313 742	324 623	277 342	6.3	5.9	6.3	6.0	7.3
$5,000 to $5,999	1 159 847	261 190	307 890	319 515	271 252	6.2	5.8	6.2	5.9	7.1
$6,000 to $6,999	836 211	199 594	217 948	241 014	177 655	4.5	4.4	4.4	4.5	4.7
$7,000 to $9,999	2 080 861	522 267	541 274	579 161	438 159	11.1	11.6	10.8	10.8	11.5
$7,000 to $7,999	819 815	196 645	213 636	235 525	174 009	4.4	4.4	4.3	4.4	4.6
$8,000 to $8,999	1 261 046	325 622	327 638	343 636	264 150	6.7	7.2	6.6	6.4	6.9
$9,000 to $9,999	(²)	(²)	(²)	(²)	(²)	(²)	(²)	(²)	(²)	(²)
$10,000 to $14,999	2 460 910	673 778	647 050	596 709	543 373	13.2	14.9	13.0	11.1	14.3
$10,000 to $11,999	2 460 910	673 778	647 050	596 709	543 373	13.2	14.9	13.0	11.1	14.3
$12,000 to $14,999	(²)	(²)	(²)	(²)	(²)	(²)	(²)	(²)	(²)	(²)
$15,000 to $24,999	2 018 611	549 307	545 203	426 769	497 330	10.8	12.2	10.9	7.9	13.1
$25,000 or more	702 609	203 220	160 675	157 816	180 896	3.8	4.5	3.2	2.9	4.8
$25,000 to $49,999	702 609	203 220	160 675	157 816	180 896	3.8	4.5	3.2	2.9	4.8
$50,000 or more	(²)	(²)	(²)	(²)	(²)	(²)	(²)	(²)	(²)	(²)
Median	$4 926	$5 564	$4 752	$3 914	$5 744	...	...	...	...	...
Mean	$7 653	$8 395	$7 407	$6 562	$8 633	...	...	...	...	...
1960										
Unrelated individuals 14 years and over	13 176 614	3 383 730	3 624 583	3 600 047	2 568 254	100.0	100.0	100.0	100.0	100.0
Less than $1,000	1 987 235	471 108	575 087	659 125	281 916	15.1	13.9	15.9	18.3	11.0
$1,000 to $1,999	1 989 224	471 579	575 663	659 785	282 198	15.1	13.9	15.9	18.3	11.0
$2,000 to $2,999	1 536 560	363 397	426 349	475 756	271 058	11.7	10.7	11.8	13.2	10.6
$3,000 to $3,999	1 103 777	259 966	283 594	299 810	260 407	8.4	7.7	7.8	8.3	10.1
$4,000 to $4,999	1 093 920	258 307	281 103	296 926	257 583	8.3	7.6	7.8	8.2	10.0
$5,000 to $5,999	633 563	180 815	164 790	162 276	125 682	4.8	5.3	4.5	4.5	4.9
$6,000 to $6,999	633 563	180 815	164 790	162 276	125 682	4.8	5.3	4.5	4.5	4.9
$7,000 to $9,999	1 561 798	459 966	413 825	366 885	321 122	11.9	13.6	11.4	10.2	12.5
$10,000 to $14,999	1 637 225	460 190	474 378	322 054	380 604	12.4	13.6	13.1	8.9	14.8
$15,000 or more	999 748	277 586	265 005	195 155	262 002	7.6	8.2	7.3	5.4	10.2
Median	$3 974	$4 485	$3 830	$3 018	$4 727	...	...	...	...	...
WHITE										
1980										
Unrelated individuals 15 years and over	25 362 410	5 675 641	6 643 457	7 255 681	5 787 631	100.0	100.0	100.0	100.0	100.0
Less than $1,000	1 809 351	434 270	426 954	573 889	374 238	7.1	7.7	6.4	7.9	6.5
$1,000 to $1,999	1 409 882	325 675	390 799	446 433	246 975	5.6	5.7	5.9	6.2	4.3
$2,000 to $2,999	2 016 308	392 776	565 986	727 208	330 338	7.9	6.9	8.5	10.0	5.7
$3,000 to $3,999	2 402 807	602 571	667 093	672 369	460 774	9.5	10.6	10.0	9.3	8.0
$4,000 to $4,999	1 965 260	466 262	516 580	495 424	486 994	7.7	8.2	7.8	6.8	8.4
$5,000 to $5,999	1 572 042	348 737	418 148	442 660	362 497	6.2	6.1	6.3	6.1	6.3
$6,000 to $6,999	1 460 508	308 878	369 170	433 846	348 614	5.8	5.4	5.6	6.0	6.0
$7,000 to $9,999	3 501 593	747 290	913 852	1 014 091	826 360	13.8	13.2	13.8	14.0	14.3
$7,000 to $7,999	1 258 612	271 343	327 581	366 574	293 114	5.0	4.8	4.9	5.1	5.1
$8,000 to $8,999	1 195 608	251 234	311 804	347 626	284 944	4.7	4.4	4.7	4.8	4.9
$9,000 to $9,999	1 047 373	224 713	274 467	299 891	248 302	4.1	4.0	4.1	4.1	4.3
$10,000 to $14,999	4 152 206	913 813	1 091 803	1 147 632	998 958	16.4	16.1	16.4	15.8	17.3
$10,000 to $11,999	1 943 290	426 818	505 530	544 625	466 317	7.7	7.5	7.6	7.5	8.1
$12,000 to $14,999	2 208 916	486 995	586 273	603 007	532 641	8.7	8.6	8.8	8.3	9.2
$15,000 to $24,999	3 660 529	818 609	969 326	923 542	949 052	14.4	14.4	14.6	12.7	16.4
$25,000 or more	1 411 924	316 760	313 746	378 587	402 831	5.6	5.6	4.7	5.2	7.0
$25,000 to $49,999	1 191 353	266 484	271 267	314 739	338 863	4.7	4.7	4.1	4.3	5.9
$50,000 or more	220 571	50 276	42 479	63 848	63 968	0.9	0.9	0.6	0.9	1.1
Median	$7 036	$6 866	$6 911	$6 622	$7 967	...	...	...	...	...
Mean	$9 695	$9 615	$9 369	$9 256	$10 700	...	...	...	...	...

²Included in preceding category.

Table 94. Income in 1979, 1969, and 1959 of Unrelated Individuals by Race: 1960 to 1980—Con.

[In 1979 dollars. Data are estimates based on a sample; see Introduction. For meaning of symbols, see Introduction. For definitions of terms, see appendixes A and B]

United States Regions	Number					Percent distribution				
	United States	Northeast	North Central	South	West	United States	Northeast	North Central	South	West
WHITE—Con.										
1970										
Unrelated individuals 14 years and over	16 297 908	4 003 257	4 525 870	4 323 478	3 445 303	100.0	100.0	100.0	100.0	100.0
Less than $1,000	1 744 459	(NA)	(NA)	(NA)	(NA)	10.7	(NA)	(NA)	(NA)	(NA)
$1,000 to $1,999	1 746 994	(NA)	(NA)	(NA)	(NA)	10.7	(NA)	(NA)	(NA)	(NA)
$2,000 to $2,999	1 783 724	(NA)	(NA)	(NA)	(NA)	10.9	(NA)	(NA)	(NA)	(NA)
$3,000 to $3,999	1 753 053	(NA)	(NA)	(NA)	(NA)	10.8	(NA)	(NA)	(NA)	(NA)
$4,000 to $4,999	1 036 618	(NA)	(NA)	(NA)	(NA)	6.4	(NA)	(NA)	(NA)	(NA)
$5,000 to $5,999	1 017 632	(NA)	(NA)	(NA)	(NA)	6.2	(NA)	(NA)	(NA)	(NA)
$6,000 to $6,999	725 826	(NA)	(NA)	(NA)	(NA)	4.5	(NA)	(NA)	(NA)	(NA)
$7,000 to $9,999	1 806 919	(NA)	(NA)	(NA)	(NA)	11.1	(NA)	(NA)	(NA)	(NA)
$7,000 to $7,999	711 613	(NA)	(NA)	(NA)	(NA)	4.4	(NA)	(NA)	(NA)	(NA)
$8,000 to $8,999	1 095 306	(NA)	(NA)	(NA)	(NA)	6.7	(NA)	(NA)	(NA)	(NA)
$9,000 to $9,999	(2)	(NA)	(NA)	(NA)	(NA)	(2)	(NA)	(NA)	(NA)	(NA)
$10,000 to $14,999	2 164 563	(NA)	(NA)	(NA)	(NA)	13.3	(NA)	(NA)	(NA)	(NA)
$10,000 to $11,999	2 164 563	(NA)	(NA)	(NA)	(NA)	13.3	(NA)	(NA)	(NA)	(NA)
$12,000 to $14,999	(2)	(NA)	(NA)	(NA)	(NA)	(2)	(NA)	(NA)	(NA)	(NA)
$15,000 to $24,999	1 844 562	(NA)	(NA)	(NA)	(NA)	11.3	(NA)	(NA)	(NA)	(NA)
$25,000 or more	673 558	(NA)	(NA)	(NA)	(NA)	4.1	(NA)	(NA)	(NA)	(NA)
$25,000 to $49,999	673 558	(NA)	(NA)	(NA)	(NA)	4.1	(NA)	(NA)	(NA)	(NA)
$50,000 or more	(2)	(NA)	(NA)	(NA)	(NA)	(2)	(NA)	(NA)	(NA)	(NA)
Median	$5 083	(NA)	(NA)	(NA)	(NA)	...	...	...	...	...
Mean	$7 928	(NA)	(NA)	(NA)	(NA)	...	...	...	...	...
1960										
Unrelated individuals 14 years and over	11 429 885	3 005 772	3 295 527	2 782 580	2 346 006	100.0	100.0	100.0	100.0	100.0
Less than $1,000	1 667 990	423 248	521 278	468 326	255 137	14.6	14.1	15.8	16.8	10.9
$1,000 to $1,999	1 669 660	423 672	521 800	468 795	255 393	14.6	14.1	15.8	16.8	10.9
$2,000 to $2,999	1 306 166	324 055	387 299	347 909	246 903	11.4	10.8	11.8	12.5	10.5
$3,000 to $3,999	958 637	228 813	258 705	232 332	238 786	8.4	7.6	7.9	8.3	10.2
$4,000 to $4,999	949 779	227 171	256 374	230 123	236 111	8.3	7.6	7.8	8.3	10.1
$5,000 to $5,999	536 098	150 458	147 520	126 956	111 165	4.7	5.0	4.5	4.6	4.7
$6,000 to $6,999	536 098	150 458	147 520	126 956	111 165	4.7	5.0	4.5	4.6	4.7
$7,000 to $9,999	1 354 253	391 823	370 753	304 409	287 268	11.8	13.0	11.3	10.9	12.2
$10,000 to $14,999	1 489 877	418 412	429 994	289 298	352 173	13.0	13.9	13.0	10.4	15.0
$15,000 or more	961 327	267 662	254 284	187 476	251 906	8.4	8.9	7.7	6.7	10.7
Median	$4 119	$4 453	$3 842	$3 461	$4 741	...	...	...	...	...
BLACK[1]										
1980										
Unrelated individuals 15 years and over	3 478 122	726 382	704 195	1 649 310	398 235	100.0	100.0	100.0	100.0	100.0
Less than $1,000	493 785	96 337	90 112	259 557	47 779	14.2	13.3	12.8	15.7	12.0
$1,000 to $1,999	260 139	44 045	47 327	148 684	20 083	7.5	6.1	6.7	9.0	5.0
$2,000 to $2,999	460 495	69 634	90 676	274 436	25 749	13.2	9.6	12.9	16.6	6.5
$3,000 to $3,999	352 020	89 144	71 763	159 314	31 799	10.1	12.3	10.2	9.7	8.0
$4,000 to $4,999	234 025	48 251	43 822	99 685	42 267	6.7	6.6	6.2	6.0	10.6
$5,000 to $5,999	196 975	37 794	34 030	96 294	28 857	5.7	5.2	4.8	5.8	7.2
$6,000 to $6,999	188 453	34 725	31 314	96 261	26 153	5.4	4.8	4.4	5.8	6.6
$7,000 to $9,999	426 887	94 822	79 476	199 483	53 106	12.3	13.1	11.3	12.1	13.3
$7,000 to $7,999	153 764	32 078	27 317	75 335	19 034	4.4	4.4	3.9	4.6	4.8
$8,000 to $8,999	144 409	32 485	27 703	65 944	18 277	4.2	4.5	3.9	4.0	4.6
$9,000 to $9,999	128 714	30 259	24 456	58 204	15 795	3.7	4.2	3.5	3.5	4.0
$10,000 to $14,999	441 837	111 005	94 705	177 965	58 162	12.7	15.3	13.4	10.8	14.6
$10,000 to $11,999	214 831	54 320	43 210	89 516	27 785	6.2	7.5	6.1	5.4	7.0
$12,000 to $14,999	227 006	56 685	51 495	88 449	30 377	6.5	7.8	7.3	5.4	7.6
$15,000 to $24,999	347 570	83 584	100 080	113 247	50 659	10.0	11.5	14.2	6.9	12.7
$25,000 or more	75 936	17 041	20 890	24 384	13 621	2.2	2.3	3.0	1.5	3.4
$25,000 to $49,999	68 161	15 737	19 465	20 763	12 196	2.0	2.2	2.8	1.3	3.1
$50,000 or more	7 775	1 304	1 425	3 621	1 425	0.2	0.2	0.2	0.2	0.4
Median	$4 738	$5 418	$5 247	$3 891	$6 099	...	...	...	...	...
Mean	$6 916	$7 468	$7 810	$5 975	$8 223	...	...	...	...	...
1970										
Unrelated individuals 14 years and over	2 122 062	471 428	430 171	1 011 431	209 032	100.0	100.0	100.0	100.0	100.0
Less than $1,000	313 951	48 994	53 668	189 806	21 483	14.8	10.4	12.5	18.8	10.3
$1,000 to $1,999	312 645	48 931	53 565	188 649	21 500	14.7	10.4	12.5	18.7	10.3
$2,000 to $2,999	237 194	43 698	46 281	125 909	21 306	11.2	9.3	10.8	12.4	10.2
$3,000 to $3,999	232 668	43 077	45 338	123 136	21 117	11.0	9.1	10.5	12.2	10.1
$4,000 to $4,999	126 924	28 559	23 323	58 357	16 685	6.0	6.1	5.4	5.8	8.0
$5,000 to $5,999	125 142	28 331	23 040	57 490	16 281	5.9	6.0	5.4	5.7	7.8
$6,000 to $6,999	97 771	24 840	18 691	44 170	10 070	4.6	5.3	4.3	4.4	4.8
$7,000 to $9,999	243 266	68 841	48 843	100 140	25 442	11.5	14.6	11.4	9.9	12.2
$7,000 to $7,999	95 860	24 624	18 411	42 938	9 887	4.5	5.2	4.3	4.2	4.7
$8,000 to $8,999	147 406	44 217	30 432	57 202	15 555	6.9	9.4	7.1	5.7	7.4
$9,000 to $9,999	(2)	(2)	(2)	(2)	(2)	(2)	(2)	(2)	(2)	(2)
$10,000 to $14,999	263 254	84 778	65 640	82 027	30 809	12.4	18.0	15.3	8.1	14.7
$10,000 to $11,999	263 254	84 778	65 640	82 027	30 809	12.4	18.0	15.3	8.1	14.7
$12,000 to $14,999	(2)	(2)	(2)	(2)	(2)	(2)	(2)	(2)	(2)	(2)
$15,000 to $24,999	147 787	44 592	46 309	36 070	20 816	7.0	9.5	10.8	3.6	10.0
$25,000 or more	21 460	6 786	5 473	5 678	3 523	1.0	1.4	1.3	0.6	1.7
$25,000 to $49,999	21 460	6 786	5 473	5 678	3 523	1.0	1.4	1.3	0.6	1.7
$50,000 or more	(2)	(2)	(2)	(2)	(2)	(2)	(2)	(2)	(2)	(2)
Median	$3 833	$5 787	$4 696	$3 012	$5 146	...	...	...	...	...
Mean	$5 677	$7 061	$6 653	$4 370	$6 859	...	...	...	...	...
1960										
Unrelated individuals 14 years and over	1 746 729	377 958	329 056	817 467	222 248	100.0	100.0	100.0	100.0	100.0
Less than $1,000	319 245	47 859	53 809	190 799	26 778	18.3	12.7	16.4	23.3	12.0
$1,000 to $1,999	319 564	47 907	53 863	190 990	26 805	18.3	12.7	16.4	23.4	12.1
$2,000 to $2,999	230 394	39 342	39 050	127 847	24 155	13.2	10.4	11.9	15.6	10.9
$3,000 to $3,999	145 140	31 153	24 889	67 478	21 621	8.3	8.2	7.6	8.3	9.7
$4,000 to $4,999	144 141	31 137	24 729	66 803	21 472	8.3	8.2	7.5	8.2	9.7
$5,000 to $5,999	97 465	30 357	17 270	35 320	14 517	5.6	8.0	5.2	4.3	6.5
$6,000 to $6,999	97 465	30 357	17 270	35 320	14 517	5.6	8.0	5.2	4.3	6.5
$7,000 to $9,999	207 545	68 143	43 072	62 476	33 855	11.9	18.0	13.1	7.6	15.2
$10,000 to $14,999	147 348	41 778	44 384	32 756	28 431	8.4	11.1	13.5	4.0	12.8
$15,000 or more	38 421	9 925	10 721	7 679	10 096	2.2	2.6	3.3	0.9	4.5
Median	$3 031	$4 732	$3 718	$2 142	$4 545	...	...	...	...	...

[1]For 1960, includes Black and other races. [2]Included in preceding category.

Table 95. Income in 1979, 1969, and 1959 of Persons by Sex and Race: 1960 to 1980

[In 1979 dollars. Data are estimates based on a sample; see Introduction. For meaning of symbols, see Introduction. For definitions of terms, see appendixes A and B]

United States Regions	Number					Percent distribution				
	United States	Northeast	North Central	South	West	United States	Northeast	North Central	South	West
TOTAL										
1980										
Persons 15 years and over	175 307 629	38 765 075	45 260 854	57 933 216	33 348 484	100.0	100.0	100.0	100.0	100.0
Without income	28 120 985	6 352 922	6 901 509	9 735 790	5 130 764	16.0	16.4	15.2	16.8	15.4
With income	147 186 644	32 412 153	38 359 345	48 197 426	28 217 720	84.0	83.6	84.8	83.2	84.6
$1 to $999 or loss	10 271 583	2 146 080	2 808 853	3 404 809	1 911 841	5.9	5.5	6.2	5.9	5.7
$1,000 to $1,999	10 468 598	2 135 775	2 710 376	3 843 334	1 779 113	6.0	5.5	6.0	6.6	5.3
$2,000 to $2,999	11 138 093	2 313 782	2 839 564	4 211 335	1 773 412	6.4	6.0	6.3	7.3	5.3
$3,000 to $3,999	10 428 856	2 480 139	2 666 715	3 399 722	1 882 280	5.9	6.4	5.9	5.9	5.6
$4,000 to $4,999	8 582 855	1 959 792	2 148 373	2 706 435	1 768 255	4.9	5.1	4.7	4.7	5.3
$5,000 to $5,999	7 763 691	1 713 483	1 926 424	2 657 275	1 466 509	4.4	4.4	4.3	4.6	4.4
$6,000 to $6,999	7 522 474	1 584 501	1 813 445	2 709 483	1 415 045	4.3	4.1	4.0	4.7	4.2
$7,000 to $9,999	19 247 318	4 196 644	4 703 905	6 774 733	3 572 036	11.0	10.8	10.4	11.7	10.7
$7,000 to $7,999	6 825 168	1 483 344	1 657 789	2 437 348	1 246 687	3.9	3.8	3.7	4.2	3.7
$8,000 to $8,999	6 641 418	1 442 331	1 620 967	2 340 132	1 237 988	3.8	3.7	3.6	4.0	3.7
$9,000 to $9,999	5 780 732	1 270 969	1 425 149	1 997 253	1 087 361	3.3	3.3	3.1	3.4	3.3
$10,000 to $24,999	61 763 176	13 881 957	16 741 690	18 490 300	12 649 229	35.2	35.8	37.0	31.9	37.9
$10,000 to $14,999	23 508 570	5 327 284	6 043 694	7 673 881	4 463 711	13.4	13.7	13.4	13.2	13.4
$15,000 to $24,999	25 296 783	5 728 897	7 216 305	7 159 342	5 192 239	14.4	14.8	15.9	12.4	15.6
$25,000 or more	12 957 823	2 825 776	3 481 691	3 657 077	2 993 279	7.4	7.3	7.7	6.3	9.0
$25,000 to $34,999	7 888 927	1 708 292	2 238 148	2 144 309	1 798 178	4.5	4.4	4.9	3.7	5.4
$35,000 to $49,999	2 923 246	636 827	738 373	855 720	692 326	1.7	1.6	1.6	1.5	2.1
$50,000 to $74,999	1 328 592	299 393	313 219	404 054	311 926	0.8	0.8	0.7	0.7	0.9
$75,000 or more	817 058	181 264	191 951	252 994	190 849	0.5	0.5	0.4	0.4	0.6
Median	$8 089	$8 270	$8 375	$7 479	$8 699	...	...	...	...	...
Mean	$11 232	$11 332	$11 389	$10 518	$12 126	...	...	...	...	...
Males 15 years and over	83 824 951	18 170 740	21 647 802	27 664 163	16 342 246	100.0	100.0	100.0	100.0	100.0
Without income	6 527 504	1 550 434	1 464 653	2 334 502	1 177 915	7.8	8.5	6.8	8.4	7.2
With income	77 297 447	16 620 306	20 183 149	25 329 661	15 164 331	92.2	91.5	93.2	91.6	92.8
$1 to $999 or loss	3 538 456	746 522	954 485	1 167 375	670 074	4.2	4.1	4.4	4.2	4.1
$1,000 to $1,999	3 249 306	668 045	812 195	1 197 722	571 344	3.9	3.7	3.8	4.3	3.5
$2,000 to $2,999	3 482 081	671 816	851 558	1 384 848	573 859	4.2	3.7	3.9	5.0	3.5
$3,000 to $3,999	3 588 160	756 267	874 569	1 292 215	665 109	4.3	4.2	4.0	4.7	4.1
$4,000 to $4,999	3 291 975	692 236	786 893	1 127 900	684 946	3.9	3.8	3.6	4.1	4.2
$5,000 to $5,999	3 184 756	656 737	747 559	1 141 850	638 610	3.8	3.6	3.5	4.1	3.9
$6,000 to $6,999	3 188 005	637 200	721 234	1 184 961	644 610	3.8	3.5	3.3	4.3	3.9
$7,000 to $9,999	8 804 123	1 847 483	2 030 233	3 249 848	1 676 559	10.5	10.2	9.4	11.7	10.3
$7,000 to $7,999	2 995 631	626 872	688 234	1 105 703	574 822	3.6	3.4	3.2	4.0	3.5
$8,000 to $8,999	3 027 691	629 291	696 476	1 121 869	580 055	3.6	3.5	3.2	4.1	3.5
$9,000 to $9,999	2 780 801	591 320	645 523	1 022 276	521 682	3.3	3.3	3.0	3.7	3.2
$10,000 to $24,999	44 970 505	9 944 000	12 404 423	13 582 942	9 039 220	53.6	54.7	57.3	49.1	55.3
$10,000 to $14,999	13 411 030	2 983 910	3 408 424	4 583 322	2 435 374	16.0	16.4	15.7	16.6	14.9
$15,000 to $24,999	19 797 764	4 418 788	5 773 292	5 694 601	3 911 083	23.6	24.3	26.7	20.6	23.9
$25,000 or more	11 761 791	2 541 302	3 222 707	3 305 019	2 692 763	14.0	14.0	14.9	11.9	16.5
$25,000 to $34,999	7 117 717	1 518 116	2 064 885	1 933 029	1 601 687	8.5	8.4	9.5	7.0	9.8
$35,000 to $49,999	2 680 524	579 737	688 508	780 285	631 994	3.2	3.2	3.2	2.8	3.9
$50,000 to $74,999	1 214 381	275 206	290 747	364 327	284 101	1.4	1.5	1.3	1.3	1.7
$75,000 or more	749 169	168 243	178 567	227 378	174 981	0.9	0.9	0.8	0.8	1.1
Median	$12 192	$12 532	$13 217	$10 909	$12 774	...	...	...	...	...
Mean	$15 124	$15 372	$15 535	$14 063	$16 079	...	...	...	...	...
Females 15 years and over	91 482 678	20 594 335	23 613 052	30 269 053	17 006 238	100.0	100.0	100.0	100.0	100.0
Without income	21 593 481	4 802 488	5 436 856	7 401 288	3 952 849	23.6	23.3	23.0	24.5	23.2
With income	69 889 197	15 791 847	18 176 196	22 867 765	13 053 389	76.4	76.7	77.0	75.5	76.8
$1 to $999 or loss	6 733 127	1 399 558	1 854 368	2 237 434	1 241 767	7.4	6.8	7.9	7.4	7.3
$1,000 to $1,999	7 219 292	1 467 730	1 898 181	2 645 612	1 207 769	7.9	7.1	8.0	8.7	7.1
$2,000 to $2,999	7 656 012	1 641 966	1 988 006	2 826 487	1 199 553	8.4	8.0	8.4	9.3	7.1
$3,000 to $3,999	6 840 696	1 723 872	1 792 146	2 107 507	1 217 171	7.5	8.4	7.6	7.0	7.2
$4,000 to $4,999	5 290 880	1 267 556	1 361 480	1 578 535	1 083 309	5.8	6.2	5.8	5.2	6.4
$5,000 to $5,999	4 578 935	1 056 746	1 178 865	1 515 425	827 899	5.0	5.1	5.0	5.0	4.9
$6,000 to $6,999	4 334 469	947 301	1 092 211	1 524 522	770 435	4.7	4.6	4.6	5.0	4.5
$7,000 to $9,999	10 443 195	2 349 161	2 673 672	3 524 885	1 895 477	11.4	11.4	11.3	11.6	11.1
$7,000 to $7,999	3 829 537	856 472	969 555	1 331 645	671 865	4.2	4.2	4.1	4.4	4.0
$8,000 to $8,999	3 613 727	813 040	924 491	1 218 263	657 933	4.0	3.9	3.9	4.0	3.9
$9,000 to $9,999	2 999 931	679 649	779 626	974 977	565 679	3.3	3.3	3.3	3.2	3.3
$10,000 to $24,999	16 792 591	3 937 957	4 337 267	4 907 358	3 610 009	18.4	19.1	18.4	16.2	21.2
$10,000 to $14,999	10 097 540	2 343 374	2 635 270	3 090 559	2 028 337	11.0	11.4	11.2	10.2	11.9
$15,000 to $24,999	5 499 019	1 310 109	1 443 013	1 464 741	1 281 156	6.0	6.4	6.1	4.8	7.5
$25,000 or more	1 196 032	284 474	258 984	352 058	300 516	1.3	1.4	1.1	1.2	1.8
$25,000 to $34,999	771 210	190 176	173 263	211 280	196 491	0.8	0.9	0.7	0.7	1.2
$35,000 to $49,999	242 722	57 090	49 865	75 435	60 332	0.3	0.3	0.2	0.2	0.4
$50,000 to $74,999	114 211	24 187	22 472	39 727	27 825	0.1	0.1	0.1	0.1	0.2
$75,000 or more	67 889	13 021	13 384	25 616	15 868	0.1	0.1	0.1	0.1	0.1
Median	$5 263	$5 374	$5 164	$5 025	$5 697	...	...	...	...	...
Mean	$6 928	$7 080	$6 786	$6 590	$7 533	...	...	...	...	...
1970										
Persons 14 years and over	149 398 189	36 622 743	41 236 848	45 959 312	25 579 286	100.0	100.0	100.0	100.0	100.0
Without income	35 292 578	8 453 271	9 569 906	11 514 088	5 755 313	23.6	23.1	23.2	25.1	22.5
With income	114 105 611	28 169 472	31 666 942	34 445 224	19 823 973	76.4	76.9	76.8	74.9	77.5
$1 to $999 or loss	10 144 708	2 215 281	2 821 229	3 445 387	1 662 811	6.8	6.0	6.8	7.5	6.5
$1,000 to $1,999	10 107 003	2 209 504	2 810 124	3 430 085	1 657 290	6.8	6.0	6.8	7.5	6.5
$2,000 to $2,999	7 877 541	1 837 105	2 161 236	2 556 630	1 322 569	5.3	5.0	5.2	5.6	5.2
$3,000 to $3,999	7 775 594	1 812 871	2 131 543	2 523 363	1 307 817	5.2	5.0	5.2	5.5	5.1
$4,000 to $4,999	5 394 258	1 246 806	1 437 960	1 746 275	963 216	3.6	3.4	3.5	3.8	3.8
$5,000 to $5,999	5 366 630	1 241 031	1 427 432	1 745 910	952 256	3.6	3.4	3.5	3.8	3.7
$6,000 to $6,999	4 941 999	1 152 271	1 265 623	1 740 285	783 820	3.3	3.1	3.1	3.8	3.1
$7,000 to $9,999	13 352 964	3 254 784	3 430 216	4 563 430	2 104 533	8.9	8.9	8.3	9.9	8.2
$7,000 to $7,999	4 885 423	1 144 324	1 251 527	1 715 290	774 281	3.3	3.1	3.0	3.7	3.0
$8,000 to $8,999	8 467 541	2 110 460	2 178 689	2 848 140	1 330 252	5.7	5.8	5.3	6.2	5.2
$9,000 to $9,999	(¹)	(¹)	(¹)	(¹)	(¹)	(¹)	(¹)	(¹)	(¹)	(¹)

¹Included in preceding category.

Table 95. Income in 1979, 1969, and 1959 of Persons by Sex and Race: 1960 to 1980—Con.

[In 1979 dollars. Data are estimates based on a sample; see Introduction. For meaning of symbols, see introduction. For definitions of terms, see appendixes A and B]

United States Regions	Number — United States	Northeast	North Central	South	West	Percent distribution — United States	Northeast	North Central	South	West
TOTAL—Con.										
1970—Con.										
Persons 14 years and over—Con.										
With income—Con.										
$10,000 or more	49 144 914	13 199 818	14 181 578	12 693 857	9 069 660	32.9	36.0	34.4	27.6	35.5
$10,000 to $14,999	18 643 312	4 966 701	5 028 045	5 537 686	3 110 880	12.5	13.6	12.2	12.0	12.2
$15,000 to $24,999	21 104 564	5 631 982	6 490 470	4 967 011	4 015 101	14.1	15.4	15.7	10.8	15.7
$25,000 or more	9 397 037	2 601 135	2 663 063	2 189 160	1 943 679	6.3	7.1	6.5	4.8	7.6
Median	$8 134	$9 163	$8 484	$7 021	$8 734	...	...	...	...	...
Mean	$10 999	$11 836	$11 217	$9 678	$11 757	...	...	...	...	...
Males 14 years and over	71 481 904	17 226 642	19 742 895	22 012 438	12 499 929	100.0	100.0	100.0	100.0	100.0
Without income	7 386 909	1 773 377	1 867 346	2 571 534	1 174 652	10.3	10.3	9.5	11.7	9.4
With income	64 094 995	15 453 265	17 875 549	19 440 904	11 325 277	89.7	89.7	90.5	88.3	90.6
$1 to $999 or loss	3 256 632	667 627	865 160	1 163 019	560 826	4.6	3.9	4.4	5.3	4.5
$1,000 to $1,999	3 257 156	668 190	865 317	1 162 777	560 872	4.6	3.9	4.4	5.3	4.5
$2,000 to $2,999	3 129 639	663 309	832 266	1 097 245	536 819	4.4	3.9	4.2	5.0	4.3
$3,000 to $3,999	3 098 477	655 840	823 451	1 086 617	532 569	4.3	3.8	4.2	4.9	4.3
$4,000 to $4,999	2 370 551	481 358	617 544	838 353	433 296	3.3	2.8	3.1	3.8	3.5
$5,000 to $5,999	2 358 147	478 599	611 959	838 732	428 857	3.3	2.8	3.1	3.8	3.4
$6,000 to $6,999	2 167 493	436 188	526 121	844 548	360 636	3.0	2.5	2.7	3.8	2.9
$7,000 to $9,999	6 120 446	1 310 106	1 460 929	2 372 146	977 265	8.6	7.6	7.4	10.8	7.8
$7,000 to $7,999	2 151 526	435 761	521 200	838 104	356 461	3.0	2.5	2.6	3.8	2.9
$8,000 to $8,999	3 968 920	874 345	939 729	1 534 042	620 804	5.6	5.1	4.8	7.0	5.0
$9,000 to $9,999	(¹)	(¹)	(¹)	(¹)	(¹)	(¹)	(¹)	(¹)	(¹)	(¹)
$10,000 or more	38 336 452	10 092 047	11 272 802	10 037 466	6 934 136	53.6	58.6	57.1	45.6	55.5
$10,000 to $14,999	11 773 560	3 022 518	3 143 347	3 779 089	1 828 605	16.5	17.5	15.9	17.2	14.6
$15,000 to $24,999	17 891 795	4 695 202	5 635 456	4 241 295	3 319 842	25.0	27.3	28.5	19.3	26.6
$25,000 or more	8 671 097	2 374 327	2 493 999	2 017 082	1 785 689	12.1	13.8	12.6	9.2	14.3
Median	$12 759	$14 022	$13 911	$10 397	$13 628	...	...	...	...	...
Mean	$14 703	$15 177	$15 832	$12 759	$15 523	...	...	...	...	...
Females 14 years and over	77 916 285	19 396 101	21 493 953	23 946 874	13 079 357	100.0	100.0	100.0	100.0	100.0
Without income	27 905 669	6 679 894	7 702 560	8 942 554	4 580 661	35.8	34.4	35.8	37.3	35.0
With income	50 010 616	12 716 207	13 791 393	15 004 320	8 498 696	64.2	65.6	64.2	62.7	65.0
$1 to $999 or loss	6 888 075	1 547 654	1 956 069	2 282 368	1 101 984	8.8	8.0	9.1	9.5	8.4
$1,000 to $1,999	6 849 847	1 541 314	1 944 807	2 267 308	1 096 418	8.8	7.9	9.0	9.5	8.4
$2,000 to $2,999	4 747 900	1 173 796	1 328 969	1 459 385	785 750	6.1	6.1	6.2	6.1	6.0
$3,000 to $3,999	4 677 118	1 157 032	1 308 092	1 436 746	775 248	6.0	6.0	6.1	6.0	5.9
$4,000 to $4,999	3 023 707	765 448	820 417	907 922	529 920	3.9	3.9	3.8	3.8	4.1
$5,000 to $5,999	3 008 483	762 432	815 474	907 178	523 399	3.9	3.9	3.8	3.8	4.0
$6,000 to $6,999	2 774 505	716 082	739 502	895 737	423 184	3.6	3.7	3.4	3.7	3.2
$7,000 to $9,999	7 232 517	1 944 678	1 969 287	2 191 284	1 127 268	9.3	10.0	9.2	9.2	8.6
$7,000 to $7,999	2 733 896	708 563	730 327	877 186	417 820	3.5	3.7	3.4	3.7	3.2
$8,000 to $8,999	4 498 621	1 236 115	1 238 960	1 314 098	709 448	5.8	6.4	5.8	5.5	5.4
$9,000 to $9,999	(¹)	(¹)	(¹)	(¹)	(¹)	(¹)	(¹)	(¹)	(¹)	(¹)
$10,000 or more	10 808 461	3 107 740	2 908 776	2 656 392	2 135 523	13.9	16.0	13.5	11.1	16.3
$10,000 to $14,999	6 869 751	1 944 182	1 884 698	1 758 596	1 282 275	8.8	10.0	8.8	7.3	9.8
$15,000 to $24,999	3 219 572	939 340	856 296	726 642	697 294	4.1	4.8	4.0	3.0	5.3
$25,000 or more	719 138	224 248	167 782	171 154	155 954	0.9	1.2	0.8	0.7	1.2
Median	$4 609	$5 227	$4 437	$4 063	$4 926	...	...	...	...	...
Mean	$6 249	$6 770	$6 083	$5 685	$6 740	...	...	...	...	...
1960										
Persons 14 years and over	126 276 556	32 561 170	36 157 258	37 948 263	19 609 865	100.0	100.0	100.0	100.0	100.0
Without income	35 822 000	9 114 028	10 247 051	11 396 765	5 064 156	28.4	28.0	28.3	30.0	25.8
With income	90 454 556	23 447 142	25 910 207	26 551 498	14 545 709	71.6	72.0	71.7	70.0	74.2
$1 to $999 or loss	9 251 534	1 983 349	2 590 414	3 397 676	1 280 094	7.3	6.1	7.2	9.0	6.5
$1,000 to $1,999	9 260 796	1 985 335	2 593 008	3 401 077	1 281 376	7.3	6.1	7.2	9.0	6.5
$2,000 to $2,999	7 246 174	1 610 554	1 996 650	2 562 822	1 076 147	5.7	4.9	5.5	6.8	5.5
$3,000 to $3,999	5 320 036	1 252 234	1 426 485	1 761 385	879 933	4.2	3.8	3.9	4.6	4.5
$4,000 to $4,999	5 300 002	1 250 584	1 420 658	1 754 499	874 260	4.2	3.8	3.9	4.6	4.5
$5,000 to $5,999	4 364 322	1 173 518	1 148 524	1 432 932	609 347	3.5	3.6	3.2	3.8	3.1
$6,000 to $6,999	4 364 321	1 173 518	1 148 524	1 432 932	609 347	3.5	3.6	3.2	3.8	3.1
$7,000 to $9,999	12 470 000	3 586 982	3 383 356	3 660 057	1 839 604	9.9	11.0	9.4	9.6	9.4
$10,000 or more	32 877 371	9 431 068	10 202 587	7 148 116	6 095 600	26.0	29.0	28.2	18.8	31.1
Median	$7 030	$8 091	$7 553	$5 279	$8 083	...	...	...	...	...
Males 14 years and over	61 315 362	15 547 376	17 588 424	18 417 937	9 761 625	100.0	100.0	100.0	100.0	100.0
Without income	6 151 125	1 522 662	1 609 402	2 226 666	792 395	10.0	9.8	9.2	12.1	8.1
With income	55 164 237	14 024 714	15 979 022	16 191 271	8 969 230	90.0	90.2	90.8	87.9	91.9
$1 to $999 or loss	3 273 414	617 476	880 197	1 339 071	436 669	5.3	4.0	5.0	7.3	4.5
$1,000 to $1,999	3 276 691	618 094	881 078	1 340 412	437 107	5.3	4.0	5.0	7.3	4.5
$2,000 to $2,999	2 956 296	581 790	787 147	1 156 429	430 930	4.8	3.7	4.5	6.3	4.4
$3,000 to $3,999	2 649 972	547 079	697 341	980 527	425 025	4.3	3.5	4.0	5.3	4.4
$4,000 to $4,999	2 643 304	546 773	695 125	978 660	422 746	4.3	3.5	4.0	5.3	4.3
$5,000 to $5,999	2 331 936	532 483	591 657	891 466	316 330	3.8	3.4	3.4	4.8	3.2
$6,000 to $6,999	2 331 936	532 483	591 657	891 466	316 330	3.8	3.4	3.4	4.8	3.2
$7,000 to $9,999	7 459 537	2 005 489	1 969 186	2 449 549	1 035 313	12.2	12.9	11.2	13.3	10.6
$10,000 or more	28 241 151	8 043 046	8 885 635	6 163 691	5 148 779	46.1	51.7	50.5	33.5	52.7
Median	$10000+	$10000+	$10000+	$7 595	$10000+	...	...	...	...	...
Females 14 years and over	64 961 194	17 013 794	18 568 834	19 530 326	9 848 240	100.0	100.0	100.0	100.0	100.0
Without income	29 670 875	7 591 366	8 637 649	9 170 099	4 271 761	45.7	44.6	46.5	47.0	43.4
With income	35 290 319	9 422 428	9 931 185	10 360 227	5 576 479	54.3	55.4	53.5	53.0	56.6
$1 to $999 or loss	5 978 120	1 365 873	1 710 218	2 058 605	843 425	9.2	8.0	9.2	10.5	8.6
$1,000 to $1,999	5 984 104	1 367 240	1 711 930	2 060 665	844 269	9.2	8.0	9.2	10.6	8.6
$2,000 to $2,999	4 289 878	1 028 764	1 209 504	1 406 393	645 217	6.6	6.0	6.5	7.2	6.6
$3,000 to $3,999	2 670 064	705 154	729 144	780 858	454 908	4.1	4.1	3.9	4.0	4.6
$4,000 to $4,999	2 656 697	703 810	725 533	775 839	451 514	4.1	4.1	3.9	4.0	4.6
$5,000 to $5,999	2 032 385	641 035	556 867	541 466	293 017	3.1	3.8	3.0	2.8	3.0
$6,000 to $6,999	2 032 385	641 035	556 867	541 466	293 017	3.1	3.8	3.0	2.8	3.0
$7,000 to $9,999	5 010 463	1 581 494	1 414 170	1 210 508	804 292	7.7	9.3	7.6	6.2	8.2
$10,000 or more	4 636 220	1 388 021	1 316 952	984 425	946 821	7.1	8.2	7.1	5.0	9.6
Median	$3 524	$4 348	$3 459	$2 560	$4 002	...	...	...	...	...

¹Included in preceding category.

Table 95. **Income in 1979, 1969, and 1959 of Persons by Sex and Race: 1960 to 1980**—Con.

[In 1979 dollars. Data are estimates based on a sample; see Introduction. For meaning of symbols, see Introduction. For definitions of terms, see appendixes A and B]

United States Regions	Number					Percent distribution				
	United States	Northeast	North Central	South	West	United States	Northeast	North Central	South	West
WHITE										
1980										
Persons 15 years and over	148 694 602	33 965 054	40 667 346	46 420 379	27 641 823	100.0	100.0	100.0	100.0	100.0
Without income	22 739 301	5 312 591	6 012 575	7 416 817	3 997 318	15.3	15.6	14.8	16.0	14.5
With income	125 955 301	28 652 463	34 654 771	39 003 562	23 644 505	84.7	84.4	85.2	84.0	85.5
$1 to $999 or loss	8 433 005	1 851 730	2 493 595	2 535 660	1 552 020	5.7	5.5	6.1	5.5	5.6
$1,000 to $1,999	8 622 093	1 867 033	2 428 099	2 869 084	1 457 877	5.8	5.5	6.0	6.2	5.3
$2,000 to $2,999	8 990 618	1 984 087	2 475 473	3 074 850	1 456 208	6.0	5.8	6.1	6.6	5.3
$3,000 to $3,999	8 667 049	2 123 818	2 354 384	2 649 350	1 539 497	5.8	6.3	5.8	5.7	5.6
$4,000 to $4,999	7 181 863	1 700 323	1 920 444	2 127 806	1 433 290	4.8	5.0	4.7	4.6	5.2
$5,000 to $5,999	6 499 808	1 493 211	1 735 201	2 076 731	1 194 665	4.4	4.4	4.3	4.5	4.3
$6,000 to $6,999	6 268 978	1 380 462	1 633 089	2 107 170	1 148 257	4.2	4.1	4.0	4.5	4.2
$7,000 to $9,999	16 174 848	3 647 298	4 230 286	5 392 573	2 904 691	10.9	10.7	10.4	11.6	10.5
$7,000 to $7,999	5 719 654	1 291 193	1 493 928	1 921 554	1 012 979	3.8	3.8	3.7	4.1	3.7
$8,000 to $8,999	5 586 621	1 256 244	1 457 475	1 866 838	1 006 064	3.8	3.7	3.6	4.0	3.6
$9,000 to $9,999	4 868 573	1 099 861	1 278 883	1 604 181	885 648	3.3	3.2	3.1	3.5	3.2
$10,000 to $24,999	55 117 039	12 604 501	15 384 200	16 170 338	10 958 000	37.1	37.1	37.8	34.8	39.6
$10,000 to $14,999	20 298 238	4 689 003	5 476 276	6 417 813	3 715 146	13.7	13.8	13.5	13.8	13.4
$15,000 to $24,999	22 618 760	5 224 636	6 594 763	6 307 849	4 491 512	15.2	15.4	16.2	13.6	16.2
$25,000 or more	12 200 041	2 690 862	3 313 161	3 444 676	2 751 342	8.2	7.9	8.1	7.4	10.0
$25,000 to $34,999	7 366 963	1 617 013	2 113 798	2 003 262	1 632 890	5.0	4.8	5.2	4.3	5.9
$35,000 to $49,999	2 784 057	609 844	712 031	816 482	645 700	1.9	1.8	1.8	1.8	2.3
$50,000 to $74,999	1 268 135	288 299	302 797	384 450	292 589	0.9	0.8	0.7	0.8	1.1
$75,000 or more	780 886	175 706	184 535	240 482	180 163	0.5	0.5	0.5	0.5	0.7
Median	$8 464	$8 505	$8 544	$8 075	$9 024	...	...	...	...	...
Mean	$11 718	$11 682	$11 622	$11 282	$12 620	...	...	...	...	...
Males 15 years and over	71 348 399	16 009 326	19 509 992	22 321 935	13 507 146	100.0	100.0	100.0	100.0	100.0
Without income	4 512 244	1 139 604	1 111 085	1 465 874	795 681	6.3	7.1	5.7	6.6	5.9
With income	66 836 155	14 869 722	18 398 907	20 856 061	12 711 465	93.7	92.9	94.3	93.4	94.1
$1 to $999 or loss	2 784 137	621 738	819 812	824 491	518 096	3.9	3.9	4.2	3.7	3.8
$1,000 to $1,999	2 571 592	563 216	701 721	867 210	439 445	3.6	3.5	3.6	3.9	3.3
$2,000 to $2,999	2 722 347	556 011	733 222	986 541	446 573	3.8	3.5	3.8	4.4	3.3
$3,000 to $3,999	2 912 505	640 682	767 475	978 592	525 756	4.1	4.0	3.9	4.4	3.9
$4,000 to $4,999	2 719 234	601 530	700 087	874 767	542 850	3.8	3.8	3.6	3.9	4.0
$5,000 to $5,999	2 640 033	573 556	671 195	883 652	511 630	3.7	3.6	3.4	4.0	3.8
$6,000 to $6,999	2 617 034	554 663	646 458	903 612	512 301	3.7	3.5	3.3	4.0	3.8
$7,000 to $9,999	7 285 690	1 599 614	1 827 605	2 524 979	1 333 492	10.2	10.0	9.4	11.3	9.9
$7,000 to $7,999	2 466 298	543 289	618 435	848 016	456 558	3.5	3.4	3.2	3.8	3.4
$8,000 to $8,999	2 507 227	545 836	626 523	874 063	460 805	3.5	3.4	3.2	3.9	3.4
$9,000 to $9,999	2 312 165	510 489	582 647	802 900	416 129	3.2	3.2	3.0	3.6	3.1
$10,000 to $24,999	40 583 583	9 158 712	11 531 332	12 012 217	7 881 322	56.9	57.2	59.1	53.8	58.3
$10,000 to $14,999	11 592 083	2 650 360	3 117 572	3 818 763	2 005 388	16.2	16.6	16.0	17.1	14.8
$15,000 to $24,999	17 867 458	4 077 517	5 335 763	5 061 764	3 392 414	25.0	25.5	27.3	22.7	25.1
$25,000 or more	11 124 042	2 430 835	3 077 997	3 131 690	2 483 520	15.6	15.2	15.8	14.0	18.4
$25,000 to $34,999	6 676 373	1 444 253	1 957 655	1 815 180	1 459 285	9.4	9.0	10.0	8.1	10.8
$35,000 to $49,999	2 562 373	557 080	665 762	748 451	591 080	3.6	3.5	3.4	3.4	4.4
$50,000 to $74,999	1 165 267	265 943	282 247	349 711	267 366	1.6	1.7	1.4	1.6	2.0
$75,000 or more	720 029	163 559	172 333	218 348	165 789	1.0	1.0	0.9	1.0	1.2
Median	$12 881	$13 035	$13 572	$11 916	$13 610	...	...	...	...	...
Mean	$15 865	$15 921	$15 910	$15 143	$16 917	...	...	...	...	...
Females 15 years and over	77 346 203	17 955 728	21 157 354	24 098 444	14 134 677	100.0	100.0	100.0	100.0	100.0
Without income	18 227 057	4 172 987	4 901 490	5 950 943	3 201 637	23.6	23.2	23.2	24.7	22.7
With income	59 119 146	13 782 741	16 255 864	18 147 501	10 933 040	76.4	76.8	76.8	75.3	77.3
$1 to $999 or loss	5 648 868	1 229 992	1 673 783	1 711 169	1 033 924	7.3	6.9	7.9	7.1	7.3
$1,000 to $1,999	6 050 501	1 303 817	1 726 378	2 001 874	1 018 432	7.8	7.3	8.2	8.3	7.2
$2,000 to $2,999	6 268 271	1 428 076	1 742 251	2 088 309	1 009 635	8.1	8.0	8.2	8.7	7.1
$3,000 to $3,999	5 754 544	1 483 136	1 586 909	1 670 758	1 013 741	7.4	8.3	7.5	6.9	7.2
$4,000 to $4,999	4 462 629	1 098 793	1 220 357	1 253 039	890 440	5.8	6.1	5.8	5.2	6.3
$5,000 to $5,999	3 859 775	919 655	1 064 006	1 193 079	683 035	5.0	5.1	5.0	5.0	4.8
$6,000 to $6,999	3 651 944	825 799	986 631	1 203 558	635 956	4.7	4.6	4.7	5.0	4.5
$7,000 to $9,999	8 889 158	2 047 684	2 402 681	2 867 594	1 571 199	11.5	11.4	11.4	11.9	11.1
$7,000 to $7,999	3 253 356	747 904	875 493	1 073 538	556 421	4.2	4.2	4.1	4.5	3.9
$8,000 to $8,999	3 079 394	710 408	830 952	992 775	545 259	4.0	4.0	3.9	4.1	3.9
$9,000 to $9,999	2 556 408	589 372	696 236	801 281	469 519	3.3	3.3	3.3	3.3	3.3
$10,000 to $24,999	14 533 456	3 445 789	3 852 868	4 158 121	3 076 678	18.8	19.2	18.2	17.3	21.8
$10,000 to $14,999	8 706 155	2 038 643	2 358 704	2 599 050	1 709 758	11.3	11.4	11.1	10.8	12.1
$15,000 to $24,999	4 751 302	1 147 119	1 259 000	1 246 085	1 099 098	6.1	6.4	6.0	5.2	7.8
$25,000 or more	1 075 999	260 027	235 164	312 986	267 822	1.4	1.4	1.1	1.3	1.9
$25,000 to $34,999	690 590	172 760	156 143	188 082	173 605	0.9	1.0	0.7	0.8	1.2
$35,000 to $49,999	221 684	52 764	46 269	68 031	54 620	0.3	0.3	0.2	0.3	0.4
$50,000 to $74,999	102 868	22 356	20 550	34 739	25 223	0.1	0.1	0.1	0.1	0.2
$75,000 or more	60 857	12 147	12 202	22 134	14 374	0.1	0.1	0.1	0.1	0.1
Median	$5 356	$5 378	$5 168	$5 292	$5 733	...	...	...	...	...
Mean	$7 030	$7 108	$6 770	$6 845	$7 624	...	...	...	...	...
1970										
Persons 14 years and over	132 459 553	33 438 218	37 969 735	37 738 884	23 312 696	100.0	100.0	100.0	100.0	100.0
Without income	30 965 411	7 672 116	8 747 226	9 336 654	5 209 415	23.4	22.9	23.0	24.7	22.3
With income	101 494 122	25 766 102	29 222 509	28 402 230	18 103 281	76.6	77.1	77.0	75.3	77.7
$1 to $999 or loss	8 742 910	2 034 738	2 599 485	2 596 096	1 512 591	6.6	6.1	6.8	6.9	6.5
$1,000 to $1,999	8 711 198	2 029 219	2 589 041	2 585 521	1 507 416	6.6	6.1	6.8	6.9	6.5
$2,000 to $2,999	6 826 269	1 677 250	1 981 301	1 971 885	1 195 832	5.2	5.0	5.2	5.2	5.1
$3,000 to $3,999	6 736 971	1 654 205	1 953 803	1 946 581	1 182 382	5.1	4.9	5.1	5.2	5.1
$4,000 to $4,999	4 651 082	1 115 904	1 311 470	1 355 504	868 204	3.5	3.3	3.5	3.6	3.7
$5,000 to $5,999	4 625 833	1 109 826	1 301 331	1 356 490	858 185	3.5	3.3	3.4	3.6	3.7
$6,000 to $6,999	4 237 754	1 016 415	1 145 496	1 371 644	704 199	3.2	3.0	3.0	3.6	3.0
$7,000 to $9,999	11 541 688	2 861 047	3 102 137	3 696 150	1 882 353	8.7	8.6	8.2	9.8	8.1
$7,000 to $7,999	4 192 633	1 008 990	1 132 637	1 355 713	695 293	3.2	3.0	3.0	3.6	3.0
$8,000 to $8,999	7 349 055	1 852 057	1 969 500	2 340 437	1 187 060	5.5	5.5	5.2	6.2	5.1
$9,000 to $9,999	(¹)	(¹)	(¹)	(¹)	(¹)	(¹)	(¹)	(¹)	(¹)	(¹)

¹Included in preceding category.

Table 95. Income in 1979, 1969, and 1959 of Persons by Sex and Race: 1960 to 1980—Con.

[In 1979 dollars. Data are estimates based on a sample; see Introduction. For meaning of symbols, see Introduction. For definitions of terms, see appendixes A and B]

United States Regions	Number					Percent distribution				
	United States	Northeast	North Central	South	West	United States	Northeast	North Central	South	West
WHITE—Con.										
1970—Con.										
Persons 14 years and over—Con.										
With income—Con.										
$10,000 or more	45 420 416	12 267 497	13 238 442	11 522 358	8 392 118	34.3	36.7	34.9	30.5	36.0
$10,000 to $14,999	16 564 321	4 435 544	4 556 515	4 773 791	2 798 471	12.5	13.3	12.0	12.6	12.0
$15,000 to $24,999	19 722 792	5 294 023	6 082 805	4 615 275	3 730 689	14.9	15.8	16.0	12.2	16.0
$25,000 or more	9 133 302	2 537 930	2 599 122	2 133 292	1 862 958	6.9	7.6	6.8	5.7	8.0
Median	$8 549	$9 163	$8 605	$7 744	$8 888	...	...	...	...	...
Mean	$11 445	(NA)	(NA)	(NA)	(NA)	...	...	...	...	...
Males 14 years and over	63 578 712	15 785 382	18 218 089	18 196 558	11 378 683	100.0	100.0	100.0	100.0	100.0
Without income	6 000 848	1 524 247	1 606 732	1 863 618	1 006 251	9.4	9.7	8.8	10.2	8.8
With income	57 577 864	14 261 135	16 611 357	16 332 940	10 372 432	90.6	90.3	91.2	89.8	91.2
$1 to $999 or loss	2 749 385	601 433	784 235	863 686	500 031	4.3	3.8	4.3	4.7	4.4
$1,000 to $1,999	2 751 153	602 098	784 584	864 361	500 110	4.3	3.8	4.3	4.8	4.4
$2,000 to $2,999	2 705 258	605 013	764 277	855 487	480 481	4.3	3.8	4.2	4.7	4.2
$3,000 to $3,999	2 678 188	598 113	756 304	846 990	476 781	4.2	3.8	4.2	4.7	4.2
$4,000 to $4,999	2 045 872	436 951	570 065	648 513	390 343	3.2	2.8	3.1	3.6	3.4
$5,000 to $5,999	2 032 471	434 010	564 668	647 453	386 340	3.2	2.7	3.1	3.6	3.4
$6,000 to $6,999	1 826 509	388 816	481 721	631 151	324 821	2.9	2.5	2.6	3.5	2.9
$7,000 to $9,999	5 167 693	1 151 244	1 328 186	1 816 647	871 616	8.1	7.3	7.3	10.0	7.7
$7,000 to $7,999	1 813 261	387 789	476 859	627 888	320 725	2.9	2.5	2.6	3.5	2.8
$8,000 to $8,999	3 354 432	763 455	851 327	1 188 759	550 891	5.3	4.8	4.7	6.5	4.8
$9,000 to $9,999	(¹)	(¹)	(¹)	(¹)	(¹)	(¹)	(¹)	(¹)	(¹)	(¹)
$10,000 or more	35 621 331	9 443 456	10 577 318	9 158 650	6 441 907	56.0	59.8	58.1	50.3	56.6
$10,000 to $14,999	10 385 660	2 693 268	2 841 440	3 213 822	1 637 130	16.3	17.1	15.6	17.7	14.4
$15,000 to $24,999	16 787 395	4 428 101	5 296 662	3 971 674	3 090 958	26.4	28.1	29.1	21.8	27.2
$25,000 or more	8 448 276	2 322 087	2 439 216	1 973 154	1 713 819	13.3	14.7	13.4	10.8	15.1
Median	$13 408	$14 378	$14 157	$11 506	$13 983	...	...	...	...	...
Mean	$15 315	(NA)	(NA)	(NA)	(NA)	...	...	...	...	...
Females 14 years and over	68 880 821	17 652 836	19 751 646	19 542 326	11 934 013	100.0	100.0	100.0	100.0	100.0
Without income	24 964 563	6 147 869	7 140 494	7 473 036	4 203 164	36.2	34.8	36.2	38.2	35.2
With income	43 916 258	11 504 967	12 611 152	12 069 290	7 730 849	63.8	65.2	63.8	61.8	64.8
$1 to $999 or loss	5 993 525	1 433 305	1 815 251	1 732 410	1 012 559	8.7	8.1	9.2	8.9	8.5
$1,000 to $1,999	5 960 046	1 427 121	1 804 457	1 721 161	1 007 306	8.7	8.1	9.1	8.8	8.4
$2,000 to $2,999	4 121 011	1 072 237	1 217 025	1 116 398	715 351	6.0	6.1	6.2	5.7	6.0
$3,000 to $3,999	4 058 783	1 056 092	1 197 499	1 099 591	705 601	5.9	6.0	6.1	5.6	5.9
$4,000 to $4,999	2 605 209	678 953	741 405	706 990	477 861	3.8	3.8	3.8	3.6	4.0
$5,000 to $5,999	2 593 360	675 816	736 663	709 037	471 845	3.8	3.8	3.7	3.6	4.0
$6,000 to $6,999	2 411 245	627 599	663 775	740 492	379 378	3.5	3.6	3.4	3.8	3.2
$7,000 to $9,999	6 373 993	1 709 802	1 773 952	1 879 502	1 010 737	9.3	9.7	9.0	9.6	8.5
$7,000 to $7,999	2 379 371	621 201	655 778	727 824	374 568	3.5	3.5	3.3	3.7	3.1
$8,000 to $8,999	3 994 622	1 088 601	1 118 174	1 151 678	636 169	5.8	6.2	5.7	5.9	5.3
$9,000 to $9,999	(¹)	(¹)	(¹)	(¹)	(¹)	(¹)	(¹)	(¹)	(¹)	(¹)
$10,000 or more	9 799 084	2 824 041	2 661 123	2 363 709	1 950 211	14.2	16.0	13.5	12.1	16.3
$10,000 to $14,999	6 178 661	1 742 276	1 715 074	1 559 970	1 161 341	9.0	9.9	8.7	8.0	9.7
$15,000 to $24,999	2 941 522	868 306	787 265	644 371	641 580	4.3	4.9	4.0	3.3	5.4
$25,000 or more	678 901	213 459	158 784	159 368	147 290	1.0	1.2	0.8	0.8	1.2
Median	$4 700	$5 126	$4 368	$4 518	$4 891	...	...	...	...	...
Mean	$6 370	(NA)	(NA)	(NA)	(NA)	...	...	...	...	...
1960										
Persons 14 years and over	113 122 902	30 398 402	33 816 919	30 739 565	18 168 016	100.0	100.0	100.0	100.0	100.0
Without income	32 102 516	8 536 383	9 558 229	9 335 306	4 672 598	28.4	28.1	28.3	30.4	25.7
With income	81 020 386	21 862 019	24 258 690	21 404 259	13 495 418	71.6	71.9	71.7	69.6	74.3
$1 to $999 or loss	7 784 354	1 842 184	2 405 441	2 359 579	1 177 150	6.9	6.1	7.1	7.7	6.5
$1,000 to $1,999	7 792 146	1 844 028	2 407 849	2 361 941	1 178 328	6.9	6.1	7.1	7.7	6.5
$2,000 to $2,999	6 149 727	1 482 513	1 846 610	1 832 880	987 723	5.4	4.9	5.5	6.0	5.4
$3,000 to $3,999	4 579 442	1 136 876	1 310 020	1 327 056	805 490	4.0	3.7	3.9	4.3	4.4
$4,000 to $4,999	4 563 191	1 135 020	1 304 629	1 323 439	800 103	4.0	3.7	3.9	4.3	4.4
$5,000 to $5,999	3 804 222	1 048 359	1 052 815	1 154 504	548 545	3.4	3.4	3.1	3.8	3.0
$6,000 to $6,999	3 804 223	1 048 359	1 052 815	1 154 504	548 545	3.4	3.4	3.1	3.8	3.0
$7,000 to $9,999	11 168 914	3 249 896	3 121 305	3 135 287	1 662 426	9.9	10.7	9.2	10.2	9.2
$10,000 or more	31 374 167	9 074 784	9 757 205	6 755 069	5 787 108	27.7	29.9	28.9	22.0	31.9
Median	$7 538	$8 298	$7 717	$6 298	$8 273	...	...	...	...	...
Males 14 years and over	55 036 177	14 541 640	16 465 496	15 012 372	9 016 669	100.0	100.0	100.0	100.0	100.0
Without income	5 160 938	1 377 768	1 436 329	1 654 020	692 821	9.4	9.5	8.7	11.0	7.7
With income	49 875 239	13 163 872	15 029 167	13 358 352	8 323 848	90.6	90.5	91.3	89.0	92.3
$1 to $999 or loss	2 710 993	569 697	812 619	934 069	394 608	4.9	3.9	4.9	6.2	4.4
$1,000 to $1,999	2 713 708	570 267	813 433	935 004	395 003	4.9	3.9	4.9	6.2	4.4
$2,000 to $2,999	2 485 019	536 088	728 987	828 816	391 127	4.5	3.7	4.4	5.5	4.3
$3,000 to $3,999	2 266 375	503 410	648 251	727 292	387 422	4.1	3.5	3.9	4.8	4.3
$4,000 to $4,999	2 260 089	502 801	646 056	726 014	385 218	4.1	3.5	3.9	4.8	4.3
$5,000 to $5,999	1 966 494	474 350	543 570	666 286	282 288	3.6	3.3	3.3	4.4	3.1
$6,000 to $6,999	1 966 494	474 350	543 570	666 286	282 288	3.6	3.3	3.3	4.4	3.1
$7,000 to $9,999	6 525 462	1 791 060	1 794 256	2 022 007	918 138	11.9	12.3	10.9	13.5	10.2
$10,000 or more	26 980 604	7 741 847	8 498 424	5 852 577	4 887 755	49.0	53.2	51.6	39.0	54.2
Median	$10000+	$10000+	$10000+	$8 776	$10000+	...	...	...	...	...
Females 14 years and over	58 086 725	15 856 762	17 351 423	15 727 193	9 151 347	100.0	100.0	100.0	100.0	100.0
Without income	26 941 578	7 158 615	8 121 900	7 681 286	3 979 777	46.4	45.1	46.8	48.8	43.5
With income	31 145 147	8 698 147	9 229 523	8 045 907	5 171 570	53.6	54.9	53.2	51.2	56.5
$1 to $999 or loss	5 073 361	1 272 487	1 592 822	1 425 510	782 542	8.7	8.0	9.2	9.1	8.6
$1,000 to $1,999	5 078 439	1 273 760	1 594 417	1 426 937	783 325	8.7	8.0	9.2	9.1	8.6
$2,000 to $2,999	3 664 706	946 425	1 117 623	1 004 064	596 596	6.3	6.0	6.4	6.4	6.5
$3,000 to $3,999	2 313 066	633 465	661 770	599 763	418 068	4.0	4.0	3.8	3.8	4.6
$4,000 to $4,999	2 303 102	632 219	658 572	597 425	414 885	4.0	4.0	3.8	3.8	4.5
$5,000 to $5,999	1 837 729	574 009	509 245	488 218	266 257	3.2	3.6	2.9	3.1	2.9
$6,000 to $6,999	1 837 729	574 009	509 245	488 218	266 257	3.2	3.6	2.9	3.1	2.9
$7,000 to $9,999	4 643 452	1 458 836	1 327 048	1 113 280	744 287	8.0	9.2	7.6	7.1	8.1
$10,000 or more	4 393 563	1 332 937	1 258 781	902 492	899 353	7.6	8.4	7.3	5.7	9.8
Median	$3 760	$4 353	$3 469	$3 280	$4 014	...	...	...	...	...

¹Included in preceding category.

Table 95. Income in 1979, 1969, and 1959 of Persons by Sex and Race: 1960 to 1980—Con.

[In 1979 dollars. Data are estimates based on a sample; see Introduction. For meaning of symbols, see Introduction. For definitions of terms, see appendixes A and B]

United States Regions	Number United States	Northeast	North Central	South	West	Percent distribution United States	Northeast	North Central	South	West
BLACK										
1980										
Persons 15 years and over	18 897 157	3 534 576	3 750 143	9 959 435	1 653 003	100.0	100.0	100.0	100.0	100.0
Without income	3 672 731	728 824	702 329	1 952 895	288 683	19.4	20.6	18.7	19.6	17.5
With income	15 224 426	2 805 752	3 047 814	8 006 540	1 364 320	80.6	79.4	81.3	80.4	82.5
$1 to $999 or loss	1 339 153	216 654	258 351	761 858	102 290	7.1	6.1	6.9	7.6	6.2
$1,000 to $1,999	1 393 000	201 398	231 277	871 365	88 960	7.4	5.7	6.2	8.7	5.4
$2,000 to $2,999	1 683 771	247 726	315 277	1 030 424	90 344	8.9	7.0	8.4	10.3	5.5
$3,000 to $3,999	1 313 250	269 930	267 801	667 773	107 746	6.9	7.6	7.1	6.7	6.5
$4,000 to $4,999	1 009 326	189 328	191 953	508 635	119 410	5.3	5.4	5.1	5.1	7.2
$5,000 to $5,999	901 480	156 764	157 138	504 382	83 196	4.8	4.4	4.2	5.1	5.0
$6,000 to $6,999	889 517	144 246	145 474	521 417	78 380	4.7	4.1	3.9	5.2	4.7
$7,000 to $9,999	2 176 063	407 250	383 343	1 195 694	189 776	11.5	11.5	10.2	12.0	11.5
$7,000 to $7,999	782 097	138 561	132 653	446 027	64 856	4.1	3.9	3.5	4.5	3.9
$8,000 to $8,999	745 015	138 496	131 199	409 279	66 041	3.9	3.9	3.5	4.1	4.0
$9,000 to $9,999	648 951	130 193	119 491	340 388	58 879	3.4	3.7	3.2	3.4	3.6
$10,000 to $24,999	4 518 866	972 456	1 097 200	1 944 992	504 218	23.9	27.5	29.3	19.5	30.5
$10,000 to $14,999	2 253 734	493 491	461 732	1 074 658	223 853	11.9	14.0	12.3	10.8	13.5
$15,000 to $24,999	1 836 843	395 385	512 980	712 453	216 025	9.7	11.2	13.7	7.2	13.1
$25,000 or more	428 289	83 580	122 488	157 881	64 340	2.3	2.4	3.3	1.6	3.9
$25,000 to $34,999	314 342	62 718	96 471	108 318	46 835	1.7	1.8	2.6	1.1	2.8
$35,000 to $49,999	70 557	14 498	17 894	27 150	11 015	0.4	0.4	0.5	0.3	0.7
$50,000 to $74,999	27 103	4 323	5 117	13 491	4 172	0.1	0.1	0.1	0.1	0.3
$75,000 or more	16 287	2 041	3 006	8 922	2 318	0.1	0.1	0.1	0.1	0.1
Median	$5 969	$6 839	$6 702	$5 324	$7 182	...	...	...	...	...
Mean	$7 905	$8 520	$8 915	$7 051	$9 398	...	...	...	...	...
Males 15 years and over	8 677 940	1 570 228	1 718 370	4 572 463	816 879	100.0	100.0	100.0	100.0	100.0
Without income	1 493 429	303 238	296 661	767 827	125 703	17.2	19.3	17.3	16.8	15.4
With income	7 184 511	1 266 990	1 421 709	3 804 636	691 176	82.8	80.7	82.7	83.2	84.6
$1 to $999 or loss	552 875	93 906	111 179	300 427	47 363	6.4	6.0	6.5	6.6	5.8
$1,000 to $1,999	496 562	77 992	88 778	291 705	38 087	5.7	5.0	5.2	6.4	4.7
$2,000 to $2,999	575 754	85 107	99 317	355 259	36 071	6.6	5.4	5.8	7.8	4.4
$3,000 to $3,999	492 731	85 773	89 326	276 785	40 847	5.7	5.5	5.2	6.1	5.0
$4,000 to $4,999	403 348	65 849	71 232	220 143	46 124	4.6	4.2	4.1	4.8	5.6
$5,000 to $5,999	378 026	58 146	61 134	221 014	37 732	4.4	3.7	3.6	4.8	4.6
$6,000 to $6,999	393 588	55 901	58 505	239 754	39 428	4.5	3.6	3.4	5.2	4.8
$7,000 to $9,999	1 036 998	171 827	157 873	616 220	91 078	11.9	10.9	9.2	13.5	11.1
$7,000 to $7,999	361 974	56 328	55 222	219 405	31 019	4.2	3.6	3.2	4.8	3.8
$8,000 to $8,999	354 057	58 168	53 821	210 391	31 677	4.1	3.7	3.1	4.6	3.9
$9,000 to $9,999	320 967	57 331	48 830	186 424	28 382	3.7	3.7	2.8	4.1	3.5
$10,000 to $24,999	2 854 629	572 489	684 365	1 283 329	314 446	32.9	36.5	39.8	28.1	38.5
$10,000 to $14,999	1 220 091	241 257	226 064	639 208	113 562	14.1	15.4	13.2	14.0	13.9
$15,000 to $24,999	1 285 409	264 437	353 950	519 046	147 976	14.8	16.8	20.6	11.4	18.1
$25,000 or more	349 129	66 795	104 351	125 075	52 908	4.0	4.3	6.1	2.7	6.5
$25,000 to $34,999	258 986	49 649	82 605	88 626	38 106	3.0	3.2	4.8	1.9	4.7
$35,000 to $49,999	58 162	12 099	15 437	21 294	9 332	0.7	0.8	0.9	0.5	1.1
$50,000 to $74,999	20 298	3 516	4 097	9 194	3 491	0.2	0.2	0.2	0.2	0.4
$75,000 or more	11 683	1 531	2 212	5 961	1 979	0.1	0.1	0.1	0.1	0.2
Median	$7 827	$8 937	$9 458	$6 988	$8 913	...	...	...	...	...
Mean	$9 728	$10 367	$11 221	$8 680	$11 257	...	...	...	...	...
Females 15 years and over	10 219 217	1 964 348	2 031 773	5 386 972	836 124	100.0	100.0	100.0	100.0	100.0
Without income	2 179 302	425 586	405 668	1 185 068	162 980	21.3	21.7	20.0	22.0	19.5
With income	8 039 915	1 538 762	1 626 105	4 201 904	673 144	78.7	78.3	80.0	78.0	80.5
$1 to $999 or loss	786 278	122 748	147 172	461 431	54 927	7.7	6.2	7.2	8.6	6.6
$1,000 to $1,999	896 438	123 406	142 499	579 660	50 873	8.8	6.3	7.0	10.8	6.1
$2,000 to $2,999	1 108 017	162 619	215 960	675 165	54 273	10.8	8.3	10.6	12.5	6.5
$3,000 to $3,999	820 519	184 157	178 475	390 988	66 899	8.0	9.4	8.8	7.3	8.0
$4,000 to $4,999	605 978	123 479	120 721	288 492	73 286	5.9	6.3	5.9	5.4	8.8
$5,000 to $5,999	523 454	98 618	96 004	283 368	45 464	5.1	5.0	4.7	5.3	5.4
$6,000 to $6,999	495 929	88 345	86 969	281 663	38 952	4.9	4.5	4.3	5.2	4.7
$7,000 to $9,999	1 139 065	235 423	225 470	579 474	98 698	11.1	12.0	11.1	10.8	11.8
$7,000 to $7,999	420 123	82 233	77 431	226 622	33 837	4.1	4.2	3.8	4.2	4.0
$8,000 to $8,999	390 958	80 328	77 378	198 888	34 364	3.8	4.1	3.8	3.7	4.1
$9,000 to $9,999	327 984	72 862	70 661	153 964	30 497	3.2	3.7	3.5	2.9	3.6
$10,000 to $24,999	1 664 237	399 967	412 835	661 663	189 772	16.3	20.4	20.3	12.3	22.7
$10,000 to $14,999	1 033 643	252 234	235 668	435 450	110 291	10.1	12.8	11.6	8.1	13.2
$15,000 to $24,999	551 434	130 948	159 030	193 407	68 049	5.4	6.7	7.8	3.6	8.1
$25,000 or more	79 160	16 785	18 137	32 806	11 432	0.8	0.9	0.9	0.6	1.4
$25,000 to $34,999	55 356	13 069	13 866	19 692	8 729	0.5	0.7	0.7	0.4	1.0
$35,000 to $49,999	12 395	2 399	2 457	5 856	1 683	0.1	0.1	0.1	0.1	0.2
$50,000 to $74,999	6 805	807	1 020	4 297	681	0.1	–	0.1	0.1	0.1
$75,000 or more	4 604	510	794	2 961	339	–	–	–	0.1	–
Median	$4 674	$5 537	$5 086	$3 984	$5 799	...	...	...	...	...
Mean	$6 276	$7 000	$6 898	$5 577	$7 489	...	...	...	...	...
1970										
Persons 14 years and over	15 129 883	2 954 754	3 056 447	7 981 485	1 137 197	100.0	100.0	100.0	100.0	100.0
Without income	3 854 931	722 196	767 566	2 105 763	259 406	25.5	24.4	25.1	26.4	22.8
With income	11 274 952	2 232 558	2 288 881	5 875 722	877 791	74.5	75.6	74.9	73.6	77.2
$1 to $999 or loss	1 272 524	166 920	204 842	830 722	70 040	8.4	5.6	6.7	10.4	6.2
$1,000 to $1,999	1 267 129	166 700	204 278	826 068	70 083	8.4	5.6	6.7	10.3	6.2
$2,000 to $2,999	956 484	148 668	168 466	570 514	68 836	6.3	5.0	5.5	7.1	6.1
$3,000 to $3,999	944 906	147 574	166 390	562 694	68 248	6.2	5.0	5.4	7.0	6.0
$4,000 to $4,999	674 470	122 012	117 909	380 031	54 518	4.5	4.1	3.9	4.8	4.8
$5,000 to $5,999	672 463	122 284	117 582	378 776	53 822	4.4	4.1	3.8	4.7	4.7
$6,000 to $6,999	641 609	126 467	112 549	359 476	43 116	4.2	4.3	3.7	4.5	3.8
$7,000 to $9,999	1 642 223	367 837	308 901	844 806	128 710	10.9	12.4	10.1	10.6	11.3
$7,000 to $7,999	630 866	126 029	111 446	350 604	42 788	4.2	4.3	3.6	4.4	3.8
$8,000 to $8,999	1 011 357	241 808	197 455	494 202	77 892	6.7	8.2	6.5	6.2	6.8
$9,000 to $9,999	(¹)	(¹)	(¹)	(¹)	(¹)	(¹)	(¹)	(¹)	(¹)	(¹)

¹Included in preceding category.

Table 95. Income in 1979, 1969, and 1959 of Persons by Sex and Race: 1960 to 1980—Con.

[In 1979 dollars. Data are estimates based on a sample; see Introduction. For meaning of symbols, see Introduction. For definitions of terms, see appendixes A and B]

United States Regions	Number					Percent distribution				
	United States	Northeast	North Central	South	West	United States	Northeast	North Central	South	West
BLACK—Con.										
1970—Con.										
Persons 14 years and over—Con.										
With income—Con.										
$10,000 or more	3 203 144	864 097	887 965	1 122 633	62 724	21.2	29.2	29.1	14.1	5.5
$10,000 to $14,999	1 860 556	501 592	448 940	740 010	170 013	12.3	17.0	14.7	9.3	15.0
$15,000 to $24,999	1 173 174	314 819	388 045	335 831	134 479	7.8	10.7	12.7	4.2	11.8
$25,000 or more	169 414	47 686	50 980	46 792	23 956	1.1	1.6	1.7	0.6	2.1
Median	$5 776	$7 916	$7 466	$4 390	$7 239	...	...	...	...	...
Mean	$7 128	(NA)	(NA)	(NA)	(NA)	...	...	...	...	...
Males 14 years and over	7 010 499	1 328 235	1 425 060	3 700 025	557 179	100.0	100.0	100.0	100.0	100.0
Without income	1 261 535	234 243	246 854	690 241	90 120	18.0	17.6	17.3	18.7	16.2
With income	5 748 964	1 093 992	1 178 206	3 009 784	466 982	82.0	82.4	82.7	81.3	83.8
$1 to $999 or loss	455 514	60 754	74 057	291 704	29 000	6.5	4.6	5.2	7.9	5.2
$1,000 to $1,999	454 345	60 656	73 890	290 790	29 009	6.5	4.6	5.2	7.9	5.2
$2,000 to $2,999	378 633	53 233	62 666	234 638	28 095	5.4	4.0	4.4	6.3	5.0
$3,000 to $3,999	374 975	52 688	61 876	232 544	27 867	5.3	4.0	4.3	6.3	5.0
$4,000 to $4,999	289 511	39 945	43 414	183 619	22 534	4.1	3.0	3.0	5.0	4.0
$5,000 to $5,999	290 725	40 096	43 239	185 119	22 271	4.1	3.0	3.0	5.0	4.0
$6,000 to $6,999	309 378	42 419	40 546	208 180	18 233	4.4	3.2	2.8	5.6	3.3
$7,000 to $9,999	864 924	144 626	123 134	541 748	55 416	12.3	10.9	8.6	14.6	9.9
$7,000 to $7,999	306 930	43 042	40 563	205 072	18 253	4.4	3.2	2.8	5.5	3.3
$8,000 to $8,999	557 994	101 584	82 571	336 676	37 163	8.0	7.6	5.8	9.1	6.7
$9,000 to $9,999	(¹)	(¹)	(¹)	(¹)	(¹)	(¹)	(¹)	(¹)	(¹)	(¹)
$10,000 or more	2 330 958	599 575	655 384	841 443	234 557	33.2	45.1	46.0	22.7	42.1
$10,000 to $14,999	1 253 083	310 887	288 118	548 503	105 575	17.9	23.4	20.2	14.8	18.9
$15,000 to $24,999	939 663	250 025	324 119	256 876	108 643	13.4	18.8	22.7	6.9	19.5
$25,000 or more	138 213	38 663	43 147	36 064	20 339	2.0	2.9	3.0	1.0	3.7
Median	$8 053	$10 822	$11 296	$6 417	$10 052	...	...	...	...	...
Mean	$8 912	(NA)	(NA)	(NA)	(NA)	...	...	...	...	...
Females 14 years and over	8 119 384	1 626 519	1 631 387	4 281 460	580 018	100.0	100.0	100.0	100.0	100.0
Without income	2 593 396	487 953	520 712	1 415 522	169 209	31.9	30.0	31.9	33.1	29.2
With income	5 525 988	1 138 566	1 110 675	2 865 938	410 809	68.1	70.0	68.1	66.9	70.8
$1 to $999 or loss	817 009	106 166	130 785	539 018	41 040	10.1	6.5	8.0	12.6	7.1
$1,000 to $1,999	812 783	106 044	130 388	535 277	41 074	10.0	6.5	8.0	12.5	7.1
$2,000 to $2,999	577 850	95 435	105 799	335 876	40 741	7.1	5.9	6.5	7.8	7.0
$3,000 to $3,999	569 932	94 886	104 514	330 151	40 381	7.0	5.8	6.4	7.7	7.0
$4,000 to $4,999	384 959	82 067	74 495	196 413	31 984	4.7	5.0	4.6	4.6	5.5
$5,000 to $5,999	381 738	82 188	74 343	193 657	31 550	4.7	5.1	4.6	4.5	5.4
$6,000 to $6,999	332 231	84 048	72 002	151 297	24 884	4.1	5.2	4.4	3.5	4.3
$7,000 to $9,999	777 300	223 211	185 766	303 060	65 263	9.6	13.7	11.4	7.1	11.3
$7,000 to $7,999	323 937	82 987	70 882	145 533	24 535	4.0	5.1	4.3	3.4	4.2
$8,000 to $8,999	453 363	140 224	114 884	157 527	40 728	5.6	8.6	7.0	3.7	7.0
$9,000 to $9,999	(¹)	(¹)	(¹)	(¹)	(¹)	(¹)	(¹)	(¹)	(¹)	(¹)
$10,000 or more	872 187	264 521	232 582	281 191	93 893	10.7	16.3	14.3	6.6	16.2
$10,000 to $14,999	607 473	190 705	160 822	191 507	64 439	7.5	11.7	9.9	4.5	11.1
$15,000 to $24,999	233 524	64 794	63 929	78 955	25 846	2.9	4.0	3.9	1.8	4.5
$25,000 or more	31 190	9 022	7 831	10 729	3 608	0.4	0.6	0.5	0.3	0.6
Median	$3 964	$6 031	$5 126	$3 069	$5 320	...	...	...	...	...
Mean	$5 271	(NA)	(NA)	(NA)	(NA)	...	...	...	...	...
1960										
Persons 14 years and over	12 087 706	2 067 582	2 226 615	7 089 014	704 495	100.0	100.0	100.0	100.0	100.0
Without income	3 398 326	551 440	653 763	2 018 179	174 944	28.1	26.7	29.4	28.5	24.8
With income	8 689 380	1 516 142	1 572 852	5 070 835	529 551	71.9	73.3	70.6	71.5	75.2
$1 to $999 or loss	1 385 550	135 473	174 219	1 025 861	50 006	11.5	6.6	7.8	14.5	7.1
$1,000 to $1,999	1 386 937	135 600	174 394	1 026 888	50 056	11.5	6.6	7.8	14.5	7.1
$2,000 to $2,999	1 031 409	122 779	141 939	720 664	46 027	8.5	5.9	6.4	10.2	6.5
$3,000 to $3,999	691 495	110 521	110 909	427 889	42 176	5.7	5.3	5.0	6.0	6.0
$4,000 to $4,999	687 869	110 718	110 507	424 673	41 970	5.7	5.4	5.0	6.0	6.0
$5,000 to $5,999	518 530	119 912	91 749	274 490	32 375	4.3	5.8	4.1	3.9	4.6
$6,000 to $6,999	518 530	119 912	91 749	274 490	32 375	4.3	5.8	4.1	3.9	4.6
$7,000 to $9,999	1 184 149	324 366	252 243	515 983	91 556	9.8	15.7	11.3	7.3	13.0
$10,000 or more	1 284 911	336 862	425 143	379 896	143 010	10.6	16.3	19.1	5.4	20.3
Median	$3 783	$6 193	$5 812	$2 470	$5 873	...	...	...	...	...
Males 14 years and over	5 713 131	952 515	1 063 373	3 346 141	351 102	100.0	100.0	100.0	100.0	100.0
Without income	908 566	138 641	163 505	562 248	44 172	15.9	14.6	15.4	16.8	12.6
With income	4 804 565	813 874	899 868	2 783 893	306 930	84.1	85.4	84.6	83.2	87.4
$1 to $999 or loss	523 792	44 974	62 194	398 739	17 885	9.2	4.7	5.8	11.9	5.1
$1,000 to $1,999	524 316	45 019	62 256	399 138	17 903	9.2	4.7	5.9	11.9	5.1
$2,000 to $2,999	437 612	42 834	53 842	322 469	18 467	7.7	4.5	5.1	9.6	5.3
$3,000 to $3,999	354 715	40 745	45 797	249 166	19 006	6.2	4.3	4.3	7.4	5.4
$4,000 to $4,999	354 382	41 032	45 792	248 600	18 958	6.2	4.3	4.3	7.4	5.4
$5,000 to $5,999	338 863	54 434	45 574	222 156	16 699	5.9	5.7	4.3	6.6	4.8
$6,000 to $6,999	338 863	54 434	45 574	222 156	16 699	5.9	5.7	4.3	6.6	4.8
$7,000 to $9,999	853 944	205 594	168 286	420 754	59 310	14.9	21.6	15.8	12.6	16.9
$10,000 or more	1 078 064	284 809	370 551	300 715	122 003	18.9	29.9	34.8	9.0	34.7
Median	$5 613	$8 283	$8 636	$4 092	$8 454	...	...	...	...	...
Females 14 years and over	6 374 575	1 115 067	1 163 242	3 742 873	353 393	100.0	100.0	100.0	100.0	100.0
Without income	2 489 760	412 799	490 258	1 455 931	130 772	39.1	37.0	42.1	38.9	37.0
With income	3 884 815	702 268	672 984	2 286 942	222 621	60.9	63.0	57.9	61.1	63.0
$1 to $999 or loss	861 758	90 490	112 025	627 122	32 120	13.5	8.1	9.6	16.8	9.1
$1,000 to $1,999	862 620	90 581	112 137	627 750	32 152	13.5	8.1	9.6	16.8	9.1
$2,000 to $2,999	593 797	79 945	88 097	398 195	27 560	9.3	7.2	7.6	10.6	7.8
$3,000 to $3,999	336 780	69 776	65 112	178 723	23 169	5.3	6.3	5.6	4.8	6.6
$4,000 to $4,999	333 487	69 686	64 715	176 073	23 012	5.2	6.2	5.6	4.7	6.5
$5,000 to $5,999	179 667	65 481	46 175	52 334	15 677	2.8	5.9	4.0	1.4	4.4
$6,000 to $6,999	179 667	65 481	46 175	52 334	15 677	2.8	5.9	4.0	1.4	4.4
$7,000 to $9,999	330 205	118 773	83 957	95 229	32 246	5.2	10.7	7.2	2.5	9.1
$10,000 or more	206 833	52 053	54 592	79 181	21 007	3.2	4.7	4.7	2.1	5.9
Median	$2 254	$4 293	$3 374	$1 823	$3 842	...	...	...	...	...

¹Included in preceding category.

Table 96. Poverty Status in 1979, 1969, and 1959 of Families and Persons by Race: 1960 to 1980

[Data are estimates based on a sample; see Introduction. For meaning of symbols, see Introduction. For definitions of terms, see appendixes A and B]

United States Regions	1980[1]			1970[1]			1960[2]		
	Total	White	Black	Total	White	Black	Total	White	Black and other races
UNITED STATES									
All Income Levels in Previous Year									
Families	59 190 133	50 644 862	6 105 698	51 168 599	45 770 351	4 863 401	45 127 642	40 872 375	4 255 267
Female householder, no husband present	8 205 279	5 488 631	2 272 097	5 539 073	4 138 756	1 334 203	4 193 760	3 304 714	889 046
Householder 65 years and over	8 823 135	7 927 492	728 165	7 043 797	6 417 376	572 519	6 104 522	5 609 163	495 359
Unrelated individuals	27 383 584	23 191 117	3 127 789	16 052 389	13 901 167	1 923 025	10 434 267	8 928 074	1 506 193
65 years and over	7 721 268	6 902 777	694 916	5 685 693	5 148 976	495 683	3 593 925	(NA)	(NA)
Persons	220 845 766	184 466 900	25 622 765	198 059 951	173 659 440	21 930 008	175 034 505	155 205 563	19 828 942
65 years and over	24 154 364	21 691 260	1 988 887	19 132 952	17 444 385	1 537 149	15 426 853	(NA)	(NA)
Income in Previous Year Below Poverty Level									
Families	5 670 215	3 566 679	1 615 952	5 481 149	3 921 514	1 450 416	8 315 419	6 255 145	2 060 274
Percent below poverty level	9.6	7.0	26.5	10.7	8.6	29.8	18.4	15.3	48.4
Female householder, no husband present	2 484 246	1 225 435	1 051 516	1 800 038	1 063 007	707 244	1 774 212	1 145 586	628 626
Householder 65 years and over	779 928	559 284	189 799	1 354 118	1 094 776	245 020	1 983 894	1 672 891	311 003
Unrelated individuals	6 860 582	5 238 332	1 240 767	5 951 538	4 933 918	916 675	4 760 860	3 915 971	844 889
Percent below poverty level	25.1	22.6	39.7	37.1	35.5	47.7	45.6	43.9	56.1
65 years and over	2 251 810	1 803 402	395 464	2 890 124	2 511 383	355 435	2 455 798	(NA)	(NA)
Persons	27 392 580	17 331 671	7 648 604	27 208 583	18 934 882	7 680 105	38 684 545	27 719 431	10 965 114
Percent below poverty level	12.4	9.4	29.9	13.7	10.9	35.0	22.1	17.9	55.3
65 years and over	3 581 729	2 774 505	700 589	5 231 912	4 425 311	759 188	5 940 836	(NA)	(NA)
NORTHEAST									
All Income Levels in Previous Year									
Families	12 731 633	11 167 719	1 136 825	12 394 267	11 342 807	982 633	11 473 451	10 779 779	693 672
Female householder, no husband present	1 987 097	1 377 922	481 068	1 458 883	1 145 336	305 550	1 143 094	981 413	161 681
Householder 65 years and over	2 017 440	1 891 641	104 799	1 756 401	1 668 057	81 722	1 592 202	1 537 187	55 015
Unrelated individuals	6 043 658	5 173 545	690 467	4 047 360	3 553 926	453 501	2 748 120	2 410 960	337 160
65 years and over	1 858 970	1 710 169	127 639	1 454 163	1 357 641	89 806	924 633	(NA)	(NA)
Persons	47 888 985	41 408 616	4 710 992	47 931 199	43 411 849	4 218 187	43 535 058	40 515 883	3 019 175
65 years and over	5 728 249	5 332 997	325 239	4 954 534	4 686 597	247 313	4 146 774	(NA)	(NA)
Income in Previous Year Below Poverty Level									
Families	1 110 969	697 374	287 093	938 352	725 419	200 906	1 359 054	1 158 680	200 374
Percent below poverty level	8.7	6.2	25.3	7.6	6.4	20.4	11.8	10.7	28.9
Female householder, no husband present	604 242	310 491	214 464	382 837	249 874	129 536	348 388	264 144	84 244
Householder 65 years and over	110 861	90 152	16 513	222 739	203 307	18 137	366 976	347 539	19 437
Unrelated individuals	1 424 140	1 109 512	246 628	1 360 503	1 182 814	161 191	125 676	985 512	40 164
Percent below poverty level	23.6	21.4	35.7	33.6	33.3	35.5	41.0	40.9	41.6
65 years and over	445 935	380 821	55 791	675 962	620 642	51 223	589 292	(NA)	(NA)
Persons	5 342 718	3 485 959	1 315 107	4 830 812	3 741 217	1 026 236	6 248 956	5 206 625	1 042 331
Percent below poverty level	11.2	8.4	27.9	10.1	8.6	24.3	14.4	12.9	34.5
65 years and over	640 984	541 092	82 627	1 073 341	985 262	81 557	1 250 123	(NA)	(NA)
NORTH CENTRAL									
All Income Levels in Previous Year									
Families	15 424 495	13 921 135	1 234 909	14 184 786	13 120 526	1 004 412	13 118 713	12 338 729	779 984
Female householder, no husband present	1 936 864	1 397 778	493 891	1 333 203	1 052 887	271 491	1 036 552	878 425	158 127
Householder 65 years and over	2 257 769	2 119 483	125 338	1 980 023	1 878 998	95 354	1 854 228	1 785 027	69 201
Unrelated individuals	6 856 468	6 070 600	660 903	4 364 871	3 926 948	405 649	2 984 172	2 686 900	297 272
65 years and over	2 104 399	1 960 285	130 803	1 671 815	1 571 097	95 663	1 126 564	(NA)	(NA)
Persons	57 383 050	50 990 312	5 178 787	55 221 915	50 478 600	4 453 116	50 532 212	47 040 998	3 491 214
65 years and over	6 255 561	5 855 384	357 643	5 415 913	5 121 070	278 567	4 697 525	(NA)	(NA)
Income in Previous Year Below Poverty Level									
Families	1 230 442	876 316	304 176	1 174 994	944 980	214 293	1 971 572	1 703 919	267 653
Percent below poverty level	8.0	6.3	24.6	8.3	7.2	21.3	15.0	13.8	34.3
Female householder, no husband present	553 078	305 530	226 335	376 593	240 782	131 204	385 473	281 696	103 777
Householder 65 years and over	150 190	127 081	20 665	322 080	293 235	27 080	551 786	520 981	30 805
Unrelated individuals	1 644 464	1 351 466	246 889	1 635 572	1 447 023	172 714	1 374 419	1 227 326	147 093
Percent below poverty level	24.0	22.3	37.4	37.5	36.8	42.6	46.1	45.7	49.5
65 years and over	563 554	492 709	65 487	855 247	788 261	63 978	774 537	(NA)	(NA)
Persons	6 009 909	4 322 507	1 430 938	5 967 632	4 750 370	1 132 428	8 953 133	7 535 383	1 417 750
Percent below poverty level	10.5	8.5	27.6	10.8	9.4	25.4	17.7	16.0	40.6
65 years and over	821 722	713 114	98 741	1 421 748	1 305 658	110 145	1 755 887	(NA)	(NA)
SOUTH									
All Income Levels in Previous Year									
Families	20 009 695	16 318 126	3 201 003	15 907 699	13 335 846	2 501 211	13 511 733	11 189 118	2 322 615
Female householder, no husband present	2 832 142	1 650 928	1 110 839	1 846 859	1 180 157	656 411	1 424 167	923 993	500 174
Householder 65 years and over	3 081 102	2 590 773	454 155	2 268 622	1 891 812	368 904	1 826 650	1 488 981	337 669
Unrelated individuals	8 129 736	6 509 069	1 425 955	4 355 740	3 442 783	885 994	2 692 031	1 991 694	700 337
65 years and over	2 442 407	2 028 581	386 627	1 588 304	1 304 485	277 886	890 992	(NA)	(NA)
Persons	73 421 320	57 691 062	13 570 903	61 051 406	49 096 673	11 636 698	53 723 049	42 485 240	11 237 809
65 years and over	8 099 873	6 824 714	1 175 995	5 817 099	4 867 750	928 704	4 339 334	(NA)	(NA)
Income in Previous Year Below Poverty Level									
Families	2 389 763	1 372 416	916 291	2 592 281	1 607 112	956 085	4 070 939	2 604 553	1 466 386
Percent below poverty level	11.9	8.4	28.6	16.3	12.1	38.2	30.1	23.3	63.1
Female householder, no husband present	937 107	368 642	537 992	760 837	355 506	398 776	815 168	415 646	399 522
Householder 65 years and over	433 590	277 111	146 383	671 742	475 232	193 399	854 823	606 675	248 148
Unrelated individuals	2 424 862	1 698 088	649 347	1 944 163	1 409 044	519 628	1 470 795	985 549	485 246
Percent below poverty level	29.8	26.1	45.5	44.6	40.9	58.6	54.6	49.5	69.3
65 years and over	972 767	696 814	260 033	970 428	741 792	224 679	675 618	(NA)	(NA)
Persons	11 284 586	6 359 813	4 414 962	12 437 667	7 179 133	5 115 169	19 104 928	11 290 358	7 814 570
Percent below poverty level	15.4	11.0	32.5	20.4	14.6	44.0	35.6	26.6	69.5
65 years and over	1 701 578	1 173 227	494 986	2 111 406	1 560 565	541 773	2 153 313	(NA)	(NA)

[1]For 1980 and 1970, excludes inmates of institutions, persons in military group quarters and in college dormitories, and unrelated individuals under 15 years in 1980 and under 14 years in 1970. [2]For 1960, excludes all persons in group quarters; includes all unrelated individuals, regardless of age.

Table 96. **Poverty Status in 1979, 1969, and 1959 of Families and Persons by Race: 1960 to 1980**—Con.

[Data are estimates based on a sample; see Introduction. For meaning of symbols, see Introduction. For definitions of terms, see appendixes A and B]

United States Regions	1980[1]			1970[1]			1960[2]		
	Total	White	Black	Total	White	Black	Total	White	Black and other races
WEST									
All Income Levels in Previous Year									
Families	11 024 310	9 237 882	532 961	8 681 847	7 971 172	375 145	7 023 745	6 564 749	458 996
Female householder, no husband present	1 449 176	1 062 003	186 299	900 128	760 376	100 751	589 947	520 883	69 064
Householder 65 years and over	1 466 824	1 325 595	43 873	1 038 751	978 509	26 539	831 442	797 968	33 474
Unrelated individuals	6 353 722	5 437 903	350 464	3 284 418	2 977 510	177 881	2 009 944	1 838 520	171 424
65 years and over	1 315 492	1 203 742	49 847	971 411	915 753	32 328	651 736	(NA)	(NA)
Persons	42 152 456	34 376 910	2 162 083	33 855 431	30 672 318	1 622 007	27 244 186	25 163 442	2 080 744
65 years and over	4 070 681	3 678 165	130 010	2 945 406	2 768 968	82 565	2 243 220	(NA)	(NA)
Income in Previous Year Below Poverty Level									
Families	939 041	620 573	108 392	775 522	644 003	79 132	913 854	787 993	125 861
Percent below poverty level	8.5	6.7	20.3	8.9	8.1	21.1	13.0	12.0	27.4
Female householder, no husband present	389 819	240 772	72 725	279 771	216 845	47 718	225 183	184 100	41 083
Householder 65 years and over	85 287	64 940	6 238	137 557	123 002	6 404	210 309	197 696	12 613
Unrelated individuals	1 367 116	1 079 267	97 903	1 011 300	895 037	63 142	789 970	717 584	72 386
Percent below poverty level	21.5	19.8	27.9	30.8	30.1	35.5	39.3	39.0	42.2
65 years and over	269 554	233 058	14 153	388 487	360 688	15 555	416 351	(NA)	(NA)
Persons	4 755 367	3 163 392	487 597	3 972 472	3 264 162	406 272	4 377 527	3 687 065	690 463
Percent below poverty level	11.3	9.2	22.6	11.7	10.6	25.0	16.1	14.7	33.2
65 years and over	417 445	346 582	24 235	625 417	573 826	25 713	781 543	(NA)	(NA)

[1]For 1980 and 1970, excludes inmates of institutions, persons in military group quarters and in college dormitories, and unrelated individuals under 15 years in 1980 and under 14 years in 1970. [2]For 1960, excludes all persons in group quarters; includes all unrelated individuals, regardless of age.

Table 97. Poverty Status in 1979 and 1969 of Families and Persons by Race: 1980 and 1970

[Excludes inmates of institutions, persons in military group quarters and in college dormitories, and unrelated individuals under 15 years in 1980 and under 14 years in 1970. Data are estimates based on a sample; see Introduction. For meaning of symbols, see Introduction. For definitions of terms, see Appendixes A and B]

United States Urban and Rural Regions	1980 Total — Total	1980 Total — White	1980 Total — Black	1980 Urban	1980 Rural	1970 Total — Total	1970 Total — White	1970 Total — Black	1970 Urban	1970 Rural
UNITED STATES										
All Income Levels in Previous Year										
Families	59 190 133	50 644 862	6 105 698	43 005 667	16 184 466	51 168 599	45 770 351	4 863 401	37 452 876	13 715 723
With Social Security income	13 086 462	11 539 900	1 247 625	9 328 315	3 758 147	10 070 743	9 089 937	896 870	7 125 886	2 944 857
With public assistance income	4 719 387	2 911 322	1 437 119	3 606 760	1 112 627	2 719 074	1 816 873	854 413	2 011 513	707 561
Householder worked in previous year	47 291 362	40 985 219	4 347 399	34 274 154	13 017 208	43 083 224	38 850 590	3 789 145	31 546 235	11 536 989
With related children under 18 years	31 953 940	25 957 243	4 238 294	22 976 039	8 977 901	29 540 540	25 815 873	3 359 019	21 490 174	8 050 366
Female householder, no husband present	8 205 279	5 488 631	2 272 097	6 845 544	1 359 735	5 539 073	4 138 756	1 334 203	4 526 572	1 012 501
Householder worked in previous year	5 130 596	3 572 036	1 320 492	4 329 040	801 556	3 388 492	2 555 978	794 023	2 830 588	557 904
With related children under 18 years	5 509 315	3 338 225	1 821 040	4 629 471	879 844	3 468 430	2 356 875	1 063 288	2 847 440	620 990
With related children under 6 years	2 132 451	1 097 746	867 800	1 820 346	312 105	1 414 146	844 225	547 388	1 180 148	233 998
Householder 65 years and over	8 823 135	7 927 492	728 165	6 294 390	2 528 745	7 043 797	6 417 376	572 519	4 901 198	2 142 599
Unrelated individuals	27 383 584	23 191 117	3 127 789	22 857 600	4 525 984	16 052 389	13 901 167	1 923 025	13 256 853	2 795 536
With Social Security income	8 074 494	7 212 072	735 382	6 304 338	1 770 156	5 384 832	4 901 426	444 460	(NA)	(NA)
With public assistance income	1 842 792	1 273 696	478 669	1 457 014	385 778	1 138 946	819 103	300 257	884 711	254 235
Worked in previous year	17 747 858	15 111 351	1 879 749	15 210 933	2 536 925	9 708 846	8 362 646	1 187 313	(NA)	(NA)
65 years and over	7 721 268	6 902 777	694 916	6 025 483	1 695 785	5 685 693	5 148 976	495 683	4 394 693	1 291 000
Persons	220 845 766	184 466 900	25 622 765	162 301 094	58 544 672	173 659 440	154 771 200	21 930 008	145 204 944	52 855 007
Related children under 18 years	62 654 136	49 583 738	9 192 010	44 511 786	18 142 350	69 014 306	58 771 200	9 323 299	49 369 823	19 644 483
65 years and over	24 154 364	21 691 260	1 988 887	17 903 658	6 250 706	19 132 952	17 444 385	1 537 149	13 926 966	5 205 986
Income in Previous Year Below Poverty Level										
Families	5 670 215	3 566 679	1 615 952	3 960 944	1 709 271	5 481 149	3 921 514	1 450 416	3 382 653	2 098 496
Percent below poverty level	9.6	7.0	26.5	9.2	10.6	10.7	8.6	29.8	9.0	15.3
Mean income deficit (in 1979 dollars)	3 076	2 851	3 434	3 102	3 014	3 053	2 825	3 627	3 120	2 963
Persons per family	3.62	3.39	3.96	3.59	3.69	3.57	3.88	4.66	3.82	3.96
With Social Security income	1 178 847	797 428	327 554	693 161	485 686	1 755 668	1 386 743	350 657	968 790	786 878
With public assistance income	1 840 830	882 681	776 268	1 441 420	399 410	1 174 533	645 904	505 803	813 295	361 238
Householder worked in previous year	2 860 666	1 940 985	680 343	1 907 045	953 621	2 835 152	1 990 240	786 632	1 660 993	1 174 159
With related children under 18 years	4 214 677	2 451 920	1 345 063	3 080 558	1 134 119	3 491 448	2 257 065	1 153 563	2 277 622	1 213 826
Female householder, no husband present	2 484 246	1 225 435	1 051 516	2 064 419	419 827	1 800 038	1 063 007	707 244	1 402 499	397 539
Householder worked in previous year	1 012 698	553 225	395 539	828 998	183 700	729 936	403 054	317 143	574 611	155 325
With related children under 18 years	2 222 439	1 071 886	959 085	1 865 733	356 706	1 499 833	840 718	633 023	1 200 360	299 473
With related children under 6 years	1 185 334	535 723	540 810	1 014 785	170 549	800 689	422 087	363 962	661 243	139 446
Householder 65 years and over	779 928	559 284	189 799	434 697	345 231	1 354 118	1 094 776	245 020	721 658	632 460
Unrelated individuals	6 860 582	5 238 332	1 240 767	5 442 506	1 418 076	5 951 538	4 933 918	916 675	4 555 322	1 396 216
Percent below poverty level	25.1	22.6	39.7	23.8	31.3	37.1	35.5	47.7	34.4	49.9
Mean income deficit (in 1979 dollars)	1 786	1 723	1 897	1 818	1 664	1 885	1 839	2 079	1 889	1 884
With Social Security income	2 291 317	1 834 349	405 208	1 638 794	652 523	2 691 630	2 358 480	310 976	(NA)	(NA)
With public assistance income	1 105 568	703 399	348 613	834 589	270 979	749 532	508 234	228 641	540 117	209 415
Worked in previous year	2 715 215	2 188 806	361 056	2 290 965	424 250	1 861 849	1 517 454	303 862	(NA)	(NA)
65 years and over	2 251 810	1 803 402	395 464	1 594 546	657 264	2 890 124	2 511 383	355 435	2 087 231	802 893
Persons	27 392 580	17 331 671	7 648 604	19 671 307	7 721 273	27 208 583	18 934 882	7 680 105	17 493 914	9 714 669
Percent below poverty level	12.4	9.4	29.9	12.1	13.2	13.7	10.9	35.0	12.0	18.4
Related children under 18 years	10 025 623	5 467 643	3 478 654	7 199 152	2 826 471	10 441 344	6 302 526	3 919 868	6 637 646	3 803 698
65 years and over	3 581 729	2 774 505	700 589	2 338 303	1 243 426	5 231 912	4 425 311	759 188	3 346 469	1 885 443
Income in Previous Year Below 125 Percent of Poverty Level										
Families	7 918 984	5 213 016	2 062 732	5 448 031	2 470 953	7 710 860	5 696 004	1 865 095	4 802 844	2 908 016
Percent below poverty level	13.4	10.3	33.8	12.7	15.3	15.1	12.4	38.3	12.8	21.2
Female householder, no husband present	3 101 393	1 598 030	1 258 521	2 558 614	542 779	2 215 959	1 348 141	832 268	1 735 364	480 595
Householder 65 years and over	1 275 534	959 684	271 441	728 890	546 644	1 926 694	1 602 301	305 666	1 078 248	848 446
Unrelated individuals	9 109 271	7 168 493	1 482 323	7 282 620	1 826 651	7 162 576	5 975 048	1 068 717	5 551 112	1 611 464
Percent below poverty level	33.3	30.9	47.4	31.9	40.4	44.6	43.0	55.6	41.9	57.6
65 years and over	3 510 636	2 932 635	502 746	2 598 686	911 950	3 503 735	3 071 386	403 827	2 577 515	926 220
Persons	37 524 156	24 745 546	9 628 991	26 707 599	10 816 557	37 024 894	26 559 351	9 675 776	23 938 916	13 085 978
Percent below poverty level	17.0	13.4	37.6	16.5	18.5	18.7	15.3	47.2	16.5	24.8
Related children under 18 years	13 292 653	7 636 923	4 264 364	9 398 798	3 893 855	14 541 271	9 316 434	4 932 411	9 256 264	5 285 007
65 years and over	5 723 766	4 618 456	951 017	3 869 710	1 854 056	6 891 970	5 913 121	918 351	4 493 991	2 397 979
NORTHEAST										
All Income Levels in Previous Year										
Families	12 731 633	11 167 719	1 136 825	9 993 288	2 738 345	12 394 267	11 342 807	982 633	9 988 980	2 405 287
With Social Security income	3 000 095	2 771 375	186 954	2 397 214	602 881	2 554 442	2 407 672	137 143	2 082 820	471 622
With public assistance income	1 129 070	716 235	300 107	983 459	145 611	663 957	468 580	195 377	587 908	76 049
Householder worked in previous year	9 888 509	8 814 035	782 734	7 642 988	2 245 521	10 505 431	9 689 437	758 162	8 410 589	2 094 842
With related children under 18 years	6 599 067	5 498 914	785 189	5 090 503	1 508 564	6 928 338	6 207 492	676 672	5 495 188	1 433 150
Female householder, no husband present	1 987 097	1 377 922	481 068	1 754 350	232 747	1 458 883	1 145 336	305 550	1 294 978	163 905
Householder worked in previous year	1 093 661	788 130	261 979	951 487	142 174	827 615	657 989	165 025	731 015	96 600
With related children under 18 years	1 233 598	742 901	384 036	1 092 132	141 466	817 549	567 898	244 089	725 073	92 476
With related children under 6 years	459 611	229 679	176 014	417 896	41 715	337 052	205 263	129 414	304 018	33 034
Householder 65 years and over	2 017 440	1 891 641	104 799	1 624 768	392 672	1 756 401	1 668 057	81 722	1 432 302	324 099
Unrelated individuals	6 043 658	5 173 545	690 467	5 182 322	861 336	4 047 360	3 553 926	453 501	3 521 007	526 353
With Social Security income	1 912 250	1 754 412	136 329	1 610 442	301 808	(NA)	(NA)	(NA)	(NA)	(NA)
With public assistance income	452 229	312 047	115 083	398 809	53 420	239 817	170 854	66 303	217 851	21 966
Worked in previous year	3 698 646	3 169 637	412 945	3 181 036	517 610	(NA)	(NA)	(NA)	(NA)	(NA)
65 years and over	1 858 970	1 710 169	127 639	1 575 160	283 810	1 454 163	1 357 641	89 806	1 235 777	218 386
Persons	47 888 985	41 408 616	4 710 992	37 871 008	10 017 977	43 411 849		4 218 187	38 579 291	9 351 908
Related children under 18 years	12 880 238	10 636 718	1 603 867	9 860 531	3 019 707	15 882 811	14 102 865	1 684 290	12 426 110	3 456 701
65 years and over	5 728 249	5 332 997	325 239	4 704 274	1 023 975	4 954 534	4 686 597	247 313	4 102 828	851 706

Table 97. Poverty Status in 1979 and 1969 of Families and Persons by Race: 1980 and 1970—Con.

[Excludes inmates of institutions, persons in military group quarters and in college dormitories, and unrelated individuals under 15 years in 1980 and under 14 years in 1970. Data are estimates based on a sample; see Introduction. For meaning of symbols, see Introduction. For definitions of terms, see Appendixes A and B]

United States Urban and Rural Regions	1980 Total — Total	White	Black	Urban	Rural	1970 Total — Total	White	Black	Urban	Rural
NORTHEAST—Con.										
Income in Previous Year Below Poverty Level										
Families	1 110 969	697 374	287 093	932 925	178 044	938 352	725 419	200 906	759 948	178 404
Percent below poverty level	8.7	6.2	25.3	9.3	6.5	7.6	6.4	20.4	7.6	7.4
Mean income deficit (in 1979 dollars)	2 986	2 807	3 264	3 015	2 838	3 025	2 897	3 483	3 099	2 724
Persons per family	3.53	3.40	3.70	3.51	3.62	3.70	3.51	4.22	3.69	3.71
With Social Security income	174 408	130 412	34 376	136 384	38 024	281 813	250 263	29 967	211 584	70 229
With public assistance income	464 837	228 365	164 400	424 211	40 626	242 812	145 621	95 130	219 625	23 187
Householder worked in previous year	451 366	324 602	91 084	347 964	103 402	391 340	311 636	74 829	299 888	91 452
With related children under 18 years	872 788	510 334	250 150	743 954	128 834	610 702	431 272	171 204	509 590	101 112
Female householder, no husband present	604 242	310 491	214 464	550 658	53 584	382 837	249 874	129 536	341 471	41 366
Householder worked in previous year	179 203	109 365	57 969	155 160	24 043	110 187	73 724	35 667	94 640	15 547
With related children under 18 years	547 915	274 325	198 705	500 490	47 425	324 267	200 244	121 052	292 466	31 801
With related children under 6 years	285 830	132 408	110 407	264 160	21 670	184 961	106 967	76 423	169 321	15 640
Householder 65 years and over	110 861	90 152	16 513	86 600	24 261	222 739	203 307	18 137	166 851	55 888
Unrelated individuals	1 424 140	1 109 512	246 628	1 214 375	209 765	1 360 503	1 182 814	161 191	1 145 168	215 335
Percent below poverty level	23.6	21.4	35.7	23.4	24.4	33.6	33.3	35.5	32.5	40.9
Mean income deficit (in 1979 dollars)	1 777	1 718	1 929	1 782	1 748	1 899	1 863	2 115	1 895	1 934
With Social Security income	448 471	380 364	59 097	371 044	77 427	(NA)	(NA)	(NA)	(NA)	(NA)
With public assistance income	263 211	165 286	80 065	231 655	31 556	131 849	90 743	39 320	116 807	15 042
Worked in previous year	505 435	420 747	63 339	429 889	75 546	(NA)	(NA)	(NA)	(NA)	(NA)
65 years and over	445 935	380 821	55 791	371 550	74 385	675 962	620 642	51 223	560 047	115 915
Persons	5 342 718	3 485 959	1 315 107	4 487 919	854 799	4 830 812	3 741 217	1 026 236	3 952 769	878 043
Percent below poverty level	11.2	8.4	27.9	11.9	8.5	10.1	8.6	24.3	10.2	9.4
Related children under 18 years	1 992 211	1 139 888	594 597	1 683 986	308 225	1 737 083	1 189 936	529 435	1 432 774	304 309
65 years and over	640 984	541 092	82 627	523 817	117 167	1 073 341	985 262	81 557	858 820	214 521
Income in Previous Year Below 125 Percent of Poverty Level										
Families	1 526 117	1 010 664	359 533	1 255 441	270 676	1 376 014	1 085 453	272 933	1 099 640	276 374
Percent below poverty level	12.0	9.0	31.6	12.6	9.9	11.1	9.6	27.8	11.0	11.5
Female householder, no husband present	737 562	394 612	254 024	666 796	70 766	490 227	324 557	161 544	436 369	53 858
Householder 65 years and over	198 892	166 603	25 803	153 367	45 525	342 885	315 728	25 329	259 557	83 328
Unrelated individuals	1 981 614	1 597 558	302 914	1 693 060	288 554	1 652 637	1 436 023	197 265	1 399 200	253 437
Percent below poverty level	32.8	30.9	43.9	32.7	33.5	40.8	40.4	43.5	39.7	48.1
65 years and over	801 030	704 289	82 798	677 316	123 714	835 199	767 632	62 878	696 800	138 399
Persons	7 343 796	5 030 945	1 644 563	6 080 536	1 263 260	6 792 101	5 334 672	1 368 511	5 477 198	1 314 903
Percent below poverty level	15.3	12.1	34.9	16.1	12.6	14.2	12.3	48.4	14.2	14.1
Related children under 18 years	2 591 606	1 563 156	720 953	2 143 710	447 896	2 554 189	1 817 561	710 379	2 050 429	503 760
65 years and over	1 155 196	1 002 868	125 992	950 942	204 254	1 456 567	1 341 967	106 487	1 169 383	287 184
NORTH CENTRAL										
All Income Levels in Previous Year										
Families	15 424 495	13 921 135	1 234 909	10 684 553	4 739 942	14 184 786	13 120 526	1 004 412	10 066 786	4 118 000
With Social Security income	3 293 310	3 034 518	232 369	2 244 397	1 048 913	2 759 493	2 586 205	164 861	1 884 026	875 467
With public assistance income	1 104 235	738 705	326 608	859 994	244 241	534 489	363 440	163 701	410 456	124 033
Householder worked in previous year	12 634 384	11 550 926	860 560	8 682 109	3 952 275	12 297 826	11 451 835	796 199	8 703 803	3 594 023
With related children under 18 years	8 387 437	7 319 720	866 400	5 768 734	2 618 703	8 192 228	7 463 624	687 528	5 813 208	2 379 020
Female householder, no husband present	1 936 864	1 397 778	493 891	1 625 034	311 830	1 333 203	1 052 887	271 491	1 099 260	233 943
Householder worked in previous year	1 240 831	937 639	277 300	1 040 968	199 863	838 252	675 518	157 840	699 744	138 508
With related children under 18 years	1 307 956	862 985	408 084	1 109 333	198 623	809 366	579 961	222 717	676 651	132 715
With related children under 6 years	525 891	303 582	203 849	457 543	68 348	329 055	206 753	118 732	282 835	46 220
Householder 65 years and over	2 257 769	2 119 483	125 338	1 508 472	749 297	1 980 023	1 884 669	95 354	1 309 504	670 519
Unrelated individuals	6 856 468	6 070 600	660 903	5 576 867	1 279 601	4 364 871	3 926 948	405 649	3 516 904	847 967
With Social Security income	2 224 845	2 066 052	144 232	1 666 344	558 501	(NA)	(NA)	(NA)	(NA)	(NA)
With public assistance income	393 055	283 215	100 751	309 710	83 345	226 211	169 290	54 435	172 974	53 237
Worked in previous year	4 420 407	3 930 632	399 623	3 699 831	720 576	(NA)	(NA)	(NA)	(NA)	(NA)
65 years and over	2 104 399	1 960 285	130 803	1 568 392	536 007	1 671 815	1 571 097	95 663	1 228 093	443 722
Persons	57 383 005	50 990 312	5 178 787	40 286 852	17 096 153	55 221 915	50 478 600	4 453 116	39 396 202	15 825 713
Related children under 18 years	16 675 529	14 319 481	1 891 973	11 297 825	5 377 704	19 686 801	17 688 292	1 887 309	13 747 308	5 939 493
65 years and over	6 255 561	5 855 384	357 643	4 377 856	1 877 705	5 415 913	5 121 070	278 567	3 752 586	1 663 327
Income in Previous Year Below Poverty Level										
Families	1 230 442	876 316	304 176	833 013	397 429	1 174 994	944 980	214 293	719 584	455 410
Percent below poverty level	8.0	6.3	24.6	7.8	8.4	8.3	7.2	21.3	7.1	11.1
Mean income deficit (in 1979 dollars)	3 050	2 905	3 375	3 020	3 111	2 895	2 705	3 695	3 065	2 633
Persons per family	3.55	3.40	3.87	3.53	3.59	3.69	3.49	4.45	3.71	3.65
With Social Security income	231 589	181 987	44 747	136 536	95 053	407 171	361 201	43 762	224 603	182 568
With public assistance income	425 710	227 236	178 371	354 533	71 177	217 861	121 666	92 243	170 541	47 320
Householder worked in previous year	640 861	511 161	104 801	388 287	252 574	601 758	504 029	91 360	339 454	262 304
With related children under 18 years	923 235	614 923	265 326	662 500	260 735	701 859	516 037	174 738	466 915	234 944
Female householder, no husband present	553 078	305 530	226 335	473 598	79 480	376 593	240 782	131 204	307 915	68 678
Householder worked in previous year	225 070	147 231	70 643	185 874	39 196	150 561	101 764	47 328	123 371	27 190
With related children under 18 years	504 226	272 885	211 418	435 180	69 046	313 865	187 898	121 870	264 411	49 454
With related children under 6 years	287 499	148 278	127 179	252 998	34 501	175 098	96 916	75 625	151 785	23 313
Householder 65 years and over	150 190	127 081	20 665	79 400	70 790	322 080	293 235	27 080	168 911	153 169
Unrelated individuals	1 644 464	1 351 465	246 889	1 299 023	345 441	1 635 572	1 447 023	172 714	1 233 365	402 207
Percent below poverty level	24.0	22.3	37.4	23.3	27.0	37.5	36.8	42.6	35.1	47.4
Mean income deficit (in 1979 dollars)	1 711	1 653	1 910	1 744	1 589	1 792	1 752	2 091	1 810	1 749
With Social Security income	589 688	512 775	71 139	415 269	174 419	(NA)	(NA)	(NA)	(NA)	(NA)
With public assistance income	251 146	168 211	76 815	198 234	52 912	162 192	118 489	41 614	119 636	42 556
Worked in previous year	671 453	581 713	68 670	565 572	105 881	(NA)	(NA)	(NA)	(NA)	(NA)
65 years and over	563 554	492 709	65 487	389 891	173 663	855 247	788 261	63 978	597 054	258 193
Persons	6 009 909	4 322 507	1 430 938	4 237 302	1 772 607	5 967 632	4 750 370	1 132 428	3 903 560	2 064 072
Percent below poverty level	10.5	8.5	27.6	10.5	10.4	10.8	9.4	25.4	9.9	13.0
Related children under 18 years	2 170 360	1 371 042	683 832	1 535 246	635 114	2 092 829	1 468 727	594 102	1 373 800	719 029
65 years and over	821 722	713 114	98 741	525 535	296 187	1 421 748	1 305 658	110 145	895 596	526 152

Table 97. Poverty Status in 1979 and 1969 of Families and Persons by Race: 1980 and 1970—Con.

[Excludes inmates of institutions, persons in military group quarters and in college dormitories, and unrelated individuals under 15 years in 1980 and under 14 years in 1970. Data are estimates based on a sample; see Introduction. For meaning of symbols, see Introduction. For definitions of terms, see Appendixes A and B]

United States Urban and Rural Regions	1980					1970				
	Total			Urban	Rural	Total			Urban	Rural
	Total	White	Black			Total	White	Black		
NORTH CENTRAL—Con.										
Income in Previous Year Below 125 Percent of Poverty Level										
Families	1 712 406	1 273 516	374 981	1 129 483	582 923	1 702 066	1 401 172	278 769	1 036 266	665 800
Percent below poverty level	11.1	9.1	30.4	10.6	12.3	12.0	10.7	27.8	10.3	16.2
Female householder, no husband present	686 696	397 360	264 566	582 094	104 602	472 622	311 624	155 302	384 730	87 892
Householder 65 years and over	264 603	228 921	32 207	141 685	122 918	485 625	446 704	36 623	264 989	220 636
Unrelated individuals	2 218 700	1 869 281	295 200	1 751 053	467 647	1 968 994	1 748 060	202 559	1 496 037	472 957
Percent below poverty level	32.4	30.8	44.7	31.4	36.5	45.1	44.5	49.9	42.5	55.8
65 years and over	912 407	815 373	89 330	654 274	258 133	1 034 736	956 522	74 615	730 548	304 188
Persons	8 235 126	6 155 966	1 753 491	5 700 507	2 534 619	8 302 475	6 727 572	1 457 521	5 360 027	2 942 448
Percent below poverty level	14.4		33.9	14.1	14.8	15.0	13.3	32.7	13.6	18.6
Related children under 18 years	2 861 070	1 901 590	813 635	1 968 807	892 263	3 039 679	2 236 461	762 873	1 942 752	1 096 927
65 years and over	1 373 275	1 216 353	142 808	900 753	472 522	1 899 416	1 753 843	138 027	1 206 194	693 222
SOUTH										
All Income Levels in Previous Year										
Families	20 009 695	16 318 126	3 201 003	13 162 648	6 847 047	15 907 699	13 335 846	2 501 211	10 201 556	5 706 143
With Social Security income	4 648 919	3 841 678	744 346	2 937 110	1 711 809	3 250 827	2 695 302	544 193	1 941 321	1 309 506
With public assistance income	1 621 927	883 801	687 929	1 018 418	603 509	951 175	528 881	415 985	533 758	417 417
Householder worked in previous year	15 793 761	13 073 903	2 309 290	10 473 614	5 320 147	12 995 175	10 995 259	1 946 166	8 395 384	4 599 791
With related children under 18 years	10 938 398	8 366 840	2 216 947	7 118 403	3 819 995	9 336 735	7 554 506	1 733 670	5 971 700	3 365 035
Female householder, no husband present	2 832 142	1 650 928	1 110 839	2 155 213	676 929	1 846 859	1 180 157	656 411	1 325 646	521 213
Householder worked in previous year	1 786 599	1 076 456	666 809	1 416 766	369 833	1 128 213	713 402	409 432	860 427	267 786
With related children under 18 years	1 931 668	1 002 445	875 594	1 494 514	437 154	1 208 495	688 788	511 898	878 566	329 929
With related children under 6 years	758 823	316 159	419 378	595 718	163 105	490 585	232 089	254 742	361 411	129 174
Householder 65 years and over	3 081 102	2 590 773	454 155	1 966 308	1 114 794	2 268 622	1 891 812	368 904	1 332 985	935 637
Unrelated individuals	8 129 736	6 509 069	1 425 955	6 404 483	1 725 253	4 355 740	3 442 783	885 994	3 299 687	1 056 053
With Social Security income	2 542 934	2 119 184	396 513	1 808 573	734 361	(NA)	(NA)	(NA)	(NA)	(NA)
With public assistance income	593 736	368 970	211 550	386 136	207 600	387 200	236 923	148 159	240 793	146 407
Worked in previous year	5 076 393	4 108 742	832 299	4 218 238	858 155	(NA)	(NA)	(NA)	(NA)	(NA)
65 years and over	2 442 407	2 028 581	386 627	1 730 467	711 940	1 588 304	1 304 485	277 886	1 093 802	494 502
Persons	73 421 320	57 691 062	13 570 903	48 818 405	24 602 915	61 051 406	49 096 673	11 636 698	39 161 060	21 890 346
Related children under 18 years	21 276 242	15 518 532	4 965 403	13 669 913	7 606 329	21 644 502	16 451 810	5 073 056	13 584 795	8 059 707
65 years and over	8 099 873	6 824 714	1 175 995	5 402 187	2 697 686	5 817 099	4 867 750	928 704	3 637 086	2 180 013
Income in Previous Year Below Poverty Level										
Families	2 389 763	1 372 416	916 291	1 438 071	951 692	2 592 281	1 607 112	956 085	1 314 025	1 278 256
Percent below poverty level	11.9	8.4	28.6	10.9	13.9	16.3	12.1	38.2	12.9	22.4
Mean income deficit (in 1979 dollars)	3 135	2 819	3 553	3 241	2 975	3 118	2 794	3 659	3 174	3 087
Persons per family	3.71	3.40	4.11	3.69	3.73	4.05	3.57	4.76	4.00	4.10
With Social Security income	640 615	390 462	234 668	323 614	317 001	878 411	609 412	264 889	398 286	480 125
With public assistance income	680 222	277 494	379 286	429 295	250 927	525 938	240 851	281 205	269 375	256 563
Householder worked in previous year	1 243 763	740 894	440 805	756 385	487 378	1 435 692	830 355	585 270	724 593	711 099
With related children under 18 years	1 690 298	871 309	736 601	1 075 749	614 549	1 645 200	883 894	740 900	886 050	759 150
Female householder, no husband present	937 107	368 642	537 792	696 603	240 504	760 837	355 506	398 786	509 943	250 894
Householder worked in previous year	428 239	173 014	241 360	330 009	98 230	352 419	134 503	215 940	254 890	97 529
With related children under 18 years	814 105	305 782	481 413	615 759	198 346	610 967	260 662	344 987	424 153	186 814
With related children under 6 years	417 698	138 516	265 402	325 128	92 570	301 611	114 305	184 596	216 857	84 754
Householder 65 years and over	433 590	277 111	146 383	207 963	225 627	671 742	475 232	193 399	290 102	381 640
Unrelated individuals	2 424 862	1 698 088	649 347	1 737 313	687 549	1 944 163	1 409 044	519 628	1 313 981	630 182
Percent below poverty level	29.8	26.1	45.5	27.1	39.9	44.6	40.9	58.6	39.8	59.7
Mean income deficit (in 1979 dollars)	1 740	1 680	1 835	1 792	1 608	1 932	1 881	2 061	1 936	1 941
With Social Security income	973 395	700 047	258 481	620 235	353 160	(NA)	(NA)	(NA)	(NA)	(NA)
With public assistance income	454 498	270 006	173 890	286 290	168 208	331 184	195 999	132 511	198 411	132 773
Worked in previous year	831 840	611 152	189 074	669 064	162 776	(NA)	(NA)	(NA)	(NA)	(NA)
65 years and over	972 767	696 814	260 033	609 471	363 296	970 428	741 792	224 679	608 450	361 978
Persons	11 284 586	6 359 813	4 414 962	7 047 547	4 237 039	12 437 667	7 179 133	5 115 169	6 571 175	5 866 492
Percent below poverty level	15.4	11.0	32.5	14.4	17.2	20.4	14.6	44.0	16.8	26.8
Related children under 18 years	4 180 249	1 973 083	1 985 152	2 619 771	1 560 478	5 085 114	2 461 653	2 583 055	2 677 337	2 407 777
65 years and over	1 701 578	1 173 717	494 986	958 490	743 088	2 111 406	1 560 565	541 773	1 103 311	1 008 095
Income in Previous Year Below 125 Percent of Poverty Level										
Families	3 351 796	2 026 482	1 187 898	1 997 495	1 354 301	3 529 124	2 279 395	1 209 377	1 827 771	1 701 353
Percent below poverty level	16.8	12.4	37.1	15.2	19.8	22.2	17.1	48.4	17.9	29.8
Female householder, no husband present	1 182 043	493 441	651 177	873 026	309 017	910 796	444 367	458 771	615 982	294 814
Householder 65 years and over	665 561	447 910	203 536	328 720	336 841	885 092	646 313	234 771	401 935	483 157
Unrelated individuals	3 032 977	2 191 512	752 109	2 194 843	838 134	2 244 872	1 640 450	586 829	1 541 007	703 865
Percent below poverty level	37.3	33.7	52.7	34.3	48.6	51.5	47.6	66.2	46.7	66.7
65 years and over	1 305 289	981 273	304 876	848 880	456 409	1 106 008	857 226	244 391	706 548	399 460
Persons	15 272 836	9 004 863	5 592 566	9 466 229	5 806 607	16 392 215	9 887 651	6 314 506	8 819 290	7 572 925
Percent below poverty level	20.8	15.6	41.2	19.4	23.6	26.8	20.1	54.3	22.5	34.6
Related children under 18 years	5 529 145	2 777 389	2 458 567	3 428 133	2 101 012	6 797 293	3 559 718	3 183 813	3 640 747	3 156 546
65 years and over	2 447 836	1 764 011	640 308	1 414 329	1 033 507	2 636 231	1 987 988	637 190	1 406 698	1 229 533

Table 97. Poverty Status in 1979 and 1969 of Families and Persons by Race: 1980 and 1970—Con.

[Excludes inmates of institutions, persons in military group quarters and in college dormitories, and unrelated individuals under 15 years in 1980 and under 14 years in 1970. Data are estimates based on a sample; see Introduction. For meaning of symbols, see Introduction. For definitions of terms, see Appendixes A and B]

United States Urban and Rural Regions	1980 Total			1980 Urban	1980 Rural	1970 Total			1970 Urban	1970 Rural
	Total	White	Black	Urban	Rural	Total	White	Black	Urban	Rural
WEST										
All Income Levels in Previous Year										
Families	11 024 310	9 237 882	532 961	9 165 178	1 859 132	8 681 847	7 971 172	375 145	7 195 554	1 486 293
With Social Security income	2 144 138	1 892 329	83 956	1 749 594	394 544	1 505 981	1 400 758	50 673	1 217 719	288 262
With public assistance income	864 155	572 581	122 475	744 889	119 266	569 453	460 945	79 350	479 391	90 062
Householder worked in previous year	8 974 708	7 546 355	394 815	7 475 443	1 499 265	7 284 792	6 714 059	288 618	6 036 459	1 248 333
With related children under 18 years	6 029 038	4 771 769	369 758	4 998 399	1 030 639	5 083 239	4 590 251	261 149	4 210 078	873 161
Female householder, no husband present	1 449 176	1 062 003	186 299	1 310 947	138 229	900 128	760 376	100 751	806 688	93 440
Householder worked in previous year	1 009 505	769 811	114 404	919 819	89 686	594 412	509 069	61 726	539 402	55 010
With related children under 18 years	1 036 093	729 894	153 326	933 492	102 601	633 020	520 228	84 584	567 150	65 870
With related children under 6 years	388 126	248 326	68 559	349 189	38 937	257 454	200 120	44 500	231 884	25 570
Householder 65 years and over	1 466 824	1 325 595	43 873	1 194 842	271 982	1 038 751	978 509	26 539	826 407	212 344
Unrelated individuals	6 353 722	5 437 903	350 464	5 693 928	659 794	3 284 418	2 977 510	177 881	2 919 255	365 163
With Social Security income	1 394 465	1 272 424	58 308	1 218 979	175 486	(NA)	(NA)	(NA)	(NA)	(NA)
With public assistance income	403 772	309 464	51 285	362 359	41 413	285 718	242 036	31 360	253 093	32 625
Worked in previous year	4 552 412	3 902 340	234 882	4 111 828	440 584	(NA)	(NA)	(NA)	(NA)	(NA)
65 years and over	1 315 492	1 203 742	49 847	1 151 464	164 028	971 411	915 753	32 328	837 021	134 390
Persons	42 152 456	34 376 910	2 162 083	35 324 829	6 827 627	33 855 431	30 672 318	1 622 007	28 068 391	5 787 040
Related children under 18 years	11 822 127	9 109 007	730 767	9 683 517	2 138 610	11 800 192	10 528 233	678 644	9 611 610	2 188 582
65 years and over	4 070 681	3 678 165	130 010	3 419 341	651 340	2 945 406	2 768 968	82 565	2 434 466	510 940
Income in Previous Year Below Poverty Level										
Families	939 041	620 573	108 392	756 935	182 106	775 522	644 003	79 132	589 096	186 426
Percent below poverty level	8.5	6.7	20.3	8.3	9.8	8.9	8.1	21.1	8.2	12.5
Mean income deficit (in 1979 dollars)	3 064	2 898	3 042	3 036	3 179	3 109	3 002	3 427	3 103	3 144
Persons per family	3.61	3.37	3.57	3.58	3.74	3.82	3.66	4.33	3.74	4.06
With Social Security income	132 235	94 567	13 763	96 627	35 608	188 273	165 867	12 039	134 317	53 956
With public assistance income	270 061	149 586	54 211	233 381	36 680	187 922	137 766	37 225	153 754	34 168
Householder worked in previous year	524 676	364 328	43 653	414 409	110 267	406 362	344 220	35 173	297 058	109 304
With related children under 18 years	728 356	455 354	92 986	598 355	130 001	533 239	425 862	66 721	415 067	118 620
Female householder, no husband present	389 819	240 772	72 725	343 560	46 259	279 771	216 845	47 718	243 170	36 601
Householder worked in previous year	180 186	123 615	25 567	157 955	22 231	116 769	93 063	18 208	101 710	15 059
With related children under 18 years	356 193	218 894	67 549	314 304	41 889	250 734	191 914	45 114	219 330	31 404
With related children under 6 years	194 307	116 521	37 822	172 499	21 808	139 019	103 899	27 318	123 280	15 739
Householder 65 years and over	85 287	64 940	6 238	60 734	24 553	137 557	123 002	6 404	95 794	41 763
Unrelated individuals	1 367 116	1 079 267	97 903	1 191 795	175 321	1 011 300	895 037	63 142	862 808	148 492
Percent below poverty level	21.5	19.8	27.9	20.9	26.6	30.8	30.1	35.5	29.6	40.7
Mean income deficit (in 1979 dollars)	1 969	1 884	2 198	1 975	1 932	1 925	1 887	2 111	1 925	1 929
With Social Security income	279 763	241 163	16 491	232 246	47 517	(NA)	(NA)	(NA)	(NA)	(NA)
With public assistance income	136 713	99 896	17 843	118 410	18 303	124 307	103 003	15 196	105 263	19 044
Worked in previous year	706 487	575 194	39 973	626 440	80 047	(NA)	(NA)	(NA)	(NA)	(NA)
65 years and over	269 554	233 058	14 153	223 634	45 920	388 487	360 688	15 555	321 680	66 807
Persons	4 755 367	3 163 392	487 597	3 898 539	856 828	3 972 472	3 264 162	406 272	3 066 410	906 062
Percent below poverty level	11.3	9.2	22.6	11.0	12.5	11.7	10.6	25.0	10.9	15.7
Related children under 18 years	1 682 803	983 630	215 073	1 360 149	322 654	1 526 318	1 182 858	213 276	1 153 735	372 583
65 years and over	417 445	346 582	24 235	330 461	86 984	625 417	573 826	25 713	488 742	136 675
Income in Previous Year Below 125 Percent of Poverty Level										
Families	1 328 665	902 354	140 320	1 065 612	263 053	1 103 656	929 984	104 016	839 167	264 489
Percent below poverty level	12.1	9.8	26.3	11.6	14.1	12.7	11.7	27.7	11.7	17.8
Female householder, no husband present	495 092	312 611	88 754	436 698	58 394	342 314	267 593	56 651	298 283	44 031
Householder 65 years and over	146 478	116 250	9 895	105 118	41 360	213 092	193 556	8 943	151 767	61 325
Unrelated individuals	1 875 980	1 510 142	132 100	1 643 664	232 316	1 296 073	1 150 515	82 064	1 114 868	181 205
Percent below poverty level	29.5	27.8	37.7	28.9	35.2	39.5	38.6	46.1	38.2	49.6
65 years and over	491 910	431 700	25 742	418 216	73 694	527 792	490 006	21 943	443 619	84 173
Persons	6 672 398	4 553 802	638 371	5 460 327	1 212 071	5 538 103	4 609 456	535 238	4 282 401	1 255 702
Percent below poverty level	15.8	13.2	29.5	15.5	17.8	16.4	15.0	33.0	15.3	21.7
Related children under 18 years	2 310 832	1 394 788	271 209	1 858 148	452 684	2 150 110	1 702 694	275 346	1 622 336	527 774
65 years and over	747 459	635 224	41 909	603 686	143 773	899 756	829 323	36 647	711 716	188 040

Table 98. **General Characteristics: 1980**

[Data are estimates based on a sample; see Introduction. For meaning of symbols, see Introduction. For definitions of terms, see appendixes A and B]

United States
Urban and Rural and Size of Place
Inside and Outside SMSA's

		Urban						Rural				
			Inside urbanized areas			Outside urbanized areas						
	United States	Total	Total	Central cities	Urban fringe	Places of 10,000 or more	Places of 2,500 to 10,000	Total	Places of 1,000 to 2,500	Rural farm	Inside SMSA's	Outside SMSA's
AGE												
Total persons	**226 545 805**	**167 054 638**	**139 182 696**	**67 035 742**	**72 146 954**	**13 480 685**	**14 391 257**	**59 491 167**	**7 034 378**	**5 617 903**	**169 430 577**	**57 115 228**
Under 5 years	16 298 350	11 743 447	9 652 021	4 774 125	4 877 896	997 979	1 093 447	4 554 903	529 167	342 183	11 931 569	4 366 781
5 to 9 years	16 654 989	11 801 266	9 764 750	4 597 605	5 167 145	960 462	1 076 054	4 853 723	533 513	380 519	12 235 838	4 419 151
10 to 14 years	18 284 837	12 906 683	10 795 325	4 879 383	5 915 942	985 593	1 125 765	5 378 154	566 798	491 872	13 554 167	4 730 670
15 to 19 years	21 178 128	15 501 112	12 758 787	6 055 200	6 703 587	1 383 523	1 358 802	5 677 016	630 412	583 122	15 707 883	5 470 245
20 to 24 years	21 293 814	16 758 790	13 896 590	7 274 649	6 621 941	1 557 707	1 304 493	4 535 024	557 376	350 464	16 317 069	4 976 745
25 to 29 years	19 471 494	14 887 055	12 626 619	6 411 871	6 214 748	1 136 131	1 124 305	4 584 439	529 529	304 168	15 019 415	4 452 079
30 to 34 years	17 709 880	13 130 101	11 182 044	5 229 291	5 952 753	947 703	1 000 354	4 579 779	485 409	304 326	13 657 730	4 052 150
35 to 39 years	13 972 227	10 074 504	8 575 152	3 764 700	4 810 452	709 798	789 554	3 897 723	391 678	325 885	10 685 301	3 286 926
40 to 44 years	11 665 328	8 391 175	7 120 830	3 149 086	3 971 744	602 033	668 312	3 274 153	338 702	328 206	8 840 064	2 825 264
45 to 49 years	11 024 925	8 032 384	6 813 437	3 047 905	3 765 532	581 799	637 148	2 992 541	321 369	350 744	8 352 506	2 672 419
50 to 54 years	11 707 376	8 678 479	7 349 643	3 377 003	3 972 640	634 886	693 950	3 028 897	349 690	389 426	8 871 601	2 835 775
55 to 59 years	11 651 267	8 691 499	7 319 426	3 458 838	3 860 588	652 676	719 397	2 959 768	361 471	400 207	8 767 488	2 883 779
60 to 64 years	10 134 804	7 457 377	6 169 949	3 023 937	3 146 012	596 465	690 963	2 677 427	354 264	354 747	7 410 032	2 724 772
65 to 69 years	8 767 959	6 410 418	5 195 904	2 655 523	2 540 381	550 678	663 836	2 357 541	340 778	287 309	6 248 116	2 519 843
70 to 74 years	6 822 149	5 047 712	4 034 462	2 118 033	1 916 429	458 292	554 958	1 774 437	284 834	197 018	4 816 389	2 005 760
75 to 79 years	4 795 045	3 613 152	2 867 052	1 549 217	1 317 835	336 000	410 100	1 181 893	211 196	119 793	3 398 534	1 396 511
80 to 84 years	2 920 554	2 241 685	1 763 194	958 849	804 345	214 770	263 721	678 869	135 215	64 780	2 076 929	843 625
85 years and over	2 192 679	1 687 799	1 297 511	710 527	586 984	174 190	216 098	504 880	112 977	43 134	1 539 946	652 733
Median	30.0	30.0	30.0	29.6	30.5	28.8	30.6	30.2	31.8	35.8	30.0	30.2
Female	**116 498 292**	**86 767 395**	**72 206 451**	**35 138 048**	**37 068 403**	**7 031 014**	**7 529 930**	**29 730 897**	**3 665 673**	**2 699 684**	**87 365 446**	**29 132 846**
Under 5 years	7 959 996	5 741 650	4 718 747	2 339 501	2 379 246	488 195	534 708	2 218 346	258 029	165 339	5 829 478	2 130 518
5 to 9 years	8 120 348	5 764 741	4 766 585	2 249 438	2 517 147	470 508	527 648	2 355 607	260 691	182 676	5 964 616	2 155 732
10 to 14 years	8 935 270	6 334 693	5 299 496	2 400 960	2 898 536	483 118	552 079	2 600 577	276 856	235 929	6 635 879	2 299 391
15 to 19 years	10 408 943	7 691 104	6 325 156	3 036 659	3 288 497	693 498	672 450	2 717 839	310 298	267 649	7 741 910	2 667 033
20 to 24 years	10 654 502	8 438 938	7 018 369	3 715 837	3 302 532	771 432	649 137	2 215 564	281 083	148 591	8 201 121	2 453 381
25 to 29 years	9 793 296	7 508 507	6 381 001	3 230 937	3 150 064	563 748	563 758	2 284 789	265 998	139 607	7 584 327	2 208 969
30 to 34 years	8 953 943	6 662 104	5 689 159	2 642 318	3 046 841	470 595	502 350	2 291 839	244 288	152 160	6 938 066	2 015 877
35 to 39 years	7 109 659	5 164 505	4 398 501	1 934 126	2 464 375	360 489	405 515	1 945 154	199 576	165 938	5 452 687	1 656 972
40 to 44 years	5 957 689	4 336 984	3 680 959	1 646 818	2 034 141	312 278	343 747	1 620 705	173 527	166 021	4 529 582	1 428 107
45 to 49 years	5 679 017	4 183 114	3 543 360	1 614 257	1 929 103	305 712	334 042	1 495 903	166 954	179 555	4 305 438	1 373 579
50 to 54 years	6 096 136	4 573 244	3 863 648	1 810 433	2 053 215	340 584	369 012	1 522 892	184 085	192 706	4 625 753	1 470 383
55 to 59 years	6 153 592	4 635 794	3 891 266	1 871 815	2 019 451	354 191	390 337	1 517 798	194 772	192 924	4 633 264	1 520 328
60 to 64 years	5 440 083	4 059 025	3 340 298	1 668 259	1 672 039	332 623	386 104	1 381 058	195 728	167 343	3 980 974	1 459 109
65 to 69 years	4 887 335	3 662 151	2 961 713	1 543 813	1 417 900	319 266	381 172	1 225 184	191 975	133 817	3 517 872	1 369 463
70 to 74 years	3 962 619	3 018 221	2 410 608	1 285 245	1 125 363	277 445	330 168	944 398	165 839	92 088	2 839 422	1 123 197
75 to 79 years	2 952 351	2 290 659	1 816 217	995 967	820 250	216 579	257 863	661 692	130 287	58 110	2 124 578	827 773
80 to 84 years	1 908 812	1 503 601	1 181 426	646 628	534 798	145 486	176 689	405 211	87 785	34 297	1 377 215	531 597
85 years and over	1 524 701	1 198 360	919 942	505 037	414 905	125 267	153 151	326 341	77 902	24 934	1 083 264	441 437
Median	31.3	31.4	31.4	31.1	31.6	30.5	32.6	31.0	33.7	36.7	31.2	31.6
CHARACTERISTICS OF PERSONS 60 YEARS AND OVER												
Persons 60 to 64 years	**10 134 804**	**7 457 377**	**6 169 949**	**3 023 937**	**3 146 012**	**596 465**	**690 963**	**2 677 427**	**354 264**	**354 747**	**7 410 032**	**2 724 772**
In families	8 267 595	5 975 219	4 947 285	2 308 358	2 638 927	473 696	554 238	2 292 376	288 056	328 596	6 005 256	2 262 339
Percent with income in 1979 below poverty level	6.6	5.3	4.9	6.6	3.5	6.6	7.4	10.1	7.7	9.9	5.3	10.2
Householder or spouse	7 811 081	5 616 435	4 636 941	2 142 765	2 494 176	451 355	528 139	2 194 646	275 630	316 611	5 647 563	2 163 518
Other relatives	456 514	358 784	310 344	165 593	144 751	22 341	26 099	97 730	12 426	11 985	357 693	98 821
Nonrelatives in households	1 745 978	1 385 701	1 146 149	670 444	475 705	113 269	126 283	360 277	61 881	26 151	1 314 019	431 959
Living alone	1 542 745	1 217 631	999 463	580 861	418 602	102 433	115 735	325 114	56 685	23 739	1 148 940	393 805
Percent with income in 1979 below poverty level	26.0	24.3	23.2	27.0	17.9	28.9	29.5	32.6	29.7	21.8	23.7	32.9
In group quarters	121 231	96 457	76 515	45 135	31 380	9 500	10 442	24 774	4 327	-	90 757	30 474
Inmate of institution	89 320	69 286	52 671	28 682	23 989	7 852	8 763	20 034	3 748	-	63 872	25 448
Home for the aged	58 441	46 209	33 718	19 020	14 698	5 733	6 758	12 232	3 140	-	40 458	17 983
Other	31 911	27 171	23 844	16 453	7 391	1 648	1 679	4 740	579	-	26 885	5 026
Persons 65 to 74 years	**15 590 108**	**11 458 130**	**9 230 366**	**4 773 556**	**4 456 810**	**1 008 970**	**1 218 794**	**4 131 978**	**625 612**	**484 327**	**11 064 505**	**4 525 603**
In families	11 184 519	8 010 305	6 488 027	3 176 667	3 311 360	682 637	839 641	3 174 214	439 834	421 258	7 883 566	3 300 953
Percent with income in 1979 below poverty level	7.5	5.8	5.3	6.9	3.8	7.6	8.2	11.7	8.8	9.5	5.8	11.6
Householder or spouse	10 229 481	7 261 964	5 836 325	2 851 805	2 984 520	637 786	787 853	2 967 517	415 080	397 392	7 128 936	3 100 545
Other relatives	955 038	748 341	651 702	324 862	326 840	44 851	51 788	206 697	24 754	23 866	754 630	200 408
Nonrelatives in households	4 061 489	3 168 059	2 530 159	1 478 314	1 051 845	295 518	342 382	893 430	170 396	63 069	2 930 430	1 131 059
Living alone	3 750 053	2 912 341	2 310 900	1 342 548	968 352	277 397	324 044	837 712	161 794	58 936	2 682 177	1 067 876
Percent with income in 1979 below poverty level	25.9	23.3	21.7	25.2	16.8	28.7	30.5	34.6	31.2	19.4	22.5	34.3
In group quarters	344 100	279 766	212 180	118 575	93 605	30 815	36 771	64 334	15 382	-	250 509	93 591
Inmate of institution	288 280	231 684	170 694	91 481	79 213	27 445	33 545	56 596	14 129	-	203 899	84 381
Home for the aged	238 962	193 937	139 565	76 412	63 153	24 165	30 207	45 025	12 850	-	166 632	72 330
Other	55 820	48 082	41 486	27 094	14 392	3 370	3 226	7 738	1 253	-	46 610	9 210
Persons 75 years and over	**9 908 278**	**7 542 636**	**5 927 757**	**3 218 593**	**2 709 164**	**724 960**	**889 919**	**2 365 642**	**459 388**	**227 707**	**7 015 409**	**2 892 869**
In families	5 248 577	3 867 870	3 129 152	1 599 428	1 529 724	329 929	408 789	1 380 707	215 299	171 145	3 742 304	1 506 273
Percent with income in 1979 below poverty level	9.4	7.2	6.3	7.8	4.8	10.0	11.1	15.6	12.4	10.6	7.0	15.2
Householder or spouse	3 956 370	2 868 142	2 267 125	1 190 130	1 076 995	265 577	335 440	1 088 228	178 730	133 633	2 734 068	1 222 302
Other relatives	1 292 207	999 728	862 027	409 298	452 729	64 352	73 349	292 479	36 569	37 512	1 008 236	283 971
Nonrelatives in households	3 528 514	2 742 407	2 127 120	1 266 584	860 536	279 168	336 119	786 107	176 813	56 562	2 481 464	1 047 050
Living alone	3 316 486	2 569 234	1 982 080	1 177 943	804 137	265 488	321 666	747 252	169 773	53 575	2 315 969	1 000 517
Percent with income in 1979 below poverty level	31.4	28.1	25.8	28.8	21.2	34.5	36.9	42.7	39.7	22.3	27.0	41.4
In group quarters	1 131 187	932 359	671 485	352 581	318 904	115 863	145 011	198 828	67 276	-	791 641	339 546
Inmate of institution	1 051 962	862 140	610 984	316 604	294 380	110 922	140 234	189 822	65 381	-	725 197	326 765
Home for the aged	993 996	815 606	574 328	299 213	275 115	106 418	134 860	178 390	63 080	-	682 724	311 272
Other	79 225	70 219	60 501	35 977	24 524	4 941	4 777	9 006	1 895	-	66 444	12 781
PERSONS IN HOUSEHOLD												
Households	**80 467 427**	**60 612 281**	**50 594 887**	**25 311 426**	**25 283 461**	**4 842 990**	**5 174 404**	**19 855 146**	**2 549 840**	**1 847 406**	**60 554 725**	**19 912 702**
1 person	18 202 015	14 899 014	12 439 783	7 333 176	5 106 607	1 215 763	1 243 468	3 303 001	597 840	213 905	14 037 907	4 164 108
2 persons	25 133 499	18 872 723	15 659 982	7 695 010	7 964 972	1 554 920	1 657 821	6 260 776	822 572	671 411	18 724 568	6 408 931
3 persons	13 957 933	10 325 506	8 645 326	4 069 794	4 575 532	817 193	862 987	3 632 427	422 037	339 291	10 501 976	3 455 957
4 persons	12 408 758	8 873 106	7 411 980	3 187 329	4 224 651	695 939	765 187	3 535 652	382 021	303 690	9 283 055	3 125 703
5 persons	6 334 903	4 486 943	3 768 728	1 661 080	2 107 648	334 751	383 464	1 847 960	193 941	181 039	4 723 840	1 611 063
6 or more persons	4 430 319	3 154 989	2 669 088	1 365 037	1 304 051	224 424	261 477	1 275 330	131 429	138 070	3 283 379	1 146 940

Table 99. **Nativity and Language: 1980**

[Data are estimates based on a sample; see Introduction. For meaning of symbols, see Introduction. For definitions of terms, see appendixes A and B]

United States Urban and Rural and Size of Place Inside and Outside SMSA's		Urban						Rural				
			Inside urbanized areas			Outside urbanized areas						
	United States	Total	Total	Central cities	Urban fringe	Places of 10,000 or more	Places of 2,500 to 10,000	Total	Places of 1,000 to 2,500	Rural farm	Inside SMSA's	Outside SMSA's
NATIVITY AND CITIZENSHIP												
Total persons	**226 545 805**	**167 054 638**	**139 182 696**	**67 035 742**	**72 146 954**	**13 480 685**	**14 391 257**	**59 491 167**	**7 034 378**	**5 617 903**	**169 430 577**	**57 115 228**
Native	212 465 899	154 139 673	127 164 565	60 610 967	66 553 598	13 009 780	13 965 328	58 326 226	6 872 139	5 544 752	156 510 392	55 955 507
Foreign born	14 079 906	12 914 965	12 018 131	6 424 775	5 593 356	470 905	425 929	1 164 941	162 239	73 151	12 920 185	1 159 721
Naturalized citizen	7 110 475	6 390 515	5 911 629	2 997 651	2 913 978	241 593	237 293	719 960	99 825	44 551	6 413 680	696 795
Not a citizen	6 969 431	6 524 450	6 106 502	3 427 124	2 679 378	229 312	188 636	444 981	62 414	28 600	6 506 505	462 926
COUNTRY OF BIRTH												
Foreign born persons	**14 079 906**	**12 914 965**	**12 018 131**	**6 424 775**	**5 593 356**	**470 905**	**425 929**	**1 164 941**	**162 239**	**73 151**	**12 920 185**	**1 159 721**
Europe	4 743 550	4 254 831	3 974 002	1 891 906	2 082 096	138 663	142 166	488 719	64 746	31 898	4 308 665	434 885
Austria	145 607	130 676	123 274	62 796	60 478	3 266	4 136	14 931	2 068	757	133 545	12 062
Czechoslovakia	112 707	99 520	93 211	42 163	51 048	2 560	3 749	13 187	1 758	932	102 504	10 203
France	120 215	106 620	98 221	46 440	51 781	4 187	4 212	13 595	1 669	695	107 741	12 474
Germany	849 384	713 764	642 650	274 688	367 962	36 112	35 002	135 620	16 719	8 236	732 230	117 154
Greece	210 998	204 116	196 194	111 788	84 406	4 814	3 108	6 882	804	264	201 886	9 112
Hungary	144 368	130 937	125 075	60 327	64 748	2 658	3 204	13 431	1 407	670	135 215	9 153
Ireland	197 817	184 361	176 644	91 095	85 549	3 519	4 198	13 456	2 116	448	186 342	11 475
Italy	831 922	788 966	753 364	363 157	390 207	19 130	16 472	42 956	6 989	1 941	786 008	45 914
Netherlands	103 136	83 133	74 691	26 047	48 644	3 722	4 720	20 003	2 213	3 452	89 525	13 611
Poland	418 128	393 538	380 148	216 157	163 991	6 195	7 195	24 590	3 442	1 466	397 566	20 562
Portugal	177 437	166 997	160 111	86 211	73 900	3 729	3 157	10 440	905	1 856	164 350	13 087
Sweden	77 157	63 862	56 131	24 627	31 504	3 821	3 910	13 295	2 416	888	63 714	13 443
United Kingdom	669 149	576 961	524 629	201 584	323 045	24 759	27 573	92 188	11 958	3 430	591 097	78 052
England	442 499	377 874	341 113	135 933	205 180	17 350	19 411	64 625	8 300	2 598	387 387	55 112
Northern Ireland	19 831	17 493	16 328	6 408	9 920	549	616	2 338	286	81	18 084	1 747
Scotland	142 001	125 312	115 409	39 353	76 056	4 626	5 277	16 689	2 273	494	127 024	14 977
Wales	13 528	11 436	10 246	3 779	6 467	535	655	2 092	353	82	11 913	1 615
Yugoslavia	152 967	142 511	136 841	68 473	68 368	2 609	3 061	10 456	1 293	728	145 686	7 281
U.S.S.R.	406 022	380 381	365 910	222 042	143 868	7 747	6 724	25 641	3 838	2 022	380 257	25 765
Asia	2 539 777	2 408 216	2 259 243	1 209 624	1 049 619	88 409	60 564	131 561	20 097	6 819	2 374 647	165 130
China	286 120	278 736	270 222	180 342	89 880	5 323	3 191	7 384	924	379	277 985	8 135
India	206 087	193 920	182 122	77 358	104 764	7 074	4 724	12 167	1 341	733	193 315	12 772
Japan	221 794	202 772	186 081	91 158	94 923	9 932	6 759	19 022	2 677	1 414	200 668	21 126
Korea	289 885	268 935	251 217	117 129	134 088	10 289	7 429	20 950	2 519	1 306	268 051	21 834
Philippines	501 440	469 378	437 057	231 615	205 442	14 454	17 867	32 062	6 223	1 184	464 124	37 316
Vietnam	231 120	220 617	205 852	114 766	91 086	8 560	6 205	10 503	2 102	439	214 817	16 303
North and Central America	4 664 903	4 292 354	3 939 067	2 240 647	1 698 420	182 432	170 855	372 549	55 922	24 838	4 277 247	387 656
Canada	842 859	700 128	617 384	239 706	377 678	40 560	42 184	142 731	19 226	7 608	700 485	142 374
Mexico	2 199 221	1 998 070	1 756 798	1 047 417	709 381	125 504	115 768	201 151	33 030	16 152	1 986 555	212 666
West Indies	1 258 363	1 241 087	1 222 442	731 045	491 397	10 391	8 254	17 276	1 953	387	1 238 308	20 055
Cuba	607 814	600 477	591 481	248 051	343 430	4 970	4 026	7 337	687	168	598 055	9 759
Dominican Republic	169 147	168 325	167 240	140 279	26 961	614	471	822	66	15	168 203	944
Jamaica	196 811	192 693	189 039	131 000	58 039	2 109	1 545	4 118	594	87	192 860	3 951
South America	561 011	543 057	527 268	294 185	233 083	9 788	6 001	17 954	1 859	788	542 167	18 844
North Africa	71 450	68 346	64 928	35 124	29 804	2 336	1 082	3 104	351	85	67 409	4 041
Other Africa	128 273	120 524	110 717	67 655	43 062	6 316	3 491	7 749	922	417	116 721	11 552
All other countries	78 896	71 075	64 640	29 579	35 061	2 765	3 670	7 821	892	481	71 577	7 319
Country not reported	886 024	776 181	712 356	434 013	278 343	32 449	31 376	109 843	13 612	5 803	781 495	104 529
YEAR OF IMMIGRATION												
Foreign born persons	**14 079 906**	**12 914 965**	**12 018 131**	**6 424 775**	**5 593 356**	**470 905**	**425 929**	**1 164 941**	**162 239**	**73 151**	**12 920 185**	**1 159 721**
1975 to 1980	3 335 024	3 143 120	2 931 375	1 727 194	1 204 181	123 134	88 611	191 904	27 590	12 400	3 101 291	233 733
1970 to 1974	2 225 339	2 096 495	1 977 791	1 119 655	858 136	63 169	55 535	128 844	17 334	7 593	2 093 049	132 290
1965 to 1969	1 807 814	1 686 040	1 591 434	846 648	744 786	49 836	44 770	121 774	15 023	6 638	1 695 297	112 517
1960 to 1964	1 327 088	1 214 963	1 132 085	553 195	578 890	44 972	37 906	112 125	13 295	5 738	1 222 508	104 580
1950 to 1959	1 911 384	1 702 142	1 577 486	756 895	820 591	65 130	59 526	209 242	23 549	13 137	1 739 800	171 584
Before 1950	3 473 257	3 072 205	2 807 960	1 421 188	1 386 772	124 664	139 581	401 052	65 448	27 645	3 068 240	405 017
LANGUAGE SPOKEN AT HOME AND ABILITY TO SPEAK ENGLISH												
Persons 5 years and over	**210 247 455**	**155 311 191**	**129 530 675**	**62 261 617**	**67 269 058**	**12 482 706**	**13 297 810**	**54 936 264**	**6 505 211**	**5 275 720**	**157 499 008**	**52 748 447**
Speak only English at home	187 187 415	135 179 597	111 553 597	51 903 416	59 650 181	11 390 530	12 235 470	52 007 818	6 081 246	4 982 329	137 685 724	49 501 691
Speak a language other than English at home	23 060 040	20 131 594	17 977 078	10 358 201	7 618 877	1 092 176	1 062 340	2 928 446	423 965	293 391	19 813 284	3 246 756
Speak English very well	12 879 004	11 092 665	9 835 278	5 353 732	4 481 546	639 243	618 144	1 786 339	251 871	177 667	10 904 001	1 975 003
Speak English well	5 957 544	5 195 867	4 637 092	2 772 120	1 864 972	283 893	274 882	761 677	115 180	84 465	5 101 950	855 594
Speak English not well or not at all	4 223 492	3 843 062	3 504 708	2 232 349	1 272 359	169 040	169 314	380 430	56 914	31 259	3 807 333	416 159
5 to 13 years	461 800	407 414	364 405	238 969	125 436	20 975	22 034	54 386	7 576	6 015	404 932	56 868
14 to 17 years	178 227	156 485	140 004	87 213	52 791	7 914	8 567	21 742	2 745	1 874	157 209	21 018
18 to 24 years	509 566	466 149	422 587	271 127	151 460	22 798	20 764	43 417	6 183	3 234	462 830	46 736
25 years and over	3 073 899	2 813 014	2 577 712	1 635 040	942 672	117 353	117 949	260 885	40 410	20 136	2 782 362	291 537
LANGUAGE SPOKEN AT HOME												
Persons 5 to 17 years	**47 493 975**	**33 601 229**	**27 985 266**	**12 845 359**	**15 139 907**	**2 633 864**	**2 982 099**	**13 892 746**	**1 494 103**	**1 260 623**	**35 065 635**	**12 428 340**
English only	42 925 646	29 657 292	24 499 199	10 766 147	13 733 052	2 407 567	2 750 526	13 268 354	1 407 645	1 197 329	31 162 285	11 763 361
Chinese	114 450	111 373	107 500	68 750	38 750	2 562	1 311	3 077	510	67	110 452	3 998
French	223 147	165 959	139 958	71 987	67 971	11 904	14 097	57 188	5 801	3 469	163 742	59 405
German	191 984	128 059	109 099	40 003	69 096	9 729	9 231	63 925	4 648	18 483	141 272	50 712
Greek	65 722	63 114	61 040	31 301	29 739	1 188	886	2 608	225	70	63 315	2 407
Italian	146 860	137 904	133 093	61 917	71 176	2 751	2 060	8 956	970	371	139 320	7 540
Philippine languages	63 189	58 873	54 782	29 413	25 369	1 657	2 434	4 316	942	115	58 285	4 904
Polish	40 934	36 304	34 642	16 088	18 554	813	849	4 630	560	368	37 704	3 230
Spanish	2 952 462	2 627 331	2 285 002	1 480 258	804 744	172 043	170 286	325 131	57 515	20 653	2 567 857	384 605
Other specified language	689 823	558 362	513 165	256 974	256 191	19 662	25 535	131 461	12 896	18 187	561 317	128 506
Unspecified language	79 758	56 658	47 786	22 521	25 265	3 988	4 884	23 100	2 391	1 511	60 086	19 672
Persons 18 years and over	**162 753 480**	**121 709 962**	**101 545 409**	**49 416 258**	**52 129 151**	**9 848 842**	**10 315 711**	**41 043 518**	**5 011 108**	**4 015 097**	**122 433 373**	**40 320 107**
English only	144 261 769	105 522 305	87 054 398	41 137 269	45 917 129	8 982 963	9 484 944	38 739 464	4 673 601	3 785 000	106 523 439	37 738 330
Chinese	516 356	502 545	483 498	314 175	169 323	12 825	6 222	13 811	1 900	396	497 516	18 840
French	1 327 604	1 034 019	840 286	462 652	377 634	96 450	97 283	293 585	37 890	16 831	949 101	378 503
German	1 394 609	1 038 096	879 389	408 974	470 415	78 371	80 336	356 513	49 809	73 281	1 055 879	338 730
Greek	335 721	321 004	306 719	162 604	144 115	8 393	5 892	14 717	1 635	596	318 872	16 849
Italian	1 471 484	1 378 624	1 304 383	625 050	679 333	39 260	34 981	92 860	14 940	4 710	1 373 423	98 061
Philippine languages	410 961	384 177	357 133	192 808	164 325	11 971	15 073	26 784	5 431	967	379 613	31 348
Polish	779 713	691 297	650 474	327 653	322 821	19 184	21 639	88 416	12 187	7 991	706 995	72 718
Spanish	8 163 732	7 380 011	6 515 919	4 131 412	2 384 507	450 376	413 716	783 721	130 415	49 539	7 177 571	986 161
Other specified language	3 852 042	3 268 699	2 989 011	1 567 758	1 421 253	137 166	142 522	583 343	77 153	71 299	3 259 740	592 302
Unspecified language	239 489	189 185	164 199	85 903	78 296	11 883	13 103	50 304	6 147	4 487	191 224	48 265

Table 100. **Fertility and Family Composition: 1980**

[Data are estimates based on a sample; see introduction. For meaning of symbols, see Introduction. For definitions of terms, see appendixes A and B]

United States Urban and Rural and Size of Place Inside and Outside SMSA's		Urban						Rural				
			Inside urbanized areas			Outside urbanized areas						
	United States	Total	Total	Central cities	Urban fringe	Places of 10,000 or more	Places of 2,500 to 10,000	Total	Places of 1,000 to 2,500	Rural farm	Inside SMSA's	Outside SMSA's
FERTILITY												
Women 15 to 24 years	**21 063 445**	**16 130 042**	**13 343 525**	**6 752 496**	**6 591 029**	**1 464 930**	**1 321 587**	**4 933 403**	**591 381**	**416 240**	**15 943 031**	**5 120 414**
Children ever born	6 670 367	4 836 249	3 862 168	2 282 530	1 579 638	469 525	504 556	1 834 118	239 488	98 606	4 702 908	1 967 459
Per 1,000 women	317	300	289	338	240	321	382	372	405	237	295	384
Women ever married	6 123 373	4 386 408	3 483 512	1 756 479	1 727 033	443 554	459 342	1 736 965	216 623	99 052	4 330 359	1 793 014
Children ever born	5 238 234	3 633 994	2 822 102	1 519 047	1 303 055	386 031	425 861	1 604 240	206 199	90 209	3 568 383	1 669 851
Per 1,000 women	855	828	810	865	755	870	927	924	952	911	824	931
Women 25 to 34 years	**18 747 239**	**14 170 611**	**12 070 160**	**5 873 255**	**6 196 905**	**1 034 343**	**1 066 108**	**4 576 628**	**510 286**	**291 767**	**14 522 393**	**4 224 846**
Children ever born	27 676 463	19 714 387	16 269 361	7 930 875	8 338 486	1 635 789	1 809 237	7 962 076	884 061	557 464	20 319 205	7 357 258
Per 1,000 women	1 476	1 391	1 348	1 350	1 346	1 581	1 697	1 740	1 732	1 911	1 399	1 741
Women ever married	15 684 467	11 493 435	9 658 608	4 435 447	5 223 161	892 545	942 282	4 191 032	456 884	266 340	11 902 678	3 781 789
Children ever born	26 480 573	18 662 577	15 328 909	7 207 554	8 121 355	1 577 977	1 755 691	7 817 996	863 267	553 670	19 320 253	7 160 320
Per 1,000 women	1 688	1 624	1 587	1 625	1 555	1 768	1 863	1 865	1 889	2 079	1 623	1 893
Women 35 to 44 years	**13 067 348**	**9 501 489**	**8 079 460**	**3 580 944**	**4 498 516**	**672 767**	**749 262**	**3 565 859**	**373 103**	**331 959**	**9 982 269**	**3 085 079**
Children ever born	34 490 834	24 331 014	20 377 378	9 184 210	11 193 168	1 843 161	2 110 475	10 159 820	1 069 035	1 002 689	25 582 936	8 907 898
Per 1,000 women	2 639	2 561	2 522	2 565	2 488	2 740	2 817	2 849	2 865	3 021	2 563	2 887
Women ever married	12 273 301	8 825 944	7 476 856	3 212 753	4 264 103	636 066	713 022	3 447 357	356 958	323 241	9 320 187	2 953 114
Children ever born	33 962 228	23 876 000	19 976 660	8 867 235	11 109 425	1 816 858	2 082 482	10 086 228	1 058 434	1 000 949	25 157 316	8 804 912
Per 1,000 women	2 767	2 705	2 672	2 760	2 605	2 856	2 921	2 926	2 965	3 097	2 699	2 982
HOUSEHOLD TYPE AND RELATIONSHIP												
Total persons	**226 545 805**	**167 054 638**	**139 182 696**	**67 035 742**	**72 146 954**	**13 480 685**	**14 391 257**	**59 491 167**	**7 034 378**	**5 617 903**	**169 430 577**	**57 115 228**
In households	220 807 382	162 242 457	135 698 584	64 995 073	70 703 511	12 701 622	13 842 251	58 564 925	6 873 407	5 617 903	165 291 191	55 516 191
Family householder: Male	49 224 032	34 748 275	28 710 293	12 507 682	16 202 611	2 837 426	3 200 556	14 475 757	1 630 411	1 541 055	35 949 637	13 274 395
Female	9 966 101	8 257 392	7 074 826	4 100 863	2 973 963	582 343	600 223	1 708 709	269 501	77 937	7 969 297	1 996 804
Nonfamily householder: Male	8 941 007	7 327 315	6 329 324	3 744 180	2 585 144	531 575	466 416	1 613 692	221 079	121 157	7 128 320	1 812 687
Female	12 336 287	10 279 299	8 480 444	4 958 701	3 521 743	891 646	907 209	2 056 988	428 849	107 257	9 507 471	2 828 816
Spouse	48 895 514	34 569 758	28 571 543	12 377 640	16 193 903	2 816 519	3 181 696	14 325 756	1 619 407	1 502 519	35 774 974	13 120 540
Child	76 076 991	54 702 309	45 861 974	21 215 202	24 646 772	4 158 279	4 682 056	21 374 682	2 338 864	2 039 966	56 776 451	19 300 540
Other relatives	9 299 544	7 165 760	6 155 401	3 484 394	2 671 007	481 256	529 103	2 133 784	250 855	180 233	7 148 241	2 151 303
Nonrelatives	6 067 906	5 192 349	4 514 779	2 606 411	1 908 368	402 578	274 992	875 557	114 441	47 779	5 036 800	1 031 106
Persons per household	2.74	2.68	2.68	2.57	2.80	2.62	2.68	2.95	2.70	3.04	2.73	2.79
Persons per family	3.27	3.24	3.25	3.23	3.27	3.18	3.21	3.34	3.22	3.30	3.27	3.26
FAMILY TYPE BY PRESENCE OF OWN CHILDREN												
Families	**59 190 133**	**43 005 667**	**35 785 119**	**16 608 545**	**19 176 574**	**3 419 769**	**3 800 779**	**16 184 466**	**1 899 912**	**1 618 992**	**43 918 934**	**15 271 199**
With own children under 18 years	30 472 339	21 892 246	18 220 344	8 296 807	9 923 537	1 742 361	1 929 541	8 580 093	952 945	725 377	22 667 714	7 804 625
With own children under 6 years	13 207 715	9 510 636	7 826 121	3 751 487	4 074 634	807 520	876 995	3 697 079	424 400	270 201	9 708 864	3 498 851
Married-couple families	**48 990 299**	**34 629 611**	**28 614 787**	**12 401 968**	**16 212 819**	**2 825 395**	**3 189 429**	**14 360 688**	**1 623 500**	**1 507 894**	**35 830 718**	**13 159 581**
With own children under 18 years	24 779 964	17 140 542	14 155 007	5 878 420	8 276 587	1 398 639	1 586 896	7 639 422	803 954	697 033	18 100 212	6 679 752
With own children under 6 years	11 253 678	7 842 285	6 406 709	2 816 010	3 590 699	679 022	756 554	3 411 393	375 042	264 231	8 139 443	3 114 235
Female householder, no husband present	**8 205 279**	**6 845 544**	**5 847 483**	**3 487 577**	**2 359 906**	**493 844**	**504 217**	**1 359 735**	**223 822**	**57 621**	**6 544 179**	**1 661 100**
With own children under 18 years	4 932 478	4 178 062	3 577 210	2 165 564	1 411 646	301 962	298 890	754 416	127 684	16 424	3 984 447	948 031
With own children under 6 years	1 705 688	1 474 753	1 255 703	839 041	416 662	113 438	105 612	230 935	42 418	3 415	1 378 815	326 873
Subfamilies	**1 386 927**	**1 039 162**	**883 511**	**498 494**	**385 017**	**74 043**	**81 608**	**347 765**	**40 633**	**24 679**	**1 049 776**	**337 151**
With own children under 18 years	1 101 539	826 179	697 476	412 116	285 360	61 638	67 065	275 360	33 015	17 268	825 553	275 986
Married-couple subfamilies	**523 728**	**383 522**	**330 336**	**156 705**	**173 631**	**24 500**	**28 686**	**140 206**	**14 897**	**13 379**	**403 494**	**120 234**
With own children under 18 years	238 340	170 539	144 301	70 327	73 974	12 095	14 143	67 801	7 279	5 968	179 271	59 069
Mother-child subfamilies	**788 033**	**601 203**	**508 230**	**315 705**	**192 525**	**45 193**	**47 780**	**186 830**	**23 346**	**9 790**	**591 780**	**196 253**
Persons under 18 years	**63 792 325**	**45 344 676**	**37 637 287**	**17 619 484**	**20 017 803**	**3 631 843**	**4 075 546**	**18 447 649**	**2 023 270**	**1 602 806**	**46 997 204**	**16 795 121**
Percent living with two parents	76.7	73.7	73.2	64.9	80.4	75.0	77.2	84.0	79.6	92.8	75.4	80.1
MARITAL HISTORY												
Ever-married persons 15 to 54 years	**84 907 133**	**61 416 481**	**51 371 179**	**23 150 092**	**28 221 087**	**4 843 187**	**5 202 115**	**23 490 652**	**2 557 740**	**1 999 980**	**63 648 631**	**21 258 502**
Never widowed or divorced	63 429 484	45 077 449	37 643 223	16 343 952	21 299 271	3 541 424	3 892 802	18 352 035	1 947 396	1 729 742	47 124 552	16 304 932
Known to have been: Widowed	2 459 126	1 815 687	1 506 757	793 339	713 418	146 102	162 828	643 439	80 462	41 928	1 808 687	650 439
Divorced	19 320 199	14 757 621	12 414 745	6 118 855	6 295 890	1 175 989	1 166 887	4 562 578	539 267	230 523	14 943 008	4 377 191
Widowed and divorced	301 676	234 276	193 546	106 054	87 492	20 328	20 402	67 400	9 385	2 213	227 616	74 060
LABOR FORCE STATUS OF FAMILY MEMBERS												
Families	**59 190 133**	**43 005 667**	**35 785 119**	**16 608 545**	**19 176 574**	**3 419 769**	**3 800 779**	**16 184 466**	**1 899 912**	**1 618 992**	**43 918 934**	**15 271 199**
Householder: Employed or in Armed Forces	43 864 484	31 990 313	26 762 793	11 720 951	15 041 842	2 512 470	2 715 050	11 874 171	1 334 594	1 279 663	33 014 498	10 849 986
Unemployed	2 026 470	1 407 597	1 153 966	630 312	523 654	117 763	135 868	618 873	71 658	24 309	1 439 171	587 299
Not in labor force	13 299 179	9 607 757	7 868 360	4 257 282	3 611 078	789 536	949 861	3 691 422	493 660	315 020	9 465 265	3 833 914
Married-couple families	**48 990 299**	**34 629 611**	**28 614 787**	**12 401 968**	**16 212 819**	**2 825 395**	**3 189 429**	**14 360 688**	**1 623 500**	**1 507 894**	**35 830 718**	**13 159 581**
Husband employed or in Armed Forces	38 178 816	27 238 509	22 676 674	9 477 760	13 198 914	2 176 747	2 385 088	10 940 307	1 189 981	1 224 803	28 414 138	9 764 678
Wife employed or in Armed Forces	20 195 937	14 682 316	12 209 706	5 148 733	7 060 973	1 194 348	1 278 262	5 513 621	634 143	534 518	15 160 045	5 035 892
Wife unemployed	1 035 222	726 282	587 512	272 116	315 396	65 592	73 178	308 940	33 956	18 659	746 381	288 841
Wife not in labor force	16 947 657	11 829 911	9 879 456	4 056 911	5 822 545	916 807	1 033 648	5 117 746	521 882	671 626	12 507 712	4 439 945
Husband unemployed	1 547 119	1 012 160	821 044	412 868	408 176	85 840	105 276	534 959	58 526	22 171	1 064 847	482 272
Wife employed or in Armed Forces	730 601	501 654	411 018	203 906	207 112	42 048	48 588	228 947	26 792	8 800	520 599	210 002
Wife unemployed	129 959	84 527	65 160	35 700	29 460	8 592	10 775	45 432	5 414	1 712	86 614	43 345
Wife not in labor force	686 559	425 979	344 866	173 262	171 604	35 200	45 913	260 580	26 320	11 659	457 634	228 925
Husband not in labor force	9 264 364	6 378 942	5 117 069	2 511 340	2 605 729	562 808	699 065	2 885 422	374 993	260 920	6 351 733	2 912 631
Wife employed or in Armed Forces	1 928 077	1 378 838	1 124 553	580 373	544 180	119 075	135 210	549 239	69 618	43 331	1 370 781	557 296
Wife unemployed	113 459	75 675	60 331	33 200	27 131	6 875	8 469	37 784	4 259	2 168	76 345	37 114
Wife not in labor force	7 222 828	4 924 429	3 932 185	1 897 767	2 034 418	436 858	555 386	2 298 399	301 116	215 421	4 904 607	2 318 221
Female householder, no husband present	**8 205 279**	**6 845 544**	**5 847 483**	**3 487 577**	**2 359 906**	**493 844**	**504 217**	**1 359 735**	**223 822**	**57 621**	**6 544 179**	**1 661 100**
Employed or in Armed Forces	4 536 099	3 855 343	3 308 845	1 819 078	1 489 767	276 594	269 904	680 756	116 021	20 573	3 698 029	838 070
Unemployed	395 094	332 061	279 470	185 132	94 338	27 087	25 504	63 033	11 064	1 095	311 144	83 950
Not in labor force	3 274 086	2 658 140	2 259 168	1 483 367	775 801	190 163	208 809	615 946	96 737	35 953	2 535 006	739 080
TYPE OF GROUP QUARTERS												
Persons in group quarters	**5 738 423**	**4 812 181**	**3 484 112**	**2 040 669**	**1 443 443**	**779 063**	**549 006**	**926 242**	**160 971**	-	**4 139 386**	**1 599 037**
Inmate of mental hospital	245 029	191 677	159 768	80 523	79 245	20 044	11 865	53 352	4 343	-	192 525	52 504
Inmate of home for the aged	1 426 371	1 162 830	826 758	440 423	386 335	148 848	187 224	263 541	85 679	-	983 832	442 539
Inmate of other institution	820 757	525 385	394 337	228 044	166 293	70 527	60 521	295 372	16 490	-	553 868	266 889
In military quarters	671 251	621 686	476 500	196 523	279 977	80 060	65 126	49 565	8 746	-	552 224	119 027
In college dormitory	1 994 282	1 847 372	1 227 164	819 716	407 448	425 297	194 911	146 910	31 494	-	1 388 494	605 788
Other, in group quarters	580 733	463 231	399 585	275 440	124 145	34 287	29 359	117 502	14 219	-	468 443	112 290

GENERAL SOCIAL AND ECONOMIC CHARACTERISTICS UNITED STATES SUMMARY 1—69

411

Table 101. Geographical Mobility and Commuting: 1980

[Data are estimates based on a sample; see Introduction. For meaning of symbols, see Introduction. For definitions of terms, see appendixes A and B]

United States Urban and Rural and Size of Place Inside and Outside SMSA's	United States	Urban Total	Urban Inside urbanized areas Total	Central cities	Urban fringe	Outside urbanized areas Places of 10,000 or more	Places of 2,500 to 10,000	Rural Total	Places of 1,000 to 2,500	Rural farm	Inside SMSA's	Outside SMSA's
NATIVITY AND PLACE OF BIRTH												
Total persons	226 545 805	167 054 638	139 182 696	67 035 742	72 146 954	13 480 685	14 391 257	59 491 167	7 034 378	5 617 903	169 430 577	57 115 228
Native	212 465 899	154 139 673	127 164 565	60 610 967	66 553 598	13 009 780	13 965 328	58 326 226	6 872 139	5 544 752	156 510 392	55 955 507
Born in State of residence	144 871 155	100 495 406	81 443 084	39 554 497	41 888 587	9 035 155	10 017 167	44 375 749	5 183 380	4 679 538	102 728 084	42 143 071
Born in different State	65 451 542	51 721 379	43 957 962	19 941 018	24 016 944	3 887 803	3 875 614	13 730 163	1 662 631	853 632	51 865 641	13 585 901
Northeast	14 818 119	12 101 189	10 810 549	3 764 740	7 045 809	604 486	686 154	2 716 930	305 666	84 060	12 516 687	2 301 432
North Central	19 186 351	14 953 529	12 410 407	5 414 939	6 995 468	1 282 972	1 260 150	4 232 822	564 391	360 846	14 781 460	4 404 891
South	23 296 807	18 447 193	15 751 243	8 459 641	7 291 602	1 368 909	1 327 041	4 849 614	545 150	268 814	18 617 565	4 679 242
West	8 150 265	6 219 468	4 985 763	2 301 698	2 684 065	631 436	602 269	1 930 797	247 424	139 912	5 949 929	2 200 336
Born abroad, at sea, etc.	2 143 202	1 922 888	1 763 519	1 115 452	648 067	86 822	72 547	220 314	26 128	11 582	1 916 667	226 535
Foreign born	14 079 906	12 914 965	12 018 131	6 424 775	5 593 356	470 905	425 929	1 164 941	162 239	73 151	12 920 185	1 159 721
RESIDENCE IN 1975												
Persons 5 years and over	210 323 291	155 370 641	129 574 934	62 290 292	67 284 642	12 491 736	13 303 971	54 952 650	6 507 038	5 276 773	157 551 738	52 771 553
Same house	112 695 416	80 766 353	67 767 131	32 268 909	35 498 222	6 002 768	6 996 454	31 929 063	3 715 007	4 060 774	82 972 382	29 723 034
Different house in United States	93 696 039	70 993 182	58 529 764	28 192 054	30 337 710	6 299 265	6 164 153	22 702 857	2 747 590	1 200 734	71 047 285	22 648 754
Same county	52 749 574	40 758 204	34 359 531	17 850 704	16 508 827	3 199 372	3 199 301	11 991 370	1 474 458	853 632	40 953 339	11 796 235
Different county	40 946 465	30 234 978	24 170 233	10 341 350	13 828 883	3 099 893	2 964 852	10 711 487	1 273 132	326 873	30 093 946	10 852 519
Same State	20 588 011	14 255 267	11 032 495	4 513 382	6 519 113	1 652 113	1 570 659	6 332 744	735 671	14 531	14 531 654	6 056 357
In Armed Forces in 1975	185 811	143 869	118 555	50 193	68 362	12 511	12 803	41 942	4 560	1 339	144 656	41 155
Attending college in 1975	2 156 579	1 741 036	1 443 670	683 603	760 067	163 768	133 598	415 543	56 245	26 912	1 692 490	464 089
Different State	20 358 454	15 979 711	13 137 738	5 827 968	7 309 770	1 447 780	1 394 193	4 378 743	537 461	162 150	15 562 292	4 796 162
In Armed Forces in 1975	811 973	664 574	536 459	236 830	299 629	64 977	63 138	147 399	19 314	4 764	631 962	180 011
Attending college in 1975	2 250 232	1 956 914	1 709 251	873 813	835 438	140 568	107 095	293 318	36 976	10 915	1 887 280	362 952
Northeast	4 585 180	3 773 993	3 309 944	1 285 600	2 024 344	222 452	241 597	811 187	92 673	16 285	3 817 296	767 884
North Central	5 198 334	4 050 367	3 279 124	1 482 123	1 797 001	394 058	377 185	1 147 967	151 612	54 630	3 909 328	1 289 006
South	6 394 116	4 958 761	4 055 825	1 864 048	2 191 777	469 337	433 599	1 435 355	162 879	47 723	4 863 232	1 530 884
West	4 180 824	3 196 590	2 492 845	1 196 197	1 296 648	361 933	341 812	984 234	130 297	43 512	2 972 436	1 208 388
Abroad	3 931 836	3 611 106	3 278 039	1 829 329	1 448 710	189 703	143 364	320 730	44 441	15 265	3 532 071	399 765
In Armed Forces in 1975	317 074	269 737	219 025	102 224	116 801	27 469	23 243	47 337	6 757	1 602	253 191	63 883
Attending college in 1975	310 861	296 013	270 955	158 791	112 164	16 851	8 207	14 848	1 800	439	283 746	27 115
SELECTED CLASSES OF MIGRANTS												
Persons 16 years and over:												
Different county in 1975	33 585 047	25 232 462	20 222 361	8 889 072	11 333 289	2 608 344	2 401 757	8 352 585	1 005 585	375 288	24 857 354	8 727 693
In Armed Forces in 1980	1 246 550	1 130 549	881 025	366 667	514 358	132 705	116 819	116 001	19 650	599	1 013 758	232 792
Inmate of institution in 1980	701 552	465 970	317 649	150 066	167 583	73 038	75 283	235 582	30 041	–	442 989	258 563
Attending college in 1980	4 826 000	4 311 135	3 281 949	1 932 093	1 349 856	706 524	322 662	514 865	67 995	15 487	3 698 843	1 127 157
Living with at least one parent	305 964	242 241	211 941	77 684	134 257	15 741	14 559	63 723	5 573	4 121	253 459	52 505
Not living with any parent	4 520 036	4 068 894	3 070 008	1 854 409	1 215 599	690 783	308 103	451 142	62 422	11 366	3 445 384	1 074 652
Different State in 1975	16 610 412	13 210 672	10 906 255	4 951 188	5 955 067	1 185 113	1 119 304	3 399 740	421 220	122 927	12 792 801	3 817 611
In Armed Forces in 1980	1 123 599	1 022 905	793 887	326 796	467 091	123 504	105 514	100 694	17 898	372	910 734	212 865
Inmate of institution in 1980	183 871	134 577	99 327	53 083	46 244	18 987	16 263	49 294	5 973	–	126 445	57 426
Attending college in 1980	2 135 255	1 924 109	1 574 159	906 169	668 090	213 134	136 816	211 146	30 571	5 224	1 736 986	398 269
Living with at least one parent	161 557	133 084	117 399	43 592	73 807	8 439	7 246	28 473	2 392	1 192	136 495	25 062
Not living with any parent	1 973 698	1 791 025	1 456 760	862 477	594 283	204 695	129 570	182 673	28 179	4 032	1 600 491	373 207
MEANS OF TRANSPORTATION TO WORK												
Workers 16 years and over	96 617 296	73 190 809	61 830 962	28 624 513	33 206 449	5 631 635	5 728 212	23 426 487	2 735 846	2 434 102	74 389 731	22 227 565
Private vehicle	81 258 496	60 674 575	50 863 150	21 654 409	29 208 741	4 849 201	4 962 224	20 583 921	2 361 373	1 518 167	62 171 165	19 087 331
Drive alone: Car	52 137 986	41 004 987	35 021 057	14 707 957	20 313 100	3 061 115	2 922 815	11 132 999	1 313 851	737 954	41 617 172	10 520 814
Truck or van	10 055 463	5 949 803	4 530 155	1 872 951	2 657 204	651 384	768 264	4 105 660	410 527	455 337	6 438 217	3 617 246
Carpool: Car	15 889 813	11 917 409	9 969 763	4 482 857	5 486 906	937 877	1 009 769	3 972 404	495 809	217 876	12 173 350	3 716 463
Truck or van	3 175 234	1 802 376	1 342 175	590 644	751 531	198 825	261 376	1 372 858	141 186	107 000	1 942 426	1 232 808
Public transportation	6 175 061	5 998 494	5 875 076	4 137 935	1 737 141	72 744	50 674	176 567	20 717	9 477	5 997 163	177 898
Bus or streetcar	3 924 787	3 785 138	3 699 111	2 605 778	1 093 333	49 125	36 902	139 649	16 106	8 741	3 786 931	137 856
Subway or elevated train	1 528 852	1 525 677	1 524 302	1 338 666	185 636	693	682	3 175	276	109	1 526 873	1 979
Railroad	554 089	527 901	522 090	100 705	421 385	1 805	4 006	26 188	3 109	465	547 928	6 161
Taxicab	167 333	159 778	129 573	92 786	36 787	21 121	9 084	7 555	1 226	162	135 431	31 902
Bicycle	468 348	418 910	331 257	172 026	159 231	51 771	35 882	49 438	12 732	2 154	369 784	98 564
Motorcycle	419 007	341 749	284 908	126 709	158 199	31 597	25 244	77 258	8 820	4 689	334 804	84 203
Walked only	5 413 248	4 249 007	3 257 508	1 952 679	1 304 829	490 271	501 228	1 164 241	250 651	16 283	3 813 903	1 599 345
Other means	703 273	481 470	384 754	192 324	192 430	46 017	50 699	221 803	24 341	38 538	479 303	223 970
Worked at home	2 179 863	1 026 604	834 309	388 431	445 878	90 034	102 261	1 153 259	57 212	652 108	1 223 609	956 254
PRIVATE VEHICLE OCCUPANCY												
Workers 16 years and over using private vehicles	81 258 496	60 674 575	50 863 150	21 654 409	29 208 741	4 849 201	4 962 224	20 583 921	2 361 373	1 518 167	62 171 165	19 087 331
Drive alone	62 193 449	46 954 790	39 551 212	16 580 908	22 970 304	3 712 499	3 691 079	15 238 659	1 724 378	1 193 291	48 055 389	14 138 060
In 2-person carpool	13 303 701	9 808 539	8 196 295	3 659 161	4 537 134	785 750	826 494	3 495 162	403 128	206 086	10 099 178	3 204 523
In 3-person carpool	3 360 781	2 328 951	1 895 543	863 646	1 031 897	195 085	238 323	1 031 830	126 107	65 252	2 407 744	953 037
In 4-person carpool	1 400 527	948 089	744 223	329 418	414 805	88 925	114 941	452 438	60 504	28 028	966 172	434 355
In 5-or-more-person carpool	1 000 038	634 206	475 877	221 276	254 601	66 942	91 387	365 832	47 256	25 510	642 682	357 356
Persons per private vehicle	1.15	1.15	1.14	1.15	1.14	1.15	1.17	1.18	1.19	1.14	1.15	1.18
TRAVEL TIME TO WORK												
Workers 16 years and over who did not work at home	94 487 095	72 213 205	61 035 269	28 263 033	32 772 236	5 546 379	5 631 557	22 273 890	2 674 706	1 780 783	73 203 593	21 283 502
Less than 10 minutes	16 871 572	12 629 987	8 627 901	3 939 265	4 688 636	1 866 615	2 135 471	4 241 585	919 589	475 487	10 761 513	6 110 059
10 to 19 minutes	31 846 602	25 052 143	20 934 785	10 205 243	10 729 542	2 368 317	1 749 041	6 794 459	717 005	524 712	24 350 911	7 495 691
20 to 29 minutes	18 849 260	14 449 684	13 244 375	5 888 399	7 355 976	552 720	652 589	4 399 576	396 509	312 406	15 788 503	3 060 757
30 to 44 minutes	15 996 009	11 991 647	10 941 521	4 764 091	6 177 430	430 279	619 847	4 004 362	376 233	276 839	13 405 553	2 590 456
45 or more minutes	10 923 652	8 089 744	7 286 687	3 466 035	3 820 652	328 448	474 609	2 833 908	265 370	191 339	8 897 113	2 026 539
Mean minutes	21.7	21.5	22.5	22.4	22.6	15.0	16.6	22.4	18.5	20.0	22.6	18.5
Workers traveling 45 or more minutes minutes	59.6	59.4	59.1	59.4	58.9	61.7	61.2	60.4	60.8	60.5	58.9	62.5

Table 102. **Educational Characteristics: 1980**

[Data are estimates based on a sample; see Introduction. For meaning of symbols, see Introduction. For definitions of terms, see appendixes A and B]

United States Urban and Rural and Size of Place Inside and Outside SMSA's		Urban						Rural				
			Inside urbanized areas			Outside urbanized areas						
	United States	Total	Total	Central cities	Urban fringe	Places of 10,000 or more	Places of 2,500 to 10,000	Total	Places of 1,000 to 2,500	Rural farm	Inside SMSA's	Outside SMSA's
SCHOOL ENROLLMENT AND TYPE OF SCHOOL												
Persons 3 years old and over enrolled in school	**62 054 304**	**46 296 314**	**38 719 094**	**18 394 843**	**20 324 251**	**3 859 735**	**3 717 485**	**15 757 990**	**1 725 204**	**1 406 681**	**47 151 325**	**14 902 979**
Nursery school	2 429 651	1 957 698	1 677 733	744 934	932 799	141 326	138 639	471 953	57 239	27 215	1 981 916	447 735
Public	894 313	697 767	579 685	299 601	280 084	56 958	61 124	196 546	27 838	12 504	683 989	210 324
Church-related	655 588	548 383	484 382	203 935	280 447	35 409	28 592	107 205	9 729	5 498	567 259	88 329
Other private	879 750	711 548	613 666	241 398	372 268	48 959	48 923	168 202	19 672	9 213	730 668	149 082
Kindergarten	3 210 098	2 309 052	1 905 226	915 387	989 839	193 264	210 562	901 046	102 780	64 393	2 369 840	840 258
Public	2 697 067	1 890 103	1 535 308	725 235	810 073	165 706	189 089	806 964	94 843	58 379	1 942 855	754 212
Church-related	346 083	286 351	252 591	131 036	121 555	20 011	13 749	59 732	4 550	3 928	291 405	54 678
Other private	166 948	132 598	117 327	59 116	58 211	7 547	7 724	34 350	3 387	2 086	135 580	31 368
Elementary (1 to 8 years)	28 775 352	20 321 342	16 923 785	7 818 515	9 105 270	1 589 718	1 807 839	8 454 010	904 108	719 329	21 245 024	7 530 328
Public	25 523 237	17 607 195	14 459 109	6 539 267	7 919 842	1 459 709	1 688 377	7 916 042	857 244	642 666	18 450 491	7 072 746
Church-related	2 812 993	2 374 645	2 159 148	1 108 965	1 050 183	115 003	100 494	438 348	37 831	64 907	2 447 560	365 433
Other private	439 122	339 502	305 528	170 283	135 245	15 006	18 968	99 620	9 033	11 756	346 973	92 149
High school (1 to 4 years)	15 260 109	10 909 152	9 171 238	4 094 540	5 076 698	812 382	925 532	4 350 957	470 694	477 370	11 407 054	3 853 055
Public	13 901 532	9 750 451	8 096 446	3 526 399	4 570 047	766 570	887 435	4 151 081	453 259	453 641	10 212 388	3 689 144
Church-related	1 063 211	930 738	869 742	458 164	411 578	35 441	25 555	132 473	10 978	16 477	958 561	104 650
Other private	295 366	227 963	205 050	109 977	95 073	10 371	12 542	67 403	6 457	7 252	236 105	59 261
College	12 379 094	10 799 070	9 041 112	4 821 467	4 219 645	1 123 045	634 913	1 580 024	190 383	118 374	10 147 491	2 231 603
Public	9 959 175	8 594 827	7 136 216	3 761 137	3 375 079	971 670	486 941	1 364 348	149 134	108 312	8 050 723	1 908 452
Persons 3 years old and over enrolled in school	**62 054 304**	**46 296 314**	**38 719 094**	**18 394 843**	**20 324 251**	**3 859 735**	**3 717 485**	**15 757 990**	**1 725 204**	**1 406 681**	**47 151 325**	**14 902 979**
3 and 4 years old	2 071 780	1 682 616	1 455 909	671 763	784 146	114 396	112 311	389 164	46 074	19 906	1 703 452	368 328
5 and 6 years old	5 392 483	3 917 565	3 257 534	1 539 014	1 718 520	314 473	345 558	1 474 918	167 140	105 780	4 028 277	1 364 206
7 to 13 years old	24 570 506	17 358 779	14 463 615	6 598 706	7 864 909	1 356 909	1 538 255	7 211 727	769 515	617 854	18 176 913	6 393 593
14 and 15 years old	7 739 575	5 463 355	4 574 006	2 049 704	2 524 302	412 830	476 519	2 276 220	241 297	226 796	5 732 600	2 006 975
16 and 17 years old	7 478 643	5 315 756	4 455 870	1 968 099	2 487 771	402 159	457 727	2 162 887	235 096	245 646	5 561 721	1 916 922
18 and 19 years old	4 514 290	3 617 062	2 889 361	1 480 902	1 408 459	428 114	299 587	897 228	108 735	98 905	3 412 522	1 101 768
20 and 21 years old	2 808 724	2 488 276	1 988 017	1 124 119	863 898	335 676	164 583	320 448	41 002	27 666	2 225 862	582 862
22 to 24 years old	2 186 802	1 961 393	1 671 520	957 894	713 626	195 349	94 524	225 409	26 714	15 359	1 828 267	358 535
25 to 34 years old	3 270 473	2 817 467	2 492 031	1 320 537	1 171 494	193 607	131 829	453 006	49 671	21 185	2 791 328	479 145
35 years old and over	2 021 028	1 674 045	1 471 231	684 105	787 126	106 222	96 592	346 983	39 960	27 584	1 690 383	330 645
Percent enrolled in school—												
3 and 4 years old	32.8	37.2	39.1	37.0	41.1	30.2	26.8	21.7	22.5	14.7	36.8	21.8
5 and 6 years old	86.3	88.2	89.0	87.7	90.2	85.2	84.2	81.5	82.6	76.1	88.1	81.3
7 to 13 years old	98.8	98.8	98.8	98.5	99.1	98.8	98.8	98.8	98.8	99.0	98.9	98.6
14 and 15 years old	97.8	97.9	97.9	97.2	98.5	97.4	97.5	97.6	97.8	97.8	98.0	97.3
16 and 17 years old	88.4	88.5	88.8	86.2	91.0	86.0	87.1	88.2	88.4	92.5	88.9	86.9
18 and 19 years old	52.3	54.7	54.2	55.1	53.2	61.5	51.8	44.5	46.0	50.7	53.1	50.3
20 and 21 years old	32.4	36.4	35.6	38.3	32.6	47.1	29.8	17.7	18.4	18.2	33.9	27.9
22 to 24 years old	17.3	19.8	20.1	22.1	18.0	23.1	12.6	8.3	8.0	7.7	18.8	12.4
25 to 34 years old	8.8	10.1	10.5	11.3	9.6	9.3	6.2	4.9	4.9	3.5	9.7	5.6
SCHOOL ENROLLMENT AND LABOR FORCE STATUS												
Persons 16 to 19 years old	**17 084 757**	**12 617 320**	**10 350 248**	**4 969 639**	**5 380 609**	**1 163 148**	**1 103 924**	**4 467 437**	**502 422**	**460 477**	**12 686 275**	**4 398 482**
Armed Forces	248 308	228 390	168 129	71 003	97 126	36 746	23 515	19 918	2 903	148	201 391	46 917
Civilian, enrolled in school	11 976 181	8 917 316	7 335 470	3 444 993	3 890 477	828 562	753 284	3 058 865	343 670	344 515	8 960 405	3 015 776
Employed	4 219 869	3 283 565	2 719 475	1 143 091	1 576 384	302 658	261 432	936 304	110 149	113 176	3 273 854	946 015
Unemployed	558 540	439 835	367 356	175 586	191 770	39 252	33 227	118 705	13 132	7 165	436 651	121 889
Not in labor force	7 197 772	5 193 916	4 248 639	2 126 316	2 122 323	486 652	458 625	2 003 856	220 389	224 174	5 249 900	1 947 872
Civilian, not enrolled in school	4 860 268	3 471 614	2 846 649	1 453 643	1 393 006	297 840	327 125	1 388 654	155 849	115 814	3 524 479	1 335 789
High school graduate	2 610 787	1 854 280	1 528 905	692 771	836 134	153 134	172 241	756 507	86 788	78 255	1 913 602	697 185
Employed	1 841 465	1 317 412	1 089 334	459 194	630 140	108 007	120 071	524 053	59 587	59 964	1 367 793	473 672
Unemployed	271 155	187 272	152 171	74 100	78 071	16 162	18 939	83 883	9 856	6 174	193 239	77 916
Not in labor force	498 167	349 596	287 400	159 477	127 923	28 965	33 231	148 571	17 345	12 117	352 570	145 597
Not high school graduate	2 249 481	1 617 334	1 317 744	760 872	556 872	144 706	154 884	632 147	69 061	37 559	1 610 877	638 604
Employed	912 107	663 857	542 841	283 372	259 469	58 863	62 153	248 250	27 377	19 254	666 250	245 857
Unemployed	345 492	252 736	205 573	119 274	86 299	23 665	23 498	92 756	10 874	3 616	249 959	95 533
Not in labor force	991 882	700 741	569 330	358 226	211 104	62 178	69 233	291 141	30 810	14 689	694 668	297 214
YEARS OF SCHOOL COMPLETED												
Male, 25 years old and over	**62 416 454**	**45 547 071**	**38 237 125**	**18 059 127**	**20 177 998**	**3 471 158**	**3 838 788**	**16 869 383**	**1 938 396**	**1 770 243**	**46 691 609**	**15 724 845**
Elementary: 0 to 4 years	2 407 672	1 569 720	1 217 509	787 630	429 879	156 676	195 535	837 952	92 354	59 980	1 538 656	869 016
5 to 7 years	4 267 377	2 767 480	2 214 522	1 308 147	906 375	246 364	306 594	1 499 897	161 659	140 267	2 819 746	1 447 631
8 years	4 892 529	3 022 280	2 370 709	1 242 220	1 128 489	282 760	368 811	1 870 249	218 777	289 973	3 119 738	1 772 791
High school: 1 to 3 years	8 862 989	6 251 242	5 203 590	2 702 725	2 500 865	485 798	561 854	2 611 747	295 224	245 894	6 461 126	2 401 863
4 years	19 422 198	13 673 949	11 341 735	5 104 131	6 237 604	1 075 424	1 256 790	5 748 249	656 508	662 464	14 241 231	5 180 967
College: 1 to 3 years	10 038 976	7 903 158	6 803 109	3 037 658	3 765 451	554 363	545 686	2 135 818	249 988	197 264	8 044 518	1 994 458
4 years	6 123 449	4 997 275	4 377 374	1 808 259	2 569 115	318 250	301 651	1 126 174	133 027	103 886	5 070 573	1 052 876
5 or more years	6 401 264	5 361 967	4 708 577	2 068 357	2 640 220	351 523	301 867	1 039 297	130 859	70 515	5 396 021	1 005 243
Percent high school graduates	67.3	70.1	71.2	66.6	75.4	66.2	62.7	59.6	60.4	58.4	70.1	58.7
Female, 25 years old and over	**70 419 233**	**52 796 269**	**44 078 098**	**21 395 653**	**22 682 445**	**4 124 263**	**4 593 908**	**17 622 964**	**2 278 716**	**1 699 500**	**52 992 442**	**17 426 791**
Elementary: 0 to 4 years	2 347 567	1 759 469	1 411 615	920 098	491 517	157 498	190 356	588 098	84 386	31 220	1 661 622	685 945
5 to 7 years	4 569 864	3 254 390	2 602 186	1 577 490	1 024 696	296 101	356 103	1 315 474	174 112	89 086	3 147 063	1 422 801
8 years	5 772 674	3 975 705	3 119 310	1 683 270	1 436 040	377 267	479 128	1 796 969	264 574	206 660	3 872 775	1 899 899
High school: 1 to 3 years	11 414 525	8 284 428	6 812 103	3 640 026	3 172 077	685 352	786 973	3 130 097	396 848	256 941	8 319 629	3 094 896
4 years	26 524 837	19 601 414	16 445 378	7 301 751	9 143 627	1 472 907	1 683 129	6 923 423	855 848	718 649	20 084 330	6 440 507
College: 1 to 3 years	10 755 999	8 513 320	7 266 164	3 305 893	3 960 271	623 774	623 382	2 242 679	291 305	237 952	8 523 178	2 232 821
4 years	5 297 050	4 276 454	3 674 079	1 643 799	2 030 280	305 395	296 980	1 020 596	135 734	106 449	4 255 343	1 041 707
5 or more years	3 736 717	3 131 089	2 747 263	1 323 326	1 423 937	205 969	177 857	605 628	75 909	52 543	3 128 502	608 215
Percent high school graduates	65.8	67.3	68.4	63.4	73.0	63.2	60.5	61.2	59.6	65.6	67.9	59.2
Persons 25 years old and over	**132 835 687**	**98 343 340**	**82 315 223**	**39 454 780**	**42 860 443**	**7 595 421**	**8 432 696**	**34 492 347**	**4 217 112**	**3 469 743**	**99 684 051**	**33 151 636**
Percent: Less than 5 years of elementary school	3.6	3.4	3.2	4.3	2.1	4.1	4.6	4.1	4.2	2.6	3.2	4.7
High school graduates	66.5	68.6	69.7	64.9	74.1	64.6	61.5	60.4	60.0	62.0	69.0	59.0
4 or more years of college	16.2	18.1	18.8	17.3	20.2	15.6	12.8	11.0	11.3	9.6	17.9	11.2
Median years of school completed	12.5	12.5	12.6	12.5	12.7	12.4	12.3	12.3	12.3	12.3	12.6	12.3
Persons 18 to 24 years old	**29 917 793**	**23 366 622**	**19 230 186**	**9 961 478**	**9 268 708**	**2 253 421**	**1 883 015**	**6 551 171**	**793 996**	**545 354**	**22 749 322**	**7 168 471**
Percent: High school graduates	76.1	77.6	77.5	75.7	79.5	79.8	75.0	70.7	72.7	75.9	76.9	73.3
4 or more years of college	6.4	7.2	7.6	7.9	7.4	5.6	4.3	3.4	4.0	3.8	7.1	4.1
Male, 18 to 24 years old	**14 988 348**	**11 611 745**	**9 539 786**	**4 874 064**	**4 665 722**	**1 126 362**	**945 597**	**3 376 603**	**395 480**	**313 243**	**11 350 161**	**3 638 187**
Percent: High school graduates	73.7	75.4	75.3	73.5	77.2	77.8	73.4	68.0	70.7	75.3	74.6	71.1
4 or more years of college	6.1	7.0	7.5	7.7	7.2	5.4	4.0	3.0	3.5	3.2	6.8	3.8
Female, 18 to 24 years old	**14 929 445**	**11 754 877**	**9 690 400**	**5 087 414**	**4 602 986**	**1 127 059**	**937 418**	**3 174 568**	**398 516**	**232 111**	**11 399 161**	**3 530 284**
Percent: High school graduates	78.4	79.7	79.7	77.8	81.8	81.8	76.6	73.6	74.6	76.8	79.2	75.7
4 or more years of college	6.6	7.4	7.8	8.0	7.6	5.8	4.6	3.8	4.6	4.6	7.3	4.5

Table 103. **Labor Force Characteristics: 1980**

[Data are estimates based on a sample; see Introduction. For meaning of symbols, see Introduction. For definitions of terms, see appendixes A and B]

United States Urban and Rural and Size of Place Inside and Outside SMSA's	United States	Urban							Rural				
			Inside urbanized areas			Outside urbanized areas						
		Total	Total	Central cities	Urban fringe	Places of 10,000 or more	Places of 2,500 to 10,000	Total	Places of 1,000 to 2,500	Rural farm	Inside SMSA's	Outside SMSA's
LABOR FORCE STATUS												
Persons 16 years and over	**171 214 258**	**127 719 450**	**106 562 061**	**51 699 068**	**54 862 993**	**10 316 276**	**10 841 113**	**43 494 808**	**5 276 910**	**4 280 684**	**128 687 395**	**42 526 863**
Labor force	106 084 668	80 245 519	67 745 804	31 780 779	35 965 025	6 187 247	6 312 468	25 839 149	3 021 376	2 566 685	81 517 906	24 566 762
Percent of persons 16 years and over	62.0	62.8	63.6	61.5	65.6	60.0	58.2	59.4	57.3	60.0	63.3	57.8
Armed Forces	1 634 851	1 472 273	1 159 959	489 633	670 326	166 396	145 918	162 578	25 877	1 723	1 334 134	300 717
Civilian labor force	104 449 817	78 773 246	66 585 845	31 291 146	35 294 699	6 020 851	6 166 550	25 676 571	2 995 499	2 564 962	80 183 772	24 266 045
Employed	97 639 355	73 754 068	62 406 577	29 011 781	33 394 796	5 612 133	5 735 358	23 885 287	2 785 277	2 473 173	75 125 252	22 514 103
Unemployed	6 810 462	5 019 178	4 179 268	2 279 365	1 899 903	408 718	431 192	1 791 284	210 222	91 789	5 058 520	1 751 942
Percent of civilian labor force	6.5	6.4	6.3	7.3	5.4	6.8	7.0	7.0	7.0	3.6	6.3	7.2
Not in labor force	65 129 590	47 473 931	38 816 257	19 918 289	18 897 968	4 129 029	4 528 645	17 655 659	2 255 534	1 713 999	47 169 489	17 960 101
Inmate of institution	2 389 482	1 806 918	1 320 880	718 486	602 394	231 696	254 342	582 564	104 686	–	1 653 009	736 473
Female, 16 years and over	**89 482 168**	**67 508 721**	**56 238 597**	**27 612 061**	**28 626 536**	**5 480 482**	**5 789 642**	**21 973 447**	**2 807 657**	**2 057 174**	**67 456 705**	**22 025 463**
Labor force	44 668 465	34 686 834	29 318 934	14 140 180	15 178 754	2 686 211	2 681 689	9 981 631	1 260 529	829 587	34 727 441	9 941 024
Percent of female, 16 years and over	49.9	51.4	52.1	51.2	53.0	49.0	46.3	45.4	44.9	40.3	51.5	45.1
Armed Forces	145 136	132 081	105 100	48 511	56 589	14 440	12 541	13 055	2 040	230	119 901	25 235
Civilian labor force	44 523 329	34 554 753	29 213 834	14 091 669	15 122 165	2 671 771	2 669 148	9 968 576	1 258 489	829 357	34 607 540	9 915 789
Employed	41 634 665	32 374 243	27 408 472	13 110 082	14 298 390	2 486 694	2 479 077	9 260 422	1 172 348	791 142	32 442 168	9 192 497
Unemployed	2 888 664	2 180 510	1 805 362	981 587	823 775	185 077	190 071	708 154	86 141	38 215	2 165 372	723 292
Percent of civilian labor force	6.5	6.3	6.2	7.0	5.4	6.9	7.1	7.1	6.8	4.6	6.3	7.3
Not in labor force	44 813 703	32 821 887	26 919 663	13 471 881	13 447 782	2 794 271	3 107 953	11 991 816	1 547 128	1 227 587	32 729 264	12 084 439
Inmate of institution	1 226 649	996 127	728 448	380 847	347 601	122 932	144 747	230 522	63 511	–	868 267	358 382
Male, 16 to 19 years	**8 676 324**	**6 343 806**	**5 208 118**	**2 469 068**	**2 739 050**	**578 361**	**557 327**	**2 332 518**	**254 564**	**251 394**	**6 423 133**	**2 253 191**
Employed	3 661 396	2 687 276	2 214 890	955 712	1 259 178	238 587	233 799	974 120	107 326	121 792	2 741 762	919 634
Unemployed	665 644	493 421	408 887	206 534	202 353	42 374	42 160	172 223	19 558	9 690	498 107	167 537
Not in labor force	4 127 525	2 959 590	2 434 970	1 244 852	1 190 118	263 936	260 684	1 167 935	125 111	119 805	3 003 732	1 123 793
Male, 20 to 24 years	**10 639 312**	**8 319 852**	**6 878 221**	**3 558 812**	**3 319 409**	**786 275**	**655 356**	**2 319 460**	**276 293**	**201 873**	**8 115 948**	**2 523 364**
Employed	7 326 856	5 619 325	4 698 283	2 319 797	2 378 486	481 767	439 275	1 707 531	203 577	168 990	5 588 914	1 737 942
Unemployed	937 065	697 554	579 257	317 685	261 572	59 469	58 828	239 511	29 278	12 987	698 707	238 358
Not in labor force	1 843 946	1 523 072	1 222 465	759 943	462 522	191 466	109 141	320 874	34 288	19 608	1 397 507	446 439
Male, 25 to 54 years	**41 961 490**	**30 765 240**	**26 111 097**	**12 100 967**	**14 010 130**	**2 258 944**	**2 395 199**	**11 196 250**	**1 181 949**	**1 006 768**	**31 990 764**	**9 970 726**
Employed	36 177 317	26 492 697	22 550 923	10 062 461	12 488 462	1 905 786	2 035 988	9 684 620	1 024 557	933 590	27 725 307	8 452 010
Unemployed	1 924 323	1 364 881	1 149 348	651 851	497 497	100 876	114 657	559 442	61 028	23 066	1 408 774	515 549
Not in labor force	3 133 594	2 259 310	1 890 773	1 172 645	718 128	188 024	180 513	874 284	84 419	49 113	2 261 111	872 483
Male, 55 to 64 years	**10 192 396**	**7 454 057**	**6 257 811**	**2 942 701**	**3 315 110**	**562 327**	**633 919**	**2 738 339**	**325 235**	**394 687**	**7 563 282**	**2 629 114**
Employed	6 963 868	5 222 435	4 425 941	1 996 002	2 429 939	382 480	414 014	1 741 433	208 814	317 201	5 297 793	1 666 075
Unemployed	292 151	206 498	173 183	88 602	84 581	15 251	18 064	85 653	10 289	6 102	212 338	79 813
Not in labor force	2 927 315	2 017 666	1 652 244	854 777	797 467	164 019	201 403	909 649	105 993	71 307	2 045 712	881 603
Male, 65 years and over	**10 262 568**	**7 327 774**	**5 868 217**	**3 015 459**	**2 852 758**	**649 887**	**809 670**	**2 934 794**	**431 212**	**368 788**	**7 137 563**	**3 125 005**
Employed	1 875 253	1 358 092	1 108 068	567 727	540 341	116 819	133 205	517 161	68 655	140 458	1 329 308	545 945
Unemployed	102 615	76 314	63 231	33 106	30 125	5 671	7 412	26 301	3 928	1 729	75 222	27 393
Not in labor force	8 283 507	5 892 406	4 696 142	2 414 191	2 281 951	527 313	668 951	2 391 101	358 595	226 579	5 732 163	2 551 344
Female, 16 to 19 years	**8 408 433**	**6 273 514**	**5 142 130**	**2 500 571**	**2 641 559**	**584 787**	**546 597**	**2 134 919**	**247 858**	**209 083**	**6 263 142**	**2 145 291**
Employed	3 312 045	2 577 558	2 136 760	929 945	1 206 815	230 941	209 857	734 487	89 787	70 602	2 566 135	745 910
Unemployed	509 543	386 422	316 213	162 426	153 787	36 705	33 504	123 121	14 304	7 265	381 742	127 801
Not in labor force	4 560 296	3 284 663	2 670 399	1 399 167	1 271 232	313 859	300 405	1 275 633	143 433	131 175	3 293 406	1 266 890
Female, 20 to 24 years	**10 654 502**	**8 438 938**	**7 018 369**	**3 715 837**	**3 302 532**	**771 432**	**649 137**	**2 215 564**	**281 083**	**148 591**	**8 201 121**	**2 453 381**
Employed	6 539 297	5 300 244	4 485 290	2 253 633	2 231 657	444 232	370 722	1 239 053	161 243	84 916	5 180 132	1 359 165
Unemployed	620 663	476 873	390 951	228 070	162 881	44 516	41 406	143 790	18 448	6 936	462 847	157 816
Not in labor force	3 433 210	2 605 767	2 098 411	1 214 215	884 196	276 282	231 074	827 443	100 473	56 715	2 508 337	924 873
Female, 25 to 54 years	**43 589 740**	**32 428 458**	**27 556 628**	**12 878 889**	**14 677 739**	**2 353 406**	**2 518 424**	**11 161 282**	**1 234 428**	**995 987**	**33 435 853**	**10 153 887**
Employed	25 991 080	19 919 945	16 984 728	7 977 653	9 007 075	1 440 322	1 494 895	6 071 135	723 094	485 814	20 284 221	5 706 859
Unemployed	1 483 440	1 103 885	920 859	497 241	423 618	87 469	95 557	379 555	44 088	19 188	1 113 389	370 051
Not in labor force	16 060 846	11 355 851	9 610 501	4 385 566	5 224 935	821 044	924 306	4 704 995	466 536	490 855	11 992 430	4 068 416
Female, 55 to 64 years	**11 593 675**	**8 694 819**	**7 231 564**	**3 540 074**	**3 691 490**	**686 814**	**776 441**	**2 898 856**	**390 500**	**360 267**	**8 614 238**	**2 979 437**
Employed	4 619 532	3 644 727	3 055 903	1 526 206	1 529 697	284 593	304 231	974 805	149 778	120 067	3 550 641	1 068 891
Unemployed	204 342	156 686	130 457	67 572	62 885	11 981	14 248	47 656	6 819	3 782	153 928	50 414
Not in labor force	6 767 306	4 891 336	4 043 371	1 945 338	2 098 033	390 099	457 866	1 875 970	233 855	236 390	4 907 522	1 859 784
Female, 65 years and over	**15 235 818**	**11 672 992**	**9 289 906**	**4 976 690**	**4 313 216**	**1 084 043**	**1 299 043**	**3 562 826**	**653 788**	**343 246**	**10 942 351**	**4 293 467**
Employed	1 172 711	931 769	745 791	422 645	323 146	86 606	99 372	240 942	48 446	29 743	861 039	311 672
Unemployed	70 676	56 644	46 882	26 278	20 604	4 406	5 356	14 032	2 482	1 044	53 466	17 210
Not in labor force	13 992 045	10 684 270	8 496 981	4 527 595	3 969 386	992 987	1 194 302	3 307 775	602 831	312 452	10 027 569	3 964 476
MARITAL STATUS AND PRESENCE OF OWN CHILDREN												
Female, 16 years and over	**89 482 168**	**67 508 721**	**56 238 597**	**27 612 061**	**28 626 536**	**5 480 482**	**5 789 642**	**21 973 447**	**2 807 657**	**2 057 174**	**67 456 705**	**22 025 463**
With own children under 6 years	13 618 762	9 806 679	8 073 534	3 902 790	4 170 744	829 706	903 439	3 812 083	437 619	277 400	10 007 953	3 610 809
In labor force	6 220 525	4 557 101	3 706 851	1 848 339	1 858 512	415 749	434 501	1 663 424	203 613	105 232	4 550 589	1 669 936
With own children 6 to 17 years only	17 016 190	12 203 034	10 244 622	4 485 635	5 758 987	920 201	1 038 211	4 813 156	521 714	449 317	12 770 800	4 245 390
In labor force	10 726 125	7 853 138	6 558 032	2 865 618	3 692 414	613 520	681 586	2 872 987	338 630	230 623	8 105 061	2 621 064
Married women 16 years and over, husband present	**49 369 352**	**34 914 522**	**28 868 751**	**12 512 651**	**16 356 100**	**2 837 989**	**3 207 782**	**14 454 830**	**1 633 040**	**1 515 148**	**36 140 843**	**13 228 509**
In labor force	24 275 765	17 551 924	14 548 993	6 312 408	8 236 585	1 440 475	1 562 456	6 723 841	778 280	612 527	18 074 837	6 200 928
With own children under 6 years	11 365 170	7 915 034	6 467 453	2 842 594	3 624 859	683 940	763 641	3 450 136	379 020	267 508	8 220 493	3 144 677
In labor force	4 990 251	3 534 266	2 854 601	1 324 650	1 529 951	327 234	352 431	1 455 985	169 598	99 419	3 589 825	1 400 426
With own children 6 to 17 years only	13 556 470	9 320 943	7 769 692	3 067 679	4 702 013	719 343	831 908	4 235 527	429 508	433 058	9 987 126	3 569 344
In labor force	8 149 334	5 695 255	4 711 906	1 873 121	2 838 785	458 490	524 859	2 454 079	269 092	219 593	6 021 241	2 128 093
CLASS OF WORKER												
Employed persons 16 years and over	**97 639 355**	**73 754 068**	**62 406 577**	**29 011 781**	**33 394 796**	**5 612 133**	**5 735 358**	**23 885 287**	**2 785 277**	**2 473 173**	**75 125 252**	**22 514 103**
Private wage and salary workers	73 772 204	56 725 246	48 426 524	22 109 843	26 316 681	4 098 615	4 200 107	17 046 958	2 016 627	1 143 522	57 969 093	15 803 111
Employees of own corporation	2 069 664	1 568 281	1 348 119	523 811	824 308	105 412	114 750	501 383	53 485	65 424	1 632 723	436 941
Federal government workers	3 762 008	3 001 501	2 617 244	1 259 657	1 357 587	195 006	189 251	760 507	90 236	51 574	3 037 597	724 411
State government workers	4 473 825	3 355 899	2 626 878	1 485 595	1 141 283	423 488	305 533	1 117 926	132 085	74 940	3 173 299	1 300 526
Local government workers	8 453 968	6 465 054	5 349 319	2 627 675	2 721 644	527 158	588 577	1 988 914	288 977	161 798	6 415 233	2 038 735
Self-employed workers	6 677 871	3 954 727	3 191 171	1 444 976	1 746 195	344 198	419 358	2 723 144	239 425	933 561	4 244 806	2 433 065
In agriculture	1 284 649	173 968	116 381	49 276	67 105	22 158	35 429	1 110 681	28 834	819 195	392 736	891 913
Unpaid family workers	499 479	251 641	195 441	84 035	111 406	23 668	32 532	247 838	17 927	107 778	285 224	214 255
In agriculture	139 760	14 101	8 768	4 083	4 685	2 152	3 181	125 659	2 063	95 647	42 196	97 564
Employed females 16 years and over	**41 634 665**	**32 374 243**	**27 408 472**	**13 110 082**	**14 298 390**	**2 486 694**	**2 479 077**	**9 260 422**	**1 172 348**	**791 142**	**32 442 168**	**9 192 497**
Private wage and salary workers	31 219 189	24 617 127	21 066 623	9 913 745	11 152 878	1 776 097	1 774 407	6 602 062	829 729	449 569	24 773 979	6 445 210
Employees of own corporation	357 325	270 221	227 210	93 037	134 173	20 187	22 824	87 104	10 644	10 099	276 053	81 272
Federal government workers	1 484 036	1 190 232	1 043 061	533 736	509 325	74 504	72 667	293 804	36 638	22 025	1 192 485	291 551
State government workers	2 363 754	1 807 111	1 424 404	813 542	610 862	222 453	160 254	556 643	67 443	38 251	1 704 809	658 945
Local government workers	4 695 676	3 554 323	2 918 443	1 411 344	1 507 099	300 372	335 508	1 141 353	163 193	105 494	3 524 140	1 171 536
Self-employed workers	1 529 190	1 016 212	809 343	377 022	432 321	95 537	111 332	512 978	61 897	117 149	1 040 859	488 331
Unpaid family workers	342 820	189 238	146 598	60 693	85 905	17 731	24 909	153 582	13 448	58 654	205 896	136 924

Table 104. Occupation of Employed Persons: 1980

United States
Urban and Rural and Size of Place
Inside and Outside SMSA's

[Data are estimates based on a sample; see Introduction. For meaning of symbols, see Introduction. For definitions of terms, see appendixes A and B]

Occupation	United States	Urban — Total	Urban: Inside urbanized areas — Total	Central cities	Urban fringe	Outside urbanized areas — Places of 10,000 or more	Places of 2,500 to 10,000	Rural — Total	Rural — Places of 1,000 to 2,500	Rural farm	Inside SMSA's	Outside SMSA's
Employed persons 16 years and over	97 639 355	73 754 068	62 406 577	29 011 781	33 394 796	5 612 133	5 735 358	23 885 287	2 785 277	2 473 173	75 125 252	22 514 103
Managerial and professional specialty occupations	22 151 648	17 998 592	15 578 293	6 820 075	8 758 218	1 252 346	1 167 953	4 153 056	529 358	276 801	18 106 882	4 044 766
Executive, administrative, and managerial occupations	10 133 551	8 247 423	7 203 652	2 990 503	4 213 149	535 537	508 234	1 886 128	232 811	114 919	8 367 923	1 765 628
Officials and administrators, public administration	361 549	272 445	223 827	100 596	123 231	22 676	25 942	89 104	14 342	8 923	367 575	93 974
Management related occupations	2 556 295	2 157 451	1 929 784	836 408	1 093 376	120 100	107 567	398 844	46 667	26 608	2 187 859	368 436
Professional specialty occupations	12 018 097	9 751 169	8 374 641	3 829 572	4 545 069	716 809	659 719	2 266 928	296 547	161 882	9 738 959	2 279 138
Engineers and natural scientists	2 150 707	1 788 557	1 606 511	583 682	1 022 829	98 926	83 120	362 150	34 350	15 938	1 872 651	278 056
Engineers	1 382 095	1 146 131	1 028 398	349 337	679 061	64 261	53 472	235 964	21 927	9 938	1 207 444	174 651
Health diagnosing occupations	643 716	547 561	484 007	217 972	266 035	33 383	30 171	96 155	12 292	6 798	547 209	96 507
Health assessment and treating occupations	1 695 436	1 379 652	1 198 202	551 111	647 091	92 675	88 775	315 784	39 059	23 692	1 385 993	309 443
Teachers, librarians, and counselors	4 675 632	3 609 740	2 947 062	1 367 801	1 579 261	341 043	321 635	1 065 892	150 895	92 030	3 530 367	1 145 265
Teachers, elementary and secondary schools	3 311 776	2 480 072	2 014 221	882 449	1 131 772	221 686	244 165	831 704	121 959	75 740	2 452 791	858 985
Technical, sales, and administrative support occupations	29 593 506	24 035 003	20 881 875	9 539 313	11 342 562	1 623 633	1 529 495	5 558 503	691 687	370 260	24 243 638	5 349 868
Health technologists and technicians	966 469	766 932	650 138	334 614	315 524	59 895	56 899	199 537	24 537	13 405	759 659	206 810
Technologists and technicians, except health	2 015 482	1 652 732	1 456 410	625 073	831 337	106 353	89 969	362 750	39 470	18 446	1 707 575	307 907
Sales occupations	9 760 157	7 826 607	6 684 116	2 887 892	3 796 224	584 012	558 479	1 933 550	250 230	119 980	8 822 926	937 231
Supervisors and proprietors, sales occupations	1 540 786	1 154 363	938 254	402 826	535 428	103 710	112 399	386 423	55 177	22 516	1 141 607	399 179
Sales representatives, commodities and finance	3 070 929	2 546 990	2 268 234	919 143	1 349 091	143 928	134 828	523 939	58 118	32 577	2 615 815	455 114
Other sales occupations	5 148 442	4 125 254	3 477 628	1 565 923	1 911 705	336 374	311 252	1 023 188	136 935	64 887	4 066 104	1 082 338
Cashiers	1 716 318	1 359 781	1 144 429	535 899	608 530	111 213	104 139	356 537	47 020	21 036	1 347 917	368 401
Administrative support occupations, including clerical	16 851 398	13 788 732	12 091 211	5 691 734	6 399 477	873 373	824 148	3 062 666	377 450	218 429	13 953 478	2 897 920
Computer equipment operators	408 475	347 059	314 940	149 847	165 093	17 593	14 526	61 416	6 575	3 513	357 109	51 366
Secretaries, stenographers, and typists	4 656 955	3 784 962	3 296 221	1 484 957	1 811 264	252 372	236 369	871 993	106 830	64 324	3 827 216	829 739
Financial records processing occupations	2 254 084	1 768 469	1 505 870	683 272	822 598	128 882	133 717	485 615	66 433	43 866	1 775 798	478 286
Mail and message distributing occupations	773 826	629 523	565 201	302 120	263 081	31 935	32 387	144 303	17 842	14 210	645 629	128 197
Service occupations	12 629 425	9 841 675	8 153 094	4 312 529	3 840 565	846 834	841 747	2 787 750	395 936	171 247	9 628 977	3 000 448
Private household occupations	589 352	448 984	362 773	225 323	137 450	42 335	43 876	140 368	20 475	10 022	428 487	160 865
Protective service occupations	1 475 315	1 188 419	1 021 077	498 280	522 797	84 603	82 739	286 896	36 712	19 193	1 191 996	283 319
Police and firefighters	598 852	489 201	420 116	192 407	227 709	35 389	33 696	109 651	14 719	4 312	491 833	107 019
Service occupations, except protective and household	10 564 758	8 204 272	6 769 244	3 588 926	3 180 318	719 896	715 132	2 360 486	338 749	148 032	8 008 494	2 556 264
Food service occupations	4 384 936	3 433 160	2 835 288	1 432 620	1 402 668	309 795	288 077	951 776	135 916	58 879	3 350 457	1 034 479
Cleaning and building service occupations	2 745 403	2 111 401	1 744 046	1 005 378	738 668	181 534	185 821	634 002	88 760	35 691	2 067 404	677 999
Farming, forestry, and fishing occupations	2 811 258	775 365	518 517	237 144	281 373	102 160	154 688	2 035 893	94 207	1 107 564	1 144 238	1 667 020
Farm operators and managers	1 298 670	123 564	66 728	28 466	38 262	21 307	35 529	1 175 106	29 892	859 676	354 264	944 406
Farm workers and related occupations	1 334 123	592 151	417 920	191 561	226 359	73 015	101 216	741 972	52 739	241 256	730 129	603 994
Precision production, craft, and repair occupations	12 594 175	8 807 832	7 294 285	3 142 463	4 151 822	710 507	803 040	3 786 343	424 023	209 732	9 317 334	3 276 841
Mechanics and repairers	3 798 598	2 634 404	2 180 809	921 980	1 258 829	210 447	243 148	1 164 194	129 046	63 780	2 807 579	991 019
Construction trades	4 247 010	2 901 728	2 399 542	1 147 147	1 252 395	234 472	267 714	1 345 282	142 433	75 786	3 117 357	1 129 653
Precision production occupations	4 255 872	3 144 530	2 658 655	1 147 473	1 511 182	237 097	248 778	1 111 342	128 686	63 734	3 298 321	957 551
Operators, fabricators, and laborers	17 859 343	12 295 601	9 980 513	4 960 257	5 020 256	1 076 653	1 238 435	5 563 742	650 066	337 569	12 684 183	5 175 160
Machine operators and tenders, except precision	5 960 505	4 045 864	3 252 947	1 680 296	1 572 651	364 837	428 080	1 914 641	201 971	105 002	4 141 903	1 818 602
Fabricators, assemblers, inspectors, and samplers	3 124 483	2 184 830	1 798 280	855 360	942 920	180 179	206 371	939 653	109 586	58 908	2 295 774	828 709
Transportation occupations	3 289 213	2 266 928	1 876 642	905 404	971 238	180 756	209 530	1 020 285	112 754	71 923	2 374 265	914 948
Motor vehicle operators	3 017 954	2 074 286	1 727 186	837 549	889 637	160 745	186 355	943 668	103 222	67 322	2 187 221	830 733
Material moving equipment operators	1 100 199	665 309	511 404	237 307	274 097	67 114	86 791	434 890	48 404	27 846	708 297	391 902
Handlers, equipment cleaners, helpers, and laborers	4 384 943	3 130 670	2 548 240	1 288 890	1 259 350	274 767	307 663	1 254 273	158 351	74 540	3 163 944	1 220 999
Construction laborers	661 411	447 236	360 079	186 296	173 783	40 514	46 643	214 175	25 028	13 331	460 916	200 495
Freight, stock, and material handlers	1 259 182	932 592	763 787	372 863	390 924	80 822	87 983	326 590	41 760	19 249	930 347	328 835

GENERAL SOCIAL AND ECONOMIC CHARACTERISTICS

UNITED STATES 5

Table 104. **Occupation of Employed Persons: 1980**—Con.

United States
Urban and Rural and Size of Place
Inside and Outside SMSA's

[Data are estimates based on a sample; see Introduction. For meaning of symbols, see Introduction. For definitions of terms, see appendixes A and B]

Occupation	United States	Urban Total	Inside urbanized areas — Total	Inside urbanized — Central cities	Inside urbanized — Urban fringe	Outside urbanized areas — Places of 10,000 or more	Outside urbanized areas — Places of 2,500 to 10,000	Rural — Total	Rural — Places of 1,000 to 2,500	Rural — Rural farm	Inside SMSA's	Outside SMSA's
Employed females 16 years and over	41 634 665	32 374 243	27 408 472	13 110 082	14 298 390	2 486 694	2 479 077	9 260 422	1 172 348	791 142	32 442 168	9 192 497
Managerial and professional specialty occupations	8 954 843	7 247 863	6 247 564	2 924 962	3 322 602	516 153	484 146	1 706 980	219 633	141 841	7 234 681	1 720 162
Executive, administrative, and managerial occupations	3 070 247	2 535 634	2 235 255	1 025 995	1 209 260	155 908	144 471	534 613	66 166	37 027	2 557 518	512 729
Officials and administrators, public administration	111 159	82 542	67 914	33 446	34 468	6 547	8 081	28 617	4 946	2 970	81 211	29 948
Management related occupations	970 779	828 100	748 959	343 243	405 716	42 410	36 731	142 679	15 658	10 262	843 501	127 278
Professional specialty occupations	5 884 596	4 712 229	4 012 309	1 898 967	2 113 342	360 245	339 675	1 172 367	153 467	104 814	4 677 163	1 207 433
Engineers and natural scientists	217 961	189 092	173 996	73 192	100 804	8 245	6 447	28 869	2 894	1 579	195 927	22 034
Engineers	63 158	54 008	48 902	19 713	29 189	2 836	2 270	9 150	880	457	55 571	7 587
Health diagnosing occupations	75 115	66 185	61 231	30 193	31 038	2 716	2 238	8 930	956	429	67 207	7 908
Health assessment and treating occupations	1 458 652	1 183 101	1 032 991	470 399	562 592	77 346	72 764	275 551	32 559	22 225	1 197 108	261 544
Teachers, librarians, and counselors	3 077 853	2 374 313	1 946 670	895 215	1 051 455	217 133	210 510	703 540	97 159	68 872	2 325 450	752 403
Teachers, elementary and secondary schools	2 371 862	1 793 974	1 464 250	651 873	812 377	160 792	168 932	577 888	80 174	58 577	1 767 630	604 232
Technical, sales, and administrative support occupations	18 971 458	15 355 631	13 294 488	6 106 547	7 187 941	1 059 554	1 001 589	3 615 827	453 576	261 069	15 458 376	3 513 082
Health technologists and technicians	808 352	633 074	532 954	270 454	262 500	50 974	49 146	175 278	21 530	12 249	628 593	179 759
Technologists and technicians, except health	494 587	413 338	365 309	170 465	194 844	26 580	21 449	81 199	9 542	4 946	420 674	73 863
Sales occupations	4 671 493	3 732 475	3 159 999	1 388 826	1 771 173	294 183	278 293	939 018	122 599	63 495	3 705 954	965 539
Supervisors and proprietors, sales occupations	429 129	320 245	260 395	114 899	145 496	29 311	32 539	108 884	14 827	7 464	315 864	113 265
Sales representatives, commodities and finance	812 867	682 994	614 713	259 085	355 628	35 684	32 597	129 503	13 322	8 195	704 264	108 233
Other sales occupations	3 429 867	2 729 236	2 284 891	1 014 842	1 270 049	229 188	215 157	700 631	94 450	47 836	2 685 826	744 041
Cashiers	1 428 066	1 117 292	933 115	428 957	504 158	94 258	89 919	310 774	41 116	18 593	1 109 932	318 134
Administrative support occupations, including clerical	12 997 076	10 576 744	9 236 226	4 276 802	4 959 424	687 817	652 701	2 420 332	299 905	180 379	10 703 155	2 293 921
Computer equipment operators	241 155	201 519	181 075	84 130	96 945	11 134	9 310	39 636	4 265	2 677	207 077	34 078
Secretaries, stenographers, and typists	4 579 938	3 717 790	3 236 175	1 450 982	1 785 193	248 448	233 167	862 148	105 479	63 796	3 761 343	818 595
Financial records processing occupations	1 991 619	1 546 545	1 309 744	583 390	726 354	115 945	120 856	445 074	60 395	41 268	1 555 951	435 668
Mail and message distributing occupations	229 096	174 077	158 616	84 961	73 655	7 245	8 216	55 019	6 848	5 256	187 790	41 306
Service occupations	7 451 845	5 642 376	4 558 861	2 395 486	2 163 375	531 292	552 223	1 809 469	266 660	123 845	5 478 384	1 973 461
Private household occupations	562 886	427 742	344 335	213 961	130 374	40 943	42 464	135 144	19 913	9 753	407 341	155 545
Protective service occupations	168 861	143 931	126 153	63 953	62 200	9 353	8 425	24 930	3 413	1 030	142 480	26 381
Police and firefighters	25 652	22 010	19 381	10 554	8 827	1 284	1 345	3 642	492	135	21 762	3 890
Service occupations, except protective and household	6 720 098	5 070 703	4 088 373	2 117 572	1 970 801	480 996	501 334	1 649 395	243 334	113 062	4 928 563	1 791 535
Food service occupations	2 905 001	2 163 592	1 726 083	833 672	892 411	218 187	219 322	741 409	108 416	50 796	2 107 741	797 260
Cleaning and building service occupations	963 370	731 661	590 446	367 472	222 974	68 645	72 570	231 709	35 023	13 639	701 799	261 571
Farming, forestry, and fishing occupations	404 269	133 289	93 269	40 513	52 756	17 064	22 956	270 980	12 325	152 233	194 424	209 845
Farm operators and managers	127 402	15 050	10 619	4 475	6 144	1 929	2 502	112 352	1 977	85 154	43 048	84 354
Farm workers and related occupations	266 717	114 032	80 126	34 621	45 505	14 499	19 407	152 685	9 515	66 692	147 232	119 485
Precision production, craft, and repair occupations	977 950	732 825	620 059	304 245	315 814	57 079	55 687	245 125	28 923	15 681	746 330	231 620
Mechanics and repairers	126 003	95 056	81 586	39 619	41 967	6 933	6 537	30 947	3 203	1 743	98 986	27 017
Construction trades	87 263	62 510	51 672	26 830	24 842	5 554	5 284	24 753	2 818	1 470	64 507	22 756
Precision production occupations	758 064	571 286	484 274	236 349	247 925	43 875	43 137	186 778	22 434	12 320	579 509	178 555
Operators, fabricators, and laborers	4 874 300	3 262 259	2 594 231	1 338 329	1 255 902	305 552	362 476	1 612 041	191 231	96 473	3 329 973	1 544 327
Machine operators and tenders, except precision	2 407 426	1 553 756	1 204 847	672 729	532 118	154 192	194 717	853 670	100 614	45 904	1 554 478	852 948
Fabricators, assemblers, inspectors, and samplers	1 238 811	868 616	705 555	335 595	369 960	79 846	83 215	370 195	44 800	22 387	896 579	342 232
Transportation occupations	286 146	182 972	152 329	63 645	88 684	12 814	16 829	103 174	9 642	10 346	209 076	77 070
Motor vehicle operators	281 133	178 097	149 181	62 040	87 141	12 483	16 433	103 036	9 463	10 312	205 407	75 726
Material moving equipment operators	61 734	41 616	32 724	16 330	16 394	4 176	4 716	20 118	2 696	1 218	43 541	18 193
Handlers, equipment cleaners, helpers, and laborers	880 183	616 299	498 776	250 030	248 746	54 524	62 999	263 884	33 479	16 618	626 299	253 884
Construction laborers	20 019	13 689	10 818	5 780	5 038	1 216	1 655	6 330	712	416	13 695	6 324
Freight, stock, and material handlers	192 687	132 280	104 575	48 269	56 306	13 022	14 683	60 407	7 446	4 068	133 905	58 782

Table 105. Industry of Employed Persons: 1980

United States
Urban and Rural and Size of Place
Inside and Outside SMSA's

[Data are estimates based on a sample; see Introduction. For meaning of symbols, see Introduction. For definitions of terms, see appendixes A and B]

Subject	United States	Urban — Total	Urban — Inside urbanized areas: Total	Urban — Inside urbanized areas: Central cities	Urban — Inside urbanized areas: Urban fringe	Urban — Outside urbanized areas: Places of 10,000 or more	Urban — Outside urbanized areas: Places of 2,500 to 10,000	Rural — Total	Rural — Places of 1,000 to 2,500	Rural — Rural farm	Inside SMSA's	Outside SMSA's
Employed persons 16 years and over	97 639 355	73 754 068	62 406 577	29 011 781	33 394 796	5 612 133	5 735 358	23 885 287	2 785 277	2 473 173	75 125 252	22 514 103
Agriculture	2 760 213	736 887	482 820	209 300	273 520	101 813	152 254	2 023 326	91 953	1 133 321	1 130 291	1 629 922
Forestry and fisheries	153 376	69 932	41 971	20 661	21 310	9 756	18 205	83 444	10 908	4 656	63 690	89 686
Mining	1 028 178	542 783	318 455	181 620	136 835	93 463	130 865	485 395	69 072	20 859	460 164	568 014
Construction	5 739 598	3 911 332	3 236 096	1 396 550	1 839 546	314 866	360 370	1 828 266	190 792	110 815	4 193 299	1 546 299
Manufacturing	21 914 754	15 852 618	13 300 016	5 714 168	7 585 848	1 219 146	1 333 456	6 062 136	682 420	331 255	16 612 877	5 301 877
Nondurable goods	8 435 543	5 933 444	4 828 391	2 275 365	2 553 026	518 451	586 602	2 502 099	294 918	139 392	6 038 356	2 397 187
Food and kindred products	1 533 548	1 077 183	841 294	436 205	405 089	118 005	117 884	456 365	61 838	39 605	1 065 967	467 581
Textile mill and finished textile products	2 246 784	1 318 109	990 023	563 570	426 453	134 747	193 339	928 675	102 594	43 105	1 313 374	933 410
Printing, publishing, and allied industries	1 531 029	1 281 663	1 130 774	525 672	605 102	77 028	73 861	249 366	33 177	13 453	1 294 938	236 091
Chemicals and allied products	1 272 484	971 788	842 285	289 562	552 723	65 276	64 227	300 696	31 110	14 266	1 043 596	228 888
Durable goods	13 479 211	9 919 174	8 471 625	3 438 803	5 032 822	700 695	746 854	3 560 037	387 502	191 863	10 574 521	2 904 690
Furniture, lumber, and wood products	1 229 394	619 804	415 933	199 671	216 262	85 226	118 645	609 590	63 160	30 806	608 325	621 069
Primary metal industries	1 307 768	961 012	819 153	324 303	494 850	65 114	76 745	346 756	38 531	15 569	1 048 392	259 376
Fabricated metal industries, including ordnance	1 424 362	1 073 513	912 468	393 834	518 634	81 780	79 265	350 849	38 790	19 120	1 141 698	282 664
Machinery, except electrical	2 766 615	2 042 107	1 727 990	696 399	1 031 591	159 463	154 654	724 508	84 735	44 627	2 171 365	595 250
Electrical machinery, equipment, and supplies	2 198 833	1 711 092	1 503 592	592 524	911 068	108 278	99 222	487 741	52 266	27 480	1 817 806	381 027
Transportation equipment	2 428 452	1 908 406	1 719 861	648 503	1 071 358	85 381	103 164	520 046	49 318	28 438	2 102 336	326 116
Transportation, communications, and other public utilities	7 087 455	5 489 324	4 756 868	2 213 035	2 543 833	352 926	379 530	1 598 131	187 315	97 730	5 653 222	1 434 233
Railroads	577 519	424 849	340 144	158 125	182 019	42 420	42 285	152 670	19 310	8 838	417 966	159 553
Trucking service and warehousing	1 546 486	1 094 765	936 722	405 117	531 605	74 434	83 609	451 721	48 799	28 180	1 184 321	362 165
Other transportation	2 149 956	1 793 139	1 641 940	799 555	842 385	70 308	80 891	356 817	40 670	27 652	1 850 990	298 966
Communications	1 440 868	1 182 311	1 039 952	477 488	562 464	75 168	67 191	258 557	27 447	12 555	1 202 259	238 609
Utilities and sanitary services	1 372 626	994 260	798 110	372 750	425 360	90 596	105 554	378 366	51 089	20 505	997 686	374 940
Wholesale trade	4 217 232	3 317 516	2 922 264	1 272 707	1 649 557	195 758	199 494	899 716	101 908	74 362	3 442 067	775 165
Retail trade	15 716 694	12 361 816	10 355 580	4 718 855	5 636 725	1 019 506	986 730	3 354 878	457 251	191 847	12 234 467	3 482 227
General merchandise stores	2 091 598	1 757 260	1 539 086	700 225	838 861	123 360	94 814	334 338	36 793	18 474	1 746 472	345 126
Food, bakery, and dairy stores	2 503 595	1 879 407	1 550 693	677 019	873 674	155 141	173 573	624 188	86 847	35 791	1 885 957	617 638
Automotive dealers and gasoline stations	1 907 506	1 366 701	1 087 626	448 016	639 610	130 710	148 365	540 805	74 559	27 640	1 373 099	534 407
Eating and drinking places	4 181 272	3 361 522	2 823 387	1 385 478	1 437 909	285 270	252 865	819 750	115 198	42 653	3 291 462	889 810
Finance, insurance, and real estate	5 898 059	4 984 033	4 468 057	2 111 744	2 356 313	258 920	257 056	914 026	116 345	61 902	5 057 726	840 333
Banking and credit agencies	2 221 438	1 834 340	1 611 220	764 760	846 460	108 299	114 821	387 098	54 008	30 648	1 836 399	385 039
Insurance, real estate, and other finance	3 676 621	3 149 693	2 856 837	1 346 984	1 509 853	150 621	142 235	526 928	62 337	31 254	3 221 327	455 294
Services	27 976 330	22 375 140	19 008 544	9 441 737	9 566 807	1 744 137	1 622 459	5 601 190	742 677	379 827	22 174 151	5 802 179
Business services	2 724 596	2 371 990	2 187 415	1 012 294	1 175 121	101 450	83 125	352 606	35 527	16 942	2 445 204	279 392
Repair services	757 081	534 150	456 780	213 519	243 261	41 193	36 177	222 931	27 450	13 876	510 953	246 128
Private households	1 374 460	993 150	844 128	385 398	458 730	71 499	77 523	381 310	39 576	11 264	1 037 001	337 459
Other personal services	2 374 304	1 877 515	1 565 060	765 304	799 756	165 304	147 151	496 789	57 575	25 375	1 816 368	557 936
Entertainment and recreation services	1 007 070	854 023	752 345	372 471	379 874	55 752	45 926	153 047	18 019	7 406	855 260	151 810
Professional and related services	19 811 819	15 743 770	13 229 221	6 582 152	6 647 069	1 311 123	1 203 426	4 068 049	549 750	298 961	15 509 365	4 302 454
Hospitals	4 424 547	3 637 809	3 150 310	1 689 857	1 460 453	252 729	234 770	786 738	96 985	47 241	3 585 407	839 140
Health services, except hospitals	2 825 918	2 176 129	1 792 263	839 370	952 893	187 460	196 406	649 789	94 922	51 241	2 147 405	678 513
Elementary and secondary schools and colleges	8 013 176	6 125 678	4 963 292	2 395 717	2 567 575	617 349	545 037	1 887 498	257 762	156 740	6 001 712	2 011 464
Other educational services	364 037	297 439	250 385	123 060	127 325	24 271	22 783	66 598	10 577	5 559	288 455	75 582
Social services, religious and membership organizations	2 115 878	1 724 289	1 461 876	781 919	679 957	137 378	125 035	391 589	57 134	20 257	1 687 661	428 217
Legal, engineering, and other professional services	2 068 263	1 782 426	1 611 095	752 229	858 866	91 936	79 395	285 837	32 370	17 643	1 798 915	269 348
Public administration	5 147 466	4 112 687	3 515 906	1 731 404	1 784 502	301 842	294 939	1 034 779	134 636	66 599	4 103 298	1 044 168

Table 105. Industry of Employed Persons: 1980—Con.

United States
Urban and Rural and Size of Place Inside and Outside SMSA's

[Data are estimates based on a sample; see Introduction. For meaning of symbols, see Introduction. For definitions of terms, see appendixes A and B]

Industry	United States	Urban: Total	Urban, Inside urbanized areas: Total	Central cities	Urban fringe	Urban, Outside urbanized areas: Places of 10,000 or more	Places of 2,500 to 10,000	Rural: Total	Rural: Places of 1,000 to 2,500	Rural farm	Inside SMSA's	Outside SMSA's
Employed females 16 years and over	41 634 645	32 374 243	27 408 472	13 110 082	14 298 390	2 486 694	2 479 077	9 260 422	1 172 348	791 142	32 442 168	9 192 497
Agriculture	493 658	176 636	124 099	51 408	72 691	22 193	30 344	317 022	15 683	168 147	249 446	244 212
Forestry and fisheries	28 392	13 993	8 569	4 360	4 209	2 346	3 078	14 399	1 912	878	12 239	16 153
Mining	124 173	94 108	75 130	47 925	27 205	9 276	9 702	30 065	4 506	1 836	88 236	35 937
Construction	479 766	366 553	315 020	132 480	182 540	25 602	25 931	113 213	12 340	6 866	383 188	96 578
Manufacturing	6 995 805	5 007 248	4 149 125	1 908 736	2 240 389	402 918	455 205	1 988 557	234 885	112 973	5 138 219	1 857 586
Nondurable goods	3 493 250	2 368 606	1 900 776	962 136	938 640	208 626	259 204	1 124 644	134 950	64 095	2 386 489	1 106 761
Food and kindred products	467 772	325 182	252 931	132 348	120 583	35 339	36 912	142 590	19 290	11 653	321 478	146 294
Textile mill and finished textile products	1 467 344	847 609	633 314	375 808	257 506	85 593	128 702	619 735	69 896	31 778	843 896	623 448
Printing, publishing, and allied industries	625 307	511 761	444 968	212 527	232 441	33 059	33 734	113 546	15 603	7 421	515 781	109 526
Chemicals and allied products	351 296	280 516	250 521	89 056	161 465	14 872	15 123	70 780	7 546	3 238	296 462	54 834
Durable goods	3 502 555	2 638 642	2 248 349	946 600	1 301 749	194 292	196 001	863 913	99 935	48 878	2 751 730	750 825
Furniture, lumber, and wood products	263 677	142 151	97 201	45 908	51 293	19 595	25 355	121 526	12 699	6 237	143 560	120 117
Primary metal industries	170 143	128 436	108 862	42 092	66 770	8 847	10 727	41 707	5 013	1 951	137 066	33 077
Fabricated metal industries, including ordnance	316 881	240 245	201 259	86 913	114 346	19 911	19 075	76 636	9 210	4 525	250 185	66 696
Machinery, except electrical	593 051	454 485	387 134	158 399	228 735	35 255	32 096	138 566	16 062	8 280	472 690	120 361
Electrical machinery, equipment, and supplies	937 616	719 370	619 820	262 987	356 833	51 564	47 986	218 246	25 491	13 014	752 098	185 518
Transportation equipment	447 249	359 053	321 674	125 562	196 112	17 706	19 673	88 196	9 673	4 909	379 892	67 357
Transportation, communications, and other public utilities	1 752 965	1 435 393	1 287 323	612 402	674 921	74 733	73 337	317 572	35 774	22 796	1 476 167	276 798
Railroads	44 764	38 353	34 325	16 423	17 902	2 107	1 921	6 411	820	527	38 467	6 297
Trucking service and warehousing	200 633	155 270	136 540	57 843	78 697	9 394	9 336	45 363	4 859	3 423	163 797	36 836
Other transportation	610 244	495 978	461 205	212 301	248 904	15 652	19 121	114 266	12 862	9 537	524 739	85 505
Communications	666 094	568 012	506 704	252 039	254 665	33 908	27 400	98 082	9 913	5 407	570 934	95 160
Utilities and sanitary services	231 230	177 780	148 549	73 796	74 753	13 672	15 559	53 450	7 320	3 902	178 230	53 000
Wholesale trade	1 133 761	925 444	833 852	361 906	471 946	45 622	45 970	208 317	23 586	19 015	960 112	173 649
Retail trade	8 004 399	6 247 385	5 192 273	2 326 547	2 865 726	535 957	519 155	1 757 014	240 872	114 841	6 168 643	1 835 756
General merchandise stores	1 468 473	1 226 540	1 070 236	482 888	587 348	87 381	68 923	241 933	26 506	14 618	1 216 989	251 484
Food, bakery, and dairy stores	1 145 676	830 713	677 690	287 200	390 490	71 189	81 834	314 963	43 506	20 678	842 673	303 003
Automotive dealers and gasoline stations	326 140	232 822	182 965	73 824	109 141	23 275	26 582	93 318	13 294	5 850	233 458	92 682
Eating and drinking places	2 491 752	1 919 406	1 564 194	736 268	827 926	181 755	173 457	572 346	82 665	33 271	1 874 866	616 886
Finance, insurance, and real estate	3 421 717	2 868 883	2 571 908	1 221 662	1 350 246	147 218	149 757	552 834	69 375	40 677	2 926 744	494 973
Banking and credit agencies	1 540 210	1 251 546	1 094 072	516 627	577 445	75 822	81 652	288 664	38 954	24 000	1 258 930	281 280
Insurance, real estate, and other finance	1 881 507	1 617 337	1 477 836	705 035	772 801	71 396	68 105	264 170	30 421	16 677	1 667 814	213 693
Services	17 097 462	13 542 884	11 396 204	5 690 265	5 705 939	1 099 477	1 047 203	3 554 578	477 795	273 193	13 361 769	3 735 693
Business services	1 216 956	1 066 192	985 983	464 836	521 147	43 933	36 276	150 764	15 820	8 616	1 095 215	121 741
Repair services	163 064	127 431	111 122	48 115	63 007	8 196	8 113	35 633	4 019	1 928	132 115	30 949
Private households	637 558	486 307	391 892	243 662	148 230	46 570	47 845	151 251	22 051	10 990	463 097	174 461
Other personal services	1 527 748	1 182 279	967 273	501 897	465 376	105 129	109 877	345 469	51 577	20 430	1 142 538	385 210
Entertainment and recreation services	407 324	343 146	299 497	144 863	154 634	24 158	19 491	64 178	7 641	3 749	342 295	65 029
Professional and related services	13 144 812	10 337 529	8 640 437	4 286 892	4 353 545	871 491	825 601	2 807 283	376 687	227 480	10 186 509	2 958 303
Hospitals	3 390 724	2 757 685	2 366 809	1 249 991	1 116 818	200 590	190 286	633 039	78 923	44 695	2 713 412	677 312
Health services, except hospitals	2 133 864	1 605 507	1 304 471	612 046	692 425	144 530	156 506	528 357	78 209	40 888	1 583 895	549 969
Elementary and secondary schools and colleges	5 185 264	3 945 435	3 207 243	1 527 711	1 679 532	385 630	352 562	1 239 829	165 461	113 468	3 883 980	1 301 284
Other educational services	259 929	210 121	174 346	91 617	82 729	18 143	17 632	49 808	8 570	4 437	203 066	56 863
Social services, religious and membership organizations	1 316 879	1 087 353	930 153	495 753	434 400	84 070	73 130	229 526	30 460	14 437	1 066 187	250 692
Legal, engineering, and other professional services	858 152	731 428	657 415	317 662	339 753	38 528	35 485	126 724	11 064	9 300	735 969	122 183
Public administration	2 102 567	1 695 716	1 454 969	752 391	702 578	121 352	119 395	406 851	55 620	29 920	1 677 405	425 162

Table 106. Labor Force Status in 1979 and Disability and Veteran Status: 1980

[Data are estimates based on a sample; see Introduction. For meaning of symbols, see Introduction. For definitions of terms, see appendixes A and B]

United States Urban and Rural and Size of Place Inside and Outside SMSA's	United States	Urban						Rural		Rural farm	Inside SMSA's	Outside SMSA's
			Inside urbanized areas			Outside urbanized areas						
		Total	Total	Central cities	Urban fringe	Places of 10,000 or more	Places of 2,500 to 10,000	Total	Places of 1,000 to 2,500			
LABOR FORCE STATUS IN 1979												
Male, 16 years and over, in labor force in 1979	**65 769 596**	**48 717 796**	**40 868 362**	**18 955 210**	**21 913 152**	**3 902 284**	**3 947 150**	**17 051 800**	**1 902 195**	**1 893 227**	**49 786 782**	**15 982 814**
Worked in 1979	64 867 639	47 987 678	40 227 559	18 548 234	21 679 325	3 856 812	3 903 307	16 879 961	1 883 334	1 886 622	49 061 081	15 806 558
50 to 52 weeks	43 113 565	31 863 873	26 931 331	11 826 401	15 104 930	2 407 762	2 524 780	11 249 692	1 230 760	1 390 688	32 935 614	10 177 951
48 to 49 weeks	2 855 305	2 177 517	1 846 331	914 341	931 990	163 691	167 495	677 788	77 769	50 597	2 218 500	636 805
40 to 47 weeks	5 356 939	3 952 307	3 311 198	1 602 201	1 708 997	314 898	326 211	1 404 632	161 385	108 637	4 046 063	1 310 876
27 to 39 weeks	4 376 379	3 182 500	2 613 010	1 324 763	1 288 247	288 769	280 721	1 193 879	138 389	98 243	3 189 494	1 186 885
14 to 26 weeks	4 804 802	3 590 144	2 938 652	1 515 394	1 423 258	344 132	307 360	1 214 658	140 420	115 194	3 535 442	1 269 360
1 to 13 weeks	4 360 649	3 221 337	2 587 037	1 365 134	1 221 903	337 560	296 740	1 139 312	134 611	123 263	3 135 968	1 224 681
Usually worked 35 or more hours per week	56 472 787	41 534 682	34 823 524	15 856 558	18 966 966	3 302 439	3 408 719	14 938 105	1 660 789	1 627 129	42 644 215	13 828 572
50 to 52 weeks	40 514 205	29 882 549	25 263 730	10 997 143	14 266 587	2 244 284	2 374 535	10 631 656	1 160 817	1 270 753	30 960 545	9 553 660
27 to 49 weeks	10 126 201	7 365 502	6 128 983	3 011 760	3 117 223	600 221	636 298	2 760 699	318 258	206 097	7 526 661	2 599 540
1 to 26 weeks	5 832 381	4 286 631	3 430 811	1 847 655	1 583 156	457 934	397 886	1 545 750	181 714	150 279	4 157 009	1 675 372
With unemployment in 1979	11 758 303	8 860 198	7 428 910	3 874 842	3 554 068	721 454	709 834	2 898 105	330 081	156 808	8 942 808	2 815 495
Percent of those in labor force in 1979	17.9	18.2	18.2	20.4	16.2	18.5	18.0	17.0	17.4	8.3	18.0	17.6
Unemployed 1 to 4 weeks	3 415 736	2 661 341	2 219 379	1 134 505	1 084 874	236 813	205 149	754 395	85 997	40 688	2 655 131	760 605
Unemployed 5 to 14 weeks	4 059 146	3 023 211	2 537 054	1 277 472	1 259 582	239 917	246 240	1 035 935	117 870	57 899	3 085 922	973 224
Unemployed 15 or more weeks	4 283 421	3 175 646	2 672 477	1 462 865	1 209 612	244 724	258 445	1 107 775	126 214	58 221	3 201 755	1 081 666
Mean weeks of unemployment	14.5	14.4	14.4	15.1	13.7	13.6	14.3	14.8	14.7	14.3	14.3	14.8
Female, 16 years and over, in labor force in 1979	**50 796 212**	**39 192 872**	**32 878 036**	**15 932 072**	**16 945 964**	**3 194 995**	**3 119 841**	**11 603 340**	**1 461 826**	**1 018 521**	**39 103 134**	**11 693 078**
Worked in 1979	49 609 602	38 253 830	32 080 998	15 443 178	16 637 820	3 124 005	3 048 827	11 355 772	1 431 994	1 006 581	38 184 748	11 424 854
50 to 52 weeks	25 228 893	19 728 561	16 829 755	8 068 280	8 761 475	1 448 908	1 449 898	5 500 332	691 127	521 946	19 815 562	5 413 331
48 to 49 weeks	2 089 867	1 674 520	1 432 738	735 067	697 671	123 318	118 464	415 347	53 689	30 712	1 661 732	428 135
40 to 47 weeks	5 186 028	4 034 375	3 400 790	1 607 903	1 792 887	321 337	312 248	1 151 653	146 328	85 158	4 033 871	1 152 157
27 to 39 weeks	5 307 659	3 978 193	3 238 807	1 566 332	1 672 475	374 539	364 847	1 329 466	172 101	114 364	3 929 750	1 377 909
14 to 26 weeks	5 923 554	4 476 609	3 665 223	1 747 091	1 918 132	417 039	394 347	1 446 945	181 027	115 531	4 444 994	1 478 560
1 to 13 weeks	5 873 601	4 361 572	3 513 685	1 718 505	1 795 180	438 864	409 023	1 512 029	187 722	138 870	4 298 839	1 574 762
Usually worked 35 or more hours per week	34 026 762	26 296 262	22 160 339	10 950 799	11 209 540	2 081 085	2 054 838	7 730 500	963 487	642 402	26 256 008	7 770 754
50 to 52 weeks	20 381 213	16 029 222	13 742 704	6 681 035	7 061 669	1 146 758	1 139 760	4 351 991	535 601	380 023	16 117 037	4 264 176
27 to 49 weeks	7 863 904	5 980 492	4 973 126	2 498 737	2 474 389	499 016	508 350	1 883 412	240 868	140 884	5 935 644	1 928 260
1 to 26 weeks	5 781 645	4 286 548	3 444 509	1 771 027	1 673 482	435 311	406 728	1 495 097	187 018	121 495	4 203 327	1 578 318
With unemployment in 1979	9 912 198	7 782 414	6 522 812	3 400 589	3 122 223	650 155	609 447	2 129 784	264 961	119 357	7 684 656	2 227 542
Percent of those in labor force in 1979	19.5	19.9	19.8	21.3	18.4	20.3	19.5	18.4	18.1	11.7	19.7	19.1
Unemployed 1 to 4 weeks	3 475 172	2 815 490	2 368 532	1 205 430	1 163 102	247 485	199 473	659 682	80 937	37 304	2 762 959	712 213
Unemployed 5 to 14 weeks	3 192 020	2 487 527	2 088 732	1 070 307	1 018 425	203 143	195 652	704 493	87 196	40 121	2 468 975	723 045
Unemployed 15 or more weeks	3 245 006	2 479 397	2 065 548	1 124 852	940 696	199 527	214 322	765 609	96 828	41 932	2 452 722	792 284
Mean weeks of unemployment	13.6	13.4	13.3	13.9	12.6	13.0	14.3	14.5	14.7	14.1	13.3	14.5
WORKERS IN FAMILY IN 1979												
Families	**59 190 133**	**43 005 667**	**35 785 119**	**16 608 545**	**19 176 574**	**3 419 769**	**3 800 779**	**16 184 466**	**1 899 912**	**1 618 992**	**43 918 934**	**15 271 199**
No workers	7 558 922	5 523 585	4 520 676	2 506 905	2 013 771	447 264	555 645	2 035 337	286 628	130 763	5 399 563	2 159 359
1 worker	19 561 999	14 104 919	11 744 749	5 574 296	6 170 453	1 113 403	1 246 767	5 457 080	621 184	592 794	14 437 334	5 124 665
2 workers	24 668 771	17 879 352	14 819 149	6 583 490	8 235 659	1 478 064	1 582 139	6 789 419	782 297	649 923	18 345 906	6 322 865
3 or more workers	7 400 441	5 497 811	4 700 545	1 943 854	2 756 691	381 038	416 228	1 902 630	209 803	245 512	5 736 131	1 664 310
Married-couple families	**48 990 299**	**34 629 611**	**28 614 787**	**12 401 968**	**16 212 819**	**2 825 395**	**3 189 429**	**14 360 688**	**1 623 500**	**1 507 894**	**35 830 718**	**13 159 581**
No workers	5 477 851	3 805 536	3 043 513	1 484 837	1 558 676	333 851	428 172	1 672 315	228 341	117 329	3 764 774	1 713 077
1 worker	14 677 486	10 101 461	8 350 666	3 622 954	4 727 712	809 246	941 549	4 576 025	484 570	545 490	10 586 771	4 090 715
2 workers	22 248 049	15 890 106	13 102 550	5 658 818	7 443 732	1 341 401	1 446 155	6 357 943	720 069	612 461	16 403 279	5 844 770
Husband and wife worked	19 459 888	13 908 613	11 406 700	4 951 270	6 455 430	1 207 797	1 294 116	5 551 275	642 451	491 457	14 296 119	5 163 769
3 or more workers	6 586 913	4 832 508	4 118 058	1 635 359	2 482 699	340 897	373 553	1 754 405	190 520	232 614	5 075 894	1 511 019
Husband and wife worked	5 449 519	3 990 952	3 376 684	1 332 679	2 044 005	293 431	320 837	1 458 567	164 000	183 651	4 174 466	1 275 053
Female householder, no husband present	**8 205 279**	**6 845 544**	**5 847 483**	**3 487 577**	**2 359 906**	**493 844**	**504 217**	**1 359 735**	**223 822**	**57 621**	**6 544 179**	**1 661 100**
No workers	1 844 009	1 544 404	1 330 207	928 072	402 135	101 903	112 294	299 605	50 447	8 913	1 463 647	380 362
1 worker	3 945 577	3 290 430	2 782 164	1 618 331	1 163 833	254 860	253 406	655 147	111 121	24 073	3 128 885	816 692
2 workers	1 777 311	1 481 568	1 273 147	692 968	580 179	104 548	103 873	295 743	46 781	17 985	1 431 996	345 315
3 or more workers	638 382	529 142	461 965	248 206	213 759	32 533	34 644	109 240	15 473	6 650	519 651	118 731
WORK DISABILITY STATUS OF NONINSTITUTIONAL PERSONS												
Male, 16 to 64 years	**70 680 243**	**52 367 038**	**44 069 230**	**20 845 439**	**23 223 791**	**4 115 069**	**4 182 739**	**18 313 205**	**2 020 690**	**1 854 722**	**53 558 318**	**17 121 925**
With a work disability	6 379 603	4 443 601	3 646 194	1 925 017	1 721 177	376 944	420 463	1 936 002	216 786	169 193	4 496 892	1 882 711
Not in labor force	3 247 100	2 220 180	1 811 966	1 027 399	784 567	186 882	221 332	1 026 920	116 000	64 192	2 228 922	1 018 178
Prevented from working	2 803 327	1 902 606	1 548 661	879 226	669 435	159 341	194 604	900 721	101 914	53 518	1 910 697	892 630
Female, 16 to 64 years	**73 986 389**	**55 638 552**	**46 795 506**	**22 551 079**	**24 244 427**	**4 373 948**	**4 469 098**	**18 347 837**	**2 146 044**	**1 713 928**	**56 325 250**	**17 661 139**
With a work disability	5 939 948	4 362 228	3 585 718	1 980 195	1 605 523	368 648	407 862	1 577 720	197 213	118 949	4 306 928	1 633 020
Not in labor force	4 376 105	3 160 264	2 589 842	1 455 663	1 134 179	266 154	304 268	1 215 841	149 653	89 832	3 127 928	1 248 177
Prevented from working	3 505 134	2 530 493	2 070 011	1 189 980	880 031	212 754	247 728	974 641	121 479	66 565	2 493 039	1 012 095
PUBLIC TRANSPORTATION DISABILITY STATUS OF NONINSTITUTIONAL PERSONS												
Persons 16 to 64 years	**144 666 632**	**108 005 590**	**90 864 736**	**43 396 518**	**47 468 218**	**8 489 017**	**8 651 837**	**36 661 042**	**4 166 734**	**3 568 650**	**109 883 568**	**34 783 064**
With a public transportation disability	2 597 631	1 926 476	1 637 439	947 444	689 995	132 930	156 107	671 155	77 826	46 742	1 927 786	669 845
With a work disability	2 392 482	1 769 481	1 499 907	870 009	629 898	124 063	145 511	623 001	72 770	42 302	1 766 553	625 929
Persons 65 years and over	**24 158 144**	**17 906 942**	**14 376 445**	**7 584 064**	**6 792 381**	**1 595 563**	**1 934 934**	**6 251 202**	**1 005 490**	**712 034**	**17 150 818**	**7 007 326**
With a public transportation disability	3 588 536	2 697 643	2 216 629	1 243 598	973 031	215 074	265 940	890 893	137 970	76 240	2 604 588	983 948
VETERAN STATUS OF CIVILIANS												
Male veterans	**27 406 299**	**20 375 479**	**17 134 300**	**7 595 807**	**9 538 493**	**1 563 141**	**1 678 038**	**7 030 820**	**834 528**	**619 597**	**20 889 396**	**6 516 903**
Percent of civilian males 16 years and over	34.2	34.6	34.8	32.1	37.2	33.4	34.1	32.9	34.1	27.9	34.8	32.2
Female veterans	**1 108 245**	**885 100**	**754 448**	**370 712**	**383 736**	**64 693**	**65 959**	**223 145**	**30 698**	**16 195**	**879 380**	**228 865**
Percent of civilian females 16 years and over	1.2	1.3	1.3	1.3	1.3	1.2	1.1	1.0	1.1	0.8	1.3	1.0
PERIOD OF SERVICE												
Civilian veterans 16 years and over	**28 514 544**	**21 260 579**	**17 888 748**	**7 966 519**	**9 922 229**	**1 627 834**	**1 743 997**	**7 253 965**	**865 226**	**635 792**	**21 768 776**	**6 745 768**
Percent of civilians 16 years and over	16.8	16.8	17.0	15.6	18.3	16.0	16.3	16.7	16.5	14.9	17.1	16.0
May 1975 or later only	975 968	767 963	638 540	350 165	288 375	68 692	60 731	208 005	26 702	9 612	748 034	227 934
Vietnam era	7 374 663	5 461 946	4 602 582	2 084 566	2 518 016	429 789	429 575	1 912 717	210 434	104 359	5 668 495	1 706 168
February 1955 to July 1964 only	3 077 097	2 201 544	1 868 823	737 510	1 131 313	156 193	176 528	875 553	90 014	75 580	2 364 724	712 373
Vietnam era and Korean conflict	662 267	504 916	429 724	183 775	245 949	39 047	36 145	157 351	16 212	9 324	520 255	142 012
Korean conflict	3 964 613	2 899 452	2 462 241	1 020 462	1 441 779	208 500	228 711	1 065 161	117 162	118 240	3 035 282	929 331
Korean conflict and World War II	788 652	624 936	537 607	234 425	303 182	43 591	43 738	163 716	20 190	10 791	634 174	154 478
World War II	10 696 714	8 063 807	6 752 055	3 042 967	3 709 088	619 033	692 719	2 632 907	346 218	285 289	8 086 164	2 610 550
World War I	491 353	376 533	296 280	155 185	141 095	35 937	44 316	114 820	22 318	10 308	349 928	141 425
Other	483 217	359 482	300 896	157 464	143 432	27 052	31 534	123 735	15 976	12 289	361 720	121 497
Civilian nonveterans 16 years and over	**141 064 863**	**104 986 598**	**87 513 354**	**43 242 916**	**44 270 438**	**8 522 046**	**8 951 198**	**36 078 265**	**4 385 807**	**3 643 169**	**105 584 485**	**35 480 378**

Table 107. Income Characteristics in 1979: 1980

[Data are estimates based on a sample; see Introduction. For meaning of symbols, see Introduction. For definitions of terms, see appendixes A and B]

United States Urban and Rural and Size of Place Inside and Outside SMSA's		Urban						Rural				
			Inside urbanized areas			Outside urbanized areas						
	United States	Total	Total	Central cities	Urban fringe	Places of 10,000 or more	Places of 2,500 to 10,000	Total	Places of 1,000 to 2,500	Rural farm	Inside SMSA's	Outside SMSA's
INCOME IN 1979												
Households	**80 467 427**	**60 612 281**	**50 594 887**	**25 311 426**	**25 283 461**	**4 842 990**	**5 174 404**	**19 855 146**	**2 549 840**	**1 847 406**	**60 554 725**	**19 912 702**
Less than $5,000	10 663 441	7 914 150	6 304 914	4 162 858	2 142 056	771 338	837 898	2 749 291	420 352	224 499	7 363 900	3 299 541
$5,000 to $7,499	6 439 024	4 735 200	3 762 996	2 289 391	1 473 605	466 532	505 672	1 703 824	253 144	151 546	4 462 955	1 976 069
$7,500 to $9,999	6 333 385	4 691 617	3 778 700	2 194 467	1 584 233	439 497	473 420	1 641 768	233 329	153 393	4 489 341	1 844 044
$10,000 to $14,999	12 342 073	9 118 361	7 452 910	4 071 677	3 381 233	801 083	864 368	3 223 712	429 276	308 503	8 907 333	3 434 740
$15,000 to $19,999	11 379 049	8 386 524	6 954 017	3 487 634	3 466 383	686 905	745 602	2 992 525	376 791	262 156	8 423 975	2 955 074
$20,000 to $24,999	10 004 409	7 445 491	6 262 778	2 838 455	3 424 323	570 845	611 868	2 558 918	307 381	218 988	7 658 084	2 346 325
$25,000 to $34,999	12 659 261	9 717 492	8 370 941	3 418 827	4 952 114	659 511	687 040	2 941 769	328 880	265 012	10 171 317	2 487 944
$35,000 to $49,999	6 954 720	5 582 302	4 972 856	1 837 146	3 135 710	303 960	305 486	1 372 418	138 027	155 908	5 898 690	1 056 030
$50,000 or more	3 692 065	3 021 144	2 734 775	1 010 971	1 723 804	143 319	143 050	670 921	62 660	107 401	3 179 130	512 935
Median	$16 841	$17 159	$17 738	$14 914	$20 790	$14 608	$14 402	$15 954	$14 220	$16 498	$17 880	$14 040
Mean	$20 306	$20 798	$21 440	$18 689	$24 194	$17 734	$17 382	$18 806	$17 001	$20 815	$21 418	$16 926
Families	**59 190 133**	**43 005 667**	**35 785 119**	**16 608 545**	**19 176 574**	**3 419 769**	**3 800 779**	**16 184 466**	**1 899 912**	**1 618 992**	**43 918 934**	**15 271 199**
Less than $5,000	4 344 476	3 033 569	2 464 927	1 625 085	839 842	269 287	299 355	1 310 907	151 057	157 794	2 932 469	1 412 007
$5,000 to $7,499	3 681 759	2 506 332	1 964 470	1 192 378	772 092	249 022	292 840	1 175 427	149 476	115 365	2 412 574	1 269 185
$7,500 to $9,999	4 064 705	2 804 814	2 213 406	1 251 087	962 319	271 522	319 886	1 259 891	161 362	125 731	2 732 545	1 332 160
$10,000 to $14,999	8 709 248	6 021 823	4 801 193	2 536 247	2 264 946	564 249	656 381	2 687 425	336 135	270 222	5 964 178	2 745 070
$15,000 to $19,999	8 937 703	6 263 518	5 076 756	2 458 695	2 618 061	555 259	631 503	2 674 185	327 295	240 364	6 356 290	2 581 413
$20,000 to $24,999	8 485 832	6 114 420	5 067 413	2 218 184	2 849 229	498 374	548 633	2 371 412	280 814	205 263	6 341 921	2 143 911
$25,000 to $34,999	11 301 814	8 522 720	7 284 592	2 872 944	4 411 648	601 012	637 116	2 779 094	307 635	252 515	8 976 053	2 325 761
$35,000 to $49,999	6 332 965	5 033 144	4 468 809	1 592 648	2 876 161	280 222	284 113	1 299 821	128 910	149 227	5 344 719	988 246
$50,000 or more	3 331 631	2 705 327	2 443 553	861 277	1 582 276	130 822	130 952	626 304	57 228	102 511	2 858 185	473 446
Median	$19 917	$20 653	$21 243	$18 379	$23 639	$18 118	$17 501	$17 995	$17 205	$17 730	$21 128	$16 592
Mean	$23 092	$23 981	$24 687	$21 869	$27 127	$20 840	$20 164	$20 730	$19 647	$22 012	$24 445	$19 201
Unrelated individuals 15 years and over	**30 041 869**	**25 320 564**	**21 076 369**	**12 410 772**	**8 665 597**	**2 335 859**	**1 908 336**	**4 721 305**	**803 873**	**267 893**	**23 656 797**	**6 385 072**
Less than $2,000	4 265 687	3 602 140	2 795 615	1 843 317	952 298	499 108	307 417	663 547	97 869	32 579	3 174 203	1 091 484
$2,000 to $2,999	2 575 125	2 020 586	1 508 265	1 035 936	472 329	284 883	227 438	554 539	99 832	19 377	1 745 559	829 566
$3,000 to $4,999	5 141 839	4 229 392	3 379 633	2 131 780	1 247 853	453 558	396 201	912 447	175 740	41 656	3 850 387	1 291 452
$5,000 to $7,999	5 032 369	4 196 551	3 458 326	2 034 638	1 423 688	390 731	347 494	835 818	153 423	50 206	3 901 292	1 131 077
$8,000 to $9,999	2 613 586	2 213 771	1 880 597	1 093 225	787 372	177 183	155 991	399 815	69 710	25 346	2 099 437	514 149
$10,000 to $14,999	4 753 467	4 095 017	3 571 699	1 980 020	1 591 679	276 662	246 656	658 450	109 553	42 927	3 950 477	802 990
$15,000 to $24,999	4 134 492	3 623 060	3 258 583	1 675 884	1 582 699	192 957	171 520	511 432	73 953	35 715	3 590 295	544 197
$25,000 to $49,999	1 292 046	1 137 526	1 038 928	514 216	524 712	51 804	46 794	154 520	19 903	16 199	1 141 113	150 933
$50,000 or more	233 258	202 521	184 723	101 756	82 967	8 973	8 825	30 737	3 890	3 888	204 034	29 224
Median	$6 695	$6 891	$7 413	$6 657	$8 572	$4 633	$5 175	$5 735	$5 494	$7 326	$7 270	$4 962
Mean	$9 282	$9 468	$9 935	$9 226	$10 949	$6 907	$7 449	$8 282	$7 737	$10 516	$9 826	$7 263
Males 15 years and over, with income	**77 297 447**	**56 924 987**	**47 501 863**	**22 415 761**	**25 086 102**	**4 606 095**	**4 817 029**	**20 372 460**	**2 357 927**	**2 123 707**	**57 878 548**	**19 418 899**
Median income	$12 192	$12 526	$12 908	$11 120	$15 021	$10 639	$10 966	$11 329	$11 057	$10 615	$12 920	$10 295
Percent year-round full-time workers	52.4	52.5	53.2	49.0	56.9	48.7	49.3	52.1	49.2	59.5	53.5	49.1
Median income	$17 363	$17 947	$18 374	$16 525	$20 116	$16 145	$15 942	$15 940	$15 723	$13 498	$18 239	$15 113
Females 15 years and over, with income	**69 889 197**	**53 838 933**	**44 785 433**	**22 381 465**	**22 403 968**	**4 450 638**	**4 602 862**	**16 050 264**	**2 201 662**	**1 353 380**	**53 105 314**	**16 783 883**
Median income	$5 263	$5 527	$5 768	$5 520	$6 033	$4 549	$4 473	$4 473	$4 379	$4 151	$5 631	$4 279
Percent year-round full-time workers	29.0	29.7	30.6	29.8	31.4	25.7	24.6	26.8	24.1	26.4	30.3	25.1
Median income	$10 380	$10 754	$11 026	$10 706	$11 318	$9 273	$8 984	$9 033	$8 875	$8 475	$10 862	$8 688
Per capita income	**$7 298**	**$7 645**	**$7 887**	**$7 166**	**$8 557**	**$6 527**	**$6 356**	**$6 322**	**$6 227**	**$6 851**	**$7 743**	**$5 977**
Persons in households	$7 412	$7 783	$8 008	$7 295	$8 664	$6 769	$6 505	$6 383	$6 314	$6 851	$7 860	$6 077
Persons in group quarters	$2 909	$2 993	$3 147	$3 050	$3 285	$2 570	$2 610	$2 477	$2 502	–	$3 069	$2 495
MEDIAN INCOME IN 1979 BY SELECTED CHARACTERISTICS												
Age of family householder:												
15 to 24 years	$12 669	$12 440	$12 570	$10 871	$14 913	$11 766	$12 320	$13 244	$12 721	$12 913	$12 901	$12 229
25 to 34 years	$19 041	$19 327	$19 721	$17 086	$21 686	$17 771	$17 539	$18 355	$17 568	$16 046	$19 834	$17 014
35 to 44 years	$23 162	$23 829	$24 302	$20 937	$26 582	$21 990	$21 378	$21 797	$21 041	$20 534	$24 321	$20 284
45 to 54 years	$25 864	$27 076	$27 746	$24 308	$30 330	$24 256	$23 368	$22 651	$22 435	$22 101	$27 388	$21 376
55 to 64 years	$21 950	$23 517	$24 329	$22 022	$26 256	$20 497	$19 321	$17 976	$18 511	$18 956	$23 686	$17 416
65 years and over	$12 295	$13 300	$13 884	$13 050	$14 692	$11 579	$11 104	$10 171	$10 563	$12 953	$13 421	$10 157
Family type by presence of own children:												
Families	**$19 917**	**$20 653**	**$21 243**	**$18 379**	**$23 639**	**$18 118**	**$17 501**	**$17 995**	**$17 205**	**$17 730**	**$21 128**	**$16 592**
With own children under 18 years	$20 337	$20 760	$21 206	$17 666	$23 905	$18 799	$18 518	$19 333	$18 475	$18 835	$21 283	$17 675
With own children under 6 years	$17 757	$18 029	$18 461	$15 474	$20 951	$16 457	$16 357	$17 188	$16 481	$15 715	$18 611	$15 907
Without own children under 18 years	$19 380	$20 528	$21 286	$19 082	$23 318	$17 362	$16 438	$16 323	$15 814	$16 903	$20 937	$15 307
Married-couple families	**$21 635**	**$22 765**	**$23 582**	**$21 261**	**$25 427**	**$20 035**	**$19 170**	**$19 045**	**$18 553**	**$17 999**	**$23 145**	**$17 798**
With own children under 18 years	$22 569	$23 734	$24 439	$21 874	$26 169	$21 245	$20 651	$20 505	$20 233	$19 154	$24 051	$19 332
With own children under 6 years	$19 630	$20 336	$20 841	$18 809	$22 222	$18 296	$17 823	$17 993	$17 602	$15 888	$20 659	$16 979
Without own children under 18 years	$20 380	$21 697	$22 536	$20 561	$24 398	$18 398	$17 240	$16 906	$16 473	$17 036	$22 049	$15 976
Female householder, no husband present	**$9 960**	**$10 140**	**$10 432**	**$9 152**	**$12 285**	**$8 844**	**$8 736**	**$9 215**	**$8 930**	**$13 278**	**$10 424**	**$8 531**
With own children under 18 years	$8 002	$8 044	$8 200	$7 093	$10 068	$7 331	$7 269	$7 801	$7 448	$9 847	$8 257	$7 163
With own children under 6 years	$5 229	$5 215	$5 241	$4 840	$6 294	$5 038	$5 120	$5 320	$5 087	$5 906	$5 292	$4 992
Without own children under 18 years	$13 811	$14 375	$14 908	$13 541	$16 825	$11 809	$11 421	$11 472	$11 408	$14 968	$14 738	$10 831
Workers in family in 1979:												
No workers	$7 791	$8 043	$8 096	$6 832	$9 732	$7 768	$7 869	$7 245	$7 624	$8 868	$8 128	$7 128
1 worker	$16 181	$16 663	$17 123	$14 691	$19 571	$14 545	$14 335	$15 018	$14 318	$14 448	$17 113	$13 616
2 workers	$23 058	$23 933	$24 613	$22 544	$26 169	$21 221	$20 846	$21 063	$20 511	$19 735	$24 353	$19 855
3 or more workers	$31 880	$33 049	$33 876	$31 376	$35 654	$29 489	$28 744	$28 775	$28 053	$27 410	$33 383	$27 188
Unrelated individuals:												
Male, 15 years and over	$8 401	$8 533	$9 077	$8 025	$10 860	$5 493	$6 576	$7 755	$7 595	$8 446	$8 989	$6 357
65 years and over	$5 327	$5 671	$5 882	$5 317	$6 838	$4 898	$4 813	$4 566	$4 781	$6 950	$5 760	$4 504
Female, 15 years and over	$5 618	$5 855	$6 293	$5 688	$7 175	$4 151	$4 551	$4 603	$4 660	$6 389	$6 126	$4 276
65 years and over	$4 633	$4 777	$4 874	$4 643	$5 307	$4 458	$4 328	$3 982	$4 175	$6 349	$4 822	$4 054
INCOME TYPE IN 1979												
Households	**80 467 427**	**60 612 281**	**50 594 887**	**25 311 426**	**25 283 461**	**4 842 990**	**5 174 404**	**19 855 146**	**2 549 840**	**1 847 406**	**60 554 725**	**19 912 702**
With earnings	65 387 819	49 053 483	41 233 317	19 849 423	21 383 894	3 841 613	3 978 553	16 334 336	1 945 414	1 722 979	49 620 595	15 767 224
Mean earnings	$20 727	$21 283	$21 893	$19 384	$24 222	$18 125	$18 008	$19 056	$17 701	$18 267	$21 823	$17 275
With wage or salary income	62 547 918	47 507 357	40 015 058	19 259 373	20 755 685	3 698 793	3 793 506	15 040 561	1 834 351	1 225 594	47 953 103	14 594 815
Mean wage or salary income	$19 796	$20 349	$20 950	$18 541	$23 186	$17 203	$17 078	$18 047	$16 787	$15 097	$20 877	$16 244
With nonfarm self-employment income	7 484 101	5 238 908	4 301 097	1 925 957	2 375 140	433 990	503 821	2 245 193	271 519	252 803	5 388 240	2 095 861
Mean nonfarm self-employment income	$13 324	$14 158	$14 560	$13 915	$15 083	$12 577	$12 089	$11 379	$11 240	$10 248	$14 160	$11 176
With farm self-employment income	2 680 184	627 856	406 460	200 780	205 680	93 459	127 937	2 052 328	92 451	1 237 591	1 004 938	1 675 246
Mean farm self-employment income	$6 479	$4 915	$4 361	$4 390	$4 333	$5 782	$6 041	$6 958	$6 386	$8 388	$5 460	$7 091
With interest, dividend, or net rental income	33 331 306	25 710 168	21 755 742	9 513 819	12 241 923	1 918 033	2 036 393	7 621 138	1 000 708	1 004 546	26 007 070	7 324 236
Mean interest, dividend, or net rental income	$2 994	$3 097	$3 137	$3 197	$3 090	$2 844	$2 907	$2 647	$2 759	$3 635	$3 060	$2 762
With Social Security income	20 837 145	15 362 962	12 295 463	6 516 843	5 778 620	1 400 124	1 667 375	5 474 183	860 353	536 887	14 739 921	6 097 224
Mean Social Security income	$4 094	$4 163	$4 209	$4 076	$4 359	$3 990	$3 974	$3 899	$3 941	$3 799	$4 190	$3 862
With public assistance income	6 425 511	4 949 346	4 100 661	2 718 496	1 382 165	393 958	454 727	1 476 165	215 385	68 081	4 714 725	1 710 786
Mean public assistance income	$2 518	$2 607	$2 691	$2 713	$2 648	$2 209	$2 197	$2 218	$2 180	$2 233	$2 650	$2 153
With all other income	19 190 069	14 396 639	11 913 482	5 813 921	6 099 561	1 177 294	1 305 863	4 793 430	647 324	303 362	14 354 208	4 835 861
Mean all other income	$4 036	$4 175	$4 282	$4 116	$4 440	$3 690	$3 639	$3 618	$3 542	$3 745	$4 197	$3 557

Table 108. **Poverty Status in 1979 of Families and Persons: 1980**

[Excludes inmates of institutions, persons in military group quarters and in college dormitories, and unrelated individuals under 15 years. Data are estimates based on a sample; see Introduction. For meaning of symbols, see Introduction. For definitions of terms, see appendixes A and B]

United States Urban and Rural and Size of Place Inside and Outside SMSA's		Urban						Rural				
			Inside urbanized areas			Outside urbanized areas						
	United States	Total	Total	Central cities	Urban fringe	Places of 10,000 or more	Places of 2,500 to 10,000	Total	Places of 1,000 to 2,500	Rural farm	Inside SMSA's	Outside SMSA's
ALL INCOME LEVELS IN 1979												
Families	**59 190 133**	**43 005 667**	**35 785 119**	**16 608 545**	**19 176 574**	**3 419 769**	**3 800 779**	**16 184 466**	**1 899 912**	**1 618 992**	**43 918 934**	**15 271 199**
With Social Security income	13 086 462	9 328 315	7 548 963	3 730 200	3 818 763	801 013	978 339	3 758 147	509 638	420 200	9 216 863	3 869 599
Income above poverty level	11 907 615	8 635 154	7 034 633	3 390 132	3 644 501	722 810	877 711	3 272 461	454 937	379 811	8 553 238	3 354 377
Below poverty level without Social Security income	3 351 110	2 266 301	1 748 410	929 117	819 293	228 769	289 122	1 084 809	158 374	83 318	2 197 453	1 153 657
With public assistance income	4 719 387	3 606 760	3 016 925	1 954 494	1 062 431	275 259	314 576	1 112 627	148 594	57 826	3 483 824	1 235 563
Income above poverty level	2 878 557	2 165 340	1 810 594	1 053 394	757 200	163 375	191 371	713 217	93 319	45 907	2 137 404	741 153
Below poverty level without public assistance income	643 169	482 669	399 126	266 847	132 279	37 647	45 896	160 500	22 002	6 577	464 255	178 914
Householder worked in 1979	47 291 362	34 274 154	28 580 151	12 651 926	15 928 225	2 730 538	2 963 465	13 017 208	1 470 665	1 404 355	35 321 403	11 969 959
With related children under 18 years	31 953 940	22 976 039	19 123 440	8 830 997	10 292 443	1 827 584	2 025 015	8 977 901	999 443	753 879	23 744 309	8 209 631
With related children 5 to 17 years	25 606 907	18 301 804	15 272 382	6 951 540	8 320 842	1 426 059	1 603 363	7 305 103	798 492	646 261	19 031 404	6 575 503
Female householder, no husband present	8 205 279	6 845 544	5 847 483	3 487 577	2 359 906	493 844	504 217	1 359 735	223 822	57 621	6 544 179	1 661 100
Householder worked in 1979	5 130 596	4 329 040	3 696 201	2 062 813	1 633 388	320 627	312 212	801 556	134 941	31 040	4 142 685	987 911
With related children under 18 years	5 509 315	4 629 471	3 952 995	2 412 955	1 540 040	338 113	338 363	879 844	145 750	21 764	4 412 997	1 096 318
With related children under 6 years	2 132 451	1 820 346	1 546 951	1 041 217	505 734	140 031	133 364	312 105	54 336	5 467	1 703 631	428 820
Householder 65 years and over	8 823 135	6 294 390	5 042 054	2 552 096	2 489 958	558 365	693 971	2 528 745	365 783	330 320	6 131 354	2 691 781
Unrelated individuals	**27 383 584**	**22 857 600**	**19 377 071**	**11 396 875**	**7 980 196**	**1 831 829**	**1 648 700**	**4 525 984**	**763 762**	**267 893**	**21 721 196**	**5 662 388**
With Social Security income	8 074 494	6 304 338	4 973 273	2 928 996	2 044 277	621 305	709 760	1 770 156	360 056	119 403	5 779 671	2 294 823
Income above poverty level	5 783 177	4 665 544	3 766 886	2 113 913	1 652 973	423 231	475 427	1 117 633	235 493	95 122	4 330 697	1 452 480
Below poverty level without Social Security income	3 379 829	2 720 437	2 182 580	1 269 915	912 665	253 572	284 285	659 392	140 952	32 503	2 514 538	865 291
With public assistance income	1 842 792	1 457 014	1 183 918	840 485	343 433	126 027	147 069	385 778	70 270	10 899	1 342 004	500 788
Income above poverty level	737 224	622 425	529 364	339 342	190 022	44 390	48 671	114 799	21 378	4 965	594 419	142 805
Below poverty level without public assistance income	448 886	379 916	324 690	216 255	108 435	26 180	29 046	68 970	12 994	2 062	364 095	84 791
Worked in 1979	17 747 858	15 210 933	13 171 995	7 588 513	5 583 482	1 151 976	886 962	2 536 925	385 003	171 594	14 595 941	3 151 917
65 years and over	7 721 268	6 025 483	4 756 532	2 806 224	1 950 308	582 677	686 274	1 695 785	350 285	119 631	5 521 850	2 199 418
Persons	**220 845 766**	**162 301 094**	**135 751 108**	**65 082 656**	**70 668 452**	**12 707 652**	**13 842 334**	**58 544 672**	**6 872 800**	**5 609 603**	**165 339 796**	**55 505 970**
Related children under 18 years	62 654 136	44 511 786	36 952 345	17 246 108	19 706 237	3 554 405	4 005 036	18 142 350	1 990 864	1 588 538	46 152 442	16 501 694
Related children 5 to 17 years	46 540 608	32 911 055	27 421 650	12 540 370	14 881 280	2 566 989	2 922 416	13 629 553	1 466 579	1 248 626	34 364 687	12 175 921
60 years and over	34 197 996	25 290 281	20 489 730	10 576 792	9 912 938	2 183 715	2 616 836	8 907 715	1 355 888	1 066 781	24 492 498	9 705 498
65 years and over	24 154 364	17 903 658	14 373 711	7 582 319	6 791 392	1 595 243	1 934 704	6 250 706	1 005 418	712 034	17 147 720	7 006 644
INCOME IN 1979 BELOW POVERTY LEVEL												
Families	**5 670 215**	**3 960 944**	**3 224 756**	**2 135 154**	**1 089 602**	**348 413**	**387 775**	**1 709 271**	**190 469**	**202 032**	**3 839 969**	**1 830 246**
Percent below poverty level	9.6	9.2	9.0	12.9	5.7	10.2	10.2	10.6	10.0	12.5	8.7	12.0
Mean income deficit	$3 076	$3 102	$3 146	$3 195	$3 050	$2 947	$2 875	$3 014	$2 817	$3 735	$3 118	$2 986
Persons per family	3.62	3.59	3.59	3.64	3.50	3.57	3.60	3.69	3.56	3.76	3.60	3.66
With Social Security income	1 178 847	693 161	514 330	340 068	174 262	78 203	100 628	485 686	54 701	40 389	663 625	515 222
With public assistance income	1 840 830	1 441 420	1 206 331	901 100	305 231	111 884	123 205	399 410	55 275	11 919	1 346 420	494 410
Householder worked in 1979	2 860 666	1 907 045	1 507 406	930 630	576 776	192 695	206 944	953 621	99 573	161 169	1 858 106	1 002 560
With related children under 18 years	4 214 677	3 080 558	2 539 820	1 705 786	834 034	260 529	280 209	1 134 119	130 810	123 533	2 970 774	1 243 903
With related children 5 to 17 years	3 331 234	2 399 684	1 980 139	1 330 543	649 596	198 904	220 641	931 550	103 899	105 134	2 326 004	1 005 230
Female householder, no husband present	2 484 246	2 064 419	1 738 842	1 230 063	508 779	161 930	163 647	419 827	69 727	10 240	1 922 402	561 844
Householder worked in 1979	1 012 698	828 998	669 972	437 791	232 181	81 339	77 687	183 700	32 411	4 609	755 882	256 816
With related children under 18 years	2 222 439	1 865 733	1 576 372	1 114 230	462 142	144 508	144 853	356 706	60 728	6 604	1 737 473	484 966
With related children under 6 years	1 185 334	1 014 785	858 341	623 365	234 976	80 041	76 403	170 549	30 849	2 437	936 913	248 421
Householder 65 years and over	779 928	434 697	316 071	202 272	113 799	50 523	68 103	345 231	38 690	32 721	418 506	361 422
Unrelated individuals	**6 860 582**	**5 442 506**	**4 375 446**	**2 946 788**	**1 428 658**	**575 807**	**491 253**	**1 418 076**	**230 676**	**66 019**	**4 995 288**	**1 865 294**
Percent below poverty level	25.1	23.8	22.6	25.9	17.9	31.4	29.8	31.3	30.2	24.6	23.0	32.9
Mean income deficit	$1 786	$1 818	$1 864	$1 851	$1 890	$1 699	$1 552	$1 664	$1 467	$1 924	$1 850	$1 616
With Social Security income	2 291 317	1 638 794	1 206 387	815 083	391 304	198 074	234 333	652 523	124 563	24 281	1 448 974	842 343
With public assistance income	1 105 568	834 589	654 554	501 143	153 411	81 637	98 398	270 979	48 892	5 934	747 585	357 983
Worked in 1979	2 715 215	2 290 965	1 863 579	1 230 294	633 285	272 449	154 937	424 250	59 499	30 752	2 085 991	629 224
65 years and over	2 251 810	1 594 546	1 173 359	786 731	386 628	187 547	233 640	657 264	125 611	26 176	1 413 557	838 253
Persons	**27 392 580**	**19 671 307**	**15 965 933**	**10 726 041**	**5 239 892**	**1 819 187**	**1 886 187**	**7 721 273**	**908 019**	**825 906**	**18 820 350**	**8 572 230**
Percent below poverty level	12.4	12.1	11.8	16.5	7.4	14.3	13.6	13.2	13.2	14.7	11.4	15.4
Related children under 18 years	10 025 623	7 199 152	5 907 393	4 027 951	1 879 442	616 887	674 872	2 826 471	315 922	313 116	6 944 664	3 080 959
Related children 5 to 17 years	7 103 217	5 028 245	4 132 189	2 806 945	1 325 244	423 145	472 911	2 074 972	224 299	234 565	4 882 337	2 220 880
60 years and over	4 615 768	3 019 072	2 252 596	1 480 603	771 993	338 255	428 221	1 596 696	232 253	123 464	2 787 997	1 827 771
65 years and over	3 581 729	2 338 303	1 717 924	1 130 745	587 179	272 364	348 015	1 243 426	191 020	84 485	2 132 702	1 449 027
INCOME IN 1979 BELOW 125 PERCENT OF POVERTY LEVEL												
Families	**7 918 984**	**5 448 031**	**4 385 501**	**2 841 532**	**1 543 969**	**496 952**	**565 578**	**2 470 953**	**280 755**	**276 286**	**5 285 778**	**2 633 206**
Percent below poverty level	13.4	12.7	12.3	17.1	8.1	14.5	14.9	15.3	14.8	17.1	12.0	17.2
Mean income deficit	$3 657	$3 717	$3 785	$3 903	$3 568	$3 492	$3 383	$3 524	$3 302	$4 231	$3 729	$3 511
Persons per family	3.59	3.57	3.57	3.62	3.49	3.52	3.54	3.64	3.50	3.72	3.58	3.60
With Social Security income	1 903 978	1 133 917	840 538	538 534	302 004	127 518	165 861	770 061	91 068	62 432	1 087 586	816 392
With public assistance income	2 273 969	1 754 687	1 457 902	1 072 496	385 406	139 675	157 110	519 282	71 475	16 723	1 642 693	631 276
Householder worked in 1979	4 294 195	2 863 248	2 255 010	1 378 363	876 647	289 798	318 440	1 430 947	153 183	221 053	2 788 490	1 505 705
With related children under 18 years	5 649 908	4 066 509	3 323 193	2 182 616	1 140 577	354 278	389 038	1 583 399	182 452	165 211	3 932 848	1 717 060
With related children 5 to 17 years	4 465 436	3 168 225	2 593 333	1 704 294	889 039	269 870	305 022	1 297 211	144 695	140 441	3 082 324	1 383 112
Female householder, no husband present	3 101 393	2 558 614	2 142 352	1 492 120	650 232	205 132	211 130	542 779	90 487	13 499	2 380 952	720 441
Householder worked in 1979	1 411 474	1 154 577	934 587	604 702	329 885	111 036	108 954	256 897	45 365	6 260	1 056 195	355 279
With related children under 18 years	2 699 304	2 255 355	1 897 367	1 319 679	577 688	177 521	180 467	443 949	75 640	8 236	2 100 545	598 759
With related children under 6 years	1 374 127	1 172 414	987 817	709 859	277 958	93 926	90 671	201 713	36 444	2 868	1 081 720	292 407
Householder 65 years and over	1 275 534	728 890	529 278	332 285	196 993	85 000	114 612	546 644	65 787	50 154	699 118	576 416
Unrelated individuals	**9 109 271**	**7 282 620**	**5 875 220**	**3 882 553**	**1 992 667**	**748 591**	**658 809**	**1 826 651**	**310 790**	**84 561**	**6 695 656**	**2 413 615**
Percent below poverty level	33.3	31.9	30.3	34.1	25.0	40.9	40.0	40.4	40.7	31.6	30.8	42.6
Mean income deficit	$2 157	$2 170	$2 199	$2 224	$2 151	$2 126	$1 958	$2 107	$1 884	$2 320	$2 191	$2 064
With Social Security income	3 657 829	2 729 444	2 074 193	1 340 949	733 244	302 950	352 301	928 385	183 657	35 689	2 447 832	1 209 997
With public assistance income	1 396 052	1 082 220	866 648	641 686	224 962	98 332	117 240	313 832	57 474	7 317	983 956	412 096
Worked in 1979	3 509 665	2 953 993	2 410 267	1 582 010	828 257	340 423	203 303	555 672	80 826	40 480	2 696 092	813 573
65 years and over	3 510 636	2 598 686	1 971 860	1 270 625	701 235	282 651	344 175	911 950	181 538	37 163	2 333 071	1 177 565
Persons	**37 524 156**	**26 707 599**	**21 551 163**	**14 163 164**	**7 387 999**	**2 497 282**	**2 659 154**	**10 816 557**	**1 293 565**	**1 112 700**	**25 619 906**	**11 904 250**
Percent below poverty level	17.0	16.5	15.9	21.8	10.5	19.7	19.2	18.5	18.8	19.8	15.5	21.4
Related children under 18 years	13 292 653	9 398 798	7 651 438	5 089 163	2 562 275	825 879	921 481	3 893 855	436 198	415 712	9 109 064	4 183 589
Related children 5 to 17 years	9 434 013	6 581 719	5 369 739	3 559 242	1 810 497	566 694	645 286	2 852 294	309 983	311 279	6 423 386	3 010 627
60 years and over	7 180 604	4 828 035	3 652 579	2 329 315	1 323 264	520 229	655 227	2 352 569	354 219	180 644	4 481 604	2 699 000
65 years and over	5 723 766	3 869 710	2 900 414	1 848 752	1 051 662	428 328	540 968	1 854 056	295 030	126 923	3 555 801	2 167 965
INCOME IN 1979 BELOW SPECIFIED POVERTY LEVEL												
Percent of persons:												
Below 75 percent of poverty level	8.3	8.2	8.1	11.4	5.0	9.5	8.7	8.6	8.2	10.5	7.7	10.1
Below 150 percent of poverty level	21.7	20.9	20.1	26.9	13.8	25.0	24.9	24.0	24.6	25.2	19.7	27.5
Below 200 percent of poverty level	31.7	30.2	29.0	37.2	21.5	36.1	36.8	35.7	36.9	36.3	28.9	40.0

Table 172. General Characteristics of Selected Ancestry Groups: 1980

[Data are estimates based on a sample; see Introduction. For meaning of symbols, see Introduction. For definitions of terms, see appendixes A and B]

United States

	English	French	German	Irish	Italian	Polish
AGE						
Total persons	23 748 772	3 068 907	17 943 485	10 337 353	6 883 320	3 805 740
Under 5 years	1 286 466	128 429	802 294	386 829	207 782	93 877
5 to 9 years	1 383 827	139 967	835 553	445 047	249 237	112 303
10 to 14 years	1 534 018	169 893	968 526	561 269	340 680	148 926
15 to 19 years	1 892 957	236 635	1 306 541	771 123	465 801	203 007
20 to 24 years	1 964 742	301 710	1 684 655	954 225	596 657	281 257
25 to 29 years	1 861 627	282 393	1 619 445	893 972	573 766	309 099
30 to 34 years	1 841 269	262 868	1 494 275	833 182	546 468	319 890
35 to 39 years	1 557 341	214 951	1 240 410	693 142	450 384	251 277
40 to 44 years	1 344 056	186 923	1 089 789	617 997	389 424	203 406
45 to 49 years	1 308 666	180 250	1 029 912	614 997	423 386	204 905
50 to 54 years	1 413 068	194 256	1 078 374	671 890	520 607	274 900
55 to 59 years	1 446 039	186 345	1 053 477	679 389	562 527	350 372
60 to 64 years	1 285 892	154 926	938 234	597 138	483 484	367 346
65 to 69 years	1 153 723	135 352	847 095	529 274	426 301	291 752
70 to 74 years	965 528	114 444	727 099	437 536	280 767	178 624
75 to 79 years	708 864	87 781	568 829	320 945	175 934	102 291
80 to 84 years	453 006	53 904	375 982	195 226	112 717	62 733
85 years and over	347 683	37 880	282 995	134 172	77 398	49 775
Median	35.4	35.3	36.0	37.3	40.1	44.5
Female	12 059 255	1 600 744	8 892 139	5 394 487	3 452 421	1 957 844
Under 5 years	625 291	63 071	388 088	187 256	100 583	45 074
5 to 9 years	670 454	67 658	403 404	215 827	120 538	54 119
10 to 14 years	743 330	83 329	466 682	270 980	165 507	71 989
15 to 19 years	916 308	118 926	635 256	378 324	226 287	97 322
20 to 24 years	939 317	150 695	814 883	470 148	288 798	136 809
25 to 29 years	889 170	139 161	759 888	439 577	273 309	149 689
30 to 34 years	886 919	129 223	695 682	413 410	262 998	154 709
35 to 39 years	763 291	108 207	584 413	352 761	217 313	122 858
40 to 44 years	664 027	94 516	520 727	318 425	189 990	100 752
45 to 49 years	653 206	92 798	491 043	318 965	209 445	103 066
50 to 54 years	716 350	102 697	522 314	352 140	262 076	142 557
55 to 59 years	749 988	100 392	522 126	361 377	285 751	182 965
60 to 64 years	676 753	85 123	473 082	322 493	250 547	193 555
65 to 69 years	630 695	77 275	445 077	297 464	229 374	159 267
70 to 74 years	552 675	68 309	401 069	260 283	157 503	102 730
75 to 79 years	435 426	55 552	335 612	205 045	102 945	63 608
80 to 84 years	298 867	36 663	239 328	132 783	65 394	43 161
85 years and over	247 202	27 149	193 465	97 229	44 063	33 614
Median	37.4	37.2	37.4	39.6	41.9	47.2
CHARACTERISTICS OF PERSONS 60 YEARS AND OVER						
Persons 60 to 64 years	1 285 892	154 926	938 234	597 138	483 484	367 346
In families	1 076 011	127 419	793 811	487 611	415 840	304 293
Percent with income in 1979 below poverty level	6.8	6.6	4.3	5.8	4.2	3.6
Householder or spouse	1 034 006	121 192	764 064	462 947	387 249	286 107
Other relatives	42 005	6 227	29 747	24 664	28 591	18 186
Nonrelatives in households	198 085	25 572	135 426	100 897	64 381	58 949
Living alone	177 998	22 572	121 286	89 377	58 927	53 564
Percent with income in 1979 below poverty level	26.5	28.9	19.6	25.3	23.7	21.1
In group quarters	11 796	1 935	8 997	8 630	3 263	4 104
Inmate of institution	9 484	1 140	5 909	4 730	2 417	2 543
Home for the aged	6 581	866	4 247	3 313	1 309	1 583
Other	2 312	795	3 088	3 900	846	1 561
Persons 65 to 74 years	2 119 251	249 796	1 574 194	966 810	707 068	470 376
In families	1 564 562	178 011	1 166 907	690 196	548 913	343 719
Percent with income in 1979 below poverty level	7.7	7.5	4.8	6.6	4.8	3.9
Householder or spouse	1 467 784	163 061	1 092 600	626 545	487 103	312 264
Other relatives	96 778	14 950	74 307	63 651	61 810	31 455
Nonrelatives in households	518 429	65 592	378 239	251 759	150 668	118 307
Living alone	484 808	60 450	353 310	233 516	142 407	110 684
Percent with income in 1979 below poverty level	26.6	28.0	19.6	24.5	21.6	19.7
In group quarters	36 260	6 193	29 048	24 855	7 487	8 350
Inmate of institution	32 081	4 609	22 677	17 086	6 205	6 005
Home for the aged	27 970	4 101	20 016	14 718	4 576	4 755
Other	4 179	1 584	6 371	7 769	1 282	2 345
Persons 75 years and over	1 509 553	179 565	1 227 806	650 343	366 049	214 799
In families	805 526	94 434	657 357	352 647	240 243	121 629
Percent with income in 1979 below poverty level	9.6	9.0	6.6	8.3	5.8	5.8
Householder or spouse	638 524	70 519	511 707	256 761	168 056	84 897
Other relatives	167 002	23 915	145 650	95 886	72 187	36 732
Nonrelatives in households	555 531	65 865	447 270	232 029	106 629	74 442
Living alone	524 113	62 019	425 049	219 012	101 831	70 474
Percent with income in 1979 below poverty level	31.7	33.0	26.9	30.4	27.6	27.0
In group quarters	148 496	19 266	123 179	65 667	19 177	18 728
Inmate of institution	137 573	17 440	111 952	58 012	18 019	16 892
Home for the aged	132 020	16 807	107 544	55 163	16 244	15 687
Other	10 923	1 826	11 227	7 655	1 158	1 836
PERSONS IN HOUSEHOLD						
Households	9 603 135	1 272 564	7 795 931	4 320 542	2 960 756	1 745 432
1 person	2 143 725	283 088	1 681 842	1 020 705	589 204	418 443
2 persons	3 295 698	397 038	2 612 630	1 392 941	959 264	595 140
3 persons	1 671 004	222 758	1 329 254	728 412	530 738	291 825
4 persons	1 446 438	198 515	1 228 422	622 724	477 656	244 629
5 persons	667 001	104 374	596 959	332 017	258 029	123 420
6 or more persons	379 269	66 791	346 824	223 743	145 865	71 975

Table 173. Fertility and Family Composition of Selected Ancestry Groups: 1980

[Data are estimates based on a sample; see Introduction. For meaning of symbols, see Introduction. For definitions of terms, see appendixes A and B]

United States	English	French	German	Irish	Italian	Polish
FERTILITY						
Women 15 to 24 years	1 855 625	269 621	1 450 139	848 472	515 085	234 131
Children ever born	655 748	96 953	425 806	245 844	93 612	50 258
Per 1,000 women	353	360	294	290	182	215
Women ever married	687 606	108 053	526 202	282 325	131 348	67 213
Children ever born	581 434	87 062	393 466	222 758	84 588	45 388
Per 1,000 women	846	806	748	789	644	675
Women 25 to 34 years	1 776 089	268 384	1 455 570	852 987	536 307	304 398
Children ever born	2 721 418	420 565	2 104 152	1 221 088	655 709	374 401
Per 1,000 women	1 532	1 567	1 446	1 432	1 223	1 230
Women ever married	1 580 712	240 337	1 288 852	732 546	443 550	251 963
Children ever born	2 677 013	415 510	2 086 291	1 207 305	649 239	370 036
Per 1,000 women	1 694	1 729	1 619	1 648	1 464	1 469
Women 35 to 44 years	1 427 318	202 723	1 105 140	671 186	407 303	223 610
Children ever born	3 651 399	567 006	2 861 494	1 786 747	962 072	537 558
Per 1,000 women	2 558	2 797	2 589	2 662	2 362	2 404
Women ever married	1 371 879	194 707	1 060 403	634 064	380 608	208 218
Children ever born	3 630 040	564 825	2 855 252	1 781 555	959 161	535 980
Per 1,000 women	2 646	2 901	2 693	2 810	2 520	2 574
HOUSEHOLD TYPE AND RELATIONSHIP						
Total persons	23 748 772	3 068 907	17 943 485	10 337 353	6 883 320	3 805 740
In households	23 187 187	2 986 744	17 464 044	10 036 664	6 761 865	3 722 598
Family householder: Male	6 245 274	812 837	5 212 294	2 667 121	1 973 836	1 101 573
Female	909 044	125 276	613 478	462 761	306 366	173 046
Nonfamily householder: Male	988 825	142 076	837 381	494 327	292 234	190 514
Female	1 459 992	192 375	1 132 778	696 333	388 320	280 299
Spouse	5 949 066	831 544	4 629 487	2 691 209	1 770 770	1 047 097
Child	6 310 238	685 814	4 080 011	2 336 109	1 600 917	698 928
Other relatives	785 667	98 524	487 331	383 309	284 007	142 088
Nonrelatives	539 081	98 298	471 284	305 495	145 415	89 053
Persons per household	2.64	2.75	2.70	2.69	2.79	2.61
Persons per family	3.12	3.27	3.19	3.23	3.25	3.13
FAMILY TYPE BY PRESENCE OF OWN CHILDREN						
Families	7 154 318	938 113	5 825 772	3 129 882	2 280 202	1 274 619
With own children under 18 years	3 373 902	491 668	2 854 607	1 509 326	1 015 787	524 864
With own children under 6 years	1 404 916	206 417	1 205 556	604 249	379 977	201 175
Married-couple families	6 236 111	805 190	5 175 656	2 643 906	1 959 729	1 093 033
With own children under 18 years	2 905 203	418 786	2 538 849	1 288 461	894 999	463 279
With own children under 6 years	1 263 212	183 365	1 113 162	543 193	351 480	186 701
Female householder, no husband present	717 014	103 199	482 891	378 681	241 248	136 432
With own children under 18 years	388 614	60 503	254 073	184 309	99 415	50 734
With own children under 6 years	119 572	19 209	75 737	51 721	24 074	12 129
Subfamilies	113 259	13 065	61 195	45 987	37 478	14 604
With own children under 18 years	85 561	8 927	41 699	33 543	20 479	8 524
Married-couple subfamilies	49 984	7 122	33 133	22 307	25 603	9 082
With own children under 18 years	22 286	2 984	13 637	9 863	8 604	3 002
Mother-child subfamilies	56 275	5 439	24 994	21 087	10 549	4 792
Persons under 18 years	5 306 807	567 894	3 321 382	1 819 347	1 054 521	466 986
Percent living with two parents	79.8	77.8	83.7	78.5	83.2	82.3
MARITAL HISTORY						
Ever-married persons 15 to 54 years	9 633 189	1 383 168	7 753 824	4 298 684	2 751 533	1 461 817
Never widowed or divorced	7 153 639	1 038 234	6 047 738	3 201 920	2 228 818	1 185 769
Known to have been: Widowed	263 892	37 823	174 399	127 321	68 451	41 708
Divorced	2 249 165	311 720	1 550 469	985 155	459 800	237 580
Widowed and divorced	33 507	4 609	18 782	15 712	5 536	3 240
LABOR FORCE STATUS OF FAMILY MEMBERS						
Families	7 154 318	938 113	5 825 772	3 129 882	2 280 202	1 274 619
Householder: Employed or in Armed Forces	5 205 600	698 044	4 426 397	2 267 415	1 647 635	907 366
Unemployed	200 091	32 049	162 796	94 717	70 514	38 556
Not in labor force	1 748 627	208 020	1 236 579	767 750	562 053	328 697
Married-couple families	6 236 111	805 190	5 175 656	2 643 906	1 959 729	1 093 033
Husband employed or in Armed Forces	4 710 853	624 669	4 046 441	2 007 328	1 482 734	814 624
Wife employed or in Armed Forces	2 434 182	321 906	2 141 487	1 044 838	715 105	414 980
Wife unemployed	109 496	16 403	93 039	49 179	37 732	21 543
Wife not in labor force	2 167 175	286 360	1 811 915	913 311	729 897	378 101
Husband unemployed	166 109	26 221	140 337	77 343	59 543	32 600
Wife employed or in Armed Forces	73 584	11 960	67 195	37 187	27 062	15 217
Wife unemployed	12 865	1 898	10 585	5 551	4 572	2 655
Wife not in labor force	79 660	12 363	62 557	34 605	27 909	14 728
Husband not in labor force	1 359 149	154 300	988 878	559 235	417 452	245 809
Wife employed or in Armed Forces	250 705	29 959	171 621	114 691	82 333	49 600
Wife unemployed	12 706	1 871	8 683	6 031	5 505	3 054
Wife not in labor force	1 095 738	122 470	808 574	438 513	329 614	193 155
Female householder, no husband present	717 014	103 199	482 891	378 681	241 248	136 432
Employed or in Armed Forces	385 173	55 934	280 906	201 048	124 047	69 005
Unemployed	27 089	4 429	16 669	13 424	8 312	4 265
Not in labor force	304 752	42 836	185 316	164 209	108 889	63 162
TYPE OF GROUP QUARTERS						
Persons in group quarters	561 585	82 163	479 441	300 689	121 455	83 142
Inmate of mental hospital	21 768	2 773	12 089	9 394	6 785	4 174
Inmate of home for the aged	181 252	23 775	140 533	79 276	25 006	24 458
Inmate of other institution	69 087	7 971	32 736	25 589	14 111	6 534
In military quarters	61 908	11 382	53 239	31 815	12 525	7 055
In college dormitory	183 968	26 167	193 578	112 494	51 433	28 600
Other, in group quarters	43 602	10 095	47 266	42 121	11 595	12 321

Table 174. **Geographical Mobility and Commuting of Selected Ancestry Groups: 1980**

[Data are estimates based on a sample; see Introduction. For meaning of symbols, see Introduction. For definitions of terms, see appendixes A and B]

United States	English	French	German	Irish	Italian	Polish
NATIVITY AND PLACE OF BIRTH						
Total persons	**23 748 772**	**3 068 907**	**17 943 485**	**10 337 353**	**6 883 320**	**3 805 740**
Native	23 075 325	2 853 663	17 088 469	10 050 701	6 008 966	3 386 649
Born in State of residence	15 541 682	1 985 855	11 905 398	6 706 367	4 516 105	2 485 101
Born in different State	7 427 635	849 461	5 109 517	3 314 524	1 466 420	892 918
Northeast	1 283 469	324 715	1 017 254	1 011 875	996 277	483 692
North Central	1 853 725	196 136	2 550 440	844 351	228 881	306 077
South	3 350 298	248 076	987 541	1 150 040	146 926	69 221
West	940 143	80 534	554 282	308 258	94 336	33 928
Born abroad, at sea, etc.	106 008	18 347	73 554	29 810	26 441	8 630
Foreign born	673 447	215 244	855 016	286 652	874 354	419 091
RESIDENCE IN 1975						
Persons 5 years and over	**22 547 664**	**2 952 618**	**17 189 247**	**9 985 026**	**6 685 447**	**3 725 841**
Same house	12 443 009	1 582 788	9 524 646	5 470 984	4 243 133	2 373 314
Different house in United States	9 896 803	1 332 824	7 526 006	4 453 223	2 389 999	1 315 711
Same county	5 398 767	763 881	4 012 753	2 374 871	1 369 545	744 531
Different county	4 498 036	568 943	3 513 253	2 078 352	1 020 454	571 180
Same State	2 307 225	289 196	1 850 958	1 059 138	542 985	288 200
In Armed Forces in 1975	20 807	3 084	17 186	10 039	3 506	1 900
Attending college in 1975	223 359	28 477	205 224	113 759	59 403	35 249
Different State	2 190 811	279 747	1 662 295	1 019 214	477 469	282 980
In Armed Forces in 1975	93 967	13 079	74 766	42 687	13 370	10 886
Attending college in 1975	220 718	26 873	197 950	114 296	58 238	38 275
Northeast	346 409	86 608	287 200	279 869	262 944	116 469
North Central	473 540	52 381	629 090	231 617	72 329	88 862
South	912 809	89 826	413 276	327 740	81 945	46 733
West	458 333	50 932	332 729	179 988	60 251	30 916
Abroad	207 852	37 006	138 595	60 819	52 315	36 816
In Armed Forces in 1975	32 773	4 817	29 970	14 828	5 116	3 822
Attending college in 1975	14 736	3 821	10 009	4 961	4 147	3 280
SELECTED CLASSES OF MIGRANTS						
Persons 16 years and over:						
Different county in 1975	3 810 448	504 551	3 109 959	1 840 291	921 859	525 629
In Armed Forces in 1980	129 062	21 384	110 615	63 236	23 286	15 207
Inmate of institution in 1980	79 959	9 109	49 737	33 623	12 557	7 473
Attending college in 1980	476 903	62 419	457 292	264 828	123 572	73 552
Living with at least one parent	26 108	1 793	14 715	12 053	8 044	3 255
Not living with any parent	450 795	60 626	442 577	252 775	115 528	70 297
Different State in 1975	1 849 045	248 707	1 467 101	898 864	433 627	260 578
In Armed Forces in 1980	116 486	19 486	100 887	57 445	21 388	14 287
Inmate of institution in 1980	20 012	2 637	12 331	9 408	3 173	1 855
Attending college in 1980	203 460	25 808	179 917	114 848	54 104	32 623
Living with at least one parent	13 777	1 065	7 367	6 523	3 418	1 596
Not living with any parent	189 683	24 743	172 550	108 325	50 686	31 027
MEANS OF TRANSPORTATION TO WORK						
Workers 16 years and over	**10 443 009**	**1 444 596**	**8 807 052**	**4 852 408**	**3 372 047**	**1 872 843**
Private vehicle	9 224 461	1 253 471	7 481 298	4 086 951	2 755 762	1 535 154
Drive alone: Car	5 767 762	766 437	4 737 669	2 648 517	1 940 561	1 062 248
Truck or van	1 407 552	188 444	1 119 729	515 489	221 108	130 246
Carpool: Car	1 632 214	238 792	1 332 070	767 163	531 828	307 730
Truck or van	416 933	59 798	291 830	155 782	62 265	34 930
Public transportation	295 513	47 439	286 641	309 904	344 904	173 055
Bus or streetcar	208 487	32 930	197 875	169 060	162 991	100 622
Subway or elevated train	44 542	9 171	44 025	84 442	128 059	46 622
Railroad	30 793	2 858	37 045	48 796	47 454	22 638
Taxicab	11 691	2 480	7 696	7 606	6 400	3 173
Bicycle	45 934	7 100	45 216	21 069	9 270	5 941
Motorcycle	48 556	8 316	44 340	20 567	8 906	4 347
Walked only	486 603	85 897	533 861	280 087	191 734	110 216
Other means	78 690	12 611	63 662	35 043	18 355	9 327
Worked at home	263 252	29 762	352 034	98 787	43 116	34 803
PRIVATE VEHICLE OCCUPANCY						
Workers 16 years and over using private vehicles	**9 224 461**	**1 253 471**	**7 481 298**	**4 086 951**	**2 755 762**	**1 535 154**
Drive alone	7 175 314	954 881	5 857 398	3 164 006	2 161 669	1 192 494
In 2-person carpool	1 418 085	207 850	1 150 085	655 815	430 427	246 269
In 3-person carpool	363 184	52 404	279 600	159 931	101 973	56 872
In 4-person carpool	155 301	21 910	116 363	64 214	38 584	24 169
In 5-or-more-person carpool	112 577	16 426	77 852	42 985	23 109	15 350
Persons per private vehicle	1.14	1.16	1.14	1.15	1.14	1.14
TRAVEL TIME TO WORK						
Workers 16 years and over who did not work at home	**10 213 987**	**1 420 412**	**8 477 789**	**4 768 680**	**3 330 843**	**1 844 282**
Less than 10 minutes	1 988 000	294 718	1 830 963	868 067	521 554	264 912
10 to 19 minutes	3 559 629	499 096	2 931 979	1 584 494	1 103 085	587 633
20 to 29 minutes	1 994 616	272 110	1 642 950	918 881	657 063	389 145
30 to 44 minutes	1 651 872	216 238	1 287 243	803 556	564 927	349 541
45 or more minutes	1 019 870	138 250	784 654	593 682	484 214	253 051
Mean minutes	20.6	20.3	19.9	22.1	23.4	23.5
Workers traveling 45 or more minutes minutes	59.7	61.1	59.4	60.3	60.5	58.9

Table 175. Educational Characteristics of Selected Ancestry Groups: 1980

[Data are estimates based on a sample; see Introduction. For meaning of symbols, see Introduction. For definitions of terms, see appendixes A and B]

United States

	English	French	German	Irish	Italian	Polish
SCHOOL ENROLLMENT AND TYPE OF SCHOOL						
Persons 3 years old and over enrolled in school	5 215 314	593 866	3 545 615	2 074 082	1 269 447	592 095
Nursery school	171 925	16 302	109 936	59 083	36 476	15 398
Public	56 081	6 169	36 772	17 866	11 356	4 825
Church-related	54 001	3 679	32 680	17 878	10 041	4 402
Other private	61 843	6 454	40 484	23 339	15 079	6 171
Kindergarten	263 785	25 632	153 820	82 030	44 355	20 022
Public	219 762	20 559	130 745	66 021	34 523	15 156
Church-related	27 577	3 241	17 509	11 541	7 898	4 029
Other private	16 446	1 832	5 566	4 468	1 934	837
Elementary (1 to 8 years)	2 416 462	257 740	1 480 969	835 704	487 645	216 571
Public	2 243 343	223 001	1 269 885	683 840	372 097	158 615
Church-related	117 525	30 326	196 856	139 650	108 783	55 023
Other private	55 594	4 413	14 228	12 214	6 765	2 933
High school (1 to 4 years)	1 282 474	152 438	873 438	510 615	325 914	141 803
Public	1 199 121	136 998	798 363	422 021	264 386	115 755
Church-related	46 921	12 125	64 673	77 224	53 797	22 667
Other private	36 432	3 315	10 402	11 370	7 731	3 381
College	1 080 668	141 754	927 452	586 650	375 057	198 301
Public	887 904	116 663	752 766	442 006	281 014	151 360
Persons 3 years old and over enrolled in school	5 215 314	593 866	3 545 615	2 074 082	1 269 447	592 095
3 and 4 years old	148 046	14 202	83 838	49 432	31 288	12 716
5 and 6 years old	431 667	43 630	258 583	138 798	79 972	35 862
7 to 13 years old	2 056 264	217 700	1 278 141	714 207	420 701	186 467
14 and 15 years old	658 356	77 122	426 020	254 677	155 897	66 630
16 and 17 years old	636 741	73 747	435 372	251 996	158 202	69 796
18 and 19 years old	379 443	47 653	308 018	183 539	117 519	51 778
20 and 21 years old	230 283	30 438	213 988	135 112	87 883	41 688
22 to 24 years old	182 028	24 990	162 159	101 353	65 219	33 641
25 to 34 years old	278 426	39 514	234 794	148 129	93 495	57 337
35 years old and over	214 060	24 870	144 702	96 839	59 271	36 180
Percent enrolled in school—						
3 and 4 years old	29.0	28.0	27.1	31.9	36.8	32.8
5 and 6 years old	83.7	85.6	83.6	86.3	90.7	88.5
7 to 13 years old	98.8	98.5	99.1	99.0	98.9	99.1
14 and 15 years old	97.3	97.2	98.2	97.9	98.4	98.6
16 and 17 years old	85.2	83.6	89.5	86.9	90.5	90.9
18 and 19 years old	48.0	44.5	52.1	53.2	56.2	56.8
20 and 21 years old	29.0	25.7	32.2	35.7	37.2	39.3
22 to 24 years old	15.6	13.6	15.9	17.6	18.1	19.2
25 to 34 years old	7.5	7.2	7.5	8.6	8.3	9.1
SCHOOL ENROLLMENT AND LABOR FORCE STATUS						
Persons 16 to 19 years old	1 537 893	195 243	1 077 879	634 878	383 793	167 916
Armed Forces	24 982	4 693	21 511	12 943	5 373	2 640
Civilian, enrolled in school	1 014 965	121 166	742 078	434 788	275 374	121 400
Employed	342 384	45 604	298 190	161 068	102 707	47 413
Unemployed	40 766	5 305	30 039	18 758	11 240	5 674
Not in labor force	631 815	70 257	413 849	254 962	161 427	68 313
Civilian, not enrolled in school	497 946	69 384	314 290	187 147	103 046	43 876
High school graduate	249 594	38 364	199 360	103 101	67 036	29 417
Employed	178 723	28 422	152 521	75 763	49 697	22 464
Unemployed	23 123	3 093	17 760	9 166	6 585	2 769
Not in labor force	47 748	6 849	29 079	18 172	10 754	4 184
Not high school graduate	248 352	31 020	114 930	84 046	36 010	14 459
Employed	100 848	14 347	53 570	35 753	16 698	6 383
Unemployed	35 010	4 446	17 534	13 788	5 400	2 539
Not in labor force	112 494	12 227	43 826	34 505	13 912	5 537
YEARS OF SCHOOL COMPLETED						
Male, 25 years old and over	7 522 193	975 208	6 162 090	3 346 908	2 472 455	1 413 839
Elementary: 0 to 4 years	251 248	35 723	84 781	86 430	95 819	34 056
5 to 7 years	535 591	85 696	306 730	211 597	190 321	93 941
8 years	597 491	95 072	672 407	273 270	221 189	141 966
High school: 1 to 3 years	1 073 230	149 845	787 632	485 618	407 016	221 878
4 years	2 267 025	320 041	2 164 958	1 078 094	785 379	448 936
College: 1 to 3 years	1 174 316	145 621	955 106	540 764	346 033	203 858
4 years	825 747	76 791	613 994	348 622	211 258	129 641
5 or more years	797 545	66 419	576 482	322 513	215 440	139 563
Percent high school graduates	67.3	62.4	70.0	68.4	63.0	65.2
Female, 25 years old and over	8 164 569	1 117 065	6 183 826	3 871 952	2 550 708	1 552 531
Elementary: 0 to 4 years	189 046	36 358	75 481	70 950	133 344	59 344
5 to 7 years	531 847	91 067	293 357	224 539	213 367	123 479
8 years	681 472	117 259	746 215	346 424	273 760	201 279
High school: 1 to 3 years	1 409 780	198 514	860 477	668 046	427 694	253 686
4 years	2 963 423	431 266	2 606 270	1 560 426	1 034 161	592 550
College: 1 to 3 years	1 269 861	147 266	896 903	555 295	252 538	169 320
4 years	696 830	59 681	439 938	266 619	122 017	83 647
5 or more years	421 706	35 654	265 185	179 653	93 827	69 226
Percent high school graduates	65.5	60.3	68.1	66.2	58.9	58.9
Persons 25 years old and over	15 686 762	2 092 273	12 345 916	7 218 860	5 023 163	2 966 370
Percent: Less than 5 years of elementary school	2.8	3.4	1.3	2.2	4.6	3.1
High school graduates	66.4	61.3	69.0	67.2	60.9	61.9
4 or more years of college	17.5	11.4	15.4	15.5	12.8	14.2
Median years of school completed	12.5	12.3	12.5	12.5	12.3	12.3
Persons 18 to 24 years old	2 755 203	408 740	2 276 187	1 299 146	805 636	372 384
Percent: High school graduates	74.1	77.4	83.2	80.4	84.2	85.8
4 or more years of college	6.0	5.2	7.1	7.5	8.5	9.7
Male, 18 to 24 years old	1 433 251	202 953	1 169 422	658 239	415 161	191 838
Percent: High school graduates	72.7	75.4	81.8	78.7	82.7	84.3
4 or more years of college	6.0	5.3	7.2	7.4	9.0	10.0
Female, 18 to 24 years old	1 321 952	205 787	1 106 765	640 907	390 475	180 546
Percent: High school graduates	75.5	79.5	84.7	82.0	85.8	87.5
4 or more years of college	6.1	5.2	7.1	7.5	8.1	9.3

Table 176. Labor Force Characteristics of Selected Ancestry Groups: 1980

[Data are estimates based on a sample; see Introduction. For meaning of symbols, see Introduction. For definitions of terms, see appendixes A and B]

United States	English	French	German	Irish	Italian	Polish
LABOR FORCE STATUS						
Persons 16 years and over	19 189 397	2 589 226	15 108 450	8 807 963	6 003 613	3 415 543
Labor force	11 304 268	1 574 871	9 472 220	5 277 552	3 671 551	2 040 213
Percent of persons 16 years and over	58.9	60.8	62.7	59.9	61.2	59.7
Armed Forces	169 486	26 599	140 393	80 174	29 297	19 007
Civilian labor force	11 134 782	1 548 272	9 331 827	5 197 378	3 642 254	2 021 206
Employed	10 533 050	1 458 415	8 874 549	4 902 405	3 435 377	1 908 699
Unemployed	601 732	89 857	457 278	294 973	206 877	112 507
Percent of civilian labor force	5.4	5.8	4.9	5.7	5.7	5.6
Not in labor force	7 885 129	1 014 355	5 636 230	3 530 411	2 332 062	1 375 330
Inmate of institution	261 562	33 496	181 371	111 470	44 311	34 466
Female, 16 years and over	9 848 145	1 366 207	7 525 525	4 653 713	3 026 496	1 770 178
Labor force	4 410 596	637 627	3 633 917	2 186 541	1 441 756	822 880
Percent of female, 16 years and over	44.8	46.7	48.3	47.0	47.6	46.5
Armed Forces	11 183	2 190	11 408	5 973	2 226	1 694
Civilian labor force	4 399 413	635 437	3 622 509	2 180 568	1 439 530	821 186
Employed	4 157 262	598 587	3 445 945	2 060 174	1 354 868	775 198
Unemployed	242 151	36 850	176 564	120 394	84 662	45 988
Percent of civilian labor force	5.5	5.8	4.9	5.5	5.9	5.6
Not in labor force	5 437 549	728 580	3 891 608	2 467 172	1 584 740	947 298
Inmate of institution	151 873	19 737	110 351	63 815	22 057	20 020
Male, 16 to 19 years	793 634	96 796	551 063	323 265	196 803	87 078
Employed	343 140	45 491	263 073	140 235	84 635	39 147
Unemployed	56 716	7 214	37 461	23 912	13 415	6 451
Not in labor force	370 671	39 923	230 984	147 234	93 774	39 171
Male, 20 to 24 years	1 025 425	151 015	869 772	484 077	307 859	144 448
Employed	728 849	111 097	642 235	344 388	219 350	102 451
Unemployed	80 730	11 174	63 823	37 644	24 511	12 004
Not in labor force	167 521	19 447	117 779	76 459	53 680	24 141
Male, 25 to 54 years	4 753 064	655 039	3 978 138	2 129 902	1 488 904	789 846
Employed	4 158 245	573 311	3 593 072	1 862 025	1 328 421	705 341
Unemployed	180 062	28 332	144 799	90 133	61 094	33 387
Not in labor force	329 309	42 532	177 571	141 568	87 842	42 148
Male, 55 to 64 years	1 305 190	155 756	996 503	592 657	509 713	341 198
Employed	883 521	105 046	719 484	392 808	362 733	236 184
Unemployed	30 767	4 844	24 924	17 033	16 901	11 257
Not in labor force	389 676	45 786	251 363	182 313	129 874	93 590
Male, 65 years and over	1 463 939	164 413	1 187 449	624 349	473 838	282 795
Employed	262 033	24 883	210 740	102 775	85 370	50 378
Unemployed	11 306	1 443	9 707	5 857	6 294	3 420
Not in labor force	1 190 403	138 087	966 925	515 665	382 152	228 982
Female, 16 to 19 years	744 259	98 447	526 816	311 613	186 990	80 838
Employed	278 815	42 882	241 208	132 349	84 467	37 113
Unemployed	42 183	5 630	27 872	17 800	9 810	4 531
Not in labor force	421 386	49 410	255 770	160 405	92 319	38 863
Female, 20 to 24 years	939 317	150 695	814 883	470 148	288 798	136 809
Employed	553 353	91 625	538 827	301 839	198 628	94 634
Unemployed	49 175	7 222	36 141	23 029	12 798	6 379
Not in labor force	332 549	50 768	234 592	142 688	76 375	35 117
Female, 25 to 54 years	4 572 963	666 602	3 574 067	2 195 278	1 415 131	773 631
Employed	2 647 007	379 480	2 154 734	1 288 225	807 500	464 375
Unemployed	123 781	19 742	92 445	64 397	44 532	24 477
Not in labor force	1 797 585	266 822	1 322 913	840 500	562 305	284 128
Female, 55 to 64 years	1 426 741	185 515	995 208	683 870	536 298	376 520
Employed	533 665	68 024	399 441	268 501	219 079	147 216
Unemployed	19 575	3 148	14 286	11 038	13 166	8 140
Not in labor force	873 110	114 316	581 356	404 176	304 012	221 138
Female, 65 years and over	2 164 865	264 948	1 614 551	992 804	599 279	402 380
Employed	144 422	16 576	111 735	69 260	45 194	31 860
Unemployed	7 437	1 108	5 820	4 130	4 356	2 461
Not in labor force	2 012 919	247 264	1 496 977	919 403	549 729	368 052
MARITAL STATUS AND PRESENCE OF OWN CHILDREN						
Female, 16 years and over	9 848 145	1 366 207	7 525 525	4 653 713	3 026 496	1 770 178
With own children under 6 years	1 361 816	204 865	1 087 876	612 158	343 126	188 289
In labor force	602 790	88 465	496 077	264 035	120 568	76 646
With own children 6 to 17 years only	1 858 866	284 514	1 452 550	906 612	563 810	297 590
In labor force	1 143 713	172 816	913 870	553 655	330 350	182 557
Married women 16 years and over, husband present	5 990 846	835 397	4 639 246	2 707 763	1 790 012	1 054 551
In labor force	2 751 262	390 180	2 255 838	1 266 342	809 292	481 143
With own children under 6 years	1 203 691	181 823	995 358	546 725	313 680	173 496
In labor force	511 373	75 875	435 655	225 630	105 320	68 626
With own children 6 to 17 years only	1 572 596	241 662	1 266 150	766 849	483 326	256 887
In labor force	924 882	140 707	761 018	446 378	270 300	151 046
CLASS OF WORKER						
Employed persons 16 years and over	10 533 050	1 458 415	8 874 549	4 902 405	3 435 377	1 908 699
Private wage and salary workers	7 790 533	1 137 975	6 677 442	3 708 074	2 630 029	1 505 543
Employees of own corporation	255 609	31 561	214 865	97 953	118 919	48 146
Federal government workers	382 356	46 224	274 457	184 408	114 676	64 498
State government workers	524 561	62 007	351 765	220 901	117 584	64 114
Local government workers	870 363	103 368	682 151	441 332	324 399	153 208
Self-employed workers	906 091	102 285	821 761	324 861	236 434	113 296
In agriculture	192 587	15 199	282 996	54 476	13 208	12 670
Unpaid family workers	59 146	6 556	66 973	22 829	12 255	8 040
In agriculture	16 198	1 059	31 721	4 502	738	1 608
Employed females 16 years and over	4 157 262	598 587	3 445 945	2 060 174	1 354 868	775 198
Private wage and salary workers	3 046 432	467 342	2 616 458	1 575 794	1 075 328	618 645
Employees of own corporation	42 492	5 553	32 646	15 684	14 179	7 617
Federal government workers	131 641	16 510	94 452	63 820	33 624	19 893
State government workers	256 996	31 262	171 743	109 624	53 720	30 871
Local government workers	490 603	54 615	365 239	223 720	144 229	75 514
Self-employed workers	191 261	23 879	153 989	70 604	39 446	24 383
Unpaid family workers	40 329	4 979	44 064	16 612	8 521	5 892

Table 177. Occupation of Employed Persons of Selected Ancestry Groups: 1980

[Data are estimates based on a sample; see Introduction. For meaning of symbols, see Introduction. For definitions of terms, see appendixes A and B]

United States

	English	French	German	Irish	Italian	Polish
Employed persons 16 years and over	10 533 050	1 458 415	8 874 549	4 902 405	3 435 377	1 908 699
Managerial and professional specialty occupations	2 572 967	287 725	2 047 112	1 187 069	798 460	450 031
Executive, administrative, and managerial occupations	1 214 954	146 282	987 340	582 363	414 500	203 666
Officials and administrators, public administration	45 836	4 660	30 974	23 243	12 787	5 942
Management related occupations	287 731	35 358	239 638	148 666	100 584	57 199
Professional specialty occupations	1 358 013	141 443	1 059 772	604 706	383 960	246 365
Engineers and natural scientists	253 428	27 990	223 218	91 013	71 283	56 136
Engineers	165 285	18 965	150 503	57 795	47 552	37 952
Health diagnosing occupations	70 816	5 488	51 515	23 277	23 433	17 690
Health assessment and treating occupations	155 820	22 387	157 303	103 121	49 161	36 836
Teachers, librarians, and counselors	557 111	54 201	404 574	230 580	149 019	80 710
Teachers, elementary and secondary schools	393 372	38 441	291 730	169 683	112 324	57 949
Technical, sales, and administrative support occupations	3 100 534	431 000	2 603 403	1 569 771	1 150 262	607 330
Health technologists and technicians	86 380	14 246	79 085	45 475	23 639	17 169
Technologists and technicians, except health	218 025	29 839	188 047	90 402	64 333	44 529
Sales occupations	1 135 090	148 907	899 562	531 311	391 219	189 913
Supervisors and proprietors, sales occupations	192 992	26 484	156 690	80 853	68 572	30 475
Sales representatives, commodities and finance	387 502	44 135	299 374	188 827	122 908	62 146
Other sales occupations	554 596	78 288	443 498	261 631	199 739	97 292
Cashiers	164 583	26 022	131 782	85 787	63 241	29 534
Administrative support occupations, including clerical	1 661 039	238 008	1 436 709	902 583	671 071	355 719
Computer equipment operators	37 266	5 920	34 579	20 021	14 839	8 931
Secretaries, stenographers, and typists	479 454	67 876	418 364	254 386	197 375	98 184
Financial records processing occupations	237 804	34 228	215 605	117 764	84 681	48 214
Mail and message distributing occupations	66 304	9 383	59 956	40 214	34 818	18 324
Service occupations	1 104 465	185 862	977 482	603 056	427 809	212 747
Private household occupations	41 514	6 048	32 575	16 305	5 917	5 005
Protective service occupations	147 361	22 122	119 703	111 138	66 429	33 154
Police and firefighters	58 790	9 205	52 956	52 431	32 121	15 269
Service occupations, except protective and household	915 590	157 692	825 204	475 613	355 463	174 588
Food service occupations	368 031	67 764	357 912	211 013	155 116	69 296
Cleaning and building service occupations	230 669	37 404	203 887	110 337	80 060	56 581
Farming, forestry, and fishing occupations	362 583	34 053	440 141	111 056	34 227	25 392
Farm operators and managers	198 842	15 553	293 054	55 019	11 147	12 390
Farm workers and related occupations	134 214	13 967	135 181	47 398	20 454	11 579
Precision production, craft, and repair occupations	1 475 470	235 338	1 295 482	639 837	477 535	268 676
Mechanics and repairers	448 791	67 527	399 370	187 576	126 521	78 313
Construction trades	512 709	82 575	433 597	237 132	161 006	71 430
Precision production occupations	461 598	77 501	438 319	198 704	186 570	116 277
Operators, fabricators, and laborers	1 917 031	284 437	1 510 929	791 616	547 084	344 523
Machine operators and tenders, except precision	648 831	97 652	484 716	243 015	189 614	132 598
Fabricators, assemblers, inspectors, and samplers	329 712	55 049	274 662	136 012	90 112	71 059
Transportation occupations	372 671	55 278	310 436	173 801	106 488	51 075
Motor vehicle operators	338 181	47 970	284 954	156 052	99 951	46 834
Material moving equipment operators	129 171	17 857	102 521	53 721	27 350	18 442
Handlers, equipment cleaners, helpers, and laborers	436 646	58 601	338 594	185 067	133 520	71 349
Construction laborers	69 694	9 417	49 837	28 643	22 804	7 105
Freight, stock, and material handlers	121 336	16 709	96 435	56 799	43 670	20 885
Employed females 16 years and over	4 157 262	598 587	3 445 945	2 060 174	1 354 868	775 198
Managerial and professional specialty occupations	946 688	111 874	738 556	472 697	258 691	159 071
Executive, administrative, and managerial occupations	323 058	43 398	254 998	166 353	99 924	54 121
Officials and administrators, public administration	12 591	1 343	8 408	6 279	2 801	1 556
Management related occupations	95 543	13 319	79 186	50 387	31 195	18 193
Professional specialty occupations	623 630	68 476	483 558	306 344	158 767	104 950
Engineers and natural scientists	18 451	2 174	17 038	9 039	5 423	4 929
Engineers	5 506	762	5 059	2 585	1 381	1 149
Health diagnosing occupations	6 056	509	5 155	2 340	1 525	1 709
Health assessment and treating occupations	130 450	18 857	136 796	92 825	38 953	30 475
Teachers, librarians, and counselors	366 757	35 520	250 644	152 513	86 100	49 057
Teachers, elementary and secondary schools	284 849	27 064	196 132	120 739	69 946	38 423
Technical, sales, and administrative support occupations	1 881 340	276 071	1 611 182	989 736	701 670	378 010
Health technologists and technicians	71 656	11 941	66 414	38 934	18 927	14 192
Technologists and technicians, except health	45 420	6 146	38 952	21 813	12 121	9 048
Sales occupations	494 430	72 646	396 805	239 966	169 844	89 209
Supervisors and proprietors, sales occupations	50 742	7 489	38 805	22 360	14 288	7 942
Sales representatives, commodities and finance	88 849	12 106	67 730	45 358	28 026	15 659
Other sales occupations	354 839	53 051	290 270	172 248	127 530	65 608
Cashiers	138 131	22 419	112 035	71 629	49 721	24 895
Administrative support occupations, including clerical	1 269 834	185 338	1 109 011	689 023	500 778	265 561
Computer equipment operators	20 898	3 420	20 433	11 827	8 115	4 891
Secretaries, stenographers, and typists	471 720	66 866	412 408	250 605	194 331	96 800
Financial records processing occupations	208 813	30 746	190 884	103 459	73 001	42 070
Mail and message distributing occupations	18 730	2 816	17 160	9 576	5 713	3 878
Service occupations	659 237	111 671	599 288	337 319	204 370	119 898
Private household occupations	39 176	5 793	31 310	15 536	5 429	4 803
Protective service occupations	13 402	2 136	11 080	9 599	6 435	3 315
Police and firefighters	1 890	310	1 603	1 425	791	486
Service occupations, except protective and household	606 659	103 742	556 898	312 184	192 506	111 780
Food service occupations	267 063	48 037	264 733	149 225	94 225	50 083
Cleaning and building service occupations	72 306	11 642	66 665	33 387	17 870	21 947
Farming, forestry, and fishing occupations	43 590	4 459	57 174	14 694	3 681	4 449
Farm operators and managers	17 392	1 489	24 922	5 229	861	1 648
Farm workers and related occupations	25 050	2 773	31 637	9 060	2 623	2 714
Precision production, craft, and repair occupations	98 661	16 552	78 884	42 618	33 660	18 124
Mechanics and repairers	12 932	1 996	9 444	5 887	2 963	2 048
Construction trades	9 580	1 547	6 965	4 158	1 789	1 011
Precision production occupations	75 201	12 869	61 956	32 312	28 818	15 018
Operators, fabricators, and laborers	527 746	77 960	360 861	203 110	152 796	95 646
Machine operators and tenders, except precision	276 797	37 178	164 201	94 849	81 806	44 581
Fabricators, assemblers, inspectors, and samplers	127 474	22 254	95 491	53 752	37 833	28 573
Transportation occupations	31 517	4 798	26 142	14 825	5 459	3 370
Motor vehicle operators	31 006	4 700	25 750	14 558	5 364	3 296
Material moving equipment operators	5 940	931	5 025	2 616	1 743	935
Handlers, equipment cleaners, helpers, and laborers	86 018	12 799	70 002	37 068	25 955	18 187
Construction laborers	2 027	333	1 323	661	405	135
Freight, stock, and material handlers	20 116	3 027	16 093	9 240	5 128	3 131

Table 178. Industry of Employed Persons of Selected Ancestry Groups: 1980

[Data are estimates based on a sample; see Introduction. For meaning of symbols, see Introduction. For definitions of terms, see appendixes A and B]

United States	English	French	German	Irish	Italian	Polish
Employed persons 16 years and over	**10 533 050**	**1 458 415**	**8 874 549**	**4 902 405**	**3 435 377**	**1 908 699**
Agriculture	356 873	31 382	447 637	107 357	30 167	23 991
Forestry and fisheries	23 332	3 941	12 020	7 411	3 197	1 314
Mining	169 152	26 691	90 897	54 466	13 877	10 037
Construction	695 338	105 275	566 357	308 356	208 802	83 846
Manufacturing	2 396 798	357 588	2 072 611	996 857	757 457	558 430
Nondurable goods	1 005 776	136 988	718 311	397 599	297 507	179 556
Food and kindred products	152 191	19 590	166 831	64 659	46 594	31 465
Textile mill and finished textile products	338 917	27 704	123 364	98 102	87 131	35 130
Printing, publishing, and allied industries	150 161	19 839	146 162	82 735	66 052	37 420
Chemicals and allied products	144 100	22 426	110 859	64 569	48 588	33 781
Durable goods	1 391 022	220 600	1 354 300	599 258	459 950	378 874
Furniture, lumber, and wood products	180 801	18 187	112 508	53 767	19 810	14 574
Primary metal industries	121 651	16 170	132 561	57 008	46 065	43 907
Fabricated metal industries, including ordnance	137 154	24 460	148 636	64 127	50 932	47 570
Machinery, except electrical	272 878	48 864	334 289	125 580	94 847	84 541
Electrical machinery, equipment, and supplies	221 913	34 965	207 052	102 086	85 237	61 570
Transportation equipment	250 905	41 007	226 135	103 009	72 320	72 096
Transportation, communications, and other public utilities	755 791	103 500	639 586	409 664	269 090	134 022
Railroads	68 400	8 202	60 969	35 848	17 704	11 078
Trucking service and warehousing	177 916	23 482	160 056	86 788	52 686	27 852
Other transportation	194 247	32 055	161 679	117 784	102 480	44 169
Communications	152 456	19 843	126 101	91 700	46 603	26 324
Utilities and sanitary services	162 772	19 918	130 781	77 544	49 617	24 599
Wholesale trade	463 722	62 154	419 568	218 441	160 236	90 045
Retail trade	1 633 455	245 157	1 387 618	777 867	626 103	289 157
General merchandise stores	206 322	30 460	177 462	104 277	82 133	45 807
Food, bakery, and dairy stores	262 137	40 407	219 155	127 294	119 852	49 218
Automotive dealers and gasoline stations	242 790	32 814	193 699	98 276	64 190	27 894
Eating and drinking places	354 060	63 061	332 972	203 048	162 467	64 756
Finance, insurance, and real estate	642 097	81 598	518 964	341 454	257 381	118 171
Banking and credit agencies	236 533	31 719	200 456	123 543	96 904	43 825
Insurance, real estate, and other finance	405 564	49 879	318 508	217 911	160 477	74 346
Services	2 859 260	373 120	2 323 908	1 379 270	923 493	506 657
Business services	263 483	34 925	215 582	138 084	101 677	59 131
Repair services	152 097	23 239	132 730	62 764	49 374	23 057
Private households	51 408	7 334	38 882	20 519	7 736	6 248
Other personal services	233 847	37 519	190 146	107 483	107 701	37 821
Entertainment and recreation services	96 883	13 901	76 090	50 602	43 077	17 502
Professional and related services	2 061 542	256 202	1 670 478	999 818	613 928	362 898
Hospitals	381 008	59 282	341 245	224 812	123 084	84 323
Health services, except hospitals	281 007	41 072	251 836	137 305	85 094	52 617
Elementary and secondary schools and colleges	897 042	100 618	695 256	398 479	264 038	139 998
Other educational services	40 325	4 261	28 948	16 262	11 298	5 996
Social services, religious and membership organizations	227 052	25 561	180 003	112 293	55 190	33 490
Legal, engineering, and other professional services	235 108	25 408	173 190	110 667	75 224	46 474
Public administration	537 232	68 009	395 383	301 262	185 574	93 029
Employed females 16 years and over	**4 157 262**	**598 587**	**3 445 945**	**2 060 174**	**1 354 868**	**775 198**
Agriculture	55 556	5 535	67 615	18 641	5 163	5 394
Forestry and fisheries	3 504	548	2 316	1 285	553	210
Mining	15 536	3 004	9 829	6 083	1 899	1 146
Construction	52 767	7 844	43 388	24 317	15 039	7 341
Manufacturing	736 848	111 192	559 376	315 371	252 198	159 126
Nondurable goods	410 818	50 384	258 485	156 991	129 985	69 393
Food and kindred products	43 946	5 509	43 926	18 471	13 088	9 918
Textile mill and finished textile products	212 389	16 771	80 350	62 860	60 367	22 011
Printing, publishing, and allied industries	59 577	7 956	57 036	31 303	23 908	14 189
Chemicals and allied products	32 256	4 768	26 687	17 606	16 505	9 763
Durable goods	326 030	60 808	300 891	158 380	122 213	89 733
Furniture, lumber, and wood products	37 039	3 741	23 657	11 878	3 718	3 340
Primary metal industries	14 137	2 328	16 330	7 544	6 239	5 210
Fabricated metal industries, including ordnance	27 902	5 485	29 997	14 597	11 980	10 916
Machinery, except electrical	52 121	11 040	58 465	28 202	20 927	15 351
Electrical machinery, equipment, and supplies	87 584	16 204	75 869	42 941	32 981	22 962
Transportation equipment	39 599	6 689	34 862	19 096	11 948	11 853
Transportation, communications, and other public utilities	161 972	23 559	136 963	95 700	54 714	32 328
Railroads	4 071	427	3 953	2 881	1 340	1 146
Trucking service and warehousing	20 436	3 007	19 277	10 336	6 322	4 024
Other transportation	52 218	8 185	45 893	29 267	20 264	10 763
Communications	60 167	8 802	48 286	40 900	20 189	12 465
Utilities and sanitary services	25 080	3 138	19 554	12 316	6 599	3 930
Wholesale trade	111 777	16 132	100 511	56 529	43 510	25 302
Retail trade	813 078	128 029	704 523	407 339	286 532	150 985
General merchandise stores	143 969	22 075	124 845	74 537	59 174	33 047
Food, bakery, and dairy stores	120 405	19 401	102 548	61 269	45 823	23 184
Automotive dealers and gasoline stations	38 804	6 049	30 983	17 731	8 610	4 619
Eating and drinking places	225 986	39 582	216 279	127 637	79 076	40 594
Finance, insurance, and real estate	334 828	48 994	289 890	186 772	140 913	69 160
Banking and credit agencies	152 164	22 744	135 323	82 213	64 984	30 362
Insurance, real estate, and other finance	182 664	26 250	154 567	104 559	75 929	38 798
Services	1 673 319	228 330	1 387 841	843 044	492 626	292 400
Business services	105 356	15 135	89 875	59 532	43 115	26 750
Repair services	16 254	2 673	14 700	8 237	5 211	2 724
Private households	45 581	6 668	35 717	18 302	6 420	5 610
Other personal services	152 381	24 302	126 172	69 634	51 342	23 183
Entertainment and recreation services	37 634	5 860	31 149	20 701	14 133	7 107
Professional and related services	1 316 113	173 692	1 090 228	666 638	372 405	227 026
Hospitals	289 139	45 089	268 175	177 830	87 399	63 690
Health services, except hospitals	206 757	33 077	195 196	108 099	57 337	35 421
Elementary and secondary schools and colleges	574 983	64 909	432 645	259 930	157 445	86 412
Other educational services	29 082	2 884	20 762	11 478	6 906	3 917
Social services, religious and membership organizations	129 009	16 218	104 209	65 627	32 889	19 771
Legal, engineering, and other professional services	87 143	11 515	69 241	43 674	30 429	17 815
Public administration	198 077	25 420	143 693	105 093	61 721	31 806

Table 179. **Labor Force Status in 1979 and Disability and Veteran Status of Selected Ancestry Groups: 1980**

[Data are estimates based on a sample; see Introduction. For meaning of symbols, see Introduction. For definitions of terms, see appendixes A and B]

United States	English	French	German	Irish	Italian	Polish
LABOR FORCE STATUS IN 1979						
Male, 16 years and over, in labor force in 1979	**7 390 335**	**991 427**	**6 231 210**	**3 313 409**	**2 351 734**	**1 290 926**
Worked in 1979	7 321 976	982 350	6 189 580	3 278 674	2 323 527	1 276 670
50 to 52 weeks	5 077 774	683 803	4 440 988	2 257 009	1 638 109	921 047
48 to 49 weeks	294 085	40 967	242 003	128 872	90 293	50 061
40 to 47 weeks	567 744	78 384	465 551	261 521	184 727	97 258
27 to 39 weeks	451 012	62 880	358 649	209 345	142 664	72 883
14 to 26 weeks	491 668	64 848	368 221	227 406	151 552	75 143
1 to 13 weeks	439 693	51 468	314 168	194 521	116 182	60 278
Usually worked 35 or more hours per week	6 467 644	882 250	5 527 225	2 908 321	2 049 104	1 142 223
50 to 52 weeks	4 799 715	649 636	4 207 699	2 136 017	1 542 312	874 200
27 to 49 weeks	1 065 387	152 542	873 620	489 699	334 562	179 442
1 to 26 weeks	602 542	80 072	445 906	282 605	172 230	88 581
With unemployment in 1979	1 103 530	160 259	866 329	541 341	367 035	192 527
Percent of those in labor force in 1979	14.9	16.2	13.9	16.3	15.6	14.9
Unemployed 1 to 4 weeks	327 004	46 001	271 476	149 703	86 814	52 377
Unemployed 5 to 14 weeks	386 346	56 253	311 967	189 255	129 435	66 465
Unemployed 15 or more weeks	390 180	58 005	282 886	202 383	150 786	73 685
Mean weeks of unemployment	14.1	14.2	13.2	14.7	15.6	15.0
Female, 16 years and over, in labor force in 1979	**5 072 446**	**725 700**	**4 151 065**	**2 489 276**	**1 592 248**	**910 557**
Worked in 1979	4 980 565	712 817	4 094 259	2 447 727	1 561 525	893 390
50 to 52 weeks	2 563 817	372 200	2 188 300	1 296 404	857 733	510 417
48 to 49 weeks	188 931	27 310	155 143	92 106	60 312	35 657
40 to 47 weeks	516 581	69 377	416 534	253 040	172 282	93 677
27 to 39 weeks	540 158	75 970	436 692	251 789	150 652	81 267
14 to 26 weeks	583 312	86 170	464 148	284 881	173 854	91 957
1 to 13 weeks	587 766	81 790	433 442	269 507	146 692	80 415
Usually worked 35 or more hours per week	3 493 067	489 026	2 727 802	1 689 160	1 024 174	598 799
50 to 52 weeks	2 098 138	297 202	1 708 712	1 048 721	665 270	400 345
27 to 49 weeks	805 309	107 699	598 277	365 780	214 779	121 181
1 to 26 weeks	589 620	84 125	420 813	274 659	144 125	77 273
With unemployment in 1979	838 045	128 354	656 702	422 781	288 993	155 862
Percent of those in labor force in 1979	16.5	17.7	15.8	17.0	18.1	17.1
Unemployed 1 to 4 weeks	302 002	44 615	251 146	149 093	83 004	49 311
Unemployed 5 to 14 weeks	270 200	40 507	211 095	137 220	98 595	51 390
Unemployed 15 or more weeks	265 843	43 232	194 461	136 468	107 394	55 161
Mean weeks of unemployment	13.3	13.8	12.4	13.4	14.7	14.3
WORKERS IN FAMILY IN 1979						
Families	**7 154 318**	**938 113**	**5 825 772**	**3 129 882**	**2 280 202**	**1 274 619**
No workers	1 025 692	119 183	715 639	421 337	303 057	174 991
1 worker	2 389 621	308 453	1 826 111	1 013 300	755 455	415 305
2 workers	2 947 488	390 284	2 520 940	1 269 471	858 153	498 465
3 or more workers	791 517	120 193	763 082	425 774	363 537	185 858
Married-couple families	**6 236 111**	**805 190**	**5 175 656**	**2 643 906**	**1 959 729**	**1 093 033**
No workers	840 056	93 341	612 007	328 696	246 774	143 497
1 worker	1 940 526	243 155	1 509 453	788 217	612 414	333 219
2 workers	2 725 694	358 809	2 343 739	1 144 337	769 914	446 935
Husband and wife worked	2 386 054	311 197	2 049 123	983 168	613 906	369 218
3 or more workers	729 835	109 885	710 457	382 656	330 627	169 382
Husband and wife worked	623 050	90 317	591 417	307 963	253 750	134 805
Female householder, no husband present	**717 014**	**103 199**	**482 891**	**378 681**	**241 248**	**136 432**
No workers	160 182	22 501	85 430	78 601	46 342	25 472
1 worker	350 596	50 784	239 199	176 477	107 675	62 205
2 workers	158 582	22 036	119 754	89 763	62 790	36 363
3 or more workers	47 654	7 878	38 508	33 840	24 441	12 392
WORK DISABILITY STATUS OF NONINSTITUTIONAL PERSONS						
Male, 16 to 64 years	**7 809 902**	**1 050 614**	**6 362 045**	**3 502 790**	**2 489 494**	**1 355 321**
With a work disability	770 670	104 328	507 414	359 150	217 615	125 804
Not in labor force	409 162	52 064	225 972	192 140	117 928	68 335
Prevented from working	357 883	45 830	193 563	169 966	105 950	60 715
Female, 16 to 64 years	**7 658 783**	**1 097 584**	**5 897 663**	**3 651 648**	**2 420 915**	**1 363 478**
With a work disability	643 884	91 572	372 819	314 534	168 694	109 384
Not in labor force	497 163	68 575	266 332	239 636	129 126	84 072
Prevented from working	402 856	55 175	203 541	196 597	109 115	68 872
PUBLIC TRANSPORTATION DISABILITY STATUS OF NONINSTITUTIONAL PERSONS						
Persons 16 to 64 years	**15 468 685**	**2 148 418**	**12 259 708**	**7 154 438**	**4 910 409**	**2 718 799**
With a public transportation disability	295 636	38 870	156 488	140 858	96 776	55 820
With a work disability	274 167	35 774	143 396	130 819	89 290	50 527
Persons 65 years and over	**3 459 150**	**407 312**	**2 667 371**	**1 542 055**	**1 048 893**	**662 278**
With a public transportation disability	531 783	63 002	355 346	248 327	140 948	92 134
VETERAN STATUS OF CIVILIANS						
Male veterans	**3 369 480**	**450 942**	**2 776 953**	**1 653 491**	**1 103 410**	**677 537**
Percent of civilian males 16 years and over	36.7	37.6	37.3	40.5	37.4	41.6
Female veterans	**119 888**	**16 631**	**85 395**	**62 136**	**29 173**	**23 468**
Percent of civilian females 16 years and over	1.2	1.2	1.1	1.3	1.0	1.3
PERIOD OF SERVICE						
Civilian veterans 16 years and over	**3 489 368**	**467 573**	**2 862 348**	**1 715 627**	**1 132 583**	**701 005**
Percent of civilians 16 years and over	18.3	18.2	19.1	19.7	19.0	20.6
May 1975 or later only	90 785	14 521	72 376	42 705	19 414	10 391
Vietnam era	799 098	122 176	733 104	395 527	203 113	133 462
February 1955 to July 1964 only	360 416	53 952	341 279	184 714	113 488	66 959
Vietnam era and Korean conflict	98 979	10 649	55 491	39 043	11 779	9 522
Korean conflict	480 184	67 986	428 083	247 136	171 276	91 049
Korean conflict and World War II	115 581	12 319	68 006	53 556	22 963	16 567
World War II	1 395 734	168 764	1 058 593	692 746	551 795	351 974
World War I	84 337	8 987	64 136	33 116	19 198	8 898
Other	64 476	8 219	41 280	27 084	19 557	12 183
Civilian nonveterans 16 years and over	**15 530 543**	**2 095 054**	**12 105 709**	**7 012 162**	**4 841 733**	**2 695 531**

Table 180. Income Characteristics in 1979 of Selected Ancestry Groups: 1980

[Data are estimates based on a sample; see Introduction. For meaning of symbols, see Introduction. For definitions of terms, see appendixes A and B]

United States	English	French	German	Irish	Italian	Polish
INCOME IN 1979						
Households	**9 603 135**	**1 272 564**	**7 795 931**	**4 320 542**	**2 960 756**	**1 745 432**
Less than $5,000	1 276 477	173 509	817 125	550 429	309 053	193 812
$5,000 to $7,499	786 135	105 542	578 571	350 374	211 918	125 643
$7,500 to $9,999	759 902	101 305	573 344	332 282	204 819	121 124
$10,000 to $14,999	1 476 097	195 645	1 159 839	640 509	415 886	240 074
$15,000 to $19,999	1 342 396	185 242	1 135 467	601 073	415 291	237 815
$20,000 to $24,999	1 172 055	165 622	1 052 215	539 446	395 366	226 431
$25,000 to $34,999	1 479 521	200 589	1 360 674	701 462	538 887	319 744
$35,000 to $49,999	829 028	99 013	743 833	396 926	312 784	186 912
$50,000 or more	481 524	46 097	374 863	208 041	156 752	91 877
Median	$16 746	$16 522	$18 307	$17 256	$19 026	$19 009
Mean	$20 606	$19 419	$21 411	$20 669	$21 989	$22 048
Families	**7 154 318**	**938 113**	**5 825 772**	**3 129 882**	**2 280 202**	**1 274 619**
Less than $5,000	481 938	60 118	264 781	181 507	103 515	49 330
$5,000 to $7,499	456 913	61 250	298 733	187 333	119 033	58 439
$7,500 to $9,999	504 254	66 410	356 242	207 754	134 731	71 468
$10,000 to $14,999	1 084 745	142 851	821 263	445 560	303 056	163 419
$15,000 to $19,999	1 089 239	150 980	911 996	470 468	338 797	185 357
$20,000 to $24,999	1 012 498	143 877	912 090	456 563	347 519	195 737
$25,000 to $34,999	1 332 304	181 151	1 233 389	627 851	495 539	291 279
$35,000 to $49,999	757 704	90 280	685 159	363 484	293 202	174 642
$50,000 or more	434 723	41 196	342 119	189 360	144 810	84 948
Median	$19 807	$19 564	$21 294	$20 719	$21 842	$22 588
Mean	$23 452	$22 175	$24 372	$23 883	$24 835	$25 734
Unrelated individuals 15 years and over	**3 231 913**	**473 617**	**2 708 627**	**1 665 327**	**894 421**	**604 029**
Less than $2,000	417 475	63 094	319 616	210 165	104 565	64 723
$2,000 to $2,999	298 130	41 887	210 795	146 702	60 587	40 658
$3,000 to $4,999	584 613	95 440	489 731	314 268	174 012	121 974
$5,000 to $7,999	541 096	83 067	479 947	286 113	150 386	104 561
$8,000 to $9,999	274 057	41 522	243 508	140 042	74 981	50 549
$10,000 to $14,999	495 007	71 769	442 308	258 745	146 312	96 647
$15,000 to $24,999	431 253	56 504	380 616	227 798	134 294	92 339
$25,000 to $49,999	157 477	17 364	120 994	69 941	42 098	28 328
$50,000 or more	32 805	2 970	21 112	11 553	7 186	4 250
Median	$6 629	$6 195	$6 954	$6 556	$7 016	$7 008
Mean	$9 582	$8 659	$9 538	$9 180	$9 678	$9 690
Males 15 years and over, with income	**8 949 067**	**1 178 103**	**7 384 226**	**4 000 477**	**2 850 846**	**1 593 881**
Median income	$12 598	$12 661	$13 907	$12 885	$14 057	$14 905
Percent year-round full-time workers	53.6	55.1	56.9	53.4	54.1	54.8
Median income	$17 594	$16 974	$18 191	$18 169	$18 940	$19 776
Females 15 years and over, with income	**7 576 721**	**1 038 670**	**5 904 300**	**3 629 991**	**2 301 427**	**1 388 283**
Median income	$5 180	$4 940	$5 387	$5 291	$5 409	$5 585
Percent year-round full-time workers	27.5	28.5	28.7	28.8	28.8	28.7
Median income	$10 013	$9 817	$10 439	$10 568	$10 912	$11 295
Per capita income	**$8 242**	**$7 958**	**$9 069**	**$8 534**	**$9 126**	**$9 790**
Persons in households	$8 370	$8 093	$9 233	$8 696	$9 240	$9 944
Persons in group quarters	$2 949	$3 052	$3 117	$3 094	$2 781	$2 883
MEDIAN INCOME IN 1979 BY SELECTED CHARACTERISTICS						
Age of family householder:						
15 to 24 years	$12 778	$14 165	$15 072	$14 024	$15 572	$16 403
25 to 34 years	$19 218	$19 482	$20 733	$20 369	$21 303	$22 281
35 to 44 years	$23 679	$23 191	$25 093	$24 453	$24 797	$25 968
45 to 54 years	$26 056	$25 093	$27 690	$27 025	$27 851	$29 025
55 to 64 years	$21 516	$20 585	$23 185	$22 138	$23 470	$24 091
65 years and over	$12 121	$10 811	$12 651	$12 237	$12 932	$13 648
Family type by presence of own children:						
Families	$19 807	$19 564	$21 294	$20 719	$21 842	$22 588
With own children under 18 years	$20 716	$20 711	$22 284	$22 050	$23 091	$24 270
With own children under 6 years	$17 950	$18 134	$19 636	$19 483	$20 461	$21 490
Without own children under 18 years	$18 777	$17 998	$20 052	$19 151	$20 679	$21 298
Married-couple families	$21 027	$20 836	$22 152	$21 986	$22 907	$23 821
With own children under 18 years	$22 244	$22 259	$23 580	$23 886	$24 567	$25 640
With own children under 6 years	$19 171	$19 377	$20 402	$20 592	$21 161	$22 141
Without own children under 18 years	$19 569	$18 663	$20 519	$19 857	$21 302	$22 030
Female householder, no husband present	$10 387	$10 053	$12 050	$11 883	$13 239	$14 152
With own children under 18 years	$8 469	$8 170	$9 693	$9 327	$9 323	$10 294
With own children under 6 years	$5 279	$5 290	$6 374	$5 832	$5 428	$5 886
Without own children under 18 years	$13 209	$13 411	$15 653	$15 136	$16 479	$16 793
Workers in family in 1979:						
No workers	$8 594	$7 530	$9 474	$8 506	$8 623	$9 398
1 worker	$16 609	$16 141	$17 969	$17 274	$18 458	$19 306
2 workers	$22 953	$22 412	$23 728	$23 639	$24 946	$26 012
3 or more workers	$31 612	$31 253	$32 827	$33 672	$34 490	$35 489
Unrelated individuals:						
Male, 15 years and over	$8 766	$8 579	$9 150	$8 578	$9 565	$9 707
65 years and over	$5 435	$4 952	$5 990	$5 524	$5 781	$6 043
Female, 15 years and over	$5 442	$4 837	$5 732	$5 371	$5 613	$5 724
65 years and over	$4 705	$4 218	$4 867	$4 562	$4 528	$4 622
INCOME TYPE IN 1979						
Households	**9 603 135**	**1 272 564**	**7 795 931**	**4 320 542**	**2 960 756**	**1 745 432**
With earnings	7 576 475	1 020 894	6 350 566	3 429 712	2 391 319	1 371 614
Mean earnings	$20 972	$20 271	$21 694	$21 452	$22 572	$22 862
With wage or salary income	7 143 537	977 610	5 975 050	3 286 644	2 295 042	1 324 151
Mean wage or salary income	$19 942	$19 376	$20 668	$20 577	$21 592	$22 012
With nonfarm self-employment income	1 002 603	115 308	799 350	373 758	296 188	140 655
Mean nonfarm self-employment income	$13 646	$13 077	$12 894	$13 846	$14 278	$14 677
With farm self-employment income	457 095	33 273	496 301	129 777	27 028	26 213
Mean farm self-employment income	$6 039	$7 354	$7 992	$5 938	$7 204	$5 620
With interest, dividend, or net rental income	4 104 911	475 824	3 905 020	1 772 792	1 412 283	941 131
Mean interest, dividend, or net rental income	$3 747	$2 704	$3 032	$2 730	$2 752	$2 784
With Social Security income	2 862 199	342 260	2 193 715	1 291 432	887 060	569 635
Mean Social Security income	$4 142	$4 085	$4 305	$4 182	$4 386	$4 340
With public assistance income	622 216	95 098	351 210	282 757	169 816	88 597
Mean public assistance income	$2 291	$2 428	$2 410	$2 372	$2 629	$2 558
With all other income	2 303 726	298 616	1 821 476	1 130 229	758 306	472 043
Mean all other income	$4 481	$3 692	$3 856	$4 261	$3 827	$3 827

Table 181. Poverty Status in 1979 of Persons and Families of Selected Ancestry Groups: 1980

[Excludes inmates of institutions, persons in military group quarters and in college dormitories, and unrelated individuals under 15 years. Data are estimates based on a sample; see Introduction. For meaning of symbols, see Introduction. For definitions of terms, see appendixes A and B]

United States	English	French	German	Irish	Italian	Polish
ALL INCOME LEVELS IN 1979						
Families	7 154 318	938 113	5 825 772	3 129 882	2 280 202	1 274 619
With Social Security income	1 792 553	208 837	1 362 100	801 966	621 643	365 927
Income above poverty level	1 630 464	191 213	1 288 257	740 668	591 423	349 916
Below poverty level without Social Security income	486 544	63 761	370 780	215 425	162 484	90 049
With public assistance income	436 029	65 154	248 346	192 497	125 255	60 985
Income above poverty level	288 034	44 207	189 556	136 001	98 206	48 807
Below poverty level without public assistance income	61 538	9 623	32 525	27 700	17 263	7 634
Householder worked in 1979	5 621 569	753 013	4 760 592	2 448 436	1 762 022	978 717
With related children under 18 years	3 519 945	508 747	2 934 121	1 571 875	1 054 110	542 718
With related children 5 to 17 years	2 843 194	407 571	2 345 845	1 277 596	869 435	446 096
Female householder, no husband present	717 014	103 199	482 891	378 681	241 248	136 432
Householder worked in 1979	435 081	63 347	314 918	226 678	136 648	76 389
With related children under 18 years	435 265	65 902	275 476	206 143	110 936	57 084
With related children under 6 years	147 866	22 594	87 790	64 084	29 796	15 152
Householder 65 years and over	1 291 920	139 718	1 010 326	548 970	425 343	248 237
Unrelated individuals	2 986 615	436 186	2 462 401	1 521 385	830 602	568 449
With Social Security income	1 107 016	139 742	863 849	512 525	272 328	210 941
Income above poverty level	788 359	97 590	661 540	369 881	207 915	162 833
Below poverty level without Social Security income	442 549	65 311	381 138	227 400	135 647	104 444
With public assistance income	196 407	31 976	108 515	96 074	46 517	29 023
Income above poverty level	77 911	14 436	53 256	41 182	24 374	14 842
Below poverty level without public assistance income	46 110	8 719	29 175	24 830	15 338	8 916
Worked in 1979	1 735 846	270 320	1 558 664	942 614	520 015	335 546
65 years and over	1 088 636	134 771	842 631	498 544	259 713	196 847
Persons	23 185 904	2 990 163	17 485 002	10 061 894	6 766 498	3 731 181
Related children under 18 years	5 193 039	551 594	3 259 892	1 779 761	1 038 134	458 379
Related children 5 to 17 years	3 921 735	425 310	2 466 166	1 398 216	832 377	365 584
60 years and over	4 734 991	560 972	3 599 090	2 133 573	1 529 924	1 026 956
65 years and over	3 458 724	407 216	2 666 895	1 541 387	1 048 869	662 195
INCOME IN 1979 BELOW POVERTY LEVEL						
Families	591 705	75 430	324 907	220 225	123 102	57 204
Percent below poverty level	8.3	8.0	5.6	7.0	5.4	4.5
Mean income deficit	$2 886	$2 758	$2 890	$2 659	$2 760	$2 694
Persons per family	3.41	3.36	3.40	3.28	3.21	3.16
With Social Security income	162 089	17 624	73 843	61 298	30 220	16 011
With public assistance income	147 995	20 947	58 790	56 496	27 049	12 178
Householder worked in 1979	304 897	38 893	195 292	110 363	56 214	26 565
With related children under 18 years	384 233	51 989	213 041	141 649	76 931	33 595
With related children 5 to 17 years	301 982	40 176	163 839	111 873	60 915	26 668
Female householder, no husband present	184 453	27 750	88 818	76 410	42 512	19 430
Householder worked in 1979	78 140	12 280	44 723	33 329	15 760	7 221
With related children under 18 years	156 818	24 515	76 861	64 908	34 479	15 338
With related children under 6 years	78 331	11 886	38 413	30 245	14 604	6 748
Householder 65 years and over	115 837	12 307	58 542	43 594	23 709	11 595
Unrelated individuals	748 382	113 643	523 961	364 061	177 019	119 359
Percent below poverty level	25.1	26.1	21.3	23.9	21.3	21.0
Mean income deficit	$1 670	$1 713	$1 651	$1 651	$1 695	$1 655
With Social Security income	318 657	42 152	202 309	142 644	64 413	48 108
With public assistance income	118 496	17 540	55 259	54 892	22 143	14 181
Worked in 1979	250 224	42 365	222 808	138 191	65 718	40 265
65 years and over	320 343	42 568	205 855	142 294	63 747	46 653
Persons	2 626 209	321 210	1 422 984	967 201	492 638	260 654
Percent below poverty level	11.3	10.7	8.1	9.6	7.3	7.0
Related children under 18 years	764 418	74 853	323 470	207 234	97 858	39 022
Related children 5 to 17 years	548 797	54 796	229 305	153 966	74 579	29 183
60 years and over	646 184	80 691	369 289	273 034	137 378	91 683
65 years and over	518 478	64 368	305 481	216 649	104 019	67 192
INCOME IN 1979 BELOW 125 PERCENT OF POVERTY LEVEL						
Families	863 135	110 499	490 305	328 120	185 295	86 161
Percent below poverty level	12.1	11.8	8.4	10.5	8.1	6.8
Mean income deficit	$3 336	$3 232	$3 248	$3 097	$3 122	$3 064
Persons per family	3.36	3.35	3.36	3.25	3.19	3.14
With Social Security income	268 691	30 406	134 670	105 630	56 521	29 271
With public assistance income	189 936	27 005	78 795	74 444	36 421	16 710
Householder worked in 1979	465 992	60 035	299 370	171 154	88 098	40 929
With related children under 18 years	534 584	72 733	306 132	199 373	108 677	47 569
With related children 5 to 17 years	420 182	56 246	235 885	157 379	86 556	38 074
Female householder, no husband present	238 215	35 717	119 808	101 709	56 155	26 426
Householder worked in 1979	110 169	17 270	65 495	48 337	23 333	11 008
With related children under 18 years	194 348	30 389	99 861	82 169	43 440	19 932
With related children under 6 years	91 453	14 006	46 825	36 149	17 272	8 155
Householder 65 years and over	192 795	21 259	105 089	74 873	43 254	21 140
Unrelated individuals	1 008 421	158 241	741 773	505 597	257 722	176 996
Percent below poverty level	33.8	36.3	30.1	33.2	31.0	31.1
Mean income deficit	$2 041	$2 022	$1 953	$1 983	$1 948	$1 888
With Social Security income	496 868	71 918	350 569	235 677	121 145	90 656
With public assistance income	147 513	24 383	74 653	71 679	32 782	20 200
Worked in 1979	323 849	55 375	290 329	182 637	85 756	53 358
65 years and over	488 160	70 482	346 395	228 581	116 958	85 377
Persons	3 706 729	463 018	2 083 661	1 401 602	730 170	389 589
Percent below poverty level	16.0	15.5	11.9	13.9	10.8	10.4
Related children under 18 years	1 042 549	103 176	457 381	288 961	136 740	54 376
Related children 5 to 17 years	748 884	75 522	325 239	215 064	104 378	41 242
60 years and over	1 004 773	132 647	620 992	440 004	240 802	159 152
65 years and over	822 934	108 681	526 459	357 820	191 681	122 820
INCOME IN 1979 BELOW SPECIFIED POVERTY LEVEL						
Percent of persons:						
Below 75 percent of poverty level	7.4	6.9	5.2	6.0	4.6	4.4
Below 150 percent of poverty level	20.8	20.4	16.1	18.4	14.6	14.0
Below 200 percent of poverty level	30.9	30.8	25.4	27.8	23.3	21.9

Table 230. **Summary of Social Characteristics for Regions, Divisions, and States: 1980**

[Data are estimates based on a sample; see Introduction. For meaning of symbols, see Introduction. For definitions of terms, see appendixes A and B]

United States Regions and Divisions States	Total persons Number	Total persons Percent foreign born	Native persons— Percent born in State of residence	Persons 5 years and over Percent living in different house in 1975	Persons 5 years and over Percent who speak a language other than English at home	Persons 3 years old and over enrolled in kindergarten or elementary school— Percent in private school	Civilian persons 16 to 19 years old—Percent not enrolled in school, not high school graduates	Persons 18 to 24 years old— Percent enrolled in school	Persons 25 years old and over Percent high school graduates	Persons 25 years old and over Percent completed 4 or more years of college	Persons 60 years and over— Percent living alone	Families— Percent with own children under 6 years	Persons under 18— Percent living with two parents	Children ever born per 1,000 women 35 to 44 years
United States	226 545 805	6.2	68.2	46.4	11.0	11.8	13.4	31.8	66.5	16.2	24.2	22.3	76.7	2 639
REGIONS AND DIVISIONS														
Northeast Region	49 135 283	9.2	76.5	38.3	14.5	15.8	10.2	35.4	67.1	17.2	24.2	20.1	76.5	2 499
New England	12 348 493	7.8	71.4	40.9	13.0	10.9	10.0	37.3	70.5	19.2	24.1	20.1	79.1	2 555
Middle Atlantic	36 786 790	9.6	78.2	37.4	15.0	17.4	10.2	34.7	66.0	16.6	24.2	20.1	75.7	2 480
North Central Region	58 865 670	3.6	74.4	44.6	6.4	12.9	11.2	31.9	68.0	14.7	25.2	23.1	79.6	2 750
East North Central	41 682 217	4.2	75.0	44.0	7.2	13.6	11.7	31.6	67.3	14.5	24.7	22.9	78.2	2 736
West North Central	17 183 453	2.0	73.1	46.1	4.6	11.2	10.1	32.7	69.6	15.3	26.1	23.6	82.9	2 787
South Region	75 372 362	3.8	67.5	47.6	8.2	9.7	16.5	29.7	60.2	15.0	23.4	22.2	74.5	2 675
South Atlantic	36 959 123	4.7	60.2	47.3	6.2	10.2	15.5	30.2	61.3	15.7	22.6	20.4	73.0	2 565
East South Central	14 666 423	1.0	77.6	44.0	1.9	10.5	17.9	29.1	55.3	12.1	24.1	22.8	74.4	2 740
West South Central	23 746 816	4.3	72.3	50.4	15.5	8.4	17.1	29.2	61.5	15.5	24.5	24.8	76.6	2 813
West Region	43 172 490	10.6	50.7	56.2	17.9	9.6	14.5	31.4	74.5	19.3	24.0	24.0	76.7	2 596
Mountain	11 372 785	4.3	46.0	57.3	14.6	5.6	15.2	30.0	75.2	18.8	23.2	26.2	80.5	2 845
Pacific	31 799 705	12.8	52.5	55.8	19.1	11.1	14.3	31.9	74.3	19.4	24.3	23.2	75.2	2 510
STATES														
New England Division														
Maine	1 124 660	3.9	75.7	43.1	10.8	5.4	10.6	30.0	68.7	14.4	24.2	22.0	80.6	2 813
New Hampshire	920 610	4.4	51.6	48.4	10.4	11.0	11.6	33.9	72.3	18.2	23.4	22.3	82.7	2 632
Vermont	511 456	4.1	64.2	45.6	6.6	6.2	9.0	36.8	71.0	19.0	24.5	23.3	81.2	2 730
Massachusetts	5 737 037	8.7	78.6	39.0	13.0	10.9	8.8	40.4	72.2	20.0	24.9	19.7	78.4	2 531
Rhode Island	947 154	8.9	74.0	39.5	16.5	16.3	13.9	38.2	61.1	15.4	24.8	19.5	78.4	2 585
Connecticut	3 107 576	8.6	63.2	41.0	14.3	12.2	10.4	34.5	70.3	20.7	22.3	19.1	78.6	2 458
Middle Atlantic Division														
New York	17 558 072	13.6	80.2	38.5	20.1	17.4	10.7	38.1	66.3	17.9	25.6	20.9	73.1	2 436
New Jersey	7 364 823	10.3	62.9	38.5	15.9	15.8	10.2	33.4	67.4	18.3	21.8	19.7	76.2	2 452
Pennsylvania	11 863 895	3.4	84.4	35.0	6.9	18.4	9.6	30.7	64.7	13.6	23.7	19.3	79.2	2 573
East North Central Division														
Ohio	10 797 630	2.8	74.6	43.3	5.2	13.2	10.4	30.9	67.0	13.7	25.0	22.3	79.4	2 691
Indiana	5 490 224	1.9	72.3	45.2	4.1	10.0	13.7	30.4	66.4	12.5	25.4	23.3	79.8	2 764
Illinois	11 426 518	7.2	74.3	44.5	11.5	15.7	12.9	31.3	66.5	16.2	25.1	22.9	75.8	2 660
Michigan	9 262 078	4.5	75.6	43.6	6.5	11.1	11.5	33.0	68.0	14.3	23.8	23.0	76.4	2 797
Wisconsin	4 705 767	2.7	79.5	43.8	5.8	18.8	9.5	32.4	69.6	14.8	24.3	23.6	83.1	2 877
West North Central Division														
Minnesota	4 075 970	2.6	76.9	44.4	5.6	11.9	7.3	35.4	73.1	17.4	25.5	24.2	85.4	2 804
Iowa	2 913 808	1.6	78.9	44.4	3.4	10.0	8.4	33.4	71.5	13.9	26.1	23.6	85.2	2 859
Missouri	4 916 686	1.7	71.4	46.0	3.1	13.7	13.9	30.5	63.5	13.9	26.6	22.0	78.3	2 676
North Dakota	652 717	2.3	74.6	48.3	11.3	8.6	8.0	32.6	66.4	14.8	25.0	26.9	87.7	3 039
South Dakota	690 768	1.4	71.7	47.1	7.8	6.8	11.1	31.4	67.9	14.0	25.8	26.4	83.5	3 109
Nebraska	1 569 825	2.0	71.6	46.9	4.8	11.3	7.8	34.0	73.4	15.5	26.5	24.8	84.2	2 846
Kansas	2 363 679	2.0	64.3	49.8	4.7	8.0	11.6	31.5	73.3	17.0	26.0	23.2	82.5	2 723
South Atlantic Division														
Delaware	594 338	3.2	53.3	43.0	5.5	19.8	11.5	34.5	68.6	17.5	22.8	21.1	75.0	2 601
Maryland	4 216 975	4.6	56.3	44.5	6.2	13.6	12.1	32.5	67.4	20.4	22.1	20.2	73.0	2 475
District of Columbia	638 333	6.4	41.1	41.8	7.9	15.7	12.7	45.5	67.1	27.5	30.0	18.0	41.6	2 161
Virginia	5 346 818	3.3	62.0	49.0	4.4	8.0	13.9	31.5	62.4	19.1	21.6	21.4	75.9	2 480
West Virginia	1 949 644	1.1	80.1	39.1	2.1	4.0	17.4	27.5	56.0	10.4	25.2	22.8	82.2	2 730
North Carolina	5 881 766	1.3	77.1	43.1	2.4	6.2	16.3	30.4	54.8	13.2	22.9	20.9	74.0	2 558
South Carolina	3 121 820	1.5	73.7	42.5	2.5	10.7	14.4	30.5	53.7	13.4	23.3	23.0	71.7	2 769
Georgia	5 463 105	1.7	72.2	47.5	2.6	9.7	17.8	26.6	56.4	14.6	24.0	23.2	71.5	2 651
Florida	9 746 324	10.9	35.0	53.8	13.2	13.5	16.8	29.1	66.7	14.9	21.6	16.9	71.5	2 541
East South Central Division														
Kentucky	3 660 777	0.9	80.0	45.6	1.8	10.1	21.5	24.5	53.1	11.1	24.4	24.0	79.2	2 739
Tennessee	4 591 120	1.1	72.7	45.8	1.9	8.3	16.7	29.9	56.2	12.6	23.2	21.3	74.8	2 555
Alabama	3 893 888	1.0	79.8	42.4	1.9	11.6	16.3	31.6	56.5	12.2	24.2	22.2	73.0	2 755
Mississippi	2 520 638	0.9	79.4	41.0	1.9	12.8	17.5	30.4	54.8	12.3	24.9	24.5	69.1	3 089
West South Central Division														
Arkansas	2 286 435	1.0	69.9	46.9	1.8	5.8	16.7	28.2	55.5	10.8	24.3	22.2	75.6	2 845
Louisiana	4 205 900	2.0	79.7	43.0	10.0	17.6	17.3	27.3	57.7	13.9	24.9	26.0	71.4	3 014
Oklahoma	3 025 290	1.9	64.2	52.4	4.0	4.2	14.3	30.3	66.0	15.1	27.0	23.1	79.1	2 646
Texas	14 229 191	6.0	72.2	52.7	21.8	6.8	17.6	29.7	62.6	16.9	23.8	25.2	77.9	2 785
Mountain Division														
Montana	786 690	2.3	58.3	52.7	5.2	4.5	10.8	31.4	74.4	17.5	26.0	25.3	83.0	2 909
Idaho	943 935	2.5	50.3	55.6	5.6	4.0	14.8	28.4	73.7	15.8	23.4	28.4	84.0	3 074
Wyoming	469 557	2.0	39.5	61.6	6.3	3.2	15.2	22.2	77.9	17.2	26.4	29.2	84.4	2 876
Colorado	2 889 964	3.9	43.5	60.2	10.6	6.9	13.1	30.7	78.6	23.0	24.8	24.3	79.8	2 550
New Mexico	1 302 894	4.0	54.0	49.7	37.8	6.9	16.5	26.3	68.9	17.6	23.4	27.2	77.0	2 998
Arizona	2 718 215	6.0	35.1	58.1	20.1	7.2	18.2	31.8	72.4	17.4	20.7	22.9	77.6	2 807
Utah	1 461 037	3.5	68.6	54.2	7.4	2.1	13.7	36.0	80.0	19.9	22.6	37.0	86.7	3 515
Nevada	800 493	6.7	23.0	65.2	9.7	4.7	18.6	20.2	75.5	14.4	23.3	21.3	74.0	2 502
Pacific Division														
Washington	4 132 156	5.8	50.9	56.3	6.9	7.6	12.9	30.8	77.6	19.0	25.3	23.3	79.3	2 598
Oregon	2 633 105	4.1	46.2	58.6	5.4	8.9	15.4	30.5	75.6	17.9	24.5	22.9	78.4	2 607
California	23 667 902	15.1	53.4	55.4	22.6	11.9	14.7	32.7	73.5	19.6	24.4	22.9	73.9	2 483
Alaska	401 851	4.0	33.3	67.8	12.5	3.3	12.9	17.4	82.5	21.1	22.4	32.7	79.9	2 683
Hawaii	964 691	14.2	67.4	50.7	25.8	16.9	7.1	27.4	73.8	20.3	14.3	25.8	78.1	2 479

Table 231. Summary of Economic Characteristics for Regions, Divisions, and States: 1980

[Data are estimates based on a sample; see Introduction. For meaning of symbols, see Introduction. For definitions of terms, see appendixes A and B]

United States Regions and Divisions States	Percent in labor force			Nonwork-ers per 100 workers	Civilian labor force— Percent unem-ployed	Employed persons 16 years and over— Percent in manufac-turing industries	Workers 16 years and over			Fami-lies— Percent with no workers in 1979	Median income in 1979 (dollars)		Per capita income in 1979 (dollars)	Income in 1979 below poverty level	
	Male, 16 years and over	Female, 16 years and over					Percent worked outside area of residence	Percent in carpools	Percent using public transpor-tation		Households	Families		Percent of persons for whom poverty status is deter-mined	Percent of families
		Total	With own children under 6 years												
United States	75.1	49.9	45.7	114	6.5	22.4	...	19.7	6.4	12.8	16 841	19 917	7 298	12.4	9.6
REGIONS AND DIVISIONS															
Northeast Region	74.2	49.1	39.1	113	6.7	25.3	...	18.5	14.2	13.8	17 310	20 651	7 475	11.2	8.7
New England	76.3	52.7	43.1	103	5.3	28.2	...	20.4	6.3	12.0	17 435	20 724	7 436	9.6	7.4
Middle Atlantic	73.5	47.9	37.8	117	7.1	24.2	...	17.8	17.1	14.4	17 267	20 626	7 488	11.7	9.2
North Central Region	76.3	50.3	45.5	112	7.4	25.9	...	18.5	4.9	11.6	17 753	20 988	7 422	10.5	8.0
East North Central	76.4	50.0	43.8	113	8.2	28.8	...	18.2	5.7	11.9	18 437	21 569	7 565	10.3	7.9
West North Central	76.2	50.9	49.7	110	5.4	19.0	...	19.3	3.1	11.0	16 310	19 589	7 074	11.0	8.2
South Region	73.9	49.1	49.8	119	5.7	20.6	...	22.5	3.3	13.3	15 318	17 857	6 725	15.4	11.9
South Atlantic	73.3	50.4	52.1	114	5.6	20.7	...	22.9	4.3	14.2	15 700	18 219	6 963	13.9	10.7
East South Central	71.8	46.2	48.7	131	7.7	25.2	...	23.5	2.0	13.7	13 623	16 155	5 893	18.7	14.8
West South Central	76.1	48.7	47.5	120	4.6	17.8	...	21.1	2.3	11.6	15 718	18 501	6 870	15.6	12.1
West Region	76.7	52.0	45.2	106	6.6	17.7	...	18.1	5.0	12.2	17 831	20 974	7 925	11.3	8.5
Mountain	77.2	51.0	43.9	114	6.0	12.2	...	20.1	2.7	11.2	16 868	19 656	7 123	11.9	8.9
Pacific	76.6	52.3	45.8	104	6.8	19.6	...	17.5	5.7	12.6	18 230	21 491	8 212	11.1	8.4
STATES															
New England Division															
Maine	73.1	47.9	45.3	122	7.6	27.3	3.1	24.6	1.5	12.8	13 816	16 167	5 768	13.0	9.8
New Hampshire	78.2	54.5	49.7	101	4.8	31.9	13.1	23.7	1.3	10.3	17 013	19 723	6 966	8.5	6.1
Vermont	75.2	51.8	48.1	111	6.3	23.9	5.0	24.9	1.4	11.2	14 790	17 205	6 178	12.1	8.9
Massachusetts	75.7	52.9	41.8	103	5.0	26.0	2.6	19.1	9.3	12.4	17 575	21 166	7 458	9.6	7.6
Rhode Island	75.3	52.4	45.0	104	7.0	32.5	8.4	21.4	4.3	13.4	16 097	19 448	6 897	10.3	7.7
Connecticut	78.3	53.6	40.8	98	4.7	31.0	4.2	19.6	5.1	11.2	20 077	23 149	8 511	8.0	6.2
Middle Atlantic Division															
New York	72.5	48.2	37.5	118	7.1	20.9	2.0	15.9	26.5	15.2	16 647	20 180	7 498	13.4	10.8
New Jersey	76.6	50.6	39.1	107	6.7	24.9	10.9	18.3	9.2	12.5	19 800	22 906	8 127	9.5	7.6
Pennsylvania	73.2	45.7	37.4	121	7.4	28.6	2.8	20.2	8.2	14.3	16 880	19 995	7 077	10.5	7.8
East North Central Division															
Ohio	76.0	48.0	42.2	117	8.0	30.1	2.0	17.3	4.0	12.1	17 754	20 909	7 285	10.3	8.0
Indiana	77.1	50.4	47.1	113	7.8	30.9	3.8	20.0	1.7	10.3	17 582	20 535	7 142	9.7	7.3
Illinois	77.3	51.6	43.3	108	7.2	25.8	2.4	17.9	12.0	11.5	19 321	22 746	8 066	11.0	8.4
Michigan	75.3	48.8	41.6	119	11.0	30.3	1.2	17.8	2.5	13.3	19 223	22 107	7 688	10.4	8.2
Wisconsin	76.4	52.7	48.6	108	6.6	28.5	2.3	19.2	3.9	11.5	17 680	20 915	7 243	8.7	6.3
West North Central Division															
Minnesota	77.1	54.0	50.4	104	5.4	20.2	1.6	19.0	5.5	10.4	17 761	21 185	7 451	9.5	7.0
Iowa	76.3	50.1	49.1	112	5.0	20.2	3.4	18.4	1.9	10.8	16 799	20 052	7 136	10.1	7.5
Missouri	74.2	49.3	50.5	115	6.9	21.9	3.9	21.8	3.8	12.8	15 581	18 784	6 917	12.2	9.1
North Dakota	75.6	47.3	47.2	119	5.3	5.8	2.6	16.4	0.7	8.8	15 293	18 023	6 417	12.6	9.8
South Dakota	75.4	49.3	50.9	117	4.9	9.6	2.0	14.3	0.4	9.9	13 156	15 993	5 697	16.9	13.1
Nebraska	78.0	51.3	49.4	107	3.7	13.8	1.8	17.8	2.5	9.8	15 925	19 122	6 936	10.7	8.0
Kansas	77.5	51.0	48.3	106	4.0	19.2	6.9	19.2	1.0	10.3	16 362	19 707	7 350	10.1	7.4
South Atlantic Division															
Delaware	76.6	51.6	48.8	108	6.3	23.6	8.8	21.3	4.1	10.7	17 846	20 817	7 449	11.9	8.9
Maryland	77.7	54.6	50.9	100	5.8	14.4	16.7	23.1	8.8	10.2	20 281	23 112	8 293	9.8	7.5
District of Columbia	69.0	58.2	62.1	96	6.8	4.5	19.1	15.7	38.0	15.5	16 211	19 099	8 960	18.6	15.1
Virginia	76.7	52.4	49.8	105	5.0	19.0	11.0	25.2	5.1	10.5	17 475	20 018	7 478	11.8	9.2
West Virginia	68.4	36.5	31.6	158	8.4	18.4	6.5	24.7	1.9	17.3	14 564	17 308	6 141	15.0	11.7
North Carolina	75.8	53.9	58.3	106	5.5	32.8	1.6	24.7	1.5	10.5	14 481	16 792	6 133	14.8	11.6
South Carolina	75.5	52.9	58.1	113	6.1	32.6	3.5	25.6	1.3	11.0	14 711	16 978	5 886	16.6	13.1
Georgia	75.8	52.3	53.9	114	5.9	24.1	2.4	22.1	3.9	11.5	15 033	17 414	6 402	16.6	13.2
Florida	67.0	45.8	50.7	126	5.1	12.6	1.2	20.3	2.7	21.8	14 675	17 280	7 270	13.5	9.9
East South Central Division															
Kentucky	71.8	43.8	41.9	135	8.5	22.5	5.9	22.8	2.5	14.5	13 965	16 444	5 978	17.6	14.6
Tennessee	73.3	48.9	51.0	119	7.4	26.7	3.2	23.2	2.5	12.7	14 142	16 564	6 213	16.5	13.1
Alabama	71.8	45.4	49.0	134	7.5	26.1	3.4	23.4	1.4	14.0	13 669	16 347	5 894	18.9	14.8
Mississippi	69.3	46.2	54.4	144	7.1	24.6	4.8	25.3	1.2	14.1	12 096	14 591	5 183	23.9	18.7
West South Central Division															
Arkansas	68.3	44.6	51.0	140	6.9	25.1	2.7	22.6	0.8	16.5	12 214	14 641	5 614	19.0	14.9
Louisiana	73.6	44.2	44.0	137	6.0	14.4	1.8	21.4	4.3	13.4	15 227	18 088	6 430	18.6	15.1
Oklahoma	74.2	47.3	47.2	120	4.1	16.7	2.1	20.3	1.0	12.9	14 750	17 668	6 858	13.4	10.3
Texas	78.4	51.0	48.1	112	4.0	17.9	0.8	21.1	2.3	10.0	16 708	19 618	7 205	14.7	11.1
Mountain Division															
Montana	75.2	49.0	44.6	117	8.3	7.4	1.0	17.3	1.1	10.3	15 420	18 413	6 589	12.3	9.2
Idaho	77.2	49.0	43.5	123	8.0	13.9	3.2	17.4	2.5	10.5	15 285	17 492	6 248	12.6	9.6
Wyoming	83.0	51.6	41.5	104	4.1	5.4	1.5	22.8	1.9	6.6	19 994	22 430	7 927	7.9	5.8
Colorado	80.0	55.2	46.4	96	5.0	14.1	1.0	20.2	4.2	9.2	18 056	21 279	7 998	10.1	7.4
New Mexico	74.3	46.5	42.5	131	7.1	7.4	1.8	20.2	1.8	12.8	14 654	16 928	6 119	17.6	14.0
Arizona	72.6	47.8	44.5	124	6.2	14.5	1.0	19.8	2.0	15.9	16 448	19 017	7 041	13.2	9.5
Utah	79.8	49.5	37.4	133	5.5	15.8	1.0	22.8	3.5	8.7	17 671	20 024	6 305	10.3	7.7
Nevada	81.1	60.1	54.1	85	5.9	5.9	1.3	19.5	1.9	8.8	18 211	21 311	8 453	8.7	6.3
Pacific Division															
Washington	76.6	50.6	42.7	108	7.4	19.5	2.6	18.9	5.3	12.1	18 367	21 696	8 073	9.8	7.2
Oregon	74.9	50.2	43.1	112	8.3	19.5	1.3	17.6	5.0	13.1	16 780	20 027	7 557	10.7	7.7
California	76.6	52.6	46.3	103	6.5	20.3	0.7	16.9	5.8	12.9	18 243	21 537	8 295	11.4	8.7
Alaska	81.7	59.7	47.4	96	9.7	6.3	0.7	21.5	3.2	4.3	25 414	28 395	10 193	10.7	8.6
Hawaii	78.3	57.8	51.5	95	4.7	7.9	2.2	23.2	8.3	9.3	20 473	22 750	7 740	9.9	7.8

Table 232. **Race by Sex for Regions, Divisions, and States: 1980**

[Data are estimates based on a sample; see Introduction. For meaning of symbols, see Introduction. For definitions of terms, see appendixes A and B]

United States Regions and Divisions States	White	Black	American Indian	Eskimo	Aleut	Japanese	Chinese	Filipino	Korean	Asian Indian	Vietnamese	Hawaiian	Guamanian	Samoan	Other	Race, n.e.c.
BOTH SEXES																
United States	189 035 012	26 482 349	1 478 523	42 098	13 715	716 331	812 178	781 894	357 393	387 223	245 025	172 346	30 695	39 520	183 835	5 767 668
Regions and Divisions																
Northeast Region	42 477 376	4 849 969	88 211	650	560	46 913	217 624	77 051	68 357	132 560	22 021	4 273	1 952	522	28 021	1 119 223
New England	11 620 483	473 924	23 747	174	181	7 474	33 113	8 311	9 327	17 010	5 199	835	572	172	6 412	141 559
Middle Atlantic	30 856 893	4 376 045	64 464	476	379	39 439	184 511	68 740	59 030	115 550	16 822	3 438	1 380	350	21 609	977 664
North Central Region	52 283 150	5 332 907	269 154	1 495	589	46 254	74 944	80 928	64 573	89 588	32 949	5 476	1 816	991	37 872	542 984
East North Central	36 222 923	4 546 044	119 178	961	425	35 789	59 581	69 958	47 895	75 051	17 238	3 442	984	389	24 091	458 268
West North Central	16 060 227	786 863	149 976	534	164	10 465	15 363	10 970	16 678	14 537	15 711	2 034	832	602	13 781	84 716
South Region	59 101 152	14 038 782	405 009	1 353	912	47 631	91 415	85 626	70 999	90 602	76 916	11 427	4 757	1 784	31 848	1 312 149
South Atlantic	28 682 645	7 650 243	130 549	698	448	25 998	50 730	58 943	44 880	50 061	26 882	5 719	2 549	900	14 311	213 567
East South Central	11 707 145	2 867 491	27 518	199	137	4 932	7 312	5 668	6 985	9 748	5 316	1 800	423	291	3 009	18 449
West South Central	18 711 362	3 521 048	246 942	456	327	16 701	33 373	21 015	19 134	30 793	44 718	3 908	1 785	593	14 528	1 080 133
West Region	35 173 334	2 260 691	716 149	38 600	11 654	575 533	428 195	538 289	153 464	74 473	113 139	151 170	22 170	36 223	86 094	2 793 312
Mountain	10 020 700	267 538	371 912	883	296	29 471	19 959	14 181	13 374	7 229	9 516	3 860	1 297	1 751	13 601	597 217
Pacific	25 152 634	1 993 153	344 237	37 717	11 358	546 062	408 236	524 108	140 090	67 244	103 623	147 310	20 873	34 472	72 493	2 196 095
States																
New England Division																
Maine	1 112 977	3 381	4 360	5	–	302	433	680	480	475	260	84	79	28	252	864
New Hampshire	910 551	4 324	1 342	22	21	356	900	286	519	742	136	76	5	12	332	986
Vermont	507 052	1 188	1 041	6	21	221	206	115	332	520	94	11	21	14	106	508
Massachusetts	5 378 403	221 029	8 996	115	87	4 290	24 882	3 180	5 369	8 943	2 847	352	251	93	2 408	75 792
Rhode Island	900 408	27 361	3 186	6	12	464	1 744	1 001	612	904	287	63	116	–	1 426	9 564
Connecticut	2 811 092	216 641	4 822	20	40	1 841	4 948	3 049	2 015	5 426	1 575	249	100	25	1 888	53 845
Middle Atlantic Division																
New York	14 033 644	2 405 818	43 508	208	271	24 754	147 250	35 630	33 260	67 636	5 849	1 950	1 017	151	13 475	743 651
New Jersey	6 154 833	924 909	10 028	131	41	10 263	23 492	24 470	13 173	30 684	2 846	579	199	112	3 565	165 498
Pennsylvania	10 668 416	1 045 318	10 928	137	67	4 422	13 769	8 640	12 597	17 230	8 127	909	164	87	4 569	68 515
East North Central Division																
Ohio	9 607 133	1 076 742	15 300	189	65	6 271	10 584	7 966	7 756	13 602	2 751	823	137	64	3 212	45 035
Indiana	5 008 817	414 489	9 495	131	65	2 503	4 491	3 507	3 940	4 746	2 137	503	119	60	2 349	32 872
Illinois	9 267 607	1 674 467	19 118	364	130	18 432	28 847	44 317	24 351	37 438	6 287	964	367	88	11 122	292 619
Michigan	7 893 278	1 197 177	44 712	102	105	6 460	10 824	11 132	8 948	15 363	4 364	894	199	90	4 367	64 063
Wisconsin	4 446 088	183 169	30 553	175	60	2 123	4 835	3 036	2 900	3 902	1 699	258	162	87	3 041	23 679
West North Central Division																
Minnesota	3 942 025	52 325	36 527	147	56	3 191	4 558	2 628	6 676	3 734	5 316	315	102	51	5 655	12 664
Iowa	2 841 326	42 228	6 311	30	1	1 024	1 973	1 058	2 057	2 424	2 101	301	95	50	2 764	10 065
Missouri	4 348 412	513 385	14 820	103	48	2 897	4 520	3 883	3 356	4 276	3 134	780	203	357	1 556	14 956
North Dakota	626 358	2 471	19 905	38	10	225	387	496	360	252	288	69	18	–	197	1 643
South Dakota	639 840	2 152	45 525	43	4	305	200	312	325	157	265	41	46	39	227	1 287
Nebraska	1 492 220	47 946	9 059	66	21	1 212	1 285	945	1 203	1 106	1 276	177	109	48	829	12 323
Kansas	2 170 046	126 356	17 829	107	24	1 611	2 440	1 648	2 701	2 588	3 331	351	259	57	2 553	31 778
South Atlantic Division																
Delaware	488 002	96 157	1 380	5	6	412	1 174	789	501	1 227	171	77	45	5	226	4 161
Maryland	3 166 142	957 418	8 946	97	32	4 656	15 037	11 763	14 783	13 788	4 162	630	323	86	2 721	16 391
District of Columbia	174 705	448 370	986	21	7	808	2 308	1 255	312	873	435	194	89	38	571	7 361
Virginia	4 236 345	1 008 665	9 867	125	77	5 173	9 495	19 111	12 797	9 046	9 451	1 033	548	194	3 721	21 170
West Virginia	1 874 618	65 041	2 317	25	15	508	1 095	1 282	489	1 936	168	85	29	32	278	1 726
North Carolina	4 460 570	1 319 054	65 808	62	90	3 594	3 229	2 869	3 694	4 855	1 966	954	388	132	1 469	13 032
South Carolina	2 147 825	947 969	6 655	83	6	1 584	1 204	3 797	1 766	2 572	1 113	467	182	57	628	5 912
Georgia	3 949 583	1 464 435	9 876	105	98	3 596	4 258	2 825	5 590	4 725	2 339	795	503	134	1 244	12 999
Florida	8 184 855	1 343 134	24 714	175	117	5 667	12 930	15 252	4 948	11 039	7 077	1 484	442	222	3 453	130 815
East South Central Division																
Kentucky	3 380 256	259 289	4 497	65	39	1 170	1 381	1 417	2 170	2 669	1 461	378	208	122	847	4 808
Tennessee	3 837 968	724 808	6 946	57	32	1 752	2 904	1 761	2 405	3 392	1 158	438	66	111	1 265	6 057
Alabama	2 873 289	996 283	9 239	45	20	1 427	1 416	1 089	1 761	2 374	1 220	583	62	38	690	4 352
Mississippi	1 615 632	887 111	6 836	32	46	583	1 611	1 401	649	1 313	1 477	401	87	20	207	3 232
West South Central Division																
Arkansas	1 889 935	373 025	12 713	40	4	697	1 184	732	596	1 194	1 900	212	65	6	646	3 486
Louisiana	2 915 310	1 238 472	12 841	46	45	1 671	3 091	2 650	2 009	3 036	10 853	626	230	69	888	14 063
Oklahoma	2 603 063	204 810	171 092	75	57	2 249	2 384	1 681	2 757	3 168	4 174	695	261	117	2 279	26 428
Texas	11 303 054	1 704 741	50 296	295	221	12 084	26 714	15 952	13 772	23 395	27 791	2 375	1 229	401	10 715	1 036 156
Mountain Division																
Montana	740 901	1 738	37 623	36	41	803	395	501	325	154	82	122	11	16	688	3 254
Idaho	904 045	2 711	10 405	98	20	3 102	701	759	635	247	443	293	42	103	396	19 935
Wyoming	446 489	3 270	8 192	52	22	757	441	194	240	104	43	87	10	27	141	9 488
Colorado	2 591 270	101 695	20 682	265	68	10 841	4 224	2 764	5 143	2 565	3 247	825	506	135	4 007	141 727
New Mexico	990 657	23 071	106 585	111	54	1 353	1 412	1 200	759	622	936	214	43	66	1 123	174 688
Arizona	2 260 288	74 159	154 175	155	60	4 629	6 681	3 799	2 543	2 078	1 756	854	346	179	1 697	204 816
Utah	1 383 997	9 691	19 994	82	27	5 508	2 913	1 138	1 397	932	1 991	913	64	1 171	4 197	27 022
Nevada	703 053	51 203	14 256	84	4	2 478	3 192	3 826	2 332	527	1 018	552	275	54	1 352	16 287
Pacific Division																
Washington	3 790 990	105 604	61 233	1 213	1 362	27 389	17 984	25 662	13 441	4 267	8 933	2 840	1 739	1 837	7 515	60 147
Oregon	2 496 398	37 454	29 783	419	267	8 580	7 918	4 800	4 998	2 265	5 743	1 555	366	97	4 636	27 826
California	18 221 353	1 818 660	227 757	2 194	1 751	268 814	325 882	358 378	102 582	59 774	85 238	24 245	17 009	18 087	52 964	2 083 214
Alaska	311 968	13 748	22 631	33 817	7 909	1 545	536	3 193	1 616	230	306	419	129	102	238	3 464
Hawaii	331 925	17 687	2 833	74	69	239 734	55 916	132 075	17 453	708	3 403	118 251	1 630	14 349	7 140	21 444

Table 232. Race by Sex for Regions, Divisions, and States: 1980—Con.

[Data are estimates based on a sample; see Introduction. For meaning of symbols, see Introduction. For definitions of terms, see appendixes A and B]

United States Regions and Divisions States	White	Black	American Indian	Eskimo	Aleut	Japanese	Chinese	Filipino	Korean	Asian Indian	Vietnamese	Hawaiian	Guamanian	Samoan	Other	Race, n.e.c.
						Asian and Pacific Islander										
MALE																
United States	92 050 198	12 508 991	729 538	21 242	6 938	328 703	410 936	377 172	149 954	193 463	127 484	83 984	15 540	20 089	93 232	2 930 049
Regions and Divisions																
Northeast Region	20 374 992	2 234 222	43 024	324	298	21 340	111 894	34 323	30 463	66 762	11 553	1 728	869	235	14 633	531 066
New England	5 575 388	225 745	11 566	95	129	3 237	16 871	3 807	3 735	8 114	2 659	412	264	64	3 439	68 215
Middle Atlantic	14 799 604	2 008 477	31 458	229	169	18 103	95 023	30 516	26 728	58 648	8 894	1 316	605	171	11 194	462 851
North Central Region	25 471 570	2 517 755	132 598	708	285	19 713	38 713	35 401	25 895	45 272	17 797	2 183	912	494	19 748	285 173
East North Central	17 642 709	2 139 558	58 831	454	216	15 605	30 758	30 831	20 285	38 432	9 176	1 221	445	195	12 631	240 361
West North Central	7 828 861	378 197	73 767	254	69	4 108	7 955	4 570	5 610	6 840	8 621	962	467	299	7 117	44 812
South Region	28 836 408	6 631 846	202 811	684	535	16 761	46 454	39 235	26 438	44 053	39 293	5 143	2 401	986	15 775	676 234
South Atlantic	13 952 854	3 615 122	65 981	313	234	8 942	25 501	27 417	17 925	24 135	13 123	2 519	1 281	512	6 632	113 928
East South Central	5 703 157	1 342 905	13 663	107	81	1 589	3 941	2 540	2 125	4 350	2 559	760	218	169	1 526	10 558
West South Central	9 180 397	1 673 819	123 167	264	220	6 230	17 012	9 278	6 388	15 568	23 611	1 864	902	305	7 617	551 748
West Region	17 367 228	1 125 168	351 105	19 526	5 820	270 889	213 875	268 213	67 158	37 376	58 841	74 930	11 358	18 374	43 076	1 437 576
Mountain	4 971 198	139 118	181 323	453	141	13 089	10 168	6 377	4 590	3 417	4 927	2 071	703	890	6 516	303 568
Pacific	12 396 030	986 050	169 782	19 073	5 679	257 800	203 707	261 836	62 568	33 959	53 914	72 859	10 655	17 484	36 560	1 134 008
States																
New England Division																
Maine	540 108	1 941	2 186	...	–	107	219	321	146	210	155	51	29	...	126	470
New Hampshire	443 280	2 370	767	...	...	127	441	132	159	304	58	53	...	...	123	527
Vermont	246 902	680	480	...	...	102	124	59	129	247	34	...	...	...	46	276
Massachusetts	2 558 848	105 416	4 383	67	44	1 971	12 668	1 252	2 171	4 352	1 442	170	102	40	1 261	36 334
Rhode Island	429 203	13 186	1 355	...	...	155	890	506	299	386	157	19	81	...	825	4 529
Connecticut	1 357 047	102 152	2 395	...	40	775	2 529	1 537	831	2 615	813	117	39	...	1 058	26 079
Middle Atlantic Division																
New York	6 710 440	1 094 458	20 893	94	110	11 716	75 885	15 579	15 378	34 621	2 982	693	470	72	6 931	348 425
New Jersey	2 963 173	430 230	5 024	56	6	4 686	11 915	10 883	5 780	15 771	1 482	225	92	52	1 883	80 215
Pennsylvania	5 125 991	483 789	5 541	79	53	1 701	7 223	4 054	5 570	8 256	4 430	398	43	47	2 380	34 211
East North Central Division																
Ohio	4 656 010	505 832	7 486	95	26	2 466	5 395	3 393	3 157	6 516	1 456	236	72	36	1 633	23 533
Indiana	2 436 435	196 243	4 659	47	35	956	2 445	1 383	1 501	2 260	1 105	208	44	50	1 242	16 815
Illinois	4 508 174	782 396	9 514	194	58	8 723	14 814	19 836	11 037	19 974	3 421	295	168	35	5 881	154 540
Michigan	3 862 082	567 686	22 227	62	49	2 718	5 595	4 873	3 535	7 948	2 299	382	96	26	2 278	33 101
Wisconsin	2 180 008	87 401	14 945	56	48	742	2 509	1 346	1 055	1 734	895	100	65	48	1 597	12 372
West North Central Division																
Minnesota	1 931 440	26 955	17 721	74	20	1 317	2 369	1 125	2 338	1 819	2 933	141	58	38	2 969	6 651
Iowa	1 380 083	21 103	3 030	30	...	415	1 064	390	662	1 170	1 205	158	32	35	1 441	5 308
Missouri	2 098 604	240 263	7 594	37	31	1 052	2 348	1 677	1 138	1 954	1 727	351	131	144	782	7 729
North Dakota	315 288	1 569	9 698	10	...	100	196	192	115	133	132	42	...	–	69	951
South Dakota	315 459	1 430	22 266	22	...	84	101	150	117	80	145	16	33	18	109	706
Nebraska	728 079	23 348	4 556	36	...	499	654	360	361	516	625	57	47	25	385	6 483
Kansas	1 059 908	63 529	8 902	45	...	641	1 223	676	879	1 168	1 854	197	155	39	1 362	16 984
South Atlantic Division																
Delaware	236 364	45 177	715	...	...	106	582	330	203	611	115	20	22	...	75	2 169
Maryland	1 543 225	453 531	4 550	40	14	1 860	7 554	5 516	6 721	6 957	1 931	282	144	47	1 275	8 344
District of Columbia	81 737	206 416	515	...	...	276	1 235	516	141	394	234	55	31	22	308	3 552
Virginia	2 083 843	483 893	5 169	64	49	1 787	4 804	9 210	5 253	4 530	4 706	577	230	102	1 745	11 767
West Virginia	910 450	30 543	1 196	...	...	189	626	616	139	899	65	22	...	5	151	843
North Carolina	2 178 782	625 467	32 484	26	46	1 230	1 753	1 213	1 207	2 208	884	343	232	95	691	7 960
South Carolina	1 057 827	447 252	3 465	22	...	426	548	1 912	578	1 223	535	177	93	17	287	3 564
Georgia	1 930 165	685 661	5 275	49	36	1 368	2 123	1 123	2 006	2 275	1 201	310	332	72	633	7 701
Florida	3 930 461	637 182	12 612	86	73	1 700	6 276	6 981	1 677	5 038	3 452	733	177	147	1 467	68 028
East South Central Division																
Kentucky	1 652 550	125 510	2 345	50	27	342	805	664	596	1 156	748	140	87	77	408	3 042
Tennessee	1 864 517	338 588	3 404	39	22	612	1 589	758	820	1 608	545	217	43	68	682	3 372
Alabama	1 396 928	462 464	4 592	9	...	454	742	451	527	996	522	227	46	12	331	2 416
Mississippi	789 162	416 343	3 322	9	22	181	805	667	182	590	744	176	42	...	105	1 728
West South Central Division																
Arkansas	919 242	174 264	6 128	–	...	214	514	228	171	504	1 069	67	55	...	327	1 986
Louisiana	1 432 733	579 935	6 847	42	18	654	1 566	1 399	663	1 458	5 615	312	117	44	435	7 429
Oklahoma	1 269 309	99 563	84 233	41	31	805	1 167	604	778	1 539	2 149	362	123	81	1 262	14 375
Texas	5 559 113	820 057	25 959	181	167	4 557	13 765	7 047	4 776	12 067	14 778	1 123	607	180	5 593	527 958
Mountain Division																
Montana	370 038	1 107	18 263	13	36	341	209	226	112	35	55	77	...	...	366	1 683
Idaho	449 576	1 686	5 158	64	...	1 433	304	364	197	91	197	147	14	50	188	11 484
Wyoming	228 651	1 812	4 061	22	...	334	206	89	62	45	23	41	...	...	72	5 087
Colorado	1 283 286	52 293	10 512	141	22	5 053	2 202	1 254	1 791	1 273	1 755	468	262	77	2 084	71 168
New Mexico	489 186	12 085	51 099	17	23	467	759	457	183	302	446	93	30	35	450	86 566
Arizona	1 109 421	38 645	75 378	91	25	1 908	3 443	1 794	844	933	768	469	211	95	681	104 037
Utah	684 723	5 668	9 725	45	...	2 668	1 576	467	503	429	1 136	458	35	576	2 096	14 592
Nevada	356 317	25 822	7 127	60	...	885	1 469	1 726	898	309	547	318	139	25	579	8 951
Pacific Division																
Washington	1 877 739	56 930	30 442	502	553	12 073	9 029	12 966	5 130	1 853	4 742	1 458	858	1 045	3 503	33 170
Oregon	1 226 106	19 695	14 922	222	116	3 547	3 838	2 260	2 041	943	3 115	836	190	77	2 489	15 553
California	8 947 589	889 931	111 522	1 141	880	125 494	163 060	176 018	47 074	30 666	44 155	12 225	8 650	9 097	26 867	1 071 735
Alaska	166 917	7 687	11 259	17 176	4 095	680	285	1 620	647	131	181	217	97	52	46	1 855
Hawaii	177 679	11 807	1 637	32	35	116 006	27 495	68 972	7 676	366	1 721	58 123	860	7 213	3 655	11 695

Table 232. Race by Sex for Regions, Divisions, and States: 1980—Con.

[Data are estimates based on a sample; see Introduction. For meaning of symbols, see Introduction. For definitions of terms, see appendixes A and B]

United States Regions and Divisions States	White	Black	American Indian	Eskimo	Aleut	Japanese	Chinese	Filipino	Korean	Asian Indian	Vietnamese	Hawaiian	Guamanian	Samoan	Other	Race, n.e.c.
FEMALE																
United States	96 984 814	13 973 358	748 985	20 856	6 777	387 628	401 242	404 722	207 439	193 760	117 541	88 362	15 155	19 431	90 603	2 837 619
Regions and Divisions																
Northeast Region	22 102 384	2 615 747	45 187	326	262	25 573	105 730	42 728	37 894	65 798	10 468	2 545	1 083	287	13 388	588 157
New England	6 045 095	248 179	12 181	79	52	4 237	16 242	4 504	5 592	8 896	2 540	423	308	108	2 973	73 344
Middle Atlantic	16 057 289	2 367 568	33 006	247	210	21 336	89 488	38 224	32 302	56 902	7 928	2 122	775	179	10 415	514 813
North Central Region	26 811 580	2 815 152	136 556	787	304	26 541	36 231	45 527	38 678	44 316	15 152	3 293	904	497	18 124	257 811
East North Central	18 580 214	2 406 486	60 347	507	209	20 184	28 823	39 127	27 610	36 619	8 062	2 221	539	194	11 460	217 907
West North Central	8 231 366	408 666	76 209	280	95	6 357	7 408	6 400	11 068	7 697	7 090	1 072	365	303	6 664	39 904
South Region	30 264 744	7 406 936	202 198	669	377	30 870	44 961	46 391	44 561	46 549	37 623	6 284	2 356	798	16 073	635 915
South Atlantic	14 729 791	4 035 121	64 568	385	214	17 056	25 229	31 526	26 955	25 926	13 759	3 200	1 268	388	7 679	99 639
East South Central	6 003 988	1 524 586	13 855	92	56	3 343	3 371	3 128	4 860	5 398	2 757	1 040	205	122	1 483	7 891
West South Central	9 530 965	1 847 229	123 775	192	107	10 471	16 361	11 737	12 746	15 225	21 107	2 044	883	288	6 911	528 385
West Region	17 806 106	1 135 523	365 044	19 074	5 834	304 644	214 320	270 076	86 306	37 097	54 298	76 240	10 812	17 849	43 018	1 355 736
Mountain	5 049 502	128 420	190 589	430	155	16 382	9 791	7 804	8 784	3 812	4 589	1 789	594	861	7 085	293 649
Pacific	12 756 604	1 007 103	174 455	18 644	5 679	288 262	204 529	262 272	77 522	33 285	49 709	74 451	10 218	16 988	35 933	1 062 087
States																
New England Division																
Maine	572 869	1 440	2 174	...	–	195	214	359	334	265	105	33	50	...	126	394
New Hampshire	467 271	1 954	575	...	...	229	459	154	360	438	78	23	...	...	209	459
Vermont	260 150	508	561	...	...	119	82	56	203	273	60	...	...	...	60	232
Massachusetts	2 819 555	115 613	4 613	48	43	2 319	12 214	1 928	3 198	4 591	1 405	182	149	53	1 147	39 458
Rhode Island	471 205	14 175	1 831	...	...	309	854	495	313	518	130	44	35	–	601	5 035
Connecticut	1 454 045	114 489	2 427	...	–	1 066	2 419	1 512	1 184	2 811	762	132	61	...	830	27 766
Middle Atlantic Division																
New York	7 323 204	1 311 360	22 615	114	161	13 038	71 365	20 051	17 882	33 015	2 867	1 257	547	79	6 544	395 226
New Jersey	3 191 660	494 679	5 004	75	35	5 577	11 577	13 587	7 393	14 913	1 364	354	107	60	1 682	85 283
Pennsylvania	5 542 425	561 529	5 387	58	14	2 721	6 546	4 586	7 027	8 974	3 697	511	121	40	2 189	34 304
East North Central Division																
Ohio	4 951 123	570 910	7 814	94	39	3 805	5 189	4 573	4 599	7 086	1 295	587	65	28	1 579	21 502
Indiana	2 572 382	218 246	4 836	84	30	1 547	2 046	2 124	2 439	2 486	1 032	295	75	10	1 107	16 057
Illinois	4 759 433	892 071	9 604	170	72	9 709	14 033	24 481	13 314	17 464	2 866	669	199	53	5 241	138 079
Michigan	4 031 196	629 491	22 485	40	56	3 742	5 229	6 259	5 413	7 415	2 065	512	103	64	2 089	30 962
Wisconsin	2 266 080	95 768	15 608	119	12	1 381	2 326	1 690	1 845	2 168	804	158	97	39	1 444	11 307
West North Central Division																
Minnesota	2 010 585	25 370	18 806	73	36	1 874	2 189	1 503	4 338	1 915	2 383	174	44	13	2 686	6 013
Iowa	1 461 243	21 125	3 281	–	...	609	909	668	1 395	1 254	896	143	63	15	1 323	4 757
Missouri	2 249 808	273 122	7 226	66	17	1 845	2 172	2 206	2 218	2 322	1 407	429	72	213	774	7 227
North Dakota	311 070	902	10 207	28	...	125	191	304	245	119	156	27	...	–	128	692
South Dakota	324 381	722	23 259	21	...	221	99	162	208	77	120	25	13	21	118	581
Nebraska	764 141	24 598	4 503	30	...	713	631	585	842	590	651	120	62	23	444	5 840
Kansas	1 110 138	62 827	8 927	62	...	970	1 217	972	1 822	1 420	1 477	154	104	18	1 191	14 794
South Atlantic Division																
Delaware	251 638	50 980	665	...	...	306	592	459	298	616	56	57	23	...	151	1 992
Maryland	1 622 917	503 887	4 396	57	18	2 796	7 483	6 247	8 062	6 831	2 231	348	179	39	1 446	8 047
District of Columbia	92 968	241 954	471	...	...	532	1 073	739	171	479	201	139	58	16	263	3 809
Virginia	2 152 502	524 772	4 698	61	28	3 386	4 691	9 901	7 544	4 516	4 745	456	318	92	1 976	9 403
West Virginia	964 168	34 498	1 121	...	...	319	469	666	350	1 037	103	63	...	27	127	883
North Carolina	2 281 788	693 587	33 324	36	44	2 364	1 476	1 656	2 487	2 647	1 082	611	156	37	778	5 072
South Carolina	1 089 998	500 717	3 190	61	...	1 158	656	1 885	1 188	1 349	578	290	89	40	341	2 348
Georgia	2 019 418	778 774	4 601	56	62	2 228	2 135	1 702	3 584	2 450	1 138	485	171	62	611	5 298
Florida	4 254 394	705 952	12 102	89	44	3 967	6 654	8 271	3 271	6 001	3 625	751	265	75	1 986	62 787
East South Central Division																
Kentucky	1 727 706	133 779	2 152	15	12	828	576	753	1 574	1 513	713	238	121	45	439	1 766
Tennessee	1 973 451	386 220	3 542	18	10	1 140	1 315	1 003	1 585	1 784	613	221	23	43	583	2 685
Alabama	1 476 361	533 819	4 647	36	...	973	674	638	1 234	1 378	698	356	16	26	359	1 936
Mississippi	826 470	470 768	3 514	23	24	402	806	734	467	723	733	225	45	...	102	1 504
West South Central Division																
Arkansas	970 693	198 761	6 585	40	...	483	670	504	425	690	831	145	10	...	319	1 500
Louisiana	1 482 577	658 537	5 994	4	27	1 017	1 525	1 251	1 346	1 578	5 238	314	113	25	453	6 634
Oklahoma	1 333 754	105 247	86 859	34	26	1 444	1 217	1 077	1 979	1 629	2 025	333	138	36	1 017	12 053
Texas	5 743 941	884 684	24 337	114	54	7 527	12 949	8 905	8 996	11 328	13 013	1 252	622	221	5 122	508 198
Mountain Division																
Montana	370 863	631	19 360	23	5	462	186	275	213	119	27	45	...	...	322	1 571
Idaho	454 469	1 025	5 247	34	...	1 669	397	395	438	156	246	146	28	53	208	8 451
Wyoming	217 838	1 458	4 131	30	...	423	235	105	178	59	20	46	...	...	69	4 401
Colorado	1 307 984	49 402	10 170	124	46	5 788	2 022	1 510	3 352	1 292	1 492	357	244	58	1 923	70 559
New Mexico	501 471	10 986	55 486	94	31	886	653	743	576	320	490	121	13	31	673	88 122
Arizona	1 150 867	35 514	78 797	64	35	2 721	3 238	2 005	1 699	1 145	988	385	135	84	1 016	100 779
Utah	699 274	4 023	10 269	37	...	2 840	1 337	671	894	503	855	455	29	595	2 101	12 430
Nevada	346 736	25 381	7 129	24	...	1 593	1 723	2 100	1 434	218	471	234	136	29	773	7 336
Pacific Division																
Washington	1 913 251	48 674	30 791	711	809	15 316	8 955	12 696	8 311	2 414	4 191	1 382	881	792	4 012	26 977
Oregon	1 270 292	17 759	14 861	197	151	5 033	4 080	2 540	2 957	1 322	2 628	719	176	20	2 147	12 273
California	9 273 764	928 729	116 235	1 053	871	143 320	162 822	182 360	55 508	29 108	41 083	12 020	8 359	8 990	26 097	1 011 479
Alaska	145 051	6 061	11 372	16 641	3 814	865	251	1 573	969	99	125	202	32	50	192	1 609
Hawaii	154 246	5 880	1 196	42	34	123 728	28 421	63 103	9 777	342	1 682	60 128	770	7 136	3 485	9 749

Table 233. Persons by Spanish Origin, Race, and Sex, for Regions, Divisions and States: 1980

[Data are estimates based on a sample; see Introduction. For meaning of symbols, see Introduction. For definitions of terms, see appendixes A and B]

United States Regions and Divisions States	Total	Spanish origin — Mexican	Puerto Rican	Cuban	Other Spanish	White	Black	Am. Indian, Eskimo, and Aleut	Asian and Pacific Islander	Race, n.e.c.	Not of Spanish origin — White	Black	Am. Indian, Eskimo, and Aleut	Asian and Pacific Islander	Race, n.e.c.
BOTH SEXES															
United States	14 603 683	8 678 632	2 004 961	806 223	3 113 867	8 432 174	390 492	101 529	175 835	5 503 653	180 602 838	26 091 857	1 432 807	3 550 605	264 015
Regions and Divisions															
Northeast Region	2 608 074	90 431	1 479 554	183 544	854 545	1 381 412	148 707	7 374	15 213	1 055 368	41 095 964	4 701 262	82 047	584 081	63 855
New England	299 498	16 496	169 358	14 005	99 639	165 116	14 248	1 222	2 218	116 694	11 455 367	459 676	22 880	86 207	24 865
Middle Atlantic	2 308 576	73 935	1 310 196	169 539	754 906	1 216 296	134 459	6 152	12 995	938 674	29 640 597	4 241 586	59 167	497 874	38 990
North Central Region	1 269 994	809 540	208 076	32 874	219 504	700 360	42 140	10 460	14 566	502 468	51 582 790	5 290 767	260 778	420 825	40 516
East North Central	1 061 545	662 948	199 351	29 175	170 071	579 172	36 116	6 489	11 199	428 569	35 643 751	4 509 928	114 075	323 219	29 699
West North Central	208 449	146 592	8 725	3 699	49 433	121 188	6 024	3 971	3 367	73 899	15 939 039	780 839	146 703	97 606	10 817
South Region	4 468 448	3 079 329	181 641	515 452	692 026	3 024 602	156 417	17 433	25 954	1 244 042	56 076 550	13 882 365	389 841	487 051	68 107
South Atlantic	1 192 138	194 308	141 926	490 139	365 765	905 872	90 312	5 189	16 169	174 596	27 776 773	7 559 931	126 506	264 804	38 971
East South Central	119 221	65 502	9 504	3 327	40 888	73 680	31 160	811	1 820	11 750	11 633 465	2 836 331	27 043	43 664	6 699
West South Central	3 157 089	2 819 519	30 211	21 986	285 373	2 045 050	34 945	11 433	7 965	1 057 696	16 666 312	3 486 103	236 292	178 583	22 437
West Region	6 257 167	4 699 332	135 690	74 353	1 347 792	3 325 800	43 228	66 262	120 102	2 701 775	31 847 534	2 217 463	700 141	2 058 648	91 537
Mountain	1 447 961	949 517	14 679	7 555	476 210	835 596	5 543	18 876	6 030	581 916	9 185 104	261 995	354 215	108 209	15 301
Pacific	4 809 206	3 749 815	121 011	66 798	871 582	2 490 204	37 685	47 386	114 072	2 119 859	22 662 430	1 955 468	345 926	1 950 439	76 236
States															
New England Division															
Maine	5 331	1 632	784	193	2 722	4 485	82	85	206	473	1 108 492	3 299	4 280	2 867	391
New Hampshire	5 248	1 044	1 141	245	2 818	4 334	135	56	64	659	906 217	4 189	1 329	3 300	327
Vermont	3 377	516	436	132	2 293	2 851	105	14	49	358	504 201	1 083	1 054	1 591	150
Massachusetts	141 380	7 874	74 910	7 009	51 587	72 440	8 421	541	892	59 086	5 305 963	212 608	8 657	51 723	16 706
Rhode Island	18 906	1 504	3 923	647	12 832	12 174	802	214	294	5 422	888 234	26 559	2 990	6 323	4 142
Connecticut	125 256	3 926	88 164	5 779	27 387	68 832	4 703	312	713	50 696	2 742 260	211 938	4 570	20 403	3 149
Middle Atlantic Division															
New York	1 660 901	40 243	978 616	79 378	562 664	822 128	107 146	4 553	8 221	718 853	13 211 516	2 298 672	39 434	322 751	24 798
New Jersey	494 096	13 913	242 367	84 325	153 491	314 604	17 978	953	2 885	157 676	5 840 229	906 931	9 247	106 498	7 822
Pennsylvania	153 579	19 779	89 213	5 836	38 751	79 564	9 335	646	1 889	62 145	10 588 852	1 035 983	10 486	68 625	6 370
East North Central Division															
Ohio	120 002	52 954	31 806	2 973	32 269	70 501	8 525	991	2 066	37 919	9 536 632	1 068 217	14 563	51 100	7 116
Indiana	86 518	57 006	12 763	1 763	14 986	51 789	2 972	337	948	30 472	4 957 028	411 517	9 354	23 407	2 400
Illinois	634 617	404 543	132 012	19 746	78 316	331 135	14 393	2 283	5 812	280 994	8 936 472	1 660 074	17 329	166 401	11 625
Michigan	157 626	107 766	12 077	3 629	34 154	87 481	8 624	1 938	1 753	57 830	7 805 797	1 188 553	42 981	60 888	6 233
Wisconsin	62 782	40 679	10 693	1 064	10 346	38 266	1 602	940	620	21 354	4 407 822	181 567	29 848	21 423	2 325
West North Central Division															
Minnesota	32 115	20 531	1 607	614	9 363	19 872	744	884	817	9 798	3 922 153	51 581	35 846	31 409	2 866
Iowa	26 274	18 851	620	389	6 414	16 899	432	307	360	8 276	2 824 427	41 796	6 035	13 487	1 789
Missouri	51 853	31 803	2 723	1 382	15 945	34 918	3 253	627	983	12 072	4 313 494	510 132	14 344	23 979	2 884
North Dakota	3 474	2 178	164	45	1 087	1 906	6	119	91	1 352	624 452	2 465	19 834	2 201	291
South Dakota	3 815	2 062	211	52	1 490	2 079	46	547	94	1 049	637 761	2 106	45 025	1 823	238
Nebraska	28 262	21 548	780	274	5 660	15 510	480	484	350	11 438	1 476 710	47 466	8 662	7 840	885
Kansas	62 656	49 619	2 620	943	9 474	30 004	1 063	1 003	672	29 914	2 140 042	125 293	16 957	16 867	1 864
South Atlantic Division															
Delaware	9 540	1 415	4 857	547	2 721	4 993	880	59	194	3 414	483 009	95 277	1 332	4 433	747
Maryland	63 196	11 896	9 301	5 247	36 752	42 521	7 737	327	2 891	9 720	3 123 621	949 681	8 748	65 058	6 671
District of Columbia	17 777	3 133	1 485	689	12 470	7 902	3 562	60	468	5 785	166 803	444 808	954	6 415	1 576
Virginia	79 722	23 937	10 030	4 665	41 090	51 003	10 378	486	4 087	13 768	4 185 342	998 287	9 583	66 482	7 402
West Virginia	13 118	6 071	826	270	5 951	11 357	513	88	355	805	1 863 261	64 528	2 269	5 547	921
North Carolina	56 039	27 334	7 693	2 327	18 685	29 917	13 703	1 702	1 140	9 577	4 430 653	1 305 351	64 258	22 010	3 455
South Carolina	33 667	17 855	3 945	1 346	10 521	15 907	12 756	295	802	3 907	2 131 918	935 213	6 449	12 568	2 005
Georgia	60 974	26 933	8 126	5 736	20 179	34 027	16 279	359	1 378	8 931	3 915 556	1 448 156	9 720	24 631	4 068
Florida	858 105	75 734	95 663	469 312	217 396	708 245	24 504	1 813	4 854	118 689	7 476 610	1 318 630	23 193	57 660	12 126
East South Central Division															
Kentucky	27 094	13 890	3 208	701	9 295	20 491	2 211	208	582	3 602	3 359 765	257 078	4 393	11 241	1 206
Tennessee	34 026	18 621	2 402	1 011	11 992	23 169	7 025	212	429	3 191	3 814 799	717 783	6 823	14 823	2 866
Alabama	33 923	19 093	2 713	1 151	10 966	18 370	12 219	217	431	2 686	2 854 919	984 064	9 087	10 229	1 666
Mississippi	24 178	13 898	1 181	464	8 635	11 650	9 705	174	378	2 271	1 603 982	877 406	6 740	7 371	961
West South Central Division															
Arkansas	16 976	10 221	717	201	5 837	10 421	3 169	261	240	2 885	1 879 514	369 856	12 496	6 992	601
Louisiana	99 699	26 687	4 429	7 331	61 252	73 401	14 052	985	940	10 321	2 841 909	1 224 420	11 947	24 183	3 742
Oklahoma	57 831	38 061	3 109	838	15 823	28 197	1 930	3 007	466	24 231	2 574 866	202 880	168 217	19 299	2 197
Texas	2 982 583	2 744 550	21 956	13 616	202 461	1 933 031	15 794	7 180	6 319	1 020 259	9 370 023	1 688 947	43 632	128 109	15 897
Mountain Division															
Montana	10 103	6 334	283	91	3 395	6 411	39	678	160	2 815	734 490	1 699	37 022	2 937	439
Idaho	36 560	27 938	383	33	8 206	16 354	41	597	318	19 250	887 691	2 670	9 926	6 403	685
Wyoming	24 535	15 256	310	38	8 931	14 986	84	374	91	9 000	431 503	3 186	7 892	1 953	488
Colorado	341 435	204 851	4 293	1 680	130 611	196 840	1 943	3 621	1 510	137 521	2 394 430	99 752	17 394	32 747	4 206
New Mexico	477 051	228 706	1 672	671	246 002	300 421	773	3 648	610	171 599	690 236	22 298	103 102	7 118	3 089
Arizona	444 102	397 940	4 061	1 069	41 032	231 563	1 749	7 929	1 674	201 187	2 028 725	72 410	146 461	22 888	3 629
Utah	60 045	36 751	1 731	284	21 279	32 775	266	1 058	622	25 324	1 351 222	9 425	19 045	19 602	1 698
Nevada	54 130	31 741	1 946	3 689	16 754	36 246	648	971	1 045	15 220	666 807	50 555	13 373	14 561	1 067
Pacific Division															
Washington	121 286	79 598	5 075	1 347	35 266	56 701	1 519	2 655	6 169	54 242	3 734 289	104 085	61 153	105 438	5 905
Oregon	66 164	44 017	1 746	974	19 427	36 999	656	1 797	1 655	25 057	2 459 399	36 798	28 672	39 303	2 769
California	4 541 300	3 613 167	93 005	63 797	771 331	2 370 578	34 574	42 002	70 816	2 023 330	15 850 775	1 784 086	189 700	1 242 157	59 884
Alaska	9 057	3 907	1 102	223	3 825	5 069	215	561	618	2 594	306 899	13 533	63 796	7 696	870
Hawaii	71 399	9 126	20 083	457	41 733	20 857	721	371	34 814	14 636	311 068	16 966	2 605	555 845	6 808

Table 233. Persons by Spanish Origin, Race, and Sex, for Regions, Divisions and States: 1980—Con.

[Data are estimates based on a sample; see Introduction. For meaning of symbols, see Introduction. For definitions of terms, see appendixes A and B]

United States Regions and Divisions States	Spanish origin										Not of Spanish origin				
	Total	Type				Race					White	Black	American Indian, Eskimo, and Aleut	Asian and Pacific Islander	Race, n.e.c.
		Mexican	Puerto Rican	Cuban	Other Spanish	White	Black	American Indian, Eskimo, and Aleut	Asian and Pacific Islander	Race, n.e.c.					
MALE															
United States	7 274 333	4 410 299	976 724	385 491	1 501 819	4 154 920	187 736	50 800	85 889	2 794 988	87 895 278	12 321 255	706 918	1 714 668	135 061
Regions and Divisions															
Northeast Region	1 243 890	45 168	704 034	87 831	406 857	664 098	69 300	3 415	7 068	500 009	19 710 894	2 164 922	40 231	286 732	31 057
New England	145 284	8 028	81 933	6 837	48 486	80 580	6 600	581	1 097	56 426	5 494 808	219 145	11 209	41 505	11 789
Middle Atlantic	1 098 606	37 140	622 101	80 994	358 371	583 518	62 700	2 834	5 971	443 583	14 216 086	1 945 777	29 022	245 227	19 268
North Central Region	652 397	421 963	105 935	16 888	107 611	356 069	20 591	5 417	6 385	263 935	25 115 501	2 497 164	128 174	199 743	21 238
East North Central	546 005	346 370	101 151	14 955	83 529	295 335	17 639	3 443	4 868	224 720	17 347 374	2 121 919	56 058	154 711	15 641
West North Central	106 392	75 593	4 784	1 933	24 082	60 734	2 952	1 974	1 517	39 215	7 768 127	375 245	72 116	45 032	5 597
South Region	2 213 689	1 538 940	95 964	244 036	334 749	1 476 223	76 005	8 925	12 356	640 180	27 360 165	6 555 841	195 105	224 183	36 054
South Atlantic	581 193	101 465	73 219	231 479	175 030	433 330	44 116	2 673	7 641	93 433	13 519 524	3 571 006	63 855	120 346	20 495
East South Central	59 551	32 165	5 420	1 659	20 307	36 316	14 965	432	850	6 988	5 666 841	1 327 940	13 419	18 927	3 570
West South Central	1 572 945	1 405 310	17 325	10 898	139 412	1 006 577	16 924	5 820	3 865	539 759	8 173 820	1 656 895	117 831	84 910	11 989
West Region	3 164 357	2 404 228	70 791	36 736	652 602	1 658 530	21 840	33 043	60 080	1 390 864	15 708 698	1 103 328	343 408	1 004 010	46 712
Mountain	725 775	481 973	8 185	4 017	231 600	414 753	2 854	9 414	2 951	295 803	4 556 445	136 264	172 503	49 797	7 765
Pacific	2 438 582	1 922 255	62 606	32 719	427 002	1 243 777	18 966	23 629	57 129	1 095 061	11 152 253	967 064	170 905	954 213	38 947
States															
New England Division															
Maine	2 740	827	365	115	1 433	2 265	31	51	122	271	537 843	1 910	2 140	1 257	199
New Hampshire	2 793	543	600	154	1 496	2 260	105	25	32	371	441 020	2 265	769	1 373	156
Vermont	1 646	213	234	73	1 126	1 411	30	6	22	177	245 491	650	497	734	99
Massachusetts	67 917	3 714	35 814	3 440	24 949	35 063	3 872	259	370	28 353	2 523 785	101 544	4 235	25 059	7 981
Rhode Island	9 630	743	2 012	340	6 535	6 256	387	92	176	2 719	422 947	12 799	1 275	3 142	1 810
Connecticut	60 558	1 988	42 908	2 715	12 947	33 325	2 175	148	375	24 535	1 323 722	99 977	2 293	9 940	1 544
Middle Atlantic Division															
New York	781 957	20 005	459 275	37 813	264 864	390 475	49 354	2 067	3 826	336 235	6 319 965	1 045 104	19 030	160 501	12 190
New Jersey	240 253	7 053	117 977	40 307	74 916	153 550	8 749	481	300	76 173	2 809 623	421 481	4 605	51 469	4 042
Pennsylvania	76 396	10 082	44 849	2 874	18 591	39 493	4 597	286	845	31 175	5 086 498	479 192	5 387	33 257	3 036
East North Central Division															
Ohio	60 628	26 828	16 528	1 606	15 666	35 308	4 245	461	923	19 691	4 620 702	501 587	7 146	23 437	3 842
Indiana	43 368	28 852	6 476	850	7 190	26 004	1 314	172	340	15 538	2 410 431	194 929	4 569	10 854	1 277
Illinois	330 814	215 479	66 278	10 210	38 847	171 248	7 032	1 299	2 590	148 645	4 336 926	775 364	8 467	81 594	5 895
Michigan	78 969	53 782	6 355	1 789	17 043	43 367	4 293	969	705	29 615	3 818 715	563 393	21 349	29 045	3 486
Wisconsin	32 226	21 429	5 514	500	4 783	19 408	755	522	310	11 231	2 160 600	86 646	14 527	9 781	1 141
West North Central Division															
Minnesota	16 209	10 706	701	329	4 473	9 867	378	433	330	5 201	1 921 573	26 577	17 382	14 777	1 450
Iowa	13 027	9 482	313	181	3 051	8 125	250	140	137	4 375	1 371 958	20 853	2 920	6 435	933
Missouri	26 260	15 992	1 615	737	7 916	17 619	1 613	339	500	6 189	2 080 985	238 650	7 323	10 804	1 540
North Dakota	1 863	1 248	84	32	499	979	4	64	26	790	314 309	1 565	9 644	964	161
South Dakota	1 941	1 105	96	42	698	967	31	295	54	594	314 492	1 399	21 997	799	112
Nebraska	14 437	11 123	415	170	2 729	7 855	191	243	138	6 010	720 224	23 157	4 355	3 391	473
Kansas	32 655	25 937	1 560	442	4 716	15 322	485	460	332	16 056	1 044 586	63 044	8 495	7 862	928
South Atlantic Division															
Delaware	4 634	732	2 455	250	1 197	2 351	408	34	74	1 767	234 013	44 769	681	1 995	402
Maryland	30 768	6 032	4 671	2 616	17 449	20 525	3 720	156	1 475	4 892	1 522 700	449 811	4 448	30 812	3 452
District of Columbia	8 211	1 616	754	361	5 480	3 581	1 641	31	199	2 759	78 156	204 775	505	3 013	793
Virginia	39 696	12 419	5 351	2 269	19 657	24 357	5 291	297	2 017	7 734	2 059 486	478 602	4 985	30 927	4 033
West Virginia	6 577	3 066	376	131	3 004	5 721	254	39	141	422	904 729	30 289	1 172	2 591	421
North Carolina	29 516	14 265	4 779	1 292	9 180	15 326	6 704	866	480	6 140	2 163 456	618 763	31 690	9 376	1 820
South Carolina	17 137	8 868	2 454	727	5 088	8 130	6 194	133	351	2 429	1 049 697	441 158	3 360	5 445	1 135
Georgia	30 912	13 502	4 804	2 717	9 789	16 867	7 757	200	689	5 399	1 913 298	677 904	5 160	10 754	2 302
Florida	413 742	40 865	47 575	221 116	104 186	336 472	12 247	917	2 215	61 891	3 593 989	624 935	11 854	25 433	6 137
East South Central Division															
Kentucky	14 226	7 173	2 061	324	4 668	10 243	1 171	150	268	2 394	1 642 307	124 339	2 272	4 755	648
Tennessee	16 584	8 896	1 247	574	5 867	11 312	3 096	104	186	1 886	1 853 205	335 492	3 361	6 756	1 486
Alabama	16 824	9 247	1 462	551	5 564	9 160	5 961	86	153	1 464	1 387 768	456 503	4 525	4 155	952
Mississippi	11 917	6 849	650	210	4 208	5 601	4 737	92	243	1 244	783 561	411 606	3 261	3 261	484
West South Central Division															
Arkansas	8 254	5 037	374	104	2 739	4 985	1 347	138	117	1 667	914 257	172 917	5 994	3 032	319
Louisiana	49 924	13 575	2 332	3 535	30 482	36 863	6 817	463	492	5 289	1 395 870	573 118	6 444	11 771	2 140
Oklahoma	30 411	20 045	1 784	494	8 088	14 669	899	1 472	212	13 159	1 254 640	98 664	82 833	8 658	1 216
Texas	1 484 356	1 366 653	12 835	6 765	98 103	950 060	7 861	3 747	3 044	519 644	4 609 053	812 196	22 560	61 449	8 314
Mountain Division															
Montana	5 108	3 197	188	39	1 684	3 212	22	331	90	1 453	366 826	1 085	17 981	1 356	230
Idaho	20 128	15 741	197	26	4 164	8 551	24	266	184	11 103	441 025	1 662	4 968	2 801	381
Wyoming	12 895	8 211	177	23	4 484	7 779	25	217	51	4 823	220 872	1 787	3 876	840	264
Colorado	170 728	104 161	2 417	967	63 183	98 136	977	1 876	786	68 951	1 185 150	51 316	8 797	15 433	2 217
New Mexico	235 847	114 883	974	353	119 637	148 384	399	1 779	234	85 051	340 802	11 686	49 360	2 988	1 515
Arizona	221 850	199 345	1 162	560	19 783	113 708	976	3 957	875	102 334	995 713	37 669	71 537	10 271	1 703
Utah	31 035	19 482	1 002	177	10 374	16 456	134	512	235	13 698	668 267	5 534	9 271	9 709	894
Nevada	28 184	16 953	1 068	1 872	8 291	18 527	297	474	496	8 390	337 790	25 525	6 713	6 399	561
Pacific Division															
Washington	63 966	42 797	2 829	778	17 562	28 481	807	1 351	3 243	30 084	1 849 258	56 123	30 146	49 414	3 086
Oregon	35 132	24 303	917	485	9 427	18 917	326	919	813	14 157	1 207 189	19 369	14 341	18 523	1 396
California	2 297 687	1 847 885	47 556	31 015	371 231	1 183 100	17 387	20 896	35 100	1 041 202	7 764 489	872 544	92 645	608 206	30 533
Alaska	4 862	2 142	665	154	1 901	2 676	105	296	325	1 460	164 241	7 582	32 234	3 631	395
Hawaii	36 935	5 128	10 639	287	20 881	10 603	361	165	17 648	8 158	167 076	11 446	1 539	274 439	3 537

Table 233. **Persons by Spanish Origin, Race, and Sex, for Regions, Divisions and States: 1980**—Con.

[Data are estimates based on a sample; see Introduction. For meaning of symbols, see Introduction. For definitions of terms, see appendixes A and B]

United States Regions and Divisions States	Spanish origin										Not of Spanish origin				
	Total	Type				Race					White	Black	American Indian, Eskimo, and Aleut	Asian and Pacific Islander	Race, n.e.c.
		Mexican	Puerto Rican	Cuban	Other Spanish	White	Black	American Indian, Eskimo, and Aleut	Asian and Pacific Islander	Race, n.e.c.					
FEMALE															
United States	7 329 350	4 268 333	1 028 237	420 732	1 612 048	4 277 254	202 756	50 729	89 946	2 708 665	92 707 560	13 770 602	725 889	1 835 937	128 954
Regions and Divisions															
Northeast Region	1 364 184	45 263	775 520	95 713	447 688	717 314	79 407	3 959	8 145	555 359	21 385 070	2 536 340	41 816	297 349	32 798
New England	154 214	8 468	87 425	7 168	51 153	84 536	7 648	641	1 121	60 268	5 960 559	240 531	11 671	44 702	13 076
Middle Atlantic	1 209 970	36 795	688 095	88 545	396 535	632 778	71 759	3 318	7 024	495 091	15 424 511	2 295 809	30 145	252 647	19 722
North Central Region	617 597	387 577	102 141	15 986	111 893	344 291	21 549	5 043	8 181	238 533	26 467 289	2 793 603	132 604	221 082	19 278
East North Central	515 540	316 578	98 200	14 220	86 542	283 837	18 477	3 046	6 331	203 849	18 296 377	2 388 009	58 017	168 508	14 058
West North Central	102 057	70 999	3 941	1 766	25 351	60 454	3 072	1 997	1 850	34 684	8 170 912	405 594	74 587	52 574	5 220
South Region	2 254 759	1 540 389	85 677	271 416	357 277	1 548 379	80 412	8 508	13 598	603 862	28 716 365	7 326 524	194 736	262 868	32 053
South Atlantic	610 945	92 843	68 707	258 660	190 735	472 542	46 196	2 516	8 528	81 163	14 257 249	3 988 925	62 651	144 458	18 476
East South Central	59 670	33 337	4 084	1 668	20 581	37 364	16 195	379	970	4 762	5 966 624	1 508 391	13 624	24 737	3 129
West South Central	1 584 144	1 414 209	12 886	11 088	145 961	1 038 473	18 021	5 613	4 100	517 937	8 492 492	1 829 208	118 461	93 673	10 448
West Region	3 092 810	2 295 104	64 899	37 617	695 190	1 667 270	21 388	33 219	60 022	1 310 911	16 138 836	1 114 135	356 733	1 054 638	44 825
Mountain	722 186	467 544	6 494	3 538	244 610	420 843	2 689	9 462	3 079	286 113	4 628 659	125 731	181 712	58 412	7 536
Pacific	2 370 624	1 827 560	58 405	34 079	450 580	1 246 427	18 699	23 757	56 943	1 024 798	11 510 177	988 404	175 021	996 226	37 289
States															
New England Division															
Maine	2 591	805	419	78	1 289	2 220	51	34	84	202	570 649	1 389	2 140	1 610	192
New Hampshire	2 455	501	541	91	1 322	2 074	30	31	32	288	465 197	1 924	560	1 927	171
Vermont	1 731	303	202	59	1 167	1 440	75	8	27	181	258 710	433	557	857	51
Massachusetts	73 463	4 160	39 096	3 569	26 638	37 377	4 549	282	522	30 733	2 782 178	111 064	4 422	26 664	8 725
Rhode Island	9 276	761	1 911	307	6 297	5 918	415	122	118	2 703	465 287	13 760	1 715	3 181	2 332
Connecticut	64 698	1 938	45 256	3 064	14 440	35 507	2 528	164	338	26 161	1 418 538	111 961	2 277	10 463	1 605
Middle Atlantic Division															
New York	878 944	20 238	519 341	41 565	297 800	431 653	57 792	2 486	4 395	382 618	6 891 551	1 253 568	20 404	162 250	12 608
New Jersey	253 843	6 860	124 390	44 018	78 575	161 054	9 229	472	1 585	81 503	3 030 606	485 450	4 642	55 029	3 780
Pennsylvania	77 183	9 697	44 364	2 962	20 160	40 071	4 738	360	1 044	30 970	5 502 354	556 791	5 099	35 368	3 334
East North Central Division															
Ohio	59 374	26 126	15 278	1 367	16 603	35 193	4 280	530	1 143	18 228	4 915 930	566 630	7 417	27 663	3 274
Indiana	43 150	28 154	6 287	913	7 796	25 785	1 658	165	608	14 934	2 546 597	216 588	4 785	12 553	1 123
Illinois	303 803	189 064	65 734	9 536	39 469	159 887	7 361	984	3 222	132 349	3 987 082	884 710	8 862	84 807	5 730
Michigan	78 657	53 984	5 722	1 840	17 111	44 114	4 331	949	1 048	28 215		625 160	21 632	31 843	2 747
Wisconsin	30 556	19 250	5 179	564	5 563	18 858	847	418	310	10 123	2 247 222	94 921	15 321	11 642	1 184
West North Central Division															
Minnesota	15 906	9 825	906	285	4 890	10 005	366	451	487	4 597	2 000 580	25 004	18 464	16 632	1 416
Iowa	13 247	9 369	307	208	3 363	8 774	182	167	223	3 901	1 452 469	20 943	3 115	7 052	856
Missouri	25 593	15 811	1 108	645	8 029	17 299	1 640	288	483	5 883	2 232 509	271 482	7 021	13 175	1 344
North Dakota	1 611	930	80	13	588	927	2	55	65	562	310 143	900	10 190	1 237	130
South Dakota	1 874	957	115	10	792	1 112	15	252	40	455	323 269	707	23 028	1 024	126
Nebraska	13 825	10 425	365	104	2 931	7 655	289	241	212	5 428	756 486	24 309	4 307	4 449	412
Kansas	30 001	23 682	1 060	501	4 758	14 682	578	543	340	13 858	1 095 456	62 249	8 462	9 005	936
South Atlantic Division															
Delaware	4 906	683	2 402	297	1 524	2 642	472	25	120	1 647	248 996	50 508	651	2 438	345
Maryland	32 428	5 864	4 630	2 631	19 303	21 996	4 017	171	1 416	4 828	1 600 921	499 870	4 300	34 246	3 219
District of Columbia	9 566	1 517	731	328	6 990	4 321	1 921	29	269	3 026	88 647	240 033	449	3 402	783
Virginia	40 026	11 518	4 679	2 396	21 433	26 646	5 087	189	2 070	6 034	2 125 856	519 685	4 598	35 555	3 369
West Virginia	6 541	3 005	450	139	2 947	5 636	259	49	214	383	958 532	34 239	1 097	2 956	500
North Carolina	26 523	13 069	2 914	1 035	9 505	14 591	6 999	836	660	3 437	2 267 197	686 588	32 568	12 634	1 635
South Carolina	16 530	8 987	1 491	619	5 433	7 777	6 662	162	451	1 478	1 082 221	494 055	3 089	7 123	870
Georgia	30 062	13 331	3 322	3 019	10 390	17 160	8 522	159	689	3 532	2 002 258	770 252	4 560	13 877	1 766
Florida	444 363	34 869	48 088	248 196	113 210	371 773	12 257	896	2 639	56 798	3 882 621	693 695	11 339	32 227	5 989
East South Central Division															
Kentucky	12 868	6 717	1 147	377	4 627	10 248	1 040	58	314	1 208	1 717 458	132 739	2 121	6 486	558
Tennessee	17 442	9 725	1 155	437	6 125	11 857	3 929	108	243	1 305	1 961 594	382 291	3 462	8 067	1 380
Alabama	17 099	9 846	1 251	600	5 402	9 210	6 258	131	278	1 222	1 467 551	527 561	4 562	6 074	714
Mississippi	12 261	7 049	531	254	4 427	6 049	4 968	82	135	1 027	820 421	465 800	3 479	4 110	477
West South Central Division															
Arkansas	8 722	5 184	343	97	3 098	5 436	1 822	123	123	1 218	965 257	196 939	6 502	3 960	282
Louisiana	49 775	13 112	2 097	3 796	30 770	36 538	7 235	522	448	5 032	1 446 039	651 302	5 503	12 412	1 602
Oklahoma	27 420	18 016	1 325	344	7 735	13 528	1 031	1 535	254	11 072	1 320 226	104 216	85 384	10 641	981
Texas	1 498 227	1 377 897	9 121	6 851	104 358	982 971	7 933	3 433	3 275	500 615	4 760 970	876 751	21 072	66 660	7 583
Mountain Division															
Montana	4 995	3 137	95	52	1 711	3 199	17	347	70	1 362	367 664	614	19 041	1 581	209
Idaho	16 432	12 197	186	7	4 042	7 803	17	331	134	8 147	446 666	1 008	4 958	3 602	304
Wyoming	11 640	7 045	133	15	4 447	7 207	59	157	40	4 177	210 631	1 399	4 016	1 113	224
Colorado	170 707	100 690	1 876	713	67 428	98 704	966	1 743	724	68 570	1 209 280	48 436	8 597	17 314	1 989
New Mexico	241 204	113 823	698	318	126 365	152 037	374	1 869	376	86 548	349 434	10 612	53 742	4 130	1 574
Arizona	222 252	198 595	1 899	509	21 249	117 855	773	3 972	799	98 853	1 033 012	34 741	74 924	12 617	1 926
Utah	29 010	17 269	729	107	10 905	16 319	132	546	387	11 626	682 955	3 891	9 774	9 893	804
Nevada	25 946	14 788	878	1 817	8 463	17 719	351	497	549	6 830	329 017	25 030	6 660	8 162	506
Pacific Division															
Washington	57 320	36 801	2 246	569	17 704	28 220	712	1 304	2 926	24 158	1 885 031	47 962	31 007	56 024	2 819
Oregon	31 032	19 714	829	489	10 000	18 082	330	878	842	10 900	1 252 210	17 429	14 331	20 780	1 373
California	2 243 613	1 765 282	45 449	32 782	400 100	1 187 478	17 187	21 104	35 716	982 128	8 086 286	911 542	97 055	633 951	29 351
Alaska	4 195	1 765	437	69	1 924	2 393	110	265	293	1 134	142 658	5 951	31 562	4 065	475
Hawaii	34 464	3 998	9 444	170	20 852	10 254	360	206	17 166	6 478	143 992	5 520	1 066	281 406	3 271

Table 234. Selected Ancestry Groups for Regions, Divisions, and States: 1980

[Data are estimates based on a sample; see Introduction. For meaning of symbols, see Introduction. For definitions of terms, see appendixes A and B]

United States Regions and Divisions States	Total persons	Single ancestry group											
		Dutch	English	French	German	Greek	Hungarian	Irish	Italian	Norwegian	Polish	Portuguese	Russian
United States	226 545 805	1 404 794	23 748 772	3 068 907	17 943 485	615 882	727 223	10 337 353	6 883 320	1 260 997	3 805 740	616 362	1 378 446
REGIONS AND DIVISIONS													
Northeast Region	49 135 283	236 765	2 984 931	1 067 743	3 298 845	273 957	295 748	3 139 662	4 372 070	79 245	1 636 106	355 118	708 965
New England	12 348 493	26 678	1 211 431	813 258	265 684	82 685	32 616	1 057 612	935 919	19 119	346 150	282 718	120 657
Middle Atlantic	36 786 790	210 087	1 773 500	254 485	3 033 161	191 272	263 132	2 082 050	3 436 151	60 126	1 289 956	72 400	588 308
North Central Region	58 865 670	584 724	4 438 223	525 996	8 188 018	143 922	225 512	2 168 162	944 750	712 496	1 461 001	11 233	193 558
East North Central	41 682 217	421 705	3 200 886	370 152	5 189 626	128 562	209 513	1 516 392	832 398	219 414	1 320 137	7 985	154 424
West North Central	17 183 453	163 019	1 237 337	155 844	2 998 392	15 360	15 999	651 770	112 352	493 082	140 864	3 248	39 134
South Region	75 372 362	295 016	12 382 681	1 067 173	3 679 277	106 096	103 405	3 593 729	756 284	84 289	414 907	27 602	235 106
South Atlantic	36 959 123	156 008	6 150 877	286 382	1 984 700	78 648	81 557	1 673 915	528 421	46 581	299 703	19 915	203 672
East South Central	14 666 423	54 019	3 332 912	106 624	557 721	8 287	6 474	901 266	58 917	8 068	24 473	2 146	8 985
West South Central	23 746 816	84 989	2 898 892	674 167	1 136 856	19 161	15 374	1 018 548	168 946	29 640	90 731	5 541	22 449
West Region	43 172 490	288 289	3 942 937	407 995	2 777 345	91 907	102 558	1 435 800	810 216	384 967	293 726	222 409	240 817
Mountain	11 372 785	82 404	1 414 542	111 583	943 700	20 600	20 522	413 282	168 877	106 047	75 508	8 399	32 047
Pacific	31 799 705	205 885	2 528 395	296 412	1 833 645	71 307	82 036	1 022 518	641 339	278 920	218 218	214 010	208 770
STATES													
New England Division													
Maine	1 124 660	3 148	259 519	147 067	20 064	2 286	835	56 335	13 516	1 948	5 802	1 095	2 351
New Hampshire	920 610	2 231	133 229	112 096	20 150	7 192	1 007	52 823	18 203	1 564	13 969	2 252	2 905
Vermont	511 456	1 807	79 019	57 160	11 617	528	771	23 353	8 769	838	5 485	340	1 824
Massachusetts	5 737 037	11 074	460 687	312 515	95 257	53 935	6 854	666 567	430 412	8 200	162 565	190 298	71 943
Rhode Island	947 154	1 247	72 365	77 050	14 011	3 198	842	71 816	118 966	1 112	18 294	61 756	6 181
Connecticut	3 107 576	7 171	206 612	107 370	104 585	15 546	22 307	186 718	346 053	5 457	140 035	26 977	35 453
Middle Atlantic Division													
New York	17 558 072	76 859	795 136	176 289	898 453	123 344	115 981	1 009 905	1 937 791	37 235	607 871	26 690	362 062
New Jersey	7 364 823	47 148	312 756	31 719	405 163	37 034	70 607	451 039	835 277	15 712	287 678	39 792	107 272
Pennsylvania	11 863 895	86 080	665 608	46 477	1 729 545	30 894	76 544	621 106	663 083	7 179	394 407	5 918	118 974
East North Central Division													
Ohio	10 797 630	52 485	1 019 608	68 575	1 430 735	28 864	102 581	422 895	258 482	7 518	186 200	2 331	35 406
Indiana	5 490 224	40 232	676 564	46 984	739 223	9 422	18 382	228 213	33 674	6 413	73 018	786	5 597
Illinois	11 426 518	66 979	650 009	65 168	1 135 212	60 516	30 373	489 307	322 914	47 876	470 517	2 677	69 935
Michigan	9 262 078	218 306	708 594	150 062	773 043	23 859	48 396	272 749	170 740	19 342	400 708	1 529	31 673
Wisconsin	4 705 767	43 703	146 111	39 363	1 111 413	5 901	9 781	103 228	46 588	138 538	189 694	662	11 813
West North Central Division													
Minnesota	4 075 970	26 833	109 486	38 943	707 161	3 380	3 970	96 187	20 853	267 853	63 518	704	11 415
Iowa	2 913 808	65 185	215 911	17 442	599 421	3 014	1 350	122 800	14 147	59 868	7 573	477	2 606
Missouri	4 916 686	24 899	527 041	51 174	633 291	5 626	6 310	242 610	52 849	6 734	5 739	146	2 762
North Dakota	652 717	2 981	14 419	7 410	170 007	308	935	12 752	1 370	97 515	28 447	947	14 021
South Dakota	690 768	14 073	29 147	5 616	179 186	455	623	21 874	1 528	47 267	2 977	132	1 145
Nebraska	1 569 825	10 334	92 699	11 790	352 873	1 226	1 230	61 614	10 892	8 167	23 554	270	2 744
Kansas	2 363 679	18 714	248 634	23 469	356 453	1 351	1 581	93 933	10 713	5 678	9 056	572	4 441
South Atlantic Division													
Delaware	594 338	2 952	77 461	3 553	34 110	1 583	1 218	36 446	22 519	739	14 228	429	2 649
Maryland	4 216 975	15 250	402 336	24 469	366 844	18 623	9 980	181 668	85 695	5 656	73 505	3 099	45 742
District of Columbia	638 333	982	27 958	2 458	10 470	1 508	1 031	12 268	4 881	615	3 022	468	5 944
Virginia	5 346 818	20 951	1 082 559	39 628	292 166	11 599	8 225	221 665	52 143	7 364	28 144	2 898	13 363
West Virginia	1 949 644	13 125	388 511	11 732	138 664	2 375	5 159	106 452	33 191	629	12 542	157	1 608
North Carolina	5 881 766	26 706	1 329 497	34 266	292 878	7 428	3 298	246 552	22 185	3 369	12 518	972	4 327
South Carolina	3 121 820	7 970	578 338	20 992	119 642	3 910	1 537	153 810	12 462	1 869	6 495	742	1 963
Georgia	5 463 105	15 844	1 132 184	31 793	152 464	5 527	3 665	282 108	21 143	3 616	13 496	1 164	8 690
Florida	9 746 324	52 228	1 132 033	117 491	577 462	26 095	47 444	432 946	274 202	22 724	135 753	9 986	119 386
East South Central Division													
Kentucky	3 660 777	15 280	931 737	24 131	245 143	1 610	2 088	230 900	14 125	1 838	7 036	350	2 975
Tennessee	4 591 120	21 040	1 046 830	26 681	164 074	2 806	2 149	289 258	17 915	2 876	8 728	827	3 769
Alabama	3 893 888	12 478	857 864	25 350	98 120	2 902	1 678	224 453	16 343	2 281	5 406	567	1 662
Mississippi	2 520 638	5 221	496 481	30 462	50 384	969	559	156 655	10 534	1 073	3 303	402	579
West South Central Division													
Arkansas	2 286 435	11 036	418 729	17 187	97 454	865	1 021	143 495	8 095	2 079	5 815	443	792
Louisiana	4 205 900	7 188	440 558	480 772	106 399	2 645	2 628	143 424	70 790	2 273	6 563	912	2 793
Oklahoma	3 025 290	20 927	400 283	24 136	178 615	1 892	1 552	158 897	11 469	4 413	7 665	785	1 942
Texas	14 229 191	45 838	1 639 322	152 072	754 388	13 759	10 173	572 732	78 592	20 875	70 688	3 401	16 922
Mountain Division													
Montana	786 690	7 993	58 456	11 607	108 658	763	1 047	40 742	6 869	36 414	4 906	320	1 625
Idaho	943 935	8 713	171 154	11 314	90 268	969	717	33 420	6 583	10 880	2 976	981	1 034
Wyoming	469 557	4 492	52 619	6 173	62 948	1 052	556	24 097	4 853	6 480	3 748	273	896
Colorado	2 889 964	20 711	257 138	27 051	309 991	4 924	5 698	108 871	51 637	19 036	20 098	1 405	10 267
New Mexico	1 302 894	6 311	120 080	9 485	61 532	1 414	1 248	45 204	11 706	3 673	5 454	559	2 247
Arizona	2 718 215	17 399	271 753	27 143	200 760	4 614	8 034	103 312	47 508	16 429	28 066	1 807	11 034
Utah	1 461 037	12 270	404 717	8 362	55 251	4 599	809	22 440	11 589	7 967	3 113	597	1 140
Nevada	800 493	4 515	78 625	10 448	54 292	2 265	2 413	35 072	28 132	5 168	7 147	2 457	4 004
Pacific Division													
Washington	4 132 156	38 719	360 608	44 561	327 907	5 583	5 540	137 816	41 324	107 819	22 370	3 577	9 326
Oregon	2 633 105	23 080	271 686	27 970	243 080	3 419	3 614	97 358	23 366	39 960	11 908	3 671	8 652
California	23 667 902	139 103	1 827 247	213 836	1 208 053	61 038	71 428	757 964	567 351	122 107	177 940	179 734	187 762
Alaska	401 851	3 097	35 592	6 109	32 424	659	710	16 535	3 967	6 904	3 039	581	1 500
Hawaii	964 691	1 886	33 262	3 936	22 181	608	744	12 845	5 331	2 130	3 061	26 447	1 530

Table 234. **Selected Ancestry Groups for Regions, Divisions, and States: 1980**—Con.

[Data are estimates based on a sample; see Introduction. For meaning of symbols, see Introduction. For definitions of terms, see appendixes A and B]

United States Regions and Divisions States	Single ancestry group—Con.				Multiple ancestry group	Ancestry not specified		Selected multiple ancestry groups					
	Scottish	Swedish	Ukrainian	Other		Total	Not reported	English and other group(s)	French and other group(s)	German and other group(s)	Irish and other group(s)	Italian and other group(s)	Polish and other group(s)
United States	1 172 904	1 288 341	381 084	43 931 068	69 737 760	38 243 367	23 182 019	25 849 263	9 835 259	31 280 661	29 828 349	5 300 372	4 422 297
REGIONS AND DIVISIONS													
Northeast Region	270 616	194 793	214 712	8 291 767	15 567 152	6 147 088	3 775 425	5 190 045	2 310 557	6 060 570	6 614 002	2 557 806	1 706 838
New England	111 826	90 322	24 418	1 255 141	4 161 027	1 511 232	927 030	1 723 697	1 178 208	828 322	1 825 116	660 591	385 708
Middle Atlantic	158 790	104 471	190 294	7 036 626	11 406 125	4 635 856	2 848 395	3 466 348	1 132 349	5 232 248	4 788 886	1 897 215	1 321 130
North Central Region	235 917	547 979	86 110	8 124 661	21 527 751	8 745 657	5 442 520	7 099 961	2 967 147	12 056 870	8 404 591	1 050 674	1 692 475
East North Central	175 091	252 136	75 459	6 513 957	14 760 182	6 334 198	3 968 314	4 977 006	2 044 673	8 197 143	5 730 444	877 659	1 418 026
West North Central	60 826	295 843	10 651	1 610 704	6 767 569	2 411 459	1 474 206	2 122 955	922 474	3 859 727	2 674 147	173 015	274 449
South Region	374 275	154 616	40 292	16 857 198	17 484 646	17 715 770	10 339 482	7 235 689	2 466 713	7 063 626	9 116 143	799 056	528 629
South Atlantic	226 264	89 329	32 327	7 949 948	8 692 306	8 458 570	4 945 627	3 704 730	988 662	3 660 856	4 310 642	488 598	361 434
East South Central	64 034	15 885	2 445	2 658 068	2 736 883	4 119 216	2 185 899	1 165 661	309 140	1 037 189	1 663 856	75 573	38 295
West South Central	83 977	49 402	5 520	6 249 182	6 055 457	5 137 984	3 207 956	2 365 298	1 168 911	2 365 581	3 141 645	234 885	128 900
West Region	292 096	390 953	39 970	10 657 442	15 158 211	5 634 852	3 624 592	6 323 568	2 090 842	6 099 595	5 693 613	892 836	494 355
Mountain	87 798	121 441	7 748	2 152 415	4 071 084	1 534 788	959 270	1 839 398	518 172	1 717 125	1 491 485	199 972	122 305
Pacific	204 298	269 512	32 222	8 505 027	11 087 127	4 100 064	2 665 322	4 484 170	1 572 670	4 382 470	4 202 128	692 864	372 050
STATES													
New England Division													
Maine	17 630	7 012	439	59 975	339 969	185 669	95 954	194 313	119 029	53 028	144 964	18 399	10 246
New Hampshire	9 750	5 373	907	63 284	340 892	132 783	82 059	172 298	125 044	63 236	139 895	27 760	20 561
Vermont	5 922	2 534	384	26 889	198 656	85 560	45 327	98 986	87 368	36 801	76 624	13 658	8 548
Massachusetts	52 609	44 900	8 465	593 954	1 893 136	673 666	429 795	747 965	525 994	323 773	897 533	319 171	174 953
Rhode Island	6 670	6 530	1 852	86 094	310 203	88 967	56 086	122 021	101 660	48 424	139 134	66 114	24 419
Connecticut	19 245	23 973	12 371	424 945	1 078 171	344 587	217 809	388 114	219 113	303 060	426 966	215 489	146 981
Middle Atlantic Division													
New York	69 805	51 255	71 248	4 023 057	4 871 762	2 303 329	1 387 601	1 525 367	658 453	1 939 516	1 967 613	874 120	570 302
New Jersey	41 225	21 092	43 266	1 484 946	2 303 009	830 088	495 964	688 841	182 194	967 805	993 269	480 355	304 494
Pennsylvania	47 760	32 124	75 780	1 528 623	4 231 354	1 502 439	964 830	1 252 140	291 702	2 324 927	1 828 004	542 740	446 334
East North Central Division													
Ohio	45 491	20 718	23 127	1 437 564	3 767 107	1 887 943	1 128 519	1 351 628	395 791	2 174 676	1 608 856	261 689	217 568
Indiana	21 949	17 400	3 278	574 851	1 746 262	1 248 249	764 751	679 571	221 354	1 036 921	789 731	52 366	82 502
Illinois	37 169	117 784	23 721	2 483 849	3 749 038	1 603 474	1 042 154	1 158 324	421 157	1 968 139	1 538 385	317 390	421 492
Michigan	59 749	53 740	22 290	1 588 017	3 537 372	1 181 909	755 929	1 327 427	721 995	1 714 828	1 249 047	173 662	424 013
Wisconsin	10 733	42 494	3 043	429 676	1 960 403	412 623	276 961	460 056	284 376	1 302 579	544 425	72 552	272 451
West North Central Division													
Minnesota	10 172	162 917	4 558	328 244	1 867 727	352 049	244 193	381 582	264 766	1 060 609	510 501	43 692	141 301
Iowa	11 321	37 720	583	166 784	1 200 720	386 886	253 080	420 045	133 659	732 203	507 220	22 597	20 277
Missouri	16 754	15 676	2 253	585 143	1 743 994	958 917	558 182	669 734	288 894	942 141	886 539	67 600	48 478
North Dakota	2 465	9 806	1 638	49 965	229 945	42 554	23 753	38 021	26 501	136 739	51 795	2 352	9 958
South Dakota	2 367	11 415	49	74 547	231 761	66 606	38 054	58 933	25 120	144 293	72 048	2 598	5 525
Nebraska	6 057	34 070	796	166 272	621 393	163 844	96 428	199 385	66 044	371 292	250 749	16 197	31 180
Kansas	11 690	24 239	774	239 749	872 029	440 603	260 516	355 255	117 490	472 450	395 295	17 979	17 730
South Atlantic Division													
Delaware	3 174	2 096	2 134	101 754	189 757	97 536	59 411	87 937	19 196	79 033	90 408	22 175	16 302
Maryland	20 745	8 424	7 056	1 011 666	1 299 717	636 500	384 280	538 932	130 259	681 241	584 203	99 558	96 204
District of Columbia	1 612	962	573	378 327	71 617	113 637	86 472	28 637	8 009	24 512	25 399	4 096	4 934
Virginia	32 373	10 805	3 647	999 318	1 322 518	1 197 452	675 913	613 068	152 095	572 133	627 404	69 987	46 950
West Virginia	8 415	2 074	871	105 289	528 768	590 082	291 445	210 304	40 019	269 392	275 820	27 724	16 096
North Carolina	45 177	6 634	1 207	1 196 292	1 099 068	1 549 392	929 294	448 511	99 944	445 771	625 169	30 355	19 431
South Carolina	18 621	4 030	678	773 907	555 587	859 267	523 411	224 741	63 080	211 223	331 007	16 012	10 445
Georgia	26 975	7 251	1 274	1 302 290	985 333	1 468 288	796 048	452 119	108 647	338 805	566 745	31 136	22 588
Florida	69 172	47 053	14 887	2 081 105	2 639 941	1 946 416	1 199 353	1 100 481	367 413	1 038 746	1 184 487	187 555	128 484
East South Central Division													
Kentucky	14 087	3 659	695	295 089	763 616	1 106 418	564 253	335 342	83 537	373 023	441 891	21 876	11 086
Tennessee	21 886	5 571	813	687 341	918 790	1 369 766	769 168	388 317	85 851	333 574	561 691	23 639	12 972
Alabama	18 188	4 542	602	893 217	659 066	1 069 169	537 032	282 112	75 118	210 122	408 583	17 494	9 498
Mississippi	9 873	2 113	335	782 421	395 411	573 863	315 446	159 890	64 634	120 470	251 691	12 564	4 739
West South Central Division													
Arkansas	7 995	4 142	278	392 600	549 370	625 039	299 129	212 810	65 869	204 106	331 666	10 860	7 306
Louisiana	9 446	3 645	694	1 038 529	957 831	928 810	652 632	310 063	453 465	339 291	414 834	94 225	11 333
Oklahoma	10 825	6 928	587	431 781	994 868	767 725	422 862	398 424	127 884	407 625	547 510	18 593	13 484
Texas	55 711	34 687	3 961	4 386 272	3 553 388	2 816 410	1 833 333	1 444 001	521 693	1 414 559	1 847 635	111 207	96 777
Mountain Division													
Montana	8 043	12 198	570	72 002	311 953	102 524	64 925	107 539	42 562	147 256	117 833	9 776	8 320
Idaho	10 747	17 110	209	85 369	348 771	142 720	77 022	175 835	43 478	141 360	119 484	9 681	5 527
Wyoming	6 056	7 496	142	46 670	167 811	73 395	40 069	68 758	20 627	75 170	64 617	6 063	4 586
Colorado	19 710	31 891	2 417	474 544	1 168 209	356 366	209 723	479 043	149 177	559 163	465 120	64 724	39 451
New Mexico	6 861	5 135	469	530 619	308 128	182 645	113 462	124 539	38 549	118 404	126 800	14 496	8 333
Arizona	17 430	21 446	2 736	657 406	889 201	392 137	257 901	373 293	127 396	390 270	359 465	50 015	37 209
Utah	13 045	19 685	288	155 348	574 697	165 120	110 944	384 573	51 919	164 860	115 039	19 651	6 904
Nevada	5 906	6 480	917	130 457	302 314	119 881	85 224	125 818	44 464	120 642	123 127	25 566	11 975
Pacific Division													
Washington	35 216	66 490	3 363	463 730	1 824 486	633 721	408 436	762 158	271 575	777 625	687 178	65 336	48 498
Oregon	24 009	36 067	1 851	229 371	1 161 044	423 099	249 762	497 780	167 987	515 838	449 154	37 403	25 285
California	137 481	160 207	26 391	7 210 405	7 715 952	2 903 903	1 914 939	3 119 307	1 093 497	2 981 456	2 967 961	576 751	287 737
Alaska	4 205	4 469	262	88 531	117 407	75 860	46 707	41 964	17 108	66 750	42 639	4 711	4 340
Hawaii	3 387	2 279	355	512 990	268 238	63 481	45 478	62 961	22 503	60 801	55 196	8 663	6 190

Table 251. Social Characteristics for American Indian Persons on Reservations and Alaska Native Villages: 1980

[Data are estimates based on a sample; see Introduction. For meaning of symbols, see Introduction. For definitions of terms, see appendixes A and B]

Reservations / Alaska Native Villages	American Indian[1]			Age				Persons 5 years and over—Percent who speak a language other than English at home	Civilian persons 16 to 19 years old—Percent not enrolled in school, not high school graduates	Persons 25 years old and over		Families—Percent with own children under 6 years	Persons under 18—Percent living with two parents	Children ever born per 1,000 women 35 to 44 years
	Total persons	Number	Percent of total persons	Under 5 years	18 years and over	65 years and over	Median			Percent high school graduates	Percent completed 4 or more years of college			
RESERVATIONS														
Acoma Pueblo, N. Mex.	2 365	2 354	99.5	307	1 294	169	20.4	82.9	46.9	55.4	–	26.9	67.0	3 591
Agua Caliente Reservation, Calif.	13 649	91	0.7	11	57	5	20.9	23.8	100.0	77.5	17.5	26.1	47.1	–
Alabama-Coushatta Reservation, Tex.	504	490	97.2	54	272	35	23.2	84.4	12.8	53.2	–	41.5	92.7	5 259
Alamo Reservation, N. Mex.	1 085	1 073	98.9	193	485	41	16.7	99.1	81.4	25.4	1.6	48.1	78.6	4 465
Allegany Reservation, N.Y.	7 630	900	11.8	75	561	105	26.9	21.7	–	54.6	4.4	25.2	53.1	3 634
Alturas Rancheria, Calif.	–	–	–	–	–	–	–	–	–	–	–	–	–	–
Annette Island Reserve, Alaska	1 105	902	81.6	115	521	54	20.6	9.8	12.2	53.5	2.1	27.0	78.7	4 864
Augustine Reservation, Calif.	–	–	–	–	–	–	–	–	–	–	–	–	–	–
Bad River Reservation, Wis.	980	694	70.8	96	395	51	22.5	7.4	14.1	63.4	7.6	37.3	56.9	3 839
Barona Rancheria, Calif.	251	183	72.9	39	101	–	18.9	4.2	–	30.4	–	51.3	92.7	3 000
Bay Mills Reservation, Mich.	306	279	91.2	42	155	3	19.5	1.3	29.3	57.7	2.9	51.6	71.8	7 500
Benton Paiute Reservation, Calif.	9	9	100.0	...	...	...	...	...	...	...	...	...	...	...
Berry Creek Rancheria, Calif.	–	–	–	–	–	–	–	–	–	–	–	–	–	–
Big Bend Rancheria, Calif.	10	4	40.0	...	...	...	...	...	...	...	...	...	...	...
Big Cypress Reservation, Fla.	360	–	–	–	–	–	–	–	–	–	–	–	–	–
Big Lagoon Rancheria, Calif.	–	–	–	–	–	–	–	–	–	–	–	–	–	–
Big Pine Rancheria, Calif.	356	265	74.4	36	133	16	18.1	–	–	94.6	–	65.2	55.3	4 286
Bishop Rancheria, Calif.	1 198	867	72.4	126	490	60	22.3	9.0	27.4	65.5	1.8	24.0	47.7	1 862
Blackfeet Reservation, Mont.	6 664	5 084	76.3	693	2 885	377	21.1	13.6	26.9	57.2	5.3	33.2	63.5	4 280
Bois Forte Reservation (Nett Lake), Minn.	400	393	98.3	59	204	29	18.6	12.3	33.3	43.8	–	51.2	40.2	6 000
Bridgeport Colony, Calif.	48	20	41.7	...	...	...	...	...	...	...	...	...	...	...
Brighton Reservation, Fla.	328	320	97.6	56	201	40	29.3	10.6	...	59.0	21.9	61.4	79.0	3 321
Burns Reservation, Oreg.	177	161	91.0	17	90	–	19.6	4.9	25.0	69.2	–	–	81.7	–
Cabazon Reservation, Calif.	723	–	–	–	–	–	–	–	–	–	–	–	–	–
Cachil Dehe Rancheria, Calif.	13	13	100.0	–	–	–	–	...	...	–	–	–	–	–
Cahuilla Reservation, Calif.	30	30	100.0	...	11	...	17.0	...	...	...	...	...	...	...
Campo Reservation, Calif.	109	98	89.9	26	59	–	18.8	45.8	100.0	–	–	–	33.3	–
Camp Verde Reservation, Ariz.	168	136	81.0	40	90	–	25.0	20.8	–	82.4	–	12.5	100.0	8 000
Canoncito Reservation, N. Mex.	1 032	1 022	99.0	108	602	30	21.1	97.0	43.1	34.2	1.8	43.5	77.1	3 527
Capitan Grande Reservation, Calif.	–	–	–	–	–	–	–	–	–	–	–	–	–	–
Carson Colony, Nev.	179	172	96.1	10	97	7	20.7	8.0	100.0	71.8	–	15.4	–	5 286
Catawba Reservation, S.C.	932	688	73.8	104	338	25	17.5	–	22.8	28.4	–	37.0	81.4	4 703
Cattaraugus Reservation, N.Y.	1 970	1 858	94.3	196	1 074	156	21.2	15.5	27.8	46.1	2.5	24.4	59.2	4 107
Cedarville Rancheria, Calif.	6	6	100.0	...	...	...	...	...	...	...	...	...	...	...
Chehalis Reservation, Wash.	352	151	42.9	49	102	22	25.6	–	–	72.5	–	54.2	85.7	...
Chemehuevi Reservation, Calif.	255	9	3.5	...	...	...	...	...	...	...	...	...	...	...
Cheyenne River Reservation, S. Dak.	1 824	1 557	85.4	252	733	63	17.2	36.2	47.1	43.1	1.8	40.8	51.0	5 667
Chitimacha Reservation, La.	1 248	159	12.7	12	92	6	21.7	4.1	57.1	75.0	–	17.8	71.6	5 000
Cochiti Pueblo, N. Mex.	1 027	796	77.5	66	440	87	20.1	60.0	26.2	65.2	4.3	19.1	75.0	3 563
Cocopah Reservation, Ariz.	407	407	100.0	33	237	33	22.8	78.6	34.8	21.7	–	33.3	55.3	4 000
Coeur d'Alene Reservation, Idaho	4 900	457	9.3	43	267	34	23.1	.6.5	–	62.0	3.8	28.8	23.7	2 250
Cold Springs Rancheria, Calif.	–	–	–	–	–	–	–	–	–	–	–	–	–	–
Colorado River Reservation, Ariz.-Calif.	7 930	1 989	25.1	292	1 108	82	21.1	24.1	38.7	50.6	4.6	45.9	58.6	3 566
Colville Reservation, Wash.	7 077	3 248	45.9	402	1 886	232	22.9	0.2	18.2	63.4	7.8	36.4	47.7	3 584
Cortina Rancheria, Calif.	–	–	–	–	–	–	–	–	–	–	–	–	–	–
Coushatta Reservation, La.	8	–	–	–	–	–	–	–	–	–	–	–	–	–
Coyote Valley Rancheria, Calif.	–	–	–	–	–	–	–	–	–	–	–	–	–	–
Crow Reservation, Mont.	5 920	4 083	69.0	586	2 251	194	20.1	77.0	17.5	53.2	7.0	33.1	63.3	4 229
Crow Creek Reservation, S. Dak.	1 780	1 484	83.4	234	706	53	17.2	24.7	62.3	46.9	2.2	43.9	61.4	4 687
Cuyapaipe Reservation, Calif.	–	–	–	–	–	–	–	–	–	–	–	–	–	–
Deer Creek Reservation, Minn.	193	–	–	–	–	–	–	–	–	–	–	–	–	–
Dresslerville Colony, Nev.	150	142	94.7	33	99	14	24.1	47.7	32.3	72.1	–	55.0	76.7	6 000
Dry Creek Rancheria, Calif.	21	18	85.7	...	...	...	...	...	...	...	...	...	...	...
Duck Valley Reservation, Idaho-Nev.	1 056	962	91.1	105	523	80	21.4	55.1	4.0	46.7	–	29.3	48.7	4 563
Duckwater Reservation, Nev.	147	147	100.0	22	125	24	30.3	29.6	–	86.0	–	60.0	–	–
Eastern Cherokee Reservation, N.C.	5 778	4 830	83.6	543	2 869	292	22.6	22.9	34.4	42.4	2.9	30.3	58.9	3 050
Eastern Pequot Reservation, Conn.	30	25	83.3	...	...	...	...	...	...	...	...	...	...	...
Ely Colony, Nev.	76	76	100.0	6	28	4	15.8	35.7	66.7	70.8	–	50.0	47.9	6 500
Enterprise Rancheria, Calif.	–	–	–	–	–	–	–	–	–	–	–	–	–	–
Fallon Colony, Nev.	66	66	100.0	–	53	26	57.7	65.2	–	24.5	–	–	100.0	–
Fallon Reservation, Nev.	263	241	91.6	28	168	9	23.9	26.3	–	37.7	12.3	–	61.6	–
Flandreau Reservation, S. Dak.	147	126	85.7	12	71	1	19.9	10.5	46.7	61.4	–	10.3	34.5	4 000
Flathead Reservation, Mont.	19 551	3 504	17.9	381	2 002	184	20.6	17.8	12.1	58.1	1.3	30.7	51.9	4 306
Fond du Lac Reservation, Minn.	2 880	471	16.4	54	250	38	20.0	11.5	4.3	47.9	3.6	40.0	64.3	3 833
Fort Apache Reservation, Ariz.	7 841	7 010	89.4	917	3 526	173	18.2	89.7	44.0	38.0	2.0	42.1	60.6	4 414
Fort Belknap Reservation, Mont.	1 945	1 711	88.0	206	949	87	20.0	4.8	37.7	53.2	6.3	30.3	59.3	5 429
Fort Berthold Reservation, N. Dak.	5 608	2 651	47.3	312	1 405	95	18.8	17.5	24.5	58.9	8.0	30.9	56.3	4 958
Fort Bidwell Reservation, Calif.	125	116	92.8	40	76	12	23.8	–	–	57.7	–	14.3	–	–
Fort Hall Reservation, Idaho	4 605	2 500	54.3	331	1 332	160	19.6	49.7	12.1	36.6	1.0	38.8	57.7	3 881
Fort Independence Reservation, Calif.	75	42	56.0	–	42	10	47.0	–	–	85.7	–	–	–	3 000
Fort McDermitt Reservation, Nev.-Oreg.	443	416	93.9	50	214	41	18.8	76.5	64.6	20.8	6.7	36.3	61.9	5 731
Fort McDowell Reservation, Ariz.	425	415	97.6	65	245	62	25.4	67.7	–	36.8	1.4	13.5	48.8	3 381
Fort Mojave Reservation, Ariz.-Calif.-Nev.	195	139	71.3	32	87	–	25.7	14.0	–	90.9	–	58.3	84.6	–
Fort Peck Reservation, Mont.	9 839	4 422	44.9	618	2 422	226	19.9	17.8	49.8	56.6	3.2	36.3	53.6	4 860
Fort Totten Reservation, N. Dak.	3 267	2 258	69.1	379	1 040	101	16.7	19.9	21.1	36.2	1.8	50.7	63.2	5 875
Fort Yuma Reservation, Ariz.-Calif.	4 667	1 097	23.5	107	637	51	23.3	33.7	11.5	47.8	0.8	16.3	63.3	4 524
Gila Bend Reservation, Ariz.	–	–	–	–	–	–	–	–	–	–	–	–	–	–
Gila River Reservation, Ariz.	7 345	6 904	94.0	859	3 784	407	19.9	50.2	47.2	37.2	2.8	33.8	54.6	4 270
Golden Hill Reservation, Conn.	–	–	–	–	–	–	–	–	–	–	–	–	–	–
Goshute Reservation, Nev.-Utah	45	45	100.0	–	14	–	13.6	44.4	–	42.9	–	–	–	6 000
Grand Portage Reservation, Minn.	294	201	68.4	22	135	15	26.3	6.7	–	65.1	6.4	45.5	56.1	5 500
Grindstone Creek Rancheria, Calif.	62	62	100.0	10	31	5	20.0	–	–	–	–	–	9.7	5 000
Hannahville Community, Mich.	205	202	98.5	42	95	4	16.9	11.9	70.8	50.8	–	50.0	60.7	10 000
Hassanamisco Reservation, Mass.	–	–	–	–	–	–	–	–	–	–	–	–	–	–

[1]Includes Eskimos and Aleuts on Annette Island Reserve and Alaska Native Villages.

Table 251. Social Characteristics for American Indian Persons on Reservations and Alaska Native Villages: 1980—Con.

[Data are estimates based on a sample; see Introduction. For meaning of symbols, see Introduction. For definitions of terms, see appendixes A and B]

Reservations Alaska Native Villages	Total persons	Number	Percent of total persons	Age: Under 5 years	Age: 18 years and over	Age: 65 years and over	Age: Median	Persons 5 years and over—Percent who speak a language other than English at home	Civilian persons 16 to 19 years old—Percent not enrolled in school, not high school graduates	Persons 25 years old and over: Percent high school graduates	Persons 25 years old and over: Percent completed 4 or more years of college	Families—Percent with own children under 6 years	Persons under 18—Percent living with two parents	Children ever born per 1,000 women 35 to 44 years
RESERVATIONS—Con.														
Havasupai Reservation, Ariz.	275	255	92.7	11	168	17	24.9	91.0	—	35.7	...	33.3	74.7	—
Hoh Reservation, Wash.	47	29	61.7	...	...	...	...	...	...	...	...	...	...	...
Hollywood Reservation, Fla.	2 435	420	17.2	71	242	16	20.6	47.9	63.9	60.5	4.2	34.1	51.1	3 476
Hoopa Valley Reservation, Calif.	2 042	1 481	72.5	214	864	99	22.4	8.8	42.7	57.0	4.3	46.1	64.5	2 913
Hoopa Valley Extension Reservation, Calif.	1 035	398	38.5	26	240	38	22.6	12.4	43.6	64.4	3.4	36.6	51.3	4 846
Hopi Reservation, Ariz.	6 834	6 606	96.7	793	3 937	646	23.1	90.1	30.4	40.3	2.5	26.2	56.3	4 713
Hopland Reservation, Calif.	13	—	—	—	—	—	—	—	—	—	—	—	—	—
Hualapai Reservation, Ariz.	924	833	90.2	125	483	18	20.1	79.2	9.0	67.7	—	58.0	72.9	5 605
Inaja-Cosmit Reservation, Calif.	—	—	—	—	—	—	—	—	—	—	—	—	—	—
Indian Township Reservation, Maine	384	333	86.7	39	153	22	16.7	90.5	21.6	30.1	—	48.3	35.6	5 000
Iowa Reservation, Kans.-Nebr.	101	31	30.7	5	21	—	21.9	—	—	73.3	—	...	100.0	5 000
Isabella Reservation, Mich.	22 907	447	2.0	73	248	30	20.7	24.1	38.2	35.4	—	33.7	65.3	5 000
Isleta Pueblo, N. Mex.	2 446	2 249	91.9	254	1 389	155	23.4	80.5	14.8	64.8	3.5	24.4	63.6	3 053
Jackson Rancheria, Calif.	—	—	—	—	—	—	—	—	—	—	—	—	—	—
Jemez Pueblo, N. Mex.	1 498	1 488	99.3	188	816	95	20.5	97.2	14.0	50.6	7.6	34.2	63.1	5 539
Jicarilla Apache Reservation, N. Mex.	1 870	1 696	90.7	232	896	55	19.1	63.7	5.6	52.7	8.8	44.8	68.6	4 518
Kaibab Reservation, Ariz.	171	47	27.5	—	30	8	44.1	80.9	—	50.0	—	—	—	9 000
Kalispel Reservation, Wash.	99	94	94.9	14	44	—	17.3	46.3	—	48.6	—	53.8	88.0	7 000
Kickapoo Reservation, Kans.	467	372	79.7	38	221	24	23.4	8.4	28.6	60.1	1.7	27.1	62.9	4 462
Kootenai Reservation, Idaho	—	—	—	—	—	—	—	—	—	—	—	—	—	—
Lac Courte Oreilles Reservation, Wis.	1 577	1 133	71.8	139	607	52	19.7	12.2	22.2	52.1	3.9	39.5	50.4	3 662
Lac du Flambeau Reservation, Wis.	2 212	1 091	49.3	121	582	59	19.6	3.4	38.7	44.2	4.4	31.6	48.5	4 404
Laguna Pueblo, N. Mex.	3 765	3 526	93.7	426	2 116	267	22.9	56.0	36.2	62.4	2.0	31.0	74.0	2 823
La Jolla Reservation, Calif.	158	158	100.0	51	86	16	25.2	—	—	90.0	—	100.0	55.6	6 000
L'Anse Reservation, Mich.	3 350	640	19.1	69	323	31	18.2	7.0	26.5	56.5	7.1	50.4	75.1	4 000
La Posta Reservation, Calif.	—	—	—	—	—	—	—	—	—	—	—	—	—	—
Las Vegas Colony, Nev.	94	89	94.7	22	47	—	18.8	17.9	50.0	56.4	—	100.0	100.0	9 000
Laytonville Rancheria, Calif.	204	204	100.0	19	132	—	19.9	—	—	73.8	26.2	48.8	77.8	—
Leech Lake Reservation, Minn.	8 529	2 612	30.6	358	1 422	187	19.6	18.0	27.1	58.6	5.5	36.9	45.9	4 493
Likely Rancheria, Calif.	—	—	—	—	—	—	—	—	—	—	—	—	—	—
Lone Pine Rancheria, Calif.	228	171	75.0	23	100	7	24.4	12.2	—	59.5	—	31.6	81.7	—
Lookout Rancheria, Calif.	—	—	—	—	—	—	—	—	—	—	—	—	—	—
Los Coyotes Reservation, Calif.	58	58	100.0	8	38	15	27.5	—	100.0	18.8	18.8	50.0	25.0	—
Lovelock Colony, Nev.	119	113	95.0	21	70	6	25.3	23.9	66.7	61.4	3.5	19.0	53.5	2 889
Lower Brule Reservation, S. Dak.	1 007	854	84.8	167	426	28	18.0	20.7	34.7	51.0	1.4	52.5	53.7	5 484
Lower Elwha Reservation, Wash.	38	38	100.0	—	24	—	34.2	—	—	75.0	33.3	—	100.0	—
Lower Sioux Community, Minn.	86	69	80.2	12	48	9	28.4	19.3	28.6	40.0	5.0	21.1	33.3	3 000
Lummi Reservation, Wash.	2 331	1 258	54.0	151	691	26	20.0	3.7	35.4	51.0	4.1	50.4	73.0	5 667
Makah Reservation, Wash.	1 288	799	62.0	117	420	14	19.6	12.5	31.3	66.2	6.3	40.0	58.8	3 644
Manchester Rancheria, Calif.	68	68	100.0	3	45	5	22.2	27.7	60.0	50.0	—	50.0	39.1	5 400
Manzanita Reservation, Calif.	—	—	—	—	—	—	—	—	—	—	—	—	—	—
Maricopa Reservation, Ariz.	427	403	94.4	42	228	19	23.1	94.5	—	18.0	—	47.3	77.1	10 750
Mattaponi Reservation, Va.	80	80	100.0	10	53	—	27.2	—	—	79.5	20.5	34.6	—	3 308
Menominee Reservation, Wis.	2 696	2 467	91.5	336	1 326	150	19.7	3.5	35.6	31.7	—	35.4	58.2	5 009
Mesa Grande Reservation, Calif.	—	—	—	—	—	—	—	—	—	—	—	—	—	—
Mescalero Apache Reservation, N. Mex.	2 086	1 945	93.2	291	991	54	18.9	62.7	32.3	54.9	2.9	47.3	63.7	3 874
Miccosukee Reservation, Fla.	190	—	—	—	—	—	—	—	—	—	—	—	—	—
Middletown Rancheria, Calif.	37	29	78.4	...	...	...	...	...	...	...	...	...	...	...
Mille Lacs Reservation, Minn.	31	30	96.8	8	13	—	15.0	36.4	100.0	50.0	—	...	17.6	8 000
Mississippi Choctaw Reservation	2 856	2 648	92.7	328	1 318	93	17.9	98.8	37.7	44.9	3.6	30.4	53.3	3 059
Moapa River Reservation, Nev.	153	153	100.0	21	86	8	20.4	35.6	100.0	50.7	7.0	20.0	31.3	2 286
Montgomery Creek Rancheria, Calif.	—	—	—	—	—	—	—	—	—	—	—	—	—	—
Morongo Reservation, Calif.	449	343	76.4	28	214	45	21.9	8.3	—	41.3	8.4	26.9	92.2	3 000
Muckleshoot Reservation, Wash.	2 974	428	14.4	68	224	—	18.8	3.9	42.6	42.8	9.7	17.0	43.1	6 000
Nambe Pueblo, N. Mex.	401	168	41.9	41	89	6	20.0	76.4	27.8	76.7	9.6	53.2	74.7	2 000
Navajo Reservation, Ariz.-N. Mex.-Utah	110 606	105 091	95.0	14 447	54 548	4 870	18.8	92.4	29.6	34.6	3.2	41.9	68.3	4 606
Nez Perce Reservation, Idaho	18 127	1 060	5.8	148	604	128	24.2	55.0	43.6	69.8	8.7	46.0	59.9	1 000
Nisqually Reservation, Wash.	238	21	8.8	...	...	...	...	...	...	...	...	...	...	...
Nooksack Reservation, Wash.	—	—	—	—	—	—	—	—	—	—	—	—	—	—
Northern Cheyenne Reservation, Mont.	3 612	3 010	83.3	444	1 492	85	17.8	44.3	20.0	54.6	2.7	43.1	53.4	4 500
Oil Springs Reservation, N.Y.	2	—	—	—	—	—	—	—	—	—	—	—	—	—
Omaha Reservation, Iowa-Nebr.	5 495	1 329	24.2	172	718	86	19.9	30.5	26.7	48.9	4.4	30.2	46.2	4 618
Oneida Reservation, Wis.	13 398	1 762	13.2	170	1 044	191	22.6	17.7	15.2	41.1	1.8	35.4	81.9	4 156
Onondaga Reservation, N.Y.	604	604	100.0	29	428	59	26.9	30.1	—	56.7	2.0	10.0	—	—
Ontonagon Reservation, Mich.	—	—	—	—	—	—	—	—	—	—	—	—	—	—
Osage Reservation, Okla.	39 327	4 727	12.0	414	2 974	493	25.6	2.6	20.0	62.7	8.1	23.2	79.5	3 165
Ozette Reservation, Wash.	—	—	—	—	—	—	—	—	—	—	—	—	—	—
Pala Reservation, Calif.	678	504	74.3	48	298	24	22.1	23.7	26.2	52.3	—	20.9	24.3	4 625
Pamunkey Reservation, Va.	39	39	100.0	—	39	—	42.5	—	—	100.0	30.8	—	—	—
Papago Reservation, Ariz.	7 331	7 052	96.2	818	4 016	478	21.6	86.7	25.3	38.7	2.1	22.8	55.2	3 613
Pascua Yaqui Reservation, Ariz.	533	471	88.4	49	216	21	15.7	100.0	23.3	10.9	—	27.0	71.8	5 478
Pauma Reservation, Calif.	—	—	—	—	—	—	—	—	—	—	—	—	—	—
Payson Community of Yavapai-Apache, Ariz.	—	—	—	—	—	—	—	—	—	—	—	—	—	—
Pechanga Reservation, Calif.	65	44	67.7	—	26	—	32.0	47.7	—	76.9	—	—	100.0	—
Penobscot Reservation, Maine	474	406	85.7	44	261	15	22.1	7.7	—	68.5	—	38.6	74.5	—
Picuris Pueblo, N. Mex.	346	124	35.8	—	93	40	46.7	100.0	13.3	20.7	—	—	6.5	10 000
Pine Creek Reservation, Mich.	—	—	—	—	—	—	—	—	—	—	—	—	—	—
Pine Ridge Reservation, S. Dak.	13 095	11 888	90.8	1 709	5 922	589	17.9	54.5	29.8	42.3	5.1	39.4	48.0	4 736
Pleasant Point Reservation, Maine	543	506	93.2	67	251	26	17.9	74.0	41.8	36.9	4.6	46.5	43.9	6 000
Pojoaque Pueblo, N. Mex.	1 219	37	3.0	6	25	—	19.9	100.0	—	100.0	—	100.0	100.0	3 000
Poospatuck Reservation, N.Y.	223	44	19.7	—	44	34	67.5	—	—	22.7	—	...	—	—
Port Gamble Reservation, Wash.	359	317	88.3	55	162	15	18.2	2.7	25.6	44.5	—	72.1	74.8	4 000
Port Madison Reservation, Wash.	3 394	153	4.5	10	92	19	26.3	1.4	—	57.7	3.8	10.9	86.9	5 000
Potawatomi Reservation, Wis.	124	124	100.0	15	69	—	19.6	11.9	40.0	39.2	—	24.2	56.4	7 000

¹Includes Eskimos and Aleuts on Annette Island Reserve and Alaska Native Villages.

Table 251. **Social Characteristics for American Indian Persons on Reservations and Alaska Native Villages: 1980—** Con.

[Data are estimates based on a sample; see Introduction. For meaning of symbols, see Introduction. For definitions of terms, see appendixes A and B]

Reservations Alaska Native Villages	Total persons	American Indian[1] Number	Percent of total persons	Age Under 5 years	18 years and over	65 years and over	Median	Persons 5 years and over— Percent who speak a language other than English at home	Civilian persons 16 to 19 years old— Percent not enrolled in school, not high school graduates	Persons 25 years old and over Percent high school graduates	Percent completed 4 or more years of college	Families— Percent with own children under 6 years	Persons under 18— Percent living with two parents	Children ever born per 1,000 women 35 to 44 years
RESERVATIONS—Con.														
Pottawatomi Reservation, Kans.	952	333	35.0	41	200	41	25.3	25.3	14.3	46.4	–	32.5	84.2	6 467
Prairie Island Community, Minn.	97	82	84.5	15	22	–	11.0	–	–	31.8	–	50.0	100.0	–
Puyallup Reservation, Wash.	25 188	900	3.6	120	487	16	18.9	3.8	42.7	49.0	3.9	46.4	56.4	2 355
Pyramid Lake Reservation, Nev.	778	699	89.8	92	430	44	22.9	21.6	29.0	52.8	–	36.1	59.1	3 821
Quileute Reservation, Wash.	334	273	81.7	44	147	–	18.9	62.4	66.7	58.6	15.7	70.2	33.3	6 000
Quinault Reservation, Wash.	1 569	974	62.1	104	542	32	19.6	5.7	50.0	42.4	1.7	41.7	62.3	6 326
Ramah Community, N. Mex.	1 218	1 170	96.1	188	702	71	21.5	99.0	28.9	39.9	8.7	37.7	50.9	3 672
Ramona Reservation, Calif.	–	–	–	–	–	–	–	–	–	–	–	–	–	–
Red Cliff Reservation, Wis.	675	586	86.8	77	305	28	18.9	7.9	25.9	42.0	0.9	27.9	69.4	4 800
Red Lake Reservation, Minn.	3 007	2 832	94.2	362	1 401	145	17.9	15.3	47.2	43.3	4.6	26.9	42.1	5 088
Reno-Sparks Colony, Nev.	448	444	99.1	50	266	21	23.3	8.1	–	54.1	3.8	33.8	43.3	4 667
Resighini Rancheria, Calif.	15	15	100.0	...	...	...	–	–	...	–	–	...	...	–
Rincon Reservation, Calif.	443	236	53.3	19	111	8	16.4	11.1	–	62.6	10.1	23.3	75.2	3 400
Roaring Creek Rancheria, Calif.	42	42	100.0	–	22	7	19.1	9.5	20.0	–	–	–	80.0	6 000
Rocky Boy's Reservation, Mont.	1 486	1 445	97.2	196	690	41	17.4	53.4	26.1	33.3	3.3	44.1	74.3	5 452
Rosebud Reservation, S. Dak.	7 328	5 688	77.6	866	2 836	254	17.9	31.6	19.7	49.7	6.5	41.9	44.4	5 363
Round Valley Reservation, Calif.	1 367	314	23.0	49	170	58	19.7	–	–	32.2	–	55.7	56.9	3 806
Rumsey Rancheria, Calif.	11	11	100.0	...	...	...	–	–	...	...	–	...	...	–
Sac and Fox Reservation, Iowa	454	454	100.0	74	256	24	20.4	81.3	9.3	48.8	9.3	44.3	55.1	7 400
Sac and Fox Reservation, Kans.-Nebr.	105	–	–	–	–	–	–	–	–	–	–	–	–	–
St. Croix Reservation, Wis.	413	360	87.2	49	212	40	21.6	32.2	59.3	25.2	0.6	16.3	43.2	2 818
St. Regis Mohawk Reservation, N.Y.	1 759	1 729	98.3	139	1 118	174	25.4	54.0	20.2	37.8	5.5	21.5	74.0	3 700
Salt River Reservation, Ariz.	4 038	2 490	61.7	338	1 352	76	19.6	42.8	45.8	49.3	5.2	31.9	52.3	3 698
San Carlos Reservation, Ariz.	6 249	6 013	96.2	759	3 212	244	19.6	82.9	32.1	43.6	0.9	40.6	59.5	4 295
Sandia Pueblo, N. Mex.	670	217	32.4	13	159	46	28.9	74.0	21.4	37.4	4.6	27.1	87.9	4 000
Sandy Lake Reservation, Minn.	–	–	–	–	–	–	–	–	–	–	–	–	–	–
San Felipe Pueblo, N. Mex.	2 282	1 787	78.3	222	941	62	18.9	99.7	24.9	45.4	1.3	29.8	36.3	4 156
San Ildefonso Pueblo, N. Mex.	1 427	478	33.5	59	317	42	25.1	83.3	–	77.9	2.5	36.3	62.1	1 000
San Juan Pueblo, N. Mex.	4 607	1 146	24.9	155	631	104	22.0	81.4	18.2	41.8	2.3	31.6	68.0	3 238
San Manuel Reservation, Calif.	31	26	83.9	...	...	...	...	...	...	...	...	...	...	...
San Pasqual Reservation, Calif.	189	144	76.2	20	87	23	19.7	37.9	–	44.4	–	65.8	100.0	3 143
Santa Ana Pueblo, N. Mex.	374	374	100.0	38	234	–	23.7	68.2	–	61.6	1.7	24.7	59.3	2 929
Santa Clara Pueblo, N. Mex.	6 702	315	4.7	52	186	15	26.6	84.8	–	71.8	25.9	62.5	67.4	4 333
Santa Rosa Rancheria, Calif.	234	173	73.9	48	63	16	8.6	6.4	–	68.1	–	...	100.0	–
Santa Rosa Reservation, Calif.	–	–	–	–	–	–	–	–	–	–	–	–	–	–
Santa Ynez Reservation, Calif.	130	–	–	–	–	–	–	–	–	–	–	–	–	–
Santa Ysabel Reservation, Calif.	203	178	87.7	–	120	13	30.0	38.2	–	43.8	9.0	19.5	82.8	3 000
Santee Reservation, Nebr.	907	430	47.4	70	216	29	18.1	19.2	24.1	57.7	6.1	47.5	52.3	2 875
Santo Domingo Pueblo, N. Mex.	2 197	2 140	97.4	246	1 168	113	19.9	99.7	26.4	48.7	4.1	31.7	54.8	3 598
San Xavier Reservation, Ariz.	828	828	100.0	89	484	33	22.6	79.0	6.5	55.5	–	29.5	61.0	3 634
Sauk-Suiattle Reservation, Wash.	–	–	–	–	–	–	–	–	–	–	–	–	–	–
Sault Ste. Marie Reservation, Mich.	–	–	–	–	–	–	–	–	–	–	–	–	–	–
Schaghticoke Reservation, Conn.	–	–	–	–	–	–	–	–	–	–	–	–	–	–
Shakopee Community, Minn.	105	76	72.4	–	62	–	38.3	15.8	–	52.0	–	–	64.3	1 000
Sheep Ranch Rancheria, Calif.	–	–	–	–	–	–	–	–	–	–	–	–	–	–
Sherwood Valley Rancheria, Calif.	–	–	–	–	–	–	–	–	–	–	–	–	–	–
Shingle Springs Rancheria, Calif.	–	–	–	–	–	–	–	–	–	–	–	–	–	–
Shinnecock Reservation, N.Y.	261	175	67.0	8	108	32	33.3	–	–	69.4	10.2	19.2	43.3	3 000
Shoalwater Reservation, Wash.	39	31	79.5	4	27	–	24.1	–	–	100.0	100.0	23.5	–	–
Sisseton Reservation, N. Dak.-S. Dak.	13 550	2 723	20.1	370	1 378	154	18.2	25.5	38.8	45.4	1.7	42.7	34.4	3 739
Skokomish Reservation, Wash.	495	342	69.1	47	164	13	17.5	–	30.4	32.0	–	45.3	65.2	4 750
Skull Valley Reservation, Utah	13	13	100.0	...	...	...	...	...	...	...	...	...	...	...
Soboba Reservation, Calif.	272	242	89.0	40	138	24	26.7	–	–	61.2	–	56.4	87.5	3 000
Sokaogon Chippewa Community, Wis.	127	107	84.3	20	68	1	23.9	12.6	14.3	40.8	2.0	33.3	53.8	5 000
Southern Paiute Reservation, Utah	1 261	228	18.1	43	112	–	13.5	30.3	–	45.7	8.5	47.2	22.4	7 125
Southern Ute Reservation, Colo.	5 639	812	14.4	95	410	39	18.2	52.0	31.5	66.8	6.3	50.3	53.2	3 737
Spokane Reservation, Wash.	1 543	1 045	67.7	120	599	40	23.1	0.8	12.6	61.4	3.7	40.7	49.8	1 812
Squaxin Island Reservation, Wash.	59	59	100.0	19	18	–	7.1	–	–	100.0	–	...	–	7 000
Standing Rock Reservation, N. Dak.-S. Dak.	8 816	4 800	54.4	716	2 442	210	18.4	34.4	41.9	46.0	4.0	40.9	53.3	5 205
Stewart's Point Rancheria, Calif.	70	62	88.6	2	35	2	20.1	3.3	16.7	–	–	–	88.9	4 100
Stockbridge Reservation, Wis.	1 269	566	44.6	68	337	58	24.5	3.8	28.1	50.2	0.7	39.5	80.3	3 552
Sulphur Bank Rancheria, Calif.	101	101	100.0	–	53	12	30.7	–	–	20.8	–	–	100.0	–
Summit Lake Reservation, Nev.	–	–	–	–	–	–	–	–	–	–	–	–	–	–
Susanville Reservation, Calif.	109	92	84.4	8	57	–	21.1	14.3	26.3	38.1	–	–	–	5 000
Swinomish Reservation, Wash.	1 434	381	26.6	49	239	27	26.3	8.1	65.0	47.1	3.4	30.9	93.7	1 421
Sycuan Reservation, Calif.	50	28	56.0	...	...	...	...	...	...	...	...	50.0	...	...
Tama Reservation, Ga.	30	16	53.3	...	...	...	...	...	...	...	...	...	...	...
Taos Pueblo, N. Mex.	1 398	729	52.1	60	498	96	26.5	86.8	26.3	63.5	2.3	13.7	66.7	5 100
Te-Moak Reservation, Nev.	79	79	100.0	17	62	13	26.3	41.9	–	62.8	–	47.1	52.9	–
Tesuque Pueblo, N. Mex.	253	229	90.5	27	134	3	23.1	88.6	–	66.7	6.7	27.0	62.1	–
Tigua Reservation, Tex.	499	–	–	–	–	–	–	–	–	–	–	–	–	–
Tonawanda Reservation, N.Y.	439	422	96.1	25	274	66	34.0	26.7	–	36.3	–	17.5	49.3	–
Torres-Martinez Reservation, Calif.	321	51	15.9	10	21	–	16.5	17.1	53.8	–	–	100.0	83.3	8 000
Trinidad Rancheria, Calif.	56	46	82.1	–	23	6	19.0	–	–	45.0	–	–	73.9	–
Tulalip Reservation, Wash.	5 036	749	14.9	107	396	31	19.3	15.3	25.0	43.8	2.0	37.1	62.9	5 432
Tule River Reservation, Calif.	452	436	96.5	71	222	19	19.3	17.8	–	50.9	–	39.6	34.1	1 913
Tunica-Biloxi Reservation, La.	53	–	–	–	–	–	–	–	–	–	–	–	–	–
Tuolumne Rancheria, Calif.	90	67	74.4	–	42	9	35.2	–	–	57.1	–	–	–	2 500
Turtle Mountain Reservation, N. Dak.	4 234	3 955	93.4	513	2 122	229	19.5	17.1	25.2	41.8	3.0	36.2	57.0	5 130
Tuscarora Reservation, N.Y.	922	881	95.6	63	623	155	36.3	28.1	8.0	50.4	7.1	28.3	34.1	3 600
Twenty-Nine Palms Reservation, Calif.	–	–	–	–	–	–	–	–	–	–	–	–	–	–
Uintah and Ouray Reservation, Utah	16 886	1 990	11.8	297	1 091	79	19.7	60.4	29.6	43.9	2.8	28.4	57.8	4 640
Umatilla Reservation, Oreg.	2 572	946	36.8	110	488	92	21.3	25.0	13.2	49.8	2.5	25.0	60.0	3 156
Upper Sioux Community, Minn.	57	53	93.0	1	38	16	32.1	44.2	–	50.0	–	16.7	86.7	–

[1]Includes Eskimos and Aleuts on Annette Island Reserve and Alaska Native Villages.

Table 251. Social Characteristics for American Indian Persons on Reservations and Alaska Native Villages: 1980—Con.

[Data are estimates based on a sample; see Introduction. For meaning of symbols, see Introduction. For definitions of terms, see appendixes A and B]

Reservations Alaska Native Villages	Total persons	American Indian[1] Number	Percent of total persons	Age Under 5 years	Age 18 years and over	Age 65 years and over	Age Median	Persons 5 years and over—Percent who speak a language other than English at home	Civilian persons 16 to 19 years old—Percent not enrolled in school, not high school graduates	Persons 25 years old and over Percent high school graduates	Persons 25 years old and over Percent completed 4 or more years of college	Families—Percent with own children under 6 years	Persons under 18—Percent living with two parents	Children ever born per 1,000 women 35 to 44 years
RESERVATIONS—Con.														
Upper Skagit Reservation, Wash.	–	997	91.0	127	589	32	20.8	78.9	56.5	16.8	2.1	48.3	86.3	4 667
Ute Mountain Reservation, Colo.-N. Mex.	1 096	138	94.5	11	71	5	19.4	27.6	26.3	45.1	–	24.0	31.3	4 000
Vermillion Lake Reservation, Minn.	146	150	88.2	16	94	–	25.0	28.4	100.0	68.0	–	62.5	26.8	4 417
Viejas Rancheria, Calif.	170	452	81.0	46	279	18	26.3	5.9	20.7	48.7	7.8	30.8	69.4	1 000
Walker River Reservation, Nev.	558													
Wampanoag Reservation, Mass.	–	2 067	85.8	256	1 117	47	19.6	20.2	50.2	50.4	7.7	35.9	64.4	5 047
Warm Springs Reservation, Oreg.	2 409													
Washoe Reservation, Nev.	79	20	100.0	–	–	–	–	6.8	27.1	41.1	4.0	36.9	62.3	4 380
Western Pequot Reservation, Conn.	20	2 585	27.3	336	1 427	193	20.3							
White Earth Reservation, Minn.	9 471													
Wind River Reservation, Wyo.	23 221	4 165	17.9	540	2 189	170	19.7	26.8	39.4	53.1	2.2	39.1	58.5	3 897
Winnebago Reservation, Nebr.	2 519	1 122	44.5	145	636	75	20.9	22.6	32.0	58.9	3.6	34.5	42.8	3 197
Winnemucca Colony, Nev.	35	35	100.0	–	17	–	13.9	74.3					100.0	
Wisconsin Winnebago Reservation	664	614	92.5	73	295	42	16.9	49.7	14.3	50.6	1.6	37.7	46.7	5 154
Woodfords Community, Calif.	296	129	43.6	7	86	11	25.8	41.8	46.2	45.6	2.9	20.0	27.9	3 800
XL Ranch Reservation, Calif.	20	20	100.0	–	–	–	–							
Yakima Reservation, Wash.	25 342	4 957	19.6	542	2 727	311	20.1	15.2	21.3	57.0	5.1	30.6	57.7	3 962
Yankton Reservation, S. Dak.	6 541	1 704	26.1	273	886	113	19.1	21.5	31.3	42.4	2.5	47.4	43.2	4 500
Yavapai Reservation, Ariz.	172	160	93.0	–	72	15	15.8	52.5	–	79.2	–	–	–	4 000
Yerington Reservation, Nev.	441	116	26.3	7	63	–	23.9	9.2	–	78.2	–	19.0	56.6	–
Yomba Reservation, Nev.	–													
Zia Pueblo, N. Mex.	602	602	100.0	85	347	35	21.1	90.5	18.7	54.7	5.0	18.1	65.5	4 591
Zuni Pueblo, N. Mex.	6 252	5 929	94.8	709	3 095	291	18.8	85.9	28.8	37.3	2.1	33.9	46.8	4 104
San Felipe/Santa Ana Joint Area, N. Mex.	–													
San Felipe/Santo Domingo Joint Area, N. Mex.	127	127	100.0	17	69	7	23.8	91.8	–	68.3	26.7	79.3	58.6	–
Other reservation lands in Montana	–													
ALASKA NATIVE VILLAGES														
Afognak	12	2	16.7	...	...	...	...	...	...	...	...	...	...	...
Akhiok	105	98	93.3	11	51	3	18.3	5.7	55.0	37.0	–	30.8	63.8	4 714
Akiachak	427	386	90.4	52	209	16	19.3	88.6	–	35.7	2.8	27.5	87.6	5 609
Akiak	175	170	97.1	...	...	...	...	87.0	–	34.0	8.0	...	–	–
Akutan	57	57	100.0	3	50	11	37.5					43.3	–	–
Alakanuk	586	565	96.4	...	...	...	...	...	...	...	...	...	...	...
Alatna	29	29	100.0	...	...	...	...	...	...	...	...	...	...	...
Aleknagik	173	152	87.9	...	...	...	...	...	...	...	...	...	...	...
Alexander	–													
Allakaket	147	144	98.0	...	...	...	–	...	...	...	...	...	...	...
Ambler	191	152	79.6	26	77	6	18.5	69.8	15.4	24.0	–	34.5	73.3	5 000
Anaktuvuk Pass	204	194	95.1	...	...	...	...	...	...	...	...	40.0	...	...
Andreafsky	122	115	94.3	...	...	...	...	...	...	...	...	...	...	...
Angoon	466	413	88.6	59	228	38	21.8	30.2	6.7	44.3	3.2	42.5	67.6	4 200
Aniak	343	213	62.1	30	121	5	21.5	13.7	–	51.2	3.5	69.2	75.0	5 857
Anvik	106	92	86.8	...	...	...	...	...	...	...	...	...	...	...
Arctic Village	106	82	77.4	...	...	...	...	...	...	...	...	22.7	89.3	4 000
Atka	93	93	100.0	8	65	8	31.3	78.8	–	23.6	–	...	...	...
Atkasook	113	109	96.5	...	...	...	...	...	...	...	...	...	...	...
Atmautluak	231	220	95.2	...	...	...	...	...	...	...	...	...	...	...
Barrow	2 207	1 720	77.9	174	1 014	73	22.3	88.7	17.0	45.6	2.2	29.9	68.6	4 545
Beaver	62	62	100.0	–	35	1	25.8	11.3	–	28.1	9.4	15.4	63.0	–
Belkofsky	7	7	100.0	...	...	...	...	...	...	...	...	...	...	...
Bethel	3 576	2 417	67.6	320	1 319	64	20.3	64.1	17.1	49.5	6.5	45.1	70.5	4 233
Bill Moore's	–													
Birch Creek	29	29	100.0	...	...	...	...	...	...	...	...	100.0	...	...
Brevig Mission	174	174	100.0	23	96	4	19.0	59.6	13.3	25.0	–	46.2	70.5	5 000
Buckland	169	165	97.6	...	...	...	15.8	36.4	–	62.5	43.8	42.9	100.0	2 571
Contwell	87	33	37.9	–	16	–						...	...	...
Chalkyitsik	110	107	97.3	...	...	...	...	...	...	...	...	...	...	...
Chefornak	228	215	94.3	...	...	...	...	...	...	...	...	52.3	...	...
Chevak	495	478	96.6	...	...	...	...	9.5	–	42.9	–	28.6	100.0	–
Chignik	123	45	36.6	3	29	–	24.4							
Chignik Lagoon	47	37	78.7	...	...	...	...	...	...	...	...	...	...	...
Chignik Lake	85	61	71.8	...	...	...	...	...	...	...	...	...	...	...
Chilkat	138	101	73.2	20	67	5	26.6	64.2	–	64.8	–	35.3	79.4	4 000
Chistochina	51	11	21.6	...	...	...	...	...	...	...	...	...	...	...
Chitina	54	33	61.1	...	...	...	...	...	...	...	...	–	–	–
Circle	55	46	83.6	...	...	...	...	...	...	...	...	...	...	...
Clark's Point	68	59	86.8	...	...	...	...	...	...	...	...	...	...	...
Copper Center	241	117	48.5	17	56	11	17.5	68.0	54.5	23.2	–	...	8.2	–
Craig	566	160	28.3	18	87	13	19.7	10.6	17.6	63.4	–	...	52.1	3 750
Crooked Creek	116	100	86.2	...	...	...	...	...	...	...	...	...	...	...
Deering	154	128	83.1	...	...	...	...	...	...	...	...	...	74.3	3 809
Dillingham	1 563	891	57.0	86	529	34	21.2	30.6	14.7	59.9	4.3	...	...	...
Dot Lake	47	15	31.9	...	...	...	...	...	...	...	...	26.7	...	...
Eagle	161	56	34.8	...	...	...	...	...	...	...	...	...	...	...
Eek	230	218	94.8	...	...	...	...	...	...	...	...	...	...	...
Egegik	77	67	87.0	...	...	...	...	...	...	...	...	...	...	...
Eklutna	51	11	21.6	...	...	...	...	...	...	...	...	...	...	...
Ekuk	–													
Ekwok	88	76	86.4	4	39	2	18.3	54.2	–	4.3	–	...	67.6	5 800
Elim	213	197	92.5	...	...	...	...	...	...	...	...	...	...	...
Emmonak	528	484	91.7	63	245	14	18.3	98.6	20.9	22.6	–	44.3	70.7	6 000
English Bay	109	104	95.4	...	...	...	...	...	...	...	...	72.2	...	...

[1] Includes Eskimos and Aleuts on Annette Island Reserve and Alaska Native Villages.

Table 251. Social Characteristics for American Indian Persons on Reservations and Alaska Native Villages: 1980—Con.

[Data are estimates based on a sample; see Introduction. For meaning of symbols, see Introduction. For definitions of terms, see appendixes A and B]

Reservations Alaska Native Villages	Total persons	American Indian[1] Number	Percent of total persons	Age Under 5 years	18 years and over	65 years and over	Median	Persons 5 years and over—Percent who speak a language other than English at home	Civilian persons 16 to 19 years old—Percent not enrolled in school, not high school graduates	Persons 25 years old and over Percent high school graduates	Percent completed 4 or more years of college	Families—Percent with own children under 6 years	Persons under 18—Percent living with two parents	Children ever born per 1,000 women 35 to 44 years
ALASKA NATIVE VILLAGES—Con.														
Evansville	118	31	26.3	–	20	2	21.6	25.8	–	35.7	–	...	54.5	–
False Pass	71	69	97.2	...	...	...	...	...	...	...	...	...	...	...
Fort Yukon	572	381	66.6	64	239	37	24.4	45.4	23.5	43.8	4.9	41.1	60.6	4 182
Gakona	59	20	33.9	...	...	...	...	...	...	...	...	–	...	...
Galena	304	214	70.4	28	124	16	20.4	18.8	...	34.9	–	57.5	21.1	5 071
Gambell	436	407	93.3	50	251	29	23.2	97.5	23.3	33.7	–	...	69.2	4 474
Georgetown	–	–	...	–	–	–	...	...	...	...	...	...	...	...
Golovin	85	85	100.0	6	54	12	24.3	36.7	60.0	37.5	–	21.1	48.4	1 000
Goodnews Bay	168	162	96.4	...	...	...	...	...	...	...	...	...	...	...
Grayling	214	187	87.4	...	...	...	...	...	...	...	...	...	...	...
Gulkana	106	29	27.4	...	...	...	...	...	...	...	...	–	...	...
Hamilton	–	–	–	–	–	–	...	...	...	...	...	–	...	...
Healy Lake	31	23	74.2	...	...	...	...	...	...	...	...	...	–	...
Holy Cross	222	212	95.5	...	...	...	...	...	...	...	...	...	...	...
Hoonah	618	525	85.0	67	296	29	21.8	21.6	6.3	39.9	–	53.6	82.5	5 000
Hooper Bay	599	577	96.3	...	...	...	...	...	...	...	...	39.1	...	...
Hughes	53	53	100.0	3	38	5	29.2	58.0	...	50.0	–	20.0	100.0	2 000
Huslia	192	183	95.3	...	...	...	...	...	...	...	...	...	...	...
Hydaburg	300	272	90.7	...	...	...	...	...	...	...	...	38.2	...	...
Igiugig	29	24	82.8	...	...	...	...	...	...	...	...	...	...	...
Iliamna	105	98	93.3	...	...	...	...	...	...	...	...	...	...	...
Inalik	130	128	98.5	...	...	...	...	...	...	...	...	42.9	...	...
Ivanof Bay	63	61	96.8	...	...	...	...	...	...	...	...	...	...	...
Kaguyak	–	–	...	...	...	...	...	...	...	...	...	...	...	...
Kake	592	508	85.8	48	300	21	25.2	37.4	–	62.5	0.8	33.7	73.6	4 375
Kaktovik	171	155	90.6	...	...	...	...	...	...	...	...	23.8	...	...
Kalskag	141	123	87.2	...	...	...	...	...	...	...	...	6.7	...	...
Kaltag	262	244	93.1	...	...	...	...	...	...	...	...	51.4	...	...
Karluk	93	93	100.0	21	46	2	17.5	16.7	–	63.2	2.6	94.1	91.5	–
Kasaan	29	20	69.0	...	...	...	...	...	...	...	...	...	...	...
Kasigluk	354	337	95.2	...	...	...	...	...	...	...	...	...	...	...
Kiana	335	315	94.0	...	...	...	...	...	...	...	...	...	...	...
King Cove	416	281	67.5	57	159	3	22.9	13.8	–	44.6	–	37.9	92.6	1 000
Kipnuk	394	377	95.7	34	229	22	22.8	99.4	–	24.9	–	...	87.2	6 357
Kivalina	245	235	95.9	34	126	14	19.6	47.3	15.8	24.7	–	...	85.3	3 500
Klawock	323	247	76.5	32	154	6	25.5	6.5	11.8	61.2	–	43.4	80.6	5 000
Knik	–	–	...	–	–	–	...	...	...	...	...	...	...	...
Kobuk	57	57	100.0	11	32	8	23.3	84.8	–	41.7	–	54.5	68.0	1 000
Kokhonok	50	41	82.0	...	...	...	...	...	...	...	...	...	...	...
Koliganek	159	151	95.0	...	...	...	...	...	...	...	...	...	...	...
Kongiganak	252	246	97.6	...	...	...	...	...	...	...	...	...	...	...
Kotlik	310	310	100.0	30	189	17	22.1	63.2	–	27.1	–	42.6	88.4	7 000
Kotzebue	2 054	1 574	76.6	188	889	102	20.9	44.0	22.7	41.2	2.6	34.9	61.6	4 500
Koyuk	176	174	98.9	...	...	...	...	...	...	...	...	41.7	...	...
Koyukuk	91	79	86.8	...	...	...	...	...	...	...	...	...	...	...
Kwethluk	484	465	96.1	49	274	36	21.6	99.5	13.3	27.4	2.0	...	75.9	4 857
Kwigillingok	319	319	100.0	41	140	6	15.2	100.0	56.5	21.6	–	57.6	75.4	3 875
Larsen Bay	134	113	84.3	...	...	...	...	...	...	...	...	42.3	...	...
Levelock	112	108	96.4	...	...	...	...	...	...	...	...	...	...	...
Lime Village	50	40	80.0	...	...	...	...	...	...	...	...	...	...	...
Lower Kalskag	234	232	99.1	...	...	...	...	...	...	...	...	...	...	...
McGrath	376	183	48.7	22	95	9	21.4	18.0	–	61.0	–	60.6	72.7	4 400
Manley Hot Springs	63	8	12.7	...	...	...	...	...	...	...	...	58.5	...	...
Manokotak	301	300	99.7	...	...	...	...	...	...	...	...	...	...	...
Marshall	255	247	96.9	...	...	...	...	...	...	...	...	...	...	...
Mary's Igloo	–	–	...	–	–	–	...	...	...	...	–	...	...	...
Mekoryuk	168	162	96.4	9	97	18	24.6	98.7	–	37.5	–	...	90.8	4 000
Mentasta Lake	31	31	100.0	–	10	4	14.4	22.6	–	60.0	–	...	100.0	6 000
Minto	137	119	86.9	...	...	...	...	...	...	...	...	...	...	...
Mountain Village	611	600	98.2	...	...	...	...	...	...	...	...	...	...	...
Naknek	317	157	49.5	11	103	4	21.8	7.5	8.7	52.3	–	...	68.5	3 389
Napaimute	–	–	–	–	–	–	...	...	...	...	...	...	...	...
Napakiak	265	261	98.5	...	...	...	...	...	...	...	...	...	...	...
Napaskiak	224	217	96.9	...	...	...	...	...	...	...	...	...	...	...
Nelson Lagoon	72	72	100.0	–	36	9	18.0	–	–	...	–	–	63.9	...
Nenana	486	238	49.0	24	142	12	21.9	17.3	–	36.7	–	27.5	83.3	5 333
Newhalen	96	78	81.3	...	...	...	...	...	...	...	...	...	...	...
New Stuyahok	345	316	91.6	...	...	...	...	...	...	...	...	45.8	...	...
Newtok	125	119	95.2	...	...	...	...	...	...	...	...	...	...	...
Nightmute	125	118	94.4	...	...	...	...	...	...	...	...	...	...	...
Nikolai	85	83	97.6	...	...	...	...	...	...	...	...	...	...	...
Nikolski	44	43	97.7	...	...	...	...	...	...	...	...	...	...	...
Ninilchik	316	63	19.9	5	38	12	25.8	24.1	–	42.4	...	33.3	100.0	...
Noatak	275	269	97.8	...	...	...	...	...	...	...	...	...	...	...
Nondalton	170	151	88.8	...	...	...	...	...	...	...	...	...	...	...
Noorvik	507	481	94.9	...	...	...	...	...	...	...	...	22.7	...	...
Northway	120	110	91.7	...	...	...	...	...	...	...	...	24.1	...	...
Nuiqsut	196	175	89.3	...	...	...	...	...	...	...	...	44.4	...	...
Nulato	402	383	95.3	...	...	...	...	...	...	...	...	...	...	...
Nunapitchuk	281	278	98.9	...	...	...	...	...	...	...	...	50.0	...	...
Ohogamiut	–	–	...	...	...	...	...	...	...	...	...	...	...	...
Old Harbor	361	324	89.8	43	188	–	21.9	21.7	10.5	29.8	2.4	44.0	50.0	4 250
Oscarville	51	51	100.0	13	16	–	8.7	21.1	–	25.0	–	...	100.0	–
Ouzinkie	173	163	94.2	...	...	...	...	...	...	...	...	...	...	...

[1]Includes Eskimos and Aleuts on Annette Island Reserve and Alaska Native Villages.

Table 251. Social Characteristics for American Indian Persons on Reservations and Alaska Native Villages: 1980—Con.

[Data are estimates based on a sample; see Introduction. For meaning of symbols, see Introduction. For definitions of terms, see appendixes A and B]

Reservations Alaska Native Villages	Total persons	American Indian[1] — Number	Percent of total persons	Age — Under 5 years	18 years and over	65 years and over	Median	Persons 5 years and over — Percent who speak a language other than English at home	Civilian persons 16 to 19 years old — Percent not enrolled in school, not high school graduates	Persons 25 years old and over — Percent high school graduates	Percent completed 4 or more years of college	Families — Percent with own children under 6 years	Persons under 18 — Percent living with two parents	Children ever born per 1,000 women 35 to 44 years
ALASKA NATIVE VILLAGES—Con.														
Paimiut	–	–	–	–	–	–	–	–	–	–	–	–	–	–
Pauloff Harbor	–	–	–	–	–	–	–	–	–	–	–	–	–	–
Pedro Bay	24	24	100.0	...	...	...	...	...	...	...	...	76.2	...	...
Parryville	106	103	97.2	...	...	...	...	...	...	...	...	...	...	...
Pilot Point	63	53	84.1	...	...	...	...	...	...	...	...	...	...	...
Pilot Station	344	335	97.4	...	...	...	...	...	...	...	...	...	...	...
Pitkas Point	85	73	85.9	...	...	...	...	...	...	...	...	...	...	...
Platinum	57	46	80.7	...	...	...	...	...	...	...	...	...	...	...
Point Hope	472	427	90.5	57	234	9	19.3	69.5	20.8	41.4	3.0	56.7	82.9	4 550
Point Lay	64	60	93.8	...	...	...	...	...	...	...	...	...	...	...
Portage Creek	62	59	95.2	...	...	...	...	...	...	...	...	...	...	...
Port Graham	157	138	87.9	...	...	...	...	...	...	...	...	...	...	...
Port Heiden	78	31	39.7	...	...	...	...	...	...	...	...	...	...	...
Port Lions	228	157	68.9	20	109	15	26.5	27.0	–	34.1	–	28.6	68.8	2 571
Quinhagak	420	409	97.4	–	16	–	17.0	24.3	–	31.3	–	...	...	...
Rampart	37	37	100.0	...	...	...	...	...	...	...	...	...	...	...
Red Devil	37	21	56.8	...	...	...	...	...	...	...	...	...	...	...
Ruby	207	196	94.7	22	105	8	18.9	32.8	33.3	32.6	5.8	32.3	62.6	6 917
Russian Mission (Kuskokwim)	108	93	86.1	...	...	...	...	...	...	...	...	...	...	...
Russian Mission (Yukon)	162	162	100.0	23	98	7	23.1	88.5	–	18.3	–	54.8	90.6	5 000
St. George	156	145	92.9	...	...	...	...	...	...	...	...	...	...	...
St. Mary's	222	170	76.6	12	123	18	29.0	94.9	–	59.6	2.9	...	74.5	–
St. Michael	231	226	97.8	...	...	...	...	...	...	...	...	...	...	...
St. Paul	648	563	86.9	59	333	22	20.8	44.6	38.3	36.3	–	...	76.5	3 833
Salamatof	341	49	14.4	5	23	–	15.8	–	28.6	75.0	–	...	100.0	3 000
Sand Point	627	351	56.0	38	221	13	22.9	3.2	–	36.8	–	40.3	86.9	3 182
Savoonga	489	473	96.7	47	272	22	21.0	94.6	8.6	25.0	1.0	31.0	81.1	4 583
Saxman	455	228	50.1	26	126	18	20.8	18.8	28.0	47.9	–	38.2	75.5	4 900
Scammon Bay	234	212	90.6	...	...	...	...	...	...	...	...	...	...	...
Selawik	360	353	98.1	...	...	...	...	...	...	...	...	...	...	...
Seldovia	479	123	25.7	...	...	...	...	...	...	...	...	...	...	...
Shageluk	112	105	93.8	...	...	...	...	...	...	...	...	...	...	...
Shaktoolik	155	152	98.1	...	...	...	...	...	...	...	...	...	...	...
Sheldon's Point	92	92	100.0	5	40	–	14.8	93.1	–	25.8	–	33.3	78.8	5 000
Shishmaref	379	332	87.6	45	171	6	19.1	56.1	26.9	50.0	2.4	56.1	67.1	4 000
Shungnak	193	170	88.1	...	...	...	...	...	...	...	...	14.7	...	...
Slana	38	–	–	–	–	–	–	–	–	–	–	–	–	–
Sleetmute	101	93	92.1	...	...	...	...	...	...	...	...	25.0	...	...
Solomon	–	–	–	–	–	–	–	–	–	–	–	–	–	–
South Naknek	144	109	75.7	21	58	5	20.3	14.8	–	48.8	7.3	50.0	80.4	2 000
Stebbins	363	354	97.5	65	145	5	14.2	49.1	24.1	31.1	–	45.5	68.9	5 800
Stevens Village	118	106	89.8	11	70	6	23.3	2.1	31.6	27.1	–	8.3	52.8	4 000
Stony River	62	46	74.2	...	...	...	...	...	...	...	...	...	...	...
Takotna	45	24	53.3	...	...	...	...	...	...	...	...	...	...	...
Tanacross	119	109	91.6	...	...	...	...	...	...	...	...	...	...	...
Tanana	368	292	79.3	27	175	16	22.1	24.9	23.5	44.4	4.8	31.1	70.9	9 000
Tatitlek	63	50	79.4	...	...	...	...	...	...	...	...	...	...	...
Tazlina	43	9	20.9	...	...	...	...	...	...	...	...	...	...	...
Telida	31	31	100.0	12	14	–	6.3	89.5	100.0	33.3	–	...	100.0	...
Teller	226	217	96.0	29	134	18	22.3	86.7	7.1	20.6	–	...	69.9	3 667
Tetlin	84	74	88.1	...	...	...	...	...	...	...	...	...	...	...
Togiak	487	453	93.0	61	266	19	22.8	95.7	10.7	25.7	–	38.7	62.0	3 714
Toksook Bay	317	303	95.6	...	...	...	...	...	...	...	...	...	...	...
Tuluksak	271	267	98.5	...	...	...	...	...	...	...	...	...	...	...
Tuntutuliak	220	215	97.7	28	100	6	16.5	98.4	13.3	23.8	–	...	78.3	4 846
Tununak	291	256	88.0	33	130	11	19.5	100.0	–	31.3	–	35.6	90.5	6 500
Twin Hills	74	70	94.6	...	...	...	...	...	...	...	...	...	...	...
Tyonek	203	184	90.6	...	...	...	...	...	...	...	...	63.0	...	...
Ugashik	8	8	100.0	...	...	...	...	...	...	...	...	...	...	...
Ukivok	–	–	–	–	–	–	–	–	–	–	–	–	–	–
Unalakleet	625	556	89.0	69	326	27	21.3	44.4	7.7	51.0	1.6	33.3	62.2	2 773
Unalaska	1 321	202	15.3	11	132	4	25.3	27.7	–	42.7	4.9	17.1	64.3	2 286
Unga	–	–	–	–	–	–	–	–	–	–	–	–	–	–
Uyak	–	–	–	–	–	–	–	–	–	–	–	–	–	–
Venetie	123	123	100.0	14	70	5	18.8	89.9	22.7	10.9	4.3	40.0	62.3	5 818
Wainwright	402	375	93.3	...	...	...	...	...	...	...	...	38.5	...	...
Wales	131	124	94.7	...	...	...	...	...	...	...	...	...	...	...
White Mountain	122	113	92.6	...	...	...	...	...	...	...	...	...	...	...
Woody Island	5	2	40.0	...	...	...	...	...	...	...	...	...	...	...
Yakutat	456	285	62.5	26	170	12	22.1	20.5	15.0	56.6	5.4	33.3	75.7	3 800

[1]Includes Eskimos and Aleuts on Annette Island Reserve and Alaska Native Villages.

Table 252. Economic Characteristics for American Indian Persons on Reservations and Alaska Native Villages: 1980

[Data include Eskimos and Aleuts on Annette Island Reserve and Alaska Native Villages. Data are estimates based on a sample; see Introduction. For meaning of symbols, see Introduction. For definitions of terms, see appendixes A and B]

Reservations / Alaska Native Villages	Male, 16 years and over	Female Total	Female, with own children under 6 years	Non-workers per 100 workers	Civilian labor force—Percent unemployed	Families Total	Families Percent with no workers in 1979	Median income: House-holds	Median income: Families Total	Median income: Families Female householder, no husband present	Per capita income in 1979 (dollars)	Poverty: Persons Total	Poverty: Persons Percent	Poverty: Families Total	Poverty: Families Female householder, no husband present
RESERVATIONS															
Acoma Pueblo, N. Mex.	76.9	44.0	53.6	184	25.8	387	10.3	13 893	14 225	10 135	2 885	696	29.7	110	62
Agua Caliente Reservation, Calif.	58.5	75.0	100.0	153	50.0	23	–	50 394	50 394	21 250	6 409	30	34.9	6	–
Alabama-Coushatta Reservation, Tex.	72.8	59.2	52.7	153	3.1	123	5.7	13 059	13 218	17 750	2 992	146	29.8	32	–
Alamo Reservation, N. Mex.	48.9	23.0	21.4	431	26.7	210	28.6	5 234	5 573	5 179	1 356	752	70.1	142	13
Allegany Reservation, N.Y.	70.6	57.3	76.6	137	33.2	234	9.0	11 458	12 269	10 125	4 228	211	23.8	47	24
Alturas Rancheria, Calif.	–	–	–	–	–	–	–	–	–	–	–	–	–	–	–
Annette Island Reserve, Alaska	76.7	46.1	27.4	153	13.4	178	–	20 781	21 563	11 429	5 973	69	7.7	9	3
Augustine Reservation, Calif.	–	–	–	–	–	–	–	–	–	–	–	–	–	–	–
Bad River Reservation, Wis.	64.9	50.3	53.4	178	19.2	161	13.7	10 909	11 858	7 045	3 229	212	30.6	40	24
Barona Rancheria, Calif.	51.3	50.0	62.5	259	–	39	–	15 114	15 114	6 250	3 634	–	–	–	–
Bay Mills Reservation, Mich.	79.6	64.3	63.2	120	15.0	62	9.7	11 875	12 778	12 500	3 544	67	24.4	14	4
Benton Paiute Reservation, Calif.	...	...	...	...	...	...	...	...	...	...	...	...	...	...	...
Berry Creek Rancheria, Calif.	–	–	–	–	–	–	–	–	–	–	–	–	–	–	–
Big Bend Rancheria, Calif.	...	...	...	...	...	...	...	...	...	...	...	...	...	...	...
Big Cypress Reservation, Fla.	–	–	–	–	–	–	–	–	–	–	–	–	–	–	–
Big Lagoon Rancheria, Calif.	...	...	...	...	...	...	...	...	...	...	...	...	...	...	...
Big Pine Rancheria, Calif.	100.0	37.5	17.2	201	22.7	69	2.9	7 043	7 331	12 250	2 889	105	39.6	24	–
Bishop Rancheria, Calif.	66.3	56.0	78.0	165	30.3	208	17.3	8 500	9 559	6 000	3 551	234	27.0	54	18
Blackfeet Reservation, Mont.	71.1	53.4	53.3	160	14.7	1 079	9.1	10 471	11 543	10 360	3 293	1 838	36.7	315	88
Bois Forte Reservation (Nett Lake), Minn.	64.9	66.7	63.6	173	15.3	82	–	9 545	9 773	4 922	3 326	133	36.4	24	24
Bridgeport Colony, Calif.	...	...	...	–	–	10	–	21 250	30 468	–	–	–	–	–	–
Brighton Reservation, Fla.	57.7	56.7	100.0	178	–	83	18.1	11 020	7 279	26 250	3 769	110	34.4	43	–
Burns Reservation, Oreg.	87.0	33.9	–	173	10.2	20	–	25 577	25 577	26 250	3 629	–	–	–	–
Cabazon Reservation, Calif.	–	–	–	–	–	–	–	–	–	–	–	–	–	–	–
Cachil Dehe Rancheria, Calif.	...	...	...	...	...	...	...	...	...	...	...	...	...	...	...
Cahuilla Reservation, Calif.	...	...	...	–	–	11	100.0	2 500–	2 500–	2 500–	...	30	100.0	11	11
Campo Reservation, Calif.	36.1	–	–	654	100.0	–	–	2 500–	2 500–	–	969	33	33.7	–	–
Camp Verde Reservation, Ariz.	76.9	77.3	–	84	–	32	–	24 107	24 375	–	11 460	–	–	–	–
Canoncito Reservation, N. Mex.	36.7	34.9	47.7	333	12.3	170	21.8	4 609	5 288	2 500–	1 673	666	65.8	108	35
Capitan Grande Reservation, Calif.	–	–	–	–	–	–	–	–	–	–	–	–	–	–	–
Carson Colony, Nev.	63.4	48.3	100.0	213	12.7	39	–	9 141	12 734	10 417	3 398	65	37.8	9	6
Catawba Reservation, S.C.	84.2	32.7	50.8	249	13.7	127	–	16 429	17 083	10 000	3 749	156	22.7	18	–
Cattaraugus Reservation, N.Y.	56.6	35.3	36.9	250	17.7	434	26.3	12 269	11 897	6 524	3 695	501	27.0	121	67
Cedarville Rancheria, Calif.	...	...	...	...	...	...	...	...	...	...	...	...	...	...	...
Chehalis Reservation, Wash.	52.3	62.1	100.0	156	18.6	48	22.9	9 350	9 821	6 250	3 674	21	13.9	11	11
Chemehuevi Reservation, Calif.	...	...	...	...	...	...	...	...	...	...	...	...	...	...	...
Cheyenne River Reservation, S. Dak.	71.6	49.2	48.0	199	13.2	282	2.8	8 898	9 697	8 667	2 563	857	55.4	134	52
Chitimacha Reservation, La.	89.8	56.0	100.0	96	–	45	–	21 103	21 103	21 250	7 355	10	6.3	–	–
Cochiti Pueblo, N. Mex.	55.1	48.7	69.7	207	4.6	157	7.6	12 545	13 259	10 329	3 211	105	13.2	14	7
Cocopah Reservation, Ariz.	54.4	39.7	44.4	239	20.8	63	–	6 937	9 792	8 542	1 741	263	64.6	32	12
Coeur d'Alene Reservation, Idaho	90.0	43.9	66.7	136	14.9	104	8.7	14 333	17 115	21 806	4 652	43	9.9	2	2
Cold Springs Rancheria, Calif.	–	–	–	–	–	–	–	–	–	–	–	–	–	–	–
Colorado River Reservation, Ariz.-Calif.	65.0	47.6	59.1	193	10.6	429	14.9	9 625	10 363	8 185	3 581	681	34.3	122	42
Colville Reservation, Wash.	72.7	49.6	46.3	157	14.5	728	12.4	13 177	12 394	7 981	4 428	1 047	32.7	238	92
Cortina Rancheria, Calif.	–	–	–	–	–	–	–	–	–	–	–	–	–	–	–
Coushatta Reservation, La.	–	–	–	–	–	–	–	–	–	–	–	–	–	–	–
Coyote Valley Rancheria, Calif.	...	...	...	...	...	...	...	...	...	...	...	...	...	...	...
Crow Reservation, Mont.	64.3	45.8	46.1	198	35.2	719	3.2	13 992	15 160	9 773	3 011	1 348	33.1	213	72
Crow Creek Reservation, S. Dak.	63.0	44.2	51.4	252	28.0	285	9.8	9 801	10 331	6 607	2 166	603	41.5	113	55
Cuyapaipe Reservation, Calif.	–	–	–	–	–	–	–	–	–	–	–	–	–	–	–
Deer Creek Reservation, Minn.	–	–	–	–	–	–	–	–	–	–	–	–	–	–	–
Dresslerville Colony, Nev.	79.4	100.0	–	49	21.1	20	–	6 827	22 273	–	4 196	14	9.9	–	–
Dry Creek Rancheria, Calif.	...	...	...	...	...	...	...	...	...	...	...	...	...	...	...
Duck Valley Reservation, Idaho-Nev.	45.5	29.4	26.0	309	13.6	174	15.5	4 328	6 296	6 146	2 254	638	67.1	109	40
Duckwater Reservation, Nev.	100.0	62.9	–	65	15.7	35	60.0	9 139	2 500–	2 500–	5 111	43	29.3	21	21
Eastern Cherokee Reservation, N.C.	67.7	57.9	70.2	147	16.0	1 206	9.3	9 287	9 849	7 441	3 066	1 623	34.0	381	148
Eastern Pequot Reservation, Conn.	–	–	–	...	–	5	–	7 031	26 250	–	–	...	...	...	...
Ely Colony, Nev.	68.0	54.5	–	230	17.4	12	–	11 667	12 500	13 750	2 500	36	47.4	3	3
Enterprise Rancheria, Calif.	–	–	–	–	–	–	–	–	–	–	–	–	–	–	–
Fallon Colony, Nev.	26.3	–	–	1 220	–	21	38.1	3 819	3 906	–	1 949	25	37.9	6	–
Fallon Reservation, Nev.	65.2	47.2	100.0	141	9.0	50	–	16 591	16 591	52 076	3 735	40	16.6	7	–
Flandreau Reservation, S. Dak.	86.5	60.0	–	125	19.6	29	–	21 250	13 125	4 000	7 231	36	28.6	10	10
Flathead Reservation, Mont.	63.0	44.8	58.1	188	20.2	688	17.0	10 439	10 826	4 247	3 129	1 401	40.5	237	149
Fond du Lac Reservation, Minn.	65.9	52.3	52.6	175	38.0	110	10.9	12 574	14 265	3 750	4 149	122	26.0	20	18
Fort Apache Reservation, Ariz.	63.9	47.0	60.3	227	16.0	1 248	12.1	9 854	10 129	4 651	2 309	2 925	42.2	496	212
Fort Belknap Reservation, Mont.	46.4	47.7	33.3	245	8.9	353	20.4	6 486	8 011	5 156	2 455	802	47.0	149	67
Fort Berthold Reservation, N. Dak.	68.7	50.8	53.9	188	24.5	492	10.2	10 817	11 045	7 415	2 730	978	37.5	190	83
Fort Bidwell Reservation, Calif.	100.0	–	–	346	34.6	28	42.9	11 042	12 083	10 833	2 610	81	69.8	16	16
Fort Hall Reservation, Idaho	59.1	41.1	51.2	242	22.1	554	23.6	9 628	10 375	4 564	3 089	1 139	46.0	241	100
Fort Independence Reservation, Calif.	–	–	–	...	–	10	50.0	11 000	12 500	–	3 756	6	14.3	–	–
Fort McDermitt Reservation, Nev.-Oreg.	61.7	29.4	–	271	46.4	91	19.8	7 500	7 917	9 219	1 982	256	61.5	47	12
Fort McDowell Reservation, Ariz.	67.7	39.3	51.6	194	27.7	89	13.5	12 768	12 768	7 250	2 843	168	41.3	25	–
Fort Mojave Reservation, Ariz.-Calif.-Nev.	100.0	17.9	28.0	153	–	48	–	16 667	16 667	–	5 506	–	–	–	–
Fort Peck Reservation, Mont.	65.6	48.9	54.0	197	25.2	954	7.7	11 516	11 500	7 500	3 268	1 478	33.7	256	126
Fort Totten Reservation, N. Dak.	54.3	37.9	33.7	315	10.5	404	7.2	10 245	10 491	6 875	2 369	1 118	50.7	191	75
Fort Yuma Reservation, Ariz.-Calif.	70.4	43.8	69.6	194	14.2	240	25.8	8 917	12 250	6 250	2 809	356	32.7	87	69
Gila Bend Reservation, Ariz.	–	–	–	–	–	–	–	–	–	–	–	–	–	–	–
Gila River Reservation, Ariz.	55.9	34.9	30.0	269	14.4	1 277	13.3	8 930	9 781	7 672	2 407	3 197	47.8	567	225
Golden Hill Reservation, Conn.	–	–	–	–	–	–	–	–	–	–	–	–	–	–	–
Goshute Reservation, Nev.-Utah	–	–	–	...	–	6	–	2 500–	8 750	8 750	1 381	45	100.0	6	6
Grand Portage Reservation, Minn.	84.9	75.7	42.1	75	20.9	55	–	13 542	14 063	7 500	5 172	28	14.4	2	2
Grindstone Creek Rancheria, Calif.	78.3	33.3	–	195	76.2	11	18.2	9 250	9 250	3 750	1 417	49	79.0	7	2
Hannahville Community, Mich.	86.2	47.9	45.5	177	41.1	36	8.3	8 750	8 571	8 250	1 879	99	49.0	16	6
Hassanamisco Reservation, Mass.	–	–	–	–	–	–	–	–	–	–	–	–	–	–	–
Havasupai Reservation, Ariz.	58.8	51.6	–	155	10.0	37	21.6	8 693	12 917	16 250	2 292	72	28.2	8	–

Table 252. Economic Characteristics for American Indian Persons on Reservations and Alaska Native Villages: 1980—Con.

[Data include Eskimos and Aleuts on Annette Island Reserve and Alaska Native Villages. Data are estimates based on a sample; see Introduction. For meaning of symbols, see Introduction. For definitions of terms, see appendixes A and B]

Reservations Alaska Native Villages	Percent in labor force				Civilian labor force— Percent unem- ployed	Families		Median income in 1979 (dollars)			Per capita income in 1979 (dollars)	Income in 1979 below poverty level			
		Female, 16 years and over							Families			Persons for whom poverty status is determined		Families	
	Male, 16 years and over	Total	With own children under 6 years	Non-workers per 100 workers		Total	Percent with no workers in 1979	House-holds	Total	Female house-holder, no husband present		Total	Percent	Total	Female house-holder, no husband present
RESERVATIONS—Con.															
Hoh Reservation, Wash.	...	...	...	...	...	6	66.7	2500—	2500—	–	–	...	...	4	–
Hollywood Reservation, Fla.	92.7	66.9	54.5	116	17.0	82	13.4	10 521	11 667	2500—	4 495	108	26.0	21	11
Hoopa Valley Reservation, Calif.	79.2	40.3	55.7	178	22.7	360	9.2	12 156	13 516	6 250	4 555	301	20.4	104	39
Hoopa Valley Extension Reservation, Calif.	38.2	27.1	21.9	368	34.1	71	18.3	4 402	4 514	2500—	2 041	219	55.0	45	33
Hopi Reservation, Ariz.	49.0	34.7	50.9	271	24.1	1 357	30.1	7 470	8 145	6 352	2 510	3 337	50.5	692	175
Hopland Rancheria, Calif.	–	–	–	–	–	–	–	–	–	–	–	–	–	–	–
Hualapai Reservation, Ariz.	73.6	62.3	79.2	137	14.5	162	16.0	11 193	11 477	8 333	2 550	238	28.6	27	5
Inaja-Cosmit Reservation, Calif.	–	–	–	–	–	–	–	–	–	–	–	–	–	–	–
Indian Township Reservation, Maine	58.7	68.6	54.8	206	25.7	60	–	10 341	15 556	6 250	3 260	91	27.8	22	17
Iowa Reservation, Kans.-Nebr.	100.0	–	–	210	–	...	...	...	...	–	6 422	1	3.2	...	...
Isabella Reservation, Mich.	64.4	48.1	28.0	202	20.3	89	6.7	12 321	12 232	8 125	2 959	126	28.5	28	5
Isleta Pueblo, N. Mex.	67.1	53.9	54.4	152	8.3	546	14.7	12 019	13 833	11 687	4 457	406	18.2	96	25
Jackson Rancheria, Calif.	–	–	–	–	–	–	–	–	–	–	–	–	–	–	–
Jemez Pueblo, N. Mex.	56.2	43.0	54.5	235	16.9	301	18.6	7 070	7 051	4 375	2 088	769	51.7	164	68
Jicarilla Apache Reservation, N. Mex.	73.4	61.0	63.1	157	15.7	395	8.6	10 981	11 788	8 125	3 408	391	23.3	87	40
Kaibab Reservation, Ariz.	100.0	68.2	–	104	–	7	–	4 333	11 250	11 250	3 010	–	–	–	–
Kalispel Reservation, Wash.	100.0	64.7	–	104	54.3	13	–	11 786	12 321	16 250	2 599	64	68.1	7	–
Kickapoo Reservation, Kans.	78.9	59.8	58.3	127	27.4	85	15.3	12 083	14 583	5 000	3 603	83	22.3	21	10
Kootenai Reservation, Idaho	–	–	–	–	–	–	–	–	–	–	–	–	–	–	–
Lac Courte Oreilles Reservation, Wis.	70.7	48.9	50.0	187	17.7	238	13.4	9 647	10 446	8 929	3 039	328	29.2	71	35
Lac du Flambeau Reservation, Wis.	62.6	50.1	62.5	200	18.4	225	13.3	11 202	11 741	7 333	3 069	270	25.0	55	30
Laguna Pueblo, N. Mex.	73.1	48.8	49.0	153	14.8	774	9.8	15 551	16 675	8 026	4 422	428	12.3	90	56
La Jolla Reservation, Calif.	63.0	26.3	33.3	259	25.0	33	–	8 409	8 977	6 250	3 298	48	30.4	10	10
L'Anse Reservation, Mich.	68.9	50.6	26.2	187	9.4	139	10.8	12 150	12 153	5 417	3 994	155	24.9	40	12
La Posta Reservation, Calif.	–	–	–	–	–	8	–	40 511	40 906	–	3 734	22	24.7	–	–
Las Vegas Colony, Nev.	78.3	51.9	33.3	178	–	43	–	11 364	12 443	11 250	4 072	19	9.3	–	–
Laytonville Rancheria, Calif.	73.6	26.7	–	196	–	–	–	–	–	–	–	–	–	–	–
Leech Lake Reservation, Minn.	60.2	45.6	55.9	219	29.8	545	11.2	8 354	9 078	6 861	3 110	1 032	40.4	196	72
Likely Rancheria, Calif.	–	–	–	–	–	–	–	–	–	–	–	–	–	–	–
Lone Pine Rancheria, Calif.	78.0	28.8	29.4	249	24.5	38	23.7	9 643	9 423	6 250	2 779	47	27.5	5	–
Lookout Rancheria, Calif.	–	–	–	–	–	–	–	–	–	–	–	–	–	–	–
Los Coyotes Reservation, Calif.	16.1	50.0	100.0	427	–	12	50.0	8 333	7 500	6 250	2 414	34	58.6	6	6
Lovelock Colony, Nev.	56.7	29.2	25.0	265	32.3	21	–	7 188	12 083	11 250	4 533	32	28.3	6	3
Lower Brule Reservation, S. Dak.	64.6	50.8	52.9	216	13.3	162	9.3	10 223	9 773	6 250	2 801	380	45.1	67	37
Lower Elwah Reservation, Wash.	55.6	–	–	280	–	10	–	22 750	23 750	–	6 837	8	21.1	–	–
Lower Sioux Community, Minn.	64.3	69.6	60.0	103	14.7	19	21.1	10 000	13 750	7 500	3 737	21	30.4	3	2
Lummi Reservation, Wash.	55.0	43.8	49.6	236	24.3	256	16.0	15 956	15 893	9 886	3 783	306	24.6	62	10
Makah Reservation, Wash.	84.1	56.2	79.2	147	7.1	205	10.2	14 432	14 851	13 333	4 694	84	10.6	17	13
Manchester Rancheria, Calif.	57.6	18.8	–	209	–	14	–	13 750	13 750	11 250	3 983	–	–	–	–
Manzanita Reservation, Calif.	–	–	–	–	–	–	–	–	–	–	–	–	–	–	–
Maricopa Reservation, Ariz.	58.8	24.8	16.1	299	–	55	–	14 038	14 904	–	2 098	85	21.1	12	–
Mattaponi Reservation, Va.	100.0	100.0	100.0	51	–	26	–	18 889	18 889	18 889	5 989	–	–	–	–
Menominee Reservation, Wis.	70.1	34.4	25.0	222	14.1	455	12.7	14 009	14 591	8 187	3 180	417	16.9	68	39
Mesa Grande Reservation, Calif.	–	–	–	–	–	–	–	–	–	–	–	–	–	–	–
Mescalero Apache Reservation, N. Mex.	68.5	53.5	57.8	200	11.3	402	7.2	10 607	11 544	6 176	2 962	688	35.6	133	83
Miccosukee Reservation, Fla.	–	–	–	–	–	–	–	–	–	–	–	–	–	–	–
Middletown Rancheria, Calif.	–	–	...	–	...	...	...	...	...	–	2 316	...	...	...	...
Mille Lacs Reservation, Minn.	85.7	50.0	–	200	30.0	...	...	11 557	11 054	8 711	2 988	14	46.7	157	53
Mississippi Choctaw Reservation	76.3	56.8	72.0	170	14.9	553	6.7	11 557	11 054	8 711	2 988	896	35.2	157	53
Moapa River Reservation, Nev.	100.0	28.4	–	303	–	40	20.0	7 353	9 000	6 528	2 992	26	17.0	8	8
Montgomery Creek Rancheria, Calif.	–	–	–	–	–	–	–	–	–	–	–	–	–	–	–
Morongo Reservation, Calif.	43.0	44.7	–	221	10.3	93	37.6	10 650	10 665	11 250	2 739	50	14.6	13	–
Muckleshoot Reservation, Wash.	53.1	48.6	25.0	251	18.9	53	28.3	7 788	4 542	4 044	1 094	287	68.8	37	18
Nambe Pueblo, N. Mex.	77.4	50.0	56.3	147	–	47	–	15 735	16 250	12 917	4 260	19	11.3	4	4
Navajo Reservation, Ariz.-N. Mex.-Utah	52.0	35.4	45.5	303	14.3	19 753	21.6	8 342	9 079	5 831	2 414	51 904	49.7	9 348	2 789
Nez Perce Reservation, Idaho	77.6	68.7	92.2	121	12.3	211	26.1	6 801	9 505	8 750	3 409	378	35.7	46	–
Nisqually Reservation, Wash.	...	...	...	...	...	5	–	30 468	30 468	–	...	–	–	–	–
Nooksack Reservation, Wash.	–	–	–	–	–	–	–	–	–	–	–	–	–	–	–
Northern Cheyenne Reservation, Mont.	53.8	56.1	65.1	233	15.7	612	17.5	8 304	9 336	5 375	2 512	1 238	41.8	255	116
Oil Springs Reservation, N.Y.	–	–	–	–	–	–	–	–	–	–	–	–	–	–	–
Omaha Reservation, Iowa-Nebr.	57.6	50.7	55.3	210	15.9	258	14.0	10 875	10 500	7 989	2 682	479	36.9	93	53
Oneida Reservation, Wis.	55.7	32.9	31.2	258	12.4	364	18.4	12 206	15 395	6 625	3 979	320	18.6	70	34
Onondaga Reservation, N.Y.	80.6	56.4	100.0	90	5.3	120	15.0	18 207	17 742	13 203	5 693	103	18.9	22	11
Ontonagon Reservation, Mich.	–	–	–	–	–	–	–	–	–	–	–	–	–	–	–
Osage Reservation, Okla.	74.8	43.6	42.5	154	3.4	1 157	14.7	14 393	15 891	8 750	5 806	865	18.5	207	82
Ozette Reservation, Wash.	–	–	–	–	–	–	–	–	–	–	–	–	–	–	–
Pala Reservation, Calif.	74.1	46.4	33.3	180	3.3	134	21.6	13 971	12 188	8 864	3 915	115	22.8	35	18
Pamunkey Reservation, Va.	100.0	–	–	160	–	12	100.0	10 250	2500—	2500—	4 202	24	61.5	12	12
Papago Reservation, Ariz.	55.9	33.1	56.5	267	13.6	1 336	15.8	7 152	8 231	8 125	2 170	3 691	54.0	661	178
Pascua Yaqui Reservation, Ariz.	74.1	29.6	82.9	293	16.7	63	28.6	9 432	9 432	2500—	1 374	374	79.4	37	8
Pauma Reservation, Calif.	–	–	–	–	–	–	–	–	–	–	–	–	–	–	–
Payson Community of Yavapai-Apache, Ariz.	–	–	–	–	–	–	–	–	–	–	–	–	–	–	–
Pechanga Reservation, Calif.	82.1	100.0	–	33	–	11	–	14 792	14 792	–	7 195	–	–	–	–
Penobscot Reservation, Maine	83.0	68.9	100.0	102	11.3	114	–	9 208	10 543	4 861	3 318	87	21.4	16	9
Picuris Pueblo, N. Mex.	54.5	–	–	313	60.0	31	–	13 365	13 365	8 750	3 219	43	34.7	11	8
Pine Creek Reservation, Mich.	–	–	–	–	–	–	–	–	–	–	–	–	–	–	–
Pine Ridge Reservation, S. Dak.	53.7	38.1	47.6	293	21.1	1 998	16.5	9 530	9 635	6 740	2 209	5 696	48.5	967	435
Pleasant Point Reservation, Maine	59.4	47.4	55.6	237	29.3	101	28.7	3 750	6 042	4 167	1 798	311	62.0	63	39
Pojoaque Pueblo, N. Mex.	66.7	–	–	208	–	5	–	4 643	16 250	–	3 225	13	35.1	–	–
Poospatuck Reservation, N.Y.	100.0	–	–	340	100.0	...	...	...	...	...	2 130	24	54.5	...	...
Port Gamble Reservation, Wash.	73.5	28.0	52.4	256	23.6	61	16.4	15 139	17 083	7 375	5 096	56	17.7	10	10
Port Madison Reservation, Wash.	52.1	36.4	–	206	8.0	46	13.0	24 000	25 227	–	8 186	17	11.1	–	–
Potawatomi Reservation, Wis.	51.4	37.2	85.7	265	–	33	33.3	4 659	3 523	2500—	3 799	73	58.9	24	13
Pottawatomi Reservation, Kans.	68.7	45.3	29.2	173	18.9	77	13.0	7 500	7 298	6 667	3 252	114	34.2	24	6
Prairie Island Community, Minn.	100.0	–	–	273	31.8	14	–	19 464	18 750	–	4 741	–	–	–	–

Table 252. **Economic Characteristics for American Indian Persons on Reservations and Alaska Native Villages: 1980**—Con.

[Data include Eskimos and Aleuts on Annette Island Reserve and Alaska Native Villages. Data are estimates based on a sample; see Introduction. For meaning of symbols, see Introduction. For definitions of terms, see appendixes A and B]

Reservations Alaska Native Villages	Percent in labor force			Non-workers per 100 workers	Civilian labor force—Percent unemployed	Families		Median income in 1979 (dollars)			Per capita income in 1979 (dollars)	Income in 1979 below poverty level			
	Male, 16 years and over	Female, 16 years and over							Families			Persons for whom poverty status is determined		Families	
		Total	With own children under 6 years			Total	Percent with no workers in 1979	Households	Total	Female householder, no husband present		Total	Percent	Total	Female householder, no husband present
RESERVATIONS—Con.															
Puyallup Reservation, Wash.	49.2	43.9	41.5	260	21.6	211	32.2	11 667	11 161	5 667	3 308	358	40.9	94	54
Pyramid Lake Reservation, Nev.	55.4	37.5	13.3	225	1.4	155	12.3	10 505	11 410	7 000	3 615	143	20.6	36	28
Quileute Reservation, Wash.	81.0	56.6	72.4	146	–	47	–	9 554	9 554	8 393	2 493	70	25.7	12	12
Quinault Reservation, Wash.	49.4	49.5	54.9	234	13.0	175	20.0	14 474	13 224	2500—	3 182	327	34.1	68	37
Ramah Community, N. Mex.	67.4	41.2	75.0	192	21.2	236	34.3	5 719	6 833	2 663	2 515	531	45.4	127	97
Ramona Reservation, Calif.	–	–	–	–	–	–	–	–	–	–	–	–	–	–	–
Red Cliff Reservation, Wis.	75.3	55.6	53.3	170	19.8	111	4.5	11 350	11 563	7 143	2 961	166	29.1	25	6
Red Lake Reservation, Minn.	67.0	45.4	27.8	215	24.6	558	8.1	12 029	12 465	8 897	4 106	812	28.9	147	90
Reno-Sparks Colony, Nev.	69.4	69.1	73.3	117	23.9	77	10.4	12 353	15 893	12 344	3 990	133	30.0	21	13
Resighini Rancheria, Calif.	...	...	...	...	...	...	...	...	...	...	...	...	...	...	...
Rincon Reservation, Calif.	100.0	23.7	–	281	22.6	43	14.0	16 923	24 375	13 750	4 687	36	15.7	7	7
Roaring Creek Rancheria, Calif.	20.0	–	–	950	100.0	...	...	–	–	–	14 042	–	–	–	–
Rocky Boy's Reservation, Mont.	54.1	37.5	47.2	289	11.3	256	4.7	15 032	15 156	7 292	2 902	515	35.6	78	39
Rosebud Reservation, S. Dak.	54.0	45.9	46.8	267	18.5	1 117	17.3	7 325	8 318	5 617	2 484	2 800	50.2	540	273
Round Valley Reservation, Calif.	34.1	6.9	–	749	–	70	–	4 142	8 300	8 750	2 710	112	35.7	27	–
Rumsey Rancheria, Calif.	...	...	...	...	...	...	...	...	...	...	...	...	...	...	...
Sac and Fox Reservation, Iowa	67.1	46.8	57.5	184	16.9	79	7.6	14 196	14 196	14 000	3 133	91	20.2	18	–
Sac and Fox Reservation, Kans.-Nebr.	–	–	–	–	–	–	–	–	–	–	–	–	–	–	–
St. Croix Reservation, Wis.	67.0	50.4	50.0	179	20.9	86	22.1	8 558	8 452	7 946	2 792	149	41.4	33	23
St. Regis Mohawk Reservation, N.Y.	63.4	33.5	27.3	195	33.4	391	15.9	12 731	14 282	13 385	3 931	357	20.6	70	15
Salt River Reservation, Ariz.	68.8	48.2	49.0	189	10.8	483	2.7	12 039	12 956	8 511	3 048	855	34.7	149	78
San Carlos Reservation, Ariz.	62.1	36.3	41.8	249	15.8	1 114	14.7	7 704	8 327	4 555	2 262	2 871	49.0	511	223
Sandia Pueblo, N. Mex.	68.6	60.5	100.0	95	9.0	59	11.9	11 250	14 250	8 750	4 403	54	24.9	20	–
Sandy Lake Reservation, Minn.	–	–	–	–	–	–	–	–	–	–	–	–	–	–	–
San Felipe Pueblo, N. Mex.	55.1	48.4	42.8	238	18.8	265	10.9	12 455	12 083	10 893	1 900	667	37.5	101	35
San Ildefonso Pueblo, N. Mex.	84.2	47.1	50.0	132	3.9	113	18.6	12 431	12 431	5 750	3 232	79	16.7	21	12
San Juan Pueblo, N. Mex.	58.5	43.0	49.3	217	14.9	282	16.7	8 525	9 139	7 917	2 253	462	41.6	81	32
San Manuel Reservation, Calif.	...	...	...	...	...	...	...	...	...	...	...	...	...	...	...
San Pasqual Reservation, Calif.	65.0	40.4	56.0	220	20.0	38	21.1	8 472	9 167	–	2 459	5	3.5	–	–
Santa Ana Pueblo, N. Mex.	80.5	52.9	68.8	121	1.2	89	–	16 000	17 250	11 324	3 515	15	4.0	3	3
Santa Clara Pueblo, N. Mex.	80.5	50.5	52.6	169	3.4	64	6.3	8 150	8 800	9 500	2 763	160	50.8	26	4
Santa Rosa Rancheria, Calif.	33.3	61.5	51.6	441	50.0	...	...	...	...	...	1 332	63	36.4	...	...
Santa Rosa Reservation, Calif.	–	–	–	–	–	–	–	–	–	–	–	–	–	–	–
Santa Ynez Reservation, Calif.	–	–	–	–	–	–	–	–	–	–	–	–	–	–	–
Santa Ysabel Reservation, Calif.	48.8	22.9	–	249	60.8	41	–	4 449	8 194	–	1 947	88	49.4	18	–
Santee Reservation, Nebr.	66.7	61.1	85.7	197	17.9	80	6.3	10 341	10 556	8 214	2 764	172	40.6	28	18
Santo Domingo Pueblo, N. Mex.	51.1	21.0	28.9	359	13.9	309	14.9	8 375	8 750	10 179	1 584	1 224	57.2	178	30
San Xavier Reservation, Ariz.	62.7	51.9	53.6	179	15.2	149	–	10 625	11 616	10 536	3 022	161	19.4	31	13
Sauk-Suiattle Reservation, Wash.	–	–	–	–	–	–	–	–	–	–	–	–	–	–	–
Sault Ste. Marie Reservation, Mich.	–	–	–	–	–	–	–	–	–	–	–	–	–	–	–
Schaghticoke Reservation, Conn.	–	–	–	–	–	–	–	–	–	–	–	–	–	–	–
Shakopee Community, Minn.	68.4	100.0	–	52	12.0	32	–	21 389	20 278	13 750	7 278	–	–	–	–
Sheep Ranch Rancheria, Calif.	–	–	–	–	–	–	–	–	–	–	–	–	–	–	–
Sherwood Valley Rancheria, Calif.	–	–	–	–	–	–	–	–	–	–	–	–	–	–	–
Shingle Springs Rancheria, Calif.	–	–	–	–	–	–	–	–	–	–	–	–	–	–	–
Shinnecock Reservation, N.Y.	73.3	48.8	100.0	173	–	52	19.2	9 556	18 864	9 437	5 570	–	–	–	–
Shoalwater Reservation, Wash.	100.0	71.4	100.0	35	26.1	17	–	25 865	25 865	6 250	10 144	–	–	–	–
Sisseton Reservation, N. Dak.-S. Dak.	61.3	47.2	52.9	229	20.8	501	14.0	7 373	7 698	5 810	2 208	1 398	54.9	238	145
Skokomish Reservation, Wash.	31.4	28.8	57.1	490	24.1	64	18.8	10 294	10 500	7 857	2 459	161	47.1	23	5
Skull Valley Reservation, Utah	...	...	...	...	...	...	...	...	...	...	...	...	...	...	...
Soboba Reservation, Calif.	67.1	28.4	47.1	256	–	39	–	7 375	11 406	11 250	3 977	85	35.1	17	8
Sokaogon Chippewa Community, Wis.	88.6	64.9	60.0	95	–	30	–	11 442	12 115	13 393	4 551	7	6.5	2	–
Southern Paiute Reservation, Utah	75.5	46.0	34.8	245	18.2	53	11.3	15 417	12 708	2 969	2 801	83	36.4	26	20
Southern Ute Reservation, Colo.	70.0	47.9	64.4	196	9.5	155	16.8	9 295	9 350	6 131	2 903	318	39.4	56	41
Spokane Reservation, Wash.	79.9	36.7	26.5	167	20.7	226	12.8	19 183	18 971	6 875	5 575	180	17.2	44	24
Squaxin Island Reservation, Wash.	...	...	...	...	...	...	...	...	...	...	755	59	100.0	...	...
Standing Rock Reservation, N. Dak.-S. Dak.	58.2	42.5	39.2	249	21.5	868	18.5	8 669	8 800	4 857	2 602	2 182	47.1	384	228
Stewart's Point Rancheria, Calif.	37.5	55.9	–	148	24.0	8	–	23 333	23 333	18 750	3 729	–	–	–	–
Stockbridge Reservation, Wis.	61.3	46.6	52.6	183	22.5	119	12.6	10 200	12 163	11 111	3 403	111	19.6	18	8
Sulphur Bank Rancheria, Calif.	...	...	...	...	...	11	100.0	10 455	11 250	–	3 433	19	18.8	–	–
Summit Lake Reservation, Nev.	–	–	–	–	–	–	–	–	–	–	–	–	–	–	–
Susanville Reservation, Calif.	27.9	64.3	100.0	207	30.0	12	–	11 250	8 750	6 250	1 933	50	54.3	4	4
Swinomish Reservation, Wash.	20.9	39.8	58.3	415	24.3	97	6.2	11 797	11 797	6 528	4 413	60	16.1	21	8
Sycuan Reservation, Calif.	...	...	...	...	...	6	–	3 625	10 000	3 750	...	...	...	3	3
Tama Reservation, Ga.	...	...	...	...	...	5	–	11 250	3 750	3 750	...	...	...	5	5
Taos Pueblo, N. Mex.	50.5	48.6	85.7	174	20.3	168	13.1	8 654	9 327	2500—	2 717	232	31.8	53	13
Te-Moak Reservation, Nev.	100.0	37.5	53.3	114	–	17	29.4	15 313	16 094	2500—	3 760	19	25.3	5	5
Tesuque Pueblo, N. Mex.	67.6	37.7	46.2	209	14.9	37	21.6	9 750	14 583	17 750	2 600	59	25.8	13	4
Tigua Reservation, Tex.	–	–	–	–	–	–	–	–	–	–	–	–	–	–	–
Tonawanda Reservation, N.Y.	55.6	45.3	–	187	12.2	103	7.8	10 893	14 028	4 868	4 426	141	33.4	31	19
Torres-Martinez Reservation, Calif.	70.0	–	–	264	50.0	7	–	23 750	23 750	–	3 157	–	–	–	–
Trinidad Rancheria, Calif.	78.6	66.7	–	171	17.6	14	21.4	16 250	16 250	–	4 003	–	–	–	–
Tulalip Reservation, Wash.	60.7	35.6	61.5	260	5.8	124	23.4	10 750	13 409	2500—	3 501	250	33.4	50	21
Tule River Reservation, Calif.	67.0	43.0	50.0	243	8.7	91	17.6	9 440	7 411	7 411	2 486	141	32.3	32	10
Tunica-Biloxi Reservation, La.	–	–	–	–	–	–	–	–	–	–	–	–	–	–	–
Tuolumne Rancheria, Calif.	34.8	52.6	–	272	–	14	13.7	13 173	12 813	–	3 030	10	19.2	–	–
Turtle Mountain Reservation, N. Dak.	56.1	47.1	52.7	225	22.3	847	23.6	9 643	10 934	5 703	3 339	1 601	40.8	319	135
Tuscarora Reservation, N.Y.	65.4	27.2	53.3	125	23.2	272	14.3	16 613	15 833	2500—	6 837	57	6.5	19	9
Twenty-Nine Palms Reservation, Calif.	–	–	–	–	–	–	–	–	–	–	–	–	–	–	–
Uintah and Ouray Reservation, Utah	62.7	36.7	39.1	245	15.9	377	15.4	13 929	14 821	11 364	2 897	493	25.6	114	28
Umatilla Reservation, Oreg.	48.5	37.1	26.5	285	19.9	212	24.5	11 019	12 037	6 852	3 003	381	40.5	63	37
Upper Sioux Community, Minn.	66.7	20.0	50.0	231	12.5	12	16.7	11 786	12 857	–	3 737	4	7.5	–	–
Upper Skagit Reservation, Wash.	–	–	–	–	–	–	–	–	–	–	–	–	–	–	–
Ute Mountain Reservation, Colo.-N. Mex.	58.4	32.9	23.8	245	20.1	205	38.0	7 935	9 323	2500—	2 543	469	47.0	96	11
Vermillion Lake Reservation, Minn.	78.0	57.7	66.7	126	26.2	25	8.0	11 875	16 563	8 438	4 176	50	36.2	5	5

Table 252. Economic Characteristics for American Indian Persons on Reservations and Alaska Native Villages: 1980—Con.

[Data include Eskimos and Aleuts on Annette Island Reserve and Alaska Native Villages. Data are estimates based on a sample; see Introduction. For meaning of symbols, see Introduction. For definitions of terms, see appendixes A and B]

Reservations / Alaska Native Villages	Percent in labor force: Male, 16 years and over	Female, 16 years and over: Total	Female: With own children under 6 years	Non-workers per 100 workers	Civilian labor force—Percent unemployed	Families: Total	Families: Percent with no workers in 1979	Median income 1979: Households	Median income 1979: Families Total	Median income 1979: Families Female householder, no husband present	Per capita income in 1979 (dollars)	Poverty: Persons Total	Poverty: Persons Percent	Poverty: Families Total	Poverty: Families Female householder, no husband present
RESERVATIONS—Con.															
Viejas Rancheria, Calif.	80.4	86.8	73.7	92	35.9	40	12.5	11 336	8 929	8 194	4 196	17	11.8	5	5
Walker River Reservation, Nev.	66.0	60.5	29.6	138	–	104	–	17 500	19 024	9 643	5 174	24	5.4	–	–
Wampanoag Reservation, Mass.	–	–	–	–	–	–	–	–	–	–	–	–	–	–	–
Warm Springs Reservation, Oreg.	64.4	58.0	62.4	175	13.3	443	6.1	15 957	16 434	10 682	3 809	463	22.6	84	28
Washoe Reservation, Nev.	–	–	–	–	–	–	–	–	–	–	–	–	–	–	–
Western Pequot Reservation, Conn.	...	...	...	...	...	...	...	...	...	...	...	...	...	...	...
White Earth Reservation, Minn.	61.1	44.6	42.0	207	25.9	499	10.8	9 380	10 382	7 958	2 803	808	31.9	132	51
Wind River Reservation, Wyo.	62.4	35.2	38.4	257	12.8	820	11.0	11 176	12 958	9 091	2 916	1 367	33.0	289	115
Winnebago Reservation, Nebr.	56.6	48.4	55.4	212	19.4	229	13.1	8 448	9 241	6 406	2 892	449	40.5	86	55
Winnemucca Colony, Nev.	100.0	100.0	–	106	52.9	9	–	6 250	6 250	–	1 719	35	100.0	9	–
Wisconsin Winnebago Reservation	69.9	48.6	61.7	236	23.5	106	14.2	9 861	10 526	8 839	2 414	193	31.5	29	16
Woodfords Community, Calif.	51.4	35.3	80.0	249	13.5	25	20.0	5 833	4 886	4 107	3 061	67	52.8	16	7
XL Ranch Reservation, Calif.	–	–	–	–	–	–	–	–	–	–	–	–	–	–	–
Yakima Reservation, Wash.	64.2	46.4	52.8	196	17.9	1 026	12.5	12 442	13 846	6 604	3 796	1 367	28.1	261	133
Yankton Reservation, S. Dak.	49.7	40.7	46.0	291	16.1	323	18.6	7 656	8 893	5 968	2 473	839	51.1	157	89
Yavapai Reservation, Ariz.	100.0	29.2	–	321	–	34	55.9	10 833	2500–	2500–	3 022	107	66.9	19	19
Yerington Reservation, Nev.	54.2	76.9	100.0	170	–	42	–	10 682	10 682	6 250	4 467	–	–	–	–
Yomba Reservation, Nev.	–	–	–	–	–	–	–	–	–	–	–	–	–	–	–
Zia Pueblo, N. Mex.	57.5	37.3	27.7	215	7.3	94	–	10 391	11 250	15 208	2 292	181	30.1	33	11
Zuni Pueblo, N. Mex.	50.9	41.4	44.2	275	24.3	997	23.2	9 848	9 835	8 560	2 112	2 488	42.1	417	127
San Felipe/Santa Ana Joint Area, N. Mex.	–	–	–	–	–	–	–	–	–	–	–	–	–	–	–
San Felipe/Santa Domingo Joint Area, N. Mex.	74.1	61.9	53.3	176	–	29	–	23 125	14 688	17 188	3 652	72	56.7	11	–
Other reservation lands in Montana	...	...	...	...	...	...	...	...	...	...	...	...	...	...	...
ALASKA NATIVE VILLAGES															
Afognak	80.0	58.6	100.0	139	65.9	13	–	8 393	8 542	3 750	1 788	57	59.4	8	–
Akhiok	46.9	18.8	20.0	354	5.1	51	–	20 357	20 268	9 643	3 028	41	10.6	9	1
Akiachak	...	...	...	...	...	...	...	...	...	...	...	...	...	...	...
Aklak	–	15.0	...	1 800	...	...	...	...	...	...	...	...	...	...	...
Akutan	...	...	...	...	...	11	27.3	5 833	7 083	6 250	1 584	47	82.5	8	...
Alakanuk	...	...	...	...	...	90	3.3	10 577	10 729	8 438	...	...	...	39	3
Alatna	...	...	...	...	...	...	...	...	...	...	...	...	...	...	...
Aleknagik	...	...	...	...	...	...	...	...	...	...	...	...	...	...	...
Alexander	...	...	...	...	...	...	...	...	...	...	...	...	...	...	...
Allakaket	...	...	...	...	...	...	...	...	...	...	...	...	...	...	...
Ambler	39.5	39.0	63.6	361	36.4	29	6.9	11 250	11 705	3 750	2 872	19	12.6	5	5
Anaktuvuk Pass	...	...	...	...	...	55	–	7 361	7 361	18 750	...	...	...	28	–
Andreafsky	...	...	...	...	...	...	...	...	...	...	...	...	...	...	...
Angoon	52.2	62.1	72.5	187	16.7	80	5.0	12 589	13 036	7 250	3 267	95	23.3	21	5
Aniak	37.2	49.1	70.8	255	10.0	39	20.5	9 250	9 844	7 917	3 567	77	36.2	12	4
Anvik	...	...	...	...	...	...	...	...	...	...	...	...	...	...	...
Arctic Village	...	...	...	...	...	22	–	11 250	13 333	8 750	2 777	18	19.4	7	–
Atka	74.5	33.3	42.9	121	64.3	...	...	...	...	...	...	...	...	...	...
Atkasook	...	...	...	...	...	...	...	...	...	...	...	...	...	...	...
Atmautluak	...	...	...	...	...	...	...	...	...	...	...	...	...	...	...
Barrow	71.9	51.5	51.7	147	7.2	308	3.9	32 146	32 515	22 500	8 808	187	11.0	34	16
Beaver	21.1	38.1	–	417	–	13	–	6 563	6 806	6 563	4 645	19	30.6	4	2
Belkofsky	...	...	...	...	...	...	...	...	...	...	...	...	...	...	...
Bethel	62.9	49.9	45.1	192	10.7	401	7.7	19 211	20 353	9 812	5 062	481	20.5	71	28
Bill Moore's	–	–	–	–	–	–	–	–	–	–	–	–	–	–	–
Birch Creek	...	...	...	...	...	5	–	3 000	2500–	11 250	...	...	...	3	–
Brevig Mission	35.3	13.6	30.8	480	6.7	26	7.7	9 844	11 250	13 750	2 299	76	43.7	11	–
Buckland	...	...	...	...	...	...	...	...	...	...	...	...	...	...	...
Cantwell	77.8	100.0	100.0	136	28.6	7	–	9 583	10 313	–	2 301	2	6.1	–	–
Cholkyitsik	...	...	...	...	...	...	...	...	...	...	...	...	...	...	...
Chefornak	...	...	...	...	...	...	...	...	...	...	...	...	...	...	...
Chevak	...	...	...	...	...	65	6.2	13 750	17 614	9 167	...	...	...	15	6
Chignik	35.7	66.7	–	200	–	14	–	31 468	31 468	–	11 816	–	...	–	–
Chignik Lagoon	...	...	...	...	...	...	...	...	...	...	...	...	...	...	...
Chignik Lake	...	...	...	...	...	...	...	...	...	...	...	...	...	...	...
Chilkat	44.1	21.2	–	359	40.9	17	29.4	6 250	25 938	–	4 011	28	27.7	7	–
Chistochina	...	...	...	...	...	5	100.0	6 250	6 250	–	...	...	...	–	–
Chitina	...	...	...	...	...	...	...	...	...	...	...	...	...	...	...
Circle	...	...	...	...	...	...	...	...	...	...	...	...	...	...	...
Clark's Point	...	...	...	...	...	...	...	...	...	...	...	...	...	...	...
Copper Center	66.7	28.3	–	333	11.1	23	–	12 917	14 583	4 375	4 504	22	18.8	6	6
Craig	51.1	60.0	70.0	202	22.6	...	...	...	...	...	5 167	46	28.8	...	...
Crooked Creek	...	...	...	...	...	...	...	...	...	...	...	...	...	...	...
Deering	...	...	...	...	...	...	...	...	...	...	...	...	...	...	...
Dillingham	61.3	42.6	37.7	207	10.7	...	...	...	...	...	7 619	250	28.5	...	...
Dot Lake	...	...	...	...	...	...	...	...	...	...	...	...	...	...	...
Eagle	...	...	...	...	...	15	–	11 250	11 250	16 250	...	...	...	6	–
Eek	...	...	...	...	...	...	...	...	...	...	...	...	...	...	...
Egegik	...	...	...	...	...	...	...	...	...	...	...	...	...	...	...
Eklutna	...	...	...	...	...	...	...	3 750	...	...	...	...	...	...	...
Ekuk	–	–	–	–	–	–	–	–	–	–	–	–	–	–	–
Ekwok	70.8	52.4	100.0	171	–	...	...	...	...	...	4 671	29	38.2	...	...
Elim	...	...	...	...	...	...	...	...	...	...	...	...	...	...	...
Emmonak	36.1	16.3	21.7	563	6.8	106	11.3	5 750	6 176	5 750	1 647	323	66.7	67	18
English Bay	...	...	...	...	...	18	–	3 929	6 000	–	...	...	...	7	–
Evansville	53.8	42.9	–	138	...	...	...	...	...	...	5 422	19	61.3	...	...
False Pass	...	...	...	...	...	...	...	...	...	...	...	...	...	...	...
Fort Yukon	31.2	41.9	51.2	314	38.0	95	10.5	8 750	8 510	7 500	3 503	166	43.8	33	11
Gakona	...	...	...	...	...	...	...	...	...	...	...	...	...	...	...
Galena	28.1	51.8	83.3	263	16.9	40	7.5	13 750	23 500	24 167	4 591	20	9.3	–	–
Gambell	33.1	31.1	29.4	357	2.2	...	...	...	...	...	2 933	175	43.0	...	...

Table 252. Economic Characteristics for American Indian Persons on Reservations and Alaska Native Villages: 1980—Con.

[Data include Eskimos and Aleuts on Annette Island Reserve and Alaska Native Villages. Data are estimates based on a sample; see Introduction. For meaning of symbols, see Introduction. For definitions of terms, see appendixes A and B]

Reservations / Alaska Native Villages	Percent in labor force			Non-workers per 100 workers	Civilian labor force—Percent unemployed	Families		Median income in 1979 (dollars)			Per capita income in 1979 (dollars)	Income in 1979 below poverty level			
	Male, 16 years and over	Female, 16 years and over				Total	Percent with no workers in 1979	Households	Families			Persons for whom poverty status is determined		Families	
		Total	With own children under 6 years						Total	Female householder, no husband present		Total	Percent	Total	Female householder, no husband present

ALASKA NATIVE VILLAGES—Con.

Reservations / Alaska Native Villages	Male 16+	Fem. Total	Fem. <6	Non-wkrs /100	% unemp	Fam. Total	Fam. % no wkrs	Househ.	Fam. Total	Fam. FH	Per capita	Pov. Total	Pov. %	Fam. Total	Fam. FH
Georgetown	—	—	—	—	—	—	—	—	—	—	—	—	—	—	—
Golovin	60.9	24.2	25.0	286	31.8	19	10.5	9 063	12 750	10 000	3 135	25	29.4	4	4
Goodnews Bay	...	...	...	...	...	...	...	...	...	...	...	...	...	...	...
Grayling	...	...	...	...	...	...	...	...	...	...	...	...	...	...	...
Gulkana	...	...	...	...	...	6	—	13 750	13 750	...	...	...	...	...	...
Hamilton	...	...	...	...	...	...	...	...	...	...	...	...	...	...	...
Healy Lake	...	...	...	...	...	...	...	...	...	...	...	...	...	...	...
Holy Cross	...	...	...	...	...	...	...	...	...	...	...	...	...	...	...
Hoonah	54.9	43.7	54.9	222	28.8	112	6.3	16 250	17 813	18 750	4 400	44	8.4	10	2
Hooper Bay	...	...	...	...	...	92	7.6	12 788	15 179	8 000	...	...	...	20	5
Hughes	21.7	40.0	—	382	—	10	—	8 750	10 000	—	3 423	33	62.3	5	—
Huslia	...	...	...	...	...	...	...	...	...	...	...	...	...	...	...
Hydaburg	...	...	...	...	...	68	11.8	13 750	16 667	6 250	...	...	...	8	3
Iguigig	...	...	...	...	...	...	...	...	...	...	...	...	...	...	...
Iliamna	...	...	...	...	...	...	...	...	...	...	...	...	...	...	...
Inalik	...	...	...	...	...	21	28.6	3 281	2 813	—	...	...	...	16	...
Ivanof Bay	...	...	...	...	...	...	...	...	...	...	...	...	...	...	...
Kaguyak	...	...	...	...	...	...	...	...	...	...	...	...	...	...	...
Kake	58.6	40.4	28.3	210	28.0	101	—	19 250	22 875	11 458	6 051	32	6.3	11	5
Kaktovik	...	...	...	...	...	21	—	39 046	43 050	—	...	...	...	...	...
Kalskag	...	...	...	...	...	15	—	6 406	7 321	6 250	...	...	...	8	2
Kaltag	...	...	...	...	...	37	—	6 420	6 691	3 750	...	...	...	22	4
Karluk	78.3	48.0	47.4	210	6.7	17	41.2	8 125	5 417	—	1 978	60	65.9	11	—
Kasaan	...	...	...	...	...	...	...	...	...	...	...	...	...	...	...
Kasigluk	...	...	...	...	...	...	...	...	...	...	...	...	...	...	...
Kiana	...	...	...	...	...	...	...	...	...	...	...	...	...	...	...
King Cove	43.8	41.7	44.8	275	6.7	58	...	21 696	21 964	3 750	7 120	59	21.7	7	7
Kipnuk	39.7	30.9	30.0	328	29.5	...	—	...	...	...	4 532	37	9.8	...	...
Kivalina	49.3	38.7	66.7	298	25.4	...	...	...	...	...	2 118	155	66.0	...	...
Klawock	66.7	50.0	57.1	155	4.1	53	—	26 944	28 036	18 750	6 337	8	3.2	—	—
Knik	—	—	—	—	—	—	—	—	—	—	—	—	—	—	—
Kobuk	64.7	64.7	33.3	159	59.1	11	—	3 000	4 250	2500—	2 317	47	82.5	9	2
Kokhanok	...	...	...	...	...	...	...	...	...	...	...	...	...	...	...
Koliganek	...	...	...	...	...	...	...	...	...	...	...	...	...	...	...
Kongiganak	...	...	...	...	...	...	...	...	...	...	...	...	...	...	...
Kotlik	37.8	22.5	40.7	392	19.0	54	7.4	18 750	19 750	—	3 340	59	19.0	12	...
Kotzebue	57.7	48.7	43.8	204	18.1	278	7.6	18 708	18 981	9 375	5 315	251	16.0	60	30
Koyuk	...	...	...	...	...	36	—	12 500	17 500	17 917	...	...	...	5	—
Koyukuk	...	...	...	...	...	...	...	...	...	...	...	...	...	...	...
Kwethluk	26.5	19.7	36.4	574	5.8	...	...	...	...	...	2 360	148	32.1	...	...
Kwigillingok	64.2	15.2	31.3	415	24.6	59	33.9	15 938	17 596	2500—	2 428	90	28.2	25	7
Larsen Bay	...	...	...	...	...	26	—	17 143	17 143	6 250	...	...	...	2	—
Levelock	...	...	...	...	...	...	...	...	...	...	...	...	...	...	...
Lime Village	...	...	...	...	...	...	...	...	...	...	...	...	...	...	...
Lower Kalskag	...	...	...	...	...	...	...	...	...	...	...	...	...	...	...
McGrath	46.2	43.6	78.9	281	16.7	33	6.1	11 250	16 250	3 750	4 728	22	12.3	6	4
Manley Hot Springs	...	...	...	...	...	—	—	—	—	—	...	...	...	...	...
Manokotak	...	...	...	...	...	53	9.4	31 320	31 320	40 255	...	...	...	14	2
Marshall	...	...	...	...	...	...	...	...	...	...	...	...	...	...	...
Mary's Igloo	—	...	—	...	...	...	...	...	...	...	...	...	...	...	...
Mekoryuk	43.8	71.9	62.5	195	23.6	...	...	...	...	...	3 324	74	45.7	...	...
Mentasta Lake	57.1	—	—	675	—	...	...	...	...	...	3 158	...	...	...	...
Minto	...	...	...	...	...	...	...	...	...	...	...	...	...	...	...
Mountain Village	...	...	...	...	...	...	...	...	...	...	...	...	...	...	...
Naknek	61.4	51.9	28.6	149	20.6	...	...	...	...	...	20 625	10	6.5	...	...
Napaimute	...	...	...	...	...	...	...	...	...	...	...	...	...	...	...
Napakiak	...	...	...	...	...	...	...	...	...	...	...	...	...	...	...
Napaskiak	...	...	...	...	...	...	...	...	...	...	...	...	...	...	...
Nelson Lagoon	...	...	...	...	...	12	33.3	4 750	10 625	2500—	1 865	22	30.6	4	4
Nenana	45.6	55.8	100.0	222	24.3	40	12.5	13 750	15 833	2500—	4 035	99	41.6	10	5
Newhalen	...	...	...	...	...	...	...	...	...	...	...	...	...	...	...
New Stuyahok	...	...	...	...	...	59	11.9	15 909	16 250	25 481	...	...	...	17	8
Newtok	...	...	...	...	...	...	...	...	...	...	...	...	...	...	...
Nightmute	...	...	...	...	...	...	...	...	...	...	...	...	...	...	...
Nikolai	...	...	...	...	...	...	...	...	...	...	...	...	...	...	...
Nikolski	...	...	...	...	...	...	...	...	...	...	...	...	...	...	...
Ninilchik	57.1	22.7	—	271	29.4	12	—	9 063	23 500	—	5 180	7	11.1	—	—
Noatak	...	...	...	...	...	...	...	...	...	...	...	...	...	...	...
Nondalton	...	...	...	...	...	...	...	...	...	...	...	...	...	...	...
Noorvik	...	...	...	...	...	75	—	11 354	11 771	7 500	...	...	...	25	5
Northway	...	...	...	...	...	29	31.0	4 271	4 271	3 750	...	...	...	15	4
Nuiqsut	...	...	...	...	...	36	—	14 688	17 500	8 750	...	...	...	3	—
Nulato	...	...	...	...	...	...	...	...	...	...	...	...	...	...	...
Nunapitchuk	...	...	...	...	...	54	—	7 312	7 692	6 875	...	...	...	28	2
Ohogamiut	—	—	—	—	—	—	—	—	—	—	—	—	—	—	—
Old Harbor	25.2	19.7	15.4	620	22.2	75	18.7	6 667	7 153	2500—	2 868	161	50.3	34	7
Oscarville	100.0	100.0	100.0	219	—	...	...	...	...	...	3 284	...	...	...	...
Ouzinkie	...	...	...	...	...	...	...	...	...	...	...	...	...	...	...
Paimiut	—	—	—	—	—	—	—	—	—	—	—	—	—	—	—
Pauloff Harbor	—	—	—	...	...	—	—	...	...	...	...	—	—	—	—
Pedro Bay	...	...	...	...	...	...	...	...	...	...	...	...	...	...	...
Perryville	...	...	...	...	...	21	19.0	7 321	7 321	...	...	...	...	11	—
Pilot Point	...	...	...	...	...	...	...	...	...	...	...	...	...	...	...
Pilot Station	...	...	...	...	...	...	...	...	...	...	...	...	...	...	...
Pitkas Point	...	...	...	...	...	...	...	...	...	...	...	...	...	...	...

Table 252. Economic Characteristics for American Indian Persons on Reservations and Alaska Native Villages: 1980—Con.

[Data include Eskimos and Aleuts on Annette Island Reserve and Alaska Native Villages. Data are estimates based on a sample; see Introduction. For meaning of symbols, see Introduction. For definitions of terms, see appendixes A and B]

Reservations / Alaska Native Villages	Percent in labor force			Non-workers per 100 workers	Civilian labor force—Percent unemployed	Families		Median income in 1979 (dollars)			Per capita income in 1979 (dollars)	Income in 1979 below poverty level			
		Female, 16 years and over							Families			Persons for whom poverty status is determined		Families	
	Male, 16 years and over	Total	With own children under 6 years			Total	Percent with no workers in 1979	Households	Total	Female householder, no husband present		Total	Percent	Total	Female householder, no husband present
ALASKA NATIVE VILLAGES—Con.															
Platinum	...	...	...	...	...	...	...	...	...	...	...	...	...	...	...
Point Hope	74.4	48.3	57.9	172	17.2	67	3.0	24 286	25 694	12 188	4 986	51	12.0	8	...
Point Lay	...	...	...	...	...	...	...	...	...	...	...	...	...	...	...
Portage Creek	...	...	...	...	...	...	...	...	...	...	...	...	...	...	...
Port Graham	...	...	...	...	...	...	...	...	...	...	...	...	...	...	...
Port Heiden	67.7	31.4	27.3	171	13.8	42	14.3	16 250	18 750	51 113	6 790	27	17.2	7	2
Port Lions	52.9	100.0	-	185	-	...	...	...	...	...	...	...	...	...	...
Quinhagak	...	...	...	...	...	...	...	...	...	...	...	...	...	...	...
Rampart	...	...	...	...	...	...	...	...	...	...	2 870	25	67.6	...	...
Red Devil	...	...	...	...	...	...	...	...	...	...	...	...	...	...	...
Ruby	49.3	50.0	46.2	227	35.0	31	6.5	7 813	14 306	6 750	3 035	45	23.0	4	4
Russian Mission (Kuskokwim)	11.1	22.9	...	853	23.5	31	25.8	2500-	3 750	-	1 516	124	76.5	20	-
Russian Mission (Yukon)	...	...	...	...	...	...	...	...	...	...	...	...	...	...	...
St. George	54.8	33.3	100.0	170	40.0	...	...	...	...	...	4 133	61	35.9	...	...
St. Mary's	...	...	...	...	...	...	...	...	...	...	...	...	...	...	...
St. Michael	33.8	21.6	28.3	447	5.8	...	...	...	...	...	5 173	69	12.5	...	...
St. Paul		42.9	100.0	444	100.0	...	...	...	...	...	4 625	2	4.1	...	...
Solamatof	52.2	22.3	21.1	277	12.9	77	3.9	52 222	60 323	6 875	23 348	28	8.0	7	4
Sand Point	27.6	29.8	28.2	444	8.0	84	21.4	7 321	8 750	6 071	2 231	198	41.9	42	7
Savoonga	...	...	...	...	...	...	...	...	...	...	...	...	...	...	...
Saxman	78.4	54.4	36.4	140	18.9	34	-	22 083	31 733	35 207	5 360	6	2.7	...	...
Scammon Bay	...	...	...	...	...	...	...	...	...	...	...	...	...	...	...
Selawik	...	...	...	...	...	...	...	...	...	...	...	...	...	...	...
Seldovia	...	...	...	...	...	...	...	...	...	...	...	...	...	...	...
Shageluk	...	...	...	...	...	...	...	...	...	...	...	...	...	...	...
Shaktoolik	...	...	...	...	...	...	...	...	...	...	...	...	...	...	...
Sheldon's Point	64.7	28.0	100.0	411	-	18	...	8 500	8 500	3 750	1 637	80	87.0	15	3
Shishmaref	36.1	28.1	47.6	482	3.5	57	22.8	9 167	9 861	7 500	2 573	106	31.9	23	5
Shungnak	...	...	...	...	-	34	-	16 250	15 000	6 875	...	...	...	8	3
Slana	...	...	...	...	...	...	...	...	...	...	...	...	...	...	...
Sleetmute	...	...	...	...	...	16	18.8	3 750	5 000	-	...	...	...	10	-
Solomon	...	...	...	...	...	...	...	...	...	...	...	...	...	...	...
South Naknek	45.8	41.7	46.2	319	34.6	22	-	26 875	30 586	18 750	9 079	6	5.5	-	-
Stebbins	65.2	51.1	73.1	298	29.2	44	11.4	12 500	13 214	14 375	2 138	115	32.5	13	2
Stevens Village	23.1	20.8	-	524	52.9	12	50.0	4 464	5 000	13 125	1 393	75	70.8	9	-
Stony River	...	...	...	...	...	...	...	...	...	...	...	...	...	...	...
Takotna	...	...	...	...	...	...	...	...	...	...	...	...	...	...	...
Tanacross	...	...	...	...	...	...	...	...	...	...	...	...	...	...	...
Tanana	18.8	49.4	58.8	363	3.2	61	8.2	10 625	15 125	10 000	3 842	68	23.5	12	3
Tatitlek	...	...	...	...	...	...	...	...	...	...	...	...	...	...	...
Tazlina	...	...	...	...	...	...	...	...	...	...	...	...	...	...	...
Telida	25.0	66.7	66.7	417	...	...	...	...	...	...	1 598	23	74.2	...	...
Teller	60.8	38.9	36.4	171	80.0	...	...	...	...	...	2 476	108	50.2	...	...
Tetlin	...	...	...	...	...	...	...	...	...	...	...	...	...	...	...
Togiak	65.3	52.4	27.8	168	81.7	93	15.1	12 292	12 250	6 500	3 494	119	26.3	24	8
Toksook Bay	...	...	...	...	...	...	...	...	...	...	...	...	...	...	...
Tuluksak	...	...	...	...	...	...	...	...	...	...	...	...	...	...	...
Tuntutuliak	70.4	50.0	52.9	226	12.1	...	...	...	...	...	3 260	57	26.5	...	...
Tununak	50.6	20.6	20.0	349	19.3	45	8.9	11 250	12 679	-	2 734	88	34.4	15	-
Twin Hills	...	...	...	...	...	...	...	...	...	...	...	...	...	...	...
Tyonek	...	...	...	...	...	46	8.7	10 750	16 000	11 500	...	...	...	9	-
Ugashik	...	...	...	...	...	...	...	...	...	...	...	...	...	...	...
Ukivok	...	...	...	...	...	...	...	...	...	...	...	...	...	...	...
Unalakleet	37.2	38.6	59.5	309	7.4	108	13.0	6 875	13 438	6 000	4 012	184	33.1	39	13
Unalaska	82.8	52.0	22.2	87	19.4	41	-	18 523	18 977	17 188	9 175	21	10.7	-	-
Unga	...	...	...	...	...	...	...	...	...	...	...	...	...	...	...
Uyak	...	...	...	...	...	...	...	...	...	...	...	...	...	...	...
Venetie	14.6	15.8	33.3	925	-	25	12.0	7 188	8 125	2500-	2 306	68	55.3	13	3
Wainwright	...	...	...	...	-	78	2.6	33 170	35 000	6 563	...	...	...	4	4
Wales	...	...	...	...	...	...	...	...	...	...	...	...	...	...	...
White Mountain	...	...	...	...	...	...	...	...	...	...	...	...	...	...	...
Woody Island	...	...	...	...	...	...	...	...	...	...	...	...	...	...	...
Yakutat	63.1	60.2	59.3	161	29.4	48	-	14 750	23 000	11 250	5 636	51	17.9	7	3

1980
Census of
Housing

VOLUME 3
SUBJECT REPORTS
CHAPTER 4

Structural Characteristics of the Housing Inventory

HC80-3-4

Issued August 1984

U.S. Department of Commerce
Malcolm Baldrige, Secretary
Clarence J. Brown, Deputy Secretary
Sidney Jones, Under Secretary
for Economic Affairs

BUREAU OF THE CENSUS
John G. Keane, Director

BL

Table 1. **Units in Structure:** 1980

[Data are estimates based on a sample; see Introduction. For meaning of symbols, see Introduction. For definitions of terms, see appendix A]

United States Regions and Divisions States	Year-round housing units				Owner-occupied housing units				Renter-occupied housing units			
	1 unit	2 to 4 units	5 or more units	Mobile home or trailer, etc.	1 unit	2 to 4 units	5 or more units	Mobile home or trailer, etc.	1 unit	2 to 4 units	5 or more units	Mobile home or trailer, etc.
United States	57 182 605	9 681 832	15 478 306	4 415 974	45 121 152	2 167 396	1 403 998	3 103 849	8 725 325	6 667 843	12 414 805	785 305
Regions and Divisions												
Northeast Region	10 222 189	3 584 651	4 322 671	402 417	8 764 611	986 815	251 084	301 363	1 012 892	2 336 922	3 747 917	69 012
New England	2 646 378	1 070 328	810 101	95 871	2 298 978	266 198	49 348	75 397	240 451	728 853	688 511	14 251
Middle Atlantic	7 575 811	2 514 323	3 512 570	306 546	6 465 633	720 617	201 736	225 966	772 441	1 608 069	3 059 406	54 761
North Central Region	15 666 522	2 562 323	3 242 135	889 551	12 900 653	551 703	260 777	644 848	1 934 345	1 772 296	2 644 587	149 997
East North Central	10 729 219	1 956 199	2 404 969	564 224	8 940 603	433 497	204 278	410 669	1 268 959	1 348 245	1 953 242	94 233
West North Central	4 937 303	606 124	837 166	325 327	3 960 050	118 206	56 499	234 179	665 386	424 051	691 345	55 764
South Region	20 486 752	2 066 704	4 386 303	2 082 789	15 406 955	373 978	566 620	1 395 863	3 664 130	1 473 408	3 206 028	399 235
South Atlantic	9 738 658	1 084 804	2 477 985	1 132 095	7 401 293	201 768	406 251	749 372	1 691 380	766 344	1 726 969	216 274
East South Central	4 110 168	385 708	540 625	411 334	3 119 540	71 592	47 466	285 303	730 330	278 636	435 030	82 988
West South Central	6 637 926	596 192	1 367 693	539 360	4 886 122	100 618	112 903	361 188	1 242 420	428 428	1 044 029	99 973
West Region	10 807 142	1 468 154	3 527 197	1 041 217	8 048 933	254 900	325 517	761 775	2 113 958	1 085 217	2 816 273	167 061
Mountain	2 908 425	355 228	704 130	443 258	2 222 297	72 058	71 590	313 947	477 508	238 197	514 190	76 363
Pacific	7 898 717	1 112 926	2 823 067	597 959	5 826 636	182 842	253 927	447 828	1 636 450	847 020	2 302 083	90 698
States												
New England Division												
Maine	282 560	67 843	42 737	35 105	233 402	17 122	1 951	27 905	29 829	44 165	35 852	4 958
New Hampshire	218 942	59 332	50 046	20 852	184 614	14 811	2 675	16 740	19 860	40 075	42 169	2 549
Vermont	128 483	35 854	18 456	13 666	102 083	8 875	1 320	10 282	14 656	23 832	14 917	2 360
Massachusetts	1 117 896	570 557	438 427	14 484	989 151	145 849	23 486	11 321	94 416	388 264	377 877	2 353
Rhode Island	197 719	103 055	59 572	2 572	171 508	23 550	2 041	1 976	19 090	69 353	50 640	432
Connecticut	700 778	233 687	200 863	9 192	618 220	55 991	17 875	7 173	62 600	163 164	167 056	1 599
Middle Atlantic Division												
New York	2 787 700	1 398 613	2 398 966	120 920	2 425 215	433 570	137 520	86 865	250 715	868 839	2 114 477	23 228
New Jersey	1 565 328	540 456	562 221	22 372	1 369 973	163 388	29 414	17 345	133 779	345 086	486 220	3 389
Pennsylvania	3 222 783	575 254	551 383	163 254	2 670 445	123 659	34 802	121 756	387 947	394 144	458 709	28 144
East North Central Division												
Ohio	2 868 288	495 556	575 099	139 121	2 396 891	89 004	32 019	105 108	353 437	355 791	478 991	22 587
Indiana	1 550 048	185 587	223 779	105 701	1 260 045	33 472	11 885	76 522	210 140	130 555	185 424	19 007
Illinois	2 545 264	687 300	957 845	114 016	2 143 933	191 358	118 788	80 683	298 435	442 653	746 860	22 664
Michigan	2 551 120	317 952	431 774	149 850	2 115 016	68 130	29 655	109 171	279 397	218 553	354 192	21 099
Wisconsin	1 214 499	269 804	216 472	55 536	1 024 718	51 533	11 931	39 185	127 550	200 693	187 775	8 876
West North Central Division												
Minnesota	1 073 678	133 009	264 815	58 791	934 640	35 385	19 187	46 526	88 930	87 337	226 115	7 102
Iowa	867 752	94 440	114 811	44 311	699 631	16 240	6 505	34 145	125 161	68 996	95 711	6 644
Missouri	1 430 384	209 585	222 806	99 801	1 128 982	36 936	15 597	67 286	199 597	147 937	178 009	19 055
North Dakota	166 188	28 486	36 235	21 840	129 491	6 471	3 299	17 254	21 394	19 010	28 507	2 238
South Dakota	194 619	23 079	30 174	21 772	146 200	4 448	2 075	15 279	30 667	15 775	23 963	4 116
Nebraska	470 298	44 027	76 262	28 246	360 027	7 402	3 901	19 594	79 030	31 483	64 295	5 668
Kansas	734 384	73 498	92 063	50 566	561 079	11 324	5 935	34 095	120 607	53 513	74 745	10 941
South Atlantic Division												
Delaware	160 684	13 784	38 442	17 391	127 290	2 229	2 583	10 975	22 024	9 301	29 837	2 842
Maryland	1 055 358	118 940	346 929	28 453	834 501	24 384	26 105	20 677	176 974	83 520	288 938	5 766
District of Columbia	97 553	32 959	145 955	390	70 081	4 735	14 919	93	21 317	25 503	116 217	278
Virginia	1 437 748	142 506	324 361	95 460	1 099 153	22 718	31 467	68 252	253 153	105 428	265 162	17 740
West Virginia	558 780	56 177	45 590	76 486	430 992	11 067	5 102	57 760	93 459	38 828	35 611	13 492
North Carolina	1 669 938	143 907	188 524	221 827	1 209 931	24 322	21 052	142 121	340 005	106 096	147 284	52 480
South Carolina	839 643	73 560	93 950	115 774	617 806	13 911	12 850	77 992	161 510	52 652	68 167	25 093
Georgia	1 414 032	163 145	281 686	154 976	1 067 133	24 340	20 384	104 575	264 837	124 256	231 856	34 271
Florida	2 504 922	339 826	1 012 548	421 338	1 944 406	74 062	271 789	266 927	358 101	220 760	543 897	64 312
East South Central Division												
Kentucky	1 000 031	110 365	136 565	108 473	775 951	20 659	10 792	77 467	168 321	78 255	109 959	21 951
Tennessee	1 294 302	134 917	199 675	108 229	999 806	25 048	15 111	70 118	219 201	98 109	164 569	26 543
Alabama	1 108 587	89 380	132 345	120 443	827 578	15 022	12 431	86 206	206 848	66 882	105 828	21 061
Mississippi	707 248	51 046	72 040	74 189	516 205	10 863	9 132	51 512	135 960	35 390	54 674	13 433
West South Central Division												
Arkansas	700 727	50 523	64 045	73 898	510 866	9 187	7 261	48 155	138 042	36 244	48 993	17 317
Louisiana	1 106 281	152 809	170 177	107 916	807 403	25 096	16 062	76 607	220 690	113 522	134 433	17 975
Oklahoma	965 985	68 636	123 994	70 907	720 695	10 225	9 658	50 028	171 026	48 809	96 165	11 955
Texas	3 864 933	324 224	1 009 477	286 639	2 847 158	56 110	79 922	186 398	712 662	229 853	764 438	52 726
Mountain Division												
Montana	208 673	34 504	31 134	40 787	155 208	7 126	2 995	29 251	37 269	21 425	23 285	7 183
Idaho	259 465	27 913	31 703	40 950	195 853	4 754	2 845	29 936	42 954	18 810	22 215	6 740
Wyoming	112 026	18 905	18 170	33 246	84 744	3 728	1 983	24 197	19 467	12 524	13 146	5 835
Colorado	767 298	84 484	249 962	67 830	591 623	17 108	25 834	49 852	125 450	57 931	181 633	11 818
New Mexico	333 800	38 406	60 193	61 090	241 273	9 107	6 816	43 372	63 112	23 889	43 187	10 710
Arizona	700 488	63 440	174 797	133 062	530 700	15 711	19 127	88 287	116 183	39 697	124 770	22 557
Utah	342 328	55 640	59 894	23 204	283 333	9 950	6 443	17 481	41 313	40 899	45 651	3 533
Nevada	184 347	31 936	78 277	43 089	139 563	4 574	5 547	31 571	31 760	23 022	60 303	7 987
Pacific Division												
Washington	1 145 939	116 419	284 061	105 261	886 054	18 995	26 528	79 745	201 079	86 396	225 151	16 562
Oregon	742 795	76 692	162 300	89 826	555 925	11 609	10 416	68 002	141 836	57 323	133 393	13 089
California	5 758 167	863 199	2 215 995	385 759	4 209 759	139 118	187 542	288 965	1 232 733	665 634	1 848 288	57 827
Alaska	80 080	23 230	34 046	16 695	58 165	4 722	2 877	10 895	13 443	14 787	23 506	3 068
Hawaii	171 736	33 386	126 665	418	116 733	8 398	26 564	221	47 359	22 880	71 745	152

STRUCTURAL CHARACTERISTICS OF THE HOUSING INVENTORY

1

Table G— 1. Gross Rent of Renter-Occupied Housing Units: 1980

Housing Units in One-Unit Detached Structures—Total

[Data are estimates based on a sample; see Introduction. For meaning of symbols, see Introduction. For definitions of terms, see appendix A]

United States

Specified renter-occupied housing units	Total	Less than $100	$100 to $149	$150 to $199	$200 to $249	$250 to $299	$300 to $349	$350 to $399	$400 to $499	$500 or more	No cash rent	Median (dollars)
Specified renter-occupied housing units	6 097 545	256 351	603 300	874 853	934 996	744 916	559 401	412 317	512 928	450 966	747 517	250
YEAR STRUCTURE BUILT												
1979 to March 1980	73 499	1 822	3 366	4 630	5 809	5 346	5 338	5 888	12 615	20 818	7 867	405
1975 to 1978	271 193	5 929	11 391	17 491	22 704	21 775	22 004	24 176	50 798	66 728	28 197	392
1970 to 1974	393 833	11 294	24 387	38 921	46 840	41 701	37 708	33 951	55 711	60 784	42 536	317
1960 to 1969	1 001 001	29 036	70 847	115 121	139 491	118 795	100 999	84 057	116 124	109 651	116 880	287
1950 to 1959	1 387 351	47 432	125 173	199 521	224 465	184 814	141 429	102 740	121 503	91 633	148 641	256
1940 to 1949	1 132 922	56 206	137 688	192 614	197 897	149 876	103 940	67 610	67 011	41 953	118 127	231
1939 or earlier	1 837 746	104 632	230 448	306 555	297 790	222 609	147 983	93 895	89 166	59 399	285 269	223
YEAR HOUSEHOLDER MOVED INTO UNIT												
1979 to March 1980	2 584 247	62 874	174 700	314 944	397 707	348 004	289 334	231 308	314 952	307 716	142 708	289
1975 to 1978	1 945 281	75 741	197 496	306 427	334 404	262 348	186 633	130 815	150 675	113 562	187 180	245
1970 to 1974	686 317	47 501	104 062	126 282	107 916	75 047	46 739	28 614	27 217	16 647	106 292	206
1960 to 1969	492 946	40 440	79 792	84 415	64 799	40 125	24 109	14 469	13 264	8 745	122 788	188
1959 or earlier	388 754	29 795	47 250	42 785	30 170	19 392	12 586	7 111	6 820	4 296	188 549	177
ROOMS												
1 room	53 066	8 453	10 586	10 473	7 419	3 545	1 916	889	678	529	8 578	165
2 rooms	159 315	24 181	31 755	32 822	22 521	13 552	7 574	4 716	3 625	1 771	16 798	173
3 rooms	544 374	62 305	114 517	123 069	88 196	46 744	23 837	14 125	13 634	7 930	50 017	179
4 rooms	1 458 160	86 381	211 058	291 180	279 685	118 864	113 896	64 557	53 866	24 024	144 649	212
5 rooms	1 721 042	46 815	143 945	238 815	287 146	243 447	186 763	136 449	158 669	92 775	186 218	260
6 rooms	1 223 405	20 278	64 408	120 690	164 376	155 952	137 639	113 387	156 092	132 224	158 359	302
7 or more rooms	938 183	7 938	27 031	57 804	85 653	92 812	87 776	78 194	126 364	191 713	182 898	362
Median	5.0	3.9	4.2	4.4	4.7	5.0	5.2	5.4	5.7	6.2	5.3	...
BEDROOMS												
None	73 056	11 042	15 221	14 939	10 266	5 097	2 847	1 538	1 209	780	10 117	167
1	811 363	84 771	160 797	185 809	139 002	75 834	38 272	21 790	18 556	9 474	77 058	183
2	2 444 944	112 470	293 955	435 048	460 426	342 555	222 971	135 524	120 614	59 736	261 645	227
3	2 146 017	39 670	111 597	200 228	271 392	264 300	241 081	204 127	291 667	239 913	282 042	309
4	514 853	6 921	18 061	32 505	45 654	48 364	45 828	41 995	69 303	115 039	91 183	367
5 or more	107 312	1 477	3 669	6 324	8 256	8 766	8 402	7 343	11 579	26 024	25 472	377
PERSONS IN UNIT												
1 person	1 274 196	119 268	217 475	236 531	183 480	110 512	63 826	39 476	36 838	26 011	240 779	188
2 persons	1 594 007	55 952	155 854	241 528	262 453	206 016	149 098	102 636	119 342	88 882	212 246	245
3 persons	1 179 739	29 785	88 400	157 559	193 571	163 872	125 982	93 734	116 192	111 005	...	270
4 persons	996 229	21 464	63 345	117 221	150 630	132 964	109 820	84 884	114 414	110 768	90 719	288
5 persons	553 400	12 668	36 943	62 393	77 044	70 994	59 587	49 126	67 884	67 291	49 470	294
6 or more persons	499 974	17 214	41 283	59 621	67 818	60 558	51 088	42 461	58 258	58 375	43 298	285
Median	2.65	1.66	2.04	2.33	2.61	2.84	3.03	3.18	3.36	3.60	2.13	...
Total persons	17 881 552	580 646	1 479 869	2 306 574	2 650 924	2 251 546	1 793 196	1 389 585	1 805 500	1 679 945	1 943 767	...
PLUMBING FACILITIES BY PERSONS PER ROOM												
Complete plumbing for exclusive use	5 860 845	179 560	550 308	853 651	926 244	740 567	557 223	411 142	511 954	450 411	679 785	255
1.01 or more persons per room	438 022	14 813	50 716	79 359	77 931	58 400	41 558	30 123	35 531	23 735	25 856	239
Lacking complete plumbing for exclusive use	236 700	76 791	52 992	21 202	8 752	4 349	2 178	1 175	974	555	67 732	107
1.01 or more persons per room	51 316	14 095	13 101	5 686	2 577	1 281	582	323	288	161	13 222	119
HOUSEHOLD INCOME IN 1979												
Less than $5,000	1 145 991	135 614	213 098	199 540	150 991	95 112	58 346	35 298	33 341	21 416	203 235	181
$5,000 to $9,999	1 274 552	64 524	174 482	242 249	221 425	150 396	95 876	61 578	60 035	33 117	170 870	216
$10,000 to $12,499	654 086	17 733	64 536	111 809	123 818	90 467	62 013	41 325	42 607	25 283	74 495	239
$12,500 to $14,999	524 690	10 368	42 638	81 275	98 022	78 240	55 583	37 649	40 813	23 800	56 302	251
$15,000 to $19,999	939 386	13 823	56 623	120 650	161 821	143 433	111 284	82 401	96 406	62 520	90 425	275
$20,000 to $24,999	649 967	7 045	27 861	63 814	94 787	93 725	81 995	65 624	86 999	69 560	58 557	305
$25,000 to $34,999	590 516	4 836	17 318	41 182	62 877	69 270	68 242	62 314	100 742	108 333	55 402	353
$35,000 to $49,999	225 866	1 586	4 736	10 426	16 038	18 619	20 061	20 222	39 940	70 118	24 100	423
$50,000 or more	92 491	822	2 008	3 908	5 197	5 654	6 001	5 906	12 045	36 819	14 131	480
Median	$12 401	$4 700	$7 258	$9 908	$11 920	$13 666	$15 324	$16 708	$19 084	$24 197	$9 989	...
Mean	$14 843	$7 090	$9 230	$11 503	$13 346	$14 943	$16 535	$18 059	$20 522	$27 204	$13 320	...
SELECTED CHARACTERISTICS												
Heating equipment	6 097 545	256 351	603 300	874 853	934 996	744 916	559 401	412 317	512 928	450 966	747 517	250
Central heating system	4 020 531	63 086	209 253	446 154	611 180	553 389	449 962	348 156	453 778	415 541	470 032	290
Air conditioning	2 489 769	51 703	187 056	327 110	376 026	308 173	244 255	183 949	241 898	221 050	348 549	271
Central system	802 915	7 591	19 720	43 097	71 868	76 357	82 522	81 012	139 863	154 676	126 209	373
Vehicles available	5 220 137	142 637	427 833	714 838	819 517	673 545	516 039	387 532	490 068	440 141	607 987	265
1	2 489 958	94 061	263 876	405 419	430 593	324 150	227 202	156 925	168 641	119 684	299 407	237
2 or more	2 730 179	48 576	163 957	309 419	388 924	349 395	288 837	230 607	321 427	320 457	308 580	293
House heating fuel	6 016 492	249 082	593 645	863 396	924 838	736 988	553 243	407 049	506 315	443 283	738 653	251
Utility gas	3 672 468	124 176	359 788	547 963	592 400	472 776	351 799	257 549	318 939	293 194	353 884	254
Bottled, tank, or LP gas	395 997	22 828	57 932	71 461	63 627	41 000	24 755	13 683	12 940	7 307	80 464	204
Electricity	774 618	19 895	49 237	88 021	109 580	96 824	82 115	67 877	96 331	81 314	83 424	291
Fuel oil, kerosene, etc.	843 419	19 245	62 779	106 678	126 282	106 886	82 339	60 523	71 087	57 909	149 691	265
Other	329 990	62 938	63 909	49 273	32 949	19 502	12 235	7 417	7 018	3 559	71 190	153
Family householder	4 392 610	129 536	364 850	598 170	696 013	579 396	446 017	329 760	411 204	353 772	483 892	264
With own children under 18 years	2 833 725	70 325	205 002	364 060	454 915	393 776	313 164	238 202	300 400	261 738	232 143	276
With own children under 6 years	1 514 720	38 629	115 621	209 878	264 863	221 790	172 586	124 539	145 999	109 985	110 830	266
Female householder, no husband present	962 322	41 706	103 157	149 453	160 607	133 219	96 840	67 380	76 216	55 416	78 332	246
With own children under 18 years	702 894	26 682	66 656	105 137	121 716	105 053	79 255	55 524	62 070	44 630	36 171	256
With own children under 6 years	275 861	12 483	29 763	44 434	51 462	42 677	31 079	19 842	20 551	11 810	11 760	244
Nonfamily householder	1 704 935	126 815	238 450	276 683	238 983	165 520	113 384	82 557	101 724	97 194	263 625	216
Income in 1979 below poverty level	1 349 295	133 060	215 184	222 298	190 971	136 194	92 620	60 928	64 455	45 300	188 285	203
Percent below poverty level	22.1	51.9	35.7	25.4	20.4	18.3	16.6	14.8	12.6	10.0	25.2	...
GROSS RENT AS PERCENTAGE OF HOUSEHOLD INCOME IN 1979												
Less than 15 percent	1 087 557	96 570	199 199	252 426	215 322	128 917	73 356	42 290	42 438	37 039	...	199
15 to 19 percent	869 556	30 451	82 179	139 935	169 518	139 521	101 836	67 930	77 106	61 080	...	255
20 to 24 percent	739 199	25 178	58 752	104 457	125 422	111 329	88 895	68 490	84 707	71 969	...	275
25 to 29 percent	558 163	22 778	43 804	72 893	91 010	76 686	64 239	51 870	71 029	63 854	...	282
30 to 34 percent	400 685	17 827	34 256	50 786	62 120	56 225	45 131	35 862	50 826	47 852	...	282
35 to 49 percent	683 206	33 045	73 190	92 874	101 894	90 507	74 962	61 663	80 593	74 478	...	272
50 percent or more	932 693	23 372	99 337	147 253	156 539	132 015	104 382	79 699	100 521	89 575	...	265
Not computed	826 486	7 130	12 583	14 229	13 171	9 916	6 600	4 513	5 708	5 119	747 517	221
Median	24.6	19.6	21.2	21.8	23.0	24.4	26.0	27.4	28.5	29.1	...	...

Table G—1. Gross Rent of Renter-Occupied Housing Units: 1980—Con.

Housing Units in One-Unit Detached Structures—Total—Con.

[Data are estimates based on a sample; see Introduction. For meaning of symbols, see Introduction. For definitions of terms, see appendix A]

United States	Total	Less than $100	$100 to $149	$150 to $199	$200 to $249	$250 to $299	$300 to $349	$350 to $399	$400 to $499	$500 or more	No cash rent	Median (dollars)
AGE OF HOUSEHOLDER												
Persons 15 years and over	6 097 545	256 351	603 300	874 853	934 996	744 916	559 401	412 317	512 928	450 966	747 517	250
15 to 19 years	86 688	3 832	10 810	17 354	17 335	11 461	6 645	4 276	4 486	3 513	6 976	223
20 to 24 years	842 024	22 027	73 732	140 708	164 173	126 907	88 772	59 460	66 754	47 136	52 355	248
25 to 29 years	1 124 602	23 981	82 303	159 918	201 735	170 128	131 045	94 471	109 496	77 948	73 577	267
30 to 34 years	877 371	18 941	59 080	108 709	138 316	120 864	100 649	78 837	101 764	88 074	62 137	284
35 to 39 years	605 509	14 498	41 125	68 628	85 700	76 473	64 587	53 174	74 728	76 565	50 031	294
40 to 44 years	444 334	12 753	32 887	53 330	60 702	55 364	43 845	36 263	50 200	53 998	44 992	286
45 to 49 years	360 321	13 229	32 443	46 943	50 778	41 081	31 668	25 150	33 777	37 745	47 507	266
50 to 54 years	339 757	16 236	37 280	49 376	48 229	37 153	26 945	19 325	25 375	26 684	53 154	242
55 to 59 years	314 246	19 346	39 993	50 732	44 373	31 302	20 821	14 705	18 508	17 750	56 716	221
60 to 64 years	279 579	21 798	42 469	46 622	37 160	24 477	16 014	10 123	11 448	9 722	59 746	199
65 to 69 years	261 469	25 325	46 462	45 919	32 281	19 286	11 359	6 745	7 119	5 250	61 723	181
70 to 74 years	221 449	24 267	41 861	36 638	24 181	13 682	7 554	4 438	4 427	3 191	61 210	169
75 years and over	340 196	40 118	62 855	49 976	30 033	16 738	9 497	5 350	4 846	3 390	117 393	158
Median	36.0	55.7	45.3	35.8	33.0	32.6	32.6	33.0	33.7	35.6	53.4	...
MARITAL STATUS OF HOUSEHOLDER												
Persons 15 years and over	6 097 545	256 351	603 300	874 853	934 996	744 916	559 401	412 317	512 928	450 966	747 517	250
Single	958 137	44 986	100 332	147 519	149 958	115 406	84 469	62 532	79 537	76 149	97 249	246
Now married, except separated	3 285 966	82 730	250 102	431 579	516 304	428 397	334 697	250 906	319 016	281 339	390 896	269
Separated	348 102	24 806	46 195	55 771	54 125	42 140	32 016	22 325	25 442	20 182	25 100	232
Widowed	642 744	70 242	118 709	106 602	71 930	43 895	25 179	15 219	15 480	11 207	164 281	174
Divorced	862 596	33 587	87 962	133 382	142 679	115 078	83 040	61 335	73 453	62 089	69 991	250
YEARS OF SCHOOL COMPLETED BY HOUSEHOLDER												
Persons 25 years old and over	5 168 833	230 492	518 758	716 791	753 488	606 548	463 984	348 581	441 688	400 317	688 186	252
Median	12.3	8.2	9.8	11.7	12.2	12.4	12.5	12.6	12.8	13.7	12.1	...
PERIOD OF SERVICE OF HOUSEHOLDER												
Civilian veterans 16 years and over	1 374 443	35 594	99 494	170 213	200 848	173 994	139 610	110 961	149 262	139 059	155 408	280
Percent of civilians 16 years and over	22.9	13.9	16.5	19.6	22.0	23.8	25.5	27.5	29.7	31.3	21.2	...
May 1975 or later only	68 151	1 710	5 177	11 215	13 600	10 214	7 902	5 232	5 819	3 683	3 599	253
Vietnam era	551 505	7 576	30 609	65 449	87 805	80 992	67 011	54 298	69 932	56 212	31 621	292
February 1955 to July 1964 only	150 639	1 931	7 604	14 539	19 674	18 374	15 497	14 282	21 886	23 460	13 392	321
Vietnam era and Korean conflict	27 619	329	1 197	2 301	3 251	3 246	3 189	2 873	4 771	4 550	1 912	340
Korean conflict	161 588	3 760	10 093	17 788	21 443	18 974	16 311	12 499	18 509	22 275	19 936	297
Korean conflict and World War II	27 502	752	2 123	3 478	3 725	2 976	2 470	1 942	3 111	3 428	3 497	282
World War II	349 432	16 895	37 202	49 902	46 763	36 106	25 157	18 555	23 745	24 189	70 918	238
World War I	17 807	1 240	2 728	2 490	1 866	1 066	792	415	405	401	6 404	185
Other	20 200	1 401	2 761	3 051	2 721	2 046	1 281	865	1 084	861	4 129	215
Civilian nonveterans 16 years and over	4 627 751	220 402	501 815	696 441	712 756	557 826	408 077	292 668	353 810	304 706	579 250	242
LABOR FORCE STATUS OF HOUSEHOLDER												
Persons 16 years and over	6 096 544	256 267	603 197	874 676	934 808	744 831	559 352	412 261	512 876	450 889	747 387	250
Labor force	4 571 768	116 307	359 163	626 237	734 842	608 086	468 667	353 211	449 578	404 921	450 756	268
Percent of persons 16 years and over	75.0	45.4	59.5	71.6	78.6	81.6	83.8	85.7	87.7	89.8	60.3	...
Armed Forces	94 350	271	1 888	8 022	21 204	13 011	11 665	8 632	9 804	7 124	12 729	286
Civilian labor force	4 477 418	116 036	357 275	618 215	713 638	595 075	457 002	344 579	439 774	397 797	438 027	268
Employed	4 126 035	102 026	323 300	564 028	651 253	543 586	418 714	318 670	412 497	379 798	412 163	270
Unemployed	351 383	14 010	33 975	54 187	62 385	51 489	38 288	25 909	27 277	17 999	25 864	249
Percent of civilian labor force	7.8	12.1	9.5	8.8	8.7	8.7	8.4	7.5	6.2	4.5	5.9	...
Not in labor force	1 524 776	139 960	244 034	248 439	199 966	136 745	90 685	59 050	63 298	45 968	296 631	196
OCCUPATION OF HOUSEHOLDER												
Employed persons 16 years and over	4 126 035	102 026	323 300	564 028	651 253	543 586	418 714	318 670	412 497	379 798	412 163	270
Managerial and professional specialty occupations	819 837	8 523	32 104	69 084	92 897	88 230	79 170	67 794	101 824	135 492	144 719	330
Executive, administrative, and managerial occupations	347 926	3 309	12 580	27 354	39 331	39 292	36 137	32 499	50 210	75 172	32 042	350
Professional specialty occupations	471 911	5 214	19 524	41 730	53 566	48 938	43 033	35 295	51 614	60 320	112 677	312
Technical, sales, and administrative support occupations	809 426	10 870	46 830	97 917	122 850	109 701	89 094	72 914	100 014	100 538	58 698	294
Technicians and related support occupations	116 068	1 445	5 951	13 871	17 447	15 633	13 042	11 354	15 483	15 352	6 490	302
Sales occupations	306 007	3 644	15 274	31 910	40 525	37 816	33 140	28 324	41 745	49 865	23 764	318
Administrative support occupations, including clerical	387 351	5 781	25 605	52 136	64 878	56 252	42 912	33 236	42 786	35 321	28 444	278
Service occupations	496 083	20 301	56 591	80 794	84 359	64 301	46 360	32 837	38 872	28 156	43 512	241
Private household occupations	31 430	3 900	6 883	5 828	4 142	2 358	1 279	766	871	520	4 883	171
Protective service occupations	71 490	1 503	5 500	9 553	12 158	10 059	8 182	5 974	7 477	5 184	5 900	270
Service occupations, except protective and household	393 163	14 898	44 208	65 413	68 059	51 884	36 899	26 097	30 524	22 452	32 729	241
Forming, forestry, and fishing occupations	141 417	9 735	17 494	21 918	18 166	13 464	8 635	5 650	6 067	3 969	36 319	209
Precision production, craft, and repair occupations	817 012	17 379	60 434	113 097	137 329	116 593	91 598	69 218	89 558	65 624	56 182	272
Operators, fabricators, and laborers	1 042 260	35 218	109 847	181 218	195 652	151 297	103 857	70 257	76 162	46 019	72 733	241
Machine operators, assemblers, and inspectors	466 051	13 929	50 364	84 390	90 241	70 118	46 480	30 796	31 016	17 660	31 057	238
Transportation and material moving occupations	322 674	9 162	28 255	50 078	58 204	47 308	34 750	24 742	29 304	18 309	22 562	255
Handlers, equipment cleaners, helpers, and laborers	253 535	12 127	31 228	46 750	47 207	33 871	22 627	14 719	15 842	10 050	19 114	229
MEANS OF TRANSPORTATION TO WORK FOR HOUSEHOLDER												
Workers 16 years and over	4 101 396	98 376	314 178	554 444	653 166	540 750	418 294	318 416	411 396	378 356	414 020	271
Private vehicle	3 559 747	78 258	266 005	480 492	576 532	480 419	373 663	285 486	369 652	334 858	314 382	273
Drive alone: Car	2 094 990	37 264	141 648	270 058	334 423	282 690	222 613	172 374	225 241	221 181	187 498	280
Drive alone: Truck or van	623 387	14 012	46 384	84 481	100 503	86 317	66 603	50 828	65 508	48 501	60 250	271
Carpool: Car	626 630	17 879	56 489	92 359	106 002	84 088	63 946	47 435	60 292	51 816	46 324	260
Carpool: Truck or van	214 740	9 103	21 484	33 594	35 604	27 324	20 501	14 849	18 611	13 360	20 310	246
Public transportation	131 062	3 966	11 538	18 663	19 163	16 857	12 891	10 012	13 974	16 433	7 565	275
Bus or streetcar	106 334	3 346	9 972	16 313	16 741	14 483	10 958	8 229	10 679	10 023	5 590	264
Subway or elevated train	7 269	20	132	337	614	814	813	779	1 300	1 926	909	500+
Railroad	8 731	15	44	191	321	549	527	603	1 484	4 088	532	500+
Taxicab	8 728	585	1 390	1 822	1 487	1 011	593	401	511	396		210
Bicycle	29 494	810	2 145	4 409	4 645	3 768	3 149	2 482	3 118	2 796	2 172	272
Motorcycle	36 615	436	1 686	4 291	6 081	5 128	4 411	3 758	4 968	3 971	1 885	297
Walked only	244 441	11 974	26 246	36 709	35 690	25 387	17 080	10 811	11 037	8 273	61 234	223
Other means	39 006	1 635	3 722	5 226	5 693	4 309	3 071	2 340	3 168	3 501	6 341	251
Worked at home	61 031	1 297	2 836	4 654	5 362	4 882	4 029	3 527	5 479	8 524	20 441	316
WORKERS IN HOUSEHOLD IN 1979												
No workers	1 049 831	116 623	188 246	174 355	129 536	83 847	50 902	31 034	29 417	19 070	226 801	181
1 worker	2 342 858	94 318	253 972	382 002	393 462	294 045	208 937	145 959	164 073	133 506	272 584	239
2 workers	2 158 617	37 396	136 797	272 219	352 572	306 999	245 916	185 849	237 549	194 291	189 029	280
3 or more workers	546 239	8 014	24 285	46 277	59 426	60 025	53 646	49 475	81 889	104 099	59 103	342

Table G—2. Gross Rent of Renter-Occupied Housing Units: 1980

Housing Units in One-Unit Attached Structures—Total

[Data are estimates based on a sample; see Introduction. For meaning of symbols, see Introduction. For definitions of terms, see appendix A]

United States	Total	Less than $100	$100 to $149	$150 to $199	$200 to $249	$250 to $299	$300 to $349	$350 to $399	$400 to $499	$500 or more	No cash rent	Median (dollars)
Specified renter-occupied housing units	1 286 132	109 105	113 008	177 938	228 980	187 003	137 751	95 751	106 020	75 572	55 004	247
YEAR STRUCTURE BUILT												
1979 to March 1980	36 974	2 353	1 890	2 306	3 005	3 382	4 396	4 283	6 519	8 045	795	359
1975 to 1978	123 594	6 034	4 228	6 127	12 960	15 329	16 825	15 440	21 750	21 341	3 560	346
1970 to 1974	194 622	15 054	10 176	14 578	26 152	29 304	26 780	21 050	27 491	18 947	5 090	299
1960 to 1969	246 372	23 066	18 192	29 726	47 324	40 102	28 215	20 133	19 676	9 910	10 028	250
1950 to 1959	206 690	21 904	21 787	35 256	43 103	29 046	18 794	10 980	9 615	4 334	11 871	221
1940 to 1949	182 460	20 481	22 743	34 286	36 748	25 110	15 924	9 097	7 934	4 214	5 923	215
1939 or earlier	295 420	20 213	33 992	55 659	59 688	44 730	26 817	14 768	13 035	8 781	17 737	224
YEAR HOUSEHOLDER MOVED INTO UNIT												
1979 to March 1980	563 384	25 044	32 819	64 768	96 946	85 473	70 936	52 289	63 880	51 600	19 629	281
1975 to 1978	430 780	37 841	37 100	60 396	81 918	66 554	46 380	32 331	32 467	19 497	16 296	244
1970 to 1974	149 440	24 608	20 276	25 710	27 198	18 872	12 379	6 551	6 033	2 864	4 949	203
1960 to 1969	93 525	15 647	14 541	17 759	16 157	12 120	5 700	3 125	2 663	1 172	4 641	190
1959 or earlier	49 003	5 965	8 272	9 305	6 761	3 984	2 356	1 455	977	439	9 489	180
ROOMS												
1 room	22 777	3 263	4 266	5 566	4 508	2 655	1 035	335	220	174	755	181
2 rooms	56 144	7 984	9 021	11 186	10 911	7 238	4 169	1 991	1 508	586	1 550	196
3 rooms	189 240	33 263	28 855	40 212	37 891	23 170	10 410	5 416	4 220	2 125	3 678	188
4 rooms	373 630	33 866	33 534	55 149	72 701	64 326	46 451	27 019	21 797	8 670	10 117	241
5 rooms	312 464	20 216	22 180	35 415	50 994	43 253	38 647	30 854	33 839	21 301	15 765	273
6 rooms	222 585	7 763	11 239	22 388	37 131	32 123	25 030	20 371	29 193	23 480	13 867	290
7 or more rooms	109 292	2 750	3 913	8 022	14 844	14 238	12 009	9 765	15 243	19 236	9 272	326
Median	4.5	3.8	3.9	4.1	4.3	4.4	4.7	4.9	5.2	5.7	5.2	...
BEDROOMS												
None	30 502	4 486	5 984	7 524	5 745	3 242	1 482	482	412	232	913	179
1	265 699	41 037	39 173	56 704	55 571	35 332	15 848	7 760	5 749	2 595	5 930	194
2	554 467	37 979	40 535	71 256	99 372	93 245	76 692	49 628	44 420	23 325	18 015	260
3	357 211	20 267	21 710	34 499	55 979	45 206	36 398	32 051	48 369	39 345	23 387	288
4	63 405	4 308	4 421	6 376	10 644	7 975	5 719	4 544	5 676	8 183	5 559	270
5 or more	14 848	1 028	1 185	1 579	1 669	2 003	1 612	1 286	1 394	1 892	1 200	284
PERSONS IN UNIT												
1 person	322 619	46 210	40 550	57 395	58 657	43 863	25 486	14 958	13 327	8 759	13 414	209
2 persons	341 128	19 775	26 002	44 943	58 176	52 631	41 907	29 216	31 486	22 889	14 103	264
3 persons	248 407	15 269	17 338	30 386	43 431	36 914	29 137	22 231	25 473	18 093	10 135	267
4 persons	189 638	11 592	12 595	21 571	36 344	27 182	21 874	14 941	19 473	14 512	9 554	265
5 persons	97 515	7 695	7 685	11 819	18 291	13 478	10 363	7 956	9 008	6 321	4 899	253
6 or more persons	86 825	8 564	8 838	11 824	14 081	12 935	8 984	6 449	7 253	4 998	2 899	245
Median	2.44	1.92	2.11	2.20	2.46	2.44	2.55	2.67	2.82	2.84	2.50	...
Total persons	3 540 022	275 035	290 461	458 294	626 547	514 586	391 485	278 105	321 311	230 916	153 282	...
PLUMBING FACILITIES BY PERSONS PER ROOM												
Complete plumbing for exclusive use	1 276 079	106 884	110 795	176 235	227 895	186 223	137 381	95 581	105 875	75 488	53 722	248
1.01 or more persons per room	101 237	10 301	12 874	18 933	19 353	14 058	9 452	5 805	5 464	2 776	2 221	219
Lacking complete plumbing for exclusive use	10 053	2 221	2 213	1 703	1 085	780	370	170	145	84	1 282	149
1.01 or more persons per room	2 492	415	487	421	281	250	114	43	68	49	364	169
HOUSEHOLD INCOME IN 1979												
Less than $5,000	282 688	75 540	43 945	46 423	42 431	27 973	15 686	8 626	7 459	3 963	10 642	168
$5,000 to $9,999	282 623	21 975	37 997	56 630	58 890	39 096	23 734	13 066	12 025	5 288	13 922	215
$10,000 to $12,499	141 206	3 968	10 497	23 233	33 727	24 351	15 358	9 345	8 679	4 220	7 828	243
$12,500 to $14,999	107 386	2 410	6 107	14 423	25 070	19 957	13 916	8 942	7 766	3 756	5 039	258
$15,000 to $19,999	179 580	2 829	7 836	19 526	34 785	34 078	27 047	18 149	18 192	9 563	7 575	281
$20,000 to $24,999	120 488	1 287	3 559	9 407	18 279	21 363	19 702	15 143	17 376	10 283	4 089	311
$25,000 to $34,999	111 275	668	2 181	6 018	11 864	14 962	16 480	15 790	21 391	18 106	3 815	355
$35,000 to $49,999	43 318	306	573	1 562	3 088	4 024	4 544	5 186	9 962	12 739	1 334	417
$50,000 or more	17 568	122	313	716	846	1 199	1 284	1 504	3 170	7 654	760	476
Median	$11 377	$3 919	$6 374	$8 750	$10 976	$12 761	$15 031	$17 043	$19 675	$25 323	$10 938	...
Mean	$13 956	$5 174	$8 211	$10 332	$12 210	$14 155	$16 204	$18 404	$21 424	$28 810	$13 317	...
SELECTED CHARACTERISTICS												
Heating equipment	1 286 132	109 105	113 008	177 938	228 980	187 003	137 751	95 751	106 020	75 572	55 004	247
Central heating system	1 047 364	79 983	71 126	125 626	184 978	159 578	121 833	87 341	98 901	72 393	45 605	262
Air conditioning	602 391	27 497	33 610	65 285	102 707	92 481	76 430	56 853	66 829	51 019	29 680	281
Central system	337 401	7 599	7 410	19 271	46 320	52 243	49 668	41 271	53 403	43 831	16 385	328
Vehicles available	975 261	35 252	63 410	122 095	179 001	153 431	119 630	86 731	98 615	72 062	45 034	271
1	596 754	30 274	49 822	89 939	120 792	95 717	66 971	43 511	44 485	27 544	27 699	247
2 or more	378 507	4 978	13 588	32 156	58 209	57 714	52 659	43 220	54 130	44 518	17 335	313
House heating fuel	1 270 065	108 260	111 090	174 871	226 037	185 234	136 660	94 946	105 144	74 737	53 086	247
Utility gas	794 785	74 313	78 702	119 818	144 518	110 602	79 164	54 397	60 627	43 414	29 230	238
Bottled, tank, or LP gas	21 627	2 462	2 882	3 819	4 056	2 760	1 766	1 001	853	434	1 594	211
Electricity	293 166	21 643	16 693	28 122	45 847	45 196	37 563	28 651	34 177	25 872	9 402	283
Fuel oil, kerosene, etc.	143 946	7 180	9 326	19 738	29 096	25 360	17 583	10 597	9 229	4 886	10 951	252
Other	16 541	2 662	3 487	3 374	2 520	1 316	584	300	258	131	1 909	167
Family householder	867 022	61 463	69 143	112 180	156 827	127 998	99 028	69 063	77 966	53 233	40 121	255
With own children under 18 years	575 202	44 929	45 175	72 024	107 600	83 952	65 198	45 364	52 328	33 899	24 733	253
With own children under 6 years	308 911	23 333	23 772	41 878	62 122	45 016	36 207	23 139	24 429	13 039	15 976	246
Female householder, no husband present	300 199	45 514	34 736	41 648	49 903	41 042	28 982	19 211	20 755	12 412	5 996	225
With own children under 18 years	230 627	36 402	25 898	30 456	38 644	31 605	22 926	15 080	16 549	9 639	3 428	227
With own children under 6 years	94 153	18 069	11 234	13 213	17 039	12 164	8 863	5 039	4 587	2 258	1 687	211
Nonfamily householder	419 110	47 642	43 865	65 758	72 153	59 005	38 723	26 688	28 054	22 339	14 883	231
Income in 1979 below poverty level	326 985	75 006	47 471	51 287	50 635	36 250	22 607	13 191	12 624	7 146	10 768	185
Percent below poverty level	25.4	68.7	42.0	28.8	22.1	19.4	16.4	13.8	11.9	9.5	19.6	...
GROSS RENT AS PERCENTAGE OF HOUSEHOLD INCOME IN 1979												
Less than 15 percent	213 475	29 743	28 451	38 797	40 983	27 966	17 450	10 937	10 936	8 212	...	212
15 to 19 percent	201 027	18 598	15 759	27 234	38 311	32 490	23 997	16 735	16 526	11 377	...	251
20 to 24 percent	185 312	19 657	13 864	23 353	33 096	27 252	22 467	15 696	17 654	12 273	...	255
25 to 29 percent	135 630	11 887	10 033	17 281	26 517	20 272	15 053	11 236	13 539	9 812	...	255
30 to 34 percent	95 706	7 017	7 351	12 089	17 186	15 418	11 364	8 626	9 605	7 050	...	264
35 to 49 percent	153 106	9 341	14 813	21 640	25 062	22 907	18 853	13 474	15 786	11 230	...	262
50 percent or more	224 408	9 210	19 714	33 703	43 629	38 022	26 938	17 959	20 726	14 507	...	258
Not computed	77 468	3 652	3 023	3 841	4 196	2 676	1 629	1 088	1 248	1 111	55 004	209
Median	25.2	21.1	23.9	24.5	25.0	26.1	26.4	26.8	27.7	27.7	...	...

Table G—2. Gross Rent of Renter-Occupied Housing Units: 1980—Con.

Housing Units in One-Unit Attached Structures—Total—Con.

[Data are estimates based on a sample; see Introduction. For meaning of symbols, see Introduction. For definitions of terms, see appendix A]

United States	Total	Less than $100	$100 to $149	$150 to $199	$200 to $249	$250 to $299	$300 to $349	$350 to $399	$400 to $499	$500 or more	No cash rent	Median (dollars)
AGE OF HOUSEHOLDER												
Persons 15 years and over	1 286 132	109 105	113 008	177 938	228 980	187 003	137 751	95 751	106 020	75 572	55 004	247
15 to 19 years	22 242	1 754	2 103	4 355	4 974	3 662	2 166	1 212	966	497	553	226
20 to 24 years	201 706	9 972	14 625	32 112	41 355	34 479	24 032	15 131	14 015	7 873	8 112	248
25 to 29 years	250 127	11 416	15 576	32 566	50 479	41 566	32 403	21 972	22 118	12 208	9 823	262
30 to 34 years	191 879	9 520	12 055	21 210	36 232	28 882	23 775	17 413	20 706	14 499	7 587	273
35 to 39 years	124 943	7 237	8 500	13 511	21 855	18 135	14 281	11 019	14 058	11 719	4 628	275
40 to 44 years	85 502	5 872	6 816	10 582	13 429	12 573	8 978	6 915	9 239	8 050	3 048	268
45 to 49 years	70 345	6 209	6 879	9 418	10 378	10 247	7 258	5 423	6 598	5 932	2 003	256
50 to 54 years	66 808	6 219	6 804	10 095	10 871	9 044	5 981	4 570	5 929	4 927	2 368	242
55 to 59 years	61 648	6 586	7 647	9 786	9 736	7 538	5 589	3 889	4 483	3 581	2 813	228
60 to 64 years	54 342	7 872	7 347	9 061	8 339	6 100	4 523	3 046	2 738	2 499	2 817	209
65 to 69 years	51 651	9 634	7 504	8 695	7 562	5 530	3 631	2 166	2 118	1 671	3 140	191
70 to 74 years	42 571	9 736	6 932	6 833	5 881	4 030	2 381	1 416	1 534	1 007	2 821	173
75 years and over	62 368	17 078	10 220	9 714	7 889	5 217	2 753	1 579	1 518	1 109	5 291	156
Median	34.4	52.1	42.7	34.7	32.4	32.4	32.2	32.7	33.8	36.2	36.5	...
MARITAL STATUS OF HOUSEHOLDER												
Persons 15 years and over	1 286 132	109 105	113 008	177 938	228 980	187 003	137 751	95 751	106 020	75 572	55 004	247
Single	277 008	22 987	25 019	41 553	52 170	43 939	29 057	19 606	20 605	15 078	6 994	244
Now married, except separated	544 385	15 648	33 147	67 758	103 579	83 240	66 722	47 523	54 191	38 729	33 848	271
Separated	112 878	13 462	13 462	17 257	18 713	15 512	10 557	7 048	7 108	4 691	1 906	222
Widowed	140 118	33 700	21 959	23 030	19 277	13 503	8 081	4 772	4 920	3 108	7 768	173
Divorced	211 743	20 146	19 421	28 340	35 241	30 809	23 334	16 802	19 196	13 966	4 488	251
YEARS OF SCHOOL COMPLETED BY HOUSEHOLDER												
Persons 25 years old and over	1 062 184	97 379	96 280	141 471	182 651	148 862	111 553	79 408	91 039	67 202	46 339	247
Median	12.4	9.2	10.5	12.0	12.3	12.5	12.7	12.8	13.2	14.7	12.5	...
PERIOD OF SERVICE OF HOUSEHOLDER												
Civilian veterans 16 years and over	216 154	7 584	14 686	26 045	34 008	32 571	27 380	20 455	25 533	20 765	7 127	284
Percent of civilians 16 years and over	17.8	7.0	13.2	15.5	16.7	18.2	20.6	22.0	24.6	27.9	19.9	...
May 1975 or later only	13 936	367	1 058	2 200	2 938	2 684	1 802	1 078	1 058	436	315	255
Vietnam era	85 484	1 383	4 038	9 093	14 392	14 246	12 822	9 372	11 243	7 216	1 679	296
February 1955 to July 1964 only	20 579	400	1 051	2 181	2 807	2 879	2 432	2 145	3 231	2 883	570	314
Vietnam era and Korean conflict	3 833	78	154	336	403	536	533	422	650	583	138	332
Korean conflict	24 127	741	1 467	2 685	3 434	3 542	2 944	2 229	2 984	3 445	656	298
Korean conflict and World War II	4 743	139	294	616	571	574	523	475	744	670	137	310
World War II	57 349	3 624	5 765	7 988	8 635	7 419	5 900	4 340	5 301	5 280	3 097	258
World War I	2 675	349	406	391	389	323	167	158	108	76	308	205
Other	3 428	503	453	555	439	368	257	236	214	176	227	210
Civilian nonveterans 16 years and over	995 303	101 366	96 790	142 027	169 954	146 382	105 420	72 699	78 432	53 590	28 643	242
LABOR FORCE STATUS OF HOUSEHOLDER												
Persons 16 years and over	1 285 928	109 059	112 966	177 882	228 958	186 996	137 739	95 732	106 020	75 572	55 004	247
Labor force	928 794	29 868	62 245	122 332	175 383	146 947	113 168	80 753	91 956	66 529	39 613	269
Percent of persons 16 years and over	72.2	27.4	55.1	68.8	76.6	78.6	82.2	84.4	86.7	88.0	72.0	...
Armed Forces	74 471	109	1 490	9 810	24 996	8 043	4 939	2 578	2 055	1 217	19 234	232
Civilian labor force	854 323	29 759	60 755	112 522	150 387	138 904	108 229	78 175	89 901	65 312	20 379	273
Employed	787 991	22 682	53 618	102 432	137 948	128 730	101 040	73 863	85 725	63 037	18 916	276
Unemployed	66 332	7 077	7 137	10 090	12 439	10 174	7 189	4 312	4 176	2 275	1 463	233
Percent of civilian labor force	7.8	23.8	11.7	9.0	8.3	7.3	6.6	5.5	4.6	3.5	7.2	...
Not in labor force	357 134	79 191	50 721	55 550	53 575	40 049	24 571	14 979	14 064	9 043	15 391	187
OCCUPATION OF HOUSEHOLDER												
Employed persons 16 years and over	787 991	22 682	53 618	102 432	137 948	128 730	101 040	73 863	85 725	63 037	18 916	276
Managerial and professional specialty occupations	170 835	1 851	5 318	12 890	21 471	25 276	22 905	20 191	27 691	27 443	5 799	334
Executive, administrative, and managerial occupations	78 692	643	1 777	5 056	8 565	10 675	10 830	9 464	13 917	15 205	2 560	353
Professional specialty occupations	92 143	1 208	3 541	7 834	12 906	14 601	12 075	10 727	13 774	12 238	3 239	318
Technical, sales, and administrative support occupations	212 596	3 940	10 831	25 250	36 855	35 486	28 641	21 912	26 343	19 384	3 954	289
Technicians and related support occupations	28 924	351	1 267	3 081	5 065	5 119	4 156	2 925	3 868	2 602	490	293
Sales occupations	65 082	1 245	3 000	5 895	8 876	9 334	8 793	7 370	10 243	8 963	1 363	320
Administrative support occupations, including clerical	118 590	2 344	6 564	16 274	22 914	21 033	15 692	11 617	12 232	7 819	2 101	274
Service occupations	118 485	8 871	13 884	19 861	22 174	18 033	12 618	7 726	7 873	4 628	2 817	234
Private household occupations	7 814	2 025	1 534	1 361	1 078	646	429	266	174	86	215	159
Protective service occupations	13 714	344	942	1 614	2 372	2 393	1 966	1 344	1 299	881	559	277
Service occupations, except protective and household	96 957	6 502	11 408	16 886	18 724	14 994	10 223	6 116	6 400	3 661	2 043	234
Farming, forestry, and fishing occupations	11 557	822	1 566	2 207	2 070	1 588	1 004	587	714	316	683	220
Precision production, craft, and repair occupations	107 300	1 694	6 108	13 333	19 827	19 096	15 464	11 113	11 707	6 493	2 465	280
Operators, fabricators, and laborers	167 218	5 504	15 911	28 891	35 551	29 251	20 408	12 334	11 397	4 773	3 198	245
Machine operators, assemblers, and inspectors	80 238	2 646	7 849	14 511	17 539	14 053	9 693	5 659	4 963	1 884	1 441	241
Transportation and material moving occupations	43 752	1 113	3 326	6 262	9 012	8 111	5 661	3 919	3 668	1 767	913	261
Handlers, equipment cleaners, helpers, and laborers	43 228	1 745	4 736	8 118	9 000	7 087	5 054	2 756	2 766	1 122	844	237
MEANS OF TRANSPORTATION TO WORK FOR HOUSEHOLDER												
Workers 16 years and over	838 416	21 216	52 922	108 606	158 626	132 943	103 335	74 735	85 764	62 900	37 369	272
Private vehicle	683 142	13 008	38 208	83 723	129 236	110 973	88 540	64 830	74 821	53 112	26 691	279
Drive alone: Car	461 288	7 466	23 971	54 431	86 527	74 976	60 159	44 690	52 506	39 217	17 345	283
Truck or van	61 368	797	2 843	6 486	11 798	10 594	8 527	6 372	6 914	3 938	3 099	284
Carpool: Car	137 822	3 898	9 758	19 548	26 549	21 644	16 891	11 754	13 508	8 944	5 328	265
Truck or van	22 664	847	1 636	3 258	4 362	3 759	2 963	2 014	1 893	1 013	919	260
Public transportation	74 926	4 482	7 403	12 271	14 070	11 646	7 462	5 105	5 580	5 253	1 654	244
Bus or streetcar	62 553	3 918	6 713	10 935	12 379	9 924	6 175	4 022	4 013	3 235	1 239	237
Subway or elevated train	6 947	137	232	656	1 061	1 063	817	680	869	1 154	278	311
Railroad	2 797	17	66	182	200	348	308	305	535	762	74	389
Taxicab	2 629	410	392	498	430	311	162	98	163	102	63	198
Bicycle	8 129	116	488	1 222	1 910	1 141	831	532	443	287	1 159	243
Motorcycle	7 689	68	247	802	1 925	1 243	930	577	639	450	808	266
Walked only	49 158	2 843	5 693	9 059	9 292	6 285	4 131	2 486	2 649	1 996	4 724	225
Other means	6 780	393	520	844	1 331	878	603	497	579	434	701	248
Worked at home	8 592	306	363	685	862	777	838	708	1 053	1 368	1 632	329
WORKERS IN HOUSEHOLD IN 1979												
No workers	258 790	67 271	40 405	40 913	37 144	26 174	14 905	8 111	7 813	4 390	11 664	169
1 worker	533 598	30 977	49 753	84 580	107 793	82 015	56 816	37 091	37 200	25 137	22 236	242
2 workers	406 693	8 406	19 039	44 661	72 483	66 429	55 963	41 612	47 459	32 477	18 164	287
3 or more workers	87 051	2 451	3 811	7 784	11 560	12 385	10 067	8 937	13 548	13 568	2 940	320

STRUCTURAL CHARACTERISTICS OF THE HOUSING INVENTORY

413

Table G— 3. Gross Rent of Renter-Occupied Housing Units: 1980

Housing Units in Structures With 2 Units—Total

[Data are estimates based on a sample; see Introduction. For meaning of symbols, see Introduction. For definitions of terms, see appendix A]

United States	Total	Less than $100	$100 to $149	$150 to $199	$200 to $249	$250 to $299	$300 to $349	$350 to $399	$400 to $499	$500 or more	No cash rent	Median (dollars)
Specified renter-occupied housing units	3 375 819	141 348	341 381	629 994	728 936	583 698	377 650	215 700	164 548	66 451	126 113	235
YEAR STRUCTURE BUILT												
1979 to March 1980	46 109	1 653	1 943	2 801	3 735	5 773	8 480	7 477	8 394	4 683	1 170	339
1975 to 1978	142 289	4 793	5 450	8 616	17 195	24 924	27 772	20 595	19 819	8 832	4 293	314
1970 to 1974	196 329	12 270	11 567	17 327	31 976	38 748	32 136	20 728	17 601	7 948	6 028	278
1960 to 1969	399 669	26 290	30 188	53 497	78 493	75 594	53 595	31 726	24 980	10 128	15 178	252
1950 to 1959	478 455	19 835	46 348	89 839	110 994	85 256	52 001	28 683	20 233	7 440	17 826	233
1940 to 1949	553 708	19 369	58 990	115 139	131 996	99 433	57 378	29 840	21 010	6 691	13 862	229
1939 or earlier	1 559 260	57 138	186 895	342 775	354 547	253 970	146 288	76 651	52 511	20 729	67 756	222
YEAR HOUSEHOLDER MOVED INTO UNIT												
1979 to March 1980	1 317 086	30 572	90 334	219 250	288 484	246 091	175 372	108 616	90 331	39 470	28 566	253
1975 to 1978	1 123 978	41 589	104 174	209 364	253 864	208 422	131 935	72 611	51 623	19 290	31 106	238
1970 to 1974	413 104	29 202	58 556	87 858	87 660	64 065	36 398	17 922	12 170	4 253	15 020	213
1960 to 1969	307 798	24 940	52 221	67 963	61 539	42 674	21 889	11 004	6 602	2 185	16 781	200
1959 or earlier	213 853	15 045	36 096	45 559	37 389	22 446	12 056	5 547	3 822	1 253	34 640	192
ROOMS												
1 room	27 883	4 532	6 456	6 765	4 193	2 093	797	432	259	113	2 243	164
2 rooms	119 861	14 894	24 997	29 282	20 997	12 179	5 876	2 978	2 035	610	6 013	179
3 rooms	609 275	52 621	116 518	172 758	129 510	68 201	29 073	12 137	7 708	2 583	18 166	187
4 rooms	1 126 880	40 653	111 247	221 395	268 643	213 044	128 906	63 909	38 272	8 933	31 878	232
5 rooms	896 081	19 890	55 830	133 402	194 426	179 632	126 757	76 230	57 237	19 950	32 727	258
6 rooms	444 110	6 604	20 561	52 795	87 567	85 107	66 052	44 063	41 471	19 607	20 283	276
7 or more rooms	151 729	2 154	5 772	13 597	23 600	23 442	20 189	15 951	17 566	14 655	14 803	300
Median	4.3	3.5	3.7	4.0	4.3	4.5	4.7	4.9	5.1	5.6	4.6	...
BEDROOMS												
None	43 217	6 045	10 303	10 824	6 775	3 500	1 499	828	486	200	2 757	168
1	940 064	71 857	166 626	261 451	206 753	113 224	50 003	21 627	13 714	4 075	30 734	191
2	1 665 240	44 872	126 875	277 866	384 981	338 200	221 970	118 501	78 160	23 285	50 530	246
3	630 670	15 255	32 389	71 592	115 913	114 613	91 675	65 364	62 015	30 435	31 419	278
4	80 371	2 872	4 277	7 034	12 939	12 388	10 588	7 883	8 398	5 896	8 096	286
5 or more	16 257	447	911	1 227	1 575	1 773	1 915	1 497	1 775	2 560	2 577	324
PERSONS IN UNIT												
1 person	1 053 593	83 992	179 035	268 875	220 328	131 342	64 633	29 927	21 123	7 722	46 616	195
2 persons	1 046 409	27 332	85 484	186 274	240 127	199 689	127 220	72 259	53 559	20 741	33 724	243
3 persons	587 329	12 299	35 650	87 515	129 404	119 203	83 977	49 064	37 391	15 228	17 598	258
4 persons	381 233	7 723	20 764	49 293	79 858	76 254	57 138	35 368	28 292	11 939	14 604	267
5 persons	173 154	4 709	10 317	21 384	34 733	33 895	25 400	16 053	13 236	6 022	7 405	267
6 or more persons	134 101	5 293	10 131	16 653	24 486	23 315	19 282	13 029	10 947	4 799	6 166	266
Median	2.11	1.34	1.45	1.75	2.10	2.30	2.48	2.62	2.70	2.81	1.99	...
Total persons	8 004 701	263 123	642 788	1 279 281	1 695 160	1 475 460	1 028 807	619 795	485 706	205 330	309 251	...
PLUMBING FACILITIES BY PERSONS PER ROOM												
Complete plumbing for exclusive use	3 280 197	129 446	327 225	612 510	712 210	572 031	370 962	212 088	162 185	65 417	116 123	236
1.01 or more persons per room	172 587	7 289	18 440	31 197	36 848	29 581	20 256	12 150	9 105	2 752	4 969	236
Lacking complete plumbing for exclusive use	95 622	11 902	14 156	17 484	16 726	11 667	6 688	3 612	2 363	1 034	9 990	198
1.01 or more persons per room	11 285	1 359	1 836	1 731	1 564	1 228	786	484	348	179	1 770	195
HOUSEHOLD INCOME IN 1979												
Less than $5,000	686 064	85 747	122 679	154 839	131 285	79 933	42 060	19 510	12 188	3 598	34 225	188
$5,000 to $9,999	762 218	32 031	105 703	181 550	176 953	116 134	63 337	31 633	19 736	5 300	29 841	213
$10,000 to $12,499	383 932	8 229	35 045	80 875	97 764	70 850	40 398	20 255	13 642	3 814	13 060	231
$12,500 to $14,999	296 113	4 842	22 059	55 018	73 758	59 809	35 675	18 850	12 875	3 565	9 662	242
$15,000 to $19,999	505 539	5 509	28 869	78 280	117 257	108 447	72 712	40 995	28 720	9 146	15 604	257
$20,000 to $24,999	331 959	2 450	13 950	42 236	67 773	72 311	55 094	33 302	25 925	9 185	9 733	274
$25,000 to $34,999	283 916	1 881	9 431	27 856	47 652	56 164	49 603	34 748	32 793	15 031	8 757	295
$35,000 to $49,999	95 471	471	2 692	6 997	12 807	15 968	15 139	12 848	14 395	10 553	3 621	323
$50,000 or more	30 607	188	953	2 343	3 687	4 082	3 632	3 559	4 274	6 279	1 610	345
Median	$11 560	$4 328	$8 001	$9 391	$11 438	$13 542	$15 472	$17 025	$19 109	$24 111	$9 822	...
Mean	$13 663	$6 058	$8 952	$11 070	$12 954	$14 890	$16 634	$18 487	$20 638	$27 760	$12 645	...
SELECTED CHARACTERISTICS												
Heating equipment	3 375 819	141 348	341 381	629 994	728 936	583 698	377 650	215 700	164 548	66 451	126 113	235
Central heating system	2 694 290	83 750	208 669	459 678	595 717	506 518	338 698	195 282	150 810	61 152	94 016	246
Air conditioning	1 280 638	39 547	104 964	206 558	263 978	234 006	167 132	99 300	78 027	32 137	54 989	250
Central system	327 818	5 826	10 994	25 101	53 406	62 458	58 348	39 239	36 516	18 280	17 650	298
Vehicles available	2 549 898	61 477	206 428	444 493	559 469	470 716	316 723	187 034	148 115	61 645	93 798	246
1	1 636 605	49 839	157 003	322 099	375 779	295 967	184 987	101 571	71 329	24 203	53 828	235
2 or more	913 293	11 638	49 425	122 394	183 690	174 749	131 736	85 463	76 786	37 442	39 970	270
House heating fuel	3 349 561	139 909	338 195	625 004	724 318	580 066	375 657	214 203	163 041	65 621	123 547	235
Utility gas	2 118 694	97 735	242 435	428 944	470 129	350 659	214 624	120 085	90 155	38 905	65 023	227
Bottled, tank, or LP gas	77 043	4 741	9 475	15 506	15 848	11 089	6 122	3 340	2 557	1 017	7 148	216
Electricity	407 304	17 931	28 956	57 843	80 648	75 473	57 345	34 853	29 065	12 048	13 142	258
Fuel oil, kerosene, etc.	701 156	13 565	48 427	113 503	151 559	139 384	95 453	54 932	40 496	13 224	30 613	253
Other	45 364	5 937	8 702	9 208	6 134	3 461	2 113	993	768	427	7 621	173
Family householder	2 057 573	53 311	148 179	324 743	455 402	402 978	276 295	160 579	117 469	42 941	75 676	251
With own children under 18 years	1 173 155	28 814	73 640	171 415	261 833	235 892	167 021	98 183	72 754	25 634	37 969	257
With own children under 6 years	665 836	15 236	41 755	103 901	157 301	135 623	93 003	51 819	34 948	10 898	21 352	251
Female householder, no husband present	606 332	27 882	54 315	102 923	137 176	116 108	74 565	42 194	29 252	8 965	13 042	241
With own children under 18 years	434 071	19 030	34 664	70 337	100 435	86 503	56 838	31 837	21 944	6 582	5 901	245
With own children under 6 years	189 264	9 159	16 161	34 374	47 134	37 722	22 354	11 654	6 706	1 637	2 363	236
Nonfamily householder	1 318 246	88 037	193 202	305 251	273 534	180 720	101 355	55 121	47 079	23 510	50 437	209
Income in 1979 below poverty level	707 712	75 989	104 591	143 185	140 615	97 597	58 704	30 380	20 593	7 385	28 673	206
Percent below poverty level	21.0	53.8	30.6	22.7	19.3	16.7	15.5	14.1	12.5	11.1	22.7	...
GROSS RENT AS PERCENTAGE OF HOUSEHOLD INCOME IN 1979												
Less than 15 percent	676 690	44 895	103 268	163 363	157 675	104 026	54 281	26 231	15 788	7 163	...	209
15 to 19 percent	539 910	19 734	48 184	99 316	123 068	107 361	69 396	36 895	26 579	9 377	...	242
20 to 24 percent	444 475	20 622	36 138	76 848	98 076	83 386	58 517	34 634	26 014	10 240	...	245
25 to 29 percent	324 996	15 199	26 878	55 169	73 246	59 861	40 356	25 594	20 550	8 143	...	245
30 to 34 percent	230 298	10 787	21 516	38 607	48 063	43 016	29 098	17 739	14 955	6 517	...	246
35 to 49 percent	396 336	15 569	45 497	71 478	81 568	68 559	48 143	29 786	25 172	10 564	...	240
50 percent or more	587 472	10 720	52 903	114 598	136 797	110 136	72 901	42 224	33 678	13 515	...	242
Not computed	175 642	3 822	6 997	10 615	10 443	7 353	4 958	2 597	1 812	932	126 113	216
Median	24.3	21.0	22.2	23.1	24.0	24.6	25.5	26.7	28.2	28.7	...	...

414

Table G— 3. Gross Rent of Renter-Occupied Housing Units: 1980—Con.

Housing Units in Structures With 2 Units—Total—Con.

[Data are estimates based on a sample; see Introduction. For meaning of symbols, see Introduction. For definitions of terms, see appendix A]

United States

	Total	Less than $100	$100 to $149	$150 to $199	$200 to $249	$250 to $299	$300 to $349	$350 to $399	$400 to $499	$500 or more	No cash rent	Median (dollars)
AGE OF HOUSEHOLDER												
Persons 15 years and over	3 375 819	141 348	341 381	629 994	728 936	583 698	377 650	215 700	164 548	66 451	126 113	235
15 to 19 years	56 978	1 901	6 585	15 411	14 591	8 469	4 587	2 021	1 470	629	1 314	213
20 to 24 years	534 499	11 106	44 901	111 259	134 581	101 054	59 784	30 455	21 185	8 152	12 022	235
25 to 29 years	646 587	10 738	42 019	111 370	152 394	131 827	86 461	48 637	34 917	12 411	15 813	250
30 to 34 years	435 282	8 188	27 256	65 038	95 685	84 679	62 368	37 167	30 386	12 613	11 902	259
35 to 39 years	263 091	6 001	18 446	38 367	53 429	49 975	36 679	22 740	20 025	8 771	6 335	261
40 to 44 years	185 720	5 550	15 737	28 906	37 379	33 031	23 915	16 124	13 058	5 685	5 648	253
45 to 49 years	162 251	5 939	15 111	28 062	32 099	28 525	19 860	12 318	10 002	4 687	6 705	245
50 to 54 years	173 675	7 428	19 687	33 254	36 026	28 471	18 512	11 278	8 465	3 849	7 850	232
55 to 59 years	184 178	9 943	22 808	38 062	38 005	28 761	17 654	10 085	7 845	3 165	8 470	223
60 to 64 years	180 570	12 242	26 375	40 191	35 798	26 161	15 194	8 228	5 617	2 294	9 448	210
65 to 69 years	177 069	16 077	30 716	38 747	34 225	23 541	12 390	6 198	4 330	1 397	9 857	198
70 to 74 years	148 705	16 501	26 828	32 749	27 158	17 423	8 913	4 814	3 290	1 172	22 091	190
75 years and over	227 214	29 734	44 912	48 578	37 566	21 781	11 333	5 635	3 958	1 626	22 091	179
Median	35.3	61.6	50.2	36.6	33.3	33.0	33.0	33.6	34.1	34.8	51.0	...
MARITAL STATUS OF HOUSEHOLDER												
Persons 15 years and over	3 375 819	141 348	341 381	629 994	728 936	583 698	377 650	215 700	164 548	66 451	126 113	235
Single	786 066	29 447	87 462	171 778	179 908	128 034	74 776	42 743	35 768	17 556	18 594	226
Now married, except separated	1 390 613	24 608	89 767	212 091	305 597	274 884	193 474	113 195	84 281	32 106	60 610	256
Separated	226 936	12 959	25 009	42 720	49 757	40 231	25 497	13 850	9 814	3 182	3 917	231
Widowed	448 075	51 020	83 022	100 149	80 216	50 378	26 351	13 287	8 794	3 200	31 658	187
Divorced	524 129	23 314	56 121	103 256	113 458	90 171	57 552	32 625	25 891	10 407	11 334	232
YEARS OF SCHOOL COMPLETED BY HOUSEHOLDER												
Persons 25 years old and over	2 784 342	128 341	289 895	503 324	579 764	474 175	313 279	183 224	141 893	57 670	112 777	236
Median	12.3	8.8	10.9	12.1	12.3	12.5	12.6	12.7	12.9	14.6	12.1	...
PERIOD OF SERVICE OF HOUSEHOLDER												
Civilian veterans 16 years and over	606 592	15 611	51 132	103 867	127 530	111 215	77 475	45 941	36 650	16 280	20 891	248
Percent of civilians 16 years and over	18.3	11.1	15.1	16.7	18.0	19.3	20.8	21.5	22.5	24.7	18.7	...
May 1975 or later only	34 874	721	2 574	6 933	9 205	7 032	4 005	1 946	1 300	488	670	237
Vietnam era	225 498	2 719	13 363	35 515	49 789	46 067	33 473	19 161	14 871	5 677	4 863	260
February 1955 to July 1964 only	52 023	863	3 633	7 666	10 025	9 457	7 251	5 000	4 475	2 068	1 585	266
Vietnam era and Korean conflict	6 770	191	507	1 010	1 079	1 067	1 126	661	566	322	241	272
Korean conflict	64 304	1 488	5 387	10 712	12 651	11 372	7 883	5 189	4 688	2 487	2 447	253
Korean conflict and World War II	11 877	383	1 082	2 212	2 273	1 996	1 447	908	765	428	383	246
World War II	190 626	7 696	21 671	35 724	38 384	31 568	20 505	12 287	9 255	4 422	9 114	233
World War I	9 960	717	1 373	2 047	1 930	1 236	803	302	291	214	1 047	208
Other	10 660	833	1 542	2 048	2 194	1 420	982	487	439	174	541	215
Civilian nonveterans 16 years and over	2 706 723	125 574	288 437	518 304	581 142	463 597	295 397	167 537	126 340	49 593	90 802	232
LABOR FORCE STATUS OF HOUSEHOLDER												
Persons 16 years and over	3 375 335	141 305	341 305	629 915	728 844	583 622	377 585	215 688	164 525	66 446	126 100	235
Labor force	2 420 055	49 468	194 097	431 830	540 853	452 117	303 138	177 701	137 627	57 187	76 037	246
Percent of persons 16 years and over	71.7	35.0	56.9	68.6	74.2	77.5	80.3	82.4	83.7	86.1	60.3	...
Armed Forces	62 020	120	1 736	7 744	20 172	8 810	4 713	2 210	1 535	573	14 407	235
Civilian labor force	2 358 035	49 348	192 361	424 086	520 681	443 307	298 425	175 491	136 092	56 614	61 630	246
Employed	2 178 618	43 228	175 389	387 904	477 798	409 819	278 319	165 133	129 283	54 293	57 452	248
Unemployed	179 417	6 120	16 972	36 182	42 883	33 488	20 106	10 358	6 809	2 321	4 178	233
Percent of civilian labor force	7.6	12.4	8.8	8.5	8.2	7.6	6.7	5.9	5.0	4.1	6.8	...
Not in labor force	955 280	91 837	147 208	198 085	187 991	131 505	74 447	37 987	26 898	9 259	50 063	204
OCCUPATION OF HOUSEHOLDER												
Employed persons 16 years and over	2 178 618	43 228	175 389	387 904	477 798	409 819	278 319	165 133	129 283	54 293	57 452	248
Managerial and professional specialty occupations	433 627	4 686	23 203	60 665	83 002	80 812	62 844	42 906	40 556	22 820	12 133	274
Executive, administrative, and managerial occupations	183 535	1 707	8 115	22 752	32 581	34 953	28 351	19 247	18 901	11 591	5 337	284
Professional specialty occupations	250 092	2 979	15 088	37 913	50 421	45 859	34 493	23 659	21 655	11 229	6 796	267
Technical, sales, and administrative support occupations	579 564	8 133	41 058	100 696	127 138	113 000	77 723	47 324	37 406	15 600	11 486	253
Technicians and related support occupations	75 771	855	4 779	12 587	16 574	14 849	10 933	6 380	5 334	2 085	1 395	258
Sales occupations	163 559	2 599	11 582	25 195	31 099	29 955	22 846	15 751	13 528	7 173	3 831	266
Administrative support occupations, including clerical	340 234	4 679	24 697	62 914	79 465	68 196	43 944	25 193	18 544	6 342	6 260	247
Service occupations	308 520	11 983	35 520	62 837	67 625	52 547	32 841	18 762	13 593	4 717	8 095	229
Private household occupations	16 128	2 216	3 705	3 417	2 676	1 492	951	461	422	108	680	176
Protective service occupations	41 662	708	2 745	6 805	8 882	8 908	6 186	3 150	2 502	708	1 068	256
Service occupations, except protective and household	250 730	9 059	29 070	52 615	56 067	42 147	25 704	15 151	10 669	3 901	6 347	228
Farming, forestry, and fishing occupations	33 306	1 673	3 722	5 431	5 729	4 194	2 424	1 566	1 153	635	6 579	220
Precision production, craft, and repair occupations	314 641	4 607	22 485	52 443	70 803	63 271	43 689	24 911	18 133	5 889	10 749	233
Operators, fabricators, and laborers	508 960	12 146	49 401	105 632	123 501	95 995	58 798	29 664	18 442	4 632	5 100	230
Machine operators, assemblers, and inspectors	266 005	6 062	26 220	57 583	66 707	50 161	29 275	14 673	8 421	1 803	5 100	230
Transportation and material moving occupations	126 278	2 439	10 387	22 412	28 975	24 689	17 209	8 913	6 468	1 754	3 032	246
Handlers, equipment cleaners, helpers, and laborers	116 677	3 645	12 794	25 637	27 819	21 145	12 314	6 078	3 553	1 075	2 617	227
MEANS OF TRANSPORTATION TO WORK FOR HOUSEHOLDER												
Workers 16 years and over	2 177 018	41 283	171 486	383 609	484 389	406 809	275 520	162 611	127 593	53 729	69 989	247
Private vehicle	1 716 730	29 291	128 743	298 884	386 386	325 011	221 732	131 243	103 495	41 623	50 322	249
Drive alone: Car	1 154 625	17 849	83 496	200 647	258 678	219 656	150 637	90 513	72 208	30 182	30 759	250
Truck or van	159 062	2 543	10 751	25 672	35 614	30 280	20 677	12 234	9 874	3 526	7 891	252
Carpool: Car	344 753	7 316	29 205	62 192	78 889	65 194	43 337	24 250	18 579	6 846	8 945	244
Truck or van	58 290	1 583	5 291	10 373	13 205	9 881	7 081	4 246	2 834	1 069	2 727	240
Public transportation	239 302	4 061	17 500	39 577	50 726	48 422	33 895	20 146	14 699	6 610	3 666	256
Bus or streetcar	156 016	3 340	14 369	30 432	35 051	29 314	18 627	10 576	8 316	3 452	2 539	241
Subway or elevated train	64 003	234	1 666	6 604	12 382	15 677	12 352	7 501	4 694	2 091	802	284
Railroad	11 587	60	285	912	1 692	2 428	2 139	1 616	1 381	883	191	308
Taxicab	7 696	427	1 180	1 629	1 601	1 003	777	453	308	184	134	217
Bicycle	16 451	323	1 439	3 173	3 639	2 704	1 812	1 018	931	494	918	239
Motorcycle	13 425	207	804	2 040	3 160	2 733	1 836	902	742	260	741	252
Walked only	157 819	6 495	20 591	35 069	35 030	23 389	13 015	6 946	5 276	2 834	9 174	217
Other means	13 644	467	1 209	2 489	2 737	2 175	1 397	844	864	371	1 091	239
Worked at home	19 647	439	1 200	2 377	2 711	2 375	1 833	1 512	1 586	1 537	4 077	272
WORKERS IN HOUSEHOLD IN 1979												
No workers	705 741	80 468	122 030	152 446	135 235	88 062	46 827	22 122	14 219	4 335	39 997	193
1 worker	1 429 261	46 070	154 748	305 322	329 794	245 431	146 576	78 896	55 416	20 038	46 970	228
2 workers	1 054 562	12 417	56 570	153 107	233 738	217 404	155 192	93 656	72 819	28 025	31 634	263
3 or more workers	186 255	2 393	8 033	19 119	30 169	32 801	29 055	21 026	22 094	14 053	7 512	295

STRUCTURAL CHARACTERISTICS OF THE HOUSING INVENTORY

415

Table G— 4. Gross Rent of Renter-Occupied Housing Units: 1980

Housing Units in Structures With 3 or 4 Units—Total

[Data are estimates based on a sample; see Introduction. For meaning of symbols, see Introduction. For definitions of terms, see appendix A]

United States	Total	Less than $100	$100 to $149	$150 to $199	$200 to $249	$250 to $299	$300 to $349	$350 to $399	$400 to $499	$500 or more	No cash rent	Median (dollars)
Specified renter-occupied housing units	3 292 024	179 384	346 425	664 661	743 260	576 191	340 333	184 998	141 242	51 329	64 201	228
YEAR STRUCTURE BUILT												
1979 to March 1980	66 913	4 771	3 669	4 596	7 779	11 290	12 232	8 492	8 792	4 180	1 112	303
1975 to 1978	205 650	11 593	9 282	15 313	34 003	43 816	34 299	22 235	21 870	8 745	4 494	285
1970 to 1974	325 332	23 949	16 167	29 180	61 521	73 217	50 781	30 913	25 468	8 271	5 865	270
1960 to 1969	515 522	31 753	29 382	67 935	115 313	113 026	72 401	39 246	28 368	8 559	9 539	254
1950 to 1959	427 925	23 089	40 886	91 434	107 590	76 379	40 606	20 822	13 427	4 024	9 668	225
1940 to 1949	470 771	23 102	55 518	119 162	119 277	74 380	38 307	17 976	11 679	3 819	7 551	214
1939 or earlier	1 279 911	61 127	191 521	337 041	297 777	184 083	91 707	45 314	31 638	13 731	25 972	206
YEAR HOUSEHOLDER MOVED INTO UNIT												
1979 to March 1980	1 419 579	46 102	110 157	262 321	322 320	269 782	175 474	99 375	81 924	31 705	20 419	244
1975 to 1978	1 092 218	59 801	109 677	218 305	255 289	199 431	113 022	60 285	43 800	14 474	18 134	229
1970 to 1974	381 458	36 751	54 838	84 136	83 888	57 872	29 018	15 032	9 564	3 180	7 179	207
1960 to 1969	252 623	24 099	43 495	61 602	53 638	33 805	15 886	7 328	4 216	1 461	7 093	195
1959 or earlier	146 146	12 631	28 258	38 297	28 125	15 301	6 933	2 978	1 738	509	11 376	185
ROOMS												
1 room	63 319	12 107	15 674	14 975	10 200	4 320	2 091	910	623	369	2 050	160
2 rooms	227 535	28 458	49 625	59 263	41 759	23 710	10 982	5 652	3 346	892	3 848	178
3 rooms	858 913	69 073	133 381	247 073	205 943	112 726	46 236	19 715	11 734	3 647	9 385	195
4 rooms	1 192 141	42 325	94 086	218 643	292 719	253 877	147 534	70 949	44 901	10 215	16 892	240
5 rooms	640 023	19 603	38 462	90 438	135 616	127 844	92 517	57 645	46 536	16 109	15 053	261
6 rooms	238 751	6 142	12 054	27 609	44 680	43 225	32 695	23 753	25 952	12 921	9 720	278
7 or more rooms	71 342	1 676	3 143	6 460	12 343	10 489	8 278	6 374	8 150	7 176	7 253	290
Median	3.9	3.2	3.3	3.6	3.9	4.1	4.3	4.4	4.7	5.2	4.5	...
BEDROOMS												
None	96 419	15 630	24 282	25 460	15 256	6 962	3 320	1 587	1 025	514	2 383	164
1	1 269 858	99 967	200 275	360 243	304 126	169 178	69 347	29 563	17 089	4 927	15 143	195
2	1 470 743	42 996	93 765	226 467	341 875	324 641	210 366	110 265	75 503	20 598	24 267	253
3	394 104	17 262	23 633	46 757	71 323	66 317	50 723	39 110	42 526	20 319	16 134	273
4	52 794	3 076	3 899	5 110	9 651	7 921	5 771	3 877	4 343	4 150	4 996	264
5 or more	8 106	453	571	624	1 029	1 172	806	596	756	821	1 278	281
PERSONS IN UNIT												
1 person	1 263 034	111 473	198 720	325 651	282 644	174 728	81 153	36 751	24 156	8 157	19 601	198
2 persons	966 221	27 953	77 243	180 314	226 501	191 382	118 617	63 128	48 791	16 639	15 653	242
3 persons	509 503	16 291	33 391	80 682	115 820	102 779	67 153	39 311	31 250	11 752	11 074	251
4 persons	308 475	11 019	18 909	44 620	67 163	61 240	41 069	25 665	20 950	8 446	9 394	256
5 persons	136 107	6 084	9 131	18 486	29 517	25 953	18 462	11 087	8 822	3 678	4 687	254
6 or more persons	108 684	6 564	9 031	14 708	21 615	20 109	13 879	9 056	7 273	2 657	3 792	251
Median	1.90	1.30	1.37	1.54	1.89	2.09	2.25	2.38	2.45	2.57	2.30	...
Total persons	7 206 514	330 013	617 819	1 261 483	1 600 304	1 343 883	850 701	492 473	390 465	148 245	171 128	...
PLUMBING FACILITIES BY PERSONS PER ROOM												
Complete plumbing for exclusive use	3 198 452	164 730	327 406	645 362	728 331	566 619	335 327	182 174	139 291	50 634	58 578	230
1.01 or more persons per room	193 091	9 881	19 390	36 718	43 537	35 367	21 192	12 191	8 545	2 598	3 672	233
Lacking complete plumbing for exclusive use	93 572	14 654	19 019	19 299	14 929	9 572	5 006	2 824	1 951	695	5 623	177
1.01 or more persons per room	12 796	1 744	2 143	2 444	1 931	1 338	915	470	365	98	1 348	188
HOUSEHOLD INCOME IN 1979												
Less than $5,000	750 405	117 740	131 842	179 535	146 450	87 306	39 509	17 743	11 091	3 292	15 897	183
$5,000 to $9,999	794 396	37 705	111 110	201 636	190 739	124 203	62 774	28 701	16 976	4 308	16 244	210
$10,000 to $12,499	385 954	8 198	34 645	85 836	104 815	73 272	37 679	18 605	12 038	3 129	7 737	229
$12,500 to $14,999	283 704	5 047	19 969	54 424	75 152	60 330	33 448	16 621	10 580	2 841	5 292	240
$15,000 to $19,999	459 533	5 427	25 712	75 943	112 321	103 160	64 079	33 899	24 440	6 667	7 885	253
$20,000 to $24,999	281 980	2 410	12 262	35 839	59 635	63 802	46 136	27 821	22 629	6 829	4 617	272
$25,000 to $34,999	231 678	1 998	8 091	23 384	40 916	47 679	40 218	27 969	26 448	11 092	3 883	291
$35,000 to $49,999	76 589	561	1 952	6 164	10 178	12 598	12 781	10 544	12 456	7 822	1 533	324
$50,000 or more	27 785	298	842	1 900	3 054	3 841	3 709	3 095	4 584	5 349	1 113	346
Median	$10 656	$4 108	$6 606	$8 726	$10 821	$12 637	$14 758	$16 479	$19 019	$23 899	$9 988	...
Mean	$12 759	$5 588	$8 404	$10 274	$12 174	$14 106	$16 172	$18 061	$21 015	$28 070	$12 911	...
SELECTED CHARACTERISTICS												
Heating equipment	3 292 024	179 384	346 425	664 661	743 260	576 191	340 333	184 998	141 242	51 329	64 201	228
Central heating system	2 650 592	129 118	231 682	495 361	603 679	500 802	302 973	166 527	128 305	47 153	44 992	237
Air conditioning	1 351 293	51 857	96 623	214 261	301 142	280 261	179 627	97 633	74 329	26 429	29 131	250
Central system	525 874	15 461	15 243	40 157	102 196	132 824	94 912	52 755	42 641	16 941	12 744	281
Vehicles available	2 379 128	67 643	194 297	440 927	548 944	459 786	285 353	159 691	125 708	46 088	50 691	242
1	1 645 016	57 848	157 123	342 849	398 056	309 167	174 812	90 807	64 045	20 693	29 616	231
2 or more	734 112	9 795	37 174	98 078	150 888	150 619	110 541	68 884	61 663	25 395	21 075	270
House heating fuel	3 260 569	177 692	342 674	657 971	736 087	572 419	338 263	183 680	139 867	50 566	61 350	229
Utility gas	1 931 907	113 499	235 278	434 523	438 827	307 128	172 315	95 210	77 443	28 188	29 496	219
Bottled, tank, or LP gas	66 744	4 246	8 607	14 597	14 812	9 629	5 265	2 420	1 800	774	4 594	212
Electricity	629 873	37 857	39 548	79 908	129 677	135 315	92 317	51 906	39 143	14 170	10 032	258
Fuel oil, kerosene, etc.	599 346	17 675	53 002	121 610	147 788	117 782	67 044	33 434	20 850	7 095	13 066	234
Other	32 699	4 415	6 239	7 333	4 983	2 565	1 322	710	631	339	4 162	175
Family householder	1 752 124	63 385	132 277	297 752	403 840	346 830	219 722	123 226	92 212	30 800	42 080	245
With own children under 18 years	1 016 468	42 075	70 472	162 503	234 698	203 829	130 509	74 564	55 431	17 541	24 846	247
With own children under 6 years	587 989	23 193	42 067	101 608	143 583	117 387	72 126	38 922	26 373	7 320	15 410	242
Female householder, no husband present	573 629	40 484	53 389	101 448	129 781	110 444	66 170	34 929	24 049	6 589	6 346	234
With own children under 18 years	430 054	32 227	37 689	73 746	97 326	84 308	51 094	26 612	18 240	4 987	3 825	236
With own children under 6 years	198 943	16 892	19 152	38 533	48 313	37 343	20 312	9 623	5 743	1 241	1 791	225
Nonfamily householder	1 539 900	115 999	214 148	366 909	339 420	229 361	120 611	61 772	49 030	20 529	22 121	209
Income in 1979 below poverty level	746 533	100 730	112 106	163 023	149 968	102 143	52 537	26 309	17 929	6 097	15 691	197
Percent below poverty level	22.7	56.2	32.4	24.5	20.2	17.7	15.4	14.2	12.7	11.9	24.4	...
GROSS RENT AS PERCENTAGE OF HOUSEHOLD INCOME IN 1979												
Less than 15 percent	603 904	50 521	92 618	148 327	137 656	87 687	45 143	21 086	14 877	5 989	...	204
15 to 19 percent	511 527	26 676	49 318	102 182	120 258	97 518	57 408	30 201	20 756	7 210	...	232
20 to 24 percent	448 270	30 352	38 204	82 576	102 837	83 885	51 248	28 905	22 586	7 677	...	235
25 to 29 percent	334 118	21 400	29 905	60 182	78 754	61 087	37 721	21 367	17 608	6 094	...	235
30 to 34 percent	237 645	13 405	22 976	42 626	52 993	45 487	27 495	15 594	12 484	4 585	...	238
35 to 49 percent	413 348	17 761	48 042	81 724	87 584	74 269	47 442	27 064	21 649	7 813	...	234
50 percent or more	617 740	14 211	56 702	133 176	148 851	116 843	68 993	38 441	29 298	11 225	...	235
Not computed	125 472	5 058	8 660	13 868	14 327	9 415	4 883	2 340	1 984	736	64 201	211
Median	25.3	21.6	23.5	24.5	25.2	26.2	26.8	27.6	28.2	28.6	...	...

Table G— 4. Gross Rent of Renter-Occupied Housing Units: 1980—Con.

Housing Units in Structures With 3 or 4 Units—Total—Con.

[Data are estimates based on a sample; see Introduction. For meaning of symbols, see Introduction. For definitions of terms, see appendix A]

United States

	Total	Less than $100	$100 to $149	$150 to $199	$200 to $249	$250 to $299	$300 to $349	$350 to $399	$400 to $499	$500 or more	No cash rent	Median (dollars)
AGE OF HOUSEHOLDER												
Persons 15 years and over	3 292 024	179 384	346 425	664 661	743 260	576 191	340 333	184 998	141 242	51 329	64 201	228
15 to 19 years	73 548	2 517	9 082	19 946	18 239	11 883	5 839	2 748	1 704	659	931	213
20 to 24 years	587 497	15 487	51 534	130 941	149 644	111 559	61 761	29 837	21 071	7 006	8 657	231
25 to 29 years	635 876	15 711	45 965	120 200	158 195	127 671	77 427	41 448	29 197	9 652	10 410	241
30 to 34 years	416 260	11 350	28 965	68 773	95 676	84 329	53 322	30 687	26 365	9 358	7 435	250
35 to 39 years	243 509	8 320	18 298	39 988	52 696	45 981	31 206	19 875	15 898	6 551	4 696	250
40 to 44 years	172 065	7 064	15 488	30 001	36 186	30 675	21 440	13 302	10 385	4 209	3 315	244
45 to 49 years	152 796	7 801	16 324	28 812	31 941	27 237	16 876	9 236	8 199	3 219	3 151	234
50 to 54 years	162 440	9 349	19 846	33 121	33 838	26 765	16 228	9 395	7 535	2 816	3 547	225
55 to 59 years	166 415	11 369	24 168	36 717	34 358	25 303	14 148	8 117	6 091	2 300	3 844	213
60 to 64 years	161 389	13 572	25 146	37 635	34 092	22 755	12 040	6 371	4 246	1 667	3 865	204
65 to 69 years	159 173	19 045	27 061	36 868	31 090	21 271	10 055	4 826	3 628	1 385	3 944	193
70 to 74 years	139 715	20 114	24 343	31 911	31 911	27 340	16 397	3 842	3 088	1 122	3 360	187
75 years and over	221 341	37 685	40 205	49 748	39 965	24 365	11 793	5 314	3 835	1 385	7 046	179
Median	34.2	60.3	46.2	34.5	32.4	32.2	32.4	33.0	33.5	34.5	40.0	...
MARITAL STATUS OF HOUSEHOLDER												
Persons 15 years and over	3 292 024	179 384	346 425	664 661	743 260	576 191	340 333	184 998	141 242	51 329	64 201	228
Single	943 218	42 658	106 411	219 859	222 731	158 072	86 397	45 254	35 841	15 131	10 864	222
Now married, except separated	1 127 935	22 872	75 670	188 393	263 089	226 526	145 840	83 449	64 230	22 706	35 160	249
Separated	243 832	18 344	29 421	48 480	54 259	43 171	24 120	12 508	8 648	2 454	2 427	223
Widowed	419 601	62 799	73 360	95 311	81 193	49 956	24 569	11 592	7 985	2 462	10 374	186
Divorced	557 438	32 711	61 563	112 618	121 988	98 466	59 407	32 195	24 538	8 576	5 376	228
YEARS OF SCHOOL COMPLETED BY HOUSEHOLDER												
Persons 25 years old and over	2 630 979	161 380	285 809	513 774	575 377	452 749	272 733	152 413	118 467	43 664	54 613	228
Median	12.4	9.2	11.1	12.2	12.4	12.6	12.7	12.9	13.4	14.8	12.3	...
PERIOD OF SERVICE OF HOUSEHOLDER												
Civilian veterans 16 years and over	540 364	18 501	52 962	101 563	116 358	97 751	63 591	36 870	30 626	11 791	10 351	240
Percent of civilians 16 years and over	16.7	10.3	15.4	15.5	16.1	17.2	19.0	20.2	22.0	23.3	19.8	...
May 1975 or later only	38 521	903	3 305	8 301	9 721	7 536	4 527	2 060	1 332	358	478	233
Vietnam era	201 318	2 859	13 792	35 485	46 765	41 019	26 951	15 466	12 380	4 042	2 559	251
February 1955 to July 1964 only	44 629	1 067	3 550	7 388	8 599	8 184	6 081	3 994	3 361	1 632	773	258
Vietnam era and Korean conflict	7 218	148	613	1 149	1 326	1 321	969	603	600	323	140	261
Korean conflict	56 184	1 941	5 664	10 471	11 584	9 400	6 492	3 952	3 724	1 599	1 357	240
Korean conflict and World War II	11 359	553	1 140	2 188	2 172	1 852	1 227	863	808	286	270	238
World War II	161 655	9 103	21 915	32 513	32 334	25 688	15 742	9 144	7 793	3 280	4 143	224
World War I	9 447	929	1 393	1 968	1 843	1 404	697	377	310	183	343	207
Other	10 033	998	1 590	2 100	2 014	1 347	879	411	318	88	288	205
Civilian nonveterans 16 years and over	2 686 419	160 647	291 263	553 202	606 038	468 932	271 367	145 431	108 727	38 904	41 908	226
LABOR FORCE STATUS OF HOUSEHOLDER												
Persons 16 years and over	3 291 419	179 336	346 358	664 569	743 105	576 095	340 284	184 953	141 199	51 329	64 191	228
Labor force	2 339 345	58 257	199 208	454 867	549 187	444 874	273 289	152 877	118 685	43 585	44 516	240
Percent of persons 16 years and over	71.1	32.5	57.5	68.4	73.9	77.2	80.3	82.7	84.1	84.9	69.3	...
Armed Forces	64 636	188	2 133	9 804	20 709	9 412	5 326	2 652	1 846	634	11 932	234
Civilian labor force	2 274 709	58 069	197 075	445 063	528 478	435 462	267 963	150 225	116 839	42 951	32 584	240
Employed	2 103 407	48 639	177 612	405 741	487 980	405 689	252 510	142 315	111 552	41 081	30 288	241
Unemployed	171 302	9 430	19 463	39 322	40 498	29 773	15 453	7 910	5 287	1 870	2 296	220
Percent of civilian labor force	7.5	16.2	9.9	8.8	7.7	6.8	5.8	5.3	4.5	4.4	7.0	...
Not in labor force	952 074	121 079	147 150	209 702	193 918	131 221	66 995	32 076	22 514	7 744	19 675	197
OCCUPATION OF HOUSEHOLDER												
Employed persons 16 years and over	2 103 407	48 639	177 612	405 741	487 980	405 689	252 510	142 315	111 552	41 081	30 288	241
Managerial and professional specialty occupations	443 653	5 008	22 672	67 595	92 721	89 625	63 981	39 843	37 430	17 353	7 425	267
Executive, administrative, and managerial occupations	186 180	1 617	7 726	23 947	36 705	37 742	29 039	18 388	18 726	8 944	3 346	278
Professional specialty occupations	257 473	3 391	14 946	43 648	56 016	51 883	34 942	21 455	18 704	8 409	4 079	258
Technical, sales, and administrative support occupations	594 037	9 577	42 126	109 336	139 908	121 388	76 143	43 519	34 697	12 473	4 870	248
Technicians and related support occupations	78 846	1 094	5 091	13 822	18 923	16 575	10 446	6 169	4 642	1 578	506	251
Sales occupations	162 425	2 683	11 062	26 459	32 737	31 763	22 178	14 136	13 526	5 933	1 948	261
Administrative support occupations, including clerical	352 766	5 800	25 973	69 055	88 248	73 050	43 519	23 214	16 529	4 962	2 416	242
Service occupations	309 443	15 225	39 936	67 743	69 507	52 427	29 671	15 917	11 082	3 560	4 375	221
Private household occupations	15 461	2 487	3 173	3 555	2 768	1 844	730	362	123	40	379	176
Protective service occupations	36 814	824	3 338	6 376	8 711	7 634	4 530	2 521	1 773	513	594	243
Service occupations, except protective and household	257 168	11 914	33 425	57 812	58 028	42 949	24 411	13 034	9 186	3 007	3 402	220
Farming, forestry, and fishing occupations	30 227	1 553	3 582	5 701	5 974	4 488	2 206	1 082	807	355	4 879	215
Precision production, craft, and repair occupations	272 088	5 094	20 275	50 798	64 058	54 822	35 278	19 727	14 089	4 100	3 847	245
Operators, fabricators, and laborers	453 959	12 182	49 021	104 568	115 812	83 339	45 231	22 227	13 447	3 240	4 892	225
Machine operators, assemblers, and inspectors	241 472	6 199	26 724	57 597	63 199	43 870	23 040	10 902	6 124	1 506	2 311	223
Transportation and material moving occupations	105 821	2 386	9 657	21 622	25 261	21 058	12 441	6 583	4 443	1 101	1 269	237
Handlers, equipment cleaners, helpers, and laborers	106 666	3 597	12 640	25 349	27 352	18 411	9 750	4 742	2 880	633	1 312	220
MEANS OF TRANSPORTATION TO WORK FOR HOUSEHOLDER												
Workers 16 years and over	2 106 131	46 410	173 548	402 363	494 336	404 215	251 585	141 231	110 459	40 761	41 223	241
Private vehicle	1 620 310	29 465	120 970	297 755	383 055	323 329	204 410	114 237	88 482	30 704	27 903	245
Drive alone: Car	1 122 873	18 253	80 342	203 734	263 752	229 087	143 861	81 003	63 375	22 698	16 768	248
Truck or van	124 664	2 294	8 909	21 628	28 933	23 572	15 764	9 597	7 432	2 225	4 310	247
Carpool: Car	325 155	7 527	27 265	63 750	79 139	62 258	38 996	20 512	15 322	5 093	5 293	239
Truck or van	47 618	1 391	4 454	8 643	11 231	8 412	5 789	3 125	2 353	688	1 532	238
Public transportation	251 122	7 100	22 652	51 014	59 967	46 782	27 211	16 208	12 863	5 552	1 773	237
Bus or streetcar	168 114	6 011	18 130	39 006	40 569	28 829	16 468	8 499	6 991	2 487	1 124	225
Subway or elevated train	66 000	530	3 034	9 113	16 073	14 878	8 684	6 164	4 568	2 428	528	263
Railroad	9 372	72	256	1 028	1 807	2 006	1 554	1 114	1 026	426	83	287
Taxicab	7 636	487	1 232	1 867	1 518	1 069	505	431	278	211	38	207
Bicycle	17 663	465	1 721	3 544	4 384	2 820	1 924	952	871	427	555	232
Motorcycle	13 092	124	733	2 122	3 010	2 530	1 813	1 137	853	261	509	256
Walked only	171 464	8 125	24 911	42 886	38 432	23 867	12 638	6 529	5 323	2 307	6 446	209
Other means	15 232	536	1 445	3 036	2 970	2 382	1 702	949	786	347	1 079	235
Worked at home	17 248	595	1 116	2 006	2 518	2 505	1 887	1 219	1 281	1 163	2 958	268
WORKERS IN HOUSEHOLD IN 1979												
No workers	726 858	107 862	123 422	165 420	143 923	91 496	43 508	19 433	12 608	4 003	15 183	188
1 worker	1 496 378	56 515	166 777	340 066	360 903	262 463	142 954	73 086	50 584	16 883	26 147	224
2 workers	919 086	12 246	49 348	142 946	212 288	194 750	131 451	75 771	61 084	20 648	18 554	259
3 or more workers	149 702	2 761	6 878	16 229	26 146	27 482	22 420	16 708	16 966	9 795	4 317	288

Table G— 5. **Gross Rent of Renter-Occupied Housing Units: 1980**

Housing Units in Structures With 5 to 9 Units—Total

[Data are estimates based on a sample; see Introduction. For meaning of symbols, see Introduction. For definitions of terms, see appendix A]

United States	Total	Less than $100	$100 to $149	$150 to $199	$200 to $249	$250 to $299	$300 to $349	$350 to $399	$400 to $499	$500 or more	No cash rent	Median (dollars)
Specified renter-occupied housing units	3 036 221	210 422	284 137	524 600	676 529	584 006	357 800	177 589	124 094	43 945	53 099	235
YEAR STRUCTURE BUILT												
1979 to March 1980	76 985	6 190	4 333	6 286	10 073	14 168	14 630	9 708	7 345	3 058	1 194	289
1975 to 1978	258 304	13 684	10 273	19 695	46 960	61 210	49 561	26 697	18 961	7 083	4 180	280
1970 to 1974	477 430	28 091	20 058	42 371	93 224	118 297	87 358	44 049	29 194	8 501	6 287	272
1960 to 1969	643 530	31 927	29 968	80 064	148 952	159 904	97 825	46 168	30 785	8 732	9 205	258
1950 to 1959	387 618	31 318	36 206	75 321	97 546	70 318	34 685	16 467	11 626	3 964	10 167	224
1940 to 1949	345 850	34 018	44 822	79 995	84 866	51 275	23 059	10 737	7 551	2 767	6 760	206
1939 or earlier	846 504	65 194	138 477	220 868	194 908	108 834	50 682	23 763	18 632	9 840	15 306	198
YEAR HOUSEHOLDER MOVED INTO UNIT												
1979 to March 1980	1 362 535	58 225	97 296	213 747	300 380	286 813	190 721	97 519	71 380	25 792	20 662	250
1975 to 1978	1 028 176	72 002	89 771	173 994	240 835	203 958	121 307	58 289	38 383	13 521	16 116	235
1970 to 1974	343 009	42 932	43 006	65 434	73 322	56 403	29 602	14 171	9 346	3 092	5 701	212
1960 to 1969	202 959	24 885	32 057	45 809	43 882	27 892	12 734	5 875	3 945	1 164	4 716	196
1959 or earlier	99 542	12 378	22 007	25 616	18 110	8 940	3 436	1 735	1 040	376	5 904	174
ROOMS												
1 room	118 064	22 551	29 839	28 357	18 792	9 577	3 764	1 409	1 172	582	2 021	160
2 rooms	293 147	31 784	54 653	73 816	62 433	37 787	16 731	6 708	4 540	1 340	3 355	190
3 rooms	816 770	62 580	85 441	186 092	217 231	149 389	65 801	25 709	14 037	3 748	6 742	216
4 rooms	1 075 745	56 647	70 277	157 130	248 451	253 143	156 305	69 370	41 265	10 481	12 676	250
5 rooms	525 014	27 248	31 721	58 831	95 564	104 903	88 877	51 953	38 652	13 345	13 920	270
6 rooms	156 739	7 706	9 319	15 963	26 001	23 153	20 851	17 956	18 451	9 106	8 233	283
7 or more rooms	50 742	1 906	2 887	4 411	8 057	6 054	5 471	4 484	5 977	5 343	6 152	292
Median	3.8	3.3	3.2	3.4	3.7	3.9	4.1	4.3	4.5	4.9	4.6	...
BEDROOMS												
None	162 856	26 465	40 027	42 205	28 050	13 825	5 548	2 018	1 633	703	2 382	166
1	1 244 669	94 544	143 066	283 062	324 323	227 382	97 984	36 943	21 024	5 751	10 590	215
2	1 288 895	60 816	72 048	160 350	264 888	297 239	218 094	107 948	68 269	19 844	19 399	263
3	292 008	23 740	23 974	33 407	51 160	39 675	32 386	28 133	30 030	14 148	15 355	258
4	39 848	4 242	4 087	4 651	7 206	5 104	3 279	2 171	2 592	2 550	3 966	234
5 or more	7 945	615	935	925	902	781	509	376	546	949	1 407	244
PERSONS IN UNIT												
1 person	1 267 516	115 789	157 728	267 710	295 967	224 559	111 775	44 658	27 455	8 629	13 246	215
2 persons	888 634	35 455	58 966	132 127	190 418	193 007	133 862	68 544	47 278	16 059	12 918	255
3 persons	419 727	23 964	28 010	60 352	89 673	84 990	58 466	32 305	23 881	8 634	9 452	252
4 persons	249 520	16 348	17 951	33 672	55 118	46 144	31 555	19 113	14 959	6 008	8 652	248
5 persons	113 804	9 048	10 298	16 052	25 990	19 375	12 501	7 197	6 074	2 607	4 662	237
6 or more persons	97 020	9 818	11 184	14 687	19 363	15 931	9 641	5 772	4 447	2 008	4 169	228
Median	1.78	1.41	1.40	1.48	1.72	1.85	2.00	2.14	2.23	2.33	2.54	...
Total persons	6 410 391	430 646	547 156	1 001 484	1 393 033	1 234 097	797 721	426 209	312 085	117 851	150 109	...
PLUMBING FACILITIES BY PERSONS PER ROOM												
Complete plumbing for exclusive use	2 930 776	187 062	257 590	506 855	661 997	574 676	353 013	175 357	122 752	43 382	48 092	237
1.01 or more persons per room	185 921	14 045	20 539	36 004	43 615	32 811	18 105	8 952	6 353	1 927	3 570	224
Lacking complete plumbing for exclusive use	105 445	23 360	26 547	17 745	14 532	9 330	4 787	2 232	1 342	563	5 007	151
1.01 or more persons per room	15 373	2 229	2 938	2 826	2 588	1 604	895	394	249	142	1 508	181
HOUSEHOLD INCOME IN 1979												
Less than $5,000	690 693	142 669	112 748	147 001	133 170	81 231	36 312	14 469	8 705	2 464	11 924	179
$5,000 to $9,999	717 544	43 341	93 764	165 902	178 287	121 365	58 697	24 473	14 141	3 692	13 882	214
$10,000 to $12,499	355 995	8 982	26 770	68 196	98 902	76 620	39 341	16 975	10 409	2 797	7 003	236
$12,500 to $14,999	258 719	4 781	15 443	41 920	68 356	62 699	34 856	14 781	8 954	2 627	4 302	248
$15,000 to $19,999	422 973	5 414	18 896	53 487	100 459	107 632	70 668	33 423	20 589	5 580	6 825	264
$20,000 to $24,999	262 583	2 636	8 904	25 888	50 934	65 554	52 059	28 161	18 937	5 607	3 903	281
$25,000 to $34,999	222 762	1 718	5 598	16 125	34 933	51 096	46 467	30 167	24 738	8 953	2 967	300
$35,000 to $49,999	76 192	585	1 341	4 371	8 729	13 574	15 265	11 330	12 672	6 907	1 418	329
$50,000 or more	28 760	296	673	1 710	2 759	4 235	4 135	3 810	4 949	5 318	875	352
Median	$10 772	$3 986	$6 305	$8 423	$10 678	$13 010	$15 621	$17 527	$19 803	$24 235	$10 265	...
Mean	$12 960	$5 248	$7 988	$9 938	$12 001	$14 490	$16 961	$19 211	$21 961	$29 222	$13 015	...
SELECTED CHARACTERISTICS												
Heating equipment	3 036 221	210 422	284 137	524 600	676 529	584 006	357 800	177 589	124 094	43 945	53 099	235
Central heating system	2 589 014	163 936	208 273	417 138	584 168	527 545	330 027	164 507	114 738	40 661	38 021	242
Air conditioning	1 500 672	54 042	77 720	188 643	327 943	357 315	244 071	121 985	78 689	25 340	24 924	263
Central system	765 906	20 638	19 401	57 225	145 393	201 727	153 464	83 097	54 265	17 584	13 112	283
Vehicles available	2 187 169	70 959	146 788	335 866	497 119	475 124	309 620	157 719	111 768	38 590	43 616	252
1	1 524 293	61 219	120 761	268 632	373 756	325 296	187 773	87 555	56 454	17 300	25 547	240
2 or more	662 876	9 740	26 027	67 234	123 363	149 828	121 847	70 164	55 314	21 290	18 069	282
House heating fuel	2 999 383	207 865	279 148	516 866	668 724	578 841	355 237	176 288	122 901	43 035	50 478	235
Utility gas	1 651 535	128 503	174 829	309 336	363 524	297 303	182 069	88 409	63 229	21 937	22 396	228
Bottled, tank, or LP gas	54 321	3 823	6 906	11 424	11 455	8 325	4 527	1 867	1 165	473	4 356	212
Electricity	802 576	45 982	40 872	90 039	171 814	191 830	127 220	66 321	43 400	14 270	10 828	262
Fuel oil, kerosene, etc.	453 022	23 864	50 145	98 274	115 676	77 646	39 855	18 818	14 058	5 743	8 943	222
Other	37 929	5 693	6 396	7 793	6 255	3 737	1 566	873	1 049	612	3 955	181
Family householder	1 495 208	90 559	114 276	225 718	328 410	298 352	198 483	104 233	73 048	24 795	37 334	245
With own children under 18 years	851 709	65 203	67 315	127 463	193 294	161 828	105 205	55 190	39 217	12 911	24 083	240
With own children under 6 years	489 044	36 754	36 980	79 224	118 786	94 091	57 476	27 717	17 797	5 071	15 148	235
Female householder, no husband present	503 248	64 814	50 685	78 850	108 373	90 413	54 828	27 112	17 454	5 006	5 703	225
With own children under 18 years	380 074	52 625	38 131	58 071	82 579	67 964	40 645	19 814	12 577	3 483	4 185	224
With own children under 6 years	175 482	28 894	17 579	29 383	41 420	30 298	15 242	6 201	3 308	772	2 385	213
Nonfamily householder	1 541 013	119 863	169 861	298 882	348 119	285 654	159 317	73 356	51 046	19 150	15 765	225
Income in 1979 below poverty level	685 438	127 185	101 641	134 598	133 936	90 510	45 677	20 713	13 432	4 591	13 155	190
Percent below poverty level	22.6	60.4	35.8	25.7	19.8	15.5	12.8	11.7	10.8	10.4	24.8	...
GROSS RENT AS PERCENTAGE OF HOUSEHOLD INCOME IN 1979												
Less than 15 percent	540 263	57 501	70 150	105 127	116 724	92 949	52 691	23 872	15 198	6 051	...	216
15 to 19 percent	484 589	33 128	39 466	78 235	108 587	101 876	65 084	31 598	20 301	6 314	...	242
20 to 24 percent	430 479	38 259	32 443	68 484	95 536	85 956	56 099	28 612	18 923	6 167	...	240
25 to 29 percent	320 197	24 078	26 165	50 664	74 478	63 936	40 211	20 997	14 847	4 821	...	240
30 to 34 percent	224 626	14 167	18 998	35 584	50 747	48 069	28 728	14 083	10 741	3 509	...	243
35 to 49 percent	376 448	18 533	40 104	65 787	81 305	72 928	47 456	25 101	18 362	6 872	...	239
50 percent or more	547 638	17 877	48 974	108 504	136 273	108 541	62 540	31 079	24 179	9 671	...	236
Not computed	111 981	6 879	7 837	12 215	12 879	9 751	4 991	2 247	1 543	540	53 099	210
Median	25.1	21.5	24.4	25.4	25.7	25.5	25.3	25.9	27.3	28.3	...	...

Table G— 5. Gross Rent of Renter-Occupied Housing Units: 1980—Con.

Housing Units in Structures With 5 to 9 Units—Total—Con.

[Data are estimates based on a sample; see Introduction. For meaning of symbols, see Introduction. For definitions of terms, see appendix A]

United States	Total	Less than $100	$100 to $149	$150 to $199	$200 to $249	$250 to $299	$300 to $349	$350 to $399	$400 to $499	$500 or more	No cash rent	Median (dollars)
AGE OF HOUSEHOLDER												
Persons 15 years and over	3 036 221	210 422	284 137	524 600	676 529	584 006	357 800	177 589	124 094	43 945	53 099	235
15 to 19 years	69 665	4 012	7 494	15 846	17 354	12 788	6 499	2 602	1 520	597	953	220
20 to 24 years	561 410	21 748	41 341	104 141	138 954	123 049	68 982	30 291	18 735	5 792	8 377	239
25 to 29 years	601 230	22 260	38 133	93 595	145 896	133 984	83 681	40 081	25 494	8 059	10 047	249
30 to 34 years	391 370	15 976	26 598	55 569	89 248	82 991	56 410	28 966	21 457	7 154	7 001	253
35 to 39 years	231 735	11 233	17 878	33 493	49 655	45 861	31 776	17 673	13 914	5 939	4 313	252
40 to 44 years	162 848	9 893	14 923	25 598	34 727	31 013	19 973	11 641	8 542	3 639	2 899	243
45 to 49 years	140 565	9 332	14 428	24 832	29 448	24 949	16 523	8 881	6 930	2 704	2 538	235
50 to 54 years	145 661	11 819	17 601	26 453	29 793	24 827	14 778	8 519	6 451	2 570	2 850	226
55 to 59 years	143 488	13 456	18 271	28 585	28 158	22 979	14 133	7 353	5 337	2 235	2 981	218
60 to 64 years	136 777	15 388	19 784	27 669	27 125	20 373	11 807	6 139	4 492	1 404	2 596	208
65 to 69 years	136 473	20 176	19 828	26 988	26 662	19 853	10 367	5 201	3 602	1 195	2 601	200
70 to 74 years	123 228	20 372	18 292	23 684	23 146	17 112	9 607	4 355	3 454	1 036	2 170	196
75 years and over	191 771	34 757	29 566	38 147	36 363	24 227	13 264	5 887	4 166	1 621	3 773	189
Median	33.7	54.6	43.6	34.4	32.0	31.3	31.7	32.7	33.8	35.3	35 2	...
MARITAL STATUS OF HOUSEHOLDER												
Persons 15 years and over	3 036 221	210 422	284 137	524 600	676 529	584 006	357 800	177 589	124 094	43 945	53 099	235
Single	970 032	55 184	90 815	181 472	230 336	194 497	108 906	51 323	35 578	13 204	8 717	233
Now married, except separated	954 478	25 857	62 014	142 181	212 412	199 117	136 934	73 147	52 476	18 706	31 634	255
Separated	225 115	26 281	27 113	39 881	48 833	39 429	21 893	10 548	6 621	2 221	2 295	219
Widowed	356 608	63 692	52 140	70 825	69 683	48 665	25 184	11 066	7 321	2 285	5 747	192
Divorced	529 988	39 408	52 055	90 241	115 265	102 298	64 883	31 505	22 098	7 529	4 706	235
YEARS OF SCHOOL COMPLETED BY HOUSEHOLDER												
Persons 25 years old and over	2 405 146	184 662	235 302	404 613	520 221	448 169	282 319	144 696	103 839	37 556	43 769	234
Median	12.5	9.6	11.1	12.2	12.5	12.8	13.0	13.5	14.1	15.3	12.4	...
PERIOD OF SERVICE OF HOUSEHOLDER												
Civilian veterans 16 years and over	484 635	21 856	44 785	77 602	99 149	94 791	64 489	36 212	27 636	10 221	7 894	247
Percent of civilians 16 years and over	16.4	10.4	15.9	15.1	15.2	16.6	18.3	20.7	22.7	23.8	19.7	...
May 1975 or later only	33 561	1 092	2 592	6 202	8 438	7 296	4 331	1 803	1 074	271	462	239
Vietnam era	180 401	4 051	12 109	26 499	39 746	39 971	27 380	14 753	10 365	3 421	2 106	258
February 1955 to July 1964 only	41 627	1 406	2 855	5 936	8 294	8 555	5 956	3 536	3 096	1 294	699	262
Vietnam era and Korean conflict	8 065	267	587	1 039	1 342	1 663	1 340	891	531	255	150	272
Korean conflict	50 846	2 109	4 862	8 097	10 220	9 327	6 667	3 997	3 356	1 339	872	249
Korean conflict and World War II	11 152	549	1 301	1 853	2 012	1 866	1 349	951	802	297	172	244
World War II	140 807	10 306	17 944	24 758	25 418	23 435	15 892	9 387	7 620	3 018	3 029	231
World War I	9 091	886	1 281	1 450	1 843	1 369	896	534	434	208	190	223
Other	9 085	1 190	1 254	1 768	1 836	1 309	678	360	358	118	214	206
Civilian nonveterans 16 years and over	2 476 819	188 346	237 417	436 633	552 337	477 200	287 187	138 721	94 163	32 705	32 110	233
LABOR FORCE STATUS OF HOUSEHOLDER												
Persons 16 years and over	3 035 741	210 381	284 112	524 494	676 402	583 925	357 771	177 558	124 084	43 942	53 072	235
Labor force	2 176 191	66 807	161 128	356 792	506 177	461 792	293 701	148 063	104 889	37 204	39 638	248
Percent of persons 16 years and over	71.7	31.8	56.7	68.0	74.8	79.1	82.1	83.4	84.5	84.7	74.7	...
Armed Forces	74 287	179	1 910	10 259	24 916	11 934	6 095	2 625	2 285	1 016	13 068	237
Civilian labor force	2 101 904	66 628	159 218	346 533	481 261	449 858	287 606	145 438	102 604	36 188	26 570	248
Employed	1 953 958	52 472	141 110	316 083	448 607	424 965	273 686	138 938	98 611	34 756	24 730	251
Unemployed	147 946	14 156	18 108	30 450	32 654	24 893	13 920	6 500	3 993	1 432	1 840	216
Percent of civilian labor force	7.0	21.2	11.4	8.8	6.8	5.5	4.8	4.5	3.9	4.0	6.9	...
Not in labor force	859 550	143 574	122 984	167 702	170 225	122 133	64 070	29 495	19 195	6 738	13 434	197
OCCUPATION OF HOUSEHOLDER												
Employed persons 16 years and over	1 953 958	52 472	141 110	316 083	448 607	424 965	273 686	138 938	98 611	34 756	24 730	251
Managerial and professional specialty occupations	474 743	4 797	17 798	54 770	96 265	110 620	83 241	46 339	38 058	16 438	6 417	277
Executive, administrative, and managerial occupations	201 726	1 602	6 362	19 976	38 042	46 097	37 078	22 353	18 755	8 164	3 297	286
Professional specialty occupations	273 017	3 195	11 436	34 794	58 223	64 523	46 163	23 986	19 303	8 274	3 120	271
Technical, sales, and administrative support occupations	587 154	9 741	33 039	88 489	138 081	136 080	89 429	46 102	31 946	10 596	3 651	258
Technicians and related support occupations	81 839	847	4 346	11 740	19 318	20 092	12 757	6 525	4 517	1 315	382	261
Sales occupations	163 361	3 019	8 055	20 191	32 266	35 523	27 913	16 645	12 944	5 276	1 529	274
Administrative support occupations, including clerical	341 954	5 875	20 638	56 558	86 497	80 465	48 759	22 932	14 485	4 005	1 740	250
Service occupations	271 312	18 318	32 947	54 909	61 264	48 978	27 447	12 347	8 620	2 681	3 801	223
Private household occupations	13 429	2 910	2 472	2 675	2 415	1 402	712	280	210	75	278	172
Protective service occupations	33 749	1 001	2 489	5 823	7 578	7 505	4 966	2 012	1 532	401	442	248
Service occupations, except protective and household	224 134	14 407	27 986	46 411	51 271	40 071	21 769	10 055	6 878	2 205	3 081	221
Farming, forestry, and fishing occupations	26 923	1 954	3 220	4 756	5 016	3 786	1 731	1 011	755	225	4 469	213
Precision production, craft, and repair occupations	224 269	4 977	15 579	35 822	52 697	51 141	32 051	16 238	10 010	2 734	3 020	229
Operators, fabricators, and laborers	369 557	12 685	38 527	77 337	95 284	74 360	39 787	16 901	9 222	2 082	3 372	227
Machine operators, assemblers, and inspectors	194 315	6 079	20 258	41 859	52 148	38 936	20 247	8 317	4 331	847	1 293	227
Transportation and material moving occupations	84 858	2 472	7 639	15 446	21 072	18 142	10 351	5 043	2 936	754	1 003	239
Handlers, equipment cleaners, helpers, and laborers	90 384	4 134	10 630	20 032	22 064	17 282	9 189	3 541	1 955	481	1 076	222
MEANS OF TRANSPORTATION TO WORK FOR HOUSEHOLDER												
Workers 16 years and over	1 973 688	49 827	137 371	316 134	460 930	426 800	273 567	138 643	98 600	34 922	36 894	250
Private vehicle	1 512 668	29 011	87 200	222 101	353 826	347 085	228 371	115 088	79 989	25 623	24 374	257
Drive alone: Car	1 081 898	17 577	57 695	154 612	252 144	252 580	167 757	85 277	60 609	19 553	14 094	260
Truck or van	104 658	2 039	6 185	14 204	24 204	23 324	15 396	7 935	5 472	1 638	4 219	258
Carpool: Car	286 872	7 966	19 897	46 764	68 721	63 102	39 879	19 726	12 382	3 926	4 509	248
Truck or van	39 240	1 429	3 423	6 479	8 757	8 079	5 339	2 150	1 526	506	1 552	243
Public transportation	243 072	10 131	23 551	47 659	60 547	45 727	25 986	13 226	10 276	4 693	1 276	233
Bus or streetcar	164 770	8 705	18 189	34 385	40 709	29 410	16 451	7 967	6 034	2 022	898	225
Subway or elevated train	61 001	855	4 178	10 949	16 329	12 846	7 035	3 627	3 037	1 836	309	244
Railroad	10 815	47	238	973	2 222	2 448	2 067	1 281	986	518	35	289
Taxicab	6 486	524	946	1 352	1 287	1 023	433	351	219	317	34	216
Bicycle	16 415	521	1 725	3 202	3 879	2 938	1 654	686	762	350	698	231
Motorcycle	11 410	92	653	1 519	2 905	2 320	1 755	830	563	239	534	256
Walked only	160 055	8 800	21 975	37 678	34 513	24 209	12 621	6 606	4 988	2 507	6 158	212
Other means	12 919	633	1 230	2 089	2 788	2 124	1 325	867	578	394	891	237
Worked at home	17 149	639	1 037	1 886	2 472	2 397	1 855	1 340	1 444	1 116	2 963	272
WORKERS IN HOUSEHOLD IN 1979												
No workers	658 581	125 468	101 263	131 181	128 309	86 862	42 646	18 362	11 374	3 660	9 456	187
1 worker	1 436 814	66 948	137 037	275 849	352 604	286 976	160 346	72 071	47 083	15 365	22 535	232
2 workers	818 008	14 441	39 132	104 733	175 736	187 258	136 613	73 334	52 250	17 529	16 982	268
3 or more workers	122 818	3 565	6 705	12 837	19 880	22 910	18 195	13 822	13 387	7 391	4 126	286

Table G— 6. **Gross Rent of Renter-Occupied Housing Units: 1980**

Housing Units in Structures With 10 to 19 Units—Total

[Data are estimates based on a sample; see Introduction. For meaning of symbols, see Introduction. For definitions of terms, see appendix A]

United States	Total	Less than $100	$100 to $149	$150 to $199	$200 to $249	$250 to $299	$300 to $349	$350 to $399	$400 to $499	$500 or more	No cash rent	Median (dollars)
Specified renter-occupied housing units	3 231 111	186 701	229 812	450 715	710 782	729 942	465 945	224 294	143 759	46 057	43 104	251
YEAR STRUCTURE BUILT												
1979 to March 1980	108 339	7 644	5 371	6 742	14 433	23 880	20 109	13 723	10 739	4 355	1 343	290
1975 to 1978	354 068	17 746	12 224	22 855	65 666	92 129	68 903	37 499	24 912	8 234	3 900	281
1970 to 1974	676 079	33 208	21 297	51 784	135 770	182 633	132 683	65 155	38 422	9 434	5 693	275
1960 to 1969	890 109	30 794	30 405	94 994	214 399	244 351	150 941	66 302	38 816	9 823	9 284	264
1950 to 1959	376 371	21 896	31 267	70 080	94 070	77 956	41 863	17 675	11 634	3 784	6 146	233
1940 to 1949	263 943	24 752	33 094	61 587	63 619	40 583	19 050	8 115	5 755	2 478	4 910	208
1939 or earlier	562 202	50 661	96 154	142 673	122 825	68 410	32 396	15 825	13 481	7 949	11 828	195
YEAR HOUSEHOLDER MOVED INTO UNIT												
1979 to March 1980	1 553 281	54 825	82 859	190 588	337 858	379 084	251 504	127 520	84 832	27 800	16 411	263
1975 to 1978	1 078 417	66 081	71 309	149 098	244 551	247 737	157 647	72 106	43 167	13 101	13 620	250
1970 to 1974	339 470	36 391	34 338	54 344	74 319	65 516	38 035	16 918	10 822	3 165	5 622	228
1960 to 1969	185 533	19 256	24 471	37 748	41 180	30 865	15 727	6 624	4 047	1 480	4 135	211
1959 or earlier	74 410	10 148	16 835	18 937	12 874	6 740	3 032	1 126	891	511	3 316	173
ROOMS												
1 room	181 193	26 982	38 386	43 722	34 770	19 660	7 813	3 379	2 241	1 490	2 750	177
2 rooms	364 470	28 981	48 006	87 356	92 329	57 634	26 636	10 921	6 407	2 289	3 911	209
3 rooms	987 385	61 180	68 601	171 552	282 329	226 577	104 096	38 900	20 435	5 412	8 303	233
4 rooms	1 088 154	43 727	47 287	105 302	224 664	300 924	200 935	88 897	52 424	12 242	11 752	269
5 rooms	469 065	19 631	20 013	32 965	62 702	105 991	104 239	60 647	40 774	13 015	9 088	295
6 rooms	108 753	4 761	5 762	7 695	11 483	15 512	18 466	17 440	16 560	7 067	4 007	319
7 or more rooms	32 091	1 439	1 757	2 123	2 505	3 644	3 760	4 110	4 918	4 542	3 293	339
Median	3.6	3.1	2.9	3.0	3.3	3.7	4.0	4.2	4.3	4.6	4.1	...
BEDROOMS												
None	244 784	30 876	49 415	65 458	49 520	26 886	10 389	4 439	2 946	1 667	3 188	181
1	1 479 843	88 602	110 937	260 050	417 839	339 580	156 015	57 195	29 383	7 945	12 297	233
2	1 282 221	47 898	50 341	104 233	217 018	336 533	270 772	134 117	81 799	22 276	17 234	282
3	196 772	16 304	15 663	17 726	23 400	24 082	26 899	26 829	27 115	10 997	7 757	294
4	22 251	2 463	2 885	2 711	2 641	2 426	1 577	1 403	2 116	2 338	1 691	242
5 or more	5 240	558	571	537	364	435	293	311	400	834	937	264
PERSONS IN UNIT												
1 person	1 482 640	113 211	131 901	254 718	374 985	320 945	163 047	62 795	35 812	11 461	13 765	231
2 persons	983 450	30 909	47 653	106 713	198 183	247 925	178 157	88 942	56 002	17 110	11 856	271
3 persons	401 976	18 103	21 817	44 728	74 044	91 843	71 511	39 004	25 633	8 324	6 969	271
4 persons	212 817	11 658	13 410	23 882	36 966	43 816	34 499	21 332	16 590	5 325	5 339	270
5 persons	84 930	6 769	7 555	11 135	15 116	14 729	11 424	7 608	5 739	2 159	2 696	252
6 or more persons	65 298	6 051	7 476	9 539	11 488	10 684	7 307	4 613	3 983	1 678	2 479	236
Median	1.64	1.32	1.37	1.38	1.45	1.68	1.89	2.05	2.14	2.18	2.16	...
Total persons	6 272 209	342 547	424 871	798 363	1 268 872	1 395 780	969 166	506 657	343 734	114 883	107 336	...
PLUMBING FACILITIES BY PERSONS PER ROOM												
Complete plumbing for exclusive use	3 128 731	164 558	205 466	435 080	697 061	718 710	459 831	221 475	142 102	45 468	38 980	253
1.01 or more persons per room	175 250	10 560	17 417	33 854	39 899	32 858	19 019	9 557	6 568	2 235	3 283	230
Lacking complete plumbing for exclusive use	102 380	22 143	24 346	15 635	13 721	11 232	6 114	2 819	1 657	589	4 124	158
1.01 or more persons per room	12 993	1 846	2 593	2 310	2 132	1 562	821	438	313	91	887	185
HOUSEHOLD INCOME IN 1979												
Less than $5,000	666 337	129 747	92 845	129 586	134 476	93 108	43 942	18 550	10 432	3 359	10 292	191
$5,000 to $9,999	727 906	36 866	76 614	143 783	189 306	147 342	73 459	29 661	15 997	3 989	10 889	227
$10,000 to $12,499	380 837	7 214	20 840	56 089	104 018	98 117	50 989	21 118	11 891	2 688	4 880	248
$12,500 to $14,999	285 739	3 995	11 936	34 044	73 247	80 697	46 481	19 326	10 230	2 467	3 316	261
$15,000 to $19,999	485 115	4 658	14 858	45 241	106 853	140 125	95 385	42 647	23 913	6 041	5 394	274
$20,000 to $24,999	306 680	2 087	6 529	20 478	55 439	85 373	68 777	36 023	22 748	5 960	3 266	289
$25,000 to $34,999	258 145	1 457	4 345	13 193	35 203	62 864	61 923	38 035	28 788	9 359	2 978	308
$35,000 to $49,999	87 614	381	1 176	3 650	9 114	17 327	19 377	14 366	14 370	6 676	1 177	330
$50,000 or more	32 738	296	669	1 658	3 126	4 989	5 612	4 568	5 390	5 518	912	346
Median	$11 453	$3 952	$6 192	$8 257	$10 760	$13 318	$15 869	$17 561	$19 869	$23 398	$10 190	...
Mean	$13 562	$5 119	$7 954	$9 765	$12 085	$14 654	$17 190	$19 175	$21 806	$28 762	$13 465	...
SELECTED CHARACTERISTICS												
Heating equipment	3 231 111	186 701	229 812	450 715	710 782	729 942	465 945	224 294	143 759	46 057	43 104	251
Central heating system	2 907 259	155 309	183 358	381 108	643 468	681 254	439 666	211 866	135 343	43 233	32 654	255
Air conditioning	2 009 126	58 494	69 132	197 935	445 873	541 097	364 169	173 797	104 768	30 672	23 189	270
Central system	1 105 641	25 899	21 519	68 358	215 771	324 094	232 327	117 147	68 677	20 379	11 470	283
Vehicles available	2 410 434	60 531	111 231	276 566	532 404	615 225	411 562	200 928	128 240	39 437	34 310	267
1	1 668 189	52 891	92 089	225 243	407 041	422 805	253 168	110 499	65 803	18 474	20 176	256
2 or more	742 245	7 640	19 142	51 323	125 363	192 420	158 394	90 429	62 437	20 963	14 134	292
House heating fuel	3 192 340	183 400	224 059	442 335	703 711	724 288	462 938	222 338	142 524	45 290	41 457	252
Utility gas	1 578 907	101 763	128 708	246 652	351 720	341 074	212 815	97 521	62 003	18 798	17 853	243
Bottled, tank, or LP gas	45 560	3 340	5 217	8 457	9 425	7 712	4 242	1 800	1 377	306	3 684	221
Electricity	1 093 522	46 399	40 545	100 702	240 115	289 043	189 915	95 993	60 970	19 003	10 837	270
Fuel oil, kerosene, etc.	438 745	27 096	43 678	77 912	96 007	82 379	54 097	26 225	17 633	6 864	6 854	235
Other	35 606	4 802	5 911	8 612	6 444	4 080	1 869	799	541	319	2 229	185
Family householder	1 425 905	69 550	87 945	169 823	277 682	326 475	238 231	124 158	80 453	24 455	27 133	264
With own children under 18 years	738 651	48 326	49 379	93 215	142 526	158 776	116 609	62 994	39 917	11 711	15 198	259
With own children under 6 years	428 543	28 636	27 793	58 161	89 319	95 423	64 973	32 144	18 287	4 842	8 965	253
Female householder, no husband present	438 434	48 119	37 302	59 365	85 085	88 761	61 211	31 218	18 479	4 684	4 210	243
With own children under 18 years	322 584	38 911	27 529	44 146	63 129	64 501	43 618	22 060	12 649	3 187	2 854	239
With own children under 6 years	145 879	22 273	12 973	22 429	31 501	28 366	15 627	6 928	3 405	866	1 511	223
Nonfamily householder	1 805 206	117 151	141 867	280 892	433 100	403 467	227 714	100 136	63 306	21 602	15 971	241
Income in 1979 below poverty level	634 446	109 160	80 150	113 792	125 844	97 693	52 317	24 451	15 225	5 187	10 627	203
Percent below poverty level	19.6	58.5	34.9	25.2	17.7	13.4	11.2	10.9	10.6	11.3	24.7	...
GROSS RENT AS PERCENTAGE OF HOUSEHOLD INCOME IN 1979												
Less than 15 percent	546 737	47 739	54 745	85 837	120 610	115 930	68 210	30 287	17 126	6 253	...	235
15 to 19 percent	531 259	29 617	30 987	66 489	116 207	131 767	87 045	39 960	23 179	6 008	...	258
20 to 24 percent	477 621	35 941	27 246	59 290	101 066	111 942	76 182	36 676	22 732	6 546	...	257
25 to 29 percent	356 723	24 061	22 066	43 741	79 961	84 171	53 612	26 567	17 545	4 999	...	255
30 to 34 percent	244 992	12 752	15 476	30 890	53 630	59 368	38 358	18 222	12 465	3 831	...	258
35 to 49 percent	401 048	15 905	32 745	57 782	87 368	88 956	59 279	30 675	21 041	7 297	...	254
50 percent or more	566 148	14 627	38 939	94 327	137 487	126 858	77 072	38 810	27 727	10 301	...	249
Not computed	106 583	6 059	7 608	12 359	14 453	10 950	6 187	3 097	1 944	822	43 104	220
Median	25.1	21.8	24.7	25.9	25.6	25.0	24.9	25.7	27.2	28.8	...	...

Table G— 6. Gross Rent of Renter-Occupied Housing Units: 1980—Con.

Housing Units in Structures With 10 to 19 Units—Total—Con.

[Data are estimates based on a sample; see Introduction. For meaning of symbols, see Introduction. For definitions of terms, see appendix A]

United States	Total	Less than $100	$100 to $149	$150 to $199	$200 to $249	$250 to $299	$300 to $349	$350 to $399	$400 to $499	$500 or more	No cash rent	Median (dollars)
AGE OF HOUSEHOLDER												
Persons 15 years and over	3 231 111	186 701	229 812	450 715	710 782	729 942	465 945	224 294	143 759	46 057	43 104	251
15 to 19 years	76 949	3 760	5 355	13 217	20 312	17 814	9 210	3 603	2 356	605	717	239
20 to 24 years	634 337	17 798	31 390	87 080	161 316	166 440	94 035	41 535	22 736	6 123	5 884	255
25 to 29 years	648 354	16 747	28 997	77 831	151 914	170 938	108 942	49 661	28 614	7 809	6 901	263
30 to 34 years	409 888	11 954	20 702	48 965	87 359	99 283	70 676	35 537	23 380	7 230	4 802	267
35 to 39 years	238 631	8 676	14 562	29 359	48 139	52 972	38 971	22 164	15 171	5 296	3 321	266
40 to 44 years	168 908	7 530	12 770	23 080	33 732	35 060	25 921	14 140	10 131	3 663	2 881	258
45 to 49 years	144 848	8 108	12 057	20 962	28 873	29 155	20 506	11 365	7 813	3 248	2 761	252
50 to 54 years	148 388	9 919	14 150	23 707	30 010	28 113	19 235	10 046	7 610	2 727	2 871	242
55 to 59 years	149 500	11 795	14 779	24 539	29 303	28 496	18 813	9 748	6 891	2 208	2 851	238
60 to 64 years	138 155	14 000	15 885	23 628	27 676	24 391	15 144	7 678	5 323	1 579	2 365	226
65 to 69 years	139 629	19 495	17 266	23 449	26 861	24 002	14 135	6 131	4 594	1 331	2 365	216
70 to 74 years	128 185	20 886	16 001	20 381	24 543	20 914	12 832	5 471	3 697	1 519	1 941	212
75 years and over	205 339	36 033	25 898	34 517	40 744	32 364	17 525	7 215	5 443	2 719	2 881	206
Median	33.1	58.8	45.5	34.8	31.3	30.5	31.5	32.4	33.9	36.2	39.9	...
MARITAL STATUS OF HOUSEHOLDER												
Persons 15 years and over	3 231 111	186 701	229 812	450 715	710 782	729 942	465 945	224 294	143 759	46 057	43 104	251
Single	1 115 734	46 994	72 493	167 780	279 750	265 586	151 125	67 170	42 715	13 732	8 389	248
Now married, except separated	952 675	21 940	50 190	108 182	187 125	228 220	168 489	88 230	58 857	18 784	22 658	271
Separated	225 855	21 089	22 602	34 154	47 742	45 164	28 639	13 739	8 185	2 210	2 331	236
Widowed	358 873	61 614	42 837	59 875	71 246	59 878	32 379	14 055	8 980	3 361	4 648	209
Divorced	577 974	35 064	41 690	80 724	124 919	131 094	85 313	41 100	25 022	7 970	5 078	252
YEARS OF SCHOOL COMPLETED BY HOUSEHOLDER												
Persons 25 years old and over	2 519 825	165 143	193 067	350 418	529 154	545 688	362 700	179 156	118 667	39 329	36 503	250
Median	12.7	9.5	11.3	12.3	12.7	12.9	13.0	13.5	14.1	15.2	12.3	...
PERIOD OF SERVICE OF HOUSEHOLDER												
Civilian veterans 16 years and over	551 447	19 558	36 548	70 057	111 362	125 360	88 758	47 157	32 335	10 941	9 371	263
Percent of civilians 16 years and over	17.3	10.5	16.0	15.7	16.0	17.3	19.3	21.3	22.8	24.0	23.3	...
May 1975 or later only	38 214	908	2 022	5 320	9 717	10 204	5 763	2 281	1 259	251	489	254
Vietnam era	207 492	2 895	8 849	23 641	44 036	53 946	37 597	19 063	11 730	3 249	2 486	271
February 1955 to July 1964 only	48 461	1 013	2 428	5 464	9 676	11 187	7 964	5 144	3 339	1 313	933	273
Vietnam era and Korean conflict	10 212	217	493	1 082	1 996	2 286	1 720	1 058	859	348	153	277
Korean conflict	57 428	1 890	4 493	7 687	11 019	11 670	8 890	5 150	3 833	1 728	1 068	263
Korean conflict and World War II	13 095	542	941	1 627	2 180	2 749	2 189	1 239	992	370	266	270
World War II	157 386	9 977	15 154	22 205	28 919	30 060	22 311	12 250	9 577	3 280	3 653	251
World War I	10 114	1 036	1 055	1 324	2 082	1 911	1 377	466	467	272	124	238
Other	9 045	1 080	1 113	1 707	1 737	1 347	947	506	279	130	199	215
Civilian nonveterans 16 years and over	2 630 991	167 005	192 138	374 753	585 821	592 014	370 062	174 093	109 571	34 630	30 904	248
LABOR FORCE STATUS OF HOUSEHOLDER												
Persons 16 years and over	3 230 652	186 655	229 788	450 605	710 713	729 845	465 905	224 260	143 750	46 052	43 079	251
Labor force	2 383 097	53 957	125 387	304 619	542 653	590 006	388 089	188 666	119 436	37 328	32 956	263
Percent of persons 16 years and over	73.8	28.9	54.6	67.6	76.4	80.8	83.3	84.1	83.1	81.1	76.5	...
Armed Forces	48 214	92	1 102	5 795	13 530	12 471	7 085	3 010	1 844	481	2 804	259
Civilian labor force	2 334 883	53 865	124 285	298 824	529 123	577 535	381 004	185 656	117 592	36 847	30 152	263
Employed	2 194 564	43 112	110 454	274 412	497 481	549 140	364 499	177 980	113 202	35 539	28 745	264
Unemployed	140 319	10 753	13 831	24 412	31 642	28 395	16 505	7 676	4 390	1 308	1 407	232
Percent of civilian labor force	6.0	20.0	11.1	8.2	6.0	4.9	4.3	4.1	3.7	3.5	4.7	...
Not in labor force	847 555	132 698	104 401	145 986	168 060	139 839	77 816	35 594	24 314	8 724	10 123	211
OCCUPATION OF HOUSEHOLDER												
Employed persons 16 years and over	2 194 564	43 112	110 454	274 412	497 481	549 140	364 499	177 980	113 202	35 539	28 745	264
Managerial and professional specialty occupations	575 101	4 036	14 360	49 157	115 273	150 199	111 967	59 921	43 824	16 588	9 776	283
Executive, administrative, and managerial occupations	254 356	1 742	5 155	18 471	46 887	64 453	51 532	28 943	21 999	8 492	6 682	290
Professional specialty occupations	320 745	2 294	9 205	30 686	68 386	85 746	60 435	30 978	21 825	8 096	3 094	278
Technical, sales, and administrative support occupations	704 846	8 021	26 207	83 356	165 481	186 213	123 973	59 855	37 185	10 935	3 620	268
Technicians and related support occupations	101 634	748	3 204	11 437	23 513	27 919	19 284	8 477	5 384	1 330	338	271
Sales occupations	198 627	2 369	7 016	19 227	39 679	49 723	37 481	21 160	14 882	5 686	1 404	280
Administrative support occupations, including clerical	404 585	4 904	15 987	52 692	102 289	108 571	67 208	30 218	16 919	3 919	1 878	262
Service occupations	285 679	15 218	27 822	50 894	63 734	57 428	36 175	16 819	9 760	2 682	5 147	236
Private household occupations	11 065	1 968	1 712	2 652	1 923	1 418	720	330	140	35	167	183
Protective service occupations	37 731	732	2 180	4 859	8 550	9 580	6 296	3 033	1 581	335	585	262
Service occupations, except protective and household	236 883	12 518	23 930	43 383	53 261	46 430	29 159	13 456	8 039	2 312	4 395	234
Farming, forestry, and fishing occupations	26 533	1 684	2 836	4 255	5 022	4 353	2 512	1 076	615	229	3 951	225
Precision production, craft, and repair occupations	242 848	3 606	10 855	28 413	55 450	64 231	42 086	20 642	11 485	2 919	3 161	267
Operators, fabricators, and laborers	359 557	10 547	28 374	58 337	92 521	86 716	47 786	19 667	10 333	2 186	3 090	244
Machine operators, assemblers, and inspectors	181 202	5 035	14 458	30 402	47 940	44 092	23 243	9 160	4 681	942	1 249	242
Transportation and material moving occupations	90 677	2 152	6 012	12 827	21 905	22 812	13 648	6 125	3 471	818	907	254
Handlers, equipment cleaners, helpers, and laborers	87 678	3 360	7 904	15 108	22 676	19 812	10 895	4 382	2 181	426	934	237
MEANS OF TRANSPORTATION TO WORK FOR HOUSEHOLDER												
Workers 16 years and over	2 187 846	40 309	107 098	271 760	498 855	549 788	364 141	177 303	112 571	35 247	30 774	265
Private vehicle	1 701 553	22 291	62 223	182 120	385 919	458 459	308 725	148 566	91 724	25 627	15 899	271
Drive alone: Car	1 240 703	13 850	41 781	129 952	282 107	336 843	227 917	110 294	69 271	19 523	9 165	272
Truck or van	112 090	1 333	4 296	11 558	24 747	29 910	19 474	10 052	5 897	1 728	3 095	271
Carpool: Car	307 541	5 889	13 437	35 687	69 842	81 785	54 674	25 050	14 832	3 726	2 619	267
Truck or van	41 219	1 219	2 709	4 923	9 223	9 921	6 660	3 170	1 724	650	1 020	260
Public transportation	266 830	8 310	22 569	49 237	66 828	53 933	32 160	16 278	11 501	4 788	1 226	239
Bus or streetcar	179 668	6 714	15 873	31 657	46 221	36 313	20 002	9 789	6 297	2 025	817	234
Subway or elevated train	67 021	1 130	5 630	11 530	17 205	13 331	8 477	4 127	3 480	1 761	350	244
Railroad	13 065	61	319	870	2 129	3 013	2 846	1 895	1 359	550	23	302
Taxicab	7 076	405	747	1 220	1 273	1 276	835	467	365	452	36	245
Bicycle	15 552	367	1 682	2 834	3 453	3 290	1 851	996	642	246	191	241
Motorcycle	11 821	102	500	1 301	2 875	2 914	2 113	973	631	236	176	268
Walked only	156 681	7 923	17 986	32 066	34 591	25 771	14 662	7 743	5 593	2 693	7 653	224
Other means	14 017	538	1 006	2 097	2 465	2 595	2 009	948	794	324	1 241	255
Worked at home	21 392	778	1 132	2 105	2 724	2 826	2 621	1 799	1 686	1 333	4 388	281
WORKERS IN HOUSEHOLD IN 1979												
No workers	650 262	118 625	86 765	116 533	127 699	98 809	52 880	22 104	13 964	5 490	7 393	200
1 worker	1 585 510	54 540	107 081	245 350	398 397	376 304	215 988	94 484	56 793	16 842	19 731	247
2 workers	877 132	10 614	30 865	79 504	168 691	231 933	175 293	92 210	58 073	17 194	12 755	281
3 or more workers	118 207	2 922	5 101	9 328	15 995	22 896	21 784	15 496	14 929	6 531	3 225	303

467

Table G— 7. Gross Rent of Renter-Occupied Housing Units: 1980

Housing Units in Structures With 20 to 49 Units—Total

[Data are estimates based on a sample; see Introduction. For meaning of symbols, see Introduction. For definitions of terms, see appendix A]

United States	Total	Less than $100	$100 to $149	$150 to $199	$200 to $249	$250 to $299	$300 to $349	$350 to $399	$400 to $499	$500 or more	No cash rent	Median (dollars)
Specified renter-occupied housing units	2 446 337	142 452	187 687	354 282	547 527	523 408	323 552	162 818	122 019	49 132	33 460	248
YEAR STRUCTURE BUILT												
1979 to March 1980	65 932	9 260	5 168	4 282	8 376	12 532	10 428	6 337	5 906	2 656	987	271
1975 to 1978	226 522	19 286	9 586	16 363	42 607	53 172	38 347	20 795	16 388	7 443	2 535	273
1970 to 1974	436 669	26 443	13 528	31 974	87 913	111 722	79 599	41 432	29 093	10 352	4 613	275
1960 to 1969	628 214	21 882	19 196	59 867	145 920	166 241	106 333	50 940	38 076	12 005	7 754	269
1950 to 1959	284 264	14 042	24 993	45 003	68 760	60 592	33 743	16 478	12 386	4 176	4 091	241
1940 to 1949	229 385	14 013	26 683	49 066	57 242	41 081	19 906	9 242	6 148	2 773	3 231	220
1939 or earlier	575 351	37 526	88 533	147 727	136 709	78 068	35 196	17 594	14 022	9 727	10 249	203
YEAR HOUSEHOLDER MOVED INTO UNIT												
1979 to March 1980	1 065 569	41 804	57 208	134 537	243 311	248 641	158 468	81 368	62 039	25 813	12 380	260
1975 to 1978	811 724	48 903	53 909	110 806	183 929	180 236	112 962	55 508	39 394	14 887	11 190	251
1970 to 1974	284 580	28 406	28 318	43 914	60 208	53 491	32 166	16 138	12 404	4 715	4 820	233
1960 to 1969	180 971	13 985	25 086	36 992	39 380	30 229	15 497	7 709	6 334	2 639	3 120	216
1959 or earlier	103 493	9 354	23 166	28 033	20 699	10 811	4 459	2 095	1 848	1 078	1 950	183
ROOMS												
1 room	191 287	23 717	38 240	48 534	38 079	21 613	9 910	3 908	2 863	2 281	2 142	184
2 rooms	341 794	28 330	39 748	79 915	86 382	55 412	26 582	11 550	7 844	2 767	3 264	212
3 rooms	854 730	57 737	56 450	134 964	239 837	194 793	93 073	38 712	23 804	7 253	8 107	236
4 rooms	725 938	22 587	36 650	66 471	141 947	186 717	131 995	67 048	47 653	14 253	10 617	274
5 rooms	259 461	7 584	12 879	18 918	34 316	54 536	52 026	32 460	28 889	12 285	5 568	299
6 rooms	55 646	1 834	2 915	4 249	5 560	8 477	7 957	7 468	8 475	6 477	2 234	323
7 or more rooms	17 481	663	805	1 231	1 406	1 860	2 009	1 672	2 491	3 816	1 528	350
Median	3.3	2.8	2.8	2.9	3.1	3.4	3.7	3.9	4.1	4.4	3.8	...
BEDROOMS												
None	262 453	27 378	49 593	73 986	55 209	29 125	12 980	5 260	3 721	2 657	2 544	186
1	1 239 311	84 051	88 194	203 442	345 435	278 179	131 774	53 767	32 809	10 083	11 577	234
2	810 332	23 341	37 204	63 049	129 837	197 818	161 730	89 612	69 452	24 459	13 830	287
3	117 290	6 616	10 998	11 587	15 031	16 217	15 439	12 898	14 666	9 583	4 255	288
4	13 243	866	1 495	1 731	1 671	1 539	1 357	1 072	1 104	1 705	703	266
5 or more	3 708	200	203	487	344	530	272	209	267	645	551	282
PERSONS IN UNIT												
1 person	1 214 603	106 011	113 455	210 763	298 901	242 164	126 230	53 982	37 243	14 725	11 129	229
2 persons	722 110	17 771	37 873	81 195	150 660	171 269	119 725	64 144	49 884	19 506	10 083	270
3 persons	263 765	8 143	15 299	31 409	53 206	59 476	42 129	23 322	18 238	7 405	5 138	268
4 persons	141 718	5 168	10 371	16 924	26 317	29 884	21 506	13 152	10 351	4 442	3 603	267
5 persons	58 513	2 583	5 519	7 519	10 602	12 146	8 123	4 487	3 667	1 899	1 968	258
6 or more persons	45 628	2 776	5 170	6 472	7 841	8 469	5 839	3 731	2 636	1 155	1 539	249
Median	1.51	1.17	1.33	1.34	1.42	1.61	1.80	1.93	1.98	2.00	2.06	...
Total persons	4 545 449	213 077	332 218	603 407	952 799	985 906	651 156	347 718	267 065	109 725	82 378	...
PLUMBING FACILITIES BY PERSONS PER ROOM												
Complete plumbing for exclusive use	2 365 218	126 879	168 047	341 420	535 472	514 043	318 245	160 777	120 600	48 628	31 107	250
1.01 or more persons per room	144 310	5 256	14 146	27 564	33 235	29 156	15 962	8 284	5 625	2 041	3 041	236
Lacking complete plumbing for exclusive use	81 119	15 573	19 640	12 862	12 055	9 365	5 307	2 041	1 419	504	2 353	166
1.01 or more persons per room	10 436	1 166	1 903	1 932	1 820	1 550	914	282	248	75	546	199
HOUSEHOLD INCOME IN 1979												
Less than $5,000	549 688	104 925	79 322	107 313	114 342	74 526	34 725	14 743	9 478	3 439	6 875	191
$5,000 to $9,999	559 864	24 925	61 960	110 271	145 673	112 156	54 744	22 740	14 544	4 345	8 506	227
$10,000 to $12,499	279 309	4 244	15 398	43 757	76 881	68 584	37 280	16 124	10 481	2 880	3 680	248
$12,500 to $14,999	208 102	2 332	9 325	27 016	54 380	54 891	31 730	14 218	9 036	2 517	2 657	259
$15,000 to $19,999	344 131	3 037	11 489	34 586	77 150	95 011	62 948	30 188	19 400	5 925	4 397	273
$20,000 to $24,999	217 678	1 444	5 176	16 061	41 097	57 368	44 760	25 088	17 819	5 903	2 962	288
$25,000 to $34,999	188 927	981	3 594	10 852	27 725	44 104	40 068	26 191	23 540	9 422	2 450	307
$35,000 to $49,999	68 708	393	933	3 116	7 600	12 891	13 051	10 065	12 132	7 377	1 150	334
$50,000 or more	29 930	171	490	1 310	2 679	3 877	4 246	3 461	5 589	7 324	783	376
Median	$11 017	$3 919	$5 940	$8 055	$10 447	$12 793	$15 235	$17 098	$19 485	$24 589	$10 916	...
Mean	$13 391	$4 943	$7 702	$9 698	$11 886	$14 307	$16 675	$18 829	$22 043	$31 451	$14 342	...
SELECTED CHARACTERISTICS												
Heating equipment	2 446 337	142 452	187 687	354 282	547 527	523 408	323 552	162 818	122 019	49 132	33 460	248
Central heating system	2 242 178	127 519	161 334	314 152	505 621	488 083	303 379	152 300	115 191	46 678	27 921	250
Air conditioning	1 420 366	47 232	50 367	144 795	322 453	358 022	234 411	120 253	87 317	35 639	19 877	269
Central system	607 900	18 776	13 901	41 250	127 489	163 906	108 097	59 790	45 243	20 865	8 583	280
Vehicles available	1 605 569	38 847	68 357	176 879	356 348	397 463	264 739	136 207	102 485	39 045	25 199	269
1	1 165 217	34 594	58 571	149 093	282 242	286 469	174 572	83 424	59 183	21 426	15 643	259
2 or more	440 352	4 253	9 786	27 786	74 106	110 994	90 167	52 783	43 302	17 619	9 556	295
House heating fuel	2 415 125	140 075	182 785	347 863	542 913	519 325	320 758	160 430	120 043	48 075	32 858	248
Utility gas	1 059 965	65 579	90 115	169 216	238 025	221 635	136 603	63 958	45 261	16 250	13 323	242
Bottled, tank, or LP gas	30 283	2 111	3 181	5 282	6 543	5 309	3 015	1 636	1 175	444	1 587	229
Electricity	744 505	39 829	26 979	65 476	160 059	186 529	120 514	64 591	50 616	20 455	9 457	270
Fuel oil, kerosene, etc.	550 966	29 392	57 374	101 105	132 188	102 047	58 963	29 552	22 395	10 598	7 352	232
Other	29 406	3 164	5 136	6 784	6 098	3 805	1 663	693	596	328	1 139	193
Family householder	1 004 984	33 829	67 090	124 082	206 119	226 668	155 041	83 502	63 183	24 827	20 643	263
With own children under 18 years	466 431	19 882	34 616	60 170	97 440	104 536	68 415	36 732	25 278	9 213	10 149	258
With own children under 6 years	265 152	11 598	18 135	36 643	60 214	61 653	37 525	18 701	11 771	3 494	5 418	253
Female householder, no husband present	295 346	20 161	28 764	41 266	64 108	62 153	38 907	20 027	13 444	4 287	2 229	244
With own children under 18 years	203 090	15 461	20 082	28 018	45 136	43 832	26 027	12 566	7 900	2 479	1 589	241
With own children under 6 years	94 612	8 857	9 280	14 454	23 882	20 464	10 180	4 093	2 164	493	745	230
Nonfamily householder	1 441 353	108 623	120 597	230 200	341 408	296 740	168 511	79 316	58 836	24 305	12 817	237
Income in 1979 below poverty level	494 737	76 462	63 754	90 252	104 518	76 758	39 693	18 358	13 038	4 919	6 985	206
Percent below poverty level	20.2	53.7	34.0	25.5	19.1	14.7	12.3	11.3	10.7	10.0	20.9	...
GROSS RENT AS PERCENTAGE OF HOUSEHOLD INCOME IN 1979												
Less than 15 percent	403 717	30 465	41 851	67 489	92 726	81 568	45 527	20 852	15 204	8 035	...	233
15 to 19 percent	378 114	22 268	23 769	51 040	83 782	88 319	55 659	27 573	18 979	6 725	...	255
20 to 24 percent	349 224	33 280	22 087	43 108	74 625	76 106	50 146	25 726	17 814	6 332	...	251
25 to 29 percent	265 859	22 610	18 563	33 492	58 504	57 783	36 810	18 858	14 132	5 107	...	250
30 to 34 percent	187 129	10 412	14 583	23 584	41 063	42 593	27 001	13 568	10 315	4 010	...	255
35 to 49 percent	315 547	10 950	29 931	47 416	67 880	66 957	43 768	23 213	18 427	7 005	...	251
50 percent or more	461 180	8 728	30 099	77 795	116 718	100 758	59 337	30 532	25 275	11 038	...	248
Not computed	85 567	3 739	5 904	10 358	12 229	9 324	5 304	2 496	1 873	880	33 460	225
Median	25.9	22.5	25.9	26.5	26.4	26.0	26.1	26.6	27.9	28.0	...	...

Table G— 7. Gross Rent of Renter-Occupied Housing Units: 1980—Con.

Housing Units in Structures With 20 to 49 Units—Total—Con.

[Data are estimates based on a sample; see Introduction. For meaning of symbols, see Introduction. For definitions of terms, see appendix A]

United States	Total	Less than $100	$100 to $149	$150 to $199	$200 to $249	$250 to $299	$300 to $349	$350 to $399	$400 to $499	$500 or more	No cash rent	Median (dollars)
AGE OF HOUSEHOLDER												
Persons 15 years and over	2 446 337	142 452	187 687	354 282	547 527	523 408	323 552	162 818	122 019	49 132	33 460	248
15 to 19 years	53 288	1 870	3 440	8 915	15 298	11 892	5 957	2 793	1 953	601	569	240
20 to 24 years	424 264	8 489	19 258	60 151	115 454	107 728	59 772	27 480	17 075	5 567	3 290	253
25 to 29 years	426 118	8 072	18 759	54 153	105 074	108 961	68 460	30 644	21 219	6 477	4 299	261
30 to 34 years	280 506	5 696	15 044	34 328	62 124	67 795	44 578	23 643	17 303	6 560	3 435	266
35 to 39 years	172 861	4 536	11 832	22 844	36 522	38 547	26 143	14 483	10 717	4 524	2 713	262
40 to 44 years	130 813	4 176	10 404	18 702	27 615	27 277	18 127	10 084	8 266	3 809	2 353	256
45 to 49 years	116 227	4 480	9 581	17 544	24 736	23 891	15 243	8 504	6 609	3 362	2 277	251
50 to 54 years	122 851	5 954	11 639	19 646	25 905	23 717	14 964	8 395	6 815	3 173	2 643	244
55 to 59 years	127 641	7 958	12 869	21 170	26 296	23 055	15 139	8 642	6 714	2 922	2 876	239
60 to 64 years	123 435	11 327	14 111	21 238	24 396	21 231	12 543	6 963	6 386	2 651	2 589	228
65 to 69 years	129 618	18 280	15 786	21 684	24 247	20 226	12 714	6 513	5 510	2 233	2 425	216
70 to 74 years	125 698	20 277	16 590	20 530	22 236	18 722	11 945	5 980	5 138	2 498	1 782	210
75 years and over	213 017	41 337	28 374	33 377	37 624	30 366	17 967	8 694	8 314	4 755	2 209	203
Median	36.1	67.4	52.4	39.3	33.1	32.4	33.1	34.3	36.6	41.1	45.2	...
MARITAL STATUS OF HOUSEHOLDER												
Persons 15 years and over	2 446 337	142 452	187 687	354 282	547 527	523 408	323 552	162 818	122 019	49 132	33 460	248
Single	855 889	30 635	59 197	135 090	220 955	193 554	108 441	51 099	36 867	13 863	6 188	245
Now married, except separated	688 935	14 796	38 111	81 196	138 703	158 840	110 916	60 361	47 707	20 230	18 075	270
Separated	167 986	11 893	18 931	28 952	37 561	32 956	18 731	9 015	6 150	2 360	1 437	231
Widowed	330 184	62 118	40 997	52 191	61 362	49 513	29 035	13 904	11 520	5 678	3 866	206
Divorced	403 343	23 010	30 451	56 853	88 946	88 545	56 429	28 439	19 775	7 001	3 894	250
YEARS OF SCHOOL COMPLETED BY HOUSEHOLDER												
Persons 25 years old and over	1 968 785	132 093	164 989	285 216	416 775	403 788	257 823	132 545	102 991	42 964	29 601	246
Median	12.6	9.2	11.2	12.2	12.6	12.8	13.0	13.5	14.2	15.4	12.3	...
PERIOD OF SERVICE OF HOUSEHOLDER												
Civilian veterans 16 years and over	416 211	14 251	30 558	55 737	86 955	89 215	60 453	32 773	26 562	11 695	8 012	259
Percent of civilians 16 years and over	17.2	10.0	16.3	15.9	16.1	17.3	18.9	20.3	21.9	24.0	24.6	...
May 1975 or later only	23 973	394	1 244	3 203	6 757	5 992	3 667	1 426	775	270	245	252
Vietnam era	133 475	1 713	5 838	15 614	30 594	34 133	22 174	11 350	7 572	2 418	2 069	267
February 1955 to July 1964 only	35 468	642	2 027	4 299	7 524	7 656	5 623	3 305	2 552	1 190	650	269
Vietnam era and Korean conflict	7 356	189	453	824	1 448	1 668	1 078	665	587	292	152	271
Korean conflict	45 488	1 236	3 296	6 376	9 153	9 645	6 246	3 587	3 282	1 687	980	261
Korean conflict and World War II	11 111	456	938	1 581	2 074	2 018	1 557	969	805	438	275	259
World War II	140 454	7 635	14 287	20 856	26 157	25 028	18 116	10 518	9 724	4 699	3 434	249
World War I	10 867	1 046	1 358	1 752	1 724	1 789	1 209	596	831	486	76	236
Other	8 019	940	1 117	1 232	1 524	1 286	783	357	434	215	131	221
Civilian nonveterans 16 years and over	2 003 451	128 102	156 796	294 948	452 269	426 884	259 754	128 451	94 553	37 091	24 603	245
LABOR FORCE STATUS OF HOUSEHOLDER												
Persons 16 years and over	2 445 988	142 436	187 667	354 231	547 395	523 360	323 527	162 805	122 006	49 130	33 431	248
Labor force	1 695 659	31 502	90 694	225 818	397 686	404 352	256 633	130 619	95 307	37 043	26 005	261
Percent of persons 16 years and over	69.3	22.1	48.3	63.7	72.7	77.3	79.3	80.2	78.1	75.4	77.8	...
Armed Forces	26 326	83	313	3 546	8 171	7 261	3 320	1 581	891	344	816	254
Civilian labor force	1 669 333	31 419	90 381	222 272	389 515	397 091	253 313	129 038	94 416	36 699	25 189	261
Employed	1 568 329	26 186	79 947	203 373	365 459	377 150	242 033	123 638	90 876	35 373	24 294	263
Unemployed	101 004	5 233	10 434	18 899	24 056	19 941	11 280	5 400	3 540	1 326	895	232
Percent of civilian labor force	6.1	16.7	11.5	8.5	6.2	5.0	4.5	4.2	3.7	3.6	3.6	...
Not in labor force	750 329	110 934	96 973	128 413	149 709	119 008	66 894	32 186	26 699	12 087	7 426	212
OCCUPATION OF HOUSEHOLDER												
Employed persons 16 years and over	1 568 329	26 186	79 947	203 373	365 459	377 150	242 033	123 638	90 876	35 373	24 294	263
Managerial and professional specialty occupations	423 487	3 218	10 090	36 043	86 312	103 157	75 233	43 502	37 012	18 522	10 398	284
Executive, administrative, and managerial occupations	192 233	1 526	3 950	14 051	35 833	45 085	33 992	21 112	18 055	10 033	8 596	290
Professional specialty occupations	231 254	1 692	6 140	21 992	50 479	58 072	41 241	22 390	18 957	8 489	1 802	280
Technical, sales, and administrative support occupations	512 718	4 882	20 795	64 970	126 128	129 595	82 206	41 065	29 933	10 324	2 820	265
Technicians and related support occupations	68 227	424	2 158	7 837	16 619	18 839	11 935	5 399	3 560	1 159	297	268
Sales occupations	141 479	1 549	4 947	13 916	29 389	34 107	24 776	13 867	12 368	5 520	1 040	280
Administrative support occupations, including clerical	303 012	2 909	13 690	43 217	80 120	76 649	45 495	21 799	14 005	3 645	1 483	257
Service occupations	213 248	8 678	20 639	37 794	50 187	43 396	25 140	12 329	8 175	2 300	4 610	237
Private household occupations	8 787	1 157	1 374	1 984	1 948	1 193	525	228	136	58	184	195
Protective service occupations	27 041	546	1 491	3 734	6 140	6 760	3 981	2 134	1 381	356	518	260
Service occupations, except protective and household	177 420	6 975	17 774	32 076	42 099	35 443	20 634	9 967	6 658	1 886	3 908	236
Farming, forestry, and fishing occupations	15 445	1 001	1 558	2 506	3 127	2 779	1 505	634	458	224	1 653	229
Precision production, craft, and repair occupations	163 967	2 215	7 800	19 856	37 652	42 003	27 915	13 563	7 980	2 322	2 661	266
Operators, fabricators, and laborers	239 464	6 192	19 065	42 204	62 053	56 220	30 034	12 545	7 318	1 681	2 152	241
Machine operators, assemblers, and inspectors	123 113	3 123	9 878	22 955	33 267	28 588	14 745	5 839	3 162	684	872	238
Transportation and material moving occupations	59 616	1 180	3 829	8 659	14 432	15 044	8 587	4 067	2 522	594	702	255
Handlers, equipment cleaners, helpers, and laborers	56 735	1 889	5 358	10 590	14 354	12 588	6 702	2 639	1 634	403	578	236
MEANS OF TRANSPORTATION TO WORK FOR HOUSEHOLDER												
Workers 16 years and over	1 552 636	24 441	77 010	200 130	363 683	375 449	240 030	122 575	89 684	34 972	24 662	263
Private vehicle	1 064 829	11 323	35 383	111 002	245 433	281 412	186 195	93 873	66 876	23 023	10 309	272
Drive alone: Car	784 855	7 084	23 773	79 586	181 336	207 390	139 184	70 573	51 513	17 922	6 494	273
Truck or van	66 895	708	2 056	6 662	14 901	18 694	12 261	5 543	3 412	1 105	1 553	272
Carpool: Car	188 194	2 699	8 253	21 774	43 575	48 998	30 988	15 786	10 890	3 608	1 623	267
Truck or van	24 885	832	1 301	2 980	5 621	6 330	3 762	1 971	1 061	388	639	261
Public transportation	300 521	5 995	24 536	56 848	77 828	61 528	34 136	18 094	13 333	6 509	1 714	240
Bus or streetcar	153 302	4 123	14 492	31 467	39 704	30 331	16 191	8 433	5 609	2 203	749	233
Subway or elevated train	126 043	1 467	9 252	23 373	34 536	26 695	14 145	7 254	5 537	2 899	885	241
Railroad	14 625	90	357	1 153	2 391	3 331	3 028	1 844	1 636	746	49	299
Taxicab	6 551	315	435	855	1 197	1 171	772	563	551	661	31	270
Bicycle	10 747	156	672	1 795	2 796	2 344	1 299	702	576	234	173	248
Motorcycle	7 541	37	213	676	1 655	2 212	1 467	633	393	142	113	276
Walked only	135 693	5 570	14 205	26 590	30 930	22 963	13 040	6 940	6 163	3 443	5 849	230
Other means	10 791	343	786	1 302	2 149	2 127	1 296	745	609	281	1 153	256
Worked at home	22 514	1 017	1 215	1 917	2 892	2 863	2 597	1 588	1 734	1 340	5 351	277
WORKERS IN HOUSEHOLD IN 1979												
No workers	597 964	102 630	83 870	106 218	116 466	88 418	47 271	21 593	18 071	8 214	5 213	202
1 worker	1 179 081	32 168	80 675	186 252	301 418	270 758	152 380	71 495	49 604	19 029	15 302	247
2 workers	585 915	6 056	19 610	54 358	117 658	148 156	109 405	59 490	44 117	16 348	10 717	280
3 or more workers	83 377	1 598	3 532	7 454	11 985	16 076	14 496	10 240	10 227	5 541	2 228	300

Table G— 8. Gross Rent of Renter-Occupied Housing Units: 1980

Housing Units in Structures With 50 or More Units—Total

[Data are estimates based on a sample; see Introduction. For meaning of symbols, see Introduction. For definitions of terms, see appendix A]

United States	Total	Less than $100	$100 to $149	$150 to $199	$200 to $249	$250 to $299	$300 to $349	$350 to $399	$400 to $499	$500 or more	No cash rent	Median (dollars)
Specified renter-occupied housing units	3 701 136	474 246	300 378	370 854	558 672	654 700	498 138	316 068	290 401	200 977	36 702	260
YEAR STRUCTURE BUILT												
1979 to March 1980	144 550	38 610	18 541	10 285	11 172	18 255	15 065	11 948	9 882	9 315	1 477	218
1975 to 1978	455 522	87 003	35 453	28 619	53 398	76 074	63 052	41 792	37 282	29 101	3 748	264
1970 to 1974	871 771	140 173	56 557	64 508	110 000	155 258	134 044	84 670	74 604	45 278	6 679	270
1960 to 1969	1 064 255	108 992	61 299	81 173	158 695	208 601	165 595	104 038	99 869	65 923	10 070	278
1950 to 1959	394 651	39 192	38 529	46 864	66 698	72 272	48 734	30 513	28 314	19 401	4 134	253
1940 to 1949	242 508	17 980	22 628	34 868	50 337	46 979	28 118	17 418	13 808	7 730	2 642	244
1939 or earlier	527 879	42 296	67 371	104 537	108 372	77 261	43 530	25 689	26 642	24 229	7 952	221
YEAR HOUSEHOLDER MOVED INTO UNIT												
1979 to March 1980	1 406 649	118 151	86 744	119 359	224 792	288 918	221 210	137 507	118 286	76 884	14 798	275
1975 to 1978	1 251 668	179 769	99 898	117 783	181 591	215 472	168 903	105 686	99 994	70 919	11 653	260
1970 to 1974	556 232	122 331	60 128	60 478	67 551	75 175	58 310	39 988	38 725	28 429	5 117	224
1960 to 1969	345 145	43 117	34 944	44 850	55 073	53 335	38 299	25 602	26 604	19 897	3 424	244
1959 or earlier	141 442	10 878	18 664	28 384	29 665	21 800	11 416	7 285	6 792	4 848	1 710	220
ROOMS												
1 room	393 775	70 765	65 170	75 054	67 634	46 115	25 520	14 265	13 619	12 310	3 323	189
2 rooms	558 678	116 443	55 340	77 482	98 035	83 967	52 161	28 708	25 614	16 816	4 112	214
3 rooms	1 304 724	211 374	94 141	126 002	233 361	259 685	161 624	86 709	75 823	47 918	8 087	246
4 rooms	938 647	49 283	55 519	61 072	118 788	196 158	175 735	114 845	97 192	58 887	11 168	296
5 rooms	386 834	20 424	24 252	23 144	32 735	57 638	68 751	55 329	57 494	40 934	6 133	323
6 rooms	92 299	4 916	4 633	6 276	6 485	9 050	11 695	13 563	16 636	16 815	2 230	357
7 or more rooms	26 179	1 041	1 323	1 824	1 634	2 087	2 652	2 649	4 023	7 297	1 649	382
Median	3.2	2.7	2.8	2.8	3.0	3.3	3.6	3.7	3.8	3.9	3.8	...
BEDROOMS												
None	502 344	83 540	76 691	96 076	91 119	62 701	35 742	19 917	18 616	14 215	3 727	196
1	1 892 271	317 318	138 447	189 729	336 726	372 261	230 230	121 931	104 698	68 247	12 684	244
2	1 074 114	51 594	58 740	62 343	110 827	198 821	208 236	145 936	134 003	88 887	14 727	311
3	205 771	18 440	22 801	17 618	17 427	18 938	22 496	26 824	31 025	25 829	4 373	312
4	22 107	3 010	3 161	4 200	2 201	1 636	1 068	1 199	1 794	3 030	808	206
5 or more	4 529	344	538	888	372	343	366	261	265	769	383	241
PERSONS IN UNIT												
1 person	1 976 699	385 540	179 163	223 929	319 267	332 206	218 023	121 059	108 387	75 486	13 639	230
2 persons	1 027 864	41 692	57 304	83 015	146 836	202 697	173 569	116 711	113 993	80 681	11 366	294
3 persons	353 428	18 075	25 731	28 039	49 685	66 709	59 081	41 365	36 865	25 020	4 832	291
4 persons	195 351	12 728	17 710	16 991	24 824	33 011	30 362	23 272	19 533	13 488	3 432	286
5 persons	82 682	7 470	11 077	9 397	10 344	12 507	10 459	8 402	7 061	4 263	1 702	259
6 or more persons	65 112	8 741	11 367	9 483	7 716	7 570	6 644	5 259	4 562	2 039	1 731	214
Median	1.44	1.12	1.34	1.33	1.37	1.49	1.68	1.82	1.82	1.81	1.91	...
Total persons	6 662 822	656 653	559 588	641 609	954 526	1 170 903	958 485	648 312	590 607	400 306	81 833	...
PLUMBING FACILITIES BY PERSONS PER ROOM												
Complete plumbing for exclusive use	3 589 156	455 441	274 478	351 101	544 436	642 826	489 858	311 120	286 512	198 764	34 620	262
1.01 or more persons per room	184 799	14 498	21 403	26 202	32 517	33 087	22 697	14 168	10 847	6 168	3 212	244
Lacking complete plumbing for exclusive use	111 980	18 805	25 900	19 753	14 236	11 874	8 280	4 948	3 889	2 213	2 082	176
1.01 or more persons per room	11 142	1 110	1 913	2 154	1 759	1 472	1 151	545	404	230	404	205
HOUSEHOLD INCOME IN 1979												
Less than $5,000	960 162	387 800	131 982	112 030	113 311	91 385	52 209	28 062	22 108	14 026	7 249	134
$5,000 to $9,999	769 051	65 099	116 646	127 648	147 899	134 693	80 757	42 080	31 023	15 017	8 189	224
$10,000 to $12,499	355 337	7 783	19 376	43 933	81 032	86 354	53 449	29 078	20 396	9 622	4 314	264
$12,500 to $14,999	269 280	4 189	10 163	25 289	55 246	70 082	48 907	25 816	18 632	8 014	2 942	277
$15,000 to $19,999	468 644	4 747	11 851	32 187	78 381	119 158	97 402	56 984	43 718	19 295	4 921	294
$20,000 to $24,999	320 881	2 197	5 206	15 239	42 084	71 548	69 252	48 500	42 955	20 397	3 503	316
$25,000 to $34,999	316 218	1 550	3 550	10 349	28 560	57 774	63 957	52 344	58 093	36 848	3 193	343
$35,000 to $49,999	148 914	599	1 091	2 898	8 730	18 067	24 072	23 873	34 382	33 829	1 373	388
$50,000 or more	92 649	282	513	1 281	3 429	5 639	8 133	9 331	19 094	43 929	1 018	490
Median	$10 854	$3 763	$5 559	$7 736	$10 559	$13 032	$15 633	$17 738	$20 940	$28 333	$11 688	...
Mean	$14 480	$4 227	$6 837	$9 379	$12 074	$14 632	$17 234	$19 769	$23 850	$36 843	$15 430	...
SELECTED CHARACTERISTICS												
Heating equipment	3 701 136	474 246	300 378	370 854	558 672	654 700	498 138	316 068	290 401	200 977	36 702	260
Central heating system	3 524 011	449 633	279 870	346 675	531 082	628 014	478 963	304 022	279 484	193 899	32 369	261
Air conditioning	2 490 642	216 203	120 655	186 250	371 186	495 962	394 759	258 785	242 570	178 562	25 710	284
Central system	1 389 789	105 116	53 788	81 956	197 006	294 349	232 574	156 462	143 603	111 037	13 898	292
Vehicles available	2 151 980	92 261	94 523	163 683	339 096	467 482	379 242	243 346	214 286	130 876	27 185	290
1	1 602 382	86 575	85 016	141 261	275 767	350 338	261 471	158 634	136 810	88 227	18 283	279
2 or more	549 598	5 686	9 507	22 422	63 329	117 144	117 771	84 712	77 476	42 649	8 902	322
House heating fuel	3 665 944	470 929	297 017	367 550	555 258	651 458	494 439	312 350	284 865	196 365	35 713	260
Utility gas	1 281 598	202 162	128 365	151 522	195 655	210 243	159 828	91 519	80 236	49 765	12 303	239
Bottled, tank, or LP gas	33 779	4 321	3 539	4 507	5 257	5 673	3 875	2 426	1 804	1 237	1 320	238
Electricity	1 297 988	174 159	77 349	87 184	182 791	258 865	201 165	129 114	108 770	66 750	11 841	273
Fuel oil, kerosene, etc.	1 003 634	82 573	83 130	117 270	165 364	170 577	125 339	86 376	90 865	75 087	8 863	265
Other	48 945	7 714	6 624	7 067	6 191	6 100	4 232	2 915	3 190	5 526	1 386	219
Family householder	1 454 030	85 192	115 113	133 176	205 591	266 935	225 710	155 479	143 705	101 662	21 467	283
With own children under 18 years	619 744	49 460	60 753	61 893	89 952	111 783	92 158	62 736	50 056	31 249	9 704	269
With own children under 6 years	324 827	27 778	27 274	32 434	52 875	63 829	49 422	30 552	22 499	13 018	5 146	265
Female householder, no husband present	407 597	53 421	53 940	43 157	58 888	68 719	51 642	33 639	27 712	13 673	2 766	244
With own children under 18 years	267 145	40 424	39 064	29 836	38 956	44 387	31 769	19 691	14 493	6 671	1 854	230
With own children under 6 years	111 706	22 386	15 540	12 615	18 828	19 431	11 404	5 703	3 599	1 171	1 029	213
Nonfamily householder	2 247 106	389 054	185 265	237 678	353 081	387 765	272 428	160 589	146 696	99 315	15 235	243
Income in 1979 below poverty level	754 577	261 369	98 162	86 036	95 433	85 415	53 296	30 447	23 517	13 925	6 977	158
Percent below poverty level	20.4	55.1	32.7	23.2	17.1	13.0	10.7	9.6	8.1	6.9	19.0	...
GROSS RENT AS PERCENTAGE OF HOUSEHOLD INCOME IN 1979												
Less than 15 percent	604 315	73 696	46 861	63 618	95 753	105 881	77 030	48 189	45 346	47 941	...	260
15 to 19 percent	577 373	82 179	35 101	49 243	84 224	110 652	86 380	52 866	47 315	29 413	...	267
20 to 24 percent	609 090	143 121	47 012	49 010	78 157	96 509	77 221	50 156	42 453	25 451	...	242
25 to 29 percent	442 742	84 286	40 060	39 132	61 188	73 595	56 336	35 202	33 833	19 110	...	247
30 to 34 percent	281 261	30 187	27 296	27 296	10 636	41 126	53 408	40 621	25 294	23 044	13 183	264
35 to 49 percent	453 320	28 379	51 505	53 836	70 045	81 384	63 684	42 447	38 681	23 359	...	264
50 percent or more	620 022	21 841	43 743	78 785	115 412	121 113	88 578	57 105	54 845	38 600	...	271
Not computed	113 009	10 557	8 800	10 124	12 767	12 158	8 288	4 809	4 884	3 920	36 702	234
Median	25.0	22.7	27.1	27.4	26.2	25.6	25.4	25.6	26.1	24.2	...	...

Table G—8. Gross Rent of Renter-Occupied Housing Units: 1980—Con.

Housing Units in Structures With 50 or More Units—Total—Con.

(Data are estimates based on a sample; see Introduction. For meaning of symbols, see Introduction. For definitions of terms, see appendix A)

United States

	Total	Less than $100	$100 to $149	$150 to $199	$200 to $249	$250 to $299	$300 to $349	$350 to $399	$400 to $499	$500 or more	No cash rent	Median (dollars)
AGE OF HOUSEHOLDER												
Persons 15 years and over	3 701 136	474 246	300 378	370 854	558 672	654 700	498 138	316 068	290 401	200 977	36 702	260
15 to 19 years	57 412	2 401	3 485	6 076	14 010	13 981	8 277	4 438	2 877	1 270	597	259
20 to 24 years	468 427	15 206	19 544	43 889	100 070	121 193	80 477	42 591	29 132	12 624	3 701	272
25 to 29 years	509 670	15 121	20 546	41 281	93 580	123 436	91 943	52 973	42 874	22 393	4 523	283
30 to 34 years	372 188	11 731	19 089	30 113	57 561	80 069	65 351	42 701	37 933	24 188	3 452	291
35 to 39 years	247 303	9 125	16 576	20 692	35 978	46 364	40 434	28 079	27 598	19 949	2 508	293
40 to 44 years	185 541	7 845	13 952	17 917	27 093	33 875	28 035	20 092	19 168	14 867	2 697	286
45 to 49 years	166 608	9 051	12 828	15 752	24 825	29 794	24 477	17 025	16 858	13 439	2 559	283
50 to 54 years	182 501	13 123	14 369	18 754	26 274	31 595	25 553	17 760	17 648	14 479	2 946	277
55 to 59 years	195 191	19 194	14 913	20 695	29 109	32 991	26 189	17 449	17 787	13 618	3 246	268
60 to 64 years	206 955	34 496	19 296	22 778	29 106	30 297	23 424	16 763	16 043	12 081	2 671	244
65 to 69 years	266 709	70 029	31 767	30 528	32 255	31 795	23 464	15 494	16 478	12 437	2 462	200
70 to 74 years	291 541	87 911	37 945	35 548	31 848	30 367	23 134	14 996	16 161	11 747	1 884	177
75 years and over	551 090	178 013	76 068	66 831	56 963	48 943	37 380	25 707	29 844	27 885	3 456	165
Median	45.3	71.6	63.9	52.6	37.0	34.3	35.4	37.7	41.2	46.9	46.7	...
MARITAL STATUS OF HOUSEHOLDER												
Persons 15 years and over	3 701 136	474 246	300 378	370 854	558 672	654 700	498 138	316 068	290 401	200 977	36 702	260
Single	1 097 818	73 011	69 621	116 129	207 132	234 547	163 897	94 894	82 778	48 367	7 442	267
Now married, except separated	1 028 903	34 787	61 797	89 968	144 913	193 810	167 790	117 054	112 087	88 173	18 524	295
Separated	237 574	36 171	28 196	26 717	38 360	40 501	27 454	16 526	13 507	8 247	1 895	235
Widowed	765 281	262 826	99 714	84 479	79 788	76 402	55 416	36 093	36 877	28 848	4 838	160
Divorced	571 560	67 451	41 050	53 561	88 479	109 440	83 581	51 501	45 152	27 342	4 003	265
YEARS OF SCHOOL COMPLETED BY HOUSEHOLDER												
Persons 25 years old and over	3 175 297	456 639	277 349	320 889	444 592	519 526	409 384	269 039	258 392	187 083	32 404	257
Median	12.6	8.9	10.7	12.2	12.6	12.9	13.2	13.6	14.6	16.1	12.4	...
PERIOD OF SERVICE OF HOUSEHOLDER												
Civilian veterans 16 years and over	608 684	32 004	38 724	57 376	89 753	111 963	93 224	64 995	63 244	48 730	8 671	287
Percent of civilians 16 years and over	16.6	6.8	12.9	15.6	16.3	17.3	18.9	20.8	21.9	24.4	24.1	...
May 1975 or later only	27 657	719	1 329	2 781	6 339	7 020	4 549	2 491	1 526	625	278	268
Vietnam era	159 673	2 223	5 181	12 144	27 251	37 468	30 701	19 547	15 458	7 902	1 798	293
February 1955 to July 1964 only	49 260	766	2 128	3 411	6 591	9 656	8 263	6 187	6 162	5 374	722	310
Vietnam era and Korean conflict	10 330	202	450	920	1 581	1 928	1 716	1 322	1 209	831	171	300
Korean conflict	64 577	1 958	3 363	5 675	9 751	11 327	10 022	7 093	7 775	6 494	1 119	298
Korean conflict and World War II	16 654	863	1 195	1 530	2 310	2 674	2 483	1 750	1 879	1 555	415	292
World War II	239 351	18 380	19 384	25 175	30 919	37 302	31 852	23 775	26 353	22 435	3 776	282
World War I	25 810	3 472	3 651	3 905	3 020	2 574	2 362	1 861	2 053	2 715	197	229
Other	15 372	3 421	2 043	1 835	1 991	2 014	1 276	969	829	799	195	207
Civilian nonveterans 16 years and over	3 060 338	442 081	261 291	310 935	460 961	533 572	399 809	247 926	225 078	151 365	27 320	254
LABOR FORCE STATUS OF HOUSEHOLDER												
Persons 16 years and over	3 700 784	474 170	300 359	370 772	558 639	654 638	498 109	316 047	290 385	200 977	36 688	260
Labor force	2 249 309	53 203	99 996	192 434	385 407	495 090	384 967	244 335	218 677	147 304	27 896	288
Percent of persons 16 years and over	60.8	11.2	33.3	51.9	69.0	75.6	77.3	77.3	75.3	73.3	76.0	...
Armed Forces	31 762	85	344	2 461	7 925	9 103	5 076	3 126	2 063	882	697	276
Civilian labor force	2 217 547	53 118	99 652	189 973	377 482	485 987	379 891	241 209	216 614	146 422	27 199	289
Employed	2 103 309	42 763	87 708	175 066	356 486	464 800	365 634	232 347	209 710	142 247	26 548	290
Unemployed	114 238	10 355	11 944	14 907	20 996	21 187	14 257	8 862	6 904	4 175	651	247
Percent of civilian labor force	5.2	19.5	12.0	7.8	5.6	4.4	3.8	3.7	3.2	2.9	2.4	...
Not in labor force	1 451 475	420 967	200 363	178 338	173 232	159 548	113 142	71 712	71 708	53 673	8 792	178
OCCUPATION OF HOUSEHOLDER												
Employed persons 16 years and over	2 103 309	42 763	87 708	175 066	356 486	464 800	365 634	232 347	209 710	142 247	26 548	290
Managerial and professional specialty occupations	672 797	4 491	10 072	30 999	84 340	134 101	122 724	87 799	97 331	87 324	13 616	327
Executive, administrative, and managerial occupations	319 065	1 828	3 990	12 489	35 428	60 077	56 154	43 143	48 091	46 941	10 924	336
Professional specialty occupations	353 732	2 663	6 082	18 510	48 912	74 024	66 570	44 656	49 240	40 383	2 692	319
Technical, sales, and administrative support occupations	715 248	9 528	25 792	60 351	130 765	168 529	130 447	79 989	68 480	38 658	2 709	289
Technicians and related support occupations	85 303	605	2 096	5 841	15 505	22 833	17 351	9 695	7 762	3 304	311	290
Sales occupations	219 939	2 646	6 362	12 878	29 901	44 315	40 399	28 341	30 407	23 667	1 023	317
Administrative support occupations, including clerical	410 006	6 277	17 334	41 632	85 359	101 381	72 697	41 953	30 311	11 687	1 375	276
Service occupations	254 825	17 185	23 981	35 020	48 029	49 459	33 491	20 736	15 342	6 217	5 365	251
Private household occupations	11 834	3 371	1 959	1 760	1 891	1 563	584	365	171	79	91	165
Protective service occupations	36 459	1 063	2 430	3 986	6 730	8 296	5 928	3 868	2 817	928	413	273
Service occupations, except protective and household	206 532	12 751	19 592	29 274	39 408	39 600	26 979	16 503	12 354	5 210	4 861	250
Farming, forestry, and fishing occupations	13 513	1 031	1 179	1 660	2 273	2 630	1 755	875	546	320	1 244	250
Precision production, craft, and repair occupations	190 303	2 327	6 654	14 415	34 546	49 381	37 384	22 174	15 396	6 045	1 981	287
Operators, fabricators, and laborers	256 623	8 201	20 030	32 621	56 533	60 700	39 833	20 774	12 615	3 683	1 633	258
Machine operators, assemblers, and inspectors	123 677	4 281	10 882	17 251	27 905	28 664	17 836	9 217	5 495	1 473	673	252
Transportation and material moving occupations	72 423	1 507	3 998	7 358	14 910	18 131	12 759	7 193	4 674	1 449	444	273
Handlers, equipment cleaners, helpers, and laborers	60 523	2 413	5 150	8 012	13 718	13 905	9 238	4 364	2 446	761	516	253
MEANS OF TRANSPORTATION TO WORK FOR HOUSEHOLDER												
Workers 16 years and over	2 079 435	39 038	83 613	171 292	354 865	463 482	362 811	230 507	207 059	139 991	26 777	291
Private vehicle	1 317 667	16 852	34 126	86 821	225 886	327 744	259 103	160 680	130 691	68 012	7 752	294
Drive alone: Car	980 505	10 764	23 168	62 177	166 962	243 697	193 623	121 862	101 074	52 189	4 989	296
Truck or van	74 240	746	1 733	4 538	12 856	20 327	15 984	8 592	6 231	2 117	1 116	291
Carpool: Car	234 595	4 458	8 099	17 873	40 943	56 463	44 152	27 228	21 393	12 670	1 316	290
Truck or van	28 327	884	1 126	2 233	5 125	7 257	5 344	2 998	1 993	1 036	331	282
Public transportation	496 019	12 364	31 488	55 710	89 007	95 101	70 555	47 581	49 355	43 178	1 680	281
Bus or streetcar	217 270	9 554	17 737	29 110	39 841	38 665	28 083	18 430	19 300	15 781	769	266
Subway or elevated train	240 059	2 324	12 461	24 510	45 046	50 884	36 491	24 507	23 666	19 434	736	285
Railroad	20 581	162	523	928	2 484	3 342	4 035	2 903	3 640	2 480	84	335
Taxicab	18 109	324	767	1 162	1 636	2 210	1 946	1 741	2 749	5 483	91	378
Bicycle	10 806	173	481	1 169	2 334	2 189	1 936	1 038	860	534	92	277
Motorcycle	8 916	40	180	614	1 730	2 256	1 913	1 144	696	206	137	290
Walked only	197 563	7 665	15 355	23 601	31 112	30 166	23 955	15 880	19 974	21 262	8 593	278
Other means	15 893	611	863	1 533	2 245	2 654	2 029	1 340	1 462	1 321	1 835	283
Worked at home	32 571	1 333	1 120	1 844	2 551	3 372	3 320	2 844	4 021	5 478	6 688	341
WORKERS IN HOUSEHOLD IN 1979												
No workers	1 241 394	402 855	180 777	154 599	140 146	122 276	85 174	52 736	53 753	42 260	6 818	161
1 worker	1 577 802	59 640	92 722	164 782	303 148	347 976	241 133	141 119	124 350	86 100	16 832	273
2 workers	767 195	9 453	21 748	44 886	103 955	166 371	151 935	104 588	93 419	60 066	10 774	310
3 or more workers	114 745	2 298	5 131	6 587	11 423	18 077	19 896	17 625	18 879	12 551	2 278	332

Table G— 9. **Gross Rent of Renter-Occupied Housing Units: 1980**

Mobile Homes or Trailers, Etc.—Total

[Data are estimates based on a sample; see Introduction. For meaning of symbols, see Introduction. For definitions of terms, see appendix A]

United States	Total	Less than $100	$100 to $149	$150 to $199	$200 to $249	$250 to $299	$300 to $349	$350 to $399	$400 to $499	$500 or more	No cash rent	Median (dollars)
Specified renter-occupied housing units	785 305	30 728	89 964	170 761	197 295	112 091	45 916	17 312	10 194	3 291	107 753	212
YEAR STRUCTURE BUILT												
1979 to March 1980	24 340	1 072	2 397	3 933	4 291	3 432	2 266	952	727	189	5 081	226
1975 to 1978	124 483	3 746	11 050	21 451	30 981	22 029	10 255	4 066	2 612	827	17 466	228
1970 to 1974	268 395	7 626	24 357	55 822	74 352	44 163	17 367	6 202	3 384	1 038	34 084	220
1960 to 1969	248 102	9 744	32 080	61 559	63 029	30 364	11 261	4 128	2 276	707	32 954	203
1950 to 1959	66 534	4 991	12 198	16 038	13 042	6 130	2 547	963	594	203	9 828	185
1940 to 1949	20 596	1 571	3 259	4 570	4 546	2 110	723	333	240	80	3 124	193
1939 or earlier	32 855	1 978	4 623	7 388	7 014	3 863	1 497	668	361	247	5 216	199
YEAR HOUSEHOLDER MOVED INTO UNIT												
1979 to March 1980	456 598	11 475	38 641	98 112	133 587	80 741	33 564	12 340	7 134	1 964	39 040	223
1975 to 1978	221 525	10 115	30 766	51 846	49 571	24 642	9 484	3 797	2 103	885	38 316	199
1970 to 1974	71 845	5 540	13 325	14 601	10 340	5 075	2 119	818	664	198	19 165	176
1960 to 1969	29 553	2 902	6 169	5 397	3 138	1 389	609	314	251	176	9 208	160
1959 or earlier	5 784	696	1 063	805	659	244	140	43	42	68	2 024	158
ROOMS												
1 room	14 877	2 521	3 304	2 572	1 452	717	294	153	101	156	3 607	147
2 rooms	43 722	5 039	9 189	10 412	7 219	3 233	1 295	575	226	141	6 393	171
3 rooms	133 473	9 239	22 889	34 255	29 399	12 736	4 597	1 562	1 010	375	17 411	188
4 rooms	367 797	9 828	38 354	85 635	104 712	54 532	20 063	6 478	3 193	1 001	44 001	213
5 rooms	177 429	3 199	13 408	31 244	45 434	32 998	14 780	5 843	3 246	871	26 406	230
6 rooms	35 297	710	2 207	5 227	7 180	5 923	3 322	1 886	1 588	440	6 814	242
7 or more rooms	12 710	192	613	1 416	1 899	1 952	1 565	815	830	307	3 121	267
Median	4.0	3.3	3.8	3.9	4.1	4.2	4.3	4.5	4.7	4.5	4.1	...
BEDROOMS												
None	17 066	2 784	3 673	3 124	1 794	943	394	189	133	166	3 866	152
1	120 480	11 307	24 002	29 886	22 175	9 906	3 995	1 522	887	455	16 345	178
2	488 711	13 729	52 148	114 029	137 020	71 636	26 295	8 667	4 598	1 494	59 095	213
3	151 413	2 703	9 689	22 869	35 172	28 521	14 313	6 544	4 120	1 010	26 472	239
4	6 767	184	381	756	1 047	962	845	372	408	118	1 694	259
5 or more	868	21	71	97	87	123	74	18	48	48	281	257
PERSONS IN UNIT												
1 person	228 782	17 447	41 341	56 596	44 592	19 099	6 804	2 424	1 553	670	38 256	182
2 persons	232 957	6 825	26 245	54 061	63 400	33 015	12 360	4 391	2 664	1 074	28 922	212
3 persons	155 181	3 050	11 795	32 369	45 528	27 519	10 850	4 020	2 368	542	17 140	224
4 persons	97 257	1 840	6 272	16 832	26 515	19 109	8 354	3 392	1 653	540	12 750	233
5 persons	43 142	849	2 439	6 867	10 914	8 365	4 472	1 862	1 172	240	5 962	239
6 or more persons	27 986	717	1 872	4 036	6 346	4 984	3 076	1 223	784	225	4 723	239
Median	2.20	1.38	1.64	2.03	2.35	2.64	2.85	2.96	2.87	2.41	2.04	...
Total persons	1 886 903	56 728	174 402	373 104	486 678	303 192	134 859	52 345	31 883	9 473	264 239	...
PLUMBING FACILITIES BY PERSONS PER ROOM												
Complete plumbing for exclusive use	767 825	27 552	87 092	168 763	196 159	111 537	45 597	17 207	10 119	3 186	100 613	213
1.01 or more persons per room	59 668	1 980	4 874	11 267	15 783	10 040	4 890	1 725	928	314	7 867	225
Lacking complete plumbing for exclusive use	17 480	3 176	2 872	1 998	1 136	554	319	105	75	105	7 140	135
1.01 or more persons per room	4 100	610	675	535	353	149	119	51	6	28	1 574	148
HOUSEHOLD INCOME IN 1979												
Less than $5,000	191 748	15 194	31 590	41 962	38 714	18 946	6 940	2 326	1 009	431	34 636	188
$5,000 to $9,999	225 816	7 374	27 200	54 111	59 679	30 010	10 743	3 664	1 751	521	30 763	207
$10,000 to $12,499	101 654	2 635	9 846	23 839	28 534	15 776	5 978	1 914	1 111	219	11 802	215
$12,500 to $14,999	69 062	1 567	6 073	14 690	19 933	11 694	4 720	1 596	978	196	7 615	221
$15,000 to $19,999	98 530	1 982	8 046	19 591	27 158	17 402	8 137	3 066	1 764	460	10 924	226
$20,000 to $24,999	50 597	909	3 937	9 114	12 667	9 849	4 614	2 153	1 371	465	5 518	234
$25,000 to $34,999	33 693	782	2 350	5 310	7 620	6 167	3 495	1 732	1 491	508	4 238	241
$35,000 to $49,999	9 563	147	626	1 485	1 976	1 641	837	664	498	280	1 409	246
$50,000 or more	4 642	138	296	659	1 014	606	452	197	221	211	848	240
Median	$9 427	$5 096	$7 184	$8 975	$10 022	$11 123	$12 206	$13 678	$15 705	$17 586	$7 954	...
Mean	$11 156	$7 663	$9 115	$10 396	$11 417	$12 593	$14 027	$15 510	$17 914	$20 948	$10 226	...
SELECTED CHARACTERISTICS												
Heating equipment	785 305	30 728	89 964	170 761	197 295	112 091	45 916	17 312	10 194	3 291	107 753	212
Central heating system	623 235	19 713	64 974	133 529	163 549	95 806	39 655	15 272	8 987	2 844	78 906	216
Air conditioning	441 624	14 128	46 935	97 889	115 707	65 545	27 289	10 154	5 697	1 837	56 443	215
Central system	167 974	4 465	14 737	28 651	40 937	29 674	14 732	6 259	3 740	1 178	23 601	230
Vehicles available	674 712	20 367	70 362	146 884	175 528	101 944	42 048	15 921	9 467	2 912	89 279	216
1	402 293	13 705	46 295	93 565	108 370	58 050	22 023	8 235	4 516	1 214	46 320	211
2 or more	272 419	6 662	24 067	53 319	67 158	43 894	20 025	7 686	4 951	1 698	42 959	223
House heating fuel	778 581	29 875	88 629	169 453	196 363	111 652	45 703	17 197	10 139	3 187	106 383	212
Utility gas	274 397	10 336	34 223	65 549	73 016	41 385	16 729	6 568	3 945	1 099	21 547	211
Bottled, tank, or LP gas	187 833	9 550	19 489	35 826	42 821	26 671	11 300	4 317	2 353	633	37 873	215
Electricity	147 559	7 362	16 895	29 240	35 623	21 241	9 796	4 044	2 503	758	20 097	214
Fuel oil, kerosene, etc.	152 070	3 763	15 482	36 052	43 015	21 354	7 444	2 024	1 185	653	21 098	212
Other	16 722	1 864	2 540	2 786	1 888	1 001	434	244	153	44	5 768	169
Family householder	501 052	12 154	44 681	102 617	135 334	82 466	34 692	13 257	7 502	2 203	66 146	221
With own children under 18 years	317 358	6 255	22 819	61 341	89 770	58 225	25 196	9 574	5 167	1 239	37 772	228
With own children under 6 years	213 856	4 241	14 947	43 227	62 863	39 004	16 011	5 840	2 955	651	24 117	226
Female householder, no husband present	103 898	3 028	10 168	22 615	29 926	18 257	7 048	2 571	1 219	346	8 720	220
With own children under 18 years	85 953	2 223	7 757	18 688	25 822	15 884	6 045	2 233	1 040	236	6 025	222
With own children under 6 years	45 413	1 354	3 970	10 450	13 824	8 460	2 965	1 052	419	45	2 874	220
Nonfamily householder	284 253	18 574	45 283	68 144	61 961	29 625	11 224	4 055	2 692	1 088	41 607	192
Income in 1979 below poverty level	206 369	12 847	27 462	43 665	47 660	25 518	10 079	3 316	1 594	581	33 647	203
Percent below poverty level	26.3	41.8	30.5	25.6	24.2	22.8	22.0	19.2	15.6	17.7	31.2	...
GROSS RENT AS PERCENTAGE OF HOUSEHOLD INCOME IN 1979												
Less than 15 percent	127 140	12 792	28 328	37 845	29 370	12 552	4 020	1 311	653	269	...	180
15 to 19 percent	99 156	3 689	12 908	27 588	30 382	15 601	5 569	2 091	1 109	219	...	209
20 to 24 percent	86 431	3 242	8 987	22 225	26 912	14 964	6 186	2 171	1 393	351	...	216
25 to 29 percent	69 479	2 624	7 069	16 568	22 062	12 371	5 208	2 070	1 154	353	...	219
30 to 34 percent	52 903	1 679	5 442	12 027	16 187	10 589	4 248	1 465	963	303	...	223
35 to 49 percent	94 070	3 207	10 536	20 473	28 626	17 999	7 843	2 976	1 892	518	...	222
50 percent or more	136 563	2 520	14 687	30 903	40 905	26 434	12 186	4 925	2 867	1 136	...	225
Not computed	119 563	975	2 007	3 132	2 851	1 581	656	303	163	142	107 753	197
Median	26.4	17.8	21.5	24.1	27.4	29.9	31.9	32.9	33.7	37.0	...	...

Table G— 9. Gross Rent of Renter-Occupied Housing Units; 1980—Con.

Mobile Homes or Trailers, Etc.—Total—Con.

[Data are estimates based on a sample; see Introduction. For meaning of symbols, see Introduction. For definitions of terms, see appendix A]

United States	Total	Less than $100	$100 to $149	$150 to $199	$200 to $249	$250 to $299	$300 to $349	$350 to $399	$400 to $499	$500 or more	No cash rent	Median (dollars)
AGE OF HOUSEHOLDER												
Persons 15 years and over	785 305	30 728	89 964	170 761	197 295	112 091	45 916	17 312	10 194	3 291	107 753	212
15 to 19 years	37 513	918	3 819	9 534	11 681	5 573	1 732	596	327	91	3 242	212
20 to 24 years	193 856	4 263	16 677	46 709	59 647	31 740	11 333	3 665	1 863	433	17 526	217
25 to 29 years	145 691	3 542	12 785	31 404	41 511	24 936	9 840	3 699	1 942	613	15 419	221
30 to 34 years	89 647	2 250	7 732	18 120	23 902	15 056	7 303	2 782	1 683	356	10 463	224
35 to 39 years	57 465	1 630	4 738	10 945	14 939	9 653	4 672	1 953	1 239	330	7 366	226
40 to 44 years	41 950	1 161	3 881	8 227	9 999	6 985	3 264	1 363	746	351	5 973	224
45 to 49 years	33 360	1 371	3 600	7 184	7 912	4 702	2 105	892	473	177	4 944	213
50 to 54 years	31 148	1 436	4 387	6 584	6 907	3 586	1 599	617	551	188	5 293	204
55 to 59 years	30 416	1 974	5 033	6 428	5 693	3 062	1 259	529	348	174	5 916	191
60 to 64 years	29 579	2 036	5 784	6 647	4 709	1 943	1 039	394	356	168	6 503	178
65 to 69 years	29 953	2 755	6 345	6 313	3 903	1 914	674	348	176	120	7 405	167
70 to 74 years	26 828	2 798	6 355	5 552	3 112	1 342	432	176	180	149	6 732	158
75 years and over	37 899	4 594	8 828	7 114	3 380	1 599	664	298	310	141	10 971	150
Median	30.9	50.8	39.2	29.6	28.3	28.8	30.0	31.3	32.9	37.3	39.9	...
MARITAL STATUS OF HOUSEHOLDER												
Persons 15 years and over	785 305	30 728	89 964	170 761	197 295	112 091	45 916	17 312	10 194	3 291	107 753	212
Single	145 356	6 832	18 462	36 365	37 440	19 282	7 137	2 653	1 612	642	14 931	205
Now married, except separated	382 124	9 067	33 433	77 268	100 885	61 191	26 307	10 164	6 018	1 819	55 972	221
Separated	49 666	1 936	5 638	11 473	14 257	7 373	2 868	1 133	426	94	4 468	212
Widowed	71 718	7 305	15 621	13 539	9 231	4 150	1 814	863	552	196	18 447	164
Divorced	136 441	5 588	16 810	32 116	35 482	20 095	7 790	2 499	1 586	540	13 935	209
YEARS OF SCHOOL COMPLETED BY HOUSEHOLDER												
Persons 25 years old and over	553 936	25 547	69 468	114 518	125 967	74 778	32 851	13 051	8 004	2 767	86 985	210
Median	12.0	9.7	11.1	12.1	12.2	12.2	12.3	12.3	12.5	12.6	10.7	...
PERIOD OF SERVICE OF HOUSEHOLDER												
Civilian veterans 16 years and over	168 501	5 320	17 179	33 090	42 724	27 159	12 739	4 760	2 945	969	21 616	221
Percent of civilians 16 years and over	22.3	17.4	19.3	20.3	23.2	25.6	28.9	28.1	29.4	29.9	20.1	...
May 1975 or later only	17 661	275	1 444	3 728	5 610	3 362	1 405	443	167	41	1 186	225
Vietnam era	70 959	1 211	4 829	13 312	20 723	13 562	6 487	2 258	1 427	347	6 803	231
February 1955 to July 1964 only	15 621	287	1 247	2 655	3 691	2 965	1 568	719	362	106	2 021	235
Vietnam era and Korean conflict	3 311	121	348	802	801	430	186	91	61	43	428	211
Korean conflict	16 012	559	1 588	3 179	3 887	2 365	1 239	500	264	113	2 318	220
Korean conflict and World War II	3 546	174	503	811	658	453	213	103	50	25	556	201
World War II	36 975	2 348	6 158	7 630	6 747	3 722	1 549	596	572	262	7 391	191
World War I	2 189	182	555	467	217	175	32	20	13	11	517	161
Other	2 227	163	507	506	390	125	60	30	29	21	396	174
Civilian nonveterans 16 years and over	585 919	25 284	71 738	130 191	141 286	78 777	31 312	12 168	7 059	2 274	85 830	208
LABOR FORCE STATUS OF HOUSEHOLDER												
Persons 16 years and over	785 121	30 711	89 947	170 688	197 242	112 091	45 907	17 306	10 194	3 291	107 744	212
Labor force	588 905	15 337	55 039	128 975	161 405	93 203	38 398	14 491	8 600	2 629	70 828	218
Percent of persons 16 years and over	75.0	49.9	61.2	75.6	81.8	83.1	83.6	83.7	84.4	79.9	65.7	...
Armed Forces	30 701	107	1 030	7 407	13 232	6 155	1 856	378	190	48	298	225
Civilian labor force	558 204	15 230	54 009	121 568	148 173	87 048	36 542	14 113	8 410	2 581	70 530	218
Employed	499 933	13 564	48 647	108 393	131 897	77 189	32 594	12 726	7 802	2 429	64 692	218
Unemployed	58 271	1 666	5 362	13 175	16 276	9 859	3 948	1 387	608	152	5 838	218
Percent of civilian labor force	10.4	10.9	9.9	10.8	11.0	11.3	10.8	9.8	7.2	5.9	8.3	...
Not in labor force	196 216	15 374	34 908	41 713	35 837	18 888	7 509	2 815	1 594	662	36 916	185
OCCUPATION OF HOUSEHOLDER												
Employed persons 16 years and over	499 933	13 564	48 647	108 393	131 897	77 189	32 594	12 726	7 802	2 429	64 692	218
Managerial and professional specialty occupations	50 647	1 713	5 106	10 212	11 824	7 208	3 413	1 615	1 221	486	7 849	218
Executive, administrative, and managerial occupations	24 925	583	2 043	4 580	5 975	3 902	1 816	1 001	652	261	4 112	227
Professional specialty occupations	25 722	1 130	3 063	5 632	5 849	3 306	1 597	614	569	225	3 737	210
Technical, sales, and administrative support occupations	75 664	1 797	7 990	17 101	20 504	12 153	4 971	2 075	1 378	609	7 086	218
Technicians and related support occupations	10 919	226	1 197	2 677	3 273	1 524	654	303	184	54	827	214
Sales occupations	27 323	681	2 700	5 799	7 160	4 452	2 035	920	449	294	2 833	221
Administrative support occupations, including clerical	37 422	890	4 093	8 625	10 071	6 177	2 282	852	745	261	3 426	217
Service occupations	62 072	2 190	7 574	14 110	16 236	9 256	4 006	1 366	987	251	6 096	213
Private household occupations	1 896	215	284	344	358	199	111	22	6	–	357	189
Protective service occupations	8 669	222	930	1 863	2 396	1 272	600	253	173	36	924	218
Service occupations, except protective and household	51 507	1 753	6 360	11 903	13 482	7 785	3 295	1 091	808	215	4 815	212
Farming, forestry, and fishing occupations	37 822	1 631	3 081	4 996	4 676	2 416	1 111	416	179	146	19 170	196
Precision production, craft, and repair occupations	110 020	2 098	9 389	23 048	31 149	19 397	8 768	3 483	2 033	481	10 174	225
Operators, fabricators, and laborers	163 708	4 135	15 507	38 926	47 508	26 759	10 325	3 771	2 004	456	14 317	217
Machine operators, assemblers, and inspectors	71 447	1 730	7 016	18 262	21 167	11 313	3 959	1 344	771	137	5 748	214
Transportation and material moving occupations	49 838	1 182	4 052	10 573	13 993	9 084	3 782	1 551	760	193	4 668	224
Handlers, equipment cleaners, helpers, and laborers	42 423	1 223	4 439	10 091	12 348	6 362	2 584	876	473	126	3 901	214
MEANS OF TRANSPORTATION TO WORK FOR HOUSEHOLDER												
Workers 16 years and over	514 967	13 226	48 058	112 315	141 043	80 847	33 513	12 620	7 771	2 402	63 172	219
Private vehicle	451 450	10 242	42 024	100 903	128 816	74 125	30 760	11 553	6 838	1 908	44 281	220
Drive alone: Car	241 111	5 404	23 251	56 590	70 983	40 085	15 853	5 719	3 458	973	18 795	218
Truck or van	80 387	1 940	7 663	15 681	19 274	12 346	5 737	2 231	1 299	383	13 833	221
Carpool: Car	93 374	1 926	8 008	20 760	29 214	16 106	6 549	2 477	1 304	346	6 684	222
Truck or van	36 578	972	3 102	7 872	9 345	5 588	2 621	1 126	777	206	4 969	221
Public transportation	7 015	455	930	1 510	1 597	1 125	486	220	277	99	316	214
Bus or streetcar	5 376	363	774	1 131	1 202	867	351	117	226	64	281	212
Subway or elevated train	796	51	56	134	187	106	93	89	37	28	15	240
Railroad	97	–	9	31	2	35	16	–	–	–	4	256
Taxicab	746	41	91	214	206	117	26	14	14	7	16	205
Bicycle	2 507	147	341	659	657	287	165	46	40	8	157	202
Motorcycle	5 405	133	536	1 188	1 633	964	379	81	74	26	391	220
Walked only	33 181	1 807	3 355	5 846	6 012	2 830	1 004	436	369	200	11 322	199
Other means	7 032	191	431	1 353	1 619	1 044	478	190	79	54	1 593	223
Worked at home	8 377	251	441	856	709	472	241	94	94	107	5 112	206
WORKERS IN HOUSEHOLD IN 1979												
No workers	144 456	13 478	29 218	31 044	22 936	10 869	4 234	1 758	948	460	29 511	174
1 worker	352 828	12 235	39 968	82 358	91 568	49 122	19 290	7 034	4 028	1 352	45 873	210
2 workers	259 461	4 495	19 119	53 268	75 823	46 275	19 564	7 096	4 178	1 155	28 488	220
3 or more workers	28 560	520	1 659	4 091	6 968	5 825	2 828	1 424	1 040	324	3 881	244

Table I— 1. **Selected Monthly Owner Costs for Mortgaged Housing Units: 1980**

Housing Units in One-Unit Detached Structures—Total

[Data are estimates based on a sample; see Introduction. For meaning of symbols, see Introduction. For definitions of terms, see appendix A]

United States	Total	Less than $200	$200 to $249	$250 to $299	$300 to $349	$350 to $399	$400 to $499	$500 to $599	$600 to $749	$750 or more	Median (dollars)
Specified owner-occupied housing units	24 657 508	2 396 268	2 799 224	3 184 040	3 048 379	2 743 779	4 224 955	2 613 091	2 015 640	1 632 132	366
YEAR STRUCTURE BUILT											
1979 to March 1980	960 454	34 544	31 076	36 421	46 937	60 901	157 345	174 335	202 246	216 649	565
1975 to 1978	3 256 569	90 391	113 863	181 138	261 676	353 423	777 985	589 923	491 947	396 223	480
1970 to 1974	3 383 512	166 003	255 980	379 404	442 091	440 476	706 501	426 701	321 286	245 070	401
1960 to 1969	6 065 645	532 844	773 076	896 704	827 091	700 802	998 822	580 533	425 745	330 028	350
1950 to 1959	5 044 879	722 351	756 427	758 094	653 350	534 225	738 292	401 755	279 578	200 807	322
1940 to 1949	2 155 631	351 415	325 941	334 200	289 253	231 294	297 654	154 426	100 053	71 395	311
1939 or earlier	3 790 818	498 720	542 861	598 079	527 981	422 658	548 356	285 418	194 785	171 960	324
YEAR HOUSEHOLDER MOVED INTO UNIT											
1979 to March 1980	3 647 176	141 612	159 257	213 674	272 261	322 372	696 116	615 774	614 605	611 505	503
1975 to 1978	8 372 220	385 883	546 500	801 905	986 429	1 063 401	1 854 269	1 188 214	885 252	660 367	420
1970 to 1974	5 344 046	490 288	683 305	858 691	811 576	672 966	886 120	444 720	290 184	206 196	339
1960 to 1969	5 526 772	903 517	1 065 877	1 021 661	771 682	542 181	625 298	290 183	180 812	125 561	289
1959 or earlier	1 767 294	474 968	344 285	288 109	206 431	142 859	163 152	74 200	44 787	28 503	261
ROOMS											
1 room	12 618	3 871	1 725	1 728	1 289	1 013	1 255	848	456	433	271
2 rooms	51 702	15 350	7 764	6 833	5 302	4 222	5 843	3 008	1 969	1 411	270
3 rooms	262 810	68 676	39 644	35 121	27 043	21 842	30 223	18 170	13 558	8 533	283
4 rooms	1 477 280	409 884	276 289	228 960	171 295	122 356	142 453	63 712	38 626	23 705	261
5 rooms	5 365 656	902 525	930 378	909 974	742 278	575 451	708 793	328 579	182 883	84 795	297
6 rooms	6 797 192	644 968	893 382	1 024 469	959 509	834 252	1 190 822	635 526	404 546	209 718	344
7 or more rooms	10 690 250	350 994	650 042	976 955	1 141 663	1 184 643	2 145 566	1 563 248	1 373 602	1 303 537	446
Median	6.3	5.3	5.7	5.9	6.1	6.3	6.5+	6.5+	6.5+	6.5+	...
BEDROOMS											
None	18 614	5 388	2 575	2 522	2 002	1 474	1 945	1 339	736	633	277
1	400 591	103 363	65 003	57 475	43 700	34 266	45 312	23 949	16 331	11 192	278
2	3 972 183	843 089	683 182	629 073	508 487	385 618	473 793	226 837	137 894	84 210	287
3	13 933 508	1 239 489	1 671 910	1 939 416	1 861 176	1 678 676	2 525 104	1 454 495	986 281	576 961	358
4	5 310 908	181 762	332 184	485 148	547 181	553 255	1 006 802	764 286	722 546	717 744	453
5 or more	1 021 704	23 177	44 370	70 406	85 833	90 490	171 999	142 185	151 852	241 392	517
PERSONS IN UNIT											
1 person	1 736 936	409 449	264 163	232 252	196 172	157 752	214 473	117 302	82 681	62 692	292
2 persons	6 092 449	811 097	809 808	812 883	720 811	623 757	937 383	581 712	448 309	346 689	342
3 persons	5 334 206	452 798	612 577	706 959	679 914	614 985	945 324	571 138	423 849	326 662	367
4 persons	6 344 301	377 254	607 333	782 173	804 620	753 796	1 196 754	750 161	588 128	484 082	390
5 persons	3 175 870	192 476	302 751	394 202	395 927	370 263	585 852	374 364	298 853	261 182	391
6 or more persons	1 973 746	153 194	202 592	255 571	250 935	223 226	345 169	218 414	173 820	150 825	378
Median	3.34	2.47	3.03	3.27	3.39	3.46	3.51	3.55	3.59	3.67	...
Total persons	83 743 165	6 789 497	8 908 637	10 661 211	10 443 886	9 523 713	14 859 448	9 298 273	7 252 637	6 005 863	...
PLUMBING FACILITIES BY PERSONS PER ROOM											
Complete plumbing for exclusive use	24 586 044	2 354 236	2 788 619	3 177 585	3 044 270	2 741 133	4 222 242	2 611 712	2 014 807	1 631 440	367
1.01 or more persons per room	728 879	119 911	118 921	122 908	98 339	74 149	94 790	49 791	31 759	18 311	301
Lacking complete plumbing for exclusive use	71 464	42 032	10 605	6 455	4 109	2 646	2 713	1 379	833	692	178
1.01 or more persons per room	15 538	9 579	2 347	1 412	780	464	440	227	149	140	173
HOUSEHOLD INCOME IN 1979											
Less than $5,000	903 890	283 730	139 196	116 180	89 947	70 061	92 285	50 118	35 019	27 354	262
$5,000 to $9,999	1 536 332	433 348	292 745	236 479	172 907	123 072	144 471	66 462	40 621	26 227	259
$10,000 to $12,499	1 176 152	233 006	221 546	201 575	154 361	113 807	135 223	60 843	35 283	20 508	283
$12,500 to $14,999	1 251 957	202 689	218 942	219 442	183 039	137 096	160 896	70 042	39 122	20 689	297
$15,000 to $19,999	3 500 634	401 790	512 397	571 781	532 250	441 624	573 575	261 399	141 043	64 775	325
$20,000 to $24,999	4 135 073	330 439	486 514	588 269	586 313	539 925	808 461	436 183	250 531	108 438	357
$25,000 to $34,999	6 345 404	343 628	597 342	762 951	783 602	761 992	1 285 181	848 472	629 750	332 486	395
$35,000 to $49,999	3 842 943	133 270	264 455	377 648	409 083	408 045	722 366	550 258	524 743	453 075	443
$50,000 or more	1 965 123	34 368	66 087	109 715	136 877	148 157	302 497	269 314	319 528	578 580	569
Median	$24 772	$15 530	$20 137	$21 908	$23 190	$24 462	$26 208	$28 777	$32 093	$41 198	...
Mean	$27 898	$17 316	$21 578	$23 654	$25 236	$26 612	$28 710	$31 894	$36 425	$50 665	...
SELECTED CHARACTERISTICS											
Heating equipment	24 657 508	2 396 268	2 799 224	3 184 040	3 048 379	2 743 779	4 224 955	2 613 091	2 015 640	1 632 132	366
Central heating system	22 245 545	1 730 934	2 375 703	2 828 385	2 775 963	2 539 525	3 977 788	2 495 115	1 940 280	1 581 852	378
Air conditioning	15 531 279	1 369 229	1 664 722	1 901 226	1 859 848	1 720 525	2 755 503	1 756 501	1 379 146	1 124 579	378
Central system	9 014 076	439 707	700 224	909 525	985 346	1 002 649	1 774 909	1 232 236	1 042 323	927 157	425
1 or more individual room units	6 517 203	929 522	964 498	991 701	874 502	717 876	980 594	524 265	336 823	197 422	321
Vehicles available	24 244 051	2 225 934	2 727 114	3 128 058	3 009 933	2 716 906	4 196 786	2 600 938	2 009 439	1 628 943	369
1	5 355 450	803 959	759 650	783 914	695 562	582 402	800 587	439 107	298 282	191 987	324
2 or more	18 888 601	1 421 975	1 967 464	2 344 144	2 314 371	2 134 504	3 396 199	2 161 831	1 711 157	1 436 956	383
House heating fuel	24 552 547	2 382 367	2 788 256	3 171 948	3 037 873	2 734 138	4 210 574	2 603 164	2 005 101	1 619 126	366
Utility gas	14 877 319	1 503 840	1 794 750	1 992 902	1 850 078	1 618 191	2 415 721	1 494 246	1 185 170	1 022 412	359
Bottled, tank, or LP gas	762 481	137 830	115 402	113 782	99 501	79 141	103 994	53 646	35 056	24 129	307
Electricity	4 397 245	342 743	411 276	484 381	503 453	499 435	855 702	553 420	431 922	314 913	396
Fuel oil, kerosene, etc.	3 703 529	237 309	337 796	455 981	477 270	450 814	724 599	451 390	325 013	243 357	388
Other	811 973	160 645	129 023	124 902	107 571	86 557	110 558	50 462	27 940	14 315	297
Family householder	22 546 762	1 953 726	2 501 545	2 910 351	2 811 280	2 546 711	3 945 828	2 450 104	1 894 129	1 533 088	372
With own children under 18 years	14 411 981	883 506	1 381 718	1 772 270	1 816 494	1 702 887	2 716 535	1 711 256	1 331 629	1 095 686	390
With own children under 6 years	5 698 530	273 505	436 755	621 576	708 683	716 018	1 191 674	756 399	566 841	427 079	407
Female householder, no husband present	1 720 908	260 488	272 242	280 065	234 957	185 630	238 311	120 656	77 569	50 990	310
With own children under 18 years	1 105 118	124 555	162 076	178 184	158 000	128 638	169 955	88 223	57 212	38 275	328
With own children under 6 years	210 769	22 789	28 501	32 359	30 643	25 850	34 548	17 839	11 028	7 212	335
Nonfamily householder	2 110 746	442 542	297 679	273 689	237 099	197 068	279 127	162 987	121 511	99 044	309
Income in 1979 below poverty level	1 104 135	288 495	171 229	152 798	121 639	95 647	125 523	67 223	46 290	35 291	280
Percent below poverty level	4.5	12.0	6.1	4.8	4.0	3.5	3.0	2.6	2.3	2.2	...
SELECTED MONTHLY OWNER COSTS AS PERCENTAGE OF HOUSEHOLD INCOME IN 1979											
Less than 15 percent	8 016 875	1 396 696	1 540 237	1 491 039	1 133 919	794 720	870 841	374 253	234 105	181 065	286
15 to 19 percent	5 091 815	316 085	480 264	695 206	768 314	717 956	1 036 716	533 211	333 033	211 030	370
20 to 24 percent	3 919 050	188 565	254 968	362 135	450 967	499 846	894 439	583 644	416 478	268 008	421
25 to 29 percent	2 550 170	121 366	149 621	192 266	229 804	261 037	549 711	423 123	359 224	264 018	457
30 to 34 percent	1 513 494	78 827	88 607	114 312	128 392	137 096	283 634	248 136	231 464	203 026	474
35 percent or more	3 446 216	273 206	271 313	314 681	324 030	321 848	572 910	439 833	432 420	495 975	436
Not computed	119 888	21 523	14 214	14 401	12 953	11 276	16 704	10 891	8 916	9 010	338
Median	19.2	13.2	14.2	15.7	17.5	19.0	21.1	23.4	25.3	27.9	...

STRUCTURAL CHARACTERISTICS OF THE HOUSING INVENTORY

Table I— 1. Selected Monthly Owner Costs for Mortgaged Housing Units: 1980—Con.

Housing Units in One-Unit Detached Structures—Total—Con.

[Data are estimates based on a sample; see Introduction. For meaning of symbols, see Introduction. For definitions of terms, see appendix A]

United States	Total	Less than $200	$200 to $249	$250 to $299	$300 to $349	$350 to $399	$400 to $499	$500 to $599	$600 to $749	$750 or more	Median (dollars)
AGE OF HOUSEHOLDER											
Persons 15 years and over	24 657 508	2 396 268	2 799 224	3 184 040	3 048 379	2 743 779	4 224 955	2 613 091	2 015 640	1 632 132	366
15 to 19 years	23 979	4 343	3 858	3 691	3 107	2 575	3 042	1 669	1 106	588	302
20 to 24 years	733 390	60 356	81 141	100 382	107 141	98 086	144 606	77 499	46 655	17 524	359
25 to 29 years	2 661 679	135 790	214 499	301 089	348 334	353 674	582 047	360 634	243 850	121 762	397
30 to 34 years	4 022 641	179 549	293 429	420 497	481 444	493 624	846 123	556 983	435 104	315 888	416
35 to 39 years	3 725 251	198 878	316 923	413 109	433 401	418 684	701 834	473 938	400 211	368 273	411
40 to 44 years	3 133 340	214 734	328 152	395 820	380 593	344 758	540 800	350 869	295 129	282 485	386
45 to 49 years	2 835 385	252 915	350 402	396 735	359 001	307 051	454 370	279 289	224 927	210 695	360
50 to 54 years	2 592 329	299 870	367 342	385 882	337 888	274 984	385 892	221 212	168 650	150 609	336
55 to 59 years	2 108 813	315 465	335 736	333 217	271 598	215 013	283 993	152 082	109 503	92 206	313
60 to 64 years	1 341 051	261 370	237 847	216 933	170 787	126 391	155 108	78 810	51 839	41 966	289
65 to 69 years	764 436	207 007	142 312	119 571	86 790	61 196	73 195	34 715	22 217	17 433	264
70 to 74 years	402 040	138 444	74 462	56 862	40 256	28 139	31 802	14 948	9 759	7 368	242
75 years and over	313 174	127 547	53 121	40 252	28 039	19 604	22 143	10 443	6 690	5 335	227
Median	41.9	52.5	47.3	44.5	42.0	40.1	38.8	38.3	38.5	39.9	...
MARITAL STATUS OF HOUSEHOLDER											
Persons 15 years and over	24 657 508	2 396 268	2 799 224	3 184 040	3 048 379	2 743 779	4 224 955	2 613 091	2 015 640	1 632 132	366
Single	838 642	102 229	95 816	107 056	103 365	94 804	140 320	84 799	62 846	47 407	356
Now married, except separated	20 509 497	1 651 175	2 185 961	2 584 439	2 536 064	2 326 936	3 660 679	2 302 025	1 797 002	1 465 216	378
Separated	419 907	52 773	51 798	56 929	53 303	45 691	67 150	39 823	28 302	24 138	345
Widowed	1 164 771	341 123	208 423	175 644	129 538	92 941	111 686	52 577	31 537	21 302	259
Divorced	1 724 691	248 968	257 226	259 972	226 109	183 407	245 120	133 867	95 953	74 069	321
YEARS OF SCHOOL COMPLETED BY HOUSEHOLDER											
Persons 25 years old and over	23 900 139	2 331 569	2 714 225	3 079 967	2 938 131	2 643 118	4 077 307	2 533 923	1 967 879	1 614 020	367
Median	12.9	12.1	12.4	12.6	12.7	12.9	13.4	14.5	15.5	16.4	...
PERIOD OF SERVICE OF HOUSEHOLDER											
Civilian veterans 16 years and over	10 540 683	881 852	1 217 964	1 413 783	1 350 018	1 206 595	1 825 152	1 105 752	846 689	692 878	367
Percent of civilians 16 years and over	43.1	36.9	43.7	44.6	44.6	44.3	43.7	42.9	42.7	43.1	...
May 1975 or later only	88 422	6 327	8 216	10 611	11 642	10 732	16 810	10 158	7 918	6 008	385
Vietnam era	3 094 603	121 832	225 694	333 935	385 501	394 820	658 139	419 373	318 094	237 215	412
February 1955 to July 1964 only	1 603 764	87 176	156 295	198 153	197 995	183 446	292 986	189 326	156 154	142 233	394
Vietnam era and Korean conflict	366 896	26 025	42 944	51 523	49 164	44 415	65 829	38 469	28 788	19 739	366
Korean conflict	1 886 082	156 170	238 366	272 827	246 208	208 554	307 442	184 848	144 800	126 867	357
Korean conflict and World War II	314 548	40 122	48 679	47 795	40 021	32 549	44 315	25 599	18 884	16 584	326
World War II	3 076 512	422 085	480 702	483 307	406 595	322 152	426 309	230 224	166 042	139 096	319
World War I	19 893	7 479	3 475	2 772	1 881	1 208	1 472	753	518	335	236
Other	89 963	14 636	13 593	12 860	11 011	8 719	11 850	7 002	5 491	4 801	318
Civilian nonveterans 16 years and over	13 904 693	1 508 733	1 572 075	1 755 949	1 678 707	1 514 642	2 354 686	1 471 050	1 134 261	914 590	364
LABOR FORCE STATUS OF HOUSEHOLDER											
Persons 16 years and over	24 656 213	2 396 042	2 799 037	3 183 907	3 048 260	2 743 632	4 224 729	2 612 973	2 015 548	1 632 085	366
Labor force	21 962 007	1 704 100	2 330 996	2 782 715	2 743 730	2 515 556	3 942 273	2 471 980	1 919 555	1 551 102	378
Percent of persons 16 years and over	89.1	71.1	83.3	87.4	90.0	91.7	93.3	94.6	95.2	95.0	...
Armed Forces	210 837	5 457	8 998	14 175	19 535	22 395	44 891	36 171	34 598	24 617	477
Civilian labor force	21 751 170	1 698 643	2 321 998	2 768 540	2 724 195	2 493 161	3 897 382	2 435 809	1 884 957	1 526 485	377
Employed	21 124 588	1 621 595	2 233 345	2 671 106	2 632 490	2 418 851	3 799 351	2 385 804	1 853 529	1 508 517	379
Unemployed	626 582	77 048	88 653	97 434	91 705	74 310	98 031	50 005	31 428	17 968	327
Percent of civilian labor force	2.9	4.5	3.8	3.5	3.4	3.0	2.5	2.1	1.7	1.2	...
Not in labor force	2 694 206	691 942	468 041	401 192	304 530	228 076	282 456	140 993	95 993	80 983	273
OCCUPATION OF HOUSEHOLDER											
Employed persons 16 years and over	21 124 588	1 621 595	2 233 345	2 671 106	2 632 490	2 418 851	3 799 351	2 385 804	1 853 529	1 508 517	379
Managerial and professional specialty occupations	6 826 378	232 336	417 165	608 792	703 056	735 771	1 341 441	989 510	891 556	906 751	451
Executive, administrative, and managerial occupations	3 696 511	126 382	220 769	313 956	359 385	382 237	714 734	548 093	508 618	522 337	460
Professional specialty occupations	3 129 867	105 954	196 396	294 836	343 671	353 534	626 707	441 417	382 938	384 414	441
Technical, sales, and administrative support occupations	4 808 464	331 126	487 573	589 469	590 086	556 511	891 136	570 533	447 162	344 868	386
Technicians and related support occupations	737 353	42 305	69 914	90 523	94 489	88 999	145 546	90 321	68 107	47 149	390
Sales occupations	2 158 012	113 873	168 973	215 636	232 307	235 261	414 893	293 784	254 362	228 923	425
Administrative support occupations, including clerical	1 913 099	174 948	248 686	283 310	263 290	232 251	330 697	186 428	124 693	68 796	347
Service occupations	1 385 969	186 962	195 907	205 182	183 655	155 215	218 439	120 714	78 784	41 111	329
Private household occupations	30 196	12 120	5 713	4 289	2 747	1 698	1 926	948	403	352	226
Protective service occupations	511 876	34 281	53 901	66 240	69 196	66 187	103 765	60 391	38 992	18 923	374
Service occupations, except protective and household	843 897	140 561	136 293	134 653	111 712	87 330	112 748	59 375	39 389	21 836	305
Farming, forestry, and fishing occupations	251 408	47 559	37 073	35 508	30 879	23 938	34 401	19 170	13 340	9 540	309
Precision production, craft, and repair occupations	4 247 626	381 200	540 086	628 837	598 482	520 295	752 479	414 517	268 801	142 929	348
Operators, fabricators, and laborers	3 604 743	442 412	555 541	603 318	526 332	427 121	561 455	271 360	153 886	63 318	319
Machine operators, assemblers, and inspectors	1 733 137	215 556	280 166	303 816	261 856	206 340	260 418	119 066	62 646	23 273	313
Transportation and material moving occupations	1 254 387	138 622	178 694	197 360	176 562	151 049	208 955	108 286	65 838	29 021	332
Handlers, equipment cleaners, helpers, and laborers	617 219	88 234	96 681	102 142	87 914	69 732	92 082	44 008	25 402	11 024	312
MEANS OF TRANSPORTATION TO WORK FOR HOUSEHOLDER											
Workers 16 years and over	20 935 250	1 581 310	2 189 344	2 625 457	2 598 773	2 396 931	3 780 676	2 386 139	1 862 641	1 513 979	381
Private vehicle	19 528 327	1 472 667	2 057 707	2 465 044	2 439 256	2 245 580	3 536 112	2 217 243	1 717 626	1 377 092	380
Drive alone: Car	11 900 289	787 725	1 140 030	1 408 971	1 427 205	1 344 658	2 185 297	1 429 368	1 154 300	1 022 735	394
Truck or van	3 734 227	368 332	485 873	544 221	510 358	445 786	646 145	356 903	238 546	138 063	346
Carpool: Car	3 076 462	227 503	321 454	390 732	389 159	359 225	566 906	357 842	274 547	189 094	379
Truck or van	817 349	89 107	110 350	121 120	112 534	95 911	137 764	73 130	50 233	27 200	339
Public transportation	658 846	34 322	45 506	60 194	63 963	67 137	121 156	94 085	86 928	85 555	446
Bus or streetcar	381 738	30 221	39 705	47 968	45 982	44 075	67 983	44 235	34 541	27 028	381
Subway or elevated train	68 174	1 066	1 935	4 440	6 618	7 634	15 482	12 023	10 927	8 049	479
Railroad	197 947	795	2 449	6 350	10 400	14 487	36 451	36 916	40 641	49 458	576
Taxicab	10 987	2 240	1 417	1 436	963	941	1 240	911	819	1 020	321
Bicycle	69 532	5 457	7 804	9 771	9 611	8 792	11 959	7 398	5 053	3 687	362
Motorcycle	113 813	8 997	11 551	15 148	14 822	14 368	21 414	13 152	9 271	5 090	372
Walked only	309 208	39 196	43 904	48 087	44 049	35 430	46 885	23 726	16 083	11 848	327
Other means	100 093	8 608	9 704	11 123	10 817	10 140	16 697	11 947	10 229	10 828	398
Worked at home	155 431	12 063	13 168	16 090	16 255	15 484	26 453	18 588	17 451	19 879	416
WORKERS IN HOUSEHOLD IN 1979											
No workers	1 344 458	432 263	238 573	190 856	138 899	99 903	119 242	56 794	37 193	30 735	250
1 worker	8 021 461	886 712	969 582	1 051 710	979 884	865 636	1 306 245	793 609	612 922	555 161	357
2 workers	11 285 099	781 916	1 119 637	1 371 229	1 395 340	1 316 867	2 118 078	1 351 761	1 044 668	785 603	387
3 or more workers	4 006 490	295 377	471 432	570 245	534 256	461 373	681 390	410 927	320 857	260 633	364

Table I— 2. **Selected Monthly Owner Costs for Mortgaged Housing Units: 1980**

Housing Units in One-Unit Attached Structures—Total

[Data are estimates based on a sample; see Introduction. For meaning of symbols, see Introduction. For definitions of terms, see appendix A]

United States	Total	Less than $200	$200 to $249	$250 to $299	$300 to $349	$350 to $399	$400 to $499	$500 to $599	$600 to $749	$750 or more	Median (dollars)
Specified owner-occupied housing units	825 966	95 209	112 814	119 003	104 203	90 169	133 757	78 220	54 376	38 215	341
YEAR STRUCTURE BUILT											
1979 to March 1980	36 480	788	799	964	1 154	2 113	6 493	7 756	8 909	7 504	576
1975 to 1978	94 605	1 771	2 266	4 126	7 200	10 344	25 878	18 885	14 577	9 558	483
1970 to 1974	91 114	4 123	4 720	8 768	10 876	12 402	21 277	14 096	9 357	5 495	421
1960 to 1969	98 858	8 405	12 624	14 648	13 757	12 859	17 968	9 449	5 603	3 545	350
1950 to 1959	119 028	16 156	21 203	20 128	17 535	13 675	16 932	7 316	3 897	2 186	306
1940 to 1949	106 102	16 290	19 030	19 500	15 358	11 360	13 412	6 082	3 203	1 867	295
1939 or earlier	279 779	47 676	52 172	50 869	38 323	27 416	31 797	14 636	8 830	8 060	289
YEAR HOUSEHOLDER MOVED INTO UNIT											
1979 to March 1980	139 293	5 558	6 374	9 173	11 459	13 568	28 700	23 477	22 274	18 710	482
1975 to 1978	267 483	13 236	19 525	29 601	35 891	36 228	59 924	35 797	23 256	14 025	399
1970 to 1974	165 306	18 182	25 813	31 564	25 253	19 922	24 926	11 229	5 273	3 144	314
1960 to 1969	174 186	32 917	42 901	35 963	23 151	15 083	14 642	5 447	2 488	1 594	266
1959 or earlier	79 698	25 316	18 201	12 702	8 449	5 368	5 565	2 270	1 085	742	240
ROOMS											
1 room	708	105	70	104	110	117	86	63	3	50	334
2 rooms	3 534	790	417	483	376	342	471	313	213	129	310
3 rooms	14 066	2 743	1 828	1 836	1 760	1 214	1 857	1 078	1 047	703	318
4 rooms	56 129	11 297	7 871	7 796	6 685	5 561	7 473	4 529	2 961	1 956	308
5 rooms	150 087	22 875	21 517	21 507	18 406	15 721	23 600	12 632	8 515	5 314	325
6 rooms	312 946	38 891	51 250	49 574	41 488	33 611	48 632	24 889	15 874	8 737	320
7 or more rooms	288 496	18 508	29 861	37 703	35 378	33 603	51 638	34 716	25 763	21 326	384
Median	6.1	5.8	6.0	6.1	6.1	6.2	6.2	6.3	6.4	6.5+	...
BEDROOMS											
None	1 090	201	106	137	150	181	128	96	15	76	334
1	21 010	4 069	3 007	2 906	2 490	1 653	2 729	1 783	1 454	919	311
2	173 370	29 186	22 754	23 507	20 610	17 918	26 295	14 719	10 518	7 863	327
3	510 602	52 627	74 341	75 355	65 318	57 071	85 396	48 853	32 219	19 422	341
4	94 469	7 204	9 995	13 334	11 937	10 426	15 193	10 344	8 437	7 599	373
5 or more	25 425	1 922	2 611	3 764	3 698	2 920	4 016	2 425	1 733	2 336	362
PERSONS IN UNIT											
1 person	105 476	20 012	13 579	13 079	11 338	10 242	15 315	9 128	7 418	5 365	327
2 persons	220 699	28 670	27 861	27 376	24 880	21 871	35 190	23 100	17 828	13 923	354
3 persons	170 753	17 594	23 554	25 236	21 567	19 420	28 561	16 214	11 107	7 500	344
4 persons	167 638	14 048	23 619	26 029	22 815	19 382	29 202	16 353	9 969	6 221	344
5 persons	90 523	8 081	13 549	15 413	12 643	10 855	14 597	7 737	4 513	3 135	333
6 or more persons	70 877	6 804	10 652	11 870	10 960	8 399	10 892	5 688	3 541	2 071	328
Median	3.01	2.46	3.14	3.25	3.24	3.17	3.07	2.92	2.67	2.49	...
Total persons	2 632 556	268 773	370 639	399 839	351 533	297 719	430 546	243 789	160 640	109 078	...
PLUMBING FACILITIES BY PERSONS PER ROOM											
Complete plumbing for exclusive use	824 156	94 417	112 521	118 763	104 036	90 119	133 627	78 147	54 334	38 192	342
1.01 or more persons per room	30 813	3 597	4 767	5 066	4 683	3 302	4 619	2 319	1 530	930	321
Lacking complete plumbing for exclusive use	1 810	792	293	240	167	50	130	73	42	23	219
1.01 or more persons per room	319	140	48	43	31	8	20	13	11	5	220
HOUSEHOLD INCOME IN 1979											
Less than $5,000	44 059	13 976	7 615	6 601	4 874	3 641	3 825	1 701	1 051	775	253
$5,000 to $9,999	66 095	16 980	12 920	11 561	7 915	5 601	6 279	2 699	1 370	770	264
$10,000 to $12,499	49 999	8 955	9 648	8 918	7 043	4 822	5 638	2 678	1 476	821	286
$12,500 to $14,999	51 478	7 798	9 196	10 012	7 811	5 400	6 238	2 762	1 621	640	294
$15,000 to $19,999	133 146	15 489	20 941	21 818	19 481	16 639	22 483	9 706	4 560	2 029	321
$20,000 to $24,999	136 908	12 343	17 770	20 456	19 158	17 683	25 900	13 566	7 188	2 844	347
$25,000 to $34,999	190 071	13 197	21 947	24 613	22 872	21 940	36 714	24 175	16 595	8 018	378
$35,000 to $49,999	106 317	5 159	10 186	11 815	11 710	10 683	19 329	14 520	12 922	9 993	417
$50,000 or more	47 893	1 312	2 591	3 209	3 339	3 760	7 351	6 413	7 593	12 325	537
Median	$22 279	$14 946	$19 042	$20 127	$21 166	$22 328	$24 274	$27 050	$30 735	$39 149	...
Mean	$25 019	$16 789	$20 663	$21 676	$22 806	$24 145	$26 655	$29 691	$34 349	$48 327	...
SELECTED CHARACTERISTICS											
Heating equipment	825 966	95 209	112 814	119 003	104 203	90 169	133 757	78 220	54 376	38 215	341
Central heating system	762 531	80 237	101 652	108 787	95 869	84 799	127 185	75 107	52 188	36 707	347
Air conditioning	561 037	52 755	70 186	76 473	70 155	64 125	100 013	59 890	41 114	26 326	359
Central system	254 445	9 881	14 949	21 815	25 238	29 048	57 874	41 388	32 424	21 828	444
1 or more individual room units	306 592	42 874	55 237	54 658	44 917	35 077	42 139	18 502	8 690	4 498	301
Vehicles available	758 331	75 431	99 427	107 288	96 680	85 106	128 515	75 647	52 932	37 305	350
1	343 162	42 995	49 860	51 770	45 749	37 840	53 388	29 684	19 232	12 644	329
2 or more	415 169	32 436	49 567	55 518	50 931	47 266	75 127	45 963	33 700	24 661	370
House heating fuel	822 536	94 792	112 522	118 624	103 898	89 854	133 144	77 912	53 990	37 800	341
Utility gas	517 539	65 698	77 988	77 611	66 060	55 628	78 025	44 320	29 814	22 375	328
Bottled, tank, or LP gas	8 546	1 785	1 249	1 290	1 095	815	1 024	546	440	302	298
Electricity	131 180	6 940	6 590	10 143	12 472	14 269	29 407	21 624	17 977	11 758	450
Fuel oil, kerosene, etc.	154 726	17 106	24 543	27 988	23 087	18 377	23 764	11 105	5 509	3 247	317
Other	10 565	3 263	2 152	1 592	1 184	765	924	317	250	118	247
Family householder	696 267	72 895	96 964	103 349	90 455	77 618	114 624	65 949	44 088	30 325	341
With own children under 18 years	404 774	32 521	53 796	61 901	55 646	49 218	71 176	39 761	24 930	15 825	349
With own children under 6 years	165 882	9 245	16 217	22 609	23 325	22 257	34 659	18 899	11 800	6 871	376
Female householder, no husband present	98 951	14 506	16 936	17 681	13 627	10 456	13 259	6 610	3 793	2 083	301
With own children under 18 years	57 316	6 242	9 032	10 256	8 297	6 769	8 509	4 362	2 554	1 295	319
With own children under 6 years	10 585	1 059	1 432	1 915	1 551	1 428	1 782	791	439	188	329
Nonfamily householder	129 699	22 314	15 850	15 654	13 748	12 551	19 133	12 271	10 288	7 890	340
Income in 1979 below poverty level	53 580	13 781	9 763	8 916	6 561	4 820	5 139	2 234	1 367	999	268
Percent below poverty level	6.5	14.5	8.7	7.5	6.3	5.3	3.8	2.9	2.5	2.6	...
SELECTED MONTHLY OWNER COSTS AS PERCENTAGE OF HOUSEHOLD INCOME IN 1979											
Less than 15 percent	252 715	53 732	57 507	47 960	31 778	20 924	22 475	9 085	5 671	3 583	266
15 to 19 percent	160 006	12 042	19 891	25 740	24 625	21 677	29 066	14 151	7 974	4 840	345
20 to 24 percent	127 034	7 394	10 605	14 373	16 469	17 385	27 375	16 938	10 697	5 798	392
25 to 29 percent	85 840	4 766	6 493	8 680	9 362	9 537	19 562	12 378	9 220	5 842	419
30 to 34 percent	53 671	3 212	3 751	5 162	5 812	5 533	10 979	8 253	6 254	4 715	429
35 percent or more	141 049	12 791	13 773	16 332	15 402	14 525	23 639	17 089	14 321	13 177	392
Not computed	5 651	1 272	794	756	755	588	661	326	239	260	300
Median	19.9	13.5	14.8	17.2	19.0	20.6	22.7	24.6	26.5	29.1	...

Table 1—2. Selected Monthly Owner Costs for Mortgaged Housing Units: 1980—Con.

Housing Units in One-Unit Attached Structures—Total—Con.

[Data are estimates based on a sample; see Introduction. For meaning of symbols, see Introduction. For definitions of terms, see appendix A]

United States	Total	Less than $200	$200 to $249	$250 to $299	$300 to $349	$350 to $399	$400 to $499	$500 to $599	$600 to $749	$750 or more	Median (dollars)
AGE OF HOUSEHOLDER											
Persons 15 years and over	825 966	95 209	112 814	119 003	104 203	90 169	133 757	78 220	54 376	38 215	341
15 to 19 years	1 014	191	118	176	143	100	178	60	24	24	308
20 to 24 years	29 485	2 155	2 959	3 829	4 183	4 063	6 279	3 186	2 054	777	370
25 to 29 years	99 795	5 094	8 037	11 752	13 637	13 323	21 903	13 005	8 918	4 126	393
30 to 34 years	132 082	7 113	11 853	16 335	16 947	16 349	26 535	17 349	11 864	7 737	392
35 to 39 years	109 791	7 853	13 015	14 986	13 476	12 579	19 593	12 142	9 255	6 892	372
40 to 44 years	91 689	8 240	13 369	13 856	11 509	9 409	14 482	8 973	6 447	5 404	345
45 to 49 years	86 510	9 762	14 203	13 785	10 893	8 838	12 821	7 154	4 854	4 200	325
50 to 54 years	83 749	11 834	14 189	13 690	10 552	8 481	10 569	6 206	4 614	3 614	310
55 to 59 years	74 130	12 211	13 234	12 254	9 311	7 473	9 157	4 801	3 014	2 675	297
60 to 64 years	50 719	10 583	10 025	8 031	6 159	4 555	5 788	2 559	1 606	1 413	280
65 to 69 years	32 579	8 393	6 053	5 351	3 650	2 828	3 461	1 343	820	680	267
70 to 74 years	18 478	5 878	3 229	2 897	1 979	1 114	1 669	860	506	346	252
75 years and over	15 945	5 902	2 530	2 061	1 764	1 057	1 322	582	400	327	241
Median	42.2	53.0	47.5	44.5	41.6	39.5	38.1	37.3	37.3	39.7	...
MARITAL STATUS OF HOUSEHOLDER											
Persons 15 years and over	825 966	95 209	112 814	119 003	104 203	90 169	133 757	78 220	54 376	38 215	341
Single	65 394	7 118	6 804	8 031	7 891	6 924	11 253	7 132	6 113	4 128	371
Now married, except separated	580 601	55 711	77 290	83 177	74 213	65 730	99 354	58 143	39 450	27 533	350
Separated	34 898	5 112	5 959	6 164	4 617	3 714	4 335	2 343	1 427	1 227	302
Widowed	61 132	16 999	11 030	9 560	7 089	4 944	6 015	2 720	1 558	1 217	263
Divorced	83 941	10 269	11 731	12 071	10 393	8 857	12 800	7 882	5 828	4 110	338
YEARS OF SCHOOL COMPLETED BY HOUSEHOLDER											
Persons 25 years old and over	795 467	92 863	109 737	114 998	99 877	86 006	127 300	74 974	52 298	37 414	340
Median	12.7	11.8	12.3	12.4	12.6	12.8	13.0	14.3	15.6	16.5	...
PERIOD OF SERVICE OF HOUSEHOLDER											
Civilian veterans 16 years and over	290 714	30 909	43 129	43 987	37 300	31 452	45 855	25 733	18 462	13 887	337
Percent of civilians 16 years and over	35.5	32.5	38.3	37.1	35.9	35.1	34.6	33.5	34.7	37.3	...
May 1975 or later only	3 207	373	350	404	411	382	565	331	231	160	359
Vietnam era	87 060	4 204	8 131	11 511	11 856	11 240	18 119	10 135	7 233	4 631	385
February 1955 to July 1964 only	39 838	3 197	5 959	6 234	5 272	4 147	6 489	3 698	2 717	2 125	343
Vietnam era and Korean conflict	6 238	400	664	783	775	602	1 086	812	646	470	391
Korean conflict	49 853	5 937	8 955	7 928	6 162	4 935	6 785	3 979	2 889	2 283	317
Korean conflict and World War II	7 830	803	1 478	1 198	904	702	1 047	682	500	516	324
World War II	92 574	15 071	16 789	15 358	11 358	9 164	11 380	5 827	4 036	3 591	297
World War I	1 010	297	201	140	152	51	49	58	47	15	252
Other	3 104	627	602	431	410	229	335	211	163	96	287
Civilian nonveterans 16 years and over	528 501	64 125	69 511	74 664	66 457	58 059	86 619	51 069	34 702	23 295	342
LABOR FORCE STATUS OF HOUSEHOLDER											
Persons 16 years and over	825 866	95 204	112 801	118 974	104 175	90 155	133 746	78 220	54 376	38 215	341
Labor force	705 633	64 322	90 679	99 760	89 804	80 392	121 492	72 630	50 981	35 573	355
Percent of persons 16 years and over	85.4	67.6	80.4	83.9	86.2	89.2	90.8	92.9	93.8	93.1	...
Armed Forces	6 651	170	161	323	418	644	1 272	1 418	1 212	1 033	524
Civilian labor force	698 982	64 152	90 518	99 437	89 386	79 748	120 220	71 212	49 769	34 540	354
Employed	674 315	60 596	86 358	94 807	85 918	77 055	116 805	69 740	48 933	34 103	356
Unemployed	24 667	3 556	4 160	4 630	3 468	2 693	3 415	1 472	836	437	300
Percent of civilian labor force	3.5	5.5	4.6	4.7	3.9	3.4	2.8	2.1	1.7	1.3	...
Not in labor force	120 233	30 882	22 122	19 214	14 371	9 763	12 254	5 590	3 395	2 642	269
OCCUPATION OF HOUSEHOLDER											
Employed persons 16 years and over	674 315	60 596	86 358	94 807	85 918	77 055	116 805	69 740	48 933	34 103	356
Managerial and professional specialty occupations	193 662	8 040	13 814	18 715	20 201	21 559	39 208	28 573	23 099	20 453	435
Executive, administrative, and managerial occupations	100 821	4 394	7 337	9 514	10 212	11 170	20 078	15 083	12 329	10 704	438
Professional specialty occupations	92 841	3 646	6 477	9 201	9 989	10 389	19 130	13 490	10 770	9 749	433
Technical, sales, and administrative support occupations	175 242	14 176	21 676	23 988	22 248	21 076	31 540	18 978	13 348	8 212	363
Technicians and related support occupations	24 627	1 516	2 550	3 108	3 055	2 967	4 863	3 206	2 024	1 338	385
Sales occupations	59 786	3 523	5 649	6 515	6 672	6 898	11 433	8 015	6 358	4 723	405
Administrative support occupations, including clerical	90 829	9 137	13 477	14 365	12 521	11 211	15 244	7 757	4 966	2 151	334
Service occupations	69 337	9 250	11 519	11 179	9 742	7 449	10 228	5 420	3 176	1 374	314
Private household occupations	1 683	586	367	262	171	114	99	63	21	–	235
Protective service occupations	25 220	2 108	3 754	3 938	3 749	3 120	4 430	2 280	1 364	477	337
Service occupations, except protective and household	42 434	6 556	7 398	6 979	5 822	4 215	5 699	3 077	1 791	897	302
Farming, forestry, and fishing occupations	4 085	633	633	563	562	382	509	359	236	208	319
Precision production, craft, and repair occupations	107 337	10 969	16 215	17 519	15 065	12 976	18 060	8 873	5 236	2 424	330
Operators, fabricators, and laborers	124 652	17 528	22 501	22 843	18 100	13 613	17 260	7 537	3 838	1 432	299
Machine operators, assemblers, and inspectors	58 159	8 762	11 289	10 532	8 516	6 202	7 727	3 030	1 585	516	293
Transportation and material moving occupations	39 620	4 606	6 695	7 044	5 834	4 427	6 016	2 927	1 463	608	313
Handlers, equipment cleaners, helpers, and laborers	26 873	4 160	4 517	5 267	3 750	2 984	3 517	1 580	790	308	295
MEANS OF TRANSPORTATION TO WORK FOR HOUSEHOLDER											
Workers 16 years and over	666 520	58 675	84 258	92 909	84 198	76 236	116 033	70 131	49 507	34 573	359
Private vehicle	549 270	46 428	68 769	76 166	69 570	63 706	97 293	58 446	41 012	27 880	361
Drive alone: Car	373 590	30 310	45 458	50 108	46 845	43 643	66 971	40 905	28 673	20 677	366
Drive alone: Truck or van	50 635	4 758	7 097	8 177	6 990	5 971	8 509	4 400	3 198	1 535	338
Carpool: Car	111 663	9 994	14 297	15 848	14 133	12 510	19 433	11 820	8 344	5 284	356
Carpool: Truck or van	13 382	1 366	1 917	2 033	1 602	1 582	2 380	1 321	797	384	343
Public transportation	85 187	8 678	11 218	11 908	10 601	9 381	14 242	8 857	6 227	4 075	351
Bus or streetcar	46 463	6 376	7 331	7 086	5 731	4 654	6 035	4 145	2 848	2 257	321
Subway or elevated train	28 114	1 760	2 809	3 502	3 771	3 543	5 959	3 265	2 383	1 122	381
Railroad	9 483	415	924	1 192	999	1 131	2 028	1 346	909	539	404
Taxicab	1 127	127	154	128	100	53	220	101	87	157	401
Bicycle	1 945	213	236	271	254	250	280	204	124	113	350
Motorcycle	2 585	156	339	438	244	218	524	340	184	142	376
Walked only	20 472	2 769	3 214	3 297	2 806	1 947	2 489	1 404	1 121	1 425	317
Other means	3 004	238	193	396	317	334	528	372	337	289	405
Worked at home	4 057	193	289	433	406	400	677	508	502	649	443
WORKERS IN HOUSEHOLD IN 1979											
No workers	64 680	20 428	11 776	9 638	6 898	5 028	5 663	2 615	1 411	1 223	251
1 worker	296 118	35 999	41 999	44 321	37 708	32 339	47 370	26 165	17 658	12 559	334
2 workers	345 937	27 712	39 216	45 323	43 797	39 660	63 233	39 178	28 293	19 525	371
3 or more workers	119 231	11 070	19 823	19 721	15 800	13 142	17 491	10 262	7 014	4 908	328

STRUCTURAL CHARACTERISTICS OF THE HOUSING INVENTORY　　　　　　　　**557**

Table J— 1. **Selected Monthly Owner Costs for Not Mortgaged Housing Units: 1980**

Housing Units in One-Unit Detached Structures—Total

[Data are estimates based on a sample; see Introduction. For meaning of symbols, see Introduction. For definitions of terms, see appendix A]

United States

	Total	Less than $50	$50 to $74	$75 to $99	$100 to $124	$125 to $149	$150 to $199	$200 to $249	$250 or more	Median (dollars)
Specified owner-occupied housing units	13 374 358	402 075	1 327 016	2 251 309	2 459 238	2 103 013	2 630 131	1 181 206	1 020 370	128
YEAR STRUCTURE BUILT										
1979 to March 1980	138 789	7 756	17 306	28 059	26 009	20 494	22 028	9 214	7 923	116
1975 to 1978	474 232	15 782	38 294	71 117	88 617	77 721	99 937	44 792	37 972	132
1970 to 1974	723 791	21 342	60 303	113 462	132 207	118 737	150 016	68 462	59 262	132
1960 to 1969	1 922 211	50 255	157 278	286 789	336 147	304 232	416 087	198 636	172 787	136
1950 to 1959	3 344 364	70 197	267 167	490 855	578 214	541 495	743 930	347 830	304 676	137
1940 to 1949	2 103 431	80 417	269 025	410 090	400 202	314 473	357 966	149 774	121 484	118
1939 or earlier	4 667 540	156 326	517 643	850 937	897 842	725 861	840 167	362 498	316 266	123
YEAR HOUSEHOLDER MOVED INTO UNIT										
1979 to March 1980	510 403	25 147	61 532	95 732	95 287	76 408	87 316	36 728	32 253	119
1975 to 1978	1 344 686	47 878	136 667	232 489	256 300	211 723	255 645	108 904	95 080	125
1970 to 1974	1 535 414	48 641	160 183	266 931	284 999	240 476	292 780	128 919	112 485	126
1960 to 1969	3 208 309	86 134	298 081	516 644	577 259	508 849	662 012	300 562	258 768	131
1959 or earlier	6 775 546	194 275	670 553	1 139 513	1 245 393	1 065 557	1 332 378	606 093	521 784	128
ROOMS										
1 room	22 471	9 135	4 070	3 081	2 115	1 482	1 464	588	536	63
2 rooms	65 021	17 516	16 077	12 280	8 053	4 461	4 280	1 312	1 042	73
3 rooms	320 125	51 201	80 286	75 023	49 020	27 457	24 367	7 702	5 069	85
4 rooms	2 024 236	139 989	394 075	500 790	401 686	259 204	227 133	67 868	33 491	99
5 rooms	3 982 711	112 913	480 514	830 688	845 215	651 638	702 699	240 380	118 664	117
6 rooms	3 671 000	51 229	249 830	557 597	708 220	653 193	840 312	365 612	245 007	135
7 or more rooms	3 288 794	20 092	102 164	271 850	444 929	505 578	829 876	497 744	616 561	168
Median	5.6	4.4	4.9	5.1	5.4	5.7	5.9	6.2	6.5+	...
BEDROOMS										
None	29 087	10 884	5 756	4 221	2 979	1 980	1 921	712	634	66
1	585 150	74 491	125 889	131 581	97 199	60 635	59 855	21 854	13 646	93
2	4 904 839	216 156	740 098	1 104 881	1 009 283	718 212	716 082	249 741	150 386	110
3	6 053 983	87 128	396 872	866 620	1 121 329	1 059 912	1 409 164	634 527	478 431	138
4	1 486 251	11 336	50 091	125 535	198 590	226 280	375 228	224 760	274 431	167
5 or more	315 048	2 080	8 310	18 471	29 858	35 994	67 881	49 612	102 842	196
PERSONS IN UNIT										
1 person	3 373 867	212 631	560 840	728 605	630 919	447 250	468 816	184 121	140 685	107
2 persons	6 051 992	118 697	528 940	1 034 365	1 180 576	1 011 253	1 222 718	523 755	431 688	129
3 persons	1 913 331	30 110	113 806	247 504	330 734	323 850	452 492	220 035	194 800	143
4 persons	1 075 902	16 791	59 881	127 054	171 543	176 289	262 091	134 562	127 691	148
5 persons	531 353	10 881	31 128	60 021	80 323	83 238	128 557	67 251	69 954	150
6 or more persons	427 913	12 965	32 421	53 760	65 143	61 133	95 457	51 482	55 552	145
Median	2.05	1.45	1.69	1.88	2.01	2.10	2.19	2.28	2.36	...
Total persons	30 571 046	729 908	2 513 545	4 619 776	5 424 623	4 896 431	6 511 728	3 073 769	2 801 266	...
PLUMBING FACILITIES BY PERSONS PER ROOM										
Complete plumbing for exclusive use	13 130 246	329 108	1 263 130	2 204 011	2 431 678	2 088 457	2 618 215	1 177 480	1 018 167	129
1.01 or more persons per room	229 325	10 190	29 694	43 949	44 391	33 693	40 315	16 264	10 829	117
Lacking complete plumbing for exclusive use	244 112	72 967	63 886	47 298	27 560	14 556	11 916	3 726	2 203	69
1.01 or more persons per room	34 561	11 583	8 283	5 938	3 586	1 980	1 925	626	640	67
HOUSEHOLD INCOME IN 1979										
Less than $5,000	2 055 450	198 737	429 293	474 040	362 043	232 661	223 204	80 943	54 529	96
$5,000 to $9,999	2 718 122	107 039	396 959	609 921	561 985	399 596	405 529	146 315	90 778	111
$10,000 to $12,499	1 182 953	28 472	129 675	237 639	249 555	195 929	210 241	80 190	51 252	120
$12,500 to $14,999	980 221	17 820	89 362	183 621	207 614	170 309	190 015	73 555	47 925	124
$15,000 to $19,999	1 718 069	23 534	125 488	284 998	353 419	309 286	369 672	150 207	101 465	131
$20,000 to $24,999	1 399 818	13 289	72 892	194 424	269 163	261 060	337 147	145 611	106 232	139
$25,000 to $34,999	1 739 713	8 693	57 527	179 889	289 741	319 028	474 628	227 964	182 243	152
$35,000 to $49,999	997 924	3 077	19 159	65 421	124 086	157 779	287 843	168 029	172 530	172
$50,000 or more	582 088	1 414	6 661	21 356	41 632	57 365	131 852	108 392	213 416	214
Median	$14 363	$5 087	$7 608	$10 439	$13 175	$15 809	$18 821	$21 896	$27 775	...
Mean	$18 919	$7 657	$10 240	$13 215	$16 037	$18 633	$21 996	$26 255	$38 335	...
SELECTED CHARACTERISTICS										
Heating equipment	13 374 358	402 075	1 327 016	2 251 309	2 459 238	2 103 013	2 630 131	1 181 206	1 020 370	128
Central heating system	10 626 450	124 779	690 518	1 542 793	1 958 494	1 817 760	2 397 047	1 113 634	981 425	139
Air conditioning	7 334 761	132 242	635 336	1 208 481	1 370 974	1 181 658	1 475 680	681 983	648 407	132
Central system	3 040 167	20 083	127 920	375 660	560 124	555 748	738 700	338 293	323 639	145
1 or more individual room units	4 294 594	112 159	507 416	832 821	810 850	625 910	736 980	343 690	324 768	121
Vehicles available	11 847 912	266 721	1 033 640	1 914 174	2 186 953	1 919 018	2 443 734	1 110 678	972 994	132
1	5 250 315	168 337	603 569	982 315	1 008 068	817 188	961 652	402 706	306 480	122
2 or more	6 597 597	98 384	430 071	931 859	1 178 885	1 101 830	1 482 082	707 972	666 514	140
House heating fuel	13 321 351	394 996	1 316 291	2 239 368	2 449 656	2 096 879	2 624 840	1 179 736	1 019 585	128
Utility gas	7 657 091	201 943	795 932	1 362 179	1 484 051	1 259 135	1 497 012	593 961	462 878	125
Bottled, tank, or LP gas	803 159	37 848	110 241	168 883	162 836	120 693	127 860	45 951	28 847	113
Electricity	1 410 557	41 018	157 822	289 210	302 208	226 952	234 442	90 966	67 939	118
Fuel oil, kerosene, etc.	2 863 806	27 750	120 692	277 486	395 863	430 261	719 440	436 835	455 479	162
Other	586 738	86 437	131 604	141 610	104 698	59 838	46 086	12 023	4 442	88
Family householder	9 845 195	184 428	749 433	1 496 852	1 800 198	1 632 499	2 132 295	983 621	865 869	136
With own children under 18 years	2 095 602	46 789	141 045	271 829	350 406	341 066	485 550	236 968	221 949	142
With own children under 6 years	465 550	19 734	48 488	78 074	86 294	71 677	88 590	38 858	33 835	125
Female householder, no husband present	1 160 973	31 465	105 887	188 514	208 441	182 070	235 349	111 901	97 346	131
With own children under 18 years	249 993	7 643	20 316	37 227	43 663	40 094	53 333	25 289	22 428	135
With own children under 6 years	36 739	2 200	4 525	6 949	6 621	5 006	6 375	2 764	2 299	118
Nonfamily householder	3 529 163	217 647	577 583	754 457	659 040	470 514	497 836	197 585	154 501	108
Income in 1979 below poverty level	1 499 034	162 578	311 949	334 416	256 587	164 092	163 067	61 924	44 421	96
Percent below poverty level	11.2	40.4	23.5	14.9	10.4	7.8	6.2	5.2	4.4	...
SELECTED MONTHLY OWNER COSTS AS PERCENTAGE OF HOUSEHOLD INCOME IN 1979										
Less than 15 percent	8 542 713	292 416	873 167	1 484 623	1 613 173	1 367 760	1 662 332	699 099	550 143	125
15 to 19 percent	1 521 993	48 905	156 981	243 058	267 223	230 984	293 496	142 633	138 713	130
20 to 24 percent	935 868	24 570	108 701	153 823	163 018	139 493	180 991	84 481	80 791	128
25 to 29 percent	611 614	8 616	68 382	110 859	105 191	89 622	117 927	58 418	52 599	129
30 to 34 percent	418 015	4 688	39 181	74 895	79 226	61 547	80 714	40 965	36 799	129
35 percent or more	1 219 150	12 214	62 679	160 553	210 258	197 543	275 784	146 518	153 601	146
Not computed	125 005	10 666	17 925	23 498	21 149	16 064	18 887	9 092	7 724	112
Median	11.4	9.1	10.5	10.6	10.8	11.1	11.8	12.9	14.1	...

Table J— 1.　Selected Monthly Owner Costs for Not Mortgaged Housing Units:　1980—Con.

Housing Units in One-Unit Detached Structures—Total—Con.

[Data are estimates based on a sample; see Introduction.　For meaning of symbols, see Introduction.　For definitions of terms, see appendix A]

United States	Total	Less than $50	$50 to $74	$75 to $99	$100 to $124	$125 to $149	$150 to $199	$200 to $249	$250 or more	Median (dollars)
AGE OF HOUSEHOLDER										
Persons 15 years and over	13 374 358	402 075	1 327 016	2 251 309	2 459 238	2 103 013	2 630 131	1 181 206	1 020 370	128
15 to 19 years	11 514	1 083	1 741	2 368	2 082	1 386	1 556	678	620	107
20 to 24 years	94 101	7 583	15 655	21 658	18 035	12 376	11 780	4 136	2 878	103
25 to 29 years	197 931	11 527	27 324	40 337	39 695	29 484	30 290	10 965	8 309	112
30 to 34 years	281 040	11 703	29 417	48 752	53 627	44 551	53 152	22 462	17 376	124
35 to 39 years	361 539	10 568	30 062	54 517	64 755	59 905	76 983	34 885	29 864	134
40 to 44 years	477 053	11 450	33 556	66 337	82 330	79 795	107 469	50 690	45 426	139
45 to 49 years	712 965	13 280	44 217	91 469	121 704	120 821	168 759	79 473	73 242	143
50 to 54 years	1 194 709	19 753	71 404	152 918	205 105	199 911	284 419	137 784	123 415	144
55 to 59 years	1 691 360	28 852	108 208	233 317	300 357	284 539	391 293	184 602	160 192	140
60 to 64 years	1 980 478	38 158	150 915	304 774	368 643	330 730	426 627	195 702	164 929	135
65 to 69 years	2 101 527	56 641	215 314	377 128	401 966	332 396	399 383	172 742	145 957	125
70 to 74 years	1 806 391	65 485	225 589	352 556	345 893	269 931	306 003	130 281	110 653	119
75 years and over	2 463 750	125 992	373 614	505 178	455 046	337 188	372 417	156 806	137 509	112
Median	64.2	69.2	68.5	66.4	64.6	63.3	62.2	61.7	61.5	...
MARITAL STATUS OF HOUSEHOLDER										
Persons 15 years and over	13 374 358	402 075	1 327 016	2 251 309	2 459 238	2 103 013	2 630 131	1 181 206	1 020 370	128
Single	647 590	42 767	86 457	118 704	113 344	88 752	106 199	50 266	41 101	117
Now married, except separated	8 479 667	145 931	625 533	1 278 924	1 557 127	1 419 938	1 852 953	850 059	749 202	136
Separated	136 365	10 904	19 975	25 116	22 414	17 309	21 622	9 910	9 115	114
Widowed	3 496 794	164 443	501 946	703 934	652 644	492 758	557 655	233 313	190 101	114
Divorced	613 942	38 030	93 105	124 631	113 709	84 256	91 702	37 658	30 851	111
YEARS OF SCHOOL COMPLETED BY HOUSEHOLDER										
Persons 25 years old and over	13 268 743	393 409	1 309 620	2 227 283	2 439 121	2 089 251	2 616 795	1 176 392	1 016 872	128
Median	12.0	8.4	9.3	10.5	11.5	12.1	12.2	12.4	12.8	...
PERIOD OF SERVICE OF HOUSEHOLDER										
Civilian veterans 16 years and over	4 273 516	66 697	269 970	584 384	760 163	724 418	989 270	466 497	412 117	141
Percent of civilians 16 years and over	32.0	16.6	20.4	26.0	30.9	34.5	37.6	39.5	40.4	...
May 1975 or later only	11 392	617	1 495	2 211	2 349	1 728	1 760	696	536	115
Vietnam era	188 044	6 163	17 339	31 742	36 525	30 982	38 158	15 507	11 628	127
February 1955 to July 1964 only	191 780	2 628	9 711	22 871	32 077	33 758	46 773	22 612	21 350	146
Vietnam era and Korean conflict	56 687	787	3 784	8 274	11 465	10 393	13 060	5 422	3 502	135
Korean conflict	464 232	5 181	21 663	51 358	77 033	79 994	120 965	57 647	50 391	149
Korean conflict and World War II	154 828	1 810	8 940	21 150	28 784	26 102	35 494	17 163	15 385	141
World War II	2 936 883	40 067	173 949	395 181	521 997	501 940	686 273	327 148	290 328	142
World War I	173 227	6 235	21 822	33 607	31 649	25 160	29 023	12 577	13 154	120
Other	96 443	3 209	11 267	17 990	18 284	14 361	17 764	7 725	5 843	122
Civilian nonveterans 16 years and over	9 091 055	335 002	1 056 231	1 665 225	1 697 152	1 376 967	1 638 933	713 925	607 620	122
LABOR FORCE STATUS OF HOUSEHOLDER										
Persons 16 years and over	13 373 606	402 032	1 326 959	2 251 139	2 459 125	2 102 928	2 629 987	1 181 158	1 020 278	128
Labor force	6 185 572	115 170	425 170	866 408	1 086 722	1 022 814	1 393 747	665 700	609 841	140
Percent of persons 16 years and over	46.3	28.6	32.0	38.5	44.2	48.6	53.0	56.4	59.8	...
Armed Forces	9 035	333	758	1 530	1 810	1 543	1 784	736	541	126
Civilian labor force	6 176 537	114 837	424 412	864 878	1 084 912	1 021 271	1 391 963	664 964	609 300	140
Employed	5 913 121	104 333	398 019	822 433	1 037 751	979 361	1 337 716	641 353	592 155	140
Unemployed	263 416	10 504	26 393	42 445	47 161	41 910	54 247	23 611	17 145	128
Percent of civilian labor force	4.3	9.1	6.2	4.9	4.3	4.1	3.9	3.6	2.8	...
Not in labor force	7 188 034	286 862	901 789	1 384 731	1 372 403	1 080 114	1 236 240	515 458	410 437	119
OCCUPATION OF HOUSEHOLDER										
Employed persons 16 years and over	5 913 121	104 333	398 019	822 433	1 037 751	979 361	1 337 716	641 353	592 155	140
Managerial and professional specialty occupations	1 240 511	9 005	42 201	106 094	161 944	181 103	301 262	186 236	252 666	170
Executive, administrative, and managerial occupations	681 442	4 102	21 520	56 909	89 813	101 244	168 077	101 877	137 900	170
Professional specialty occupations	559 069	4 903	20 681	49 185	72 131	79 859	133 185	84 359	114 766	170
Technical, sales, and administrative support occupations	1 309 832	14 573	73 938	168 720	225 218	220 316	310 461	154 897	141 709	145
Technicians and related support occupations	124 691	1 668	6 904	16 487	21 340	21 197	30 215	15 364	11 516	144
Sales occupations	559 099	5 894	29 829	65 367	89 706	89 117	131 953	70 227	77 006	150
Administrative support occupations, including clerical	626 042	7 011	37 205	86 866	114 172	110 002	148 293	69 306	53 187	140
Service occupations	634 518	20 251	67 922	115 544	123 070	101 558	120 542	50 149	35 482	123
Private household occupations	42 736	3 595	8 432	10 183	7 751	5 386	4 719	1 682	988	98
Protective service occupations	113 452	1 986	7 772	16 238	20 342	18 833	26 199	12 204	9 878	139
Service occupations, except protective and household	478 330	14 670	51 718	89 123	94 977	77 339	89 624	36 263	24 616	122
Farming, forestry, and fishing occupations	174 711	8 888	21 335	30 946	31 632	26 063	31 380	14 105	10 362	121
Precision production, craft, and repair occupations	1 281 840	20 567	82 464	185 416	240 052	225 688	301 673	131 833	94 147	137
Operators, fabricators, and laborers	1 271 709	31 049	110 159	215 713	255 835	224 633	272 398	104 133	57 789	128
Machine operators, assemblers, and inspectors	633 072	12 548	50 855	105 697	127 378	112 796	140 727	54 831	28 240	129
Transportation and material moving occupations	399 305	9 154	33 089	65 676	80 257	72 035	86 494	32 843	19 757	129
Handlers, equipment cleaners, helpers, and laborers	239 332	9 347	26 215	44 340	48 200	39 802	45 177	16 459	9 792	121
MEANS OF TRANSPORTATION TO WORK FOR HOUSEHOLDER										
Workers 16 years and over	5 734 126	99 888	384 237	796 568	1 005 495	949 316	1 298 657	623 450	576 515	140
Private vehicle	5 187 849	85 605	342 920	720 399	914 490	864 656	1 183 002	565 835	510 942	140
Drive alone: Car	3 106 343	42 861	182 185	388 341	506 073	502 488	730 999	376 865	376 531	147
Truck or van	1 099 579	21 674	86 333	183 574	227 190	198 015	234 547	91 169	57 077	129
Carpool: Car	750 171	13 403	51 359	105 284	132 249	125 446	173 768	81 655	67 007	140
Truck or van	231 756	7 667	23 043	43 200	48 978	38 707	43 688	16 146	10 327	121
Public transportation	171 031	2 987	9 268	17 971	22 590	23 911	38 129	22 231	33 944	162
Bus or streetcar	120 791	2 602	7 960	15 718	20 011	20 598	29 197	13 160	11 545	142
Subway or elevated train	15 055	17	143	351	617	1 049	3 540	3 715	5 623	224
Railroad	27 711	28	89	405	510	1 268	4 365	4 823	16 223	250+
Taxicab	7 474	340	1 076	1 497	1 452	996	1 027	533	553	114
Bicycle	15 350	405	1 375	2 500	2 985	2 622	3 186	1 311	966	129
Motorcycle	12 532	476	1 243	2 547	2 726	2 047	2 076	789	628	118
Walked only	229 050	6 748	19 524	36 177	43 601	38 817	48 594	20 044	15 545	130
Other means	31 769	1 380	3 442	5 522	5 501	4 775	5 830	2 673	2 646	125
Worked at home	86 545	2 287	6 465	11 452	13 602	12 488	17 840	10 567	11 844	144
WORKERS IN HOUSEHOLD IN 1979										
No workers	5 148 136	243 579	730 519	1 055 031	991 553	742 570	813 294	323 940	247 650	114
1 worker	4 347 023	110 984	395 676	723 759	811 959	699 412	867 218	390 049	347 966	130
2 workers	2 750 724	38 355	161 636	369 086	494 329	477 741	644 653	300 840	264 084	141
3 or more workers	1 128 475	9 157	39 185	103 433	161 397	183 290	304 966	166 377	160 670	161

Table J— 2. **Selected Monthly Owner Costs for Not Mortgaged Housing Units: 1980**

Housing Units in One-Unit Attached Structures—Total

[Data are estimates based on a sample; see Introduction. For meaning of symbols, see Introduction. For definitions of terms, see appendix A]

United States	Total	Less than $50	$50 to $74	$75 to $99	$100 to $124	$125 to $149	$150 to $199	$200 to $249	$250 or more	Median (dollars)
Specified owner-occupied housing units _____	**571 598**	**10 581**	**39 229**	**91 395**	**121 274**	**108 475**	**123 792**	**46 946**	**29 906**	**130**
YEAR STRUCTURE BUILT										
1979 to March 1980 _____	4 955	220	614	989	978	549	921	410	274	117
1975 to 1978_____	11 673	395	850	1 846	2 033	1 970	2 473	1 147	959	134
1970 to 1974_____	15 801	671	1 601	2 857	2 818	2 484	3 139	1 390	841	125
1960 to 1969_____	29 049	1 348	2 660	3 875	4 977	5 112	6 804	2 464	1 809	133
1950 to 1959_____	69 583	1 479	3 967	8 855	15 029	14 103	16 973	5 485	3 692	135
1940 to 1949_____	73 746	1 794	5 469	11 528	15 561	14 679	15 180	5 936	3 599	129
1939 or earlier_____	366 791	4 674	24 068	61 445	79 878	69 578	78 302	30 114	18 732	130
YEAR HOUSEHOLDER MOVED INTO UNIT										
1979 to March 1980 _____	19 751	1 100	2 037	3 237	3 686	2 937	3 860	1 622	1 272	124
1975 to 1978_____	42 939	1 541	3 791	6 942	8 232	7 475	8 537	3 774	2 647	128
1970 to 1974_____	47 025	1 486	4 006	7 759	9 023	8 197	9 902	3 919	2 733	129
1960 to 1969_____	106 033	1 780	6 603	14 558	20 900	20 895	25 208	9 800	6 289	136
1959 or earlier_____	355 850	4 674	22 792	58 899	79 433	68 971	76 285	27 831	16 965	129
ROOMS										
1 room _____	935	328	145	168	143	79	48	16	8	74
2 rooms _____	2 618	526	621	547	367	208	236	51	62	82
3 rooms _____	11 457	1 577	2 297	2 342	1 891	1 243	1 346	421	340	95
4 rooms _____	54 006	2 872	8 918	13 926	11 189	7 151	6 697	1 877	1 376	103
5 rooms _____	114 960	2 619	12 271	25 625	27 361	19 338	18 215	6 137	3 394	116
6 rooms _____	243 413	1 792	10 926	36 155	56 263	52 868	56 907	19 051	9 451	133
7 or more rooms _____	144 209	867	4 051	12 632	24 060	27 588	40 343	19 393	15 275	154
Median _____	5.9	4.5	5.1	5.6	5.8	6.0	6.1	6.3	6.5+	...
BEDROOMS										
None _____	1 337	416	236	233	185	108	126	25	8	77
1_____	20 587	2 323	3 746	4 460	3 423	2 369	2 588	972	706	99
2_____	159 423	4 934	19 804	37 538	36 280	25 081	23 250	7 660	4 876	112
3_____	314 483	2 443	13 240	43 138	70 059	67 204	76 697	27 065	14 637	136
4_____	54 343	331	1 674	4 612	8 654	9 944	15 382	7 694	6 052	156
5 or more _____	21 425	134	529	1 414	2 673	3 769	5 749	3 530	3 627	169
PERSONS IN UNIT										
1 person _____	161 934	5 330	18 989	36 438	36 399	26 758	24 940	7 966	5 114	114
2 persons _____	226 458	2 788	13 806	37 794	52 371	44 526	47 833	16 792	10 548	129
3 persons _____	88 085	1 008	3 157	9 805	17 467	18 514	23 269	9 537	5 328	142
4 persons _____	48 282	577	1 526	3 945	8 416	9 970	14 141	5 862	3 845	149
5 persons _____	24 546	280	734	1 831	3 635	4 841	7 445	3 319	2 461	156
6 or more persons _____	22 293	598	1 017	1 582	2 986	3 866	6 164	3 470	2 610	159
Median _____	2.05	1.49	1.55	1.74	1.96	2.12	2.27	2.42	2.43	...
Total persons_____	1 325 809	21 190	70 668	173 110	261 035	257 419	322 196	132 649	87 542	...
PLUMBING FACILITIES BY PERSONS PER ROOM										
Complete plumbing for exclusive use _____	566 965	9 523	38 181	90 367	120 541	108 029	123 605	46 849	29 870	131
1.01 or more persons per room _____	10 130	461	896	1 222	1 718	1 637	2 318	1 159	719	137
Lacking complete plumbing for exclusive use _____	4 633	1 058	1 048	1 028	733	446	187	97	36	80
1.01 or more persons per room _____	874	336	167	165	103	57	34	4	8	65
HOUSEHOLD INCOME IN 1979										
Less than $5,000 _____	95 823	4 495	12 973	21 119	20 584	14 808	14 189	4 706	2 949	111
$5,000 to $9,999 _____	122 895	2 627	11 087	26 048	28 896	21 812	21 363	7 255	3 807	119
$10,000 to $12,499_____	51 212	866	3 414	9 290	11 889	9 981	10 376	3 316	2 080	125
$12,500 to $14,999_____	42 252	563	2 652	6 916	9 366	8 303	9 377	3 212	1 863	130
$15,000 to $19,999_____	74 750	727	3 803	10 455	17 001	15 325	17 423	6 406	3 610	134
$20,000 to $24,999_____	59 730	430	2 313	7 499	12 467	12 864	15 382	5 485	3 290	139
$25,000 to $34,999_____	71 838	555	1 796	6 910	13 422	15 706	20 320	8 029	5 100	146
$35,000 to $49,999_____	37 368	233	869	2 431	5 805	7 327	11 296	5 599	3 808	159
$50,000 or more _____	15 730	85	322	727	1 844	2 349	4 066	2 938	3 399	181
Median _____	$13 439	$6 317	$7 487	$9 689	$12 346	$14 799	$16 855	$18 741	$20 914	...
Mean _____	$17 055	$9 571	$10 909	$12 597	$15 312	$17 483	$19 588	$22 533	$27 823	...
SELECTED CHARACTERISTICS										
Heating equipment _____	**571 598**	**10 581**	**39 229**	**91 395**	**121 274**	**108 475**	**123 792**	**46 946**	**29 906**	**130**
Central heating system _____	507 590	5 946	28 796	78 062	109 467	99 869	114 534	43 409	27 507	133
Air conditioning _____	**314 345**	**3 922**	**14 643**	**42 018**	**65 361**	**63 731**	**76 492**	**29 294**	**18 884**	**137**
Central system_____	66 034	1 005	3 148	7 946	12 218	13 210	17 219	6 376	4 912	141
1 or more individual room units _____	248 311	2 917	11 495	34 072	53 143	50 521	59 273	22 918	13 972	136
Vehicles available _____	**421 843**	**6 234**	**23 368**	**58 869**	**87 293**	**84 170**	**99 260**	**38 400**	**24 249**	**135**
1_____	262 236	4 401	16 695	41 790	57 905	51 583	56 539	20 631	12 692	130
2 or more _____	159 607	1 833	6 673	17 079	29 388	32 587	42 721	17 769	11 557	144
House heating fuel _____	**570 144**	**10 400**	**38 892**	**91 137**	**121 019**	**108 336**	**123 601**	**46 882**	**29 877**	**130**
Utility gas _____	343 530	6 449	26 657	61 808	77 789	65 067	68 408	23 269	14 083	125
Bottled, tank, or LP gas _____	9 062	546	1 155	1 911	1 784	1 311	1 411	569	375	113
Electricity _____	30 943	1 118	3 165	5 923	6 838	4 957	5 316	2 107	1 519	119
Fuel oil, kerosene, etc. _____	168 476	952	4 998	15 937	30 446	34 756	47 009	20 596	13 782	148
Other _____	18 133	1 335	2 917	5 558	4 162	2 245	1 457	341	118	97
Family householder _____	**398 145**	**4 998**	**19 535**	**53 025**	**82 548**	**79 769**	**96 378**	**37 903**	**23 989**	**137**
With own children under 18 years _____	78 133	1 496	3 318	7 301	13 311	15 698	21 362	9 420	6 227	147
With own children under 6 years _____	17 440	646	1 196	2 271	3 139	3 388	3 905	1 689	1 206	136
Female householder, no husband present _____	77 186	1 092	4 133	10 382	15 506	14 955	18 454	7 903	4 761	138
With own children under 18 years _____	14 230	407	775	1 482	2 505	2 511	3 737	1 790	1 023	144
With own children under 6 years _____	2 420	150	169	289	461	393	550	231	177	134
Nonfamily householder _____	**173 453**	**5 583**	**19 694**	**38 370**	**38 726**	**28 706**	**27 414**	**9 043**	**5 917**	**115**
Income in 1979 below poverty level _____	67 795	3 711	8 357	13 542	13 626	10 574	10 969	4 250	2 766	115
Percent below poverty level _____	11.9	35.1	21.3	14.8	11.2	9.7	8.9	9.1	9.2	...
SELECTED MONTHLY OWNER COSTS AS PERCENTAGE OF HOUSEHOLD INCOME IN 1979										
Less than 15 percent _____	340 929	8 227	25 484	57 152	75 452	66 523	71 799	24 061	12 231	127
15 to 19 percent_____	66 678	947	4 771	10 706	13 338	12 091	14 222	6 254	4 349	132
20 to 24 percent_____	42 922	375	3 825	7 128	8 811	7 325	9 150	3 596	2 712	130
25 to 29 percent_____	29 026	216	1 900	5 162	6 002	5 106	6 056	2 577	2 007	131
30 to 34 percent_____	20 436	70	915	3 524	4 488	3 735	4 535	1 904	1 265	133
35 percent or more _____	64 696	273	1 767	6 574	11 992	12 551	16 608	7 999	6 932	148
Not computed _____	6 911	473	567	1 149	1 191	1 144	1 422	555	410	127
Median _____	12.4	7.5	10.7	11.6	11.6	11.8	13.0	14.6	17.9	...

Table J— 2. **Selected Monthly Owner Costs for Not Mortgaged Housing Units: 1980**—Con.

Housing Units in One-Unit Attached Structures—Total—Con.

[Data are estimates based on a sample; see Introduction. For meaning of symbols, see Introduction. For definitions of terms, see appendix A]

United States	Total	Less than $50	$50 to $74	$75 to $99	$100 to $124	$125 to $149	$150 to $199	$200 to $249	$250 or more	Median (dollars)
AGE OF HOUSEHOLDER										
Persons 15 years and over	571 598	10 581	39 229	91 395	121 274	108 475	123 792	46 946	29 906	130
15 to 19 years	560	16	53	85	140	87	90	57	32	122
20 to 24 years	4 339	374	451	777	765	639	859	279	195	119
25 to 29 years	9 115	357	871	1 498	1 907	1 552	1 728	835	367	124
30 to 34 years	12 039	416	931	1 534	2 340	2 282	2 839	1 034	663	134
35 to 39 years	13 994	348	801	1 787	2 446	2 715	3 540	1 418	939	140
40 to 44 years	18 250	326	825	1 965	3 201	3 655	4 669	2 155	1 454	144
45 to 49 years	27 853	475	1 230	2 967	4 705	5 778	7 402	3 184	2 112	145
50 to 54 years	49 039	549	1 854	5 458	9 712	9 827	13 098	5 183	3 358	143
55 to 59 years	71 603	702	3 158	9 129	14 874	15 014	17 903	6 735	4 088	138
60 to 64 years	85 254	1 061	4 291	12 522	18 599	17 754	19 452	6 962	4 613	134
65 to 69 years	90 989	1 383	6 249	16 248	21 286	16 564	18 400	6 808	4 051	125
70 to 74 years	79 783	1 574	7 122	15 385	17 761	14 472	14 967	5 047	3 455	122
75 years and over	108 780	3 000	11 393	22 040	23 538	18 136	18 845	7 249	4 579	119
Median	64.6	67.4	69.1	67.5	65.5	63.6	62.5	61.9	61.9	...
MARITAL STATUS OF HOUSEHOLDER										
Persons 15 years and over	571 598	10 581	39 229	91 395	121 274	108 475	123 792	46 946	29 906	130
Single	48 422	1 447	4 525	9 519	10 201	7 730	8 908	3 605	2 487	121
Now married, except separated	303 619	3 602	14 511	40 267	63 475	61 513	73 769	28 207	18 275	137
Separated	13 399	456	929	1 897	2 579	2 539	2 924	1 305	770	133
Widowed	176 077	4 075	16 229	34 311	38 989	31 398	32 594	11 531	6 950	121
Divorced	30 081	1 001	3 035	5 401	6 030	5 295	5 597	2 298	1 424	123
YEARS OF SCHOOL COMPLETED BY HOUSEHOLDER										
Persons 25 years old and over	566 699	10 191	38 725	90 533	120 369	107 749	122 843	46 610	29 679	130
Median	11.0	8.9	9.0	9.8	10.7	11.3	11.8	12.1	12.4	...
PERIOD OF SERVICE OF HOUSEHOLDER										
Civilian veterans 16 years and over	162 767	1 891	7 183	20 638	33 897	33 567	40 483	15 238	9 870	138
Percent of civilians 16 years and over	28.5	18.0	18.3	22.6	28.0	30.9	32.7	32.5	33.0	...
May 1975 or later only	475	34	59	70	66	68	95	55	28	128
Vietnam era	6 725	174	423	964	1 112	1 407	1 717	554	374	137
February 1955 to July 1964 only	6 798	57	160	677	1 260	1 376	2 066	699	503	148
Vietnam era and Korean conflict	1 451	–	65	216	261	314	384	121	90	140
Korean conflict	16 556	159	575	1 575	2 968	3 540	4 437	2 041	1 261	146
Korean conflict and World War II	4 941	67	277	629	906	1 095	1 059	611	297	139
World War II	114 953	1 130	4 515	14 461	24 988	23 978	28 794	10 308	6 779	138
World War I	6 301	136	598	1 199	1 284	1 046	1 165	502	371	124
Other	4 567	134	511	847	1 052	743	766	347	167	119
Civilian nonveterans 16 years and over	408 488	8 625	32 022	70 722	87 322	74 897	83 202	31 674	20 024	127
LABOR FORCE STATUS OF HOUSEHOLDER										
Persons 16 years and over	571 569	10 581	39 229	91 388	121 256	108 475	123 788	46 946	29 906	130
Labor force	247 229	3 338	11 424	30 519	49 186	49 574	62 091	24 578	16 519	140
Percent of persons 16 years and over	43.3	31.5	29.1	33.4	40.6	45.7	50.2	52.4	55.2	...
Armed Forces	314	65	24	28	37	11	103	34	12	132
Civilian labor force	246 915	3 273	11 400	30 491	49 149	49 563	61 988	24 544	16 507	140
Employed	234 428	3 049	10 623	28 712	46 573	47 097	59 118	23 557	15 699	140
Unemployed	12 487	224	777	1 779	2 576	2 466	2 870	987	808	134
Percent of civilian labor force	5.1	6.8	6.8	5.8	5.2	5.0	4.6	4.0	4.9	...
Not in labor force	324 340	7 243	27 805	60 869	72 070	58 901	61 697	22 368	13 387	123
OCCUPATION OF HOUSEHOLDER										
Employed persons 16 years and over	234 428	3 049	10 623	28 712	46 573	47 097	59 118	23 557	15 699	140
Managerial and professional specialty occupations	38 961	390	1 310	3 601	5 879	7 263	10 422	5 365	4 731	155
Executive, administrative, and managerial occupations	20 808	158	587	1 929	3 195	4 004	5 576	2 913	2 446	155
Professional specialty occupations	18 153	232	723	1 672	2 684	3 259	4 846	2 452	2 285	155
Technical, sales, and administrative support occupations	60 939	514	2 379	7 369	12 419	12 151	15 659	6 416	4 032	141
Technicians and related support occupations	5 242	56	187	693	1 144	1 056	1 271	515	320	138
Sales occupations	18 567	140	631	2 178	3 394	3 384	4 983	2 232	1 625	147
Administrative support occupations, including clerical	37 130	318	1 561	4 498	7 881	7 711	9 405	3 669	2 087	139
Service occupations	32 755	517	1 981	4 636	6 538	6 475	7 732	2 945	1 931	135
Private household occupations	1 969	63	169	416	393	296	391	119	122	121
Protective service occupations	6 719	68	337	680	1 293	1 470	1 815	679	377	142
Service occupations, except protective and household	24 067	386	1 475	3 540	4 852	4 709	5 526	2 147	1 432	134
Farming, forestry, and fishing occupations	2 256	136	265	388	377	360	458	143	129	122
Precision production, craft, and repair occupations	42 578	559	1 783	4 693	8 845	8 775	11 331	4 193	2 399	140
Operators, fabricators, and laborers	56 939	933	2 905	8 025	12 515	12 073	13 516	4 495	2 477	133
Machine operators, assemblers, and inspectors	29 513	397	1 515	4 374	6 693	6 396	6 905	2 117	1 116	132
Transportation and material moving occupations	15 681	274	798	1 878	3 292	3 253	3 931	1 450	805	137
Handlers, equipment cleaners, helpers, and laborers	11 745	262	592	1 773	2 530	2 424	2 680	928	556	132
MEANS OF TRANSPORTATION TO WORK FOR HOUSEHOLDER										
Workers 16 years and over	226 139	2 940	10 236	27 470	44 877	45 368	57 151	22 981	15 116	140
Private vehicle	171 793	2 219	7 840	20 000	34 299	35 243	44 311	17 122	10 759	140
Drive alone: Car	117 109	1 287	4 986	13 100	23 084	24 015	30 700	12 191	7 746	142
Truck or van	15 269	414	1 039	2 010	3 087	2 982	3 734	1 209	794	134
Carpool: Car	35 360	407	1 478	4 235	7 280	7 547	8 951	3 408	2 054	139
Truck or van	4 055	111	337	655	848	699	926	314	165	128
Public transportation	34 274	389	1 237	4 380	6 513	6 451	8 455	3 951	2 898	143
Bus or streetcar	22 281	323	1 034	3 473	4 947	4 447	5 025	1 820	1 212	133
Subway or elevated train	9 456	30	144	706	1 247	1 553	2 679	1 755	1 342	170
Railroad	1 904	–	45	126	216	375	594	286	262	166
Taxicab	633	36	14	75	103	76	157	90	82	154
Bicycle	467	26	73	48	86	67	63	73	31	125
Motorcycle	309	20	36	43	41	64	70	20	15	131
Walked only	16 098	220	885	2 595	3 452	2 992	3 400	1 492	1 062	132
Other means	902	36	42	134	171	97	276	63	83	143
Worked at home	2 296	30	123	270	315	454	576	260	268	148
WORKERS IN HOUSEHOLD IN 1979										
No workers	228 587	6 245	23 108	47 809	51 937	39 392	39 177	12 968	7 951	118
1 worker	184 680	2 747	10 974	28 545	40 250	36 146	40 495	15 598	9 925	132
2 workers	107 393	1 239	3 931	12 098	21 377	22 301	28 233	11 158	7 056	142
3 or more workers	50 938	350	1 216	2 943	7 710	10 636	15 887	7 222	4 974	158

CODE (Leave blank)	Citizenship of the foreign born	IN WHAT PLACE DID THIS PERSON LIVE ON APRIL 1, 1935?			On a farm (Yes or No)	CODE (Leave blank)								Number of hours worked	Duration of unemployment	OCCUPATION
		City, town, or village having 2,500 or more inhabitants. Enter "R" for all other places.	COUNTY	STATE (or Territory or foreign country)			21	22	23	24	25	E		26	27	28
C	16	17	18	19	20	D										
		Same House			No		Yes	–	–	–			1	40	–	Foreman
		Same House			No		No	No	No	No	H			–	–	
		Same House			No		No	No	No	No	S			–	–	
		Same House			No		Yes	–	–	–				–	–	Labor

Allen, Michael J. *Until the Last Man Comes Home : POWs, MIAs, and the Unending Vietnam War.* Chapel Hill: U of North Carolina, 2009. Web. Dec. 2015.

Bell, Taylor H. A. *Sweet Charlie, Dike, Cazzie, and Bobby Joe: High School Basketball in Illinois.* Urbana: U of Illinois, 2004. Print.

Bennett, Alison Muir., and Clare Davis. *The Hitchhiker's Guide to the Oceans: Crewing around the World.* London: Adlard Coles, 1990. Print.

Brown, Frank. *A Day in the Life of the National Hockey League.* San Francisco, CA: CollinsPublishersSan Francisco, 1996. Print.

Cooney, Joan Ganz. *The First Year of Sesame Street: A History and Overview—Final Report.* New York: Childrens Television Workshop, 1970. Print.

Deletant, Dennis. *Romania under Communist Rule.* Iasi, Romania: Center for Romanian Studies in Cooperation with the Civic Academy Foundation, 1999. Print.

Freed, Les, and Sarah Ishida. *The History of Computers.* Emeryville, CA: Ziff-Davis, 1995. Print.

Gart, Galen. *First Pressings : Rock History as Chronicled in Billboard Magazine.* Milford N.H.: Big Nickel Productions, 1986. Print.

Gillon, Edmund Vincent., and Clay Lancaster. *Victorian Houses: A Treasury of Lesser-known Examples.* New York: Dover Publications, 1973. Print.

Hargreaves, Margaret Barnwell. *Learning under Stress: Children of Single Parents and the Schools.* Metuchen, NJ: Women's Action Alliance, 1991. Print.

Heineman, Kenneth J. *Campus Wars: The Peace Movement at American State Universities in the Vietnam Era.* New York: New York UP, 1993. Print.

Hulin, Belinda, Renee Skelton, Ellen Appelbaum, Scott Cameron, Miranda Barry, Jordan D. Brown, Jeffrey Nelson, Robin Warsaw, Donna Nitzberg, Lisa Jo. Rudy, Sheila Sweeny Higginson, and Amy Bernstein. *Harcourt Social Studies: Florida.* Orlando: Harcourt, n.d. Print.

Hunt, Andrew E. *The Turning: A History of Vietnam Veterans Against the War.* New York: New York UP, 1999. Print.

Kaufman, Will. *American Culture in the 1970s.* Edinburgh: Edinburgh UP, 2009. Print.

Kinnear, Karen L. *Single Parents: A Reference Handbook.* Santa Barbara, CA: ABC-CLIO, 1999. Print.

Legal Advocacy for Older Persons at Risk Involving Religious Organizations, Social Workers, and Eldercare Coalitions: Final Report. Washington, DC (1800 M St., N.W., Washington 20036): Association, 1993. Print.

López-Garza, Marta C., and David R. Diaz. *Asian and Latino Immigrants in a Restructuring Economy: The Metamorphosis of Southern California.* Stanford, CA: Stanford UP, 2001. Print.

McConnell, John, and John C. Munday. *Earth Day: Vision for Peace, Justice, and Earth Care: My Life and Thought at Age 96.* Eugene, OR: Resource Publications, 2011. Print.

Miller, Jim. *Flowers in the Dustbin: The Rise of Rock and Roll, 1947-1977.* New York: Simon & Schuster, 1999. Print.

Otto, Steve. *Memoirs of a Drugged-up, Sex-crazed Yippie: Tales from the 1970s Counter-culture: Drugs, Sex, Politics and Rock and Roll.* Bloomington, IN: AuthorHouse, 2005. Print.

Palley, Marian Lief, and Howard A. Palley. *The Politics of Women's Health Care in the United States.* New YOrk: Palgrave Macmillan, 2014. Print.

Participation by the United States in the United Nations Environment Program: Hearings, Ninety-third Congress, First Session, on H.R. 5696, April 5 and 10, 1973. Washington: U.S. Govt. Print. Off., 1973. Print.

Plutnik, Adam. *Standing Eight : The Inspiring Story of Jesus "El Matador" Chavez, Who Became Lightweight Champion of the World*. Cambridge: De Capo, 2006. Print.

Rantala, Judy Austin. *Laos: Caught in the Web: The Vietnam War Years*. Bangkok, Thailand: Orchid, 2004. Print.

A Report of the Department of Health & Rehabilitative Services Medical and Dental Conference, September 8 & 9, 1972, Tampa, Florida. Tallahassee, FL: Florida Rural Development Committee and Florida Dept. of Health and Rehabilitative Services, 1983. Print.

School Desegregation in Texas: The Implementation of United States v. State of Texas: A Report. Austin: School, 1982. Print.

Sesame Street at Five: The Changing Look of a Perpetual Experiment. New York: n.p., 1974. Print.

Small, Edgar C. *History of Nebraska*. Forest County, PA: Forest, 1988. Print.

Spencer, Peter D. *The Structure and Regulation of Financial Markets*. Oxford: Oxford UP, 2000. Print.

Stacewicz, Richard. *Winter Soldiers: An Oral History of the Vietnam Veterans Against the War*. New York: Twayne, 1997. Print.

Sulick, Michael J. *American Spies Espionage against the US from the Cold War to the Present*. Ely: IT Governance Pub., 2010. Print.

Thimmesh, Catherine, and Melissa Sweet. *Girls Think of Everything: Stories of Ingenious Inventions by Women*. Boston: Houghton Mifflin, 2000. Print.

Twiname, Eric. *Start to Win: The Classic Text*. London: Adlard Coles Nautical, 2009. Print.

Villarino, José. *Mexican and Chicano Music*. New York: McGraw-Hill Companies, 1999. Print.

Welaratna, Usha. *Beyond the Killing Fields: Voices of Nine Cambodian Survivors in America*. Stanford, CA: Stanford UP, 1993. Print.

Ziegler, Louis W., and Herbert S. Wolfe. *Citrus Growing in Florida*. Gainesville: Ues of Florida, 1975. Print.

City, town, or village having 2,500 or more inhabitants. Enter "R" for all other places.	COUNTY	STATE (or Territory or foreign country)	On a farm? (Yes or No)	CODE (Leave blank)						CODE	Number of hours worked during week of March 24-30, 1940		OCCUPATION
17	18	19	20	D	21	22	23	24	25	E	26	27	28
Same House			No		Yes	—	—	—	—	1	40	—	Foreman
Same House			No		No	No	No	No	H				
Same House			No		No	No	No	No	S				
Same House			No		Yes	—	—	—	—			—	Laborer

This index covers content in Section One: Profiles.

This index covers content in Section One: Profiles.

2016 Title List

Visit www.GreyHouse.com for Product Information, Table of Contents, and Sample Pages.

General Reference

An African Biographical Dictionary
America's College Museums
American Environmental Leaders: From Colonial Times to the Present
Encyclopedia of African-American Writing
Encyclopedia of Constitutional Amendments
Encyclopedia of Gun Control & Gun Rights
An Encyclopedia of Human Rights in the United States
Encyclopedia of Invasions & Conquests
Encyclopedia of Prisoners of War & Internment
Encyclopedia of Religion & Law in America
Encyclopedia of Rural America
Encyclopedia of the Continental Congress
Encyclopedia of the United States Cabinet, 1789-2010
Encyclopedia of War Journalism
Encyclopedia of Warrior Peoples & Fighting Groups
The Environmental Debate: A Documentary History
The Evolution Wars: A Guide to the Debates
From Suffrage to the Senate: America's Political Women
Global Terror & Political Risk Assessment
Nations of the World
Political Corruption in America
Privacy Rights in the Digital Era
The Religious Right: A Reference Handbook
Speakers of the House of Representatives, 1789-2009
This is Who We Were: 1880-1900
This is Who We Were: A Companion to the 1940 Census
This is Who We Were: In the 1910s
This is Who We Were: In the 1920s
This is Who We Were: In the 1940s
This is Who We Were: In the 1950s
This is Who We Were: In the 1960s
This is Who We Were: In the 1970s
U.S. Land & Natural Resource Policy
The Value of a Dollar 1600-1865: Colonial Era to the Civil War
The Value of a Dollar: 1860-2014
Working Americans 1770-1869 Vol. IX: Revolutionary War to the Civil War
Working Americans 1880-1999 Vol. I: The Working Class
Working Americans 1880-1999 Vol. II: The Middle Class
Working Americans 1880-1999 Vol. III: The Upper Class
Working Americans 1880-1999 Vol. IV: Their Children
Working Americans 1880-2015 Vol. V: Americans At War
Working Americans 1880-2005 Vol. VI: Women at Work
Working Americans 1880-2006 Vol. VII: Social Movements
Working Americans 1880-2007 Vol. VIII: Immigrants
Working Americans 1880-2009 Vol. X: Sports & Recreation
Working Americans 1880-2010 Vol. XI: Inventors & Entrepreneurs
Working Americans 1880-2011 Vol. XII: Our History through Music
Working Americans 1880-2012 Vol. XIII: Education & Educators
World Cultural Leaders of the 20th & 21st Centuries

Education Information

Charter School Movement
Comparative Guide to American Elementary & Secondary Schools
Complete Learning Disabilities Directory
Educators Resource Directory
Special Education: A Reference Book for Policy and Curriculum Development

Health Information

Comparative Guide to American Hospitals
Complete Directory for Pediatric Disorders
Complete Directory for People with Chronic Illness
Complete Directory for People with Disabilities
Complete Mental Health Directory
Diabetes in America: Analysis of an Epidemic
Directory of Drug & Alcohol Residential Rehab Facilities
Directory of Health Care Group Purchasing Organizations
Directory of Hospital Personnel
HMO/PPO Directory
Medical Device Register
Older Americans Information Directory

Business Information

Complete Television, Radio & Cable Industry Directory
Directory of Business Information Resources
Directory of Mail Order Catalogs
Directory of Venture Capital & Private Equity Firms
Environmental Resource Handbook
Food & Beverage Market Place
Grey House Homeland Security Directory
Grey House Performing Arts Directory
Grey House Safety & Security Directory
Grey House Transportation Security Directory
Hudson's Washington News Media Contacts Directory
New York State Directory
Rauch Market Research Guides
Sports Market Place Directory

Statistics & Demographics

American Tally
America's Top-Rated Cities
America's Top-Rated Smaller Cities
America's Top-Rated Small Towns & Cities
Ancestry & Ethnicity in America
The Asian Databook
Comparative Guide to American Suburbs
The Hispanic Databook
Profiles of America
"Profiles of" Series – State Handbooks
Weather America

Financial Ratings Series

TheStreet Ratings' Guide to Bond & Money Market Mutual Funds
TheStreet Ratings' Guide to Common Stocks
TheStreet Ratings' Guide to Exchange-Traded Funds
TheStreet Ratings' Guide to Stock Mutual Funds
TheStreet Ratings' Ultimate Guided Tour of Stock Investing
Weiss Ratings' Consumer Guides
Weiss Ratings' Guide to Banks
Weiss Ratings' Guide to Credit Unions
Weiss Ratings' Guide to Health Insurers
Weiss Ratings' Guide to Life & Annuity Insurers
Weiss Ratings' Guide to Property & Casualty Insurers

Bowker's Books In Print® Titles

American Book Publishing Record® Annual
American Book Publishing Record® Monthly
Books In Print®
Books In Print® Supplement
Books Out Loud™
Bowker's Complete Video Directory™
Children's Books In Print®
El-Hi Textbooks & Serials In Print®
Forthcoming Books®
Large Print Books & Serials™
Law Books & Serials In Print™
Medical & Health Care Books In Print™
Publishers, Distributors & Wholesalers of the US™
Subject Guide to Books In Print®
Subject Guide to Children's Books In Print®

Canadian General Reference

Associations Canada
Canadian Almanac & Directory
Canadian Environmental Resource Guide
Canadian Parliamentary Guide
Canadian Venture Capital & Private Equity Firms
Financial Post Directory of Directors
Financial Services Canada
Governments Canada
Health Guide Canada
The History of Canada
Libraries Canada
Major Canadian Cities

Grey House Publishing | Salem Press | H.W. Wilson | 4919 Route, 22 PO Box 56, Amenia NY 12501-0056

2016 Title List

Visit www.SalemPress.com for Product Information, Table of Contents, and Sample Pages.

Science, Careers & Mathematics

Ancient Creatures
Applied Science
Applied Science: Engineering & Mathematics
Applied Science: Science & Medicine
Applied Science: Technology
Biomes and Ecosystems
Careers in Building Construction
Careers in Business
Careers in Chemistry
Careers in Communications & Media
Careers in Environment & Conservation
Careers in Healthcare
Careers in Hospitality & Tourism
Careers in Human Services
Careers in Law, Criminal Justice & Emergency Services
Careers in Manufacturing
Careers in Physics
Careers in Sales, Insurance & Real Estate
Careers in Science & Engineering
Careers in Technology Services & Repair
Computer Technology Innovators
Contemporary Biographies in Business
Contemporary Biographies in Chemistry
Contemporary Biographies in Communications & Media
Contemporary Biographies in Environment & Conservation
Contemporary Biographies in Healthcare
Contemporary Biographies in Hospitality & Tourism
Contemporary Biographies in Law & Criminal Justice
Contemporary Biographies in Physics
Earth Science
Earth Science: Earth Materials & Resources
Earth Science: Earth's Surface and History
Earth Science: Physics & Chemistry of the Earth
Earth Science: Weather, Water & Atmosphere
Encyclopedia of Energy
Encyclopedia of Environmental Issues
Encyclopedia of Environmental Issues: Atmosphere and Air Pollution
Encyclopedia of Environmental Issues: Ecology and Ecosystems
Encyclopedia of Environmental Issues: Energy and Energy Use
Encyclopedia of Environmental Issues: Policy and Activism
Encyclopedia of Environmental Issues: Preservation/Wilderness Issues
Encyclopedia of Environmental Issues: Water and Water Pollution
Encyclopedia of Global Resources
Encyclopedia of Global Warming
Encyclopedia of Mathematics & Society
Encyclopedia of Mathematics & Society: Engineering, Tech, Medicine
Encyclopedia of Mathematics & Society: Great Mathematicians
Encyclopedia of Mathematics & Society: Math & Social Sciences
Encyclopedia of Mathematics & Society: Math Development/Concepts
Encyclopedia of Mathematics & Society: Math in Culture & Society
Encyclopedia of Mathematics & Society: Space, Science, Environment
Encyclopedia of the Ancient World
Forensic Science
Geography Basics
Internet Innovators
Inventions and Inventors
Magill's Encyclopedia of Science: Animal Life
Magill's Encyclopedia of Science: Plant life
Notable Natural Disasters
Principles of Astronomy
Principles of Chemistry
Principles of Physics
Science and Scientists
Solar System
Solar System: Great Astronomers
Solar System: Study of the Universe
Solar System: The Inner Planets
Solar System: The Moon and Other Small Bodies
Solar System: The Outer Planets
Solar System: The Sun and Other Stars
World Geography

Literature

American Ethnic Writers
Classics of Science Fiction & Fantasy Literature
Critical Insights: Authors
Critical Insights: Film
Critical Insights: Literary Collection Bundles
Critical Insights: Themes
Critical Insights: Works
Critical Survey of Drama
Critical Survey of Graphic Novels: Heroes & Super Heroes
Critical Survey of Graphic Novels: History, Theme & Technique
Critical Survey of Graphic Novels: Independents/Underground Classics
Critical Survey of Graphic Novels: Manga
Critical Survey of Long Fiction
Critical Survey of Mystery & Detective Fiction
Critical Survey of Mythology and Folklore: Heroes and Heroines
Critical Survey of Mythology and Folklore: Love, Sexuality & Desire
Critical Survey of Mythology and Folklore: World Mythology
Critical Survey of Poetry
Critical Survey of Poetry: American Poets
Critical Survey of Poetry: British, Irish & Commonwealth Poets
Critical Survey of Poetry: Cumulative Index
Critical Survey of Poetry: European Poets
Critical Survey of Poetry: Topical Essays
Critical Survey of Poetry: World Poets
Critical Survey of Shakespeare's Plays
Critical Survey of Shakespeare's Sonnets
Critical Survey of Short Fiction
Critical Survey of Short Fiction: American Writers
Critical Survey of Short Fiction: British, Irish, Commonwealth Writers
Critical Survey of Short Fiction: Cumulative Index
Critical Survey of Short Fiction: European Writers
Critical Survey of Short Fiction: Topical Essays
Critical Survey of Short Fiction: World Writers
Critical Survey of Young Adult Literature
Cyclopedia of Literary Characters
Cyclopedia of Literary Places
Holocaust Literature
Introduction to Literary Context: American Poetry of the 20th Century
Introduction to Literary Context: American Post-Modernist Novels
Introduction to Literary Context: American Short Fiction
Introduction to Literary Context: English Literature
Introduction to Literary Context: Plays
Introduction to Literary Context: World Literature
Magill's Literary Annual 2015
Magill's Survey of American Literature
Magill's Survey of World Literature
Masterplots
Masterplots II: African American Literature
Masterplots II: American Fiction Series
Masterplots II: British & Commonwealth Fiction Series
Masterplots II: Christian Literature
Masterplots II: Drama Series
Masterplots II: Juvenile & Young Adult Literature, Supplement
Masterplots II: Nonfiction Series
Masterplots II: Poetry Series
Masterplots II: Short Story Series
Masterplots II: Women's Literature Series
Notable African American Writers
Notable American Novelists
Notable Playwrights
Notable Poets
Recommended Reading: 600 Classics Reviewed
Short Story Writers

2016 Title List

Visit www.SalemPress.com for Product Information, Table of Contents, and Sample Pages.

SALEM PRESS

History and Social Science

The 2000s in America
50 States
African American History
Agriculture in History
American First Ladies
American Heroes
American Indian Culture
American Indian History
American Indian Tribes
American Presidents
American Villains
America's Historic Sites
Ancient Greece
The Bill of Rights
The Civil Rights Movement
The Cold War
Countries, Peoples & Cultures
Countries, Peoples & Cultures: Central & South America
Countries, Peoples & Cultures: Central, South & Southeast Asia
Countries, Peoples & Cultures: East & South Africa
Countries, Peoples & Cultures: East Asia & the Pacific
Countries, Peoples & Cultures: Eastern Europe
Countries, Peoples & Cultures: Middle East & North Africa
Countries, Peoples & Cultures: North America & the Caribbean
Countries, Peoples & Cultures: West & Central Africa
Countries, Peoples & Cultures: Western Europe
Defining Documents: American Revolution
Defining Documents: Civil Rights
Defining Documents: Civil War
Defining Documents: Emergence of Modern America
Defining Documents: Exploration & Colonial America
Defining Documents: Manifest Destiny
Defining Documents: Postwar 1940s
Defining Documents: Reconstruction
Defining Documents: 1920s
Defining Documents: 1930s
Defining Documents: 1950s
Defining Documents: 1960s
Defining Documents: 1970s
Defining Documents: American West
Defining Documents: Ancient World
Defining Documents: Middle Ages
Defining Documents: Vietnam War
Defining Documents: World War I
Defining Documents: World War II
The Eighties in America
Encyclopedia of American Immigration
Encyclopedia of Flight
Encyclopedia of the Ancient World
Fashion Innovators
The Fifties in America
The Forties in America
Great Athletes
Great Athletes: Baseball
Great Athletes: Basketball
Great Athletes: Boxing & Soccer
Great Athletes: Cumulative Index
Great Athletes: Football
Great Athletes: Golf & Tennis
Great Athletes: Olympics
Great Athletes: Racing & Individual Sports
Great Events from History: 17th Century
Great Events from History: 18th Century
Great Events from History: 19th Century
Great Events from History: 20th Century (1901-1940)
Great Events from History: 20th Century (1941-1970)
Great Events from History: 20th Century (1971-2000)
Great Events from History: Ancient World
Great Events from History: Cumulative Indexes
Great Events from History: Gay, Lesbian, Bisexual, Transgender Events

Great Events from History: Middle Ages
Great Events from History: Modern Scandals
Great Events from History: Renaissance & Early Modern Era
Great Lives from History: 17th Century
Great Lives from History: 18th Century
Great Lives from History: 19th Century
Great Lives from History: 20th Century
Great Lives from History: African Americans
Great Lives from History: American Women
Great Lives from History: Ancient World
Great Lives from History: Asian & Pacific Islander Americans
Great Lives from History: Cumulative Indexes
Great Lives from History: Incredibly Wealthy
Great Lives from History: Inventors & Inventions
Great Lives from History: Jewish Americans
Great Lives from History: Latinos
Great Lives from History: Middle Ages
Great Lives from History: Notorious Lives
Great Lives from History: Renaissance & Early Modern Era
Great Lives from History: Scientists & Science
Historical Encyclopedia of American Business
Issues in U.S. Immigration
Magill's Guide to Military History
Milestone Documents in African American History
Milestone Documents in American History
Milestone Documents in World History
Milestone Documents of American Leaders
Milestone Documents of World Religions
Music Innovators
Musicians & Composers 20th Century
The Nineties in America
The Seventies in America
The Sixties in America
Survey of American Industry and Careers
The Thirties in America
The Twenties in America
United States at War
U.S.A. in Space
U.S. Court Cases
U.S. Government Leaders
U.S. Laws, Acts, and Treaties
U.S. Legal System
U.S. Supreme Court
Weapons and Warfare
World Conflicts: Asia and the Middle East
World Political Yearbook

Health

Addictions & Substance Abuse
Adolescent Health & Wellness
Cancer
Complementary & Alternative Medicine
Genetics & Inherited Conditions
Health Issues
Infectious Diseases & Conditions
Magill's Medical Guide
Psychology & Behavioral Health
Psychology Basics

Grey House Publishing | Salem Press | H.W. Wilson | 4919 Route, 22 PO Box 56, Amenia NY 12501-0056

2016 Title List

Visit www.HWWilsonInPrint.com for Product Information, Table of Contents and Sample Pages

Current Biography
Current Biography Cumulative Index 1946-2013
Current Biography Monthly Magazine
Current Biography Yearbook: 2003
Current Biography Yearbook: 2004
Current Biography Yearbook: 2005
Current Biography Yearbook: 2006
Current Biography Yearbook: 2007
Current Biography Yearbook: 2008
Current Biography Yearbook: 2009
Current Biography Yearbook: 2010
Current Biography Yearbook: 2011
Current Biography Yearbook: 2012
Current Biography Yearbook: 2013
Current Biography Yearbook: 2014
Current Biography Yearbook: 2015

Core Collections
Children's Core Collection
Fiction Core Collection
Graphic Novels Core Collection
Middle & Junior High School Core
Public Library Core Collection: Nonfiction
Senior High Core Collection
Young Adult Fiction Core Collection

The Reference Shelf
Aging in America
American Military Presence Overseas
The Arab Spring
The Brain
The Business of Food
Campaign Trends & Election Law
Conspiracy Theories
The Digital Age
Dinosaurs
Embracing New Paradigms in Education
Faith & Science
Families: Traditional and New Structures
The Future of U.S. Economic Relations: Mexico, Cuba, and Venezuela
Global Climate Change
Graphic Novels and Comic Books
Immigration
Immigration in the U.S.
Internet Safety
Marijuana Reform
The News and its Future
The Paranormal
Politics of the Ocean
Racial Tension in a "Postracial" Age
Reality Television
Representative American Speeches: 2008-2009
Representative American Speeches: 2009-2010
Representative American Speeches: 2010-2011
Representative American Speeches: 2011-2012
Representative American Speeches: 2012-2013
Representative American Speeches: 2013-2014
Representative American Speeches: 2014-2015
Representative American Speeches: 2015-2016
Rethinking Work
Revisiting Gender
Robotics
Russia
Social Networking
Social Services for the Poor
Space Exploration & Development
Sports in America
The Supreme Court
The Transformation of American Cities

U.S. Infrastructure
U.S. National Debate Topic: Surveillance
U.S. National Debate Topic: The Ocean
U.S. National Debate Topic: Transportation Infrastructure
Whistleblowers

Readers' Guide
Abridged Readers' Guide to Periodical Literature
Readers' Guide to Periodical Literature

Indexes
Index to Legal Periodicals & Books
Short Story Index
Book Review Digest

Sears List
Sears List of Subject Headings
Sears: Lista de Encabezamientos de Materia

Facts About Series
Facts About American Immigration
Facts About China
Facts About the 20th Century
Facts About the Presidents
Facts About the World's Languages

Nobel Prize Winners
Nobel Prize Winners: 1901-1986
Nobel Prize Winners: 1987-1991
Nobel Prize Winners: 1992-1996
Nobel Prize Winners: 1997-2001

World Authors
World Authors: 1995-2000
World Authors: 2000-2005

Famous First Facts
Famous First Facts
Famous First Facts About American Politics
Famous First Facts About Sports
Famous First Facts About the Environment
Famous First Facts: International Edition

American Book of Days
The American Book of Days
The International Book of Days

Junior Authors & Illustrators
Eleventh Book of Junior Authors & Illustrations

Monographs
The Barnhart Dictionary of Etymology
Celebrate the World
Guide to the Ancient World
Indexing from A to Z
The Poetry Break
Radical Change: Books for Youth in a Digital Age

Wilson Chronology
Wilson Chronology of Asia and the Pacific
Wilson Chronology of Human Rights
Wilson Chronology of Ideas
Wilson Chronology of the Arts
Wilson Chronology of the World's Religions
Wilson Chronology of Women's Achievements

Grey House Publishing | Salem Press | H.W. Wilson | 4919 Route, 22 PO Box 56, Amenia NY 12501-0056